P9-AGK-889

HANDBOOK OF PERSONALITY

Theory and Research

SECOND EDITION

HANDBOOK OF PERSONALITY

Theory and Research

SECOND EDITION

Edited by

Lawrence A. Pervin
Rutgers University

Oliver P. John
University of California, Berkeley

THE GUILFORD PRESS
New York / London

© 1999 The Guilford Press
A Division of Guilford Publications, Inc.
72 Spring Street, New York, NY 10012
http://www.guilford.com

All rights reserved

No part of this book may be reproduced, translated, stored in a retrieval system, or transmitted, in any form or by any means, electronic, mechanical, photocopying, microfilming, recording, or otherwise, without written permission from the Publisher.

Printed in the United States of America

This book is printed on acid-free paper.

Last digit is print number: 9 8 7 6 5 4 3 2 1

Library of Congress Cataloging-in-Publication Data

Handbook of personality: theory and research / edited by Lawrence A. Pervin, Oliver P. John. — 2nd ed.
p. cm.
Includes bibliographical references and index.
ISBN 1-57230-483-9
1. Personality. I. Pervin, Lawrence A. II. John, Oliver P.
BF698.H335 1999 99-25807
155.2—DC21 CIP

About the Editors

Lawrence A. Pervin (PhD, Harvard University, 1962) is Professor of Psychology at Rutgers University. A fellow of the American Psychological Association and American Psychological Society, Dr. Pervin is the author of three personality texts, *Personality: Theory and Research* (7th edition, coauthored with Oliver P. John), *Current Controversies and Issues in Personality,* and *The Science of Personality.* He is the founding editor of *Psychological Inquiry,* and has served on the editorial boards of the *Psychological Review,* the *Journal of Personality and Social Psychology,* and the *European Journal of Personality.* His clinical experience includes an ongoing private practice in psychotherapy. He is the editor of two books in the field, has published scores of articles and reviews in leading journals here and abroad, and has contributed to four major psychology reference works.

Oliver P. John (PhD, University of Oregon, 1986) is Associate Professor of Psychology at the University of California, Berkeley, where he has served as acting director of the Institute of Personality and Social Research. He has published widely on trait and cognitive approaches to personality, and recently was cited as one of the top 25 impact authors in psychology for the 1990–1994 period. Dr. John has served as Associate Editor of *Personality and Social Psychology Bulletin,* and on the editorial boards of *Psychological Science* and the *Journal of Research in Personality.* He lectures frequently in the United States and Europe on various aspects of personality theory and research.

Contributors

Albert Bandura, PhD, Department of Psychology, Stanford University, Stanford, CA

Nicole B. Barenbaum, PhD, Department of Psychology, University of the South, Sewanee, TN

Roy F. Baumeister, PhD, Department of Psychology, Case Western Reserve University, Cleveland, OH

David M. Buss, PhD, Department of Psychology, University of Texas, Austin, TX

Charles S. Carver, PhD, Department of Psychology, University of Miami, Coral Gables, FL

Avshalom Caspi, PhD, Social, Genetic and Developmental Psychiatry Research Centre, Institute of Psychiatry, London, UK, and University of Wisconsin, Madison, WI

Corrine Cather, graduate student, Department of Psychology, Rutgers—The State University of New Jersey, New Brunswick, NJ

Jonathan M. Cheek, PhD, Department of Psychology, Wellesley College, Wellesley, MA

Lee Anna Clark, PhD, Department of Psychology, University of Iowa, Iowa City, IA

Richard J. Contrada, PhD, Department of Psychology, Rutgers—The State University of New Jersey, New Brunswick, NJ

Paul T. Costa, Jr., PhD, Gerontology Research Center, National Institute on Aging, National Institutes of Health, Baltimore, MD

Susan E. Cross, PhD, Department of Psychology, Iowa State University, Ames, IA

Glen O. Gabbard, MD, Department of Psychiatry, Menninger School of Medicine, Topeka, KS

Sandra Graham, PhD, Department of Psychology, University of California, Los Angeles, CA

Jeffrey A. Gray, PhD, Institute of Psychiatry, University of London, London, UK

James J. Gross, PhD, Department of Psychology, Stanford University, Stanford, CA

Oliver P. John, PhD, Department of Psychology and Institute of Personality and Social Research, University of California, Berkeley, CA

John F. Kihlstrom, PhD, Department of Psychology, University of California, Berkeley, CA

Michael Lewis, PhD, Institute for the Study of Child Development, Robert Wood Johnson Medical School, University of Medicine and Dentistry of New Jersey, New Brunswick, NJ

Brian R. Little, PhD, Department of Psychology, Carleton University, Ottawa, Ontario, Canada

David Magnusson, PhD, Department of Psychology, Stockholm University, Stockholm, Sweden

Hazel R. Markus, PhD, Department of Psychology, Stanford University, Stanford, CA

Dan P. McAdams, PhD, Program in Human Development and Social Policy, School of Education and Social Policy, Northwestern University, Evanston, IL

Robert R. McCrae, PhD, Gerontology Research Center, National Institute on Aging, National Institutes of Health, Baltimore, MD

Walter Mischel, PhD, Department of Psychology, Columbia University, New York, NY

Julie K. Norem, PhD, Department of Psychology, Wellesley College, Wellesley, MA

Ann O'Leary, PhD, Department of Psychology, Rutgers—The State University of New Jersey, New Brunswick, NJ

Daniel J. Ozer, PhD, Department of Psychology, University of California, Riverside, CA

Lawrence A. Pervin, PhD, Department of Psychology, Rutgers—The State University of New Jersey, Piscataway, NJ

Alan D. Pickering, PhD, Department of Psychology, St. George's Hospital Medical School, University of London, London, UK

Robert Plomin, PhD, Social, Genetic and Developmental Psychiatry Research Centre, Institute of Psychiatry, London, UK

Brent W. Roberts, PhD, Department of Psychology, University of Tulsa, Tulsa, OK

Richard W. Robins, PhD, Department of Psychology, University of California, Davis, CA

Michael F. Scheier, PhD, Department of Psychology, Carnegie Mellon University, Pittsburgh, PA

Yuichi Shoda, PhD, Department of Psychology, University of Washington, Seattle, WA

Dean Keith Simonton, PhD, Department of Psychology, University of California, Davis, CA

Sanjay Srivastava, graduate student, Department of Psychology and Institute of Personality and Social Research, University of California, Berkeley, CA

Krista K. Trobst, PhD, Gerontology Research Center, National Institute on Aging, National Institutes of Health, Baltimore, MD

Wim van den Brink, MD, PhD, Amsterdam Institute for Addiction Research, University of Amsterdam, Amsterdam, The Netherlands

Roel Verheul, PhD, Amsterdam Institute for Addiction Research, University of Amsterdam, Amsterdam, The Netherlands

David Watson, PhD, Department of Psychology, University of Iowa, Iowa City, IA

Bernard Weiner, PhD, Department of Psychology, University of California, Los Angeles, CA

Drew Westen, PhD, Department of Psychiatry, Harvard Medical School and The Cambridge Hospital, Cambridge, MA

Thomas A. Widiger, PhD, Department of Psychology, University of Kentucky, Lexington, KY

Jerry S. Wiggins, PhD, Gerontology Research Center, National Institute on Aging, National Institutes of Health, Baltimore, MD

David G. Winter, PhD, Department of Psychology, University of Michigan, Ann Arbor, MI

Preface

Publication of the second edition of this handbook comes a decade after publication of the first edition and as we approach the new millennium. Thus, it is a time of looking back and looking forward—looking back both to see our roots and to assess progress made and looking forward to see what the future may hold. In a sense, such consideration relates to a central issue in the study of personality, that is, the dialectic between continuity and change in personality functioning across situations and over time.

The second edition of the handbook itself reflects both continuity and change. The basic structure of the book remains the same, with an introductory chapter on the history of the field, a section on major theoretical perspectives, a section on the interface with other fields, and a section on specific research topics. Within each of these sections there again is evidence of continuity and change. For example, the section on theoretical perspectives continues to have chapters on the psychoanalytic, trait, social cognitive, and interactional perspectives. And the section on the interface with other fields continues to have chapters on the relation of personality to biology, developmental psychology, social psychology, clinical psychology, and anthropology. Finally, specific chapters cover such important content areas as the self, motivation, the unconscious, attribution, emotion, health, and assessment. As another indicator of continuity, 10 of the 28 chapters in the current edition are authored by the same individuals as in the first edition. In addition, two authors from the first edition return to contribute chapters in new areas. Thus, there is evidence of continuity to the field of personality psychology over the past decade.

At the same time, the second edition reflects evidence of change in the field as well as in major contributors to this change. In the theoretical perspectives section, a new chapter appears on evolutionary psychology, a new chapter is devoted to the influential five-factor model of personality, and there is a comprehensive presentation of the social cognitive theory of Albert Bandura. In the section on the interface with other fields, a new chapter focuses specifically on the important emerging area of the relation between neuroscience and personality. Finally, there are new chapters on temperament, personal narratives, self-regulatory processes, creativity, and interpersonal processes. The last reflects the critical point made by Robert Carson in his otherwise extremely positive *Contemporary Psychology* review of the first edition. In all, 17 of the 28 chapters represent totally new contributions. Many of these reflect the contributions of a younger cohort of researchers, trained during the 1980s and 1990s, who are leading the field in new directions. At the same time, we note with sadness the passing of several influential pioneers in the field of personality psychology, among them Raymond Cattell, Jack Digman, Hans Eysenck, David McClelland, and Warren Norman, some of whom made valuable contributions to the first edition.

A final note concerning continuity and change—the editors, one from the old, one for the new. It has been a delight for us to work together on this project. It has offered us the opportunity to reflect upon the status of the field, what is of major importance and what of lesser importance, what shows promise for the future and what may be a passing fad. We have tried to be unbiased in this regard and to use the best wisdom available to us personally as well as to others with whom we consulted. We apologize for areas neglected or given less attention than some might think is deserved. We approached the task of estimating the future with the full humility expressed in Samuel Goldwyn's comment that "Only a fool would make predictions, especially about the future," and we are keenly aware of the great diversity of views expressed in the 1996 special issue on the future of the field in the *Journal of Research in Personality.*

We have been fortunate in having the cooperation of the many contributors to this volume. Once more it seemed important to ensure that chapters delivered on time were not out of date by the time the full manuscript was turned in. In this case the lag between arrival of the first and last chapters represented just a few months. This, in conjunction with the effort of The Guilford Press to put the book on a fast production track, has enabled us to feel confident that the contributions are current. In this regard we are indebted to the editor-in-chief of The Guilford Press, Seymour Weingarten, and to the members of the the Guilford staff who were so diligent in seeing the book through the various phases of the publication process.

The first edition of this handbook was greeted with considerable enthusiasm. With the publication of the second edition we hope to be able to continue in the tradition of the distinguished contributions from our related disciplines, the *Handbook of Social Psychology* and the *Handbook of Developmental Psychology.*

LAWRENCE A. PERVIN
Princeton, NJ

OLIVER P. JOHN
Berkeley, CA

Contents

PART THREE. INTERFACE WITH OTHER FIELDS

PART FOUR. CONTENT AREAS

PART ONE
INTRODUCTION

Chapter 1

History of Modern Personality Theory and Research

David G. Winter
University of Michigan

Nicole B. Barenbaum
University of the South

Why would you want to read this chapter? To be sure, any science has a history; but the history of a science, while a legitimate field of scholarly inquiry, is usually quite separate from the science itself. Few chemists are concerned with Johann Becher's now-discredited phlogiston theory or Dmitri Mendeleyev's life and how he came to construct the periodic table of the elements. If psychological science is concerned with what is true *now*, why bother with what people used to think was true? Why, then, a history of personality psychology?

USES OF A HISTORICAL PERSPECTIVE

We suggest three important reasons for personality psychologists to know something of their history. First, origins are intrinsically interesting, even compelling. As Freud (1908/1959b) once suggested, the question "Where did I come from?" may be the child's "first grand problem of life" (p. 212). Origins are often a critical part of adult identity (witness people's interest in genealogy). In fact, the history of psychology is of increasing interest to psychologists, as manifest in the new APA journal, *History of Psychology*. In this chapter, then, we offer an outline of the "family history" of personality psychology.

Second, the study of history can help us avoid making the same journeys over the same terrain, repeating the mistakes of the past. If we know what has gone before, we may discover that some questions have been asked before, perhaps even answered! As the philosopher Santayana (1906) cautioned, "Progress, far from consisting in change, depends on retentiveness. . . . When experience is not retained . . . infancy is perpetual. Those who cannot remember the past are condemned to repeat it" (p. 284).

Further, any discipline is the way it is because its early workers formulated certain questions and framed certain key concepts. By understanding how our field evolved and was constructed—by particular psychologists, in particular social contexts—we gain a broader perspective on contemporary questions and issues. For example, Gordon Allport's decision to ratify "trait" as the key concept for the newly emerging field of personality (Allport, 1927) had important consequences in framing such later issues as the ways in which personality is measured, stability versus change, the roles of "personality" and "situation" in the explanation of behavior, and the relationship between trait and other personality constructs such as motive (Winter, John, Stewart, Klohnen, & Duncan, 1998).

Finally, no science is divorced from its surrounding social conditions and values-climate. For example, any attempt to study the psychology of personality presumes the belief that "personality" is important and worth explaining. This belief, in turn, rests on a philosophical individualism and a view of the individual as cause or agent. Because Americans are particularly likely to hold such individualistic beliefs and reluctant to acknowledge the importance of collectivities (Bellah, Madsen, Sullivan, Swidler, & Tipton, 1985), it is not surprising that "personality" has been a major focus of psychological inquiry as well as popular culture in the United States (see Susman, 1979). One observer suggested that "no country in the world is so driven by personality as this one" and that Americans have a "hunger to identify with larger-than-life personalities" ("Only spectacular crimes," 1994). Our historical account, therefore, will emphasize developments in the United States. It should be taken as building upon earlier historical handbook chapters by Burnham (1968), Pervin (1990), McAdams (1997) and Runyan (1997)—and, indeed, on those entire earlier handbooks.

NINETEENTH-CENTURY INTELLECTUAL ANTECEDENTS OF PERSONALITY PSYCHOLOGY

The modern psychological study of personality, which began to flourish during the early decades of the 20th century, has roots in three 19th-century intellectual themes: a deep belief in *individualism,* a pervasive *concern with irrationality and the unconscious,* and a strong *emphasis on measurement.* Although these three themes are by no means fully consistent with each other and not every personality psychologist emphasized all three, they did shape (and limit) the emerging field of personality psychology in important ways that can still be recognized.

Individualism and the "Skin-Bounded" Individual

Personality psychology evolved and flourished in the Western philosophical–political climate of individualism—the belief that individuals are important and unique. Such a discipline would be unlikely to develop in a homogeneous society in which everyone lived through the same small set of life cycles. Thus the cultural historian Burckhardt (1860/1954) concluded that in the Middle Ages, people were conscious of themselves "only as a member of a race, people, party, family, or corporation—only through some general category" (p. 101). After the Renaissance, however, people recognized themselves as *individuals.*

From the individualist perspective, "persons," the very subject matter of personality psychology, are construed as single bodies, bounded by skin. Anything else (objects and environments, intimate partners, other people, family, solidary groups, communities, institutions, cultures) is construed as "outside," wholly external to the autonomous skin-bounded individual person. From this perspective, they only exist and are understood as internal representations, objects of contractual relations, or encroachments on the individual.[1]

The individualistic perspective, however, leads to a paradox: Often we do not seem so very different from each other. For example, the many studies of bogus personality feedback (Dickson & Kelly, 1985) suggest that people readily accept uniform, standardized feedback as an accurate description of their own "individual" selves. And Singer (1995), after studying thousands of college students' self-stories, was "overwhelmed by the narrative *similarities* they bring to the important events in their lives" (p. 452, emphasis added). Further, an excessively individualistic perspective can blind psychologists to the importance of collective aspects of personality such as groups, social identities, and cultural symbols.

The Unconscious

In revolt against the 18th-century "age of reason," the 19th-century Romantic movement exalted the role of unconscious and irrational emotions, spontaneity, and impulsivity in literature, the arts, and philosophy. In personality psychology, this influence was most obvious in psychoanalysis, particularly Freud's concepts of id and primary process. The notion of an unconscious still survives today, albeit in a muted and less grandiose form, in the claim that many important processes are *implicit* or automatic—that is, they operate outside of conscious awareness (Kihlstrom, 1990, and Chapter 17, this volume; see also Bargh, 1982; Greenwald & Banaji, 1995; Nisbett & Wilson, 1977). Still, an exclusive focus on unconscious or implicit forces may lead to a neglect or underestimation of the importance of rational planning and directed behavior (see Cantor & Zirkel, 1990).

Emphasis on Measurement

In devoting an extraordinary amount of attention to issues of measurement and psychometrics, personality psychology tried to follow in the footsteps of the prestigious "exact sciences" that had developed so rapidly in the late 19th century. The modern emphasis on precision and measurement was prefigured in the writings of British scientist and statistician Sir Francis Galton (1884): "The character which shapes our conduct is a definite and durable 'something,' and therefore . . . it is reasonable to attempt to measure it" (p. 179).[2] In the early 20th century, American experimental psychologist E. L. Thorndike (1914) insisted that "if a thing exists, it exists in some *amount;* and if it exists in some amount, it can be *measured"* (p. 141; emphasis in original).

The prestige of Binet and the early intelligence "tests" also increased the concern with measurement in personality psychology. A rapidly developing assessment technology led to a number of paper and pencil "tests" of personality, modeled after the early intelligence tests and consisting of questionnaire "items" intended to measure the "traits" of personality. Later on, personality psychologists expanded their measurement technology to include ratings and behavior observations.

The emphasis on measurement also fit with the imperative, strongly felt by personality psychology in its beginning decades, to be *useful,* to furnish assistance to a corporate culture and a government suddenly confronted by dramatic changes and the need to "manage" and control an American population that had suddenly become larger, more diverse, and "difficult" (Parker, 1991). This point is nicely illustrated by the example of Woodworth's Personal Data Sheet, which was probably the first personality test based on the IQ test model of adding "scores" on discrete individual "items" to get a total. By the time the United States finally entered the war in April 1917, the experience of other armies suggested that many soldiers were vulnerable to "shell shock" or "war neurosis." (Nowadays this would probably be called posttraumatic stress disorder.) The American Psychological Association quickly set up a committee charged with developing a diagnostic test of "susceptibility to shock," which was conceived as one aspect of a more general emotional instability (Camfield, 1969, pp. 126, 131–132). Acting without the benefit of much prior knowledge or technique, Robert Woodworth collected a long list of symptoms from the case histories of "neurotic subjects" and turned them into a series of 116 simple questions that could be answered Yes or No (for example, "Do you usually feel well and strong?" or "Has your family always treated you right?"). Overall scores, calculated by summing scores of the individual items, differentiated "normal" soldiers from diagnosed neurotics or returned "shell shock" cases (Woodworth, 1919, 1932, p. 374). The resulting Personal Data Sheet was the first objective, self-report "inventory" purporting to measure a personality characteristic, in this case what was later labeled Neuroticism.

A focus on measurement was obviously beneficial to any science that aspired to prestige by developing along the traditional positivistic path blazed by 19th-century physics. Conversely, it was a handicap insofar as it constrained the scope of investigation and explanation to that which was easily measured, thereby neglecting more subtle and complex personality characteristics and processes. For example, self-report questionnaires constructed on the IQ-test "item" model are sensitive only to conscious (rather than implicit) sentiments. They are usually based on the atomistic assumption that a complex whole can be broken down into a series of small component parts, each of which is equal to every other and all of which combine in additive (rather than interactive or nonlinear) ways. In this respect, the "measurement imperative" of personality psychology sometimes resembled the famous joke about the drunken man who had lost his keys on the dark side of the street but looked for them on the (other) lighted side, "because that's where the light is."

THE TWO TASKS OF PERSONALITY PSYCHOLOGY

From its earliest days, American personality psychology involved two related but contrasting endeavors: (1) the *study of individual differences,* or the dimensions along which people differ from each other, and (2) the *study of individual persons as unique, integrated wholes* (see, e.g., Lamiell, 1997; McAdams, 1997; Murphy, 1932; Sanford, 1963). These two endeavors have been variously labeled as "analytic" versus "structural," or "quantitative" versus "qualitative," respectively. According to one early commentator (Young, 1928):

> A review of the whole gamut of personality studies . . . reveals two essentially distinct approaches to the data. One of these, which has been developed by recent psychology, concerns itself with a . . . cross-sectional treatment of personality in terms of traits, attitudes and habits. The other, which has arisen from a number of sources, especially psychiatry, treats personality from a functional, historical–genetic standpoint. (p. 431)

Much of the difference between these two approaches is also captured by the "nomothetic–idiographic" dichotomy—terms first used by Windelband (1894/1904), later adopted by Allport (1937),[3] and still a lively topic at the end of the century (West, 1983; see also Lamiell, 1998).

The Psychometric "Analysis" Approach

Discussing the analytic or quantitative approach, Murphy (1932) characterized its view of personality as the "sum of all of an individual's traits" (p. 386). In his view, psychologists who measured and studied the intercorrelations of separate personality traits conceived of personality "as the answer to a complicated arithmetical problem" (p. 386). The practical goal of personality research was to predict, modify, and control behavior, with individual differences conceived as coefficients to be supplied to linear, additive prediction equations.[4]

Influence of Intelligence Testing

We have called this the "psychometric" approach because, according to an early reviewer, it "owes its prominence to the work of Galton, Pearson, Cattell, Thorndike and Terman with their investigations of individual differences, particularly in the field of intelligence" (Young, 1928, p. 431). During the first two decades of the 20th century, psychologists had developed "mental tests" for selection, diagnosis, and placement, as psychologists tried to demonstrate their usefulness in solving urgent practical problems associated with immigration, labor unions, and schools, as well as the 1917–1918 national war mobilization (Danziger, 1990; Parker, 1991; Vernon, 1933; see Schaffer, 1991, pp. 133–139, on the effects of World War I in particular).

In the post-World War I period, however, many critics questioned the predictive utility of intelligence tests in various applied settings (Parker, 1991) and suggested that measures of personality or character traits were needed to improve the prediction of military, managerial, industrial, and educational performance (see, e.g., Fernald, 1920; Poffenberger, 1922; Pressey, 1921). Still, these newer "character tests" were based on the mental test model in preference to other, less "efficient" methods (Parker, 1991). The content of trait measures also reflected practical demands: "Ascendance–Submission" and "Extraversion–Introversion," considered relevant to selecting business managers and military officers, received the greatest attention (Danziger, 1990; Parker, 1991).

"Mental Hygiene" and Personality

Yet another important influence on the psychometric approach to personality during the 1920–1930 period was the so-called mental hygiene movement. This well-funded alliance of psychiatrists, educators, and social workers viewed individual maladjustment as the root cause of a wide variety of social and personal problems (S. Cohen, 1983; see also Parker, 1991). With its "personality" focus, the movement enlisted psychologists to supply a "scientific" basis for the therapeutic efforts of mental hygiene workers. As Danziger (1990) noted, "in practice this generally came down to the construction and application of scales that would subject 'personality' to the rigors of measurement and so convert it from merely an object of social intervention to an object of science" (p. 164).

"Science" or "Servant"?

The continuing concern of personality psychologists to demonstrate the practical usefulness of their work on measuring individual differences suggests the need for viewing history from a political and moral perspective. In fact, most of the "practical social problems" personality psychologists tried to solve were problems faced (and framed) by elite groups: selecting managers who could maximize profits; selecting military officers who could win wars; controlling an increasingly diverse population in the country's schools, factories, crowded cities, and prisons; and controlling "deviant" behavior, at least to the extent of promoting labels suggesting individual pathology instead of social problems. Not surprisingly, the "solutions" supplied by personality psychologists tended to leave existing power relations intact or even reinforced, because the intellectual roots of personality psychology—radical individualism, supported by the mystique of "science"—were quite compatible with the ideological stance of the ruling elites who financed the research. Thus the practically oriented psychometric approach to personality psychology runs the danger of becoming a technology that deliberately or unwittingly functions mainly to serve the interests of the powerful.[5]

The Psychiatric and Historical "Interpretation" Approach

Murphy (1932) contrasted the psychometric approach to personality with the psychiatric focus on "personality as a whole," observing that psychiatric conceptions "added much to the richness of the term 'personality'" by introducing topics such as dissociation and unconscious mental processes (p. 387). Young (1928) was especially enthusiastic about this historical-interpretive approach (though he noted that at the time of his writing, it "has had very little attention from the psychologist," p. 437): "[It] has arisen from the study of literary biography, from historical biography, but especially from psychiatry and sociology. Here we find the great biographers, the psychoanalysts led by Freud, Jung and Adler, the invaluable work of Healy [a neurologist] and latterly the sociological reformulation of W. I. Thomas" (p. 431).

Mainstream psychologists ignored or criticized biographical and case study methods and were (at least initially) quite hostile toward psychoanalysis (Danziger, 1990, 1997, especially p. 125). Given their concern for scientific respectability via sophisticated quantitative techniques, it is not surprising that they viewed the case study methods of psychiatrists and psychoanalysts as part of an "old-fashioned and unscientific" medical tradition (Hale, 1971, p. 115).

Discussing the case study literature in their review of personality, Allport and Vernon (1930) noted the contributions of psychiatrists and sociologists (rather than psychologists) and echoed the prevailing view that the method was "unsatisfactory." However, they went on to suggest that "the concrete individual has eluded study by any other approach" and concluded with the hope that "in the future there will undoubtedly be attempts to standardize the case-study in some way which will reduce its dependence upon the uncontrolled artistry of the author" (p. 700).

The whole-person or interpretive approach to personality had been especially prominent in German psychology during the first three decades of the 20th century. Influenced by the philosopher Dilthey's view of psychology as a "human science" (*Geisteswissenschaft*), it emphasized the ways in which personality characteristics and other psychological processes were organized or patterned within the unique individual. Writing for an American audience about the German qualitative approach to the "undivided" personality, Allport summarized this perspective: "More fundamental than differential psychology [i.e., the psychometric focus on dimensions of difference among people], by far, is the problem of the nature, the activity, and the unity of the *total personality*" (Allport, 1923, p. 614; emphasis in original). Allport traced the German emphasis on structured "wholes" in Gestalt psychology, the personalistic psychology of William Stern, and Eduard Spranger's method of "intuitive understanding" (*Verstehen*) (Allport, 1923, 1924a, 1924b, 1929).

However, Allport's early attempts to introduce this approach to personality to American psychologists apparently met with little response. Vernon (1933) noted that most American psychometrists were either unaware of the German qualitative approach or else found it scientifically unacceptable.

The Uneasy Coalition between "Analysis" and "Interpretation" Approaches

For the past 70 years, the two approaches to personality psychology—the study of individual personality *differences* and the study of individual *persons*—have existed in an uneasy coalition or truce. As part of their efforts to broaden (and systematize) personality, Allport (1937) and

Murray (1938) tried to move the field toward studying persons as integrated wholes, but as several later commentators noted, personality psychologists generally avoided studies of individual lives through most of the century (see, e.g., Carlson, 1971; McAdams & West, 1997; Runyan, 1997).

Even Allport and Murray seemed ambivalent about case studies. As a journal editor and professor, Allport *advocated* studying individual persons (see, e.g., Allport, 1924b, 1929, 1937, 1942) and tried (unsuccessfully) to develop a set of systematic rules for writing life histories (Allport, 1967; see also Barenbaum, 1997a, 1997c; Garraty, 1981). Yet he himself actually published only one case study (Allport, 1965), and much of his research involved nomothetic traits (Allport, 1928; Vernon & Allport, 1931). Situated within Harvard's scientifically oriented academic department of psychology, Allport opted for a moderate, eclectic approach that included both analytic and interpretive methods (see Nicholson, 1997a, but also Pandora, 1997).

Situated as a maverick in opposition to the "scientistic" Harvard department (Robinson, 1992), Murray still needed to justify his foundation support on the basis of the "scientific" status of his work (see also Triplet, 1983, 1992). Although Murray's group developed elaborate *procedures* for the intensive study of individual persons, their book (Murray, 1938) actually included only one case.[6] Later, in establishing an assessment program for the wartime Office of Strategic Services (OSS), Murray modified his "diagnostic council" method even more in the direction of more quantitative assessments (McLeod, 1992).

From a historical perspective, it is easy to see that the psychometric tradition was already well established in psychology by the time that personality emerged as a separate field, so that this prior "triumph of the aggregate" (Danziger, 1997, p. 68) led to an early dominance of the "individual differences" tradition over the "study of individuals" tradition. For example, when the American Psychological Association took over publication of the *Journal of Abnormal and Social Psychology* (from the psychiatrically oriented American Psychopathological Association) in 1925, the publication pattern changed dramatically (Danziger, 1990):

> What was given up was an earlier tradition of detailed study of individuals. . . . Whereas in 1924[,] 80 percent of the empirical papers published were based on the study of individual cases, that proportion dropped to 25 percent in the following year. Their place was taken by statistical studies based on group data, as was required by the prevailing Galtonian paradigm for psychological measurement. (p. 165)

The marginal status of studies of individual persons in personality psychology, then, really continues an early trend. Yet interest in individual cases has continued to survive—at first mainly among students and associates of Allport and Murray (e.g., Polansky, 1941; Rosenzweig, 1943; White, 1952), but in recent years among a much broader and larger array of personality psychologists (Runyan, 1997, p. 42; see the review by McAdams & West, 1997; also the collections edited by Franz & Stewart, 1994, and McAdams & Ochberg, 1988).[7]

1921–1946: THE CRITICAL FORMATIVE ERA OF PERSONALITY PSYCHOLOGY IN THE UNITED STATES

We suggest that while the "official" emergence of personality psychology is often dated by the appearance of the "canonical" texts by Allport (1937), Murray (1938),[8] and Stagner (1937), it really began at least 15 years earlier. The 1921–1938 period was a time of intense research activity; the years between 1938 and 1946 were really the consolidation of "modern" personality concepts and methods, as well as the widespread institutional recognition of personality as a specialty within psychology departments (Danziger, 1990; 1997; Parker, 1991). We first review the period before the canonical texts, then discuss the latter period in terms of the influence of three major figures who had substantial and enduring impact on the field: Gordon Allport (1897–1967), Henry Murray (1893–1988), and Raymond Cattell (1905–1998).

Origins: The Decade of the 1920s

The first American review of the psychological literature on "personality and character" appeared in 1921 (Allport, 1921).[9] Most of the various sources cited by Allport involved *traits,* which suggests that the trait concept had already achieved a theoretical dominance by that time (Danziger, 1990; Parker, 1991). The article focused primarily on the distinction between "personality" and "character," two concepts that had been used interchangeably by American psychologists up to that time. In agreement with the behaviorists, Allport suggested that the latter term, defined as "the personality evaluated according to prevailing standards of conduct" (p. 443), was not an appropriate topic for psychological study. Allport continued to advocate the use of "personality" in preference to "character" (1927; Allport & Vernon, 1930); this soon became standard practice, not only for reasons of scientific respectability but also on account of a cultural shift from moralism to pragmatism (Nicholson, 1998).

A "Personality" Journal

Before the 1920s, the term "personality" had been used primarily in discussions of abnormal psychology, which was considered to be the province of the medical specialty of psychiatry (Parker, 1991). Another indication that the field of personality was emerging as a separate and autonomous area of *psychological* research was the 1921 expansion of the *Journal of Abnormal Psychology* into the *Journal of Abnormal Psychology and Social Psychology*[10] with Floyd Allport as an additional editor "in cooperation with" Morton Prince. In a joint editorial, they noted that psychopathologists and social psychologists shared an interest in the "dynamics of human nature" and invited contributions on a number of topics, including "the foundation-study of human traits" and "the personality of the individual" (Prince & Allport, 1921, p. 2). The lead article of the first issue of the expanded journal was the study of personality traits by the Allport brothers (Allport & Allport, 1921).

Seven years later, Prince and Moore (1928) introduced a special issue of the *Journal of Abnormal and Social Psychology* devoted to personality with the observation that "the rapidly increasing number of manuscripts dealing with problems of temperament, character and personal traits shows that an extraordinary pressure of investigation is being directed toward this subject which until quite recently numbered but a few brief pages in any standard textbook of psychology." They noted the "necessity of ever widening approaches and more manifold studies," and concluded with a prophetic reference to "the complex task that faces the author of a Psychology of Personality ten years hence" (p. 117).

Institutional Developments

By the end of the 1920s there were several institutional indicators of the widespread interest in personality as a field of psychology. During the period 1923–1928, the American Psychological Association responded to its members' increasing interest in personality by scheduling convention sessions on "character" and "personality," sometimes in the practical context of vocational guidance or selection (Parker, 1991). Similar developments occurred at other conferences and meetings. Support for personality research came from a variety of foundations. Other signs of recognition of the new discipline included the founding of the journal *Character and Personality* (later renamed *Journal of Personality*) in 1932, and the 1934 addition of "personality" as a category in the *Psychological Abstracts* (Parker, 1991).

Allport: Defining and Systematizing the Field of Personality

Gordon Allport's early efforts to define and systematize the field of personality included what he later described as "perhaps the first American dissertation written explicitly on the question of component traits of personality" (Allport, 1967, p. 9).[11] Trained in social ethics as well as psychology, Allport attempted in his 1922 dissertation to define "a sound conception of human personality" on which to base "effective social service," arguing that "sound theory must underlie application" (Allport, 1967, p. 7). Rejecting as superficial many of the existing trait measures derived from exclusively practical concerns, he adopted a behavioristic definition of traits as "systems of habits" and designed measures of those traits he saw as basic components of personality.

As a postdoctoral student in Germany (1922–1923), Allport encountered psychological approaches to personality that "converted" him from his "semifaith in behaviorism" (1967, p. 12). From that time onward, he advocated structural approaches such as Gestalt psychology, Spranger's intuitive method, and Stern's personalistic emphasis on the uniqueness and unity of personality (see, e.g., Allport, 1923, 1924a, 1924b, 1929). Stern was especially influential in shaping Allport's views (Allport, 1967): "From Stern in particular I learned that a chasm exists between the common variety of differential psychology (which he himself had largely invented . . .) and a truly personalistic psychology that focuses upon the organization, not the mere profiling, of an individual's traits" (p. 10). Allport was particularly impressed with Stern's "repudiation" of his earlier view of "personality as a sum-total of traits" in favor of an emphasis on "the total personality" (Allport, 1924a, p. 359), and Stern's influence is especially reflected in many of Allport's later (1937) views (e.g., the very definition of "trait," the concept of functional autonomy of motives, and the distinction between idiographic and nomothetic methods; see Barenbaum, 1997b).

Returning from Europe in 1924, Allport continued his efforts to define a systematic psychology of personality. Having accepted an offer to teach social ethics at Harvard, he taught what he later described as "probably the first course on the subject [of personality] offered in an American college" (Allport, 1967, p. 9). With the title "Personality and Social Amelioration," the course was first offered in 1924 in the Department of Social Ethics. The following year it was cross-listed in psychology under a new title, "Personality: Its Psychological and Social Aspects" (Nicholson, 1997b, pp. 734–735). During his time at Dartmouth (from 1926 to 1930) and later at Harvard (in the psychology department), Allport refined his definition of traits (1931) and attempted to synthesize analytic and interpretive methods of studying personality. He experimented with case methods in teaching (1929) and developed the *Study of Values,* an instrument based on Spranger's sixfold conception of value (Vernon & Allport, 1931).

Although personality research had proliferated during the 1920s, Allport and other commentators noted a continuing lack of attention to the development of personality theory. According to Allport and Vernon (1930), "experimental approaches in recent years have far outgrown an adequate philosophical and theoretical background, especially in America" (p. 702). In a similar vein, Murphy (1932) commented that "those who have occupied themselves with the measurement of personality traits have in general been even less concerned with the theory of personality than most intelligence testers have been with theories of intelligence" (p. 386). Vernon (1933) attributed this lack of attention to American psychologists' preoccupation with applied issues: "The preliminary study of fundamental theoretical problems seems to have been neglected for the sake of practical results" (p. 166).

Allport's 1937 text, like his early reviews, attempted to define and systematize the field of personality psychology in order to provide "co-ordinating concepts and theories" (1937, p. ix). His survey of existing definitions of personality and methods of studying it led to a renewed emphasis on *trait* as the fundamental unit of study for personality. Traits, Allport suggested, were neuropsychic systems with dynamic or motivational properties. At the same time Allport's focus throughout was on "the manifest individuality of mind" (p. vii), which implied both idiographic and nomothetic methods. Although some critics considered this focus on the individual unscientific (Bills, 1938; Skaggs, 1945), most reviewers immediately recognized Allport's "precise, well-integrated, and thoughtful review" of the field of personality and his "coherent defense of the individual as a proper subject for scientific study" (Jenkins, 1938, p. 777). Even those who took issue with Allport's views agreed that the book would be influential (Guilford, 1938; Hollingworth, 1938; Jenkins, 1938).

Allport's influence on the emerging field of personality psychology and his anticipation of issues of enduring significance in personality theory and research are well known (see, e.g., Craik, Hogan, & Wolfe, 1993). We have discussed above his efforts to reconcile analytic and interpretive approaches and his emphasis on the structure and organization of the individual personality. Further, on account of his pioneering contribution to the lexical study of traits (Allport & Odbert, 1936), as well his insistence that "a theory of personality requires more than a descriptive taxonomy" of traits, John and Robins (1993) claim Allport as the "father and critic of the Five-Factor Model" (pp. 225, 215). (We mention below the influence of Allport's concepts of motivation and the self.) Cohler (1993) has succinctly summarized Allport's importance to the field of personality:

> Allport's primary contribution to the study of the person may be less a matter of theoretical notions, methodological prescriptions, or empirical work than of his uncanny ability to comprehend the major issues in the field. As early as his first papers, Allport was aware of the fundamental problems confronting those who wished to study persons, such as the problem of distinguishing between text and interpretation, the advantages and drawbacks of individual difference formulations in the study of personality structure, the fact that traits as well as environments were ever-changing, and the challenges of accounting for continuity and change in lives over time. (p. 142)

Murray: Expanding Disciplinary Boundaries

Henry Murray came to the study of personality by way of psychoanalysis and abnormal psychology. Trained originally in medicine and in biochemistry, Murray chose a career in "depth psychology" after encountering the work of Jung and Freud. Only after accepting a position as assistant director of Morton Prince's Harvard Psychological Clinic in 1926, however, did he realize that the academic psychology of the time had very little in common with psychoanalysis (Murray, 1940; Murray, 1967; Robinson, 1992; Triplet, 1992). At a time when psychologists were struggling to define and delimit the disciplinary boundaries of their field, Murray's unorthodox and divergent interests were not acceptable to proponents of a strictly scientific psychology; in fact, they almost cost him his position at Harvard (Triplet, 1983).

Murray's eclectic, multimethod approach reflected his medical training and the nonpositivist philosophy of science of Whitehead and Henderson (Laughlin, 1973; Robinson, 1992), as well as the theories of Freud and Jung. Yet at the same time, Murray's background in biochemistry permeated his work; for example, in the explicit analogy between his classification of the "variables of personality" and the periodic table of chemistry (1938, pp. 142–143). The difficulty of such an eclectic enterprise is perhaps indicated by Murray's numerous revisions of his system of personality variables (Murray, 1951, 1968, 1977) and by the tentative titles he used for these works (e.g., "Preparations for the Scaffold of a Comprehensive System"; Murray, 1959).

While *Explorations in Personality* was praised in a representative mainstream review (Elliott, 1939) as "by far the most comprehensive attempt to bring Freudian psychology and experimental psychology into line with each other" (p. 453), the tenor of the review was decidedly mixed. On the one hand, Elliott noted that as a practicing psychoanalyst, Murray was "unique among those who hold a major position in psychology in a leading American university" (p. 453). He was impressed with the new tests and procedures (especially the Thematic Apperception Test) and with Murray's analysis of the variables of personality and environment. On the other hand, Elliott suggested that psychoanalysis was unproven and unscientific and criticized Murray for overlooking existing work in experimental and differential psychology as well as for insufficient use of statistics. He considered the book's single case study too speculative.

According to Triplet (1983, 1992), Murray's work had a profound effect on the expansion of the disciplinary boundaries of personality psychology. By demonstrating the use of experimental techniques to investigate psychoanalytic concepts, by teaching courses on abnormal and dynamic psychology in a prestigious academic psychology department, and by inspiring a large number of graduate students, Murray played an important part in expanding the definition of personality psychology to include psychoanalytic theories that had earlier "had pariah status in academia" (Smith, 1990, p. 537). While he advocated the interpretive study of lives, his most enduring legacy was probably the catalog of "variables of personality" (the title of Chapter 3 of *Explorations*; see Danziger, 1997) and the Thematic Apperception Test (Morgan & Murray, 1935).

Murray's diagnostic council method was generally overlooked, however (McLeod, 1992). Although variants of the approach were used in later assessment settings such as the Office of Strategic Services (OSS), and the Institute for Personality Assessment and Research (IPAR) at the University of California (MacKinnon, 1975), as well as in organizations such as AT&T (Bray, 1982), the practical demands of assessment even in those well-financed settings led assessors to base decisions "on statistical averages of ratings, rather than on discussion" (McLeod, 1992, p. 10). Perhaps only when executives of the very highest levels (and salaries) were to be assessed, could the full range of person-focused techniques be financially justified.

Cattell and the Measurement Imperative

The third major figure in the formative years of American personality psychology was Raymond Cattell. Cattell was born and educated in England (with an undergraduate degree in chemistry and a doctorate in psychology). He was greatly influenced by his assistantships at the University of London with Charles Spearman,[12] who first developed the technique of factor analysis, and later at Columbia University with E. L. Thorndike. Most of his professional career was spent at the University of Illinois, where he introduced many conceptual refinements and elaborated methodological developments, especially concerning the use of correlation, factor analysis, and other multivariate techniques, into the field of personality. Taking seriously Thorndike's famous dictum about measurement as well as the early work on intelligence testing, Cattell prefaced his first major book on personality with the assertion that "it is on measurement that all further scientific advance depends" (1946, p. iv). He went on to argue that "the ideal of a science of personality description [is] to build its traits upon a foundation of objective test measurements, as has been done to a very large extent in the analysis of abilities" (p. 210).

Kinds of Data

In reviewing the extant literature on personality measurement, Cattell first distinguished among different types of data (1946, pp. 10, 210–213; chaps. 9–11): ratings by skilled judges (R data), self-ratings (S data), and measurements on tests or experimental situations (T data). (Later he added life-outcome or L data to the list; see Cattell, 1957.) He believed that in the long run, T data were the soundest; but since for the foreseeable future objective tests could not measure everything of importance, he preferred ratings (1946, p. 294).

Kinds of Personality Traits

Like Allport, Cattell adopted trait as the fundamental conceptual unit of personality; but at the same time he also, in the spirit of Murray, distinguished motivational or "dynamic traits" (also called ergic traits or ergs) from stylistic or "temperament traits," as well as "ability traits." In his view, each kind of trait had its own pattern of correlational relationships among its component variables and the external situation: Thus, dynamic trait variables "change most in response to change of incentives" and showed complex higher-order correlations, while temperament trait variables "change least in response to any change in the field" (1946, p. 167). Cattell's major contribution to personality was his analysis of temperament traits via mathematical and statistical techniques.

The Search for Personality Coherence through Factor Analysis

Given the enormous array of data available to the personality psychologist—"too many variables, and too many influences behind these variables" (1946, p. 272)—Cattell turned to correlation and other multivariate techniques for clarification. Believing that the essence of a trait was *covariation* or correlation, he concluded that the "most potent method of attacking the tangle is to work out correlation coefficients between the inconveniently multitudinous variables abounding in the subject and to seek some smaller number of 'behind the scenes' or underlying variables, known as factors" (p. 272).

Cattell's first major investigation of personality (1945) used peer ratings of 208 men on 35 trait-word clusters derived from the exhaustive Allport and Odbert (1936) list of 4,504 traits. After carrying out a factor analysis of these data, Cattell studied various rotations and finally settled on an oblique rotation that yielded 12 factors, which were also consistent with cluster studies carried out by other investigators. (The rotations process, which could now be done on a personal computer in seconds, took 6 months!) He concluded that these 12 factors represented "the established primary traits" (1946, Chaps. 10–12).

Cattell thus introduced or established many conceptions and techniques that are an enduring part of contemporary personality psychology. His distinction between different kinds of data (especially the difference between R and S data, on the one hand, and T data, on the other) re-emerged in the 1970s dispute about the cross-situational and temporal consistency of personality (Block, 1977; Epstein, 1979). His formulation and defense of the "lexical hypothesis," that "language covers all aspects [of personality] that are important for other human beings" (1946, pp. 215–216),[13] prefigured the adjective-based trait assessments widely used over the next several decades. Finally, his discussion and examples of rotated factor analyses set the stage for an entire approach to personality, though there would be considerable controversy about his particular methods and assumptions. For example, Eysenck preferred orthogonal rather than oblique rotations, and so he argued that Cattell's 12 oblique factors were really equivalent to his own three orthogonal "superfactors" of Extraversion, Neuroticism, and Psychoticism (Eysenck & Eysenck, 1985). Yet in spite of Cattell's general influence, few personality psychologists adopted his full views about personality measurement as outlined in his "specification equation" for predicting behavior (Cattell, 1957, pp. 302–306).

Psychometric Technology

We have seen that the prestige and apparent success of intelligence testing at the beginning of the 20th century convinced many personality psychologists that personality could (and should) be measured in a similar way, by scales of "items." While factor analysis was the apotheosis of this ideal, the same general conviction guided the construction of numerous other scales, inventories, and questionnaires not based on factor analysis: omnibus instruments such as the Bernreuter Personality Inventory, Minnesota Multiphasic Personality Inventory, California Personality Inventory (CPI; Gough, 1957; 1987), Adjective Check List, and Personality Research Form (PRF; Jackson, 1974), as well as countless scales designed to measure particular personality characteristics.

As statistical methods of scale construction and refinement became increasingly sophisticated, the psychometric rule book expanded to include matters such as test–retest reliability, internal and cross-situational consistency (Cronbach, 1951), convergent–discriminant validity (Campbell & Fiske, 1959), correction for attenuation, and the distinction between "trait" and "state." Some psychologists protested that psychometric rules unduly constrained personality theorizing and research because they did not take account of nonlinear, interactive, or functionally substitutable (but not correlated) relationships among components of a concept (see Atkinson, 1982; Fleming, 1982; Winter et al., 1998). At the end of the century, the increased popularity of chaos theory and associated mathematical concepts (e.g., Vallacher & Nowak, 1997) suggested possible alternatives to the classical psychometric rules.

THE FOURFOLD FLOWERING OF PERSONALITY PSYCHOLOGY: TRAITS, MOTIVES, COGNITIONS, AND CONTEXT

By 1946, shortly after the end of World War II, the main concepts and issues of personality psychology were established. For almost all personality psychologists, traits were viewed as a major element of personality. Many would say traits were the *only* personality element (e.g., A. Buss, 1989); others, however, argued for the fundamental distinctiveness and importance of motives as well (see Winter et al., 1998). Rating scales and questionnaires were firmly established as the preferred method of personality measurement, especially for traits.

Our account of the next 50 years of personality psychology is framed in terms of the four elements or classes of theory and variables and theories introduced by Winter (1996): traits, motives, cognitions, and social context. The articles in the special issue of the *Journal of Personality* on "levels and domains in personality" (Emmons & McAdams, 1995) offer a similar scheme for organizing personality variables.

PERSONALITY TRAITS

In personality psychology, the concept of *trait* has been used to denote consistent intercorrelated patterns of behavior, especially expressive or stylistic behavior (see Winter et al., 1998, pp. 232–233). Our discussion of traits will be organized around four rather disparate topics, because these reflect the main lines of theorizing and research about traits. Perhaps the most frequently studied topic has been the number, nature, and organization of "basic" traits. Personality psychologists have used three different strategies. In approximate order of popularity, they are: factor analysis and related mathematical techniques; rational or a priori theorizing, often involving the construction of typologies; and the idiographic approach, which essentially ignores the question of "basic" traits. After discussing developments in each of these three strategies, we turn to another frequently studied topic, namely the relation between traits and biology.

Factor Analytic Study of Traits

With the availability of cheap, powerful computers, factor analysis became the method of choice for understanding traits. By the end of the century, many personality psychologists had reached a working consensus that the trait domain could be described, at least at the broadest and most abstract level, by five orthogonally rotated factors or clusters of traits (see John, 1990; also Chapter 4, this volume; McCrae & Costa, Chapter 5, this volume; Wiggins, 1996), measured in a variety of alternative ways (see Goldberg, 1992): Extraversion or Surgency, Agreeableness, Conscientiousness, Neuroticism, and Openness (often called the five-factor model or

"Big Five"). Nevertheless, Eysenck and his followers (Eysenck & Eysenck, 1985) have continued to argue that the three factors measured by the Eysenck Personality Questionnaire (EPQ)—Extraversion, Neuroticism, and Psychoticism—are sufficient (see the exchange between Costa & McCrae, 1992a, 1992b; and Eysenck, 1992a, 1992b). Block (1995) challenged many of the underlying assumptions (going back to Cattell's earliest studies) of factor-analytic techniques in general as well as the five-factor model in particular.

Alternative Analyses of Traits

Rationally and Empirically Constructed Scales

Still, the five-factor model of traits had not achieved complete hegemony at the end of the century. Several personality psychologists developed trait measures based on alternative methods: Gough (1957) developed the CPI by using contrasting groups to construct scales for positive lay or "folk" concepts such as "achievement," "sociability," or "dominance." In a later revision (Gough, 1987), he used clustering techniques to construct three "vectors" that bore some resemblance to Eysenck's three factors. Scales of the PRF were labeled with the names of the Murray needs, although they appeared to function essentially as traits.

Typologies

From time to time, personality psychologists have proposed certain syndromes or types, or coherently organized bundles of personality characteristics that define an interesting pattern. The Myers–Briggs Type Indicator (Myers, 1962; see also Thorne & Gough, 1991), which in the last decades of the century became one of the most widely used personality tests, was developed on the basis of Jung's (1923/1971) typological combination of traits (Extraversion–Introversion) and predominant "functions" (thinking, feeling, sensing, and intuiting).

Jung's typology and Gough's vectors are both comprehensive, that is, presumed to cover all people. Other personality psychologists have used types and typologies in a more limited way, to formalize observations about interesting cases or summarize complex data patterns. For example, Freud wrote about the anal type (1908/1959a) and various character types (1916/1957). Murray (1955/1981) described an "Icarus" type. In recent years, psychologists have used Q-sort methods and inverse (P) factor analysis to define types: for example, Block's (1971) account of how personality develops over time, Wink's (1992) description of different forms of narcissism, and York & John's (1992) use of Rank's theory to interpret patterns of adult women's lives.

The Idiographic Approach

In spite of the popularity and prestige of factor analysis, the idiographic approach, which rejects the need to search for underlying "basic" trait factors and instead draws upon the broad lexicon for whatever trait adjectives fit a particular person, has continued to survive (West, 1983; Winter, 1996, Chap. 11).

Biological Basis of Traits

From the time of Galen's famous theory of humors, people have speculated about links between personality, or mind, and biology, or body. For example, Freud anchored his theory in biology, and Murray (1938) defined needs as "physico-chemical" forces in the brain (p. 124). In the mid-20th-century, Eysenck began a sustained effort to link the trait factors of Extraversion, Neuroticism, and Psychoticism to individual differences in nervous system structures and functioning. Early on (Eysenck, 1957, 1967), he used Pavlovian concepts of excitation and inhibition; later (Eysenck & Eysenck, 1985; Eysenck, 1990), he turned to arousal and such brain structures as the reticular formation and the limbic system. Gray (1981, 1987; see also Pickering & Gray, Chapter 10, this volume) proposed an alternative factor structure of traits and a correspondingly different conception of their biological bases.

Cloninger (1991, 1998) proceeded in the opposite direction, using individual differences in chemically defined neural pathways to define scales reflecting personality traits. Heritability studies flourished as a way to estimate genetic contributions to trait differences. For all of the progress and excitement, though, definitive and replicable results linking personality and biology still remained somewhat elusive at the end of the century (see D. Buss, 1990; Zuckerman, 1991; and Winter, 1996, Chap. 14).

MOTIVATIONAL CONCEPTS IN PERSONALITY

The personality construct of *motive* is based on the fundamental postulate that most behavior is oriented toward a *goal* and shows intelligent variation in moving toward the goal (or away from it, with avoidance motives), in response to incentives, circumstances, opportunities, obstacles, and other current goals. Thus motives contrast with traits, for as Murray (1938, pp. 56–58) pointed out, a given motive may be associated with an indefinitely large number of quite different actions; correspondingly, the same action may serve multiple and varied goals (see also Pervin, 1983; 1989; Little, Chapter 20, this volume). Thus the concept of "alpha," which is so essential for consistency-based trait concepts, has little meaning for motives. In one form or another, the distinction between motives and traits appears in the theorizing of many personality psychologists (see Pervin, 1994; Winter et al., 1998).

Motive Concepts in the Psychoanalytic Tradition

Nature and Organization of Motives

Freud placed motivation at the center of personality. He argued that all behavior was motivated and grouped human motives into a few broad, general classes (rather than the long lists of specific "instincts" compiled by 19th-century biologists and psychologists): self-preservation; libidinal or sexual motives; and aggressive motives or "death instinct" (see Freud 1916–1917/1961–1963, 1920/1955, and 1933/1964). While such a grouping had roots in Western thought as far back as Empedocles (5th century B.C.E.), Freud's vigorous insistence on the libidinal (and later, aggressive) motivational roots of human behavior led him to impressive accomplishments in the analysis of surprising and unusual behavior, as well as cultural symbols. (Analysis of symbolism, often by psychologists who departed from psychoanalytic theory, e.g., Jung, von Franz, Henderson, Jacobi, & Jaffe, 1964, also made important contributions to cultural studies and the humanities.)

Many post-Freudian theorists rephrased Freud's dualistic motivational theory. For example, Bakan's (1966) concepts of "agency" and "communion" stimulated a good deal of empirical research (Helgeson, 1994; Wiggins, 1991; Wiggins & Trobst, Chapter 26, this volume), whereas Winter (1996, Chap. 5) linked Freud's libidinal and aggressive motive groupings to the TAT-measured affiliation and power motives.

Drawing eclectically on psychoanalytic theory and its neo-Freudian variants and basing his conclusions on an intensive study of a group of normal adult males, Murray (1938) constructed an empirically based catalog of 20 needs or motives[14] that has been widely accepted by later personality psychologists, either as a general list measured by questionnaires, such as the PRF, or as the basis for elaborate research programs measuring particular motives (e.g., McClelland, Atkinson, Clark, & Lowell, 1953, on the achievement motive; see also C. Smith, 1992).

Related Personality Concepts Deriving from Psychoanalytic Motivational Theory

Freud's claim that all behavior was motivated naturally entailed the concept of unconscious motives, or motives that were out of awareness. To explain *why* motives might become unconscious, Freud postulated the structures of id, ego, and superego; to answer the question of *how,* he introduced the notion of defense mechanisms that transform libidinal and aggressive motives in varied ways so as to render them "safe," thereby reducing anxiety. Anna Freud (1937/1946) elaborated the nature and operation of the defense mechanisms more fully.

Over the years, psychologists have carried out a good deal of experimental research to evaluate psychoanalytic theory and especially defense mechanisms such as repression (see e.g., Cramer, 1991; Eriksen & Pierce, 1968; Fisher & Greenberg, 1977; and Sears, 1943). The concept of an "unconscious," however, remained controversial, especially to such behaviorist psychologists as Skinner (1953).[15] However, advances in the study of cognition suggested ways to understand or translate psychoanalytic concepts in terms of sophisticated mechanisms of information processing (Erdelyi, 1974, 1985; see also Kihlstrom, 1990, and Chapter 17, this volume). At the same time, the research program on subliminal psychodynamic activation by Silverman and his colleagues (Weinberger & Silverman, 1990) provided a striking demonstration of unconscious processes as well as specific psychodynamic motives. Some psychologists preferred more theoretically neutral concepts, such as "implicit" psychological mechanisms (Greenwald & Banaji, 1995), to describe these "unconscious" effects.

Intrinsic Motivation

As a reaction against what he considered to be the excessive psychoanalytic (and behaviorist) search for childhood motivational origins of adult behavior, Allport introduced the notion of the "functional autonomy" of motives (1937), by which he meant that the motives actually influencing here-and-now adult behavior are not (or are not any longer) derived from original "primitive" or "primary" drives, such as libido or childhood experiences. More formally, functional autonomy presumes an "acquired system of motivation in which the tensions involved are not of the same kind as the antecedent tensions from which the acquired system developed" (Allport, 1961, p. 229).

From the beginning, the concept of functional autonomy was criticized, and it is fair to say that personality psychologists have not accepted it. However, Allport's argument certainly anticipated several important motivational developments in the latter decades of the 20th century: (1) the notion that age-graded tasks derived from cultural imperatives create "motivation" through such mechanisms as "life tasks," "goals," or "personal projects" (Cantor & Zirkel, 1990); (2) the concept of intrinsic motivation (Deci, 1975), which holds that activity can generate its own motivation; (3) Rogers's (1959) concept of actualization as a motivational force, i.e., that capacities create motivation; and even (4) the notion that personality develops by discontinuous "stages," or nonlinear reorganizations of what has gone before.

Measuring Motives through Thematic Apperception

Among the many novel assessment procedures introduced in Murray's *Explorations in Personality,* the Thematic Apperception Test or TAT (Morgan & Murray, 1935) is undoubtedly the most famous and widely used. Although psychologists developed many ways to interpret and score the TAT (see Gieser & Stein, in press), the empirically derived measures of motivation pioneered by McClelland deserve special mention (see Winter, 1998), though they have sometimes been completely ignored by some reviewers of personality assessment (e.g., Rorer, 1990, p. 698). Having been trained at Yale University during the ascendancy of Hull's rigorous behaviorism, McClelland and his associates used experimental procedures to arouse such motives as hunger and, later, achievement (McClelland et al., 1953), affiliation, and power (see C. Smith, 1992). Motive scoring systems were defined by observing the changes in thematic apperception produced by arousal.

Application to Cognate Fields

Using these thematic apperceptive measures, McClelland expanded the application of personality psychology into other social sciences. The achievement motive, for example, emerged as a major personality impetus to entrepreneurship and economic growth (McClelland, 1961; Spangler, 1992), whereas the power motive is related to charisma and management success (Winter, 1996, Chap. 5). Under certain circumstances, power motivation is associated with sympathetic nervous system arousal and thereby cardiovascular problems, lowered immune system functioning, and infectious diseases (McClelland, 1989). High power and low affiliation motives are linked to aggression and war (Winter, 1993).

Psychometric Critique

The early popularity of TAT-based motive measures diminished somewhat in reaction to criticisms about (1) low internal consistency and temporal reliability, and (2) the consistent lack of correlation between TAT measures and questionnaire measures of the presumed "same" construct. For a variety of reasons (see Atkinson, 1982; Winter, 1996, Chap. 5), many methodological canons traditionally applied to measures of traits are not fully appropriate to motive concepts and thematic apperceptive measures. Weinberger and McClelland (1990) argued that TAT and direct questionnaire measures reflected two fundamentally different motive systems—one unconscious or "implicit," the other conscious and self-attributed. The meta-analysis by Spangler (1992) supports this conclusion.

COGNITIONS AND PERSONALITY

The "cognitive revolution" of the late 1950s and early 1960s had major effects on personality (see Blake & Ramsey, 1951, for an early review). Kelly (1955) developed a cognitive theory of personality, based on the person's construct system and dispensing completely with motivation. Although his direct influence was confined to clinical psychology and consumer psychology (Jankowicz, 1987), his *indirect* effect on personality was great. Several measures involving cognitive style and cognitive complexity were inspired by Kelly's ideas (Winter, 1996, pp. 198–210),[16] and Mischel, a former Kelly student, used cognitive concepts to broaden learning theories of personality (Mischel & Shoda, 1995; see also Cantor, 1990).

Attributional Style

The development of causal attribution theory in social psychology led to a parallel concern with attributional style (or explanatory style) as a personality variable (see Weiner, 1990; Weiner & Graham, Chapter 24, this volume). Although attributions are surely related to emotions and motivation, the relationships are complex and probably run in both directions. The explanatory style concept has generated considerable research on depression, performance, health and other significant life outcomes (see Winter, 1996, pp. 269–277).

"Self"-Related Personality Variables

Although as far back as the 1930s Allport called attention to the importance of the self[17] for personality integration and functioning, the advent of the cognitive revolution brought a proliferation of "self-" related variables in personality psychology (see Markus & Cross, 1990; Robins, Norem, Cheek, Chapter 18, this volume): the self-concept (Wylie, 1974–1979), self-esteem (Rosenberg, 1979), self-monitoring (Snyder, 1987), and self-awareness (Carver & Scheier, 1981). Classic early 20th-century concepts of the role of the "generalized other" (George Herbert Mead) and the "looking-glass self" (Charles Horton Cooley) were blended in with later conceptions to create the symbolic interactionism approach (see Gergen & Gordon, 1968). With the advent of postmodernism and the notion of multiple selves (Gergen, 1991) came the related personality concept of a "dialogical self" (Hermans, Kempen, & van Loon, 1992).

Erikson's (1950/1963) psychosocial elaboration of psychoanalysis was most fully developed around the concept of ego identity (Erikson, 1959/1980), which involved congruence between people's inner sense of self and the external social definition they receive. Using the identity concept, Erikson analyzed the lives of historical figures, such as Luther (1958) and Gandhi (1969). Meanwhile, Marcia and his colleagues (Marcia, Waterman, Matteson, Archer, & Orlofsky, 1993) developed methods for measuring different aspects of the identity concept. Given its conceptual status as a bridge between the individual and society, identity also proved particularly useful in analyzing *social identity*, or the role that social variables, such as gender, race, class, and nationality play in the formation of personality (see Gurin, Miller, & Gurin, 1980; Tajfel, 1982). McAdams (1985) has suggested a "life story" model of identity, with power and intimacy motivation, as well as ego development, as component variables.

Finally, coincident with the "self psychology" of Kohut (1985) and perhaps Lasch's (1979) analysis of the late-century United States as a "culture of narcissism," came increased research interest in the psychoanalytic concept of narcissism (John & Robins, 1994; Wink, 1992).

The Social–Political Context of "Cognitive" Research in Personality

Research trends always develop in particular social and political contexts. Since cognitive personality theory focuses on internal processes that are in principle modifiable, rather than on objective conditions of existence, as the major mediators (if not "causes") of behavior and well-being, it is especially congenial to an individualist (rather than collectivist or contextual) perspective. If we only need to change people's *perceptions,* then the existing *realities* of status, power, and oppression will continue without critique or challenge. Thus Sampson (1981) observed that the emphasis on cognition arose at the height of the Cold War, just after the apogee of McCarthyism—a time in the United States when it was dangerous to challenge the social order and advocate change. In popular culture, this was the heyday of Norman Vincent Peale's best-selling *The Power of Positive Thinking* (1952), a quasi-religious exhortation to subjective self-transformation instead of political action.

THE SOCIAL CONTEXT OF PERSONALITY

In many different (though apparently unrelated) ways, personality psychologists have long been concerned about context. Early in the 20th century, personality came under the sway of behaviorism and the prestige of experimental research on learning. Later, the culture and personality movement stressed the broader social matrix in which personality is formed. In the late 1960s and 1970s, the situationist critique of personality caused a major crisis in the field and led to a re-examination of fundamental postulates and research methods. Finally in the 1980s and 1990s, the rise of "cultural psychology" and the influence of feminist and other critical perspectives from the humanities, as well as a more global perspective, showed signs of generating new interest in the social and cultural macrocontexts of personality.

The Influence of Behaviorism

Even as the early personality psychologists were developing questionnaire measures of certain socially important traits, the early behaviorists, such as Watson, were trying to reduce personality to conditioning and instrumental learning processes. Watson and Rayner's (1920) famous "Little Albert" demonstration had an enduring influence, despite its many methodological faults and lack of consistent replication (see Harris, 1979; Winter, 1996, pp. 531–534). At Yale University during the 1930s and 1940s, the Institute of Human Relations under the leadership of Hull tried to bring about a synthesis of psychoanalytic theory and an experimental psychology self-consciously striving for immaculate purity of method (see Morawski, 1986). One result was a series of experimental studies of psychoanalytic concepts (Sears, 1943); another was the Miller–Dollard learning-based theory of personality (Dollard & Miller, 1950; Miller & Dollard, 1941). At the behaviorist extreme, Skinner (1953) proposed to dispense with personality theory and constructs altogether, in favor of the concept of reinforcement history.

The Rise and Fall of Culture and Personality

The culture and personality movement was born in the 1930s, as anthropologists and psychoanalysts became interested in each other's disciplines (see Inkeles & Levinson, 1954; Kluckhohn, 1954). The underlying theoretical notion was that a culture's distinctive pattern of childrearing, derived from its broader characteristics and values, formed distinctive personalities in its children; thus the adults in each culture would have similar or "modal" adult personalities (see Benedict, 1946, for a culture and personality study of Japan). Early financial support came from such sources as the Social Sciences Research Council's Committee on Personality and Culture to support cross-cultural studies (e.g., Mead, 1937).[18] Later, during World War II, culture and personality research contributed to the Allied war effort with studies of enemies (and allies), as well as methodological handbooks (see examples cited in Inkeles & Levinson, 1954).

After the war, culture and personality studies of particular cultures were collected in interdisciplinary readers (Kluckhohn, Murray, & Schneider, 1953; see also Y. Cohen, 1961; and LeVine, 1982). Interdisciplinary programs, such as Harvard's Department of Social Relations evolved to support the enterprise. The development of the Human Relations Area Files (Murdock, 1982) made possible cross-cultural research on personality (e.g., Whiting & Child, 1953). By the late 1950s, however, the culture and personality movement seemed to have run its course. With the hot war won and the Cold War dominated by political scientists and economists operating in an atmosphere of suspicion and orthodoxy, the intellectual climate had clearly changed. Moreover, the methodological and conceptual critiques leveled by Inkeles and Levinson (1954) met with no real response. Culture and personality research, they argued, oversimplified "culture" by assuming uniformity and homogeneity, while neglecting social structure. The field relied almost exclusively on impressionistic or small-sample methods. By the early 1960s, culture and personality had almost disappeared, although some researchers continued to develop new methods and carry out cross-national personality research (e.g., Barrett & Eysenck, 1984; McClelland, 1961). House (1981) offered a sophisticated delineation of the distinctive influences of social structure and culture in relation to personality.

Mischel's Critique and Personality's Response

Although its title, *Personality and Assessment,* was innocent enough, Mischel's book (1968) had the effect of a bombshell. Reviewing the field, Mischel claimed that the usefulness of broad dispositional personality variables had been seriously overstated, because (1) such variables did not show cross-situational or temporal consistency, and (2) they were not highly correlated with behavioral outcomes.[19] The term "personality coefficient" was derisively applied to any correlation "between .20 and .30 which is found persistently when virtually any personality dimension inferred from a questionnaire is related to almost any conceivable external criterion. . . . Generally such correlations are too low to have value for most individual assessment purposes" (Mischel, 1968, pp. 77–78). In place of the usual array of personality variables, Mischel advocated the use of a highly specific, almost idiographic, version of social learning theory. Later Mischel and Shoda (1995; see also Mischel and Shoda, Chapter 7, this volume) emphasized cognitive variables, so that his theory, along with that of Bandura (1989; see also Chapter 6, this volume), became known as social cognitive theory.

After some initial confusion and disorientation, personality psychologists found their bearings and replied (see Winter, 1996, Chap. 16). Block (1977) criticized Mischel's review of the literature as selective and partial, weighted heavily with studies involving one-shot experimental responses (Cattell's T data). Epstein (1979) showed that aggregating one-shot dependent variables across situations produced stronger relationships to personality. Funder and Ozer (1983) demonstrated that classic "situational" findings from social psychology, when expressed as correlations, were of the same magnitudes as "personality coefficients." Studies showed individual differences in consistency and in the explanatory power of situational versus personality variables (see Winter, 1996, pp. 582–584), and demonstrated interaction between personality and situation—either cross-sectional (Magnusson & Endler, 1977) or temporal (Caspi, Elder, & Bem, 1987). Researchers measured the precise nature of situations (Bem & Funder, 1978) and used context variables as moderators in relating personality to behavior and outcome. Moreover, as D. Buss (1987) pointed out, personality can affect situations, through processes of selection, evocation, and manipulation.

Cultural and Cross-Cultural Psychology

During the last decade of the century, perhaps as a response to the increasing globalization of economic, social, and intellectual life, personality psychology began to be influenced by the perspectives of cultural psychology (see Cole, 1996; Cross & Markus, Chapter 15, this volume; Shweder, 1991; Shweder & Sullivan, 1990). Some researchers studied psychological processes in particular cultures; others sought a more comprehensive cross-cultural framework (see Berry, Dasen, & Saraswathi, 1997). Hofstede (1980) identified four dimensions along which cultures can be compared: individualism–collectivism, power distance, orientation to uncertainty, and gendering of male–female relations. So far, though, only the first dimension has received much attention from personality psychologists interested in culture, as for example in the discussion of "self" by Markus and Kitayama (1991).

FUTURE DIRECTIONS AND THE "LESSONS OF HISTORY" FOR PERSONALITY PSYCHOLOGY

What lessons have we learned from our survey of the last century of personality psychology? What are the likely directions of future advance? Predictions are always perilous, but we permit ourselves two observations about likely future trends during the next few decades.

Importance of Context

First, we believe that personality psychology will need to pay increased attention to matters of context. Whatever the evolutionary origins, genetic basis, or physiological substrate of any aspect of personality, both its *level* and *channels of expression* will be strongly affected, in complex ways, by the multiple dimensions of social context: not only the immediate situational context, but also the larger contexts of age cohort, family, institution, social class, nation/culture, history, and (perhaps supremely) gender. We suggest that varying the social macrocontext will "constellate," or completely change, all other variables of personality—much as in the classic demonstrations of gestalt principles of perception.

To give a simple illustration (see Winter, 1996, p. 586): Personality variables, such as surgency, conscientiousness, power motivation, or attributional style may (or may not) have evolutionary, genetic, or physiological aspects. But consider how differently these variables would have been expressed on the morning of June 6, 1944, by (1) a white 20-year-old American man storming "Utah" Beach during the World War II Normandy invasion, and (2) a middle-aged Japanese American woman held in an "internment camp" for U.S. citizens and residents of Japanese ancestry, in the Utah (U.S.) desert.

Most macrocontexts involve power differentials or hegemony. As a kind of "force-field" (see Lewin, 1935), social power therefore affects the formation and expression of personality. This would be obvious in many other social sciences and humanities, influenced as they have been by Foucault, deconstructionism, feminist theory, and critical theory. Although psychology has been largely isolated from these intellectual currents, we believe that the field of personality can continue to ignore them only at its peril.

Complexity of Perspective

Personality is inherently complex, the result of many interacting forces ranging from biology to history. The postmodernist perspective merely emphasizes this complexity. To consider just one personality variable: Just as there is not a single "text" in literature, so also there may not be a single "self" but rather many selves. We suggest the following analogy: Personality may come to be seen as a series of interacting elements, all existing like a series of Windows computer applications. Over time, different personality "applications" are installed, opened, moved between foreground and background, modified, closed, even deleted. Although the sum total of available "personality" elements may have limits that are specifiable (though perhaps unique for each person), the current "on-line" personality may be complex and fluid.

In other fields of science, recognition of increased complexity has led to the development of "chaos theory" or "complexity theory," which is now being taken up by psychologists (e.g., Vallacher & Nowak, 1997). Because two basic postulates of personality psychology are (1) complexity of interaction among elements and (2) that earlier experience affects later behavior in ways that are at least somewhat irreversible (or reversible with greater difficulty than acquisition), the field seems ideally situated to take advantage of these new theoretical and methodological tools.

Diversity of People, Diversity of Personality Psychologists

A final "lesson" from the history of personality involves the background and training of many of its great figures over the past century. Consider that Freud started as a neurologist; Murray, as a surgeon with a doctorate in biochemistry; and Cattell, with an extensive background in statistics. Rogers enrolled in theological seminary before he turned to psychology, Eysenck originally planned to study physics, and Kelly was first an aeronautical engineer and then taught public speaking. Even Gordon Allport blended his studies of psychology with social ethics.

As a field, therefore, personality has been enormously enriched by the experiences and perspectives that these people brought from their original fields and interests. As our society increasingly recognizes the diversity of the persons we claim to interpret and analyze, personality psychology needs to insure that its theorists and researchers in the 21st century are drawn from a diverse (academic and extraacademic) background and that they are given diverse experiences *as a part of* their professional training.

NOTES

1. This is only one possible construction; in many cultures (China, for example) it would be unusual, if not impossible, to conceive of a skin-bounded individual body without at the same time considering the family (or kin-group, tribe, neighborhood, and nation).

2. Galton's work is one of the major foundations of correlation and psychological testing. It served his convictions that most human abilites were innate and that British civilization was inherently superior, and his advocacy of eugenics. These uncomfortable sociopolitical facts must be noted, because by shaping the ways in which questions are framed and the putatively "adequate" methods of answering them are evaluated, they may continue to exert subtle effects long after being overtly discarded. Thus the conceptions of "intelligence" implied by the methods of Galton and others influenced (from today's perspective, seriously impeded) our understanding of the *family* of multiple "intelligences."

3. Allport later tried (without success) to replace these terms with "dimensional" and "morphogenic," respectively (1962, p. 407).

4. Cattell's "specification equation" is perhaps the most fully developed example (1957, pp. 302–306) of such prediction equations.

5. The history of research on the authoritarian personality is illustrative and instructive in this respect. Conceived originally as a *critique* of existing structures of social and economic power, it became transformed into a measure of individual pathology as it moved "from Berlin to Berkeley" (Samelson, 1993).

6. Even Murray's biographical study of Melville remained largely unpublished (Robinson, 1992).

7. One extraordinary recent example is Nasby and Read's (1997) 283-page case study of Dodge Morgan, integrating analytic and interpretive approaches, published as an entire issue of the *Journal of Personality*.

8. See, for example, M. Smith (1990, p. 539).

9. A review of several studies of "character and temperament" had appeared 5 years earlier (Thurstone, 1916).

10. In 1925, when it was taken over by APA, it was renamed *Journal of Abnormal and Social Psychology*.

11. Although Allport's dissertation appears to have been the first on *personality* traits, a dissertation on character traits had appeared the previous year (Filter, 1921).

12. Like Galton and other early measurement theorists, Cattell endorsed the principles of eugenics (1987). His views on this topic—for example, that from an evolutionary perspective, democracy might be an "injustice and an unethical procedure" because it fosters the "parasitism" of the "less gifted" upon the "brains" of the "intelligent management and inventor types" (p. 113)—aroused considerable controversy when they became widely known in the late 1990s.

13. To this assertion, however, Cattell added an amusing postscript: "If machines had tongues they might rate human beings according to certain machine-handling traits . . . not . . . observable by or important to other human beings, while among dogs there might well be terms much concerned with the way human beings use their feet" (1946, p. 216).

14. Murray studied several additional needs less formally.

15. Some behaviorists simply ridiculed such concepts as the unconscious, whereas others tried to translate them; for example, as "behavior that has become unverbalizable, due to conflicting reinforcement contingencies."

16. Loevinger's concept and measure of ego development (1976), although directly drawn from psychoanalysis, shares substantial construct and empirical validity with cognitive complexity measures.

17. Later (e.g., Allport, 1961) the *proprium* or "essential selfhood."

18. Perhaps this support reflected a realization, on the part of significant elite groups, of growing U.S. world power and influence. In an analogous way, the waxing of the British Empire in the 19th century was associated with support for the emergence of anthropology as a discipline.

19. Mischel was not alone in these criticisms: Peterson (1965) and Vernon (1964) raised similar points at about the same time.

REFERENCES

Allport, F. H., & Allport, G. W. (1921). Personality traits: Their classification and measurement. *Journal of Abnormal Psychology and Social Psychology, 16,* 6-40.

Allport, G. W. (1921). Personality and character. *Psychological Bulletin, 18,* 441–455.

Allport, G. W. (1923). The Leipzig Congress of Psychology. *American Journal of Psychology, 34,* 612-615.

Allport, G. W. (1924a). The standpoint of Gestalt psychology. *Psyche, 4,* 354–361.

Allport, G. W. (1924b). The study of the undivided personality. *Journal of Abnormal and Social Psychology, 19,* 132–141.

Allport, G. W. (1927). Concepts of trait and personality. *Psychological Bulletin, 24,* 284–293.

Allport, G. W. (1928). A test for ascendance–submission. *Journal of Abnormal and Social Psychology, 23,* 118–136.

Allport, G. W. (1929). The study of personality by the intuitive method: An experiment in teaching from *The Locomotive God. Journal of Abnormal and Social Psychology, 24,* 14–27.

Allport, G. W. (1931). What is a trait of personality? *Journal of Abnormal and Social Psychology, 25,* 368–372.

Allport, G. W. (1937). *Personality: A psychological interpretation.* New York: Henry Holt.

Allport, G. W. (1942). *The use of personal documents in psychological science.* New York: Social Science Research Council.

Allport, G. W. (1961). *Pattern and growth in personality.* New York: Holt, Rinehart & Winston.

Allport, G. W. (1962). The general and the unique in psychological science. *Journal of Personality, 30,* 405–422.

Allport, G. W. (1965). *Letters from Jenny.* New York: Harcourt, Brace & World.

Allport, G. W. (1967). Gordon W. Allport. In E. G. Boring & G. Lindzey (Eds.), *A history of psychology in autobiography* (Vol. 5, pp. 1–25). New York: Appleton-Century-Crofts.

Allport, G. W., & Odbert, H. S. (1936). Trait-names: A psycho-lexical study. *Psychological Monographs, 47*(1, Whole No. 211), 1–171.

Allport, G. W., & Vernon, P. E. (1930). The field of personality. *Psychological Bulletin, 27,* 677–730.

Atkinson, J. W. (1982). Motivational determinants of thematic apperception. In A. J. Stewart (Ed.), *Motivation and society* (pp. 3–40). San Francisco: Jossey-Bass.

Bakan, D. (1966). *The duality of human existence.* Chicago: Rand McNally.

Bandura, A. (1989). Human agency in social cognitive theory. *American Psychologist, 44,* 1175–1184.

Barenbaum, N. B. (1997a). The case(s) of Gordon Allport. *Journal of Personality, 65,* 743–755.

Barenbaum, N. B. (1997b, April). The general and the unique: William Stern's "considerable influence" on Gordon Allport. In J. T. Lamiell (Chair), *William*

Stern's critical personalism in contemporary psychology. Symposium conducted at the meeting of the Eastern Psychological Association, Washington, DC.

Barenbaum, N. B. (1997c, June). *"The most revealing method of all": Gordon Allport and case studies.* Paper presented at the annual meeting of Cheiron, Richmond, VA.

Bargh, J. A. (1982). Attention and automaticity in the processing of self-relevant information. *Journal of Personality and Social Psychology, 43,* 425–436.

Barrett, P., & Eysenck, S. B. (1984). The assessment of personality factors across 25 countries. *Personality and Individual Differences, 5,* 615–632.

Bellah, R. N., Madsen, R., Sullivan, W. M., Swidler, A., & Tipton, S. M. (1985). *Habits of the heart: Individualism and commitment in American life.* Berkeley and Los Angeles: University of California Press.

Bem, D. J., & Funder, D. C. (1978). Predicting more of the people more of the time: Assessing the personality of situations. *Psychological Review, 85,* 485–501.

Benedict, R. (1946). *The chrysanthemum and the sword: Patterns of Japanese culture.* Boston: Houghton Mifflin.

Berry, J. W., Dasen, P. R., Saraswathi, T. S. (Eds.). (1997). *Handbook of cross-cultural psychology: Vol. 2. Basic processes and human development.* Boston: Allyn & Bacon.

Bills, A. G. (1938). Changing views of psychology as science. *Psychological Review, 45,* 377–394.

Blake, R. R., & Ramsey, G. V. (Eds.). (1951). *Perception: An approach to personality.* New York: Ronald Press.

Block, J. (1971). *Lives through time.* Berkeley, CA: Bancroft Books.

Block, J. (1977). Advancing the psychology of personality: Paradigmatic shift or improving the quality of research? In D. Magnusson & N. S. Endler (Eds.), *Personality at the crossroads: Current issues in interactional psychology* (pp. 37–63). Hillsdale, NJ: Erlbaum.

Block, J. (1995). A contrarian view of the five-factor approach to personality. *Psychological Bulletin, 117,* 187–215.

Bray, D. W. (1982). The assessment center and the study of lives. *American Psychologist, 37,* 180–189.

Burckhardt, J. (1954). *The civilization of the Renaissance in Italy.* New York: Modern Library. (Original work published 1860)

Burnham, J. C. (1968). Historical background for the study of personality. In E. F. Borgatta & W. W. Lambert (Eds.), *Handbook of personality theory and research* (pp. 3–81). Chicago: Rand McNally.

Buss, A. H. (1989). Personality as traits. *American Psychologist, 44,* 1378–1388.

Buss, D. M. (1987). Selection, evocation, and manipulation. *Journal of Personality and Social Psychology, 53,* 1214–1221.

Buss, D. M. (Ed.). (1990). Biological foundations of personality: Evolution, behavioral genetics, and psychophysiology [Special issue]. *Journal of Personality, 58*(1).

Camfield, T. M. (1969). *Psychologists at war: The history of American psychology and the First World War.* Unpublished doctoral dissertation, University of Texas, Austin.

Campbell, D. T., & Fiske, D. W. (1959). Convergent and discriminant validity by the multitrait–multimethod matrix. *Psychological Bulletin, 56,* 81–105.

Cantor, N. (1990). From thought to behavior: "Having" and "doing" in the study of personality and cognition. *American Psychologist, 45,* 735–750.

Cantor, N., & Zirkel, S. (1990). Personality, cognition, and purposive behavior. In L. Pervin (Ed.), *Handbook of personality: Theory and research* (pp. 135–164). New York: Guilford Press.

Carlson, R. (1971). Where is the person in personality research? *Psychological Bulletin, 75,* 203–219.

Carver, C. S., & Scheier, M. F. (1981). *Attention and self-regulation: A control theory approach to human behavior.* New York: Springer-Verlag.

Caspi, A., Elder, G. H., Jr., & Bem, D. J. (1987). Moving against the world: Life-course patterns of explosive children. *Developmental Psychology, 23,* 308–313.

Cattell, R. B. (1945). The description of personality. III: Principles and findings in a factor analysis. *American Journal of Psychology, 58,* 69–90.

Cattell, R. B. (1946). *Description and measurement of personality.* Yonkers-on-Hudson, NY: World Book.

Cattell, R. B. (1957). *Personality and motivation structure and measurement.* Yonkers-on-Hudson, NY: World Book.

Cattell, R. B. (1987). *Beyondism: Religion from science.* New York: Praeger.

Cloninger, C. R. (1991). Brain networks underlying personality development. In B. J. Carroll & J. E. Barrett (Eds.), *Psychopathology and the brain* (pp. 183–208). New York: Raven Press.

Cloninger, C. R. (1998). The genetics and psychobiology of the seven-factor model of personality. In K. R. Silk (Ed.), *Biology of personality disorders* (pp. 63–92). Washington, DC: American Psychiatric Press.

Cohen, S. (1983). The mental hygiene movement, the development of personality and the school: The medicalization of American education. *History of Education Quarterly, 23,* 123–149.

Cohen, Y. A. (1961). *Social structure and personality: A casebook.* New York: Holt, Rinehart & Winston.

Cohler, B. J. (1993). Describing lives: Gordon Allport and the "science" of personality. In K. H. Craik, R. Hogan, & R. N. Wolfe (Eds.), *Fifty years of personality psychology* (pp. 131–146). New York: Plenum Press.

Cole, M. (1996). *Cultural psychology: A once and future discipline.* Cambridge, MA: Harvard University Press.

Costa, P. T., & McCrae, R. R. (1992a). Four ways five factors are basic. *Personality and Individual Differences, 13,* 653–665.

Costa, P. T., & McCrae, R. R. (1992b). "Four ways five factors are *not* basic": Reply. *Personality and Individual Differences, 13,* 861–865.

Craik, K. H., Hogan, R., & Wolfe, R. N. (Eds.). (1993). *Fifty years of personality psychology.* New York: Plenum Press.

Cramer, P. (1991). *The development of defense mechanisms: Theory, research, and assessment.* New York: Springer-Verlag.

Cronbach, L. J. (1951). Coefficient alpha and the internal structure of tests. *Psychometrika, 16,* 297–334.

Danziger, K. (1990). *Constructing the subject: Historical origins of psychological research.* New York: Cambridge University Press.

Danziger, K. (1997). *Naming the mind: How psychology found its language.* Thousand Oaks, CA: Sage.

Deci, E. L. (1975). *Intrinsic motivation.* New York: Plenum Press.

Dickson, D. H., & Kelly, I. W. (1985). The "Barnum effect" in personality assessment: A review of the literature. *Psychological Reports, 57,* 367–382.

Dollard, J., & Miller, N. E. (1950). *Personality and psychotherapy: An analysis in terms of learning, thinking, and culture.* New York: McGraw-Hill.

Elliott, R. M. (1939). The Harvard *Explorations in personality* [Review of the book *Explorations in personality: A clinical and experimental study of fifty men of college age]. American Journal of Psychology, 52,* 453–462.

Emmons, R. A., & McAdams, D. P. (1995). Levels and domains in personality [Special issue]. *Journal of Personality, 63*(3).

Epstein, S. (1979). The stability of behavior: I. On predicting most of the people much of the time. *Journal of Personality and Social Psychology, 37,* 1097–1126

Erdelyi, M. H. (1974). A new look at the New Look: Perceptual defense and vigilance. *Psychological Review, 81,* 1–25.

Erdelyi, M. H. (1985). *Psychoanalysis: Freud's cognitive psychology.* New York: Freeman.

Eriksen, C. W., & Pierce, J. (1968). Defense mechanisms. In E. F. Borgatta & W. W. Lambert (Eds.), *Handbook of personality theory and research* (pp. 1007–1040). Chicago: Rand McNally.

Erikson, E. H. (1958). *Young man Luther.* New York: Norton.

Erikson, E. H. (1963). *Childhood and society* (2nd ed.). New York: Norton. (Original work published 1950)

Erikson, E. H. (1969). *Gandhi's truth.* New York: Norton.

Erikson, E. H. (1980). *Identity and the life cycle.* New York: Norton. (Original work published 1959)

Eysenck, H. J. (1957). *The dynamics of anxiety and hysteria.* London: Routledge & Kegan Paul.

Eysenck, H. J. (1967). *The biological basis of personality.* Springfield, IL: Charles C Thomas, Publisher.

Eysenck, H. J. (1990). Biological dimensions of personality. In L. Pervin (Ed.), *Handbook of personality: Theory and research* (pp. 244–276). New York: Guilford Press.

Eysenck, H. J. (1992a). Four ways five factors are *not* basic. *Personality and Individual Differences, 13,* 667–673.

Eysenck, H. J. (1992b). A reply to Costa and McCrae: P or A and C—the role of theory. *Personality and Individual Differences, 13*(8), 867–868.

Eysenck, H. J., & Eysenck, M. W. (1985). *Personality and individual differences: A natural science approach.* New York: Plenum Press.

Fernald, G. G. (1920). Character vs. intelligence in personality studies. *Journal of Abnormal Psychology, 15,* 1–10.

Filter, R. O. (1921). An experimental study of character traits. *Journal of Applied Psychology, 5,* 297–317.

Fisher, S., & Greenberg, R. P. (1977). *The scientific credibility of Freud's theories and therapy.* New York: Basic Books.

Fleming, J. (1982). Projective and psychometric approaches to measurement: The case of fear of success. In A. J. Stewart (Ed.), *Motivation and society* (pp. 63–96). San Francisco: Jossey-Bass.

Franz, C. E., & Stewart, A. J. (Eds.). (1994). *Women creating lives: Identities, resilience, and resistance.* Boulder, CO: Westview Press.

Freud, A. (1946). *The ego and the mechanisms of defense.* New York: International Universities Press. (Original work published 1937)

Freud, S. (1955). Beyond the pleasure principle. In J. Strachey (Ed.), *The standard edition of the complete psychological works of Sigmund Freud* (Vol. 18, pp. 7–64). London: Hogarth Press. (Original work published 1920)

Freud, S. (1957). Some character types met with in psycho-analytic work. In J. Strachey (Ed.), *The standard edition of the complete psychological works of Sigmund Freud* (Vol. 14, pp. 309–333). London: Hogarth Press. (Original work published 1916)

Freud, S. (1959a). Character and anal erotism. In J. Strachey (Ed.), *The standard edition of the complete psychological works of Sigmund Freud* (Vol. 9, pp. 169–175). London: Hogarth Press. (Original work published 1908)

Freud, S. (1959b). On the sexual theories of children. In J. Strachey (Ed.), *The standard edition of the complete psychological works of Sigmund Freud* (Vol. 9, pp. 209–226). London: Hogarth Press. (Original work published 1908)

Freud, S. (1961–1963). Introductory lectures on psychoanalysis. In J. Strachey (Ed.), *The standard edition of the complete psychological works of Sigmund Freud* (Vols. 15–16). London: Hogarth Press. (Original work published 1916–1917)

Freud, S. (1964). New introductory lectures on psychoanalysis. In J. Strachey (Ed.), *The standard edition of the complete psychological works of Sigmund Freud* (Vol. 22, pp. 5–182). London: Hogarth Press. (Original work published 1933)

Funder, D. C., & Ozer, D. J. (1983). Behavior as a function of the situation. *Journal of Personality and Social Psychology, 44,* 107–112.

Galton, F. (1884). Measurement of character. *Fortnightly Review, 36,* 179–185.
Garraty, J. A. (1981). Gordon Allport's rules for the preparation of life histories and case studies. *Biography, 4,* 283–292.
Gergen, K. J. (1991). *The saturated self: Dilemmas of identity in contemporary life.* New York: Basic Books.
Gergen, K. J., & Gordon, C. (Eds.). (1968). *The self in social interaction.* New York: Holt, Rinehart & Winston.
Gieser, L., & Stein, M. I. (Eds.). (in press). *Evocative images: The Thematic Apperception Test and the art of projection.* Washington, DC: APA Books.
Goldberg, L. R. (1992). The development of markers for the Big-Five factor structure. *Psychological Assessment, 4,* 26–42.
Gough, H. G. (1957). *California Psychological Inventory: Manual.* Palo Alto, CA: Consulting Psychologists Press.
Gough, H. G. (1987). *California Psychological Inventory: Administrator's guide.* Palo Alto, CA: Consulting Psychologists Press.
Gray, J. A. (1981). A critique of Eysenck's theory of personality. In H. J. Eysenck (Ed.), *A model for personality* (pp. 246–276). New York: Springer.
Gray, J. A. (1987). Perspectives on anxiety and impulsivity: A commentary. *Journal of Research in Personality, 21,* 493–509.
Greenwald, A. G., & Banaji, M. R. (1995). Implicit social cognition: Attitudes, self-esteem, and stereotypes. *Psychological Review, 102,* 4–27.
Guilford, J. P. (1938). [Review of the book *Personality: A psychological interpretation*]. *Journal of Abnormal and Social Psychology, 33,* 414–420.
Gurin, P., Miller, A. H., & Gurin, G. (1980). Stratum identification and consciousness. *Social Psychology Quarterly, 43,* 30–47.
Hale, N. G. (1971). *Freud and the Americans: The beginnings of psychoanalysis in the United States, 1876–1917.* New York: Oxford University Press.
Harris, B. (1979). Whatever happened to Little Albert? *American Psychologist, 34,* 151–160.
Helgeson, V. S. (1994). Relation of agency and communion to well-being: Evidence and potential explanations. *Psychological Bulletin, 116*(3), 412–428.
Hermans, H. J. M., Kempen, H. J. G., & van Loon, R. J. P. (1992). The dialogical self: Beyond individualism and rationalism. *American Psychologist, 47,* 23–33.
Hofstede, G. H. (1980). *Culture's consequences: International differences in work-related values.* Beverly Hills, CA: Sage.
Hollingworth, H. L. (1938). [Review of the book *Personality: A psychological interpretation*]. *Psychological Bulletin, 35,* 103–107.
House, J. S. (1981). Social structure and personality. In M. Rosenberg & R. H. Turner (Eds.), *Social psychology: Sociological perspectives* (pp. 525–561). New York: Basic Books.
Inkeles, A., & Levinson, D. J. (1954). National character: The study of modal personality and sociocultural systems. In G. Lindzey (Ed.), *Handbook of social psychology* (Vol. 2, pp. 977–1020). Cambridge, MA: Addison-Wesley.
Jackson, D. N. (1974). *The Personality Research Form.* Port Huron, MI: Research Psychologists Press.
Jankowicz, A. D. (1987). Whatever became of George Kelly? Applications and implications. *American Psychologist, 42*(5), 481–487.
Jenkins, J. G. (1938). [Review of the book *Personality: A psychological interpretation*]. *American Journal of Psychology, 51,* 777–778.
John, O. P. (1990). The "Big Five" factor taxonomy: Dimensions of personality in the natural language and in questionnaires. In L. A. Pervin (Ed.), *Handbook of personality: Theory and research* (pp. 66–100). New York: Guilford Press.
John, O. P., & Robins, R. W. (1993). Gordon Allport: Father and critic of the five-factor model. In K. H. Craik, R. Hogan, & R. N. Wolfe (Eds.), *Fifty years of personality psychology* (pp. 215–236). New York: Plenum Press.
John, O. P., & Robins, R. W. (1994). Accuracy and bias in self-perception: Individual differences in self-enhancement and the role of narcissism. *Journal of Personality and Social Psychology, 66,* 206–219.
Jung, C. G. (1971). *Psychological types.* In H. Read, M. Fundham, G. Adler, & W. McGuire (Eds.), *The collected works of C. G. Jung* (Vol. 6, pp. 1–495). Princeton: Princeton University Press. (Original work published 1923)
Jung, C. G., von Franz, M.-L., Henderson, J. L., Jacobi, J., & Jaffe, A. (1964). *Man and his symbols.* Garden City, NY: Doubleday.
Kelly, G. A. (1955). *The psychology of personal constructs.* 2 vols. New York: Norton.
Kihlstrom, J. F. (1990). The psychological unconscious. In L. Pervin (Ed.), *Handbook of personality: Theory and research* (pp. 445–464). New York: Guilford Press.
Kluckhohn, C. (1954). Culture and behavior. In G. Lindzey (Ed.), *Handbook of social psychology* (Vol. 2, pp. 921–976). Cambridge, MA: Addison-Wesley.
Kluckhohn, C., Murray, H. A., & Schneider, D. M. (1953). *Personality in nature, society, and culture.* New York: Knopf.
Kohut, H. (1985). *Self psychology and the humanities.* New York: Norton.
Lamiell, J. T. (1997). Individuals and the differences between them. In R. Hogan, J. Johnson, & S. Briggs (Eds.), *Handbook of personality psychology* (pp. 117–141). San Diego: Academic Press.
Lamiell, J. T. (1998). "Nomothetic" and "idiographic": Contrasting Windelband's understanding with contemporary usage. *Theory and Psychology, 8,* 23–38.
Lasch, C. L. (1979). *The culture of narcissism.* New York: Norton.
Laughlin, C. D. (1973). Discussion: The influence of Whitehead's organism upon Murray's personology. *Journal of the History of the Behavioral Sciences, 9,* 251–257.

LeVine, R. A. (1982). *Culture, behavior and personality* (2nd ed.). Chicago: Aldine.

Lewin, K. (1935). *A dynamic theory of personality.* New York: McGraw-Hill.

Loevinger, J. (1976). *Ego development: Conceptions and theories.* San Francisco: Jossey-Bass.

MacKinnon, D. W. (1975). IPAR's contribution to the conceptualization and study of creativity. In I. A. Taylor & J. W. Getzels (Eds.), *Perspectives in creativity* (pp. 60–89). Chicago: Aldine.

Magnusson, D., & Endler, N. S. (1977). *Personality at the crossroads: Current issues in interactional psychology.* Hillsdale, NJ: Erlbaum.

Marcia, J. E., Waterman, A. S., Matteson, D. R., Archer, S. L., & Orlofsky, J. L. (1993). *Ego identity: A handbook for psychosocial research.* New York: Springer-Verlag.

Markus, H., & Cross, S. (1990). The interpersonal self. In L. Pervin (Ed.), *Handbook of personality: Theory and research* (pp. 576–608). New York: Guilford Press.

Markus, H. R., & Kitayama, S. (1991). Culture and the self: Implications for cognition, emotion, and motivation. *Psychological Review, 98,* 224–253.

McAdams, D. P. (1985). *Power, intimacy, and the life story.* Homewood, IL: Dorsey.

McAdams, D. P. (1997). A conceptual history of personality psychology. In R. Hogan, J. Johnson, & S. Briggs (Eds.), *Handbook of personality psychology* (pp. 3–39). San Diego: Academic Press.

McAdams, D. P., & Ochberg, R. L. (Eds.). (1988). Psychobiography and life narratives [Special issue]. *Journal of Personality, 56*(1).

McAdams, D. P., & West, S. G. (1997). Introduction: Personality psychology and the case study. *Journal of Personality, 65,* 757–783.

McClelland, D. C. (1961). *The achieving society.* Princeton, NJ: Van Nostrand.

McClelland, D. C. (1989). Motivational factors in health and disease. *American Psychologist, 44,* 675–683.

McClelland, D. C., Atkinson, J. W., Clark, R. A., & Lowell, E. L. (1953). *The achievement motive.* New York: Appleton-Century-Crofts.

McLeod, J. (1992). The story of Henry Murray's diagnostic council: A case study in the demise of a scientific method. *Clinical Psychology Forum, 44,* 6–12.

Mead, M. (Ed.). (1937). *Cooperation and competition among primitive peoples.* New York: McGraw-Hill.

Miller, N. E., & Dollard, J. (1941). *Social learning and imitation.* New Haven, CT: Yale University Press.

Mischel, W. (1968). *Personality and assessment.* New York: Wiley.

Mischel, W., & Shoda, Y. (1995). A cognitive–affective system theory of personality: Reconceptualizing situations, dispositions, dynamics, and invariance in personality structure. *Psychological Review, 102,* 246–268.

Morawski, J. (1986). Organizing knowledge and behavior at Yale's Institute of Human Relations. *Isis, 77,* 219–242.

Morgan, C. D., & Murray, H. A. (1935). A method for investigating fantasies: The Thematic Apperception Test. *Archives of Neurology and Psychiatry, 34,* 289–306.

Murdock, G. P. (Ed.). (1982). *Outline of cultural materials* (5th ed.). New Haven, CT: Human Relations Area Files.

Murphy, G. (1932). *An historical introduction to modern psychology* (4th rev. ed.). New York: Harcourt, Brace.

Murray, H. A. (1938). *Explorations in personality.* New York: Oxford University Press.

Murray, H. A. (1940). What should psychologists do about psychoanalysis? *Journal of Abnormal and Social Psychology, 35,* 150–175.

Murray, H. A. (1951). Toward a classification of interactions. In T. Parsons & E. A. Shils (Eds.), *Toward a general theory of action* (pp. 434–464). Cambridge, MA: Harvard University Press.

Murray, H. A. (1959). Preparations for the scaffold of a comprehensive system. In S. Koch (Ed.), *Psychology: Study of a science* (Vol. 3, pp. 7–54). New York: McGraw-Hill.

Murray, H. A. (1967). Henry A. Murray. In E. G. Boring & G. Lindzey (Eds.), *A history of psychology in autobiography* (Vol. 5, pp. 283–310). New York: Appleton-Century-Crofts.

Murray, H. A. (1968). Components of an evolving personological system. In D. L. Sills (Ed.), *International encyclopedia of the social sciences* (Vol. 12, pp. 5–13). New York: Macmillan-Free Press.

Murray, H. A. (1977). Indispensables for the making, testing, and remaking of a personological system. In R. W. Rieber & K. Salzinger (Eds.), *The roots of American psychology: Historical influences and implications for the future* (pp. 323–331). New York: New York Academy of Sciences.

Murray, H. A. (1981). An American Icarus. In: E. S. Shneidman (Ed.), *Endeavors in psychology: Selections from the personology of Henry A. Murray* (pp. 535–556). New York: Harper & Row. (Original work published 1955)

Myers, I. (1962). *The Myers–Briggs Type Indicator.* Princeton, NJ: Educational Testing Service.

Nasby, W., & Read, N. W. (1997). The life voyage of a solo circumnavigator: Integrating theoretical and methodological perspectives. *Journal of Personality, 65,* 785–1068.

Nicholson, I. A. M. (1997a). Humanistic psychology and intellectual identity: The "open" system of Gordon Allport. *Journal of Humanistic Psychology, 37*(3), 61–79.

Nicholson, I. A. M. (1997b). To "correlate psychology and social ethics": Gordon Allport and the first course in American personality psychology. *Journal of Personality, 65,* 733–742.

Nicholson, I. A. M. (1998). Gordon Allport, character, and the "culture of personality," 1897–1937. *History of Psychology, 1,* 52–68.

Nisbett, R. E., & Wilson, T. D. (1977). Telling more than we can know: Verbal reports on mental processes. *Psychological Review, 84,* 231–259.

Only spectacular crimes grab headlines in L.A. (1994, February 19). *Toronto Globe and Mail,* p. A12.

Pandora, K. (1997). *Rebels within the ranks: Psychologists' critique of scientific authority and democratic realities in New Deal America.* Cambridge: Cambridge University Press.

Parker, J. D. A. (1991). *In search of the person: The historical development of American personality psychology.* Unpublished doctoral dissertation, York University, Toronto.

Peale, N. V. (1952). *The power of positive thinking.* New York: Prentice-Hall.

Pervin, L. A. (1983). The stasis and flow of behavior: Toward a theory of goals. In M. M. Page (Ed.), *Nebraska Symposium on Motivation 1982* (pp. 1–53). Lincoln: University of Nebraska Press.

Pervin, L. A. (Ed.). (1989). *Goal concepts in personality and social psychology.* Hillsdale, NJ: Erlbaum.

Pervin, L. A. (1990). A brief history of modern personality theory. In L. Pervin (Ed.), *Handbook of personality: Theory and research* (pp. 3–18). New York: Guilford Press.

Pervin, L. A. (1994). A critical analysis of current trait theory. *Psychological Inquiry, 5,* 103–113.

Peterson, D. R. (1965). Scope and generality of verbally defined personality factors. *Psychological Review, 72,* 48–59.

Poffenberger, A. T. (1922). Measures of intelligence and character. *Journal of Philosophy, 19,* 261–266.

Polansky, N. A. (1941). How shall a life-history be written? *Character and Personality, 9,* 188–207.

Pressey, S. L. (1921). A group scale for investigating the emotions. *Journal of Abnormal Psychology and Social Psychology, 16,* 55–64.

Prince, M., & Allport, F. H. (1921). Editorial announcement. *Journal of Abnormal Psychology and Social Psychology, 16,* 1–5.

Prince, M., & Moore, H. T. (1928). Editorial: The current number. *Journal of Abnormal Psychology and Social Psychology, 23,* 117.

Robinson, F. G. (1992). *Love's story told: A life of Henry A. Murray.* Cambridge, MA: Harvard University Press.

Rogers, C. R. (1959). A theory of therapy, personality, and interpersonal relationships, as developed in the client-centered framework. In S. Koch (Ed.), *Psychology: A study of a science* (Vol. 3, pp. 184–256). New York: McGraw-Hill.

Rorer, L. G. (1990). Personality assessment: A conceptual survey. In L. A. Pervin (Ed.), *Handbook of personality: Theory and research* (pp. 693–720). New York: Guilford Press.

Rosenberg, M. (1979). *Conceiving the self.* New York: Basic Books.

Rosenzweig, S. (1943). The ghost of Henry James: A study in thematic apperception. *Character & Personality, 12,* 79–100.

Runyan, W. M. (1997). Studying lives: Psychobiography and the conceptual structure of personality psychology. In R. Hogan, J. Johnson, & S. Briggs (Eds.), *Handbook of personality psychology* (pp. 41–69). San Diego: Academic Press.

Samelson, F. (1993). The authoritarian character from Berlin to Berkeley and beyond: The odyssey of a problem. In W. F. Stone, G. Lederer, & R. Christie (Eds.), *Strength and weakness: The authoritarian personality today* (pp. 22–43). New York: Springer.

Sampson, E. E. (1981). Cognitive psychology as ideology. *American Psychologist, 36,* 730–743.

Sanford, R. N. (1963). Personality: Its place in psychology. In S. Koch (Ed.), *Psychology: A study of a science* (Vol. 5, pp. 488–592). New York: McGraw-Hill.

Santayana, G. (1906). *The life of reason: Or the phases of human progress. I. Introduction and reason in common sense.* New York: Scribner's.

Schaffer, R. (1991). *America in the Great War: The rise of the war welfare state.* New York : Oxford University Press.

Sears, R. R. (1943). *Survey of objective studies of psychoanalytic concepts: A report prepared for the Committee on Social Adjustment.* New York: Social Science Research Council.

Shweder, R. A. (1991). *Thinking through cultures: Expeditions in cultural psychology.* Cambridge, MA: Harvard University Press.

Shweder, R. A., & Sullivan, M. A. (1990). The semiotic subject of cultural psychology. In L. Pervin (Ed.), *Handbook of personality: Theory and research* (pp. 399–416). New York: Guilford Press.

Singer, J. A. (1995). Seeing one's self: Locating narrative memory in a framework of personality. *Journal of Personality, 63,* 429–457.

Skaggs, E. B. (1945). Personalistic psychology as science. *Psychological Review, 52,* 234–238.

Skinner, B. F. (1953). *Science and human behavior.* New York: Macmillan.

Smith, C. P. (Ed.). (1992). *Motivation and personality: Handbook of thematic content analysis.* New York: Cambridge University Press.

Smith, M. B. (1990). Personology launched [Review of the book *Explorations in personality: A clinical and experimental study of fifty men of college age*]. *Contemporary Psychology, 35,* 537–539.

Snyder, M. (1987). *Public appearances, private realities: The psychology of self-monitoring.* New York: Freeman.

Spangler, W. D. (1992). Validity of questionnaire and TAT measures of need for achievement: Two meta-analyses. *Psychological Bulletin, 112,* 140–154.

Stagner, R. (1937). *Psychology of personality.* New York: McGraw-Hill.

Susman, W. I. (1979). "Personality" and the making of twentieth-century culture. In J. Higham & P. K. Conklin (Eds.), *New directions in American intellectual history* (pp. 212–226). Baltimore: Johns Hopkins University Press.

Tajfel, H. (Ed.). (1982). *Social identity and intergroup relations.* London: Cambridge University Press.

Thorndike, E. L. (1914). Units and scales for measuring educational products. *Proceedings of a Conference on*

Educational Measurements. Indiana University Bulletin, 12(10), 128–141.

Thorne, A., & Gough, H. G. (1991). *Portraits of type: An MBTI research compendium.* Palo Alto, CA: Consulting Psychologists Press.

Thurstone, L. L. (1916). Character and temperament. *Psychological Bulletin, 13,* 384–388.

Triplet, R. G. (1983). *Henry A. Murray and the Harvard Psychological Clinic, 1926–1938: A struggle to expand the disciplinary boundaries of academic psychology.* Unpublished doctoral dissertation, University of New Hampshire, Durham.

Triplet, R. G. (1992). Henry A. Murray: The making of a psychologist? *American Psychologist, 47*(2), 299–307.

Vallacher, R. R., & Nowak, A. (1997). The emergence of dynamical social psychology. *Psychological Inquiry, 8,* 73–99.

Vernon, P. E. (1933). The American v. the German methods of approach to the study of temperament and personality. *British Journal of Psychology, 24,* 156–177.

Vernon, P. E. (1964). *Personality assessment: A critical survey.* New York: Wiley.

Vernon, P. E., & Allport, G. W. (1931). A test for personal values. *Journal of Abnormal and Social Psychology, 26,* 231–248.

Watson, J. B., & Rayner, R. (1920). Conditioned emotional reactions. *Journal of Experimental Psychology, 3,* 1–14.

Weinberger, J., & McClelland, D. C. (1990). Cognitive versus traditional motivational models: Irreconcilable or complementary? In E. T. Higgins & R. M. Sorrentino (Eds.), *Handbook of motivation and cognition* (Vol. 2, pp. 562–597). New York: Guilford Press.

Weinberger, J., & Silverman, L. H. (1990). Testability and empirical verification of psychoanalytic dynamic propositions through subliminal psychodynamic activation. *Psychoanalytic Psychology, 7,* 299–339.

Weiner, B. (1990). Attribution in personality psychology. In L. Pervin (Ed.), *Handbook of personality: Theory and research* (pp. 465–485). New York: Guilford Press.

West, S. G. (1983). Personality and prediction: Nomothetic and idiographic approaches [Special issue]. *Journal of Personality, 51*(3).

White, R. W. (1952). *Lives in progress.* New York: Holt, Rinehart & Winston.

Whiting, J. W. M., & Child, I. L. (1953). *Child training and personality: A cross-cultural study.* New Haven, CT: Yale University Press.

Wiggins, J. S. (1991). Agency and communion as conceptual coordinates for the understanding and measurement of interpersonal behavior. In D. Cicchetti (Ed.), *Thinking clearly about psychology: Essays in honor of Paul E. Meehl: Vol. 2. Personality and psychopathology* (pp. 89–113). Minneapolis: University of Minnesota Press.

Wiggins, J. S. (Ed.). (1996). *The five-factor model of personality: Theoretical perspectives.* New York: Guilford Press.

Windelband, W. (1904). *Geschichte und Naturwissenschaft* [History and natural science] (3rd ed.). Strassburg: Heitz. (Original work delivered 1894.)

Wink, P. (1992). Three types of narcissism in women from college to mid-life. *Journal of Personality, 60,* 7–30.

Winter, D. G. (1993). Power, affiliation and war: Three tests of a motivational model. *Journal of Personality and Social Psychology, 65,* 532–545.

Winter, D. G. (1996). *Personality: Analysis and interpretation of lives.* New York: McGraw-Hill.

Winter, D. G. (1998). "Toward a science of personality psychology": David McClelland's development of empirically derived TAT measures. *History of Psychology, 1,* 130–153.

Winter, D. G., John, O. P., Stewart, A. J., Klohnen, E. C., & Duncan, L. E. (1998). Traits and motives: Toward an integration of two traditions in personality research. *Psychological Review, 105,* 230–250.

Woodworth, R. S. (1919). Examination of emotional fitness for warfare. *Psychological Bulletin, 15,* 59–60.

Woodworth, R. S. (1932). Robert S. Woodworth. In C. Murchison (Ed.), *A history of psychology in autobiography* (Vol. 2, pp. 359–380). Worcester, MA: Clark University Press.

Wylie, R. C. (1974–1979). *The self-concept.* Lincoln, NE: University of Nebraska Press.

York, K. L., & John, O. P. (1992). The four faces of Eve: A typological analysis of women's personality at midlife. *Journal of Personality and Social Psychology, 63,* 494–508.

Young, K. (1928). The measurement of personal and social traits. *Journal of Abnormal and Social Psychology, 22,* 431–442.

Zuckerman, M. (1991). *Psychobiology of personality.* New York: Cambridge University Press.

PART TWO
THEORETICAL PERSPECTIVES

Chapter 2

Human Nature and Individual Differences: The Evolution of Human Personality

David M. Buss
University of Texas, Austin

Personality psychology aspires to be the grandest, most integrative branch of the psychological sciences. Its content is not restricted to particular sub-sets of psychological phenomena, such as information processing, social interaction, or deviations from normality. Personality psychologists historically have attempted to synthesize and integrate these diverse phenomena into a larger unifying theory that includes the whole person in all the myriad modes of functioning (McAdams, 1997; Pervin, 1990). Moreover, personality theorists have attempted to conceptualize the place of whole persons within the broader matrix of groups and society. The central argument of this chapter is that these theoretical goals cannot be attained without an explicit consideration of the causal processes that gave rise to the mechanisms of mind that define human nature.

Although there has been much debate about the definition of personality, two major themes have pervaded nearly all efforts at grand personality theorizing—human nature and individual differences (Buss, 1984). Human nature deals with the common characteristics of humans—the shared motives, goals, and psychological mechanisms that are either universal or nearly universal. Proposed species-typical motives range from the sexual and aggressive instincts postulated by Freud (1905/1953) to the motives to get along and get ahead postulated by Hogan (1983). A proper conceptualization of human nature, however, is much larger than the forces that impel people out of bed in the morning and motivate them in their daily quests. Human nature also includes the species-typical ways in which humans make decisions (e.g., selection of mates and habitats), the ways in which humans respond to environmental stimuli (e.g., fears of snakes and heights are more typical than fears of cars or electrical outlets), and even the ways in which people influence and manipulate the world around them. No other branch of psychology except personality psychology aspires to this broad conceptualization of human nature.

Personality psychology is also the only branch of psychology for which individual differences play a prominent role. Indeed, some leading personality psychologists define the field of personality psychology as that branch of psychology concerned with identifying the most important individual differences (e.g., Goldberg, 1981;

Norman, 1963; Wiggins, 1979). Individuals differ in an infinite number of ways that either go unnoticed or are not sufficiently noteworthy to warrant much discussion. Some individuals have belly buttons turned in, others have belly buttons turned out. Some lead with their left foot, others with their right. Some prefer blondes, others prefer brunettes. One key function of personality theory is to identify the most important ways in which individuals differ from among the infinite dimensions of possible difference.

These two themes—human nature and individual differences—ideally should not occupy separate and isolated branches of the field of personality psychology (Buss, 1984). Most grand theories of personality have incorporated propositions about ways in which human nature and individual differences are systematically linked. In Freud's (1953) theory of psychoanalysis, for example, all humans were presumed to progress through the universal stages of oral, anal, phallic, latency, and genital. Different environmental events occurring during these stages, however, produced systematic individual differences. Over-indulgence at the oral stage might lead to an oral fixation, leading to an adult who talks a lot, chews gum, and feels "hungry" for the attention of others. An overly strict mode of toilet training might lead to a different personality, such as an adult who was compulsively neat. In this manner, the theory's specification of human nature—the universal progression through the psychosexual stages—was coherently linked with the major ways in which individuals were proposed to differ.

Over the past few decades, the field of personality has retreated somewhat from its grander goals. Most actual research on personality psychology deals with individual differences, not with human nature or with the links between human nature and individual differences (e.g., McCrae & John, 1992). In this sense, personality may have ceded the study of human nature to other branches of psychology, such as cognitive and social psychology, which typically concentrate exclusively on shared characteristics or human nature and neglect individual differences.

One of the central arguments of this chapter is that the grand goals of personality psychology should be reclaimed. An analogy might help to clarify this argument. Suppose that invisible Martian scientists were assigned the task of studying the large metallic vehicles that earthlings use for transportation. One group of scientists was assigned the task of figuring out "car nature," the basic design that is common to all cars. They might conclude that all cars have tires, a steering mechanism, a method of braking, and an engine that provides propulsion. The second group of scientists, in contrast, was assigned the task of determining the major ways in which cars differ from one another. They conclude that some have large tires, others small tires; some have rack-and-pinion steering, others do not; some have antilock brakes, others do not; some have a six-cylinder engine, whereas others make due with four cylinders.

The second group of scientists is faced with the task of determining which individual differences are the really important ones and separating these from the trivial ones. Cars differ in the color of the engine wires, for example, but are these differences really important (Tooby & Cosmides, 1990a)? The Martian scientists who study car differences conclude that they cannot really accomplish their task—identifying in a nonarbitrary fashion the most important individual differences—without talking to the first group of scientists who are responsible for developing a theory of "car nature." From a collaboration between these two groups, they arrive at a non-arbitrary criterion for determining which car differences are really important: Those differences that affect the basic functioning of the car, that is, those that affect the component parts that contribute to what cars are designed to do. Using this criterion, they decide that "differences in the colors of the engine wires" is really a trivial dimension of individual differences, because these differences have no impact on the functioning of the car's engine. But they include differences in engine cylinder number, tire size, and breaking mechanism because these differences have a profound effect on what the car is designed to do, affecting its power, propulsion, ability to hug the road, and ability to stop. The key point is that it would be illogical to have two entirely separate "car theorists," one dealing with car nature and one dealing with car differences. The two are inextricably bound, and their integration provides the basis for a nonarbitrary theory that includes both car nature and the major ways in which cars differ.

People are not cars, and the analogy breaks down at a certain point. Cars are designed by humans, for example, but humans were designed by a different causal process. But the central point of the analogy may be expressed as a syllogism: (1) If humans have a human nature and (2) if the components of that nature were "designed" to perform certain functions, then (3) a nonarbitrary means for identifying the most important individual differences involves discovering those differences that affect the performance of those functions. In order to establish the veracity of the first two premises, we must examine the causal processes that "designed" humans and ask whether this process has produced a human nature with an identifiable set of functions.

THE EVOLUTIONARY PROCESS

Scientists over the past two centuries have proposed a delimited set of theories about the causal process responsible for the design of humans and other life forms. One theory is that of "divine creation," the idea that a deity created humans in all of their glorious nature. Another theory is that extraterrestrial organisms planted the seeds of life on earth, and that these seeds were transformed by some evolutionary process over millions of years into humans. Neither divine creation nor seeding theory have many proponents among modern scientists. Indeed, only one theory of origins, albeit with modifications and extensions, has had held sway among scientists over the past century and a half—the theory of evolution by selection.

Natural and Sexual Selection

Although it is widely misunderstood, the theory of evolution by selection is remarkably simple in form as applied to all organic forms. First, individuals differ in a variety of ways. Second, some of these variants are heritable, that is, reliably passed down from parents to children. Third, some of these variants are correlated with survival and reproduction recurrently over generations. Fourth, those variants that contribute to greater reproduction, however indirectly, are passed down to succeeding generations in greater numbers than those that do not lead to greater relative reproduction. Fifth, over generations, those variants that contribute to reproduction recurrently tend to displace those that do not, eventually spreading to most or all members of the species. This selective process, occurring over vast expanses of time and space, is responsible for the origins of the basic "design" of all organisms.

Selection, of course, is not the only causal process that produces change over time. Genetic drift, sudden catastrophes, such as a meteorite hitting the earth, and other processes certainly produce change and must be included in any complete history of the evolution of species. Natural selection, however, is generally regarded as the most important causal process, because it is the *only known causal process* that can produce *complex functional design*. A meteorite may have caused the extinction of dinosaurs and perhaps even opened up new niches for the explosive evolution of mammals, but such catastrophic events cannot create the complex functional design that characterized dinosaurs or any other organisms. Whereas unpredictable catastrophes are important in understanding the evolution of life on earth, no known causal process other than natural selection can produce the complex functional design that characterizes each species (see Buss, Haselton, Shackelford, Bleske, & Wakefield, 1998, for a more detailed discussion of these issues).

Darwin envisioned two classes of evolved variants—one playing a role in survival and one playing a role in reproductive competition (Darwin, 1859/1958). Among humans, for example, our sweat glands help us to maintain a constant body temperature and thus presumably help us to survive (or more accurately, helped our ancestors to survive). Our tastes for sugar and fat presumably helped to guide our ancestors to eat certain foods and to avoid others, and thus helped them to survive. Other inherited attributes aid more directly in reproductive competition and were said to be sexually selected (Darwin, 1871/1981). The elaborate songs and brilliant plumage of various bird species, for example, help to attract mates and hence to reproduce, but they do nothing to enhance the individual's survival. In fact, these characteristics may be detrimental to survival by carrying large metabolic costs or by alerting predators.

In summary, although differential reproductive success of inherited variants is the crux of Darwin's theory of natural selection, he conceived of two classes of variants that might evolve—those that help organisms to survive (and thus indirectly help them to reproduce) and those that more directly help organisms in reproductive competition. The theory of natural selection unified all living creatures, from single-celled amoebas to multicellular mammals, into one grand tree of descent. It also provided for the first time a scientific theory to account for the exquisite design and functional nature of the component parts of each of these species.

In its modern form, the evolutionary process of natural selection has been refined in the form of inclusive fitness theory (Hamilton, 1964). Hamilton reasoned that classical fitness—a measure of an individual's direct reproductive success in passing on genes through the production of offspring—was too narrow to describe the process of evolution by selection. He proposed that natural selection will favor characteristics that cause an organism's genes to be passed on, regardless of whether the organism produces offspring directly. If a person helps his or her brother, sister, or niece to become an ancestor, for example, by sharing resources, offering protection, or helping in times of need, then he or she contributes to the reproductive success of genes "for" brotherly, sisterly, or niecely assistance (assuming that such helping is partly heritable). In other words, parental care—investing in one's own children—is merely a special case of caring for kin who carry copies of one's genes in their bodies. Thus, the notion of classical fitness was expanded to inclusive fitness.

Technically, inclusive fitness is not a property of an individual organism but rather a property of its actions or effects (Hamilton, 1964; see also Dawkins, 1982). Inclusive fitness can be viewed as the sum of an individual's own reproductive success (classical fitness) plus the effects the individual's actions have on the reproductive success of his or her genetic relatives, weighted by the degree of genetic relatedness.

It is critical to keep in mind that evolution by natural selection is not forward looking or intentional. The giraffe does not notice the juicy leaves stirring high in the tree and "evolve" a longer neck. Rather, those giraffes that happen to have slightly longer necks than other giraffes have a slight advantage in getting to those leaves. Hence, they survive better and are more likely to live to pass on genes for slightly longer necks to offspring. Natural selection acts only on those variants that happen to exist. Evolution is not intentional and cannot look into the future to foresee distant needs.

Products of Evolutionary Processes

In each generation, the process of selection acts as a sieve (Dawkins, 1996). Variants that interfere with successful solutions to adaptive problems are filtered out. Variants that are tributary to the successful solution to an adaptive problem pass through the selective sieve. Iterated over thousands of generations, this filtering process tends to produce characteristics that interact with the physical, social, or internal environment in ways that promote the reproduction of the individuals who possess the characteristics or the reproduction of the individual's genetic relatives (Dawkins, 1982; Hamilton, 1964; Tooby & Cosmides, 1990a; Williams, 1966). These characteristics are called "adaptations."

There has been much debate about the precise meaning of adaptation, but a provisional working definition may be offered. An adaptation may be defined as an inherited and reliably developing characteristic that came into existence through natural selection because it helped to solve a problem of reproduction during the period of its evolution (after Tooby & Cosmides, 1992). An adaptation must have genes "for" that adaptation. Those genes are required for the passage of the adaptation from parents to offspring. Adaptations, therefore, are by definition inherited.

An adaptation must develop reliably among species members in all "normal" environments. Environmental events during ontogeny always have the potential for disrupting the emergence of an adaptation in a particular individual, and thus the genes "for" the adaptation do not invariantly result in its intact phenotypic manifestation. To qualify as an adaptation, the characteristics must reliably emerge in reasonably intact form at the appropriate time during an organism's life, however, and be characteristic of most or all members of a species (with some exceptions, such as characteristics that are sex-linked or exist in only a subset of members of a species due to frequent-dependent selection).

Adaptations, of course, need not be present at birth. Many adaptations develop long after birth. Bipedal locomotion is a reliably developing characteristic of humans, but most humans do not begin to walk until a year after birth. The beards of men and the breasts of women are reliably developing, but they do not start to develop until puberty.

The characteristics that make it through the filtering process in each generation generally do so because they contribute to the successful solution of adaptive problems—solutions that are either necessary for reproduction or that enhance relative reproductive success. Solutions to adaptive problems can be direct, such as a fear of dangerous snakes that solves a survival problem or a desire to mate with particular members of one's species that helps to solve a reproductive problem. They can be indirect, as in a desire to ascend a social hierarchy, which many years later might give an individual better access to more desirable mates. Or they can be even more indirect, such as when a person helps a brother or sister, which eventually helps that sibling to reproduce.

Each adaptation has its own period of evolution. Initially, a mutation occurs in a single individual. Most mutations hinder reproduction, disrupting the existing design of the organism. If the mutation is helpful to reproduction, however, it will become integrated into the existing design of the organism and passed down to the next generation in greater numbers. In the next generation, therefore, more individuals will possess the characteristic that was initially a mutation in a single individual. Over many generations, if it continues to be successful, the characteristic will spread to the entire population, so that every species member will have it.

An adaptation's "environment of evolutionary adaptedness" (EEA) refers to the cumulative selection processes that constructed it piece by piece until it came to characterize the species. There is no single EEA that can be localized in time and space for all the adaptations that characterize a species. The EEA is best described as a statistical aggregate of selection pressures over a particular period of time responsible for the emergence of an adaptation (Tooby & Cosmides, 1992). Each adaptation, therefore, has it's own EEA. The human eyes, for example, have an EEA that is distinct from the EEA of concealed ovulation or the EEA of male sexual jealousy.

The hallmarks of adaptation are features that define "special design"—complexity, economy, efficiency, reliability, precision, and functionality (Williams, 1966). These qualities are conceptual criteria subject to empirical testing and potential falsification for a particular hypothesis about an adaptation. Because in principle there are an infinite number of alternative hypotheses to account for an particular constellation of findings, the evaluation of a specific hypothesis about an adaptation is a probability statement about the likelihood that the complex, reliable, and functional features of special design could not have arisen as an incidental byproduct of another characteristic or by chance alone (Tooby & Cosmides, 1992). As more and more functional features of special design are predicted and subsequently documented for a hypothesized adaptation, each pointing to the successful solution to a specific adaptive problem, the alternative hypotheses of chance and incidental by-product become increasingly improbable.

Although adaptations are generally considered to be the primary products of the evolutionary process, they are not the only products (see Tooby & Cosmides, 1992; Buss et al., 1998). The evolutionary process also produces "by-products of adaptations" and a residue of "noise". By-products are characteristics that do not solve adaptive problems and tend not to have functional design. They are carried along with characteristics that do have functional design because they happen to be coupled with those adaptations.

Consider the humanly designed light bulb. A light bulb is designed to produce light. Light production is its function. The design features of a light bulb—the conducting filament, the vacuum surrounding the filament, and the glass encasement—are all tributary to the production of light and part of its functional design. Light bulbs, however, also produce heat. Heat is a by-product of light production. It is carried along not because the bulb was designed to produce heat, but rather because heat tends to be a reliable incidental consequence of light production.

A naturally occurring example of a by-product of adaptation would be the human belly button. There is no evidence that the belly button, per se, helped human ancestors to survive or reproduce. A belly button is not good for catching food, detecting predators, avoiding snakes, locating good habitats, or choosing mates. It does not seem to be involved directly or indirectly in the solution to an adaptive problem. Rather the belly button is a by-product of something that is an adaptation—namely, the umbilical cord that formerly provided the food supply to the growing fetus. The hypothesis that something is a by-product of an adaptation requires the identification of the adaptation of which it is a by-product and the cause for it being coupled with that adaptation (Tooby & Cosmides, 1992). In other words, the hypothesis that something is a by-product, just like the hypothesis that something is an adaptation, must be subjected to rigorous standards of scientific confirmation and potential falsification.

The third and final product of the evolutionary process is "noise" or "random effects." Noise can be produced by mutations that neither contribute to, nor detract from, the functional design of the organism. The glass encasement of a light bulb, for example, often contains perturbations from smoothness due to imperfections in the materials and the process of manufacturing that do not affect the functioning of the bulb. In self-reproducing systems, these neutral effects can be carried along and passed down to succeeding generations, as long as they do not impair the functioning of the mechanisms that are adaptations.

In summary, the evolutionary process produces three products—adaptations, by-products of adaptations, and a residue of noise. In principle, we can analyze the component parts of a species and conduct empirical studies to determine which of these parts are adaptations, which are by-products, and which represent neutral noise. Evolutionary scientists differ in their estimates of the relative sizes of these three categories of products. Some argue that even uniquely human qualities, such as language, are merely incidental by-products of large brains (e.g., Gould, 1991). Others argue that qualities such as language show evidence of special design that render it highly improbable that it is anything other than a well-designed adaptation for communication and conspecific manipulation (Pinker, 1994). It is equally incumbent on both sides of this argument to formulate hypotheses in a precise, testable, and potentially falsifiable manner so that the different positions can be adjudicated empirically.

EVOLUTIONARY CONSEQUENCES FOR HUMAN NATURE

One important consequence of a careful consideration of the products of the evolutionary process is that the core of human nature largely consists of primarily of adaptations and by-products of those adaptations, along with a residue of random noise. This section addresses the core of human nature from an evolutionary psychological perspective. First, I argue that all species, including humans, have a nature that can be described and explained. Second, I provide a definition of evolved psychological mechanisms—the core units that compose human nature. Third, I explore two illustrations of evolved psychological mechanisms. And fourth, I suggest some ways in which evolutionary thinking can provide a nonarbitrary foundation for a personality theory that specifies the core of human nature.

Humans Have a Human Nature

All species have a nature. It is part of lion's nature to walk on four legs, display a large furry mane, hunt other animals for food, and live on the Savannah. It is part of butterfly nature to enter a flightless pupae state, wrap itself in a cocoon, and emerge to soar, fluttering gracefully in search of food and mates. It is part of a porcupine's nature to defend itself with quills, a skunk's nature to defend itself with a spray of acrid liquid smell, a stag's nature to defend itself with antlers, and a turtle's nature to defend itself with a shell. All species have a nature, but that nature is different for each species. Each species has faced at least somewhat unique selection pressures during its evolutionary history, and therefore has evolved at least some unique adaptive solutions.

Humans also have a nature—qualities that define us as a unique species—and all psychological theories imply the existence of a human nature. For Freud, human nature consisted of raging sexual and aggressive impulses. For William James, human nature consisted of dozens or hundreds of instincts. Even the most ardently environmentalist theories, such as Skinner's theory of radical behaviorism, assume that humans have a nature—in this case, consisting of a few highly general learning mechanisms (Symons, 1987). All psychological theories require as their core a specification of, or fundamental premises about, human nature.

Because evolution by selection is the only known causal process that is capable of producing the fundamental components of that human nature, all psychological theories are implicitly or explicitly evolutionary (Symons, 1987). Although many psychologists fail to specify their assumptions about the evolution of human nature (hence keeping those assumptions implicit), not one has ever proposed a psychological theory that has presumed some other causal process to be responsible for creating human nature.

If humans have a nature and if evolution by selection is the causal process that produced that nature, then the next question is: What insights into human nature can be provided by examining our evolutionary origins? Can examining the *process* of evolution tell us anything about the *products* of that process in the human case?

Whereas the broader field of evolutionary biology is concerned with the evolutionary analysis of grandly integrated parts of an organism, evolutionary psychology focuses more narrowly on those parts that are psychological—the analysis of the human mind as a collection of evolved mechanisms, the contexts that activate those mechanisms, and the behavior generated by those mechanisms. And so the next section explores the subclass of adaptations that make up the human mind—evolved psychological mechanisms.

The Nature of Evolved Psychological Mechanisms

An "evolved psychological mechanism" is a set of processes inside an organism that has the following properties (see Buss, 1991, 1995a, 1999; Tooby & Cosmides, 1992):

An evolved psychological mechanism exists in the form that it does because it solved a specific problem of survival or reproduction recurrently over evolutionary history. This means that the form of the mechanism, its set of design features, is like a key made to fit a particular lock (Tooby & Cosmides, 1992). Just as the shape of the key must be coordinated to fit the internal features of the lock, the shape of the design features of a psychological mechanism must be coordinated with the features required to solve an adaptive problem of survival or reproduction. Failure to mesh with the adaptive problem meant failure to pass through the selective sieve of evolution.

An evolved psychological mechanism is designed to take in only a narrow slice of information. Consider the human eye. Although it seems as though we open our eyes and see nearly everything, in fact the eye is sensitive only to a narrow range of input from the broad spectrum of electromagnetic waves. We do not see X-rays, which are shorter than those in the visual spectrum. We do not see radio waves, which are longer than those in the visual spectrum. In fact, our eyes are designed to process input from only a very narrow wedge of waves—waves within the visual spectrum.

Even within the visual spectrum, our eyes are designed to process a narrower subset of information (Marr, 1982). Our eyes have specific edge-detectors that pick up contrasting reflections from objects. Our eyes have specific motion detectors that pick up movement. Our eyes have specific cones designed to pick up specific information about the colors of objects. So the eye is not an all-purpose seeing device. It is designed to process only narrow slices of information—waves within a particular range of frequency, edges, motion, and so on—from among the much larger domain of potential information.

Similarly, the psychological mechanism of a predisposition to learn to fear snakes is designed to take in only a narrow slice of information—slithery movements from self-propelled elongated objects. Our evolved preferences for food, landscapes, and mates are all designed to take in only a limited subset of information from among the infinite array of information that could potentially constitute input.

The input of an evolved psychological mechanism tells an organism the particular adaptive problem it is facing. The input of seeing a slithering snake tells you that you are confronting a particular survival problem, namely physical damage and perhaps death if bitten. The differing smells of potentially edible objects—rancid and rotting versus sweet and fragrant—tell you that you are facing an adaptive survival problem of food selection. The input, in short, lets the organism know what adaptive problem it is dealing with. This occurs almost invariably out of consciousness. Humans do not smell a cooking pizza and think "Aha, I am facing an adaptive problem of food selection!" Instead, the smell unconsciously triggers food selection mechanisms, and no consciousness or awareness of the adaptive problem is necessary.

The input of an evolved psychological mechanism is transformed through decision rules into output. Upon seeing a snake, you can decide to attack it, run away from it, or freeze. Upon smelling a fragrant pizza just out of the oven, you can devour it or walk away (perhaps if you are on a diet). The decision rules are a set of procedures—"if . . . then . . ." statements—for channeling an organism down one path or another.

The output of an evolved psychological mechanism can be physiological activity, information to other psychological mechanisms, or manifest behavior. Upon seeing a snake, you may get autonomically aroused or frightened (physiological output), you may use this information to evaluate your behavioral options, such as freezing or fleeing (information to other psychological mechanisms), and the consequence of this evaluation is an action, such as running away (behavioral output).

Consider another example—sexual jealousy. Let's say that you go to a party with your romantic partner and then leave the room to get a drink. When you return, you spot your partner talking animatedly to another person. They stand very close to each other, look deeply into each other's eyes, and you notice that they are starting to touch each other.

These cues might trigger a reaction we can call sexual jealousy. The cues act as input to the mechanism, signaling to you an adaptive problem—the threat of losing your partner. This input is then evaluated according to a set of decision rules. One option is to ignore them and feign indifference. Another is to threaten the rival. A third option is to get enraged and hit your partner. Still another option would be to re-evaluate your relationship. Thus, the output of a psychological mechanism can be "physiological" (arousal), "behavioral" (confronting, threatening, hitting), or "input" into other psychological mechanisms (reevaluating the status of your relationship).

The output of an evolved psychological mechanism is directed toward the solution to a specific adaptive problem. Just as the cues to a partner's potential infidelity signal the presence of an adaptive problem, the output of the sexual jealousy mechanism is geared toward solving that problem. The threatened rival may leave the scene. Your romantic partner may be deterred from flirting with others. Or your reevaluation of the relationship may cause you to cut your losses and move into a potentially better relationship. Any of these might help with the solution to your adaptive problem.

Stating that the output of a psychological mechanism leads to solutions to specific adaptive problems does not imply that the solutions will always be optimal or invariably successful. The rival may not be deterred by your threats. Your partner may have a fling with your rival despite your display of jealousy. The main point is *not* that the output of a psychological mechanism *always* leads to a successful solution, but rather that the output of the mechanism *on average* tended to solve the adaptive problem in the environment in which it evolved better than outputs from alternative designs present in the population during those periods.

An important point to keep in mind is that a mechanism that led to a successful solution in the evolutionary past may or may not lead to a successful solution now. Our strong taste preferences for fat, for example, were clearly adaptive in our evolutionary past because fat was a valuable source of calories but very scarce (Symons, 1987). Now, however, with hamburger and pizza joints on every street corner, fat is no longer a scarce resource. Thus, our strong taste for fatty substances now causes us to overconsume fat. This leads to clogged arteries and heart attacks and hinders our survival. The central point is that evolved mechanisms exist in the form that they do because they led to success on average during the period in which they evolved. Whether they are currently adaptive—that is, currently lead to increased survival and reproduction—is an empirical matter that must be determined on a case-by-case basis.

In summary, an evolved psychological mechanism is a set of procedures within the organism that is designed to take in a particular slice of information and transform that information via decision rules into output that historically helped with the solution to an adaptive problem. The psychological mechanism exists in current organisms because it led, on average, to the successful solution of a specific adaptive problem for the ancestors of the current species of organism.

Two Illustrations of Evolved Psychological Mechanisms: Fear of Spiders and Landscape Preferences

At this early stage in the development of the field of evolutionary psychology, no psychological mechanism has been completely described. We do not know all of the decision rules, the precise range of events that trigger their activation, or the complete range of outputs of any mechanism. Nonetheless, two illustrations of *possible* psychological mechanisms will help to convey the scientific goals of this enterprise.

Let's consider the fear of spiders and preferences for certain landscapes. An evolved fear of spiders exists in the form that it does because it solved a specific problem of survival in human ancestral environments (Marks, 1987). The fear is triggered only by a narrow range of inputs, such as certain shapes and movements associated with spiders. Once a spider is perceived as dangerous and within striking range, this information is transformed via decision rules that might activate physiological arousal and perhaps the implementation of a host of behavioral options. The options—such as stomping on the spider, fleeing, or yelling for help—would presumably have lowered the odds of receiving a deadly spider bite in ancestral environments. Thus, the output of the fear-of-spiders mechanism solves an ancestral adaptive problem. It is not by chance that human fears and phobias tend to be concentrated heavily toward environmental events that threatened human survival. Fears of snakes, spiders, heights, darkness, and strangers provide a window for viewing the survival hazards that our human ancestors faced (Marks, 1987).

Preferences are evolved psychological mechanisms of a different sort than fears. Preferences motivate an organism to seek things rich in the "resource providing potential" needed for survival or reproduction (Orians & Heerwagen, 1992). Landscape preferences provide an illustration. Studies of landscape preferences show that savanna-like environments are consistently preferred to other environments. In particular, people like landscapes that provide food, water, and safety. They like places that offer protection from hazards such as bad weather or landslides. And they like places that offer freedom from predators, parasites, toxic foods, and unfriendly humans (Orians & Heerwagen, 1992). Furthermore, people prefer places where they can see without being seen, places containing multiple views for surveillance, and places containing multiple ways of moving through space for escape.

As a human walks through a variety of places searching for a place to stay for a while, some particular landscapes fail to fulfill these evolved preferences. Those that do fulfill our evolved preferences for certain features of landscapes trigger a set of cognitive procedures or decision rules, depending in part upon other contextual input, such as one's state of hunger or thirst, the size of one's group, and one's knowledge about the presence of hostile humans in the vicinity. Eventually, these procedures produce output in the form of a behavioral decision to remain in the habitat or to continue one's search for a better habitat. These behavioral decisions presumably led their possessors to survive and reproduce better than those lacking them, or those who possessed alternative preferences that were less effective at securing resources and reducing risk.

Although psychological mechanisms such as landscape preferences clearly differ in important ways from mechanisms such as spider fears, they share critical ingredients that qualify them as evolved psychological mechanisms: They exist due to a history of natural selection, they are triggered only by a narrow range of information; they are characterized by a particular set of decision rules, and they produce behavioral output that solved an adaptive problem in ancestral times.

Given the infinite courses of action a human could pursue in principle, evolved psychological mechanisms are necessary for channeling action into the narrow pockets of adaptive choices. Psychological mechanisms are necessary for seeking and extracting particular forms of information. Decision rules are necessary for producing action based on that information.

Describing the Human Mind: Important Properties of Evolved Psychological Mechanisms

This section examines several important properties of evolved psychological mechanisms. They provide nonarbitrary criteria for "carving the mind at its natural joints" and tend to be problem-specific, numerous, and complex. These features combine to yield the tremendous flexibility of behavior that characterizes modern humans.

Evolved Psychological Mechanisms Provide Nonarbitrary Criteria for "Carving the Mind at Its Joints"

A central premise of evolutionary psychology is that the main nonarbitrary way to identify, describe, and understand psychological mechanisms is to articulate their functions—the specific adaptive problems they were designed by selection to solve.

Consider the human body. In principle, the mechanisms of the body could be described in an infinite number of ways. Why do anatomists identify as separate mechanisms the liver, the heart, the hand, the nose, and the eyes? What makes these divisions nonarbitrary compared with alternative ways of dividing the human body? The answer is function. The liver is recognized as a mechanism that performs functions different from those performed by the heart or hand. The eyes and the nose, although they are close to each other on the face, perform different functions and operate according to different input (electromagnetic waves in the visual spectrum versus odors). If an anatomist tried to lump the eyes and the nose into one category, it would be seen as ludicrous. Understanding the component parts of the body requires the identification of function. Function provides the only sensible nonarbitrary way to understand these component parts.

Evolutionary psychologists believe that similar principles should be used for understanding the mechanisms of the mind. Although the mind could be divided in an infinite number of ways, most of these ways would simply be arbitrary. A powerful nonarbitrary analysis of the human mind is one that rests on function. If two components of the mind perform different functions, then they can be regarded as separate mechanisms (although they may interact with other mechanisms in interesting ways).

Evolved psychological mechanisms tend to be problem-specific. Imagine giving directions to someone to get from New York City to a specific street address in San Francisco, California. If you gave some general directions such as "head west," the person might end up as far south as Texas or as far north as Alaska. The general direction would not reliably get the person to the right state.

Now let's suppose that the person did get to the right state. The "go west" direction now would be entirely useless, since west of California is ocean. The general direction would not provide any guidance to get to the right city within California, let alone the right street address. To get to the right state, city, street, and location on that street, you need to give more specific instructions. Furthermore, although there are many ways to get to a particular street address, some paths will be far more efficient and timesaving than others.

The search for a specific street address across country is a good analogy for what is needed to reach a specific adaptive solution. Adaptive problems, like street addresses, are specific—don't get bitten by that snake, select a habitat with running water and places to hide, avoid eating food that is poisonous, select a mate who is fertile, and so on. There is no such thing as a "general adaptive problem" (Symons, 1992). All problems are specific.

Because adaptive problems are specific, their solutions tend to be specific as well. Just as general instructions fail to get you to the correct location, general solutions fail to get you to the right adaptive solution. Consider two adaptive problems—selecting the right foods to eat (a survival problem) and selecting the right mates with whom to have children (a reproductive problem). What counts as a "successful solution" is quite different for these two adaptive problems. Successful food selection involves identifying objects that have calories, contain particular vitamins and minerals, and do not contain poisonous substances. Successful mate selection involves, among other things, identifying a partner who is fertile and who will be a good parent.

What might a general solution be to these two selection problems, and how effective would it be at solving them? One general solution would be "select the first thing that comes along." This would be disastrous, since it might lead to eating poisonous plants or marrying an infertile person. If anyone ever had developed such a general solution to these adaptive problems in human evolutionary history, he or she failed to become one of our ancestors.

To solve these selection problems in a reasonable way, one needs more specific guidance about the qualities of foods and qualities of mates that are important. Fruit that looks fresh and ripe, for example, will signal better nutrients than fruit that looks rotten. People who look young and healthy will be more fertile, on average, than people who look old and unhealthy. We need "specific selection criteria"—qualities that are part of our selection mechanisms—in order to solve these selection problems successfully.

The specificity of mechanisms is further illustrated by errors in selection. If you make an error in food selection, then you have an array of mechanisms that are tailored to correcting that error. When you place a piece of bad food in your mouth, it may taste terrible, in which case you would spit it out. You may gag on it if makes its way past your taste buds. And if it makes its way all the way down to your stomach, you may vomit—a specific mechanism designed to get rid of toxic or detrimental ingested substances. But if you make an error in mate selection, you do not spit, gag, or throw up (at least not usually!). You correct your error in other ways—by leaving, selecting someone else, or simply telling the person that you don't want to see him or her anymore.

In summary, problem specificity of adaptive mechanisms is favored over generality because (1) general solutions fail to guide the organism to the correct adaptive solutions; (2) general solutions, even if they do work, lead to too many errors and thus are costly to the organism; and (3) what constitutes a "successful solution" differs from problem to problem (criteria for successful food selection differ from criteria for successful mate selection). The adaptive solutions, in short, must have dedicated procedures and content-sensitive elements in order to solve adaptive problems successfully.

Humans possess many evolved psychological mechanisms. Humans, like most organisms, face a large number of adaptive problems. The problems of survival alone number in the dozens or hundreds—problems of thermal regulation (getting too cold or too hot), avoiding predators and parasites, ingesting life-sustaining foods, and so on. Then there are problems of mating, such as selecting, attracting, and keeping good mates and getting rid of bad mates. There are also problems of parenting, such as breast feeding, weaning, socializing, deciding on the varying needs of different children, and so on. Then there are the problems of investing in kin, such as brothers, sisters, nephews, and nieces; dealing with social conflicts; defending yourself against aggressive groups; grappling with the social hierarchy; and dozens more.

Because specific problems require specific solutions, numerous specific problems will require numerous specific solutions. Just as our bodies contain thousands of specific mechanisms—a heart to pump blood, lungs for oxygen uptake, a liver to filter out toxins—the mind, according to this analysis, must also contain hundreds or thousands of specific mechanisms. Because a large number of different adaptive problems cannot be solved with just a few mechanisms, the human mind must contain a large number of evolved psychological mechanisms.

The specificity, complexity, and numerosity of evolved psychological mechanisms gives humans behavioral flexibility. The definition of a psychological mechanism, including the key components of input, decision rules, and output, highlights why adaptations are not rigid "instincts" that show up invariably in behavior. Recall the example of callous-producing mechanisms that have evolved to protect the structures beneath the skin. You can design your environment so that you don't experience repeated friction. In this case, your callus-producing mechanisms will not be activated. The activation of the mechanisms is dependent on contextual input coming from the environment. In the same way, all psychological mechanisms require input for their activation.

Psychological mechanisms are not like rigid instincts for another important reason—the decision rules. Decision rules are *if . . . then . . .* procedures, such as "if the snake hisses, then run for your life" or "if the person I'm attracted to shows interest, then smile and decrease distance." For most mechanisms, these decision rules permit at least several possible response options. Even in the simple case of encountering a snake, you can attack it with a stick, freeze and hope it will go away, or run away. In general, the more complex the mechanism, the more response options there will be.

Consider a carpenter's tool box. The carpenter gains flexibility not by having one "highly general tool" that can be used to cut, poke, saw, screw, twist, wrench, plane, balance, and hammer. Instead, the carpenter gains flexibility by having a large number of highly specific tools in the tool box. These highly specific tools can then be used in many combinations that would not be possible with one highly "flexible" tool. Indeed, it is difficult to imagine what a "general" tool would even look like, since there is no such thing as a "general carpenter's problem." In a similar fashion, humans gain their flexibility from having a large number of complex, specific, functional psychological mechanisms.

With each new mechanism that is added to the mind, an organism can perform a new task that it could not previously perform. A bird has feet that enable it to walk. Adding wings to a bird enables it to fly. Adding a beak to a bird enables it to break the shells of seeds and nuts and get at their nutritious core. With each new specific mechanism that is added, the bird can do a new task that it could not do without it. Having both feet and wings gives the bird the flexibility to both walk and fly.

This leads to a conclusion that is contrary to our intuitions. Most people's intuitions are that having a lot of innate mechanisms causes behavior to be rigid and inflexible. But just the opposite is the case. The more mechanisms we have, the greater the range of behaviors we can perform, and hence the greater the flexibility of behavior.

In summary, an evolutionary perspective provides some broad specifications of human nature. First, it suggests a nonarbitrary foundation for describing the contents of human nature—contents described by the evolved psychological mechanisms of humans. Second, it suggests that human nature is likely to be extremely complex, consisting of a large number of evolved psychological mechanisms rather than one or a few simple drives, motives, or goals. Third, because evolved psychological mechanisms tend to be problem-specific and hence activated only in particular contexts, it suggests that human nature will express itself in variable and context-dependent ways, rather than as invariant impulses as implied by some personality theories. Fourth, it suggests that human behavioral flexibility comes not from having highly general psychological mechanisms, but rather from having a large number of specific psychological mechanisms that are activated and concatenated in varying complex sequences, depending on the adaptive problem being confronted. These implications render the study of human nature a difficult and daunting task, but also one that is tractable, since progress can be made sequentially and cumulatively by uncovering each evolved psychological mechanism along with the adaptive problem that it was designed to solve.

Implications for Human Motives, Goals, and Strivings

This evolutionary analysis has profound implications for personality theories of human nature. It provides an incisive heuristic that guides theorists to the sorts of motives, goals, and strivings that commonly characterize humans. At the most general level, it suggests that, at some fundamental level of description, the *only* directional tendencies that can have evolved are those that historically contributed to the survival and reproduction of human ancestors. For a variety of reasons outlined by Symons (1992) and Tooby and Cosmides (1990b), what might seem like the most obvious candidate for a human motive—the goal of maximizing inclusive fitness—cannot have evolved. Because what constitutes fitness differs for different species, sexes, times, and contexts, evolution by selection cannot produce a domain-general motive of fitness maximization. It's not just that people never list "maximization of gene replication" as a personal project when asked to list what they are striving toward in their lives (Little, 1983). It's that no such goal can evolve even in principle, consciously or unconsciously. Stated differently, the *products* of the evolutionary process—the specific adaptations and by-products that characterize humans—should not be confused with the evolutionary *process* that fashioned them. Differential gene replication caused by differences in design features is the process by which adaptations get created. But the adaptations themselves do not include a desire to maximize gene replication.

Status Striving

What can evolve are *specific* motives, goals, and strivings, the attainment of which recurrently led to reproductive success over human evolutionary history. Consider one candidate for a universal human motive—*striving for status* (Buss, 1995b; Hogan, 1983; Maslow, 1970). Why would status striving be a universal evolved motive in humans? A variety of sources of evidence can be brought to bear on why status striving is a good candidate. First, among closely related species, such as chimpanzees, that form status hierarchies, those who are high in status tend to out-reproduce those who are lower. They do so because they gain preferential access to the resources needed for survival such as choice food, and they also gain preferential access to desirable mates. Among chimpanzees, for example, the dominant males tend to monopolize the matings with females during estrus, while the copulations of less dominant males, when they occur, take place outside of the peak period of fecundity (de Waal, 1982).

Second, the cross-cultural and historical evidence suggests that high status males, such as kings, emperors, and despots, routinely use their status to gain increased sexual access to females (Betzig, 1986). Kings and despots routinely stocked their harems with young, attractive, nubile women and had sex with them frequently. The Moroccan emperor Moulay Ismail the Bloodthirsty, for example, acknowledged having sired 888 children (actually, the number is probably double this, since only male children were acknowledged). His harem had 500 women. But when a woman reached the age of 30, she was banished from the emperor's harem, sent to a lower-level leader's harem, and replaced by a younger woman. Roman, Babylonian, Egyptian, Incan, Indian, and Chinese emperors acted in a similar manner, using their status to enjoin their trustees to scour the land for as many young pretty woman as could be found (Betzig, 1992).

Third, the cross-cultural evidence suggests that the children of high status individuals tend to receive better health care, and hence they survive longer and are more healthy than the children of lower status individuals. Among the Ache Indians, a hunter–gatherer group residing in Paraguay, tribal members take great pains to remove splinters and thorns from the feet of the children of high status males (Hill & Hurtado, 1996). Choice food, choice territory, and choice mates all flow with greater abundance to those high in status among hunters and gatherers around the world (e.g., Chagnon, 1983; Hart & Pilling, 1960; Hill & Hurtado, 1996).

If the attainment of high status recurrently led to increased reproductive success over human evolutionary history, then selection would have fashioned a human motive of status striving. The evolutionary analysis, however, does not stop there, because specific and testable hypotheses about status striving can be derived. One key hypothesis pertains to a sex difference in the strength of the status striving motive. Men and women differ in a fundamental fact of their reproductive biology—women bear the burdens (and pleasures) of heavy obligatory parental investment, because a minimum of nine months of pregnancy, with all the metabolic costs that entails, are required to produce a single child. Men, on the other hand, can produce a child from a single low-cost act of sexual intercourse. This fundamental sex difference has led to profound sex differences in sexual strategies (Buss, 1994; Symons, 1979; Williams, 1975). The key difference relevant to status striving is this: The reproductive payoff to men of gaining sexual access to multiple partners historically has been far greater than the reproductive payoff for women. Because status leads to increased sexual access to partners, men are predicted to be higher in status striving than women.

This evolutionary reasoning produces a specific and testable prediction—men in every culture around the world should have a greater desire for status, on average, than women. Among the many possible empirical tests that could be conducted are the following:

1. Men should be willing to take greater risks than women in order to achieve high status.
2. In the allocation of their effort across various adaptive problems, men should allocate more time and effort to status striving than women.
3. Men who lose status should engage in more desperate measures than women who lose status in order to staunch the loss.
4. The psychological pain that men experience after a status loss should be greater than the psychological pain women experience after a comparable status loss.

These are easily testable predictions, but to my knowledge, none of these predictions has been examined empirically in a systematic fashion across cultures.

There are several key implications from this evolutionary analysis of status striving. First, evolutionary psychology provides a heuristic, guiding theorists and researchers toward motives and goals that may form the building blocks of human nature. Second, the evolutionary predictions derived are testable and hence potentially falsifiable, contradicting a common but mistaken idea that evolutionary hypotheses are not testable. Third, this evolutionary analysis suggests that the building blocks of human nature will differ for men and women, principally because the sexes have faced recurrently different adaptive problems over the long expanse of human evolutionary history.

Mating Motivation

A second prime candidate for human nature is a universal mating motivation. At first blush, this may seem so obvious as to hardly warrant much comment, but first blushes can be misleading. Despite the obvious importance of sex and sexuality in the everyday lives of people (Buss, 1994), few personality theories explicitly consider sex. Freud, of course, was a major exception. Indeed, sexual motivation was the primary driving force in psychoanalytic theory, providing the raw energy that fueled nearly all other forms of human activity, from sports to cultural innovation (Freud, 1905/1953). Since Freud's theory, however, personality theories have minimized sexual and mating motivations. Evolutionary personality psychology appears to be the only large theoretical framework that predicts that sexual motivation will be a fundamental component of human nature (Buss, 1991). Even personality frameworks that restrict their focus to individual differences typically exclude individual differences in sexuality, despite their prevalence and importance in the everyday lives of persons (Schmitt & Buss, 1999).

Evolutionary analysis provides a compelling rationale for the importance of sexuality. Evolution by selection occurs through differential reproduction caused by differences in design (Symons, 1992). Reproductive differences, in other words, are the engine of the evolutionary process. Therefore, anything that resides in close proximity to reproduction and affects the probability of reproduction is likely to be a special target of the selective process. Perhaps nothing lies closer to the reproductive engine than sexuality and mating.

Consider what it would have taken human ancestors to succeed in reproduction. The first task is mate attraction, successfully enticing a member of the opposite sex to become one's mate. This task is more difficult than it might seem, for it includes at a minimum selecting the "right" mates on whom to deploy one's attraction tactics (e.g., those that are reproductively valuable rather than sterile) as well as embodying the desires of the targeted member of the opposite sex sufficiently to succeed in attraction (Buss, 1994). Embodying or fulfilling the desires of the targeted other might include a prolonged effort at attaining a modicum of social status, establishing a favorable reputation among one's peers, and displaying physical cues of desirability.

Successful attraction is not enough. To produce viable offspring, human ancestors would also have had to be motivated to engage in sex with the targeted person. Although this may appear to flow naturally and effortlessly for some, it actually entails a complex set of properly sequenced and contingent behaviors in order to culminate in the successful merging of the male sperm and female egg. Mating motivation also entails the intricate tasks of besting intrasexual competitors in successful attraction tactics (Buss, 1988a; Schmitt & Buss, 1996), perhaps derogation of intrasexual competitors to make them seem less desirable (Buss & Dedden, 1990), and successful mate retention (Buss, 1988b; Buss & Shackelford, 1997). Mating motivation is a multifaceted venture, entailing a host of subtasks, any of which can result in a failure. As descendants of ancestors who succeeded in all of these mating tasks, modern humans have inherited the mating motivations and strategies that led to their success. Personality theories that fail to include mating motivation, broadly conceived, must be viewed as woefully inadequate, from the perspective of evolutionary psychology.

Like status striving, however, evolutionary analysis provides a powerful rationale for predicting sex differences in the nature of mating motivation. Due to the asymmetries in obligatory parental investment, for example, men are predicted to have a greater desire than women for a larger number of sex partners, and a large body of empirical evidence supports this prediction (Buss & Schmitt, 1993; Kenrick, Sadalla, Groth, & Trost, 1990). Furthermore, a large body of cross-cultural evidence supports the specific predictions that men will be more motivated to seek young and physically attractive mates, whereas women will be more motivated to seek mates who offer a willingness and ability to accrue and commit resources (Buss, 1989a; Kenrick & Keefe, 1992). Personality theories that include mating motivation, in short, must also include specific premises about the ways in which mating motivation is known to differ between the sexes, corresponding to sex differences in the adaptive problems faced over human evolutionary history.

Universal Emotions

Another core feature of human nature proposed by evolutionary psychology involves universal mechanisms of emotion (Buss, 1989b; Nesse, 1990; Tooby & Cosmides, 1990b). A large body of cross-cultural evidence already exists to suggest that certain forms of emotional expression are universal (Ekman, 1973). Evolutionary analysis suggests that certain emotions will be universal, designed to solve specific adaptive problems. One candidate for such a universal emotion is jealousy.

Jealousy has been hypothesized to be a universal emotion that evolved to solve the problem of mate retention (Daly, Wilson, & Weghorst, 1982; Buss, Larsen, Westen, & Semmelroth, 1992). Threats to a valued sexual or romantic mating relationship are hypothesized to activate the emotion of jealousy, which then motivates action designed to reduce the threat. Jealousy may motivate actions that range from vigilance to violence, with three potential goals—to ward off intrasexual competitors, to induce one's mate to stay in the relationship and not stray, and to enhance one's value to one's mate as an inducement to remain in the relationship (Buss & Shackelford, 1997). Although jealousy and the mate retention tactics it produces clearly fail some of the time in their adaptive function, the hypothesis is that they succeeded, on average, relative to nonjealous counterparts over evolutionary time.

Like status striving and sexual motivation, evolutionary analysis provides a powerful basis for predicting sex differences. These are not sex differences in the presence or intensity of jealousy, since both sexes have faced the adaptive problem of mate retention. And indeed, the empirical evidence suggests that the sexes do not differ in measures such as the frequency and intensity of jealousy experienced (Buunk & Hupka, 1987).

An evolutionary analysis, however, suggests that the sexes might differ in the events that activate jealousy. Specifically, because fertilization occurs internally within women and not within men, men over evolutionary history have faced the adaptive problem of "paternity uncertainty." Because a partner's sexual intercourse with another man would have been the primary threat to paternity certainty, and hence to successful reproduction, men's jealousy is hypothesized to be specially keyed to signals of sexual infidelity by a partner. Ancestral women, in contrast, faced a different adaptive problem—the loss of a mate's time, energy, effort, attention, investment, and commitment, all of which could get re-channeled to a rival woman and her children. Because a man's emotional involvement with another woman is a leading cue to such redirection of commitments, women's jealousy is predicted to be keyed to signals of emotional involvement more than to sexual infidelity per se, although the two signals are clearly correlated in nature.

Much empirical evidence supports these predicted sex differences. In forced-choice dilemmas, men more than women report that they would experience greater distress at a partner's sexual infidelity, whereas women more than men report that they would experience greater distress as a result of a partner's emotional infidelity (Buss, et al., 1992). These results have been replicated by different researchers (Weiderman & Allgeier, 1993), have been replicated across methods that include psychophysiological recordings (Buss et al., 1992), and have been replicated across Western and non-Western cultures (Buunk, Angleitner, Oubaid, & Buss, 1996). All of these empirical findings suggest that jealousy is a universal and universally sex-differentiated emotion that is a good candidate for inclusion in a personality theory of human nature.

Jealousy is clearly not the only candidate. Others include fear, rage, envy, disgust, sadness, and others. As Ekman (1994) notes, the empirical evidence suggest that these emotions are universal across human cultures, have been adaptive phylogenetically, occur in common eliciting contexts despite individual differences and cultural differences, are likely to be present in closely related primate species, and can be activated quickly, prior to awareness, mobilizing action designed to respond to specific adaptive challenges. There is no reason why theories of personality should fail to include these emotions as candidates for the core of human nature.

Parental Motivation

From an evolutionary perspective, offspring are vehicles for parents. They are a means by which their parent's genes get transported to succeeding generations. Without these vehicles, an individual's genes would perish forever. Given the supreme importance of offspring as genetic vehicles, it is reasonable to expect that natural selection will favor powerful mechanisms in parents to ensure the survival and reproductive success of their children. Aside from the problems of mating, perhaps no other adaptive problems are as paramount as making sure that one's offspring survive and thrive. Indeed, without the success of offspring, all the effort that an organism invested in mating would be reproductively meaningless. Evolution, in short, should produce a rich repertoire of parental mechanisms specially adapted to caring for offspring.

Despite the paramount importance of parental care from an evolutionary perspective, it has been a relatively neglected topic within the field of human personality psychology. When the evolutionary psychologists Martin Daly and Margo Wilson prepared a chapter on the topic for the 1987 Nebraska Symposium on Motivation, they scanned the 34 previous volumes in the series in search of either psychological research or theories on parental motivation. Not a single one of the 34 volumes contained even a paragraph on parental motivation (Daly & Wilson, 1995). And despite the widespread everyday knowledge that mothers tend to love their children, the very phenomenon of powerful parental love appears to have baffled psychologists at a theoretical level. One prominent psychologist who has written books on the topic of love noted that "The needs that lead many of us to feel unconditional love for our children also seem to be remarkably persistent, for reasons that are not at present altogether clear" (Sternberg, 1986, p. 133). From an evolutionary perspective, however, the reasons for deep parental love do seem clear, or at least understandable. It is reasonable to expect that selection has designed precisely such psychological mechanisms—parental mechanisms of motivation designed to ensure the survival and reproductive success of the invaluable vehicles that transport an individual's genes into the next generation.

The evolution of parenting motivation has produced in humans mechanisms that are far from unconditional. Empirical evidence suggests than parents invest more in children when they are higher in phenotypic quality, have a high probability of genetic relatedness to parents, and have the ability to convert such aid into reproduction (see Buss, 1999, for a summary of the empirical evidence). Mothers, by virtue of internal fertilization, are 100% sure that the offspring they bear are genetically their own. Fathers can never be sure. This analysis leads to the prediction that maternal love will tend to be stronger than paternal love, on average. Although there is circumstantial evidence to support this prediction, such as the higher rates of child abandonment by men compared with women, this hypothesis remains to be tested rigorously in studies of parental feeling and behavior. The incidence of physical abuse of children, to take another example, is roughly 40 times higher in step-families compared with genetically intact families, supporting the prediction that genetic relatedness affects feelings of parental love (Daly & Wilson, 1988). Moreover, the evolutionary theory of parent–offspring conflict suggests that children will generally desire a higher level of parental investment that parents are willing to give, since parents are motivated to distribute their investments across offspring (Trivers, 1974).

Parental motivation, as a core feature of human nature, appears to be absent from most or all personality theories, although Freud clearly signaled the importance of relationships with parents in the development of personality. Evolutionary psychology provides a heuristic for the inclusion of this neglected component of human nature.

Other Motivational Candidates for Human Nature

Status striving, mating motivation, jealousy, emotions, and parental motivation are merely a few of the most obvious candidates for a comprehensive theory of human nature. Others include the desire to form friendships or dyadic reciprocal alliances (Bleske & Buss, 1999), the desire to help and invest in kin (Burnstein, Crandall, & Kitayaman, 1994), and the motivation to form and join larger coalitions (Tooby & Cosmides, 1988). An evolutionary perspective leads us to anticipate the evolution of many complex psychological mechanisms underlying each of these forms of social relationships. One clear implication is that evolutionary psychology provides a nonarbitrary theoretical foundation for postulating fundamental human motivations, such as "sex and aggression," or "love and power," or "getting along and getting ahead." At the same time, it suggests that the postulation of only one or a few such motivational tendencies will grossly underestimate the complexity of human nature.

THE EVOLUTION OF INDIVIDUAL DIFFERENCES

According to this analysis, individual differences cannot be divorced from, or considered apart from, the foundations of human nature. Just as the fundamental mechanisms of cars yield the major dimensions along which cars differ, the fundamental psychological mechanisms of humans yield the major dimensions along which human personality differs. Personality models of individual differences, according to this reasoning, must have as a foundation a specification of human nature.

This section offers some suggestions for a nonarbitrary evolutionary framework of individual differences (see Buss & Greiling, 1999). First, the major ways of treating individual differences from an evolutionary psychological perspective are discussed. Second, specific examples of adaptive individual differences stemming from species-typical motives and strivings are presented to illustrate these conceptions.

Major Forms of Individual Differences

Individual differences can emerge from a variety of heritable and nonheritable sources. Evidence from behavioral genetic studies of personality strongly suggests that both are important. Personality characteristics commonly show evidence of moderate heritability, typically ranging from 30% to 50% (Bouchard & McGue, 1990; Loehlin, Horn, & Willerman, 1990; Plomin, DeFries, & McClearn, 1990). Simultaneously, these studies provide the strongest evidence of environmental sources of variance, ranging from 50% to 70%. A conceptual taxonomy of sources of adaptively patterned individual differences is presented below, based on environmental and heritable sources, as well as interactions between these sources (Buss & Greiling, 1999). The routes to adaptively patterned individual differences are presented descriptively with illustrative cases that are sometimes speculative.

Early Experiential Calibration

Individuals who share a common evolved psychology can experience different early environmental events that channel them into alternative strategies. According to this conception, each person comes equipped with two or more potential strategies within their repertoire. From this species-typical menu, one strategy is selected based on early environmental experiences. These early experiences, in essence, "lock in" a person to one strategy to the exclusion of others that could have been pursued had the environmental input been different.

Belsky, Steinberg, and Draper (1991), for example, propose the critical event of early father presence versus father absence as a calibrator of alternative sexual strategies. Individuals growing up in father-absent homes during the first 5 to 7 years of life, according to this theory, develop the expectations that parental resources will not be reliably or predictably provided and adult pair bonds will not be enduring. Accordingly, such individuals cultivate a sexual strategy marked by early sexual maturation, early sexual initiation, and frequent partner switching—a strategy designed to produce a large number of offspring with low levels of investment in each. Extraverted and impulsive personality traits may accompany this strategy. Other individuals are perceived as untrustworthy, relationships as transitory. Resources sought from brief sexual liaisons are opportunistically attained and immediately extracted.

Individuals marked by a reliably investing father during the first 5 to 7 years of life, according to the theory, develop a different set of expectations about the nature and trustworthiness of others. People are seen as reliable and trustworthy, and relationships are expected to be enduring. These early environmental experiences channel individuals toward a long-term mating strategy, marked by delay of sexual maturation, a later onset of sexual activity, a search for long-term securely attached adult relationships, and heavy investment in a small number of children.

All theories of environmental influence, including this one, ultimately rest on a foundation of evolved psychological mechanisms, whether they are acknowledged as such or not (Tooby & Cosmides, 1990a). Contrary to views that perpetuate the false dichotomies of nature/nurture or genetic/environmental, evolved psychological mechanisms are necessarily entailed by theories of environmental influence (Tooby & Cosmides, 1990). In this particular case, the implicit psychological mechanisms are specifically designed to take as *input* information about the presence and reliability of paternal resources, to *process* that input via an evolved set of decision rules, to *develop* one of two possible psychological models of the social world, and to pursue one of two alternative mating strategies as *output* of the mechanisms. It is possible, of course, that mechanisms of this sort may permit three or more alternative strategies from a larger menu of options.

There are two key points to draw from the Belsky et al. (1991) theory of adaptively patterned individual differences. First, the individual variation lies not on a single dimension or trait, but rather represents a coherent constellation of covarying qualities, including reproductive physiology (e.g., early age of menarche), psychological models of the social world (e.g., others as untrustworthy), and overt behavior (e.g., transitory sexual liaisons).

Second, the individual differences that result from early experiential calibration are adaptively patterned, the result of evolved mechanisms that assess the social environment and select one strategy from the menu. In one case, reproductive success historically was attained through a high reproductive rate, with perhaps a concomitant decrease in the survival and reproduction of any one offspring. In the other case, reproductive success historically was attained through a lower reproductive rate marked by heavy investment in the survival and reproduction of fewer offspring. The evolution of these environment-contingent strategies presumably resulted from a long and recurrent evolutionary history in which different individuals confronted radically different rearing environments. Environmental variation over human evolutionary history presumably selected for developmentally flexible mechanisms that take as input the nature of the rearing environment as a key cue to the expected adult environment.

Enduring Situational Evocation

Many human adaptations respond to immediately encountered environmental contingencies rather than being "set in plaster" by early environmental events. The physiological mechanism that results in calluses, for example, responds to immediately experienced friction to the skin. Individuals differ recurrently in the degree to which they pursue activities that result in frequent repeated friction to the skin. The stable individual differences in calluses, in this example, are properly understood as adaptively patterned differences stemming from enduring environmental differences in the evocation of the callous-producing mechanism. These enduring individual differences, like those set by early experiential calibration, are the result of a specific form of interaction between environments and evolved mechanisms.

A similar form of adaptively patterned individual differences can occur with psychological factors. Consider a man who is married to a woman who has higher perceived "mate value" on the mating market than he does (Frank,

1988; Tooby & Cosmides, 1990a; Walster, Traupmann, & Walster, 1978). Even if his social environment is not populated with interested same-sex rivals, his enduring relationship with his wife may lower his threshold for jealousy compared with the man who is equal to, or higher than, his wife in perceived mate value (Tooby & Cosmides, 1990a). As a consequence, he may get jealous more easily (Tooby & Cosmides, 1990a), and engage in mate guarding efforts, such as monitoring his wife's activities with greater vigilance and striving to sequester her more intensely (Buss, 1988a). He may become more easily suspicious about her interactions with others and more enraged when observing her conversing casually with other men. Some empirical evidence supports these suggestions, indicating that the more desirable partner is indeed more susceptible to defecting (Walster et al., 1978; Hatfield, Traupmann, Sprecher, Utne, & Hay, 1985). From an adaptationist perspective, a mechanism for adjusting one's threshold for jealousy could have resulted from thousands of selective events in the evolutionary past in which a mate value discrepancy, on average, was statistically associated with a greater likelihood of a partner's infidelity or defection (Tooby & Cosmides, 1990a).

Individual differences in jealousy, in this example, are enduring over time and adaptively patterned. They rest on a foundation of evolved psychological mechanisms shared by all but differentially activated in some. Were the enduring environment to change—for example, if the man got divorced and remarried a woman of equal or lower mate value—then the enduring pattern of psychological and behavioral jealousy would presumably change (Tooby & Cosmides, 1990a).

In sum, enduring adaptive individual differences result from evocations produced by the enduring situations inhabited. These relatively enduring situations may include one's overall desirability as a mate on the mating market (Gangestad & Simpson, 1999), age, and the ratio of men to women in the local population (Pedersen, 1991). Future research could profitably explore these and other features of enduring environments as sources of relatively stable individual differences.

Strategic Specialization

From an evolutionary perspective, competition is keenest among those pursuing the same strategy. As one niche becomes more and more crowded with competitors, success can suffer compared with those seeking alternative niches (Maynard Smith, 1982; Wilson, 1994). Selection can favor mechanisms that cause some individuals to seek niches where the competition is less intense and hence where the average payoff may be higher.

Mating provides some clear examples. If most women pursue the man with the highest status or greatest resources, then some women would achieve more success by courting males outside of the arenas in which competition is keenest. In a mating system in which both polygyny and monogamy are possible, for example, a woman might be better off securing all of the resources of a lower status monogamous man rather than having to settle for a fraction of the resources of a high status polygynous man.

The ability to exploit a niche will depend on the resources and personal characteristics an individual brings to the situation, whether environmental or heritable in origin (Buss, 1989a; Gangestad & Simpson, 1999). One variable that is not heritable is birth order. It is possible that first borns and second borns have faced, on average, recurrently different adaptive problems over human evolutionary history. Sulloway (1996), for example, argues that first borns occupy a niche characterized by strong identification with parents and other existing authority figures. Second borns, in contrast, have less to gain by authority identification and more to gain by overthrowing the existing order. According to Sulloway, birth order influences niche specialization. Second borns develop a different personality marked by greater rebelliousness, lower levels of conscientiousness, and higher levels of openness to new experiences (Sulloway, 1996). Birth order differences show up strongly among scientists, where second borns tend to be strong advocates of scientific revolutions; first borns tend to strenuously resist such revolutions (Sulloway, 1996).

Whether or not the details of Sulloway's arguments turn out to be correct, the example illustrates strategic niche specialization. Individual differences are adaptively patterned, but they are *not* based on heritable individual differences. Rather, birth order, a nonheritable individual difference, provides input (presumably through interactions with family members) into a species-typical mechanism that canalizes strategic niche specialization.

Adaptive Self-Assessment

According to Tooby and Cosmides (1990a), selection operates through the attainment of goal states. Any feature of the individual's world—*including one's own personal characteristics*—that influences the successful attainment of those goal states may be assessed and evaluated by evolved psychological mechanisms (Tooby & Cosmides, 1990a, p. 59). Evolved mechanisms, in this view, are not only attuned to recurrent features of the external world, such as the reliability of parental provisioning, but can also be attuned to the evaluation of self. Tooby and Cosmides (1990a) coined the term "reactive heritability" to describe evolved psychological mechanisms designed to take as input heritable qualities as a guide to strategic solutions.

Suppose that all men have an evolved decision rule of the form: Pursue an aggressive strategy when aggression can be successfully implemented to achieve goals, but pursue a cooperative strategy when aggression cannot be successfully implemented (modified from Tooby & Cosmides, 1990a, p. 58). Evolved decision rules are undoubtedly more complex than this. But given this simplified rule, those who happen to be mesomorphic (muscular) in body build can more successfully carry out an aggressive strategy than those who are ectomorphic (skinny) or endomorphic (rotund). Heritable individual differences in body build provide input into the decision rule, thereby producing stable individual differences in aggression and cooperativeness. In this example, the proclivity toward aggression is not directly heritable, but rather would be "reactively heritable" in the sense that it is a secondary consequence of heritable body build that provides input into species-typical mechanisms of self-assessment and decision making.

Similar models of heritable adaptive input can be developed for individual differences in mating strategies. A recent study assessed the physical appearance of teenage boys on two dimensions—the degree to which their faces looked dominant or submissive and physically attractive (Mazur, Halpern, & Udry, 1994). Only photographs were available for the judgments of these features, with a dominant person being defined as someone who "tells other people what to do, is respected, influential, and often a leader" (p. 90). The teenagers who were judged to be more facially dominant and physically attractive were discovered to have had more heterosexual experience with "heavy petting" and sexual intercourse. Furthermore, dominant facial appearance predicted cumulative coital experience, even after statistically controlling for facial attractiveness and puberty development.

Although speculative, these findings may illustrate heritable adaptive input, on the assumption that facial features involved in appearing dominant and attractive are partially heritable. Males could all have an evolved psychological mechanism that takes as input a self-assessment (Tooby & Cosmides, 1990a) of the degree to which one appears dominant and attractive : "If high on these dimensions, pursue a short-term sexual strategy; if low, pursue a long-term sexual strategy" (see also Gangestad & Simpson, 1992, 1999). In this example, of course, one cannot rule out third variables, such as testosterone, which may simultaneously produce a more dominant looking face and a higher sex drive.

According to the conception of adaptive self-assessment of heritable qualities, stable individual differences in the pursuit of short-term and long-term sexual strategies are not directly heritable. But they represent adaptive individual differences based on self-assessment of heritable information.

Frequency-Dependent Adaptive Strategies

In general, the process of directional selection tends to use up heritable variation. Heritable variants that are more successful tend to replace those that are less successful, resulting in species-typical adaptations that show little or no heritable variation in the presence or absence of basic functional components (Williams, 1966).

There is a major exception to this trend—frequency-dependent selection. In some contexts, two or more heritable variants can be sustained in equilibrium. The most obvious example is biological sex. In sexually reproducing species, the two sexes represent frequency-dependent suites of covarying adaptive complexes. If one sex becomes rare relative to the other, success increases for the rare sex, and hence selection favors parents who produce offspring of the less common sex. Typically, the sexes are maintained in approximately equal ratio through the process of frequency-dependent selection. Frequency dependent selection requires that the payoff of each strategy decreases as its frequency increases, relative to other strategies, in the population.

Alternative adaptive strategies can also be maintained *within sex* by frequency-dependent selection. Among the bluegill sunfish, for example, three different male mating strategies are observed—a "parental" strategy that defends the nest, a "sneak" strategy that matures to only a small body size, and a "mimic" strategy that resembles the female form (Gross, 1982). The sneakers gain sexual access to the female eggs by avoiding detection due to their small size, while the mimics gain access by resembling females and thus avoiding aggression from the parental males. As the parasitizing strategists increase in frequency, however, their success decreases—their existence depends upon the parentals who become rarer as the parasites become more common, rendering the parasite strategies more difficult to pursue. Thus, heritable alternative strategies within sex are maintained by the process of frequency-dependent selection. Theoretically, these heritable individual differences can persist in the population indefinitely through frequency-dependent selection, unlike the process of directional selection, which tends to drive out heritable variation.

Gangestad and Simpson (1990) argue that individual differences in women's mating strategies have been caused (and are presumably maintained) by frequency-dependent selection. They start with the observation that competition tends to be most intense among individuals pursuing the same mating strategy (Maynard Smith, 1982). This lays the groundwork for the evolution of alternative strategies.

According to Gangestad and Simpson, women's mating strategies should center on two key qualities of potential mates—the "parental investment" a man could provide and his "genetic fitness." A man who is able and willing to invest in her and her children can be an extraordinarily valuable reproductive asset. Similarly, independent of a man's ability to invest, women could benefit by selecting men who are themselves in good condition and are highly attractive to other women. Such men may carry genes for good health, physical attractiveness, or sexiness which are then passed on to the woman's own sons or daughters.

There may be a tradeoff, however, between selecting a man for his parenting abilities and selecting him for his genetic fitness. Men who are highly attractive to women, for example, may be reluctant to commit to any one woman. Thus, a woman seeking a man for his genetic fitness may have to settle for a short-term sexual relationship without parental investment.

These different selection foci, according to Gangestad and Simpson (1990), produce two alternative female mating strategies. Women seeking a high-investing mate are predicted to adopt a "restricted" sexual strategy marked by delayed intercourse and a prolonged courtship. This would enable a woman to assess the man's level of commitment to her, detect the existence of prior commitments to other women or children, and simultaneously signal to the man her sexual fidelity and hence assure him of his paternity in future offspring.

Women "seeking" a man for the quality of his genes (no consciousness of goal state is implied by this formulation), on the other hand, have less reason to delay intercourse. A man's level of commitment to her is less relevant, prolonged assessment of his prior commitments is less necessary, and so there is less need for delaying intercourse. Indeed, if the man is pursuing a short-term sexual strategy, any delay on her part may deter him from seeking sexual intercourse with her, thus defeating the raison d'etre of the mating strategy.

According to this theory, the two mating strategies of women—restricted and unrestricted—evolved and are maintained by frequency-dependent selection. As the number of *unrestricted* females in the population increases, the number of "sexy sons" also increases. As their numbers increase, the competition between these sons increases, and hence the success of the unrestricted strategy decreases. Conversely, as the number of *restricted* females in the population increases, the competition for men who are able and willing to invest exclusively in them and their children increases, and the fitness of that strategy commensurably declines.

There are many complicating factors with this theory, and the authors recognize that it must be described and tested more formally. Furthermore, the theory requires evidence that (1) the key elements of each strategy must covary in an organized coherent fashion; (2) the covarying suite of elements must fulfill stringent criteria for adaptation, such as efficiency, economy, and precision for solving the respective adaptive problems; and (3) the adaptive payoff of each strategy decreases as it becomes more common in the population. Pending these further tests, it remains a viable theory of individual differences produced and maintained by frequency-dependent selection.

Mealey (1995) proposes a theory of primary psychopathy based on frequency-dependent selection. Psychopathy (sometimes called sociopathy or antisocial personality disorder) represents a cluster of traits marked by irresponsible and unreliable behavior, egocentrism, impulsivity, an inability to form lasting relationships, superficial social charm, and a deficit of social emotions, such as love, shame, guilt, and empathy (Cleckley, 1982; American Psychiatric Association, 1994). Psychopaths pursue a deceptive or "cheating" strategy in their social interactions. Psychopathy is more common among men than women, forming roughly 3%–4% of the former and less than 1% of the latter (DSM-IV, American Psychiatric Association, 1994).

Psychopaths pursue a social strategy characterized by exploiting the reciprocity mechanisms of others. After feigning cooperation, psychopaths typically defect. This cheating strategy might be pursued by men who are unlikely to out-compete other men in a more traditional or mainstream status hierarchy (Mealey, 1995).

According to the theory, a psychopathic strategy can be maintained by frequency-dependent selection. As the number of cheaters increases, and hence the average cost to the cooperative hosts increases, mechanisms would presumably evolve to detect cheating and to inflict costs on those pursuing a cheating strategy. As the prevalence of psychopaths increases, therefore, the average payoff of the psychopath strategy decreases. As long as the frequency of psychopaths is not too large, it can be maintained amidst a population composed primarily of cooperators (Mealey, 1995).

There is some evidence, albeit indirect, that is at least consistent with Mealey's theory of psychopathy. First, behavioral genetics studies suggest that psychopathy may be moderately heritable, at least as indicated by the MMPI Psychopathic Deviate scale (Willerman, Loehlin, & Horn, 1992). Second, some psychopaths appear to pursue an exploitative short-term sexual strategy, which could be the primary route through which genes for psychopathy increase or are maintained (Rowe, 1995). Psychopathic men tend to be more sexually precocious, have sex with a larger number of women, have more illegitimate children, and are more likely to separate from their wives than nonpsychopathic men (Rowe, 1995). This short-term, opportunistic, exploitative sexual strategy would be expected to rise in populations marked by high mobility, where the reputational costs associated with such a strategy would be least likely to be incurred (Wilson, 1995).

There are several challenges to this theory, such as whether it represents a type or a continuum (Baldwin, 1995; Eysenck, 1995), whether its frequency is sufficiently large to be maintained by frequency-dependent selection, and whether it represents a recently evolved cluster in modern populations or an ancient evolved strategy (Wilson, 1995; but see Mealey's, 1995, response to these challenges).

Despite these complications, Mealey's theory of psychopathy and Gangestad and Simpson's theory of sociosexuality nicely illustrate the possibility that heritable alternative strategies can be maintained by frequency-dependent selection. Frequency-dependent selection offers a potential explanation for integrating the cumulative results from behavioral genetic studies (e.g., Willerman et al., 1992) and the findings on the sexual strategies apparently pursued by psychopaths (Rowe, 1995) with an evolutionary analysis of adaptive individual differences.

Two final comments on frequency-dependent strategies. First, frequency-dependent strategies need not occur through heritable differences. They can occur through local situation-dependent shifts, whereby individuals adjust their strategy according to the frequency of those pursuing various strategies. Second, the logic of frequency dependent selection does not require typological thinking or discrete strategies. It can also produce continuous heritable variation.

Traversing the Social Landscape of Individual Differences

Other individuals compose one of the primary environments within which humans function (Alexander, 1987). Other individuals are crucial for solving adaptive problems. The presence of large individual differences, whether adaptively patterned or not, defines a major part of the human adaptive landscape (Buss, 1991). Attending to those individual differences can facilitate solutions to adaptive problems. Ignoring those individual differences can be disastrous. Failure to assess differences in whether others are pursuing cooperative or defecting social strategies, for example, can result in resources pilfered, reputations damaged, and pregnancies unwanted.

Over evolutionary time, those individuals who attended to and acted on individual differences in others that were adaptively consequential would have survived and reproduced more successfully than those who were oblivious to adaptively consequential differences in others. It has been proposed that humans have evolved difference-detecting assessment mechanisms that facilitated successful adaptive solutions (Buss, 1989b, 1996).

These mechanisms would have been critical in assessing individual differences for the goals of mate selection, coalition formation, and dyadic alliance building. The formation of these different relationships and the attendant adaptive problems entailed by them may require assessment specificity. That is, different individual differences in the social landscape may be relevant to some problems and irrelevant to others. Individual differences in sexual fidelity, for example, are more critical to assessing the viability of a long-term mate than a coalition partner (Shackelford & Buss, 1996). Despite some degree of domain-specificity, some dimensions of individual differences, such as those captured by the five-factor model of personality, may be important because they are relevant to a host of different adaptive problems, and hence they transcend the particulars of specific relationships (MacDonald, 1995).

Because individual differences are so critical to solving adaptive problems, individuals often attempt to manipulate others' perceptions and reputations of their own and competitors' standings on relevant dimensions of differences. In mate competition, for example, men tend to impugn the surgency, agreeableness, and emotional stability of their rivals (Buss & Dedden, 1990). Thus, derogation of competitors becomes a verbal form of trait usage as manipulation, exploiting the difference-detecting mechanisms of others in the service of mate competition. Simultaneously, men will exaggerate their own positive traits in self-presentation to a woman, striving to appear to fulfill characteristics that she desires in a mate (Buss, 1988b).

Whatever the origins of individual differences—whether they are adaptively patterned or not adaptively patterned—they represent important vectors in the human adaptive landscape. When the individual differences of others in one's social environment are adaptively patterned, however, it may be especially important to detect and act on them because they are more likely to represent coherent and hence predictable suites of covarying qualities rather than randomly varying or single-dimension attributes.

Ultimately, comprehensive theories of personality and individual differences will require accounts of both the adaptive and nonadaptive differences, as well as the difference-detecting mechanisms humans have evolved to grapple with the varying terrain of the human adaptive landscape.

CONCLUSIONS

Theories of personality, according to the arguments presented in this chapter, ideally should include both a specification of human nature and an account of the major ways in which individuals differ. Evolutionary psychology provides a powerful heuristic for the discovery of both. Because the evolutionary process is the only known creative process capable, in principle, of producing complex organic mechanisms, all theories of human nature must at some level be anchored in the basic principles of evolution by selection. Theories of personality inconsistent with these evolutionary principles stand little or no chance of being correct (Buss, 1991).

The products of the evolutionary process define the contents of the nature of all species, and human nature is no exception. These products are primarily adaptations, by-products of adaptations, and a residue of noise. Because by-products can only be understood by first describing the adaptations from which the by-products flow, adaptations must form the core nature of all animals, including human nature.

For a variety of reasons, many adaptations are species-typical, with important exceptions, such as those that are sex-linked or caused by processes such as frequency-dependent selection or variation in selection pressure over time and space (see also Wilson, 1994). The core of personality theory, therefore, must be defined by the adaptive mechanisms that are characteristic of most members of our species—in other words, a species-typical human nature. The mechanisms of human nature cannot be fully understood without identifying the adaptive problems they were designed to solve. These adaptive solutions exist in the present because in the past they contributed, either directly or indirectly, to the successful reproduction of ancestors who carried them. Modern humans are the end product of a long and unbroken chain of ancestors who succeeded in solving the adaptive problems necessary for, or that enhanced, survival and reproduction. As the descendants of these successful ancestors, modern humans carry with them the adaptive mechanisms that led to their success.

The most obvious candidates for the human nature component of personality theory are those that are closely linked with the engine of the evolutionary process—differential reproductive success. These candidates include status striving, which gives humans access to the resources of survival and reproduction; mating motivations, which propel reproduction; parenting motivations, which increase the survival and success of the "vehicles" produced by mating unions; universal emotions, such as jealousy, which protect those reproductive resources already acquired; and a host of others, such as the ability to discern the motives and beliefs of other minds (Haselton & Buss, 1997).

Personality theories would be incomplete without an account of the major ways in which individuals differ. Theories of individual differences, however, cannot be divorced from theories of human nature, any more than a theory of "car differences" could be divorced from a theory of "universal car nature." Although some individual differences may be random, and hence independent of the basic functioning of human nature, the most important individual differences are those that stem from the workings and nature of the species-typical mechanisms.

Major individual differences can originate, in principle, from environmental sources of variation, genetic sources of variation, or a combination of the two. It may seem ironic to some that the environmentally based individual differences are most easily handled within this evolutionary psychological framework. Individual differences can result from varying environmental input into species-typical mechanisms. All individuals possess callus-producing mechanisms but differ in the thickness and distribution of calluses because of individual differences in experiences of friction to the skin. Similarly, all individuals may possess a psychological mechanisms of jealousy but differ in the degree to which they enduringly occupy an environment filled with threats to one's romantic relationship, perhaps because they are mated with someone who is habitually flirtatious or who is higher in "mate value" and so gives off signals of defection (Tooby & Cosmides, 1990a).

Enduring environments experienced, however, are not the only source of individual differences. Early experience during childhood, for example, can potentially calibrate or set thresholds on species-typical mechanisms. Children growing up without an investing father, for example, may select a short-term mating strategy in adulthood, whereas those with an investing father may opt for a long-term mating strategy. In this example, the species-typical mating mechanism contains a fixed "menu" of alternatives. Which alternative is selected from this menu is influenced by early experience.

Individual differences can also derive from strategic specialization. Indeed, selection will sometimes favor the evolution of strategies whereby organisms seek out niches that contain less competition. These forms of strategic specialization may be influenced by environmental factors, such as early training in a particular domain; by heritable factors, such as natural athletic or verbal ability; or by a combination of the two.

Frequency-dependent selection is one selective force that can create heritable individual differences that are adaptively patterned. Like the other forms of major individual differences, those due to frequency-dependent selection will be most likely to occur in domains that are closely linked with the engine of the evolutionary process, that is differential reproduction. The proposal by Gangestad and Simpson (1990) for individual differences in sociosexuality is one example Another is hypothesized by Mealey (1995), who proposed that psychopathy has evolved as a frequency-dependent social and sexual strategy that can exist in low levels, essentially parasitizing off of the more common long-term cooperative strategy. These and other forms of frequency-dependent selection require further empirical documentation, but they represent an exciting and promising form of adaptive individual differences for future personality theory.

Not all individual differences, of course, will be adaptively patterned. Some might occur because of random environmental forces, genetic noise, genetic defects, and other factors. The evolutionary psychology framework, however, suggests that the most important individual differences will be those linked with the major adaptive mechanisms that define human nature.

Given this early stage in the development of evolutionary personality psychology, no pretense is made that we have arrived at, or even approximated, the ultimate theory of personality. This chapter has merely offered some suggestions for ingredients that might be contained within a future theory of personality. Evolutionary psychology, however, does offer something lacking in all existing nonevolutionary theories of personality—a nonarbitrary anchoring for a specification of the basic psychological machinery that humans share, as well as for the major ways in which humans differ.

REFERENCES

Alexander, R. D. (1987). *The biology of moral systems*. New York: Aldine de Gruytor.

American Psychiatric Association. (1994). *Diagnostic and statistical manual of mental disorders* (4th ed.). Washington, DC: Author.

Baldwin, J. D. (1995). Continua outperform dichotomies. *Behavioral and Brain Sciences, 18,* 543–544.

Belsky, J., Steinberg, L., & Draper, P. (1991). Childhood experience, interpersonal development, and reproductive strategy: An evolutionary theory of socialization. *Child Development, 62,* 647–670.

Betzig, L. L. (1986). *Despotism and differential reproduction: A Darwinian view of history*. Hawthorne, NY: Aldine.

Betzig, L. (1992). Roman polygyny. *Ethology and Sociobiology, 13,* 309–349.

Bleske, A., & Buss, D. M. (1999). *Functions of friendship*. Manuscript submitted for publication.

Bouchard, T. J., & McGue, M. (1990). Genetic and rearing environmental influences on adult personality: An analysis of adopted twins reared apart. *Journal of Personality, 58,* 263–292.

Burnstein, E., Crandall, C., & Kitayama, S. (1994). Some neo-Darwinian decision rules for altruism: Weighing cures for inclusive fitness as a function of the biological importance of the decision. *Journal of Personality and Social Psychology, 67,* 773–789.

Buss, D. M. (1984). Evolutionary biology and personality psychology: Toward a conception of human nature and individual differences. *American Psychologist, 39,* 1135–1147.

Buss, D.M. (1988a). The evolution of human intrasexual competition: Tactics of mate attraction. *Journal of Personality and Social Psychology, 54,* 616–628.

Buss, D. M. (1988b). From vigilance to violence: Tactics of mate retention. *Ethology and Sociobiology, 9,* 291–317.

Buss, D.M. (1989a). Sex differences in human mate preferences: Evolutionary hypotheses testing in 37 cultures. *Behavioral and Brain Sciences, 12,* 1–49.

Buss, D. M. (1989b). Conflict between the sexes: Strategic interference and the evocation of anger and upset. *Journal of Personality and Social Psychology, 56,* 735–747.

Buss, D.M. (1991). Evolutionary personality psychology. *Annual Review of Psychology, 42,* 459–492.

Buss, D. M. (1994). *The evolution of desire: Strategies of human mating*. New York: Basic Books.

Buss, D. M. (1995a). Evolutionary psychology: A new paradigm for psychological science. *Psychological Inquiry, 6,* 1–49.

Buss, D. M. (1995b). *Human prestige criteria*. Paper presented to the Human Behavior and Evolution Society Annual Meeting, University of California, Santa Barbara, CA (June 29).

Buss, D. M. (1996). Social adaptation and five major factors of personality. In J. S. Wiggins (Ed.), *The five factor model of personality: Theoretical perspectives (pp. 180–208).* New York: Guilford Press.

Buss, D. M. (1999). *Evolutionary psychology: The new science of the mind*. Boston: Allyn & Bacon.

Buss, D. M., & Dedden, L. A. (1990). Derogation of competitors. *Journal of Social and Personal Relationships, 7,* 395–422.

Buss, D. M., & Greiling, H. (1999). Adaptive individual differences. *Journal of Personality, 67,* 209–242.

Buss, D. M., Haselton, M. G., Shackelford, T. K., Bleske, A. L., & Wakefield, J. C. (1998). Adaptations, exaptations, and spandrels. *American Psychologist, 53,* 533–548.

Buss, D. M., Larsen, R. J., Westen, D., & Semmelroth, J. (1992). Sex differences in jealousy: Evolution, physiology, and psychology. *Psychological Science, 3,* 251–255.

Buss, D. M., & Schmitt, D. P. (1993). Sexual strategies theory: An evolutionary perspective on human mating. *Psychological Review, 100,* 204–232.

Buss, D. M., & Shackelford, T. K. (1997). From vigilance to violence: Mate retention tactics in married couples. *Journal of Personality and Social Psychology, 72,* 346–361.

Buunk, A. P., Angleitner, A., Oubaid, V., & Buss, D. M. (1996). Sex differences in jealousy in evolutionary and cultural perspective: Tests from the Netherlands, Germany, and the United States. *Psychological Science,* 7, 359–363.

Chagnon, N. (1983). *Yanomamö: The fierce people* (3rd ed.). New York: Holt, Rinehart & Winston.

Cleckley, H. (1982). *The mask of sanity*. New York: New American Library.

Daly, M., & Wilson, M. (1988). *Homicide*. Hawthorne, NY: Aldine.

Daly, M., & Wilson, M. (1995). Discriminative parental solicitude and the relevance of evolutionary models to the analysis of motivational systems. In M.S. Gazzaniga (Ed.), *The cognitive neurosciences* (pp. 1269–1286). Cambridge, MA: MIT Press.

Daly, M., Wilson, M., & Weghorst, S. J. (1982). Male sexual jealousy. *Ethology and Sociobiology, 3,* 11–27.

Darwin, C. (1958). *The origin of the species*. London: Murray. (Original work published 1859)

Darwin, C. (1981). *The descent of man and selection in relation to sex*. London: Murray. (Original work published 1871)

Dawkins, R. (1982). *The extended phenotype*. San Francisco: W.H. Freeman.

Dawkins, R. (1996). *Climbing mount improbable*. New York: W.W. Norton.

de Waal, F. (1982). *Chimpanzee politics: Sex and power among apes*. Baltimore, MD: The Johns Hopkins University Press.

Ekman, P. (1973). Cross-cultural studies of facial expression. In P. Ekman (Ed.), *Darwin and facial expression: A century of research in review* (pp. 169–222). New York: Academic Press.

Ekman, P. (1994). All emotions are basic. In P. Ekman & R. J. Davidson (Eds.), *The nature of emotion* (pp. 15–19). New York: Oxford University Press.

Eysenck, H. J. (1995). Psychopathology: Type or trait? *Behavioral and Brain Sciences, 18,* 355–356.

Frank, R. (1988). *Passions within reason.* New York: Norton.

Freud, S. (1953). Three essays on the theory of sexuality. In J. Strachey (Ed. and Trans.), *The standard edition of the complete psychological works of Sigmund Freud* (Vol. 7, pp. 126–243). London: Hogarth Press. (Original work published 1905)

Gangestad, S. W., & Simpson, J. A. (1990). Toward an evolutionary history of female sociosexual variation. *Journal of Personality, 58,* 69–96.

Gangestad, S. W., & Simpson, J. A. (1999). The evolution of human mating: Trade-offs and strategic pluralism. Manuscript submitted for publication.

Goldberg, L. R. (1981). Language and individual differences: The search for universals in personality lexicons. In L. Wheeler (Ed.), *Review of personality and social psychology* (pp. 141–165). Beverly Hills, CA: Sage.

Gross, M. R. (1982). Sneakers, satellites and parentals: Polymorphic mating strategies in North American sunfishes. *Zeitschrift fur Tierpsychologie, 60,* 1–26.

Gould, S. J. (1991). Exaptation: A crucial tool for evolutionary psychology. *Journal of Social Issues, 47,* 43–65.

Hamilton, W. D. (1964). The genetical evolution of social behavior. I and II. *Journal of Theoretical Biology, 7,* 1–52.

Hart, C.W., & Pilling, A.R. (1960). *The Tiwi of North Australia.* New York: Hart, Rinehart & Winston.

Haselton, M. B., & Buss, D. M. (1997). *Errors in mind reading: Design flaws or design features?* Paper presented to the Ninth Annual Meeting of the Human Behavior and Evolution Society, University of Arizona, Tucson, AZ (June 4–8).

Hatfield, E., Traupmann, J., Sprecher, S., Utne, M., & Hay, J. (1985). Equity and intimate relations: Recent research. In W. Ickes (Ed.), *Compatible and incompatible relationships* (pp. 91–117). New York: Springer-Verlag.

Hill, K., & Hurtado, A. M. (1996). *Ache life history.* New York: Aldine De Gruyter.

Hogan, R. (1983). A socioanalytic theory of personality. In M. M. Page (Ed.), *Nebraska Symposium on Motivation.* Lincoln: University of Nebraska Press.

James, W. (1962). *Principles of psychology.* New York: Dover. (Original work published 1890)

Johnson, J. (1969). Organic psychosyndromes due to boxing. *British Journal of Psychiatry, 115,* 45–53.

Kenrick, D. T., & Keefe, R. C. (1992). Age preferences in mates reflect sex differences in reproductive strategies. *Behavioral and Brain Sciences, 15,* 75–133.

Kenrick, D. T., Sadalla, E. K., Groth, G., & Trost, M. R. (1990). Evolution, traits, and the stages of human courtship: Qualifying the parental investment model. *Journal of Personality, 58,* 97–116.

Loehlin, J. C., Horn, J. M., & Willerman, L. (1990). Heredity, environment, and personality change: Evidence from the Texas Adoption Project. *Journal of Personality, 58,* 221–244.

MacDonald, K. (1995). Evolution, the Five-Factor Model, and Levels of Personality. *Journal of Personality, 63,* 525–568.

Marks, I. (1987). *Fears, phobias, and rituals: Panic, anxiety, and their disorders.* New York: Oxford University Press.

Marr, D. (1982). *Vision.* San Francisco: W. H. Freeman.

Maynard Smith, J. (1982). *Evolution and the theory of games.* Cambridge, UK: Cambridge University Press.

Mazlow, A. H. (1970). *Motivation and personality* (2nd ed.). New York: Harper & Row.

Mazur, A., Halpern, C., & Udry, J. R. (1994). Dominant looking male teenagers copulate earlier. *Ethology and Sociobiology, 15,* 87–94.

McAdams, D. P. (1997). A conceptual history of personality psychology. In R. Hogan, J. Johnson, & S. Briggs (Eds.), *Handbook of personality psychology* (pp. 3–39). New York: Academic Press.

McCrae, R. R., & John, O. P. (1992). An introduction to the five-factor model and its applications. *Journal of Personality,* 60, 175–215.

Mealey, L. (1995). The sociobiology of sociopathy: An integrated evolutionary model. *Behavioral and Brain Sciences, 18,* 523–599.

Nesse, R. M. (1990). Evolutionary explanations of emotions. *Human Nature, 1,* 261–289.

Norman, W. T. (1963). Toward an adequate taxonomy of personality attributes: Replicated factor structure in peer nomination personality ratings. *Journal of Abnormal and Social Psychology, 66,* 574–583.

Orians, G. H., & Heerwagen, J. H. (1992). Evolved responses to landscapes. In J. Barkow, L. Cosmides, & J. Tooby (Eds.), *The adapted mind* (pp. 555–579). New York: Oxford University Press.

Pedersen, F. A. (1991). Secular trends in human sex ratios: Their influence on individual and family behavior. *Human Nature, 3,* 271–291.

Pervin, L. A. (1990). Personality theory and research: Prospects for the future. In L. A. Pervin (Ed.), *Handbook of personality: Theory and research* (pp. 723–727). New York: Guilford Press.

Pinker, S. (1994). *The language instinct.* New York: Morrow.

Plomin, R., DeFries, J. C., & McClearn, G. E. (1990). *Behavioral genetics: A primer* (2nd ed.). New York: Freeman.

Rowe, D.C. (1995). Evolution, mating effort, and crime. *Behavioral and Brain Sciences, 18,* 573–574.

Schmitt, D. P., & Buss, D. M. (1996). Strategic self-promotion and competitor derogation: Sex and context effects on perceived effectiveness of mate attraction tactics. *Journal of Personality and Social Psychology,* 70, 1185–1204.

Schmitt, D. P., & Buss, D. M. (1999). *Individual differences in sexuality description: A lexical analysis of neglected personality dimensions.* Manuscript submitted for publication.

Shackelford, T. K., & Buss, D. M. (1996). Betrayal in mateships, friendships, and coalitions. *Personality and Social Psychology Bulletin, 22,* 1151–1164.

Sternberg, R. (1986). A triangular theory of love. *Psychological Review, 93,* 119–135.
Sulloway, F. (1996). *Born to rebel.* New York: Pantheon.
Symons, D. (1999). *The evolution of human sexuality.* New York: Oxford University Press.
Symons, D. (1987). If we're all Darwinians, what's the fuss about. In C. Crawford, D. Krebs, & M. Smith (Eds.), *Sociobiology and psychology* (pp. 121–145). Hillsdale, NJ: Erlbaum.
Symons, D. (1992). On the use and misuse of Darwinism in the study of human behavior. In J. Barkow, L. Cosmides, & J. Tooby (Eds.), *The adapted mind* (pp. 137–159). New York: Oxford University Press.
Tooby, J., & Cosmides, L. (1988). *The evolution of war and its cognitive foundations.* (Technical Report #88–1). Santa Barbara, CA: Institute for Evolutionary Studies.
Tooby, J., & Cosmides, L. (1990a). On the universality of human nature and the uniqueness of the individual: The role of genetics and adaptation. *Journal of Personality, 58,* 17–68.
Tooby, J., & Cosmides, L. (1990b). The past explains the present: Emotional adaptations and the structure of ancestral environments. *Ethology and Sociobiology, 11,* 375–424.
Tooby, J., & Cosmides, L. (1992). Psychological foundations of culture. In J. Barkow, L. Cosmides, & J. Tooby (Eds.), *The adapted mind* (pp. 19–136). New York: Oxford University Press.
Trivers, R. (1974). Parent–offspring conflict. *American Zoologist, 14,* 249–264.
Walster, E., Traupmann, J., & Walster, G. W. (1978). Equity and extramarital sexuality. *Archives of Sexual Behavior, 7,* 127–141.
Wiederman, M. W., & Allgeier, R. R. (1993). Gender differences in sexual jealousy: Adaptationist or social learning explanation? *Ethology and Sociobiology, 14,* 115–140.
Wiggins, J. S. (1979). A psychological taxonomy of trait descriptive terms: The interpersonal domain. *Journal of Personality and Social Psychology, 37,* 395–412.
Willerman, L., Loehlin, J. C., & Horn, J. M. (1992). An adoption and a cross-fostering study of the Minnesota Multiphasic Personality Inventory (MMPI) Psychopathic Deviate scale. *Behavior Genetics, 22,* 515–529.
Williams, G. C. (1966). *Adaptation and natural selection.* Princeton, NJ: Princeton University Press.
Williams, G. C. (1975). *Sex and evolution.* Princeton, NJ: Princeton University Press.
Williams, G.C. (1992). *Natural selection.* New York: Oxford University Press.
Wilson, D. S. (1994). Adaptive genetic variation and human evolutionary psychology. *Ethology and Sociobiology, 15,* 219–235.
Wilson, D. S. (1995). Sociopathy within and between small groups. *Behavioral and Brain Sciences, 18,* 577.

Chapter 3
Psychoanalytic Approaches to Personality

Drew Westen
Harvard Medical School and The Cambridge Hospital
Glen O. Gabbard
Menninger School of Medicine

Perhaps the greatest challenge in trying to summarize the state of psychoanalysis as a theory of personality roughly a century after its inception is to delineate precisely what one means by "psychoanalysis." Sixty years ago, such a definition would have been relatively clear. Psychoanalysis was a well-guarded fortress, and most psychologists had little interest in scaling its walls. The password to enter was relatively unambiguous: Those who considered themselves psychoanalytic believed in the importance of unconscious processes, conflicts and defenses, the Oedipus complex, and the centrality of the sexual drive in the development of personality and neurosis; those who did not consider themselves psychoanalytic believed in none of these things.

Psychologists who were caught in the moat—who accepted some of Freud's premises but rejected aspects of theory important to him, such as the centrality of sexuality or the Oedipus complex—would by and large depart the stronghold or be cast out as heretics, and their work would never be cited again in psychoanalytic literature. This ragtag army of the not-quite-analytic-enough came to be identified under the broader rubric of "psychodynamic," which included those who believed in the importance of unconscious processes and conflicting forces within the mind but did not necessarily hold to the theory of libido and the pre-eminence of the Oedipus complex.

As we will see, the distinction between psychodynamic and psychoanalytic has virtually disappeared since the 1980s, as previously "forbidden" ideas have entered the pale, and as mainstream psychoanalytic theorists and clinicians have come to reject many of the propositions that Freud considered defining of the approach to the mind he created, notably the centrality of the Oedipus complex and the sexual drive—or the concept of drive at all. Today most of the major psychoanalytic journals publish papers from radically differing theoretical perspectives, including object relations theory, self psychology, relational perspectives, constructivist perspectives, and various postmodern views, many of which would have been anathema to Freud. Hence the use of the plural in the title of this chapter, "Psychoanalytic *Approaches* to Personality," reflecting the pluralism that characterizes contemporary psychoanalysis (Hamilton, 1996; Wallerstein, 1988).

Psychoanalysis has thus become less easy to define because its boundaries are more permeable. Perspectives that would at one time have been relegated to the wider ranks of the psychodynamic, such as more interpersonal approaches, are now part of mainstream psychoanalytic literature. Another factor rendering psychoanalytic approaches less distinct is that contemporary psychology has come to accept many of the postulates that once clearly demarcated psychoanalysis from other points of view. The cognitive revolution ushered in an interest in mental events, which had been largely extinguished by the behaviorists (with occasional spontaneous recoveries). Of particular importance is the burgeoning literature on unconscious processes (called "implicit processes," largely to ward off any association with the Freudian unconscious) in cognitive and social psychology. This development began with implicit memory and cognition (Bowers & Meichenbaum, 1984; Kihlstrom, 1987; Schacter, 1992) but has begun to spread, as we predicted in the first edition of this handbook (Westen, 1990a), to the realms of affect and motivation as well. Indeed, the fall of the "Berlin Wall" between psychology and psychoanalysis actually may have occurred without fanfare in 1987 when E. Tory Higgins and John A. Bargh, two leading experimental social psychologists, criticized exclusive reliance on the "faulty computer" metaphor for explaining errors in social cognition and called instead for a conception of mental processes that would have been familiar to Freud, and certainly to contemporary psychoanalytic theorists and clinicians:

> It may be that people are not motivated solely to be accurate or correct. Indeed, people are likely to have multiple and conflicting motivations when processing information such that not all of them can be fully satisfied. . . . If one abandons this assumption [that people are motivated to be accurate], then an alternative perspective of people as "creatures of compromise" may be considered, a perspective suggesting that people's judgments and inferences must be understood in terms of the competing motivations that they are trying to satisfy. (Higgins & Bargh, 1987, p. 414)

Although substantial differences remain between the views of psychologists and psychoanalytic theorists, the differences are now more subtle, so that mutual dismissal and slinging of epithets require considerably more finesse than was once the case.

What, then, is a psychoanalytic approach? Freud (1923/1961) defined psychoanalysis as (1) a theory of the mind or personality, (2) a method of investigation of unconscious processes, and (3) a method of treatment. In this discussion, we focus on psychoanalysis as a theory of personality, although discussions of method and treatment invariably arise because much of the evidence for psychoanalytic theory has stemmed from its distinct methods of inquiry (and because clinical observation has been the basis of most of the evolution in psychoanalytic theory—something we believe is changing, a point to which we will return).

At this writing, psychoanalytic perspectives on personality are probably best categorized prototypically rather than through any particular set of defining features. Psychoanalytic approaches are those that take as axiomatic the importance of unconscious cognitive, affective, and motivational processes; conflicting mental processes; compromises among competing psychological tendencies that may be negotiated unconsciously; defense and self-deception; the influence of the past on current functioning; the enduring effects of interpersonal patterns laid down in childhood; and the role of sexual, aggressive, and other wishes and fears (such as the need for self-esteem and the need for relatedness to others) in consciously and unconsciously influencing thought, feeling, and behavior. The degree to which an approach matches this prototype is the degree to which it can be considered psychoanalytic.

This chapter proceeds as follows. The first section provides a brief discussion of the evolution of psychoanalytic theory. The next section turns to current issues and controversies in psychoanalysis, focusing on two central issues of particular relevance to personality theory: the nature of motivation, and how we know when we understand a person. The third section addresses the enduring contributions of psychoanalysis to the study of personality. The fourth section describes emerging points of contact and integration with other areas of psychology, focusing on efforts to integrate psychodynamic thinking with research in cognitive neuroscience and evolutionary psychology. The final section suggests directions for the future.

THE EVOLUTION OF PSYCHOANALYTIC THEORY

Freud's models of the mind, and the early revisionist theories of Adler, Jung, and the neo-Freudians, should be well known to readers of this volume and hence are described only briefly here. Freud developed a series of models and theories that he never attempted to integrate fully. Freud's psychological theorizing was, however, from the start guided by his interest and his database: He was interested first and foremost in understanding psychopathology, and his primary data were the things that patients wittingly and unwittingly told about themselves in clinical hours. Of the greatest importance methodologically were free associations (which held the promise of revealing associational networks and mental transformations of ideas and feelings) and transference phenomena (in which patients revealed interpersonal cognitive-affective-behavioral patterns that the analyst could observe directly).

Fundamental to Freud's thinking about the mind was a simple assumption: If there is a discontinuity in consciousness—something the person is doing but cannot report or explain—then the relevant mental processes necessary to "fill in the gaps" must be unconscious (see Rapaport, 1944/1967). This deceptively simple assumption was at once both brilliant and controversial. Freud was led to this assumption by patients, first described in the *Studies on Hysteria* (Breuer & Freud, 1893–1895/1955), who had symptoms with no organic origin. The patients were making every conscious effort to stop these symptoms but could not. Freud's logic was simple: If the "force" behind the symptom is psychological but not conscious, that leaves only one possible explanation: The source of the symptom must be unconscious. Opposing the conscious will, Freud reasoned, must be an unconscious counterwill of equal or greater magnitude. The interplay of these forces was what he described as "psychodynamics." (See Erdelyi, 1985, for a vivid and readable account of Freud's discovery of psychodynamics.)

The Topographic Model

Freud's first model of the mind, his topographic model, divided mental processes into conscious, preconscious, and unconscious. Conscious thoughts are those of which the person is immediately aware; preconscious thoughts are those of which the person is not currently aware but can readily bring to consciousness (such as a phone number); unconscious mental processes are those that are actively kept unconscious by repression because of their content. This model was first fully elaborated in *The Interpretation of Dreams* (1900/1953), in which Freud also distinguished the manifest content of a dream (the consciously recalled, often seemingly bizarre plot line) from the latent content (the underlying unconscious meaning, which Freud argued is an unconscious wish). The concept of latent wishes being transformed through various mental mechanisms to produce seemingly unintelligible, but psychologically meaningful mental products became Freud's paradigm for symptom formation as well.

The Drive–Instinct and Energy Models

From his early publications onward, Freud was concerned with the nature of human motivation, and he attempted to bring together a psychological theory of adaptive and maladaptive mental processes with mechanistic and materialist conceptions of psychic energy, instinct, and drive rooted in the scientific thinking of his age (see Sulloway, 1979). His drive–instinct and energy models, which for our purposes we largely describe as a single model (though see Compton, 1981a, 1981b; Rapaport & Gill, 1959), evolved throughout his career, but always preserved their emphasis on (1) the conservation of psychic energy, and (2) the biological and animal origins of human motivation. Freud assumed that mental processes must be powered by energy, and that this energy must follow the same laws as other forms of energy in nature. A psychological motive to which energy has been attached can be consciously or unconsciously suppressed, but it cannot be destroyed. The act of suppression will itself require expenditure of energy, and the motive, if fueled by enough force, will likely be expressed by conversion to another form no longer under conscious control, such as a symptom, a dream, a joke, a slip of the tongue, behavior, ideology—the possible outlets are boundless.[1]

Freud also argued that basic human motivations are little different from those of other animals. The major differences between humans and animals in this respect stem from (1) social requirements for inhibition of impulses in humans; (2) the capacity of humans to express their motives in symbolic and derivative forms; and (3) the greater capacity of humans either to obtain or to inhibit their desires, based on their capacity to adapt to their environment.

Freud was dualistic in his instinct theory throughout much of his career, at first juxtaposing self-preservation and preservation of the species (through sex) as the two basic motives (e.g., Freud, 1914/1957), and later asserting that sex and aggression are the basic human instincts from which all other motives ultimately flow. Freud's notion of the sexual drive, or libido, is broader than common usage of the term, and is similar to its Platonic prototype: For Plato, Eros is a rich and malleable kind of desire, which has both physical and sublime expressions. Likewise, libido, for Freud, refers as much to pleasure seeking, sensuality, and love as it does to sexual desire.

Ultimately Freud came to view life as a struggle between life and death instincts, although this was Freud at his most metaphysical, and "classical" analysts today tend to equate drive theory with Freud's dual instinct theory of sex and aggression (e.g., Brenner, 1982). Perhaps what is most compelling about Freud's instinct theory is the notion that certain motives are simply rooted in the organism, and that there is nothing people can do but to try to adapt to them, enjoy them or inhibit them when appropriate, and extrude them from their experience of self when they are too threatening to acknowledge as their own.

The Developmental Model

Although Freud's drive theory was dualistic, his primary focus was on the sexual drive, which he at times equated more generally with psychic energy. In his *Three Essays on the Theory of Sexuality* (1905/1953b), in which he articulated his developmental or "genetic" model (as in genesis, not behavioral genetics), he argued that the development of personality could be understood in terms of the vicissitudes of the sexual drive (broadly understood). From this springs his argument that stages in the development of libido are psychosexual stages—that is, stages in the development of both sexuality and personality.

Freud's psychosexual stages represent the child's evolving quest for pleasure and realization of the limitations of pleasure seeking. According to Freud, a drive has a source (a body zone), an aim (discharge), and an object (something with which to satisfy it). The sources or body zones on which libido is centered at different periods follow a timetable that is biologically determined, although the various modes of pleasure seeking associated with these zones have profound social implications as well. Freud's stages should be understood both concretely and metaphorically: They relate to specific bodily experiences, but these experiences are viewed as exemplars of larger psychological and psychosocial conflicts and concerns (see Erikson's [1963] elaborations of Freud's developmental theory).

In the oral stage, the child explores the world with its mouth, experiences considerable gratification and connection with people through its mouth, and exists in a state of dependency. The anal stage is characterized by the child's discovery that the anus can be a source of pleasurable excitation; by conflicts with socialization agents over compliance and defiance (the "terrible twos"), which Freud described in terms of conflicts over toilet training; and by the formation of attitudes toward order and disorder, giving and withholding, and messiness and cleanliness. The phallic stage is characterized by the child's discovery of the genitals and masturbation, an expanding social network, identification (particularly with same-sex parents), oedipal conflicts, and the castration complex in boys and penis envy in girls. In the latency stage, sexual impulses undergo repression, and the child continues to identify with significant others and to learn culturally acceptable sublimations of sex and aggression. Finally, in the genital stage, conscious sexuality resurfaces, genital sex becomes the primary end of sexual activity, and the person becomes capable of mature relatedness to others.

These are among Freud's most controversial formulations, some of which are no longer central to contemporary psychoanalytic thinking. The extent to which one finds them credible depends in part upon whether one has observed such phenomena in a clinical or child care setting and how literally or metaphorically one chooses to take them. That little children masturbate or can be coy or competitive with their parents is manifestly obvious to anyone who has spent time with young children. For example, a friend's 3-year-old announced at the dinner table, "Daddy, I'm going to eat you up so I can have Mommy all to myself!" Experimental evidence provides surprising support for some of Freud's more classical psychosexual hypotheses as well, such as the Oedipus complex (see Fisher & Greenberg, 1996; Westen, 1998a).

Many of Freud's psychosexual hypotheses have not, however, fared as well, and are better understood metaphorically or discarded altogether. On the other hand, knowing which ones to discard is not always an easy task. Freud's concept of penis envy, seemingly his most outlandish and gender-biased concept, provides a good example. Freud had a tendency to generalize from small and unrepresentative samples, but he was not simply inventing concepts off the top of his head without basis in clinical data. At its most metaphorical, penis envy can refer to the envy developed by a little girl in a society in which men's activities seem more interesting and valued (see Horney, 1967). Given the concreteness of childhood cognition, it would not be surprising if a 5-year-old symbolized this in terms of having or not having a penis. At a less metaphorical level, even those of us who were initially hostile to the concept of penis envy have often been astonished to hear patients unacquainted with Freudian theory talk about childhood fantasies that their vagina was a wound or physical defect. If the reader will forgive an anecdote (we cannot help it—we are psychoanalytic, and we break into anecdotes at the slightest provocation), prior to entering psychology a coworker of one of us (D. W.) told the author that her 6-year-old daughter had cried the night before in the bathtub because her younger brother, with whom she was bathing, had "one of those things" and she did not. The author has always wondered about the impact of the mother's tongue-in-cheek reply to her daughter, "Don't worry, you'll get one someday." The coworker, incidentally, had never heard of penis envy.

The Structural Model

Whereas Freud's first model, the topographic model, categorized mental processes by their quality vis-à-vis consciousness, his last basic model, the structural model (see Freud, 1923/1961, 1933/1964b), categorized mental processes by their "functions" or purposes (Jahoda, 1977). With the introduction of this tripartite model of id, ego, and superego, Freud's understanding of conflict shifted from conflict between consciousness and the unconscious to conflict between desires and the dictates of conscience or reality.

The id is the reservoir of sexual and aggressive energy and, like the topographic unconscious, operates on the basis of primary process thought (i.e., associative, wishful, illogical, nonvoluntary thought). The superego is the person's conscience and is established through identification. The ego is the structure that must somehow balance the demands of desire, reality, and morality. To do this, the ego marshals mechanisms of defense as well as creative compromises among competing forces. Like the conscious and preconscious of the topographic model, the ego is characterized by the use of secondary process thought (controlled, rational, voluntary, planful thinking). As Bettelheim (1983) observes, in the original German Freud's structural model was phrased in much more colloquial terms—the *I*, the *it*, and the *above-me*—so that Freud could actually speak to his patients about feeling that some moralistic part standing above the self was judging the self, or that an impulse felt like an impersonal, uncontrolled force, as in, "It just came over me."

Developments in Psychoanalysis

Both during and since Freud's time, psychoanalysis has changed in significant ways. The first challenges to psychoanalysis from within were posed by the early revisionists, Adler and Jung, and by later neo-Freudians, who ultimately became challengers from without. The major developments since Freud's time within psychoanalysis are ego psychology, object relations theory and related developments (self psychology and relational theories), and evolving concepts of conflict and compromise in classical psychoanalysis. Despite some efforts at integration across these perspectives (e.g., Kernberg, 1984; Pine, 1990; Westen, 1998b), these approaches remain in many respects distinct and sometimes competing propositions about the mind and personality, which have yet to be thoroughly integrated and contribute to the pluralism of contemporary psychoanalytic thinking.

Early Revisionists and Neo-Freudians

Because Adler, Jung, and later neo-Freudians are not, strictly speaking, psychoanalytic, we touch upon their work only briefly here. Adler (1929, 1939) and Jung (1971) were among the first prominent analysts to split with Freud, largely because they felt, to use Jung's phrasing, that Freud viewed the brain "as an appendage to the genital glands." Adler, for example, placed a greater focus on more conscious, everyday motives and experiences such as needs for achievement, as well on social motivation and the striving for superiority.

Since Adler and Jung's time, the ranks of the "psychodynamic" have become swollen with fallen analysts. Psychodynamic theorists such as Horney (1950), Fromm (1947, 1962), and Sullivan (1953) maintained aspects of the psychoanalytic approach but placed much greater emphasis on the role of social forces in the genesis of personality. These later theorists also rejected Freud's view of libido as the primary motivational force in human life. For example, Fromm criticized Freud's theory primarily on four interrelated grounds, all of which have considerable merit. First, he argued, Freud underestimated the extent to which humans are historically and culturally situated, so that basic motivations cannot be seen as entirely biologically determined. Second, humans are innately social creatures, and Freud's psychosexual stages are as much reflections of psychosocial dilemmas (giving or receiving, complying or defying) as they are of an unfolding ontogenetic blueprint (see also Erikson, 1963). Third, Freud treated acts of benevolence, altruism, and pursuit of ideals largely as reaction formations against their opposites, whereas Fromm proposed that humans have innately prosocial tendencies as well. Finally, Freud's psychology is a psychology of want—that is, of the need to reduce tensions; Fromm proposed that humans have other kinds of motivation as well, such as a need for relatedness to others, a need to be active and creative, and a need for a coherent sense of identity and meaning in life. Fromm, like Erikson, stressed conflicts specific to particular historical time periods and modes of production. He argued, foreshadowing Mahler (Mahler, Pine, & Bergman, 1975), that particularly in the present age a central conflict is between autonomy and individuation on the one hand, and the fear of aloneness and loss of connectedness on the other. Today, many theorists *within* mainstream psychoanalysis would agree with Fromm's criticisms.

Ego Psychology

Although psychoanalytic theory evolved considerably during Freud's lifetime, in many ways it remained an "id psychology," focusing on the vicissitudes of the libidinal drive and the person's attempts to deal with impulses. A significant shift in psychoanalytic theory began to occur at about the time of Freud's death, with the development of ego psychology, which focuses on the functions and development of the ego (see Blanck & Blanck, 1974, 1979). During the same period in which Anna Freud (1936) was delineating various mechanisms of defense postulated to be used by the ego to cope with internal and external forces, Heinz Hartmann (1939/1958) and his colleagues were beginning to describe the interaction of motivational processes with ego functions. Perhaps the central point of their work was that motivational forces must be harnessed and employed by mental processes involved in thought and adaptation to the environment with a developmental history of their own; these ego functions interact with, but are not reducible to, drives.

Hartmann argued that the infant has inborn primary ego apparatuses, such as perceptual abilities, that are present from the start and are not derivative of conflict. Alongside drive development as adumbrated by Freud is the development of a conflict-free ego sphere that may become entangled in conflicts but is primarily an evolutionary endowment for purposes of adaptation. Hartmann and his colleagues (see Hartmann, Kris, & Loewenstein, 1946) were, to a significant extent, cognitive psychologists, and they actively read and attempted to integrate into psychoanalytic theory the work of Piaget and Wemer. Hartmann (1939/1958) discussed means–end problem solving and the impact of automaticity of thought processes on cognitive development and adaptation in ways that would be familiar to contemporary cognitive psychologists (e.g., Anderson, 1993).

Many other psychoanalysts have contributed to ego psychology as well. Rapaport (1951) and his colleagues systematically observed and described the organization and pathology of thinking in ways that have yet to be integrated into contemporary information-processing models. Menninger, Mayman, and Pruyser (1963) made a seminal (and relatively underappreciated) contribution to the understanding of adaptive functions and coping processes from a psychoanalytic point of view, elaborating the concept of levels of ego functioning and dyscontrol. In a work that has probably been equally unappreciated for its contributions to ego psychology, Redl and Wineman (1951) distinguished a vast number of quasi-independent ego functions in their study of delinquent adolescents who manifested deficits in many domains of ego control. Bellak, Hurvich, and Gediman (1973) developed a taxonomy of ego functions that they operationalized for systematic empirical investigation. Erikson's (1963, 1968) contributions have been crucial as well: his elaboration of stages of psychosocial/ego development parallel to Freud's psychosexual stages, his explication of processes of identity crisis and formation, and his elucidation of interactions of personality development with historical and cultural forces. Work in ego psychology contrinues to this day (e.g., Busch, 1995, 1999; Gray 1994).

Object Relations Theory, Self Psychology, and Relational Theories

Undoubtedly the major development in psychoanalysis since Freud has been the emergence of object relations theories and related approaches to personality (see Eagle, 1984; Greenberg & Mitchell, 1983; Guntrip, 1971; Mitchell, 1988; Scharf & Scharf, 1998). Like most psychoanalytic terms, "object relations" carries many meanings, although, most broadly, the term denotes enduring patterns of interpersonal functioning in intimate relationships and the cognitive and affective processes mediating those patterns.

Object Relations Theories. Although classical psychoanalytic theory focused on the vicissitudes of libido and aggression, from the start clinical practice has been oriented toward the "objects" of drives, and toward the individual's thoughts and feelings about those objects. Interest in object relations grew as clinicians began confronting patients with personality disorders who were unable to maintain satisfying relationships, and who seemed to be haunted by their fears and fantasies about the dangers of intimate relations with others and by unrealistic, often malevolent representations of significant others (Fairbairn, 1952; Guntrip, 1971; Klein, 1948). In contrast to classical psychoanalytic theory, object relations theory stresses the impact of actual deprivation in infancy and early childhood, the importance of self-representations and representations of others (called "object representations") in mediating interpersonal functioning, and the primary need for human relatedness that begins in infancy.

Psychoanalytic theory has seen a gradual shift from viewing objects as the repositories of drives (Freud, 1905/1953), to objects as fantasy figures (Klein, 1948; Fairbairn, 1952), to objects as psychic representations of real people (Sandler & Rosenblatt, 1962). Alongside this shift has been a continuing debate about whether human social motivation is best conceived of as motivated by the desire for sexual/sensual pleasure or the desire for human contact and relatedness. Fairbairn (1952) and Sullivan (1953) clearly specified interpersonal alternatives to Freud's theories of motivation and psychic structure, with Fairbairn asserting that libido is object seeking and not pleasure seeking, and Sullivan developing a comprehensive model of the structure and development of personality that emphasized the distortions in personality and self-concept necessitated by the avoidance of interpersonally generated anxiety.

Two major developments in object relations theory in the 1960s were Sandler and Rosenblatt's (1962) paper on the representational world and Bowlby's (1969) enunciation of his theory of attachment. Following Jacobson (1954) and others, Sandler and Rosenblatt described the cognitive-affective structure of the "representational world"—that is, of people's representations of the self and others—in ways that could still profitably be assimilated by researchers studying social cognition. In the 1962 paper, for example, they described the self-concept as a self-schema, and elaborated the importance of distinguishing momentary from prototypic self-representations. Bowlby (1969, 1973, 1982) elaborated on Sandler and Rosenblatt's concept of "internal working models" of people and relationships but added a powerful reformulation of motivational constructs such as "instinct" by integrating psychoanalytic thinking with control theory and ethology. He argued that attachment is a primary motivational system in humans as in other species, and that its evolutionary significance is the provision of security to immature members of the species. He suggested, further, that the expectations of relationships and the patterns of affective experience and regulation shaped in the first relationships are central determinants of later interpersonal functioning. As will be seen later, his theory has led to an enormous body of empirical research and a corroboration of many of these ideas. Also of considerable importance in the 1960s and 1970s was Mahler's research (Mahler et al., 1975), based on observation of infants and young children, in which she and her colleagues traced the development of separation–individuation—that is, of the child's struggle to develop a sense of autonomy and independent selfhood while maintaining an attachment to (or, in Mahler's theory, libidinal investment in) the primary caretaker.

Although numerous theorists have proposed models of object relations (e.g., Jacobson, 1964; Masterson, 1976), one of the major contemporary theories is Kernberg's (1975, 1976, 1984) attempt to wed drive theory, ego psychology, and object relations theory. From the perspective of personality theory, one of Kernberg's central contributions (Kernberg, 1975, 1984) has been his development of a model of levels of personality organization. According to Kernberg, personality oganization—that is, the enduring ways people perceive themselves and others, behave interpersonally, pursue their goals, and defend against unpleasant feelings—can be understood on a continuum of pathology. Individuals whose personality is organized at a psychotic level have difficulty knowing what is inside or outside their heads and tend to be tremendously interpersonally alienated. Individuals with a borderline level of personality organization can clearly distinguish inner and outer (that is, they do not hallucinate), but they have difficulty maintaining consistent views of themselves and others over time, and they are prone to severe distortions in the way they perceive reality—particularly interpersonal reality—when the going gets tough. People at a neurotic to normal level of personality organization may have all kinds of conflicts, concerns, and problems (such as low self-esteem, anxiety, and so forth), but they are generally able to love and to work effectively.

Kernberg proposes a model of normal and pathological development that attempts to account for these different levels of personality organization. The basic logic of Kernberg's developmental model is that development proceeds from a lack of awareness in infancy of the distinction between self and other, to a differentiation of representations based on affective valence (i.e., "good" vs. "bad" people and experiences) in the toddler years, to an eventual construction of mature representations that integrate ambivalent feelings by age 5 or 6. Kernberg formulated his theory to account for phenomena observed in the treatment of severe personality disorders, notably the tendency of these patients toward "splitting" (the separation of good and bad representations, so that the person cannot see the self or others at a particular time with any richness or complexity). The preschooler scolded by his or her mother who yells, "Mommy, I hate you! You don't love me!" is evidencing this normal developmental incapacity to retrieve memories of interactions with the mother associated with a different affective tone; later, according to Kernberg, splitting can be used defensively to maintain idealizations of the self or significant others, or to protect the other from the individual's own aggressive impulses.

Self Psychology. Whereas Kernberg retains many elements of the classical theory of drive, conflict, and defense, self psychology, developed by Heinz Kohut (1966, 1971, 1977, 1984), represents a much more radical departure. Kohut originally developed his theory as an attempt to explain the phenomenology and symptomatology of patients with narcissistic personality disorders (Kohut, 1966). Whereas in his early work Kohut defined the "self" as other analysts had since Hartmann (1950)—as a collection of self representations (and hence an ego structure, as cognition is an ego function)—later Kohut (1971, 1977) came to view a psychology of the self as complementary to the classical theory of drive and defense. By the end of his life, Kohut (1984; Kohut & Wolf, 1978) argued that defects in the self, not conflicts, are central to psychopathology, and that classical psychoanalysis has been superseded by self psychology. "Self" in this later work refers to a psychic structure on a par with, or superordinate to id, ego, and superego. Kohut describes this structure as bipolar, with ambitions on one side, ideals on the other, and talents and skills driven by these two poles "arched" between them.

Although Kohut's terminology can be confusing, the thrust of his argument is that having a core of ambitions and ideals, talents and skills with which to try to actualize them, and a cohesive and positive sense of self is what mental health is all about. The extent to which children develop these is determined, according to Kohut, by the extent to which their caretakers in the first years of life themselves are healthy along these dimensions, and can thus respond empathically when their children need them and can impart their own sense of security and self-esteem to their children. For Kohut. ambitions, ideals, and the need for self-esteem are three primary motivational systems in humans.

Kohut's developmental theory, like that of most psychoanalytic theorists, proposes that the infant begins in a state of relatively poor differentiation of self and other, characterized by fragmented, unintegrated representations; he calls this the stage of the fragmented self. At some time in the second year a "nuclear self," or core sense of self, emerges, with the bipolar structure described above. What he means by this is that, on the one hand, the child is driven by a fantasied sense of the self as omnipotent and omniscient, which Kohut calls the grandiose self. On the other hand, the child endows her parents with a similar greatness, creating what Kohut calls the idealized parent imago. If the child's primary caretakers are unempathic, chronically responding to their own needs instead of those of the infant, the child will develop defects in one or both poles of the self. This may lead to symptoms such as grandiosity, poor self-esteem, a desperate need to be attended to and admired, and severe problems in establishing a cohesive sense of identity.

Relational Theories. Perhaps the most important recent development in psychoanalysis is the emergence of relational theories (Aron, 1996; Mitchell, 1988, 1993, 1997), which in many respects are an outgrowth of both object relations theories within psychoanalysis and the interpersonal theory of Harry Stack Sullivan (1953). Like both of these theoretical viewpoints, relational theories stress the importance of motives for relatedness and tend to downplay the importance of sexual and aggressive drives or wishes. They also emphasize the importance of internalization of interpersonal interactions in the development of personality, arguing that the child's fundamental adaptations are to the interpersonal world, and that the building blocks of personality are the ideas and images the child forms of the self and significant others. We will discuss these theories in greater detail below.

Developments in Classical Psychoanalysis

Alongside these various developments have come changes in the classical model since Freud's time. Although these have been many, some of the major changes have come about through the systematizing and revisionist efforts of Charles Brenner (1982). Freud developed many models of the mind and never made a concerted attempt to reconcile them, with the result that some psychoanalysts continued to speak in the language of the topographic model, whereas others spoke more in the language of Freud's later structural model. Arlow and Brenner (1964) made an important contribution by translating accounts of phenomena explained by the topographic model, such as dreams, into structural terms, and by demonstrating the superiority and comprehensiveness of the structural model. Since that time, Brenner in particular has been reformulating many basic Freudian constructs while attempting to preserve what is most important in the classical theory. Brenner's attempts at reformulation are set forth most succinctly in *The Mind in Conflict* (1982), which expresses the classical theory, as revised by decades of psychoanalytic practice, probably as clearly and persuasively as it could be expressed. (For a review of the development of Brenner's work, see also Richards, 1986.)

Brenner's major contribution has been his elaboration of the concept of compromise formation. Freud proposed that neurotic symptoms represent compromises among competing forces in the mind, particularly impulses, superego prohibitions, and the constraints of reality. In *The Interpretation of Dreams* (1900/1953a), Freud proposed that compromise is crucial in dream formation as well. Brenner's extension of Freud's theory was to suggest that all psychological events are compromise formations that include various elements of wishes, anxiety, depressive affect, defense, and superego prohibitions. For example, the academic who derives pleasure from his or her work may simultaneously be gratifying wishes to be superior to competitors, shaped in the oedipal years, which are satisfied by feelings of intellectual superiority; gratifying wishes to be admired, which are achieved by being surrounded by a cadre of graduate students (probably an illusory gratification); allaying anxiety by mastering intellectual domains of uncertainty and solving small problems in the discipline; warding off depressive affect by bolstering self-esteem through publishing papers, making presentations, and winning the esteem of colleagues; and satisfying superego mandates by being disciplined in scientific method and seeking truth.

From the perspective of personality theory, Brenner's list of ingredients involved in compromise formations probably requires some tinkering (Westen, 1985, 1998a). Notably absent are the need to see things as they really are, as well as cognitive processes leading to relatively veridical perception and cognition, which surely get expressed in beliefs along with more dynamic processes. Nevertheless, the basic point is that people are always synthesizing momentary compromises among multiple and competing mental processes. Some of these compromises are relatively stable and enduring, whereas others exist only briefly, because the "balance of forces" within the person is constantly changing in response to thoughts, feelings, fantasies, and environmental events.

CURRENT CONTROVERSIES IN PSYCHOANALYSIS

Currently psychoanalysis is in a state of flux, with no single theory in the ascendant. Indeed, in some ways, the 1990s have seen a flight from theory, as analysts have increasingly recognized the limitations of Freud's models of the mind but have begun to despair of the possibility of any comprehensive alternative. The loss of consensus and faith in Freud's models of the mind within psychoanalysis began to take shape in the 1970s with a growing disenchantment with drive theory, energy concepts, aspects of the structural model, the distance of concepts such as "libidinal cathexis" and "drive fusion" from observable psychological events, and the persistent tendency in psychoanalytic literature for Freud's structures to be reified (as if "the ego" feels or chooses something). An influential group of psychoanalytic theorists began to suggest abandonment of much of Freud's theoretical superstructure, denoted his "metapsychology," in favor of the more experience-near concepts (e.g., repression, defense, conflict) that constitute what has been called the "clinical theory" of psychoanalysis (Klein, 1976; Schafer, 1976).

The positive side of this "cultural revolution" within psychoanalysis is that it ultimately changed the nature of psychoanalytic discourse, which once required rigid adherence to particular dogmas and led maverick theorists to hide their innovations in classical garb. The negative side of this quiet revolution is that psychoanalytic practice is now guided less by an explicit set of theoretical propositions about personality and psychopathology than by an implicit one. Indeed, psychoanalytic theory today is less about personality and more about clinical technique and the nature of subjectivity. Nevertheless, a number of interrelated issues are at the forefront of thinking in contemporary psychoanalysis and have substantial relevance to personality psychology. Here we address two of these issues: The nature of motivation, and what it means to know a person.

The Nature of Motivation

Freud's theory of motivation has always been both the heart and the Achilles' heel of psychoanalytic theory. Psychoanalysis is, above all else, a theory of the complexities of human motivation and the ways in which motives interact, conflict, and attain surreptitious expression. Despite multiple changes in his motivational theories throughout his career, Freud was unflagging in his view of sexuality as the primary instinct in humans that draws them to each other and motivates much of their behavior, and in his corresponding implication of sexuality in the etiology of neurosis. As an inveterate biologist who never entirely relinquished his wish to ground his theory in physiology (Sulloway,1979), Freud maintained a theory of psychic energy in his latest models of the mind that was a clear descendent of a purely physiological theory he developed in 1895 but abandoned and chose never to publish (Freud, 1895/1966; see Pribram & Gill, 1976).

The Demise of the Classical Freudian Theory of Motivation

The libido theory was, as noted earlier, the point of contention that drove many of Freud's adherents from the fold in the early part of the 20th century. By the 1980s, fealty to Freud's theory of motivation was becoming "optional" for maintaining good standing in analytic circles, and by the 1990s, most psychoanalysts and psychoanalytic psychologists had abandoned much of Freud's theory of motivation, including his dual-instinct theory, his model of a displaceable psychic energy, his drive-discharge model of motivation, and the notion of a primary aggressive drive (see Gill, 1976; Holt, 1976; Rubenstein, 1976; Shevrin, 1984). The reasons are complex and many, but perhaps the most important were the recognition that not all motives can be reduced to sex and aggression; that motives for intimacy are not uniformly reducible to sexual desire; that not all motives (particularly aggressive motives) build up and require discharge; and that Freud's energy concepts (the notion of a displaceable psychic energy), though powerful metaphors, were too unwieldy and scientistic.

Although most psychoanalytic theorists today recognize that the time has come to replace Freud's theory of motivation, no coherent theory has yet emerged to replace it. Even before Freud's death, Melanie Klein (1948) argued for the importance of motives such as envy. Fairbairn (1952) and other object relations theorists argued for the importance of relatedness to others, which Bowlby (1969) developed into a more systematic theory of attachment-related motivation years later, and which relational theorists (Mitchell, 1988) tend to view as the primary motive in humans. Robert White (1959) emphasized the need to be effective or to attain mastery, and he reinterpreted Freud's psychosexual stages along these lines. Kohut (1971) emphasized the needs for self-esteem and for a sense of cohesion, and described what could go wrong in development to lead some people to have difficulty regulating their self-esteem or to be vulnerable to feelings of fragmentation. Whereas many theorists have attempted to replace Freud's relatively simple two-motive theory with equally reductionist theories, others have offered more complex formulations. For example, Lichtenberg (1989) has proposed that human motivation involves five motivational systems: physiological regulation, attachment, exploration/assertion, withdrawal or antagonism in response to aversive events, and sensual/sexual pleasure.

Most contemporary psychoanalytic approaches to motivation, particularly in clinical practice, continue to retain some key features of Freud's theory, at least implicitly, such as the recognition of the importance of unconscious motives. Nevertheless, the psychoanalytic theory of motivation would profit from greater acquaintance with both evolutionary theory and relevant psychological research (Westen, 1997). For example, rather than speculating about how many motives humans have, psychoanalytically oriented researchers might instead try to develop a relatively comprehensive list of motives as expressed in clinical sessions, everyday interactions, and ethnographies, and use statistical aggregation procedures such as factor analysis to see which ones, empirically, cluster together. Knowing something about the neural pathways that mediate different psychological motive systems, and considering their possible evolutionary functions, might also be useful in deciding to what extent various motives should be considered part of the same system or relatively independent of each other. The notion that the desires for sex and for relatedness to others are transformations of the same underlying drive makes little sense in light of what we now know about the distinct functions of different hypothalamic regions and neural circuits linking cortical and subcortical brain structures.

Affect and Motivation

If any consensus is beginning to emerge in the psychoanalytic literature, it is probably a deceptively simple one that has always implicitly guided clinical practice, and was anticipated in the psychological literature by Tomkins (1962) and others: that affect is a primary motivational mechanism in humans (see Pervin, 1984; Plutchik, 1980; Sandler, 1987; Spezzano, 1993; Westen, 1985, 1997). In other words, people are drawn to actions, objects, and representations associated with positive feelings or the anticipation of positive feelings, and are repulsed by those associated with negative feelings or the likely activation of negative feelings.

This simple formula has a number of complications and ramifications that are—or, we believe, will soon be—the focus of increased attention. Four are of particular significance. First, these affect-driven motivational pulls need not be conscious. As we will see, experimental research supports the proposition that people often respond simultaneously to multiple such pulls in various directions. Second, precisely how to integrate an affect theory of motivation with phenomena such as eating and sex, which have traditionally been understood in both psychology and psychoanalysis in terms of drives, is not yet entirely clear. One possibility, for example, is that drive states may take on motivational significance only to the extent that they lead to feeling states such as sexual arousal or hunger, or to the extent that they become associatively linked with experiences of pleasure.

Third, a shift to thinking of motives in terms of affects and efforts at affect regulation—that is, the selection of behaviors and mental processes based on their emotional consequences—allows one to avoid choosing among overly reductionistic single-motive or dual-motive systems that are unlikely to do justice to the complexity of human motivation. Fairbairn (1952), for example, brought something very important into psychoanalysis by challenging the view that the desire for relationships is really just a derivative of the sexual drive. He argued, instead, that things are the other way around: libido (desire) is object seeking (desirous of relationships) not pleasure seeking (desirous of sex).

Yet the antinomy between pleasure seeking and object seeking is only an antinomy in the context of Freud's specific meaning of libido, which confounds pleasure seeking with sexual pleasure seeking. People have a number of desires for connectedness with others, from wishes for physical proximity and security to desires for affiliation, intimacy, and a sense of belongingness. These are clearly mediated by affective systems—that is, characterized by pleasure seeking (and pain avoidance)—just as surely as are sexual desires. As Bowlby elucidated (1969, 1973), the child's attachment behavior is mediated by feelings such as separation distress, pleasure at being held in the mother's arms, or relief at reunion. There is no a priori reason a person cannot be simultaneously motivated by several motive systems, each mediated by pleasurable and unpleasurable feelings, including both attachment and sensual/sexual gratification (Westen, 1985, 1997).

A fourth ramification is that a shift to an affect theory of motivation has the salutary effect of permitting much more coherent thinking about interactions of affect and cognition in psychoanalysis than has previously been the case, and is likely to allow much more (and more useful) contact with research on affect and cognition in empirical psychology (see Westen, 1999a). One example is the growing recognition that motives involve representations of desired, feared, or valued outcomes associatively linked with various feeling states. A prime example is the concept of *wish,* which has begun to replace the concept of *drive* in even classical analytic circles (Brenner, 1982; Dahl, 1983; Holt, 1976; Sandler & Sandler, 1978; Westen, 1985, 1997). "Wish" is an experience-near construct that does not rely on 19th-century energy concepts and is intuitively much more compelling.

Wishes may arise through interaction of biological and environmental events, as affects become associated in "preprogrammed" and learned ways with various cognitive representations and structures. For example, in the second half of the first year, separation from a primary attachment figure (we will use the example of the mother) may trigger a distress response that is genetically determined (given, of course, the proper environmental input, referred to in the psychoanalytic literature as an "average expectable environment"). When the return of the mother repeatedly quells this distress, the association of her representation with regulation of an aversive affective state creates an affect-laden representation of a desired state that is activated when the mother has been out of sight for a period of time and sets in motion a wish for proximity.

Implications for Personality Theory

Although the links may not be readily apparent, these trends in psychoanalysis are of considerable relevance to personality psychology more broadly. The debate about drive theory and its potential successors is a debate about the nature of human motivation, which branches into questions about the role of affect and cognition in motivation, the extent to which motives endure over time, the circumstances under which motives and affects are chronically elicited in ways that bear the signature of an individual's personality, and the interaction of nature and nurture in generating the motives that underlie human behavior. Trait approaches to personality tend to remain silent on motivational issues. Social learning and social-cognitive approaches tend to emphasize conscious, cognitive, rational, and environmentally induced motivations, and to study them without reference to their developmental vicissitudes. Each of these approaches could profitably wrestle with some of these issues facing psychoanalysis.

From a psychoanalytic standpoint, what is crucial to any reconceptualization of the concept of motivation are several elements of classical Freudian theory that remain central, if implicitly, in psychoanalytically oriented *clinical* thinking about motives and are too easily forgotten: Motives can (1) be active consciously or unconsciously; (2) combine and interact in complex ways; (3) conflict with equally compelling wishes, fears, or internal standards in which a person has invested emotionally; (4) be rooted in the biology of the organism and hence not readily "shut off"; and (5) feel "it-like" (Freud's clinical concept of the "id," or "it"), or like nonself, precisely because they are peremptory and cannot be readily eliminated. As we will see, many of these features of psychoanalytic approaches to motivation, particularly the focus on unconscious motivational processes and on conflict and compromise, have considerable empirical support.

On the other hand, one of the major dangers inherent in a theory that begins with the assumption that *everything is motivated* is its potential to overestimate the role of motivation and underestimate the importance of expectations derived in part from social learning. The pervasive expectations of malevolence in borderline patients, which have been documented in several studies (e.g., Lerner & St. Peter, 1984; Westen, Lohr, Silk, Gold, & Kerben, 1990; Nigg, Lohr, Westen, Gold, & Silk, 1992), were for years interpreted from within the classical framework as projections of aggression. Although this is clearly part of the picture, research over the last decade has documented extremely high frequencies of childhood abuse, particularly sexual abuse, in the histories of patients with borderline personality disorder (Herman et al., 1989; Zanarini, 1997). The malevolent object world of the patient with borderline personality disorder is thus likely to reflect in part real experiences of abuse. Where dynamic explanations are essential, however, is in recognizing the extent to which such expectations can be perpetuated by ways the person subsequently behaves, which themselves may reflect motives, affect regulation strategies, and interpersonal patterns shaped in the context of abusive or neglectful child-rearing experiences. These patterns (such as readily switching to a malevolent view of someone who is being momentarily frustrating, and hence behaving impulsively or responding angrily) can in turn elicit precisely what the person fears, leading to further and confirmatory experiences of rejection or abuse (see Wachtel, 1997, on "cyclical psychodynamics"). Perhaps the take-home message is that a theory of personality must take seriously both cognition and conation. Any effort to reduce one consistently to the other is likely to be an oversimplification.

What Does It Mean to Know a Person?

Alongside these theoretical issues, a growing controversy has emerged over the epistemological status of psychoanalytic data and theory—that is, the kind of knowledge (if any) that psychoanalysis as a theory and a method affords. What does it mean to know, and know about, a person? To what extent are the narratives the patient constructs in psychotherapy or psychoanalysis (1) a record of the historical past; (2) an index of the patient's current ways of experiencing the self, others, and the past; or (3) an index of the efforts of two people to come to terms with the person's past and present in the context of a particular relationship?

As we will see, these issues, too, are of import for the study of personality, given the tendency of many researchers to take patients' self-reports of their personality as an index of who they are, rather than as compromise formations that reflect an amalgam of their efforts to perceive themselves accurately, to regulate their self-esteem, to avoid warded-off representations of self that remind them of significant others from the past (McWilliams, 1994, 1998), to approach idealized representations of significant others, to manage guilt or shame, and so forth.

Psychoanalytic Constructions: Narrative or Historical Truth?

Questions such as these first came to the fore as theorists began to wrestle with the extent to which real events influence psychic events, and the correlative question of the extent to which actual historical events in the life of a patient are psychoanalytically knowable or useful. Freud initially believed hysteria to result from sexual abuse, but the extremely high prevalence of reports of childhood seductions by his patients eventually led him to believe that many of these reports must represent childhood fantasies. It is now clear that Freud, in so shifting directions, vastly underestimated the prevalence of actual abuse. However, this shift was important theoretically, because it inaugurated Freud's focus on "psychic reality" as opposed to "actual reality." This focus has been a cornerstone of psychoanalytic thinking, most systematically adhered to in more classical circles (Arlow, 1985). The point is that the way a person reacts to an event is determined by the way he or she experiences it, which in turn is crucially influenced by motives, fantasies, and affect-laden ideas. In many ways, the shift in Freud's thinking parallels the similar shift in cognitive-behavioral thinking that occurred in the 1960s, as researchers shifted from viewing stimuli as causes to focusing on the influence on behavior of the way environmental events are construed and expected by the organism.[2]

The concept of psychic reality raises some challenging questions about the extent to which what matters psychologically is what actually happens or how the person construes what happens. Complicating things considerably is that it is often exceedingly difficult to know where to place a patient's accounts of present and past relationships on the continuum from relatively accurate to relatively inaccurate or distorted—or, for that matter, where to place the patient's accounts of his or her *past* psychic reality (e.g., "I used to think I was . . .").

Spence (1982) opened a Pandora's box by advancing an elegant argument that what happens in psychoanalytic treatment is not an act of archaeology, or recovering the past, but an act of mutual storymaking, in which patient and analyst construct a compelling narrative that provides the patient with an integrated view of his of her history and helps explain seemingly inexplicable aspects of the patient's life. Juxtaposed with historical truth is what Spence called narrative truth, which "depends on continuity and closure and the extent to which the fit of the pieces takes on an aesthetic finality. Narrative truth is what we have in mind when we say that such and such is a good story" (p. 31).

Spence made an important distinction between therapeutic gains that may accrue from coming to understand oneself better, and gains that may accrue from coming to *believe* that one has done so. He also gave voice to an emerging trend in the practice of psychoanalysis and psychoanalytic psychotherapy away from an archaological search for hidden memories—or for psychic boils in need of lancing—and toward a more interactive therapeutic stance focused on the here-and-now, including the here-and-now of the interaction between patient and therapist.

On the other hand, Spence introduced a relativistic position into psychoanalysis that is philosophically problematic and has grown moreso in the intervening decades since publication of his book. In arguing that reconstructions of the past are constructions and as such include elements of fiction, he seemed to conclude that they are therefore *nothing but* fiction. The intermingling of reality with the observer's own cognitive structure is, however, true of all science and all cognition. As Morris Eagle (personal communication) has observed, the problem may not be so much Spence's argument but his affording the status of "truth" to narrative truth. One could surely concoct an aesthetically pleasing story in which the Holocaust never happened, but most of us are outraged by neo-Nazi revisionists who claim truth status for this narrative. Coherence of structure and veridicality are two essential elements of a good theory, not criteria for competing brands of truth.

Science or Hermeneutics?

The question of the nature of truth in psychoanalysis—veridical reconstruction versus narrative coherence—dovetails with a question about precisely what kind of discipline psychoanalysis is or should be. Freud was quite clear—at least most of the time—in his view that psychoanalysis is a science just like any other natural science (Freud, 1940/1964a), although he evidenced an indifferent or disparaging attitude toward experimentation that has probably set the field back by decades. Many analysts and psychoanalytic psychologists remain committed to the view that psychoanalysis, like other sciences, seeks general laws and attempts to establish causal connections among events—in this case, psychological events, such as thoughts, feelings, and behaviors (Blight, 1981; Brenner, 1980; Holt, 1985; Holzman, 1985).

On the other hand, others within psychoanalysis have suggested that psychoanalysis is not a science but is instead a hermeneutic discipline, aimed at the *interpretive understanding* of human actions (Habermas, 1971; Ricoeur, 1971; Spence, 1982). In this view, the crucial difference between humans and the objects of natural science such as planets or molecules is that humans confer meanings on their experiences, and that these meanings in turn influence what they do. Thus, as a social scientist (or, in this case, a psychoanalyst), what one endeavors to do is not to attribute *causes* but to interpret behavior and understand people's *reasons* for doing what they are doing—that is, their intentions. In psychoanalysis, these reasons are presumed often to be unconscious.

Many psychoanalysts have argued against this approach (see Edelson, 1985), contending that it trivializes psychoanalysis and ignores many of its factual assertions about stages of development, psychological mechanisms, and the like, which can and should be tested just as the hypotheses of any approach to human mental life and behavior can and should be tested. As Holzman (1985) observes, psychoanalysis has, from the start, been replete with causal theories (symptoms are caused by problematic compromise formations; attempting to repress a wish can lead to its unconscious expression or displacement; people may fail to remember traumatic events because doing so would be painful and hence leads to inhibition of memory, etc.). Furthermore, reasons themselves have their causes (people have sexual fantasies because sexual motivation is rooted in their biology; narcissistic patients may consider a situation only in terms of its relevance to their own needs because they did not experience appropriate empathy as a child, etc.). Grunbaum (1984) offered a trenchant critique of the hermeneutic account of psychoanalysis, arguing, among other things, that reasons are simultaneously causes. Whether an event is physical or psychological makes no difference to an account of causality: To be causal, an event *X* must simply *make a difference* to the occurrence of another event *Y*, and intentions can do this as well as material causes can (see also Edelson, 1984, 1985; Holt, 1981).

In some respects, we suspect the controversy over whether psychoanalysis should be a scientific or interpretative/hermeneutic enterprise reflects to some extent a failure to consider the circumstances under which scientific and interpretive thinking are useful. There can be little doubt that one of the most important legacies of psychoanalysis for psychology is the recognition that meaning often does not lie on the surface of people's actions or communications and hence requires interpretation. To put it another way more congenial to contemporary thinking in cognitive neuroscience, the crux of psychoanalysis as an interpretive approach is in the exploration and mapping of a patient's associational networks, which are, by virtue of both mental architecture and efforts at affect regulation, not available to introspection (Westen, 1998, 1999, in press-b,c). What skilled clinicians do, and what skilled clinical supervisors teach, is a way of listening to the manifest content of a patient's communications and recognizing patterns of thought, feeling, motivation, and behavior that seem to co-occur and become activated under particular circumstances. This is one of the major reasons we believe psychoanalysis has a great deal to offer personality psychology in terms of methods of inquiry, which aim less at asking people to *describe themselves* than to *express themselves,* and in so doing to *reveal themselves*.

On the other hand, the implicit principles that underlie psychoanalytic interpretative efforts are in fact empirical propositions, such as the view that people often reveal their characteristic ways of experiencing themselves and others in the therapeutic relationship, that their conscious beliefs can reflect transformations of unconscious beliefs distorted by their wishes, that their behaviors and beliefs can reflect compromises among multiple competing motives, and so forth. As we will see, many of these broad assumptions have received considerable empirical support, but this does not absolve clinicians or theorists from the need to test the more specific theoretical assumptions that underlie their interpretations with their patients. These interpretations are frequently guided by theories of motivation, emotion, or development that lead particular clinicians to offer interpretations from a Freudian, Kleinian, object-relational, interpersonal, self-psychological, relational, or other point of view. Given the multitude of ways a clinician can interpret a particular piece of clinical data, it is surely not a matter of indifference whether some or all of the theoretical propositions underlying his preferred theoretical orientation are empirically inaccurate.

Postmodern Views

By the late 1980s and early 1990s, these questions about the scientific status of psychoanalysis converged with "postmodern" approaches in the humanities that radically challenge the nature of knowledge and the scientific pursuit of it. According to these thinkers, Freud and the classical psychoanalysis that he developed are exemplars of modernity, that is, a positivist search for an objective truth. In the case of psychoanlaysis, this search manifests itself in a quest for objective truth about a patient observed dispassionately by the analyst. A variety of contemporary schools of thought have challenged this traditional view of the psychoanalytic enterprise, some of them under the banner of postmodernism and some of them simply reflecting greater humility than psychoanalysis of old. These postmodern approaches go under a number of names, including mutuality, intersubjectivity, social constructivism, relativism, and perspectivism, all of which regard absolute objectivity as a myth (Aron, 1996; Gill, 1994; Greenberg, 1991; Hoffman, 1991, 1998; Levine, 1994; Mitchell, 1993, 1997; Natterson, 1991; Ogden, 1994; Renik, 1993, 1998; Stolorow, Brandschaft, & Atwood, 1987).

A common theme in this literature is that the perceptions of the patient are inevitably colored by the subjectivity of the analytic interpreter. Inherent in postmodernism is a skepticism about any fundamental truths. In this regard the concept of *essentialism*—the idea that people (or things) have objective "essences"— is often a foil for the postmodernists. Reality itself is viewed as growing out of social and linguistic constructions. Postmodernists doubt that any theories or ideas are an accurate reflection of an objective reality "out there" (Aron, 1996; Holland, 1993; Leary, 1994).

These postmodern perspectives are often referred to collectively as two-person theories or two-person psychologies. They are distinguished from the one-person psychology inherent in older views of psychoanalytic technique and observation that viewed the patient (the one person) as an object to be known, rather than as a person whose personality is expressed, interpreted, and shaped in interaction with significant others, notably the analyst or therapist. Although radically postmodern ideas certainly have their advocates, most psychoanalytic theorists and clinicians do not approach the extreme form of postmodernism known as relativism, in which the possibility of truth is denied entirely. Rather, they approach the analytic situation with a combination of realism and perspectivism that acknowledges the presence of an external reality but emphasizes that each participant in the analytic dyad brings his or her own perspective to bear on that reality (Gabbard, 1997a).

Among the most influential of these two-person theories is Stephen Mitchell's (1993, 1997) relational-conflict model. Unlike Freud's model of intrapsychic conflict between structural agencies, such as the ego, superego, and id, Mitchell views conflicts as relational configurations. Conflict is inherent in relationships, and these conflicted relationships are internalized from early in life and re-experienced in adulthood, as people seek interactions with others that actualize often competing and sometimes destructive prototypes from earlier in life. Mitchell acknowledges his debt to theorists from the British School of object relations, such as Fairbairn and Winnicott. He was also influenced by American interpersonalists such as Sullivan, who emphasized the role of actual relationships in shaping and maintaining personality processes. Like object relations approaches, Mitchell's approach, and that of all postmodern theorists, share the view that object seeking (seeking relationships) is more fundamental in the realm of human motivation than the pursuit of instinctual (sexual and aggressive) pleasure.

Ogden (1994) emphasizes an "analytic third" that is intersubjectively created by analyst and analysand. In this variant of intersubjectivity, a third subjectivity is created in the "potential space" between the two subjectivities of analyst and patient. Benjamin (1990), on the other hand, regards intersubjectivity as a developmental achievement involving the full recognition of separateness and autonomy in the other party. In other words, a genuine relationship is one in which both parties recognize both their separateness and their interdependence. A goal of some psychoanalytic treatments is thus for the person to learn to treat others, including the analyst, as separate subjects rather than as objects to be used by the patient for the gratification of the patient's needs. Benjamin states it succinctly: "Where objects were, subjects must be" (1990, p. 34). Other theorists, such as Stolorow and Atwood (1992), emphasize less the recognition of autonomy than the inevitable intersubjectivity that arises when two people come together for an emotionally significant purpose, a prime example of which is the therapeutic situation. Similarly, Hoffman's (1983, 1991, 1998) social constructivist, or dialectical-constructivist, approach focuses on the replacement of a positivist orientation with a constructivist view in which the analyst's personal involvement is seen as having a continuous effect on what the analyst understands about the patient and the interaction—as well as on the way the patient experiences the analyst and the analytic situation.

Postmodern and relational theorists, like some psychologists and feminist scholars, have also questioned the objectivity of time-honoted categories such as self and gender. Some have offered notions of "multiple selves," emphasizing the fluidity and contextual construction of self-representations. Schafer (1989), for example, describes the experiential self as "the set of varying narratives that seem to be told *by* a cast of varied selves *to* and *about* a cast of varied selves" (p. 157). Mitchell (1993) and Aron (1995) have also argued for a set of multiple self-representations that may be discontinuous with one another and are highly influenced by the relational context. Similarly, many theorists have come to regard a major feature of personality, gender, as a more fluid construct than once supposed (Aron, 1995; Benjamin, 1995; Gabbard & Wilkinson, 1996; Harris, 1991). Whereas classical psychoanalytic theory tended to emphasize same-gender identifications (or warded off cross-gender identifications), theorists emphasize the multiplicity of identifications with male and female figures that occur over the course of development.

Some analysts have argued that sounding the death knell for objectivity in psychoanalysis is premature. Cavell (1998) and Gabbard (1997a) both argue that there is room for both objectivity and subjectivity within psychoanalytic theory. Cavell (1998) avers that whereas meaning may be constructed, truth is not. Our perception of truth may change, but not the truths themselves. Gabbard (1997a) stresses the derivation of the term "objectivity" from the word "object," referring to something external to the thinking mind of the subject. He points out that through the influence of the patient's behavior, the analyst begins to experience what other people experience in relationship to the patient. Hence the analyst's position as a person external to the patient provides the analyst the opportunity to present a *different* view of the patient's experience.

Indeed, there is something naive about many of the critiques of "modernism" in psychoanalysis, in two senses. First, they fail to recognize the extent to which "postmodern" concerns have been influential in the social sciences at least since the "premodern" writing of Karl Marx, who similarly viewed modernist "objectivity" as a myth, and a motivated one at that. There is something deeply ironic about postmodernism attacking the work of Sigmund Freud, an heir to Marx and the German philosophical tradition that emphasized the distinction between the manifest and the latent, and a thinker who emphasized, perhaps above all, the ubiquity of self-deception in people's conscious beliefs and ideologies. Second, many contemporary postmodern approaches are, like much of postmodern writing, vulnerable to many of the problems that rendered "premodern" relativism (e.g., of early 20th-century anthropology) untenable. For example, if nothing is objectively true, then the statement that "nothing is true" is just one more assertion among competing assertions, all of which should ultimately be discarded because none is true. Further, no analyst actually believes, or could believe, such a radically relativistic point of view and survive in the world (or make an honest living). If no knowledge is privileged, or at least probabilisitically more likely than other points of view, then analysts should be just as happy to become behaviorists and tell a different set of stories to their patients. Or better yet, they should become barbers, because there is nothing about their training or knowledge that renders their potential co-constructions any more useful than those of the patient's barber as barber and patient chat away, co-constructing an intersubjective field.

There is probably a reason that postmodernism has taken hold in the humanities, anthropology, and psychoanalysis (but not in mainstream psychology), because each of these disciplines shares a methodological feature: the lack of any solid rules for choosing among competing hypotheses. Researchers can interpret empirical findings with quantifiable effect sizes and significance levels in different ways, but quantitative data place constraints on the cognitive concoctions of curious minds. No serious reader of the literature on the behavioral genetics of schizophrenia, for example, could come away with the conclusion that genetics play little role in the etiology of the disorder. There is in fact a reality expressed by heritability coefficients, open as it may be to multiple interpretations, but the interpretations made by a person with expertise and a sound mind are constrained by the data, just as are interpretations in clinical practice.

Implications for Personality Theory

The points of controversy currently enlivening the psychoanalytic scene are not, strictly speaking, only psychoanalytic concerns; many of them point to fundamental issues for personality theory more generally. From the perspective of personality psychology, one way to describe the changing psychoanalytic landscape is to suggest that psychoanalytic *theory* is increasingly catching up with psychoanalytic *practice* in recognizing the extent to which personality lies in person-by-situation interactions. Personality is not something people carry with them and express everywhere; rather, personality processes are essentially *if . . . then . . .* contingencies (Mischel & Shoda, 1995), in which particular circumstances—including external situations as well as conscious and unconscious configurations of meaning—elicit particular ways of thinking, feeling, or behaving.

From a methodological standpoint, this means that we cannot assume that what we see in any research situation—whether a more traditional laboratory experiment or the "laboratory" of the clinical consulting room—is a "pure specimen" of behavior independent of its context. The increasing focus in psychoanalytic writing on countertransference and the role of the analyst's own history, feelings, beliefs, and subjectivity on the way he or she interprets data (e.g., Tansey & Burke, 1989; Renik, 1993, 1998) suggests a more self-critical attitude that might be useful in personality psychology as well. Researchers' choice of theories, hypotheses, and methods are not independent of their own affective, motivational, and cognitive biases, which should routinely be a part of their own empirical inquiries. In a recent study, Westen and Morrison (1999) found that psychodynamic and cognitive-behavioral clinicians perceived their patients very similarly in terms of clinically significant personality problems, except two:

Cognitive-behavioral clinicians saw fewer problems with emotional constriction and rigidity. Whether this reflects underdiagnosis on their part or overdiagnosis by analytic clinicians (or simply different postmodern readings of the same "texts"), it does not seem unlikely that researchers gravitate toward theories and methods that suit their own emotional styles, not to mention express their loyalty to authority figures, such as dissertation advisers, from their own past. Some of the most virulent attacks on Freud would be difficult to understand—most dead people do not draw such passion—without considering such affective biases and loyalties. Similarly, the personal demands of handing research participants questionnaires versus engaging them in in-depth interviews about poignant personal experiences are very different, and it would be surprising if a preference for one or another were completely orthogonal to interpersonal needs, attachment styles, and so forth.

The infusion of postmodernism into psychoanalysis also has implications for personality psychology. Just as analysts can no longer assume the objectivity of their interpretive frames and must pay more attention to the interpretive frames of their actively constructing subjects, so, too, personality psychologists need to think more carefully about the circumstances under which asking participants to describe themselves using statements constructed by the observer—that is, questionnaires—does justice to the subjectivity, and hence the personality, of the observed.

Another implication of the "two-person" point of view in psychoanalysis is that a central aspect of personality is a set of characteristic internal object relations—ways of representing and feeling about the self, others, and relationships—that evoke specific responses in others (Gabbard, 1997c, in press-b; Sandler, 1976). A central aspect of personality, then, may be the attempt to actualize certain patterns of relatedness that reflect implicit and explicit wishes and action patterns forged in childhood and shaped through subsequent interactions.

ENDURING CONTRIBUTIONS AND EMPIRICAL RESEARCH

Psychoanalysis has made a number of enduring contributions to psychology, and particularly to personality theory. Some of these take the form of testable propositions that have stood the test of time; others are better conceived as guiding assumptions that are theoretically or methodologically useful. With respect to testable propositions, when one considers not only research generated by psychoanalytic researchers but also experimental findings in other research traditions that corroborate, dovetail with, or refine basic psychoanalytic hypotheses, one finds that the empirical basis of psychoanalytic concepts is far better documented, and that psychoanalytic thinking is far more widely applicable, than is typically assumed. Westen (1998a, in press-a) has reviewed the empirical data on five basic postulates of contemporary psychodynamic thinking that have stood the test of time:

1. Much of mental life is unconscious, including thoughts, feelings, and motives.
2. Mental processes, including affective and motivational processes, operate in parallel, so that individuals can have conflicting feelings toward the same person or situation that motivate them in opposing ways and often lead to compromise solutions.
3. Stable personality patterns begin to form in childhood, and childhood experiences play an important role in personality development, particularly in shaping the ways people form later social relationships.
4. Mental representations of the self, others, and relationships guide people's interactions with others and influence the ways they become psychologically symptomatic.
5. Personality development involves not only learning to regulate sexual and aggressive feelings but also moving from an immature, socially dependent state to a mature interdependent one.

We will not repeat that review here, but will instead briefly describe what we believe are a set of fundamental insights, concepts, and ways of orienting to the data of personality that psychoanalytic approaches continue to offer.

Unconscious Processes

The most fundamental assumption of psychoanalytic theory, which once provided the major distinction between it and every other approach to personality, is that much of mental life, including thought, feeling, and motivation, is unconscious. Freud was not, of course, the first to recognize unconscious processes; he was in many respects the end of the line of a long tradition of

German philosophy that focused on "the unconscious" (Ellenberger, 1970; Weinberger, in press). Yet he was the first and only theorist to base an entire approach to personality on the notion that much of what people consciously think and feel and most of their conscious choices are determined outside of awareness. He was also the first to try to describe the nature of unconscious processes systematically.

During the 1940s and 1950s, and into the 1960s, researchers associated with the "New Look" in perception (see Bruner, 1973; Erdelyi, 1974, 1985) studied the influence of motives, expectations, and defenses on perception. As early as 1917, Poetzl (1917/1960) had demonstrated, using tachistoscopic presentation of stimuli, that subliminal stimuli could influence subsequent dream content. A basic idea behind New Look research was that considerable cognitive processing goes on before a stimulus is ever consciously perceived. These investigators argued, further, that the emotional content of subliminally perceived stimuli can have an important impact on subsequent thought and behavior. The evidence is now clear that both of these suppositions are correct (Dixon, 1971, 1981; Weinberger, in press).

The research of the New Look was, oddly, dismissed by most psychologists in the late 1950s just as the information-processing perspective, which could have assimilated its findings, began to emerge (see Erdelyi, 1974). Since then, this work has rarely been cited. However, in 1977, Nisbett and Wilson (1977b) demonstrated that people have minimal access to their cognitive processes; that they often "tell more than they know" about these psychological events; and that the explanations people typically offer about why they did or thought as they did involve application of general attributional knowledge rather than access to their own cognitive processes. One study reported by Nisbett and Wilson documented that subjects are unaware of the activation of associational networks. After learning the word pair *ocean–moon,* for example, participants were more likely to respond with "Tide" to a question about laundry detergents, even though they had no conscious idea that a network was active and had influenced their response.

In 1980, Shevrin and Dickman marshaled evidence from several fields of research—notably work on selective attention, subliminal perception, and cortical evoked potentials—to argue that a concept of unconscious psychological processes is both necessary for and implicit in much psychological research and theory. Within four years, two prominent psychologists not identified with psychoanalysis (Bowers & Meichenbaum, 1984) edited a volume entitled *The Unconscious Reconsidered* and stated unequivocally that unconscious processes pervasively influence thought, feeling, and behavior. Unconscious processes became a fully respectable area of research with the publication in *Science* of John Kihlstrom's (1987) article on the "cognitive unconscious."

Today, the notion that much of memory and cognition is unconscious is no longer a matter of much debate (Holyoak & Spellman, 1993; Roediger, 1990; Schacter, 1992, 1995; Squire, 1987). Two important forms of implicit memory—that is, memory expressed in behavior rather than in conscious recollection—are associative memory and procedural memory. Associative memory can be observed in priming experiments, as described above, in which prior exposure to the same or related information facilitates the processing of new information. Procedural memory, which refers to "how to" knowledge of procedures or skills useful in various activities, can be seen in everyday activities, such as playing a complex piece of music on the piano, which requires the performer to move her fingers far faster than she can consciously remember how the piece goes or how to play it. Various literatures on thinking have similarly come to distinguish implicit and explicit thought and learning processes (Holyoak & Spellman, 1993; Jacoby & Kelly, 1992; Kihlstrom, 1990; Lewicki, 1986; Reber, 1992; Seger, 1994; Underwood, 1996). These literatures have demonstrated that people can learn to respond to regularities in the environment (such as the tendency of people in a culture to respond in certain ways to people of higher or lower status) without any awareness of these regularities, and that patients with damage to the neural systems involved in conscious recollection or manipulation of ideas can nevertheless respond to environmental contingencies (such as associations between stimuli with pleasure or pain) even without explicit knowledge of those contingencies. In general, for the past decade, cognitive psychology has witnessed a radical shift from serial processing models to parallel processing models that share a central assmption with psychoanalytic theory: that most mental processes occur outside of awareness in parallel rather than one at a time in consciousness.

As we argued in the last edition of this handbook (Westen, 1990a), if serial processing models are inadequate for describing cognitive processes, we have little reason to presume their adequacy for describing affective and motivational processes. Whereas in the early 1990s researchers were largely clear in limiting unconscious processes to unconscious cognition, today the landscape regarding affect and motivation is shifting, just as it did 10 years earlier for cognition. In fact, research has been amassing for years suggesting the importance of unconscious emotional processes, but the zeitgeist did not support this concept until recently, with the growing recognition of the importance of implicit processes more generally (see Greenberg & Safran, 1987; Westen, 1985, 1998).

For example, Broadbent (1977) found many years ago that neutral words were more easily perceived than were unpleasant words, suggesting preconscious processing of the affective significance of stimuli. Moray found that words paired with electric shocks in a classical conditioning procedure altered galvanic skin response (suggesting an emotional reaction) when presented to the unattended ear in a dichotic listening task; although participants never consciously perceived the word that had been "tagged" with fear, presentation of the stimulus produced an emotional response that could be measured physiologically (see Moray, 1969). Subsequent studies have shown that conditioned emotional responses can be both acquired and elicited outside of awareness (see, e.g., Ohman, 1994; Wong, Shevrin, & Williams, 1994). Heinemann and Emrich (1971), studying cortical evoked potentials, found that emotion-laden words presented subliminally elicited significantly greater alpha rhythms than did neutral words even before subjects reported seeing anything, suggesting differential processing of emotional and neutral material outside of awareness. Studies of amnesic patients demonstrate that these patients can retain affective associations without any conscious recollection of having seen the stimulus about which they nevertheless have retained feelings (e.g., Johnson, Kim, & Risse, 1985). Perhaps the most convincing evidence of unconscious affect comes from recent attitude research, which finds that people's implicit and explicit attitudes—including the emotional components of those attitudes—can be very different (e.g., Fazio Jackson, Dunton, & Williams, 1995; Greenwald & Banaji, 1995; Greenwald, McGhee, & Schwartz, 1998). Although many of the studies described above have been conducted by researchers with little interest in psychodynamic ideas, the idea that affective processes activated outside of awareness can influence thought and behavior has been the basis of two major programs of psychoanalytically inspired research using subliminal activation since the 1980s (see Shevrin, Bond, Brakel, Hertel, & Williams, 1996; Silverman & Weinberger, 1985; Weinberger & Silverman, 1988).

The situation is no different with unconscious motivation, which was once seen by most psychologists as a contradiction in terms. At this writing, research is rapidly amassing in support of this key psychoanalytic concept as well. In a classic paper, McClelland, Koestner, and Weinberger (1989) reviewed decades of research on self-report and Thematic Apperception Test (TAT) measures of motivation. They found that these two ways of measuring motives—one explicit and the other implicit—rarely correlate with one another, but each has predictable external correlates. For example, over the long run, motives assessed from TAT stories are highly predictive of entrepreneurial or managerial success, whereas self-report measures are not. On the other hand, self-report measures are highly predictive of achievement when people's conscious motives are aroused with instructions such as "You should work really hard on this and do the best you can." These and other data suggest that when conscious motives are activated, they guide behavior. When they are not, which is much of the time, unconscious motives guide behavior. More recently, Bargh (1997; Bargh & Barndollar, 1996) has conducted an extraordinary series of experiments demonstrating unconscious motives, using priming procedures to prime implicit motives just as cognitive psychologists have used these procedures to prime implicit memories.

These propositions about unconscious (implicit) cognitive, affective, and motivational processes have methodological implications that have also not yet been fully appreciated. The methods used in most studies of personality, which tend to rely heavily on self-report data, were crafted long before the 1990s, when what might be called the "second cognitive revolution" ushered in this new wave of research on unconscious cognitive processes. Self-report methods implicitly presume that people are aware of most of what is important about their personalities—either that they have direct access to it or that they are likely to observe enough of their own behaviors to hold empirically viable views of themselves. If psychoanalytic theory turns out to have been right that (1) much of what we think and do is determined unconsciously and (2) affective and motivational processes can be unconscious, this will likely require a paradigm shift in the way we study personality. We suspect, in fact, that in the first decade of the 21st century, personality researchers studying individual differences will routinely include implicit and explicit measures of the same contructs, and that these implicit and explicit measures will generally show small to moderate correlations with one another but will independently predict relevant criterion variables.

The Inner World

By 1914, Freud had begun to recognize the extent to which the people who inhabit our minds—ghosts from the past as well as goblins from the present—influence who we are and what we do. As described earlier, this emphasis on "internal objects"—mental representations of the self, others, and relationships—became the cornerstone of object relations theories of personality.

As with unconscious processes, this view is no longer so distinctive of psychoanalytic approaches. George Kelly's (1955) approach to personality had similar elements, as do contemporary social-cognitive approaches. One of the features that remains distinctive about object relations approaches, however, is the presumed complexity of these representations and the pervasiveness of the cognitive, affective, and behavioral precipitates of childhood attachment relationships in adult relationship patterns.

Empirical Studies of Object Relations

Object relations theory has served as the major impetus to psychoanalytically inspired research since the 1980s, much of it relying on projective data. Although in previous eras this would have disqualified such research from serious consideration in the minds of many personality psychologists, social-cognitive research (Bargh, 1984; Higgins, King, & Mavin, 1982) suggests that chronically activated or accessible categories developed through experience are readily employed in the processing of social stimuli; in turn, this suggests that the characters subjects see in the Rorschach or the TAT are likely to bear the imprint of enduring cognitive-affective processes and structures. Indeed, the recent explosion of research on implicit processes, and the emergence of research on individual differences in implicit associations (e.g., Greenwald et al., 1998), suggests that measures applied to projective data may have considerably more validity than once presumed (Westen, Feit, & Zittel, 1999).

Mayman (1967, 1968) argued that the affective quality and cognitive structure of representations of self and others may be examined through projective tests. He hypothesized that the extent to which individuals describe characters who are psychologically rich, differentiated, and interacting in benign ways should predict relative psychological health and capacity for intimacy. Research since Mayman's initial studies, primarily by Mayman and his students (e.g., Krohn & Mayman, 1974; Shedler, Mayman, & Manis, 1993; Urist, 1980) and by Blatt at Yale, has consistently confirmed this hypothesis. Blatt and his colleagues (Blatt, Brenneis, & Schimeck, 1976; Blatt & Lerner, 1983, 1991) have carried out an extensive program of research measuring several dimensions of object relations from Rorschach responses. They have found predicted differences among various clinical and normal populations, as well as developmental changes through adolescence. Blatt has also developed a scale for assessing dimensions of object relations from free-response descriptions of significant others (Blatt, Auerbach, & Levy, 1997; Blatt, Wein, Chevron, & Quinlan, 1979; Levy, Blatt, & Shaver, 1998), which assesses dimensions such as the cognitive or conceptual level of representations and the degrees of ambivalence and malevolence expressed toward the person. Blatt's methods reflect an attempt to integrate psychoanalytic object relations theories with Wernerian and Piagetian cognitive-developmental theories. Blatt has also developed an approach to depression grounded in object relations theory, which distinguishes self-critical and dependent styles (Blatt & Zuroff, 1992).

Another program of research, developed by Westen and colleagues, reflects an integration of object relations theory and research in social cognition (e.g., Westen, 1990b, 1991; Westen, Lohr, et al., 1990). In this research they have used TAT stories and individuals' descriptions of salient interpersonal episodes to assess *working representations*—that is, momentarily active representations that shape thought and behavior, rather than the conscious, prototypical representations elicited by questions such as "Describe yourself" or "Do you think people can usually be trusted?" Most of this research has focused on five dimensions: complexity of representations of people; affective quality of relationship paradigms (the extent to which the person expects malevolence and pain or benevolence and pleasure in relationships); capacity for emotional investment in relationships; capacity for emotional investment in ideals and moral standards; and social causality (the ability to tell logical and coherent narratives about interpersonal events, reflecting an understanding of why people do what they do). More recently, Westen and colleagues have added four additional variables: self-esteem, identity and coherence of sense of self, regulation of interpersonal aggression, and dominant interpersonal concerns (thematic content) (see Conklin & Westen, in press; Westen, 1999b). A number of studies have found predicted differences among various patient groups (e.g., Fowler, Hilsenroth, & Handler, 1996; Hibbard, Hilsenroth, Hibbard, & Nash, 1995; Porcerelli, Hill, & Dauphin, 1995; Westen, Lohr, Silk, Gold, & Kerber, 1990), and developmental studies have documented developmental differences between 2nd and 5th graders and between 9th and 12th graders, as predicted (Westen, Klepser, Ruffins, et al., 1991).

Attachment Research and Internal Working Models

A major development in the empirical study of object relations is attachment research, based on Bowlby's (1969, 1973, 1982) integration of psychoanalysis, ethology, and systems theory. Ainsworth (1979; Ainsworth, Blehar, Waters, & Wall, 1978) developed a procedure for measuring different styles of secure and insecure attachment in infancy. Subsequent research has found these to be predictive of later adjustment and interpersonal styles in the school years (see Bretherton, 1985; Sroufe & Fleeson, 1986), and to be influenced substantially by the quality of the primary caretakers' relatedness to the child (see De Wolff & van IJzendoorn, 1997; Howes, Hamilton, & Philipsen, 1998; Ricks, 1985; Steele, Steele, and Fonagy, 1996).

A quantum leap in our understanding of the ramifications of early attachment was made possible by the development of instruments for assessing adult attachment, particularly the Adult Attachment Interview (AAI), created by Main and her colleagues (Main & Goldwin, 1991). This interview elicits information about the way individuals recall separation and attachment experiences as they describe significant events with attachment figures. Transcripts are coded for four styles of responding, which are analogous to infant attachment classifications: secure or autonomous; anxious or preoccupied with attachment; avoidant or dismissive of attachment; and unresolved with respect to loss or trauma. AAI attachment classification of parents (in relation to their own attachment figures) has proven highly predictive of the attachment status of their children, providing important data on the intergenerational transmission of attachment (Fonagy, Steele, & Steele, 1991; Main, Kaplan, & Cassidy, 1985; Main, 1990; Steele, Steele, & Fonagy, 1996). Self-report measures of adult attachment have also produced important findings in dozens of studies (e.g., Mikulincer, 1998a, 1998b; Mickelson, Kessler, & Shaver, 1997), although narrative and self-report measures tend, as in other areas of research, not to be highly correlated, and researchers are just beginning to tease apart what the two types of instruments may be measuring (see Brennan, Clark, & Shaver, 1998).

Although Bowlby's work was once outside the mainstream of psychoanalytic thought, the recent surge of empirical work on attachment is having a significant impact on psychoanalytic theories of development. A prime example is the work of Fonagy and colleagues (Fonagy, Moran, Steele, Steele, & Higgitt, 1991), who have developed a scale for assessing "reflective self-function," designed to be used with AAI data, which assesses the individual's capacity to understand and reflect upon psychological states. Empirical research using both the standard AAI classification system and Fonagy's measure have supported many of Bowlby's ideas about links between attachment and adult psychopathology (Fonagy et al., 1996). For example, Fonagy's work suggests a link between serious maltreatment in childhood and difficulties with reflective self-function. According to Fonagy, abused children may learn to avoid thinking about their abusive caregivers' inner worlds so as not to have to consider why the caregiver would wish to harm them. As a result, these children grow up with an incapacity to understand mental states in themselves and others. This research dovetails with research on object relations in adults and adolescents with borderline personality disorder and with histories of abuse, who show deficits, for example, in the complexity of their representations or the understanding of social causality (Nigg et al., 1992; Westen, Lohr, et al., 1990).

Transference

One of Freud's most important discoveries, of relevance to object relations theory, was his concept of "transference," the displacement of thoughts, feelings, wishes, and interactional patterns from childhood figures onto people in adulthood (Freud, 1912/1958). Two programs of research have provided important insight into transferential processes. Luborsky and colleagues (Luborsky, Crits-Christoph, & Mellon, 1986; Luborsky & Crits-Christoph, 1996) have analyzed core conflictual relationship themes in patients' narratives, particularly as assessed from psychotherapy transcripts. Among other findings, Luborsky and colleagues have demonstrated, as Freud proposed, that core relationship themes expressed toward the therapist are associated with similar themes that occur outside of the treatment relationship.

Andersen and colleagues have approached transferential processes in an entirely different way, using methods and concepts from social cognition to study transference processes experimentally. For example, Andersen and Cole (1991) asked participants to describe significant others and then embedded descriptions from their responses in descriptions of fictional characters. When subsequently asked to describe the characters, participants mistakenly attributed traits to the characters that were part of their schemas of the significant other but were not originally included in the character's description. More recently, she and her colleagues have documented the transference of affect from significant others to descriptions of unknown others allegedly seated next door (Andersen and Baum, 1994), have shown that these affective evaluations lead to transference of motives (Andersen, Reznik, & Manzella, 1996), and have demonstrated unconscious transferential processes of this sort through *subliminal* presentation of significant-other descriptors (Glassman & Andersen, in press).

Methodological Implications

Some of the central claims of psychoanalytic object relations theories—such as the theory that as adults we live with representations, motives, defenses, and interpersonal strategies forged in significant relationships from the past, and that many of these psychological processes emerge in our behavior without our knowledge of them—have substantial methodological implications. One of the most important is that people are likely to reveal important aspects of their inner worlds through their associations, ways of interacting with others (particularly with people who are emotionally significant), and narratives about themselves and significant interpersonal events. As we have seen, several bodies of research are now converging on the finding that what people reveal about their internal experience of the self and others explicitly through conscious self-reports and what they reveal implicitly through narratives or other tasks that provide access to their associational networks are often very different. Enduring object relational patterns can also be ascertained through the patterns of feeling and behavior people draw from *others*—for example, in the role relationships in which they manage to get others to engage (Sandler, 1976; Wachtel, 1997)—which is a central feature of contemporary views of countertransference (Tansey & Burke, 1989). What this means is that we may need to broaden substantially the ways we assess personality, relying on multiple methods and measures rather than those that are relatively quick and easily administered, which may provide a window to only one aspect of people's experience of the self and others.

The Bodily, the Animal, and the Uncomfortable

Psychoanalysis repeatedly leads one to think about what one does not wish to think about. It is an approach to personality that one does not care to discuss with one's mother. Motivation and fantasy are rich and sometimes aggressive, socially grossly inappropriate, or perverse, and any theory that is entirely comfortable to discuss is probably missing something very important about what it means to be human.

A good example is social learning research on the influence of television aggression on children's behavior. This research is important and suggestive, but it fails to ask a crucial question: Why is it that aggressive television shows appeal to people so much? Would Freud be surprised to learn that the two variables that censors keep an eye on in television shows and movies are sex and aggression? One can read a thousand pages of the best social-cognitive work on personality and never know that people have genitals–or, for that matter, that they have bodies–let alone fantasies.

One of us (D. W.) once evaluated a patient who had been treated for his "poor social skills" and difficulties in his marriage for a year by a cognitive-behavioral therapist, who sent a glowing report of his progress in his treatment. Within the first session, however, the patient disclosed that he had had active fantasies of raping and murdering her, which were clearly tied to a core sexual fantasy that was troubling him in his relationship with his wife. His therapist did not know about this fantasy, because, the patient noted with a sly shrug, "she never asked." Psychoanalysis is the only theory of personality that suggests why one might want to ask.

Another example is Freud's psychosexual hypotheses. No doubt, many of his theories of development were off-base, such as his view that penis envy is *the* central psychological event in a young girl's personality development (see Fisher & Greenberg, 1985, 1996). On the other hand, Freudian psychosexual theory can often provide a compelling explanation of phenomena from everyday life about which competing theories can offer no rival explanations. For example, if readers try generating for themselves a list of all the profanities they can call a person, they will notice an overrepresentation of Freud's erogenous zones. Indeed, the *worst* name a person in our culture can call another person has a distinctly Oedipal ring (Sophocles, circa 500 B.C.E.), and we doubt this term came to the United States via the Viennese doctor.

Defensive Processes

From the start, a central assumption of psychoanalytic theory and technique has focused on the pervasive nature of human self-deception. Whether this takes the form of simple ablation of material from consciousness (as in repression and denial), turning feelings or beliefs into their opposite (as in reaction formation), manipulating arguments or perceptions so that they point to the desired conclusion, or sundry other ways, from a psychodynamic point of view, every act of cognition is simultaneously an act of affect regulation (Westen & Feit, 1999).

A wealth of research now provides incontrovertible evidence for the existence of defensive processes, by which people adjust their conscious thoughts and feelings in an effort to maximize positive affect and minimize negative affect (see Conte & Plutchik, 1995; Haan, 1977; Paulhus, Fridhandler, & Hayes, 1997; Perry & Cooper, 1987; Plutchik, 1998; Vaillant, 1992; Westen, 1998a). In the 1950s and 1960s, Blum and his students (see Blum, 1968) used hypnotic procedures, typically in combination with a projective task in which subjects responded to pictures of a cartoon dog ("Blacky") in various psychoanalytically relevant situations, to test hypotheses about defensive processes. For example, in a fascinating unpublished doctoral dissertation, Hedegard (1969) induced anxiety hypnotically and asked participants before and after anxiety induction to choose captions to the Blacky pictures. Supporting the notion that defenses form a hierarchy of relative adaptiveness, Hedegard found that higher levels of anxiety elicited less mature defenses.

The concept of hierarchical levels of defenses, originally developed by Anna Freud (1936), has been refined and studied empirically by Vaillant (1977, 1992), who has made some of the major empirical contributions to the concept of defense. Theoretically, defenses involving rigidly held and gross distortions of reality are viewed as more pathological, and hence are expected to be used with much greater frequency by individuals with severe character pathology or by relatively healthy people in times of severe stress (e.g., bereaved individuals who imagine the presence of recently deceased love ones). For example, individuals with narcissistic personality disorders may find even minor inadequacies so intolerable that they must externalize the causes of any failure or deny any idea that threatens their tenuous self-esteem. Recent research, in fact, supports such a view, linking particular defensive styles to particular types and levels of personality disturbance (Perry & Cooper, 1989; Vaillant & Drake, 1985; Westen, Muderrisoglu, Fowler, Shedler, & Koren, 1997; Westen & Shedler, 1999a).

Other researchers studying defensive processes have converged on a defensive style that has adverse impact on physical health. Weinberger and colleagues (Weinberger, Schwartz, & Davidson, 1979; Weinberger, 1995) have studied individuals who simultaneously report a low level of distress on the Taylor Manifest Anxiety scale and a high level of social desirability, defensiveness, or over-control as measured by the Marlowe–Crowne scale (Crowne & Marlow, 1964). These "repressors" (low anxiety, high social desirability) are distinguished from other subjects by, among other things, greater reaction time when confronted with sexual and aggressive verbal stimuli; more difficulty retrieving unpleasant childhood memories; and health risks linked to hyperreactivity to potentially stressful events (e.g., Bonnano & Singer, 1995; Brown et al., 1996; Davis & Schwartz, 1987). Shedler, Mayman, & Manis (1993) have isolated a related group of individuals who report minimal emotional disturbance on standard self-report measures such as Eysenck's Neuroticism scale but whose narratives of early experience (early memories) manifest distress or a lack of narrative coherence. In a series of studies, Shedler and colleagues found that, when presented with a stressful or mildly threatening task (such as telling TAT stories), these individuals were hyperreactive on a combined index of heart rate and blood pressure used by cardiologists and empirically related to heart disease. Furthermore, although these individuals self-reported less subjective anxiety, their verbal productions revealed signicantly more manifestations of anxiety (laughing, sighing, stuttering, blocking, avoiding the content of the stimulus, etc.) than individuals whose narratives and self-reports were concordant—that is, who were either genuinely distressed or genuinely nondistressed.

Conflict and Ambivalence

Another enduring contribution of psychoanalysis is the concept of intrapsychic conflict. From the start, Freud emphasized that nothing about the mind requires that any given stimulus be associated exclusively or primarily with one feeling, and that our experiences with anyone of significance to us are likely to be mixed. What led Freud to this view was not only his clinical experience, in which he observed people who seemed to be in turmoil when their wishes came into conflict with their moral standards, but a remarkably modern, modular view of the mind as comprising relatively independent dynamisms that can be operative outside of awareness.

A substantial body of research has begun to emerge across a number of areas of psychology documenting the importance of conflict and ambivalence in human psychology (see Westen, 1998a). For example, many attitude researchers in social psychology (Cacioppo, Gardner, & Berntson, 1997; Priester and Petty, 1996) now suggest that attitudes may be better conceived as including two distinct evaluative dimensions, positive and negative, than as bipolar (and hence measurable using Likert scales running from negative to postive). The reason is that the same attitude object can engender both positive and negative feelings, which can be relatively independent and can vary in strength. Low positive/low negative attitudes tend to have minimal impact on behavior because they leave the person neutrally inclined toward a person, product, political issue, or other attitude object. Low positive/low negative attitudes are, empirically, very different from high positive/high negative (ambivalent) attitudes, which nonetheless yield similar, moderate scores on traditional bipolar attitude measures. For example, when people have fallen out of love and mourned the end of the relationship, their feelings toward each other may be relatively neutral. Months earlier, their feelings may have been intensely ambivalent, leading to the experience of tremendous conflict, psychosomatic symptoms, anxiety, and so forth. In both cases, the person's attitude might be expressed as midway between positive and negative, but surely this would mask the difference between having "gotten over" the relationship and being in the midst of psychological turmoil about it.

The literature on ambivalence is consistent with research suggesting that positive and negative affect are only moderately negatively correlated—that is, that people who often feel good may also often feel bad—and are mediated by different neutral circuits (see, e.g., Davidson, 1992; Gray, 1990). Indeed, several literatures are independently converging on the notion that positive and negative interpersonal interactions, and their attendant feelings, are only moderately correlated and have distinct correlates. Developmental research suggests that supportive and harsh parenting, for example, do not appear to be opposite ends of a continuum. Rather, they correlate only imperfectly with each other and each predict unique components of the variance in children's adjustment (Pettit, Bates, & Dodge, 1997). Some parents can be harsh but can also be loving; others, who might receive a similar rating on the overall affective quality of their parenting, can be distant but not overtly punishing. These distinct parenting styles are likely to have very different consequences. Similarly, in-group favoritism and out-group denigration are not simply opposite sides of the same coin (Brewer & Brown, 1998). In most situations, in-group favoritism is more common than out-group derogation. Indeed, a subtle form of racism or group antagonism may lie less in the presence of hostile feelings than in the absence of the positive feelings that normally bind people together (Pettigrew & Meertens, 1995).

Positivity and negativity in dyadic relationships also appear to be distinct. In children, warm, positive interactions are only somewhat negatively correlated with negative or conflictual interactions; some durable friendships are more passionate all the way around (Hartup, 1998). A recent study of couples (Arkowitz-Westen, 1998) similarly found only a moderate negative correlation between acceptance and mutual validation in marital couples and the extent to which their relationship was permeated by hostility and cycles of negative reciprocity, in which conflicts escalate rather than resolve. Indeed, acceptance and negative reciprocity *independently* contributed to measures of relationship satisfaction. (Further, in support of research described earlier documenting a distinction between implicit and explicit affective processing, acceptance coded from videotapes of couples' interactions with each other—that is, as expressed in their behavior—accounted for variance in couples' satisfaction above and beyond *self-reported* acceptance.)

The Concept of Personality Structure

Central to psychoanalytic approaches to personality is the concept of personality organization or structure. A search for simple behavioral regularities is likely to miss much about human beings that is important because qualitatively different behaviors can stem from the same structure (see Sroufe & Waters, 1977). Several studies using Q-sort methods have attempted to operationalize this construct (Block, 1971; Block & Block, 1980; Westen & Shedler, 1999b). A study from Jack Block's longitudinal project is instructive in this respect. Shedler and Block (1990) found a systematic relationship between patterns of drug use at age 18, personality as assessed by Q-sort at age 18, personality as assessed in childhood, and quality of parenting as assessed at age 5. The investigators did not find a simple linear relation between drug use (from none to plenty) on the one hand, and personality charactersitics or parenting styles on the other. Participants who had experimented with marijuana were the *most* well-adjusted in the sample, compared with those who had never tried the drug (who were described by Q-sort as relatively anxious, emotionally constricted, and lacking in social skills) and those who abused marijuana (who were observed to be alienated and impulsive). Mothers of both the abstainers and the abusers had been previously rated as more cold and unresponsive than mothers of those who later experimented with marijuana.

As the authors point out, in the context of a relatively intact, flexible personality structure that permits experimentation and individuation in adolescence, drug use may be relatively healthy, depending on the historical and cultural moment. Educational or social learning approaches that focus on peer pressure as a primary cause of adolescent drug abuse and attempt to teach teenagers about the problems with drugs may be missing the point (and have proven, empirically, to be of little value in the long run; see Klepp, Kelder, & Perry, 1995) because of their focus on discrete behaviors divorced from the personality structure in which they are embedded. The learning of behaviors occurs within the context of a personality structure, including characteristic ways of coping with and defending against impulses and affects; perceiving the self and others; obtaining satisfaction of one's wishes and desires; responding to environmental demands; and finding meaning in one's activities, values, and relationships. Educational and social learning approaches also seriously underestimate the extent to which underlying personality dispositions influence what are often treated as "independent variables," such as the peers with whom adolescents choose to associate and by whom they are pressured, which in turn influence subsequent responses (see Wachtel, 1987).

Viewing the Present in the Context of the Past

Axiomatic for psychoanalytic accounts of any mental or behavioral event is that current psychological processes must be viewed in the context of their development. Psychological experience is assumed to be so rich, and current thoughts, feelings, and actions are presumed to be so densely interconnected with networks of association at various levels of consciousness developed over time, that studying an adult form without its developmental antecedents is like trying to make sense of current politics without any knowledge of their history.

This does not mean that psychoanalytic theory is wedded to a psychosocial determinism that is difficult to maintain in the face of research in behavioral genetics (e.g., Plomin, DeFries, McClearn, & Rutter, 1997). Nothing about a psychodynamic theory of the development of any adult psychological tendency, such as positive self-esteem or the tendency to split representations, requires that temperamental factors play little or no role. Indeed, we suspect this is an area in which psychoanalytic thinking will grow more complex in the years ahead as it assimilates empirical findings on heritability. For example, having a primary caregiver with an anxious attachment style may be much more problematic for a child with an anxious temperament, whose own anxiety is likely to amplify anxious signals from the caregiver.

What a psychoanalytic account emphasizes, however, is that matters are not as simple as "anxious parents predict anxious children." Rather, the way the child responds to caregiver anxiety, based on both prior experience and genetic proclivities, depends on the meanings the child constructs about interpersonal interactions with caregivers, which in turn affect the child's ways of coping, defending, and responding behaviorally. These ways of experiencing and responding to the interpersonal world will then form the psychological context for future interpersonal experiences. Thus, a child with an anxious mother who develops internal working models of attachment relationships as anxiety provoking may respond by pushing people away in an effort to regulate affect. This affect regulation strategy may in turn push other people away as the child ventures out into the world, such as in interactions with peers. The child may then feel rejected by peers, reinforcing a view of relationships as fraught with distress (see Wachtel, 1997, on cyclical psychodynamics).

The Clinical Database

That psychoanalysts seriously shot themselves in the foot by never evolving from case study methods as their primary mode of knowledge generation and hypothesis testing is beyond doubt. Throughout the 20th century, for example, psychoanalysts have offered a plethora of competing developmental theories, few of which have even been subjected to empirical scrutiny, and some of which are empirically unfalsifiable (or already falsified, such as most of Melanie Klein's speculations about infancy, which fly in the face of research on infant cognition). On the other hand, no other method allows the depth of observation of a single personality offered by the psychoanalytic method of intensive interviewing, observation, and interaction with a person aimed at coming to understand the individual's associative networks, meaning structures, affective proclivities, ways of regulating affect, and so forth.

Clinical observation casts a broad net for observing psychologically meaningful phenomena, particularly in the "context of discovery," where theories and hypotheses are spawned. The laboratory may be much more useful in the "context of justification," where hypotheses are tested, but in the context of discovery, it is much less valuable. The reason for its relative lack of value in observing new phenomena and creating broader networks of ideas is precisely the reason for its strength in the context of justification: The experimenter exercises as much control as possible, limiting participants' responses to a small number in which the investigator is interested.

Indeed, one could make a strong case that the quest for relative certainty at the level of hypothesis testing in psychology (exemplified by decades of preoccupation with p values) leads to the certainty of falsehood at the level of theory. If psychologists base their theoretical frameworks exclusively on well-replicated experiments, they create a collective "availability bias" that leads them to understate the importance of processes and variables that, for technological, practical, or ethical reasons, are relatively inaccessible to the scientific community. We need not, of course, choose between relatively rich theories containing numerous specific falsehoods or relatively impoverished theories containing numerous likely truths that, when aggregated, produce a narrow and distorted view. One way to avoid this is to consider psychological data as forming an evidentiary hierarchy, in which experimental demonstrations are especially convincing forms of evidence, and nonreplicable clinical observations are less compelling but important sources of data for theory building. This is particularly important for the field of personality, which deals with phenomena of considerable complexity, many of which cannot be easily brought into a laboratory for systematic investigation.

The Interpretation of Meaning

Perhaps above all, psychoanalytic approaches offer an approach to interpreting what people mean by their communications and actions that allows the psychologist to understand human behavior in ways that may not seem intuitive or obvious to a layperson. This may well be the reason the vast majority of clinicians, whose work requires that they understand personal meanings, rely exclusively or in part on psychodynamic conceptualizations (Pope, Tabachnick, & Keith-Spiegel, 1987), whereas most experimentalists remain dubious of psychodynamic propositions. Learning to listen psychoanalytically and to interpret meanings in this manner requires years of experience and supervision, just as does learning to design and conduct valid experiments.

Of course, the "art" inherent in interpretation is precisely what has let the postmodern cat out of the bag in psychoanalysis. This does not mean, however, that meaning cannot be coded with some reliability, or that there are no principles that can be used to recognize salient themes (see Alexander, 1988; Demorest & Siegel, 1996, Westen & Shedler, 1999a). In everyday life, we decode meaning all the time, and much of the time lay observers reach considerable consensus on what they have observed. The same is true when researchers apply coding systems to narratives in an effort to quantify either thematic content or structural aspects of the narrative that provide insight into what the person may be implicitly thinking or feeling—that is, meaning. From a methodological standpoint, the recognition that humans inherently attach meaning to their experiences, and that these meanings affect the way they behave, once again suggests limits to approaches that take people's responses—even their responses to highly structured stimuli, such as questionnaires—at face value.

PSYCHOANALYSIS AND PSYCHOLOGY: EMERGING AREAS OF INTEGRATION

As recently as the early 1980s, psychoanalysis and empirical psychology had little contact. The contact remains too sparse on both sides, but it is steadily increasing (see Barron, Eagle, & Wolitzky, 1992). Here we briefly describe two potentially important domains in which integration is increasingly occurring: cognitive science and neuroscience, and evolutionary approaches to psychology.

Cognitive Science, Neuroscience, and Psychoanalysis

Freud's "cognitive psychology" was extensive (see Erdelyi, 1985). His distinction between primary process thought, which is organized by associations rather than by logic, and secondary process thought, which is more rational and directed by conscious concerns, is similar in many respects to contemporary distinctions between controlled and automatic information processing and serial and parallel processing. However, an important difference between psychoanalytic and contemporary cognitive approaches to thought and memory is that the former were tied from the start to considerations of affect, cognitive-affective interaction, and consciousness. For psychoanalysis, it is axiomatic that cognition is largely if not entirely in the service of affective and motivational processes, and that needs, wishes, and conflicts are involved in categorizing and selecting information to be consciously perceived and processed. As we will see, the recent shift from a computer metaphor to a brain metaphor in cognitive science may allow a rapprochement between psychodynamic ideas about motivated cognition and information-processing models of perception, thought, and memory. The reason is that brains, unlike computers, process fears, wishes, and other feelings.

Thought Disorder and the Menninger Group

A major impetus for psychoanalytic investigations of thinking in the middle of the 20th century was the attempt to understand disordered thought in patients with schizophrenia. Rapaport and his colleagues (see Allison, Blatt, & Zimet, 1968; Rapaport, 1951; Rapaport, Gill, & Schafer, 1945–1946) painstakingly analyzed the verbatim psychological testing protocols of hundreds of institutionalized patients, in an attempt to categorize the pathologic processes characterizing schizophrenic thought. For example, they found, from examination of Rorschach responses, that psychotic patients frequently contaminated one percept with another; that is, they superimposed one percept on another without recognizing the impossibility of the superimposition. Such patients were also found to make logical errors and category errors of various sorts, and to suffer from associative intrusions (see Coleman, Levy, Lenzenweger, & Holzman, 1996; Johnson & Holzman, 1979). Subsequent research on thought disorder in patients with borderline personality disorder has found more attenuated forms of thought disturbance, such as egocentric or fanciful elaborations and intrusions of aggressive content into perceptions (see Gartner, Hurt, & Gartner, 1987). To our knowledge, no one has to date integrated these various observations with contemporary cognitive models, although they may provide insight into the nature of both well-ordered and disordered cognitive processes.

Information Processing and Psychoanalysis

A growing number of psychoanalytically oriented researchers and clinicians have attempted to bring psychoanalytic theory together with contemporary cognitive science. In a rarely cited but important book, Blum (1961) developed a model of cognitive–dynamic interactions, based on systematic experimental research using hypnosis. Relying upon a computer model similar to the emerging models that guided the cognitive revolution in the 1960s, Blum described networks of association, which he related to neural circuits; elaborated a theory of spreading activation (which he described as "reverberation" from an activated node in a network to related representations); described networks linking cognitive and affective representations; discussed cognitively controlled inhibitory mechanisms responsible for repression; and used an experimental paradigm for exploring cognitive–affective interactions that predated similar work in cognitive psychology by 20 years.

Beginning in the 1960s, several theorists have attempted to bring together psychodynamic concepts of motivation and affect with various maintstream approaches to cognition. Shared by all of these approaches was an attention to cognitive-affective interactions. For example, a number of theorists attempted to wed psychoanalytic and Piagetian notions, exploring the interaction of the child's developing understanding of the self, others, and the world with evolving wishes and fears (e.g., Basch, 1977; Fast, 1985; Greenspan, 1979; Wolff, 1960). Others have offered potential integrations of psychoanalytic concepts of conflict, defense, and motivation with information-processing approaches to cognition, focusing on concepts such as networks of association and cognitive–affective schemas (Bucci, 1997; Erdelyi, 1985; Horowitz, 1987, 1988, 1998; Peterfreund, 1971; Shevrin et al., 1996; Bonanno & Singer, 1995; Singer & Salovey, 1993; Westen, 1985, 1994, 1999a).

Of particular importance today for potential integrations of psychodynamic and cognitive approaches is the rise of connectionist models in cognitive science (Rumelhart, McClelland, & the PDP Research Group, 1986; Smith, 1998). These models diverge from the information-processing models that dominated cognitive psychology for three decades in multiple respects: (1) they assume that most information processing occurs outside of awareness, in parallel; (2) they view representations as distributed throughout a network of neural units, each of which attends to some part of the representation; (3) they view knowledge as residing in associative links established through repeated coactivation, such that activation of one node in a network can either *facilitate* or *inhibit* nodes associatively linked to it; (4) they propose an equilibration model of cognition involving parallel constraint satisfaction, in which the brain simultaneously and unconsciously processes multiple features of a stimulus or situation; and (5) they rely on the metaphor of mind as brain, rather than mind as computer.

These models are of particular relevance because they suggest that conscious perception, memory, and thought occur through the collaboration and competition of multiple processes outside of awareness. Whereas connectionist models focus on parallel satisfaction of *cognitive* constraints—that is, "data" as represented by processing units within the brain—psychoanalytic theories of conflict and compromise focus on the way thoughts and behaviors reflect a similar equilibration process involving *feelings* and *motives* (see Westen, 1998a, 1999; Westen & Feit, 1999). An integrated model might suggest, instead, that most of the time our beliefs and inferences reflect a process of parallel constraint satisfaction that includes both cognitive *and* affective constraints, such that we tend to make judgments or inferences that best fit the data only to the extent that we are indifferent about the solutions to which our minds equilibrate. In everyday life, we are rarely so indifferent. Thus, our judgments and beliefs tend to reflect the activation and inhibition of neural networks not only by the data of observation but also by their affective meaning. In other words, we see ourselves and others as accurately as we can within the constraints imposed by our wishes, fears, and values.

Neuroscience and Psychoanalysis

A growing area of interface with psychoanalysis is neuroscience. Freud was himself a neurologist, and his theories were developed in the context of his understanding of the nervous system (Pribram & Gill, 1976). His structural model of the mind is in many ways compatible with contemporary conceptualizations of the structure and evolution of the nervous system. Freud viewed the ego and superego as regulatory structures superimposed on the more phylogenetically and ontogenetically primitive id, and argued that our fundamental motivational structures are little different from those of other animals. From a neuropsychological perspective, the primitive brainstem of humans is indeed difficult to distinguish from the brain stem of many other animals; the central differences between humans and other animals lie in the evolution of the cerebrum, and particularly the cortex. The nervous system does appear to be organized hierarchically, with progressive regulation and inhibition of primitive motivational and behavioral tendencies exercised through development of higher cortical centers (see Kolb & Wishaw, 1990; Luria, 1962).

Increasing understanding of the relations among hypothalamic, limbic, and cortical structures in motivation (see LeDoux, 1995) is likely to lead to a better understanding of the relation between drive, affect, and conditioning on the one hand, and motivational states mediated by more complex cognitive processes on the other. Work in this area was just beginning when it was summarized in the first edition of this handbook (e.g., Cooper, 1984; Hadley, 1983; Miller, 1986; Reiser, 1984; Schwartz, 1987; Winson, 1985). The extraordinary advances in understanding of neural functioning that have come about in the 1990s because of the development of more and more sophisticated neuroimaging techniques promise to expand this area of inquiry tremendously within the early years of the 21st century (e.g., Miller, 1997; Pribram, 1998; Schore, 1994; Solms, 1996).

Evolutionary Psychology and Psychoanalysis

One of the major developments today in contemporary psychology is the return of evolutionary thinking (Buss, Haselton, Shackelford, Bleske, & Wakefield, 1998), which dominated functionalist theories and approaches to motivation at the turn of the 20th century and has now been invigorated by developments in Darwinian thinking since the rise of "sociobiology" in the 1960s (Williams, 1966) and 1970s (Trivers, 1971; Wilson, 1976). In some respects, a link between psychoanalysis and evolutionary theory is natural, given that Freud was born the year of the publication of the *Origin of Species* (1859) and was deeply influenced by Darwinian thinking. Freud, like Darwin, was writing at a time prior to the recognition of the importance for natural selection of Gregor Mendel's work on genetics, but his drive theory reflected his understanding of the importance of sexual motivation and intraspecific competition, particularly for mates. Yet Freud never thought to evaluate his ideas systematically in relation to Darwinian thinking, proposing concepts such as the "death instinct" that were evolutionarily untenable.

The first evolutionary approaches in psychoanalysis were arguably the writings of the ego psychologists, who emphasized the development of ego functions that foster adaptation to the natural and social environments (Hartmann, 1939/1958). For many years, however, the primary psychoanalytic voices heralding an integration of psychoanalysis and evolutionary thinking were Robert Plutchik (1980, 1998), John Bowlby (1973), and Robert LeVine (1982). Plutchik proposed an evolutionary theory of emotion and defense, which stressed the adaptive nature of human emotions and the way individuals develop defenses to cope with particular emotions. Bowlby focused on attachment-related motives and emotions, drawing links between the primate literature on imprinting and the psychoanalytic literature on the effects of maternal deprivation and disturbances in the attachment relationship on subsequent development. Bowlby explicitly argued for the origin of object-relational strivings in the infant's immaturity and need for security. LeVine (1982), in work that has not yet been fully integrated into the mainstream, came at evolutionary theory from a different angle, focusing on the natural selection of cultural practices.

Since that time, evolutionary thinking has begun to creep into the psychoanalytic literature, though only slowly. One of the first thoroughgoing attempts to wed psychodynamic and evolutionary accounts was Westen's (1985) book on personality and culture, which drew on the work of Plutchik, Bowlby, and LeVine, and explicitly addressed the implications of then-recent work in sociobiology for personality theory. Westen argued that emotions were naturally selected adaptations that themselves perform the function of "naturally selecting" thoughts, behaviors, and other mental processes that foster adaptation. In this view, emotions and sensory feeling states evolved to lead people toward ways of thinking and behaving that maximize survival and reproduction and lead them away from pain-inducing acts that, in aggregate, tend to be maladaptive. Mental processes and behaviors associated with pain tend to be punished, whereas those leading to pleasure and goal-attainment are reinforced. From this point of view, pathology of affect regulation and motivation often involves the maladaptive use of mechanisms "designed" by nature to foster adaptation (such as avoidance of thoughts or stimuli associated with anxiety). Further, Westen proposed two constellations of motives—self-oriented and other-oriented—derived from evolutionary theory, which resemble concepts such as Bakan's distinction of motives for agency and communion and Blatt's body of theory and research on introjective and anaclitic modes (see Guisinger & Blatt, 1994). More recently, Slavin and Kriegman (1992) and Badcock (1994) have been developing self-consciously evolutionary approaches to psychoanalysis, and Wakefield (1992) has applied evolutionary theory to concepts of dysfunction in clinical psychology.

So what might a psychodynamic account of personality look like 100 years after Freud began his inquiries and nearly 150 years after Darwin's *Origin of Species*? Here we briefly outline the directions an evolutionarily informed psychodynamic point of view might take. Humans are organisms endowed through natural selection with motives, feelings, cognitive processes, and behaviors—and the capacity to develop these processes through learning—that foster survival, adaptation, reproduction, and concern for the well-being of significant others. Biologically, we are all endowed with processes that serve self-preservative, sexual, and social functions that we cannot escape because they are built into our brains and our guts. We need to eat, to drink, to have sex, to form attachments and affiliative relationships with others, to nurture the next generation, and to experience ourselves and be viewed by others as important and worthwhile. Pursuit of these motives often entails expressing aggression or seeking dominance because status, sexual access to attractive others, and in some ecological circumstances, survival, necessarily engender clashes between relationship seeking on the one hand, and self-interest or the interest of others in whose welfare we are emotionally invested on the other. To what extent aggression and sadism can be gratifying in and of themselves, and if so why we evolved that way, remains unclear. The motives that drive people reflect universal biology, biologically and environmentally influenced gender differences, individual differences in genotype, culturally normative experiences, and idiosyncratic personal experience and associations. Thus, the strength of various motivations, and the extent to which they are compatible with one another, vary across individuals.

Conflict between motives is built into human life for at least three reasons. First, naturally selected motive systems at times inevitably come into conflict. Whether the conflict is a struggle between two good friends over the affection of a potential love object or the conflict between two siblings for their mother's attention, there is no innate requirement of human motives that they be harmonious. A second and related factor is our tendency to internalize the needs and motives of significant others as our own. We care about the welfare of people with whom we interact closely, particularly those to whom we are attached, so that their motives become, to a greater or lesser extent, our motives. Once inside us, either as wishes for their happiness and relief of their pain, or as the set of moral standards Freud called the superego, these motives will inevitably conflict at times with our own personal desires. Third, one of the primary mechanisms that evolved in humans and other animals to register the effects of prior experience is associative learning. In the course of daily life, we associate any frequently encountered person or stimulus with whatever emotions the person or object engenders. Thus, over time, our representations of anything or anyone who is significant in our lives will be ambivalent, and different situations and associations will trigger different, and sometimes conflicting, affective reactions.

Organisms survived for millions of years without consciousness. Precisely when consciousness as we think of it arose evolutionarily is unknown and depends substantially on how one defines it. Yet millions of years before the evolution of consciousness, organisms learned to avoid aversive stimuli and seek rewarding ones that fostered survival and reproduction. With the development of limbic structures, most adaptively significant learning came to involve feeling states of pleasure, pain, and more specific emotions. Nothing in the architecture of the human brain requires that these feeling states be conscious in order for us to associate them with stimuli or to develop motives to avoid or approach stimuli associated with them. With the evolution of the neocortex, the capacity to form associations expanded dramatically, as did the ability to plan, remember, and make conscious choices and decisions. Yet most associations, cognitive patterns, decisions, and plans occur outside awareness; we simply could not attend to all the motives relevant to adaptation at any given moment because we have limited attentional capacity. The function of consciousness is to focus attention on stimuli that are potentially adaptively significant and require more processing than can be carried out unconsciously and automatically. Often this means that consciousness is drawn to anomalies, affectively significant stimuli, and stimuli that are salient because of their familiarity or unfamiliarity.

Consciousness of feeling states is a useful guide to the potential significance of environmental events, internal processes, and possible courses of action. The downside of conscious emotion, however, is that we can experience emotional pain. Where possible, people tend to respond at any given moment by trying to solve problems of adaptation directly. Under three circumstances, however, they tend, instead, to alter their conscious cognitive or affective states or keep certain mental contents out of awareness that are nonetheless adaptively significant. First, when circumstances do not allow control over painful circumstances, people turn to coping and defensive strategies that protect them from the conscious experience of mental and physical pain, such as dissociation during sexual abuse or torture, or denial in the face of abandonment by a love object. Second, people routinize many affect-regulatory procedures, just as they routinize other forms of procedural knowledge (such as tying their shoes), during childhood. To the extent that childhood cognition places limits on the affect-regulatory procedures that become selected and routinized, and to the extent that these routinized procedures interfere with learning of more adaptive procedures, people will regulate their affects using unconscious procedures that prevent certain ideas, feelings, or motives from becoming conscious. Third, to the extent that consciousness of a thought, feeling, or desire conflicts with other powerful goals, such as moral standards or wishes, defensive distortion of conscious representations is likely to result.

Humans are not born as adults. They have a longer apprenticeship at the hands of parental figures than members of other species, and their experience in these hands influences their beliefs, expectations, feelings, motives, and behaviors. Their caretaking environment is not independent of their actions; what they experience involves a transaction between their own innate tendencies and the personalities and situational constraints of their caregivers. Cognitively and affectively, children reorganize continuously throughout development, as people do throughout their lives. Yet every decision that works—that solves a problem of adaptation, lends order where previously there was subjective disorder, or regulates an affect—becomes a conservative dynamic, a schema in the Piagetian sense. Often, however, cognitive, affective, and motivational "decisions" that resist accommodation prevent psychological development along different pathways. A child who learns to fear intimacy in his interactions with his avoidant/dismissing mother is likely to bring his characteristic working models of self and relationships, along with the motives and affect-regulatory strategies associated with them, into other relationships. This in turn constrains the reactions of others and the consequent feedback that might disconfirm expectations and challenge procedures that are maladaptive or at least nonoptimal.

Humans are also born into bodies. Our feelings, wishes, fears, and representations of self are, from the start, tied to our physical existence. And physical experiences are frequently linked to emotionally salient interpersonal encounters. The nurturant touch of a caretaker, or the gleam in a proud parent's eyes, is an intensely pleasurable experience. It is natural—and perhaps naturally selected—that children would at times want to be the *only* apple of their parents' eyes and would wish they could eliminate the competition—even though they may also be deeply attached to the competitors for their parent's love. Requirements to control one's body—to eat on schedule, to defecate in particular places at particular times, or to sit at a desk for hours a day in school—begin early in life and cannot avoid creating conflicts of obedience versus disobedience or identification with respected others versus pursuit of one's own desires. And with the development of full-blown sexual wishes at puberty, children must negotiate a remarkably complex process of directing sexual and loving feelings toward particular others and avoiding sexual feelings toward some who are loved, with whom mating would be biologically disadvantageous—all without the aid of conscious attention. An affective aversion to incest is probably one more example of "prepared" emotional potentialities—in this case, a spontaneous feeling of disgust—that render certain assocations between affects and representations more likely than others, just as humans and other animals are more likely to associate nausea with tastes than with sounds (on taste and nausea, see Garcia & Koelling, 1966).

Humans, like all other primates, are social animals, for whom survival and reproduction require considerable good will from others, including caretakers, family, potential mates, friends, and coalition partners. Most of our wishes can only be attained interpersonally, which means that much of life involves an *external* negotiation with significant others to adjudicate and balance conflicting desires and an *internal* negotiation among competing feelings and motives associated with those we care about or need. From birth, our survival depends on the benevolence of others whose subjectivity and individuality we scarcely understand. For the young child, caretaking others are a given—ground, not figure—and their help, nurturance, and selflessness is expected and generally unacknowledged. At the same time, these important people in our lives invariably frustrate us, because they have competing needs and demands on their time and energy, because as young children we have only a limited understanding of their thoughts and motives, and because their own imperfections often lead them to respond in ways that are emotionally destructive. Thus, the fundamental templates for our later social representations are always ambivalent—associated with love and hate—which is why there is no one who can elicit our anger or aggression more than the ones we most love.

These templates—internal working models of the self, relationships, and others; wishes, fears, and emotions associated with them; and modes of relating and regulating affects—are by no means unalterable or monolithic. From early in life, children develop multiple working models even of the same caregiver, and they form significant relationships with siblings and others in their environment that establish templates for future relationships. Once again, however, it is important to bear in mind that routinized cognitive, affective, and affect-regulatory "decisions" can not only foster development, by directing behavior in adaptive directions selected through learning, but also derail it, as they lock people into patterns maintained by avoidance of consciously or unconsciously feared alternatives, or lead them to behave in ways that lead to confirmation of their beliefs and fears (Wachtel, 1997).

This is just an outline of what an evolutionarily influenced psychodynamic model of personality might look like, but we believe it is an important start. In any case, psychoanalytic theorists would do well in the future to weigh evolutionary considerations whenever they propose theories of motivation, development, or personality, because personality processes, like other psychological processes, likely bear the clear imprint of natural selection.

DIRECTIONS FOR THE FUTURE

True to our stripes as psychoanalytically oriented clinicians and personality psychologists, we are probably better at interpreting the past than at predicting future behavior, so we describe only briefly here what we believe to be four directions that psychoanalysis, and psychoanalytic approaches to personality in particular, will (and, we think, must) take in the future. Either our prognostic skills were uncharacteristically accurate or our schemas are rigid, because these are essentially the same as those we proposed in the last edition of this handbook.

An Expanded Empiricism and the End of Splendid Isolation

As we have seen, many prominent analysts are now calling for psychoanalysis to upgrade its credentials as an empirical science. As suggested above, this process is in some respects already underway, although it is considerably obstructed by many institutional processes both within psychoanalysis (such as a disregard for, or indifference to, experimental work among many analysts, and a lack of research training at psychoanalytic institutes) and within academic psychology departments (such as disrespect for clinical data, a general suspicion or dismissal of psychoanalytic ideas, and a decreasing presence of psychodynamically oriented faculty in clinical psychology programs).

Examination of Microstructures and Processes

Perhaps the most important contribution of a mind like Freud's or Piaget's is to pose big questions and big solutions. The historian H. R. Trevor-Roper once said something to the effect that the function of a genius is not to provide answers but to pose questions that time and mediocrity will resolve. Freud, like Piaget, drew the big picture, and proposed broad stages and structures that could account for an astonishing array of observable phenomena.

Scientific progress seems to require a dialectic not only between abstract theory and detailed observation but also between the holistic purview of thinkers such as Freud and Piaget and the more atomistic view characteristic of most academic psychology, at least in North America. The time is overdue in psychoanalysis for a move toward exploration of microprocesses, just as researchers in cognitive development have moved toward mapping the specific processes involved in cognitive development that produce some of the phenomena Piaget observed and carrying out the painstaking work of refining and eliminating inadequate aspects of his theoretical superstructure (Brainerd, 1978; Case, 1992; Flavell, 1992; Fischer & Bidell, 1998). Whereas the psychoanalytic assessment of personality today largely involves assessment of level of object relations, level of ego functioning, and dynamic conflicts, assessment in the future will require a much more differentiated understanding of each of those domains.

For example, when theorists speak of "internalized object relations" or "internalization of the mother," it is often difficult to know precisely what they mean. Frequently notions of internalization rely upon Freud's antiquated copy theory of perception (Schimek, 1975), as if somehow children store veridical percepts of important objects alongside their fantasy constructions. Equally problematic are classical analytic models of internalization that view the "taking in" of objects as some kind of act of oral incorporation.

One can, in fact, distinguish several legitimate but distinct ways in which one can speak of internalization:

1. Formation of a person schema or object representation, with or without access to consciousness.
2. Formation of a relationship schema—that is, a representation of a relationship or set of relationships, with or without access to consciousness.
3. Formation of dynamic relationship paradigms and object-related fantasies—that is, cognitive-affective structures linking interpersonal wishes and fears with representations and action tendencies, and motivating interpersonal behavior—again, which may be conscious or unconscious.
4. Various forms of procedural knowledge, in which the individual learns to relate in particular ways, expects to feel particular things in relationships, or learns to regulate affect in relationships, typically without consciousness of these processes.
4. Modeling, in which the person develops the competence to imitate some aspect of another's behavior.
5. Internalization of function, in which functions previously carried out by an external object become self-regulating functions, such as self-soothing in the face of pain or threat, and do not necessarily entail representation of specific people.
6. Moral internalization, in which moral injunctions become valued or emotionally invested in as moral ideals.
7. Identification narrowly defined, which combines formation of an object representation, modeling and behavioral imitation, establishment of a motivational structure of "ideal object" to emulate, and adjustment of the self-concept or specific self-representations to reflect the altered ideal and behavior.

As can be seen, these various processes are not isomorphic. Any theorist who wishes to speak coherently of internalization of objects or internalized object relations must be able to specify precisely which processes he or she means in a particular instance.

Attention to Activating Conditions

Psychoanalysis is above all a dynamic theory, which in its sophisticated forms rarely posits trait-like phenomena that express themselves across all situations. Psychoanalytic research and theories of object relations and the self, however, must be careful to avoid static conceptions of processes, stages, and levels of functioning viewed as always operative (Westen, 1990b). Future psychoanalytic research must pay careful attention to the activating conditions of various processes. We do not know, for example, whether borderline patients are uniformly unable to form relatively rich, differentiated representations of people, or whether they use less mature split representations and make illogical attributions under certain conditions, such as poorly modulated affect or conflicts centered around separation or aggression. In many respects, a renewed emphasis on dynamics leads both to more classically psychoanalytic conceptions of conflict and compromise, and to contemporary currents in personality psychology focusing on conditions under which personality dispositions can be expected to be expressed, such as Mischel's *if . . . then . . .* contingencies (Mischel & Shoda, 1995).

A Cognitive–Affective Theory

Finally, we suspect that a shift that has been occurring since the 1980s will continue, namely that basic theoretical concepts in psychoanalysis will be denoted by terms such as "thoughts," "feelings," "wishes," "actions," and "compromise formations," rather than by more obscure terms lacking clear empirical referents, such as "countercathexis," "symbiotic fusion," "drive derivative," and the like.

CONCLUSION

A story is told of a student who asked his mentor, "Professor, what is science?" The professor paused and finally answered, "Science is looking for a black cat in a dark room." Momentarily satisfied, the student began to turn away, but then another question came to him. "Professor," he asked, "what is philosophy?" The academic furrowed his brow and after some thought replied, "Philosophy is looking for a black cat in a dark room where there *is* no black cat." Once again the student, satisfied that his question was answered, took leave of his mentor, only to return to ask one further question: "Professor, what is psychoanalysis?" "Psychoanalysis," the professor responded after a moment of deep contemplation, "is looking for a black cat in a dark room where there is no black cat—and finding one anyway."

Although, as we have attempted to show, the cat has actually been there lurking in the dark more often than has been supposed, one can have little doubt that in the history of psychoanalysis, clinicians and theorists have mistaken more than one shadow for substance, and more than one of our own eyelashes for a feline whisker. The alternative, which personality psychologists who rely exclusively on more conservative methods have chosen, is to turn on the light, see what can be seen, and assume that what goes on in the dark is unknowable or unimportant. If psychoanalysis has, and will continue to have, anything to offer the psychology of personality, it is the insight that we need not be in the dark about processes that are not manifestly observable, and that in the shadows sometimes lies the substance.

ACKNOWLEDGMENTS

We thank the following people for their comments on drafts of the first or second editions of this chapter: Marie Jahoda, Stanley Messer, Christopher Peterson, Lawrence Pervin, George Rosenwald, and Paul Wachtel.

NOTES

1. Although, as we will see, Freud's theory of psychic energy has increasingly fallen into disrepute in psychoanalysis because of the many ways it is problematic (Holt, 1976), certain aspects of it are intuitively appealing and even have empirical support. One is the notion that actively keeping knowledge from onself may require expenditure of considerable psychic energy, and that this may have both psychological and physiological costs (Shedler, Mayman, & Manis, 1993; Weinberger, 1990).

2. The concept of psychic reality is closely tied to another issue that has come to the fore in the last decade in psychoanalysis, namely the role of actual events, particularly traumatic events, in shaping personality. Although Freud never entirely abandoned the idea that actual childhood seduction was a common and pathogenic phenomenon, he certainly emphasized the role of fantasy in his psychoanalytic writing. Simon (1992) noted that cases of actual incest were remarkably absent from much of the psychoanalytic literature until the decade of the 1980s. More recently, psychoanalytic thought has been heavily influenced by the rediscovery of the relatively high prevalence of incest and other forms of childhood abuse. A by-product of the increased interest in traumatic experiences in childhood has been a widespread controversy about the veridicality of recovered memories in clinical practice. Critics of psychoanalysis (Crews, 1995, 1996) have tended to blame Freud for the so-called recovered memory therapists who supposedly encourage patients to believe in the absolute accuracy of memories of childhood seductions. These attacks are based on the assumption that Freud's model of treatment in the 1890s was never superseded by advances in theory or technique. In fact, Freud abandoned the cathartic abreaction model of de-repressing pathogenic memories before the turn of the century. Indeed, there is great irony in the linkage of recovered memory therapists to Freud, because in actuality he was the first to recognize the

fallibility of recovered memories of childhood sexual abuse (Lear, 1998).

REFERENCES

Adler, A. (1929). *The science of living.* Garden City, NY: Doubleday/Anchor.

Adler, A. (1939). *Social interest.* New York: G. P. Putnam.

Ainsworth, M. D. S. (1979). Infant–mother attachment. *American Psychologist, 34,* 932–937.

Ainsworth, M. D. S., Blehar, M. C., Waters, E., & Wall, S. (1978). *Patterns of attachment: A psychological study of the strange situation.* Hillsdale, NJ: Erlbaum.

Alexander, I. (1988). Personality, psychological assessment, and psychobiography. *Journal of Personality, 56,* 265–294.

Allison, J., Blatt, S. J., & Zimet, C. N. (1968). *The interpretation of psychological tests.* New York: Harper & Row.

Anderson, J. R. (1983). *The architecture of cognition.* Cambridge, MA: Harvard University Press.

Anderson, J. R. (1985). *Cognitive psychology and its implications* (2nd ed.). San Francisco: Freeman.

Anderson, J. (1993). Problem solving and learning. *American Psychologist, 48,* 35–44.

Andersen, S., & Baum, A. (1994). Transference in interpersonal relations: Inferences and affect based on significant-other representations. *Journal of Personality, 62,* 460–497.

Andersen, S., & Cole, S. (1991). Do I know you? The role of significant others in general social perception. *Journal of Personality and Social Psychology, 59,* 384–399.

Andersen, S., Reznik, I., & Manzella, L. (1996). Eliciting facial affect, motivation, and expectancies in transference: Significant-other representations in social relations. *Journal of Personality and Social Psychology, 71,* 1108–1129.

Arkowitz-Westen, L. (1998). *The roles of negative reciprocity and acceptance in couples: Predicting relationship quality.* Unpublished doctoral dissertation, University of Nevada, Reno.

Arlow, J. (1985). The concept of psychic reality and related problems. *Journal of the American Psychoanalytic Association, 33,* 521–535.

Arlow, J., & Brenner, C. (1964). Psychoanalytic concepts and the structure model. *Journal of the American Psychoanalytic Association* (Monograph No. 3).

Aron, L. (1995). The internalized primal scene. *Psychoanalytic Dialogues, 5,* 195–237.

Aron, L. (1996). *A meeting of minds: Mutuality in psychoanalysis.* Hillside, NJ: Analytic Press.

Badcock, C. (1994). *PsychoDarwinism: The new synthesis of Darwin and Freud.* London: HarperCollins.

Bargh, J. (1997). The automaticity of everyday life. R. S. Wyer Jr. (Ed.), *The automaticity of everyday life: Advances in social cognition* (Vol. 10, pp. 1–61). Mahwah, NJ: Erlbaum.

Bargh, J. (1984). Automatic and conscious processing of social information. In R. S. Wyer & T. K. Srull (Eds.), *Handbook of social cognition* (Vol. 3, pp. 1–43). Hillsdale, NJ: Erlbaum.

Bargh, J. & Barndollar, K. (1996). Automaticity in action: The unconscious as repository of chronic goals and motives. In P. M. Gollwitzer & J. Bargh (Eds.), *The psychology of action: Linking cognition and motivation to behavior* (pp. 457–481). New York: Guilford Press.

Barron, J. W., Eagle, M. N., & Wolitzky, D. L. (Eds.). (1992). *The interface of psychoanalysis and psychology.* Washington, DC: American Psychological Association.

Basch, F. M. (1977). Developmental psychology and explanatory theory in psychoanalysis. *Annual of Psychoanalysis, 5,* 229–263.

Bellak, L., Hurvich, M., & Gediman, H. K. (1973). *Ego functions in schizophrenics, neurotics, and normals.* New York: Wiley.

Benjamin, J. (1990). An outline of intersubjectivity: The development of recognition. *Psychoanalytic Psychology, 7,* 33–46.

Benjamin, J. (1995). *Like subjects, love objects: Essays on recognition and sexual difference.* New Haven, CT: Yale University Press.

Bettelheim, B. (1983). *Freud and man's soul.* New York: Knopf.

Blanck, G., & Blanck, R. (1974). *Ego psychology: Theory and practice.* New York: Columbia University Press.

Blanck, G., & Blanck, R. (1979). *Ego psychology II: Psychoanalytic developmental psychology.* New York: Columbia University Press.

Blatt, S., Auerbach, J., & Levy, K. (1997). Mental representations in personality development, psychopathology, and the therapeutic process. *Review of General Psychology, 1,* 351–374.

Blatt, S. J., Brenneis, C. B., & Schimek, J. G. (1976). Normal development and psychopathological impairment of the object on the Rorschach. *Journal of Abnormal Psychology, 85,* 364–373.

Blatt, S. J., & Lerner, H. (1983). Investigations in the psychoanalytic theory of object relations and object representations. In J. Masling (Ed.), *Empirical studies in psychoanalytic theories* (Vol. 1, pp. 189–249). Hillsdale, NJ: Erlbaum.

Blatt, S., & Lerner, H. (1991). Psychodynamic perspectives on personality theory. In M. Hersen & A. Kazdin (Eds.), *The clinical psychology handbook* (2nd ed). New York: Pergamon Press.

Blatt, S. J., Wein, S., Chevron, E. S., & Quinlan, D. M. (1979). Parental representations and depression in normal young adults. *Journal of Abnormal Psychology, 78,* 388–397.

Blatt, S., & Zuroff, D. (1992). Interpersonal relatedness and self-definition: Two prototypes for depression. *Clinical Psychology Review, 12,* 527–562.

Blight, J. (1981). Must psychoanalysis retreat to hermeneutics? Psychoanalytic theory in the light of Popper's evolutionary epistomology. *Psychoanalysis and Contemporary Thought, 4,* 146–206.

Block, J. (1971). *Lives through time.* Berkeley, CA: Bancroft.

Block, J., & Block, J. (1980). The role of ego-control and ego-resiliency in the organization of behavior. In W. A. Collins (Ed.), *Minnesota Symposium on Child Development* (Vol. 13). Hillsdale, NJ: Erlbaum.

Blum, G. S. (1961). *A model of the mind.* New York: Wiley.

Blum, G. S. (1968). Assessment of psychodynamic variables by the Blacky pictures. In P. McReynolds (Ed.), *Advances in psychological assessment* (Vol. 1). Palo Alto, CA: Science and Behavior Press.

Bonanno, G. A., & Singer, J. L. (1995). Repressive personality style: Theoretical and methodological implications for health and pathology. In J. L. Singer (Ed.), *Repression and dissociation: Implications for personality theory, psychopathology, and health* (pp. 435–470). Chicago: University of Chicago Press.

Bowers, K., & Meichenbaum, D. (Eds.). (1984). *The unconscious reconsidered.* New York: Wiley.

Bowlby, J. (1969). *Attachment and loss: Vol. 1. Attachment.* New York: Basic Books.

Bowlby, J. (1973). *Attachment and loss: Vol. 2. Separation.* New York: Basic Books.

Bowlby, J. (1982). Attachment and loss: Retrospective and prospect. *American Journal of Orthopsychiatry, 52,* 664–678.

Brainerd, C. J. (1978). The stage question in cognitive-developmental theory. *Behavioral and Brain Sciences, 2,* 173–213.

Brennan, K., Clark, C. L., & Shaver, P. (1998). Self-report measurement of adult attachment: An integrative overview. In J. A. Simpson & W. Rholes (Eds.), *Attachment theory and close relationships* (pp. 46–76). New York: Guilford Press.

Brenner, C. (1980). Metapsychology and psychoanalytic theory. *Psychoanalytic Quarterly, 49,* 189–214.

Brenner, C. (1982). *The mind in conflict.* New York: International Universities Press.

Bretherton, I. (1985). Attachment theory: Retrospect and prospect. In I. Bretherton & E. Waters (Eds.), Growing points of attachment theory and research. *Monographs of the Society for Research in Child Development, 50*(1–2, Serial No. 209), 3–35.

Breuer, J., & Freud, S. (1955). Studies on hysteria. In J. Strachey (Ed. and Trans.), *The standard edition of the complete psychological works of Sigmund Freud* (Vol. 2, pp. 1–305). London: Hogarth Press. (Original work published 1893–1895).

Brewer, M., & Brown, R. J. (1998). Intergroup relations. In D. T. Gilbert, S. T. Fiske, & G. Lindzey (Eds.), *Handbook of social psychology* (Vol. 2, pp. 554–594). New York: McGraw-Hill.

Broadent, D. E. (1977). The hidden preattentive processes. *American Psychologist, 32,* 109–118.

Brown, L. L., Tomarken, A., Orth, D., Loosen, P., Kalin, N, and Davidson, R. (1996). Individual differences in repressive-defensiveness predict basal salivary cortisol levels. *Journal of Personality and Social Psychology, 70,* 362–371.

Bruner, J. S. (1973). *Beyond the information given: Studies in the psychology of knowing.* New York: Norton.

Bucci, W. (1997). *Psychoanalysis and cognitive science: A multiple code theory.* New York: Guilford Press.

Busch, F. (1995). *The ego at the center of clinical technique.* Northvale, NJ: Jason Aronson.

Busch, F. (1999). *Rethinking clinical technique.* Northvale, NJ: Jason Aronson.

Buss, D., Haselton, M., Shackelford, T., Bleske, A., & Wakefield, J. (1998). Adaptations, exaptations, and spandrels. *American Psychologist, 53,* 533–548.

Cacioppo, J., Gardner, W., & Berntson, G. (1997). Beyond bipolar conceptualizations and measures: The case of attitudes and evaluative space. *Personality and Social Psychology Review, 1,* 3–25.

Case, R. (1992). Neo-Piagetian theories of child development. In R. J. Sternberg, C. A. Berg, et al. (Eds.), *Intellectual development* (pp. 161–196). New York: Cambridge University Press.

Cavell, M. (1998). Triangulation, ones own mind and objectivity. *International Journal of Psycho-Analysis, 79,* 449–467.

Coleman, M. J., Levy, D. L., Lenzenweger, M. F., & Holzman, P. S. (1996). Thought disorder, perceptual aberrations, and schizotypy. *Journal of Abnormal Psychology, 105,* 469–473.

Compton, A. (1981a). On the psychoanalytic theory of instinctual drives: III. The implications of libido and narcissism. *Psychoanalytic Quarterly, 50,* 345–362.

Compton, A. (1981b). On the psychoanalytic theory of instinctual drives: IV. Instinctual drives and the ego –id–superego model. *Psychoanalytic Quarterly, 50,* 363–392.

Conklin, A., & Westen, D. (in press). Clinical uses of the TAT. In Dorfman, W. I. & Hersen, M. (Eds.). *Understanding psychological assessment.* New York: Plenum Press.

Conte, H. R., & Plutchik, R., Eds. (1995). Ego defenses: Theory and measurement. New York: Wiley.

Cooper, A. (1984). Psychoanalysis at one hundred years: Beginnings of maturity. *Journal of the American Psychoanalytic Association, 32,* 245–267.

Crews, F. (1995). *The memory wars: Freuds legacy in dispute.* New York: New York Review of Books.

Crowne, D. P., & Marlowe, D. (1964). *The approval motive: Studies in evaluative dependence.* New York: Wiley.

Dahl, H. (1983). On the definition and measurement of wishes. In j. Masling (Ed.), *Empirical studies of psychoanalytic theories* (Vol. 1). Hillsdale, NJ: Erlbaum.

Davidson, R. (1992). Emotion and affective style: Hemispheric substrates. *Psychological Science, 3,* 39–43.

Davis, P., & Schwartz, G. (1987). Repression and the inaccessibility of affective memories. *Journal of Personality and Social Psychology, 52,* 155–162.

Demorest, A. P., & Siegel, P. F. (1996). Personal influences on professional work: An empirical case study of B. F. Skinner. *Journal of Personality, 64,* 243–261.

De Wolff, M., & van IJzendoorn, M. (1997). Sensitivity and attachment: A meta-analysis on parental antecedents of infant attachment. *Child Development, 68,* 571–591.

Dixon, N. F. (1971). *Subliminal perception: The nature of controversy*. New York: McGraw-Hill.

Dixon, N. F. (1981). *Preconscious processing*. New York: Wiley.

Eagle, M. (1984). *Recent developments on psychoanalysis*. New York: McGraw-Hill.

Edelson, M. (1984). *Hypothesis and evidence in psychoanalysis*. Chicago: University of Chicago Press.

Edelson, M. (1985). The hermeneutic turn and the single case study in psychoanalysis. *Psychoanalysis & Contemporary Thought, 8,* 567–614.

Ellenberger, H. F. (1970). *The discovery of the unconscious: The history and evolution of dynamic psychiatry.* New York : Basic Books.

Erdelyi, M. (1974). A "new look" at the New Look in perception. *Psychological Review, 81,* 1–25.

Erdelyi, M. (1985). *Psychoanalysis: Freud's cognitive psychology*. San Francisco: Freeman.

Erikson, E. (1963). *Childhood and society* (rev. ed.). New York: Norton.

Erikson, E. (1968). *Identity: Youth and crises*. New York: Norton.

Fairbairn, W. R. D. (1952). *Psychoanalytic studies of the personality*. London: Routledge & Kegan Paul.

Fast, I. (1985). *Event theory*. Hillsdale, NJ: Erlbaum.

Fazio, R., Jackson, J. R., Dunton, B., & Williams, C. J. (1995). Variability in automatic activiation as an unobtrusive measure of racial attitudes: A bona fide pipeline? *Journal of Personality and Social Psychology, 69,* 1013–1027.

Fischer, K., & Bidell, T. (1998). Dynamic development of psychological structures in action and thought. In W. Damon (Ed.), R. M. Lerner (Vol. Ed.), *Handbook of child psychology* (5th ed.). *Vol. 1. Theoretical models of human development* (pp. 467–562). New York: Wiley.

Fisher, S., & Greenberg, R. P. (1977). *The scientific credibility of Freud's theories and therapy*. New York: Columbia University Press.

Fisher, S., & Greenberg, R. (1985). *The scientific credibility of Freud's theories and therapy.* New York: Columbia University Press.

Fisher, S., & Greenberg, R. P. (1996). *Freud scientifically reappraised: Testing the theories and therapy.* New York: Wiley.

Flavell, J. (1992). Cognitive development: past, present, and future. *Developmental Psychology, 28,* 998–1005.

Fonagy, P., Leigh, T., Steele, M., Steele, H., Kennedy, R., Mattoon, G., Target, M., & Gerber A. (1996). The relationship of attachment status, psychiatric classification, and response to psychotherapy. *Journal of Consulting and Clinical Psychology, 64,* 22–31.

Fonagy, P., Moran, G. S., Steele, M., Steele, H., & Higgitt, A. C. (1991). The capacity for understanding mental states: The reflective self in parent and child and its significance for security of attachment. *Infant Mental Health Journal, 13,* 200–216.

Fonagy, P., Steele, H., & Steele, M. (1991). Maternal representations of attachment during pregnancy predict the organization of infant-mother attachment at one year of age. *Child Development, 62,* 891–905.

Fowler, C., Hilsenroth, M., & Handler, L. (1996). Two methods of early memories data collection: An empirical comparison of the projective yield. *Assessment, 3,* 63–71.

Freud, A. (1936). *The ego and the mechanisms of defense.* New York: International Universities Press.

Freud, S. (1953a). The interpretation of dreams. In J. Strachey (Ed. and Trans.), *The standard edition of the complete psychological works of Sigmund Freud* (Vol. 4, pp. 1–338; Vol. 5, pp. 339–621). London: Hogarth Press. (Original work published 1900)

Freud, S. (1953b). Three essays on the theory of sexuality. In J. Strachey (Ed. and Trans.), *The standard edition of the complete psychological works of Sigmund Freud* (Vol. 7, pp. 123–245). London: Hogarth Press. (Original work published 1905)

Freud, S. (1957). Mourning and melancholia. In J. Strachey (Ed. and Trans.), *The standard edition of the complete psychological works of Sigmund Freud* (Vol. 14, pp. 237–260). London: Hogarth Press. (Original work published 1917)

Freud, S. (1957). On narcissism. In J. Strachey (Ed. and Trans.), *The standard edition of the complete psychological works of Sigmund Freud* (Vol. 14, pp. 67–102). London: Hogarth Press. (Original work published 1914)

Freud, S. (1957). The unconscious. In J. Strachey (Ed. and Trans.), *The standard edition of the complete psychological works of Sigmund Freud* (Vol. 14, pp. 159–215). London: Hogarth Press. (Original work published 1915)

Freud, S. (1958). The dynamics of transference. In J. Strachey (Ed. and Trans.), *The standard edition of the complete psychological works of Sigmund Freud* (Vol. 12, pp. 97–108). London: Hogarth Press. (Original work published 1912)

Freud, S. (1961). The ego and the id. In J. Strachey (Ed. and Trans.), *The standard edition of the complete psychological works of Sigmund Freud* (Vol. 19, pp. 1–66). London: Hogarth Press. (Original work published 1923)

Freud, S. (1964a). An outline of psycho-analysis. In J. Strachey (Ed. and Trans.), *The standard edition of the complete psychological works of Sigmund Freud* (Vol. 23, pp. 139–207). London: Hogarth Press. (Original work published 1940)

Freud, S. (1964b). New introductory lectures on psychoanalysis. In J. Strachey (Ed. and Trans.), *The standard edition of the complete psychological works of Sigmund Freud* (Vol. 22, pp. 1–182). London: Hogarth Press. (Original work published 1933)

Freud, S. (1966). Project for a scientific psychology. In J. Strachey (Ed. and Trans.), *The standard edition of the complete psychological works of Sigmund Freud* (Vol. 1, pp. 281–397). London: Hogarth Press. (Original work written in 1895, published 1950)

Fromm, E. (1947). *Man for himself: An inquiry into the psychology of ethics*. New York: Holt, Rinehart & Winston.

Fromm, E. (1962). *The sane society.* Greenwich, CT: Fawcett Books.

Gabbard, G. O. (1997a). A reconsideration of objectivity in the analyst. *International Journal of Psycho-Analysis, 78,* 15–26.

Gabbard, G. O. (1997b). Challenges in the analysis of adult patients with histories of childhood sexual abuse. *Canadian Journal of Psychoanalysis, 5,* 1–25.

Gabbard, G. O. (1997c). Finding the "person" in personality disorders. *American Journal of Psychiatry, 154,* 891–893.

Gabbard, G. O. (in press-a). How does treatment help? In O. Kernberg (Ed.), *The analytic hour: The good, the bad, and the ugly.* Connecticut: International Universities Press.

Gabbard, G. O. (in press-b). Psychoanalysis and psychoanalytic psychotherapy. In J. Livesley (Ed.), *Handbook of personality disorders.* New York: Guilford Press.

Gabbard, G. O., & Wilkinson, S. M. (1996). Nominal gender and gender fluidity in the psychoanalytic situation. *Gender and Psychoanalysis, 1,* 463–481.

Garcia, J., & Koelling, R. (1966). Relation of cue to consequence in avoidance learning. *Psychonomic Science, 4,* 123–124.

Gartner, J., Hurt, S. W., & Gartner, A. (1987, September). *Psychological test signs of borderline personality disorder: A review of the empirical literature.* Paper presented at the annual convention of the American Psychological Association, New York.

Gill, M. M. (1976). Metapsychology is not psychology. In M. M. Gill & P. S. Holzman (Eds.), Psychology versus metapsychology: Psychoanalytic essays in memory of George S. Klein. *Psychological Issues, 9*(4, Monograph No. 36).

Gill, M. M. (1994). *Psychoanalysis in transition: A personal view.* Hillsdale, NJ: Analytic Press.

Glassman, N. S., & Andersen, S. (in press). Activating transference without awareness: Using significant-other representations to go beyond the subliminally given information. *Journal of Personality and Social Psychology.*

Gray, J. A. (1990). Brain systems that mediate both emotion and cognition. *Cognition and Emotion, 4,* 269–288.

Gray, P. (1994). *The ego and the analysis of defense.* Northvale, NJ: Jason Aronson.

Greenberg, J. (1991). *Oedipus and beyond: A clinical theory.* Cambridge, MA: Harvard University Press.

Greenberg, J. R., & Mitchell, S. A. (1983). *Object relations in psychoanalytic theory.* Cambridge, MA: Harvard University Press.

Greenberg, L. S., & Safran, J. D. (1987). *Emotion in psychotherapy.* New York: Guilford Press.

Greenspan, S. (1979). *Intelligence and adaptation.* New York: International University Press.

Greenwald, A., & Banaji, M. (1995). Implicit social cognition: Attitudes, self-esteem, and stereotypes. *Psychological Review, 102,* 4–27.

Greenwald, A., McGhee, D., & Schwartz, J. (1998). Measuring individual differences in implicit cognition: The implicit association test. *Journal of Personality and Social Psychology, 74,* 1464–1480.

Grunbaum, A. (1984). *The foundations of psychoanalysis: A philosophical critique.* Berkeley, CA: University of California Press.

Guisinger, S., & Blatt, S. J. (1994). Individuality and relatedness: Evolution of a fundamental dialectic. *American Psychologist, 49,* 104–111.

Guntrip, H. (1971). *Psychoanalytic theory, therapy, and the self.* New York: Basic Books.

Haan, N. (1977). *Coping and defending.* New York: Academic Press.

Habermas, J. (1971). Knowledge and human interests (J. J. Shapiro, Trans.). London: Heinemann.

Hadley, J. L. (1983). The representational system: A bridging concept for psychoanalysis and neurophysiology. *International Journal of Psycho-Analysis, 10,* 13–30.

Hamilton, V. (1996). *The analysts preconscious.* Hillsdale, NJ: Analytic Press.

Harris, A. (1991). Gender as contradiction. *Psychoanalytic Dialogues, 1,* 197–224.

Hartmann, H. (1950). Comments on the psychoanalytic theory of the ego. *Psychoanalytic Study of the Child, 5,* 74–96.

Hartmann, H. (1958). *Ego psychology and the problem of adaptation.* New York: International Universities Press. (Original work published 1939.)

Hartmann, H., Kris, E., & Loewenstein, R. (1946). Comments on the formation of psychic structure. *Psychoanalytic Study of the Child, 2,* 11–38.

Hartup, W. (1996). The company they keep: Friendships and their developmental significance. *Child Development, 67,* 1–13.

Hedegard, S. (1969). *A molecular analysis of psychological defenses.* Unpublished doctoral dissertation, University of Michigan, Ann Arbor, Michigan.

Heinemann, L., & Emrich, H. (1971). Alpha activity during inhibitory brain processes. *Psychophysiology, 7,* 442–450.

Herman, J., Perry, J. C., & van der Kolk, B. A. (1989). Childhood trauma in borderline personality disorder. *American Journal of Psychiatry, 146,* 490–495.

Hibbard, S., Hilsenroth, M., Hibbard, J. K., & Nash, M. (1995). A validity study of two projective object representations measures. *Psychological Assessment, 7,* 432–439.

Higgins, E. T., & Bargh, J. A. (1987). Social cognition and social perception. *Annual Review of Psychology, 38,* 369–425.

Higgins, E. T., King, G. A., & Mavin, G. H. (1982). Individual construct accessibility and subjective impressions and recall. *Journal of Personality and Social Psychology, 43,* 35–47.

Hoffman, I. Z. (1983). The patient as interpreter of the analysts experience. *Contemporary Psychoanalysis, 19,* 389–422.

Hoffman, I. Z. (1991). Discussion: Toward a social constructivist view of the psychoanalytic situation. *Psychoanalytic Dialogues, 1,* 74–105.

Hoffman, I. Z. (1998). *Ritual and spontaneity in the psychoanalytic process: A dialectical–constructivist view.* Hillsdale, NJ: Analytic Press.

Holland, N. N. (1993). Post-modern psychoanalysis. In I. Hassan & S. Hassan (Eds.), *Innovation/renovation: New perspectives on the humanities* (pp. 291–309). Madison, WI: University of Wisconsin Press.

Holt, R. R. (1976). Drive or wish? In M. M. Gill & P. S. Holzman (Eds.), Psychology versus metapsychology: Psychoanalytic essays in memory of George S. Klein. *Psychological Issues, 9*(4, Monograph No. 36).

Holt, R. R. (1981). The death and transfiguration of metapsychology. *International Review of Psycho-Analysis, 8,* 129–143.

Holt, R. R. (1985). The current status of psychoanalytic theory. *Psychoanalytic Psychology, 2,* 289–315.

Holzman, P. (1985). Psychoanalysis: Is the therapy destroying the science? *Journal of the American Psychoanalytic Association, 33,* 725–770.

Holyoak, K., & Spellman, B. (1993). Thinking. *Annual Review of Psychology, 44,* 265–315.

Horney, K. (1950). *Neurosis and human growth.* New York: Norton.

Horney, K. (1967). *Feminine psychology.* New York: Norton.

Horowitz, M. J. (1987). *States of mind: Configurational analysis of individual psychology* (2nd ed). New York: Plenum Press.

Horowitz, M. J. (1988). *Introduction to psychodynamics: A Synthesis.* New York: Basic Books.

Horowitz, M. (1998). *Cognitive psychodynamics: From conflict to character.* New York: Wiley.

Howes, C., Hamilton, C. E., & Philipsen, L. (1998). Stability and comorbidity of child- caregiver and child-peer relationships. *Current Directions in Psychological Science, 69,* 418–426.

Jacobson, E. (1954). The self and the object world. *Psychoanalytic Study of the Child, 9,* 75–127.

Jacoby, L., & Kelly, C. M. (1992). A process-dissociation framework for investigating unconscious influences: Freudian slips, projective tests, subliminal perception, and signal detection theory. *Current Directions in Psychological Science, 1,* 174–179.

Jahoda, M. (1977). *Freud and the dilemmas of psychology.* London: Hogarth Press.

Johnston, M. H., & Holzman, P. S. (1979). *Assessing schizophrenic thinking.* San Francisco: Jossey-Bass.

Johnson, M. K., Kim, J. K., & Risse, G. (1985). Do alcoholic Korsakoff's syndrome patients acquire affective reactions? *Journal of Experimental Psychology: Learning, Memory, and Cognition, 11,* 22–36.

Jung, C. G. (1971). *The portable Jung* (J. Campbell, Ed.). New York: Viking.

Kelly, G. A. (1955). *Psychology of personal constructs.* New York: Norton.

Kernberg, O. (1975). *Borderline conditions and pathological narcissism.* New York: Jason Aronson.

Kernberg, O. (1976). *Object relations theory and clinical psychoanalysis.* New York: Jason Aronson.

Kernberg, O. (1984). *Severe personality disorders: Psychotherapeutic strategies.* New Haven, CT: Yale University Press.

Kihlstrom, J. F. (1987). The cognitive unconscious. *Science, 237,* 1445–1452.

Kihlstrom, J. (1990). The psychological unconscious. In L. Pervin (Ed.), *Handbook of personality: Theory and research* (pp. 445–464). New York: Guilford Press.

Klepp, K.-I., Kelder, S. H., & Perry, C. L. (1995). Alcohol and marijuana use among adolescents: Long-term outcomes of the class of 1989 study. *Annals of Behavioral Medicine, 17,* 19–24.

Klein, G. S. (1976). Freud's two theories of sexuality. In M. M. Gill & P. S. Holzman (Eds.), Psychology versus metapsychology: Psychoanalytic essays in memory of George S. Klein. *Psychological Issues, 9*(4, Monograph No. 36).

Klein, M. (1948). *Contributions to psycho-analysis,* 1921–1945. London: Hogarth Press.

Kohut, H. (1966). Forms and transformations of narcissism. *Journal of the American Psychoanalytic Association, 14,* 243–272.

Kohut, H. (1971). *The analysis of the self: A systematic psychoanalytic approach to the treatment of narcissistic personality disorders.* New York: International Universities Press.

Kohut, H. (1977). *The restoration of the self.* New York: International Universities Press.

Kohut, H. (1984). *How does analysis cure?* (A. Goldberg, Ed., with collaboration of P. E. Stepansky). Chicago: University of Chicago Press.

Kohut, H., & Wolf, E. (1978). The disorders of the self and their treatment: An outline. *International Journal of Psycho-Analysis, 59,* 413–425.

Kolb, B., & Wishaw, I. Q. (1990). *Fundamentals of human neuropsychology* (3rd ed.). San Francisco: Freeman.

Krohn, A., & Mayman, M. (1974). Object representations in dreams and projective tests. *Bulletin of the Menninger Clinic, 38,* 445–466.

Lear, J. (1998). *Open minded: Working out the logic of the soul.* Cambridge, MA: Harvard University Press.

Leary, K. (1994). Psychoanalytic "problems" and post-modern "solutions." *Psychoanalytic Quarterly, 63,* 433–465.

LeDoux, J. (1995). Emotion: Clues from the brain. *Annual Review of Psychology, 46,* 209–235.

Levine, H. B. (1994). The analysts participation in the analytic process. *International Journal of Psycho-Analysis, 75,* 665–676.

LeVine, R. (1982). *Culture, behavior, and personality* (2nd ed.). Chicago: Aldine.

Levy, K. N, Blatt, S., & Shaver, P. (1998). Attachment styles and parental representations. *Journal of Personality and Social Psychology, 74,* 407–419.

Lewicki, P. (1986). *Nonconscious social information processing.* New York: Academic Press.

Lichtenberg, J. (1989). *Psychoanalysis and motivation.* Hillsdale, NJ: Analytic Press.

Loevinger, J. (1966). The meaning and measurement of ego development. *American Psychologist, 21,* 195–206.

Luborsky, L., & Crits-Christoph, P. (1990). *Understanding transference: The core conflictual relationship theme method.* New York: Basic Books.

Luborsky, L., & Crits-Christoph, P. (1996). *Understanding transference: The core conflictual relationship theme method* (2nd ed.). Washington, DC: American Psychological Association Press.

Luborsky, L., Crits-Christoph, P., & Mellon, J. (1986). Advent of direct measures of the transference concept. *Journal of Consulting and Clinical Psychology, 54,* 39–47.

Luria, A. (1962). *The role of speech in the regulation of normal and abnormal behaviors.* New York: Liveright Books.

Mahler, M., Pine, F., & Bergman, A. (1975). *The psychological birth of the human infant: Symbiosis and individuation.* New York: Basic Books.

Main, M. (1990). Cross-cultural studies of attachment organization: Recent studies, changing methodologies, and the concept of conditional strategies. *Human Development, 33,* 48- 61.

Main, M. & Goldwin, R. (1991). *Adult attachment classification system, version 5.* Unpublished manuscript, Berkeley: University of California.

Main, M., Kaplan, N., & Cassidy, J. (1985). Security in infancy, childhood, and adulthood: A move to the level of representation. In I. Bretherton & E. Waters (Eds.), Growing points of attachment theory and research. *Monographs of the Society for Research in Child Development,* 50(1–2, Serial No. 209), 67–104.

Masterson, J. F. (1976). *Psychotherapy of the borderline adult: A developmental approach.* New York: Brunner/Mazel.

Mayman, M. (1967). Object-representation and object relationships in Rorschach responses. *Journal of Projective Techniques and Personality Assessment, 31,* 17–24.

Mayman, M. (1968). Early memories and character structure. *Journal of Projective Techniques and Personality Assessment, 32,* 303–316.

McClelland, D. C., Koestner, R., & Weinberger, J. (1989). How do self-attributed and implicit motives differ? *Psychological Review, 96,* 690–702.

McWilliams, N. (1994). *Psychodynamic diagnosis: Understanding personality structure in clinical context.* New York: Guilford Press.

McWilliams, N. (1998). Relationship, subjectivity, and inference in diagnosis. In J. Barron & D. Wolitzky (Eds.), *Making diagnosis meaningful: Enhancing evaluation and treatment of psychological disorders* (pp. 197–226). Washington, DC: American Psychological Association Press.

Menninger, K., Mayman, M., & Pruyser, P. (1963). *The vital balance: The life process in mental health and illness.* New York: Viking.

Mickelson, K., Kessler, R. C., & Shaver, P. (1997). Adult attachment in a nationally representative sample. *Journal of Personality and Social Psychology, 73,* 1092–1106.

Mikulincer, M. (1998a). Adult attachment style and affect regulation: Strategic variations in self-appraisals. *Journal of Personality and Social Psychology, 75,* 420–435.

Mikulincer, M. (1998b). Adult attachment style and individual differences in functional versus dysfunctional experiences of anger. *Journal of Personality and Social Psychology, 74,* 513- 524.

Miller, L. (1997). Freud and consciousness: The first one hundred years of neuropsychodynamics in theory and clinical practice. *Seminars in Neurology, 17,* 171–177.

Miller, L. (1986, December). In search of the unconscious. *Psychology Today, 20*(12), 60–64.

Mischel, W., & Shoda, Y. (1995). A cognitive-affective system theory of personality: Reconceptualizing situations, dispositions, dynamics, and invariance in personality structure. *Psychological Review, 102,* 246–268.

Mitchell, S. A. (1988). *Relational concepts in psychoanalysis: An integration.* Cambridge, MA: Harvard University Press.

Mitchell, S. A. (1993). *Hope and dread in psychoanalysis.* New York: Basic Books.

Mitchell, S. A. (1997). *Autonomy and influence in psychoanalysis.* Hillsdale, NJ: Analytic Press.

Moray, N. (1969). *Attention: Selective processes in vision and hearing.* London: Hutchinson.

Morrison, K., & Westen, D. (1999). How empirically valid are empirically validated therapies? Unpublished manuscript, Harvard Medical School.

Natterson, J. (1991). *Beyond countertransference: The therapists subjectivity in the therapeutic process.* Northvale, NJ: Jason Aronson.

Nigg, J., Lohr, N. E., Westen, D., Gold, L., & Silk, K. R. (1992). Malevolent object representations in borderline personality disorder and major depression. *Journal of Abnormal Psychology, 101,* 61–67.

Nisbett, R., & Wilson, T. (1977). Telling more than we can know: Verbal reports on mental processes. *Psychological Review, 84,* 231–259.

Ogden, T. H. (1994). The analytic third: Working with intersubjective clinical facts. *International Journal of Psycho-Analysis, 75,* 3–19.

Ohman, A. (1994). "Unconscious anxiety": Phobic responses to masked stimuli. *Journal of Abnormal Psychology, 103,* 231–240.

Paulhus, D., Fridhandler, B., & Hayes, S. (1997). Psychological defense: Contemporary theory and research. In R. Hogan, J. Johnson, & S. R. Briggs (Eds.), *Handbook of personality psychology* (pp. 543–579). San Diego: Academic Press.

Perry, J. C., & Cooper, S. H. (1987). Empirical studies of psychological defense mechanisms. In R. Michels & J. O. Cavenar Jr. (Eds.), *Psychiatry.* Philadelphia: Lippincott.

Perry, J. C., & Cooper, S. H. (1989). An empirical study of defense mechanisms: I. Clinical interview and life vignette ratings. *Archives of General Psychiatry, 46,* 444–460.

Pervin, L. A. (1984). The stasis and flow of behavior: Toward a theory of goals. In M. M. Page (Ed.), *Personality: Current theory and research* (pp. 1–53). Lincoln, NE: University of Nebraska Press.

Peterfreund, E. (1971). Information, systems, and psychoanalysis: An evolutionary biological approach to psychoanalytic theory. *Psychological Issues, 7*(1/2, Monograph No. 25/26).

Pettigrew, T., & Meertens, R. (1995). Subtle and blatant prejudice in Western Europe. *European Journal of Social Psychology, 25,* 57–75.

Pettit, G., Bates, J., & Dodge, K. (1997). Supportive parenting, ecological context, and children's adjustment: A seven-year longitudinal study. *Child Development, 68,* 908–923.

Pine, F. (1985). *Developmental theory and clinical process.* New Haven: CT: Yale University Press.

Pine, F. (1988). The four psychologies and their place in clinical work. *Journal of the American Psychoanalytic Association,* 571–596.

Pine, F. (1990). *Drive, ego, object, and self: A synthesis for clinical work.* New York: Basic Books.

Plomin, R., DeFries, J. C., McClearn, G. E., & Rutter, R. (1997). Behavioral genetics (3rd ed.). New York: W. H. Freeman.

Plutchik, R. (1980). A general psychoevolutionary theory of emotion. In R. Plutchik & H. Kellerman (Eds.), *Emotion: Vol. 1. Theories of emotion.* New York: Academic Press.

Plutchik, R. (1998). Emotions, diagnoses and ego defenses: A psychoevolutionary perspective. In W. Flack & J. D. Laird (Eds). *Emotions in psychopathology: Theory and research* (pp. 367–379). New York: Oxford University Press.

Poetzl, O. (1960). The relationship between experimentally induced dream images and indirect vision. *Psychological Issues, 2*(Monograph No. 7), 41–120. (Original work published in 1917.)

Pope, K. S., Tabachnick, B. A., & Keith-Spiegel, P. (1987). Ethics of practice: The beliefs and behaviors of psychologists as therapists. *American Psychologist, 42,* 993–1006.

Porcerelli, J., Hill, K., & Dauphin, V. B. (1995). Need-gratifying object relations and psychopathology. *Bulletin of the Menninger Clinic, 59,* 99–104.

Pribram, K. (1998). A century of progress? *Annals of the New York Academy of Sciences, 843,* 11–17.

Pribram, K. H., & Gill, M. M. (1976). *Freud's "Project" re-assessed: Preface to contemporary cognitive theory and neuropsychology.* New York: Basic Books.

Priester, J. R., & Petty, R. E. (1996). The gradual negative threshold model of ambivalence: Relating positive and negative bases of attitudes to subjective ambivalence. *Journal of Personality and Social Psychology, 71,* 431–449.

Rapaport, D. (1951). *Organization and pathology of thought: Selected sources.* New York: Columbia University Press.

Rapaport, D. (1967). The scientific methodology of psychoanalysis. In M. Gill (Ed.), *The collected papers of David Rapaport.* New York: Basic Books. (Original work published 1944)

Rapaport, D., & Gill, M. M. (1959). The points of view and assumptions of metapsychology. *International Journal of Psycho-Analysis, 40,* 153–162.

Rapaport, D., Gill, M., & Schafer, R. (1945–1946). *Diagnostic psychological testing* (2 vols.). Chicago: Year Book Medical.

Reber, A. (1992). The cognitive unconscious: An evolutionary perspective. *Consciousness and Cognition, 1,* 93–133.

Redl, R. A., & Wineman, D. (1951). *Children who hate.* New York: Collier.

Renik, O. (1993). Analytic interaction: Conceptualizing technique in light of the analyst's irreducible subjectivity. *Psychoanalytic Quarterly, 62,* 553–571.

Renik, O. (1998). The analysts subjectivity and the analysts objectivity. International Journal of Psycho-Analysis, 79, 487–497.

Reiser, M. F. (1984). *Mind, brain, body.* New York: Basic Books.

Richards, A. (1986). Introduction. In A. Richards & M. S. Willick (Eds.), *Psychoanalysis, the science of mental conflict: Essays in honor of Charles Brenner* (pp. 1–27). Hillsdale, NJ: Erlbaum.

Ricks, M. H. (1985). The social transmission of parental behavior: Attachment across generations. In I. Bretherton & E. Waters (Eds.), Growing points of attachment theory and research. *Monographs of the Society for Research in Child Development, 50*(1–2, Serial No. 209), 211–227.

Ricoeur, P. (1971). *Freud and philosophy: An essay on interpretation* (D. Savage, Trans.). New Haven, CT: Yale University Press.

Roediger, H. L. (1990). Implicit memory: Retention without remembering. *American Psychologist, 45*(9), 1043–1056.

Rubenstein, B. (1976). On the possibility of a strictly clinical theory: An essay on the philosophy of psychoanalysis. In M. M. Gill & P. S. Holzman (Eds.), Psychology versus metapsychology: Psychoanalytic essays in memory of George S. Klein. *Psychological Issues, 9*(4, Monograph No. 36).

Rumelhart, D. E., McClelland, J. L., & the PDP Research Group. (1986). *Parallel distributed processing: Explanations on the microstructures of cognition* (2 vols.). Cambridge, MA: MIT Press.

Sandler, J. (1976). Countertransference and role-responsiveness. *International Review of Psycho-Analysis, 3,* 43–47.

Sandler, J. (1987). *From safety to superego: Selected papers of Joseph Sandler.* New York: Guilford Press.

Sandler, J. (1991). Character traits and object relationships. *Psychoanalytic Quarterly, 50,* 694–708.

Sandler, J., & Rosenblatt, B. (1962). The concept of the representational world. *Psychoanalytic Study of the Child, 17,* 128–145.

Sandler, J., & Sandler, A. (1978). On the development of object relationships and affects. *International Journal of Psycho-Analysis, 59,* 285–296.

Schacter, D. L. (1986). The psychology of memory. In J. E. LeDoux & W. Hirst (Eds.), *Mind and brain: Dialogues in cognitive neuroscience.* New York: Cambridge University Press.

Schacter, D. (1992). Understanding implicit memory: A cognitive neuroscience approach. *American Psychologist, 47,* 559–569.

Schacter, D. (1995). Implicit memory: A new frontier for cognitive neuroscience. In M. Gazzaniga (Ed.), *The cognitive neurosciences* (pp. 815–824). Cambridge, MA: MIT Press.

Schafer, R. (1976). *A new language for psychoanalysis.* New Haven, CT: Yale University Press.

Schafer, R. (1989). Narratives of the self. In A. M. Cooper, O. F. Kernberg, & E. S. Person (Eds.), *Psychoanalysis: Toward the second century* (pp. 153–167). New Haven, CT: Yale University Press.

Scharf, J. S., & Scharf, D. (1998). *Object relations individual therapy.* New York: Jason Aronson.

Schimek, J. (1975). A critical re-examination of Freud's concept of unconscious mental representation. *International Review of Psycho-Analysis, 2,* 171–187.

Schore, A. (1994). *Affect regulation and the origin of the self: The neurobiology of emotional development.* Mahwah, NJ: Erlbaum.

Schwartz, A. (1987). Drives, affects, and behavior—and learning: Approaches to a psychobiology of emotion and to an integration of psychoanalyic and neurobiologic thought. *Journal of the American Psychoanalytic Association, 35,* 467–506.

Seger, C. A. (1994). Implicit learning. *Psychological Bulletin, 115,* 163–196.

Shapiro, D. (1965). *Neurotic styles.* New York: Basic Books.

Shedler, J., & Block, J. (1990). Adolescent drug use and psycholoical health: A longitudinal inquiry. *American Psychologist, 45,* 612–630.

Shedler, J., Mayman, M., & Manis, M. (1993). The illusion of mental health. *American Psychologist, 48,* 1117–1131.

Shevrin, H. (1984). The fate of the five metaphysical principles. *Psychoanalytic Inquiry, 4,* 33–58.

Shevrin, H., Bond, J., Brakel, L., Hertel, R., & Williams, W. J. (1996). *Conscious and unconscious processes: Psychodynamic, cognitive, and neurophysiological convergences.* New York: Guilford Press.

Shevrin, H., & Dickman, S. (1980). The psychological unconscious: A necessary assumption for all psychological theory? *American Psychologist, 35,* 421–434.

Silverman, L. H., & Weinberger, J. (1985). Mommy and I are one: Implications for psychotherapy. *American Psychologist, 12,* 1296–1308.

Simon, H. (1990). Invariants of human behavior. *Annual Review of Psychology, 41,* 1–19.

Singer, J. A., & Salovey, P. (1993). *The remembered self: Emotion and memory in personality.* New York: Free Press.

Slavin, M. O., & Kriegman, D. (1992). *The adaptive design of the human psyche: psychoanalysis, evolution, and the therapeutic process.* New York: Guilford Press.

Smith, E. R. (1998). Mental representation and memory. In D. T. Gilbert, S. T. Fiske, & G. Lindzey (Eds.), *Handbook of social psychology* (Vol. 1, pp. 391–445). New York: McGraw-Hill.

Solms, M. (1996). Towards an anatomy of the unconscious. *Journal of Clinical Psychoanalysis, 5,* 331–367.

Spence, D. P. (1982). *Narrative truth and historical truth: Meaning and interpretation in psychoanalysis.* New York: Norton.

Spezzano, C. (1993). *Affect in psychoanalysis: A clinical synthesis.* Hillsdale, NJ: Analytic Press.

Squire, L. R. (1987). *Memory and brain.* New York: Oxford University Press.

Steele, H., Steele, M., & Fonagy, P. (1996). Associations among attachment classifications of mothers, fathers, and their infants. *Child Development, 67,* 541–555.

Stolorow, R., & Atwood, G. (1992). *Contexts of being.* Hillsdale, NJ: Analytic Press.

Stolorow, R., Brandchaft, B., & Atwood, G. (1987). *Psychoanalytic treatment: An intersubjective approach.* Hillsdale, NJ: Analytic Press.

Stroufe, L. A., & Fleeson, J. (1986). Attachment and the construction of relationships. In W. W. Hartup & Z. Rubin (Eds.), *Relationships and development.* Hillsdale, NJ: Erlbaum.

Stroufe, L. A., & Waters, E. (1977). Attachmet as an organizational construct. *Child Development, 48,* 1184–1199.

Sullivan, H. S. (1953). *The interpersonal theory of psychiatry.* New York: Norton.

Sulloway, F. J. (1979). *Freud: Biologist of the mind.* New York: Basic Books.

Tansey, M. J., & Burke, W. F. (1989). *Understanding countertransference: From projective identification to empathy.* Hillsdale, NJ: Analytic Press.

Tomkins, S. (1962). *Affect, imagery, consciousness* (Vol. 1). New York: Springer.

Trivers, R. (1971). The evolution of reciprocal altruism. *Quarterly Review of Biology, 46,* 35–57.

Underwood, G. (Ed.). (1996). *Implicit cognition.* New York: Oxford University Press.

Urist, J. (1980). Object relations. In R. W. Woody (Ed.), *Encyclopedia of clinical assessment* (Vol. 2, pp. 821–833). San Francisco: Jossey-Bass.

Vaillant, G. E. (1977). *Adaptation to life.* Boston: Little Brown.

Vaillant, G. (Ed.). (1992). *Ego mechanisms of defense: A guide for clinicians and researchers.* Washington, DC: American Psychiatric Association Press.

Vaillant, G. E., & Drake, R. E. (1985). Maturity of defenses in relation to *DSM-III* Axis II personality disorder. *Archives of General Psychiatry, 42,* 597–601.

Wachtel, P. (1987). *Action and insight.* New York: Guilford Press.

Wachtel, P. (1997). *Psychoanalysis, behavior therapy, and the relational world.* Washington, DC: American Psychological Association Press.

Wakefield, J. (1992). The concept of mental disorder: On the boundary between biological facts and social values. *American Psychologist, 47,* 373–388.

Wallerstein, R. S. (1988). One psychoanalysis or many? *International Journal of Psycho-Analysis, 69,* 5–22.

Weinberger, D. A. (1995). The construct validity of the repressive coping style. In J. L. Singer (Ed.), *Repression and dissociation: Implications for personality theory, psychopathology, and health* (pp. 337–386). Chicago: University of Chicago Press.

Weinberger, D. A., Schwartz, G. E., & Davidson, R. J. (1979). Low-anxious, high-anxious, and repressive coping styles: Psychometric patterns and behavioral and psychological responses to stress. *Journal of Abnormal Psychology, 88,* 369–380.

Weinberger, J., & Silverman, L. (1988). *Testability and empirical verification of psychoanalytic dynamic propositions through subliminal psychodynamic activation.* Unpublished manuscript, H. A. Murray Center, Harvard University, Cambridge, Mass.

Westen, D. (1985). *Self and society: Narcissism, collectivism, and the development of morals.* New York: Cambridge University Press.

Westen, D. (1990a). Psychoanalytic approaches to personality. In L. Pervin (Ed.), *Handbook of personality: Theory and research* (pp. 21–65). New York: Guilford Press.

Westen, D. (1990b). Toward a revised theory of borderline object relations: Implications of empirical research. *International Journal of Psycho-Analysis, 71,* 661–693.

Westen, D. (1991). Social cognition and object relations. *Psychological Bulletin, 109,* 429–455.

Westen, D. (1994). Toward an integrative model of affect regulation: Applications to social-psychological research. *Journal of Personality, 62,* 641–647.

Westen, D. (1997). Toward an empirically and clinically sound theory of motivation. *International Journal of Psycho-Analysis, 78,* 521–548.

Westen, D. (1998a). The scientific legacy of Sigmund Freud. Toward a psychodynamically informed psychological science. *Psychological Bulletin, 124,* 333–371.

Westen, D. (1998b). Case formulation and personality diagnosis: Two processes or one? In James Barron (Ed.), *Making diagnosis meaningful* (pp. 111–138). Washington, DC: American Psychological Association Press.

Westen, D. (1999a). Psychodynamic theory and technique in relation to research on cognition and emotion: Mutual implications. In T. Dalgleish & M. Power (Eds.), *Handbook of cognition and emotion* (pp. 727–746). New York: Wiley.

Westen, D. (1999b). *Social Cognition and Object Relations Scales (SCORS) for narrative data and projective stories.* Unpublished manual, Harvard Medical School.

Westen, D. (in press). The scientific status of unconscious processes: Is Freud really dead? *Journal of the American Psychoanalytic Association.*

Westen, D., & Feit, W. (1999). All the president's women: Affective constraint satisfaction in ambiguous social cognition. Unpublished data, Harvard Medical School.

Westen, D., Feit, A., & Zittel, C. (1999). Methodological issues in research using projective techniques. In P. C. Kendall, J. N. Butcher, & G. Holmbeck (Eds.), *Handbook of research methods in clinical psychology,* 2nd ed. (pp. 224–240). New York: Wiley.

Westen, D., Klepser, J., Ruffins, S., Silverman, M., Lifton, N., & Boekamp, J. (1991). Object relations in childhood and adolescence: The development of working representations. *Journal of Consulting and Clinical Psychology, 59,* 400–409.

Westen, D., Lohr, N., Silk, K., Gold, L., & Kerber, K. (1990). Object relations and social cognition in borderlines, major depressives, and normals: A TAT analysis. *Psychological Assessment: A Journal of Consulting and Clinical Psychology, 2,* 355–364.

Westen, D., Ludolph, P., Lerner, H., Ruffins, S., & Wiss, F. C. (1990). Object relations in borderline adolescents. *Journal of the American Academy of Child and Adolescent Psychiatry, 29,* 338–348.

Westen, D., Ludolph, P., Misle, B., Ruffins, S., & Block, J. (1990). Physical and sexual abuse in female adolescents with borderline personality disorder. *American Journal of Orthopsychiatry, 60,* 55–66.

Westen, D., Muderrisoglu, S., Fowler, C., Shedler, J., & Koren, D. (1997). Affect regulation and affective experience: Individual differences, group differences, and measurement using a Q-sort procedure. *Journal of Consulting and Clinical Psychology, 65,* 429–439.

Westen, D., & Shedler, J. (1999a). Revising and assessing Axis II, Part I: Developing a clinically and empirically valid assessment method. *American Journal of Psychiatry, 156,* 258–272.

Westen, D., & Shedler, J. (1999b). Revising and assessing Axis II, Part II: Toward an empirically based and clinically useful classification of personality disorders. *American Journal of Psychiatry, 156,* 273–285.

White, R.W. (1959). Motivation reconsidered: The concept of competence. *Psychological Review, 66,* 297–333.

Williams, G. C. (1966). *Adaptation and natural selection: A critique of some current evolutionary thought.* Princeton: Princeton University Press.

Wilson, E. O. (1978). *On human nature.* New York: Bantam.

Winson, J. (1985). *Brain and psyche: The biology of the unconscious*. New York: Anchor/Doubleday.

Wolff, P. H. (1960). The developmental psychologies of Jean Piaget and psychoanalysis. *Psychological Issues, 2* (Monograph 5).

Wong, P., Shevrin, H., & Williams, W. J. (1994). Conscious and nonconscious processes: An ERP index of an anticipatory response in a conditioning paradigm using visually masked stimuli. *Psychophysiology, 31,* 87–101.

Zanarini, M. (1997). Role of sexual abuse in the etiology of borderline personality disorder. Washington, DC: American Psychiatric Press.

Zeanah, C. H., & Zeanah, P. D. (1989). Intergenerational transmission of maltreatment: Insights from attachment theory and research. *Psychiatry, 52,* 177–196.

Chapter 4

The Big Five Trait Taxonomy: History, Measurement, and Theoretical Perspectives

Oliver P. John and Sanjay Srivastava
University of California, Berkeley

Taxonomy is always a contentious issue because the world does not come to us in neat little packages

—GOULD (1981, p. 158)

Personality has been conceptualized from a variety of theoretical perspectives, and at various levels of abstraction or breadth (John, Hampson, & Goldberg, 1991; McAdams, 1995). Each of these levels has made unique contributions to our understanding of individual differences in behavior and experience. One frequently studied level is personality traits (John & Gosling, in press). However, the number of personality traits, and scales designed to measure them, has escalated without an end in sight (Goldberg, 1971). Researchers, as well as practitioners in the field of personality assessment, have been faced with a bewildering array of personality scales from which to choose, with little guidance and no overall rationale at hand. To make matters worse, scales with the same name often measure concepts that are not the same, and scales with different names often measure concepts that are quite similar. Although diversity and scientific pluralism are useful, the systematic accumulation of findings and the communication among researchers has become difficult amidst the Babel of concepts and scales.

Many personality researchers had hoped that they might devise the structure that would transform the Babel into a community speaking a common language. However, such an integration was not to be achieved by any one researcher or by any one theoretical perspective. As Allport once put it, "each assessor has his own pet units and uses a pet battery of diagnostic devices" (1958, p. 258).

What personality psychology needed was a descriptive model, or taxonomy, of traits. One of the central goals of scientific taxonomies is the definition of overarching domains within which large numbers of specific instances can be understood in a simplified way. Thus, in personality psychology, a taxonomy would permit researchers to study specified domains of personality characteristics, rather than examining separately the thousands of particular attributes that make each human being individual and unique. Moreover, a generally accepted taxonomy would greatly facilitate the accumulation and communication of empirical findings by offering a standard vocabulary, or nomenclature.

After decades of research, the field is finally approaching consensus on a general taxonomy of personality traits, the "Big Five" personality dimensions. These dimensions do not represent a particular theoretical perspective but were derived from analyses of the natural language terms people use to describe themselves and others. Rather than replacing all previous systems, the Big Five taxonomy serves an integrative function because it can represent diverse systems of personality description in a common framework. It thus provides a starting place for vigorous research and theorizing that can eventually lead to an explication and revision of the descriptive taxonomy in causal and dynamic terms.

In this chapter, we first review the history of the Big Five, including the discovery of the five dimensions, research replicating and extending the model, its convergence with research in the questionnaire tradition, and the development of several instruments to measure the Big Five. Then, we compare three of the most frequently used instruments and report data regarding their reliability and convergent validity. Finally, we address a number of critical issues, including how the Big Five taxonomy is structured hierarchically, whether the five dimensions predict important life outcomes, how they develop, how they combine into personality types, and whether they are descriptive or explanatory concepts.

THE LEXICAL APPROACH AND DISCOVERY OF THE BIG FIVE

One starting place for a shared taxonomy is the natural language of personality description. Beginning with Klages (1926), Baumgarten (1933), and Allport and Odbert (1936), various psychologists have turned to the natural language as a source of attributes for a scientific taxonomy. This work, beginning with the extraction of all personality-relevant terms from the dictionary, has generally been guided by the lexical hypothesis (see John, Angleitner, & Ostendorf, 1988; Saucier & Goldberg, 1996b). The lexical hypothesis posits that most of the socially relevant and salient personality characteristics have become encoded in the natural language (e.g., Allport, 1937). Thus, the personality vocabulary contained in the dictionaries of a natural language provides an extensive, yet finite, set of attributes that the people speaking that language have found important and useful in their daily interactions (Goldberg, 1981).

Allport and Odbert's Psycholexical Study: Traits, States, Activities, and Evaluations

Following Baumgarten's (1933) work in German, Allport and Odbert (1936) conducted a seminal lexical study of the personality-relevant terms in an unabridged English dictionary. They included all the terms that could be used to "distinguish the behavior of one human being from that of another" (p. 24) Their complete list amounted to almost 18,000 terms. At the time, the staggering size of this list seemed "like a semantic nightmare" (Allport, 1937, pp. 353–354). Allport and Odbert thought that organizing these thousands of personality attributes into a satisfactory taxonomy would keep psychologists "at work for a life time" (1936, p. vi). Indeed, this task has occupied personality psychologists for more than 60 years. (For detailed reviews of the history of the lexical approach, see John et al., 1988; John, 1990).

Allport and Odbert (1936) tried to bring some order to the semantic nightmare they had created. What kinds of person descriptors are included in the dictionary? Allport and Odbert identified four major categories. The first category included personality traits (e.g., sociable, aggressive, and fearful), which they defined as "generalized and personalized determining tendencies—consistent and stable modes of an individual's adjustment to his environment" (p. 26). The second category included temporary states, moods, and activities, such as afraid, rejoicing, and elated. The third category consisted of highly evaluative judgments of personal conduct and reputation, such as excellent, worthy, average, and irritating. Although these terms presuppose some traits within the individual, they do not indicate the specific attributes that gave rise to the individual's evaluation by others or by society in general. The last category included physical characteristics, capacities and talents, terms of doubtful relevance to personality, and terms that could not be assigned to any of the other three categories.

Norman (1967) subsequently elaborated Allport and Odbert's initial classification and divided the domain into seven content categories: stable "biophysical" traits, temporary states, activities, social roles, social effects, evaluative terms, anatomical and physical terms, as well as ambiguous and obscure terms not considered useful for personality descriptive purposes. These categories illustrate that the personality lexicon in the natural language includes a wealth of concepts. Individuals can be described by their enduring *traits* (e.g., irrascible), by the *internal states* they typically experience (furious), by the *physical states* they endure (trembling), by the *activities* they engage in (screaming), by the *effects* they have on others (frightening), by the *roles* they play (murderer), and by social *evaluations* of their conduct (unacceptable, bad). Moreover, individuals differ in their anatomical and morphological characteristics (short) and in the personal and societal evaluations attached to these appearance characteristics (cute).

Both Allport and Odbert (1936) and Norman (1967) classified the terms culled from the dictionary into mutually exclusive categories. An inspection of the classifications quickly shows that the categories overlap and have fuzzy boundaries, leading some researchers to conclude that distinctions between classes of personality descriptors are arbitrary and should be abolished (Allen & Potkay, 1981). In contrast, Chaplin, John, and Goldberg (1988) argued for a prototype conception in which each category is defined in terms of its clear cases rather than its boundaries; category membership need not be discrete but can be defined as continuous. Chaplin and colleagues (1988) applied this prototype conception to traits, states, and activities. Although the classification of a few descriptors was difficult, the core of each category was distinct from the others and could be differentiated by a set of conceptually derived attributes. Prototypical *states* were seen as temporary, brief, and externally caused. Prototypical *traits* were seen as stable, long lasting, and internally caused, and needed to be observed more frequently and across a wider range of situations than states before they were attributed to an individual. These findings closely replicated the earlier classifications and confirmed that the conceptual definitions of traits and states are widely shared.

Identifying the Major Dimensions of Personality Description: Cattell's Early Efforts

Allport and Odbert's (1936) classifications provided some initial structure for the personality lexicon. However, to be of practical value, a taxonomy must provide a systematic framework for distinguishing, ordering, and naming individual differences in people's behavior and experience (John, 1989). Aiming for such a taxonomy, Cattell (1943) used the Allport and Odbert list as a starting point for his multidimensional model of personality structure. Because the size of that list was too overwhelming for research purposes, Cattell (1943, 1945a, 1945b) began with the subset of 4,500 trait terms. Most taxonomic research has focused on the personality trait category, although the other categories are no less important. For example, the emotional-state and social-evaluation categories have recently received considerable attention (Almagor, Tellegen & Waller, 1995; Benet-Martinez & Waller, 1997).

Using both semantic and empirical clustering procedures as well as his own reviews of the personological literature available at the time (for reviews, see John et al., 1988; John, 1990), Cattell reduced the 4,500 trait terms to a mere 35 variables. That is, Cattell eliminated more than 99% of the terms Allport (1937) had so tenaciously defended. This drastic reduction was dictated primarily by the data-analytic limitations of his time, which made factor analyses of large variable sets prohibitively costly and complex. Using this small set of variables, Cattell conducted several oblique factor analyses and concluded that he had identified 12 personality factors, which eventually became part of his 16 Personality Factors (16PF) questionnaire (Cattell, Eber, & Tatsuoka, 1970).

Cattell also claimed that his factors showed excellent correspondence across methods, such as self-reports, ratings by others, and objective tests; however, these claims have not gone unquestioned (e.g., Becker, 1960; Nowakowska, 1973). Moreover, reanalyses of Cattell's own correlation matrices by others have not confirmed the number and nature of the factors he proposed (e.g., Tupes & Christal, 1961[1]). Digman and Takemoto-Chock (1981) concluded that Cattell's "original model, based on the unfortunate clerical errors noted here, cannot have been correct" (p. 168), although the second-order factors of the 16PF show some correspondence between Cattell's system and the subsequently derived Big Five dimensions.

THE BIG FIVE FACTORS IN PERSONALITY TRAIT RATINGS

Discovery of the Big Five in Cattell's Variable List

Cattell's pioneering work, and the availability of a relatively short list of variables, stimulated other researchers to examine the dimensional structure of trait ratings. Several investigators were involved in the discovery and clarification of the Big Five dimensions. Fiske (1949) constructed much simplified descriptions from 22 of Cattell's variables; the factor structures derived from self-ratings, ratings by peers, and ratings by psychological staff members were highly similar and resembled what would be later known as the Big Five. To clarify these factors, Tupes and Christal (1961) reanalyzed correlation matrices from eight different samples, ranging from airmen with no more than high school education to first-year graduate students, and included ratings by peers, supervisors, teachers, or experienced clinicians in settings as diverse as military training courses and sorority houses. In all the analyses, Tupes and Christal found "five relatively strong and recurrent factors and nothing more of any consequence" (1961, p. 14).

This five-factor structure has been replicated by Norman (1963), Borgatta (1964), and Digman and Takemoto-Chock (1981) in lists derived from Cattell's 35 variables. These factors are typically labeled:

I. Extraversion or Surgency (talkative, assertive, energetic)
II. Agreeableness (good-natured, cooperative, trustful)
III. Conscientiousness (orderly, responsible, dependable)
IV. Emotional Stability versus Neuroticism (calm, not neurotic, not easily upset)
V. Intellect or Openness (intellectual, imaginative, independent-minded)

These factors eventually became known as the "Big Five" (Goldberg, 1981)—a title chosen not to reflect their intrinsic greatness but to emphasize that each of these factors is extremely broad. Thus, the Big Five structure does not imply that personality differences can be reduced to only five traits. Rather, these five dimensions represent personality at the broadest level of abstraction, and each dimension summarizes a large number of distinct, more specific personality characteristics.

Testing the Big Five in a Comprehensive Set of English Trait Terms

After a period of dormancy during the 1970s and early 1980s, research on the Big Five, and on issues of personality structure more generally, has increased dramatically since the mid-1980s. Factor structures resembling the Big Five were identified in numerous sets of variables (e.g., Botwin & Buss, 1989; Conley, 1985; De Raad, Mulder, Kloosterman, & Hofstee, 1988; Digman & Inouye, 1986; Field & Millsap, 1991; Goldberg, 1981, 1990; John, 1990; McCrae & Costa, 1985c, 1987; Peabody & Goldberg, 1989; Saucier & Goldberg, 1996a). However, a number of these studies were influenced by Cattell's selection of variables (Block, 1995), making it important to test the comprehensiveness and generality of the Big Five in more comprehensive variable sets. To update the Allport and Odbert list and to rectify the imperfections of Cattell's reduction steps, Norman (1967) compiled an exhaustive list of personality descriptive terms, which he sorted into 75 semantic categories. Goldberg (1990; see also 1981, 1982) used this list to clarify the nature and composition of these broad factors and to test their stability and generalizability across methodological variations and data sources. Using Norman's (1967) listing, Goldberg (1990) constructed an inventory of 1,710 trait adjectives that participants could use to rate their own personality. He then scored Norman's semantic categories as scales and factor analyzed their intercorrelations in the self-rating data. The first five factors represented the Big Five and replicated across a variety of different methods of factor extraction and rotation. Moreover, Goldberg (1990) demonstrated that the first five factors remained virtually invariant when more than five were rotated.

To ensure independence from any a priori classification, Goldberg (1990) conducted two additional studies using abbreviated sets of more common terms. In one study, Goldberg obtained self and peer ratings of 475 very common trait adjectives which he had grouped into 131 sets of "tight synonym" clusters. In four samples, the five-factor structures were very similar to each other and to the structure obtained in the more comprehensive list of 1,710 terms, and the results in the self-rating data were virtually indistinguishable from those in the peer ratings. Most important, however, were the results from the search for replicable additional factors. In a more recent study, Saucier and Goldberg (1996a) selected 435 trait adjectives rated by subjects as highly familiar terms; a factor analysis of these adjectives closely replicated the Big Five. Furthermore, a thorough search for factors beyond the Big Five showed that the Big Five were the only consistently replicable factors (Saucier, 1997).

Assessing the Big Five with Trait Descriptive Adjectives

Goldberg (1990, 1992) distilled his extensive taxonomic findings into several published adjective lists. One of them is a 50-item instrument using the so-called "transparent format" (Goldberg, 1992), which is excellent for instructional purposes (Pervin & John, 1997). For each factor, this measure presents 10 bipolar adjective scales (e.g., quiet–talkative) grouped together under the factor name, thus making the constructs being measured transparent to the research participants. The list used more commonly in research is the set of 100 unipolar trait descriptive adjectives (TDA). Goldberg (1992) conducted a series of factor analytic studies to develop and refine the TDA as an optimal representation of the five-factor space in English, selecting for each Big Five scale only those adjectives that uniquely defined that factor. These scales have impressively high internal consistency, and their factor structure is easily replicated.[2]

Another adjectival measure of the Big Five was developed by Wiggins (1995; Trapnell & Wiggins, 1990). In his 20-year program of research on the interpersonal circumplex, Wiggins (1979) has used personality trait adjectives to elaborate both the conception and the measurement of the two major dimensions of interpersonal behavior, Dominance (or Agency) and Nurturance (or Communion). Noting that the first dimension closely resembles the Extraversion factor in the Big Five, and the second dimension the Agreeableness factor, Wiggins extended his circumplex scales by adding adjective measures for the other three of the Big Five factors (Trapnell & Wiggins, 1990). The resulting Interpersonal Adjective Scales (Wiggins, 1995) have excellent reliabilities and converge well with other measures; they have been used by researchers who want to measure the specific octants of the interpersonal circle as well as the Big Five.

The circumplex approach has also been applied to a perennial problem in lexical research on personality factors. One important task is to spell out, with much more precision, those characteristics that fall in the fuzzy regions *between* the factors. Using 10 two-dimensional circumplexes, Hofstee, De Raad, and Goldberg (1992) have devised a novel empirical approach to represent the space formed by each pair of factors. This approach specifies facets that reflect various combinations of two factors. The facets differ in whether they are more closely related to one or the other factor. For example, there are two facets that reflect high Agreeableness and high Conscientiousness, but they differ in which of the two factors is given prominence. Thus, the *responsibility* facet represents agreeable Conscientiousness, whereas the *cooperation* facet represents conscientious Agreeableness (Hofstee, Kiers, De Raad, Goldberg, & Ostendorf, 1997).

Cross-Language and Cross-Cultural Studies

The results reviewed so far suggest that the Big Five structure provides a replicable representation of the major dimensions of trait description in English. The five-factor structure seems to generalize reliably across different types of samples, raters, and methodological variations when comprehensive sets of variables are factored. Generalizability across languages and cultures is another important criterion for evaluating personality taxonomies (John, Goldberg, & Angleitner, 1984).

Taxonomic research in other languages and cultures can determine the usefulness of a taxonomy across cultural contexts and test for universals and variations in the encoding of individual differences across languages and cultures (Goldberg, 1981). The existence of cultural universals would be consistent with an evolutionary interpretation of the way individual differences have become encoded as personality categories into the natural language: If the tasks most central to human survival are universal, the most important individual differences, and the terms people use to label these individual differences, would be universal as well (Buss, 1996; Hogan, 1983; see also Buss, Chapter 2, this volume). Similarly, if cross-cultural research reveals a culturally specific dimension, variation on that dimension may be uniquely important within the particular social context of that culture (Yang & Bond, 1990).

Although central from the vantage point of the lexical approach, cross-language research is difficult and expensive to conduct, and until the 1990s it was quite rare. In the initial comprehensive taxonomic studies, English was the language of choice, primarily because the taxonomers were American (for reviews, see John et al., 1984; John et al., 1988).

Initial Studies in Dutch and German

The first two non-English taxonomy projects involved Dutch and German, languages closely related to English. The Dutch project has been carried out by Hofstee, De Raad, and their colleagues at the University of Groningen in the Netherlands (De Raad, Mulder, Kloosterman, & Hofstee, 1988; Hofstee et al., 1997; see also De Raad, Perugini, et al., 1998, for reviews). The conclusions from the Dutch projects are generally consistent with those from the American English research: Only five factors were replicable across different selections of trait adjectives and across different subject samples. Those five factors were similar to the English Big Five, although in Dutch the fifth factor emphasizes Unconventionality and Rebelliousness rather than Intellect and Imagination as found in English.

The dictionary-based German taxonomy project was begun in Bielefeld by Angleitner, Ostendorf, and John (1990), who carried out a "psycholexical" study of the German personality vocabulary. Their study was explicitly based on the prototype conception and improved on the earlier studies of English in several respects. In particular, 10 independent judges classified all the terms, thus providing a continuous measure of prototypicality and an assessment of the reliability and validity of the judgments. The resulting German personality lexicon is more convenient to use than the unwieldy Allport and Odbert lists because continuous prototypicality values are available for each term in 13 different content categories. Thus, it is easy to select subsets of prototypical traits, states, social evaluations, and so on from the total pool for further studies. Angleitner and colleagues' (1990) research served as a blueprint for several taxonomic efforts in other languages.

Ostendorf (1990) selected the most prototypical trait adjectives from the German taxonomy, and his factor analyses of about 450 traits yielded the clearest replication of the Big Five so far. In addition to the prototypical traits representing the distillation of the German trait lexicon, Ostendorf also included German translations of several English Big Five instruments. Thus, Ostendorf's study is a good example of the combined emic–etic design, which allows researchers to establish empirically the similarity of indigenous (emic) factors to the factors translated from other languages and cultures (etic). Correlational analyses allowed Ostendorf to demonstrate substantial convergence between the emic German dimensions and the etic Big Five measures in the same sample of German subjects.

However, this combined emic–etic strategy is difficult to implement and not consistently used in research. Thus, conclusions about factor similarity are often made by "eyeballing" the item content of the factors in the indigenous language and comparing it to the typical factor definitions in English. That leaves much leeway to the investigators in "seeing" a factor that another investigator might not see. For example, the Hebrew factor defined primarily by traits such as sophisticated, sharp, knowledgeable, articulate, and impressive would lead some researchers to see an Intellect factor, whereas Almagor and colleagues (1995) interpreted it as Positive Valence.

Underestimating Cross-Language Congruence

One of the difficulties in cross-language research involves translations. Often, researchers working within their indigenous language have to translate their concepts into English to communicate their findings and much slippage occurs in the translation process. For example, one wonders why "temperamental" was a definer of Extraversion in German until one realizes that the German trait was probably *temperamentvoll*, which has nothing to do with temper but means "full of life and energy," as in vivacious. Similarly, *frizzante* (translated as sparkling) was not related to brilliant intellect, but instead seems to mean something like the English word "bubbly."

An initial study of German–English bilinguals, which provided support for cross-language generalizability (John et al., 1984), directly addressed the issue of translation equivalence. The unique advantage of the bilingual design is that sample differences can be controlled and that translation checks can be made at the level of individual items because the same subject provides descriptions in both languages (see also Benet-Martinez & John, 1998). Using a careful back-translation procedure, John and colleagues (1984) found acceptable levels of translation equivalence between English and German trait adjectives, with a mean correlation of .52 across a two-week interval between administrations. However, several translations proved to be inadequate, with item-translation correlations approaching zero. These findings suggest that mistranslations that cannot be detected in monolingual investigations will lead to severe underestimations of cross-language generality.

To permit empirical estimates of factor similarity across monolingual investigations, Hofstee, De Raad, and their colleagues have used translations of terms as a way to compare factor solutions across languages. For example, Hofstee and colleagues (1997) identified 126 words that they could translate across previous lexical studies in English, Dutch, and German and used them to assess factor congruence coefficients among all pairs of factors in the three languages. Their findings are illuminating in that they showed considerable congruence across these three Germanic languages. With the exception of the fifth factor in Dutch and English, the pairwise congruence coefficients all exceeded .70. Strangely, the authors interpreted these levels of cross-language congruence as "disappointing" (Hofstee et al., 1997, p. 27). This interpretation contradicts Ostendorf's (1990) own conclusions, which were drawn from the emic–etic comparisons in his well-designed study.

We are more optimistic about these findings. The empirically observed levels of factor congruence reported by Hofstee and colleagues (1997) can be interpreted only if one assumes that the translations are perfectly equivalent and that the factor structures in each language are perfectly stable. What happens when we correct the cross-language congruence coefficients at least for the imperfect reliability of the factor structures reported by Hofstee and colleagues? The corrected English–German congruence coefficients range from .84 to .93, impressive values given that they are not corrected for the imperfect translations; moreover, the correspondence for the fifth factor was .93, suggesting that the Intellect/Openness factor was defined almost identically in English and German. The corrected English–Dutch and German–Dutch congruence coefficients were very similar to each other, and suggested the same conclusions: Congruence was substantial for the first four factors (.88 to .97) but not the fifth (.50 to .53). In short, our reexamination suggests that translation-based comparisons across languages are heuristically useful but should not be interpreted in terms of absolute effect sizes. These results also suggest that the fifth factor in Dutch is defined differently in the other two languages, and explanations for this finding need to be sought.

Rules for Including Trait Descriptors in Taxonomic Studies

In all likelihood, some of the differences observed among the factor structures in the three languages also result from the different inclusion rules followed by the taxonomy teams. The selection criterion used by the Dutch researchers favored terms related to temperament, excluded terms related to intellect, talents, and capacities, and included a number of extremely negative evaluative terms, such as perverse, sadistic, and criminal. The German team explicitly included intellect and talent descriptors but omitted attitudes and evaluative terms, which were included as categories separate from traits. Finally, the American English taxonomy included attitudinal terms such as liberal, progressive, and provincial, along with a number of intellect terms. Given the diverse range of traits related to the fifth factor, it is less surprising that the German and English factors shared the intellect components, whereas the Dutch factor included some imagination-related traits (e.g., inventive, original, imaginative) but otherwise emphasized unconventionality and was thus interpreted initially as a "Rebelliousness" factor. An Italian taxonomy (Caprara & Perugini, 1994) found a similar fifth factor interpreted as Unconventionality: Not surprisingly, these Italian researchers had followed the Dutch selection procedures rather than the German procedures, which would have represented more Intellect terms in the taxonomy.

Szirmak and De Raad (1994) examined Hungarian personality descriptors and found strong support for the first four of the Big Five but failed to obtain a factor resembling the fifth of the Big Five; instead, when they forced a five-factor solution, the Agreeableness factor split into two factors. An Intellect/Openness factor emerged only when six factors were rotated. Again, this finding may be due to the selection rules that included a "trait versus state rating."

Evidence in Non-Germanic Languages

The personality lexicon has recently been studied in a wide range of additional languages, such as Chinese (Yang & Bond, 1990), Czech (Hrebickova & Ostendorf, 1995), Hebrew (Almagor et al., 1995), Hungarian (Szirmak & De Raad, 1994), Italian (De Raad, Di Blas, & Perugini, 1998), Polish (Szarota, 1995), Russian (Shmelyov & Pokhilko, 1993), and Turkish (Somer &

Goldberg, 1999). A recent review (De Raad, Perugini, et al., 1998) has compared many of the European studies, using translations to estimate factor similarity quantitatively. Most generally, factors similar to the Big Five have been found in many other languages but often, more than five factors needed to be rotated and sometimes two indigenous factors corresponded to one of the Big Five. Overall, the evidence is least compelling for the fifth factor, which appears in various guises, ranging from pure Intellect (in German) to Unconventionality and Rebelliousness (in Dutch and Italian).

Extensions into cultures different from the industrialized West have also begun to appear. Whereas early studies used translations of English-language measures (Bond, 1979, 1983; Bond & Forgas, 1984; Bond, Nakazato, & Shiraishi, 1975; Guthrie & Bennett, 1971; Nakazato, Bond, & Shiraishi, 1976; White, 1980), more recent studies have used emic and combined emic–etic designs. For example, extensive studies of Filipino samples have provided some support for the generality of the Big Five (Church & Katigbak, 1989; Church, Reyes, Katigbak, & Grimm, 1997). Church and Katigbak (1989) had subjects generate behavioral exemplars, and Church and colleagues (1997) derived a comprehensive list of personality descriptors following the methods proposed by the German taxonomy team. Both studies suggest that the structure of the Filipino personality lexicon is quite similar to the Big Five, although more than five factors needed to be extracted to produce all of the Big Five dimensions. As the authors caution, "this does not mean that there are no unique concepts in either language. However, at a higher level of generality, similar structural dimensions emerge" (Church & Katigbak, 1989, p. 868).

Bond and collaborators (Yang & Bond, 1990; Yik & Bond, 1993) have recently followed up on their earlier etic work in Chinese. They drew their emic items from free descriptions and from indigenous personality questionnaires. By including translations of Big Five marker items from English, they were able to use regression analyses to compare the emic factor space with the etic (i.e., imported) Big Five. Their results suggest that although the Chinese language does not cleanly reproduce the English Big Five and several differences remain, the indigenous Chinese dimensions do overlap considerably with the Big Five dimensions.

In summary, the cross-language research suggests that the Big Five can be replicated in Germanic languages. The evidence for non-Western languages and cultures is more complex, and Factor V generally shows the weakest replicability. Thus, strong conclusions about the linguistic universality of the lexically derived Big Five would be premature. Most generally, we agree with De Raad, Perugini, and colleagues (1998) who concluded that the findings in seven languages support "the general contours of the Big Five model as the best working hypothesis of an omnipresent trait structure" (p. 214).

THE BIG FIVE IN PERSONALITY QUESTIONNAIRES

While researchers in the lexical tradition were accumulating evidence for the Big Five, the need for an integrative framework became more pressing among researchers who studied personality with questionnaire scales. Joint factor analyses of questionnaires developed by different investigators had shown that two broad dimensions, Extraversion and Neuroticism, appear in one form or another in most personality inventories. Beyond these "Big Two" (Wiggins, 1968), however, the various questionnaire-based models had shown few signs of convergence. For example, Eysenck (1991) observed that "Where we have literally hundreds of inventories incorporating thousands of traits, largely overlapping but also containing specific variance, each empirical finding is strictly speaking only relevant to a specific trait. . . . This is not the way to build a unified scientific discipline" (p. 786).

Costa and McCrae's Research

The situation began to change in the early 1980s when Costa and McCrae were developing the NEO Personality Inventory (eventually published in 1985) to measure three broad personality dimensions: Neuroticism, Extraversion, and Openness to Experience. Costa and McCrae (1976) had begun their work with cluster analyses of the 16PF (Cattell, Eber, & Tatsuoka, 1970) which, as we described above, originated in Cattell's early lexical work. Their analyses again yielded the ubiquitous Extraversion and Neuroticism dimensions, but also convinced Costa and McCrae of the importance of Openness, which originated from several of Cattell's primary factors (e.g., imaginative, experimenting).

In 1983 Costa and McCrae realized that their NEO system closely resembled three of the Big Five factors, but did not encompass traits in the Agreeableness and Conscientiousness domains. They therefore extended their model with preliminary scales measuring Agreeableness and Conscientiousness. In several studies, McCrae and Costa (1985b, 1985c, 1987) demonstrated that their five questionnaire scales converged with adjective-based measures of the Big Five, although their conception of Openness seemed broader than the Intellect or Imagination factor emerging from the lexical analyses (Saucier & Goldberg, 1996a). A series of influential papers showed that these five factors could also be recovered in various other personality questionnaires, as well as in self-ratings on Block's (1961/1978) California Adult Q-set (see Costa & McCrae, 1992; McCrae & Costa, 1990).

The Revised NEO Personality Inventory

The initial NEO Personality Inventory (Costa & McCrae, 1985) included scales to measure six facets of Neuroticism, Extraversion, and Openness but did not include any facet scales for the newly added Agreeableness and Conscientiousness. In 1992, Costa and McCrae published the 240-item NEO Personality Inventory, Revised (NEO PI-R; Costa & McCrae, 1992), which permits differentiated measurement of each Big Five dimension in terms of six specific facets per factor (Costa & McCrae, 1995). Table 4.1 shows the six facets defining each of the factors, as well as a highly correlated trait adjective to illustrate the links with the lexical research. The NEO PI-R was developed in samples of middle-aged and older adults, using both factor analytic and multimethod validational procedures of test construction. The scales have shown substantial in-

TABLE 4.1. Costa and McCrae's (1992) NEO PI-R Facets

Big Five dimensions		Facet (and correlated trait adjective)[a]
E	Extraversion versus introversion	Gregariousness (sociable)
		Assertiveness (forceful)
		Activity (energetic)
		Excitement-seeking (adventurous)
		Positive emotions (enthusiastic)
		Warmth (outgoing)
A	Agreeableness versus antagonism	Trust (forgiving)
		Straightforwardness (not demanding)
		Altruism (warm)
		Compliance (not stubborn)
		Modesty (not show-off)
		Tender-mindedness (sympathetic)
C	Conscientiousness versus lack of direction	Competence (efficient)
		Order (organized)
		Dutifulness (not careless)
		Achievement striving (thorough)
		Self-discipline (not lazy)
		Deliberation (not impulsive)
N	Neuroticism versus emotional stability	Anxiety (tense)
		Angry hostility (irritable)
		Depression (not contented)
		Self-consciousness (shy)
		Impulsiveness (moody)
		Vulnerability (not self-confident)
O	Openness versus closedness to experience	Ideas (curious)
		Fantasy (imaginative)
		Aesthetics (artistic)
		Actions (wide interests)
		Feelings (excitable)
		Values (unconventional)

[a]These traits from the Adjective Check List (listed in parentheses following each facet) correlated substantially with scores on that facet in a study of self-ratings (Costa & McCrae, 1992, p. 49).

ternal consistency, temporal stability, and convergent and discriminant validity against spouse and peer ratings (Costa & McCrae, 1992; McCrae & Costa, 1990). Moreover, the factor structure of the 30-facet scales replicates very closely in a broad range of languages and cultures (McCrae & Costa, 1997).

For many research applications, the NEO PI-R is rather lengthy. To provide a shorter measure, Costa and McCrae (1992) developed the 60-item NEO-FFI, an abbreviated version based on an item factor analysis of the 1985 version of the NEO PI (Costa & McCrae, 1985). The 12-item scales of the FFI include the items that loaded highest on each of the five factors in that analysis. The item content of the scales was adjusted somewhat to ensure adequate content coverage of the facets; however, these scales do not equally represent each of the six facets defining each factor. For example, the Agreeableness scale includes five items from the Altruism facet, three from Compliance, two from Trust, one from Tender-Mindedness, one from Straightforwardness, and none from Modesty. The reliabilities reported in the manual (Costa & McCrae, 1992) are adequate, with a mean of .78 across the five scales. The NEO-FFI scales are substantially correlated with the NEO PI-R scales, suggesting that they inherit a substantial portion of the validity of the longer scales.

A PROTOTYPE APPROACH TO DEFINING THE BIG FIVE ACROSS STUDIES

So far, we have reviewed both Goldberg's (1990) lexically based research and Costa and McCrae's (1992) questionnaire-based research on the Big Five. Despite these extensive studies, the Big Five structure has not been accepted as a taxonomic superstructure by all researchers in the field (e.g., Block, 1995; Eysenck, 1992, 1997; McAdams, 1992; Pervin, 1994). One problem, it seems, is the perception that there is no *single* Big Five, which is evident in questions such as "*which* Big Five?" or "*whose* Big Five?" (John, 1989). For example, across studies the Extraversion factor has appeared as confident self-expression, surgency, assertiveness, social extraversion, and power (see John, 1990, Table 3.1). Agreeableness has been labeled social adaptability, likability, friendly compliance, agreeableness, and love. The Conscientiousness factor has appeared under the names dependability, task interest, will to achieve, impulse control, and work. Neuroticism versus Emotional Stability has also been called emotionality, ego strength (vs. anxiety), dominant–assured, satisfaction, and affect. Finally, Openness has also been labeled inquiring intellect, culture, intelligence, intellect, intellectual interests, and intellectance.

Of course, some variation from study to study is to be expected with dimensions as broad and inclusive as the Big Five. Differences in factor solutions are likely to arise when researchers differ in the variables they include, thus representing different parts of the factor's total range of meaning. Moreover, researchers differ in their preferences for factor labels even when the factor content is quite similar. The fact that the labels differ does not necessarily mean that the factors are different, too. Thus, there may be more commonality than meets the eye.

A prototype approach may help identify these commonalities across studies. Natural categories typically have fuzzy and partially overlapping definitions (Rosch, 1978), and the Big Five are no exception. Fuzzy categories may still be useful if they can be defined in terms of prototypical exemplars. Similarly, the Big Five may be defined with prototypical traits that occur consistently across studies.

How might one integrate the findings from a large and varied set of factor analytic investigations, each using somewhat different sets of variables, analytic procedures, and factor interpretations? One approach is to conceptually map the five dimensions into a common language. To abstract the common elements in these findings, John (1989, 1990) used human judges, and the 300 terms included in the Adjective Check List (ACL; Gough & Heilbrun, 1983) served as the standard language.

Conceptually Derived Prototype Descriptions of the Big Five

A set of 10 judges first formed a detailed understanding of the Big Five dimensions by reviewing the factor solutions and interpretations of all the important articles published on the Big Five by that time. The judges then independently sorted each of the 300 items in the ACL into one of the Big Five domains, or, if that was not possible, into a sixth "other" category. Interjudge agreement was substantial; coefficient alpha reliabilities ranged from .90 for Factor IV to .94 for Factor V, suggesting that the raters had formed a consensually shared understanding of the five dimensions. As shown in Table 4.2, 112 of the 300 ACL terms were assigned to one of the Big Five with almost perfect agreement (i.e., by at least 90% of the judges). These terms form a relatively narrow, or "core," definition of the five factors because they include only those traits that appeared consistently across studies.

As with any rationally constructed measure, the validity of these categorizations must be tested empirically. The results from a factor analysis of the 112 terms are also included in Table 4.2. If the initial prototypes adequately capture the composition of the Big Five, the 112 terms should clearly define five factors, and each term should load only on its respective factor. Most research on the Big Five has been based on self- and peer ratings, typically by college students. This study used judgments by psychologists based on intensive observations and interviews, thus testing the degree to which the Big Five can capture the personality judgments formulated by psychologists and addressing the criticism that the Big Five merely captures the personality conceptions of lay persons (Block, 1995).

Validation of the Prototypes in Observer Data

The ACL was initially developed at the Institute of Personality Assessment and Research (now the Institute of Personality and Social Research, or IPSR) in Berkeley, California, as a procedure to help staff members describe the personalities of individuals examined in assessment programs (Gough & Heilbrun, 1983, p. 1). John (1990) used a sample of 140 men and 140 women who had participated in groups of 10 to 15 in one of the IPSR assessment weekends. As each subject had been described on the ACL by 10 staff members, a factor analysis using these aggregated observer judgments could be performed. The varimax rotated factor loadings, shown in Table 4.2 for each adjective for its hypothesized factor, provide a compelling confirmation of the initial prototypes. With one exception, each item loaded on its hypothesized factor in the expected direction; for 98 of the 112 items the highest loading was also on that factor, and most of the loadings were substantial.

Note that the items defining each of the factors cover a broad range of content. For example, the Extraversion factor includes traits such as active, adventurous, assertive, dominant, energetic, enthusiastic, outgoing, sociable, and show-off. In light of the enormous breadth of the five factors, the heterogeneity of the previous factor labels is more easily understood. Different investigators have focused on different components, or facets, of the total range of meaning subsumed by each factor. In this study, the Extraversion factor includes at least five distinguishable components: Activity level (active, energetic), Dominance (assertive, forceful, bossy), Sociability (outgoing, sociable, talkative), Expressiveness (adventurous, outspoken, noisy, show-off), and Positive emotionality (enthusiastic, spunky). Note that these five components are similar to five of the six facets Costa and McCrae (1992) included in their definition of the Extraversion domain—Activity, Assertiveness, Gregariousness, Excitement-seeking, and Positive Emotions. Their sixth facet, Warmth, is here considered a component of Agreeableness (Factor II); all 10 judges interpreted past research to imply that Warmth is part of Factor II, and the empirical loading of .82 confirmed this interpretation. In addition to Warmth (affectionate, gentle, warm), Factor II covers themes such as Tender-Mindedness (sensitive, kind, soft-hearted, sympathetic), Altruism (generous, helping, praising), and Trust (trusting, forgiving), as contrasted with Hostility, Criticality, and Distrust; again, note the convergence with Costa and McCrae's (1992) facets. More generally, the definitions of the Big Five in Table 4.2 seem to capture the prototypical traits found in other studies.

The Prototypical Definition of Factor V: Culture, Intellect, or Openness?

The findings in Table 4.2 also address a recurrent issue in the literature, namely, how the fifth factor should be defined. Most of the deviations from the hypothesized structure (marked by asterisks in Table 4.2), involved Factor V. Many items referring to aspects of culture (i.e., civilized, polished, dignified, foresighted, logical) loaded more highly on Factor III (Conscientiousness) than on Factor V, thus further discrediting a Culture interpretation of Factor V. The items that did load substantially on the fifth factor include both the "open" characteristics (e.g., artistic, curious, original, wide interests) highlighted by McCrae and Costa (1985b, 1985c) and the "intellectual" characteristics (intelligent, insightful, sophisticated) emphasized by Digman and Inouye (1981), Peabody and Goldberg (1989), and Goldberg (1990).

How do these findings compare with other research? Goldberg's (1990, 1992) detailed lexical

TABLE 4.2. Initial and Validated Big Five Prototypes: Consensually Selected ACL Marker Items and Their Factor Loadings in Personality Descriptions Obtained from 10 Psychologists Serving as Observers

Extraversion		Agreeableness		Conscientiousness		Neuroticism		Openness/Intellect	
Low	High	Low	High	Low	High	Low	High	Low	High
–.83 Quiet	.85 Talkative	–.52 Fault-finding	.87 Sympathetic	–.58 Careless	.80 Organized	–.39 Stable*	.73 Tense	–.74 Commonplace	.76 Wide interests
–.80 Reserved	.83 Assertive	–.48 Cold	.85 Kind	–.53 Disorderly	.80 Thorough	–.35 Calm*	.72 Anxious	–.73 Narrow interests	.76 Imaginative
–.75 Shy	.82 Active	–.45 Unfriendly	.85 Appreciative	–.50 Frivolous	.78 Planful	–.21 Contented*	.72 Nervous	–.67 Simple	.72 Intelligent
–.71 Silent	.82 Energetic	–.45 Quarrelsome	.84 Affectionate	–.49 Irresponsible	.78 Efficient	.14 Unemotional*	.71 Moody	–.55 Shallow	.73 Original
–.67 Withdrawn	.82 Outgoing	–.45 Hard-hearted	.84 Soft-hearted	–.40 Slipshot	.73 Responsible		.71 Worrying	–.47 Unintelligent	.68 Insightful
–.66 Retiring	.80 Outspoken	–.38 Unkind	.82 Warm	–.39 Undependable	.72 Reliable		.68 Touchy		.64 Curious
	.79 Dominant	–.33 Cruel	.81 Generous	–.37 Forgetful	.70 Dependable		.64 Fearful		.59 Sophisticated
	.73 Forceful	–.31 Stern*	.78 Trusting		.68 Conscientious		.63 High-strung		.59 Artistic
	.73 Enthusiastic	–.28 Thankless	.77 Helpful		.66 Precise		.63 Self-pitying		.59 Clever
	.68 Show-off	–.24 Stingy*	.77 Forgiving		.66 Practical		.60 Temperamental		.58 Inventive
	.68 Sociable		.74 Pleasant		.65 Deliberate		.59 Unstable		.56 Sharp-witted
	.64 Spunky		.73 Good-natured		.46 Painstaking		.58 Self-punishing		.55 Ingenious
	.64 Adventurous		.73 Friendly		.26 Cautious*		.54 Despondent		.45 Witty*
	.62 Noisy		.72 Cooperative				.51 Emotional		.45 Resourceful*
	.58 Bossy		.67 Gentle						.37 Wise
			.66 Unselfish						.33 Logical*
			.56 Praising						.29 Civilized*
			.51 Sensitive						.22 Foresighted*
									.21 Polished*
									.20 Dignified*

Note. These 112 items were selected as initial prototypes for the Big Five because they were assigned to one factor by at least 90% of the judges. The factor loadings, shown for the hypothesized factor, were based on a sample of 140 males and 140 females, each of whom had been described by 10 psychologists serving as observers during an assessment weekend at the Institute of Personality Assessment and Research at the University of California at Berkeley (John, 1990).

*Potentially misclassified items (i.e., loading more highly on a factor different from the one hypothesized in the original prototype definition).

analyses suggest an interpretation closer to Intellectual Interests or even Openness than to the original interpretation as Culture (Norman, 1963). In Goldberg's (1990) factor analysis of Norman's 75 categories, Factor V was defined by Originality, Wisdom, Objectivity, Knowledge, Reflection, and Art, thus involving facets of Openness related to ideas, fantasy, and aesthetics (Costa & McCrae, 1992). When the 133 synonym clusters were factored, the two clusters labeled Intellectuality (intellectual, contemplative, meditative, philosophical, and introspective) and Creativity (creative, imaginative, inventive, ingenious, innovative) had the highest loadings, followed by Intelligence, Versatility, Wisdom, Perceptiveness, Art, Logic, Curiosity, and Nonconformity. The variables related to Cultural Sophistication (cultured, refined, worldly, cosmopolitan, urbane) did not load consistently on Factor V, and Dignity (mannerly, dignified, formal) loaded more highly on Conscientiousness than on Factor V. Nonconformity (nonconforming, unconventional, rebellious) loaded positively, and Conventionality (traditional, conventional, unprogressive) loaded negatively on Factor V in all four samples. These findings are inconsistent with the Culture interpretation and instead favor an Openness interpretation (McCrae, 1996). The finding that Unconventionality and Nonconformity load on Factor V is also consistent with the definition of this factor in Dutch and Italian (De Raad, Perugini, et al., 1998).

Indeed, Peabody and Goldberg (1989) concluded that the initial interpretation of Tupes and Christal's (1961) fifth factor as Culture was a historical accident. Peabody and Goldberg compared their representative variable selection with Cattell's and found that his selection underrepresented traits related to intellectual interests and overrepresented traits related to Culture. Even in Norman's (1963) studies, only one of the four variables included as a marker of Factor V was a measure of Cultural Sophistication: "polished, refined versus crude, boorish." The other three variables ("Artistically sensitive versus insensitive"; "Intellectual versus unreflective, narrow"; "Imaginative versus simple, direct") have more to do with creativity, cognitive complexity, and broad interests (i.e., Openness) than with being cultured, well-educated, and from an upper-class background. In 1963 as much as today, Factor V seems to encompass a broad range of intellectual, creative, and artistic inclinations, preferences, and skills found foremost in highly original and creative individuals (Barron, 1968; Helson, 1967; Gough, 1979; MacKinnon, 1965).

An alternative label for Factor V is Intellect. For example, Peabody and Goldberg (1989) included both *controlled* aspects of intelligence (perceptive, reflective, intelligent) and *expressive* aspects (imaginative, curious, broad-minded). The Intellect interpretation emphasizes thinking and reasoning but omits aspects of thought and experience that reflect personal orientations and attitudes, such as aesthetic and artistic interests, nonconformity, and progressive values. Indeed, the fifth factor is *not* a measure of intelligence, and it has only small positive correlations with measures of IQ and scholastic aptitude (e.g., Helson, 1985; John, Caspi, Robins, Moffitt, & Stouthamer-Loeber, 1994; McCrae & Costa, 1985c). Moving away from a narrow Intellect interpretation, Saucier (1994b) has suggested the label Imagination, which is somewhat closer to Openness and emphasizes that fantasy, ideas, and aesthetics, rather than intelligence, are most central to this factor.

In our view, Intellect is one part of a broader personality factor that McCrae and Costa (1985b, 1987) have described as Openness to Experience. Nonetheless, there is still some debate about the best interpretation of the fifth factor, and a special issue of the *European Journal of Personality* was devoted to this topic (see De Raad, 1994).

The Big Five Inventory (BFI): Measuring the Core Features of the Big Five with Short Phrases

To address the need for a short instrument measuring the prototypical components of the Big Five that are common across studies, John, Donahue, and Kentle (1991) constructed the Big Five Inventory (BFI; see also Benet-Martinez & John, 1998). The 44-item BFI was developed to represent the prototype definitions developed through expert ratings and subsequent factor analytic verification in observer personality ratings (see Table 4.2). The goal was to create a brief inventory that would allow efficient and flexible assessment of the five dimensions when there is no need for more differentiated measurement of individual facets. There is much to be said in favor of brevity; as Burisch (1984) observed, "Short scales not only save testing time, but also avoid subject boredom and fatigue . . . there are subjects . . . from whom you won't get any response if the test looks too long" (p. 219).

The BFI does not use single adjectives as items because such items are answered less consistently than when they are accompanied by definitions or elaborations (Goldberg & Kilkowski, 1985). Instead, the BFI uses short phrases based on the trait adjectives known to be prototypical markers of the Big Five (John, 1989, 1990). One or two prototypical trait adjectives served as the item core to which elaborative, clarifying, or contextual information was added. For example, the Openness adjective "original" became the BFI item "Is original, comes up with new ideas," and the Conscientiousness adjective "persevering" served as the basis for the item "Perseveres until the task is finished." Thus the BFI items (which are reprinted here in the Appendix) retain the advantages of adjectival items (brevity and simplicity) while avoiding some of their pitfalls (ambiguous or multiple meanings and salient desirability).

Although the BFI scales include only eight to ten items, they do not sacrifice either content coverage or good psychometric properties. For example, the nine-item Agreeableness scale includes items related to at least five of the six facets postulated by Costa and McCrae (1992)—namely, Trust (forgiving, trusting), Altruism (helpful and unselfish), Compliance (not quarrelsome), Modesty (not faultfinding with others), and Tender-Mindedness (considerate and kind). In U.S. and Canadian samples, the alpha reliabilities of the BFI scales typically range from .75 to .90 and average above .80; three-month test–retest reliabilities range from .80 to .90, with a mean of .85. Validity evidence includes substantial convergent and divergent relations with other Big Five instruments as well as with peer ratings.

MEASUREMENT: COMPARING THREE BIG FIVE INSTRUMENTS

So far, we have discussed Goldberg's (1992) TDA, Costa and McCrae's (1992) NEO questionnaires, and the BFI. In addition, a variety of other measures are available to assess the Big Five in English. Most of them were developed for specific research applications. Digman (e.g., 1963, 1989) constructed several different adjective sets to study teacher ratings of personality in children and adolescents. Big Five scales have also been constructed using items from existing instruments. For example, John and colleagues (1994) developed scales to measure the Big Five in adolescents using personality ratings on the California Child Q-sort obtained from their mothers. In their behavior genetic research, Loehlin, McCrae, Costa, and John (1998) used Big Five scales specifically constructed from the California Psychological Inventory (Gough, 1987) and the Adjective Check List (Gough & Heilbrun, 1983). Another broad-band personality inventory that provides scores for the Big Five is the Hogan Personality Inventory (Hogan, 1986). Extraversion is represented by the Sociability and Ambition scales, Agreeableness is represented by Likeability, Conscientiousness by Prudence (vs. impulsivity), Neuroticism by low scores on Adjustment, and Openness by Intellectance (see Table 4.5 later on in this chapter). The availability of so many different instruments to measure the Big Five makes clear that there is no single instrument that represents *the* gold standard.

Comparing the TDA, NEO-FFI, and BFI

In general, the NEO questionnaires represent the best-validated Big Five measures in the questionnaire tradition. Goldberg's (1992) 100-item TDA is the most commonly used measure consisting of single adjectives. Finally, the BFI has been used frequently in research settings in which subject time is at a premium and the short-phrase item format provides more context than Goldberg's single adjective items but less complexity than the sentence format used by the NEO questionnaires.

How well do these different Big Five measures converge? Moreover, are the five dimensions really independent? Critics have suggested that some of the Big Five dimensions are highly intercorrelated (Block, 1995; Eysenck, 1992). How high are these intercorrelations, and do they involve the same dimensions across instruments?

A number of studies have reported on the psychometric characteristics of each instrument, and a few studies have compared two instruments with each other (e.g., Benet-Martinez & John, 1998; Goldberg, 1992; McCrae & Costa, 1987). However, no published studies have compared all three. To provide such a comparison, we summarize findings from a large data set of self-reports on all three measures. The sample consisted of 462 undergraduates (61% female) at the University of California, Berkeley, who completed the TDA, the NEO-FFI, and the BFI. We analyzed the data in a multitrait–multimethod (MTMM) design in which the methods are three self-report instruments rather than different data sources (for a recent review, see John & Benet-Martinez, in press).

Although we expected the convergent validities across the three instruments to be substantial, we have already noted some subtle but important differences in the definitions of Extraversion and Openness. The NEO definition of Extraversion in terms of six facets was already in place before Costa and McCrae added domain scales for Agreeableness and Conscientiousness in 1985 and facet scales for these two factors in 1992. The Warmth facet scale, included in Extraversion (see Table 4.1), also correlates with their Agreeableness domain scale (Costa & McCrae, 1992). In contrast, Goldberg (1992) and John (1990) found that trait adjectives related to Warmth correlate more highly with Agreeableness than with Extraversion, suggesting that Warmth should be included on Agreeableness (see Table 4.2). The other potential difference involves the fifth factor. As described above, Goldberg (1992) interprets it as Intellect or Imagination (Saucier, 1992), thus emphasizing Openness to Ideas and to Fantasy over the other four facets. Similarly, the BFI Openness scale does not include items related to Costa and McCrae's (1992) Values and Actions facets. In college student samples, preliminary BFI items intended to measure liberal versus conservative values (for the Values facet), and behavioral flexibility (for the Action facet) failed to cohere with the other items on the BFI Openness scale (John et al., 1991).

Reliability of the Three Instruments

The coefficient alpha reliabilities are given in Table 4.3. Overall, the reliabilities were impressive for these relatively short scales. Not surprisingly, the longer TDA scales had the highest alphas (mean of .89), followed by the BFI (.83) and the NEO-FFI (.79). Across instruments, Extraversion, Conscientiousness, and Neuroticism were measured most reliably, whereas Agreeableness and Openness tended to be less reliable. The scale with the lowest reliability was the NEO-FFI Openness scale, replicating a finding in a different sample (Benet-Martinez & John, 1998). A number of NEO-FFI Openness items did not correlate well with the total scale in this student sample. These less reliable items included both of the items from the Action facet, as well as both of the Values items. It is possible that on liberal college campuses, items involving trying new and foreign foods (Action) and looking to religious authorities for decisions on moral issues (reverse scored on Values) do not discriminate as well as in Costa and McCrae's (1992) samples of older adults. In contrast, the three items from the Ideas facet (e.g., intellectual curiosity) and the three items from the Aesthetics facet (e.g., experiential effects of poetry or art) had the strongest item-total correlations. Finally, in contrast to the heavy representation of imagination items on the TDA, only one item related to imagination (from the Fantasy facet) was included on the NEO-FFI Openness scale.[3]

Convergent and Discriminant Validity across the Three Instruments

As a first test of cross-instrument convergence, we examined the full 15 × 15 MTMM correlation matrix formed by the five factors crossed with the three instruments.[4] In general, the cross-instrument validity correlations, computed between pairs of instruments and shown in Table 4.3, were substantial. Across all five factors, the mean of the convergent validity correlations across instruments was .75. As shown in Table 4.3, the BFI and TDA showed the strongest convergence (mean r = .81), followed by the BFI and NEO-FFI (mean r = .73), and finally the TDA and NEO-FFI (mean r = .68).[5]

To determine the extent to which the validity correlations simply reflect the imperfect reliability of the scales rather than substantive differences among the instruments, we corrected for attenuation using alpha. As shown in Table 4.3, the corrected validity correlations averaged .91. However, this excellent overall result masks some important differences. Across instruments, the first three of the Big Five (Extraversion, Agreeableness, and Conscientiousness) showed mean validities clearly exceeding .90, suggesting virtual equivalence among the instruments. Neuroticism (.88) and Openness (.83) were lower. Focusing on the pairwise comparisons between instruments, the BFI and the TDA shared virtually all of their reliable variance (corrected mean r = .95). Convergence between the BFI and the NEO-FFI was also substantial (mean = .93); however, the correlations for Extraversion and for Openness did not reach .90, suggesting that the conceptualizations of these factors are not fully equivalent across these two instruments. A similar pattern was observed for the TDA and the NEO-FFI but the convergent correlations were generally lower (mean = .83) and fell below

TABLE 4.3. Reliability and Convergent Validity Coefficients for the TDA, NEO-FFI, and BFI

	Extraversion	Agreeableness	Conscientiousness	Neuroticism	Openness	Mean
			Reliabilities			
TDA	.92	.90	.90	.85	.88	.89
BFI	.88	.79	.82	.84	.81	.83
NEO	.78	.78	.83	.85	.70	.79
Mean	.87	.83	.85	.85	.81	**.84**
			Uncorrected pairwise convergent validities			
BFI-TDA	.90	.78	.81	.76	.75	.81
BFI-NEO	.69	.76	.79	.76	.64	.73
TDA-NEO	.67	.68	.77	.70	.56	.68
Mean	.78	.74	.79	.74	.66	**.75**
			Corrected pairwise convergent validities			
BFI-TDA	.99	.93	.94	.90	.89	.95
BFI-NEO	.83	.97	.96	.90	.85	.92
TDA-NEO	.79	.81	.89	.82	.71	.81
Mean	.93	.92	.94	.88	.83	**.91**
			Standardized validity coefficients from CFA (Model 6)			
BFI	.94	.92	.92	.90	.92	.92
TDA	.95	.85	.87	.83	.79	.87
NEO	.68[a]	.83	.86	.84	.70	.79
Mean	.90	.87	.89	.86	.83	**.87**

Note. $N = 462$. BFI, Big Five Inventory; TDA, Trait Descriptive Adjectives, NEO, NEO Five Factor Inventory. Grand means are shown in **bold**. All means are based on Fisher r-to-Z transformations.

[a]The NEO Extraversion scale had a cross-loading on Agreeableness in Model 6 (see Figure 4.1).

.80 for Extraversion and Openness. In short, the NEO-FFI showed greater convergence with the BFI than with the TDA, but it defined Extraversion and Openness somewhat differently than those two instruments.

Overall, discriminant correlations were low; absolute values averaged .21 for the TDA, .17 for the NEO-FFI, and .20 for the BFI. Moreover, none of the discriminant correlations reached .40 on any of the instruments, and the largest correlations were .39 for the TDA, .38 for the NEO-FFI, and .33 for the BFI. Averaged across instruments, only four of the 10 discriminant correlations exceeded .20: the mean correlation was .28 between Agreeableness and Conscientiousness, –.28 between Agreeableness and Neuroticism, –.27 between Extraversion and Neuroticism, and .24 between Extraversion and Conscientiousness. Thus, there was little support for Eysenck's (1992) contention that Agreeableness and Conscientiousness are highly correlated "primary" traits that combine into a broader dimension contrasting Eysenck's Psychoticism with what might be called "good character." Together the findings show that the Big Five are fairly independent dimensions that can be measured with convergent and discriminant validity.

Confirmatory Factor Analysis (CFA) of the Multitrait–Multimethod Matrix

As a more formal test of convergent and discriminant validity, we used a series of nested CFA models to estimate latent factors representing the Big Five, their intercorrelations, and method factors representing the unique characteristics of each instrument. The most basic model (see Model 1 in Table 4.4) specified five uncorrelated latent trait factors and no method factors. This model showed marginal fit. Allowing intercorrelations among the Big Five factors significantly improved model fit (Model 2) suggesting that some of the Big Five intercorrelations were consistent across all three instruments.

TABLE 4.4. Nested Confirmatory Factor Analyses of the Multitrait–Multimethod Matrix Formed by the Three Big Five Instruments

Model	χ^2	*df*	CFI	$\Delta\chi^2$
1. Uncorrelated Big Five, no method factors	783	90	.863	—
2. Correlated Big Five, no method factors	583	80	.900	200*
3. Correlated Big Five, no method factors, cross-loading of NEO-Extraversion on Agreeableness	496	79	.917	87*
4. Model 3 plus NEO method factor	484	74	.919	12*
5. Model 4 plus TDA method factor	323	69	.950	160*
6. Model 5 plus BFI method factor	296	64	.954	28*
6a. Model 6 plus cross-loading of TDA—Intellect on Conscientiousness	274	63	.958	22*

Note. $N = 462$. CFI, comparative fit index (Bentler, 1990); $\Delta\chi^2$, increase in overall fit; BFI, Big Five Inventory; NEO, NEO Five Factor Inventory; TDA, trait descriptive adjectives.

* $p < .05$.

As we noted earlier, the NEO-FFI includes items related to warmth in Extraversion, whereas the BFI and TDA include them in Agreeableness. We examined this hypothesis directly by modifying our model and testing the improvement in model fit. By adding a cross-loading of the NEO Extraversion scale on the latent Agreeableness factor, we achieved a significant improvement in fit (see Model 3). As shown in Figure 4.1, the NEO-FFI Extraversion scale still loaded substantially on the Extraversion factor but also had a secondary loading on Agreeableness.[6]

The next three models were increasingly complex, adding method factors specific to each instrument. In Model 4 we added a method factor for the NEO-FFI, producing a small improvement in fit; as shown in Figure 4.1, this method factor primarily represented instrument-specific variance related to Openness. Model 5 added a TDA method factor, yielding a sizeable improvement; this method factor represented a positive correlation between Agreeableness and Intellect observed on the TDA but not on the BFI and the NEO-FFI. Model 6 added a BFI method factor, modeling a moderate negative correlation between Neuroticism and Openness on the BFI that was not observed on the TDA and the NEO. In short, these method factors capture specific differences in the ways the Big Five dimensions are conceptualized on each of the instruments. Figure 4.1 shows the parameter estimates for Model 6, which accounts for trait variance, method variance, and the expected cross-loading of NEO Extraversion on the Agreeableness factor.

We also explored how we could improve fit further. When we examined the residual matrix to see what relationships were still unexplained by our model, we found that the largest unexplained covariances were between the TDA fifth factor scale (Intellect) and the three Conscientiousness scales. McCrae and Costa (1985c, 1987) had previously noted that Goldberg's conceptualization of Factor V as Intellect is related to Conscientiousness, whereas the Openness conceptualization on the NEO-FFI and BFI is not. When we respecified our model with a cross-loading of the TDA Intellect scale on the Conscientiousness factor (Model 6a), we did observe an improvement in fit, but it was very small and the estimated cross-loading was only .15. In our view, such small gains in fit do not justify the added complexity required by the more detailed model, leading us to prefer the more parsimonious model represented in Figure 4.1.

Table 4.3 summarizes the standardized validity coefficients from the CFA. They average .92 for the BFI, .87 for the TDA, and .79 for the NEO-FFI, suggesting that the canonical representation achieved by the CFA is captured most closely by the BFI, which was developed to capture the core characteristics of the Big Five. The parameter estimates for Model 6 (see Figure 4.1) suggest three major conclusions that are consistent with the preceding analyses. First, all fifteen scales had substantial loadings on the five latent factors, with an average loading of .87, suggesting that all three measures generally tap the same five dimensions. Second, the substantial size of these loadings did not leave

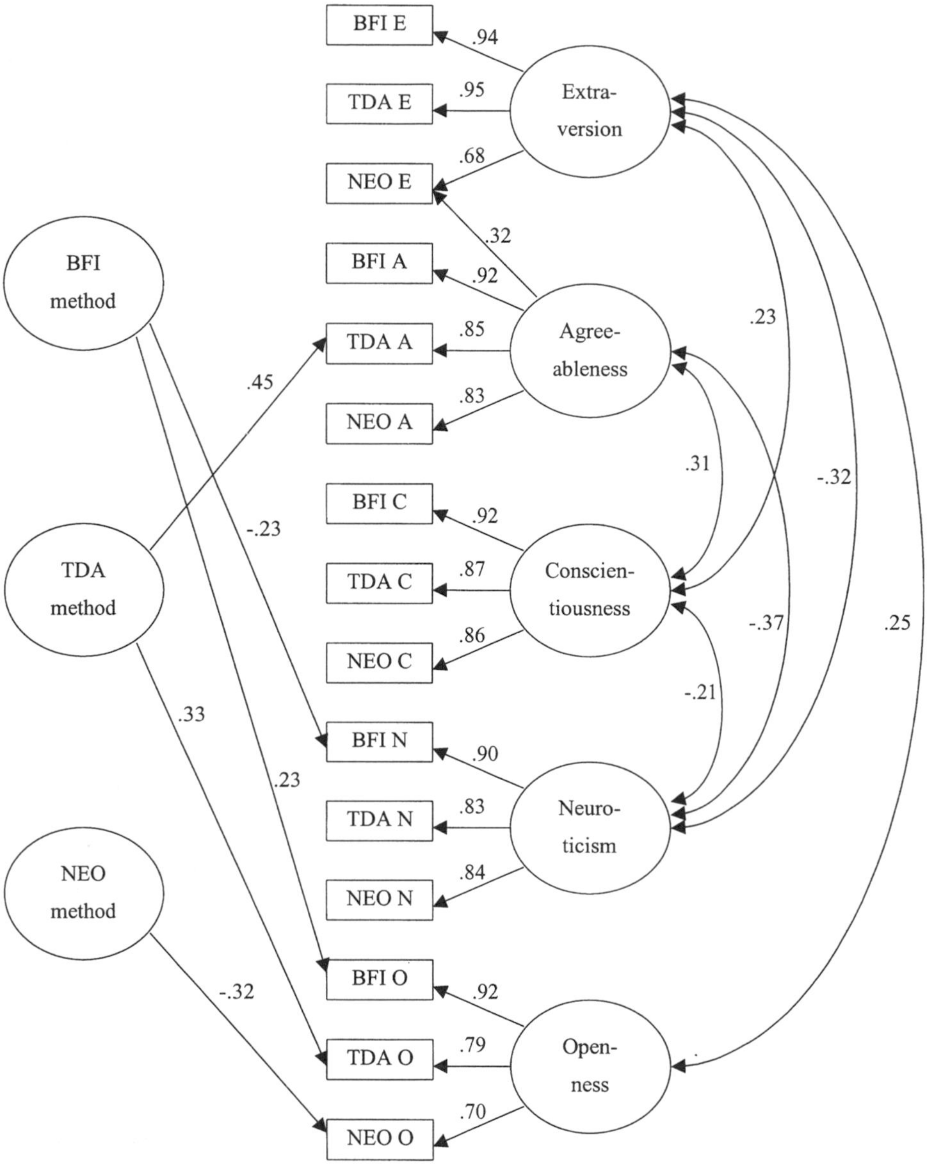

FIGURE 4.1. Standardized parameter estimates for the final multitrait–multimethod model (Model 6 in Table 4.3). Method effects and trait intercorrelations less than .20 and error terms are not shown.

much systematic variance for general instrument factors; instead, the three latent method factors we did uncover related to specific scale intercorrelations that were unique to each instrument. Nonetheless, in all cases the loadings on these method factors were considerably smaller than the substantive trait loadings, suggesting that the measures are more similar than different. The third conclusion involves the size of the intercorrelations among the latent Big Five dimensions, which remained low even when disattenuated for unreliability by CFA; none of them reached .40. Overall, then, the CFA results show that five latent, modestly correlated personality factors capture the major sources of variance in our MTMM design, and three smaller method factors represent trait-specific variance for each instrument.

A Joint Item Factor Analysis of the Three Instruments

To elaborate the shared meanings of the five factors across measures, we examined the highest-loading items for each factor in a joint item-level factor analysis, which included all 44 BFI items, 60 NEO-FFI items, and 100 TDA items. For Extraversion, the top-loading items were "Is outgoing, sociable" from the BFI, "Quiet" (reverse-scored) from the TDA, and "I really enjoy talking to people" from the NEO. Items referring to assertiveness, activity level, and positive emotions also had substantial loadings. For Agreeableness, item examples included "Is considerate and kind to almost everyone" from the BFI, "Unkind" (reversed) from the TDA, and "Some people think of me as cold and calculating" (reversed) from the NEO. For Conscientiousness, key items were "Does a thorough job" from the BFI, "Disorganized" (reversed) from the TDA, and the NEO item "I am a productive person who always gets the job done." Exemplars of the Neuroticism factor include "Worries a lot" from the BFI, "Nervous" from the TDA, and "I often feel tense and jittery" from the NEO. The top loadings on the joint Openness factor were particularly instructive: although Goldberg labeled his scale Intellect (or Imagination), the TDA item "Creative" had the strongest loading on the joint factor. The highest-loading BFI item was "Values artistic, aesthetic experiences," and the best NEO items were "I often enjoy playing with theories or abstract ideas" and "I have a lot of intellectual curiosity." These item examples for Openness make two points. First, the factor clearly involves Openness rather than intellectual ability or skill. Second, the aspects of the Openness factor shared across the three instruments involve openness to ideas, fantasy, and aesthetics.

Big Five Measurement: Conclusions and Limitations

One of the limitations of the findings presented here is that we did not examine external (or predictive) validity. Both the NEO questionnaires and the BFI have been shown to predict peer ratings; such evidence still needs to be obtained for the TDA scales. Future research needs to compare the validity of all three instruments using peer ratings and other external criteria. One of the advantages of the BFI is its efficiency, taking only about 5 minutes of administration time, compared with about 15 minutes for the NEO-FFI and the TDA. Moreover, the BFI items are shorter and easier to understand than the NEO-FFI items (Benet-Martinez & John, 1998). The 100 adjectives on the TDA are even shorter; however, single-trait adjectives can be ambiguous in their meanings (see note 3).

When should researchers use each of these instruments? When participant time is not at a premium, participants are well educated and test savvy, and the research question calls for the assessment of multiple facets for each of the Big Five, then the full 240-item NEO PI-R would be most useful. Otherwise, the 44-item BFI would seem to offer a measure of the core attributes of the Big Five that is at least as efficient and easily understood as the 60-item NEO-FFI and the 100-item TDA.

FACTOR NAMES, NUMBERS, OR INITIALS: WHICH SHALL WE USE?

Problems with the English Factor Labels

Now that we have considered both the history of the Big Five and their measurement, it is time to revisit the names or labels assigned to the factors. Although the constructs that will eventually replace the current Big Five may be different from what we know now, labels are important because they imply particular interpretations and thus influence the directions that theorizing might take. Norman's (1963) factor labels have been used frequently in later research, but Norman offered little in the way of a theoretical rationale for the selection of these particular labels. Norman's labels differ vastly in their breadth or inclusiveness (Hampson, Goldberg & John, 1987); in particular, Conscientiousness and Culture are much too narrow to capture the enormous breadth of these two dimensions. Moreover, as noted above, researchers quickly abandoned Culture as a label for Factor V, in favor of Intellect or Imagination (Saucier & Goldberg, 1996a) or Openness to Experience (McCrae & Costa, 1985b). Neither label is truly satisfactory, however, because Intellect is too narrow and Openness, while broad enough, is somewhat vague.

Agreeableness is another problematic label. For one, it refers to the behavioral tendency to *agree* with others, thus incorrectly implying submissiveness, which is more closely related to the introverted pole of Factor I. Agreeableness is also too detached, too neutral a label for a factor supposed to capture intensely affective characteristics, such as love, compassion, and sympathy. Freud viewed love and work as central; following this lead, we could call Factor II simply Love (Peabody & Goldberg, 1989).

However, Work is too narrow a label for Factor III. Even Conscientiousness is too narrow because it omits a central component that Peabody and Goldberg (1989) called "favorable impulse control." Thus, Responsibility or even Degree of Socialization (see Gough, 1987) might be labels more appropriate for Factor III than is Conscientiousness.

More could be said about the many shortcomings of the traditional labels (see also Block, 1995), but better labels are hard to come by. The unsurpassed advantage of the traditional labels is that they are commonly known and used, thus preventing Babel from taking over the literature on the Big Five. Moreover, before any new names are devised, the definition of the factors in terms of facets or components must be elaborated and sharpened. At this point, it seems premature to settle the scope and theoretical interpretation of the factors by devising new names.

Preliminary Definitions

Because the traditional labels are so easily misunderstood, short definitions of the five dimensions may be useful here (cf., Costa & McCrae, 1992; John, 1990; Tellegen, 1985). Briefly, Extraversion implies an *energetic approach* to the social and material world and includes traits such as sociability, activity, assertiveness, and positive emotionality. Agreeableness contrasts a *prosocial and communal orientation* toward others with antagonism and includes traits such as altruism, tender-mindedness, trust, and modesty. Conscientiousness describes *socially prescribed impulse control* that facilitates task- and goal-directed behavior, such as thinking before acting, delaying gratification, following norms and rules, and planning, organizing, and prioritizing tasks. Neuroticism contrasts emotional stability and even-temperedness with *negative emotionality*, such as feeling anxious, nervous, sad, and tense. Finally, Openness to Experience (versus closed-mindedness) describes the breadth, depth, originality, and complexity of an individual's *mental and experiential life*.

The numbering convention from I to V, favored by Saucier and Goldberg (1996b) and Hofstee and colleagues (1997), is useful because it reflects the relative size of the factors in lexical studies. Factor I and II, which primarily summarize traits of interpersonal nature, tend to account for the largest percentage of variance in personality ratings, followed by Factor III, whereas the last two factors are by far the smallest in lexical studies (De Raad, Perugini, Hrebickova, & Szarota, 1998). However, the Roman numerals are hard to remember, and the order of the factors is not invariant across studies. Thus, we favor the mnemonic convention suggested by the initials given below. They evoke multiple associations that represent more fully than a single word the broad range of meaning captured by each of the factors:

- E Extraversion, Energy, Enthusiasm (I)
- A Agreeableness, Altruism, Affection (II)
- C Conscientiousness, Control, Constraint (III)
- N Neuroticism, Negative Affectivity, Nervousness (IV)
- O Openness, Originality, Open-Mindedness (V)

The reader intrigued by anagrams may have noticed that these letters form the OCEAN of personality dimensions.

CONVERGENCE BETWEEN THE BIG FIVE AND OTHER STRUCTURAL MODELS

McCrae and Costa's (1985a, 1985b, 1985c; 1987) findings, like evidence for cross-instrument convergence presented above, show that the factor-analytic results from the lexical tradition converge surprisingly well with those from the questionnaire tradition. This convergence has led to a dramatic change in the acceptance of the five factors in the field. With regard to their empirical status, the findings accumulated since the mid-1980s show that the five factors replicate across different types of subjects, raters, and data sources, in both dictionary-based and questionnaire-based studies. Indeed, even skeptical reviewers were led to conclude that "agreement among these descriptive studies with respect to *what* are the appropriate dimensions is impressive" (Revelle, 1987, p. 437; see also Briggs, 1989; McAdams, 1992; Pervin, 1994). The finding that it doesn't matter whether Conscientiousness is measured with trait adjectives, short phrases, or questionnaire items suggests that the Big Five dimensions have the same conceptual status as other personality constructs. For example, Loehlin and colleagues (1998) found that all five factors show substantial and about equal heritabilities, regardless of whether they are measured with questionnaires or with adjective scales derived from the lexical approach.

One of the apparent strengths of the Big Five taxonomy is that it can capture, at a broad level of abstraction, the commonalities among most of the existing systems of personality traits, thus providing an integrative descriptive model for research. Table 4.5 summarizes the personality dimensions proposed by a broad range of personality theorists and researchers. These dimensions, although by no means a complete tabulation, emphasize the diversity of current conceptions of personality. However, they also point to some important convergences. First, almost every one of the theorists includes a dimension akin to Extraversion. Although the labels and exact definitions vary, nobody seems to doubt the fundamental importance of this dimension (Guilford, 1974, 1975). The second almost universally accepted personality dimension is Emotional Stability, as contrasted with Neuroticism, Negative Emotionality, and Proneness to Anxiety (Tellegen, 1982, 1985). Interestingly, however, not all the researchers listed in Table 4.5 include a separate measure for this dimension. This is particularly true of the interpersonal researchers, such as Wiggins (1979) and Bales (1970), as well as the questionnaires aimed primarily at the assessment of basically healthy, well-functioning adults, such as Gough's (1987) CPI, the Myers–Briggs Type Indicator (Myers & McCaulley, 1985), and even Jackson's (1984) PRF. In contrast, all of the temperament-based models include Neuroticism. There is somewhat less agreement on the third dimension, which appears in various guises, such as Control, Constraint, Super-Ego Strength, and Work Orientation as contrasted with Impulsivity, Psychoticism, and Play Orientation. The theme underlying most of these concepts involves the control, or moderation, of impulses in a normatively and socially appropriate way (cf. Block & Block, 1980). However, Table 4.5 also points to the importance of Agreeableness and Openness, which are neglected by temperament-oriented theorists such as Buss and Plomin (1975) and Eysenck (1985). In a comprehensive taxonomy, even at the broadest level, we need a "place" for an interpersonal dimension related to Communion, Feeling Orientation, Altruism, Nurturance, Love Styles, and Social Closeness, as contrasted with Hostility, Anger Proneness, and Narcissism. The existence of these questionnaire scales, and the cross-cultural work on the interpersonal origin and consequences of personality, stress the need for a broad domain akin to Agreeableness, Warmth, or Love.

Similar arguments apply to the fifth and last factor included in the Big Five. For one, there are the concepts of Creativity, Originality, and Cognitive Complexity, which are measured by numerous questionnaire scales (Barron, 1968; Helson, 1967, 1985; Gough, 1979). Although these concepts are cognitive, or, more appropriately, *mental* in nature, they are clearly different from IQ. Second, limited-domain scales measuring concepts such as Absorption, Fantasy Proneness, Need for Cognition, Private Self-Consciousness, Independence, and Autonomy would be difficult to subsume under Extraversion, Neuroticism, or Conscientiousness. Indeed, the fifth factor is necessary because individual differences in intellectual and creative functioning underlie artistic interests and performances, inventions and innovation, and even humor. Individual differences in these domains of human behavior and experience cannot be, and fortunately have not been, neglected by personality psychologists.

Finally, the matches between the Big Five and other constructs sketched out in Table 4.5 should be considered with a healthy dose of skepticism. Some of these correspondences are indeed based on solid research findings. Others, however, are conceptually derived and seem plausible, but await empirical confirmation. All of these matches reflect broad similarities, ignoring some important, implicative, and useful differences among the concepts proposed by different investigators. Nonetheless, at this stage in the field, we are more impressed by the newly apparent similarities than by the continuing differences among the various models. Indeed, the Big Five are useful primarily because of their integrative and heuristic value, a value that becomes apparent in Table 4.5. The availability of a taxonomy, even one that is as broad and incomplete as the Big Five, permits the comparison and potential integration of dimensions that, by their names alone, would seem entirely disparate.

TABLE 4.5. The Big Five and Dimensions of Similar Breadth in Questionnaires and in Models of Personality and Interpersonal Behavior

Theorist	Extraversion I	Agreeableness II	Conscientiousness III	Neuroticism IV	Openness/Intellect V
Bales	Dominant-Initiative	Social-Emotional Orientation	Task Orientation$_R$ [a]		—
Block	Undercontrol	Overcontrol		Resiliency$_R$ [b]	
Buss & Plomin	Activity	—	Impulsivity$_R$	Emotionality	—
Cattell	Exvia (vs. Invia)	Pathemia (vs. Cortertia)	Superego Strength	Adjustment$_R$ (vs. Anxiety)	Independence
Comrey Scales (Noller et al.)	Extraversion and Activity	Femininity (vs. Masculinity)	Orderliness and Social Conformity	Emotional Stability$_R$	Rebelliousness
Eysenck	Extraversion	Psychoticism$_R$ [c]		Neuroticism	—
Gough					
CPI Vectors	Externality	—	Norm-Favoring	Self-Realization$_R$ [d]	
CPI Scales	Sociability	Femininity	Norm-Favoring	Well-being	Achievement via Independence
Guilford	Social Activity	Paranoid-Disposition$_R$	Thinking Introversion	Emotional Stability$_R$	—
Hogan	Sociability	Likeability	Prudence (vs. Impulsivity)	Adjustment$_R$	Intellectance
Jackson	Outgoing, Social Leadership	Self-Protective Orientation$_R$	Work Orientation	Dependence	Aesthetic-Intellectual
MMPI Personality Disorder Scales	Histrionic	Paranoid$_R$	Compulsive	Borderline	Schizotypal
Myers–Briggs	Extraversion (vs. Introversion)	Feeling (vs. Thinking)	Judging (vs. Perception)	—	Intuition (vs. Sensing)
Tellegen	Positive Emotionality		Constraint	Negative Emotionality	Absorption
	Agentive	Communal			
Wiggins [e]	Dominance	Nurturance	(Conscientiousness)	(Neuroticism)	(Openness)

Note. Based on John (1990) and McCrae and John (1992). Subscript "R" indicates that the dimension was reverse-scored in the direction *opposite* to that of the Big Five label listed above.

[a]This dimension contrasts a work-directed, emotionally neutral orientation with an erratic, emotionally expressive orientation (Bales & Cohen, 1979), and thus seems to combine elements of both Conscientiousness and Neuroticism.

[b]Resiliency seems to subsume aspects of both Openness and low Neuroticism, because an ego-resilient individual is considered both intellectually resourceful and effective in controlling anxiety (Block & Block, 1980). However, Robins, John, and Caspi (1994) found that in adolescents, ego-resiliency is related to all of the Big Five dimensions in the well-adjusted direction. Ego control was related to Extraversion, Conscientiousness, and Agreeableness, with undercontrol similar to Extraversion and overcontrol similar to Conscientiousness and Agreeableness.

[c]High scores on the EPQ Psychoticism scale are associated with low scores on both Agreeableness and Conscientiousness (Goldberg & Rosolack, 1994; McCrae & Costa, 1985a).

[d]The third vector scale on the CPI (Gough, 1987) measures levels of psychological integration and realization, and should reflect aspects of both low Neuroticism (e.g., Well-being) and high Openness (e.g., Achievement via Independence).

[e]Wiggins (1979) originally focused on Dominance and Nurturance, which define the interpersonal circumplex. Trapnell and Wiggins (1990) added adjective scales for Conscientiousness, Neuroticism, and Openness (see also Wiggins, 1995).

CRITICAL ISSUES AND THEORETICAL PERSPECTIVES

The Big Five provides a descriptive taxonomy that organizes the myriad natural-language and scientific trait concepts into a single classificatory framework. However, like any scientific model, it has limitations. Several critics have argued that the Big Five does not provide a complete *theory* of personality (e.g., Block, 1995; Eysenck, 1997; McAdams, 1992; Pervin, 1994). We agree. The Big Five taxonomy was never intended as a comprehensive personality theory; it was developed to account for the structural relations among personality traits (Goldberg, 1993). Thus, like most structural models it provides an account of personality that is primarily descriptive rather than explanatory, emphasizes regularities in behavior rather than inferred dynamic and developmental processes, and focuses on variables rather than on individuals or types of individuals (cf. John & Robins, 1993, 1998). Nonetheless, the Big Five trait taxonomy provides a conceptual foundation that helps examine these theoretical issues. In this section, we begin with the hierarchical structure defined by the Big Five, and then review whether the Big Five dimensions predict important life outcomes, how they develop, how they combine into personality types, and how different researchers view their conceptual status.

Hierarchy, Levels of Abstraction, and the Big Five

A frequent objection to the Big Five is that five dimensions cannot possibly capture all of the variation in human personality (Block, 1995; Briggs, 1989; McAdams, 1992; Mershon & Gorsuch, 1988), and that they are much too broad. However, the objection that five dimensions are too few overlooks the fact that personality can be conceptualized at different levels of abstraction or breadth. Indeed, many trait domains are hierarchically structured (Hampson, John, & Goldberg, 1986).

The advantage of categories as broad as the Big Five is their enormous bandwidth. Their disadvantage, of course, is their low fidelity. In any hierarchical representation, one always loses information as one moves up the hierarchical levels. For example, categorizing something as a "guppy" is more informative than categorizing it as a "fish," which in turn is more informative than categorizing it as an "animal." Or, in psychometric terms, one necessarily loses item information as one aggregates items into scales, and one loses scale information as one aggregates scales into factors (John, Hampson, & Goldberg, 1991).

The Big Five dimensions represent a rather broad level in the hierarchy of personality descriptors. In that sense, they are to personality what the categories "plant" and "animal" are to the world of biological objects—extremely useful for some initial rough distinctions but of less value for predicting specific behaviors of a particular object. The hierarchical level a researcher selects depends on the descriptive and predictive tasks to be addressed (Hampson et al., 1986). In principle, the number of specific distinctions one can make in the description of an individual is infinite, limited only by one's objectives.

Norman, Goldberg, McCrae and Costa, and Hogan all recognized that there was a need in personality, just as in biology, "to have a system in which different levels of generality or inclusion are recognized" (Simpson, 1961, p. 12). A complete trait taxonomy must include middle-level categories, such as Assertiveness, Orderliness, and Creativity, and even narrower descriptors, such as talkative, punctual, and musical (John et al., 1991). Therefore Norman and, more extensively, Goldberg (1982, 1990) have developed between 40 and 75 middle-level categories subordinate to the Big Five dimensions (for a review, see John et al., 1988). However, as Briggs (1989) noted, Norman's and Goldberg's middle-level categories have not been investigated systematically nor have they been included in an assessment instrument. At this point, Costa and McCrae's (1992) 30 facets represent the most elaborated and empirically validated model. Hofstee and colleagues' (1992) circumplex-based approach, which defines facets as pairwise combinations of two factors, is another promising direction to pursue. However, the two approaches differ notably in the facets they propose, indicating the need for further conceptual and empirical work to achieve a consensual specification of the Big Five factors at this lower level of abstraction.

Predicting Important Life Outcomes

External validity and predictive utility are topics that in the past have received conspicuously little attention from researchers working in the Big Five tradition. However, one of the criteria for the usefulness of a structural model is its success in predicting important outcomes in people's lives. Eysenck (1991) argued that "little is known about the social relevance and importance of Openness, Agreeableness, and Conscientiousness. . . . What is lacking is a series of large-scale studies which would flesh out such possibilities" (p. 785). According to Eysenck (1991), the validity of the Big Five should be examined against socially relevant criteria such as criminality, mental illness, academic aptitude and achievement, and work performance.

A large study of adolescents has addressed this challenge, examining three of Eysenck's criteria: juvenile delinquency, childhood psychopathology, and academic performance (see John et al., 1994; Robins et al., 1994). The findings suggest that the Big Five can help us understand theoretically, socially, and developmentally significant life outcomes. For example, low Agreeableness and low Conscientiousness predict juvenile delinquency. In terms of psychopathology, Neuroticism and low Conscientiousness predict internalizing disorders. Conscientiousness and Openness predict school performance. These findings suggest that the Big Five dimensions can be used as indicators of risk for subsequent maladjustment. Huey and Weisz's (1997) findings suggest that these links between personality and life outcomes hold up in a clinical sample as well. Researchers may eventually use Big Five profiles to identify children at risk and ultimately design appropriate interventions, such as teaching children low in Conscientiousness relevant behaviors and skills (e.g., strategies for delaying gratification).

The literature on adults also provides evidence for the external validity of the Big Five. For example, in studies of job performance (for reviews see Barrick & Mount, 1991; Mount, Barrick, & Stewart, 1998), the Big Five have been found to relate to important outcomes in the workplace. Conscientiousness has emerged as the only general predictor of job performance, although other dimensions relate to more specific aspects of job performance. For example, Agreeableness and Neuroticism predict performance in jobs in which employees work in groups, whereas Extraversion predicts success in sales and management positions. These trait-by-job interactions help researchers develop a more fine-grained understanding of how different traits are instrumental to performance in various job environments.

The availability of the Big Five taxonomy has also renewed interest in the links between personality and adult psychopathology (e.g., Wiggins & Pincus, 1989); findings from this burgeoning literature have been reviewed in Costa and Widiger (1994). The Big Five has also helped bring order to the many, often confusing, findings linking personality traits to physical health (see Adams, Cartwright, Ostrove, & Stewart, 1998; Friedman, Hawley, & Tucker, 1994; Friedman, Tucker, Schwartz, & Tomlinson-Keasey, 1995); the accumulated evidence now suggests that the regular and well-structured lives led by individuals high in Conscientiousness are conducive to better health outcomes and longevity, whereas antagonistic hostility (i.e., low Agreeableness) and negative affect (i.e., high Neuroticism) appear to be risk factors.

The emerging nomological network for each of the Big Five now includes an ever-broadening range of life outcome variables, such as leadership (Extraversion), helping others and donating to charity (Agreeableness), school and college grades (Conscientiousness), vulnerability to depression (Neuroticism), creative performance (Openness), and so on. These findings have been summarized in several recent reviews (Graziano & Eisenberg, 1997; Hogan & Ones, 1997; McCrae, 1996; Watson & Clark, 1997).

In interpreting these findings, it is important to realize that although personality traits are stable, people can change their patterns of behavior, thought, and feeling as a result of therapy and intervention programs (Heatherton & Weinberger, 1994). Thus, the links between the Big Five and important life outcomes point to behavioral domains that people can target for personal development and change; for example, people can improve how conscientiously they adhere to a diet, exercise regimen, or medical treatment plan (Friedman et al., 1994).

The Big Five and Personality Development

Historically, personality psychology has concerned itself with a range of developmental issues that are relevant to the Big Five—the antecedents of adult personality traits, how traits develop, the timelines for the emergence and peak expression of traits, their stability or change throughout the life span, and the effects of traits on other aspects of personal development. Some critics have suggested that Big Five researchers have not paid enough attention to issues of personality development in childhood and adolescence (Pervin, 1994). This criticism has some merit: Although the Big Five taxonomy has influenced research on adult development and aging (Field & Millsap, 1991; Helson & Stewart, 1994; McCrae & Costa, 1990), there has been little research on personality structure in childhood. Developmental and temperament psychologists have studied a number of important traits (e.g., sociability, fearful distress, shyness, impulsivity) but they tend to study one trait at a time, in isolation from the others, and the available research has not been integrated in a coherent taxonomic framework. Until this work is done, however, research on personality development across the life span is likely to remain fragmented (Halverson, Kohnstamm, & Martin, 1994).

The adult personality taxonomy defined by the Big Five can offer some promising leads. In our view, the Big Five should be examined in developmental research for two reasons (John et al., 1994). Theoretically, it may be necessary to examine the developmental origins of the Big Five: Given that the Big Five emerge as basic dimensions of personality in adulthood, researchers need to explain how they develop. Practically, the Big Five taxonomy has proven useful as a framework for organizing findings on adult personality in areas as diverse as behavioral genetics and industrial psychology. Thus, extension of the Big Five into childhood and adolescence would facilitate comparisons across developmental periods.

Work on these issues has now begun, and researchers are drawing on existing models of infant and child temperament (see Clark & Watson, Chapter 16, this volume) to make connections to the Big Five dimensions in adulthood. A book edited by Halverson and colleagues (1994) summarizes these recent efforts. Some research suggests that the Big Five may provide a good approximation of personality structure in childhood and adolescence (Digman, 1989; Graziano & Ward, 1992). Extending Digman's (1989) earlier work on Hawaiian children, Digman and Shmelyov (1996) examined both temperament dimensions and personality dimensions in a sample of Russian children. Based on analyses of teachers' ratings, they concluded that the Big Five taxonomy offers a useful model for describing the structure of temperament. Studies using free-response techniques found that the Big Five can account for a substantial portion of children's descriptions of their own and others' personalities (Donahue, 1994), as well as teachers' and parents' descriptions of children's personality (Kohnstamm, Halverson, Mervielde, & Havill, 1998).

Two large-scale studies suggest that the picture may be more complicated. John et al. (1994) tested whether the adult Big Five structure would replicate in a large and ethnically diverse sample of adolescent boys. This research used the California Child Q-set (CCQ; Block & Block, 1969), a comprehensive item pool for the description of children and adolescents that was not derived from the adult Big Five and does not represent any particular theoretical orientation. Factor analyses identified five dimensions that corresponded closely with a priori scales representing the adult Big Five. However, two additional dimensions emerged in this study: "Irritability" was defined by items that involve negative affect expressed in age-inappropriate behaviors, such as whining, crying, tantrums, and being overly sensitive to teasing. "Activity" was defined by items involving physical activity, energy, and high tempo, such as running, playing, and moving and reacting quickly. In several Dutch samples of boys and girls aged 3 to 16 years, van Lieshout and Haselager (1994) also found the Big Five plus two factors similar to Irritability and Activity, thus supporting the generalizability of these dimensions across cultures and the two sexes. These replicated findings suggest that the structure of personality traits may be more differentiated in childhood than in adulthood. Specifically, the two additional dimensions may originate in temperamental features of childhood personality (i.e., irritable distress and activity level) that become integrated into adult personality structure over the course of adolescence (John et al., 1994).

These studies illustrate how the Big Five can help stimulate research that connects and integrates findings across long-separate research traditions. These studies also provide some initial insights about the way personality structure may develop toward its adult form. Yet, a great deal of work still lies ahead. Change in personality structure should be studied with reference to maturational changes, social-contextual transitions, and age-specific life tasks. Longitudinal research can help map changes in the dimensional structure of personality and discover how temperamental characteristics observed in infancy and early childhood manifest themselves during adolescence and adulthood. Finally, studies need to examine the antecedents of the Big Five and their relations to other aspects of personality functioning in childhood and adolescence. In this way, the Big Five can help connect research on adult personality with the vast field of social development (Caspi, 1997).

Personality Types and Dynamics

The emergence of the Big Five has also rekindled interest in personality types. Note that the Big Five dimensions provide a model of personality structure that represents the covariation among personality traits *across* individuals. However, "personality structure" can also refer to the organization of traits *within* the individual (Allport, 1958). Person-centered research focuses on the particular configuration, patterning, and dynamic organization of the individual's total set of characteristics (cf. York & John, 1992; see also Magnusson, Chapter 8, this volume), and asks how multiple variables are organized within the individual and how this organization defines particular types, or categories, of people.

Calls for person-centered research have been made repeatedly for the past 50 years (e.g., Carlson, 1971). More recently, Pervin (1994) noted that trait researchers focus on individual differences rather than on the individuals themselves, and that "little attention is given to the question of pattern and organization," a "neglected area" of research (pp. 36–37). Until recently, the study of personality types has been held back by the lack of generally accepted procedures for deriving personality types empirically (see Robins, John, and Caspi, 1998, for a review). Thus, with the exception of Block's (1971) pioneering study, *Lives Through Time,* little systematic research was done on personality typology.

With the advent of the Big Five, however, researchers again became interested in studying the ways in which personality traits combine into coherent patterns within individuals and in identifying types of individuals that share the same basic personality profile. A series of recent studies has renewed the search for replicable personality types.

As shown in Table 4.6 (see next page), these studies varied greatly in the sex and age of the participants, their birth cohort and country of origin, as well as the type of data, instrument, and procedures used to derive the types. Nonetheless, three types recurred across all eight studies. In terms of their Big Five profiles, the type labeled Resilients showed a high level of adjustment and effective functioning on all five factors. In contrast, the types interpreted as Overcontrollers and Undercontrollers represent two different ways in which poor psychological adjustment can be manifested. The Overcontrollers had elevated scores on Agreeableness and Conscientiousness but scored low on Extraversion, whereas the Undercontrollers scored particularly low on Agreeableness and Conscientiousness and had elevated scores on Neuroticism.

Together, these studies demonstrate that replicable and generalizable personality types can be identified empirically. Validational studies further indicated that the unique constellation of traits associated with each type has important consequences for a wide range of life outcomes (Robins et al., 1998). These findings also suggest an integration of the Big Five dimensions with Block's (1971; Block & Block, 1980) dynamic conceptualization of personality functioning in terms of ego resilience and ego control. Block's dynamic constructs can be used to define the three replicable types, each of which captures a unique Big Five profile. More generally, the studies summarized in Table 4.6 show that the Big Five taxonomy is not only compatible with person-centered research but can help interpret personality types identified with different methods and in different cultures. Moreover, the Big Five need typological and dynamic elaboration if they are to fully account for personality structure. Conversely, person-centered typological research can make use of, and be informed by, the nomothetic Big Five dimensions, thus helping researchers develop dynamic accounts of personality functioning.

Theoretical Perspectives on the Big Five: Description and Explanation

Over the years, researchers have articulated a number of different perspectives on the conceptual status of the Big Five dimensions. Because the Big Five were first discovered in lexical research intended to provide a taxonomy of trait terms in the natural language, the factors were initially interpreted as dimensions of trait description or attribution (John et al., 1988). Subsequent research, however, has shown that the lexical factors converge with dimensions derived in other personality research traditions, that they have external or predictive validity (as reviewed above), and that all five of them show about equal amounts of heritability (Loehlin et al., 1998). Thus, it seems unlikely that these five dimensions are merely psycholexical artifacts or language phenomena. Given the evidence that

TABLE 4.6. Toward a Generalizable Personality Typology: Summary of Eight Studies Replicating Three Basic Types

	Studies in the United States			
	Block (1971)	York & John (1992)	Robins, John, Caspi, Moffitt, & Stouthamer-Loeber (1996)	Klohnen & Block (1996)
Personality types				
Type 1	Ego-Resilients	Individuated	Resilients	Resilients
Type 2	Vulnerable Overcontrollers	Traditional	Overcontrollers	Overcontrollers
Type 3	Unsettled Undercontrollers	Conflicted	Undercontrollers	Undercontrollers
Facets of generalizability				
Participants	84 boys/men	103 women	300 boys	106 men and women
Age	Both 13 and 35 years	43 years	12–13 years	23 years
Birth cohort	1920s	1937–1939	Late 1970s	1960s
Region	San Francisco area	San Francisco area	Pittsburgh	San Francisco area
Data source	Clinical judgments from data archives	Clinical judgments from data archives	Caregivers' reports	Interviewer's assessments
Instrument	Adult Q-set	Adult Q-set	Child Q-set	Adult Q-set
Type derivation	Q-factors across two time periods	Replicated Q-factors	Replicated Q-factors	Q-factors

	International replications			
	Caspi & Silva (1995)	van Lieshout, Haselager, Riksen-Walraven, & van Aken (1995)	Pulkkinen (1996)	Hart, Hofman, Edelstein, & Keller (1997)
Personality types				
Type 1	Well-adjusted	Resilients	Resilients/Individuated	Resilients
Type 2	Inhibited	Overcontrollers	Introverts/Anxious	Overcontrollers
Type 3	Undercontrolled	Undercontrollers	Conflicted/Under-controlled	Undercontrollers
Facets of generalizability				
Participants	1,024 boys and girls	79 boys and girls	275 men and women	168 boys and girls
Age	3 years	7, 10, and 12 years	26 years	7 years
Birth cohort	1972–1973	Early 1970s	1960s	1970
Region	New Zealand	The Netherlands	Finland	Iceland
Data source	Examiners' observations during a testing session	Teacher reports	Self-reports	Interviewer's assessments
Instrument	Behavior ratings	Child Q-set	Scale scores	Child Q-set
Type derivation	Replicated clusters	Cluster analysis	Cluster analysis	Replicated Q-factors

Note. Based on Robins et al. (1996) and Robins et al. (1998).

the Big Five dimensions refer to real individual differences, we need to ask how these differences should be conceptualized. A recent volume (Wiggins, 1996) addressed this issue, and we briefly summarize some of the major theoretical perspectives on the Big Five.

Researchers in the lexical tradition tend to take an agnostic stance regarding the conceptual status of traits. For example, Saucier and Goldberg (1996b) argued that their studies of personality description do not address issues of causality or the mechanisms underlying behavior. Their interest is primarily in the language of personality. This level of self-restraint may seem dissatisfactory to psychologists who are more interested in personality itself. However, the findings from the lexical approach are informative because the lexical hypothesis is essentially a functionalist argument about the trait concepts in the natural language. These concepts are of interest because language encodes the characteristics that are central, for cultural, social, or biological reasons, to human life and experience. Thus, Saucier and Goldberg argue that lexical studies define an agenda for personality psychologists because they highlight the important and meaningful psychological phenomena (i.e., phenotypic characteristics) that personality psychologists should study and explain. In other words, lexical researchers view issues such as the accuracy of self-descriptions and the causal origin of traits (i.e., genotypes) as open questions that need to be answered empirically. However, there may exist important characteristics that people may not be able to observe and describe verbally; if so, the agenda specified by the lexical approach may be incomplete and would need to be supplemented by more theoretically driven approaches (Block, 1995; Tellegen, 1993).

Several theories conceptualize the Big Five as relational constructs. In interpersonal theory (Wiggins & Trapnell, 1996), the theoretical emphasis is on the individual in relationships. The Big Five are taken to describe "the relatively enduring pattern of recurrent interpersonal situations that characterize a human life" (Sullivan, 1953, pp. 110–111), thus conceptualizing the Big Five as descriptive concepts. Wiggins and Trapnell emphasize the interpersonal motives of Agency and Communion, and interpret all of the Big Five dimensions in terms of their interpersonal implications. Because Extraversion and Agreeableness are the most clearly interpersonal dimensions in the Big Five, they receive conceptual priority in this model.

Socioanalytic theory (Hogan, 1996) focuses on the social functions of self- and other-perceptions. According to Hogan, trait concepts serve as the "linguistic tools of observers" (p. 172) used to encode and communicate reputations. This view implies that traits are socially constructed to serve interpersonal functions. Because trait terms are fundamentally about reputation, individuals who self-report their traits engage in a symbolic-interactionist process of introspection (i.e., the individual considers how others view him or her). Hogan emphasizes that individuals may distort their self-reports with self-presentational strategies; another source of distortion are self-deceptive biases (cf. Paulhus & John, 1998) which do not reflect deliberate impression management but honestly held, though biased, beliefs about the self.

The evolutionary perspective on the Big Five holds that humans have evolved "difference-detecting mechanisms" to perceive individual differences that are relevant to survival and reproduction (Buss, 1996, p. 185; see also Botwin, Buss, & Shackelford, 1997). Buss views personality as an "adaptive landscape" in which the Big Five traits represent the most salient and important dimensions of the individual's survival needs. The evolutionary perspective equally emphasizes person-perception and individual differences: Because people vary systematically along certain trait dimensions, and because knowledge of others' traits has adaptive value, humans have evolved a capacity to perceive those individual differences that are central to adaptation to the social landscape. The Big Five summarize these centrally important individual differences.

McCrae and Costa (1996; see also Chapter 5, this volume) view the Big Five as causal personality dispositions. Their five-factor theory (FFT) is an explanatory interpretation of the empirically derived Big Five taxonomy. The FFT is based on the finding that all of the Big Five dimensions have a substantial genetic basis (Loehlin et al., 1998) and must therefore derive, in part, from biological structures and processes, such as specific gene loci, brain regions (e.g., the amygdala), neurotransmitters (e.g., dopamine), hormones (e.g., testosterone), and so on (Plomin & Caspi, Chapter 9, this volume); it is in this sense that traits have causal status. McCrae and Costa distinguish between "basic tendencies" and "characteristic adaptations." Personality traits are basic tendencies that refer to the abstract underlying potentials of the individual; whereas attitudes, roles, relationships, and goals are characteristic adaptations that reflect the interactions between basic tendencies and environmental demands accumulated over time. According to McCrae and Costa, basic tendencies remain stable across the life course, whereas characteristic adaptations can undergo considerable change. From this perspective, then, a statement such as "Paul likes to go to parties *because* he is extraverted" is not circular, as it would be if "extraverted" were merely a description of typical behavior (Wiggins, 1997). Instead, the concept "extraverted" stands in for biological structures and processes that remain to be discovered. This view is similar to Allport's (1937) account of traits as neuropsychic structures and Eysenck's view of traits as biological mechanisms (Eysenck & Eysenck, 1985).

The idea that personality traits have a biological basis is also fundamental to Gosling's (1999) proposal for a comparative approach to personality that studies individual differences in both human and nonhuman animals. Although scientists are reluctant to ascribe personality traits, emotions, and cognitions to animals, evolutionary theory predicts cross-species continuities not only for physical but also for behavioral traits; for example, Darwin (1998/1872) argued that emotions exist in both human and nonhuman animals. A recent review of 19 studies of personality factors in 12 nonhuman species showed substantial evidence for cross-species continuities (Gosling & John, 1999). Chimpanzees, various other primates, nonprimate mammals, and even guppies and octopuses all showed reliable individual differences in Extraversion and Neuroticism, and all but guppies and octopuses varied in Agreeableness as well, suggesting that these three Big Five factors may capture fundamental dimensions of individual differences across species. Further evidence suggests that elements of Openness (such as curiosity and playfulness) are present in at least some nonhuman animals. In contrast, only humans and our closest relatives, chimpanzees, appear to show systematic individual differences in Conscientiousness. Given the relatively complex social-cognitive functions involved in this dimension (i.e., following norms and rules, thinking before acting, and controlling impulses), it makes sense that Conscientiousness may have appeared rather recently in our evolutionary history. The careful application of ethological and experimental methodology and the high interobserver reliability in these studies make it unlikely that these findings reflect anthropomorphic projections. Rather, these surprising cross-species commonalities suggest that personality traits are caused, in part, by biological mechanisms that are shared by many species.

In conclusion, researchers hold a diversity of perspectives on the conceptual status of the Big Five, ranging from purely descriptive concepts to biologically based causal concepts. This diversity may seem to suggest that researchers cannot agree about the definition of the trait concept and that the field is in disarray (e.g., Pervin, 1994). It is important to recognize, however, that the various theoretical perspectives are not mutually exclusive. For example, although Saucier and Goldberg (1996b) caution against drawing inferences about genotypes from lexical studies, the lexical hypothesis does not preclude the possibility that the Big Five are embodied in biological structures and processes. In our view, "what is a trait?" is fundamentally an empirical question. Research in diverse areas such as behavior genetics (Plomin & Caspi, Chapter 9, this volume), molecular genetics (Lesch, Bengel, Heils, & Sabol, 1996), personality stability and change (Costa & McCrae, 1994; Helson & Stewart, 1994), and accuracy and bias in interpersonal perception (Kenny, 1994; Robins & John, 1997; see also Robins, Norem, & Cheek, Chapter 18, this volume) will be instrumental in building and refining a comprehensive theoretical account of the Big Five.

CONCLUSIONS AND IMPLICATIONS

At the beginning of this chapter, we argued that a personality taxonomy should provide a systematic framework for distinguishing, ordering, and naming types and characteristics of individuals. Ideally, that taxonomy would be built around principles that are causal and dynamic, exist at multiple levels of abstraction or hierarchy, and offer a standard nomenclature for scientists working in the field of personality. The Big Five taxonomy does not yet meet this high standard. In contrast to the biological taxonomies, the Big Five taxonomy provides descriptive concepts that still need to be explicated theoretically, and a nomenclature that is still rooted in vernacular English.

The Big Five structure has the advantage that everybody can understand the words that define the factors, and disagreements about their meanings can be reconciled by establishing their most common usage. Moreover, the natural language is not biased in favor of any existing scientific conceptions; although the atheoretical nature of the Big Five dimensions makes them less appealing to some psychologists, it also makes them more palatable to researchers that reject dimensions cast in a theoretical mold different from their own. Whatever the inadequacies of the natural language for scientific systematics, broad dimensions inferred from folk usage are *not* a bad place to start a taxonomy. Even in animal taxonomy, as G. G. Simpson has pointed out, "the technical system evolved from the vernacular" (1961, pp. 12–13).

Obviously, a system that initially derives from the natural language does not need to reify such terms indefinitely. Indeed, several of the dimensions included among the Big Five, most notably Extraversion and Neuroticism, have been the target of various physiological and mechanistic explanations (Rothbart, 1991; see also Clark & Watson, Chapter 16, this volume). Similarly, Block and Block's (1980) notion of Ego Control might shed some light on the mechanisms underlying Conscientiousness and Extraversion. Tellegen's (1985) interpretation of Extraversion and Neuroticism as persistent dispositions toward thinking and behaving in ways that foster, respectively, positive and negative affective experiences promises to connect the Big Five with individual differences in affective functioning which, in turn, may be studied in more tightly controlled laboratory settings. In a sense, the Big Five differentiate domains of individual differences that have similar surface manifestations. However, the structures and processes underlying them have only begun to be explicated. Explication in explanatory and mechanistic terms will change the definition and assessment of the Big Five dimensions as we know them today.

As Allport concluded, "scalable dimensions are useful dimensions, and we hope that work will continue until we reach firmer agreement concerning their number and nature" (1958, p. 252). As Allport had hoped, the work on scalable dimensions has continued since, and researchers have now reached a firmer consensus about them: There are five replicable, broad dimensions of personality, and they may be summarized by the broad concepts of Extraversion, Agreeableness, Conscientiousness, Neuroticism, and Openness to Experience. In our view, the Big Five taxonomy is a major step ahead, a long-due extension and improvement over earlier factor systems that tended to compete with each other, rather than establish commonalities and convergences. The Big Five taxonomy captures, at a broad level of abstraction, the commonalities among most of the existing systems of personality description, and provides an integrative descriptive model for personality research.

ACKNOWLEDGMENTS

This chapter summarizes and updates previous reviews by John (1990) and John and Robins (1993, 1998). The preparation of this chapter was supported in part by Grant No. MH49255 from the National Institutes of Mental Health to Oliver P. John, and by an NSF Predoctoral Fellowship to Sanjay Srivastava. The support and resources provided by the Institute of Personality and Social Research are also gratefully acknowledged. We are grateful to Samuel D. Gosling, James J. Gross and Richard W. Robins for their comments and suggestions on a previous draft of this chapter.

NOTES

1. This historically important report, available only as an obscure Air Force technical report, was reprinted in a special issue on the Big Five in the *Journal of Personality* (Tupes & Christal, 1992).

2. Saucier (1994a) abbreviated the 100-item TDA to a set of 40 "mini-markers" to obtain an even shorter measure.

3. The other scale with a relatively lower reliability was the TDA Emotional Stability scale. In an attempt to measure the stable pole of his scale (which after all is called Emotional Stability), Goldberg (1992) included adjectives such as imperturbable, unexcitable, undemanding, unemotional, and unenvious as factor markers. Note that these adjectives are negations of emotionality, rather than affirmations of stability, and as such they were answered less reliably even in our verbally sophisticated sample, probably because these words are less familiar and more difficult to understand. More generally, the problem is that English has few adjectives denoting emotional stability, and those that do often fail to uniquely define the emotionally stable pole of Neuroticism (e.g., stable, calm, contented, and unemotional failed to load highly negatively on the Neuroticism factor in John, 1990, as shown here in Table 4.2). On the BFI, the problem of measuring the stable pole was solved through the use of phrases, such as "Is emotionally stable, not easily upset" and "Remains calm in tense situations," which provide sufficient context to clarify the attribute being measured.

4. The full matrix is available from the authors.

5. These values are lower-bound estimates, probably because the participants in the introductory psychology subject pool had little motivation to complete the instruments with utmost care. For example, Benet-Martinez and John (1998; Study 2) found somewhat higher mean alpha coefficients for both BFI (.85) and NEO-FFI (.82), as well as higher mean convergent validity correlations (.77). Similarly, a reanalysis of data from Gross and John (1998) showed a mean convergent validity correlation across all three instruments of .79, which is slightly higher than the .75 we found here. On the other hand, Goldberg (1992) reported much lower convergent validity correlations between his TDA scales and the longer NEO PI, averaging .61 compared to the .68 found here.

6. To test more directly whether this cross-loading is indeed due to the placement of warmth, we examined the three warmth-related items included in the BFI and the TDA. Interestingly, all three items had a stronger correlation with Agreeableness than with Extraversion on the NEO-FFI, and the total warmth scale formed from the three items correlated .59 with Agreeableness and .45 with Extraversion. When

APPENDIX: THE BIG FIVE INVENTORY (BFI)

Here are a number of characteristics that may or may not apply to you. For example, do you agree that you are someone who *likes to spend time with others*? Please write a number next to each statement to indicate the extent to which you agree or disagree with that statement.

1. Disagree strongly
2. Disagree a little
3. Neither agree nor disagree
4. Agree a little
5. Agree strongly

I See Myself as Someone Who . . .

____1. Is talkative
____2. Tends to find fault with others
____3. Does a thorough job
____4. Is depressed, blue
____5. Is original, comes up with new ideas
____6. Is reserved
____7. Is helpful and unselfish with others
____8. Can be somewhat careless
____9. Is relaxed, handles stress well
____10. Is curious about many different things
____11. Is full of energy
____12. Starts quarrels with others
____13. Is a reliable worker
____14. Can be tense
____15. Is ingenious, a deep thinker
____16. Generates a lot of enthusiasm
____17. Has a forgiving nature
____18. Tends to be disorganized
____19. Worries a lot
____20. Has an active imagination
____21. Tends to be quiet
____22. Is generally trusting
____23. Tends to be lazy
____24. Is emotionally stable, not easily upset
____25. Is inventive
____26. Has an assertive personality
____27. Can be cold and aloof
____28. Perseveres until the task is finished
____29. Can be moody
____30. Values artistic, aesthetic experiences
____31. Is sometimes shy, inhibited
____32. Is considerate and kind to almost everyone
____33. Does things efficiently
____34. Remains calm in tense situations
____35. Prefers work that is routine
____36. Is outgoing, sociable
____37. Is sometimes rude to others
____38. Makes plans and follows through with them
____39. Gets nervous easily
____40. Likes to reflect, play with ideas
____41. Has few artistic interests
____42. Likes to cooperate with others
____43. Is easily distracted
____44. Is sophisticated in art, music, or literature

Please check: Did you write a number in front of each statement?

BFI scale scoring ("R" denotes reverse-scored items):

Extraversion: 1, 6R, 11, 16, 21R, 26, 31R, 36; Agreeableness: 2R, 7, 12R, 17, 22, 27R, 32, 37R, 42; Conscientiousness: 3, 8R, 13, 18R, 23R, 28, 33, 38, 43R; Neuroticism: 4, 9R, 14, 19, 24R, 29, 34R, 39; Openness: 5, 10, 15, 20, 25, 30, 35R, 40, 41R, 44

Note. Copyright © 1991 by Oliver P. John. Reprinted with permission.

warmth was partialled out, the discriminant validity correlations between Extraversion on the NEO-FFI and Agreeableness on the BFI and TDA were reduced substantially, from .36 to .08 for the BFI and from .41 to .12 for the TDA. Even the correlation between Extraversion and Agreeableness on the NEO-FFI itself was reduced from .25 to –.02. These results are consistent with those from the CFA: reclassifying warmth as a facet of Agreeableness would reduce the overlap between Extraversion and Agreeableness, even within the NEO-FFI, and improve both convergent and discriminant validity.

REFERENCES

Adams, S. H., Cartwright, L. K., Ostrove, J. M., & Stewart, A. J., (1998). Psychological predictors of good health in three longitudinal samples of educated midlife women. *Health Psychology, 17,* 412–420.

Allen, B. P., & Potkay, C. R. (1981). On the arbitrary distinction between states and traits. *Journal of Personality and Social Psychology, 41,* 916–928.

Allport, G. W. (1937). *Personality: A psychological interpretation.* New York: Holt.

Allport, G. W. (1958). What units shall we employ? In G. Lindzey (Ed.), *Assessment of human motives* (pp. 238–260). New York: Rinehart.

Allport, G. W., & Odbert, H. S. (1936). Trait-names: A psycho-lexical study. *Psychological Monographs, 47,* No. 211.

Almagor, M., Tellegen, A., & Waller, N. G. (1995). The Big Seven model: A cross-cultural replication and further exploration of the basic dimensions of natural language trait descriptors. *Journal of Personality and Social Psychology, 69,* 300–307.

Angleitner, A., Ostendorf, F., & John, O. P. (1990). Towards a taxonomy of personality descriptors in German: A psycho-lexical study [Special Issue: Personality language]. *European Journal of Personality, 4,* 89–118.

Bales, R. F. (1970). *Personality and interpersonal behavior.* New York: Holt, Rinehart, & Winston.

Bales, R. F., & Cohen, S. P. (1979). *SYMLOG: A system for the multiple level observation of groups.* New York: The Free Press.

Barrick, M. R., & Mount, M. K. (1991). The Big Five personality dimensions and job performance: A meta-analysis. *Personnel Psychology, 44,* 1–26.

Barron, F. (1968). *Creativity and personal freedom.* Princeton, NJ: Van Nostrand.

Baumgarten, F. (1933). 'Die Charktereigenschaften.' [The character traits]. In *Beitraege zur Charakter- und Persoenlichkeitsforschung* (Whole No. 1). Bern, Switzerland: A. Francke.

Becker, W. C. (1960). The matching of behavior rating and questionnaire personality factors. *Psychological Bulletin, 57,* 201–212.

Benet-Martinez, V., & John, O. P. (1998). *Los Cinco Grandes* across cultures and ethnic groups: Multitrait-multimethod analyses of the Big Five in Spanish and English. *Journal of Personality and Social Psychology, 75,* 729–750.

Benet-Martinez, V., & Waller, N. G. (1997). Further evidence for the cross-cultural generality of the Big Seven Factor model: Indigenous and imported Spanish personality constructs. *Journal of Personality, 65,* 567–598.

Bentler, P. E. (1990). Comparative fit indexes in structural models. *Psychological Bulletin, 107,* 238–246.

Block, J. (1961). *The Q-sort method in personality assessment and psychiatric research* (Reprint Ed., 1978). Palo Alto, CA: Consulting Psychologists Press.

Block, J. (1971). *Lives through time.* Berkeley, CA: Bancroft Books.

Block, J. (1995). A contrarian view of the five-factor approach to personality description. *Psychological Bulletin, 117,* 187–215.

Block, J., & Block, J. H. (1969). *The California Child Q-set.* Palo Alto, CA: Consulting Psychologists Press.

Block, J. H., & Block, J. (1980). The role of ego-control and ego-resiliency in the organization of behavior. In W. A. Collins (Ed.), *Minnesota symposia on child psychology* (Vol. 13, pp. 39–101). Hillsdale, NJ: Erlbaum.

Bond, M. H. (1979). Dimensions used in perceiving peers: Cross-cultural comparisons of Hong Kong, Japanese, American and Filipino university students. *International Journal of Psychology, 14,* 47–56.

Bond, M. H. (1983). Linking person perception dimensions to behavioral intention dimensions: The Chinese connection. *Journal of Cross-Cultural Psychology, 14,* 41–63.

Bond, M. H., & Forgas, J. P. (1984). Linking person perception to behavior intention across cultures: The role of cultural collectivism. *Journal of Cross-Cultural Psychology, 15,* 337–352.

Bond, M. H., Nakazato, H., & Shiraishi, D. (1975). Universality and distinctiveness in dimensions of Japanese person perception. *Journal of Cross-Cultural Psychology, 6,* 346–357.

Borgatta, E. F. (1964). The structure of personality characteristics. *Behavioral Science, 9,* 8–17.

Botwin, M. D., & Buss, D. M. (1989). Structure of act-report data: Is the five-factor model of personality recaptured? *Journal of Personality and Social Psychology, 56,* 988–1001.

Botwin, M. D., Buss, D. M., & Shackelford, T. K. (1997). Personality and mate preferences: Five factors in mate selection and marital satisfaction. *Journal of Personality, 65,* 107–136.

Briggs, S. R. (1989). The optimal level of measurement for personality constructs. In D. M. Buss and N. Cantor (Eds.), *Personality psychology: Recent trends and emerging directions* (pp. 246–260). New York: Springer.

Burisch, M. (1984). Approaches to personality inventory construction. *American Psychologist, 39,* 214–227.

Buss, A. H., & Plomin, R. (1975). *A temperament theory of personality development.* New York: Wiley.

Buss, D. M. (1996). Social adaptation and five major factors of personality. In J. S. Wiggins (Ed.), *The five-factor model of personality: Theoretical perspectives* (pp. 180–207). New York: Guilford Press.

Caprara, G. V., & Perugini, M. (1994). Personality described by adjectives: The generalizability of the Big Five to the Italian lexical context. *European Journal of Personality, 8,* 357–369.

Carlson, R. (1971). Where is the person in personality research? *Psychological Bulletin, 75,* 203–219.

Caspi, A. (1998). Personality development across the life course. In W. Damon (Series Ed.) & N. Eisenberg (Vol. Ed.), *Handbook of child psychology: Social, emotional, and personality development* (5th ed., pp. 311–388). New York: Wiley.

Caspi, A., & Silva, P. A. (1995). Temperamental qualities at age 3 predict personality traits in young adulthood: Longitudinal evidence from a birth cohort. *Child Development, 66,* 486–498.

Cattell, R. B. (1943). The description of personality: Basic traits resolved into clusters. *Journal of Abnormal and Social Psychology, 38,* 476–506.

Cattell, R. B. (1945a). The description of personality: Principles and findings in a factor analysis. *American Journal of Psychology, 58,* 69–90.

Cattell, R. B. (1945b). The principal trait clusters for describing personality. *Psychological Bulletin, 42,* 129–161.

Cattell, R. B., Eber, H. W., & Tatsuoka, M. M. (1970). *Handbook for the Sixteen Personality Factor Questionnaire (16PF).* Champaign, IL: IPAT.

Chaplin, W. F., John, O. P., & Goldberg, L. R. (1988). Conceptions of states and traits: Dimensional attributes with ideals as prototypes. *Journal of Personality and Social Psychology, 54,* 541–557.

Church, T. A., & Katigbak, M. S. (1989). Internal, external, and self-report structure of personality in a non-western culture: An investigation of cross-language and cross-cultural generalizability. *Journal of Personality and Social Psychology, 57,* 857–872.

Church, A. T., Reyes, J. A. S., Katigbak, M. S., & Grimm S. D. (1997). Filipino personality structure and the Big Five model: A lexical approach. *Journal of Personality, 65,* 477–528.

Comrey, A. L. (1970). *Manual for the Comrey Personality Scales.* San Diego, CA: Educational and Industrial Testing Service.

Conley, J. J. (1985). Longitudinal stability of personality traits: A multitrait–multimethod–multioccasion analysis. *Journal of Personality and Social Psychology, 49,* 1266–1282.

Costa, P. T., & McCrae, R. R. (1976). Age differences in personality structure: A cluster analytic approach. *Journal of Gerontology, 31,* 564–570.

Costa, P. T., & McCrae, R. R. (1995). Domains and facets: Hierarchical personality assessment using the Revised NEO Personality Inventory. *Journal of Personality Assessment, 64,* 21–50.

Costa, P. T., & McCrae, R. R. (1985). *The NEO Personality Inventory manual.* Odessa, FL: Psychological Assessment Resources.

Costa, P. T., & McCrae, R. R. (1989). *NEO PI/FFI manual supplement.* Odessa, FL: Psychological Assessment Resources.

Costa, P. T., & McCrae, R. R. (1992). *NEO PI-R Professional manual.* Odessa, FL: Psychological Assessment Resources.

Costa, P. T., & McCrae, R. R. (1994). Set like plaster: Evidence for the stability of adult personality. In T. F. Heatherton & J. L Weinberger (Ed.), *Can personality change?* (pp. 21–40). Washington, DC: American Psychological Association.

Costa, P. T., & Widiger, T. A. (Eds.). (1994). *Personality disorders and the five-factor model of personality.* Washington, DC: American Psychological Association.

Darwin, C. (1998). *The expression of emotions in man and animals,* 3rd ed., P. Ekman, Ed. New York: Oxford. (Original work published 1872.)

De Raad, B. (1994). An expedition in search of a fifth universal factor: Key issues in the lexical approach. *European Journal of Personality, 8,* 229–250.

De Raad, B., Di Blas, L., & Perugini, M. (1998). Two independently constructed Italian trait taxonomies: Comparisons among Italian and between Italian and Germanic languages. *European Journal of Personality, 12,* 19–41.

De Raad, B., Mulder, E., Kloosterman, K., & Hofstee, W. K. (1988). Personality-descriptive verbs. *European Journal of Personality, 2,* 81–96.

De Raad, B., Perugini, M., Hrebickova, M., & Szarota, P. (1998). Lingua franca of personality: Taxonomies and structures based on the psycholexical approach. *Journal of Cross-Cultural Psychology, 29,* 212–232.

Digman, J. M. (1963). Principal dimensions of child personality as seen in teachers' judgments. *Child Development, 34,* 43–60.

Digman, J. M. (1989). Five robust trait dimensions: Development, stability, and utility. Special Issue: Long-term stability and change in personality. *Journal of Personality, 57,* 195–214.

Digman, J. M., & Inouye, J. (1986). Further specification of the five robust factors of personality. *Journal of Personality and Social Psychology, 50,* 116–123.

Digman, J. M., & Shmelyov, A. G. (1996). The structure of temperament and personality in Russian children. *Journal of Personality and Social Psychology, 71,* 341–351.

Digman, J. M., & Takemoto-Chock, N. K. (1981). Factors in the natural language of personality: Re-analysis and comparison of six major studies. *Multivariate Behavioral Research, 16,* 149–170.

Donahue, E. M. (1994). Do children use the Big Five, too? Content and structural form in personality description. *Journal of Personality, 62,* 45–66.

Eysenck, H. J. (1986). Models and paradigms in personality research. In A. Angleitner, A. Furnham, & G. Van Heck (Eds.) *Personality psychology in Europe, Vol. 2: Current Trends and Controversies* (pp. 213–223). Lisse, The Netherlands: Swets & Zeitlinger.

Eysenck, H. J. (1991). Dimensions of personality: 16, 5, or 3?—Criteria for a taxonomic paradigm. *Personality and Individual Differences, 12,* 773–790.

Eysenck, H. J. (1992). Four ways five factors are not basic. *Personality and Individual Differences, 13,* 667–673.

Eysenck, H. J. (1997). Personality and experimental psychology: The unification of psychology and the possibility of a paradigm. *Journal of Personality and Social Psychology, 73,* 1224–1237.

Eysenck, H. J., & Eysenck, M. W. (1985). *Personality and individual differences: A natural science approach.* New York: Plenum Press.

Field, D., & Millsap, R. E. (1991). Personality in advanced old age: Continuity or change? *Journals of Gerontology, 46,* 299–308.

Fiske, D. W. (1949). Consistency of the factorial structures of personality ratings from different sources. *Journal of Abnormal and Social Psychology, 44,* 329–344.

Friedman, H. S., Hawley, P. H., & Tucker, J. S. (1994). Personality, health, and longevity. *Current Directions in Psychological Science, 3,* 37–41.

Friedman, H. S., Tucker, J. S., Schwartz, J. E., & Tomlinson-Keasey, C. (1995). Psychosocial and behavioral predictors of longevity: The aging and death of the "Termites." *American Psychologist, 50,* 69–78.

Goldberg, L. R. (1971). A historical survey of personality scales and inventories. In P. McReynolds (Ed.), *Advances in psychological assessment* (Vol. 2, pp. 293–336). Palo Alto, CA: Science and Behavior Books.

Goldberg, L. R. (1981). Language and individual differences: The search for universals in personality lexicons. In L. Wheeler (Ed.), *Review of personality and social psychology,* (Vol. 2, pp. 141–165). Beverly Hills, CA: Sage.

Goldberg, L. R. (1982). From Ace to Zombie: Some explorations in the language of personality. In C. D. Spielberger & J. N. Butcher (Eds.), *Advances in personality assessment* (Vol. 1, pp. 203–234). Hillsdale, NJ: Erlbaum.

Goldberg, L. R. (1990). An alternative "description of personality": The Big-Five factor structure. *Journal of Personality and Social Psychology, 59,* 1216–1229.

Goldberg, L. R. (1992). The development of markers for the Big-Five factor structure. *Psychological Assessment, 4,* 26–42.

Goldberg, L. R. (1993). The structure of phenotypic personality traits. *American Psychologist, 48,* 26–34.

Goldberg, L. R., & Kilkowski, J. M. (1985). The prediction of semantic consistency in self-descriptions: Characteristics of persons and of terms that affect the consistency of responses to synonym and antonym pairs. *Journal of Personality and Social Psychology, 48,* 82–98.

Goldberg, L. R., & Rosolack, T. K. (1994). The Big Five factor structure as an integrative framework: An empirical comparison with Eysenck's P-E-N model. In C. F. Halverson, G. A. Kohnstamm, & R. P. Martin (Eds.), *The developing structure of temperament and personality from infancy to adulthood.* Hillsdale, NJ: Erlbaum.

Gosling, S. D. (1999). *From mice to men: What can animal research tell us about personality?* Manuscript submitted for publication.

Gosling, S. D., & John, O. P. (1999). Personality dimensions in non-human animals: A cross-species review. *Current Directions in Psychological Science, 8,* 69–75.

Gough, H. G. (1979). A creative personality scale for the Adjective Check List. *Journal of Personality and Social Psychology, 37,* 1938–1405.

Gough, H. G. (1987). *The California Psychological Inventory administrator's guide.* Palo Alto, CA: Consulting Psychologists Press.

Gough, H. G., & Heilbrun, A. B., Jr. (1983). *The Adjective Check List manual.* Palo Alto, CA: Consulting Psychologists Press.

Gould, S. J. (1981). *The mismeasure of man.* New York: Norton.

Graziano, W. G., & Eisenberg, N. (1997). Agreeableness: A dimension of personality. In R. Hogan, J. A. Johnson, & S. R. Briggs (Eds.), *Handbook of personality psychology* (pp. 795–824). San Diego, CA: Academic Press.

Graziano, W. G., & Ward, D. (1992). Probing the Big Five in adolescence: Personality and adjustment during a developmental transition. *Journal of Personality, 60,* 425–439.

Gross, J. J., & John, O. P. (1998). Mapping the domain of expressivity: Multimethod evidence for a hierarchical model. *Journal of Personality and Social Psychology, 74,* 171–190.

Guilford, J. P. (1974). Rotation problems in factor analysis. *Psychological Bulletin, 81,* 498–501.

Guilford, J. P. (1975). Factors and factors of personality. *Psychological Bulletin, 82,* 802–814.

Guthrie, G. M., & Bennett, A. B., Jr. (1971). Cultural differences in implicit personality theory. *International Journal of Psychology, 6,* 305–312.

Halverson, C. F., Kohnstamm, G. A., & Martin R. P. (1994). *The developing structure of temperament and personality from infancy to adulthood.* Hillsdale, NJ: Erlbaum.

Hampson, S. E., Goldberg, L. R., & John, O. P. (1987). Category-breadth and social-desirability values for 573 personality terms. *European Journal of Personality, 1,* 241–258.

Hampson, S. E., John, O. P., & Goldberg, L. R. (1986). Category breadth and hierarchical structure in personality: Studies of asymmetries in judgments of trait implications. *Journal of Personality and Social Psychology, 51,* 37–54.

Hart, D., Hofman, V., Edelstein, W., & Keller, M. (1997). The relation of childhood personality types to adolescent behavior and development: A longitudinal study of Icelandic children. *Developmental Psychology, 33,* 195–205

Heatherton, T. F., & Weinberger, J. L. (Eds.). (1994). *Can personality change?* Washington, DC: American Psychological Association.

Helson, R. (1967). Personality characteristics and developmental history of creative college women. *Genetic Psychology Monographs, 76,* 205–256.

Helson, R. (1985). Which of those young women with creative potential became productive? Personality in college and characteristics of parents. In R. Hogan and W. H. Jones (Eds.), *Perspectives in personality theory, measurement, and interpersonal dynamics* (Vol. 1, pp. 49–80). Greenwich, CT: JAI Press.

Helson, R., & Stewart, A. (1994). Personality change in adulthood. In T. F. Heatherton & J. L. Weinberger (Eds.), *Can personality change?* (pp. 21–40). Washington, DC: American Psychological Association.

Hofstee, W. K., De Raad, B., & Goldberg, L. R. (1992). Integration of the Big Five and circumplex approaches to trait structure. *Journal of Personality and Social Psychology, 63,* 146–163.

Hofstee, W. K., Kiers, H. A., De Raad, B., Goldberg, L. R., & Ostendorf, F. (1997). A comparison of Big-Five structures of personality traits in Dutch, English, and German. *European Journal of Personality, 11,* 15–31.

Hogan, R. (1983). A socioanalytic theory of personality. In M. Page (Ed.) *Nebraska symposium on motivation, 1982: Personality—Current theory and research.* Lincoln, NE: University of Nebraska Press.

Hogan, J., & Ones, D. S. (1997). Conscientiousness and integrity at work. In R. Hogan, J. A. Johnson, and S. R. Briggs (Eds.), *Handbook of personality psychology* (pp. 849–870). San Diego, CA: Academic Press.

Hogan, R. (1986). *Hogan Personality Inventory manual.* Minneapolis, MN: National Computer Systems.

Hogan, R. (1996). A socioanalytic perspective on the five-factor model. In J. S. Wiggins (Ed.), *The five-factor model of personality: Theoretical perspectives* (pp. 180–207). New York: Guilford Press.

Hrebickova, M., & Ostendorf, F. (1995). Lexikalni pristup k osobnosti. V: Klasifikace pridavnych jmen do kategorii osobnostni deskripce. [Lexical approach to personality: V. Classification of adjectives into categories of personality description]. *Ceskoslovenska Psychologie, 39,* 265–276.

Huey, S.J., & Weisz, J. R. (1997). Ego control, ego resiliency, and the five-factor model as predictors of behavioral and emotional problems in clinic-referred children and adolescents. *Journal of Abnormal Psychology, 106,* 404–415.

Jackson, D. N. (1984). *Personality Research Form manual* (3rd ed). Port Huron, MI: Research Psychologists Press.

John, O. P. (1989). Towards a taxonomy of personality descriptors. In D. M. Buss & N. Cantor (Eds.), *Personality psychology: Recent trends and emerging directions* (pp. 261–271). New York: Springer.

John, O. P. (1990). The "Big Five" factor taxonomy: Dimensions of personality in the natural language and in questionnaires. In L. A. Pervin (Ed.), *Handbook of personality: Theory and research* (pp. 66–100). New York: Guilford Press.

John, O. P., Angleitner, A., & Ostendorf, F. (1988). The lexical approach to personality: A historical review of trait taxonomic research. *European Journal of Personality, 2,* 171–203.

John, O. P., & Benet-Martinez, V. (in press). Measurement: Reliability, construct validation, and scale construction. In H. T. Reis & C. M. Judd (Eds.), *Handbook of research methods in social psychology.* Cambridge, UK: Cambridge University Press.

John, O. P., Caspi, A., Robins, R. W., Moffitt, T. E., & Stouthamer-Loeber, M. (1994). The "Little Five": Exploring the nomological network of the five-factor model of personality in adolescent boys. *Child Development, 65,* 160–178.

John, O. P., Donahue, E. M., & Kentle, R. L. (1991). *The Big Five Inventory—Versions 4a and 54.* Berkeley, CA: University of California, Berkeley, Institute of Personality and Social Research.

John, O. P., Goldberg, L. R., & Angleitner, A. (1984). Better than the alphabet: Taxonomies of personality-descriptive terms in English, Dutch, and German. In H. Bonarius, G. van Heck, and N. Smid (Eds.), *Personality psychology in Europe: Theoretical and empirical developments* (pp. 83–100). Berwyn, PA: Swets North America Inc.

John, O. P., & Gosling, S. D. (in press). Personality traits. In A. E. Kazdin (Ed.), *Encyclopedia of psychology.* Washington, DC: American Psychological Association.

John, O. P., Hampson, S. E., & Goldberg, L. R. (1991). Is there a basic level of personality description? *Journal of Personality and Social Psychology, 60,* 348–361.

John, O. P., & Robins, R. W. (1993). Gordon Allport: Father and critic of the five-factor model. In K. H. Craik, R. T. Hogan, & R. N. Wolfe (Eds.), *Fifty years of personality research* (pp. 215–236). New York: Plenum Press.

John, O. P., & Robins, R. W. (1998). Recent trends in Big Five research: Development, predictive validity, and personality types. In J. Bermudez et al. (Eds.), *Personality Psychology in Europe* (Vol. 6, pp. 6–16). Tilburg, The Netherlands: Tilburg University Press.

Kenny, D. A. (1994). *Interpersonal perception: A social relations analysis.* New York: Guilford Press.

Klages, L. (1926). *The science of character* (Translated 1932). London: George Allen and Unwin. (Original work published 1926.)

Klohnen, E. C., & Block, J. (1996). Unpublished data, Department of Psychology, Berkeley, California.

Kohnstamm, G. A., Halverson, C. F., Mervielde, I., & Havill, V. L. (Eds.). (1998). *Parental descriptions of child personality: Developmental antecedents of the Big Five?* Mahwah, NJ: Erlbaum.

Lesch, K. P., Bengel, D., Heils, A., & Sabol, S. Z. (1996). Association of anxiety-related traits with a polymorphism in the serotonin transporter gene regulatory region. *Science, 274,* 1527–1531.

Loehlin, J. C., McCrae, R. R., Costa, P. T., Jr., & John, O. P. (1998). Heritabilities of common and measure-specific components of the Big Five personality factors. *Journal of Research in Personality, 32,* 431–453.

MacKinnon, D. W. (1965). Personality and the realization of creative potential. *American Psychologist, 20,* 273–281.

McAdams, D. P. (1992). The five-factor model in personality: A critical appraisal. *Journal of Personality, 60,* 329–361.

McAdams, D. P. (1995). What do we know when we know a person? *Journal of Personality, 63,* 365–396.

McCrae, R. R. (1996). Social consequences of experiential openness. *Psychological Bulletin, 120,* 323–337.

McCrae, R. R., & Costa, P. T. (1985a). Comparison of EPI and psychoticism scales with measures of the five-factor model of personality. *Personality and Individual Differences, 6,* 587–597.

McCrae, R. R., & Costa, P. T. (1985b). Openness to experience. In R. Hogan & W. H. Jones, *Perspectives in personality* (Vol. 1, pp. 145–172). Greenwich, CT: JAI Press.

McCrae, R. R., & Costa, P. T. (1985c). Updating Norman's adequate taxonomy: Intelligence and personality dimensions in natural language and in questionnaires. *Journal of Personality and Social Psychology, 49,* 710–721.

McCrae, R. R., & Costa, P. T. (1987). Validation of the five-factor model of personality across instruments and observers. *Journal of Personality and Social Psychology, 52,* 81–90.

McCrae, R. R., & Costa, P. T. (1990). *Personality in adulthood.* New York: Guilford Press.

McCrae, R. R., & Costa, P. T. (1996). Toward a new generation of personality theories: Theoretical contexts for the five-factor model. In J. S. Wiggins (Ed.), *The five- factor model of personality: Theoretical perspectives* (pp. 51–87). New York: Guilford Press.

McCrae, R. R., & Costa, P. T. (1997). Personality trait structure as a human universal. *American Psychologist, 52,* 509–516.

McCrae, R. R., & John, O. P. (1992). An introduction to the five-factor model and its applications. *Journal of Personality, 60,* 175–215.

Mershon, B., & Gorsuch, R. L. (1988). Number of factors in the personality sphere: Does increase in factors increase predictability of real-life criteria? *Journal of Personality and Social Psychology, 55,* 675–680.

Mount, M. K., Barrick, M. R., & Stewart, G. L. (1998). Five-factor model of personality and performance in jobs involving interpersonal interactions. *Human Performance, 11,* 145–165.

Myers, I. B., & McCaulley, M. H. (1985). *Manual: A guide to the development and use of the Myers–Briggs Type Indicator.* Palo Alto, CA: Consulting Psychologists Press.

Nakazato, H., Bond, M. H., & Shiraishi, D. (1976). Dimensions of personality perception: An examination of Norman's hypothesis. *Japanese Journal of Psychology, 47,* 139–148.

Norman, W. T. (1963). Toward an adequate taxonomy of personality attributes: Replicated factor structure in peer nomination personality ratings. *Journal of Abnormal and Social Psychology, 66,* 574–583.

Norman, W. T. (1967). *2,800 personality trait descriptors: Normative operating characteristics for a university population.* Department of Psychology, University of Michigan, Ann Arbor, MI.

Nowakowska, M. (1973). The limitations of the factor-analytic approach to psychology with special application to Cattell's research strategy. *Theory and Decision, 4,* 109–139.

Ostendorf, F. (1990). *Sprache und Persoenlichkeitsstruktur: Zur Validitaet des Fuenf-Faktoren-Modells der Persoenlichkeit* [Language and personality structure: On the validity of the five factor model of personality.] Regensburg, Germany: S. Roderer Verlag.

Paulhus, D. L., & John, O. P. (1998). Egoistic and moralistic biases in self-perception: The interplay of self-deceptive styles with basic traits and motives. *Journal of Personality, 66,* 1025–1060.

Peabody, D. & Goldberg, L. R. (1989). Some determinants of factor structures from personality-trait descriptors. *Journal of Personality and Social Psychology, 57,* 552–567.

Pervin, L. A. (1994). A critical analysis of current trait theory. *Psychological Inquiry,* 5, 103–113.

Pervin, L. A., & John, O. P. (1997). *Personality: Theory and research* (7th ed.). New York: Wiley.

Pulkkinen, L. (1996). Female and male personality styles: A typological and developmental analysis. *Journal of Personality and Social Psychology, 70,* 1288–1306.

Revelle, W. (1987). Personality and motivation: Sources of inefficiency in cognitive performance. *Journal of Research in Personality, 21,* 436–452.

Robins, R. W., & John, O. P. (1997). The quest for self-insight: Theory and research on accuracy and bias in self-perception. In R. Hogan, J. A. Johnson, & S. R. Briggs (Ed.), *Handbook of personality psychology* (pp. 649–679). San Diego, CA: Academic Press.

Robins, R. W., John, O. P., & Caspi, A. (1994). Major dimensions of personality in early adolescence: The Big Five and beyond. In C. F. Halverson, J. A. Kohnstamm, & R. P. Martin (Eds.), *The developing structure of temperament and personality from infancy to adulthood* (pp. 267–291). Hillsdale, NJ: Erlbaum.

Robins, R. W., John, O. P., & Caspi, A. (1998). The typological approach to studying personality. In R. B. Cairns, J. Kagan, & L. Bergman (Eds.), *The individual in developmental research: Essays in honor of Marian Radke-Yarrow* (pp. 135–160). Beverly Hills, CA: Sage

Robins, R. W., John, O. P., Caspi, A., Moffitt, T. E., & Stouthamer-Loeber, M. (1996). Resilient, overcontrolled, and undercontrolled boys: Three replicable personality types? *Journal of Personality and Social Psychology, 70,* 157–171.

Rosch, E. (1978). Principles of categorization. In E. Rosch & B. B. Lloyd (Eds.), *Cognition and categorization* (pp. 27–48). Hillsdale, NJ: Erlbaum.

Rothbart, M. (1991). Temperament and development. In G. A. Kohnstamm, L. Bates, and M. K. Rothbart (Eds.), *Handbook of temperament in childhood*. Sussex, UK: Wiley.

Saucier, G. (1992). Openness versus intellect: Much ado about nothing? *European Journal of Personality, 6,* 381–386.

Saucier, G. (1994a). Mini-Markers: A brief version of Goldberg's unipolar Big-Five markers. *Journal of Personality Assessment, 63,* 506–516.

Saucier, G. (1994b). Trapnell versus the lexical factor: More ado about nothing? *European Journal of Personality, 8,* 291–298.

Saucier, G. (1997). Effects of variable selection on the factor structure of person descriptors. *Journal of Personality and Social Psychology, 73,* 1296–1312.

Saucier, G., & Goldberg, L. R. (1996a). Evidence for the Big Five in analyses of familiar English personality adjectives. *European Journal of Personality, 10,* 61–77.

Saucier, G., & Goldberg, L. R. (1996b). The language of personality: Lexical perspectives on the five-factor model. In J. S. Wiggins (Ed.), *The five-factor model of personality: Theoretical perspectives* (pp. 21–50). New York: Guilford Press.

Shmelyov, A. G., & Pokhil'ko, V. I. (1993). A taxonomy-oriented study of Russian personality-trait names. *European Journal of Personality, 7,* 1–17.

Simpson, G. G. (1961). *Principles of animal taxonomy*. New York: Columbia University Press.

Somer, O., & Goldberg, L. R. (1999). The structure of Turkish trait-descriptive adjectives. *Journal of Personality and Social Psychology, 76,* 431–450.

Sullivan, H. S. (1953). *The interpersonal theory of psychiatry*. New York: Norton.

Szarota, P. (1995). Polska Lista Przymiotnikowa (PLP): Narzedzie do diagnozy Pieciu Wielkich czynnikow osobowosci [Polish Adjective List: An instrument to assess the five-factor model of personality]. *Studia Psychologiczne, 33,* 227–256.

Szirmak, Z., & De Raad, B. (1994). Taxonomy and structure of Hungarian personality traits. *European Journal of Personality, 8,* 95–117.

Tellegen, A. (1982). *Brief manual for the Differential Personality Questionnaire*. Unpublished manuscript, University of Minnesota.

Tellegen, A. (1985). Structures of mood and personality and their relevance to assessing anxiety, with an emphasis on self-report. In A. H. Tuma & J. D. Maser (Eds.), *Anxiety and the anxiety disorders* (pp. 681–716). Hillsdale, NJ: Erlbaum.

Tellegen, A. (1993). Folk concepts and psychological concepts of personality and personality disorder. *Psychological Inquiry, 4,* 122–130.

Trapnell, P. D., & Wiggins, J. S. (1990). Extension of the Interpersonal Adjective scales to include the Big Five dimensions of personality. *Journal of Personality and Social Psychology, 59,* 781–790.

Tupes, E. C., & Christal, R. C. (1961). *Recurrent personality factors based on trait ratings* (Tech. Rep.). Lackland Air Force Base, TX: USAF.

Tupes, E. C., & Christal, R. C. (1992). Recurrent personality factors based on trait ratings. *Journal of Personality, 60,* 225–251.

van Lieshout, C. F. M., & Haselager, G. J. T. (1994). The Big Five personality factors in Q-sort descriptions of children and adolescents. In C. F. Halverson, G. A. Kohnstamm, and R. P. Martin (Eds.), *The developing structure of temperament and personality from infancy to adulthood* (pp. 293–318). Hillsdale, NJ: Erlbaum.

van Lieshout, C. F. M., Haselager, G. J. T., Riksen-Walraven, J. M., & van Aken, M. A. (1995, April). *Personality development in middle childhood.* Paper presented at the Society for Research in Child Development, Indianapolis, Indiana.

Watson, D., & Clark, L. A. (1997). Extraversion and its positive emotional core. In R. Hogan, J. A. Johnson, and S. R. Briggs (Eds.), *Handbook of personality psychology* (pp. 767–793). San Diego, CA: Academic Press.

White, G. M. (1980). Conceptual universals in interpersonal language. *American Anthropologist, 82,* 759–781.

Wiggins, J. S. (1968). Personality structure. In P. R. Farnsworth (Ed.), *Annual review of psychology* (Vol. 19, pp. 320–322). Palo Alto: Annual Reviews.

Wiggins, J. S. (1979). A psychological taxonomy of trait-descriptive terms: The interpersonal domain. *Journal of Personality and Social Psychology, 37,* 395–412.

Wiggins, J. S. (1995). *Interpersonal Adjective Scales: Professional manual.* Odessa, FL: Psychological Assessment Resources.

Wiggins, J. S. (1997). In defense of traits. In R. Hogan, J. A. Johnson, & S. R. Briggs (Ed.), *Handbook of personality psychology* (pp. 649–679). San Diego, CA: Academic Press.

Wiggins, J. S. (Ed.). (1996). *The five-factor model of personality: Theoretical perspectives.* New York: Guilford Press.

Wiggins, J. S., & Pincus, A. L. (1989). Conceptions of personality disorders and dimensions of personality. *Psychological Assessment, 1,* 305–316.

Wiggins, J. S., & Trapnell, P. D. (1996). A dyadic-interactional perspective on the five-factor model. In J. S. Wiggins (Ed.), *The five-factor model of personality: Theoretical perspectives* (pp. 180–207). New York: Guilford Press.

Yang, K.-S., & Bond, M. H. (1990). Exploring implicit personality theories with indigenous or imported constructs: The Chinese case. *Journal of Personality and Social Psychology, 58,* 1087–1095.

Yik, M. S., & Bond, M. H. (1993). Exploring the dimensions of Chinese person perception with indigenous and imported constructs: Creating a culturally balanced scale. *International Journal of Psychology, 28,* 75–95.

York, K. L., & John, O. P. (1992). The four faces of Eve: A typological analysis of women's personality at midlife. *Journal of Personality and Social Psychology, 62,* 494–508.

Chapter 5

A Five-Factor Theory of Personality

Robert R. McCrae and Paul T. Costa, Jr.
Gerontology Research Center, National Institute on Aging

EMPIRICAL AND CONCEPTUAL BASES OF A NEW THEORY

In a narrow sense, the Five-Factor Model (FFM) of personality is an empirical generalization about the covariation of personality traits. As Digman and Inouye (1986) put it, "If a large number of rating scales is used and if the scope of the scales is very broad, the domain of personality descriptors is almost completely accounted for by five robust factors" (p. 116). The five factors, frequently labeled Neuroticism (N), Extraversion (E), Openness (O), Agreeableness (A), and Conscientiousness (C), have been found not only in the peer rating scales in which they were originally discovered (Tupes & Christal, 1961/1992) but also in self-reports on trait descriptive adjectives (Saucier, 1997), in questionnaire measures of needs and motives (Costa & McCrae, 1988), in expert ratings on the California Q-Set (Lanning, 1994), and in personality disorder symptom clusters (Clark & Livesley, 1994). Much of what psychologists mean by the term *personality* is summarized by the FFM, and the model has been of great utility to the field by integrating and systematizing diverse conceptions and measures.

In a broader sense, the FFM refers to the entire body of research that it has inspired, amounting to a reinvigoration of trait psychology itself. Research associated with the FFM has included studies of diverse populations (McCrae, Costa, del Pilar, Rolland & Parker, 1998), often followed over decades of the lifespan (Costa & McCrae, 1992c); employed multiple methods of assessment (Funder, Kolar, & Blackman, 1995); and even featured case studies (Costa & McCrae, 1998b; McCrae, 1993–94). As Carlson (1984) might have predicted, these diverse research strategies have paid off handsomely in substantive findings: The FFM "is the Christmas tree on which findings of stability, heritability, consensual validation, cross-cultural invariance, and predictive utility are hung like ornaments" (Costa & McCrae, 1993, p. 302). After decades of floundering, personality psychology has begun to make steady progress, accumulating a store of replicable findings about the origins, development, and functioning of personality traits (McCrae, 1992).

But neither the model itself nor the body of research findings with which it is associated constitutes a theory of personality. A theory organizes findings to tell a coherent story, to bring into focus those issues and phenomena that can and should be explained. As Mayer (1998) argued, personality may be viewed as a system, and an adequate theory of personality must provide a definition of the system, a specification of its components, a model of their organization and interaction, and an account of the system's development. Five-Factor Theory (FFT; McCrae & Costa, 1996) represents an effort to construct such a theory that is consistent with current knowledge about personality. In this chapter we summarize and elaborate it.

The FFM and Trait Theory

Although the FFM is not a theory of personality, McCrae and John (1992) argued that it implicitly adopts the basic tenets of *trait theory*—that individuals can be characterized in terms of relatively enduring patterns of thoughts, feelings, and actions; that traits can be quantitatively assessed; that they show some degree of cross-situational consistency; and so on. The hundreds of studies of personality correlates that employ measures of the FFM both presume and confirm that personality traits exist.

It is therefore somewhat surprising that, in a recent volume on the theoretical basis of the FFM (Wiggins, 1996), some of the psychologists most closely associated with the FFM explicitly disavowed a trait perspective. Saucier and Goldberg (1996) stated that their "lexical perspective is not an instance of 'trait theory'," which they describe as "a rubric that may have no meaning outside introductory personality texts" (p. 25). They are concerned only with the phenotypic level of personality and do not even presume that trait descriptive adjectives refer to temporally stable attributes. Hogan (1996), who advocates a socioanalytic perspective, argued that personality attributes are not neuropsychic structures within the individual but "categories that people use to evaluate one another" that "reveal the amount of status and acceptance that a person has been granted" (p. 173). Responses to personality questionnaires, according to Hogan, are not veridical self-descriptions but strategic self-presentations; socioanalytic theory does not presume that there is any "link between item endorsements and other behavior" (p. 176). Wiggins and Trapnell (1996) follow Sullivan in seeing the locus of personality not within the individual, but in patterns of interpersonal relationships; their major conceptual orientation is guided by the metatheoretical concepts of agency and communion.

Perhaps these positions can be understood historically as reactions to the disrepute into which traits had fallen in the 1970s. Today, however, they seem needlessly modest: Why restrict theoretical ambitions to the phenotypic level? Why not hypothesize temporal stability for traits when stability is already well documented? Why doubt neuropsychic structures exist when the heritability of traits has been amply replicated? Why locate personality in interpersonal space when we can understand interpersonal behavior as a result of characteristics within the individual (Côté & Moskowitz, 1998)? FFT is unabashedly a trait theory, making full use of the empirical results of the last two decades that constitute the FFM in the broader sense.

Personality traits are recognized by laypersons, who have a rich vocabulary for describing themselves and others (e.g., *anxious, bold, curious, docile, efficient*), and traits have been formally studied by psychologists from Francis Galton to Gordon Allport to Hans Eysenck. Despite theoretical distinctions, on an empirical level other individual difference variables (including needs, types, and folk concepts) appear to be closely related to traits (Costa & McCrae, 1988; McCrae & Costa, 1989; McCrae, Costa, & Piedmont, 1993). In fact, most psychological questionnaires measure some form of personality trait.

Traits (under one name or another) have proven so very interesting to personality psychologists because they explain much of what defines the individual person—the chosen focus of personologists. Universal characteristics—like the need for oxygen or the capacity for language—tell us much about the species but nothing about the individual. Conversely, specific behaviors, transient moods, and biographical details tell us about the individual-in-context but may not permit generalizable insights. From the perspective of trait theory, these two levels appear to yield only truisms and trivia. By contrast, traits point to more-or-less consistent and recurrent patterns of acting and reacting that simultaneously characterize individuals and differentiate them from others; and they allow the discovery of empirical generalizations about how others with similar traits are likely to act and react.

As a practical matter, trait psychologists do routinely ignore the universal and the particular in their research. Except when dealing with very unusual populations, trait researchers do not bother to remind readers that their subjects could understand the questionnaires, had self-concepts on which to base their self-reports, and continued to breathe normally for the duration of the testing session. Nor, except in the occasional case study, do they give concrete instances of how traits are expressed in specific times and circumstances.

But a theory of personality cannot afford to ignore these two levels of explanation. Part of making sense of trait findings requires putting them into a broader context and showing how they in turn form the context for specific behaviors and individual lives. In Mayer's (1998) terminology, the trait system must be identified in terms of its boundaries with other systems, higher and lower. These links will form a recurrent theme in this chapter.

Assumptions about Human Nature

The trait perspective, like every psychological theory, is based on a set of assumptions about what people are like and what a theory of personality ought to do. Most of these assumptions—for example, that explanations for behavior are to be sought in the circumstances of this life, not karma from a previous one—are implicit. FFT explicitly acknowledges four assumptions about human nature (cf. Hjelle & Siegler, 1976)—*knowability, rationality, variability,* and *proactivity;* all of these appear to be implicit in the standard enterprise of trait research.

Knowability is the assumption that personality is a proper object of scientific study. In contrast to some humanistic and existential theories that celebrate human freedom and the irreducible uniqueness of the individual, FFT assumes that there is much to be gained from the scientific study of personality in individuals and groups.

Scientific study does not necessarily imply experimentation, and we do not agree with Eysenck (1997) that a persuasive paradigm for personality psychology must involve a unification of correlational and experimental methods. Science proceeds by many methods and works best when the method is dictated by the nature of the problem rather than academic fashion and prestige. In particular, correlational methods can capitalize on natural experiments, especially in longitudinal, twin, and cross-cultural studies. Yang, McCrae, and Costa (1998), for example, looked at the impact of China's Cultural Revolution on personality formation—an experimental maniupulation whose scope, intensity, and duration could never be matched in the laboratory.

Rationality is the assumption that, despite errors and biases (e.g., Robins & John, 1997), people are in general capable of understanding themselves and others (Funder, 1995). In this respect, psychology is an unusual science. Physicians would not ask their patients to estimate their own white blood cell count, because patients could not be expected to possess such information. But trait psychologists routinely—and properly—ask people how sociable or competitive or irritable they are and interpret the answers (suitably aggregated and normed) as meaning what they say. Psychologists are able to do this because with respect to personality traits, laypersons are extraordinarily sophisticated judges who employ a trait language evolved over centuries to express important social judgments (cf. Saucier & Goldberg, 1996).

The assumption of rationality does not mean that FFT is merely folk psychology. Lay understanding is largely limited to the phenotypic level, whereas FFT attempts to account for the genotypic level and its operations. People understand whether someone is arrogant or modest, but they do not intuitively know the heritability of modesty, or its lifespan developmental course, or its evolutionary significance. Trait psychology is thus like representational art: Viewers recognize the face or flower, although they may know nothing about the laws of perspective or the techniques of overpainting.

Variability asserts that people differ from each other in psychologically significant ways—an obvious premise for differential psychology. Note, however, that this position sets trait theories apart from all those views of human nature, philosophical and psychological, that seek a single answer to what human nature is really like. Are people basically selfish or altruistic? Creative or conventional? Purposeful or lazy? Within FFT, those are all meaningless questions; *creative* and *conventional* define opposite poles of a dimension along which people vary.

Proactivity refers to the assumption that the locus of causation of human action is to be sought in the person. It goes without saying that people are not absolute masters of their destinies, and that (consistent with the premise of variability) people differ in the extent to which they control their lives. But trait theory holds that it is worthwhile to seek the origins of behavior in characteristics of the person. People are neither passive victims of their life circumstances nor empty organisms programmed by histories of reinforcements. Personality is actively involved in shaping people's lives.

It is important to recognize that proactivity of personality is not equivalent to proactivity of the person; one's proactive basic tendencies are not necessarily the same as one's conscious goals. Failure to adhere to a diet may be as much an expression of one's personality as success in dieting; anxiety and depression may be one's own natural, albeit noxious, way of life.

A UNIVERSAL PERSONALITY SYSTEM

Personality traits are individual difference variables; to understand them and how they operate, it is necessary to describe personality itself, the dynamic psychological organization that coordinates experience and action. Previously (Costa & McCrae, 1994; McCrae & Costa, 1996), we have described our account of this as a "model of the person," but to distinguish it from the five-factor model, it would perhaps be better to call it the FFT *personality system* and to describe it in the terms that Mayer (1998) used for his systems framework. It is represented schematically in Figure 5.1.

Components of the Personality System

The personality system consists of components that correspond to the definitions of FFT and dynamic processes that indicate how these components are interrelated—the basic postulates of FFT. The definitions would probably seem reasonable to personologists from many different theoretical backgrounds; the postulates distinguish FFT from most other theories of personality and reflect interpretations of empirical data.

The core components of the personality system, indicated in rectangles, are designated as *basic tendencies, characteristic adaptations,* and the *self-concept* (actually a subcomponent of characteristic adaptations, but one of sufficient interest to warrant its own box). The elliptical peripheral components, which represent the interfaces of personality with adjoining systems, are labeled *biological bases, external influences,* and the *objective biography*. Figure 5.1 can be interpreted cross-sectionally as a diagram of how

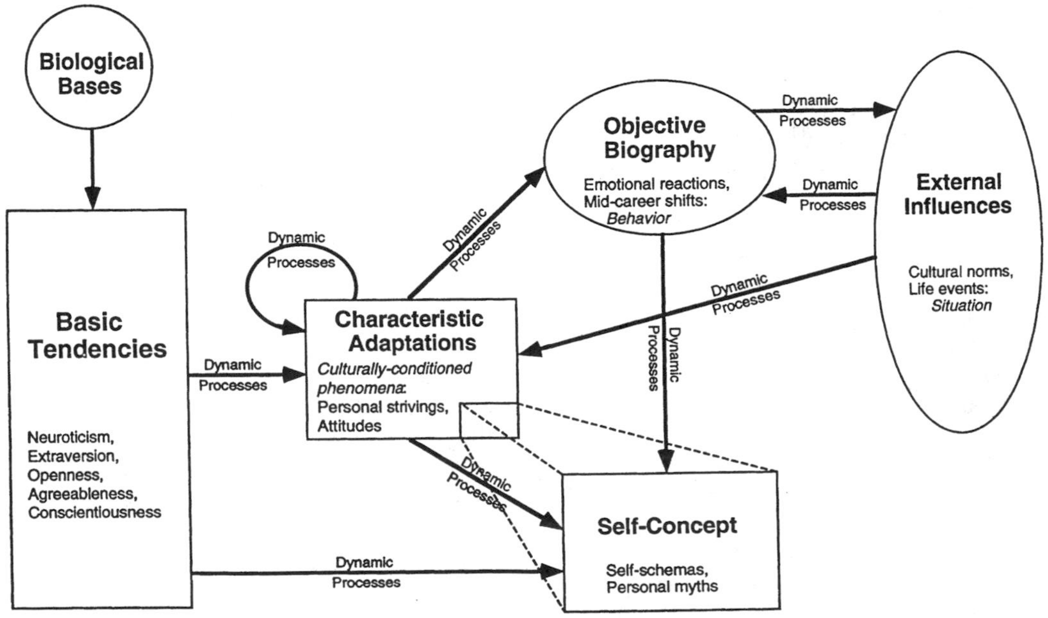

FIGURE 5.1. A representation of the five-factor theory personality system. Core components are in rectangles; interfacing components are in ellipses. Adapted from McCrae and Costa (1996).

TABLE 5.1. Some Examples of FFT Personality System Components

Basic tendencies	Characteristic adaptations	Objective biography
Neuroticism		
N3: Depression (a tendency to experience dysphoric effect—sadness, hopelessness, guilt)	Low self-esteem, irrational perfectionistic beliefs, pessimistic attitudes	"Betty" (very high N3) feels guilty about her low-prestige job (Bruehl, 1994).
Extraversion		
E2: Gregariousness (a preference for companionship and social stimulation)	Social skills, numerous friendships, enterprising vocational interests, participation in sports, club memberships	J.-J. Rousseau (very low E2) leaves Paris for the countryside (McCrae, 1996).
Openness to Experience		
O4: Actions (a need for variety, novelty, and change)	Interest in travel, many different hobbies, knowledge of foreign cuisine, diverse vocational interests, friends who share tastes	Diane Ackerman (high O4) cruises the Antarctic (McCrae, 1993–1994).
Agreeableness		
A4: Compliance (a willingness to defer to others during interpersonal conflict)	Forgiving attitudes, belief in cooperation, inoffensive language, reputation as a pushover.	Case 3 (very low A4) throws things at her husband during a fight (Costa & McCrae, 1992b).
Conscientiousness		
C4: Achievement Striving (strong sense of purpose and high aspiration levels)	Leadership skills, long-term plans, organized support network, technical expertise	Richard Nixon (very high C4) runs for President (Costa & McCrae, in press).

personality operates at any given time; in that case the external influences constitute the situation, and the objective biography is a specific instance of behavior, the output of the system. Figure 5.1 can also be interpreted longitudinally to indicate personality development (in basic tendencies and characteristic adaptations) and the unfolding of the life course (objective biography).

It may be helpful to consider some of the substance of personality to flesh out the abstractions in Figure 5.1. Table 5.1 presents some examples. For each of the five factors, an illustrative trait is identified in the first column of the table. The intrapsychic and interpersonal adaptations that develop over time as expressions of these facet traits are illustrated in the second column, and the third column mentions an instance of behavior from an individual characterized by the high or low pole of the facet.

At present, FFT has relatively little to say about the peripheral components of the personality system. Biological bases certainly include genes and brain structures, but the precise mechanisms—developmental, neuroanatomical, or psychophysiological—are not yet specified. Similarly, FFT does not detail types of external influences or aspects of the objective biography. Like most theories of personality, FFT presumes that "situation" and "behavior" are more or less self-evident.

What FFT does focus attention on is the distinction between basic tendencies (abstract psychological potentials) and characteristic adaptations (their concrete manifestations). Somewhat similar distinctions have been made by others—for example, in the familiar contrast of genotypic and phenotypic traits (Wiggins, 1973/1997) and in McAdams's (1996) distinction between Level 1 and Level 2 personality variables. FFT, however, insists on a distinction that other theories usually make only in passing, and it assigns traits exclusively to the category of basic tendencies. In FFT, traits are not patterns of behavior (Buss & Craik, 1983), nor are they the plans, skills, and desires that lead to patterns of behavior (Johnson, 1997). They are directly accessible neither to public observation nor to private introspection. Instead, they are deeper psychological entities that can only be *inferred* from behavior and experience. Self-reports of personality traits are based on such inferences, just as observer ratings are.

Although it smacks of obfuscation, there are good reasons to uncouple personality traits from the more observable components of personality. Characteristic adaptations—habits, attitudes, skills, roles, relationships—are influenced both by basic tendencies and by external influences. They are *characteristic* because they reflect the enduring psychological core of the individual, and they are *adaptations* because they help the individual fit into the ever-changing social environment. Characteristic adaptations and their configurations inevitably vary tremendously across cultures, families, and portions of the lifespan. *But personality traits do not:* The same five factors are found in all cultures studied so far (McCrae & Costa, 1997b); parent–child relations have little lasting effect on personality traits (Rowe, 1994; see also Fraley, 1998, on the precipitous drop in the continuity of attachment); and traits are generally stable across the adult lifespan (McCrae & Costa, 1990). These well-replicated empirical generalizations make sense only if personality traits are insulated from the direct effects of the environment. Human nature is proactive because personality traits are endogenous basic tendencies (McCrae, Costa, Ostendorf, et al., 1998).

Operation of the System

The welter of arrows in Figure 5.1 indicate some of the most important paths by which personality components interact. The plural *processes* is used because many quite distinct processes may be involved in each pathway. For example, the arrow from objective biography to self-concept implies that we learn who we are in part from observing what we do. But interpreting what we have done may involve social comparison, selective attention, defensive denial, implicit learning, or any number of other cognitive–affective processes. (Evolutionary psychologists such as Buss, 1991, have also emphasized that there are likely to be a very large number of evolved psychological mechanisms for specific problems in adaptation.)

One implication is that personality theories that posit a small handful of key dynamic processes (repression, learning, self-actualization, getting ahead and getting along) are unlikely to prove adequate. Another is that psychologists who prefer to study processes instead of traits—"doing" instead of "having" (Cantor, 1990)—face the challenging prospect of identifying the most important of these many processes to study. There is as yet nothing like an adequate taxonomy of processes, and although evolutionary theory points to certain adaptive functions for which mechanisms must presumably have evolved, the evolutionary significance of much of human behavior is not clear (Buss, Haselton, Shackelford, Bleske, & Wakefield, 1998). FFT acknowledges the issue of multiple dynamic processes and specifies important categories of processes that share a common function in the organization of the personality system. It does not, however, detail the specifics. A complete theory of personality will ultimately include subtheories that elaborate on such specific topics (cf. Mayer, 1998).

Table 5.2 lists the 16 postulates originally proposed to specify how the personality system operates (McCrae & Costa, 1996). They are intended to be empirically testable, and in fact most of them are based on a body of empirical literature. Although it may generate novel predictions, FFT was designed primarily to make understandable what was already known.

The most radical of these postulates is 1b, *Origin,* which flatly declares that traits are endogenous basic tendencies. This postulate is based chiefly on results from studies of behavior genetics, which consistently point to a large role played by genetic factors and little or no role for common environmental factors (Riemann, Angleitner, & Strelau, 1997). Future research may well force some modification of this postulate; culture (McCrae, Yik, Trapnell, Bond, & Paulhus, 1998) or birth order (Sulloway, 1996) may be shown to affect trait levels. But as stated, Postulate 1b parsimoniously summarizes most of what is now known and offers a clear alternative to most older theories of personality, which emphasize the importance of culture and early life experience in forming personality. Today, even clinicians have begun to recognize that the standard environmental theories of personality are inadequate (Bowman, 1997).

Postulates 1b and 1d recently inspired a novel twin study (Jang, McCrae, Angleitner, Riemann, & Livesley, 1998). FFT clearly implies that N, E, O, A, and C are heritable, a claim long since supported in the cases of N and E, and more recently with respect to O, A, and C (Loehlin, McCrae, Costa, & John, 1998; Riemann, Angleitner, & Strelau, 1997). But are the specific facet traits that define the five factors also specifically heritable; or are they better interpreted as characteristic adaptations, the environmentally molded forms in which the heritable factors are manifested? One could easily suppose that

TABLE 5.2. Five-Factor Theory Postulates

1. Basic tendencies

1a. *Individuality.* All adults can be characterized by their differential standing on a series of personality traits that influence patterns of thoughts, feelings, and actions.
1b. *Origin.* Personality traits are endogenous basic tendencies.
1c. *Development.* Traits develop through childhood and reach mature form in adulthood; thereafter they are stable in cognitively intact individuals.
1d. *Structure.* Traits are organized hierarchically from narrow and specific to broad and general dispositions; Neuroticism, Extraversion, Openness to Experience, Agreeableness, and Conscientiousness constitute the highest level of the hierarchy.

2. Characteristic adaptations

2a. *Adaptation.* Over time, individuals react to their environments by evolving patterns of thoughts, feelings, and behaviors that are consistent with their personality traits and earlier adaptations.
2b. *Maladjustment.* At any one time, adaptations may not be optimal with respect to cultural values or personal goals.
2c. *Plasticity.* Characteristic adaptations change over time in response to biological maturation, changes in the environment, or deliberate interventions.

3. Objective biography

3a. *Multiple determination.* Action and experience at any given moment are complex functions of all those characteristic adaptations that are evoked by the situation.
3b. *Life course.* Individuals have plans, schedules, and goals that allow action to be organized over long time intervals in ways that are consistent with their personality traits.

4. Self-concept

4a. *Self-schema.* Individuals maintain a cognitive–affective view of themselves that is accessible to consciousness.
4b. *Selective perception.* Information is selectively represented in the self-concept in ways that (i) are consistent with personality traits; and (ii) give a sense of coherence to the individual.

5. External influences

5a. *Interaction.* The social and physical environment interacts with personality dispositions to shape characteristic adaptations and with characteristic adaptations to regulate the flow of behavior.
5b. *Apperception.* Individuals attend to and construe the environment in ways that are consistent with their personality traits.
5c. *Reciprocity.* Individuals selectively influence the environment to which they respond.

6. Dynamic processes

6a. *Universal dynamics.* The ongoing functioning of the individual in creating adaptations and expressing them in thoughts, feelings, and behaviors is regulated in part by universal cognitive, affective, and volitional mechanisms.
6b. *Differential dynamics.* Some dynamic processes are differentially affected by basic tendencies of the individual, including personality traits.

Note. Adapted from McCrae and Costa (1996).

people inherit only a global tendency to be Open to Experience and become open to Aesthetics, or to Ideas, or to Values as a result of individual learning experiences. But behavior genetic analyses of specific facet scores (from which the variance accounted for by the five factors had been partialled) showed that in almost all cases, specific variance was significantly heritable. It appears that the genetic blueprint for personality includes detailed specifications of dozens, perhaps hundreds, of traits.

Postulate 1c is also ripe for minor revision. At the time it was proposed, there was little convincing evidence of systematic personality change after age 30. Newer analyses, especially cross-cultural analyses (McCrae, Costa, Lima, et al., 1999), suggest that cross-sectional decreases in N, E, and O and increases in A and C continue at a very modest pace throughout adulthood. Strikingly similar results from cross-cultural studies of adult age differences in personality do, however, strongly support the basic idea that change in the level of personality traits is part of an intrinsic, endogenous maturational process that belongs in the category of basic tendencies.

In our view, Postulate 1d, which asserts that the five factors form "the highest level of the hierarchy," is still tenable. Digman (1997) has proposed a yet-higher level with superfactors α and β—the former contrasting N with A and C, the latter combining E and O. Digman argued that these factors represent some of the broadest concepts traditionally found in personality theory: α is associated with socialization and communion, β with personal growth and agency. But an alternative explanation is that these superfactors represent only evaluative artifacts (Costa & McCrae, 1992a). That view is strengthened by the demonstration that evaluation occurs not on a single dimension of good to bad, but along two independent dimensions of positive and negative valence (Waller, 1999). Those two in turn are related to the five substantive factors in ways that could account for Digman's structure (McCrae & Costa, 1995a): α corresponds to the low pole of negative valence and β to positive valence. Eliminate the evaluative biases in personality assessment, and Postulate 1d stands. From this perspective, Digman's (1997) major contribution is in showing links at the evaluative level between substantive factors of personality and broad theoretical concepts: C and A, for example, are related to socialization not because they result from particular patterns of childrearing, but because they facilitate the goals of socialization, namely disciplined, prosocial behavior. C, A, and socialization have the same value.

Postulate 2a states the obvious claim that traits affect the way one adapts to the world. A recent example is found in analyses of the need for closure (Kruglanski & Webster, 1996). This tendency to "seize" the first credible answer and to "freeze" on one's initial decisions was shown to be strongly inversely related to Openness to Experience. It is easy to imagine the paths by which such habits of thought might develop:

> Lacking a need for change and uncertainty, closed people come to prefer a simple, structured, familiar world. Through experience they discover that tradition, conventionality, and stereotypes offer tried-and-true answers that they can adopt without much thought. They begin to think of themselves as conservative, down-to-earth people, and they seek out like-minded friends and spouses who will not challenge their beliefs. Thus, basic tendencies of closedness develop into preferences, ideologies, self-construals, and social roles; these characteristic adaptations habitualize, legitimatize, and socially support a way of thinking that expresses a high need for closure. (Costa & McCrae, 1998a, p. 117)

According to FFT, the personality system represented in Figure 5.1 is a universal of human nature. All people have basic tendencies, characteristic adaptations, and a self-concept, and they are related to biology and to society in the same basic ways. FFT adopts this system as a framework for explaining the operation of personality; it does not explain why the system exists. Various hypotheses might be offered, most probably based on Darwinian evolution (Buss, 1991); rudimentary forms of this system might be seen in animals (Gosling & John, in press). More formally, the FFT personality system includes the two features that characterize many dynamic systems: A distinctive core that is preserved, and mechanisms for adapting to a changing environment. Species that did not reproduce or adapt to their environments are now extinct; personality traits that did not endure over time and transcend situational influences would never have been recognized in lay lexicons or psychological theories.

INDIVIDUAL DIFFERENCES IN PERSONALITY

Consider as a thought experiment the possibility of a utopian community—call it Walden Three—based on the findings of trait psychology. Because individual differences can lead to misunderstanding and conflict (McCrae, 1996), its founders decide to people their society with clones from a single individual; to ensure happiness, they choose an adjusted extravert (Costa & McCrae, 1980). We will let medical ethicists and social philosophers debate the wisdom of this plan and turn our attention to the consequences for personality psychology.

In one respect nothing will have changed. The personality system is universal, and the denizens of Walden Three would still have needs, plans, skills, habits, relationships; they would still interact with the world in ways that external observers would recognize as reflecting their sociability and emotional stability—they would be happy people.

But personality psychologists who attempted to study them by the usual methods would reach startling conclusions. Except for error of measurement, everyone would score the same on every personality scale, and with no variance there could be no covariance. Traits would appear to have no longitudinal stability, no heritability, no five-factor structure. Indigenous psychologists might conclude that traits were a myth, and if asked, residents of Walden Three would probably attribute their behavior solely to situational causes ("Why did you go to that party?" "I was invited!").

What this thought experiment demonstrates is the curious relation of trait psychology to individual differences. On the one hand, it might be argued that personality psychology is not about individual differences; it is about how basic tendencies of a certain class affect thoughts, feelings, and actions. Employers seek conscientious employees not because they differ from lazy and careless employees, but because they work hard and well (Barrick & Mount, 1991). On the other hand, it is only the existence of individual differences in personality that reveals that hard work and carefulness are in part the result of heritable and enduring dispositions. Variation in personality traits across individuals is the ultimate natural experiment that illuminates the workings of personality.

Theoretical Approaches to Individual Differences

Postulate 1d of FFT states that "Traits are organized hierarchically from narrow and specific to broad and general dispositions; Neuroticism, Extraversion, Openness to Experience, Agreeableness, and Conscientiousness constitute the highest level of the hierarchy." This is the only postulate in which the FFM is even mentioned; otherwise the theory could just as well be adopted by proponents of a three- or seven- or *N*-factor model.

And Postulate 1d does not offer to explain the FFM, it merely asserts it. Shouldn't a five-factor theory explain why there are five factors and not six? And why these factors and not others? That would be an impressive feat, but it is not essential to scientific understanding. The speed of light is crucial to the theory of special relativity, but that theory gives no clue as to why $c \approx$ 300,000 km/sec.

Postulate 1d reflects the position of McCrae and John (1992), who explained the recurrent finding of five robust factors by saying, "we believe it is an empirical fact, like the fact that there are seven continents or eight American presidents from Virginia" (p. 194). McCrae and John were not trying to make a dogmatic pronouncement about the true number of factors (although the quote seems sometimes to have been interpreted that way; see, e.g., Block, 1995). Instead, they hoped to offer an alternative to the seductive but ultimately unpersuasive notion that the number somehow reflected the information-processing capacities of human raters (Goldberg, 1983; Miller, 1956). There is nothing magic about the number five; it is simply what the data seem to show.

Without further rationale, Postulate 1d is vulnerable to empirical falsification. The continent of Atlantis may rise again from the sea, and Virginian Pat Robertson may be elected president, and trait researchers may discover another factor or factors of personality of comparable scope to N, E, O, A, and C. At that point it will be time to modify FFT.

Although they could not explain the number 8, historians could certainly give some reasons why natives of Virginia were disproportionately chosen as U.S. presidents and could give very specific reasons for the selection of Washington, Jefferson, and Madison. Can personality psychologists explain why people differ in levels of N, E, O, A, or C?

Given that personality traits have a biological basis and that human beings are the products of evolution, it is natural to seek answers in evolutionary psychology. Buss (1996) made a strong case for the relevance of personality traits to social adaptation. People with different personality traits go about the tasks of survival and reproduction in different ways. For example, to retain their mates, extraverts show off, agreeable men express affection, and men low in C try to make their mates jealous. Personality traits influence the ability to make strategic alliances and to compete with others for resources. Personality, and specifically the five major factors, are of central relevance to the tasks people have evolved to solve. Because of this, people have learned to attend to individual differences in personality and to base their choices of leaders, friends, and mates in part on inferred personality characteristics.

This does not in itself explain the evolution of the FFM, however. Normally, natural and sexual selection are invoked to explain a specieswide characteristic, not variation within the species. If Extraversion is useful in forming the social bonds that lead to reproductive success, why haven't we all become extraverts?

One answer is that, relatively speaking, we all *are* extraverts—we all live in social groups (or did in the early stages of our development), all respond to human companionship (Baumeister & Leary, 1995), all are active and energetic enough to get through life. Similarly, we might argue that we have all evolved to be sufficiently open to experience to allow us to learn about our environments and sufficiently neurotic to make us respond to threats and losses. Variation within the normal range on these traits may have no real implications for survival, and they may persist solely because they are not selected out. In this case, evolution may explain the basic psychological mechanisms on which people vary but not the variation itself, which is mere noise from an evolutionary perspective.

A second possibility is that individual differences in personality reflect different but equally effective adaptational strategies. Agreeableness makes it easier to acquire allies, but antagonism sharpens one's ability to compete with enemies; open exploration leads to new resources, but closed conventionality exploits the tried-and-true. It is clearly to the advantage of social groups to have a variety of talents and dispositions at their disposal, and it may be to the advantage of individuals to occupy different niches in the social environment. (Sulloway, 1996, has recently used this "principle of divergence" in his theory of birth order differences in personality.) Useful diversity might have evolved if "adaptive optima for some strategies have fluctuated over time or place" (Buss, 1991, p. 475).

Such scenarios do not make a compelling case for the value of evolutionary explanations of personality traits. As Buss (1991) acknowledged, "general evolutionary theory broadly outlines what is *unlikely* to have evolved . . . [but] it can rarely specify what must have evolved" (p. 465). More focused predictions can be made for particular adaptive domains, such as social exchange and hierarchy formation. Unfortunately, it is often difficult to understand the adaptive function of personality traits. Evolutionary psychology has yielded valuable insights into sexual behavior, but its relevance to an understanding of aesthetic sensitivity is more dubious.

One complication in formulating evolutionary hypotheses is that we do not yet know to which evolutionary era they must be pegged. Buss (1991) sought to analyze personality by identifying "*adaptive problems confronted by ancestral human populations*" (p. 476; italics in original), but recent evidence (King & Figueredo, 1997) suggests that the FFM can also be glimpsed in chimpanzees. This suggests that precursors of these personality factors may have evolved in ancestors common to some or all primates. Indeed, for all we know, Extraversion evolved when fish first formed schools. Identifying the relevant adaptive problems may require much more data from comparative personality psychology.

Subtheories of the Five Factors

The postulates of FFT deal uniformly with all five factors, and thus must offer quite general propositions. It would be entirely possible to construct more specific subtheories to deal with each of the five factors separately. Conceptual analyses of the individual factors have been offered in several articles (Costa & McCrae, 1998b; Costa, McCrae, & Dembroski, 1989; McCrae & Costa, 1997a; Watson & Clark, 1997); formal theorizing could be guided by Figure 5.1. The agenda might be as follows:

1. Define the basic tendencies involved for the factor and its defining facet traits.
2. Identify specific biological bases, from genes to brain structures and functions.
3. Identify dynamic processes, like defenses, cognitive styles, or planning and scheduling, that are differentially affected by the factor (see Postulate 6b).
4. Catalog the characteristic adaptations—interests, roles, skills, self-image, psychiatric symptoms—associated with the factor and explain how they reflect common basic tendencies.
5. Account for the lifespan development of the factor, its objective reflection in the life course, and its subjective representation in life narratives.

Different parts of this agenda appeal to different psychologists. Factor analysts are concerned with identifying the facet traits and interpreting the resulting factors (Hofstee, Kiers, De Raad, Goldberg, & Ostendorf, 1997). Psychobiologists emphasize the identification of underlying biological mechanisms (Eysenck, 1967). Clinicians might be most concerned with problematic characteristic adaptations (see Postulate 2b), which they might be able to modify (Harkness & Lilienfeld, 1997).

Perhaps because they ground psychology in a more basic science, theories that offer biological explanations for traits seem particularly desirable, and we encourage research on which such theories could be based. In our present state of relative ignorance, however, theories of biological mechanisms may be premature. For example, Cloninger's neurohormonal theory of personality, which staked so much on the initial findings in the molecular genetics of personality (Cloninger, Adolfsson, & Svrakic, 1996), was surely shaken by subsequent failures to replicate (Malhotra et al., 1996; Vandenbergh, Zonderman, Wang, Uhl, & Costa, 1997).

Steps 1 through 3 of the above agenda are presumably universal to all human beings. Steps 4 and 5, however, deal with the interaction of the person and the environment and speak only to particular contexts. How Conscientiousness is expressed in Italy is likely to be very different from how it is expressed in Iran. Ethnographic methods might be needed to identify the culturally prescribed forms in which personality factors are manifested, and comparative cross-cultural studies could illuminate links between personality and culture (McCrae, 1998).

FIVE-FACTOR THEORY AND THE INDIVIDUAL

Although it is doubtless true that every person is in some respects like no other person (Kluckhohn & Murray, 1953), FFT (like most personality theories) has nothing to say about this aspect of the person. It is, from a scientific perspective, error variance. This most emphatically does not mean that personality is irrelevant to understanding the individual.

In the typical application in clinical or personnel psychology, the individual case is understood by inferring personality traits from one set of indicators and using the resulting personality profile to interpret a life history or predict future adjustment. This is not circular reasoning, because if valid personality measures are used, the traits identified carry surplus meaning that allows the interpreter to go beyond the information given (McCrae & Costa, 1995b). If respondents tell us that they are cheerful and high-spirited, we detect Extraversion and can guess with better-than-chance accuracy that they will be interested in managerial and sales positions. However, it would be much harder to predict their current occupation: Just as the theory of evolution is better at explaining how existing species function than it is at predicting which species will evolve, so personality profiles are more useful in understanding a life than in making specific predictions about what a person will do. This is not a limitation of FFT; it is an intrinsic feature of complex and chaotic systems.

Postulate 3a, *Multiple determination,* points out that there is rarely a one-to-one correspondence between characteristic adaptations and behaviors; the same is of course equally true for the traits that underlie characteristic adaptations. Consequently, interpreting individual behaviors even when the personality profile is well known is a somewhat speculative art. Consider the case of Horatio, Lord Nelson (Costa & McCrae, 1998b; Southey, 1813/1922). In the course of his campaigns against Napoleon's France, he spent many months defending the woefully corrupt court of Naples against a democratic insurrection that had been encouraged by the French. Why would so heroic a figure take on so shabby a task?

We know from a lifetime of instances that Nelson was a paragon of dutifulness, and we might suspect that he was simply following orders—certainly he would have rationalized his conduct as devotion to the war against France. But we also know that Nelson was fiercely independent in his views of what constituted his duty: "I always act as I feel right, without regard to custom" (Southey, 1813/1922, p. 94). He might equally well have supported the insurrection and won its allegiance to the English cause.

We should also consider another trait Nelson possessed: He was excessively low in modesty. Great as his naval achievements were, he never failed to remind people of them. His sympathies were thus with the aristocracy, and he was flattered by the court of Naples, which ultimately named him Duke Di Bronte.

Together, diligence (C), independence (O), and vanity (low A) go far to explain this episode of behavior.

To be sure, there are other factors, including Nelson's relationship to the English ambassador's wife, Lady Hamilton (Simpson, 1983). That notorious affair itself reflects Nelson's independence and vanity, but seems strikingly incongruent with his dutifulness. At the level of the individual, the operations of personality traits are complex and often inconsistent (a phenomenon Mischel and Shoda, 1995, have recently tried to explain).

The Subjective Experience of Personality

A number of writers (e.g., Hogan, 1996) have suggested that the FFM does not accurately represent personality as it is subjectively experienced by the individual. Daniel Levinson dismissed the whole enterprise of trait psychology as a concern for trivial and peripheral aspects of the person (Rubin, 1981). McAdams (1996) has referred to it as the "psychology of the stranger," because standing on the five factors is the sort of thing one would want to know about a stranger to whom one has just been introduced. Ozer (1996) claims that traits are personality as seen from the standpoint of the other, not the self.

We believe this last position represents a slight confusion. Individuals, who have access to private thoughts, feelings, and desires, and who generally have a more extensive knowledge of their own history of behavior, have a quite different perspective on their own traits than do external observers. What they nonetheless share with others is the need to infer the nature of their own traits and to express their inference in the comparative language of traits. We have no direct intuition of our trait profile; we can only guess at it from its manifestations in our actions and experience. (One possible reason for the increasing stability of personality as assessed by self-reports from age 20 to age 30—see Siegler et al., 1990—is that we continue to learn about ourselves in this time period.)

The fact that traits must be inferred does not, however, mean that they are or seem foreign. When adults were asked to give 20 different answers to the question "Who am I?," about a quarter of the responses were personality traits, and many others combined trait and role characteristics (e.g., "a loving mother"). Traits seem to form an important component of the spontaneous self-concept (McCrae & Costa, 1988); even children use trait terms to describe themselves (Donahue, 1994).

Sheldon, Ryan, Rawsthorne, and Ilardi (1997) brought a humanistic perspective to this issue by assessing sense of authenticity in individuals as they occupied different social roles. They also asked for context-specific self-reports of personality (e.g., how extraverted respondents were as students and as romantic partners). They found that individuals who described themselves most consistently across roles also claimed the highest feelings of authenticity. They concluded that "more often than not, one's true self and one's trait self are one and the same" (p. 1392).

CONCLUSION

Five-factor theory is an attempt to make sense of the explosion of findings that researchers have reported in the wake of the FFM. FFT is a contemporary version of trait theory, based on the assumptions that people are knowable, rational, variable, and proactive. FFT explains personality functioning as the operation of a universal personality system, with defined categories of variables and classes of dynamic processes that indicate the main causal pathways. The five personality factors—Neuroticism, Extraversion, Openness, Agreeableness, and Conscientiousness—form the substantive nucleus of the system; FFT traces their ramifications throughout the personality system. FFT provides a framework in which to understand the development and operation of psychological mechanisms (such as need for closure) and the behavior and experience of individual men and women.

FFT is a Grand Theory in the sense that it attempts to provide an overview of the functioning of the whole person across the complete lifespan. To do so it necessarily omits many specifics that a complete theory of personality would include. We have described in some detail the need for and possible form of subtheories of each of the individual factors. Also needed are subtheories that catalog the contents of characteristic adaptations and systematize dynamic processes, more formal treatment of the self-concept, theories of psychopathology and psychotherapy; theories of personality perception and assessment; and an account of the basic executive mechanism—the operating system—that coordinates the ongoing flow of behavior and experience. Much is already known about all these topics; the theorist's task is to organize the information and integrate it into the overall scheme of FFT.

Historically, personality psychology has been characterized by elaborate and ambitious theories with only the most tenuous links to empirical findings, and theorists have often been considered profound to the extent that their visions of human nature departed from common sense. Freud's glorification of the taboo, Jung's obscure mysticism, Skinner's denial of that most basic experience of having a mind—such esoteric ideas set personality theorists apart from normal human beings and suggested they were privy to secret knowledge. By contrast, FFT is closely tied to the empirical findings it summarizes, and its vision of human nature, at least at the phenotypic level, is not far removed from folk psychology. If that makes it a rather prosaic Grand Theory, so be it. What matters is how far it takes us in understanding that endlessly fascinating phenomenon, personality.

REFERENCES

Barrick, M. R., & Mount, M. K. (1991). The Big Five personality dimensions and job performance: A meta-analysis. *Personnel Psychology, 44,* 1–26.

Baumeister, R. F., & Leary, M. R. (1995). The need to belong: Desire for interpersonal attachments as a fundamental human motivation. *Psychological Bulletin, 117,* 497–529.

Block, J. (1995). A contrarian view of the five-factor approach to personality description. *Psychological Bulletin, 117,* 187–215.

Bowman, M. (1997). *Individual differences in posttraumatic response: Problems with the adversity–distress connection.* Mahwah, NJ: Erlbaum.

Bruehl, S. (1994). A case of borderline personality disorder. In P. T. Costa, Jr., & T. A. Widiger (Eds.), *Personality disorders and the five-factor model of personality* (pp. 189–197). Washington, DC: American Psychological Association.

Buss, D. M. (1991). Evolutionary personality psychology. *Annual Review of Psychology, 42,* 459–491.

Buss, D. M. (1996). Social adaptation and the five major factors of personality. In J. S. Wiggins (Ed.), *The five-factor model of personality: Theoretical perspectives* (pp. 180–207). New York: Guilford Press.

Buss, D. M., & Craik, K. H. (1983). The act frequency approach to personality. *Psychological Review, 90,* 105–126.

Buss, D. M., Haselton, M. G., Shackelford, T. K., Bleske, A. L., & Wakefield, J. C. (1998). Adaptations, exaptations, and spandrels. *American Psychologist, 53,* 533–548.

Cantor, N. (1990). From thought to behavior: "Having" and "doing" in the study of personality and cognition. *American Psychologist, 45,* 735–750.

Carlson, R. (1984). What's social about social psychology? Where's the person in personality research? *Journal of Personality and Social Psychology, 47,* 1304–1309.

Clark, L. A., & Livesley, W. J. (1994). Two approaches to identifying dimensions of personality disorder: Convergence on the five-factor model. In P. T. Costa Jr. & T. A. Widiger (Eds.), *Personality disorders and the five-factor model of personality* (pp. 261–278). Washington, DC: American Psychological Association.

Cloninger, C. R., Adolfsson, R., & Svrakic, N. M. (1996). Mapping genes for human personality. *Nature Genetics, 12,* 3–4.

Costa, P. T., Jr., & McCrae, R. R. (1980). Influence of extraversion and neuroticism on subjective well-being: Happy and unhappy people. *Journal of Personality and Social Psychology, 38,* 668–678.

Costa, P. T., Jr., & McCrae, R. R. (1988). From catalog to classification: Murray's needs and the five-factor model. *Journal of Personality and Social Psychology, 55,* 258–265.

Costa, P. T., Jr., & McCrae, R. R. (1992a). Reply to Eysenck. *Personality and Individual Differences, 13,* 861–865.

Costa, P. T., Jr., & McCrae, R. R. (1992b). *Revised NEO Personality Inventory (NEO-PI-R) and NEO Five-Factor Inventory (NEO-FFI) professional manual.* Odessa, FL: Psychological Assessment Resources.

Costa, P. T., Jr., & McCrae, R. R. (1992c). Trait psychology comes of age. In T. B. Sonderegger (Ed.), *Nebraska Symposium on Motivation: Psychology and aging* (pp. 169–204). Lincoln: University of Nebraska Press.

Costa, P. T., Jr., & McCrae, R. R. (1993). Bullish on personality psychology. *The Psychologist, 6,* 302–303.

Costa, P. T., Jr., & McCrae, R. R. (1994). "Set like plaster"? Evidence for the stability of adult personality. In T. Heatherton & J. Weinberger (Eds.), *Can personality change?* (pp. 21–40). Washington, DC: American Psychological Association.

Costa, P. T., & McCrae, R. R. (1998a). Trait theories of personality. In D. F. Barone, M. Hersen, & V. B. V. Hasselt (Eds.), *Advanced personality* (pp. 103–121). New York: Plenum Press.

Costa, P. T., Jr., & McCrae, R. R. (1998b). Six approaches to the explication of facet-level traits: Examples from conscientiousness. *European Journal of Personality, 12,* 117–134.

Costa, P. T., Jr., & McCrae, R. R. (in press). Theories of personality and psychopathology: Approaches derived from philosophy and psychology. In H. I. Kaplan & B. J. Saddock (Eds.), *Comprehensive textbook of psychiatry* (7th ed.). Baltimore: Williams & Wilkins.

Costa, P. T., Jr., McCrae, R. R., & Dembroski, T. M. (1989). Agreeableness vs. antagonism: Explication of a potential risk factor for CHD. In A. Siegman & T. M. Dembroski (Eds.), *In search of coronary-prone behavior: Beyond Type A* (pp. 41–63). Hillsdale, NJ: Lawrence Erlbaum.

Côté, S., & Moskowitz, D. S. (1998). On the dynamic covariation between interpersonal behavior and affect: Prediction from Neuroticism, Extraversion, and Agreeableness. *Journal of Personality and Social Psychology, 75,* 1032–1046.

Digman, J. M. (1997). Higher-order factors of the Big Five. *Journal of Personality and Social Psychology, 73,* 1246–1256.

Digman, J. M., & Inouye, J. (1986). Further specification of the five robust factors of personality. *Journal of Personality and Social Psychology, 50,* 116–123.

Donahue, E. M. (1994). Do children use the Big Five, too? Content and structural form in personality description. *Journal of Personality, 62,* 45–66.

Eysenck, H. J. (1967). *The biological basis of personality.* Springfield, IL: Charles C Thomas.

Eysenck, H. J. (1997). Personality and experimental psychology: The unification of psychology and the pos-

sibility of a paradigm. *Journal of Personality and Social Psychology, 73,* 1224–1237.
Fraley, R. C. (1998). *Attachment continuity from infancy to adulthood: Meta-analysis and dynamic modeling of developmental mechanisms.* Unpublished manuscript, University of California, Davis.
Funder, D. C. (1995). On the accuracy of personality judgment: A realistic approach. *Psychological Review, 102,* 652–670.
Funder, D. C., Kolar, D. C., & Blackman, M. C. (1995). Agreement among judges of personality: Interpersonal relations, similarity, and acquaintanceship. *Journal of Personality and Social Psychology, 69,* 656–672.
Goldberg, L. R. (1983, June). *The magical number five, plus or minus two: Some considerations on the dimensionality of personality descriptors.* Paper presented at a Research Seminar, Gerontology Research Center, Baltimore, MD.
Gosling, S. D., & John, O. P. (in press). Personality dimensions in non-human animals: A cross-species review. *Current Directions in Psychological Science.*
Harkness, A. R., & Lilienfeld, S. O. (1997). Individual differences science for treatment planning: Personality traits. *Psychological Assessment, 9,* 349–360.
Hjelle, L. A., & Siegler, D. J. (1976). *Personality: Theories, basic assumptions, research and applications.* New York: McGraw-Hill.
Hofstee, W. K. B., Kiers, H. A. L., De Raad, B., Goldberg, L. R., & Ostendorf, F. (1997). A comparison of Big Five structures of personality traits in Dutch, English, and German. *European Journal of Personality, 11,* 15–31.
Hogan, R. (1996). A socioanalytic perspective on the five-factor model. In J. S. Wiggins (Ed.), *The five-factor model of personality: Theoretical perspectives* (pp. 163–179). New York: Guilford Press.
Jang, K. L., McCrae, R. R., Angleitner, A., Riemann, R., & Livesley, W. J. (1998). Heritability of facet-level traits in a cross-cultural twin study: Support for a hierarchical model of personality. *Journal of Personality and Social Psychology, 74,* 1556–1565.
Johnson, J. A. (1997). Units of analysis for the description and explanation of personality. In R. Hogan, J. A. Johnson, & S. R. Briggs (Eds.), *Handbook of personality psychology* (pp. 73–93). New York: Academic Press.
King, J. E., & Figueredo, A. J. (1997). The five-factor model plus dominance in chimpanzee personality. *Journal of Research in Personality, 31,* 257–271.
Kluckhohn, C., & Murray, H. A. (1953). Personality formation: The determinants. In C. Kluckhohn, H. A. Murray, & D. M. Schneider (Eds.), *Personality in nature, society, and culture* (pp. 53–67. New York: Knopf.
Kruglanski, A. W., & Webster, D. M. (1996). Motivated closing of the mind: "Seizing" and "freezing." *Psychological Review, 103,* 263–283.
Lanning, K. (1994). Dimensionality of observer ratings on the California Adult Q-Set. *Journal of Personality and Social Psychology, 67,* 151–160.
Loehlin, J. C., McCrae, R. R., Costa, P. T., Jr., & John, O. P. (1998). Heritabilities of common and measure-specific components of the Big Five personality factors. *Journal of Research in Personality, 32,* 431–453.
Malhotra, A. K., Virkkunen, M., Rooney, W., Eggert, M., Linnoila, M., & Goldman, D. (1996). The association between the dopamine D4 receptor (D4DR) 16 amino acid repeat polymorphism and novelty seeking. *Molecular Psychiatry, 1,* 388–391.
Mayer, J. D. (1998). A systems framework for the field of personality. *Psychological Inquiry, 9,* 118–144.
McAdams, D. P. (1996). Personality, modernity, and the storied self: A contemporary framework for studying persons. *Psychological Inquiry, 7,* 295–321.
McCrae, R. R. (1992). The five-factor model: Issues and applications [Special issue]. *Journal of Personality, 60*(2).
McCrae, R. R. (1993–1994). Openness to Experience as a basic dimension of personality. *Imagination, Cognition and Personality, 13,* 39–55.
McCrae, R. R. (1996). Social consequences of experiential openness. *Psychological Bulletin, 120,* 323–337.
McCrae, R. R. (1998, August). Trait psychology and the revival of personality-and-culture studies. In P. T. Costa Jr. (Chair), *Personality traits and culture: New perspectives on some classic issues.* Symposium conducted at the Annual Convention of the American Psychological Association, San Francisco.
McCrae, R. R., & Costa, P. T., Jr. (1988). Age, personality, and the spontaneous self-concept. *Journal of Gerontology: Social Sciences, 43,* S177–S185.
McCrae, R. R., & Costa, P. T., Jr. (1989). Reinterpreting the Myers-Briggs Type Indicator from the perspective of the five-factor model of personality. *Journal of Personality, 57,* 17–40.
McCrae, R. R., & Costa, P. T., Jr. (1990). *Personality in adulthood.* New York: Guilford Press.
McCrae, R. R., & Costa, P. T., Jr. (1995a). Positive and negative valence within the five-factor model. *Journal of Research in Personality, 29,* 443–460.
McCrae, R. R., & Costa, P. T., Jr. (1995b). Trait explanations in personality psychology. *European Journal of Personality, 9,* 231–252.
McCrae, R. R., & Costa, P. T., Jr. (1996). Toward a new generation of personality theories: Theoretical contexts for the five-factor model. In J. S. Wiggins (Ed.), *The five-factor model of personality: Theoretical perspectives* (pp. 51–87). New York: Guilford Press.
McCrae, R. R., & Costa, P. T., Jr. (1997a). Conceptions and correlates of Openness to Experience. In R. Hogan, J. A. Johnson, & S. R. Briggs (Eds.), *Handbook of personality psychology* (pp. 269–290). Orlando, FL: Academic Press.
McCrae, R. R., & Costa, P. T., Jr. (1997b). Personality trait structure as a human universal. *American Psychologist, 52,* 509–516.
McCrae, R. R., Costa, P. T., Jr., del Pilar, G. H., Rolland, J. P., & Parker, W. D. (1998). Cross-cultural assessment of the five-factor model: The Revised NEO Personality Inventory. *Journal of Cross-Cultural Psychology, 29,* 171–188.

McCrae, R. R., Costa, P. T., Jr., Lima, M. P., Simões, A., Ostendorf, F., Angleitner, A., Marusic, I., Bratko, D., Caprara, G. V., Barbaranelli, C., Chae, J. H., & Piedmont, R. L. (1999). Age differences in personality across the adult lifespan: Parallels in five cultures. *Developmental Psychology, 35,* 466–477.

McCrae, R. R., Costa, P. T., Jr., Ostendorf, F., Angleitner, A., Hrebickova, M., Avia, M. D., Sanz, J., Sánchez-Bernardos, M. L., Kusdil, M. E., Woodfield, R., Saunders, P. R., & Smith, P. B. (1998). *Nature over Nurture: Temperament, Personality, and Lifespan Development.* Unpublished manuscript. Gerontology Research Center.

McCrae, R. R., Costa, P. T., Jr., & Piedmont, R. L. (1993). Folk concepts, natural language, and psychological constructs: The California Psychological Inventory and the five-factor model. *Journal of Personality, 61,* 1–26.

McCrae, R. R., & John, O. P. (1992). An introduction to the five-factor model and its applications. *Journal of Personality, 60,* 175–215.

McCrae, R. R., Yik, M. S. M., Trapnell, P. D., Bond, M. H., & Paulhus, D. L. (1998). Interpreting personality profiles across cultures: Bilingual, acculturation, and peer rating studies of Chinese undergraduates. *Journal of Personality and Social Psychology, 74,* 1041–1058.

Miller, G. E. (1956). The magical number seven, plus-or-minus two: Some limits on our capacity for processing information. *Psychological Review, 63,* 81–97.

Mischel, W., & Shoda, Y. (1995). A cognitive–affective system theory of personality: Reconceptualizing situations, dispositions, dynamics, and invariance in personality structure. *Psychological Review, 102,* 246–268.

Ozer, D. J. (1996). The units we should employ. *Psychological Inquiry, 7,* 360–363.

Riemann, R., Angleitner, A., & Strelau, J. (1997). Genetic and environmental influences on personality: A study of twins reared together using the self-and peer report NEO-FFI scales. *Journal of Personality, 65,* 449–475.

Robins, R. W., & John, O. P. (1997). Effects of visual perspective and narcissism on self-perceptions: Is seeing believing? *Psychological Science, 8,* 37–42.

Rowe, D. C. (1994). *The limits of family influence: Genes, experience, and behavior.* New York: Guilford Press.

Rubin, Z. (1981). Does personality really change after 20? *Psychology Today, 15,* 18–27.

Saucier, G. (1997). Effects of variable selection on the factor structure of person descriptors. *Journal of Personality and Social Psychology, 73,* 1296–1312.

Saucier, G., & Goldberg, L. R. (1996). The language of personality: Lexical perspectives on the five-factor model. In J. S. Wiggins (Ed.), *The five-factor model of personality: Theoretical perspectives* (pp. 21–50). New York: Guilford Press.

Sheldon, K. M., Ryan, R. M., Rawsthorne, L. J., & Ilardi, B. (1997). Trait self and true self: Cross-role variation in the Big-Five personality traits and its relations with psychological authenticity and subjective well-being. *Journal of Personality and Social Psychology, 73,* 1380–1393.

Siegler, I. C., Zonderman, A. B., Barefoot, J. C., Williams, R. B., Jr., Costa, P. T., Jr., & McCrae, R. R. (1990). Predicting personality in adulthood from college MMPI scores: Implications for follow-up studies in psychosomatic medicine. *Psychosomatic Medicine, 52,* 644–652.

Simpson, C. (1983). *Emma: The life of Lady Hamilton.* London: The Bodley Head.

Southey, R. (1922). *Life of Nelson.* New York: Dutton. (Original work published 1813)

Sulloway, F. J. (1996). *Born to rebel: Birth order, family dynamics, and creative lives.* New York: Pantheon Books.

Tupes, E. C., & Christal, R. E. (1992). Recurrent personality factors based on trait ratings. *Journal of Personality, 60,* 225–251. (Original work published 1961)

Vandenbergh, D. J., Zonderman, A. B., Wang, J., Uhl, G. R., & Costa, P. T., Jr. (1997). No association between Novelty Seeking and dopamine D4 receptor (D4DR) exon III seven repeat alleles in Baltimore Longitudinal Study of Aging participants. *Molecular Psychiatry, 2,* 417–419.

Waller, N. G. (1999). Evaluating the structure of personality. In C. R. Cloninger (Ed.), *Personality and psychopathology.* (pp. 155–197). Washington, DC: American Psychiatric Press.

Watson, D., & Clark, L. A. (1997). Extraversion and its positive emotional core. In R. Hogan, J. A. Johnson, & S. R. Briggs (Eds.), *Handbook of personality psychology* (pp. 767–793). New York: Academic Press.

Wiggins, J. S. (Ed.). (1996). *The five-factor model of personality: Theoretical perspectives.* New York: Guilford Press.

Wiggins, J. S. (1997). In defense of traits. In R. Hogan, J. A. Johnson, & S. R. Briggs (Eds.), *Handbook of personality psychology* (pp. 97–115). San Diego: Academic Press. (Original work presented 1973)

Wiggins, J. S., & Trapnell, P. D. (1996). A dyadic-interactional perspective on the five-factor model. In J. S. Wiggins (Ed.), *The five-factor model of personality: Theoretical perspectives* (pp. 88–162). New York: Guilford Press.

Yang, J., McCrae, R. R., & Costa, P. T., Jr. (1998). Adult age differences in personality traits in the United States and the People's Republic of China. *Journal of Gerontology: Psychological Sciences, 53B,* P375–P383.

Chapter 6
Social Cognitive Theory of Personality

Albert Bandura
Stanford University

Many psychological theories have been proposed over the years to explain human behavior. The view of human nature embodied in such theories and the causal processes they postulate have considerable import. What theorists believe people to be determines which aspects of human functioning they explore most thoroughly and which they leave unexamined. The conceptions of human nature in which psychological theories are rooted is more than a theoretical issue. As knowledge gained through inquiry is applied, the conceptions guiding the social practices have even vaster implications. They affect which human potentialities are cultivated, which are underdeveloped, and whether efforts at change are directed mainly at psychosocial, biological, or sociostructural factors. This chapter addresses the personal determinants and mechanisms of human functioning from the perspective of social cognitive theory (Bandura, 1986).

The recent years have witnessed a resurgence of interest in self-referent phenomena. Self processes have come to pervade diverse domains of psychology because most external influences affect human functioning through intermediary self processes rather than directly. The self system thus lies at the very heart of causal processes. To cite but a few examples, personal factors are very much involved in regulating attentional processes, schematic processing of experiences, memory representation and reconstruction, cognitively based motivation, emotion activation, psychobiologic functioning and the efficacy with which cognitive and behavioral competencies are executed in the transactions of everyday life.

AN AGENTIC VIEW OF PERSONALITY

In the agentic sociocognitive view, people are self-organizing, proactive, self-reflecting, and self-regulating, not just reactive organisms shaped and shepherded by external events. To be agentic is to be an intentional doer selecting, constructing, and regulating one's own activity to realize certain outcomes (Bandura, 1997). People have the power to influence their own actions to produce certain results. The capacity to exercise control over one's thought processes, motivation, affect, and action operates through mechanisms of personal agency. Human agency has been conceptualized in at least three different ways–as autonomous agency, mechanically reactive agency, or emergent interactive agency. The notion that humans operate as entirely independent agents has few serious advocates, although it is sometimes invoked in caricatures of cognitive theories of human behavior (Skinner, 1971). The tools for the exercise of agency are derived, in large part, from experiences, but what is created by their generative use is not reducible to those experiences. Human action, being socially situated, is the product of a dynamic interplay of personal and situational influences.

A second approach to the self system is to construe it as mechanically reactive agency. It is an internal system through which external influences operate mechanistically on action, but individuals exert no motivative, self-reflective, self-reactive, creative, or directive influence on the process. The self system is merely a repository for implanted structures and a conduit for external influences. The more dynamic models operating holistically include multilevel neural networks. However, a diverse mix of parallel distributed neural activity cannot remain fragmented. It requires an integrative system. Given the proactive nature of human functioning, such a system must have agentic capabilities as well as integrative reactive ones. Agentic functions get lodged in a hidden network operating without any consciousness. Consciousness is the very substance of phenomenal and functional mental life. It provides the information base for thinking about events, planning, constructing courses of action, and reflecting on the adequacy of one's thinking and actions. There is an important difference between *being conscious* of the experiences one is undergoing and *consciously producing* given experiences. For example, consciousness of one's heart rate and consciously, intentionally doing things known to elevate one's heart rate illustrate the difference between passive undergoing and agentic doing. The purposive accessing and deliberative processing of information to fashion efficacious courses of action represent the functional consciousness. Consciousness cannot be reduced to a nonfunctional epiphenomenon of the output of a mental process realized mechanically at nonconscious lower levels. In the connectionist line of theorizing, sensory organs deliver up information through their diverse pathways to the hidden network acting as the cognitive agent that does the construing, planning, motivating, and regulating. However, stripped of consciousness and agentic capability of decision and action, people are mere automatons undergoing actions devoid of any subjectivity, conscious regulation, phenomenological life, or personal identity.

As Green and Vervaeke (1996) note, originally connectionists regarded their conceptual models as approximations of cognitive activities. But more recently, many connectionists have become eliminative materialists, likening cognitive factors to the phlogiston of yesteryear. In their view, people do not act on beliefs, goals, aspirations, and expectations. Rather, activation of their network structure makes them do things. The phlogiston argument is sophistry. The phlogiston notion neither provided any evidential grounds for its existence nor had any explanatory or predictive value. In a critique of eliminativism, Greenwood (1992) notes that cognitions are contentful psychological factors that are logically independent of the explanatory propositions in which they figure. Cognitive factors do quite well in accounting for variance in human behavior and guiding successful interventions. To make their way successfully through a complex world, people have to make sound judgments about their capabilities, anticipate the probable effects of different events and actions, ascertain sociostructural opportunities and constraints, and regulate their behavior accordingly. These belief systems represent a working model of the world that enables people to achieve desired results and avoid untoward ones. Reflective and forethoughtful capabilities are, therefore, vital for survival and progress. Agentic factors that are explanatory, predictive, and of demonstrated functional value may be translatable, refinable, and modeled in another theoretical language but not eliminatable (Rottschaefer, 1985, 1991).

In social cognitive theory, people are agentic operators in their life course not just onlooking hosts of internal mechanisms orchestrated by environmental events. They are sentient agents of experiences rather than simply undergoers of experiences. The sensory, motor, and cerebral systems are tools people use to accomplish the tasks and goals that give meaning and direction to their lives (Bandura, 1997; Harré & Gillet, 1994). Agentic action shapes brain development and fosters brain cell growth subserving learning, memory, and other aspects of functioning throughout the life course (Diamond, 1988; Kolb & Whishaw, 1998). It is not just exposure to stimulation, but agentic action in exploring, manipulating, and influencing the environment that counts. By regulating their own motivation and the activities they pursue, people produce the experiences that form the neurobiological substrate of symbolic, social, psychomotor and other skills.

Social cognitive theory subscribes to a model of emergent interactive agency (Bandura, 1986, 1997). Persons are neither autonomous agents nor simply mechanical conveyers of animating environmental influences. Mental events are brain activities not immaterial entities existing apart from neural systems. However, materialism does not imply reductionism of psychology to biology. Knowing how the biological machinery works tells one little about how to orchestrate that machinery psychosocially for diverse purposes. For example, knowledge of the brain circuitry involved in learning says little about how best to devise conditions of learning in terms of levels of abstractness, novelty, and challenge; how to provide incentives to get people to attend to, process, and organize relevant information; in what modes to present information; and whether learning is better achieved independently, cooperatively, or competitively. The optimal conditions must be specified by psychological principles and are not derivable from neurophysiological theory because the latter does not contain the relevant psychosocial factors in its subject matter. To use an analogy, the agentic software is not reducible to the biological hardware. Each is governed by its own set of principles requiring explication in its own right.

In a nondualistic mentalism, thought processes are emergent brain activities that are not ontologically reducible (Sperry, 1993). Emergent properties differ qualitatively from their constituent elements. To use Bunge's (1977) analogy, the unique emergent properties of water such as fluidity, viscosity, and transparency are not simply the aggregate properties of its microcomponents of oxygen and hydrogen. Through their interactive effects they are transformed into new phenomena.

One must distinguish between the physical basis of thought and its functional properties. Cognitive processes are not only emergent brain activities; they also exert determinative influence. The human mind is generative, creative, proactive, and self-reflective—not just reactive. The dignified burial of the dualistic Descartes brings to the fore the more formidable explanatory challenge for a physicalistic theory of human agency. It must explain how people operate as thinkers of the thoughts that serve determinative functions. They construct thoughts about future courses of action to suit ever-changing situations, assess their likely functional value, organize and deploy strategically the selected options, and evaluate the adequacy of their thinking based on the effects their actions produce. In the theory enunciated by Sperry (1993), cognitive agents regulate their actions by cognitive downward causation as well as undergo upward activation by sensory stimulation. In the exercise of personal agency, people actuate the brain processes for realizing selected intentions. Theorists seeking explanations of human behavior at the neurophysiological level must address agentic activities such as forethought, intention, aspiration, proaction, creativity, self-appraisal, and self-reflection and their functional neural circuitry.

Triadic Reciprocal Causation

Human behavior has often been explained in terms of one-sided determinism. In such modes of unidirectional causation, behavior is depicted as being shaped and controlled by environmental influences or driven by internal dispositions. Social cognitive theory explains psychosocial functioning in terms of triadic reciprocal causation (Bandura, 1986). The term "causation" is used to mean functional dependence between events. In this model of reciprocal causality, internal personal factors in the form of cognitive, affective, and biological events; behavioral patterns; and environmental events all operate as interacting determinants that influence one another bidirectionally.

In triadic causation there is no fixed pattern for reciprocal interaction. Rather, the relative contribution of each of the constituent classes of influence depends on the activities, situational circumstances, and sociostructural constraints and opportunities. The environment is not a monolithic entity. Social cognitive theory distinguishes among three types of environmental structures (Bandura, 1997): the imposed environment, selected environment, and constructed environment. Gradations of environmental changeability require the exercise of increasing levels of personal agency. The imposed physical and sociostructural environment is thrust upon people whether they like it or not. Although they have little control over its presence, they have leeway in how they construe it and react to it.

There is a major difference between the potential environment and the environment people actually experience. For the most part, the environment is only a potentiality whose rewarding and punishing aspects do not come into being until the environment is selectively activated by appropriate courses of action. Which part of the potential environment becomes the actual experienced environment thus depends on how people behave. The choice of associates, activities, and milieus constitutes the selected environment. The environments that are created do not exist as a potentiality waiting to be selected and activated; rather, people construct social environments and institutional systems through their generative efforts. The construal, selection, and construction of environments affect the nature of the reciprocal interplay among personal, behavioral, and environmental factors.

Unidirectional causality emphasizing either dispositionalism or situationalism eventually gave way to reciprocal models of causation. Nowadays almost everyone is an interactionist. The major issues in contention center on the type of interactionism espoused. At least three different interactional models have been posed, two of which subscribe to one-way causation in the link to behavior. These alternative causal structures are represented schematically in Figure 6.1. In the unidirectional model, persons (P) and environments (E) are treated as independent influences that combine in unspecified ways to produce behavior (B). The major weakness with this causal model is that personal and environmental influences do not function as independent determinants. They affect each other. People create, alter, and destroy environments. The changes they produce in environmental conditions, in turn, affect them personally. The unidirectional causality with regard to behavior is another serious deficiency of this model of interactionism.

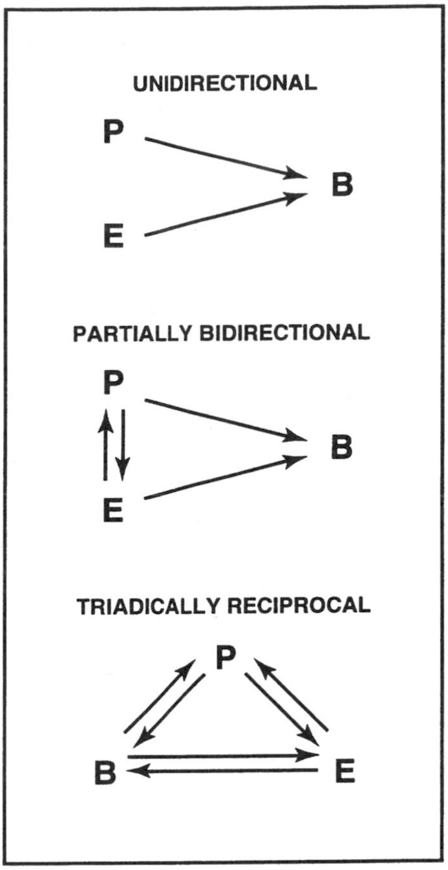

FIGURE 6.1. Schematization of the interplay of constituent determinants in alternative interactional causal models. B represents behavior; P, the internal personal factors in the form of cognitive, affective, and biological events; and E, the external environment.

The partially bidirectional conception of interaction, which is now widely adopted in personality theory, acknowledges that persons and environments affect each other. But this model treats influences relating to behavior as flowing in only one direction. The person-environment interchange undirectionally produces behavior, but the behavior itself does not affect the ongoing transaction between the person and the environment. A major limitation of this interactional causal model is that behavior is not procreated by an intimate interchange between a behaviorless person and the environment. Such a feat would be analogous to immaculate conception. Except through their social stimulus value, people cannot affect their environment other than through their actions. Their behavior plays a dominant role in how they influence situations, which in turn affect their thoughts, emotional reactions, and behavior. In short, behavior is an interacting determinant rather than a detached by-product of a behaviorless person–environment interchange.

As noted earlier, social cognitive theory conceptualizes the interactional causal structure as triadic reciprocal causation. It involves a dynamic interplay among personal determinants, behavior, and environmental influences. Efforts to verify every possible interactant simultaneously would produce experimental paralysis. However, because of the time lags in the operation of the triadic factors, one can gain understanding of how different segments of reciprocal causation function.

Different subspecialties of psychology center their inquiry on selected segments of triadic reciprocality. Cognitive psychologists examine the interactive relation between thought and action as their major sector of interest. This effort centers on the P→B segment of triadic causation. The programs of research clarify how conceptions, beliefs, self-percepts, aspirations, and intentions shape and direct behavior. What people think, believe, and feel affects how they behave. The natural and extrinsic effects of their actions (B→P), in turn, partly influence their thought patterns and affective reactions.

Social psychologists examine mainly the segment of reciprocality between the person and the environment in the triadic system (E→P). This line of inquiry adds to our understanding of how environmental influences in the form of social persuasion, modeling, and tuition alter cognitions and affective proclivities. The reciprocal element in the person–environment segment of causation (P→E) is of central interest to the subspecialty of person perception. People evoke different reactions from their social environment by their physical characteristics—such as their age, size, race, sex, and physical attractiveness—even before they say or do anything. They similarly activate different reactions depending on their socially conferred roles and status. The social reactions so elicited, in turn, affect the recipients' conceptions of themselves and others in ways that either strengthen or weaken the environmental bias.

Of all the different segments in the triadic causal structure, historically the reciprocal interplay between behavior and environmental events has received the greatest attention. Indeed, ethological, transactional, and behavioristic theories focus almost exclusively on this portion of reciprocity in the explanation of behavior. In the transactions of everyday life, behavior alters environmental conditions (B→E), and behavior is, in turn, altered by the very conditions it creates (E→B). The bidirectional relation between behavior and environment is not disembodied from thought, however. Consider coercive parent–child interactions. In discordant families, coercive actions by one member tend to elicit coercive counteractions from the partner in mutually escalating aggression (Patterson, 1976). But about half the time coercion does not produce coercive counteractions. To understand fully the interactive relation between behavior and social environment, the analysis must be extended temporally and broadened to include cognitive determinants operating in the triadic interlocking system. This requires tapping into what people are thinking as they perform actions and experience their effects. Counterresponses to antecedent acts are influenced not only by their immediate effects but also by people's judgments of eventual outcomes should they stick to that course of action. Thus, aggressive children although immediately punished, will continue or even escalate their coercive behavior when they expect persistence eventually to gain them what they seek (Bandura & Walters, 1959). But the same momentary punishment will serve as an inhibitor, rather than as an escalator, of coercion when the children expect that the continuance of the aversive conduct will be ineffective. Thus, in acting on their environment, people think about where their actions are likely to lead and what they eventually produce. Forethought partly governs the form the reciprocal interplay between behavior and environment takes.

Combining knowledge of the various subsystems of causality increases understanding of the superordinate causal system. Some progress has been made in clarifying how the triadic determinants operate together and how their patterning and relative strength change in the causal structure over time. These studies involve microanalyses of triadic reciprocal causation in which people manage a dynamic computerized environment (Bandura & Jourden, 1991; Bandura & Wood, 1989; Wood & Bandura, 1989). Each of the major interactants in the triadic causal structure—personal, behavioral, and environmental—functions as an important constituent in the transactional system. The personal determinant is indexed by self-beliefs of efficacy, cognized goals, quality of analytic thinking, and affective self-reactions. The options that are actually executed in the management of the organizational environment constitute the behavioral determinant. The properties of the organizational environment, the level of challenge it prescribes, and its responsiveness to behavioral interventions represent the environmental determinant. The constituent factors in the ongoing transactional system are measured repeatedly to verify the dynamics of the triadic causal system over time. The findings clarify the way in which the interlocked set of determinants operate as a whole and change in their relative contribution with experience.

Fortuitous Determinants in Causal Structures

There is an element of fortuity in people's lives. The role of fortuitous determinants in causal structures remains ever dormant in psychological theorizing even though it is often a critical factor in the paths lives take (Bandura, 1982b, 1998a). People are often brought together through a fortuitous constellation of events that set in motion reciprocal interplays of influences that shape the course of their lives. Indeed, some of the most important determinants of life paths often arise through the most trivial of circumstances. In these instances, seemingly minor events have important and enduring impact on the courses that lives take. Consider an example that illustrates prospectively the branching power of fortuitous events in the formation of a marital partnership. Some years ago I delivered a presidential address to the Western Psychological Association on the psychology of chance encounters and life paths (Bandura, 1982b). At the convention the following year an editor of one of the publishing houses explained that he had entered the lecture hall as it was rapidly filling up and seized an empty chair near the entrance. In the coming week he will be marrying the woman who happened to be seated next to him. With only a momentary change in time of entry, seating constellations would have altered and this intersect would not have occurred. A marital partnership was thus fortuitously formed at a talk devoted to fortuitous determinants of life paths! A flight delayed by an unexpected storm creates a fortuitous intersect by two people who found themselves seated next to each other at the airport that eventuates in a marriage, geographic relocation, and a shift in career trajectory, none of which would have occurred if the original flight had departed on time (Krantz, 1998).

A fortuitous event in socially mediated happenstances is defined as an unintended meeting of persons unfamiliar with each other. Although the separate chains of events in a chance encounter have their own causal determinants, their intersection occurs fortuitously rather than by design (Nagel, 1961). It is not that a fortuitous event is uncaused but, rather, there is a lot of randomness to the determining conditions of its intersections. The profusion of separate chains of events in everyday life provides numerous opportunities for such fortuitous intersects. People are often inaugurated into marital partnerships, occupational careers, or untoward life paths through fortuitous circumstances. A happenstance meeting launches a new life trajectory. Had the chance encounter not occurred, the participants lives would have taken quite different courses. The power of most fortuitous influences lies not in the properties of the events themselves but in the interactive processes they initiate. These branching processes are in accord with chaos theory, in which minor events set in motion cyclic processes that eventuate in major changes (Robertson & Combs, 1995).

Of the myriad fortuitous elements encountered in daily life, many of them touch people only lightly; others leave more lasting effects; and still others thrust people into new life trajectories. Psychological science cannot foretell the occurrence of fortuitous intersects except in a very general way. Personal proclivities, the social circles in which one moves, and the kinds of people who populate those settings make some types of intersects more probable than others. However, social cognitive theory provides a conceptual scheme for predicting the nature, scope, and strength of the impact that chance encounters will have on human lives based on the reciprocal interplay of personal attributes and the characteristics of the social milieus into which one is inaugurated (Bandura, 1982b).

The personal determinants of the impact of fortuitous encounters operate by converting chance meetings into ongoing relationships. People's attributes, interests, and skills will affect whether they can gain sufficient social acceptance and satisfaction to sustain involvement with those they happened to encounter. Emotional ties also play an influential role. Interpersonal attraction seals chance encounters into lasting bonds. Values and personal standards similarly come into play. Fortuitous meetings are more apt to last if the persons involved have similar value commitments and evaluative standards than if they clash.

The social determinants of the impact of fortuitous encounters concern the holding and shaping power of the milieus into which people are fortuitously inaugurated. Individuals become attached to groups that provide valued benefits and rewards but forsake those that have little to offer. Fortuitous induction into a group also provides a new symbolic environment designed to foster affinity, solidarity, and shape ideological perspectives on life. The belief system of milieus and their reach and degree of closedness operate as other formative environmental factors. Chance encounters have the greatest potential for abruptly branching people into new trajectories of life when they induct them into a relatively closed milieu (Bromley & Shupe, 1979; Winfrey, 1979). A totalistic environment supplies a pervading new reality—new kinships, strongly held group beliefs and values, all-encompassing codes of conduct, and substantial rewarding and coercive power to alter the entire course of personal lives.

People can make chance happen by pursuing an active life that increases the number of fortuitous encounters they are likely to experience. Indeed, Austin (1978) highlights the role of action in chance occurrences. In the proactive sociocognitive view, chance favors the inquisitive, venturesome, and persistent. By selecting advantageous activities and milieus, people can make chance occurrences work for them.

Social scientists underplay fortuitous determinants in their theoretical schemes, but such factors figure significantly in their prescriptions for personal development (Bandura, 1995, 1997; Hamburg, 1992; Masten, Best, & Garmezy, 1990; Rutter, 1990). On the utilization side, the proactive efforts center on cultivating personal attributes that enable people to make the most of opportunities that arise unexpectedly from time to time. Pasteur put it well when he noted, "Chance favors only the prepared mind." On the nullifying side, people are equipped with self-protective capabilities that enable them to resist social traps leading down detrimental paths and to extricate themselves from such predicaments should they become enmeshed in them. At the societal level, they create social systems that provide opportunity structures for beneficial fortuities and institute safeguards that set limits on coercive control in detrimental fortuities. Mastering the tools of personal agency does not necessarily assure a desired future—but these types of personal and institutional measures give people a greater hand in shaping their own destinies.

Personal Determinants versus Individual Differences

The field of personality has traditionally relied heavily on all-purpose measures of personal attributes in efforts to explain how personal factors contribute to psychosocial functioning. In this "one size fits all" approach, the items are decontextualized by deleting information about the situations with which people are dealing. For example, they are asked to judge their aggressiveness in an environmental void without reference to the form of aggression, who the protagonists are, their power status, the type and level of provocation, the social setting, and other conditional circumstances that can strongly influence behavioral outcomes that affect one's proneness to act aggressively. The more general the items, the more respondents have to try to guess what the unspecified situational particulars might be. The predictiveness of indefinite global measures will depend on the extent to which the visualized activities and contextual factors on which the mental averaging is performed happen to overlap with those being studied.

The everyday realities that people must manage are structured and operate conditionally. Thus, for example, behaving assertively with indifferent store clerks will bring more attentive service, whereas confrontive assertiveness toward police officers will get one roughed up or arrested. As a consequence, people will behave assertively with clerks but compliantly with police. A shapeless overall rating is ill-equipped to explain and predict the variation in assertiveness under these different circumstances. Given the highly conditional nature of human functioning, it is unrealistic to expect personality measures cast in nonconditional generalities to shed much light on the contribution of personal factors to psychosocial functioning in different task domains under diverse circumstances across all situations. Indeed, personality measures that capture the contextualized and multifaceted nature of personal causation within an agentic model have greater explanatory and predictive power and provide more effective guides for personal change than do global trait measures (Bandura, 1997). The convenience of all-purpose global tests of personal determinants is gained at the cost of explanatory and predictive power.

A major movement in psychology is away from global structures to more domain-linked knowledge structures, self-conceptions, and competencies. Even in the field of cognitive development, the bulwark of global structuralism (Piaget, 1950) is being abandoned for more specialized cognitive competencies (Feldman, 1980; Flavell, 1978). It is ironic that, at a time when other subfields of psychology are becoming contextualized and discarding global personal structures for more particularized ones, much of the field of personality is seeking the personal causes of human behavior in omnibus conglomerate traits severed from the social realities of everyday life.

The multifaceted dynamic nature of personal causation raises the broader issue of how personal determinants are conceptualized and measured. The influence of personal factors on human functioning is often insufficiently recognized because the issue tends to be construed in static terms of individual differences rather than personal determination of action. The issue of major interest for the science of personality is not how differences between individuals on a behavioral continuum correlate with behavior, but rather how personal factors operate in causal structures in producing and regulating behavior under the highly contingent conditions of everyday life. Consider a situation in which a personal factor is essential for certain types of performances but is developed to the same high level in different individuals. The difference among individuals is negligible and would, therefore, not correlate with performance because of constricted variability. However, the personal competence is, in fact, vital for successful performance. For example, all librarians know how to read well and do not differ in this respect, but possessing the ability to read is indispensable for performing the librarianship role.

Low correlations between "individual differences" in a personal determinant and performance resulting from curtailed variability are often misinterpreted as evidence that personal factors exert little causal impact. Personal determinants operate as multifaceted dynamic factors in causal structures rather than as static entities that people possess in differing amounts. These alternative perspectives on personal causation reflect more than differences in semantic labeling. The individual differences approach is rooted in trait theory, whereas the personal determinants approach is founded on an agentic model of functional relations between dynamic personal factors that govern the quality of human adaptation and change.

Social cognitive theory does not cede the construct of "disposition" to trait theory. Dynamic dispositions must be distinguished from static trait dispositions. For example, individuals who have a resilient sense of efficacy in a given domain are disposed to behave differently in that realm of activity from those who are beset by self-doubt. Efficacy beliefs are patterned differently across individuals and spheres of activity. The issue in contention is not whether people have personal dispositions but how they are conceptualized and operationalized. In social cognitive theory, an efficacious personality disposition is a dynamic, multifaceted belief system that varies across different activity domains and under different situational demands rather than being a decontextualized conglomerate. The patterned individuality of efficacy beliefs represents the unique dispositional makeup of efficaciousness for any given person. In social cognitive theory, dispositions are personal factors such as self-beliefs, aspirations, and outcome expectations that regulate behavior rather then descriptors of habitual behavior.

DISCARDING DUALISTIC CONCEPTIONS OF PERSONALITY

Theorizing in personality often contains a variety of dualities that social cognitive theory rejects. It will be recalled from the earlier discussion that the theory casts off mind–body dualism. Mental events are brain activities rather than immaterial entities that exist apart from brain processes. There are other forms, the dualistic conceptions of which are discussed briefly in the sections that follow.

Duality of Self as Agent and Object

One common dichotomy separates self into agent and object. People are said to be agents when they act on the environment but objects when they reflect and act on themselves. Social cognitive theory questions such a dualistic view of self. Proaction does not operate isolatedly from self-reaction. The dual functions of the self typically operate interactively. In their daily transactions, people formulate courses of action, anticipate their likely effects, and act on their judgments. While acting on their environment, they are also evaluating and reacting to themselves. They monitor and analyze how well their thinking and corresponding actions have served them and change their strategies accordingly. One is just as much an agent in monitoring and reflecting on one's experiences and exerting self-influence as in acting on the environment. It is simply a shift in perspective of the same agent between self and environment. Even when individuals are the object of external influence, they are not just passive recipients of stimulus inputs.

They act agentically on that influence in cognitive, affective, and behavioral ways that enhance, neutralize, or subvert it. Rather than splitting the self into object and agent, social cognitive theory treats this static dichotomy as a dynamic system of interlocking functions.

Social cognitive theory also rejects the fractionation of human agency into multiple selves. A theory of personality cast in terms of multiple selves plunges one into deep philosophical waters. It requires a regress of selves to a presiding overseer self that selects and manages the collection of selves to suit given purposes. Actually, there is only one self that can visualize different futures and select courses of action designed to attain desired futures and avoid aversive ones. Actions are regulated by a person not by a cluster of selves doing the choosing and guiding.

The fractionation of agency into different types of selves poses additional conceptual problems. Once one starts fractionating the self, where does one stop? For example, an athletic self can be split into an envisioned tennis self and a golfing self. These separable selves would, in turn, have their subselves. Thus, a golfing self can be subdivided into different facets of the athletic ability to include a driving self, a fairway self, a sand-trapped self, and a putting self. How does one decide where to stop fractionating selves? Here, too, there is only one self that can strive to perfect different sets of competencies required for an envisioned pursuit. Diversity of action arises not from a collection of agentive selves but from the different options considered by the one and the same agentive self. It is the person who is doing the thinking, regulating, and reflecting, not a homunculus, overseeing self.

People striving to realize an envisioned future guide and motivate their efforts through a set of self-regulatory mechanisms. These are governed by appraisal of personal capabilities for different pursuits, long-range aspiration merged with working proximal subgoals that lead to its fulfillment, positive and negative outcome expectations for different life courses, the value placed on those envisioned outcomes, and the perceived environmental constraints and opportunity structures. These represent some of the influential sociocognitive determinants of the courses that lives take. One and the same person exercises these self-influences differentially for different purposes, in different activity domains, and in different social contexts.

Duality of Structure and Process of the Self System

The affinity to global dispositional constructs has also fostered a disjoined duality of process and structure that pervades the field of personality. This dualistic view is also reflected in the dichotomization of personality theories as embodying structuralism or functionalism. Theories that specify how human agency is exercised are often mistakenly depicted solely as process theories. Trait approaches are said to be structural theories. Social cognitive theory rejects this false separateness of structural and process theories. Regulatory processes operate through guiding self structures rather than disembodied from them. Self structures do not emerge autonomously and give rise to behavior divorced from any operational processes. Developed self structures are translated into actions through regulatory functions. The experiences produced by regulatory processes operating on the environment, in turn, shape self structures. In short, both the structure of a self system and the regulatory processes must work together in human functioning.

To illustrate the interdependence of structure and process consider the self-regulation of moral conduct. Social cognitive theory provides a detailed account of how moral standards are constructed through cognitive processing of diverse sources of information conveyed by modeled moral commitments, direct instruction in moral precepts, and the evaluative reactions of others to conduct that has ethical and moral significance (Bandura, 1991b). The nature and pattern of the acquired moral standards represent an enduring cognitive structure for judging the moral status of conduct in situations containing many morally relevant decisional ingredients. One does not have a full set of moral standards on Monday, none on Tuesday, and a new set on Wednesday. The standards of conduct are enduring unless they happen to be altered by powerful experiences. Moral structure is translated into action via self-regulatory mechanisms operating through a set of agentive subfunctions. These include self-monitoring of conduct; judging the conduct in relation to one's moral standards and the circumstances under which it occurs; and applying evaluative self-sanctions depending on whether the conduct measures up to or violates the internal standards. In short, processes do not operate in a vacuum without structural properties that provide the substance and direction for those processes. People do not run around mindlessly engaging in structure-free processing of experiences.

A social cognitive theory combining moral rule structures and self-regulative processes operating through them is no less a structural theory of personality than, for example, the psychoanalytic approach in which a superego is posited as a structural feature of personality that controls conduct. The major differences between these two theories are in globality of constructs, explicitness of acquisitional and regulative mechanisms, and explanatory and predictive power, not in whether one theory postulates a structure and the other does not (Bandura, 1973, 1991b).

Moral rule structures do not operate as invariant internal regulators of conduct. Self-regulatory mechanisms do not operate unless they are activated, and there are many processes by which self-sanctions can be disengaged from internal standards to perpetrate inhumane conduct (Bandura, 1986, 1991b). Selective activation and disengagement of internal control thus permits different types of conduct with the same moral standards. Many inhumanities are perpetrated by people who, in other aspects of their lives and other circumstances, behave in considerate, compassionate ways (Bandura, 1991b; Kelman & Hamilton, 1989; Reich, 1990; Sanford & Comstock, 1971). Consideration of the conjoint operation of moral rule structures, self-regulatory mechanisms, and contextual influences helps to explain this seeming paradox where more global structures alone do not (Gillespie, 1971). We shall return to the issue of selective self-regulation later.

The nature and regulative function of self-conceptions provides a further illustration in which relinquishment of global measures is sometimes misconstrued as abandonment of structure. Self-appraisal has traditionally been conceptualized in personality theory in terms of the self-concept (Rogers, 1959; Wylie, 1974). Such self theories are concerned, for the most part, with global self-images. A global self-conception does not do justice to the multifaceted structure of self-belief systems. They can vary substantially across different life domains and operate dynamically in concert with other psychosocial determinants. Thus, people's self-conceptions as parents may differ from their occupational self-conception and, even in the occupational realm, their self-conceptions are likely to differ for different facets of occupational competency. Composite self-images are not equal to the task of predicting with any degree of accuracy such intraindividual variability. Social cognitive theory approaches the structure of self-belief systems in more refined, domain-linked ways that have greater explanatory and predictive power (Bandura, 1986, 1997; Pajares & Kranzler, 1995; Pajares & Miller, 1994, 1995).

A multifaceted approach does not mean that there is no structure or generality to human functioning. Given that no two situations are ever identical, life would be unbearably burdensome if one had to figure out anew how to behave in every situation one encounters. Conversely, life would be exceedingly costly and perilous if people remained blissfully inattentive to situational factors signifying appropriate courses of action and indifferent to the personal and social effects of what they do. In short, neither isolated specificity nor obtuse indiscriminativeness is adaptive (Bandura, 1986, 1997).

Trait theorists framed the issue of human adaptiveness in terms of "consistency" with misleading connotations that perpetuated the search for behavioral fixedness. Consistency not only implies virtues of steadfastness and principled conduct, but it sets up the contrast as "inconsistency," implying instability or expediency. In fact, action devoid of discriminative forethought would produce disastrous results. Nevertheless, the inverted value implications diverted attention from analyses of the dynamic nature of human adaptation to an elusive search for how to extract consistency from variability and efforts to explain how the same global disposition can spawn highly variable conduct (Bandura, 1986).

Much ink has been spilt in fruitless debates about whether behavior is characterized by uniformity or specificity. In fact, as already noted, adaptive functioning requires both generalization and differentiation of action. Therefore, social cognitive theory addresses the determinants and mechanisms governing both generality and specificity of action rather than championing only variability. Whether people behave uniformly or variably depends heavily upon the functional equivalence of the environments. Thus, if acting intelligently in diverse settings has functional value, people will be consistently intelligent in situations that otherwise differ markedly. By contrast, if directives to subordinates improve performance but giving commands to bosses brings rebukes, people will behave authoritatively with subordinates but diplomatically with bosses. Nor is consistency across expressive modalities a blessing. If people acted on every thought that entered their minds, or if their affect ruled every action, they would get themselves into very serious trouble. Here, too, they have to regulate their actions and affective expressions discriminatively. In their conditional conception of dispositions, Mischel and Shoda (1995) document that individuals exhibit stable but discriminative patterns of social behavior. These behavioral signatures of personality are functionally related to conditional influences that facilitate or deter certain styles of behavior. The particular organization of conditional relations characterizes the uniqueness and coherence of personality for any given individual.

Behavior patterns are not necessarily locked in temporally either. Otherwise, people would not alter their behavior over the course of their development to suit their age and the changing demands of life. Changes over the life course take diverse forms across spheres of functioning rather than follow a consistent, unidirectional course (Baltes, Lindenberger, & Staudinger, 1998; Bandura, 1982b). Whether social behavior is invariant or changes over time depends partly on the degree of continuity of environmental conditions over the time span that affect the functional value of different forms of behavior. However, environments are diverse rather than monolithic. In the agentic constructivist perspective of social cognitive theory, people have a hand in promoting continuities in their life. They do so by selecting environments compatible with their values, attributes, and aspirations and by constructing social environments through their actions (Bandura, 1986, 1997; Snyder, 1981). For example, we are all acquainted with problem-prone individuals who, by their aversive conduct, breed negative social milieus wherever they go. In contrast, those skilled in bringing out the best in others create beneficial social milieus. Through selection and construction of environments, personality patterns can become self-perpetuating.

Protracted disputes continue to be fought under the banners of the idiographic view that people behave idiosyncratically as though they have no processes in common, or the nomothetic view that people's behavior follows general principles that allegedly grant no individuality. These disputes often fail to distinguish between what one thinks, feels, values, and can do from the basic mechanisms by which these personal proclivities are developed and regulated. People obviously differ in their makeup because they come with different biological endowments and experience different admixtures of influences. But cultures provide numerous common direct and modeling influences that create many similar proclivities. An ideographic psychology solely of uniqueness would be a feeble scientific enterprise devoid of generalizability and operative utility. With regard to mechanisms, all people learn through modeling and the effects of their actions. Indeed, in many cultures the word for "teach" is the same as the word for "show" (Reichard, 1938). People regulate their motivation and actions anticipatorily by judgments of their capabilities, goal aspirations, outcome expectations, and perceived environmental opportunity structures and impediments (Bandura, 1986, 1997). Thus, there is diversity in sociostructural arrangements and the forms that lives take in different social milieus, but there is universality in the basic acquisitional and regulative mechanisms.

Continuity has meaning when applied to distinct styles of behavior, but it takes on considerable indefiniteness when judged in terms of broad categories of adaptation. One can always find linkages between early and later endeavors as, for example, between pursuit of scholarship in childhood and professional careers in adulthood. However, at this level of generality, continuity can be achieved through a variety of life paths. Personal lives, whether marked by continuities or discontinuities have their particular characters. The rapid pace of social and technological changes increasingly requires new forms of adaptation throughout the life course (Bandura, 1997). Broad adaptational categories mask personal changes over time. As in the explanation of both generality and specificity of behavior across contextual variations, a comprehensive theory must also explain both temporal continuities and change.

The dualistic thinking is also reflected in suggestions that the processes of sociocognitive theories be combined with trait theory, such as in the five-factor taxonomy, to form the comprehensive theory of personality. According to trait structuralists, factor analyses of everyday descriptors of behavior culled from dictionaries and personality questionnaires will yield the supertraits that constitute the basic structure of personality. Some of the trait theorists rallied with missionary zeal around the "Big Five" global supertraits of Extraversion, Agreeableness,

Conscientiousness, Neuroticism, and Openness to Experience as the universal features of personality structure. McCrae and Costa (1996), the leading proponents of this approach, relied on the computer to find the supertraits in the mixture of common descriptors, and on bootstrapping to fill them out with additional variants of the descriptors. They dismiss conceptually guided approaches to personality as "armchair theories," as though theoretical propositions are never subjected to empirical verification or translated into social applications. The epistemological issue in that metaphorical armchair, which incidentally has served other scientific disciplines remarkably well, centers on whether personologists or machines do the conceptualizing. The essentially atheoretical strategy of research, the shrinking of personal characteristics to a few global traits, the empirical status of the extracted traits, and the exaggerated claims of consensuality regarding the fivefold taxonomy drew sharp critiques (Block, 1995; Carlson, 1992; Endler & Parker, 1992; Eysenck, 1991; Kroger & Wood, 1993; McAdams, 1992). Although the fivefold clustering is presented as a "model," a descriptive classification of habitual behavior is not a conceptual model, which must specify a system of postulates governing the phenomenon of interest.

Seeking the structure of personality by factor analyzing a limited collection of behavioral descriptors essentially reduces to a psychometric method in search of a theory. In an earlier expedition in the unabridged dictionary, Gordon Allport came up with thousands of trait descriptors. This vast collection required severe pruning to reduce them to a small, manageable lot. The products of factor analysis are predetermined by what one puts into it. The prepruning and the methods of factor extraction used largely preordain the clusters that will be found. Adding a few more classes of trait descriptors yields more supertraits (Almagor, Tellegen, & Waller, 1995). An even more inclusive collection of descriptors with built-in assemblages of redundancies would probably yield still more clusters. Moreover, sets of descriptors of sociocognitive belief systems and other self-regulatory factors that constitute the personality structures governing human behavior would produce factors quite different than descriptors of habitual behaviors.

Not surprisingly, there are disputes among trait theorists about how many supertraits there are. Proponents of the fivefold taxonomy assert that there are five supertraits (McCrae & Costa, 1997), but others contend that there are two (Digman, 1997), or three (Eysenck, 1991), or six (Jackson, Ashton, & Tomes, 1996), or seven (Tellegen & Waller, 1987), and still others find even more basic traits (Barrett & Kline, 1982). Variations in the claimed size of the trait collection have fueled semantic debates about what constitutes a trait, how broad it should be, and whether traits should be analyzed as untiered groupings or as tiered groupings with cardinal traits subsuming secondary ones (Guastello, 1993). This controversy is reminiscent of the debates of yesteryear about the correct number of instincts or cardinal motives.

Trait theorists disagree not only over how many supertraits there are but what factors belong in them and what they should be called (Block, 1995). To add further to classificatory fuzziness, some of the trait descriptors show up in more than one trait cluster, creating significant intertrait correlations. The traits are measured by either single-word descriptors or brief phrases stripped of any contextual conditions. Actions severed from context depict a socially disembodied reclusive personality. We know that the same behavior can mean different things in different contexts. For example, the item "prefer to do things alone" is a rejective behavior in a marital relationship but self-sufficiency in a physical fitness routine. Killing is a heroic act deserving commendation on the battlefield but a homicidal act demanding imprisonment in civilian life. The behavioral descriptors that form the trait terms may, therefore, shift from one cluster to another depending on the contexts in which the behavior is performed and the purposes it is designed to serve.

The Big-Five adherents spend much time comparing lists of descriptors used by different trait theorists, seeking analogues of the competitors' supertraits to the fivefold clusters, and explaining misfitting ones and how they might be subsumed under the five clusters. Formal goodness-of-fit tests, however, reveal a poor fit of the empirical data to five distinct personality features (Parker, Bagby, & Summerfeldt, 1993). The substantial intercorrelations among some of the supertraits refute their distinctiveness. McCrae and his colleagues argue that the fivefold taxonomy is correct, but the statistical methods are at fault (McCrae, Zonderman, Costa, Bond, & Paunonen, 1996). The view that the supertraits are distinct yet have overlapping defining traits does not provide an adequately specified conceptual model required for definitive tests of goodness of fit. The discounting and refitting of discordant findings convey the impression that the fivefold taxonomy has become the procrustean bed of trait theorizing. Some personologists suggest that trait theorists should seek better representation of the diversity of personal characteristics by adding clusters of theoretically distinct items rather than reiterating a fivefold clustering within a stripped-down assemblage of items (Jackson, Paunonen, Fraboni, & Goffin, 1996).

Development of a comprehensive theory of personality requires an integrated conceptual scheme that not only classifies behaviors but specifies their determinants and the key mechanisms through which they operate and the modes by which desired ones can be fostered and undesired ones altered. Theory guides the development of appropriate measures, specifies the conditions for empirical verification of its core propositions, and informs effective psychosocial programs of change.

The so-called supertraits are essentially clusters of habitual behaviors. People are asked to rate whether they are courteous, methodical, curious, fearful, get into arguments, and the like. It comes as no surprise, for example, that a collection of behaviors that resemble one another, such as being organized, dutiful, disciplined, and effortful form a behavioral cluster dubbed "conscientiousness." Some of the clusters cohere better than others depending on the degree of redundancy of behavioral descriptors representing them. However, descriptive behavioral clusters tell us little about the determinants and regulative structures governing the behaviors that make up a particular cluster.

In trait analyses, the behavioral descriptors tend to get reified as causes of behavior. Consider conscientiousness as an example. In measuring this factor, individuals rate things such as whether they "are a productive person who always get the job done," "work hard to accomplish my goals," and "perform the tasks assigned to me conscientiously." Conscientious behavior is said to affect how well people perform on a job. One can, of course, use past conscientious performance as a predictor of future conscientious job performance. But conscientious behavior is neither a personality structure nor a cause of itself.

The proponents of taxonomies founded on behavioral descriptors locate the personality structure in the wrong place. As shown in Figure 6.1, the determinative personality structures are in the self system, not in the behavioral expressions. To continue with the above example, the personal determinants of job performance include, among other things, people's knowledge structures, their skills, self-beliefs of efficacy to manage given activities and environmental demands, and self-regulatory capabilities operating though goals and outcome expectancies rooted in a value structure (Bandura, 1986, 1997; Feather, 1982; Locke & Latham, 1990). These are the personality structures and processes operating within the self system that regulate the level of motivation, performance attainments, and affective states. If clusters of behavior are the personality structure, then even the lowest organisms have at least a twofold personality characterized by approach and avoidance proclivities.

The paucity of guiding theory in seeking the structure of personality through factor analyses of behavioral descriptors is further revealed in the ambiguity about the sources of the supertraits. They are said to be "set like plaster" by innate endowment and unspecified experiences into terminal entities by early adulthood and remain essentially unchangeable thereafter (Costa & McCrae, 1994). The apparent fixedness of personal attributes throughout adulthood most likely has more to do with the insensitivity of nonconditional global measures than with unchangeableness of personal factors over the life course. Global measures of personal attributes mask significant patterns of changes with age that domain-linked measures reveal (Brandstädter, Krampen, & Heil, 1996; Lachman, 1986; McAvay, Seeman, & Rodin, 1996). Adding conditional factors to personality assessments further increases their sensitivity to variability in the way individuals behave in different social contexts (Matsumoto, Kudoh, & Takeuchi, 1996).

Each of the supertraits is a conglomerate of facets. For example, the supertrait Openness to Experience includes such diverse activities as endorsement of daydreaming, rejection of religious authority, excitement over art and poetry, support of controversial speakers, and trying foreign foods. An individual may display high intellectual curiosity and openness to technical and commercial ideas but not care much about exotic foods or what the glitterati decree is modern art. By contrast, another individual may support diverse artistic endeavors but act like a Luddite toward technological innovations. Efforts to understand the nature, origin, and predictiveness of scientific curiosity, for example, should not clutter the personal determinant with preferences for exotic foods. It is not that a general disposition predicts behavior, but that a few of the behavioral descriptors in the conglomerate mixture may provide some overlap with the particular behavior being predicted to yield a correlate. Global conglomerates do not lend themselves to causal analyses because human experiences do not occur at the level of averaged behavioral conglomerates or life circumstances reduced to a nondescript average.

Nor are conglomerate measures equipped to explain the wide variations in behavior by the same individual in a given domain of activity under different situational circumstances. Trait theorists sought to remedy the weak predictiveness of trait indices by averaging ratings of behavior across situations and occasions, which presumably provides a truer measure of the trait (Epstein, 1983). However, aggregation does not produce much predictive gain when actual behavior in different situations rather than self-reports of behavior is measured (Rushton, Brainerd, & Pressley, 1983). No amount of aggregation will elevate correlations between a given form of behavior toward different individuals in response to different situational conditions that social sanctions have disjoined. Aggressive acts by delinquents toward parish priests and toward rival gang members will correlate poorly, however much averaging one does. In a world characterized by contingency, one can lose rather than gain predictive power by trying to predict behavior from an average value that typifies neither situation. The situational averaging solution reminds one of the nonswimmer who drowned while crossing a river that averaged only three feet in depth.

Other efforts to boost correlates included aggregating differing forms of conduct, such as physical aggression, verbal aggression, and antagonistic conduct into a conglomerate index. Mixing behaviors obscures the understanding of psychological functioning, as does the mixing of situations. To be able to predict through aggregation that individuals will sometime, somewhere, do something within a wide assortment of acts is of no great interest. For example, people want to know whether adolescent offenders are likely to commit physical assaults, not whether sometime, somewhere, they may speak offensively or behave antagonistically, or do something else untoward.

There is little evidence that the repackaging of traits in a fivefold format has produced any better prediction of human behavior than do the traditional trait measures (Pervin, 1994), which are not much to rave about. The inflated self-congratulatory claims of breakthrough stand in stark contrast to the paucity of empirical reality tests of predictiveness. It is the replication of fivefold clustering rather than evidence of predictive power that seems to be racing the pulse of adherents to this taxonomic view of personality. It should be noted in passing that the standard correlate of omnibus trait measures is not .30, as commonly assumed. When it comes to predicting particular forms of behavior, global measures are weaker or nonsignificant predictors. Gains in social consensus among trait theorists about the number of supertraits without gains in predictive power hardly constitutes an advance in the field of personality.

Job productivity is often cited as a domain in which the predictive utility of the fivefold approach has been demonstrated. In commenting on behavioral description versus prediction, Hough (1992) notes that the fivefold supertraits are not only too general and heterogeneous in facets but lack relevant factors to be useful in accounting for job performance. Innumerable studies have shown that personal goals are consistent predictors of job productivity (Locke & Latham, 1990). Barrick, Mount, and Strauss (1993) found that conscientiousness was related to actual sales productivity but neither extraversion, which presumably should make for good sellers, nor any of the other supertraits had any predictive value. Even the relationship between conscientiousness and sales performance disappears when the influence of the goals employees set for themselves is removed. Given the view that personality is essentially unchangeable after early adulthood, this taxonomic approach offers little hope of self-betterment along the life course for those who happened to have gotten off to a poor start. Once cast into a nonconscientious mold by innate endowment and experience, one remains ever nonconscientious thereafter. To continue with the productivity example, goal theory offers a much more optimistic view of human changeableness with sound conceptual and empirical backing on how to instill goals and how they work. Teaching people how to regulate their motivation and activities through goal setting enables them to achieve sizeable increases in productivity regardless of their age or sphere of activity (Bandura, 1991a; Locke & Latham, 1990).

A comparative test conducted by Caprara and his associates further illustrates the benefit in predictiveness and social utility of personality factors linked to modifiable determinants and explanatory mechanisms (Caprara, Barbaranelli, & Pastorelli, 1998). They tested the longitudinal predictiveness of the big five factors and three aspects of perceived self-efficacy (social, academic, and self-regulatory) for four different forms of adolescent functioning. In a stepwise regression analysis, perceived academic and self-regulatory efficacy predicted academic achievement, peer preference, and degree of internalization problems and externalization problems that take the form of transgressive and aggressive conduct. Except for a relationship between openness to experience and academic achievement, the big five factors proved unpredictive. Social cognitive theory provides explicit guidelines on how to build a resilient sense of efficacy, which adds to the social utility of the theory. Perceived self-efficacy operates in concert with other sociocognitive factors in a multifaceted causal structure. The addition of goal aspirations, outcome expectations, and perceived opportunities and impediments would further enhance the predictive power of the theory.

The value of a psychological theory is judged not only by its explanatory and predictive power but also by its operative power to guide change in human functioning. A descriptive taxonomy of aggregated behaviors offers no guidance on how to effect personal or social change. Social cognitive theory provides a large body of particularized knowledge on how to develop the cognitive structures and enlist the processes of the self system that govern human adaptation and change (Bandura, 1986, 1997). It lends itself readily to applications because the factors it posits are empirically anchored in indices of functioning and are amenable to change. The determinants and mechanisms through which they operate are spelled out so the theory provides explicit guidelines on how to structure conditions that foster personal and social change.

One could argue that a taxonomic scheme is not designed to be explanatory or prescriptive for change. However, trait theorists often make conflicting claims. On the one hand, their classification scheme is portrayed as simply a descriptive taxonomy. Once the major classes of behavior are firmly established, their origins and functions could be examined. On the other hand, behavioral characteristics are often reified as dynamic causal factors. This creates a serious problem of circularity: Behavior becomes the cause of behavior. Even as descriptive taxonomies, global traits cannot shed much light on the nature of personal causation because personal determinants operate conditionally at a particular contextualized level, not at a socially detached conglomerate level.

Duality of Social Structure and Personal Agency

Human adaptation and change are rooted in social systems. Therefore, personal agency operates within a broad network of sociostructural influences. In these agentic transactions, people are producers as well as products of social systems. Social structures are devised to organize, guide, and regulate human affairs in given domains by authorized rules and sanctions. For the most part, social structures represent authorized social practices carried out by human beings occupying designated roles (Giddens, 1984). Within the rule structures, there is a lot of personal variation in their interpretation, enforcement, adoption, circumvention, or active opposition (Burns & Dietz, in press). It is not a dichotomy between a disembodied social structure and personal agency but a dynamic interplay between individuals and those who preside over the institutionalized operations of social systems. Social structures are created by human activity. The structural practices, in turn, impose constraints and provide resources and opportunity structures for personal development and functioning. Given this dynamic bidirectionality of influence, social cognitive theory rejects a dualism between personal agency and social structure.

Sociostructural theories and psychological theories are often regarded as rival conceptions of human behavior or as representing different levels and proximity of causation. Human behavior cannot be fully understood solely in terms of sociostructural factors or psychological factors. A full understanding requires an integrated perspective in which sociostructural influences operate through psychological mechanisms to produce behavioral effects. However, the self system is not merely a conduit for external influences. The self is socially constituted but, by exercising self-influence, human agency operates generatively and proactively on social systems, not just reactively.

In the theory of triadic reciprocal causation, sociostructural and personal determinants are treated as cofactors within a unified causal structure (Bandura, 1997). Diverse lines of research lend support to this interdependent multicausality. For example, poverty is not a matter of multilayered or distal causation. Lacking the money to provide for the subsistence of one's family impinges pervasively on everyday life in a very specific, proximal way. Elder and his colleagues show that economic hardship, by itself, has no direct influence on parents' efficacy to promote their children's development (Elder & Ardelt, 1992). Families that feel overwhelmed by the hardships experience high subjective strain, whereas those that feel they can make it through tough times experience less emotional strain. In intact households, subjective strain impairs parental efficacy by increasing marital discord. For single parents, subjective strain weakens parents' sense of efficacy both directly and by creating feelings of despondency. Thus the impact of both economic conditions and family structure operate through self processes.

Similarly, socioeconomic status does not directly affect children's academic development. Rather, it does so by influencing parents' educational aspirations for their children (Bandura, Barbaranelli, Caprara, & Pastorelli, 1996b). Parental aspirations and belief in their educational parenting efficacy, in turn, influence their children's scholastic performances by raising educational aspirations and beliefs in scholastic capabilities. Different facets of perceived self-efficacy operating in concert with other psychosocial factors contribute to academic achievement through different mediated paths. Multifaceted measures thus provide a refined view of causal structures that global measures of perceived efficacy cannot provide.

A similar integrated causality governs occupational trajectories of youth (Bandura, Barbaranelli, Caprara, & Pastorelli, 1999). Socioeconomic status has no direct effect on either occupational efficacy or career considerations. Rather, it has an indirect impact by influencing parents' beliefs in their efficacy to promote their children's educational development and the aspirations they hold for them. Parental efficacy and aspirations raise children's educational aspirations and their sense of academic, social, and self-regulatory efficacy. The patterning of children's perceived efficacy influences the types of occupational activities they believe they can do, which, in turn, is linked to the kinds of jobs they would choose for their life's work. In other aspects of family functioning, the impact of socioeconomic status on child outcomes is entirely mediated through parents' child management practices (Baldwin, Baldwin, Sameroff, & Seifer, 1989).

Similar paths of multicausality mediated through self processes are evident in the functioning of educational systems as well as familial systems. Schools that have many poor students and those of disadvantaged minority status generally do poorly academically. However, these sociodemographic characteristics exert their impact on schools' level of achievement largely by shaping teachers' beliefs in their collective efficacy to motivate and educate their students (Bandura, 1993). Schools that have teachers who believe strongly in their collective instructional efficacy do well academically regardless of the sociodemographic characteristics of the student bodies. In verifying the path of influence from sociostructural conditions through familial and self-regulatory processes, these types of studies clarify how personal agency operates within a broad network of sociostructural influences.

FUNDAMENTAL HUMAN CAPABILITIES

In social cognitive theory, people are neither driven by global traits nor automatically shaped and controlled by the environment. As we have already seen, they function as contributors to their own motivation, behavior, and development within a network of reciprocally interacting influences. Persons are characterized within this theoretical perspective in terms of a number of fundamental capabilities. These are reviewed in the sections that follow.

Symbolizing Capability

Social cognitive theory assigns a central role to cognitive, vicarious, self-regulatory, and self-reflective processes in human development and functioning (Bandura, 1986). The extraordinary capacity to represent events and their relationships in symbolic form provides humans with a powerful tool for comprehending their environment and for creating and managing environmental conditions that touch virtually every aspect of their lives. Symbols serve as the vehicle of thought.

Most environmental events exert their effects through cognitive processing rather than directly. Cognitive factors partly determine which environmental events are observed, what meaning is conferred on them, what emotional impact and motivating power they have, and how the information they convey is organized and preserved for future use. Through the medium of symbols, people transform transient experiences into cognitive models that serve as guides for reasoning and action. People transcend time and place in communicating with others at any distance. By symbolizing their experiences, people give structure, meaning, and continuity to their lives.

Knowledge provides the substance and thinking operations provide the tools for cognitive problem solving. Rather than solve problems solely by performing actions and suffering the consequences of missteps, people usually test possible solutions in thought. They generate alternative solutions to problems, and discard or retain them based on estimated outcomes without having to go through a laborious behavioral search. The remarkable flexibility of symbolization also enables people to create novel and fanciful ideas that transcend their sensory experiences. One can easily *think* of cows jumping over the moon even though these feats are physically impossible. The other distinctive human capabilities are founded on this advanced capacity for symbolization. However, in keeping with the interactional perspective, social cognitive theory specifies the social origins of thought and the mechanisms through which social factors exert their influence on cognitive functioning (Bandura, 1986).

Although the capacity for symbolization vastly expands human capabilities, if put to faulty use it can also breed personal distress. Many human dysfunctions and torments stem from problems of thought. This is because, in their thoughts, people often dwell on painful pasts and on perturbing futures of their own invention. They burden themselves with stressful arousal through anxiety-provoking rumination. They debilitate their own efforts by self-doubting and other self-defeating ideation. They constrain and impoverish their lives through phobic thinking. They drive themselves to despondency by harsh self-evaluation and dejecting modes of thinking. Further, they often act on misconceptions that get them into trouble. Thought can thus be a source of human failings and distress as well as a source of human accomplishments.

Vicarious Capability

A comprehensive theory of personality must explain the acquisition of competencies, attitudes, values, and emotional proclivities, not just the enactments of behaviors that get dubbed as traits. There are two basic modes of learning. People learn by experiencing the effects of their actions and through the power of social modeling. Psychological theories have focused almost exclusively on learning from positive and negative response consequences. Natural endowment provides humans with enabling biological systems but few inborn skills. Skills must be developed over long periods and altered to fit changing conditions over the life course. If knowledge and skills had to be shaped laboriously by response consequences without the benefit of modeled guidance, a culture could never transmit its language, social practices, mores, and adaptive competencies. Mistakes can produce costly or even fatal consequences. The prospects for survival would, therefore, be slim indeed if one had to rely solely on trial-and-error experiences. Moreover, the constraints of time, resources, and mobility impose severe limits on the situations and activities that can be directly explored for the acquisition of new knowledge and skills. Fortunately, the tedious and hazardous trial-and-error learning can be short cut by social modeling.

Humans have evolved an advanced capacity for observational learning that enables them to expand their knowledge and competencies rapidly through the information conveyed by the rich variety of models. Virtually all behavioral, cognitive, and affective learning from direct experience can be achieved vicariously by observing people's actions and the consequences for them (Bandura, 1986; Rosenthal & Zimmerman, 1978).

Much human learning occurs either designedly or unintentionally from the models in one's immediate environment. However, a vast amount of knowledge about people, places, and styles of thinking and behaving is gained from the extensive modeling in the symbolic environment of the electronic mass media. A major significance of symbolic modeling lies in its tremendous scope and multiplicative power. Unlike learning by doing, which requires shaping the actions of each individual through repeated consequences, in observational learning a single model can transmit new ways of thinking and behaving simultaneously to many people in widely dispersed locales. Video and computer delivery systems feeding off telecommunications satellites are now rapidly diffusing new ideas, values, and styles of conduct worldwide.

Most psychological theories were cast long before the advent of revolutionary advances in the technology of communication. As a result, they give insufficient attention to the increasingly powerful role that the symbolic environment plays in contemporary societies. For example, television has vastly expanded the range of models to which members of society are exposed day in and day out. By drawing on these modeled patterns of thought and behavior, observers transcend the bounds of their immediate environment. Because the symbolic environment occupies a major part of people's everyday lives, the study of human development and acculturation in the electronic era must be broadened to include electronic acculturation. At the societal level, symbolic modes of modeling are transforming how social systems operate and serving as a major vehicle for sociopolitical change (Bandura, 1997; Braithwaite, 1994).

Observational learning, which can take the form of behavioral, cognitive, valuational, and affective change, is governed by four component subfunctions (Figure 6.2). "Attentional processes" determine what people observe in the profusion of modeling influences and what information they extract from what they notice. People cannot be much influenced by observed events if they do not remember them. A second major subfunction governing observational learning concerns "representational processes." Retention involves an active process of transforming and restructuring the information conveyed by modeled events into rules and conceptions for memory representation. In the third subfunction—"the behavioral production process"—symbolic conceptions are translated into appropriate courses of action. This is achieved through a conception matching process in which behavioral enactments are structured until they match the conception of the activity.

Behavior operates under hierarchical levels of control. Cognitive guidance is important in early and intermediate phases of competency development. Once proficient modes of behavior become routinized, they are regulated largely by lower sensorimotor systems and no longer require higher cognitive control (Carroll & Bandura, 1990). However, when routinized behavior patterns fail to produce desired results, cognitive control again comes into play in the search for better solutions. Control reverts to lower control systems after an adequate means is found and becomes the habitual way of doing things.

"Automatization" should not me equated with "unconsciousness" as is commonly done. Routinization of complex skills involves at least three major subprocesses (Bandura, 1986). The first process is "mergerization." Initially, considerable thought is given to what to do at each step of a skilled activity and how to coordinate the subparts. Once the segments are fully integrated and routinized through repeated practice, there is no longer any need to think about the mechanics of the habitual routine. Thought is freed for other purposes. The second subprocess involves "distributed consciousness." Attention can be distributed across activities using noncompeting modalities. This process of automization involves a shift in the locus of attention from the execution of the action to its observable correlated effects. Thus, one can drive an automobile while conversing with others or thinking of something else, but vigilantly tracking the flow of traffic and where the car is going and making necessary corrective adjustments. Initially, people figure out what best suits certain types of situations. When highly predictable relations exist between situations and the actions they require, eventually the situation rather than prior judgment prescribes action. This third subprocess of automaticity involves routinized linkage of habitual behavior patterns to recurrent contexts. In short, routinization does not mean that people operate as unconscious automatons.

Partial disengagement of thought from proficient action has considerable functional value because it frees cognitive activity for matters requiring attention. If one had to think before carrying out every routine activity, it would consume most of one's attention and create a monotonously dull inner life. Efficient functioning requires a mix of routinized and mindful action. As a result of routinization, people often react with fixed ways of thinking unreflectively and with habitual ways of behaving unthinkingly. Nonconscious information processing and routinization of thought and action should be distinguished from an unconscious mind acting as a concealed agent orchestrating behavior in an unwitting host organism. To reify, from evidence of automatic and routinized responses, a subterranean agent steering perceptions and actions is to commit a serious metaphysical transgression.

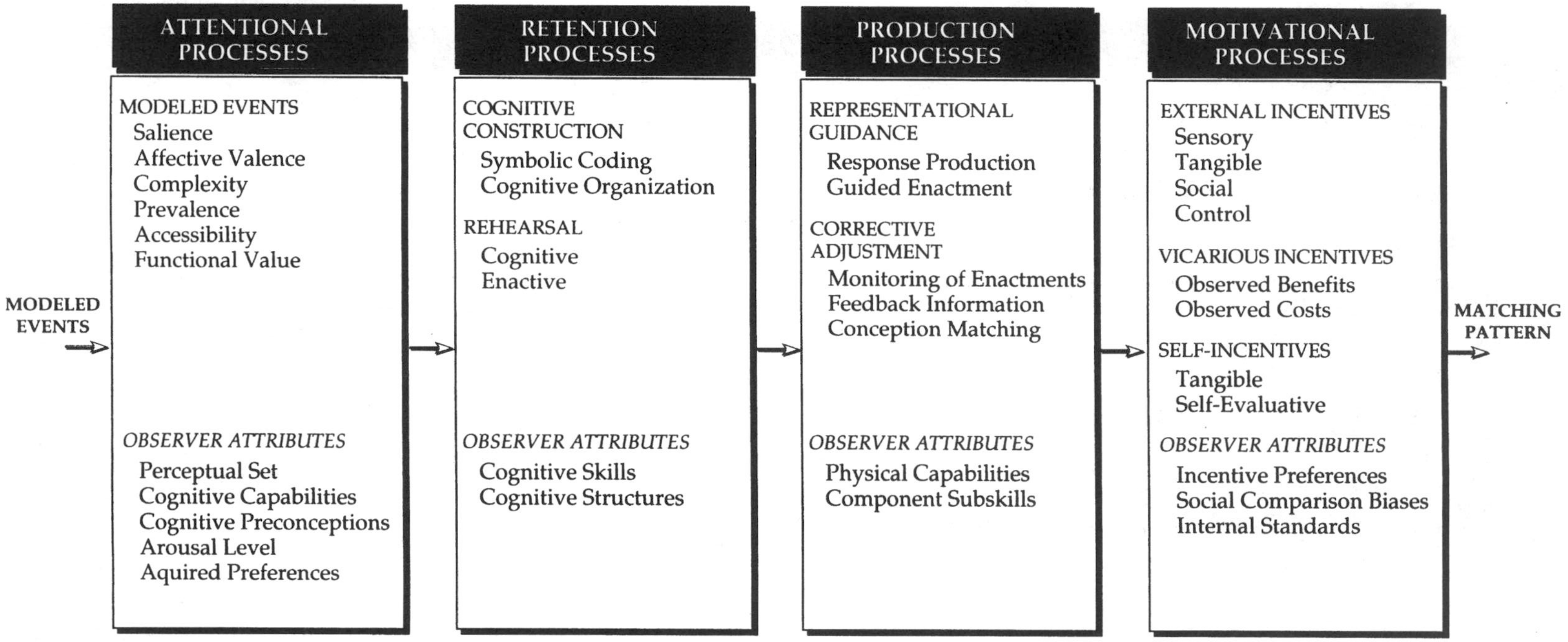

FIGURE 6.2. Four subprocesses governing observational learning (Bandura, 1986).

The fourth subfunction in modeling concerns "motivational processes." Social cognitive theory distinguishes between acquisition and performance because people do not perform everything they learn. Performance of observationally learned behavior is influenced by three major types of incentive motivators—direct, vicarious, and self-produced. People are more likely to adopt modeled styles of behavior if they produce valued outcomes than if they have unrewarding or punishing effects. The observed cost and benefits accruing to others influence the adoption of modeled patterns in much the same way as do directly experienced consequences. People are motivated by the successes of others who are similar to themselves, but they are discouraged from pursuing courses of behavior that they have seen often result in aversive consequences. The evaluative reactions people generate to their own behavior also regulate which observationally learned activities they are most likely to pursue. People express what they find self-satisfying and reject what they personally disapprove.

Abstract and Creative Modeling

Modeling is not simply a process of response mimicry as commonly believed. Modeled judgments and actions may differ in specific content but embody the same rule. For example, a model may deal with moral dilemmas that differ widely in the nature of the activity but apply the same moral standard to the activity. Modeled activities thus convey rules for generative and innovative behavior. This higher-level learning is achieved through abstract modeling. Once observers extract the rules underlying the modeled activities they can generate new behaviors that go beyond what they have seen or heard.

Creativeness rarely springs entirely from individual inventiveness. A lot of modeling goes on in creativity. By refining preexisting innovations, synthesizing them into new ways, and adding novel elements to them, something new is created. When exposed to models of differing styles of thinking and behaving, observers vary in what they adopt from the different sources and thereby create new blends of personal characteristics that differ from the individual models (Bandura, Ross, & Ross, 1963). Modeling influences that exemplify new perspectives and innovative styles of thinking also foster creativity by weakening conventional mind sets (Belcher, 1975; Harris & Evans, 1973).

Motivational, Emotional, and Valuational Effects

In addition to cultivating new competencies, modeling influences can alter incentive motivation (Bandura, 1986). Seeing others achieve desired outcomes by their efforts can instill motivating outcome expectations in observers that they can secure similar benefits for comparable performances. These motivational effects rest on observers' judgments that they have the efficacy to produce the modeled level of attainments and that comparable accomplishments will bring them similar beneficial outcomes. By the same token, seeing others punished for engaging in certain activities can instill negative outcome expectations that serve as disincentives.

People are easily aroused by the emotional expressions of others. If the affective reactions of models only aroused observers fleetingly, it would be of limited psychological import. What gives significance to vicarious emotional influence is that observers can acquire lasting attitudes and emotional and behavioral proclivities toward persons, places, or things that have been associated with modeled emotional experiences. They learn to fear the things that frightened models, to dislike what repulsed them, and to like what gratified them (Bandura, 1992; Berger, 1962; Duncker, 1938). Fears and intractable phobias are ameliorated by modeling influences that convey information about coping strategies for exercising control over the things that are feared. The stronger the instilled sense of perceived coping efficacy, the bolder the behavior (Bandura, 1997; Williams, 1992). Values can similarly be developed and altered vicariously by repeated exposure to modeled preferences.

During the course of their daily lives, people have direct contact with only a small sector of the physical and social environment. In their daily routines, they travel the same routes, visit the same familiar places, and see the same group of friends and associates. As a result, their conceptions of the wider social reality are greatly influenced by symbolic representations of society, mainly by the mass media (Gerbner, 1972). To a large extent, people act on their images of reality. The more their conceptions of the world around them depend on portrayals in the media's symbolic environment, the greater is the media's social impact (Ball-Rokeach & DeFleur, 1976).

To sum up, modeling influences serve diverse functions—as tutors, motivators, social prompters, emotion arousers, and shapers of values and conceptions of reality. The vast body of knowledge on vicarious processes is being widely applied for personal development, therapeutic purposes, and social change (Bandura, 1986, 1997; Bandura & Rosenthal, 1978; Rogers, Vaughan, Swalehe, Rao, & Sood, 1996; Singhal & Rogers, 1989).

Forethought Capability

Another distinctive human characteristic is the capacity for forethought. The ability to bring anticipated outcomes to bear on current activities promotes foresightful behavior. It enables people to transcend the dictates of their immediate environment and to shape and regulate the present to fit a desired future. Much human self-directedness is the product of forethought. The future time perspective manifests itself in many different ways. People set goals for themselves, anticipate the likely consequences of prospective actions, and plan courses of action likely to produce desired outcomes and avoid detrimental ones (Bandura, 1991a; Feather, 1982; Locke & Latham, 1990; Markus & Nurius, 1986; Pervin, 1989). Through the exercise of forethought, people motivate themselves and guide their actions anticipatorily. When projected over a long-time course on matters of value, a forethoughtful perspective provides direction, coherence, and meaning to one's life. As people progress in their life course they continue to plan ahead, reorder their priorities, and structure their lives accordingly.

The capacity for intentional purposive action is rooted in symbolic activity. Future events cannot, of course, be causes of current motivation and action because they have no actual existence. However, by being represented cognitively in the present, foreseeable future events are converted into current motivators and regulators of behavior. In this form of anticipatory self-guidance, behavior is motivated and directed by anticipated outcomes rather than being pulled by an unrealized future state.

Outcome Expectations

People regulate their behavior partly by outcome expectations. Courses of action that are likely to produce positive outcomes are generally adapted and used; those that bring unrewarding or punishing outcomes are usually discarded. Response consequences do not automatically shape and control actions, as claimed by radical behaviorists. Rather, people construct outcome expectations from observed conditional relations between environmental events and between given actions and outcomes (Bandura, 1986). In social cognitive theory, "reinforcement" is a form of incentive motivation operating through outcome expectations rather than an automatic strengthener of responses.

Because outcomes exert their influence through forethought, they have little or no motivational or behavioral impact until people discover how outcomes are linked to actions in their environment. This is no easy matter. In everyday life, actions usually produce mixed effects: The outcomes may occur immediately or far removed in time; the same behavior may have different effects depending on where, when, and toward whom it is performed, and many situational factors affect behavioral outcomes. Such causal ambiguity provides a fertile ground for misjudgment. When belief about the effects of actions differs from actuality, behavior is weakly controlled by its actual consequences until repeated experience instills realistic beliefs. Yet it is not always one's beliefs that change in the direction of social reality. Acting on erroneous beliefs can alter how others behave, thus shaping the social reality in the direction of the misbeliefs (Snyder, 1980).

External consequences are not the only kind of outcomes that influence human behavior. As noted earlier, people profit from the successes and mistakes of others as well as from their own experiences. As a general rule, they do things they have seen succeed and avoid those they have seen fail. However, observed outcomes exert their influence through perceived similarity that one is likely to experience similar outcomes for similar courses of action and that one possesses the capabilities to achieve similar performances.

Observed outcomes can also affect the level of motivation by altering the value of external outcomes through social comparison processes. People weigh their own outcomes by those accruing to others for similar performances. For example, the same monetary raise is likely to be viewed negatively by someone who has seen colleagues compensated more generously, but viewed positively if colleagues have been compensated less well. The relational properties of incentives affect not only motivation and performance but personal satisfaction and discontent. Equitable outcomes foster a sense of well-being; inequitable ones breed discontent and resentment (Bandura, 1973; Martin, 1981).

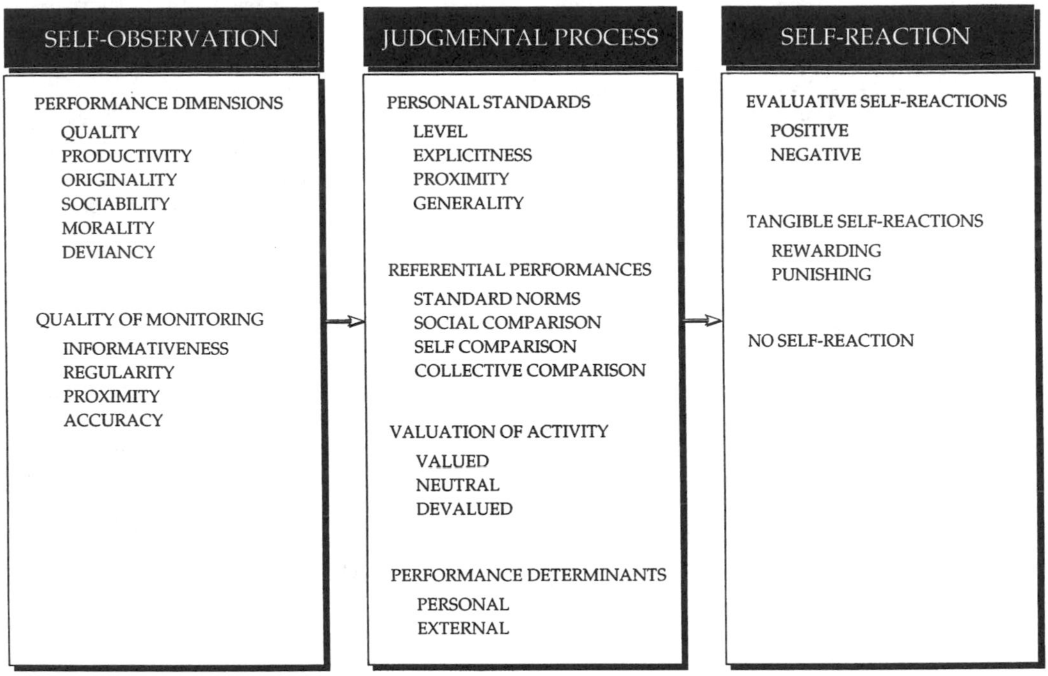

FIGURE 6.3. Structure of the system of self-regulation of motivation and action through internal standards and self-reactive influence (Bandura, 1986).

Self-Regulatory Capability

People are not only knowers and performers guided by outcome expectations—they are also self-reactors with a capacity for self-direction. This capability is grounded in a self-regulatory structure. Successful development requires the substitution of internal regulation and direction for external sanctions and demands. Once the capability for self-direction is developed, self-demands and self-sanctions serve as major guides, motivators, and deterrents. In the absence of internal standards and self-sanctions, people would behave like weather vanes, constantly shifting direction to conform to whatever momentary influence happened to impinge upon them.

Subfunctions of Self-Regulation

The self-regulation of motivation, affect, and action operates through a set of psychological subfunctions (Figure 6.3). They include self-observation, judgmental, and self-reaction subfunctions. People cannot influence their own motivation and actions very well if they do not pay adequate attention to their thought processes and performances, to the conditions under which they occur, and to the immediate and distal effects they produce. Therefore, success in self-regulation partly depends on the fidelity, consistency, and temporal proximity of self-observation (Kazdin, 1974). Depending on people's values and the functional significance of different activities, they attend selectively to certain aspects of their functioning and ignore those that are of little import to them.

Observing one's pattern of behavior is the first step toward doing something to affect it; but in itself, such information provides little basis for self-directed reactions. Actions give rise to self-reactions through a judgmental function that includes several subsidiary processes. Personal standards for judging and guiding one's actions play a major role in self-motivation and in the exercise of self-directedness (Bandura, 1991a; Bandura & Cervone, 1986; Locke & Latham, 1990). Whether a given performance is regarded favorably or negatively will depend on the personal standards against which it is evaluated. Once people commit themselves to a valued goal, they seek self-satisfaction from fulfilling it, and are prompted to intensify their efforts by discontent with substandard performances. The anticipated affective self-reactions serve as incentive motivators for personal accomplishments.

For most activities, there are no absolute measures of adequacy. People must, therefore, evaluate their performances in relation to the attainments of others (Festinger, 1954; Goethals & Darley, 1977). The referential comparisons may take the form of performance attainments of others in similar situations, standard norms based on representative groups, one's own past attainments, or comparative group performance in societies organized around collectivistic principles (Bandura, 1986; Bandura & Jourden, 1991). Another factor in the judgmental component of self-regulation concerns the valuation of activities. The more relevant performances are to one's value preferences and sense of personal adequacy, the more likely self-evaluative reactions are to be elicited in that activity. Self-reactions also vary depending on how people perceive the determinants of their behavior (Weiner, 1986). They are most likely to take pride in their accomplishments when they ascribe their successes to their own abilities and efforts. They respond self-critically to faulty performances for which they hold themselves responsible but not to those they perceive as due to unusual circumstances, to insufficient capabilities, or to unrealistic demands.

Motivation based on personal standards involves a cognitive comparison process between the standards and perceived performance attainments. The motivational effects do not stem from the standards themselves but rather from several self-reactive influences. These include perceived self-efficacy to fulfill one's standards, affective self-evaluation of one's attainments, and adjustment of proximal subgoals depending on the progress one is making (Bandura 1991a; Bandura & Cervone, 1986).

Performance judgments set the occasion for self-reactive influence. Self-reactions provide the linking mechanism by which standards regulate courses of action. The self-regulatory control is achieved by creating incentives for one's own actions and by anticipative affective reactions to one's own behavior depending on how it measures up to personal standards. Thus, people pursue courses of action that give them self-satisfaction and a sense of self-worth, but they refrain from behaving in ways that result in self-censure.

Some of the self-motivating incentives may be tangible outcomes, as when people get themselves to do things they would otherwise put off or avoid altogether by making tangible rewards dependent upon performance attainments. However, most people value their self-respect and the self-satisfaction derived from a job well done more highly than they do material rewards. The self-regulation of behavior by self-evaluative reactions is a uniquely human capability. Self-evaluation gives direction to behavior and creates motivators for it.

Most theories of self-regulation are founded on a negative feedback system (Carver & Scheier, 1981; Lord & Hanges, 1987; Powers, 1973). In this view, negative discrepancy between one's perceived performance and an adopted standard motivates action to reduce the disparity. However, self-regulation by negative discrepancy tells only half the story and not necessarily the more interesting half. People are proactive, aspiring organisms. Human self-motivation relies on both discrepancy production and discrepancy reduction. It requires proactive control as well as reactive control. People initially motivate themselves through proactive control by setting themselves valued performance standards that create a state of disequilibrium and then mobilizing their effort on the basis of anticipatory estimation of what it would take to reach them. Feedback control comes into play in subsequent adjustments of effort expenditure to achieve desired results. After people attain the standard they have been pursuing, those who have a strong sense of efficacy generally set a higher standard for themselves. The adoption of further challenges creates new motivating discrepancies to be mastered.

Interplay between Personal and External Outcomes

After self-regulatory capabilities are developed, behavior usually produces two sets of consequences: self-evaluative reactions and external outcomes, which may operate as complementary or opposing influences on behavior (Bandura, 1986). External outcomes are most likely to wield influence when they are compatible with self-evaluative ones. This condition exists when externally rewardable actions are a source of self-satisfaction and self-pride and when externally punishable ones bring self-censure. Behavior is also highly susceptible to external influences in the absence of countervailing internal standards. People with weak commitment to personal standards adopt a pragmatic orientation, tailoring their behavior to fit whatever the situation seems to call for (Snyder, 1987). They become adept at reading social cues and varying their self-presentation accordingly.

People commonly experience conflicts of outcomes when they are rewarded socially or materially for behavior they personally devalue. When self-devaluative consequences outweigh the force of external rewards, the consequences have little sway. There is no more devastating consequence than self-contempt. But if the allure of rewards outweigh self-censure, the result can be cheerless compliance. However, people possess sociocognitive skills for reconciling perturbing disparities between personal standards and conduct. The mechanisms by which losses of self-respect for devalued conduct are reduced is considered shortly.

Another type of conflict of outcomes arises when individuals are punished for activities they value highly. Principled dissenters and nonconformists often find themselves in such predicaments. The relative strength of self-approval and external censure determine whether the courses of action will be pursued or abandoned. There are individuals, however, whose sense of self-worth is so strongly invested in certain convictions that they will submit to prolonged maltreatment rather than accede to what they regard as unjust or immoral. Sir Thomas More, who was beheaded for refusing to compromise his resolute convictions, is a notable example from history. It is not uncommon for people to endure severe abuse, as Gandhi, Martin Luther King, and Nelsen Mandela did, for unyielding adherence to ideological and moral principles.

Another common situation is one in which both the external support and reward for given activities are minimal or lacking, and individuals have to sustain their efforts largely through self-encouragement. For example, innovators persevere despite repeated failures in endeavors that provide neither rewards nor recognition for long periods, if at all during their lifetime. Innovative pursuits that clash with existing preferences bring criticism and social rejection. To persist, innovators must be sufficiently convinced of their efficacy and the worth of their pursuit to self-reward their efforts, and not be much concerned with the opinions of others (Shepherd, 1995; White, 1982).

Disengagement of Moral Self-Regulatory Agency

In development of competencies and aspirational pursuits, the self-regulatory standards selected as a mark of adequacy are progressively raised as knowledge and skills are acquired and challenges are met. In many areas of social and moral behavior, the self-regulatory standards have greater stability. People do not change from week to week what they regard as right or wrong or good or bad. After people adopt a standard of morality, their negative self-sanctions for actions that violate their personal standards, and their positive self-sanctions for conduct faithful to their moral standards serve as the regulatory influences (Bandura, 1991b). These self-referent processes provide the motivational as well as the cognitive regulators of moral conduct. Self-sanctions keep conduct in line with personal standards. The exercise of moral agency has dual aspects—"inhibitive" and "proactive" (Bandura, in press). The inhibitive form of morality is manifested in the power to refrain from behaving inhumanely, whereas the proactive form is expressed in the power to behave humanely.

Moral standards do not function as fixed internal regulators of conduct, as implied by theories of internalization that posit global entities such as conscience and superego as constant overseers of conduct. There are many social and psychological maneuvers by which moral self-reactions can be selectively disengaged from inhumane conduct (Bandura, 1991b). Figure 6.4 shows that the disengagement may center on the conduct itself, on the sense of personal agency for the actions taken, the consequences that flow from actions, or on the victims of mistreatment.

One set of disengagement practices operates on the cognitive construal of the conduct itself. In this process of "moral justification," detrimental conduct is made personally and socially acceptable by portraying it as serving socially worthy or moral purposes. People can then act on a moral imperative. Voltaire put it well when he said, "Those who can make you believe absurdities can make you commit atrocities." Over the centuries, much destructive conduct has been perpetrated by ordinary, decent people in the name of righteous ideologies, religious principles, and nationalistic imperatives (Kelman & Hamilton, 1989; Rapoport & Alexander, 1982; Reich, 1990; Sanford & Comstock, 1971).

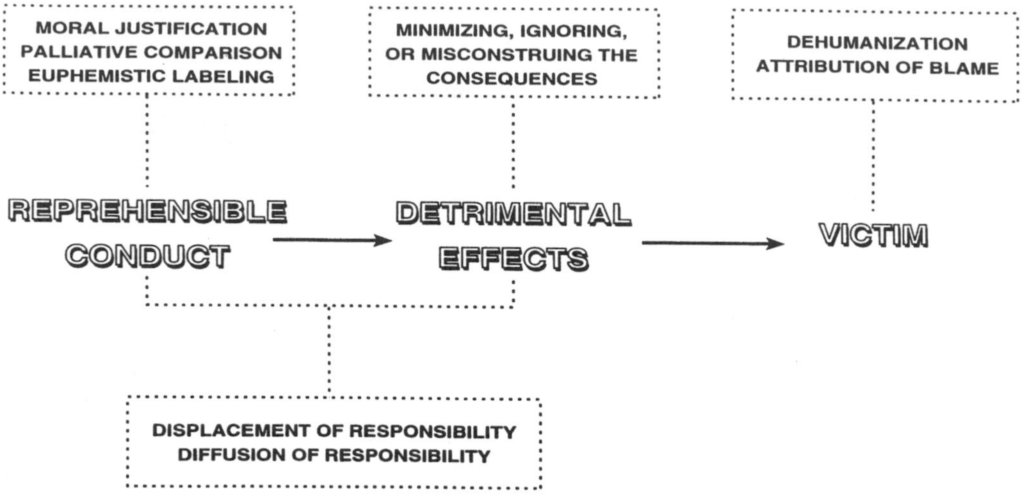

FIGURE 6.4. Mechanisms through which moral self-sanctions are selectively activated or disengaged from reprehensible conduct at different points in the self-regulatory process (Bandura, 1986).

Language shapes thought patterns on which actions are based. Activities can take on very different appearances depending on what they are called. Not surprisingly, "sanitizing euphemistic language" is widely used to make harmful conduct respectable and to reduce personal responsibility for it (Bolinger, 1982; Lutz, 1987). How behavior is viewed is also colored by what it is compared against. The more flagrant the inhumanities against which one's destructive conduct is contrasted, the more likely it will lose its repugnancy or even appear benevolent. "Exonerating comparison" relies heavily on moral justification by utilitarian arguments that one's injurious actions will prevent more human suffering than they cause. For example, the massive destruction in Vietnam was morally justified on utilitarian grounds that the U.S. military intervention was saving the populous from communist enslavement.

Cognitive restructuring of harmful conduct through moral justification, sanitizing language, and exonerating comparison is the most effective psychological mechanism for disengaging moral control. Investing harmful conduct with high moral purpose not only eliminates self-censure, but it engages self-approval in the service of destructive exploits as well. What was once morally condemnable becomes a source of self-pride.

Moral control operates most strongly when people acknowledge that they are contributors to harmful outcomes. The second set of disengagement practices operates by obscuring or minimizing the agentive role in the harm one causes. This is achieved by "displacement and diffusion of responsibility." People will behave in ways they normally repudiate if a legitimate authority accepts responsibility for the effects of their conduct (Diener, 1977; Milgram, 1974; Zimbardo, 1995). Disclaim of personal agency removes self-condemning reactions to one's harmful conduct. As C. P. Snow insightfully observed, "More hideous crimes have been committed in the name of obedience than in the name of rebellion." The exercise of moral control is also weakened when personal agency is obscured by diffusing responsibility for detrimental behavior by group decision making, subdividing injurious activities into seemingly harmless parts, and exploiting the anonymity of collective action.

Additional ways of weakening moral control operate by disregarding or distorting harm caused by one's conduct (Klass, 1978). As long as the harmful effects are ignored, minimized, distorted or disbelieved, there is little reason for self-censure to be activated. The final set of disengagement practices operates on the recipients of detrimental acts. Blaming one's adversaries or compelling circumstances can serve self-exonerative purposes. In this process, people view themselves as faultless victims driven to harmful conduct by provocation. Through "ascription of blame," injurious conduct becomes a justifiable defensive reaction to perceived provocations and mistreatments. Victims get blamed for bringing the suffering on themselves (Ferguson & Rule, 1983).

The strength of moral self-censure depends partly on how the perpetrators view the people they mistreat. To perceive another as human activates empathetic and vicarious emotional reactions through perceived similarity (Bandura, 1992). Self-censure for cruel conduct can be disengaged by "dehumanization" that strips people of human qualities. Once dehumanized, they are no longer viewed as persons with feelings, hopes, and concerns but as subhuman objects. If dispossessing one's foes of humanness does not weaken self-censure, it can be eliminated by attributing demonic or bestial qualities to them. It is easier to brutalize people when they are viewed as low animal forms (Bandura, Underwood, & Fromson, 1975; Haritos-Fatouros, 1988; Keen, 1986).

Psychological research tends to emphasize how easy it is to get good people to perform cruel deeds through dehumanization and other self-exonerative means (Milgram, 1974). What is rarely noted is the striking evidence that most people refuse to behave cruelly, even with strong authoritarian commands, toward people who are humanized (Bandura et al., 1975). The affirmation of common humanity can bring out the best in others.

Developmental research sheds some light on how the mechanisms of moral disengagement promote antisocial and destructive conduct. They weaken self-censure for harmful conduct, reduce prosocialness, and foster cognitive and emotional reactions conducive to antisocial conduct (Bandura, Barbaranelli, Caprara, & Pastorelli, 1996a). Facility in moral disengagement combined with a low sense of efficacy to resist peer pressure for transgressive activities foster heavy engagement in antisocial conduct (Kwak & Bandura, 1997).

Growing Primacy of Self-Regulation

The accelerated pace of social and technological changes has placed a premium on people's capabilities to exert a strong hand in their own development and functioning through the life course. For example, information technologies are transforming the educational system. In the past, students have had to rely heavily on classroom teachers for their knowledge. Students now have the best libraries, museums and multimedia instruction at their fingertips through the global Internet for educating themselves. Efficacious self-regulators gain knowledge, skills, and intrinsic interests in intellectual matters (Bandura, 1997; Zimmerman, 1990). Weak self-regulators do not achieve much progress in self-development. As in the case of modeling, sociocognitive principles of self-regulation provide explicit guidelines for educational development (Schunk, 1989, 1996).

Recent years have witnessed a major change in the conception of health from a disease model to a health model. Viewed from this perspective, human health is heavily dependent on lifestyle habits and environmental conditions. It emphasizes health enhancement, not just disease prevention. By exercising control over health habits, people can live longer and healthier. New health promotion systems structured around self-regulatory principles are reducing major health risks, slowing the rate of biological aging and enhancing health (Bandura, 1998b).

Self-regulation is also becoming a key factor in occupational life. In the past, employees learned a given trade and performed it much the same way throughout their lifetime in the same organization. Much of the world of work is now being structured so that employees assume operational control in flexible self-managed teams. In the modern workplace, knowledge and technical skills are quickly outmoded unless they are updated to fit the new technologies. Employees have to take charge of their self-development over the full course of their worklife. Efficacious innovativeness and adaptability have become a premium at the organizational level as well. These new realities place increasing demands on individual and collective efficacy to shape personal destinies and the national life of societies.

A favorable self-regulatory system provides a continuing source of motivation, self-directedness, and personal satisfaction. However, a dysfunctional self system can also breed much human misery. For people who adopt stringent personal standards, most of their accomplishments bring them a sense of failure and self-disparagement (Bandura, 1997; Rehm, 1988). In its more extreme forms, harsh standards of self-evaluation give rise to despondency, chronic discouragement, feelings of worthlessness, and lack of purposefulness. Effective treatments must remedy each of the dysfunctional aspects of the self system. They correct self-belittling interpretative biases, promote adoption of attainable subgoals that provide a sense of accomplishment, and get clients to be more self-rewarding (Rehm, 1981). High aspirations do not produce self-demoralization as long as current attainments are measured against attainable subgoals of progress rather than against lofty ultimate goals.

The preceding discussion portrays the personal misery that can result from stringent self-evaluative standards. Deficient or deviant standards also create problems, although the adverse effects are more likely to be social than personal. Unprincipled individuals who pursue an ethic of expediency and those who pride themselves on excelling at antisocial activities readily engage in injurious conduct unless deterred by external sanctions.

Self-Reflective Capability

The capability to reflect upon oneself and the adequacy of one's thoughts and actions is another exclusively human attribute that figures prominently in social cognitive theory. People are not only agents of action but self-examiners of their own cognitive, affective, and behavioral functioning. Effective functioning requires reliable ways of distinguishing between accurate and faulty thinking. In verifying the adequacy of thought by self-reflective means, people generate ideas and act upon them or predict occurrences from them. They then judge from the results the accuracy and functional value of their thinking and try to improve it if necessary.

Thought Verification by Self-Reflectiveness

The process of thought verification involves comparing how well one's thoughts match some indicator of reality. There are four modes of thought verification: enactive, vicarious, persuasory, and logical. Enactive verification relies on the closeness of the fit between one's thoughts and the results of the actions they spawn. Good matches lend validity to the thoughts; mismatches refute them. In the vicarious mode of thought verification, seeing the effects of other people's actions provides the check on the correctness of one's own thinking. Vicarious thought verification is not simply a supplement to enactive validation. Symbolic modeling vastly expands the range of verification experiences that cannot be attained by personal action because of the constraints of time, resources, and mobility.

Some spheres of life involve highly specialized knowledge requiring dependence on experts or metaphysical ideas that are not amenable to empirical confirmation. When experiential verification is difficult or unfeasible, people evaluate the soundness of their views by checking against the beliefs of others, to whom they give credence. Thoughts are also verified by inferential means. In logical verification, people can check for fallacies in their thinking by deducing from knowledge that is known and what necessarily follows from it.

Such metacognitive activities usually foster dependable thought, but they can produce faulty thought patterns as well. Forceful actions arising from erroneous beliefs often create social environments that confirm the misbeliefs (Snyder, 1980). Readers are undoubtedly familiar with problem-prone individuals who manage to create perturbing environments wherever they go. Thus, for example, individuals prone to misattribute hostile intent to others act in inimical ways that create their own self-validating hostile realities (Rausch, 1965). In contrast, those who are prosocially oriented create amicable social environments that bring out the best in others. Verification of thought by comparison with distorted media versions of social reality can foster shared misconceptions of people, places, or things. Public fear of criminal victimization provides one example of vicarious biasing of public consciousness. Heavy viewers of televised fare populated with villainous and violent characters view their social environment as more dangerous and mistrustful than do light viewers. (Hawkins & Pingree, 1991; Signorielli & Morgan, 1989).

Social verification can foster bizarre views of reality if the shared beliefs of the reference group with which one affiliates are eccentric and the group is encapsulated from outside social ties and influences (Bandura, 1982a). This is most strikingly illustrated in cultist beliefs (Hall, 1987). Similarly, deductive reasoning will be flawed if the propositional knowledge on which it is based is faulty or biases intrude on reasoning processes (Falmagne, 1975).

Perceived Self-Efficacy

Among the self-referent thoughts that influence human motivation, affect, and action, none is more central or pervasive than people's judgments of personal efficacy (Bandura, 1997). Perceived self-efficacy is concerned with people's beliefs in their capabilities to perform in ways that give them some control over events that affect their lives. Efficacy beliefs form the foundation of human agency. Unless people believe that they can produce desired results by their actions, they have little incentive to act or to persevere in the face of difficulties.

Sources of Self-Efficacy

Self-efficacy beliefs are constructed from four principal sources of information. The most authentic and influential source is "mastery experiences." This can be achieved by tackling problems in successive, attainable steps. Successes build a robust belief in one's efficacy. Failures undermine it, especially in earlier phases of self-development. Moreover, if people have only easy successes, they are readily discouraged by failure or setbacks. Development of resilient self-efficacy requires experiences in overcoming obstacles through perseverant effort.

The second way of creating and strengthening beliefs of personal efficacy is through "vicarious experiences." If people see others like themselves succeed by sustained effort, they come to believe that they, too, have the capacity to succeed. Conversely, observing the failures of others instills doubts about one's own ability to master similar activities. Competent models also build efficacy by conveying knowledge and skills for managing environmental demands.

"Social persuasion" is the third way of strengthening people's beliefs in their efficacy. If people are persuaded that they have what it takes to succeed, they exert more effort and are more perseverant than if they harbor self-doubts and dwell on personal deficiencies when problems arise. However, effective social persuaders do more than convey faith in people's capabilities. They arrange activities for others in ways that bring success and avoid placing people prematurely in situations in which they are likely to fail.

People also rely on their "physical and emotional states" to judge their capabilities. They read their tension, anxiety, and depression as signs of personal deficiency. In activities that require strength and stamina, they interpret fatigue, windedness, and aches and pains as indictors of low physical efficacy. Thus, the fourth way of altering efficacy beliefs is to enhance physical status, reduce negative emotional states, and correct misinterpretations of somatic sources of information.

Cognitive Processing of Efficacy Information

Information that is relevant for judging personal efficacy is not inherently informative. It is only raw data. Experiences become informative through cognitive processing of efficacy information and self-reflective thought. The information conveyed by events must be distinguished from how that information is selected, weighted, and integrated into self-efficacy judgments. A host of factors, personal, social, and situational, affect how experiences are interpreted.

The cognitive processing of efficacy information involves two separate functions. The first is the types of information people attend to and use as indicators of personal efficacy. Sociocognitive theory specifies the set of efficacy indicators that are distinctive for each of the four major modalities of influence (Bandura, 1997). For example, the judgments people make about their efficacy based on performance attainments may vary depending on their interpretive biases, the difficulty of the task, how hard they worked at it, how much help they received, the conditions under which they performed, their emotional and physical state at the time, their rate of improvement over time, and selective biases in how they monitor and recall their attainments.

The particular indicators people single out provide the information base on which the self-appraisal process operates. The second function involves the combination rules or heuristics people use to integrate efficacy information conveyed enactively, vicariously, socially, and physiologically. This involves a complex process of self-persuasion concerning one's capabilities.

Diverse Effects of Self-Efficacy

Beliefs of personal efficacy regulate human functioning through four major processes (Bandura, 1997): cognitive, motivational, emotional, and choice processes. The cognitive pathway takes a variety of forms. A major function of thought is to enable people to predict events and to exercise control over those that are important to them. People of high perceived efficacy show greater cognitive resourcefulness, strategic flexibility, and effectiveness in managing their environment (Bouffard-Bouchard, Parent, & Larivée, 1991; Wood & Bandura, 1989). They also set cognized

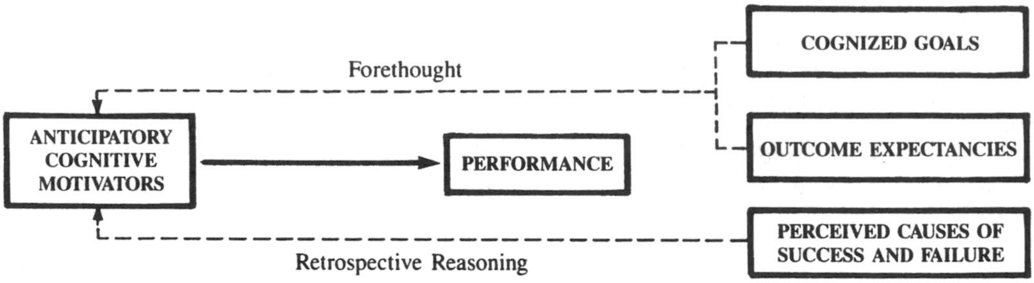

FIGURE 6.5. Schematic representation of conceptions of cognitive motivation based on cognized goals, outcome expectancies, and causal attributions.

challenges for themselves and visualize success scenarios that provide positive guides for performance. Those who doubt their efficacy visualize failure scenarios that undermine performances by dwelling on things that can go wrong. In appraising situations, people who are assured in their efficacy focus on the opportunities worth pursuing rather than dwell on risks (Krueger & Dickson, 1993, 1994). They take a future time perspective in structuring their lives (Eppel, Bandura, & Zimbardo, 1999).

Efficacy beliefs play a central role in the self-regulation of motivation. Most human motivation is cognitively generated. There are three forms of cognitive motivators, around which different theories have been built (Figure 6.5): "causal attributions," "outcome expectancies," and "cognized goals." The corresponding theories are attribution theory, expectancy-value theory, and goal theory. Efficacy beliefs play a key role in each of these motivational systems.

The causal attributions people make for their performances affect their motivation (Weiner, 1986). Efficacy beliefs influence causal attributions, regardless of whether the activities involve cognitive attainments, interpersonal transactions, physical performances, or management of health habits (Bandura, 1997). People who regard themselves as highly efficacious ascribe their failures to insufficient effort, inadequate strategies, or unfavorable circumstances. Those of low efficacy attribute their failures to low ability. The effects of causal attributions on achievement strivings are mediated almost entirely through efficacy beliefs (Relich, Debus, & Walker, 1986; Schunk & Gunn, 1986; Schunk & Rice, 1986).

We have seen in the earlier discussion of self-regulatory capabilities that much human motivation and behavior are regulated anticipatorily by the outcomes expected for given actions (Feather, 1982). However, there are many activities that, if done well, produce valued outcomes, but they are not pursued by people who doubt they can do what it takes to succeed. Such exclusions of large classes of options are made rapidly on efficacy grounds with little thought of costs and benefits. Rational models of decision making that exclude efficacy judgment sacrifice explanatory and predictive power (Bandura, 1997). Perceived self-efficacy not only sets the slate of options for consideration, but also regulates their implementation. Making decisions in no way ensures that the needed courses of action will be executed successfully, especially in the face of difficulties. A psychology of decision making requires a psychology of action grounded in enabling and sustaining efficacy beliefs (Bandura, 1997; Harré, 1983).

The capacity to exercise self-influence by personal challenge through goal setting and evaluative reaction to one's own performances provides another major cognitive mechanism of motivation and self-directedness. Efficacy beliefs play a key role in this form of cognitive motivation as well. It is partly on the basis of efficacy beliefs that people choose which goal challenges to undertake, how much effort to invest and how long to persevere in the face of difficulties (Bandura, 1991a; Locke & Latham, 1990). When faced with obstacles, setbacks, and failures, those who doubt their abilities slacken their efforts, give up, or settle for mediocre solutions. Those who have strong belief in their capabilities redouble their effort and figure out better ways to master the challenges. In short, people of high perceived efficacy set motivating goals for themselves, expect their efforts to produce favorable outcomes, ascribe failures to factors that are potentially controllable through ingenuity and effort, view obstacles as surmountable, and figure out ways to overcome them.

People's beliefs in their coping efficacy affect how much stress, anxiety, and depression they experience in threatening or taxing situations. There are four major ways in which efficacy beliefs regulate emotional states (Bandura, 1997): by influencing how threats are cognitively processed, by supporting coping actions that alter the threats, by exercising control over perturbing thought patterns, and by alleviating aversive affective states.

Efficacy beliefs influence how threats and taxing demands are perceived and cognitively processed. People who believe they can manage threats and adversities view them as less inimical and are not distressed by them. Those who believe they cannot control them experience high anxiety, dwell on their coping deficiencies, view many aspects of their environment as fraught with danger, magnify possible risks, and worry about perils that rarely happen. By such thinking, they distress themselves and impair their functioning (Bandura, 1997; Sanderson, Rapee, & Barlow, 1989).

People who have a high sense of coping efficacy lower their stress and anxiety by acting in ways that transform threatening environments into benign ones. The stronger the sense of efficacy, the bolder people are in tackling the problems that breed stress and anxiety and the greater is their success in shaping the environment to their liking (Bandura, 1997; Williams, 1992).

People have to live with a psychic environment that is largely of their own making. Many human distresses result from failures to control disturbing, ruminative thoughts. Control of one's thought processes is, therefore, a key factor in self-regulation of emotional states. The process of efficacious thought control is summed up well in the proverb: "You cannot prevent the birds of worry and care from flying over your head. But you can stop them from building a nest in your hair." What causes distress is not the sheer frequency of disturbing thoughts, but the perceived inability to turn them off (Kent, 1987; Kent & Gibbons, 1987).

In addition, people can exercise control over their affective states by palliative means without altering the causes of their emotional arousal. They do things that bring relief from unpleasant emotional states when these arise. Belief that one can relieve unpleasant emotional states makes them less aversive (Arch, 1992a, 1992b).

Perceived inefficacy to control things one values also produces depression in varied ways. One route is through unfulfilled aspirations. People who impose on themselves standards of self-worth they judge they cannot attain drive themselves to depression (Bandura, 1991a; Kanfer & Zeiss, 1983). Depression, in turn, weakens people's beliefs in their own efficacy, creating a downward cycle (Kavanagh & Bower, 1985).

A second route to depression is through a low sense of social efficacy to develop social relationships that bring satisfaction to one's life and make chronic stressors easier to bear. A low sense of social efficacy contributes to depression both directly and by curtailing development of social supports (Bandura, Pastorelli, Barbaronelli, & Caprara, 1999; Holahan & Holahan, 1987a, 1987b). Perceived efficacy and social support operate bidirectionally in human adaptation and change. Supportive relationships, in turn, can enhance personal efficacy. Indeed, social support has beneficial effects only to the extent that it raises perceived coping efficacy (Cutrona & Troutman, 1986; Major, Mueller, & Hildebrandt, 1985).

The third route to depression is through thought-control efficacy. Much human depression is cognitively generated by dejecting, ruminative thought (Nolen-Hoeksema, 1991). A low sense of efficacy to control ruminative thought contributes to the occurrence, duration, and recurrence of depressive episodes (Kavanagh & Wilson, 1989).

So far, the analysis of pathways of influence has focused on how efficacy beliefs enable people to create beneficial environments and to exercise control over them. People are partly the product of their environments. By choosing their environments, they can have a hand in what they become. Beliefs of personal efficacy can, therefore, play a key role in shaping the courses lives take by influencing the types of activities and environments people choose to get into (Lent, Brown, & Hackett, 1994). In self-development through choice processes, destinies are shaped by selection of environments known to cultivate valued potentialities and lifestyles.

To sum up, people with a low sense of efficacy avoid difficult tasks, which they view as threats. They have low aspirations and weak commitment to the goals they choose to pursue. They turn inward on their self-doubts instead of thinking about how to perform successfully under pressure. When faced with difficulties, they dwell on obstacles, the negative consequences of failure, and their personal deficiencies. Failure makes them lose faith in themselves because they take it as evidence of their inherent incapability. They slacken their efforts or give up quickly in the face of obstacles. They are slow to recover their sense of efficacy after failures or setbacks and easily fall victim to stress and depression.

People with high perceived self-efficacy, by contrast, approach difficult tasks as challenges to be mastered rather than threats to be avoided. They develop interest in what they do, set challenges for themselves, and sustain strong commitments to them. They concentrate on how to perform successfully rather than on disruptive personal concerns when they encounter problems. They attribute their failures to lack of knowledge or skill, faulty strategies, or insufficient effort, all of which are remediable. They redouble their efforts in the face of obstacles and soon recover their self-assurance after setbacks. This outlook sustains motivation, reduces stress, and lowers vulnerability to depression.

That self-efficacy beliefs yield functional dividends is amply documented by meta-analyses centered on different spheres of functioning (Gillis, 1993; Holden, 1991; Holden, Moncher, Schinke, & Barker, 1990; Stajkovic & Luthans, 1998). Because social cognitive theory articulates the ways in which a strong sense of efficacy can be instilled and delineates the operative mechanisms, this knowledge has been extensively applied to enhance human functioning in diverse spheres of life (Bandura, 1995, 1997; Maddux, 1995; Schwarzer, 1992). These wide-ranging applications include education, health, psychopathology, athletics, organizational innovations, and large-scale social change.

DIFFERENT FORMS OF AGENCY

The exercise of human agency can take different forms. It includes production of effects through "direct personal agency"; through "proxy agency" relying on the efforts of intermediaries; and by collective agency, operating through shared beliefs of efficacy, pooled understandings, group aspirations, incentive systems, and collective action. Each of these expressions of agency is rooted in belief in the power to make things happen.

Proxy Agency

The preceding analyses addressed the direct exercise of personal agency. In many spheres of life, people do not have direct control over social conditions and institutional practices that affect their lives. Under these circumstances, they seek their well-being and security through the exercise of proxy agency rather than through direct control. In this socially mediated mode of agency, people try to get those who wield influence and power to act on their behalf to get what they want (Bandura, 1997). Moreover, people often turn to proxy control in areas in which they can exert direct influence because they have not developed the means to do so, they believe others can do it better, or they do not want to saddle themselves with some of the burdensome aspects of direct control.

Personal control is neither universally desired nor universally exercised, as is commonly assumed. There is an onerous side to direct personal control that can dull the appetite for it. The exercise of control requires mastery of knowledge and skills attainable only through long hours of arduous work. Moreover, maintaining proficiency under ever-changing conditions of life demands continued investment of time, effort, and resources. The prolific composer, Irving Berlin, put it succinctly when he said, "The toughest thing about success is that you've got to keep on being a success."

In addition to the hard work of continual self-development, in many situations the exercise of personal control carries heavy responsibilities, stressors, and risks. People are not too eager to shoulder the burdens of responsibility. All too often, they surrender control to intermediaries in areas over which they can command some direct influence. They do so to free themselves of the performance demands and onerous responsibilities that personal control entails. Part of the price of proxy agency is a vulnerable security that rests on the competence, power, and favors of others.

Perceived Efficacy in Collective Agency

Conceptions of human agency have been confined to individual agency. However, people do not live their lives as isolates. They work together to produce the outcomes they desire but cannot accomplish on their own. Social cognitive theory, therefore, extends the conception of mechanisms of human agency to collective agency. People's shared beliefs in their collective power to produce desired outcomes is a crucial ingredient of collective agency. Group performance is the product of interactive and coordinative dynamics of its members. Therefore, perceived collective efficacy is not simply the sum of the efficacy beliefs of individual members. Rather, it is an emergent group-level property. A group, of course, operates through the behavior of its members. It is people acting collectively on a shared belief, not a disembodied group mind that is doing the cognizing, aspiring, motivating, and regulating. Personal and collective efficacy differ in the unit of agency, but in both forms, efficacy beliefs serve similar functions and operate through similar processes. The stronger the beliefs people hold about their collective capabilities, the more they achieve (Bandura, 1993; Hodges & Carron, 1992; Little & Madigan, 1994; Prussia & Kinicki, 1996; Sampson, Raudenbush, & Earls, 1997).

The patterning of perceived collective political efficacy and trust in the governmental system predicts the form and level of political participation and social activism. People who believe that they can achieve desired changes through citizen action and regard their governmental system as trustworthy and socially responsive display high involvement in conventional models of political action (Craig, 1979; Finkel, 1985; Pollock, 1983; Zimmerman & Rappaport, 1988). In contrast, those who believe they can produce political change through tenacious collective action but view the governmental systems and its leaders as fundamentally unresponsive and untrustworthy favor more confrontive and coercive tactics outside the traditional political channels. The politically apathetic have a low sense of efficacy that they can influence governmental functioning through collective initiatives and are disaffected from the political system as not acting in their interest (Bandura, 1997).

Some people live their lives in individualistically oriented social systems, whereas others do so in collectivistically oriented systems (Triandis, 1995). Some writers inappropriately equate self-efficacy with individualism and pit it against collectivism (Schooler, 1990). In fact, a high sense of personal efficacy contributes just as importantly to group-directedness as to self-directedness. If people are to work together successfully, the members of a group have to perform their roles with a high sense of efficacy. Personal efficacy is valued not because of reverence for individualism but because a strong sense of efficacy is vital for successful functioning, regardless of whether it is achieved individually or by group members working together.

Cross-cultural research on organizational functioning corroborates the universal functional value of efficacy beliefs (Earley, 1993, 1994). Beliefs of personal efficacy contribute to productivity by members of collectivist cultures just as they do by those raised in individualistic cultures. But cultural context shapes how efficacy beliefs are developed, the purposes to which they are put, and the social arrangements through which they are best expressed. People from individualistic cultures, such as the United States, feel most efficacious and perform best under an individual-oriented system. Those from collectivistic cultures, such as Hong Kong and China, judge themselves most efficacious and work most productively under a group-oriented system.

Cultures are not static, uniform entities, as the stereotypic portrayals would lead one to believe. Collectivistic systems, founded on Confucianism, Buddhism, or Marxism, favor a communal ethic but they differ from each other in the values, meanings, and customs they promote (Kim, Triandis, Kâgitçibasi, Choi, & Yoon, 1994). Nor are so-called individualistic cultures a uniform lot. Americans, Italians, Germans and the British differ in their particular brands of individualism. Even within an individual-oriented culture, such as in the United States, the New England brand of individualism is quite different from the Californian version, as well as from the Texan brand.

There is substantial heterogeneity among individuals in communality within both individualistic and collectivistic cultures and even greater intraindividual variation in communality across social relationships with family members, friends, and colleagues (Matsumoto, Kudoh, & Takeuchi, 1996). There are generational and socioeconomic variations in collectivistic cultures with younger and more affluent members adopting more individualistic orientations. Moreover, people express their cultural orientations conditionally rather than invariantly depending on incentive conditions (Yamagishi, 1988).

There are collectivists in individualistic cultures, and individualists in collectivistic cultures. Regardless of cultural background, people achieve the greatest personal efficacy and productivity when their personal orientation is congruent with the social system (Earley, 1994). Thus, American collectivists do better under a group-oriented system, Chinese individualists do better under an individual-oriented system. The personal orientation rather than the cultural orientation is a major carrier of the effects. Both at the societal and individual level of analysis, a strong perceived efficacy fosters high group effort and performance attainments.

Cultures are no longer insular. Global market forces are restructuring national economies and shaping the political and social life of societies. Advanced telecommunications technologies are disseminating ideas, values, and styles of behavior transnationally at an unprecedented rate. These new realities call for broadening the scope of cross-cultural analyses beyond the focus on social forces operating within the boundaries of given societies to the forces impinging upon them from abroad. With growing international imbeddedness and interdependence of societies, the issues of interest center on how national and global forces interact to shape the nature of cultural life.

Underminers of Collective Efficacy in Changing Societies

Life in the societies of today is increasingly shaped by transnational interdependencies (Keohane & Nye, 1977; Keohane, 1993). Because of extensive global interconnectedness, what happens economically and politically in one part of the world can affect the welfare of vast populations elsewhere. The transnational forces, which are hard to disentangle let alone control, challenge the efficacy of governmental systems to exert a determining influence on their own economic and national life. As the need for efficacious collective effort grows, so does the sense of collective powerlessness. Many of the contemporary conditions of life undermine the development of collective efficacy.

Some of the transnational market forces may erode or undermine valued cultural aspects of life when they are disregarded or considered detractors from profitability. Social bonds and common commitments that lack marketability are especially vulnerable to erosion by global market forces. There are no handy social mechanisms or global agencies through which people can shape and regulate transnational practices that affect their lives. As nations wrestle with the loss of control, the public expresses disillusionment and cynicism over whether their leaders and institutions can work for them to improve their lives.

Under the new realities of growing transnational control, nation states increase their controlling leverage by merging into larger regional units such as the European Union. Other regional nation states will similarly be forced to merge into larger blocks, otherwise they will have little bargaining power in transnational relations. These regional marriages do not come without a price. Paradoxically, to gain international control, nations have to negotiate reciprocal pacts that require some loss of national autonomy and changes in traditional ways of life (Keohane, 1993). Some sectors of the society gain from the pacts, others lose.

Modern life is increasingly regulated by complex technologies that most people neither understand nor believe they can do much to influence. The very technologies that people create to control their life environment can become a constraining force that, in turn, controls how they think and behave. The social machinery of society is no less challenging. Bureaucracies thwart effective social action. Many of the bureaucratic practices are designed more to benefit the people who run the social systems than to serve the public. Social change does not come easily because beneficiaries build their privileges into protective institutional structures and processes. Those who exercise authority and control wield their power to maintain their advantages. Long delays between action and noticeable results discourage efforts at change.

Social efforts to change lives for the better require merging diverse self-interests in support of common core values and goals. Disagreements among different constituencies create additional obstacles to successful collective action. The recent years have witnessed growing social fragmentation into separate interest groups, each exercising its own power. Pluralism is taking the form of antagonistic factionalism. In addition, mass migration of people fleeing tyranny or seeking a better life is changing cultural landscapes. Societies are thus becoming more diverse and harder to unite around a national vision and purpose.

The magnitude of human problems also undermines perceived efficacy to find effective solutions for them. Profound global changes, arising from burgeoning populations, deforestation, desertification of croplands, ozone depletion, and rapid extinction of species by razing their habitats are destroying the intertwined ecosystems that sustain life. Worldwide problems of growing magnitude instill a sense of paralysis that there is little people can do to reduce such problems. Global effects are the products of local actions. The strategy of "Think globally, act locally" is an effort to restore in people a sense of efficacy, that they can make a difference. Macrosocial applications of sociocognitive principles via the electronic media illustrate how small collective efforts can have huge impacts on such urgent global problems as the soaring population growth (Singhal & Rogers, 1989; Vaughn, Rogers, & Swalehe, 1995; Westoff & Rodriguez, 1995).

PERSONALITY AS INTEGRATED SELF SYSTEM

Sociocognitive theories are commonly misconstrued as atomistic, without an overreaching "personality." The umbrella term "personality" represents a complex of interacting attributes, not a self-contained entity describable by a few pithy terms creating the illusion of a high-order structure. Personality is multifaceted, richly contextualized, and conditionally expressed in the diverse transactions of everyday life. The totality of an individual's cognitive, behavioral, and affective proclivities is not shrinkable to a few static descriptive categories.

Unity of Agency and Personal Identity

People express their individuality and give structure, meaning, and purpose to their lives by acting on their beliefs about themselves, their values, personal standards, aspirations, and construals of the world around them. These multiform belief systems, self structures, and self-referent processes through which one's "personality" is manifested in its totality function in concert not isolatedly. It is through coordinative and integrative activity that the diverse sources of influence produce unity of experience and action. The self embodies all of the endowments, belief systems, and distributed structures and functions through which personal agency is exercised rather than residing as a discrete entity in a particular place. In short, the self is the person, not a homunculian subpart. "Personality" is the integrated self system within which the previously identified constituents operate in complex mutual interaction in the management of diverse and changing environmental circumstances. The various constituents must be orchestrated in an integrated way because, whatever options are considered, the choices finally made and the actions taken at a given time require unity of agency. Given but a single body, one cannot perform incompatible acts simultaneously. People may, of course, exhibit contradictory behavior, but these are instances of the same being doing discordant things on different occasions not different selves doing their separate things.

Personal identity refers to self-characterizations that tell what one is. Social cognitive theory and research not only examine the individual properties of these key constituents of the self system but how they contribute to personal identity and functioning within the organized multifaceted system of determinants (Bandura, 1997). The exercise of agency through the interrelated self structures and regulatory processes shapes the kind of life people live and what they consider themselves to be. The personal identity they create for themselves derives, in large part, from how they live their life and reflect upon it. The continuity of personal identity resides more in psychological factors and the experiential continuity of the course of life followed than in physical constancy. An amnesiac remains the same physically but has lost a sense of personal identity. Continuing self-identity is preserved in memories that give temporal coherence to life (McAdams, 1996), in continuance of belief and value commitments that link the present to the past and shape the course of future events, and in the connectedness of human relationships and one's life work over time.

Continuing self-identity is not solely a product of an intrapsychic autobiographical process that preserves a sense of personal continuity over time. Others perceive, socially label, and treat one as the same person over the course of life. Personal identity is partially constructed from one's social identity as reflected in how one is treated by significant others. In keeping with the model of triadic reciprocal causation, a sense of selfhood is the product of a complex interplay of social and personal construal processes. Others, of course, have only a limited sample of a given person's social life and know even much less of that individual's experiential life. Consequently, the social identity conveyed by others is more heavily dependent on the sameness of physical characteristics, social roles, and habitual behaviors that are publicly observable than on personal uniqueness and experiential factors.

Identity formation is an ongoing process, not one characterized by fixedness in time. Moreover, the self-view is multifaceted rather than monolithic. There are many aspects to the self. They are not equally salient, valued, or functional in different spheres of life or under different circumstances. In a dynamic, multifaceted model, continuity of personal identity requires neither high consistency among different aspects of self nor invariance across different social environments or domains of functioning. For given individuals, their personal identities are likely to be composed of unique amalgams of identities with national, social, political, ethnic, occupational, and familial aspects of life depending on their value commitments. Thus, for a particular individual, a strong occupational identity may coexist with a moderate ethnic identity and a weak political identity without any felt discordance because these aspects differ in the value placed on them. Another individual, with dissimilar value commitments, may exhibit a quite different constellation of identities, combining a strong ethnic and political identity with a weak occupational identity. Similarly, a person's self-view with parents may differ significantly from the self-view in relationships with peers because these social worlds tap somewhat different aspects of the self. In each case, however, it is one and the same person manifesting a multifaceted personal identity. It is the temporal stability of the patterned self-view rather than high coherence of aspects that defines one's personal uniqueness and sense of continuity. Theories that construe personal identity as a fixed monolith are discordant with a vast body of evidence.

With further experiences over time, people evolve and integrate some new aspects into their self-identity. This raises the issue of how they extract continuity from variability across time, activity domains, and social contexts. To the extent that they consider mainly core aspects or focus on different aspects of themselves as relevant in different life situations, they can change in particulars but preserve a sense of continuity in their view of themselves. However, if they undergo major life changes, they consider themselves to be different persons from whom they were in the past. Taken as a whole, the findings of diverse lines of research on the various personal properties subsumed under the spacious construct of "personality," attest to the explanatory, predictive and operative efficacy of theories that specify multiform personal structures operating conditionally through self-regulatory mechanisms within the contextual influences in which people construct and conduct their lives (Bandura, 1986, 1997). The oft-repeated query, "Where is the person in the personality theory?," is essentially a call for a disembodied homuncular self. Self-referent cognitive processes are embedded in a whole organism with the totality of attributes and regulative proclivities representing the distinctive personhood.

The Nature of Human Nature

Social cognitive theory acknowledges the influential role of evolutionary factors in human adaptation and change, but rejects one-sided evolutionism in which social behavior is the product of evolved biology but social and technological innovations that create new environmental selection pressures for adaptiveness have no effect on biological evolution. In the bidirectional view of evolutionary processes, evolutionary pressures fostered changes in biological structures and upright posture conducive to the development and use of tools, which enabled an organism to manipulate, alter, and construct new environmental conditions. Environmental innovations of increasing complexity, in turn, created new selection pressures for the evolution of specialized biological systems for functional consciousness, thought, language, and symbolic communication.

All too often, the multicausality of human behavior is misleadingly framed in terms of partitioning behavioral variance into percent nature and percent nurture. This causal dualism is mistaken for several reasons. It disregards the *interdependence* of nature and nurture. Socially constructed nurture has a hand in shaping nature. It also fails to address fundamental issues concerning the operational nature of human nature. Human evolution provides bodily structures and biological potentialities, not behavioral dictates. Psychosocial influences operate through these biological resources in the construction and regulation of human behavior acting in the service of diverse purposes. Having evolved, the advanced biological capacities can be used to create diverse cultures–aggressive ones, pacific ones, egalitarian ones or autocratic ones. As Stephen J. Gould (1987) notes, biology sets constraints that vary in nature, degree, and strength across different spheres of functioning, but in most domains of human functioning biology permits a broad range of cultural possibilities. He argues cogently that evidence favors a potentialist view over a determinist view. In this insightful analysis, the major explanatory battle is not between nature and nurture as commonly portrayed, but whether nature operates as a determinist or as a potentialist. Gould makes the further interesting point that biological determinism is often clothed in the language of interactionism, to make it more palatable. The bidirectional biology–culture coevolution is acknowledged but then the major causation of human behavior is ascribed to evolved biology. The cultural side of this two-way causation, in which genetic makeup is shaped by the adaptational pressures of socially constructed environments, receives little notice. Biological determinism is also often clothed in the language of changeability: The malleability of evolved proclivities is acknowledged but determinative potency is then ascribed to them with caution against efforts to change existing sociostructural arrangements and practices allegedly ruled by evolved dispositions. Such efforts are regarded as not only doomed to failure but socially harmful because they go against the dictates of nature (Wilson, 1998). In Wilson's view, biology has culture on a "tight leash"; in Gould's (1987) view, biology has culture on a "loose leash." The conception of the operational nature of human nature affects the relative explanatory weight given to genetic mismatch and to the counterforce of entrenched vested interests for resistance to sociostructural changes. Biological determinists favor heavily the rule of nature, whereas biological potentialists see human nature as permitting a range of possibilities that gives greater saliency to the rule of distributed opportunities, privileges, and power. Thus, a biological determinist view highlights inherent constraints and limitations. A biological potentialist view of human nature emphasizes multiform human possibilities.

Psychological evolutionists often take a more extreme deterministic stance regarding the dictates of nature (Buss, 1985) than do many biological evolutionists (Dobzhansky, 1972); Fuasto-Sterling, 1992; Gould, 1987). Psychological evolutionists are also quick to invoke evolved behavioral traits as cultural universals; whereas biological evolutionists emphasize functional relations between organism and situated environment that underscore the diversifying selection influence of variant ecological contexts. Ancestral origin of bodily structures and biological potentialities and the determinants governing contemporary social practices are quite different matters. Because evolved potentialities can serve diverse purposes, ancestral origin dictates neither current social function nor singular sociostructural arrangements. The conceptual, methodological, and ideological aspects of psychological evolutionism have been addressed elsewhere in analysis of the factors governing gender development and differentiations (Bussey & Bandura, in press).

Theories that heavily attribute human social behavior to the rule of nature are disputed by the remarkable cultural diversity. Consider aggression, which is presumably genetically programmed as a biological universal and more so for males than for females. There are three types of cultural diversity that challenge the view that people are inherently aggressive. The first concerns intercultural diversity. There are fighting cultures that breed aggression by modeling it pervasively, attaching prestige to it, and according it functional value for gaining social status, material benefits, and social control. There are pacific cultures in which interpersonal aggression is a rarity because it is devalued, rarely modeled, and has no functional value (Alland, 1972; Bandura, 1973; Sanday, 1981). Is the genetic makeup of the Germans who perpetrated unprecedented barbarity really different from the genetic makeup of peaceable Swiss residing in the German canton of Switzerland? People possess the biological potentiality for aggression, but the answer to the differential aggressiveness in the latter case lies more in ideology than in biology.

The second form of variability concerns intracultural diversity. The Unites States is a relatively violent society, but American Quakers and Hutterites, who adopt pacifism as a way of life, eschew aggressive conduct. The third form of variability that challenges the view that aggression is coded in the genes involves rapid transformation of warring societies into peaceful ones. For ages the Vikings plundered other nations. After a prolonged war with Russia that exhausted Sweden's resources, the populace rose up and collectively forced a constitutional change that prohibited kings from starting wars (Moerk, 1995). This political act promptly transformed a fighting society into a peaceable one that has served as a mediator for peace among warring nations. This rapid cultural metamorphosis underscores the power of the dictates of nurture. Sweden ranks at the very bottom of all forms of violence within the society, with virtually no incidence of domestic violence.

A biologically universalistic view has problems not only with cultural diversity but with the rapid pace of social change. The process of biological selection moves at a snails pace, whereas societies have been undergoing major changes in sexual mores, family structures, social and occupational roles, and institutional practices. Ancestral origin and the determinants governing contemporary social practices are quite different matters. Because evolved potentialities can serve diverse purposes, ancestral origin dictates neither current function nor a singular sociostructural arrangement. Social systems and practices are being changed by social means rather than by reliance on the protracted process of biological selection. Dobzhansky (1972) reminds us that the human species has been selected for learnability and plasticity of behavior adaptive to remarkably diverse habitats and socially constructed environments, not for behavioral fixedness. The pace of social change gives testimony that biology, indeed, permits a range of possibilities.

Seen from the social cognitive perspective, human nature is characterized by a vast potentiality that can be fashioned by direct and vicarious experience into a variety of forms within biological limits. To say that a major distinguishing mark of humans is their endowed plasticity is not to say that they have no nature or that they come structureless (Midgley, 1978). The plasticity, which is intrinsic to the nature of humans, depends upon specialized neurophysiological structures and mechanisms that have evolved over time. These advanced neural systems are specialized for channeling attention, detecting the causal structure of the world around one, transforming that information into abstract form, integrating it, and using it for adaptive purposes. The evolved morphology and special-purpose systems facilitate acquisitional processes. Social cognitive theory does not assume an equipotential mechanism of learning (Bandura, 1986). In addition to biological biases, some things are more easily learnable because the properties of the events can facilitate or impede acquisitional processes. The evolved informative processing systems provide the capacity for the very characteristics that are distinctly human—generative symbolization, forethought, evaluative self-regulation, reflective self-consciousness, and symbolic communication.

Although neurophysiological systems have been shaped by evolutionary pressures, people are not just reactive products of selection pressures. They are producers of new selection pressures. Through agentic action, they devise ways of adapting flexibly to remarkably diverse environments; they circumvent environmental constraints, redesign and construct environments to their liking, create styles of behavior that enable them to realize desired outcomes, and pass on the effective ones to others by social modeling and other experiential means. Indeed, growth of knowledge has greatly enhanced human power to control, transform, and create environments of increasing complexity. We build physical technologies that drastically alter how we live our daily lives; we create mechanical devices that compensate immensely for our sensory and physical limitations; we develop medical and psychological methods that enable us to exert some measure of control over our physical and psychosocial lives; through contraceptive ingenuity that disjoined sex from procreation, humans have outwitted and taken control over their evolved reproductive system; we have created biotechnologies to change the genetic makeup of plants and animals, and are now even cloning clones; and we are exploring methods that could alter the genetic codes of humans. People have changed little genetically over recent decades, but they have changed markedly through rapid cultural and technological evolution in their thinking, styles of behavior, and the roles they perform. There is much genetic homogeneity across cultures but vast diversity in belief systems and conduct. Given this variability, genetic coding that characterizes humans underscores the power of the environment orchestrated through agentic action. As people devise ever more powerful technologies that transform environments, the psychosocial side of coevolution is gaining ascendancy. By creating ever more complex environments, humans are becoming major agents of their own evolution.

Most patterns of human behavior are organized by individual experience and retained in neural codes rather than having been provided ready-made by inborn programming. Although human behavior is fashioned largely through experience, innately determined factors enter into every form of behavior to varying degrees. Genetic factors affect behavioral potentialities, which, through their actualization, can influence the kinds of environments that are experienced and constructed. The experiences produced by agentic action shape the nature of brain development and quality of functioning. Both experientially derived factors and genetically determined ones interact, often in intricate synergistic ways, to determine behavior. The level of psychological and biological development, of course, limits what can be acquired at any given time.

Humans have an unparalleled capacity to become many things. The qualities that are cultivated and the life paths that realistically become open to them are partly determined by the nature of the societal systems to which their development is entrusted. Social systems that cultivate generalizable competencies, instill a robust sense of efficacy, create opportunity structures, provide aidful resources, and allow room for self-directedness increase the chances that people will realize what they wish to become.

ACKNOWLEDGMENTS

Preparation of this chapter and some of the cited research were supported by grants from the Grant Foundation, the Spencer Foundation, and the Johann Jacobs Foundation. Some sections of this chapter include revised, updated, and expanded material from the books *Social Foundations of Thought and Action: A Social Cognitive Theory* (Bandura, 1986) and *Self-Efficacy: The Exercise of Control* (Bandura, 1997).

REFERENCES

Alland, A., Jr. (1972). *The human imperative*. New York: Columbia University Press.

Almagor, M., Tellegen, A., & Waller, N. G. (1995). The big seven model: A cross-cultural replication and further exploration of the basic dimensions of natural language trait descriptors. *Journal of Personality and Social Psychology, 69,* 300–307.

Arch, E. C. (1992a). Affective control efficacy as a factor in willingness to participate in a public performance situation. *Psychological Reports, 71,* 1247-1250.

Arch, E. C. (1992b). Sex differences in the effect of self-efficacy on willingness to participate in a performance situation. *Psychological Reports, 70,* 3–9.

Austin, J. H. (1978). *Chase, chance, and creativity: The lucky art of novelty*. New York: Columbia University Press.

Baldwin, C., Baldwin, A., Sameroff, A., & Seifer, R. (1989, April). *The role of family interaction in the prediction of adolescent competence*. Paper presented at the Biennial Meeting of the Society for Research in Child Development, Kansas City, MO.

Ball-Rokeach, S., & DeFleur, M. (1976). A dependency model of mass media effects. *Communication Research, 3,* 3–21.

Baltes, P. B., Lindenberger, U., & Staudinger, U. M. (1998). Life-span theory in development psychology. In R. M. Lerner (Ed.), *Handbook of child psychology* (5th ed.): *Vol. 1. Theoretical models of human development* (Editor-in-Chief: William Damon, pp. 1029–1143). New York: Wiley.

Bandura, A. (1973). *Aggression: A social learning analysis*. Englewood Cliffs, NJ: Prentice Hall.

Bandura, A. (1982a). Self-efficacy mechanism in human agency. *American Psychologist, 37,* 122–147.

Bandura, A. (1982b). The psychology of chance encounters and life paths. *American Psychologist, 37,* 747-755.

Bandura, A. (1986). *Social foundations of thought and action: A social cognitive theory*. Englewood Cliffs, NJ: Prentice Hall.

Bandura, A. (1991a). Self-regulation of motivation through anticipatory and self-regulatory mechanisms. In R. A. Dienstbier (Ed.), *Nebraska symposium on motivation: Vol. 38. Perspectives on motivation* (pp. 69–164). Lincoln, NE: University of Nebraska Press.

Bandura, A. (1991b). Social cognitive theory of moral thought and action. In W. M. Kurtines & J. L. Gewirtz (Eds.), *Handbook of moral behavior and development* (Vol. A, pp. 45–103). Hillsdale, NJ: Erlbaum.

Bandura, A. (1992). Social cognitive theory and social referencing. In S. Feinman (Ed.), *Social referencing and the social construction of reality in infancy* (pp. 175–208). New York: Plenum Press.

Bandura, A. (1993). Perceived self-efficacy in cognitive development and functioning. *Educational Psychologist, 28,* 117-148.

Bandura, A. (Ed.). (1995). *Self-efficacy in changing societies*. New York: Cambridge University Press.

Bandura, A. (1997). *Self-efficacy: The exercise of control*. New York: Freeman.

Bandura, A. (1998a). Exploration of fortuitous determinants of life paths. *Psychological Inquiry, 9,* 95–99.

Bandura, A. (1998b). Health promotion from the perspective of social cognitive theory. *Psychology and Health, 13,* 623–649.

Bandura, A. (in press). Moral disengagement in the perpetration of inhumanities. [Special Issue on Evil]. *Personality and Social Psychology Review*.

Bandura, A., Barbaranelli, C., Caprara, G. V., & Pastorelli, C. (1996a). Mechanisms of moral disengagement in the exercise of moral agency. *Journal of Personality and Social Psychology, 71,* 364–374.

Bandura, A., Barbaranelli, C., Caprara, G. V., & Pastorelli, C. (1996b). Multifaceted impact of self-efficacy beliefs on academic functioning. *Child Development, 67,* 1206–1222.

Bandura, A., Barbaranelli, C., Caprara, G.V., & Pastorelli, C. (1999). *Efficacy beliefs as shapers of aspirations and occupational trajectories*. Submitted for publication.

Bandura, A., & Cervone, D. (1986). Differential engagement of self-reactive influences in cognitive motivation. *Organizational Behavior and Human Decision Processes, 38,* 92–113.

Bandura, A., & Jourden, F. J. (1991). Self-regulatory mechanisms governing the impact of social comparison on complex decision making. *Journal of Personality and Social Psychology, 60,* 941–951.

Bandura, A., Pastorelli, C., Barbaranelli, C., & Caprara, G. V. (1999). Self-efficacy pathways to childhood depression. *Journal of Personality and Social Psychology, 76,* 258–269.

Bandura, A., & Rosenthal, T. L. (1978). Psychological modeling: Theory and practice. In S. L. Garfield & A. E. Bergin (Eds.), *Handbook of psychotherapy and behavior change* (2nd ed., pp. 621–658). New York: Wiley.

Bandura, A., Ross, D., & Ross, S. A. (1963). A comparative test of the status envy, social power, and secondary reinforcement theories of identificatory learning. *Journal of Abnormal and Social Psychology, 67,* 527–534.

Bandura, A., Underwood, B., & , Fromson, M. E. (1975). Disinhibition of aggression through diffusion of responsibility and dehumanization of victims. *Journal of Research in Personality, 9,* 253–269.

Bandura, A., & Walters, R. H. (1959). *Adolescent aggression.* New York: Ronald Press.

Bandura, A., & Wood, R. E. (1989). Effect of perceived controllability and performance standards on self-regulation of complex decision making. *Journal of Personality and Social Psychology, 56,* 805–814.

Barrett, P., & Kline, P. (1982). An item and radial parcel factor analysis of the 16 PF questionnaire. *Personality and Individual Differences, 3,* 259–270.

Barrick, M. R., Mount, M. K., & Strauss, J. P. (1993). Conscientiousness and performance of sales representatives: Test of the mediating effects of goal setting. *Journal of Applied Psychology, 76,* 715–722.

Belcher, T. L. (1975). Modeling original divergent responses: An initial investigation. Journal of *Educational Psychology, 67,* 351–358.

Berger, S. M. (1962). Conditioning through vicarious instigation. *Psychological Review, 69,* 450–466.

Block, J. (1995). A contrarian view of the five-factor approach to personality description. *Psychological Bulletin, 117,* 187–215.

Bolinger, D. (1982). *Language: The loaded weapon.* London: Longman.

Bouffard-Bouchard, T., Parent, S., & Larivée, S. (1991). Influence of self-efficacy on self-regulation and performance among junior and senior high school age students. *International Journal of Behavioral Development, 14,* 153–164.

Braithwaite, J. (1994). A sociology of modeling and the politics of empowerment. *British Journal of Sociology, 45,* 445–479.

Brandstädter, J., Krampen, G., & Heil, F. E. (1996). Personal control and emotional evaluation of development in partnership relations during adulthood. In M. M. Baltes & P. B. Baltes (Eds.), *The psychology of control and aging* (pp. 265–296). Hillsdale, NJ: Erlbaum.

Bromley, D. G., & Shupe, A. D. (1979). *"Moonies" in America: Cult, church, and crusade.* Beverly Hills: Sage.

Bunge, M. (1977). Emergence and the mind. *Neuroscience, 2,* 501–509.

Burns, T. R., & Dietz, T. (in press). Human agency and evolutionary processes: Institutional dynamics and social revolution. In B. Wittrock (Ed.), *Agency in social theory.* Thousand Oaks, CA.: Sage.

Buss, D. M. (1985). Psychological sex differences: Origins through sexual selection. *American Psychologist, 50,* 164–168.

Bussey, K. & Bandura, A. (in press). Social cognitive theory of gender development and differentiation. *Psychological Review.*

Caprara, G. V., Barbaranelli, C., & Pastorelli, C. (1998, July). *Comparative test of longitudinal predictiveness of perceived self-efficacy and big five factors.* Paper presented at the 9th Conference on Personality, University of Surrey, United Kingdom.

Carlson, R. (1992). Shrinking personality: One cheer for the big five. *Contemporary Psychology, 37,* 644–645.

Carroll, W. R., & Bandura, A. (1990). Representational guidance of action production in observational learning: A causal analysis. *Journal of Motor Behavior, 22,* 85–97.

Carver, C. S., & Scheier, M. F. (1981). *Attention and self-regulation: A control-theory approach to human behavior.* New York: Springer-Verlag.

Costa, P. T., Jr., & McCrae, R. R. (1994). "Set like plaster?" Evidence for the stability of adult personality. In T. Heatherton & J. Weinberger (Eds.), *Can personality change?* (pp. 21–40). Washington, DC: American Psychological Association.

Craig, S. C. (1979). Efficacy, trust, and political behavior: An attempt to resolve a lingering conceptual dilemma. *American Politics Quarterly, 7,* 225–239.

Cutrona, C. E., & Troutman, B. R. (1986). Social support, infant temperament, and parenting self-efficacy: A mediational model of postpartum depression. *Child Development, 57,* 1507–1518.

Diamond, M. C. (1988). *Enriching heredity.* New York: The Free Press.

Diener, E. (1977). Deindividuation: Causes and consequences. *Social Behavior and Personality, 5,* 143–156.

Digman, J. M. (1997). Higher-order factors of the big five. *Journal of Personality and Social Psychology, 73,* 1246–1256.

Dobzhansky, T. (1972). Genetics and the diversity of behavior. *American Psychologist, 27,* 523–530.

Duncker, K. (1938). Experimental modification of children's food preferences through social suggestion. *Journal of Abnormal Social Psychology, 33,* 489–507.

Earley, P. C. (1993). East meets West meets Mideast: Further explorations of collectivistic and individualistic work groups. *Academy of Management Journal, 36,* 319–348.

Earley, P. C. (1994). Self or group? Cultural effects of training on self-efficacy and performance. *Administrative Science Quarterly, 39,* 89–117.

Elder, G. H., & Ardelt, M. (1992, March 18–20). *Families adapting to economic pressure: Some consequences for parents and adolescents.* Paper presented at the Society for Research on Adolescence, Washington, DC.

Endler, N. S., & Parker, J. D. A. (1992). Interactionism revisited: Reflections on the continuing crisis in the personality area. *European Journal of Personality, 6,* 177–198.

Eppel, E. S., Bandura, A., & Zimbardo, P. G. (1999). Escaping homelessness: Influence of self-efficacy and time perspective on coping with homelessness. *Journal of Applied Social Psychology, 29,* 595–596.

Epstein, S. (1983). The stability of behavior across time and situations. In R. Zucker, J. Aronoff, & A. I. Rabin (Eds.), *Personality and the prediction of behavior* (pp. 209–268). San Diego, CA: Academic Press.

Eysenck, H. J. (1991). Dimensions of personality: 16, 5 or 3?—Criteria for a taxonomic paradigm. *Personality and Individual Differences, 12,* 773–790.

Falmagne, R. J. (1975). *Reasoning: Representation and process in children and adults.* Hillsdale, NJ: Erlbaum.

Fausto-Sterling, A. (1992). *Myths of gender: Biological theories about women and men* (2nd ed.). New York: Basic Books.

Feather, N. T. (Ed.). (1982). *Expectations and actions: Expectancy-value models in psychology.* Hillsdale, NJ: Erlbaum.

Feldman, D. H. (1980). *Beyond universals in cognitive development.* Norwood, NJ: Ablex.

Ferguson, T. J., & Rule, B. G. (1983). An attributional perspective on anger and aggression. In R. G. Geen & E. I. Donnerstein (Eds.), *Aggression: Theoretical and empirical,* (Vol. 1, pp. 41–74). New York: Academic Press.

Festinger, L. (1954). A theory of social comparison processes. *Human Relations, 7,* 117-140.

Finkel, S. E. (1985). Reciprocal effects of participation and political efficacy: A panel analysis. *American Journal of Political Science, 29,* 891–913.

Flavell, J. H. (1978). Developmental stage: Explanans or explanadum? *Behavioral and Brain Sciences, 2,* 187–188.

Gerbner, G. (1972). Communication and social environment. *Scientific American, 227,* 153–160.

Giddens, A. (1984). *The constitution of society: Outline of the theory of structuration.* Cambridge, UK: Polity Press; Berkeley, CA: University of California Press.

Gillespie, W. H. (1971). Aggression and instinct theory. *International Journal of Psycho-Analysis, 52,* 155–160.

Gillis, A. J. (1993). Determinants of a health-promoting lifestyle: An integrative review. *Journal of Advance Nursing, 18,* 345–353.

Goethals, G. R., & Darley, J. M. (1977). Social comparison theory: Attributional approach. In J. M. Suls & R. L. Miller (Eds.), *Social comparison processes: Theoretical and empirical perspectives* (pp. 259–278). Washington, DC: Hemisphere.

Gould, S. J. (1987). *An urchin in the storm.* New York: Norton.

Green, C. D., & Vervaeke, J. (1996). What kind of explanation, if any, is a connectionist net? In C. W. Tolman, F. Cherry, R. van Hezewijk, & I. Lubek (Eds.), *Problems of theoretical psychology* (pp. 201–208). North York, ON: Captus.

Greenwood, J. D. (1992). Against eliminative materialism: From folk psychology to Völkerpsychologie. *Philosophical Psychology, 5,* 349–367.

Guastello, S. J. (1993). A two-(and-a-half)-tiered trait taxonomy. *American Psychologist, 48,* 1298–1299.

Hall, J. R. (1987). *Gone from the promised land: Jonestown in American cultural history.* New Brunswick, NJ: Transaction Books.

Hamburg, D. A. (1992). *Today's children: Creating a future for a generation in crisis.* New York: Times Books.

Haritos-Fatouros, M. (1988). The official torturer: A learning model for obedience to the authority of violence. *Journal of Applied Social Psychology, 18,* 1107–1120.

Harré, R. (1983). *Personal being: A theory for individual psychology.* Oxford: Blackwell.

Harré, R., & Gillet, G. (1994). *The discursive mind.* Thousand Oaks, CA: Sage.

Harris, M. B., & Evans, R. C. (1973). Models and creativity. *Psychological Reports, 33,* 763–769.

Hawkins, R. P., & Pingree, S. (1991). Divergent psychological processes in constructing social reality from mass media content. In N. Signorielli & M. Morgan (Eds.), *New directions in media effects research: Vol. 108. Cultivation analysis* (pp. 35–50). Beverly Hills, CA: Sage.

Hodges, L., & Carron, A. V. (1992). Collective efficacy and group performance. *International Journal of Sport Psychology, 23,* 48–59.

Holahan, C. K., & Holahan, C. J. (1987a). Life stress, hassles, and self-efficacy in aging: A replication and extension. *Journal of Applied Social Psychology, 17,* 574–592.

Holahan, C. K., & Holahan, C. J. (1987b). Self-efficacy, social support, and depression in aging: A longitudinal analysis. *Journal of Gerontology, 42,* 65–68.

Holden, G. (1991). The relationship of self-efficacy appraisals to subsequent health related outcomes: A meta-analysis. *Social Work in Health Care, 16,* 53–93.

Holden, G., Moncher, M. S., Schinke, S. P., & Barker, K. M. (1990). Self-efficacy of children and adolescents: A meta-analysis. *Psychological Reports, 66,* 1044–1046.

Hough, L. M. (1992). The "Big Five" personality variables—Construct confusion: Description versus prediction. *Human Performance, 5,* 139–155.

Jackson, D. N., Ashton, M. C., & Tomes, J. L. (1996). The six-factor model of personality: Facets from the big five. *Personality and Individual Differences, 21,* 391–402.

Jackson, D. N., Paunonen, S. V., Fraboni, M., & Goffin, R. D. (1996). A five-factor versus six-factor model of personality structure. *Personality and Individual Differences, 20,* 33–46.

Kanfer, R., & Zeiss, A. M. (1983). Depression, interpersonal standard-setting, and judgments of self-efficacy. *Journal of Abnormal Psychology, 92,* 319–329.

Kavanagh, D. J., & Bower, G. H. (1985). Mood and self-efficacy: Impact of joy and sadness on perceived capabilities. *Cognitive Therapy and Research, 9,* 507–525.

Kavanagh, D. J., & Wilson, P. H. (1989). Prediction of outcome with a group version of cognitive therapy for depression. *Behaviour Research and Therapy, 27,* 333–347.

Kazdin, A. E. (1974). Comparative effects of some variations of covert modeling. *Journal of Behavior Therapy and Experimental Psychiatry, 5,* 225–232.

Keen, S. (1986). *Faces of the enemy.* San Francisco: Harper & Row.

Kelman, H. C., & Hamilton, V. L. (1989). *Crimes of obedience: Toward a social psychology of authority and responsibility.* New Haven, CT: Yale University Press.

Kent, G. (1987). Self-efficacious control over reported physiological, cognitive and behavioural symptoms of dental anxiety. *Behaviour Research and Therapy, 25,* 341–347.

Kent, G., & Gibbons, R. (1987). Self-efficacy and the control of anxious cognitions. *Journal of Behavior Therapy & Experimental Psychiatry, 18,* 33–40.

Keohane, R. O. (1993). Sovereignty, interdependence and international institutions. In L. Miller & M. Smith (Eds.), *Ideas and ideals: Essays on politics in honor of Stanley Hoffman* (pp. 91–107). Boulder, CO: Westview.

Keohane, R. O., & Nye, J. S. (1977). *Power and interdependence: World politics in transition.* Boston: Little, Brown.

Kim, U., Triandis, H. D., Kâgitçibasi, C., Choi, S., & Yoon, G. (1994). *Individualism and collectivism: Theory, method, and applications.* Thousand Oaks, CA: Sage.

Klass, E. T. (1978). Psychological effects of immoral actions: The experimental evidence. *Psychological Bulletin, 85,* 756–771.

Kolb, B., & Whishaw, I. Q. (1998). Brain plasticity and behavior. *Annual Review of Psychology, 49,* 43–64.

Krantz, D. L. (1998). Taming chance: Social science and everyday narratives. *Psychological Inquiry. 9,* 87–94.

Kroger, R. O., & Wood, L. M. (1993). Reification, "faking," and the big five. *American Psychologist, 48,* 1297–1298.

Krueger, N. F., Jr., & Dickson, P. R. (1993). Self-efficacy and perceptions of opportunities and threats. *Psychological Reports, 72,* 1235–1240.

Krueger, N., Jr., & Dickson, P. R. (1994). How believing in ourselves increases risk taking: Perceived self-efficacy and opportunity recognition. *Decision Sciences, 25,* 385–400.

Kwak, K., & Bandura, A. (1997). *Role of perceived self-efficacy and moral disengagement in antisocial conduct.* Unpublished manuscript, Osan College, Seoul, Korea.

Lachman, M. E. (1986). Personal control in later life: Stability, change, and cognitive correlates. In M. M. Baltes & P. B. Baltes (Eds.), *The psychology of control and aging* (pp. 207–236). Hillsdale, NJ: Erlbaum.

Lent, R. W., Brown, S. D., & Hackett, G. (1994). Toward a unifying social cognitive theory of career and academic interest, choice, and performance. *Journal of Vocational Behavior, 45,* 79–122.

Little, B. L., & Madigan, R. M. (1994, August). *Motivation in work teams: A test of the construct of collective efficacy.* Paper presented at the annual meeting of the Academy of Management, Houston, TX.

Locke, E. A., & Latham, G. P. (1990). *A theory of goal setting and task performance.* Englewood Cliffs, NJ: Prentice Hall.

Lord, R. G., & Hanges, P. J. (1987). A control system model of organizational motivation: Theoretical development and applied implications. *Behavioral Science, 32,* 161–178.

Lutz, W. D. (1987). Language, appearance, and reality: Doublespeak in 1984. In P. C. Boardman (Ed.), *The legacy of language: A tribute to Charlton Laird* (pp. 103–119). Reno, NV: University of Nevada Press.

Maddux, J. E. (Ed.). (1995). *Self-efficacy, adaptation, and adjustment: Theory, research and application.* New York: Plenum Press.

Major, B., Mueller, P., & Hildebrandt, K. (1985). Attributions, expectations, and coping with abortion. *Journal of Personality and Social Psychology, 48,* 585–599.

Markus, H., & Nurius, P. (1986). Possible selves. *American Psychologist, 41,* 954–969.

Martin, J. (1981). Relative deprivation: A theory of distributive injustice for an era of shrinking resources. In B. Staw & L. Cummings (Eds.), *Research in organizational behavior* (Vol. 3, pp. 53–107). Greenwich, CT: JAI Press.

Masten, A. S., Best, K. M., & Garmezy, N. (1990). Resilience and development: Contributions from the study of children who overcome adversity. *Development and Psychopathology,* 2, 425–444.

Matsumoto, D., Kudoh, T., & Takeuchi, S. (1996). Changing patterns of individualism and collectivism in the United States and Japan. *Culture & Psychology, 2,* 77–107.

McAdams, D. P. (1992). The five-factor model in personality: A critical appraisal. *Journal of Personality, 60,* 329–361.

McAdams, D. P. (1996). Personality, modernity, and the storied self: A comtemporary framework for studying persons. *Psychological Inquiry, 7,* 295–321.

McAvay, G. J., Seeman, T. E., & Rodin, J. (1996). A longitudinal study of change in domain-specific self-efficacy among older adults. *Journal of Gerontology: Psychological Sciences, 51B,* 243–253.

McCrae, R. R., & Costa, P. T. (1996). Toward a new generation of personality theories: Theoretical contexts for the five-factor model. In J. S. Wiggins (Ed.), *Five-factor model of personality: Theoretical perspectives* (pp. 51–87). New York: Guilford Press.

McCrae, R. R., & Costa, P. T. (1997). Personality trait structure as a human universal. *American Psychologist, 52,* 509–516.

McCrae, R. R., Zonderman, A. B., Costa, P. T., Bond, M. H., & Paunonen, S. V. (1996). Evaluating replicability of factors in the Revised NEO Personality Inventory: Confirmatory factor analysis versus procrustes rotation. *Personality and Social Psychology, 70,* 552–566

Midgley, M. (1978). *Beast and man: The roots of human nature.* Ithaca, NY: Cornell University Press.

Milgram, S. (1974). *Obedience to authority: An experimental view.* New York: Harper & Row.

Mischel, W., & Shoda, Y. (1995). A cognitive-affective system theory of personality: Reconceptualizing situations, dispositions, dynamics, and invariance in personality structure. *Psychological Review, 102,* 246–268.

Moerk, E. L. (1995). Acquisition and transmission of pacifist mentalities in Sweden. *Peace and Conflict: Journal of Peace Psychology, 1,* 291–307.

Nagel, E. (1961). *The structure of science.* New York: Harcourt, Brace & World.

Nolen-Hoeksema, S. (1991). Responses to depression and their effects on the duration of depressive episodes. *Journal of Abnormal Psychology, 100,* 569–582.

Pajares, F., & Kranzler, J. (1995). Self-efficacy beliefs and general mental ability in mathematical problem solving. *Contemporary Educational Psychology, 20,* 426–443.

Pajares, F., & Miller, M. D. (1994). Role of self-efficacy and self-concept beliefs in mathematical problem solving: A path analysis. *Journal of Educational Psychology, 86,* 193–203.

Pajares, F., & Miller, M. D. (1995). Mathematics self-efficacy and mathematics performances: The need for specificity of assessment. *Journal of Counseling Psychology, 42,* 190–198.

Parker, J. D. A., Bagby, R. M., & Summerfeldt, L. J. (1993). Confirmatory factor analysis of the Revised NEO Personality Inventory. *Personality and Individual Differences, 15,* 463–466.

Patterson, G. R. (1976). The aggressive child: Victim and architect of a coercive system. In E. J. Mash, L. A. Hamerlynck, & L. C. Handy (Eds.), *Behavior modification and families* (pp. 267-316). New York: Brunner/Mazel.

Pervin, L. A. (1989). *Goal concepts in personality and social psychology.* Hillsdale, NJ: Erlbaum.

Pervin, L. A. (1994). A critical analysis of current trait theory. *Psychological Inquiry, 5,* 103–113.

Piaget, J. (1950). *The psychology of intelligence.* New York: International Universities Press.

Pollock, P. H. (1983). The participatory consequences of internal and external political efficacy. *Western Political Quarterly, 36,* 400–409.

Powers, W. T. (1973). *Behavior: The control of perception.* Chicago: Aldine.

Prussia, G. E., & Kinicki, A. J. (1996). A motivational investigation of group effectiveness using social cognitive theory. *Journal of Applied Psychology, 81,* 187–199.

Rapoport, D. C., & Alexander, Y. (Eds.). (1982). *The morality of terrorism: Religious and secular justification.* Elmsford, NY: Pergamon.

Rausch, H. L. (1965). Interaction sequences. *Journal of Personality and Social Psychology, 2,* 487–499.

Rehm, L. P. (1981). A self-control therapy program for treatment of depression. In J. F. Clarkin & H. Glazer (Eds.), *Depression: Behavioral and directive treatment strategies* (pp. 68–110). New York: Garland Press.

Rehm, L. P. (1988). Self-management and cognitive processes in depression. In L. B. Alloy (Ed.), *Cognitive processes in depression* (pp. 143–176). New York: Guilford Press.

Reich, W. (Ed.), (1990). *Origins of terrorism: Psychologies, ideologies, theologies, states of mind.* Cambridge, UK: Cambridge University Press.

Reichard, G. A. (1938). Social life. In F. Boas (Ed.), *General anthropology* (pp. 409–486). Boston: Heath.

Relich, J. D., Debus, R. L., & Walker, R. (1986). The mediating role of attribution and self-efficacy variables for treatment effects on achievement outcomes. *Contemporary Educational Psychology, 11,* 195–216.

Robertson, R. & Combs, A. (Eds.). (1995). *Chaos theory in psychology and the life sciences.* Hillsdale, NJ: Erlbaum.

Rogers, C. R. (1959). A theory of therapy, personality, and interpersonal relationships, as developed in the client-centered framework. In S. Koch (Ed.), *Psychology: A study of a science (Vol. III). Formulations of the person and the social context* (pp. 184–256). New York: McGraw-Hill.

Rogers, E. J., Vaughan, P. W., Swalehe, R. M. A., Rao, N., & Sood, S. (1996). *Effects of an entertainment-education radio soap opera on family planning and HIV/AIDS prevention behavior in Tanzania.* Unpublished manuscript, Department of Communication and Journalism, University of New Mexico, Albuquerque.

Rosenthal, T. L., & Zimmerman, B. J. (1978). *Social learning and cognition.* New York: Academic.

Rottschaefer, W. A. (1985). Evading conceptual self-annihilation: Some implications of Albert Bandura's theory of the self-system for the status of psychology. *New Ideas Psychology, 2,* 223–230.

Rottschaefer, W. A. (1991). Some philosophical implications of Bandura's social cognitive theory of human agency. *American Psychologist, 46,* 153–155.

Rushton, J. P., Brainerd, C. J., & Pressley, M. (1983). Behavioral development and construct validity: The principle of aggregation. *Psychological Bulletin, 94,* 39–53.

Rutter, M. (1990). Psychosocial resilience and protective mechanisms. In J. Rolf, A. S. Masten, D. Cicchetti, K. H. Neuchterlein, & S. Weintraub (Eds.), *Risk and protective factors in the development of psychopathology* (pp. 181–214). New York: Cambridge University Press.

Sampson, R., Raudenbush, S., & Earls, F. (1997). Neighborhood and violent crime: A multilevel study of collective efficacy. *Science, 277,* 918–924.

Sanday, P. R. (1981). The socio-cultural context of rape: A cross-cultural study. *Journal of Social Issues, 37,* 5–27.

Sanderson, W. C., Rapee, R. M., & Barlow, D. H. (1989). The influence of an illusion of control on panic attacks induced via inhalation of 5.5% carbon dioxide-enriched air. *Archives of General Psychiatry, 46,* 157–162.

Sanford, N., & Comstock, C. (1971). *Sanctions for evil.* San Francisco: Jossey-Bass.

Schooler, C. (1990). Individualism and the historical and social-structural determinants of people's concerns over self-directedness and efficacy. In J. Rodin, C. Schooler, & K. W. Schaie (Eds.), *Self-directedness: Cause and effects throughout the life course* (pp. 19–58). Hillsdale, NJ: Erlbaum.

Schunk, D. H. (1989). Self-efficacy and cognitive skill learning. In C. Ames and R. Ames (Eds.), *Research on motivation in education. Vol. 3. Goals and cognitions* (pp. 13–44). San Diego: Academic Press.

Schunk, D. H. (1996). Goal and self-evaluative influences during children's cognitive skill learning. *American Educational Research Journal, 33,* 359–382.

Schunk, D. H., & Gunn, T. P. (1986). Self-efficacy and skill development: Influence of task strategies and attributions. *Journal of Educational Research, 79,* 238–244.

Schunk, D. H., & Rice, J. M. (1986). Extended attributional feedback: Sequence effects during remedial reading instruction. *Journal of Early Adolescence, 6,* 55–66.

Schwarzer, R. (1992). Self-efficacy in the adoption and maintenance of health behaviors: Theoretical approaches and a new model. In R. Schwarzer (Ed.), *Self-efficacy: Thought control of action* (pp. 217–243). Washington, DC: Hemisphere.

Shepherd, G. (Ed.). (1995). *Rejected: Leading economists ponder the publication process.* Sun Lakes, AZ: Thomas Horton.

Signorielli, N., & Morgan, M. (Eds.). (1989). *Cultivation analysis: New directions in media effects research.* Newbury Park, CA: Sage.

Singhal, A., & Rogers, E. M. (1989). Pro-social television for development in India. In R. E. Rice & C. K. Atkin (Eds.), *Public communication campaigns* (2nd ed., pp. 331–350). Newbury Park, CA: Sage.

Skinner, B. F. (1971). *Beyond freedom and dignity.* New York: Knopf.

Snyder, M. (1980). Seek, and ye shall find: Testing hypotheses about other people. In E. T. Higgins, C. P. Herman, & M. P. Zanna (Eds.), *The Ontario symposium on personality and social psychology. Social cognition, Vol. 1.* (pp. 105–130). Hillsdale, NJ: Erlbaum.

Snyder, M. (1981). On the self-perpetuating nature of social stereotypes. In D. L Hamilton (Ed.), *Cognitive processes in stereotyping and intergroup behavior* (pp. 182–212). Hillsdale, NJ: Erlbaum.

Snyder, M. (1987). *Public appearances/private realities: The psychology of self-monitoring.* New York: Freeman.

Sperry, R. W. (1993). The impact and promise of the cognitive revolution. *American Psychologist, 48,* 878–885.

Stajkovic, A. D., & Luthans, F. (1998). Self-efficacy and work-related performance: A meta-analysis. *Psychological Bulletin, 124,* 240–261.

Tellegen, A., & Waller, N. G. (1987, August). *Re-examining basic dimensions of natural language trait descriptors.* Paper presented at the 95th Annual Convention of the American Psychological Association, New York.

Triandis, H. C. (1995). *Individualism and collectivism.* Boulder, CO: Westview.

Vaughan, P. W., Rogers, E. M., & Swalehe, R. M. A. (1995). *The effects of "Twende Na Wakati," an entertainment-education radio soap opera for family planning and HIV/AIDS prevention in Tanzania.* Unpublished manuscript, University of New Mexico, Albuquerque.

Weiner, B. (1986). *An attributional theory of motivation and emotion.* New York: Springer-Verlag.

Westoff, C. F., & Rodriguez, G. (1995). The mass media and family planning in Kenya. *International Family Planning Perspectives, 21,* 26–31.

White, J. (1982). *Rejection.* Reading, MA: Addison-Wesley.

Williams, S. L. (1992). Perceived self-efficacy and phobic disability. In R. Schwarzer (Ed.), *Self-efficacy: Thought control of action* (pp. 149–176). Washington, DC: Hemisphere.

Wilson, E. O. (1998). *Consilience: The unity of knowledge.* New York: Knopf.

Winfrey, C. (1979, February 25). Why 900 died in Guyana. *The New York Times Magazine,* p. 39.

Wood, R. E., & Bandura, A. (1989). Social cognitive theory of organizational management. *Academy of Management Review, 14,* 361–384.

Wylie, R. C. (1974). *The self-concept: A review of methodological considerations and measuring instruments* (rev. ed.). Lincoln, NE: University of Nebraska Press.

Yamagishi, T. (1988). The provision of a sanctioning system in the United States and Japan. *Social Psychology Quarterly, 51,* 265–271.

Zimbardo, P. G. (1995). The psychology of evil: A situationist perspective on recruiting good people to engage in anti-social acts. *Japanese Journal of Research in Social Psychology, 11,* 125–133.

Zimmerman, B. J. (1990). Self-regulating academic learning and achievement: The emergence of a social cognitive perspective. *Educational Psychology Review, 2,* 173–201.

Zimmerman, B. J. & Rappaport, J. (1988). Citizen participation, perceived control, and psychological empowerment. *American Journal of Community Psychology, 16,* 725–750.

Chapter 7

Integrating Dispositions and Processing Dynamics within a Unified Theory of Personality: The Cognitive–Affective Personality System

Walter Mischel
Columbia University
Yuichi Shoda
University of Washington

What units shall we use? That was the question Gordon Allport (1937) asked more than half a century ago, and it remains the most urgent and crucial challenge that personality psychologists still face now: How should one conceptualize personality dispositions? What is personality structure and what is meant by "personality processes and dynamics"? Indeed, what is "personality"? How does it interact with the "situation"? How should these constructs be formulated and assessed? For most of the 20th century, the field has struggled for answers to these questions. Happily, in the last decade basic debates in the search for the nature of personality are being replaced by findings and reconceptualizations that promise to resolve paradoxes and to overcome problems that have frustrated and divided the study of personality almost since its inception. This chapter focuses on the key implications of these developments for building a unifying personality theory. The question is: In light of these advances is it possible to integrate within a unitary framework the dispositional (trait) and processing (social cognitive–affective–dynamic) approaches that have so long been split virtually into two separate fields (e.g., Mischel & Shoda, 1994, 1998)?

PERSONALITY DISPOSITIONS AND PROCESSING DYNAMICS: COMPETING APPROACHES OR TWO SIDES OF ONE SYSTEM?

In the first approach, dispositional or trait theory, in recent years led by the five-factor model (FFM) approach (e.g., McCrae & Costa, 1996), a few broad, stable traits, factors, or behavioral dispositions are the basic units for characterizing and understanding individuals and the differences among them. The fundamental goal is to characterize all people in terms of a comprehensive but small set of such stable "behavioral dispositions" or factors on which they differ. These factors are assumed to remain invariant across situations and to determine a broad range of important behaviors (e.g., Allport, 1937; Funder, 1991; Goldberg, 1993; Wiggins & Pincus, 1992).

The second or "processing approach" construes personality as a system of mediating units (e.g., encodings, expectancies, goals, motives) and psychological processes or cognitive–affective dynamics, conscious and unconscious, that interact with the situation (e.g., Cervone & Shoda, 1999; Mischel, 1973, 1990). In this view, in the last 30 years, the basic concern has been with discovering general principles about how the mind operates and influences social behavior as the person interacts with social situations, conceptualized within a broadly social–cognitive theoretical framework (e.g., Bandura, 1986; Cantor, 1994; Cantor & Kihlstrom, 1987; Higgins, 1990, 1996a, 1996b; Mischel, 1973, 1990; Mischel & Shoda, 1995; Pervin, 1990, 1994). In contrast, the dispositional approach focuses on the broad, stable characteristics that differentiate individuals consistently, and its advocates seek evidence for the breadth and durability of these differences across diverse situations (e.g., Hogan, Johnson, & Briggs, 1997).

Each approach has its strengths and its distinctive vulnerabilities (Mischel, 1998). As trait psychologists are quick to note, although the general principles that emerge from research on social cognition and social learning are valuable, one can challenge their relevance for understanding some of the most essential aspects of personality. Perhaps the most common critique by traditional personality psychologists of social–cognitive processing approaches is that they contain lists of seemingly disconnected personality processes and they simply do not explain (or often do not even address) the coherent functioning of the whole person (Mischel, 1999). Thus, although these principles, both singly and collectively, advance our understanding of basic social–cognitive–motivational processes, they must be applied in concert to understand the individual as an organized coherent functioning system—the fundamental unit of analysis to which personality psychology has been committed since its inception (Allport, 1937). In addition, processing approaches also have been criticized for ignoring "what people are like" in general terms, neglecting the stable dispositional differences between individuals and thus miss the essence of the personality construct. In this vein, Funder (1994), for example, urges a return to a neo-Allportian global dispositional approach in which people are characterized in broad dispositional terms with the language of traits.

On the other side, however, dispositional-trait approaches are vulnerable to the criticism that they do not adequately consider, or even address, the psychological processes and dynamics that underlie behavioral dispositions (e.g., Block, 1995; Mischel, 1968; Pervin, 1994). Nor do they deal with the complex interplay between situations and behavioral tendencies that, empirically, has been shown to violate some of the most basic assumptions of the dispositional-trait approach regarding the structure of consistency, as in the failure to obtain evidence for the cross-situational consistency of behavior and the resulting paradigm crisis (e.g., Hartshorne & May, 1928; Mischel, 1968, 1990; Mischel & Peake, 1982a; Newcomb, 1929; Pervin, 1994; Shoda, Mischel & Wright, 1989, 1994).

In the present view, it is certainly essential for personality psychology to take serious account of important stable differences between people. The question is not the existence of such differences but rather how to capture (1) the nature of the stability and consistency that exists in the behavioral expressions of individual differences relevant to personality and (2) the psychological processes and structures that underlie those expressions and that function in a coherent fashion. Thus the stable differences between people in their behavioral tendencies and qualities of temperament or other social–cognitive–affective characteristics and behavior patterns need to be captured, but they also need to be understood and explained in terms of the psychological processes that characterize the intraindividual dynamics of persons and not just described in trait terms.

In short, a comprehensive theory of personality needs to encompass two goals. It needs to identify the stable qualities and behavior patterns that characterize different individuals and types. But it also needs to clarify the intraindividual dynamics and psychological processes and structures that underlie these patterns and that regulate and constrain their experiential and behavioral manifestations as individuals interact with different types of psychological situations. Advances in theory and research in the last few decades have led to the development of at least the framework for such a unifying theory of personality (Cervone & Shoda, 1999; Mischel & Shoda, 1995, 1998; Shoda & Mischel, 1998), and that is the focus of the present chapter. Its main goal is to show that personality dispositions and the psychological processes that underlie them are two aspects of the same personality system and therefore need to be integrated within a unifying theory rather than split into alternative or even competing fields. That goal may now be becoming feasible in light of recent findings on the nature of the consistencies and coherence that characterize individuals (e.g., Shoda et al., 1994).

FRAMEWORK FOR A COGNITIVE–AFFECTIVE PERSONALITY SYSTEM

A theoretical integration that reconciles dispositions and the psychological processes that underlie them within a comprehensive theory of personality needs at its foundation a processing model of the personality system at the level of the individual (Mischel & Shoda, 1995). In such a model, person variables are important and it is valuable to understand the basic psychological processes underlying, for example, how people construe or encode situations and themselves, their self-efficacy expectations and beliefs, their goals, and so on, as has long been recognized (e.g., Mischel, 1973). But these variables do not function singly and in isolation; rather, they are components that are dynamically interconnected within an organized system of relationships, a unique network that functions as an organized whole and that interacts with the social–psychological situations in which the system is activated and contextualized (e.g., Shoda & Mischel, 1998).

An adequate personality system also must account for intraindividual coherence and stability as well as for plasticity and discriminativeness in behavior across situations. It must encompass the individual's characteristic dispositions as well as the dynamic mediating processes that underlie them. Moreover, it needs to incorporate not only social–cognitive–motivational and affective determinants but also biological and genetic antecedents. And this system must be able to deal with the complexity of human personality and the cognitive–affective dynamics, conscious and unconscious—both "cool" and "hot," cognitive and emotional, rational and impulsive—that underlie the individual's distinctive, characteristic internal states and external behavioral expressions (see Metcalfe & Jacobs, 1998; Metcalfe & Mischel, 1999). In such a system the individual is not conceptualized as a bundle of mediating variables and procedural-decision rules but rather in terms of a complex multilevel parallel and a distributed (rather than serial, centralized) social information processing system (e.g., Kunda & Thagard, 1996; Read & Miller, 1998; Shultz & Lepper, 1996) that operates at various levels of awareness (e.g., Westen, 1990). The recently proposed Cognitive–Affective Personality System, or CAPS theory (Mischel & Shoda, 1995, 1998; Shoda & Mischel, 1998), was developed in part to move personality psychology in this direction.

Two Basic Assumptions

With the above ambitious goals, but also with a commitment to parsimony, CAPS theory makes two fundamental assumptions.

1. *Individual differences in chronic accessibility.* CAPS theory assumes, first, that people differ in the *chronic accessibility,* that is, the ease, with which particular cognitive and affective mental representations or units, called CAUs, become activated. These CAUs refer to the cognitions and affects or feelings that are available to the person. Such mediating units were conceptualized initially in terms of five relatively stable person variables on which individuals differ in processing self-relevant information, such as the individual's encodings or construal (of self, other people, situations) and expectancies (Mischel, 1973). In the years since that formulation, research developments (reviewed in Mischel & Shoda, 1995) suggest a set of CAUs, largely based on the person variables previously proposed, that are represented in the personality system, as summarized in Table 7.1. Namely, encodings or construals, efficacy and outcome expectancies, beliefs, goals and values, affects and feeling states, as well as competencies and self-regulatory plans and strategies, exemplify the types of units in the system that interact as the individual selects, interprets and generates situations.

The cognitive–affective units in the system are not conceptualized as isolated, static components. They are organized, for example, into subjective equivalent classes, as illustrated in theory and research on encoding, person prototypes

TABLE 7.1. Types of Cognitive–Affective Units in the Personality Mediating System

1. *Encodings*: Categories (constructs) for the self, people, events, and situations (external and internal).
2. *Expectancies and beliefs*: About the social world, about outcomes for behavior in particular situations, about self-efficacy.
3. *Affects*: Feelings, emotions, and affective responses (including physiological reactions).
4. *Goals and values*: Desirable outcomes and affective states; aversive outcomes and affective states; goals, values, and life projects.
5. *Competencies and self-regulatory plans*: Potential behaviors and scripts that one can do, and plans and strategies for organizing action and for affecting outcomes and one's own behavior and internal states.

Note. From Mischel and Shoda (1995). Copyright 1995, by the American Psychological Association. Reprinted by permission.

and personal constructs, (e.g., Cantor & Mischel, 1977, 1979; Cantor, Mischel, & Schwartz, 1982; Forgas, 1983a, 1983b; Higgins, King, Mavin, 1982; Kelly, 1955; Linville & Clark, 1989; Vallacher & Wegner, 1987). Some aspects of the organization of relations among the cognitions and affects, such as evaluative–affective associations and interconcept relations (e.g., Cantor & Kihlstrom, 1987; Murphy & Medin, 1985), are common among members of a culture, whereas others may be unique for an individual (e.g., Rosenberg & Jones, 1972). But whether common or unique, cognitive–affective representations are not unconnected discrete units that are simply elicited as discrete "responses" in isolation: Rather, these cognitive representations and affective states interact dynamically and influence each other reciprocally. It is the organization of the relationships among them that forms the core of the personality structure and that guides and constrains their effects.

2. *Individual differences in the stable organization of relations among units (interconnections).* Thus the CAPS model makes a second assumption: Individual differences reflect not only the accessibility of particular cognitions and affects but also the distinctive "organization of relationships" among them (see Figure 7.1 which shows a schematic, greatly simplified CAPS system). This organization constitutes the basic stable "structure of the personality system"and underlies the behavioral expressions that characterize the individual. It is this organization that guides and constrains the activation of the particular cognitions, affects, and actions that are available within the system.

As Figure 7.1 illustrates, when the individual perceives certain features of a situation a characteristic pattern of cognitions and affects (shown schematically as circles) becomes activated through this distinctive network of connections. Mediating units in the system become activated in relation to some situation features (positive connections) but are deactivated or inhibited in relation to others (negative connections, shown as broken lines), which decreases the activation and is not affected by the rest. The CAPS is a system that interacts continuously and dynamically with the social world in which it is contextualized. The interactions with the external word involve a two-way reciprocal interaction: The behaviors that the personality system generates impact on the social world, partly shaping and selecting, the interpersonal situations the person subsequently faces and that, in turn, influence the person (e.g., Bandura, 1986; Buss, 1987; Mischel, 1973).

Multiple Levels in the Analysis of Personality

We can now consider within the CAPS framework the conceptualization of the basic constructs of "personality disposition" and "personality processes and dynamics" and indeed of "personality" itself—terms that often are assumed intuitively to be self-evident but that within the field have become extraordinarily unclear, causing much unnecessary debate and confusion. The confusion reflects the many possible meanings of these constructs and their referents that depend on the level of analysis: when the level is unspecified, which is usually the case, misunderstandings become almost inevitable.

Several levels—both psychosocial and biosocial—in the analysis of personality stability and invariance have been distinguished (e.g., Mischel, 1999), and CAPS theory addresses each level. By definition, the interests of psychologists focus on the psychosocial levels of analysis that in turn can be divided into four aspects, as depicted in Figure 7.2. At a first level is the psychological processing system of personality with its structures and the "processing dynamics" that become activated within it. Second, the expressions and manifestations of the system are visible at the level of the individual's characteristic

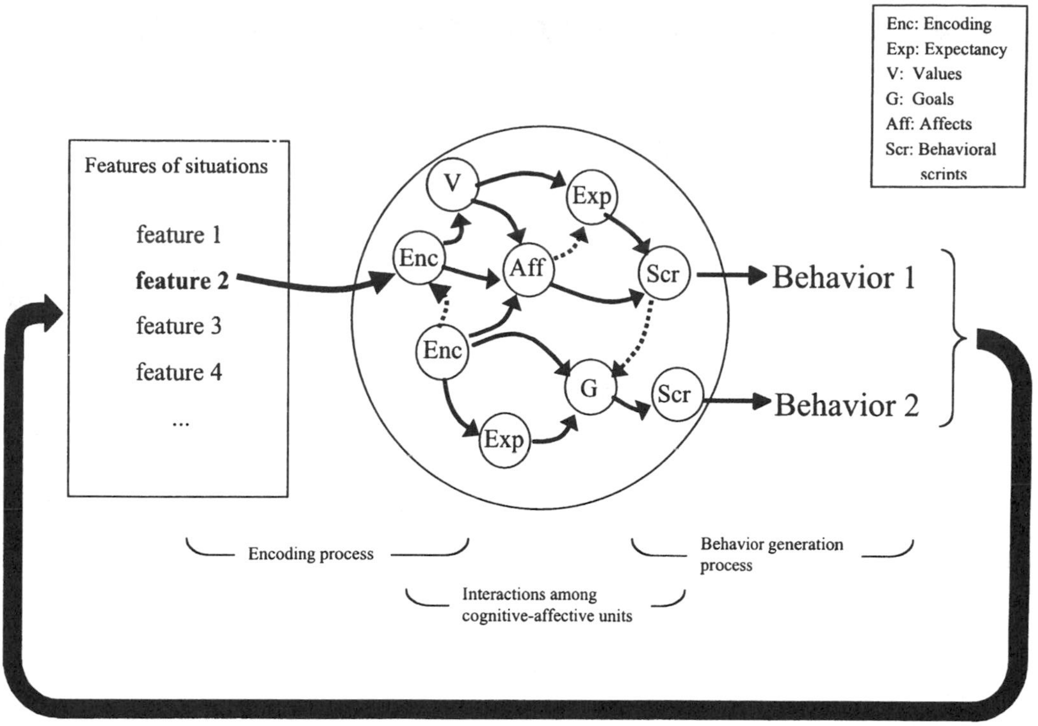

FIGURE 7.1. Cognitive–Affective Personality System (CAPS). Situational features activate a given mediating unit which activates specific subsets of other mediating units through a stable network of relations that characterize an individual, generating a characteristic pattern of behavior in response to different situations. The relation may be positive (solid line), which increases the activation, or negative (dashed line), which decreases the activation. Adapted from Mischel and Shoda (1995).

"behavior" as it unfolds in vivo across situations and over time (shown in the situation–behavior, *if . . . then . . .* profile data in the figure). At a third level are the "perceptions" of personality and of the person's behavior, including the individual's self-perceptions (as schematicized by the eye shown in Figure 7.2, see next page). A fourth level consists of the stable personal environment of situations that come to characterize the individual's life space (depicted as the inputs into the system). In addition, at the biosocial level or substrate are the *pre*-dispositions, consisting of genetic–biochemical, somatic structures and states, as well as the cumulative social learning and sociocultural influences, that constitute the person's total history and current endowment. All of these levels, and the interactions among them, are relevant to personality, and each is discussed from the CAPS framework in the remainder of this chapter.

LEVEL 1: PROCESSING DYNAMICS OF PERSONALITY

At the processing system level, CAPS theory conceptualizes dispositions as having distinctive cognitive–affective processing structures that underlie and generate characteristic processing dynamics (Mischel & Shoda, 1995). In this section we define and illustrate these dynamics and discuss how they operate.

Processing Dynamics Defined

The "processing dynamics" of a disposition consist of an organized pattern and sequence of activation among cognitive–affective mediating units in CAPS that is generated when these persons experience situations with relevant features (e.g., rejection cues, failure cues, achievement cues). As an example (in highly simplified form)

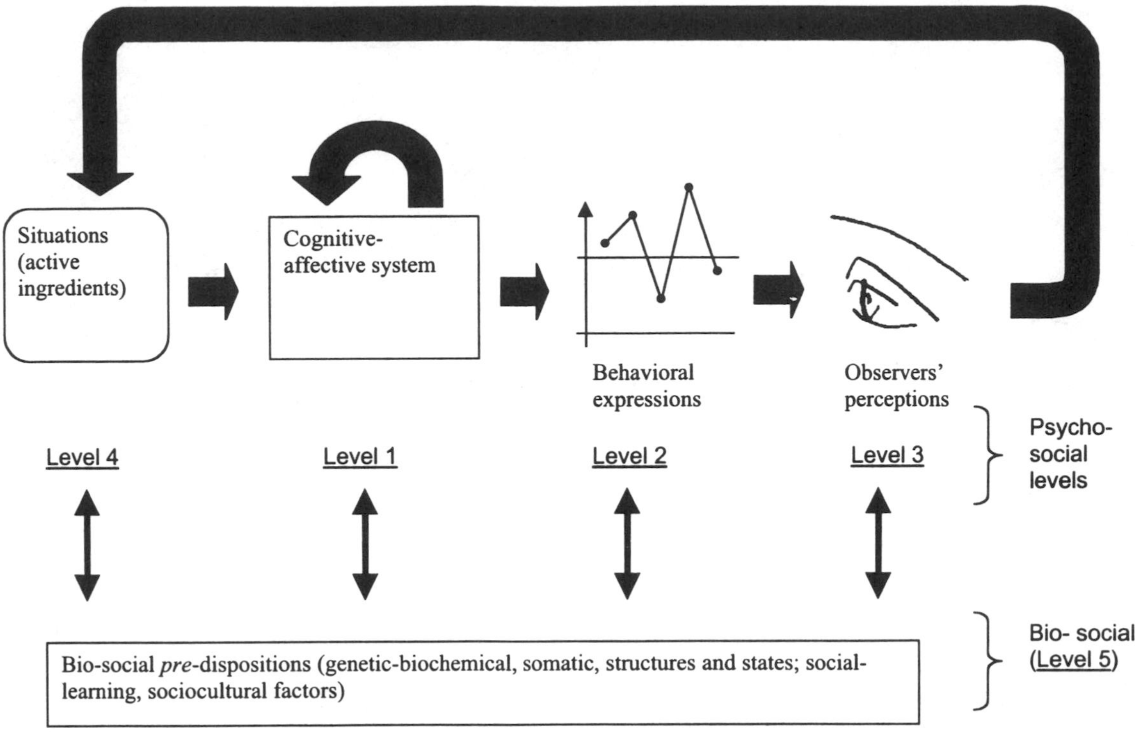

FIGURE 7.2. Personality stability and invariance: Five levels of analysis. Adapted from Mischel and Shoda (1995).

of the processing dynamics for a disposition or personality prototype (Cantor & Mischel, 1979), consider the construct of "rejection sensitivity" (e.g., Downey, Freitas, Michaelis, & Khouri, 1997; Feldman & Downey, 1994). Many of these rejection sensitive persons have had histories of exposure to family violence and rejection. Later in life, when they encounter what could be perceived as uncaring behavior from a romantic partner (e.g., he or she is attentive to someone else), they easily experience thoughts like "she doesn't love me," which in turn trigger expectations of rejection, abandonment, and associated emotions. These expectations and affects interact and combine to lead the person to readily perceive rejection even in ambiguous situations, which tend to activate behavioral scripts for hostility (Ayduk, Downey, Testa, Yin, & Shoda, in press). A wide range of controlling and coercive behaviors may be enacted and often are blamed on the behavior of the partner rather than seen as self-generated. These behaviors in turn tend to elicit the partner rejection that is most feared. Over time this process increasingly erodes the relationship in a self-defeating pattern that ultimately confirms and maintains rejection expectations and strengthens the vicious cycle (Downey et al., 1997).

Role of the Situation in Personality Dynamics

As the rejection sensitivity example indicates, CAPS theory incorporates the situation into the conception of the personality processing dynamics that characterize the individual and the type: the situation activates the processing dynamics and in part defines them. But although the situation plays an important role in this model, it is not conceptualized like the simple stimulus in early behaviorism that mechanically and inevitably pulls responses from an organism's repertoire. In CAPS theory it is the person, or more precisely, the personality system that is sensitized to particular features of situations and ready to scan for, and potentially overreact to, them in an organized predictable pattern. In the example of rejection sensitive people, this is seen in their tendency to scan for and find potential rejection cues even in ambiguous situations, which then triggers their vulnerable characteristic pattern of reactions.

Most important, CAPS theory distinguishes between "nominal situations" and the "active ingredients" or psychological features of situations (Shoda et al., 1994). Nominal situations refer to the particular places and activities in the setting, for example, woodworking activities in a summer camp, or arithmetic tests and dining halls, or playgrounds in a school setting (e.g., Hartshorne & May, 1928; Newcomb, 1929). Individual differences in relation to such specific nominal situations, even if highly stable, necessarily would be of limited generalizability. But if situations are redefined to capture their basic psychological features (the active ingredients that impact on the person's behavior), it becomes possible to predict behavior across a broad range of contexts that contain the same psychological features (Shoda et al., 1994).

For example, situations that include such psychological features as criticism or lack of attention from a partner tend to be those in which rejection sensitive people become consistently more upset than others even when those features occur in diverse nominal situations. People differ characteristically in the particular situational features (e.g., being teased, being frustrated, being approached socially, feeling rejected) that are the salient active ingredients for them and that thus activate their characteristic and relatively predictable patterns of cognitions and affects in those situations, that is, their distinctive processing dynamics (Mischel & Shoda, 1995). Although some individuals readily respond aggressively to such ambiguous stimuli as having milk spilled on them in the cafeteria line, others do not (Dodge, 1986). There also are internal feedback loops within the system through which self-generated stimuli (as in thinking, fantasy, daydreaming) activate the individual's personality dynamics, triggering characteristic cognitive–affective–behavioral reaction patterns (e.g., Shoda & Mischel, 1998).

The pattern of activation among cognitions and affects that exists at a given time in this system is the "personality state" and it depends on the particular context and the psychological situations experienced by the individual at that moment. Whereas the personality system and its structure may remain stable across diverse situations, the personality state can easily change when the situational features that are activated change (e.g., Mischel, Shoda, & Rodriquez, 1989). But the change is not random. Rather, it is guided by the personality system, which mediates the "relationships" between the types of situations encountered and the cognitive, affective, and behavioral reaction patterns—the dynamics—that become activated. Thus, if the situations change, so do the reaction patterns to them, but the "relationship" between the situations and the reaction patterns is stable as long as the personality system remains unchanged. This assumption leads CAPS theory to predict characteristic, predictable patterns of "variation" in the individual's characteristic behavior across situations—that is, the sorts of stable situation–behavior, *if . . . then . . .* profiles that in fact are found in empirical studies of the structure of social behavior in relation to situations and over time (Mischel & Shoda, 1995; Shoda et al., 1994). These patterns are discussed further in a later section on the behavioral expressions of the personality system.

Hot and Cool Processing Subsystems and Their Dynamic Interactions

The characteristic reactions of the personality system to situations sometimes are immediate, automatic, emotional, and virtually reflexive, but sometimes they are highly mediated and reflective, involving higher-order cognitive processes, as when the individual exerts effortful control strategies to prevent impulsive responses to "hot" trigger stimuli. To deal with these phenomena within a CAPS framework, and to incorporate the long-neglected but crucial role of emotion into the personality system, a distinction has been made between two subsystems, one "a hot" emotional "go" system, and one a "cool" cognitive "know" system, that closely interact (Metcalfe & Mischel, 1999).

The "cool cognitive system" is specialized for complex spatio-temporal and episodic representation and thought. It is cognitive, emotionally neutral, contemplative, flexible, integrated, coherent, spatio-temporal, slow, episodic, strategic—the seat of self-regulation and self-control. The "hot system" is specialized for quick emotional processing and responding based on unconditional or conditional trigger features, as when rejection sensitive people become abusive to their partners as automatic reactions to perceived rejection cues. It is conceptualized as the basis of emotionality, fears as well as passions—impulsive and reflexive—initially controlled by innate releasing stimuli (and thus literally under "stimulus control"), it is fundamental for emotional (classical) conditioning, and it undermines efforts at self-control and reflective thought and planfulness (Metcalfe & Mischel, 1999).

The balance between the hot and cool systems is determined by stress, developmental level, and the individual's self-regulatory dynamics. Whereas stress—both chronic and situational—enhances the hot system and attenuates the cool system, with increasing development and maturation the cool system becomes more developed and active, and the impact of the hot system becomes attenuated. The interactions between these systems allow prediction and explanation of findings on diverse phenomena involving the interplay of emotion and cognition, including goal-directed delay of gratification and the operation of "willpower" and self-directed change. Thus strategic interventions may be used to influence the interaction of the hot and cool systems to overcome the power of stimulus control as people attempt to purposefully prevent powerful stimuli from eliciting their impulsive immediate responses and dispositional vulnerabilities.

Dynamic, Transactional System: The Active/Proactive Person

To recapitulate, the personality system, at least within its cool subsystem, is capable of being active and indeed proactive, as well as reactive. It thus can anticipate, interpret, rearrange, and change situations as well as react to them, not only responding to the environment but also generating, selecting, and modifying situations in reciprocal transactions.

In CAPS theory, the features of situations that activate the person's processing dynamics not only are encountered in the external environment but also are generated within the personality system through thought, planning, fantasy, and imagination (e.g., Antrobus, 1991; Gollwitzer, 1996; Klinger, 1996; Mischel et al., 1989; Nolen-Hoeksema, Parker, & Larson, 1994). And they encompass not just social and interpersonal situations (as when lovers "reject" or peers "tease and provoke") but also intrapsychic situations, as in mood states (e.g., Isen, Niedenthal, & Cantor, 1992; Schwarz, 1990) and in the everyday stream of experience and feeling (e.g., Bolger & Eckenrode, 1991; Emmons, 1991; Smith & Lazarus, 1990; Wright & Mischel, 1988).

The proactive rather than merely reactive operations of the system take many forms. These include self-induced motivational changes by means of various mental framing operations (as in a "promotion versus prevention" focus, as illustrated in research by Higgins, 1996c, 1997, 1998); by the operation of different types of goals and the person's own theories (e.g., Grant & Dweck, 1999); by cognitive transformations of the situation itself to reframe it strategically, for example by focusing on different features within it (e.g., Metcalfe & Mischel, 1999; Mischel, 1974, 1996); and by the operation of self-regulatory and control processes in the service of long-term goals and life projects (e.g., as reviewed in Mischel, Cantor & Feldman, 1996).

Purposeful Change

CAPS theory also suggests ways in which individuals may be able to facilitate goal-directed change in their own reaction tendencies. For example, if they understand their own processing dynamics people may become able to anticipate the events and conditions that will activate certain cognitions and affects in them. Such metacognitive knowledge may help them to recognize some of the key internal or external stimuli that activate or deactivate their problematic emotional, cognitive, and behavioral dynamics and to modify them if they prove to be maladaptive or dysfunctional. Such knowledge (a goal to which therapy might be directed) could help them to influence their personality states and behaviors (e.g., Mischel & Mischel, 1983; Rodriguez, Mischel, & Shoda, 1989), for example, by avoiding some situations and selecting or generating others, to the degree that they know their own processing dynamics and the features of situations that activate them.

Under many conditions people also may be able to reconstrue or reframe the situation with alternative encodings, that altering their own thoughts and feelings in relation to particular problem-producing situations that cannot themselves be changed. For example, self-generated changes in the mental representations of a stimulus by cognitively focusing on its potentially affect-arousing "hot," consummatory features, versus on its more abstract, "cool," or informative features "in imagination" may dramatically influence self-regulatory behaviors of considerable long-term personal significance (Mischel et al., 1989). This is seen experimentally when 4 year olds are primed to focus on "hot," consummatory features of rewards—such as the pretzel's crunchy salty taste—they want them immediately and further delay to obtain them becomes extremely difficult. In contrast, a focus on the abstract features (e.g., how the pretzels are "like little logs") makes it easy to continue to wait in order to get them. By influencing the stimuli-as-encoded, or by focusing attention on selected mental representations, individuals can exert some control over their own cognitions and affects. They can select, structure, influence, and reinterpret or cognitively and emotionally transform situations to which they are exposed, and thus they are not merely passive victims of the situations or stimuli that are imposed on them (e.g., Mischel, 1996; Mischel et al., 1996).

LEVEL 2: BEHAVIORAL EXPRESSIONS OF PERSONALITY

CAPS theory suggests that the second level of personality may be seen in the behavioral expressions of the processing system. The nature of the consistencies or coherences in these behavioral expressions of personality has been the focus of concern and intense debate in personality psychology for decades. This "consistency controversy" historically underlies much of the divisiveness between the two main approaches to personality that still persists. The resolution of these issues is therefore an essential prerequisite for development of the integrative, unifying approach addressed in the present chapter and is discussed next.

The Classic Consistency Problem

The belief that people are characterized by pervasive cross-situational consistencies in their behavior has been perhaps the most basic and intensely disputed assumption of personality psychology for most of this century, defining much of the field's agenda (e.g., Mischel, 1968; Mischel & Shoda, 1995, 1998; Pervin, 1994). On the one hand, a belief in the consistency of personality is intuitively evident, captured as a fundamental principle in theories of impression-formation: perceivers expect consistency in the traits and behaviors of the perceived (e.g., Hamilton & Sherman, 1996). It is also the case, however, that the history of research in the pursuit of consistency at the behavioral level has long yielded perplexing results, marked by years of continuing disputes about the extent and nature of consistency and predictability in the individual's behavior across situations and findings and claims in the form of the classic "personality paradox" that such consistency is much less than our intuitions predict and that the situation or context plays a crucial role in the regulation and structure of behavioral consistency (e.g., Bem & Allen, 1974; Krahe, 1990; Mischel, 1968; Mischel & Peake, 1982a, 1982b; Mischel & Shoda, 1998; Nisbett, 1980; Nisbett & Ross, 1980; Pervin, 1994; Ross & Nisbett, 1991; Shweder, 1975; Shweder & D'Andrade, 1980).

The Consistency Controversy Briefly Revisited

Throughout this consistency controversy, which arose early in the century (e.g., Hartshorne & May, 1928) and continued over the years (e.g., Cervone & Shoda, in press; Mischel, 1999; Pervin, 1994; Ross & Nisbett, 1991), the virtually unquestioned basic assumption was that personality consists of broad traits, expressed across many different situations as generalized, global behavior tendencies. Given this assumption, the failure to find strong support for cross-situational consistency at the behavioral level, especially when juxtaposed with evidence for the importance of the situation (e.g., Ross & Nisbett, 1991), was often read as a basic threat to the construct of personality itself, creating an unfortunate and prolonged "person versus situation" debate and a paradigm crisis in the area (e.g., Bem & Allen, 1974; Krahe, 1990; Magnusson & Endler, 1977; Mischel, 1968, 1994; Pervin, 1990, 1994).

After years of debate, culminating in the Carleton College study (Mischel & Peake, 1982a), consensus was reached about the state of the data: The average cross-situational consistency coefficient is nonzero but not by much (Bem, 1983; Epstein, 1983; Funder, 1983). But there was and is deep disagreement about how to in-

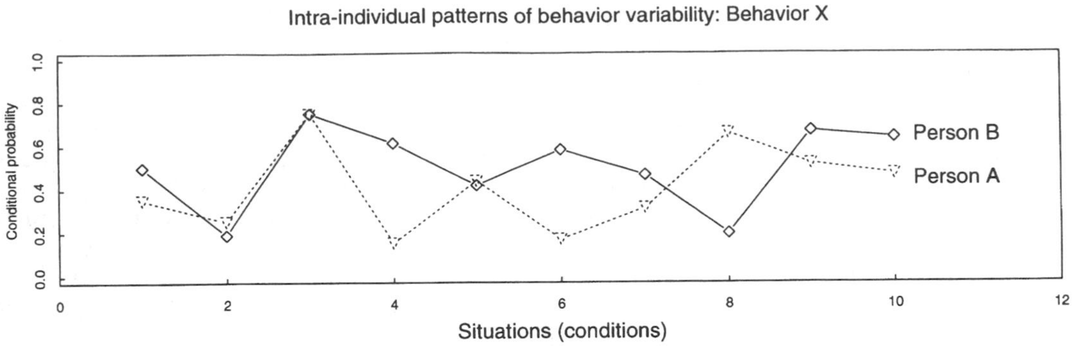

FIGURE 7.3. Typical individual differences in the conditional probability of a type of behavior in different situations. From Mischel and Shoda (1995). Copyright © 1995 by the American Psychological Association. Reprinted by permission.

terpret the data and proceed in the study of personality (e.g., as discussed in Pervin, 1994; Mischel & Shoda, 1995, 1998). The classic dispositional or trait approach generally has focused on the broad stable characteristics that differentiate individuals consistently on the whole, seeking evidence for the breadth and durability of these differences across diverse situations. Its most widely accepted strategy acknowledges the low cross-situational consistency in behavior found from situation to situation; it then systematically removes the situation by aggregating the individual's behavior on a given dimension (e.g., "conscientiousness") over many different situations (e.g., home, school, work) to estimate an overall "true score" (as discussed in Epstein, 1979, 1980; Mischel & Peake, 1982a), treating the variability across situations as "error."

Alternative Conception of Stability: Incorporating the Situation

CAPS theory proposes a fundamentally different conception of personality invariance. In this approach, personality is construed as a relatively stable system of social–cognitive–affective mediating processes whose expressions are manifested in predictable patterns of situation–behavior relations: They therefore cannot be properly assessed unless the situation is incorporated into the conception and analysis of personality coherence (e.g., Mischel, 1973; Mischel & Shoda, 1995, 1998). Moreover, the relationship between the behavioral expressions within situations and the underlying variables or processes is not necessarily one of direct correspondence. The research challenge is to identify the meaningful patterns that characterize the person's behavior across seemingly diverse situations and that are expressions of the social–cognitive and motivational processes that underlie that patterning and that can explain it (e.g., Gollwitzer & Bargh, 1996; Cervone & Shoda, 1999: Higgins & Kruglanski, 1996; Vansteelandt & Van Mechelen, 1998). In the analysis of the nature of personality invariance and its behavioral expressions, process models in general and CAPS theory specifically suggest that clues about the person's underlying qualities—the construals and goals, the motives and passions, that drive the individual—may be seen in *when* and *where* a type of behavior is manifested, not only in its overall frequency (Mischel, 1973; Mischel & Shoda, 1995, 1998).

Consider the differences between two people, A and B, whose behavior in a particular domain, for example, their helping behavior across situations, is shown on the horizontal axis of Figure 7.3. In the traditional approach to behavioral dispositions, the observed variability within each person on a dimension is seen as "error" and averaged out to get the best approximation of the underlying stable "true score," so the question simply becomes: Is person *A* different overall in the level of helping behavior than person *B*? This question is important, and perhaps the best first question to ask in the analysis of personality invariance. But it may also be its premature end if we ignore the profile information about *when* and *where A* and *B* differ in their unique pattern with regard to the particular dimension of behavior. These differences in their pattern of variability in relation to situations may be a possible key to understanding individuality and personal-

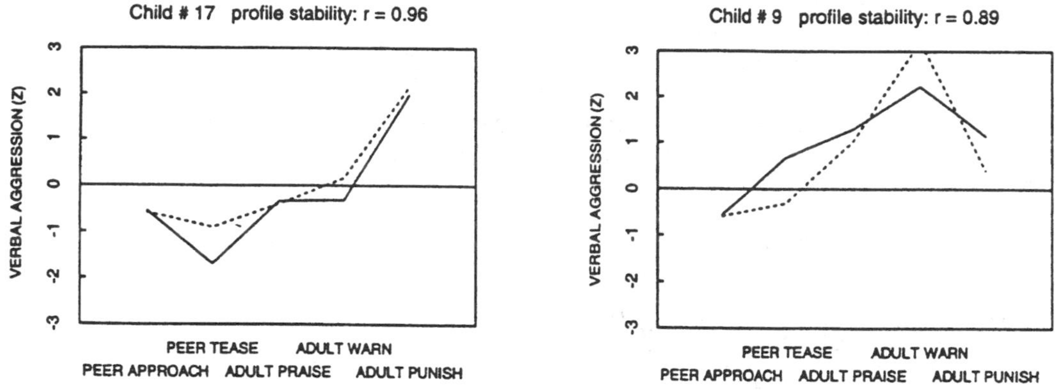

FIGURE 7.4. Illustrative intraindividual profiles of verbal aggression across five types of psychological situations. The two lines indicate the profiles based on two different, nonoverlapping samples of occasions in which the child encountered each type of psychological sitaution, shown as Time 1 (solid) and Time 2 (broken). From Shoda, Mischel, and Wright (1994). Copyright © 1994 by the American Psychological Association. Reprinted by permission.

ity coherence and their underlying motivations and personality systems. In that case, these patterns are potential signatures that need to be identified and harnessed rather than deliberately removed.

The Conditional Contextualized Expression of Dispositions

As noted in the discussion of the assumptions of the CAPS model and its processing operations, in this theory variation in the person's behavior in relation to changing situations in part constitutes a potentially meaningful reflection of the personality system itself. Empirical evidence to support this expectation comes from a series of studies of social behavior as it unfolds in vivo in relation to situations. In these studies, the social behavior (e.g., "verbal aggression," "compliance") of children was systematically observed in relation to the interpersonal situations in which the behavior occurred in vivo in a residential summer camp setting. The results provided clear evidence for the contextualized expression of dispositions (e.g., Mischel & Shoda, 1995; Shoda et al., 1993a, 1994). Some children were found to be consistently more verbally aggressive than others when warned by an adult, for example, but were much less aggressive than most peers when peers approached them positively. In contrast, another group of children with a similar overall average level of aggression were distinguished by a striking and opposite pattern: They were more aggressive than any other children when peers approached them positively but were exceptionally unaggressive when warned by an adult.

It is noteworthy that in classic trait approaches to behavioral dispositions, such intraindividual variations in a type of behavior across situations (after the main effects of situations are removed by standardization) is assumed to reflect only intrinsic unpredictability or measurement error. From that perspective, thus, the stability of the intraindividual pattern of variation should on average be zero. The obtained findings yielding highly significant intraindividual stability coefficients for these profiles obviously contradict this expectation. They reveal that meaningfully patterned behavioral expressions of personality, contextualized within particular situations, characterize individuals. They yield distinctive profiles of variability for particular types of behavior that form behavioral signatures of personality that have a meaningful shape as well as elevation or overall mean level, as illustrated in Figure 7.4.

These profiles indicate the situations in which a given individual becomes particularly angry or depressed, anxious or relieved, revealing a stable pattern, such as: he *A* when *X*, but *B* when *Y*, and does *A* most when *Z*. When properly analyzed and assessed, these patterns of intraindividual variation of behavior across situations seem to reflect the structure and organization of the underlying personality system, such as how the situations are encoded and the expectations, affects and goals that become activated within them (Mischel & Shoda, 1995). Although it had long been assumed that a focus on the role of the situation undermined the search for personality consistency, in fact, by focusing on the effects of the situation on the organization of behavior in depth and detail it became possible to find this second type of personality stability, hopefully enriching rather than undermining the personality construct. The surprise is not simply that this type of behavioral signature of personality exists, but rather that it has so long been treated as error and deliberately removed by averaging behavior over diverse situations to remove their role. Ironically, although such aggregation was intended to capture personality, it actually can delete data that reflect the individual's most distinctive qualities and unique intraindividual patterning.

Furthermore, the CAPS analysis shows that it is not necessary to have separate units or constructs to represent overall levels of behavior; the CAPS system can account for stable mean level differences in particular types of behavior, as well as stable patterns of variability in that behavior, across situations. This was seen, for example, in computer simulation of person–situation interactions within the CAPS model in which individual differences were represented only in terms of the connections among the internal representations that were common to all individuals (patterns of activation pathways determining the links between features of situations and the outcomes generated by the system).

As predicted, an individual's unique configuration in the personality system was manifested in the uniqueness of the *if . . . then . . .* profiles that unfolded as the individual interacts with situations containing different psychologically active features. Interestingly, however, some individuals in this simulation consistently produced higher levels of the behavior in question, whereas the predicted behavior profiles of others were consistently low in elevation (Mischel & Shoda, 1995; Shoda & Mischel, 1998). What is noteworthy is that such stable differences in global behavior tendencies—usually interpreted as directly reflecting the underlying disposition—were predicted and obtained even though the CAPS representation of personality did not contain any unit that directly represented chronic individual differences in generalized behavioral dispositions independent of situation features. This simulation thus showed that to account for stable differences in the overall levels of behavior observed does not require positing mediating units that correspond directly to behavioral dispositions. Individual differences in global behavioral tendencies, or traits as traditionally defined, and processing dynamics within an interactive model like CAPS are not intrinsically incompatible: The CAPS system yields both types of behavioral expressions without additional assumptions.

To recapitulate, the personality system is expressed at the level of behavior in the pattern with which a type of behavior varies over a set of situations, as well as in the average level of the behavior aggregated across situations (that is, its overall act frequency). Predictable variability in relation to context in CAPS theory is a potential key to the individual's stability and coherence, a sign of the underlying system that generates it. Personality assessment then can move beyond characterization of the person's overall average types of behavior to a more precise level of contextualized specific prediction of who is likely to do what when, that is, in relation to particular types of diagnostic situations (Shoda et al., 1994).

To illustrate again with the example of the rejection sensitive person, a defining situation–behavior profile for this disposition—its behavioral signature—may include both being more prone than others to anger, disapproval, and coercive behaviors in certain types of situations in intimate relationships and being more supportive, caring, and romantic than most people, for example, in initial encounters with potential partners who are not yet committed to them or later in the relationship when they are about to lose the partner (Downey et al., 1997). The profile analysis of these individuals suggests that the same rejection sensitive man who coerces and abuses his partner also can behave in exceedingly tender and loving ways (e.g., Walker, 1979) in seemingly similar situations that have different "active ingredients" or psychological trigger features (e.g., Mischel & Shoda, 1995). In semantic terms, he is both hurtful and kind, caring and uncaring, violent and gentle.

Traditional analyses of such "inconsistencies" in personality lead to the questions: "Which one of these two people is the real one? What is simply the effect of the situation?" In contrast, CAPS theory allows the same person to have contradictory facets that are equally genuine.

The surface contradictions become comprehensible when one analyzes the network of relations among cognitions and affects and how they interact with situations. The research problem becomes to understand when and why different cognitions and affects become activated predictably in relation to different features of situations, external and internal. The theory views the individual's distinctive patterns of variability not necessarily as internal contradictions but as the potentially predictable expressions of a stable underlying system that itself may remain quite unchanged in its organization. The challenge is to discriminate, understand, and predict when each aspect will be activated and the dynamics that underlie the pattern. For example, are the caring and uncaring behaviors two scripts in the service of the same goal? If so, how are they connected to, and guided by, the person's self-conceptions and belief system in relation to the psychological features of situations that activate them?

Identifying Common Dispositions, Types, and Dynamics

The stable situation–behavior profiles generated by the system lend themselves not only to the idiographic study of persons in their life contexts but also provide a nomothetic route to characterize groups or types of persons. Such a personality type consists of people who share a common organization of relations among mediating units in the processing of certain situation features, (e.g., Shoda et al., 1994). One can identify these individuals by finding the common *if . . . then . . .* patterns of behavior variation that they share. Conversely, identifying similarities among people in their underlying dynamics should allow prediction of the common *if . . . then . . .* patterns they are likely to manifest behaviorally.

The specification of the diagnostic *if . . . then . . .* profiles that characterize exemplars of a hypothesized disposition constitutes the first assessment task in research on dispositions from this perspective. It calls for measurement not only of characteristic mean levels of relevant behaviors but also of the distinctive behavioral signatures—the *if . . . then . . .* profiles that define the disposition. These distinctive *if . . . then . . .* patterns in turn provide clues to infer the hypothetical processing dynamics that generate them. By observing these *if . . . then . . .* patterns, perceivers—whether lay persons or professional observers—can more accurately predict the behaviors of the perceived presumably because context allows the underlying meanings and motivation to be inferred (Shoda et al., 1989).

LEVEL 3: THE PERCEPTION OF PERSONALITY

The behavioral manifestations of a disposition may be easily and reliably encoded by observers as indicators of person prototypes or exemplars, (e.g., Cantor et al., 1982; Wright & Mischel, 1987, 1988), and of traits and types in everyday psycholexical terms, both by lay perceivers (e.g., Jones, 1990) and psychologists (e.g., John, 1990; Goldberg, 1993; McCrae & Costa, 1996). These perceptions depend not just on the average levels of different types of behavior displayed by a person, but also on the situations in which they are contextualized, that is, on the *if . . . then . . .*, situation–behavior patterns of the person's variability across situations; for example, "She *A* when *X* but *B* when *Y*. . . ." For example, judgments by observers of how well individuals fit particular dispositional prototypes (e.g., the "friendly" child, the "withdrawn" child, the "aggressive" child) are related clearly to the shape of the observed situation–behavior pattern or profile, as well as to their average level of prototype-relevant behaviors (Shoda et al., 1993a, 1994). If the pattern of variability is changed, so are the personality judgments (Shoda et al., 1989). A "friendly person," for example, is perceived as such not just because of his average level of friendliness but also because of the stable pattern of *if . . . then . . .* relationships, as in "friendly with people he knows personally but not with casual acquaintances at work." (Shoda & Mischel, 1993).

The processing dynamics and structure of personality are inferred (regardless of accuracy) not only by professional psychologists but also by lay perceivers in their intuitive theories of personality: At least some of the time, some perceivers surely try to infer the beliefs, goals, and affects of the people they want to understand to see how these qualities underlie their behavior (Shoda & Mischel, 1993). Given that the expressions of the personality system are reflected in the shape as well as in the elevation of the *if . . . then . . .*, situation–behavior profiles generated by the system, the perceiver (whether lay person or psychologist) needs such information to infer the underlying structure and dynamics and generate a theory about the person. In the relatively rare studies in which such data are made available to perceivers, they seem to be linked to the social perceptions and inferences that are formed and suggest the lay perceiver may be an intuitive interactionist at least some of the time (e.g., Chiu, 1994; Dweck, Hong, & Chiu, 1993; Kruglanski, 1989, 1990; Read & Miller, 1993; Shoda et al., 1993a; Wright & Mischel, 1987, 1988).

Global behavioral dispositions in recent years have often become equated with personality itself, as Pervin (1994) has noted. Such an equation of personality with behavioral dispositions easily leads one to construe personality and situation as mutually exclusive and indeed opposing influences (discussed in Shoda & Mischel, 1993). If one makes such an equation, it makes sense to assume that perceivers dichotomize observed behavior into its situational versus dispositional components with the goal of partialling out the effect of the situation in order to discover the "true" score of the perceived. But then the information on behavioral variability and *if . . . then . . .* , situation–behavior profiles that CAPS theory sees as an essential personality signature is considered as due to situations and not reflective of personality. Because such information is assumed to be extraneous to personality it usually is not made available to the perceiver in research on personality inferences, and its potential role remains unexplored systematically. That in turn, can easily create the incorrect conclusion that perceivers are invariably trait theorists. If they are given the opportunity and the necessary information, however, lay perceivers also seem to view personality like intuitive social cognitive theorists, quite congruent with a CAPS conception (Shoda & Mischel, 1993).

In the culture and language the word "personality," as well as the concept, often seems to be virtually synonymous with generalized behavior tendencies, usually described by adjectives. But although personality is commonly equated with generalized behavior tendencies, intuitive perceivers do not necessarily consider only situation-free behavior tendencies when they attempt to understand people and themselves. Even if traits appear to be the preferred language for the psychology of the stranger (McAdams, 1994), perceivers may make goal-based inferences (Read, Jones, & Miller, 1990), for example, as well as other assessments of underlying motives and feeling, particularly when they try to understand themselves and their intimates or have an empathic orientation (e.g., Hoffman, Mischel, & Mazze, 1981). The popular equation between personality and generalized behavior tendencies need not distract researchers from clarifying when and how the intuitive perceiver might make inferences about cognitive–affective dynamics and their nonobvious behavioral expressions, guided by an implicit or intuitive interactionist theory of personality (e.g., Chiu, 1994; Dweck, Chiu, & Hong, 1995; Shoda & Mischel, 1993; Shoda et al., 1989). The CAPS perspective suggests, however, that such implicit personality theories cannot be glimpsed without research paradigms that make available to the perceiver the *if . . . then . . .* , situation–behavior relations that constitute the personality signatures of the perceived.

Perceived Consistencies and Their Behavioral Roots: The Locus of Self-Perceived Consistency and Dispositional Judgments

The profiles of situation–behavior relations that characterize persons—their behavioral signatures of personality—also appear to be an important locus of self-perception of consistency and coherence. This was found in a reanalysis by Mischel and Shoda (1995) of the Carleton College field study (Mischel & Peake, 1982a). In that study college students were repeatedly observed on campus in various situations relevant to their conscientiousness in the college setting (such as in the classroom, in the dormitory, in the library, assessed over repeated occasions in the semester). Students who perceived themselves as consistent did not show greater overall cross-situational consistency than those who did not. But for individuals who perceived themselves as consistent, the average situation–behavior profile stability correlation was near .5, whereas it was trivial for those who viewed themselves as inconsistent. So it is the stability in the situation–behavior profiles (e.g., conscientious about homework but not about punctuality), not the cross-situational consistency of behavior that underlies the perception of consistency with regard to a type of behavior or disposition.

The Personality Paradox Demystified

The types of *if . . . then . . .* , situation–behavior relations that a dynamic personality system like CAPS necessarily generates has important implications for the field, particularly the classic "personality paradox" (Bem & Allen, 1974). As Bem and Allen noted over two decades ago, on the one hand, the person's behavior across situations yields only modest cross-situational consistency coefficients (Hartshorne & May, 1928; Newcomb, 1929), but on the other hand, personality theory's fundamental assumption, and our intuition, insist that personality surely is stable (e.g., Bem & Allen, 1974; Krahe, 1990; Heatherton & Weinberger, 1994; Mischel, 1968; Moskowitz, 1982, 1994). Indeed, such discriminative facility is an index of adaptive behavior and constructive functioning, whereas consistency regardless of subtle contextual cues can be a sign of rigidity (Chiu, Hong, Mischel, & Shoda, 1995).

This paradox dissolves, however, by recognizing that the variability of behaviors within individuals across situations is neither all "error" nor "due to the situation rather than to the person." Instead, it is at least partly an essential expression of the enduring but dynamic personality system itself and its stable underlying organization. Thus the person's behaviors in a domain will necessarily change from one type of situation to another because when the *if* changes, so will the *then,* even when the personality structure remains entirely unchanged. Just how the individual's behavior and experience change across situations is part of the essential expression of personality (Mischel & Shoda, 1995) and becomes a key focus for personality assessment. From this perspective, the person's ability to make subtle discriminations among situations and to take these cues into account in the self-regulation of behavior in order to adapt it to changing situational requirements, is a basic aspect of social competence, not a reflection of inconsistency (Chiu et al., 1995, Shoda et al., 1993a). This type of discriminative facility seems to be a component of social intelligence, a sensitivity to the subtle cues in the situation that influences behavior. Such discriminative facility, for example, by encoding spontaneously social information in conditional versus global dispositional terms, was found to predict the quality of the person's social interaction (Chiu et al., 1995).

In sum, relatively stable situation–behavior profiles reflect characteristic intraindividual patterns in how the person relates to different psychological conditions or features of situations, forming a sort of behavioral signature of personality (Shoda et al., 1994). The stability of these situation–behavior profiles in turn predicts the self-perception of consistency and is linked to the dispositional judgments made about the person by others (Shoda et al., 1993a, 1994). These expectations and findings are congruent with classic processing theories, most notably Freud's conception of psychodynamics. In that view, peoples' underlying processing dynamics and qualities—the construals and goals, the motives and passions, that drive them—may be reflected not only in how often they display particular types of behavior but also in when and where, and thus, most importantly, *why* that behavior occurs. In short, the CAPS model expects that the stable patterns of situation–behavior relationships that characterize persons provide potential keys to their dynamics. They are informative roads to the underlying system that produces them, not sources of error to be eliminated systematically by aggregating out the situation.

LEVEL 4: SITUATIONAL SIGNATURES OF PERSONALITY: THE STABLE PERSONAL SPACE

Although different models of personality hypothesize different mediating processes, there is wide agreement among researchers, ranging from behavior geneticists (e.g., Plomin, DeFries, McClearn, & Rutter, 1997) to social cognitive interactionists (e.g., Bandura, 1986; Mischel & Shoda, 1995), that individuals' characteristics and behaviors influence the environments or situations that they subsequently experience. As was discussed above, these characteristics and behaviors are perceived and encoded by people who observe them, as well as by themselves, and they have important consequences for the psychological world that comes to characterize their lives with considerable stability. For example, the dispositional inferences observers make about an individual in turn may influence their reactions (e.g., by avoiding contact) and thus influence that individual's future interpersonal space. Thus people select, influence, and even generate their own interpersonal situations and are influenced by them in an interactive process (e.g., Bolger & Shilling, 1991; Bolger, DeLongis, Kessler, & Shilling, 1989; Buss, 1987; Ross & Nisbett, 1991; Snyder, 1983; Snyder & Gangestad, 1982). Ultimately this results in a degree of stability or equilibrium in the situations the person characteristically experiences. Such stability "belongs" neither to the person nor to the situation in isolation, but is a reflection of the enduring pattern of reciprocal interactions between the individual and his or her distinctive interpersonal world that dynamically influence each other. To illustrate, suppose at a summer camp John is praised on average four times an hour by the counselor but ignored by his peers, while Susan is teased twice by her peers and praised only once by the counselor. If such different patterns of interpersonal encounters are characteristic and stable for each individual across different activities and contexts, they constitute an aspect of behavioral coherence that needs to be incorporated into the conception and assessment of personality consistency (Mischel & Shoda, 1995).

LEVEL 5: *PRE*-DISPOSITIONS AT THE BIOCHEMICAL-GENETIC AND SOCIAL HISTORY SUBSTRATE: INTERACTIONS AMONG LEVELS

Biological and genetic history, as well as social learning history, developmental processes, and cultural–social influences, impact importantly on the developing personality system and the structures and dispositions that emerge within it. People differ in diverse biochemical–genetic–somatic factors that may be conceptualized as *pre*dispositions, with emphasis on the "pre" to make clear that they are biological precursors that may manifest indirectly as well as directly at the other levels of analysis in diverse and complex forms. These *pre*dispositions ultimately influence such personality-relevant qualities as sensory and psychomotor sensitivities and vulnerabilities, skills and competencies, temperament (including activity level and emotionality), chronic mood, and affective states. These in turn interact with social cognitive, social learning and cultural–societal influences, mediated by, and conjointly further influencing, the system—and the person—that emerges.

Individuals differ with regard to virtually every aspect of the biological human repertoire and genetic heritage, and these differences can have profound predisposing implications for the personality processing system and its behavioral expressions that ultimately develop (e.g., Plomin et al., 1997). Such differences may occur, for instance, in sensory, perceptual, cognitive, and affective systems, in metabolic clocks and hormones, in neurotransmitters—in short, in the person's total biochemical–genetic–somatic heritage. These *pre*dispositions interact with conditions throughout development and play out in ways that influence what the person thinks, feels, and does and the processing dynamics and behavioral signatures that come to characterize the individual. Even small differences between persons at the biochemical–somatic level (e.g., in sensory-perceptual sensitivity, in allergy and disease proneness, in energy levels) may manifest ultimately as considerable differences in their experiences and behavior and in what comes to be perceived as their personalities.

Consequently, a comprehensive approach to personality ultimately requires addressing not only the structure and organization of the cognitive–affective–behavioral processing system at the psychological level but also its biochemical–genetic predisposing foundations (Plomin et al., 1997; Saudino & Plomin, 1996) and their interactions with social learning and cultural–societal sources of influence (Mischel 1998). Genetically influenced individual differences presumably at least indirectly affect how people construe or encode—and shape their environments, which in turn produce important person–context interactions throughout the life course (Plomin, 1994; Saudino & Plomin, 1996). Given these considerations, in CAPS theory, both biochemical and social cognitive influences, heritable and learned, are expected to affect the availability of cognitive–affective units and their organization, that is, the personality system. For example, variables of temperament or reactivity, such as activity, irritability, tension, distress, and emotional lability, visible early in life (Bates & Wachs, 1994), seem to have important, albeit complexly interactive links to emotional and attentional processing and self-regulation (e.g., Rothbart, Derryberry, and Posner, 1994), and thus should influence the organization of relations among the mediating units in the system. Because this system, in turn, generates the specific, *if . . . then . . .* situation–behavior relations manifested, the theory predicts that individual differences in genes and early social learning history will be seen not only in the mean level of behaviors, but in the behavioral signatures of personality, that is, the stable configuration of *if . . . then . . .*, situation–behavior relations. When the system changes, either due to modification in the biological substrates or due to developmental changes and significant life events, the effects will also be manifested at the behavioral level, visible as a change in the relationships between the *ifs* and the *thens* in the person's characteristic situation–behavior profiles.

SUMMARY

In sum, although it has been widely assumed and asserted that process-oriented approaches to personality ignore or deny stable personality dispositions (e.g., Funder, 1991; Goldberg, 1993), in fact, in CAPS theory they have a significant role in the personality system itself. As was seen, dispositions are defined by a characteristic cognitive–affective processing structure that underlies, and generates, distinctive processing dynamics. The processing structure of the disposition consists of a characteristic set of cognitions, affects, and behavioral strategies in an organization of inter-relations that guides and constrains their activation. The processing dynamics of the disposition refer to the patterns and sequences of activation among the mediating units that are generated when these individuals encounter or construct situations with relevant features. The dynamics of personality occur in relation to particular types of situational features (e.g., certain interpersonal encounters), including those that are self-generated within the system, as when people think or ruminate about situations. The behavioral manifestations of a disposition and its processing dynamics are seen in the elevations and shapes of the situation–behavior profiles—the dispositional signature—that distinguishes its exemplars, as well in the overall level of different types of behaviors or act frequencies generated over time. Individuals who have similar organizations of relations among cognitions and affects that become activated in relation to a particular distinctive set of situational features may be said to have a particular processing disposition. Distinctive dispositions are characterized by distinctive processing dynamics that become activated and, over time and contexts, will generate the situation–behavior profiles that have the characteristic elevations and shapes that identify the dispositional exemplars.

It should be clear that in this approach personality psychologists can analyze both the distinctive *if . . . then . . .* profiles that characterize the disposition's exemplars and illuminate the dynamic processes underlying them as two aspects of the same system. The antecedents of this system are multifaceted, encompassing the genetic–biochemical substrate—humans are biological creatures—as well as the contextualized interplay of person and psychological contexts—humans are social–cognitive beings, interacting throughout the life course.

TOWARD A CUMULATIVE SCIENCE: RECONCILING THE TWO APPROACHES WITHIN A UNIFIED FIELD AND FRAMEWORK?

The question this chapter posed was: Can the two approaches to personality—dispositional-trait and processing-dynamic—be reconciled and integrated within a unifying framework? The present analysis suggests that at this point in the development of the field they probably can be, and probably should be, if personality psychology is to develop into a cumulative science.

Clarifying the Goals and Agenda of the Field

At present it is not at all clear that an integration between approaches will occur, however, probably more because of the field's history, traditions, and sociology and because of differences in the underlying philosophies implied by different conceptions of personality than for scientific reasons. Thus to make the possible real, many old "hot" reflexes and treasured assumptions will have to be overcome. One of the most pernicious of these is the preemptive definition of personality psychology as a science of personality "traits," conceptualized as causal, genotypic entities that correspond to phenotypic behavioral dispositions. That automatically makes narrowly defined "traits" *the* target of investigation—as well as the bases for explanations. If personality psychology is to become a cumulative science, we must orient the goals of the field to the phenomena that demand explanation, rather than be governed by any set of explanatory constructs. These phenomena can be analyzed at each of the alternative and presumably complementary levels outlined above, allowing an ultimately more comprehensive and cumulative science conception of personality and its diverse manifestations and antecedents. Seen that way, many of the differences between the two major approaches of the field currently may reflect different goals and preferences in the level of analysis pursued more than fundamental incompatibilities.

Trends toward Integration

There are some indications that moves toward an integration may be under way (Mischel & Shoda, 1998). Certainly CAPS theory attempts to take account of overall important differences between people in such qualities as temperament, chronic mood and affective states, and skills and is compatible with data pointing to the substantial genetic contributions to personality, as noted above. Far from denying the importance of individual differences in personality and behavior, researchers within the CAPS framework, and in related processing approaches, have been identifying diagnostic situations in which such differences, for example with regard to aggressive tendencies or self-control abilities, may become particularly visible (e.g., Baumeister, Heatherton, & Tice, 1993; Mischel et al., 1989; Mischel et al., 1996; Shoda, Mischel, & Peake, 1990; Vansteelandt & Van Mechelen, 1998; Wright & Mischel, 1987, 1988). Furthermore, the stable correlates and consequences of individual differences in such social–cognitive person variables as the goals and personal projects pursued over time (e.g., Cantor, 1994; Cantor & Fleeson, 1994), the person's beliefs and goal structures (Weary & Edwards, 1994), the person's own implicit theories about personality (e.g., Dweck & Leggett 1988, Grant & Dweck, 1999), and the type of focus primed in goal pursuit, such as gain-oriented versus loss-avoidant (Higgins, 1996b, 1996c) are central to the agenda of current processing approaches.

In the same vein, analyses of cognitive–attentional processes during self-control efforts in young children in the 1990s also have identified dramatic threads of long-term continuity and stability in the course of development (e.g., Mischel et al., 1989; Mischel et al., 1996). For example, significant and substantial links have been found between seconds of delay of gratification in certain diagnostic laboratory situations in preschool and behavioral outcomes years later in adolescence and early adulthood showing levels of stability and meaningful networks of associated developmental outcomes that are clearly indicative of long-term personality coherence (e.g., Mischel et al., 1989; Shoda et al., 1990).

It is also noteworthy that at least some dispositional theorists increasingly seem to take account of the contextualized, situation-bound expressions of traits and try to include motivational and processing-dynamic concepts in their models (e.g., Revelle, 1995). Such research is helping to specify the specific boundary conditions within which traits become activated (e.g., Stemmler, 1997). For many researchers, a quiet but dramatic transformation may be occurring in how personality dispositions are defined. That move seems to be away from the global and situation-free trait construct, criticized 30 years earlier for its empirically unviable assumption of cross-situational consistency (Mischel, 1968), to: "likelihood and rates of change in behavior in response to particular situational cues" (Revelle, 1995, p. 315)—a definition free of the cross-situational consistency requirement and acceptable to any processing theorist.

We hope that this chapter makes it evident that personality psychologists do not have to choose between the study of dispositions or processes, but can analyze both the distinctive behavior patterns that characterize the exemplars of a disposition (defined in terms of characteristic behavior patterns) and the psychological processes and mediating units that underlie those. A theoretical integration and the building of a cumulative science of personality seem achievable, at least in the abstract, and the realization of that prospect could become an exciting time for the field.

REFERENCES

Allport, G. (1937). *Personality: A psychological interpretation.* New York: Holt.

Antrobus, J. (1991). Dreaming: Cognitive processes during critical activation and high afferent thresholds. *Psychological Review, 98,* 96–121.

Ayduk, O. N., Downey, G., Testa, S., Yin, Y., & Shoda, Y. (in press). Does rejection elicit hostility in rejection sensitive women? *Social Cognition.*

Bandura, A. (1986). *Social foundations of thought and action: A social cognitive theory.* Englewood Cliffs, NJ: Prentice-Hall.

Bates, J. E., & Wachs, T. D. (1994). *Temperament: Individual differences at the interface of biology and behavior.* Washington, DC: American Psychological Association.

Baumeister, R. F., Heatherton, T. F., & Tice, D. (1993). When ego threats lead to self-regulation failure: Negative consequences of high self-esteem. *Journal of Personality and Social Psychology, 64,* 141–156.

Bem, D. J. (1983). Further deja vu in the search for cross-situational consistency: A response to Mischel & Peake. *Psychological Review, 90,* 390–393.

Bem, D. J., & Allen, A. (1974). On predicting some of the people some of the time: The search for cross-situational consistencies in behavior. *Psychological Review, 81,* 506–520.

Block, J. (1995). A contrarian view of the five-factor approach to personality description. *Psychological Bulletin, 117,* 187–215.

Bolger, N., DeLongis, A., Kessler, R. C., & Schilling, E. A. (1989). Effects of daily stress on negative mood. *Journal of Personality and Social Psychology, 57,* 808–818.

Bolger, N., & Eckenrode, J. (1991). Social relationships, personality, and anxiety during a major stressful event. *Journal of Personality and Social Psychology, 61,* 440–449.

Bolger, N., & Schilling, E. A. (1991). Personality and the problems of everyday life: The role of neuroticism in exposure and reactivity to daily stressors. *Journal of Personality, 59,* 355–386.

Buss, D. M. (1987). Selection, evocation, and manipulation. *Journal of Personality and Social Psychology, 53,* 1214–1221.

Cantor, N. (1994). Life task problem-solving: situational affordances and personal needs. Presidential address of the Society for Personality and Social Psychology (Division 8 of the American Psychological Association, 1993, Toronto, Canada), *Personality and Social Psychology Bulletin, 20,* 235–243.

Cantor, N., & Fleeson, W. (1994). Social intelligence and intelligent goal pursuit: A cognitive slice of motivation. In W. Spaulding (Ed.), *Nebraska Symposium on Motivation: Vol. 41. Integrative views of motivation, cognition, and emotion* (pp. 125–179). Lincoln: University of Nebraska Press.

Cantor, N., & Kihlstrom, J. F. (1987). *Personality and social intelligence.* Englewood Cliffs, NJ: Prentice Hall.

Cantor, N., & Mischel, W. (1977). Traits as prototypes: Effects on recognition memory. *Journal of Personality and Social Psychology, 35,* 38–48.

Cantor, N., & Mischel, W. (1979). Prototypes in person perception. In L. Berkowitz (Ed.), *Advances in experimental social psychology* (Vol. 12, pp. 3–52). New York: Academic Press.

Cantor, N., Mischel, W., & Schwartz, J. (1982). A prototype analysis of psychological situations. *Cognitive Psychology, 14,* 45–77.

Cervone, D., & Shoda, Y. (Eds.). (1999). *The coherence of personality: Social-cognitive bases of consistency, variability, and organization.* New York: Guilford Press.

Chiu, C. (1994). *Bases of categorization and person cognition.* Unpublished doctoral dissertation, Columbia University.

Chiu, C., Hong, Y., Mischel, W., & Shoda, Y. (1995). Discriminative facility in social competence: Conditional versus dispositional encoding and monitoring-blunting of information. *Social Cognition, 13,* 49–70.

Dodge, K. A. (1986). A social information processing model of social competence in children. In M. Perlmutter (Ed.), *The Minnesota Symposium on Child Psychology* (Vol. 18, pp. 77–125). Hillsdale, NJ: Erlbaum.

Downey, G., Freitas, A., Michaelis, B., & Khouri, H. (1997). The self-fulfilling prophecy in close relationships: Rejection sensitivity and rejection by romantic partners. *Journal of Personality and Social Psychology, 75,* 545–560.

Dweck, C. S., Chiu, C., & Hong, Y. (1995). Implicit theories and their role in judgments and reactions: A world from two perspectives. *Psychological Inquiry, 6,* 267–285.

Dweck, C. S., Hong, Y., Chiu, C. (1993). Implicit theories: Individual differences in the likelihood and meaning of dispositional inference. *Personality and Social Psychology Bulletin, 19,* 644–656.

Dweck, C. S., & Leggett, E. L. (1988). A social-cognitive approach to motivation and personality. *Psychological Review, 95,* 256–273.

Emmons, R. A. (1991). Personal strivings, daily life events, and psychological and physical well-being. *Journal of Personality, 59,* 453–472.

Epstein, S. (1979). The stability of behavior: On predicting most of the people much of the time. *Journal of Personality and Social Psychology, 37,* 1097–1126.

Epstein, S. (1980). The stability of behavior: II. Implications for psychological research. *American Psychologist, 35,* 790–806.

Epstein, S. (1983). Aggregation and beyond: Some basic issues on the prediction of behavior. *Journal of Personality, 51,* 360–392.

Feldman, S., & Downey, G. (1994). Rejection sensitivity as a mediator of the impact of childhood exposure to family violence on adult attachment behavior. *Development and Psychopathology, 6,* 231–247.

Forgas, J. P. (1983a). Episode cognition and personality: A multidimensional analysis. *Journal of Personality, 51,* 34–48.

Forgas, J. P. (1983b). Social skills and the perception of interaction episodes. *British Journal of Clinical Psychology, 22,* 195–207.

Funder, D. C. (1983). Three issues in predicting more of the people: A reply to Mischel & Peake. *Psychological Review, 90,* 283–289.

Funder, D. C. (1991). Global traits: A neo-Allportian approach to personality. *Psychological Science, 2,* 31–39.

Funder, D. C. (1994). Explaining traits. *Psychological Inquiry, 5,* 125–127.

Goldberg, L. R. (1993). The structure of phenotypic personality traits. *American Psychologist, 48,* 26–34.

Gollwitzer, P. M. (1996). The volitional benefits of planning. In P. M. Gollwitzer & J. A. Bargh (Eds.), *The psychology of action: Linking cognition and motivation to behavior* (pp. 297–312). New York: Guilford Press.

Gollwitzer, P. M., & Bargh, J. A. (Eds.). (1996). *The psychology of action: Linking cognition and motivation to behavior.* New York: Guilford Press.

Grant, H., & Dweck, C. (1999). A goal analysis of personality and personality coherence. In D. Cervone & Y. Shoda (Eds.), *The coherence of personality: Social-cognitive bases of consistency, variability, and organization.* New York: Guilford Press.

Hamilton, D. L., & Sherman, S. J. (1996). Perceiving persons and groups. *Psychological Review, 103,* 336–355.

Hartshorne, H., & May, M. A. (1928). *Studies in the nature of character: Vol. 1. Studies in deceit.* New York: Macmillan.

Heatherton, T. F., & Weinberger, J. L. (Eds.). (1994). *Can personality change?* Washington, DC: American Psyhcological Association.

Higgins, E. T. (1990). Personality, social psychology, and person–situation relations: Standards and knowledge activation as a common language. In L. A. Pervin (Ed.), *Handbook of personality: Theory and research* (pp. 301–338). New York: Guilford Press.

Higgins, E. T. (1996a). Knowledge activation: Accessibility, applicability and salience. In E. T. Higgins & A. W. Kruglanski (Eds.), *Social psychology: Handbook of basic principles* (pp. 133–168). New York: Guilford Press.

Higgins, E. T. (1996b). Ideals, oughts, & regulatory focus: Affect and motivation from distinct pains and pleasures. In P. M. Gollwitzer and J. A. Bargh (Eds.), *The psychology of action: Linking cognition and motivation to behavior* (pp. 91–114). New York: Guilford Press.

Higgins, E. T. (1996c). Emotional experiences: The pains and pleasures of distinct regulatory systems. In R. D. Kavanaugh, B. Zimmerberg, & S. Fein (Eds.), *Emotion: Interdisciplinary perspectives* (pp. 203–241). Mahwah, NJ: Erlbaum.

Higgins, E. T. (1997). Beyond pleasure and pain. *American Psychologist, 52,* 1280–1300.

Higgins, E. T. (1998). Promotion and prevention: Regulatory focus as a motivational principle. In M. P. Zanna (Ed.), Advances in experimental social psychology (Vol. 30, pp. 1–46). New York: Academic Press.

Higgins, E. T., King, G. A., & Mavin, G. H. (1982). Individual construct accessibility and subjective impressions and recall. *Journal of Personality and Social Psychology, 43,* 35–47.

Higgins, E. T., & Kruglanski, A. W. (Eds.). (1996). *Social psychology: Handbook of basic principles.* New York: Guilford Press.

Hoffman, C., Mischel, W., & Mazze, K. (1981). The role of purpose in the organization of information about behavior: Trait-based versus goal-based categories in person cognition. *Journal of Personality and Social Psychology, 40,* 211–225.

Hogan, R., Johnson, J., & Briggs, S. (1997). *Handbook of Personality Psychology.* New York: Academic Press.

Isen, A. M., Niedenthal, P. M., & Cantor, N. (1992). An influence of positive affect on social categorization. *Motivation and Emotion, 16,* 65–78.

John, O. P. (1990). The "Big Five" factor taxonomy: Dimensions of personality in the natural language and in questions. In L. A. Pervin (Ed.), *Handbook of personality: Theory and research* (pp. 66–100). New York: Guilford Press.

Jones, E. E. (1990). *Interpersonal perception.* New York: Macmillan.

Kelly, G. (1955). *The psychology of personal constructs.* New York: Basic Books.

Klinger, E. (1996). Emotional influences on cognitive processing, with implications for theories of both. In P. M. Gollwitzer & J. A. Bargh (Eds.), *The psychology of action: Linking cognition and motivation to action* (pp. 168–189). New York: Guilford Press.

Krahe, B. (1990). *Situation cognition and coherence in personality: An individual-centered approach.* Cambridge, UK: Cambridge University Press.

Kruglanski, A. W. (1989). *Lay epistemics and human knowledge: Cognitive and motivational bases.* New York: Plenum Press.

Kruglanski, A. W. (1990). Lay epistemic theory in social–cognitive psychology. *Psychological Inquiry, 1,* 181–197.

Kunda, Z., & Thagard, P. (1996). Forming impressions from stereotypes, traits, and behaviors: A parallel-constraint-satisfaction theory. *Psychological Review, 103,* 284–308.

Linville, P. W., & Clark, L. F. (1989). Can production systems cope with coping? *Social Cognition, 7,* 195–236.

Magnusson, D., & Endler, N. S. (Eds.). (1977). *Personality at the crossroads: Current issues in interactional psychology.* Hillsdale, NJ: Erlbaum.

McAdams, D. P. (1994). A psychology of the stranger. *Psychological Inquiry, 5,* 145–148.

McCrae, R. R., & Costa, P. T. (1996). Toward a new generation of personality theories: Theoretical contexts for the five-factor model. In J. S. Wiggins (Ed.), *The five-factor model of personality: Theoretical perspectives* (pp. 51–87). New York: Guilford Press.

Metcalfe, J., & Jacobs W. J. (1998). Emotional memory: The effects of stress on "cool" and "hot" memory systems. In D. L. Medin (Ed.), *The psychology of learning and motivation: Vol. 38. Advances in research and theory* (pp. 187–222). San Diego, CA: Academic Press.

Metcalfe, J., & Mischel, W. (1999). A hot/cool system analysis of delay of gratification: Dynamics of willpower. *Psychological Review, 106,* 3–19.

Mischel, W. (1968). *Personality and assessment.* New York: Wiley.

Mischel, W. (1973). Toward a cognitive social learning reconceptualization of personality. *Psychological Review, 80,* 252–283.

Mischel, W. (1974). Processes in delay of gratification. In L. Berkowitz (Ed.), *Advances in experimental social psychology* (Vol. 7, pp. 249–292). New York: Academic Press.

Mischel, W. (1984). Convergences and challenges in the search for consistency. *American Psychologist, 39,* 351–364.

Mischel, W. (1990). Personality dispositions revisited and revised: A view after three decades. In L. A. Pervin (Ed.), *Handbook of personality: Theory and research* (pp. 111–134). New York: Guilford Press.

Mischel, W. (1994). On the predictability of behavior and the structure of personality. In R. A. Zucker, J. Aronoff, & A. I. Rabin (Eds.), *Personality and the prediction of behavior* (pp. 269–305). New York: Academic Press.

Mischel, W. (1996). From good intentions to willpower. In P. M. Gollwitzer & J. A. Bargh (Eds.), *The psychology of action: Linking cognition and motivation to action* (pp. 197–218). New York: Guilford Press.

Mischel, W. (1998). *Introduction to Personality* (6th ed.). Fort Worth, TX: Harcourt Brace

Mischel, W. (1999). Personality coherence and dispositions in a cognitive–affective processing system (CAPS) approach. In D. Cervone & Y. Shoda (Eds.), *The coherence of personality: Social–cognitive bases of consistency, variability, and organization.* New York: Guilford Press.

Mischel, W., Cantor, N., & Feldman, S. (1996). Principles of self-regulation: The nature of willpower and self-control. In E. T. Higgins & A. W. Kruglanski (Eds.), *Social psychology: Handbook of basic principles* (pp. 329–360). New York: Guilford Press.

Mischel, W., & Mischel, H. N. (1983). The development of children's knowledge of self-control strategies. *Child Development, 54,* 603–619.

Mischel, W., & Peake, P. K. (1982a). Beyond deja vu in the search for cross-situational consistency. *Psychological Review, 89,* 730–755.

Mischel, W., & Peake, P. K. (1982b). In search of consistency: Measure for measure. In M. P. Zanna, E. T. Higgins, & C. P. Herman (Eds.), *Consistency in social behavior: The Ontario Symposium* (Vol. 2, pp. 187–207). Hillsdale, NJ: Erlbaum.

Mischel, W., & Shoda, Y. (1994). Personality psychology has two goals: Must it be two fields? *Psychological Inquiry, 5,* 156–158.

Mischel, W., & Shoda, Y. (1995). A cognitive–affective system theory of personality: Reconceptualizing situations, dispositions, dynamics, and invariance in personality structure. *Psychological Review, 102,* 246–268.

Mischel, W., & Shoda, Y. (1998). Reconciling processing dynamics and personality dispositions. *Annual Review of Psychology, 49,* 229–258.

Mischel, W., Shoda, Y., & Rodriguez, M. L. (1989, May). Delay of gratification in children. *Science, 244,* 933–938.

Moskowitz, D. S. (1982). Coherence and cross-situational generality in personality: A new analysis of old problems. *Journal of Personality and Social Psychology, 43,* 754–768.

Moskowitz, D. S. (1994). Cross-situational generality and the interpersonal circumplex. *Journal of Personality and Social Psychology, 66,* 921–933.

Murphy, G. L., & Medin, D. L. (1985). The role of theories in conceptual coherence. *Psychological Review, 92,* 289–316.

Newcomb, T. M. (1929). *Consistency of certain extrovert–introvert behavior patterns in 51 problem boys.* New York: Columbia University, Teachers College, Bureau of Publications.

Nisbett, R. E. (1980). Evolutionary psychology, biology, and cultural evolution. *Motivation and Emotion, 14,* 255–263.

Nisbett, R. E., & Ross, L. D. (1980). *Human inference: Strategies and shortcomings of social judgment.* Englewood Cliffs, NJ: Prentice Hall.

Nolen-Hoeksema, S., Parker, L. E, & Larson, J. (1994). Ruminative coping with depressed mood following loss. *Journal of Personality and Social Psychology, 67,* 92–104.

Pervin, L. A. (Ed.). (1990). *Handbook of personality: Theory and research.* New York: Guilford Press.

Pervin, L. A. (1994). A critical analysis of trait theory. *Psychological Inquiry, 5,* 103–113.

Plomin, R. (1994). *Genetics and experience: The developmental interplay between nature and nurture.* Newbury Park, CA: Sage.

Plomin, R., DeFries, J. C., McClearn, G. E., & Rutter, M. (1997). *Behavioral genetics* (3rd ed.). New York: W. H. Freeman.

Read, S. J., Jones, D. K., Miller, L. C. (1990). Traits as goal-based categories: The importance of goals in the coherence of dispositional categories. *Journal of Personality and. Social Psychology, 58,* 1048–1061

Read, S. J., & Miller, L. C. (1993). Rapist or "regular guy": Explanatory coherence in the construction of mental models of others. *Personality and Social Psychology Bulletin, 19,* 526–540.

Read, S. J., & Miller, L. C. (Eds.). (1998). *Connectionist models of social reasoning and social behavior.* Mahwah, NJ: Erlbaum.

Revelle, W. (1995). Personality processes. *Annual Review of Psychology, 46,* 295–328.

Rodriguez, M., Mischel, W., & Shoda, Y. (1989). Cognitive person variables in the delay of gratification of older children at-risk. *Journal of Personality and Social Psychology, 57,* 358–367.

Rosenberg, S., & Jones, R. (1972). A method for investigating and representing a person's implicit theory of personality. *Journal of Personality and Social Psychology, 22,* 372–386.

Ross, L., & Nisbett. R. E. (1991). *The person and the situation: Perspectives of social psychology.* New York: McGraw-Hill.

Rothbart, M. K., Derryberry, D., & Posner, M. I. (1994). A psychobiological approach to the development of temperament. In J. E. Bates & T. D. Wachs (Eds.), *Temperament: Individual differences at the interface of biology and behavior* (pp. 83–116). Washington, DC: American Psychological Association.

Saudino, K. J., & Plomin, R. (1996). Personality and behavioral genetics: Where have we been and where are we going? *Journal of Research in Personality, 30,* 335–347.

Schwarz, N. (1990). Feelings and information: Informational and motivational functions of affective states. In R. M. Sorrentino & E. T. Higgins (Eds.), *Handbook of motivation and cognition: Foundations of social behavior* (Vol. 2, pp. 527–561). New York: Guilford Press.

Shoda, Y., & Mischel, W. (1993). Cognitive social approach to dispositional inferences: What if the perceiver is a cognitive–social theorist? *Personality and Social Psychology Bulletin [Special issue on Dispositional Inferences], 19,* 574–585.

Shoda, Y., & Mischel, W. (1998). Personality as a stable cognitive–affective activation network: Characteristic patterns of behavior variation emerge from a stable personality structure. In S. Read & L. C. Miller (Eds.), *Connectionist models of social reasoning and social behavior* (pp. 175–208). Mahwah, NJ: Erlbaum.

Shoda, Y., Mischel, W., & Peake, P. K. (1990). Predicting adolescent cognitive and self-regulatory competencies from preschool delay of gratification: Identifying diagnostic conditions. *Developmental Psychology, 26,* 978–986.

Shoda, Y., Mischel, W., & Wright, J. C. (1989). Intuitive interactionism in person perception: Effects of situation–behavior relations on dispositional judgments. *Journal of Personality and Social Psychology, 56,* 41–53.

Shoda, Y., Mischel, W., & Wright, J. C. (1993a). Links between personality judgments and contextualized behavior patterns: Situation-behavior profiles of personality prototypes. *Social Cognition, 4,* 399–429.

Shoda, Y., Mischel, W., & Wright, J. C. (1993b). The role of situational demands and cognitive competencies in behavior organization and personality coherence. *Journal of Personality and Social Psychology, 56,* 41–53.

Shoda, Y. Mischel, W., & Wright, J. C. (1994). Intra-individual stability in the organization and patterning of behavior: Incorporating psychological situations into the idiographic analysis of personality. *Journal of Personality and Social Psychology, 65,* 674–687.

Shweder, R. A. (1975). How relevant is an individual difference theory of personality? *Journal of Personality, 43,* 455–485.

Shweder, R. A., & D'Andrade, R. G. (1980). The systematic distortion hypothesis. In R. A. Shweder (Ed.), *Fallible judgment in behavioral research: New directions for methodology of behavioral science* (pp. 37–58). San Francisco: Jossey-Bass.

Shultz, T. R., & Lepper, M. R. (1996). Cognitive dissonance reduction as constraint satisfaction. *Psychological Review, 103,* 219–240.

Smith, C. A., & Lazarus, R. S. (1990). Emotion and adaptation. In L. A. Pervin (Ed.), *Handbook of personality: Theory and research* (pp. 609–637). New York: Guilford Press.

Snyder, M. (1983). The influence of individuals on situations: Implications for understanding the links between personality and social behavior. *Journal of Personality, 51,* 497–516.

Snyder, M., & Gangestad, S. (1982). Choosing social situations: Two investigations of self-monitoring processes. *Journal of Personality and Social Psychology, 43,* 123–135.

Stemmler, G. (1997). Selective activation of traits: Boundary conditions for the activation of anger. *Personality and Individual Differences, 22,* 213–233.

Vallacher, R. R., & Wegner, D. M. (1987). What do people think they're doing? Action identification and human behavior. *Psychological Review, 94,* 3–15.

Vansteelandt, K., & Van Mechelen, I. (1998). Individual differences in situation–behavior profiles: A triple typology model. *Journal of Personality and Social Psychology, 75,* 751–765.

Walker, L. E. (1979). *The battered women.* New York: Harper & Row.

Weary, G., & Edwards, J. A. (1994). Individual differences in causal uncertainty. *Journal of Personality and Social Psychology, 67,* 308–318.

Westen, D. (1990). Psychoanalytic approaches to personality. In L. A. Pervin (Ed.), *Handbook of personality: Theory and research* (pp. 21–65). New York: Guilford Press.

Wiggins, J. S., & Pincus, A. L. (1992). Personality: Structure and assessment. *Annual Review of Psychology, 43,* 473–504.

Wright, J. C., & Mischel, W. (1987). A conditional analysis of dispositional constructs: The local predictability of social behavior. *Journal of Personality and Social Psychology, 53,* 1159–1177.

Wright, J. C., & Mischel. W. (1988). Conditional hedges and the intuitive psychology of traits. *Journal of Personality and Social Psychology, 3,* 454–469.

Chapter 8

Holistic Interactionism: A Perspective for Research on Personality Development

David Magnusson
Stockholm University

Although a lot of research referring to personality is being conducted and reported, a review of recent articles in relevant journals (Van Heck, 1997) reveals the difficulty in arriving at a formulation that can serve a scientific purpose. The view advocated here is that what exists and can be the target of scientific analysis is an active and purposeful organism, functioning and developing as a total, integrated being (Magnusson & Törestad, 1993). With reference to this view, the task for personality research is to contribute knowledge about how and why individuals think, feel, act, and react in real life situations.

The formulations above imply that our main concern is the individual. However, an individual cannot be understood separately from the environment in which he or she lives. Ryff (1987) argued that contemporary sociology worked with an oversocialized conception of mankind, whereas contemporary psychology worked with an overpsychologized conception of human nature. A basic proposition for the presentation and discussion here is that the individual is an active, purposeful part of an integrated, complex, dynamic, and adaptive person–environment system. Furthermore, within this person–environment system, the individual develops and functions as an integrated, complex, dynamic, and adaptive organism. The implication for future psychological research is that theorizing and empirical work, instead of focusing on a context-free individual, have to center on a person who functions and develops as an active part of an integrated person–environment system.

When considering what this definition implies for the goal of personality research, it is essential to be aware of some limitations. Among all the factors involved in the functioning and development of an individual, there is a large domain or factor space to which scientific inquiry does not have access. This applies, above all, to factors concerned with existential and ethical questions. Such questions play an essential, for some individuals a dominant role in forming their inner and outer life. Empirical research can never answer such questions as: Does God exist? Is there a given meaning to my life? Which way of acting is more ethical than another? Why should I act in one way rather than another? Empirical research can indeed contribute knowledge about the role of the answers to such questions for individuals and societies but can never provide an objective answer to the ethical and existential issues per se with reference to empirical research.

This proposition has a consequence for the theoretical scope of the statistical–mathematical models which we apply in our endeavors to understand and explain psychological processes. In the final analyses, aimed at understanding the functioning and development of the total undivided person, the implication is that there will always be remaining variance that such models are incapable of explaining.

TWO PERSPECTIVES

In principle, the basic question of how and why individuals think, feel, act, and react as they do can be analyzed and investigated from three different perspectives: a current, synchronic perspective, a developmental, diachronic perspective, and an evolutionary perspective. This chapter concerns the first two perspectives, the synchronic and the diachronic. The evolutionary perspective is dealt with in Chapter 2.

In a synchronic perspective, models analyze and explain why individuals function as they do in terms of their current psychological and biological dispositions. The accounts are framed independently of the developmental processes that might have led to the present state of affairs. Developmental models, on the other hand, analyze and explain current functioning in terms of an individual's developmental history. Such models are concerned with the ontogeny of relevant aspects of the individual, the timing and expression of significant environmental events in his or her past and present, and the ways these factors operate in an interactive process to produce current functioning.

The focus of this presentation is individual development. However, the two perspectives cross-fertilize; we need both. For a full understanding of current individual functioning we need to understand the developmental background, and for a full understanding of developmental processes we need to understand how the individual functions at each stage of the life course.

Current Functioning

Figure 8.1 presents a summarized description of what happens psychologically and biologically in a particular situation with its distinctive features, that is, it gives a current perspective on individual functioning. The figure shows the main elements of the process in which an individual is involved in a situation that he/she interprets as threatening or demanding. (It should be emphasized that the figure presents a correct but simplified picture of a very complex process, involving a number of physiological, behavioral, cognitive, and noncognitive factors. Its purpose here is to illustrate a basic principle in individual functioning.)

The cognitive act of interpreting the situation stimulates, via the amygdala and the hypothalamus, the excretion of adrenaline from the adrenal glands, which in turn triggers a complex network of other physiological processes. The cognitive–physiological interplay is accompanied by emotional states of fear, anxiety, generally experienced arousal in this specific situation, or any combination of these (cf. Öhman, Flykt, & Lundqvist, in press). In the next stage of the process these emotions affect the individual's interpretation of sequences of changes in the situational conditions and, thereby, his or her physiological reactions and the adaptive behavioral responses during the next stage of the process.

The process described in Figure 8.1 illustrates how perceptual–cognitive–emotional, biological, and behavioral aspects of an individual's functioning and the perceived and interpreted aspects of the environment are involved in a continuous process of dynamic interaction in a current situation.[1] The outcomes of such situation-individual encounters will set the stage for subsequent actions and reactions to psychologically similar situations, as interpreted by the individual in his or her perceptual–cognitive system. An illustration of the application of this perspective is given in the discussion of stress research by Appley and Turnball (1986).

A Developmental Perspective

An empirical study from our longitudinal research program in Stockholm illustrates the developmental perspective (Magnusson, 1988; Stattin & Magnusson, 1990). A cohort of all boys and girls in one community in Sweden was followed from the age of 10 to adulthood. At the age of 14.5, girls maturing very early reported a much higher alcohol consumption than later maturing girls. However, in the follow-up of the same girls at the age of 26–27, no systematic relation was found between age of menarche and frequency of drinking. Thus, high alcohol con-

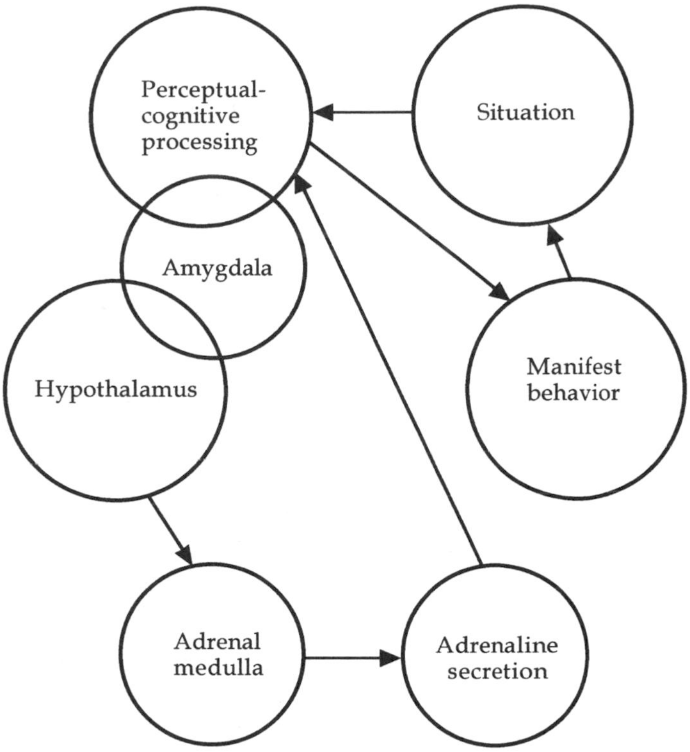

FIGURE 8.1. A simplified picture of envionmental, cognitive–emotional, physiological, and behavioral factors for an individual in a threatening situation.

sumption at age 14 among early maturing girls was not a precursor of alcohol abuse at adult age.

However, very early biological maturation did have long-term consequences in other respects. As adults, the early maturing girls married earlier, had more children, completed less education, and acquired a lower job status than average or late maturing girls. These effects could not be attributed to early maturation per se; rather they were the net result of many interrelated factors, linked to biological maturation during adolescence: self-perception, self-evaluation and, above all, the social characteristics of close friends in puberty. The short-term deviances in norm-breaking behavior and the long-term consequences for family life, education, and job status were observed only among early maturing girls who perceived themselves as more mature than their agemates and who affiliated in early adolescence with older males or with peers who were out of school and working.

Caspi and Moffit (1991), replicating the study for a sample of New Zealand girls, found the same early maturation deviance, but only if the girls were enrolled in a coeducational school. Presumably the opportunities for association with older boys were greater in the coeducational setting than in all-girl schools. It is less clear how very early maturation is linked to norm-breaking behavior among girls in American schools (Cairns & Cairns, 1994). Silbereisen and Kracke (1997), using self-reports of different aspects of maturational timing from two rather large samples of German adolescents, have emphasized the role of peer affiliation in the development process.

What these studies demonstrate is that the biological age for onset of sexual maturity plays a role in but does not alone account for the short- and long-term consequences observed. The rate of biological maturation, which to some extent is influenced by environmental factors, provides predisposing conditions for a process in which mental, biological, behavioral, and social factors are involved.

EXPLANATORY MODELS IN PSYCHOLOGICAL RESEARCH

A central concept in scientific psychology is that of causality, which implies the need for explanatory models. At a metatheoretical level it is possible to identify three such models for the study of causal relations in traditional psychological research: a mentalistic, a biological, and an environmental model. Identifying them helps to place the holistic approach in a historical perspective. The main distinction concerns the focus of each with regard to the dominant factors presumed to guide individual processes of current functioning and development. Few researchers adhere explicitly and strictly to only one approach; it is a matter of where the researcher places the center of gravity. However, in practice each of these approaches exerts a strong influence, which is one indication of the fragmentation that characterizes much psychological research.

The *mentalistic* model emphasizes mental factors as central to understanding why individuals function and develop as they do. According to this view, the main explanation for an individual's current functioning and development is to be found in the intrapsychic structures and processes of perceptions, thoughts, memories, emotions, values, goals, plans, conflicts, and so forth.

When *biological* models for current functioning are applied, an individual's thoughts, feelings, actions, and reactions are assumed to be determined basically by his or her biological equipment and how it functions. Primary determining factors in current individual functioning are assumed to be found in the physiological system, in the brain and the autonomic nervous system. The major determining guiding factors in developmental processes are genetic and maturational. In its extreme version this model implies that individual differences in the course of development have their roots in genes, with little role played by environmental and mental factors.

The *environmental* model locates the main causal factors for individual functioning in the environment. It is reflected in theories and models of human behavior at all levels of generality for environmental factors: macrosocial theories, theories about the role of the "sick family," and S-R models for various aspects of individual functioning, to give a few examples.

One aspect of an environmental approach to *current* functioning is to be found in traditional experimental psychological research. Within this orientation, laws and principles for individual functioning are studied in terms of reactions to variation in the intensity of one or several aspects of the physical environment, most often in a laboratory setting. The trend in personality research to assign the dominant determinant of behavior to situations and situational conditions has been discussed and criticized in terms of "situationism" (see Forgas & Van Heck, 1992). An overview and appraisal of the situationist position was presented by Krahé (1990).

In research on individual *development,* various environmental streams can be identified. The most extreme view was expressed by Watson (1930) in his discussion of individual development in a behavioristic perspective (see also Skinner, 1971). Another line, which strongly influenced developmental psychology during the sixties and seventies is rooted in sociology. The sociological influence is reflected in the vast amount of research on children growing up in environments that differ with respect to general geographical or social characteristics such as rural versus urban cultures and various levels of social class, or with respect to more specific characteristics, such as one versus two parent families, home versus day care, mother's employment status, and so forth (cf. Bronfenbrenner & Crouter, 1983, and their discussion of "the new demography").

The distinctions between the three approaches are not merely of theoretical interest. Each of the explanatory models has had and still has implications in discussions about and applications of appropriate methods for prevention and treatment in clinical psychology. A case in point is the current discussion concerning the appropriate treatment of mental problems and mental illness. Each approach recommends different methods for curing patients and forestalling maladaptation. The mentalistic approach sees the main cause of an individual's suffering, from depression or schizophrenia, for example, as the malfunctioning of intrapsychic thought processes. The natural treatment is then psychological therapy. According to the biological approach, an individual's thoughts, emotions, and actions can be influenced basically by changing his or her biological processes, and the appropriate therapy is therefore psychopharmacological treatment. The environmental approach holds that the genesis and development of various aspects of mental illness can be influenced, treated, and prevented by changing the environment through the removal, addition or improvement of external conditions.

There is, of course, nothing wrong per se with each of the explanatory models. Each of them has something essential to contribute to understanding and explaining individual functioning and development. The problem arises when each one claims complete supremacy as the only relevant model for explaining all aspects of current and developmental processes of individuals or for forming, through political decisions, the environments that individuals have to deal with and adapt to. It is easy to find examples of the suffering that this rigid claim of supremacy has caused societies and individuals. In clinical practice, for instance, a dominant opinion for a time among some psychologists was that all autistic reactions are caused by environmental factors, particularly in the family, and can thus be treated by changing the family environment. Recent research on this issue has moved towards a scientifically sounder attitude (Yeung-Courchesne & Courchesne, 1997).

An analysis of the two empirical illustrations that were presented earlier demonstrates that none of the three explanatory models is able by itself to explain individual current functioning and individual developmental processes. Any general model that seeks to contribute to the goal for psychological research must incorporate perceptual, cognitive–emotional, biological, behavioral and environmental factors into a single integrated model. These factors function simultaneously and need to be placed in a coherent theoretical framework, in which the total individual is the organizing principle.

The negative effects of the lack of a unified and unifying theoretical framework for psychological research have accumulated over the years and thus, also, the arguments for formulating such a framework (see, e.g., Lykken, 1991, Magnusson, 1995, and Richters, 1997). The aim of this chapter is to show how conditions have changed in recent decades and now enable us to formulate an effective general theoretical framework for conducting empirical research on specific issues.

THE HOLISTIC MODEL IN A HISTORICAL PERSPECTIVE

Making the individual the organizing principle for understanding and explaining individual functioning and development, that is a holistic perspective, has ancient roots. According to a well-known assumption, individuals could be classified into four temperamental types: sanguine, phlegmatic, melancholic, and choleric. Each type was assumed to be dominated by one of the four basic body fluids: blood, phlegm, black bile, and yellow bile. Galen, in the second century A.D., suggested that nine combinations of bodily fluids and the four elements of the physical world—soil, water, fire, and air—could be identified and used to describe individual differences. These notions were still current in scientific discussions about temperament during the 19th century (cf. Kagan, 1994).

Early in the history of psychology, a holistic perspective was forcefully claimed by prominent psychologists. In France, Binet and Henri (1895) discussed the elemental/holistic duality in understanding children's cognitive functioning and problem-solving at the end of the 19th century. In Germany, the holistic view was fundamental to Stern's (1911, 1917) person-oriented theory. In his presentation of Gestalt psychology, Wertheimer (1925) expressed the basic principle in words that are central in a modern holistic view: "there are wholes, the behavior of which is not determined by that of their individual elements, but where the part processes are themselves determined by the intrinsic nature of the whole." Brunswik (1929) likewise argued that the general Gestalt principle that the whole is more than the sum of the parts holds for the functioning of the total individual. Lewin's (1926, 1927) discussion of types and a typological approach belongs to the holistic tradition. In the United States, Gordon Allport was the leading advocate. In 1924, he summarized his position thus:

> An increasing number of investigators are engaging in the problem of classifying and measuring the traits of personality with the result that the advance in method is rapid and gratifying. But with analyzing, testing, and correlating most of these investigators become blind to the true nature of the problem before them. They lose sight of the forest in their preoccupation with individual trees. What they want is an adequate representation in psychological terms of the total personality; what they get is a series of separate measurements which pertain only to isolated and arbitrarily defined traits. (Allport, 1924, p. 132)

Later, using formulations which anticipated modern theories, Allport wrote "Of the several sciences devoted to the study of life-processes, none, peculiarly enough, recognizes as its central fact that life processes actually occur only in unified, complex, individual form" (Allport, 1937, p. 3). The Kraepelinian approach to psychiatric diagnoses from the turn of the last century, which is still influential in psychiatric thinking and practice, the typologies (e.g., Jung's categorical typology and its transformation into a dimensional typology by Sheldon), and clinical diagnoses reflect a holistic approach in psychological practice and research.

In spite of the strong formulations by leading scientists, for a long time there was little, if any, impact on empirical psychological research. Sanford (1965) strongly criticized the state of the art and proposed a holistic perspective for research in general psychology. In 1971, Rae Carlson asked, after having reviewed the leading journals in the field: "Where is the person in personality research?" Still in 1975, Cronbach described and analyzed the separation between what he designated the "two worlds of scientific psychology" with respect to problem formulation, methods, and statistics.

The slight influence of a holistic view on postwar empirical research had to do with structural features that dominated the existing paradigm: the dominance of S-R models with reference to behavioristic theory, the use of the experiment as the ultimate criterion of the discipline's scientific status, regardless of the character of the phenomena, and the misuse of theory due to misunderstanding the role of theory in natural sciences.

One reason for this state of affairs was the lack of a holistic integrated model for individual functioning and development that could serve as the common theoretical framework for theorizing and empirical research on psychological phenomena. The traditional holistic view was empty; it lacked specific content about the functioning and interplay of basic psychological and biological elements operating in the processes of the integrated organism. What went on between the stimulus and the response was regarded as unknown and inaccessible for scientific inquiry; it was concealed in the black box. The reason for this state of affairs was formulated in 1943 by Clark Hull, who drew a distinction between molar behavior and specific properties of living organisms and argued that "any theory of behavior is at present, and must be for some time to come, a molar theory. This is because neuroanatomy and physiology have not yet developed to a point such that they yield principles which may be employed as postulates in a system of behavior theory" (p. 275). Thus, the elements of the processes could not be discussed and analyzed scientifically.

However, over time an increasing number of voices have been raised in defence of the neglected perspective, proposing models that help to overcome the limitations of the empty holistic model and discuss the research strategy and methodological consequences for empirical research (see, e.g., Baltes, Lindenberger, & Staudinger, 1997; Block, 1971; Cairns & Valsiner, 1984; Caprara, 1992; Emde, 1994; Magnusson, 1988; Wapner & Demick, 1998). Cairns (1979) presented a coherent holistic perspective that is still up to date. Building on the Russian tradition and referring to the contributions by Lomov (1984) in this field, the methodological and theoretical aspects of a holistic approach were discussed by Rusalov (1989). The recent development of this issue has two characteristics. First, the main contributions come from research on social development and personality. Second, the application of a holistic view was dominated for a long time, and still is to some extent, by theoretical discussions, with fewer examples of empirical studies carried through with explicit reference to a holistic view.

Contributions to a Modern Holistic Perspective

The situation for a holistic perspective in research on psychological phenomena has now changed, mainly due to influences from four main interrelated sources: (1) cognitive research, (2) research on biological aspects of individual functioning and development, (3) the development of modern models for dynamic complex processes, and (4) longitudinal research. Together, research in these areas has contributed by filling the empty holistic view with substantive content and providing a basis for the development of methodological tools and research strategies, which are compatible with the nature of the phenomena with which we are concerned.

1. As indicated above, a consequence of the postwar dominance of S-R models was the neglect of mental processes. Since the sixties, however, research on cognitive processes has been the most rapidly developing field in psychological theorizing and research. Research on information processing, memory and decision-making has made dramatic progress. Among other things, it has laid the basis for research on artifi-

cial intelligence. The recent examples of integration of cognitive and brain research indicates a promising development towards a more insightful understanding and explanation of mental and behavioral processes. This movement is reflected in the evolution of "cognitive neuroscience" (Posner & Raichle, 1994).

For further progress, research on emotions, values, goals, motivation, and other noncognitive aspects of intrapsychic structures and processes should be planned and implemented in a holistic frame of reference. These aspects of the integrated organism are crucial for understanding and explaining almost all other aspects of positive as well as negative facets of individual functioning and developmental processes. How these noncognitive aspects develop and function in the integrated processes of interaction with cognitive, biological, behavioral, and social factors defines an essential and promising research domain (Damasio, 1994; Edelman & Tononi, 1996).

2. In recent decades, research in biological and medical sciences has advanced at an increasing pace. Developments in these fields have helped to fill the holistic model with new content from three main interrelated directions of interest for understanding and explaining psychological processes.

The first contribution concerns detailed knowledge about the brain, how it develops from conception and onwards over the lifespan in a process of interaction between constitutional factors and context factors, and how it functions at each stage of development, as an active organ, selecting, interpreting and integrating information from the environment. Through the application of techniques from molecular biology and biophysics to unicellular model systems and nowadays even on transgene organisms, new ways have been opened for understanding the mechanisms that regulate the growth, division and development of new forms of cells. Access to advanced techniques for brain-imaging has made it possible to investigate the current functioning of the brain, while an individual is performing a mental task. This research has shown how multiple brain regions, operating in synchronic interaction, are involved in complex, adaptive perceptual–cognitive–emotional processes.

The rapid development of research on brain functioning and its role for understanding mental processes has helped bridge the gap between biological and psychological models that has obstructed a deeper understanding and explanation of mental and behavioral processes (Damasio & Damasio, 1996). An issue of *Science* (March, 1997) summarized and discussed the far-reaching implications of the new scenery, both for theoretical models and for application, in such central areas for psychological inquiry as learning, memory, reasoning, intelligence, perception, language, and mental illnesses.

The second contribution from research in medicine and biology lies in new insights into the role of internal biological structures and processes in the total functioning and development of individuals. Research into the role of biochemicals in the individual's way of dealing with situational–environmental conditions, such as stress, and in developmental processes, such as those underlying the development of antisocial behavior, is developing at an increasing pace. Research in this field has enriched our understanding of processes underlying individual differences in personality (cf. Klinteberg, Schalling, Levander, & Oreland, 1988), problem behaviors (Susman, 1993), temperament (Kagan, 1994), antisocial development (Magnusson, 1996a), depression (Depue, 1995; Hettema, 1995), and suicidal behavior (Åsberg, 1997).

The third contribution comes from recent research on the role of genes in individual development processes. For a long time, this line of research was dominated by investigations into the relative contributions of environmental and hereditary factors to distributions of measurements, at group level, of different individual characteristics, such as intelligence. The interpretation of recent findings has been promoted by the introduction of theoretical models that emphasize the interdependence of genetic factors and environmental factors in the developmental processes of individuals (e.g., Magnusson, 1988; Rose, 1995; Rutter et al., 1997). An important step toward understanding the role of genes was the discovery of DNA and the genetic code in the sixties. This discovery opened up new windows for mapping the individual genome structure and for research on the mechanisms by which genetic factors operate.

3. The third source for the application of a holistic perspective in research on individual functioning and development lies in the general modern models that have been developed in the natural sciences for the study of complex, dynamic processes. For natural reasons, the most influential for psychology has been the general systems theory. A review of developmental re-

search within a system theoretical framework was presented by Thelen (1995) and Thelen and Smith (1998) (see also Ford & Lerner, 1992; Gottlieb, 1996; Sameroff, 1983). A holistic system view for research on aging was recently presented by Baltes and Smith (1997) with reference to the Berliner longitudinal program.

The formulations of these models have theoretical, methodological, and research strategy implications for psychological research.

First, the models emphasize the holistic, integrated nature of dynamic, complex processes. This has two theoretical and methodological implications for empirical investigation. First, no single factor determines normal processes. As soon that it might happen, the processes will stop or go astray, as, for example, in Huntington's disease. Thus, one aspect of integrated dynamic processes is the restriction they impose on the functioning of single variables operating in the system. Second, and related to the first point, the models confirm and provide a theoretical basis for the following old proposition: The psychological significance of a certain variable for the functioning of an individual cannot be understood by studying that variable in isolation, outside its context with other, simultaneously operating variables in the individual. The totality has properties that cannot be derived by summing results from studies on single variables in isolation. The limitations of results from studies of single variables taken out of context were demonstrated empirically by Magnusson, Andersson, and Törestad (1993).

Second, the models emphasize the interactive character of the processes at all levels of the dynamic, integrated person–environment system. This emphasis draws attention to the concept of context. The role of context is essential for understanding individual development and functioning at all levels of the total system, from the cellular level to the individual's interaction with the environment (Edelman, 1987; Hinde, 1996). The basic role of context in developmental processes has been recognized for a long time by researchers focusing on social and personality development of individuals (e.g., Sarbin, 1976). A recent review of this issue was presented by Magnusson and Stattin (1997). In cognitive research there is a growing awareness and consideration of the role of contextual factors, demonstrated in research on "situated cognition" (e.g., Choi & Hannafin, 1995) and on memory (e.g., Erngrund, Mäntylä, & Nilsson, 1996).

Third, the models provide a theoretical basis for the development of methodological tools for the investigation of the interactive, dynamic processes underlying individual functioning and development. In natural sciences, they have initiated the development of mathematical and methodological tools appropriate for studying such processes (Kelso, 1995). There is a growing interest and application of such models and methods in developmental research. Examples are van Geert's (1994) application of a nonlinear dynamic model for the redefinition of Vygotsky's "zone of proximal development" and the application by Gottman, Guralnick, Wilson, Swanson, and Murray (1997) of a nonlinear dynamic mathematical model to the study of emotions.

However, when methodologies that were originally developed for the study of dynamic, complex processes are considered for research on developmental phenomena, a word of caution is appropriate. There are, indeed, certain similarities between the structures and processes studied in the natural sciences and those investigated in psychological research (Edelman, 1992). Thus, under specific circumstances methods used in natural sciences are applicable in research on psychological phenomena. But there are also essential differences, particularly with reference to the functioning of the total organism.

A fundamental characteristic of developmental processes is that besides being dynamic and complex, they are also adaptive; individual development involves adaptational processes over time. In these individual processes, a guiding element is *intentionality,* which is linked to *emotions* and *values* and the fact that the individual learns from experience. This does not imply that data reflecting different aspects of individuals' complex, adaptive processes are in principle inaccessible to strong methodological analyses. It simply represents a challenge to develop and apply strong methods for analyzing such data, taking into consideration the specific nature of the phenomena being investigated.

4. The fourth main source for enrichment of the holistic perspective lies in the revival of longitudinal research. This underscores the holistic nature of personality and social development in human beings in ways that previously could only have been speculated about. Inadequacies of the piecemeal or variable-oriented approach to the study of developmental issues become obvious in well-planned longitudinal studies that track individuals over time and contexts. Such a de-

sign is necessary for understanding developmental processes for a number of reasons. One is that operating factors necessarily shift over time, both with respect to which factors operate, their distinct character per se, and their significance and role in the total integrated, interactive processes of the individual. It is only the organism that remains distinct and identifiable.

The contributions from cognitive research, from biological and medical sciences, from modern models for dynamic complex processes, and from longitudinal research have enriched the old holistic view in ways that make it a fruitful theoretical framework for planning, implementing, and interpreting empirical studies on specific psychological issues. The modern holistic view now offers a stable platform for further scientific progress in psychology, enabling us to fall into step with recent developments in other disciplines in the life sciences. It is now possible to meet the challenges of the old theoretical formulations with appropriate methodological tools within a solid theoretical frame of reference.

The Role of a Holistic Perspective in Psychological Inquiry

A characteristic feature of scientific progress in empirical sciences is specialization. When specialization in a subfield of the natural sciences has reached a certain level, it becomes apparent that further progress lies in integration with what has been achieved in neighboring disciplines. In recent decades, significant developments have occurred at the interface of biology, chemistry and physics. The role of the integrative phases of this iterative process of specialization and integration in natural sciences and medicine is explicitly manifested in the areas for Nobel prizes in these disciplines during the last 40 years.

In the natural sciences, the iterative process of specialization and integration has been facilitated by the existence of a general theoretical framework for theorizing and empirical inquiry, a general model of nature. This model has provided a foundation for continuous progress in two interrelated respects. First, it has served as the common theoretical framework for planning, implementing and interpretating studies on specific problems. Second, it has enabled researchers concerned with very different levels of the physical world (e.g., nuclear physicists and astrophysicists) to communicate with and understand each other. As a result, new discoveries in different fields and at different levels of the physical world can be integrated in and contribute to a deeper understanding of the same general system of structures and processes.

The situation in psychology is different. For a long time it was characterized by increasing specialization but very little integration. In 1981, Toulmin described the relations between subfields as "sectarian rivalry" rather than constructive collaboration. As part of a broader trend, major steps in psychology have now been taken for fruitful collaboration with researchers in neighboring, relevant disciplines. The integration of cognitive and brain research, described earlier, is one of an increasing number of examples. In order to be fully productive, these integrative efforts need to be planned and organized within a single integrated theoretical framework, using a holistic theoretical approach. We need a general, integrated model of humans and environments that can serve the same purposes in psychological research as the general model of nature serves in natural sciences: to form a common theoretical framework for planning and implementation of studies on specific problems and provide a common conceptual space as a prerequisite for effective communication even among researchers concerned with very different issues. It also serves as a theoretical framework for planning and implementation of effective methods and strategies for effective prevention and treatment in applied psychology.

To prevent misunderstanding of this claim, let me add five interrelated comments.

First, the adoption of a holistic view does not, of course, imply that specific mental, behavioral, and biological aspects of individual functioning cannot or should not be the object of empirical research. The warning by Mayr (1976) with respect to biology is equally applicable to psychology: "The past history of biology has shown that progress is equally inhibited by an anti-intellectual holism and a purely atomistic reductionism" (p. 72).

Second, the role and functioning of a holistic model are not to offer a hypothesis or an explanation for all problems. The Newtonian model did not answer every question about the structure and functioning of the physical world, but it served the two purposes summarized above. In empirical research on a specific problem, the holistic perspective has two functions: as a theoretical framework for the identification and formulation of the research problem (discussing the problem in such a framework has consequences for the manner in which the problem is investigated) and as the framework for interpretating and discussing the significance of the empirical results. Interpreted and integrated within a holistic framework, results from studies on specific problems at different levels of the total system (1) gain a surplus meaning, and (2) contribute more effectively than otherwise to the understanding of the total organism's functioning.

Third, a holistic, integrated model does not imply that the entire system of an individual should be studied in every research endeavor. The acceptance of a common model of nature has never implied that the whole universe should be investigated in every study in the natural sciences.

Fourth, no single researcher can be an expert on all problems at all levels of individual functioning and development. Researchers in cognition and antisocial behavior are concerned with different kinds of problems and may apply different methods for observation and data treatment. A common theoretical framework enables them to communicate and gain from each other more effectively.

Fifth, the application of a general model of human beings and environments is not tantamount to criticism of what has and is being done in psychological research. Current research is clearly contributing real knowledge about psychological phenomena. Within the holistic framework general principles for scientific invetsigation are applicable. Criticism of particular fields of today's research or of specific studies is relevant and constructive only when it refers to approaches that are more concerned with piecemeal theories, methods and statistics than with real problems (Cairns, 1986; Cairns & Rodkin, 1998; Magnusson, 1992).

Controversies

Taken seriously, a holistic interactionistic view has far-reaching implications for theory building as well as for planning, implementing, and interpreting empirical research. It is also consistent with progress in other scientific disciplines concerned with dynamic, complex processes. In psychology, however, the interactionistic perspective has often been dismissed, most of the time in superficial terms without arguments, sometimes due to misunderstanding. In a discussion of models for the interplay of genetic and environmental factors in developmental processes, Plomin (1986) explicitly formulated an attitude that is not uncommon: "If interactionism were to be believed, it would imply that 'main effects' cannot be found because everything interacts with everything else" (p. 249). Two comments are pertinent.

First, the formulation reflects a misunderstanding of complex, dynamic, and adaptive processes. In a holistic interactionistic perspective, everything does not interact with everything else; interaction is only one of the basic principles underlying the adapative processes of individual functioning and development. Second, operating factors do not interact in a random way. The manner in which structures function and processes proceed in a current perspective and the manner in which they change across time are organized and specific. In addition, of course, the interactive nature of such processes does not exclude the investigation of main effects in terms of data in empirical investigations.

Another common misunderstanding of the interactionistic view is that it conflicts with the trait concept. The discussion of the interactionistic and trait positions as conflicting is one of the many nonintellectual pseudo-issues that can occupy researchers in psychology for decades and prevent them from devoting time and energy to the analysis and investigation of real, central psychological problems. It has even happened that trait theorists have found it necessary to defend "the existence" of traits against what they regard as criticism from those who argue for an interactionistic view. In order to preempt a discussion of what is really a pseudo-issue, it must be emphasized that there is no contradiction between trait theories and an interactionistic view on the existence of enduring, latent individual dispositions: The essential argument concerns the trait concept's explanatory contribution to understanding individual functioning in specific situations and to understanding the developmental processes of individuals. What Allport (1937) defined as "bona fide structures in each personality that account for the consistency of its behavior" (p. 37) form an essential basis for coherence in the individual's interaction with situations of different character and for lawful continuity in the individual's interaction with the environment over time. A theoretical contribution to this discussion was presented recently by Mischel and Shoda (1995), who analyzed traits in terms of processing dispositions with reference to social, cognitive, and biological models.

THE MODERN HOLISTIC APPROACH: THE INDIVIDUAL AS ORGANIZING PRINCIPLE FOR PSYCHOLOGICAL INQUIRY

Summarizing, a modern holistic view emphasizes an approach to the individual and the person–environment system as organized wholes, functioning as integrated totalities. At each level, the totality derives its characteristic features and properties from the interaction of the elements involved, not from the effect of each isolated part on the totality. Each aspect of the structures and processes that are operating (perceptions, plans, values, goals, motives, biological factors, conduct, etc.), as well as each aspect of the environment, takes on meaning from its role in the total functioning of the individual (Magnusson, 1990). A certain element derives its significance, not from its structure but from its role in the system of which it forms a part.

From the above description it will be seen that a holistic perspective for psychological research is something else and more than the sum of pieces of knowledge that have been collected separately and without reference to a common theoretical framework. The essential feature of the perspective is that it constitutes a *synthesis* of all available knowledge that is relevant for understanding and explaining why individuals think, feel, act, and react as they do in real life and how they develop in these respects.

Individual Developmental Processes within Organized Structures

The basis for the claim that the processes of individual functioning and development are accessible to systematic, scientific inquiry is that these processes are not random; they occur in a specific way within organized structures and are guided by specific principles.

Organization is a characteristic of individual structures and processes at all levels; it is a characteristic of mental structures and processes, of behavior, of biological structures and processes, and of the functioning and development of the total, integrated individual. In this connection it is interesting to note that already "Allport was concerned with synthesis, organization, patterning and the 'unity of personality'" and that he "increasingly became concerned with personality as a dynamic system" (Pervin, 1993, p. 70). The orderly organization of behavior in a developmental perspective was emphasized and discussed by Fentress (1989). Baltes and Graf (1996) have raised the issue of whether the differences between early development and aging are essentially a discontinuity in organizational directionality, from more to less.

For understanding and explaining the structural organization of the functioning and development of individual organisms, a relevant principle is "self-organization," well documented in the development of biological systems. Self-organizing ability is a characteristic of open systems and refers to a process by which new structures and "patterns" emerge from existing ones. The fundamental role of self-organization was expressed by the Nobel laureate Jacob (1989): "Finality in the living world thus originates from the idea of organism, because the parts have to produce each other, because they have to associate to form the whole, because, as Kant said, living beings must be 'self-organized.'"

Self-organization is a guiding principle from the beginning of fetal development. Within subsystems, the operating components organize themselves to maximize the functioning of that subsystem with respect to its purpose in the total system (e.g., Hess & Mikhailov, 1994). At a higher level subsystems organize themselves in order to fulfill their role in the functioning of the totality. We find this principle in the development and functioning of the brain, the coronary system, and the immune system. Referring to the concept of self-organization, Schore (1997) discussed the organization of the brain and its role in the predisposition to psychiatric disorders. Derryberry and Rothbart (1997) used the concept for a discussion of temperament. The principle can be applied to the development and functioning of the sensory and cognitive systems, and to manifest behavior (see Carlson, Earls, & Todd, 1988). Its role for understanding developmental processes was discussed by Thelen (1989).

Developmental Processes

Individual development refers to progressive or regressive changes in the structures and/or the functioning of systems at different levels across the entire life span—from conception to death.

Two concepts are central in this definition: time and change. While development always has a temporal dimension, the passage of time is not equivalent to development. For example, a salient individual characteristic, such as a claustrophobic fear, which originated at the age of 8 and remains unaltered at the age of 12 has not "developed" over this period. But, if the disorder has become more severe from age 8 to 12, there will have been a negative, or regressive, development ("change"). And the characteristic feature of developmental change does not lie in a single variable per se, in isolation from other aspects of the system in which it functions; developmental change means restructuring and transformation of systems of interdependent, operating factors at different levels of the functioning of the integrated organism.

Individual developmental processes are rooted in constitutional factors. Such factors, inherited or not, form the potentialities and set the boundaries for the developmental processes. At each stage of development, organized structures of mental and biological elements are the results of previous processes and form, at the same time, the basis for current processes (Magnusson, 1993; Caprara, 1996).

Both individuals and environments change over time in a process of reciprocal interaction: The individual changes as a result of biological maturation (e.g., growth; myelinization of the brain) and cognitive–emotional experiences gained in the interaction with the environment; the environment, with which the individual interacts, changes as a consequence of societal changes at different levels and of the individual's direct and indirect actions in and on it (e.g., choosing a new job or moving to a new environment). As a consequence of the simultaneous changes of the person and his or her environment, the nature of the interaction processes changes over the life span, partly as a result of the interaction process itself. For example, the interaction between an infant and its family is not the same as that individual's interaction with his or her family in puberty, middle age, or retirement. The interaction process per se will thus precipitate development.

Stability and Change

A characteristic of all changes during the life span of an individual is *lawful continuity*; the functioning of an individual at any given stage of development is related to earlier and later stages. This implies that change in the process of human ontogeny is understandable in the light of the individual's previous life history, the active current processes of the individual, characterized by intentionality, emotions, and values; and the environmental influences operating at the time of the change. The significance of a "chance event" may be completely different for the developmental processes of two different individuals, since it is embedded in two different integrated, time related processes. The present has a past and a future for each individual. This tenet holds true even for changes that are so abrupt that they seem to break a stable direction of development. The issues of whether individual development is characterized by continuity or discontinuity, and by homotypic or heterotypic continuity, should be seen and discussed in that perspective. The need for a theoretical framework for understanding heterotypic continuity was emphasized by Pulkkinen (1998). Moffit (1993) discussed this issue with reference to the developmental process behind antisocial behavior.

Individuals' paths through life differ. This implies, among other things, a process of "personality crystallization"; that is, the developmental processes of individuals whose systems organization differ at a certain point in time—as a result of different constitutional factors, maturation, and experiences—will take partly different directions in the next step. Each step underpins future developmental alternatives and eventually more stable "types" will emerge. If this view is correct, it should show up in more distinct homogenization within categories of individuals and a clearer differentiation between categories of individuals over time. Among other things, this means less change with age; development itself slows down. Individual strategies for coping with the restrictions that follow from loss of mental and physical resources in aging were discussed by Baltes (1987) in terms of "selective optimization with compensation" (see also Baltes & Baltes, 1990).

Models for dynamic complex processes discussed above in "Contributions to a Modern Holistic Perspective" are applicable to this discussion. For the effective application of the models, it is essential to consider the specific character of the processes that are our concern in the study of psychological phenomena.

The total individual system and its subsystems of biological, mental, and behavioral structures have properties that imply that they are less chaotic than the processes studied in meteorology, for which chaos theory was first developed. As emphasized earlier, an essential feature of the processes of individual functioning and development is that, besides being complex and dynamic, they are adaptive. The adaptational process of an individual over time involves two opposing forces: maturation and experiences, which drive change, and resistance to change. In the face of environmental challenges, physiological systems maintain a dynamic balance. In the context of maintaining the organism's functional balance and avoiding being open to accidental, irregular stimulation from the environment, an essential feature of the organismic system is its inbuilt resistance to change; once a mental, biological, or behavioral structure has been established during the developmental process, it becomes resistant to transformation into new structures. Biological systems defend themselves against inappropriate causes of change, which might lead to malfunction or destruction of the system. For example, in the normal functioning and development of the brain, a number of events, which might lead to a detrimental butterfly effect, are ignored, and only those that contribute to effective current functioning and the development of new functional structures are accepted.

That developmental processes are stable does not mean that they are static; stability of living organisms' way of developing rather implies adaptive ability to change. Referring to the ability to achieve stability through change, the concept of "homeostasis" has been supplemented by the concept of "allostasis" (Schulkin, McEwen, & Gold, 1994). This concept is central in the Allostatic Load Model in research on the long-term impact of the physiological response to stress (McEwen & Stellar, 1993). The allostatic principle functions so that the autonomic nervous system, the hypothalamic–pituitary–adrenal axis, and the cardiovascular, metabolic, and immune systems protect the body by responding adequately to internal and external stress. With reference to their "process theory," Sabelli and Carlson-Sabelli (1991) emphasized the role of harmonious and conflicting interactions between opposites in normal development and psychopathology. Recently, the cell biologist Ingber (1998) suggested the principle of "tensegrity" (originally an architectural model for the construction of buildings in which structures stabilize themselves by balancing forces of internal tension and compression) as a basic principle for the developmental organization of biological structures.

Much developmental research on stability and change has centered on stability and change in quantitative terms, and a common issue has been whether or not individual development is characterized by more of the same. It should be recognized that the process of developmental change in an individual is characterized by both quantitative and qualitative change. Individual development is not a process of accumulation of outcomes; it is rather a process of restructuring subsystems and the whole system within the boundaries set by biological and social constraints. If one aspect changes, it affects related parts of the subsystem and sometimes the whole organism; for example, if one of the necessary operating factors in the coronary system totters, the whole coronary system and the whole organism may be affected and "remodelled." Referring to animal research, Waddington (1969) discussed this phenomena:

> That is to say, if by some experimental intervention we change the conditions of a developing system, e.g., by cutting a piece off an embryo or otherwise altering it, there is usually a very strong tendency for the disturbed processes to change in such a way that they eventually come back to a further point along the trajectory they had originally been following. We see this in many sorts of phenomena, in regeneration and regulation of defects. (p. 96)

This implies that patterns are states of systems that are adaptive to developmental changes. Factors and operating mechanisms involved in "remodelling" the coronary system have become a central area of scientific study (e.g., Sharpe, et al., 1991). At a more general level, the restructuring of structures and processes in the individual is embedded in and part of the restructuring of the total individual–environment system.

With reference to the importance of understanding change in developmental processes, it is interesting to note that the main concern in traditional empirical research on individual development has been mostly the study of stability. In one of the most frequently cited studies in the field, Olweus (1979) presented an overview of results showing that the correlations for the stability of rank orders of individuals with respect to data for a certain personality variable across time were of the same size as usually found for the stability of rank orders with respect to data for intelligence. The same kind of stability coefficients were presented by Backteman and Magnusson (1981) for personality characteristics. So far, so good. A problem arises, however, when these coefficients are taken to say something about the developmental processes of individuals. In fact, they are not much help in understanding and explaining what happens with individuals over time. What is sorely needed is empirical work that concentrates on the study of the change processes of individual development, taking into consideration their specific character. To reach that goal we have to develop appropriate research strategies and methodologies.

Causality

As discussed in the introductory part of this chapter, a central concept in scientific work is causality. Three views on causality in psychological research can be distinguished in a historical perspective: (1) unidirectional causality, (2) classical interactionism (Endler & Magnusson, 1976), and (3) modern holistic interactionism (Magnusson & Stattin, 1997). Each has its specific implications for theory building and for implementation and interpretation.

1. Characteristic for all three overriding explanatory models (described in "Explanatory Models in Psychological Research") is their unidirectional view of causality. In the mentalistic model, behavior is caused by intrapsychic perceptual, cognitive, and emotional processes. In the biological model, individual functioning and development are driven by biological factors. The driving force in the environmental model is the characteristic features of the individual's environment; the individual is the target of environmental influences.

2. The central idea of classical interactionism was early expressed in the formula $B = f(P, E)$; that is, behavior in a wide sense is the result of the interplay of individual and environmental factors (Lewin, 1954). This implies that the focus of interest is the interface of person–environment relations. In a later overview of the state of the art of this perspective, Endler and Magnusson (1976) emphasized (1) that an individual and his or her environment form a total system in which the individual functions as the active, purposeful agent, and (2) that a main characteristic of the causal relations is reciprocity rather than unidirectionality. The process character of the person–environment relation was discussed by Bronfenbrenner (1988) in terms of process–person–context models.

Classical interactionist formulations for current individual functioning were presented by Pervin (1968), adopting the term "transactional," and by Bandura (1978), using the term "reciprocal determinism." Strelau's (1983) "regulative theory of temperament" also stresses person–environment interaction. Particularly during the 1970s and 1980s, the explicit formulations of a classical interactionist model had a strong twofold impact on personality research, along with implications for planning, implementing, and interpreting developmental research. First, the issue of cross-situational consistency in individual functioning became a central topic for theoretical debate (Magnusson, 1976; Magnusson & Endler, 1977). Second, this debate led, as a consequence, to an interest in theoretical taxonomies and empirical analyses of situational characteristics (Forgas & Van Heck, 1992; Magnusson, 1981).

In recent decades the role of person–environment reciprocal interaction for individual development has become accepted theoretically by most developmentalists. Various labels for this view have been adopted by leading researchers in personality and developmental research. Baltes, Reese, and Lipsitt (1980) used "dialectic–dualistic," Bronfenbrenner and Crouter (1983) "process–person–context" model, Cairns (1979) "developmental synthesis," and Lerner and Kauffman (1985) "developmental contextualism" for their discussions of an interactionist view of individual development. Oyama (1989) critically discussed what is here designated classical interactionism and suggested the term "constructivist interactionism" for her approach. A main reference for empirical developmental research in the framework of classical interactionism has been the "goodness of fit" model (Lerner, 1983), a concept launched by Stern (see Kreppner, 1992).

3. In two interrelated ways, holistic interactionism differs from classical interactionism. First, in holistic interactionism, behavior is not regarded as an outcome variable; it is a certain aspect of individual functioning and development and an integrated part in the total dynamic interaction process. Second, as demonstrated in Figure 8.1, interactional processes, current and developmental, are not restricted to the level of person–environment interaction. Dynamic in-

teraction is also a central characteristic of the processes going on *within* the individual. This has consequences for the appraisal of causality in holistic interactionism. Developmental processes are multidetermined; the characteristic feature of these processes is not simple, once-and-for-all established x–y relations; most often x and y are aspects of the same process. What initiates a specific process and what maintains it over time may vary. An intrapsychic factor may trigger an interaction process in the individual in which biological and environmental factors also are involved. Similarly, mental and environmental factors can become active and operate in an interaction process that was originally triggered by biological factors. The initiation of personbound interaction processes of mental, behavioral, and biological factors may lie in environmental conditions, as illustrated in Figure 8.1. The reciprocity is also a characteristic of the individual–environment dynamic interaction process. Environmental factors influence an individual's physical and mental well-being; at the same time, the character or the individual's interaction with the environment is influenced by his or her characteristic mental, behavioral, and biological ways of functioning.

Comments

Linked to the unidirectional view on causality is the use of the concepts of dependent and independent variables and of predictor and criterion in empirical research. A consequence of the modern interactionistic view is that those concepts acquire a relative meaning in experimental designs. A certain kind of variable, be it biological, mental, behavioral, or environmental, can be the independent variable in one study and the dependent variable in another and even serve as both independent and dependent variable in the same study. The same for predictor and criterion; what is the predictor in one study can be the criterion measure in another.

METHODOLOGICAL ISSUES

Empirical research has the basic task of contributing appropriate answers to relevant questions. One necessary condition for achieving this is that the data used to elucidate certain phenomena and the method by which the data are processed match the character of the phenomena under investigation. The formulation of a holistic, interactionistic model has specific implications for the choice of data and the application of methodological tools.

One feature of the traditional approach to psychological research is methodological "monism" or even, in Koch's (1981) terminology, methodological "fetishism." The experimental method has been perceived as *the* method for the collection of data to such an extent that mainstream psychology has been referred to as "experimental psychology," that is, defined with reference to method. References to the use of experiments have even been used as the criterion for psychology as a scientific discipline. In natural sciences the experiment has been the classical study design, and it is interesting to note how even in such fields the supremacy of the experimental method in research on dynamic processes is now being questioned. A debate in *Science* on the relevance of experiments in ecological research was introduced with the following formulation: "Ecological experiments have become quite good at isolating causes and effects. But there's a debate brewing over whether these results reveal anything about the natural world" (Roush, 1995, p. 313). From the foregoing discussion it should be clear that a particular methodology cannot be applied regardless of the level of structures and processes at which a research problem has been formulated. There is no single "scientific" method that can be used for effective research on all types of problems (Magnusson, 1992).

Research on individual development is primarily based on quantitative data reflecting individual functioning at various levels. The discussion here on methodological issues and the discussion on data treatment refer to this tradition. However, important knowledge for our understanding of psychological processes would be obtained by extending the arsenal of methods to include qualitative methods, frequently and successfully applied in ethnographic research. Another complement to the standard data collection techniques is the narrative approach, in which individuals' stories of their own lives are analyzed (Sarbin, 1986). The application of this approach was exemplified by Manturzewska (1990) in her study of the life-span development of professional musicians. With reference to Tomkins's (1979) "script theory," Carlson (1988) advocated the usefulness of psychobiographical inquiry in several areas of personality research. The type of interview data collected by Cairns and Cairns (1994) in their longitudinal study of adolescence yield information that cannot be obtained in other ways.

The limited space here does not allow a comprehensive presentation and discussion of the methodological consequences of a holistic interactionistic framework for the planning, implementation, and interpretation of empirical studies on specific issues. Two contrasting but complementary approaches to the use of data in order to understand psychological mechanisms and principles in individual functioning and development are discussed briefly: the variable approach and the person approach, referring to concepts coined by Block (1971). Both are useful tools in empirical research. However, they make different assumptions and give distinctly different answers to psychological questions. The merits and limitations of each of these approaches were analyzed and discussed by Bergman (1998), Bergman and Magnusson (1991), and Magnusson (1998).

Individual Differences in Organization of Operating Factors

For the discussion of individual differences, two aspects of the organization of structures and processes are central.

First, individuals differ to some extent in the way in which operational factors are organized and function within subsystems. Individuals also differ in subsystem organization and function. Factors within systems operate in terms of *patterns*; the organization of structures and processes in terms of patterns is a characteristic at all levels and for all aspects of the organism. For example, Stryker (1994) emphasized the role of patterns of neural activity in the developing nervous system and how these patterns of activity vary among individuals, and Weiner (1989) suggested that even the oscillations produced by the natural pacemakers of the heart, the stomach, and the brain are patterned (cf. also Kelso, 1995).

Second, both the number of ways in which operating factors in a certain subsystem can be organized in patterns, in order to allow the subsystem to play its functional role in the totality, and the number of ways in which subsystems can be organized to form the total pattern for the total organism are *restricted*. Only a limited number of patterned states are functional for each subsystem and for the totality (cf. Bergman & Magnusson, 1991; Sapolsky, 1994). This view suggests that each individual can be referred to one of a limited number of more or less homogeneous categories of individuals for systems at different levels. An empirical illustration was presented by Gramer and Huber (1994) in a study of cardiovascular responses in what was assumed to be a stressful situation. They found that the subjects could be assigned to one of three groups on the basis of their distinct patterns of values for systolic blood pressure, diastolic blood pressure, and heart rate. Mills et al. (1994) studied patterns of adrenergic receptors and adrenergic agonists underlying responses to a laboratory task and identified four distinct groups of individuals. Using data for problem behaviors, Magnusson and Bergman (1988, 1990) distinguished eight groups of boys with characteristic patterns at 13 years of age. The main results of that study were replicated by Pulkkinen (1992a) and Pulkkinen and Tremblay (1992). In the Swedish study the groupings of boys formed the basis for the study of their life trajectories up to adulthood in a longitudinal perspective. The same approach was used by Pulkkinen (1992b) for the longitudinal study of aggressively inclined girls over a 12-year period.

The two propositions lead to the conclusion that subsystems and individuals can be understood as complex sets of categories, which Meehl (1992) defined as "natural classes," that is, really existing classes or categories as distinct from "arbitrary classes," the product of some method of classification.

Thus, the important information about an individual lies in the special organization of operating mental, biological, and behavioral factors at all levels of individual functioning in terms of patterns. One implication of this conclusion is that each subsystem must be analyzed in terms of its role in the total functioning of the individual and the total functioning of the person–environment system, as well as in terms of the manner in which it affects and is affected by other subsystems.

In this connection a special case is the proposition that a certain class of complex, dynamic systems that characterize individuals has inherent restrictions in terms of states that cannot occur. Lewin (1931) discussed boundary conditions in terms of "region of freedom of movement" and Valsiner (1984) drew attention to the fact that the range of an individual's actual behavior constitutes only a fraction of what is theoretically possible. The identification of "white spots," that is patterns that occur very seldom or not at all, can be of importance for understanding functional systems, sometimes even more important than finding typical, developmental sequences. What cannot occur demarcates what can occur, and both aspects have to be accounted for in sound theoretical explanation of some phenomena (Bergman & Magnusson, 1997). This reasoning may be of particular relevance for the study of psychopathology, because it is at the boundaries of what can occur that "normal" development leaves the track.

It should be noted that the view of individual differences summarized above does not imply a renewal of the classical concept of typologies. Classical typologies have little, if anything, in common with the categorization of individuals in terms of patterns of relevant variables with reference to a modern holistic view. In contrast to the view advocated here, main characteristics of the classical typologies are that they are static, do not consider the influence of contextual factors in life-span development, are not interested in processes, and do not allow for developmental changes.

The Variable Approach

Traditional psychological research is dominated by a variable approach. For research in personality, the dominance of this approach was demonstrated recently in a review of articles published in five prominent journals during the period 1993–1995 (Endler & Speer, 1998). In the variable approach, the focus of interest is the variable, interrelations among variables, and their relations to specified criteria (R-R, and S-R-relations). The problems are formulated in terms of variables, and the results are interpreted and generalizations made in such terms. The approach is evident in many contexts, for example, in correlational studies of relations between variables, in studies of the stability of single variables over time, in studies of the links between environmental factors and various aspects of individual functioning, and in studies of the developmental background to adult functioning. Commonly used statistical models include comparisons between means, correlation and regression analysis, and factor analysis modeling. The dominance of a variable approach is manifested in the widespread application of structural equation modeling in the search for causal relations (see, e.g., Hoyle, 1995).

At a metatheoretical level, the variable approach is closely linked to the unidirectional view of causality in what Overton (1997) designated "split models" of developmental change, as opposed to "relational models." In that perspective, two interrelated factors often contribute to misinterpretation of results from variable oriented studies; the tendency towards reification of the variable concept, and the tendency to overestimate the role of independent variables as causes; that is as actors in the processes being studied.

Data Treatment

In a variable approach the lawfulness of processes in individual functioning and development is studied in terms of statistical relations between variables *across individuals at group level.* For the correct use of analytical results, it is essential to be aware of a basic assumption: The measures for relations between variables studied across individuals are assumed to reflect and be valid for the functional relations between the same variables in the individual, internally integrated processes of mental, biological, and behavioral factors. In practice, this assumption is seldom met.

The basis for this treatment of empirical data is a statistical model with certain specifications. A number of statistical models have been developed for different cases. The most common is the linear model, which serves as a starting point for the application of a number of statistical methods, such as Pearson correlations, multiple correlations, ANOVA, and LISREL (see Bergman, 1988a; Nesselroade & Ford, 1987). Although nonlinear models and methods actually utilize more of the valid covariance among variables being studied, they are applied much less frequently than linear models and methods.

Correctly applied under certain, specified conditions and taking into consideration the specific nature of the psychological phenomena under study, research using a variable approach yields valuable information. This is the case particularly in the first stage of the two-step process of empirical research, when the aim is to identify possible operating factors in the psychological processes that are the ultimate concern. However, the need to match methods and phenomena tends to be neglected. This neglect takes two interrelated forms. First, psychological individual-related problems are formulated and analyzed with reference to a statistical model, with little or no reference to an explicitly formulated view regarding the nature of the phenomena to which the data refer. Such is often the case, for example, in discussions and applications of causal models and causal relations (see, e.g., von Eye & Clogg, 1994; Hellvik, 1988). Second, the statistical models are tested with reference to data sets, the relevance of which is taken for granted without reference to the character of the real phenomena. An example can be found in the literature on structural equation modeling (see, e.g., Hoyle, 1995). The importance of basing statistical analyses on careful analysis of the phenomena involved in sociological process(es) was emphasized by Cox (1990) and further discussed by Goldthorpe (1998) in his analysis of causation as generative processes.

The Person Approach

The theoretical basis for person-oriented research, which statistical models have to match, is the holistic, integrated view, summarized in an earlier section; the person is conceptualized as an integrated, hierarchically organized totality, rather than as a summation of variables. The person approach as a theoretical framework for empirical research, using this perspective, was discussed by Magnusson and Allen (1983), and Magnusson (1985, 1988). The goal of empirical research, using the theoretical person-oriented perspective, is to identify (1) the distinctive configurations of operating factors, at different levels of the total hierarchical system, which characterize each individual's psychological processes in a current perspective, (2) how these change over time in the developmental process of individuals, and (3) the guiding mechanisms in the process of systems stability and change. The advantage of the person approach is that—unlike the case with the variable approach—generalizations of empirical results refer directly to persons, not to variables.

Data Treatment

With reference to the earlier discussion of individual differences, in operationalization individual differences are investigated empirically in terms of *patterns* of data for relevant operating factors at the level of the system being studied. A number of methods are more or less natural for this purpose: cluster analytical techniques (Bergman, 1993; Bock, 1987; Manly, 1994), Q-sort technique (Block, 1971; Ozer, 1993), latent profile analysis (LPA) (Gibson, 1959), configural frequency analysis (CFA) (von Eye, 1990; Krauth & Lienert, 1982), latent transition analysis (Collins & Wugalter, 1992), log-linear modeling (Bishop, Feinberg, & Holland, 1975), and multivariate P-technique factor analysis (Cattell, Cattell, & Rhymer, 1947; Nesselroade & Featherman, 1989; Nesselroade & Ford, 1987). The characteristic features of these and other methods are discussed by Bergman (1998). More and more empirical studies on developmental phenomena, using a pattern approach, are being reported. Applications of methods for pattern analyses were recently exemplified by Bergman and Magnusson (1997) for research on psychopathology, and by Stattin and Magnusson (1996) for research on antisocial behavior. Pattern analysis is equally applicable as a tool in studies of what constitutes normal and good development.

Pattern analysis is a *tool* (not a theory) for the study of the organization of operating factors in a current and a developmental perspective. For the study of developmental issues, to date the approach has primarily been applied in studies linking patterns observed at different ages, that is, patterns for current individual functioning. An important challenge for further progress in research on developmental processes is to develop and apply appropriate and effective process oriented methodological tools for the study of systems over time (Bergman, 1995; Bergman & Magnusson, 1990).

Theoretically, a perfect classification of objects or organisms presupposes two conditions: the total system of categories must be (1) complete, and (2) mutually exclusive, that is, all objects and individuals must be classifiable and each object and organism can belong to only one category (Bailey, 1994). As discussed by Bergman (1988b), when classification concerns individuals, these prerequisites are rarely, if ever, met. The results of categorizing individuals with existing methodological tools for pattern analysis must be interpreted in the light of the following characteristics.

First, the number of categories obtained in a pattern analysis depends on the criteria for deciding which number of clusters gives the best solution. This problem is the same in principle as the one of deciding about the number of factors to be identified in factor analysis. To deal with this problem, York and John (1992) proposed a replication approach that retains only those person factors that show high generalizability across two half samples.

Second, the number of factors that operate in a system and that have to be considered in a correct pattern analysis is restricted. The character of such factors varies with systems and levels of systems. The number and content of categories of individuals obtained in a pattern analysis depend on the number and character of the variables that form the basis for the individual patterns. Thus, the more correctly the variables chosen as the basis for a pattern analysis cover the system under investigation, the more relevant will be the categorization of individuals. The identification of possible operating factors in the system is therefore a first basic step in the preparation of a pattern analysis. For this purpose the variable approach is a valuable tool.

Third, the categories obtained in pattern analyses are never totally homogeneous in the sense that all individuals belonging to a certain cluster have identical profiles. Neither are categories totally exclusive. To some extent, clusters overlap. York and John (1992) dealt with this problem by discussing categories of individuals in terms of prototypes, implying, among other things, (1) that some individuals are more prototypical than others, and (2) that some individuals can be representatives of more than one prototype. (See also Robins, John, & Caspi, 1998, for a further discussion of this approach, and Robins et al., 1996, for a cross-cultural replication of the results obtained by York & John, 1992.)

Fourth, individuals may have such special configurations of values that they do not belong to any of the categories obtained in the pattern analysis. Individuals with such profiles may be of special interest in some connections (Bergman, 1988b). Kagan, Snidman, and Arcus (1998) have emphasized the importance of studying extreme cases, or what they describe as "outliers."

These characteristics of pattern analysis as a methodological approach to the study of systems and system changes imply that, so far, we have only taken the first but necessary step on a road full of problems. The present state of affairs shows that we still have a long way to go. The development of appropriate and effective person-oriented methodological tools for the study of mechanisms and principles in developmental processes has to overcome extremely difficult problems. Two of the most obvious requirements, when the study is concerned with processes over considerable time (e.g., through adolescence or aging), are that the sample of individuals must be reasonably large and observations must be made sufficiently frequently.

Comments

The basic difference in terms of data between a person approach and a variable approach lies in the interpretation of an observation, operationalized as a number indicating an individual's position on a latent dimension. In the "variable approach" each single datum for individual *A* on a certain latent dimension *k* derives its psychological meaning from its position relative to positions for other individuals *B*, *C*, *D*, and so on, on the same dimension. In the "person approach," each single datum for individual *A* derives its psychological meaning from its place in a pattern of data for the same individual, representing his or her positions on the latent dimensions *k*, *l*, *m*, *n*, and so on, which are operating simultaneously in the system under investigation. This difference in the role of a datum for a single observation follows from the different theoretical models underlying the two approaches. These basic characteristics of the two approaches should be considered when choosing the most appropriate method for data treatment in each specific case, with reference to the nature of the phenomena being studied and to the question being posed.

RESEARCH: STRATEGIC CONSIDERATIONS

The holistic theoretical framework has distinct research strategy implications.

Cross-Sectional and Longitudinal Designs

In the study of many of the issues that are essential for understanding and explaining psychological phenomena, a cross-sectional approach has been and is an indispensable tool. Recent advances in research on cognition, memory, and neuropsychology offer good illustrations. The main advantages are, however, linked to the study of psychological phenomena in a current perspective. When the purpose is to understand

and explain developmental processes of individuals, the equally indispensable tool is the longitudinal design, that is, a design in which the same individuals are observed over time. This proposition follows logically from the description of individual development as a series of interrelated processes. It follows from the definition of development that such central issues as stability and change and causal mechanisms in individual development processes cannot be investigated without observing the individual over time.

The importance and fruitfulness of a longitudinal approach to the study of developmental phenomena has been demonstrated in systematically planned studies over crucial time periods. In a historical perspective it is notable that interest in longitudinal research has followed the same trend as interest in a holistic perspective in psychological research. After the introduction of the well-known longitudinal programs—the Berkeley Growth Study, initiated by Nancy Bayley in 1928; the Guidance Study, started by Jean W. Macfarlane in 1928; and the Oakland Growth Study, initiated by Harold E. Jones and Herbert Stoltz in 1931—decades passed before systematic longitudinal research programs for the study of individual development were planned and implemented.

Prediction as the Ultimate Criterion for Scientific Success?

One of the most frequent concepts in presentations of empirical studies is prediction. This reflects the concept's central role in the mental world of the researchers.

For the following discussion, two different meanings of prediction must be distinguished. When used in the presentation of empirical studies, the term means statistical prediction, that is, it is used to express the relation between a predictor and its criterion or between an independent and a dependent variable in statistical terms. Of course, statistical prediction is a relevant concept in a research design that is appropriate for research on properly analyzed phenomena. The concept of prediction is also applicable in numerous practical situations to which psychological methods are being applied; for example, in personnel selection or decision making. In such situations, the certainty with which predictions are made, that is, the probability that certain events will occur, is of basic interest. In these examples, statistical prediction is a useful *tool* for estimating the certainty of a certain outcome. When and where prediction is a useful tool depends, among other things, on the character of the phenomena: "Predictability is one thing in a cloud chamber where two particles collide at the end of a race around an accelerator. It is something else altogether in the simplest tub of boiling fluid, or in the earth's weather, or in the human brain" (Gleick, 1987, p. 7). The problem arises when high prediction becomes the overriding *goal* in psychological research, a criterion of the discipline's scientific status.

The goal of scientific work in general is to formulate the basic principles for how and why various domains of the total space of phenomena function as they do at various levels of complexity. In natural sciences, principles are formulated in precise laws that sometimes permit high predictions of process outcomes. The formulation of such laws has contributed to the high scientific status of the disciplines in natural sciences. Other sciences readily adopted the goals and values espoused by physicists without considering whether or not the character of the phenomena involved is congruent with the model that physics provides. For example, Pearson (1892) in *The Grammar of Science* advocated that the paradigm of natural sciences applies to all fields of scientific endeavor, including social sciences.

Even in psychology accurate prediction has been widely accepted as a main criterion of the validity of a scientific law, ever since J. B. Watson (1913) defended the status of psychology as a natural science with reference to the formulation that "prediction and control of behavior" are the goals of scientific psychology. Fostered by the development and application of technically sophisticated statistical tools, prediction has survived as a central goal for psychological research, including research on human ontogeny, even in areas in which it is not very appropriate. The psychological significance of single variables or composites of variables in individual development is often estimated by how well they predict later outcomes.

Accurate prediction of individuals' life courses as the ultimate goal for developmental research can be questioned for two interrelated reasons. The first concerns characterizing individual functioning and development as complex, adaptive processes; the second concerns the type of laws that direct these processes.

One of the fundamental propositions of modern models for dynamic complex processes is that such processes are in principle unpredictable. Research on human functioning and development belongs to the "life sciences." Crick, who started his career as a physicist and then worked in molecular biology (in which he shared the Nobel prize for the discovery of DNA), discussed the kinds of laws sought in different disciplines in "What Mad Pursuit" (Crick, 1988). He concluded that the character of the phenomena studied in biological systems is such that the same kind of universally valid, strong laws that are formulated in physics cannot be found in biology. What can be found are principles and mechanisms guiding the processes of living organisms.

Crick's conclusions are as relevant for research on psychological phenomena as they are for research in biology. Given the complex, often nonlinear interplay of mental, biological, and behavioral subsystems within the individual and the complex interplay between the individual and an environment, operating in a probabilistic manner, it is unrealistic to hope for accurate prediction of individual functioning across situations of differing character (Magnusson, Gerzén, & Nyman, 1968) or over the life course of single individuals (Magnusson, 1988).

In this perspective, the ultimate criterion for success in our scientific endeavors is not how well we can predict individual behavior across situations of different character or over the life course, but how well we succeed in explaining and understanding the processes underlying individual functioning and development. In this view, the overriding scientific task of empirical psychology is twofold:

1. To identify the factors operating in human functioning and ontogeny, at different levels of structures and processes.
2. To identify and understand the mechanisms and principles by which these factors operate.

These points represent steps in the empirical research process. The identification of possible operating factors comes first; it is a prerequisite for step 2, the study of how the factors involved at the level under study operate together in a simultaneous process.

So far, the overwhelming number of empirical studies in developmental and personality research have contributed to identifying operating factors, although few have addressed the mechanisms by which such factors work. An example from the study of deviant behavior illustrates the point. A large number of empirical studies indicate that low sympathetic physiological activity/reactivity is a correlate of various kinds of antisocial behavior (Susman, 1993). However, we still lack research showing the mechanisms by which this physiological factor operates in the development process leading to adult criminal activity in some individuals but not in others.

Generalization of Results

One characteristic of Western psychological research is its *ethnocentrism*. We take for granted that results can be generalized to hold for the rest of the world and forget that they refer to cultural conditions that apply to only, at best, a sixth of the global population. When studies performed in a Western country on relations among relevant variables for the specific problem are replicated in other parts of the world, different relations are often found. A fairly common conclusion is that at least one of the two results must be questioned. Of course, differences in empirical results can be caused by bad planning and other irrelevant factors. But most of the time, differences in results have their causes in differences in the contextual factors that make up the total integrated process(es) of which the specific phenomena being studied form an element. And as said earlier, each element of a complex, adaptive process gets its meaning from the role it plays in the process to which it belongs. This circumstance emphasizes the role of cross-cultural research for a full understanding and explanation of why individuals function and develop as they do in real life. The same conclusion holds for generalization across generations, as demonstrated in the research presented by Elder and his colleagues (see, e.g., Elder, Modell, & Parke, 1993).

Matching Strategy to Phenomena

One element in the complex, adaptive processes of individual functioning and development that makes the identification of operating mechanisms extremely difficult is the fact that subsystems operate interdependently but often at different spatial and temporal scales and at different levels. This circumstance has implications for the choice of research strategies that are appropriate and effective as tools for understanding and explaining the dynamic, adaptive processes of individual functioning and development. Then we have to combine research strategies operating at different time perspectives and at different levels: (1) cross-sectional and longitudinal designs, (2) studies of perceptual–cognitive processes at the microlevel and studies of manifest behavior and of the person in his or her environment at a macrolevel, and (3) an experimental and an observational approach. Maurer (1998) concluded that the characteristics of ecological dynamic processes require both holistic and reductionistic perspectives on process-based explanations. In my opinion, this conclusion is also valid for research on psychological phenomena.

Processes and Outcomes

A characteristic of most psychological research in its search for causal relations is its focus on outcomes (Horowitz, 1987). This is reflected in the view of unidirectional causality in the traditional application of the classical experiment. In much empirical developmental research, the interest lies in the relation between a factor operating early in an individual's life, regarded as the predictor, and a later outcome variable, treated as the criterion. Such research has contributed significant knowledge and will continue to do so. But in the context of a holistic, interactionistic framework, an essential task for further research is to develop research strategies and methodologies that focus on the process rather than on outcomes. Binet (see Cairns & Ornstein, 1979) made the point that the most effective techniques for describing outcomes may not be effective for analyzing the processes leading to the outcome. Thus, one of the most important challenges for the future is the development and application of research strategies that focus on processes within a holistic frame of reference.

TIMELINESS OF THE HOLISTIC VIEW

In this chapter it has been argued that in order to make a better contribution than hitherto to the goal of research on individual development, we have to plan, implement, and interpret empirical studies on individual functioning and development in a theoretical framework, taking into consideration and integrating overriding interaction processes at two levels: the person-bound interaction process of mental, biological, and behavioral factors and the continuously ongoing process of person–environment interaction.

The acceptance and application of a holistic view are not confined to psychology. This is part of a more general, dominant trend in scientific disciplines concerned with dynamic, complex processes: biology, meteorology, ecology, and life sciences in general. A striking example on the importance of applying a holistic view for the study of complex, adaptive systems is the program for the study of global change, including the human aspects (IGBP, 1998). In that program, a holistic view forms the theoretical frame of reference for the planning and implementation of empirical work, from studies on air bubbles trapped in ice to studies at the global level. The need for a holistic general model of human beings and society as a theoretical framework for developmental research was demonstrated by the contributions from leading scientists in adequate scientific disciplines to a Nobel symposium on individual development in a life-span perspective, organized under the auspicies of the Swedish Royal Academy of Sciences (Magnusson, 1996b).

Taken seriously, the research strategy consequence of this proposition is that in order to understand and explain why individuals think, feel, act, and react as they do, contributions from personality and developmental psychology are not enough. Rather, knowledge is needed from all scientific fields that are concerned with different aspects of the processes involved in individual development: developmental psychology, neuroscience, molecular biology, genetics, physiology, social psychology, sociology, anthropology, and other neighbouring disciplines. For developmental research, this conclusion has led to the establishment of a new discipline, *developmental science* with its special need for theory, methods, and research strategy. The domain of this discipline is located at the interface of behavioral sciences, humanities, social sciences, biology and medicine, as illustrated in Figure 8.2 (Cairns, Elder, & Costello, 1996; Magnusson, 1996c; Magnusson & Cairns, 1996).

The establishment of developmental science as a field for scientific inquiry with its common demands on theory, methodology, and research strategy, does not mean that psychology loses its identity as a scientific discipline. The development of new scientific disciplines at the interface of physics, chemistry, and biology, for example, did not diminish their own identity. Rather, the adoption of a general theoretical framework that is compatible with those in neighboring disciplines enables us to participate in and profit

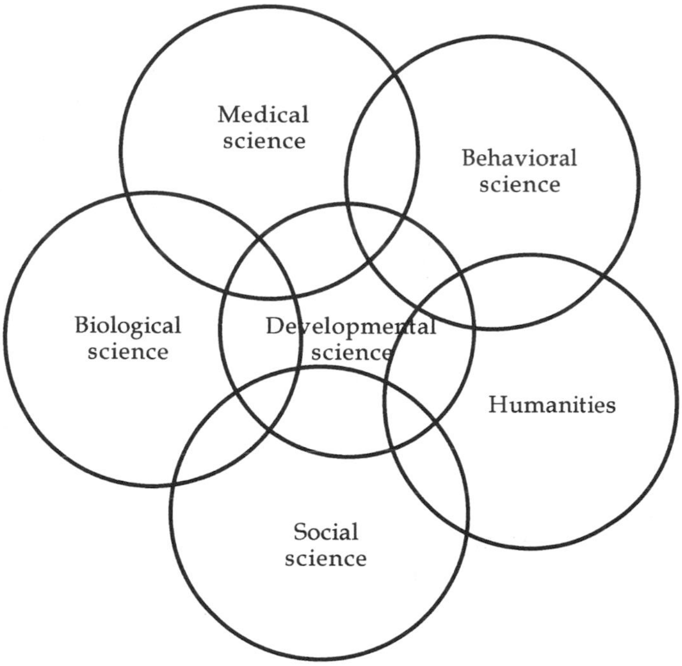

FIGURE 8.2. An illustration of the location of developmental science in the interface of behavioral, social, biological, and medical sciences.

from effective collaboration with them; our contributions will be enriched, not reduced, by participating in that collaboration. As an active partner in this wider scientific context, we can contribute unique knowledge to the understanding and explanation of why individuals think, feel, act, and react as they do, and how they develop in these respects, which is the ultimate goal for psychology as a scientific discipline.

ACKNOWLEDGMENTS

Preparation of this chapter was financially supported by the Swedish Council for Social Research and the Swedish Council for Planning and Coordination of Research. I thank Lars R. Bergman, Robert B. Cairns, Joseph Mahoney, Håkan Stattin, and the editors for valuable comments on an earlier version.

NOTES

1. It should be clear that here and in the following text the term "interaction" refers to dynamic interaction as a basic principle in the processes of individual functioning and development. This meaning should be distinguished from statistical interaction in experimental designs for the study of individual differences (cf. Olweus, 1977).

REFERENCES

Allport, G. W. (1924). The study of the undivided personality. *Journal of Abnormal and Social Psychology, 19,* 131–141.

Allport, G. W. (1937). *Personality: A psychological interpretation.* New York: Holt.

Appley, M. H., & Turnball, R. (1986). *Dynamics of stress. Physiological, psychological, and social perspectives.* New York: Plenum Press.

Åsberg, M. (1997). Neurotransmitters and suicidal behavior: The evidence from cerebrospinal fluid studies. In D. M Stoff (Ed.), *Annals of the New York Academy of Sciences: Vol. 836. The neurobiology of suicide: From the bench to the clinic* (pp. 158–181). New York: New York Academy of Sciences.

Backteman, G., & Magnusson, D. (1981). Longitudinal stability of personality characteristics. *Journal of Personality, 49,* 148–160.

Bailey, K. D. (1994). *Typologies and taxonomies.* Belmont, CA: Sage.

Baltes, P. B. (1987). Theoretical propositions of life-span developmental psychology: On the dynamics between growth and decline. *Developmental Psychology, 23,* 611–626.

Baltes, P. B., & Baltes, M. M. (1990). *Successful aging: Perspectives from the behavioral sciences.* New York: Cambridge University Press.

Baltes, P. B., & Graf, P. (1996). Psychological aspects of aging: Facts and frontiers. In D. Magnusson (Ed.), *The life-span development of individuals: Behavioral, neurobiological and psychosocial perspectives* (pp. 426–460). Cambridge, UK: Cambridge University Press.

Baltes, P. B., Lindenberger, U., & Staudinger, U. M. (1997). Life-span theory in developmental psychology. In R. M. Lerner (Vol. Ed.) and W. Damon (Ed.-in-Chief), *Handbook of child psychology: Vol. 1. Theoretical models of human development* (pp. 1029–1143). New York: Wiley.

Baltes, P. B., Reese, H. W., & Lipsitt, L. P. (1980). Life-span developmental psychology. In M. R. Rosenzweig & L. W. Porter (Eds.), *Annual review of psychology* (Vol. 31, pp. 65–110). Palo Alto, CA: Annual Reviews.

Baltes, P. B., & Smith, J. (1997). A systemic-wholistic view of psychological functioning in very old age: Introduction to a collection of articles from the Berlin aging study. *Psychology and Aging, 12,* 395–409.

Bandura, A. (1978). The self system in reciprocal determinism. *American Psychologist, 33,* 344–358.

Bergman, L. R. (1988a). Modeling reality: Some comments. In M. Rutter (Ed.), *Studies of psychosocial risk* (pp. 354–366). Cambridge, UK: Cambridge University Press.

Bergman, L. R. (1988b). You can't classify all of the people all of the time. *Multivariate Behavioral Research, 23,* 425–441.

Bergman, L. R. (1993). Some methodological issues in longitudinal research: Looking forward. In D. Magnusson & P. Casaer (Eds.), *Longitudinal research on individual development: Present status and future perspectives* (pp. 217–241). Cambridge, UK: Cambridge University Press.

Bergman, L. R. (1995). Describing individual development using i-state sequence analysis. *Reports from the Department of Psychology,* Stockholm University, No. 805.

Bergman, L. R. (1998). A pattern-oriented approach to studying individual development: Snapshots and processes. In R. B. Cairns, L. R. Bergman, & J. Kagan (Eds.), *Methods and models for studying the individual* (pp. 83–121). Thousand Oaks, CA: Sage.

Bergman, L. R ., & Magnusson, D. (1990). General issues about data quality in longitudinal research. In D. Magnusson & L. R. Bergman (Eds.), *Data quality in longitudinal research* (pp. 1–31). Cambridge, UK: Cambridge University Press.

Bergman, L. R., & Magnusson, D. (1991). Stability and change in patterns of extrinsic adjustment problems. In D. Magnusson, L. R. Bergman, G. Rudinger, & B. Törestad (Eds.), *Problems and methods in longitudinal research: Stability and change* (pp. 323–346). Cambridge, UK: Cambridge University Press.

Bergman, L. R., & Magnusson, D. (1997). A person-oriented approach in research on developmental psychopathology. *Development and Psychopathology, 9,* 291–319.

Binet, A., & Henri,V. (1895). La psychologie individuelle. *L'Année Psychologique, 2,* 411–465.

Bishop, Y. M. M., Feinberg, S. E., & Holland, P. W. (1975). *Discrete multivariate analysis: Theory and practice.* Cambridge, MA: MIT Press.

Block, J. (1971). *Lives through time.* Berkeley, CA: Bancroft Books.

Bock, H. H. (1987). *Classification and related methods of data analysis.* Amsterdam: North-Holland.

Bronfenbrenner, U. (1988). Interacting systems in human development: Research paradigms. Present and future. In N. Bolger, A. Caspi, G. Downey, & M. Moorehouse (Eds.), *Persons in context: Developmental processes* (pp. 25–49). Cambridge, UK: Cambridge University Press.

Bronfenbrenner, U., & Crouter, A. C. (1983). The evolution of environmental models in developmental research. In P. Mussen (Series Ed.) & W. Kessen (Vol. Ed.), *Handbook of child psychology. Vol. 1. History, theories and methods* (4th ed., pp. 357–414). New York: Wiley.

Brunswik, E. (1929). Prinzipienfragen der Gestalttheorie. In E. Brunswik, C. Bühler, H. Hetzer, L. Kardos, E. Köhler, J. Krug, & A. Willwohl (Eds.), *Beiträge zur Problemgeschichte der Psychologie* (pp. 78–149). Jena: Verlag von Gustav Fischer.

Cairns, R. B. (1979). *Social development: The origins and plasticity of interchanges.* San Francisco, CA: Freeman.

Cairns, R. B. (1986). Phenomena lost: Issues in the study of development. In J. Valsiner (Ed.), *The individual subject and scientific psychology* (pp. 79–112). New York: Plenum Press.

Cairns, R. B., & Cairns, B. D. (1994). *Lifelines and risks. Pathways of youth in our time.* Hemel Hempstead: Harvester Wheatsheaf.

Cairns, R. B., Elder, G. H. Jr., & E. J. Costello (Eds.) (1996). *Developmental science.* Cambridge, UK: Cambridge University Press.

Cairns, R. B., & Ornstein, P. A. (1979). Developmental Psychology. In E. Hearst (Ed.), *The first century of experimental psychology* (pp. 459–510). Hillsdale, NJ: Erlbaum.

Cairns, R. B., & Rodkin, P. C. (1998). Phenomena regained: From configurations to pathways. In R. B. Cairns, L. R. Bergman, & J. Kagan (Eds.), *Methods and models for studying the individual* (pp. 245–263). Thousand Oaks, CA: Sage

Cairns, R. B., & Valsiner, J. (1984). Child Psychology. *Annual Review of Psychology, 35,* 553–577.

Caprara, G. V. (1992). Reflections on the recent history and the present challenges of personality psychology. *European Journal of Personality, 6,* 345–358.

Caprara, G. V. (1996). Structures and processes in personality research. *European Psychologist, 1,* 14–26.

Carlson, R. (1971). Where is the person in personality research? *Psychological Bulletin, 5,* 203–219.

Carlson, R. (1988). Exemplary lives: The uses of psychobiography for theory development. *Journal of Personality, 56,* 105–138.

Carlson, M., Earls, F., & Todd, R. D. (1988). The importance of regressive changes in the development of the nervous system: Towards a neurobiological theory of child development. *Psychiatric Developments, 1,* 1–22.

Caspi, A., & Moffit, T. (1991). Individual differences are accentuated during periods of social change: The sample case of girls at puberty. *Journal of Personality and Social Psychology, 61,* 157–168.

Cattell, R. B., Cattell, A. K. S, & Rhymer, R. M. (1947). P-technique demonstrated in determining psychophysiological source traits in a normal individual. *Psychometrika, 12,* 267–288.

Choi, J. I., & Hannafin, M. (1995). Situated cognition and learning environments: Roles, structures, and implications for design. *Educational Technology Research and Development, 43,* 53–69.

Collins, L. M., & Wugalter, S. E. (1992). Latent class models for stage-sequential dynamic latent variables. *Multivariable Behavioral Research, 27,* 131–157.

Cox, D. R. (1990). Role of models in statistical analysis. *Statistical Science, 5,* 169–174.

Crick, F. (1988). *What mad pursuit: A personal view of scientific discovery.* New York: Basic Books.

Cronbach, L. (1975). Beyond the two disciplines of scientific psychology. *American Psychologist, 30,* 116–127.

Damasio, A. R . (1994). *Descartes' error. Emotion, reason and the human brain.* New York: Putnam.

Damasio, A. R., & Damasio, H. (1996). Advances in cognitive neuroscience. In D. Magnusson (Ed.), *The life-span development of individuals: Behavioral, neurobiological and psychosocial perspectives* (pp. 265–274). Cambridge, UK: Cambridge University Press.

Depue, R. A. (1995). Neurobiological factors in personality and depression. *European Journal of Personality, 9,* 413–439.

Derryberry, D., & Rothbart, M. K. (1997). Reactive and effortful processes in the organization of temperament. *Development and Psychopathology, 9,* 633–652.

Edelman, G. (1987). *Neural Darwinism: The theory of neuronal group selection.* New York: Basic Books.

Edelman, G. (1992). *Bright air, brilliant fire.* London: Penguin Press.

Edelman, G. M., & Tononi, G. (1996). Selection and development. The brain as a complex system. In D. Magnusson (Ed.), *The life-span development of individuals: Behavioral, neurobiological and psychosocial perspectives* (pp. 179–404). Cambridge, UK: Cambridge University Press.

Elder, G. H., Jr., Modell, J., & Parke, R. H. (Eds.). (1993). *Children in time and place: Developmental and historical insights.* New York: Cambridge University Press.

Emde, R. N. (1994). Individuality, context, and the search for meaning. *Child Development, 65,* 719–737.

Endler, N. S., & Magnusson, D. (1976). Toward an interactional psychology of personality. *Psychological Bulletin, 83,* 956–979.

Endler, N. S., & Speer, R. L. (1998). Personality psychology: Research trends for 1993–1995. *Journal of Personality, 66,* 956–979.

Erngrund, K., Mäntylä, T., & Nilsson, L. G. (1996). Adult age differences in source recall: A population-based study. *Journals of Gerontology, 51B*(6) 335–345.

Eye von, A. (1990). *Introduction to configural frequency analysis. The search for types and antitypes in cross-classifications.* New York: Cambridge University Press.

Eye von, A., & Clogg, C. C. (1994). *Latent variables analysis. Applications for developmental research.* London: Sage.

Fentress, J. C. (1989). Developmental roots of behavioral order: Systemic approaches to the examination of core developmental issues. In M. R. Gunnar & E. Thelen (Eds.), *Systems and Development* (pp. 35–75). Hillsdale, NJ: Erlbaum.

Ford, D.H., & Lerner, R. M. (1992). *Developmental systems theory: An integrative approach.* London: Sage.

Forgas, J. P., & van Heck, G. L. (1992). The psychology of situations. In G. V. Caprara & G. L. van Heck (Eds.), *Modern personality psychology* (pp. 418–455). New York: Harvester.

Geert van, P. (1994). Vygotskian dynamics of development. *Human Development, 37,* 346–365.

Gibson, W. A. (1959). Three multivariate models: Factor analysis, latent structure analysis and latent profile analysis. *Psychometrika, 24,* 229–252.

Gleick, J. (1987). *Chaos: Making a new science.* New York: Penguin Books.

Goldthorpe, J. H. (1998). Rational action theory for sociology. *British Journal of Sociology, 49,* 167–192.

Gottlieb, G. (1996). A systems view of psychobiological development. In D. Magnusson (Ed.), *The life-span development of individuals: Behavioral, neurobiological and psychosocial perspectives.* (pp. 76–103). Cambridge, UK: Cambridge University Press.

Gottman, J. M., Guralnick, M. J., Wilson, B., Swanson, C. C., & Murray, J. D. (1997). What should be the forms of emotion regulation in children? A nonlinear dynamic mathematical model of children's peer interaction in groups. *Development and Psychopathology, 9,* 421–452.

Gramer, M., & Huber, H. P. (1994). Individual variability in task-specific cardiovascular response patterns during psychological challenge. *German Journal of Psychology, 18,* 1–17.

Hellvik, O. (1988). *Introduction to causal analysis. Exploring survey data by crosstabulation.* Oslo: Norwegian University Press.

Hess, B., & Mikhailov, A. (1994). Self-organization in living cells. *Science, 264,* 223–224.

Hettema, J. (1995). Personality and depression: A multilevel perspective. *European Journal of Psychology, 9,* 401–412.

Hinde, R. A. (1996). The interpenetration of biology and culture. In D. Magnusson (Ed.), *The life-span development of individuals: Behavioral, neurobiological and psychosocial perspectives* (pp. 359–375). Cambridge, UK: Cambridge University Press.

Horowitz, F. D. (1987). *Exploring developmental theories: Toward a structural model of development.* Hillsdale, NJ: Erlbaum.

Hoyle, R. H. (1995). The structural equation modeling approach. Basic concepts and fundamental issues. In R. H. Hoyle (Ed.), *Structural equation modeling. Concepts, issues, and applications* (pp. 1–15). Thousand Oaks: Sage.

Hull, C. L. (1943). The problem of intervening variables in molar behavior theory. *Psychological Review, 50,* 273–291.

IGBP: The International Geosphere–Biosphere Programme. (1998). *A study of global change.* Stockholm: Sweden: IGBP secretariat, the Royal Swedish Academy of Sciences.

Ingber, D. E. (1998). The architecture of life. *Scientific American, 278,* 30–39.

Jacob, F. (1989). *The logic of life: A history of heredity and the possible and the actual.* London: Penguin.

Kagan, J. (1994). *Galen's prophecy: Temperament in human nature.* New York: Basic Books.

Kagan, J., Snidman, N., & Arcus, D. (1998). The value of extreme groups. In R. B. Cairns, L. R. Bergman, & J. Kagan (Eds.), *Methods and models for studying the individual* (pp. 65–80). Thousand Oaks, CA: Sage.

Kelso, J. A. (1995). *Dynamic patterns: The self-organization of brain and behavior.* Cambridge, MA: MIT Press.

af Klinteberg, B., Schalling, D., Levander, S. E., & Oreland, L. (1988). Personality and neuropsychological correlates of platelat monoamine oxidase (MAO) activity in female and male subjects. *Pharmacological Research Communciation, 20,* 147–148.

Koch, S. (1981). The nature and limits of psychological knowledge: Lessons of a century qua "science." *American Psychologist, 36,* 257–269.

Krahé, B. (1990). *Situation cognition and coherence in personality: An individual centered approach.* European Monographs in Social Psychology. Cambridge, UK: Cambridge University Press.

Krauth, J., & Lienert, G. A. (1982). Fundamentals and modifications of configural frequency analysis (CFA). *Interdisciplinaria, 3,* (1).

Kreppner, K. (1992). William L. Stern, 1871–1938: A neglected founder of developmental psychology. *Developmental Psychology, 28,* 539–547.

Lerner, R. M. (1983). A "goodness of fit" model of person-interaction. In D. Magnusson & V. L. Allen (Eds.), *Human development. An interactional perspective* (pp. 279–294). New York: Academic Press.

Lerner, R. M., & Kauffman, M. B. (1985). The concept of development in contextualism. *Developmental Review, 5,* 309–333.

Lewin, K. (1926). Untersuchungen zur Handlungs- und Affekt-Psychologie. I und II. *Psychologische Forschung, 7,* 294–329, 330–385.

Lewin, K. (1927). *Gesetz und Experiment in der Psychologie* (pp. 375– 421). (Sonderdruck des Symposium.) Berlin-Schlachtensee: Weltkreis.

Lewin, K. (1931). Environmental forces. In C. Murchison (Ed.), *A handbook of child psychology* (pp. 590–625). Worcester, MA: Clark University Press.

Lewin, K. (1954). Behavior and development as a function of the total situation. In L. Carmichael (Ed.), *Manual of child psychology* (2nd ed., pp. 918–983). New York: Wiley.

Lomov, B. F. (1984). *Methodological and theoretical problems of psychology.* Moscow: Nauka.

Lykken, D.T. (1991). What's wrong with psychology anyway? In D. Cicchetti & W. M. Grove (Eds.), *Thinking clearly about psychology* (Vol. 1, pp. 3–39). Minneapolis: University of Minnesota Press.

Magnusson, D. (1976). The person and the situation in an interactional model of behavior. *Scandinavian Journal of Psychology, 17,* 253–271.

Magnusson, D. (1981). *Toward a psychology of situations. An interactional perspective.* Hillsdale, NJ: Erlbaum.

Magnusson, D. (1985). Implications of an interactional paradigm for research on human development. *International Journal of Behavioral Development, 8,* 115–137.

Magnusson, D. (Ed.). (1988). *Paths through life: Vol. 1. Individual development from an interactional perspective.* Hillsdale, NJ: Erlbaum.

Magnusson, D. (1990). Personality development from an interactional perspective. In L. Pervin (Ed.), *Handbook of personality* (pp. 193–222). New York: Guilford Press.

Magnusson, D. (1992). Back to the phenomena: Theory, methods and statistics in psychological research. *European Journal of Personality, 6,* 1–14.

Magnusson, D. (1993). Human ontogeny: A longitudinal perspective. In D. Magnusson & P. Casaer (Eds.), *Longitudinal research on individual development: Present status and future perspectives* (pp. 1–25). Cambridge, UK: Cambridge University Press.

Magnusson, D. (1995). Individual development: A holistic integrated model. In P. Moen, G. H. Elder, & K. Lüscher (Eds.), *Linking lives and contexts: Perspectives on the ecology of human development* (pp. 19–60). Washington, DC: APA Books.

Magnusson, D. (1996a). The patterning of antisocial behavior and autonomic reactivity. In D. M. Stoff & R. B. Cairns (Eds.), *The neurobiology of clinical aggression* (pp. 291–308). Hillsdale, NJ: Erlbaum.

Magnusson, D. (1996b). *The life-span development of individuals: Behavioral, neurobiological and psychosocial perspectives. A synthesis*. Cambridge, UK: Cambridge University Press.

Magnusson, D. (1996c). Towards a developmental science. In D. Magnusson (Ed.), *The life-span development of individuals: Behavioral, neurobiological and psychosocial perspectives. A synthesis* (pp. xv–xvii). Cambridge, UK: Cambridge University Press.

Magnusson, D. (1998). The logic and implications of a person approach. In R. B. Cairns, L. R. Bergman, & J. Kagan (Eds.), *Methods and models for studying the individual* (pp. 33–63). Thousand Oaks, CA: Sage.

Magnusson, D., & Allen, V. L. (1983). Implications and applications of an interactional perspective for human development. In D. Magnusson & V. L. Allen (Eds.), *Human development: An interactional perspective* (pp. 369–387). New York: Academic Press.

Magnusson, D., Andersson, T., & Törestad, B. (1993). Methodological implications of a peephole perspective on personality. In D.C. Funder, R.D. Parke, C. Tomlinson-Keasey, & K. Widaman (Eds.), *Studying lives through time. Personality and development* (pp. 207–220). Washington, DC: APA.

Magnusson, D., & Bergman, L. R. (1988). Individual and variable-based approaches to longitudinal research on early risk factors. In M. Rutter (Ed.), *Studies of psychosocial risk: The power of longitudinal data* (pp. 45–61). Cambridge, UK: Cambridge University Press.

Magnusson, D., & Bergman, L. R. (1990). A pattern approach to the study of pathways from childhood to adulthood. In L. N. Robins & M. Rutter (Eds.), *Straight and devious pathways from childhood to adulthood* (pp. 101–115). Cambridge. UK: Cambridge University Press.

Magnusson, D., & Cairns, R. B. (1996). Developmental science: Principles and illustrations. In R. B. Cairns, G. H. Elder Jr., & E. J. Costello (Eds.), *Developmental science* (pp. 7–30). New York: Cambridge University Press.

Magnusson, D., & Endler, N. S. (1977). Interactional psychology: Present status and future prospects. In D. Magnusson & N. S. Endler (Eds.), *Personality at the crossroads: Current issues in interactional psychology* (pp. 3–31). Hillsdale, NJ: Erlbaum.

Magnusson, D., Gerzén, M., & Nyman, B. (1968). The generality of behavioral data: 1. Generalization from observation on one occasion. *Multivariate Behavioral Research, 3,* 415–422.

Magnuson, D., & Stattin, H. (1997). Person-context interaction theories. In R. M. Lerner (Vol. ed.) & W. Damon (Ed.-in-Chief), *Handbook of child psychology: Vol. 1. Theoretical models of human development* (pp. 685–759). New York: Wiley.

Magnusson, D., & Törestad, B., (1993). A holistic view of personality: A model revisited. *Annual Review of Psychology, 44,* 427–452.

Manly, B. F. (1994). *Multivariate statistical methods. A primer* (2nd ed.). London: Chapman & Hall.

Manturzewska, M. (1990). A biographical study of the life-span development of professional musicians. *Psychology of Music, 18,* 112–139.

Maurer, B. A. (1998). Ecological science and statistical paradigms: At the threshold. *Science, 279,* 52–53.

Mayr, E. (1976). *Evolution and the diversity of life*. Cambridge, MA: Harvard University Press.

McEwen, B. S., & Stellar, E. (1993). Stress and the individual: mechanisms leading to disease. *Archives of Internal Medicine, 151,* 2093–2101.

Meehl, P. E. (1992). Factors and taxa, traits and types, differences of degree and differences in kind. *Journal of Personality, 60* (1) 117–174.

Mills, P., Dimsdale, J. E., Nelesen, R. A., Jasievicz, J., Ziegler, G., & Kennedy, B. (1994). Patterns of adrenergic receptors and adrenergic agonists underlying cardiovascular responses to a psychological challenge. *Psychological Medicine, 56,* 70–86.

Mischel, W., & Shoda, Y. (1995). A cognitive–affective system theory of personality: Reconceptualizing situations, dispositions, dynamics, and invariance in personality structure. *Psychological Review, 102,* 246–268.

Moffit, T. E. (1993). Adolescence-limited and life-course-persistent antisocial behavior: A developmental taxonomy. *Psychological Review, 100,* 674–701.

Nesselroade, J. R., & Featherman, D. L. (1989). Intraindividual variability in older adults' depression scores: Some implications for developmental theory and longitudinal research. In D. Magnusson, L. R. Bergman, G. Rudinger, & B. Törestad (Eds.), *Problems and methods in longitudinal research: Stability and change* (pp. 47–66). Cambridge, UK: Cambridge University Press.

Nesselroade, J. R., & Ford, D. H. (1987). Methodological considerations in modeling living systems. In M. E. Ford & D. H. Ford (Eds.), *Humans as self-constructing living systems: Putting the framework to work* (pp. 47–79). Hillsdale, NJ: Erlbaum.

Öhman, A., Flykt, A., & Lundqvist, D. (in press). Unconscious emotion: Evolutionary perspectives, psychophysiological data and neuropsychological mechanisms. In R. Lane, L. Nadel, G. Ahern, A. Kazniak, S. Rapscak, & G. E. Schwartz (Eds.), *The cognitive neuroscience of emotion*. New York: Oxford University Press.

Olweus, D. (1977). A critical analysis of the "modern" interactionist postition. In D. Magnusson & N. S. Endler (Eds.), *Personality at the crossroads: Current issues in interactional psychology* (pp. 221–233). Hillsdale, NJ: Erlbaum.

Olweus, D. (1979). Stability of aggressive reaction patterns in males: A review. *Psychological Bulletin, 86,* 852–857.

Overton, W. F. (1997). Developmental psychology: Philosophy, concepts, and methodology. In R. M. Lerner (Vol. ed.) & W. Damon (Ed.-in-Chief), *Handbook of child psychology: Vol. 1. Theoretical models of human development* (pp. 107–188). New York: Wiley.

Oyama, S. (1989). Ontogeny and the central dogma: Do we need the concept of genetic programming in order to have an evolutionary perspective. In M. R.

Gunnar & E. Thelen (Eds.), *The Minnesota Symposia on Child Psychology: Vol. 22. Systems and development* (pp. 1–34). Hillsdale, NJ: Erlbaum.

Ozer, D. J. (1993). The Q-sort method and the study of personality development. In D. C. Funder, R. D. Parke, C. Tomlinson-Keasey, & K. Widaman (Eds.), *Studying lives through time: Personality and development* (pp.147–168). Washington, DC: American Psychological Association.

Pearson, K. P. (1892). *The grammar of science* (2nd ed.). London: Adam and Charles Black.

Pervin, L. (1968). Performance and satisfaction as a function of individual environment fit. *Psychological Bulletin, 69,* 56–68.

Pervin, L. A. (1993). Pattern and organization: Current trends and prospects for the future. In K. H. Craik, R. Hogan, & R. N. Wolfe (Eds.), *Fifty years of personality psychology* (pp. 69–84). New York: Plenum Press.

Plomin, R. (1986). Behavioral genetic methods. *Journal of Personality, 54,* 226–261.

Posner, M. J., & Raichle, M. E. (1994). *Images of mind.* New York: Scientific American Library.

Pulkkinen, L. (1992a). Life-styles in personality development. *European Journal of Personality, 6,* 139–155.

Pulkkinen, L. (1992b). The path to adulthood for aggressively inclined girls. In K. Björkqvist & P. Niemelä (Eds.), *Of mice and women: Aspects of female aggression.* San Diego, CA: Academic Press.

Pulkkinen, L. (1998). Levels of longitudinal data differing in complexity and the study of continuity in personality characteristics. In R. B. Cairns, L. R. Bergman, & J. Kagan (Eds.), *Methods and models for studying the individual* (pp. 161–183). Thousand Oaks, CA: Sage.

Pulkkinen, L., & Tremblay, R. E. (1992). Patterns of boys' social adjustment in two cultures and at different ages: A longitudinal perspective. *International Journal of Behavioral Development, 15,* 527–553.

Richters, J. E. (1997). The Hubble hypothesis and the developmentalist's dilemma. *Development and Psychopathology, 9,* 193–229.

Robins, R. W., John, O. P., & Caspi, A. (1998). The typological approach to studying personality. In R. B. Cairns, L. R. Bergman, & J. Kagan (Eds.), *Methods and models for studying the individual* (pp. 135–158). Thousand Oaks, CA: Sage.

Robins, R. W., John, O. P., Caspi, A., Moffitt, T. E., & Stouthamer-Loeber, M. (1996). Resilient, overcontrolled, and undercontrolled boys: Three replicable personality types. *Journal of Personality and Social Psychology, 70,* 157–171.

Rose, S. (1995). The rise of neurogenetic determinism. *Nature, 373,* 380–382.

Roush, W. (1995). When rigor meets reality. *Science, 269,* 313–315.

Rusalov, V. M. (1989). The natural prerequisites of development of human individuality. *Studia Psychologica, 31,* 53–68.

Rutter, M. (1995). Causal concepts and their testing. In M. Rutter & D. J. Smith (Eds.), *Psychosocial disorders in young people: Time trends and their causes* (pp. 7–34). Chichester, UK: Wiley.

Rutter, M., Dunn, J., Plomin, R., Simonoff, E., Pickles, A., Maugham, B., Ormel, J., Meyer, J., & Eaves, L. (1997). Integrating nature and nurture: Implications of person–environment correlations and interactions for developmental psychopathology. *Development and Psychopathology, 9,* 335–364.

Ryff, C. D. (1987). The place of personality and social structure research in social psychology. *Journal of Personality and Social Psychology, 53,* 1192–1202.

Sabelli, H. C., & Carlson-Sabelli, L. (1991). Process theory as a framework for comprehensive psychodynamic formulations. *Genetic, Social, and General Psychology Monographs, 117,* 5–27.

Sameroff, A. J. (1983). Developmental systems: Contexts and evolution. In P. H. Mussen (Series Ed.) & W. Kessen (Vol. Ed.), *Handbook of child psychology: Vol. 1. History, theory and methods* (4th ed., pp. 237–294). New York: Wiley.

Sanford, N. (1965). Will psychologists study human problems? *American Psychologist, 20,* 192–202.

Sapolsky, R. M. (1994). On human nature. *The Sciences, 34* (6),14–16.

Sarbin, T. R. (1976). Contextualism: A world view of modern psychology. In A. W. Landfield (Ed.), *Nebraska Symposium on Motivation. Personal construct psychology*. Lincoln/London: University of Nebraska Press.

Sarbin, T. R. (1986). The narrative as the root metaphor for psychology. In T. R. Sarbin (Ed.), *Narrative psychology: The storied nature of human conduct* (pp. 3–21). New York: Praeger.

Schore, A.N. (1997). Early organization of the nonlinear right brain and development of a predisposition to psychiatric disorders. *Development and Psychopathology, 9,* 595–631.

Schulkin, J., McEwen, B. S., & Gold, P. W. (1994). Allostasis, amygdala, and anticipatory angst. *Neuroscientific Biobehavioral Review, 18,* 385–396.

Sharpe, N., Smith, H., Murphy, J., Greaves, S., Hart, H., Gamble, G. (1991). Early prevention of left ventricular dysfunction after myocardial infarction with angiotensin-converting-enzyme inhibition. *Lancet, 337,* 872–876.

Silbereisen, R. K., & Kracke, B. (1997). Self-reported maturational timing and adaptation in adolescence. In G. Schulenberg, J. Maggs, & K. Hurrelmann (Eds.), *Health risks and developmental transitions during adolescence* (pp. 85–109). Cambridge, UK: Cambridge University Press.

Skinner, B. F. (1971). *Beyond freedom and dignity.* New York: Knopf.

Stattin, H., & Magnusson, D. (1990). *Paths through life: Vol. 2. Pubertal maturation in female development.* Hillsdale, NJ: Erlbaum.

Stattin, H., & Magnusson, D. (1996). Antisocial behavior—a holistic perspective. *Development and Psychopathology, 8,* 617–645.

Stern, W. (1911). *Die Differentielle Psychologie in Ihren Methodischen Grundlagen* Differential psychology in its methodological basis. Leipzig: Verlag von Johann A. Barth.

Stern, W. (1917). *Die Psychologie und der Personalismus.* Leipzig: Barth.

Strelau, J. (1983). *Temperament–Personality–Activity.* New York: Academic Press.

Stryker, M. P. (1994). Precise development from imprecise rule. *Science, 263,* 1244–1245.

Susman, E. J. (1993). Psychological, contextual, and psychobiological interactions: A developmental perspective on conduct disorder. Special Issue: Toward a developmental perspective on conduct disorder. *Development and Psychopathology, 5,* 181–189.

Thelen, E. (1989). Selforganization in developmental processes: Can systems approaches work? In M. R. Gunnar & E. Thelen (Eds.), *Systems and development* (pp. 77–117). Hillsdalc, NJ: Erlbaum.

Thelen, E. (1995). Motor development. A new synthesis. *American Psychologist, 50,* 79–95.

Thelen, E., & Smith, L. B. (1998). Dynamic systems theory. In R. M. Lerner (Vol. ed.) & W. Damon (Ed.-in-Chief), *Handbook of child psychology: Vol. 1. Theoretical models of human development* (pp. 563–634). New York: Wiley.

Tomkins, S. (1979). Script theory: Differential magnification of affects. In H. Howe & R. Dienstbier (Eds.), *Nebraska symposium on motivation* (pp. 201–236). Lincoln, NE: University of Nebraska.

Toulmin, S. (1981). Toward reintegration: An agenda for psychology's next century. In R. A. Kasschau & Ch. N. Cofer (Eds.), *Psychology's next century: Enduring issues* (pp. 264–286). New York: Praeger.

Valsiner, J. (1984). Two alternative epistemiological frameworks in psychology: The typological and variational modes of thinking. *The Journal of Mind and Behavior, 5,* 449–470.

Van Heck, G. L. (1997). Personality and physical health: Toward an ecological approach to health related personality research. *European Journal of Psychology, 11,* 415–443.

Waddington, C. H. (1969). The importance of biological ways of thought. In A. Tiselius & S. Nilsson (Eds.), The place of values in a world of facts. *The proceedings from the fourteenth Nobel symposium* (pp. 95–103). New York: Wiley.

Wapner, S., & Demick, J. (1998). Developmental analysis: A holistic, developmental, systems-oriented perspective. In R. M. Lerner (Vol. ed.) & W. Damon (Ed.-in-Chief), *Handbook of child psychology: Vol. 1. Theoretical models of human development* (pp. 761–805). New York: Wiley.

Watson, J. B. (1913). Psychology as the behaviorist views it. *Psychological Review, 20,* 158–177.

Watson, J. B. (1930). *Behaviorism* (2nd ed). New York: Norton.

Weiner, H. (1989). The dynamics of the organism: Implications of recent biological thought for psychosomatic theory and research. *Psychosomatic Medicine, 51,* 608–635.

Werner, E. E., & Smith, R. S. (1992). *Overcoming the odds: High risk children from brith to adulthood.* Ithaca and London, Cornell University Press.

Wertheimer, M. (1925). Gestalt theory. In W. D. Ellis (Ed.) *A sourcebook of Gestalt psychology* (pp. 1–12). London: Routledge & Kegan Paul.

Yeung-Courchesne, R., & Courchesne, E. (1997). From impass to insight in autism research. From behavioral symptoms to biological implications. *Development and Psychopathology, 9,* 389–419.

York, K. L., & John, O. P. (1992). The four faces of Eve: A typological analysis of women's personality at midlife. *Journal of Personality and Social Psychology, 63,* 494–508.

PART THREE
INTERFACE WITH OTHER FIELDS

Chapter 9

Behavioral Genetics and Personality

Robert Plomin
Institute of Psychiatry, London

Avshalom Caspi
Institute of Psychiatry, London
University of Wisconsin–Madison

Shakespeare first brought the words "nature" and "nurture" together in *The Tempest* (1611/1974) when Prospero, speaking of Caliban says:

> A devil, a born devil, on whose nature
> Nurture can never stick; on whom my pains
> Humanely taken, all, all lost, quite lost . . .
> (IV.i.188–190)

The idea of nurture in conflict with nature provided the impetus for the alliterative phrase "nature–nurture," coined by Francis Galton (1865) more than a century ago at the birth of behavioral genetics. Joining these two words created a fission that exploded into the longest-lived controversy in science. As in Shakespeare, the hyphen in nature–nurture connoted the implicit conjunction "versus." We now know that the appropriate conjunction is "and."

We begin with an overview of research showing a genetic contribution to personality, but the primary purpose of this chapter is to show how behavioral genetics can move beyond heritability to ask questions of central importance to the field of personality. One example at the heart of the nature–nurture controversy is that behavioral genetic theory and methods are as informative about environmental influences as they are about genetic influences. In addition to documenting the influence of genetics, behavioral genetic research provides the best available evidence for the importance of the environment and has led to two discoveries with far-reaching implications about how the environment works to affect personality development. Another exciting new direction for genetic research on personality is the attempt to identify specific genes responsible for genetic influence on personality.

The chapter focuses on these three broad topics of heritability, environment, and molecular genetics. We do this using the somewhat provocative format of stating what we know in the form of propositions. These should not be read as laws but rather as hypotheses that try to distill what we know in concise statements that we hope will serve as lightning rods to attract future research.

Space limitations have made it necessary to slight two topics of great importance to personality: developmental genetic analysis and multivariate genetic analysis. Developmental genetic analyses have yielded interesting patterns of change in the magnitude of genetic and environmental influence during the life course, and longitudinal analyses suggest that genetic factors contribute largely to continuity rather than change (e.g., Plomin, 1986) during the fast-moving era of infancy (e.g., Saudino, DeFries, & Plomin, 1996) and in adulthood (Loehlin, Horn, & Willerman, 1990; McGue, Bacon, & Lykken, 1993; Pogue-Geile & Rose, 1985), although there is some indication of genetic change on personality in childhood (Goldsmith & Gottesman, 1981; Matheny, 1989; Matheny, 1989; Plomin & Nesselroade, 1990). Multivariate genetic analyses have investigated personality structure in relation to its genetic and environmental origins (e.g., Loehlin, 1992), as well as exploring situational differences (Saudino, 1997) and the relations between personality and psychopathology (e.g., Nigg & Goldsmith, 1998).

Considerations of space have also made it necessary to assume that the reader has some general acquaintance with the theory and methods of behavioral genetics, which are available in a general textbook on behavioral genetics (Plomin, DeFries, McClearn, & Rutter, 1997) and in books that focus on genetics and personality (Cattell, 1982; Eaves, Eysenck, & Martin, 1989; Loehlin, 1992). We must also leave aside important general issues about personality that are not specific to behavioral genetic research. However, one of these issues must be mentioned at the outset, the ontological status of personality traits. We unreservedly take sides with Allport, who argued for a realist conception of traits as explanatory concepts: "Personality is and does something. . . . It is what lies behind specific acts and within the individual" (Allport, 1937, p. 48). However, traits are hypothetical constructs rather than observable entities, and their usefulness needs to be demonstrated through a process of construct validation (Meehl, 1986; Zuroff, 1986). Traits are not an end, but rather they are "place-holders" in an evolving search for social, psychological, and biological processes that provide fuller explanations of behavior (Caspi, 1998). We believe that behavioral genetics can contribute importantly to this search.

HERITABILITY

Twin Studies Using Self-Report Personality Questionnaires Consistently Suggest Moderate Heritability

More than two decades ago, a landmark study involving nearly 800 pairs of adolescent twins and dozens of personality traits reached an important conclusion that has stood the test of time (Loehlin & Nicholls, 1976): Nearly all personality traits assessed by self-report questionnaire show moderate genetic influence in twin studies in the sense that identical twin correlations are consistently greater than fraternal twin correlations. Extraversion and Neuroticism are by far the most widely studied traits. For five large twin studies in five different countries, with a total sample size of 24,000 pairs of twins, average correlations for identical twins and for fraternal twins, respectively, are .51 and .18 for Extraversion and .46 and .20 for Neuroticism (Loehlin, 1992). Heritability is a statistic that describes the effect size of genetic influence and refers to the proportion of observed (phenotypic) variance that can be explained by genetic variance. Doubling the difference between identical and fraternal twin correlations, which assumes a simple model of additive genetic effects (Plomin et al., 1997), estimates heritability as about 60% for Extraversion and about 50% for Neuroticism. (As indicated in the next section, these are overestimates because heritability should not exceed the identical twin correlation.)

Explaining 50% of the variance is an astounding achievement in personality research, which has been pushing against a glass ceiling of explaining more than 10% of the variance, as indexed by correlations of .30. Because behavior is multiply determined, it is unlikely that any single factor can explain more than 10% of the variance (Caspi, 1998). However, the advantage of the "anonymous" components-of-variance approach of behavioral genetics is that it examines the net effect of genetic and environmental influences, regardless of how many factors are involved. When we try to identify specific genes or specific environmental factors that account for genetic and environmental components of variance, we run up against the same issue: We can realistically expect to account for only a small proportion of variance with any one genetic or environmental factor.

Across dozens of self-report personality questionnaires, twin correlations are consistently greater for identical twins than for fraternal twins for other traits in addition to Extraversion and Neuroticism (e.g., Caspi, 1998; Goldsmith, 1983; Loehlin, 1992). For example, when scales were organized according to the Big Five scheme, Agreeableness, Conscientiousness, and Openness to Experience showed identical twin correlations of about .45 and fraternal twin cor-

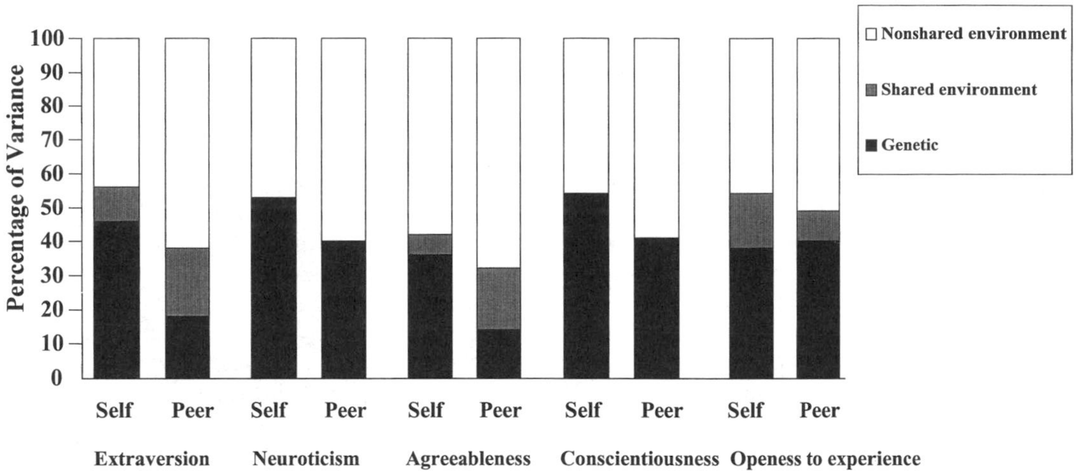

FIGURE 9.1. Genetic (black), shared environment (gray), and nonshared environment (white) components of variance for self-report ratings and peer ratings for the Big Five personality traits. Components of variance were calculated from identical twin (660 pairs) and same-sex fraternal twin (200 pairs) correlations presented by Riemann et al. (1997). Heritability was estimated by doubling the difference between the identical and fraternal twin correlations with the proviso that heritability cannot exceed the identical twin correlation. Shared environment was estimated as the difference between the identical twin correlation and heritability. The remainder of the variance was attributed to nonshared environment, which includes error of measurement. These estimates differ somewhat from the model-fitting results reported by Riemann et al. because their results were presented for best-fitting models in which parameters were dropped unless they were significant. As a result, shared environment, which the twin method has little power to detect, was not significant and thus not included in the best-fitting models presented by Riemann et al., and heritability estimates sometimes exceeded identical twin correlations.

relations of about .20, suggesting heritability estimates of about 40% (Loehlin, 1992). Two more recent twins studies report similar results (Beer & Rose, 1995; Jang, Livesley, & Vernon, 1996). It is surprising to find that the many traits that have been studied all show moderate genetic influence—no personality trait assessed by self-report questionnaire has reliably shown low or no heritability. Can this be true? One way to explore this issue is to use measures other than self-report questionnaires to investigate whether this result is somehow due to self-report measures (Saudino, 1997).

Twin Studies Using Measures Other Than Self-Report Personality Questionnaires Also Suggest Moderate Heritability

A recent study of adult twins in Germany and Poland compared twin results for self-report questionnaires and ratings by peers for measures of the Big Five personality factors for nearly a thousand pairs of twins (Riemann, Angleitner, & Strelau, 1997). Each twin's personality was rated by two different peers. The average correlation between the two peer ratings was .61, a result indicating substantial agreement concerning each twin's personality. The averaged peer ratings correlated .55 with the twins' self-report ratings, a result indicating moderate validity of self-report ratings. Figure 9.1 shows the results of twin analyses for self-report data and peer ratings averaged across two peers. The results for self-report ratings are similar to other studies. The exciting result is that peer ratings also show significant genetic influence, although somewhat less than self-report ratings. Moreover, multivariate genetic analysis indicates that the same genetic factors are largely involved in self-report and peer ratings, which provides strong evidence for genetic validity of self-report ratings. Another interesting result is that some shared environmental influence was detected for both self and peer ratings for Extraversion, Agreeableness, and Openness to Experience, although these estimates were not statistically significant. An earlier study used twin reports about each other and also found similar evidence for genetic influence on personality traits, whether assessed by self-report or by the cotwin (Heath, Neale, Kessler, Eaves, & Kendler, 1992).

Genetic researchers interested in personality and temperament in childhood were forced to use measures other than self-report questionnaires. For the past 20 years, this research has primarily relied on ratings by parents. However, twin studies using parent ratings have yielded an odd result: Correlations for identical twins are high, and correlations for fraternal twins are very low, sometimes even negative (Saudino & Cherny, in press-a; Saudino, McGuire, Reiss, Hetherington, & Plomin, 1995). It is likely that these results are due to contrast effects in which parents of fraternal twins contrast the twins. For example, parents might report that one twin is the active twin and the other is the inactive twin, even though, relative to other children that age, the twins are not really very different from each other (Neale & Stevenson, 1989). It has been suggested that some parental rating measures attenuate this problem (Goldsmith, Buss, & Lemery, 1997).

Other measures of children's personality, especially behavioral ratings by observers, show more reasonable patterns of twin correlations (Braungart, Plomin, DeFries, & Fulker, 1992; Cherny, Fulker, Corley, Plomin, & DeFries, 1994; Emde, Plomin, et al., 1992; Goldsmith & Campos, 1986; Matheny, 1980; Plomin, Emde et al., 1993; Plomin & Foch, 1980; Plomin, Foch, & Rowe, 1981; Saudino & Cherny, in press-b; Saudino et al., 1996; Wilson & Matheny, 1986). For example, genetic influence has been found in observational studies of young twins for a dimension of fearfulness called behavioral inhibition (Matheny, 1989; Robinson, Kagan, Reznick, & Corley, 1992), for shyness observed in the home and the laboratory (Cherny et al., 1994), and for activity level measured using actometers that record movement (Saudino & Eaton, 1991). Because evidence for genetic influence is so widespread even for observational measures, it is interesting that observer ratings of personality in the first few days of life have found no evidence for genetic influence (Riese, 1990) and that individual differences in smiling in infancy also show no genetic influence (Plomin, 1987).

More systematic genetic research is needed that explicitly incorporates different sources of personality data (Goldsmith, 1993). These multiple data sources can be summarized with the acronym STORI (Moffitt, 1991): self-reports, including questionnaires and interviews; tests and objective laboratory measurements; observational assessments; records, such as family, educational, occupational, and marital histories, as well as records from such agencies as schools, hospitals, and the police; and informant ratings by peers, parents, teachers, and other observers. Multivariate genetic analysis, which analyzes the covariance between measures rather than the variance of each measure considered separately (Plomin et al., 1997), has begun to be applied across multiple sources of personality data. An interesting finding appears to be emerging from these studies that suggests genetic validity from cross-source assessments of personality: Genetic factors largely account for what is in common across ratings in the home and laboratory (Cherny et al., 1994), across teacher and tester ratings (Schmitz, Saudino, Plomin, Fulker, & DeFries, 1996), and across parent and laboratory ratings (Goldsmith, Lemery, Buss, & Campos, in press).

Adoption Studies Suggest Less Genetic Influence Than Twin Studies

Although adoption studies are far fewer and much smaller than twin studies of personality, it is noteworthy that they suggest less genetic influence than twin studies. Nonadoptive parents and their offspring correlate only .16 for Extraversion and .13 for Neuroticism, modest correlations that are similar to the results of the largest family study of personality (Ahern, Johnson, Wilson, McClearn, & Vandenbergh, 1982). Taken at face value, these correlations suggest upper-limit estimates of heritabilities of about 30% for Extraversion and 15% for Neuroticism. Adoptive relatives (genetically unrelated individuals adopted together) are not at all similar. For example, adoptive parents and their adopted children correlate .01 for Extraversion and .05 for Neuroticism (Loehlin, 1992). These are important data because they indicate that shared family environment does not contribute importantly to familial resemblance.

Similar results have been reported recently from the Colorado Adoption Project for sociability and emotionality, which are major components of Extraversion and Neuroticism, respectively (Plomin, Corley, Caspi, Fulker, &

DeFries, 1998). Self-reported questionnaires were administered to parents once and to children yearly from 9 to 16 years of age. A direct test of genetic influence comes from biological parents and their adopted-away offspring. Across the 7 years of assessment, their correlations averaged .03 for sociability and –.01 for emotionality. Adoptive parent–adoptee correlations were .06 and .02, respectively. Parents rearing their own biological children (called nonadoptive parents) yielded parent–offspring correlations of .13 and .04, respectively. Model-fitting analyses of the parent–offspring data for 16-year-olds, when the adopted children were nearly the same age as their biological mothers at time of testing, yielded heritability estimates of 30% for sociability and 0% for emotionality. Sibling data also yielded similar results: Sibling correlations, assessed when each child was the same age, averaged .11 for nonadoptive siblings and –.04 for adoptive siblings for sociability and .04 and .08, respectively, for emotionality. These sibling adoption data suggest heritabilities of about 20% for sociability and 0% for emotionality. Similar results were reported earlier in this same study for parental ratings of children from 1 to 7 years of age (Plomin, Coon, Carey, DeFries, & Fulker, 1991) and in other adoption studies of young children rated by their parents (Scarr, Webber, Weinberg, & Wittig, 1981; Loehlin, Horn, & Willerman, 1981; Loehlin, Willerman, & Horn, 1982).

Several factors might contribute to the discrepancy between twin and adoption results (Plomin et al., 1998). For example, a special environmental effect might boost identical twin similarity, called identical twin assimilation. Studies of twins adopted apart yield mixed support for this hypothesis. A Swedish study yielded correlations for identical twins reared apart of .30 for Extraversion and .25 for Neuroticism, considerably lower than the study's correlations of .54 and .41, respectively, for identical twins reared together (Pedersen, Plomin, McClearn, & Friberg, 1998). For fraternal twins, there was little difference between correlations for twins reared apart and twins reared together. Although these results provide strong support for the hypothesis of identical twin assimilation, a similar study in Minnesota found Neuroticism correlations for twins reared apart that were similar to correlations for twins reared together (Tellegen et al., 1988).

Another possible explanation of the lower heritability estimates in adoption studies is nonadditive genetic effects. Traditionally, it has been assumed that genetic effects on personality are inherited in an additive manner, as appears to be the case for physical characteristics such as height and weight. Additive genetic effects refer to independent effects of genes that "add up" to influence a trait, in contrast to nonadditive genetic effects in which genes interact. Identical twins are identical for all genetic effects whether additive or nonadditive. Fraternal twins, however, resemble each other 50% on average for additive effects of genes, but nonadditive effects only contribute slightly to the resemblance of fraternal twins and other first-degree relatives (Plomin et al., 1997). Doubling the difference between identical and fraternal twin correlations assumes a model of additive genetic effects. For the twin correlations given earlier, this model is violated because the fraternal twin correlation (.18 for Extraversion) is less than half the identical twin correlation (.51). For this reason, doubling the difference between these correlations yields a heritability estimate (66%) that is greater than the identical twin correlation, which provides an upper-limit bound for heritability. Twin analyses of personality now tend to consider nonadditive genetic models (e.g., Finkel & McGue, 1997). Nonadditive genetic variance could explain why correlations for other first-degree relatives, including those in adoption studies, are relatively low.

These comparisons between twin and adoption results rely on data from self-report questionnaires and parental ratings because there are not as yet sufficient comparative data available for other measures. Tester ratings of temperament in infancy in one study of nonadoptive and adoptive siblings (Braungart, Plomin, DeFries, & Fulker, 1992) and in two twin studies (Matheny, 1980; Plomin et al., 1993) yielded results too disparate to draw conclusions about nonadditive genetic variance. Comparative data from multiple sources are needed.

This is an important issue in relation to attempts to identify specific genes responsible for genetic influence, which assume additive effects of genes. If genetic effects involve interactions among a large number of genes, it will be more difficult to identify individual genes in such complex systems. With 30,000 genes expressed in the brain, two- and three-way interactions alone could yield millions of possible interactions (Frankel & Schork, 1996). It is also possible to examine interactions between one or two DNA markers rather than simply examining the additive effects of each marker. Nonadditive genetic effects will be proven only when such gene–gene interactions are found. One molecular genetic study of personality has reported such interactions between DNA markers (Cloninger, 1997), although replication is required.

Until recently, behavioral genetic research has had the limited goal of asking whether and to what extent genetic factors are important in the origins of individual differences in personality. This is a reasonable first step toward understanding etiology, a first step that has yet to be taken in some areas of personality and in many other areas of psychology. Nonetheless, at least for self-report questionnaires of personality, it seems clear that genetic factors contribute importantly to individual differences in personality. Indeed, we are aware of no personality trait assessed by self-report questionnaire that has been reliably demonstrated to show no genetic influence. The future of behavioral genetic research lies in going beyond heritability. One important direction for research lies at the interface between nature and nurture.

ENVIRONMENT

Genetic research is changing the way we think about the environment as it relates to personality. The major topics of this section are two of the most important discoveries from genetic research and they concern nurture rather than nature. At the outset, three reminders about the environment are warranted. First, genetic research provides the best available evidence for the importance of environmental factors. Heritability rarely exceeds 50% and thus "environmentality" is rarely less than 50%. Second, in quantitative genetic theory (e.g., Falconer & Mackay, 1996), the word *environment* includes all influences other than inheritance, a much broader use of the word than is usual in psychology. By this definition, environment includes, for instance, prenatal events and such biological events as nutrition and illness, not just family socialization factors. Third, genetic research describes *what is* rather than predicts *what could be*. Even for a highly heritable trait, the behavior of individuals could be altered dramatically, for example, in a laboratory experiment or some other environmental intervention. Moreover, behavioral genetic studies have not studied severe environments such as neglectful or abusive environments.

Most Environmental Influence on Personality Is of the Nonshared Variety

From Freud onward, most theories about how the environment works in personality development implicitly assume that offspring resemble their parents because parents provide the family environment for their offspring. Similarly, siblings resemble each other because they share that family environment. Twin and adoption research during the past two decades has dramatically altered this view. The reason why genetic designs, such as twin and adoption methods, were devised was to address the possibility that some of the widespread resemblance between family members may be due to shared heredity rather than to shared family environment. The surprise is that genetic research consistently shows that family resemblance for personality is almost entirely due to shared heredity rather than to shared family environment. The environment is important, but it is not shared by family members. This remarkable finding means that environmental influences that affect personality development operate to make children growing up in the same family no more similar than children growing up in different families. Because such environmental factors, whatever they may be, are not shared by family members, they have been called *nonshared* (Plomin & Daniels, 1987; Rowe & Plomin, 1981). At the outset, we emphasize that this does *not* mean that the family environment is unimportant for two reasons. First, children growing up in the same family lead surprisingly separate lives (Dunn & Plomin, 1990), which means that family environment can make siblings different. Second, even common family experiences like divorce can be experienced differently by siblings.

As indicated earlier, genetically unrelated adoptive relatives hardly correlate at all for personality. This is a direct test of the importance of shared environment—resemblance between adoptive relatives can only be caused by shared environment because they are unrelated genetically. Twin studies of personality also indicate that twin resemblance is due entirely to genetic factors. For example, differences within pairs of identical twins, who correlate only about .50 for self-report personality questionnaires, can only be due to nonshared environment and error of measurement. For self-report personality questionnaires, genetics typically accounts for about 40% of the variance, shared environment for 0%, and nonshared environment plus error of measurement accounts for the remaining 60% of the variance. Such questionnaires are usually at least 80% reliable, which means that about 20 percent of the variance may be due to error of measurement. Thus, systematic nonshared environmental variance excluding error of measurement accounts for about 40% of the variance (Plomin, Chipuer, & Neiderhiser, 1994).

The implication of nonshared environment is that specific environmental influences on personality should not be sought in familywide risk factors but rather in the ways these risk factors impinge differentially on different children in the same family. The key to identifying specific nonshared environmental factors relevant to personality development is to ask what makes children growing up in the same family so different. Such research begins by assessing aspects of the environment specific to each child rather than aspects shared by siblings. Many measures of the environment used in studies of personality development are general to a family rather than specific to a child. For example, whether or not their parents have been divorced is the same for two children in the family. Assessed in this family-general way, divorce cannot be a source of differences in siblings' outcomes. However, research on divorce has shown that divorce affects children in a family differently (Hetherington & Clingempeel, 1992). If divorce is assessed in a child-specific way (for example, the children's different perceptions about the stress caused by the divorce), it could well be a source of differential sibling outcome. Even when environmental measures are specific to a child, they can be shared by two children in a family. Research on siblings' experiences is needed to assess the extent to which their experiences are shared or nonshared.

Some family structure variables, such as birth order and sibling age spacing, are by definition nonshared environmental factors. A meta-analysis of studies of birth order and personality found that first-borns are more conforming and traditional, more conscientious, and more neurotic than later-borns, differences which have been interpreted in evolutionary terms of differential parental investment (Sulloway, 1996). Research on more dynamic aspects of nonshared environment has found that children growing up in the same family lead surprisingly separate lives (Dunn & Plomin, 1990; Hetherington, Reiss, & Plomin, 1994). Siblings perceive their parents' treatment of them quite differently, although parents report they treat their children similarly. Observational studies tend to back up the children's perspective.

A recently reported behavioral genetic study, called the Nonshared Environment and Adolescent Development (NEAD) project, focused on family factors (Reiss et al., 1995; Reiss, Neiderhiser, Hetherington, & Plomin, in press). During two 2-hour visits to 720 families with sibling offspring (including twins, siblings, half-siblings, and genetically unrelated siblings) ranging in age from 10 to 18 years, a large battery of questionnaire and interview measures of the family environment was administered to both parents and offspring, and parent–child interactions were videotaped during a session when problems in family relationships were discussed. Sibling correlations for children's reports of their family environments were modest, as were observational ratings of child-to-parent interactions and parent-to-child interactions, indicating nonshared experiences. The next step was to ask whether these nonshared experiences are related to sibling outcomes. As in other studies (Daniels, Dunn, Furstenberg, & Plomin, 1985; Hetherington et al., 1994; McGuire, Dunn, & Plomin, 1995; Reitsma-Street, Offord, & Finch, 1985), NEAD found that these nonshared experiences were strongly related to adolescent problem behaviors, such as antisocial behavior and depression. Although studies of this type have focused on adjustment rather than personality, the first report on personality found that sibling differences in family experiences were related to sibling differences in personality (Vernon, Jang, Harris, & McCarthy, 1997).

A final hurdle in the hunt for nonshared environment is to investigate the direction of effects. That is, are nonshared family experiences the cause or the effect of sibling differences in personality? One way to disentangle cause and effect is by means of longitudinal analysis. In NEAD, the adolescent siblings and their families were studied again three years later. If differential parental treatment causes sibling differences, differential parental treatment at the first time of assessment would be expected to predict changes in sibling's behavior over the three-year period. Although no evidence for this direction of effects was found, it was not a strong test because sibling behavior was quite stable over the three years, leaving little room to find change in the siblings' behavior.

Another test is to investigate genetic mediation because genetics makes siblings different as well as similar. In NEAD, when associations between family environment and adolescent outcome were embedded in analyses using its genetically sensitive design, some evidence for modest nonshared environmental effects independent of genetic effects was found, a result similar to another study of this type (Rodgers, Rowe, & Li, 1994). But the surprise, and the topic of the next section, was that the associations between family environment and adolescent problem behaviors were largely mediated by genetic factors (Pike, McGuire, Hetherington, Reiss, & Plomin, 1996). That is, parents largely respond to genetic differences between their children rather than cause those differences environmentally. Correlating identical twin differences in experience with identical twin differences in outcome is a direct test of nonshared environment independent of genetics. An NEAD analysis of identical twin differences also found some evidence for nonshared environmental effects independent of genetics (Pike et al., 1996). Nonshared environment need not be limited to family environment. Experiences outside the family as siblings make their own way in the world are even more likely candidates for nonshared environmental influence. For example, peers (Harris, 1995) and adult experiences, such as spouses (Caspi, Herbener, & Ozer, 1992) and life events (Plomin, 1994), may be sources of nonshared environment. It is also possible that nonsystematic factors, such as accidents and illnesses, initiate differences between siblings. Compounded over time, small differences in such experiences might lead to large differences in outcome. No matter how difficult it may be to find specific nonshared environmental factors, it should be emphasized that nonshared environment is the way the environment works for personality.

The finding of the importance of nonshared environment has aroused several reactions, which are discussed elsewhere (Caspi, 1998). The first reaction, however, is disbelief, because, for a long time, research has documented associations between measures of parenting and measures of children's personality. However, this research has not shown that the direction of effects is from parenting environment to children's personality. Parenting behavior might be associated with children's personality for genetic reasons, as discussed in the following section.

There are few exceptions to this sweeping conclusion, but these exceptions may be important for advancing understanding of how the environment works. One exception has been reported at the edge of the field of personality research, where research has shown substantial shared environmental influence for juvenile delinquency (Rowe, 1983b; Rowe, 1986; Rowe, Rodgers, & Meseck Bushey, 1992). Shared environmental effects typically refer to such factors as social class or child-rearing practices that are shared by members of a sibling pair and that serve to make siblings similar to one each other. However, it may be that with regard to delinquency the shared-environment effect may not necessarily reflect criminogenic home environments as provided by parents but mutual influence within twin pairs, in the sense that siblings may be partners in crime.

A second possible exception concerns Positive Emotionality or positive affect. Several twin studies of adults have reported some shared environmental influence for self reports of Positive Emotionality (Tellegen et al., 1988) and Agreeableness (Bergeman et al., 1993; Riemann et al., 1997). Studies of infants consistently show no genetic influence and strong shared environmental influence for smiling (Plomin, 1987). Shared environmental influence has also been suggested for positive affect in childhood (Goldsmith, Lemery, Buss, & Compos, in press). These findings, coupled with a substantial shared environmental influence for self-reports of attitudes toward love and romantic relationships (Waller & Shaver, 1994), suggest that growing up in the same environment may lead siblings to develop similar expectations about interpersonal relationships.

Some commentators have noted that most behavioral genetic studies only estimate an anonymous component of variance attributed to nonshared environment; they do not actually measure environmental factors directly (Hoffman, 1991). More behavioral genetic studies are needed like the NEAD study that directly measure whether specific environmental factors make children in the same family similar to one another. Some studies at the edge of personality research have begun to do so. For example, a twin study of psychiatric disorders reported that childhood parental loss through divorce or death is associated with increased adult risk for depression and anxiety among siblings (Kendler, Neale, Kessler, Heath, & Eaves, 1992). Thus, parental loss appears to be a specific shared environmental factor that makes children who grow up in the same family similar to each other. Such studies illustrate the important etiological contributions that can be made by behavioral genetic studies that directly assess environmental influences. Still, the interpretation of even this shared environmental effect is not straightforward because, as discussed in the next section, parental loss is not purely an environmental variable. For example, both divorce and death have been linked to heritable personality traits, such as Neuroticism, and it could be that the ostensible environmental effect of parental loss on offspring anxiety and depression is a spurious function of parental Neuroticism (Brody & Crowley, 1995). More sophisticated adoption designs (Plomin, 1994) or extended family-twin designs (Kendler, 1996) can be used to test these competing accounts. However, the simple point we wish to make here is that social scientists increasingly appreciate that behavioral genetic research designs that incorporate measures of the environment are better suited to establishing unambiguous inferences about environmental influence than are research designs that do not use genetic controls.

Environmental Measures Show Genetic Influence, in Part Due to Personality

The second finding that is changing the way we think about the environment seems paradoxical at first glance: Measures widely used as measures of the environment show as much genetic influence as measures of personality. However, this finding seems more reasonable with the realization that measures of psychological environments, unlike the weather for example, are actually measures of behavior. For example, measures of the family environment usually involve parenting behavior. Parenting behavior can show genetic influence for two reasons: Genetic characteristics of parents, such as their personality, might be reflected in their parenting, and parenting behavior might reflect genetic characteristics, such as personality, of their children. More generally, environmental measures can show genetic influence because people create their own experiences in part for genetic reasons. This topic has been called the *nature of nurture* (Plomin & Bergeman, 1991), although in genetics it is known technically as *genotype–environment correlation* because it refers to experiences that are correlated with genetic propensities.

This finding emerged in the 1980s when genetic researchers began to investigate environmental measures in twin and adoption studies. The pioneering research in this area was two twin studies of adolescents' perceptions of their family environment (Rowe, 1981; 1983a). Both studies found substantial genetic influence on adolescents' perceptions of their parents' acceptance and affection and no genetic influence on perceptions of parents' control. Since then, more than a dozen other studies of twins and adoptees have reported genetic influence on questionnaires of family environment (Plomin, 1994). These include studies of adult twins reared apart, who were asked to rate the family environment in which they were reared (Plomin, McClearn, Pedersen, Nesselroade, & Bergeman, 1988). Even though members of each twin pair were reared in different families, identical twins reared apart rated their family environments more similarly than did fraternal twins reared apart. This evidence for genetic influence emerged in relation to the rearing family's warmth (cohesion, expressiveness) and the family's emphasis on personal growth (achievement, culture) but, again, not for control. How can genetic effects emerge when the reared-apart twins rate different families? Although subjective processes of perception are likely to be involved, it is also possible that members of the two families were responding similarly to genetically influenced characteristics of the separated twins.

Evidence for genetic influence is not limited to self-report measures of the environment. Several observational studies of the family environment also show genetic influence in infancy (Braungart, Fulker, & Plomin, 1992; Dunn & Plomin, 1986; Lytton, 1977; Lytton, 1980), middle childhood (Rende, Slomkowski, Stocker, Fulker, & Plomin, 1992), and adolescence (O'Connor, Hetherington, Reiss, & Plomin, 1995). An interesting aspect of two of these studies (Lytton, 1977; Lytton, 1980; O'Connor et al., 1995) was that parent-initiated interactions and child-initiated interactions were rated separately. Genetic effects emerged primarily for child-initiated interactions, as would be expected because the genetic designs hinged on the children rather than the parents. That is, a child-based genetic design can only detect genetic factors in parents' behavior that reflect genetically based behavioral differences among children.

The complementary design is a parent-based genetic design in which the parents are twins or adoptees. In this design, genetic influence can be detected for parents' perceptions and behavior independent of their effect on their offspring, which means that parent-initiated interactions should show greater genetic influence than child-initiated interactions. The first study of this type involved adult twins who were parents and found evidence for genetic influence for most dimensions of current family environments, this time for parental control as well as for other dimensions (Plomin, McClearn, Pedersen, Nesselroade, & Bergeman, 1989). In contrast to the results of the child-based genetic designs, three other studies of parent-based designs have also found genetic influence on parental control as well as on other dimensions of parenting (Losoya, Callor, Rowe, & Goldsmith, 1997; Perusse, Neale, Heath, & Eaves, 1992), although one such study found significant genetic influence for warmth but not control (Kendler, 1996). One explanation for finding genetic influence on parental control in parent-based genetic designs but not in child-based genetic designs is that parental control might involve genetically influenced characteristics of parents to a greater extent than it involves genetically influenced characteristics of children.

Genetic influence on environmental measures also extends beyond the family environment. For example, genetic influence has been found for characteristics of children's peer groups (e.g., Manke, McGuire, Reiss, Hetherington, & Plomin, 1995), work environments (Hershberger, Lichtenstein, & Knox, 1994), social support (Bergeman, Plomin, Pedersen, McClearn, & Nesselroade, 1990; Kendler, 1977; Kessler, Kendler, Heath, Neale, & Eaves, 1992), and life events (Kendler, Neale, Kessler, Heath, & Eaves, 1993b; McGuffin, Katz, & Rutherford, 1991; Plomin, Lichtenstein, Pedersen, McClearn, & Nesselroade, 1990), including accidents in childhood (Phillips & Matheny, 1995), divorce (McGue & Lykken, 1992), exposure to drugs (Tsuang et al., 1992), and exposure to trauma (Lyons et al., 1993). One study found little genetic influence on adults' retrospective perceptions of their classroom environments (Vernon et al., 1997).

A key issue for personality researchers is the extent to which personality contributes to genetic influence on measures of the environment. The first investigation of this issue compared correlations between measures of family environment and children's development in nonadoptive families and adoptive families (Plomin, Loehlin, & DeFries, 1985). Evidence for genetic mediation was found in that the correlations were greater in nonadoptive families in which parents and offspring are genetically related than in adoptive families where parents and offspring are not related genetically. This method assesses passive genotype–environment correlation, which occurs when children passively inherit from their parents environments that are correlated with their genetic propensities. Evidence for this type of genetic mediation was found whenever an environmental measure correlated with children's development. Most of these correlations involved cognitive development and problem behaviors, but some involved personality. For example, correlations between parental warmth and infants' low emotionality and high sociability showed genetic mediation. However, when measures of the environment are not phenotypically correlated with personality, they cannot show genetic mediation, and this is often the case (Neiderhiser, 1994).

A second method correlates biological parents' traits with adoptive families' environments. If biological parents' traits correlate with the environment of their adopted-away children, this suggests that the environmental measure reflects genetically influenced characteristic of the adopted children. This is called evocative or reactive genotype–environment correlation, because it occurs when individuals evoke reactions from other people on the basis of their genetic propensities. Applications of this method in infancy and early childhood yielded only slightly more than a chance number of significant results. Nonetheless, some of the results were interesting in relation to personality (Plomin & DeFries, 1985; Plomin, DeFries, & Fulker, 1988). For example, adoptive parents were more responsive to adopted children whose biological mothers were more active and impulsive. Another example is that adoptive parents were less affectionate to their adopted children whose biological mothers were less emotionally stable.

It has been predicted that the evocative form of genotype–environment correlation becomes more important as children experience environments outside the family (Scarr & McCartney, 1983). In line with this hypothesis, a recent adoption study using this method found evidence for evocative genotype–environment correlation for antisocial behavior in adolescence (Ge et al., 1996). Adoptive parents were more negative in their parenting to adoptees whose biological parents were antisocial. Moreover, this effect was shown to be mediated by the adolescent adoptees' own antisocial behavior.

A third method for detecting specific genotype–environment correlation is the most general in that it can detect any type of genotype–environment correlation—passive, evocative or a third type called active, which occurs when individuals select, modify, construct, or reconstruct experiences that are correlated with their genetic propensities. This method involves multivariate genetic analysis of the correlation between an environmental measure and a trait. Multivariate genetic analysis can estimate the extent to which genetic effects on the environmental measure overlap with genetic effects on the trait measure. Genetic overlap between an environmental measure and a measure of personality suggests that genetic effects on the personality trait are responsible for genetic effects on the environmental measure.

Using this multivariate genetic approach, a striking example of the contribution of personality to genetic influence on an environmental measure comes from an observational study of family environment and temperament in infancy (Saudino & Plomin, 1997). In this case, genetic effects on tester ratings of infant temperament (task orientation, which includes attention span and goal directedness) entirely accounts for genetic influence on an observational measure of aspects of the family environment relevant to children's cognitive development. In adolescence, multivariate genetic analyses also found substantial genetic mediation of correlations between measures of family environment and adolescents' depression and antisocial behavior (Pike et al., 1996). In adulthood, genetic influence on personality has also been reported to contribute to genetic influence on parenting in two studies (Chipuer, Plomin, Pedersen, McClearn, & Nesselroade, 1993; Losoya et al., 19997) but not in another (Vernon et al., 1997). Finally, genetic effects on the Big Five personality traits completely explain genetic influences on life events in a sample of older women (Saudino, Pedersen, Lichtenstein, McClearn, & Plomin, 1997).

This finding of genetic influence on environmental measures does not mean that experience is entirely driven by genes—most of the variance is not genetic. The main implication is that associations between environmental measures and personality cannot be assumed to be caused environmentally (Rowe, 1994). It seems more likely that the direction of effects is in the other direction: Genetic influences on personality contribute to genetic effects on measures of the environment. These findings support a current shift from thinking about passive models of how the environment affects individuals toward models that recognize the active role we play in selecting, modifying, and creating our own environments (Plomin, 1994). It seems likely that personality contributes importantly in this construction of experience.

The two topics of this section, nonshared environment and personality-mediated genetic influence on environmental measures, are examples of a major trend for research at the interface between nature and nurture. Some of the most important questions in genetic research involve the environment and some of the most important questions for environmental research involve genetics (Rutter et al., 1997). Genetic research will profit if it includes sophisticated measures of the environment, environmental research will benefit from the use of genetic designs, and the field of personality will be advanced by collaboration between geneticists and environmentalists. These are ways in which some personality researchers are putting the nature–nurture controversy behind them and bringing nature and nurture together in the study of development in order to understand the processes by which genotypes eventuate in phenotypes (Reiss, 1997).

MOLECULAR GENETIC ANALYSIS: THE IDENTIFICATION OF SPECIFIC GENES CORRELATED WITH PERSONALITY

One of the most exciting directions for genetic research on personality involves the use of molecular genetic techniques to identify some of the specific genes responsible for genetic influence on personality (Hamer & Copeland, 1998). Finding genes for personality will revolutionize genetic research by providing direct measures of specific genotypes of individuals, which will facilitate more incisive analyses of genetics and personality. Ultimately it will focus attention on causal processes from cells to social systems that will elucidate how genes affect personality development. From a practical perspective, the availability of specific genes associated with personality will make it possible for any personality researcher to incorporate genes in their ongoing research, because, as we shall explain, it is relatively easy and inexpensive to use genes once they have been identified. Space does not permit a detailed explanation of basic molecular genetic concepts or methods, but introductory material is available elsewhere (e.g., Plomin et al., 1997). In addition, the topics raised in this section are discussed in greater detail elsewhere (Plomin & Caspi, 1998).

The search for genes for personality is difficult because, unlike classical single-gene disorders in which a single gene is necessary and sufficient to produce the disorder, there is no evidence for such major effects of genes for personality. For quantitative traits like personality, genetic influence is much more likely to involve multiple genes of varying but small effect size, which greatly increases the difficulty of detecting such genes. Genes for complex traits influenced by multiple genes and multiple environmental factors are known as *quantitative trait loci* (QTLs) (Plomin, Owen, & McGuffin, 1994). The goal is not to find *the* gene for a particular personality trait, but rather *some* of the many genes that make contributions of varying effect sizes to the variance of the trait. Perhaps one gene will be found that accounts for 5% of the variance, 5 other genes might each account for 2% of the variance, 10 other genes might each account for 1% of the variance, and many other genes might have effects so small that we can never detect them. If the effects of these QTLs are independent, together these QTLs would account for 25% of the variance, or half of the heritable variance for the trait. All of the genes that contribute to the heritability of the trait may never be identified if some of their effect sizes are very small.

Researchers attempting to find QTLs for personality have investigated allelic association using DNA markers that are in or near genes thought to be relevant to the trait. Allelic association refers to a correlation between alleles of a DNA marker and trait scores across unrelated individuals (Owen, Holmans, & McGuffin, 1997). That is, allelic association occurs when individuals with a particular allele for the marker have higher scores on the trait. Genes thought to be relevant to a particular trait are often called *candidate genes*, which is something of a misnomer. For cardiovascular disease, the several cholesterol-related genes were good candidate genes because it was known that cholesterol is importantly involved in the processes leading to heart disease. However, for personality, much less is known about relevant physiological mechanisms, which means that few specific genes can be suggested as candidates. The phrase *candidate gene* has been corrupted to include any genes that might conceivably be related to personality—innocent bystanders rather than real culprits that are identified in a line-up of relevant physiological mechanisms. The problem with this loose use of the phrase *candidate gene* is that any gene expressed in the brain—which includes at least a third of all genes—could be considered as a candidate gene, so the phrase loses its meaning.

Although we should not fool ourselves by pretending that any gene expressed in the brain is a true candidate gene, it nonetheless makes sense to attempt to associate known genes with personality, especially for those with functional DNA markers known to have a physiological effect. The dopamine system, for example, is likely to have widespread effects throughout personality and psychopathology, so that it is reasonable to investigate whether the five genes for dopamine receptors and dopamine promoters and transporters show associations, even though these cannot be considered as specific candidate genes. This could of course be branded as a "fishing expedition." Although a fishing expedition is generally considered to be a bad thing, the QTL perspective suggests that a fishing expedition may be appropriate because there are so many fish to be caught—provided that we have nets with sufficiently fine mesh to catch small fish.

DRD4 and Novelty Seeking

In this section, we focus on the first reported QTL association with personality. Whether or not this association proves to be true in the long run, it serves as an example of attempts to identify specific genes associated with personality. An excellent popular account of this area of research is *Living with Our Genes* (Hamer & Copeland, 1998).

1996 was a watershed for molecular genetic research on personality (Hamer, 1997). Using a candidate gene approach, an allelic association between Novelty Seeking and a gene for a particular dopamine receptor (*dopamine D4, DRD4*) was reported in three tests in two independent studies in the prestigious molecular genetics journal *Nature Genetics* (Cloninger, Adolfsson, & Svrakic, 1996). Novelty Seeking is one of the four traits included in a theory of temperament developed by Cloninger (e.g., Cloninger, Svrakic, & Przybeck, 1993), although it is very similar to the impulsive sensation-seeking dimension studied by Zuckerman (1979, 1994). Individuals high in Novelty Seeking as measured by Cloninger's Tridimensional Personality Questionnaire (TPQ) are characterized as impulsive, exploratory, fickle, excitable, quick-tempered, and extravagant. Cloninger's theory predicts that Novelty Seeking involves genetic differences in dopamine transmission.

The DRD4 marker consists of 7 alleles involving 2, 3, 4, 5, 6, 7, or 8 repeats of a 48 base-pair sequence in exon III of the gene on chromosome 11 that codes for the D4 receptor of dopamine. The gene is expressed primarily in the brain limbic system. The number of repeats changes the length of the third cytoplasmic loop of the receptor, which has been shown to affect the receptor's efficiency in vitro (Asghari et al., 1994, 1995). The shorter alleles (2, 3, 4, or 5 repeats) code for a receptor that is more efficient in binding dopamine than the larger alleles (6, 7, or 8 repeats). For this reason, the DRD4 alleles are usually grouped as *short* (about 85% of alleles) or *long* (15% of alleles). Alleles are doled out two at a time as genotypes of individuals, who inherit one allele from their mother and one from their father. For DRD4, genotypes have usually been analyzed by comparing individuals who have two short alleles (about 70% of genotypes) versus one or two long alleles (30% of genotypes). The theory is that individuals with the long-repeat DRD4 allele are dopamine deficient and seek novelty to increase dopamine release.

In the original studies, individuals with at least one long-repeat DRD4 allele showed significantly higher Novelty-Seeking scores than individuals without a long-repeat allele. The first study included 124 Ashkenazi and non-Ashkenazi adults who were staff and students of Beersheva University in Israel using the TPQ (Ebstein et al., 1996). The other three TPQ scales (Reward Dependence, Persistence, Harm Avoidance) showed no significant differences between the two groups. The effect size for Novelty Seeking was 0.5 standard deviation units, accounting for 6% of the variance.

A replication study, published simultaneously, included 315 American adults and siblings (Benjamin, Patterson, Greenberg, Murphy, & Hamer, 1996). The NEO-PI-R personality questionnaire (Costa & McCrae, 1992) was used to predict Novelty Seeking because Novelty Seeking is not one of the NEO dimensions. Again, novelty seeking was associated with the long-repeat DRD4 allele, with an effect size accounting for 4% of the variance. The two NEO-PI-R scales thought to relate most to Novelty Seeking (Extraversion and Conscientiousness) both showed significant associations with DRD4, but the other three NEO-PI-R scales (Neuroticism, Openness, and Agreeableness) did not.

This replication study also included an additional test for association within pairs of siblings. For 60 sibling pairs who differed in short versus long DRD4 genotypes, the sibling with the long-repeat allele had a significantly higher Novelty-Seeking score than the sibling without a long-repeat allele. In addition to providing a nearly independent replication of the population association, finding an association within families is important because it eliminates the possibility that association is an artifact of ethnic stratification in that siblings are of the same ethnic group.

Ebstein, Nemanov, Klotz, Gritsenko, & Belmaker (1997) have conducted a replication study using an independent sample of 94 university staff and students in Jerusalem. Although the difference was not quite statistically significant, when this Jerusalem sample was combined with the previous sample from Beersheva (Ebstein et al., 1996), the difference was significant in the expected direction. An important additional finding is that TPQ Novelty Seeking differs significantly for individuals with and without DRD4 long repeats in both of the major ethnic groups (Ashkenazi and non-Ashkenazi Jews). In addition to the Ebstein et al. (1997) replication study, the association between Novelty Seeking and long-repeat DRD4 alleles has also been replicated by another group who studied 153 female student nurses in Japan (Ono et al., 1997).

These five positive findings are offset by six studies that failed to find significant associations. However, two of these studies showed trends in the expected direction. One was a study of 126 Swedish individuals (average age of 41) that used Impulsiveness and Monotony avoidance scales from a Swedish personality questionnaire (Jönsson et al., 1997). The other was a study of the top and bottom 100 individuals on a NEO-PI-R index of Novelty Seeking who were selected from 1143 American participants in the Baltimore Longitudinal Study of Aging (mean age of 61 years) (Vandenbergh, Zonderman, Wang, Uhl, & Costa, 1997). Three studies found no association: a study of 193 Finnish males assessed for TPQ Novelty Seeking (Malhotra et al., 1996); a TPQ study in the United States of about 200 young adult twin individuals (Pogue-

Geile, Ferrell, Deka, Debski, & Manuck, 1998); a small German study of 58 adults (Gebhardt et al., 1997); and a small American study (Gelernter et al., 1997).

A possible explanation for these inconsistent results is lack of power to detect small effects (Plomin & Caspi, 1998). If the true effect size is 1% rather than 6%, as in the original report (Ebstein et al., 1996), or 4%, as in the first replication study (Benjamin et al., 1996), samples larger than 300 subjects are needed to detect the effect with 80% power, even with a one-tailed *p* of .05 (Cohen, 1988). With sample sizes on the order of 150 as in the extant studies, power is only about 50% to detect an effect size of 1%, which means that such an effect would be detected as significant in only half the studies, which is close to the obtained result. In addition, systematic moderators, such as age and sex, might cloud the results for these diverse samples (Ebstein & Belmaker, 1997). For example, the four reports that yielded a significant association studied young adults from 18 to 32 years (Ebstein & Belmaker, 1997); one of the studies that did not find a significant association included much older subjects (Vandenbergh et al., 1997), although another study with negative results included young adults (Pogue-Geile et al., 1998). Concerning sex, the Ebstein, Nemanov, Klotz, Gritsenko, & Belmaker study (1997) reported a significant effect for females but not males (although the difference between females and males was not statistically significant), and one of the other studies that yielded a significant replication included only females (Ono et al., 1997); one of the studies that did not replicate included only males (Malhotra et al., 1996). Although one of the original studies (Benjamin et al., 1996) showing a significant association primarily (95%) included males, it might be relevant that half the subjects were homosexual. Such great diversity of samples makes the trend toward replication more impressive.

Much more research is underway that will soon make it clear whether DRD4 long-repeat alleles are in fact associated with Novelty Seeking. (We predict that this will be considerably clearer by the time our paper is actually published, too late for us to keep up with this fast-moving field.) An important issue is the file drawer problem in which negative results are not published (Rosenthal, 1980). Because DRD4 is the first major association with personality, negative as well as positive results are currently being published. However, as we become more accustomed to reports about QTL associations, it is likely that it will be increasingly difficult to publish negative results. This would be a mistake because the literature could soon become cluttered with false (or just weak) positive results. Moreover, progress is often made by examining patterns of discrepant results, such as the possible importance of age and sex mentioned above in relation to DRD4 and Novelty Seeking. We encourage researchers to publish failures to replicate and editors to embrace such reports. However, at the same time we also encourage researchers to conduct studies with at least 80% power to detect the expected effect size. For example, at least 300 unselected subjects are needed if the expected effect size accounts for 1% of the variance. The best way not to replicate a finding is to lack power to detect it!

Also relevant are numerous recent reports of DRD4 associations with other behaviors relevant to Novelty Seeking. For example, three studies found a significantly higher frequency of long-repeat DRD4 alleles in heroin addicts (Kotler et al., 1997; Li et al., 1997; Mel, Kramer, Gritsenko, Kotler, & Ebstein, 1997). Alcoholics show some DRD4 associations, but the results are more mixed (Ebstein & Belmaker, 1997). Associations have also been reported between the long-repeat allele of DRD4 and attention-deficit hyperactivity disorder (Bailey et al., 1997; LaHoste et al., 1996; Sunohara, Swanson, et al., 1996; Sunohara, Barr, et al., 1997; Swanson et al., 1998; Asherson, Curran, Simonoff, & Taylor, 1997; Castellanos et al., 1997), Tourette syndrome (Grice et al., 1996), smoking (Lerman et al., 1998), panic disorder (Benjamin, Gulman, Osher, Segman, & Ebstein, 1997), lowered risk for depression (Serretti et al., 1996), and better retention in a fear conditioning task as assessed by skin conductance (Annas, 1997).

Other QTL Associations with Personality

Although DRD4 was the first DNA marker associated with personality and has been studied much more than other markers, associations between several other markers and personality have been reported. For example, an association between Neuroticism and a functional marker in the control region of a gene involved in serotonin function (5-HTTLPR) was reported in *Science* in two samples as well as in a within-family comparison (Lesch et al., 1996). Although one small study has reported results in the expected direction for TPQ Harm Avoidance (Ricketts et al., 1997), three other studies have so far failed to replicate the finding (Ball et al., 1997; Ebstein et al., 1997; Jönsson et al., 1997). As another example, TPQ Reward Dependence and Persistence have been reported to be related to a DNA marker in a gene for a serotonin receptor (HTR2C); Reward Dependence was also associated with an interaction between HTR2C and two dopamine receptor DNA markers (Ebstein et al., 1997). The gene for the D2 receptor of dopamine (DRD2), which has been associated with drug abuse in several studies (e.g., Noble, 1996), has also been reported to be associated with personality (Compton, Anglin, Khalsa-Denison, & Paredes, 1996). Intense molecular genetic research on psychopathology is likely to identify other genes that are also relevant to personality (Plomin et al., 1997).

Moreover, two new techniques will take allelic association beyond examining a few "candidate" genes. One technique, called DNA pooling, makes it possible to screen the genome systematically for allelic association using thousands of closely spaced DNA markers (Daniels et al., 1998). DNA pooling combines DNA from all individuals within a group (for example, individuals high on a particular personality trait) and comparing this pooled DNA to DNA pooled from another group (individuals low on the personality trait). The pooled DNA for the two groups can be genotyped and compared as if they were just two individuals. In terms of genotyping effort, in a study of 200 highs and 200 lows, DNA pooling requires only two genotypings per marker rather than 400 genotypings. This means that 3,500 markers needed for a systematic genome screen will require only 7,000 genotypings as compared to 1,400,000 genotypings if traditional individual genotyping were used. DNA pooling is only relevant when selected groups are investigated, such as groups high and low on a personality trait. Unselected samples require individual genotyping because there are no groups to compare.

A second advance will make it even more feasible to conduct a systematic genome scan for allelic association. It is called "DNA chip" technology because it integrates DNA analysis with the electronic circuits of silicon "chips" (Livak, Marmaro, & Todd, 1995). DNA chips the size of a credit card can genotype thousands of DNA markers in a few minutes with a few drops of blood from an individual. Combining DNA chips with DNA pooling means that an entire genome scan for allelic association can be conducted for a particular personality trait in a few minutes.

Using QTLs Associated with Personality

The pace of molecular genetics research leads us to predict that by the turn of the century personality researchers will routinely use DNA markers as a tool in their research. This is a safe prediction because it is already happening in research on dementia and cognitive decline in the elderly. In 1993, a gene on chromosome 19 called apolipoprotein E was found to predict risk for the cognitive decline of late-onset Alzheimer's disease (Corder et al., 1993), a finding replicated in scores of studies. If one copy of a particular allele of the apolipoprotein E gene is inherited, risk for late-onset dementia is about five times greater as compared to other alleles. It has quickly become standard practice for research on cognitive decline in the elderly to take advantage of the genetic risk information provided by the DNA marker for apolipoprotein E. This has happened even for researchers who are primarily interested in psychosocial risk mechanisms because they are now able to study gene-environment interaction and correlation using measured genotypes.

Although it is difficult and expensive to find genes associated with complex traits, it is relatively easy and inexpensive to use genes once they have been identified. For example, blood is no longer needed to obtain DNA. Simply rubbing a Q-tip on the inside of the mouth provides enough DNA to genotype hundreds of DNA markers. This also means that DNA can be obtained by mail and that parents can collect it from their children (Freeman, Ball, Powell, Craig, & Plomin, 1997). Once DNA is extracted, it can be stored indefinitely until genes of interest are identified. Costs for materials and labor in extracting DNA and genotyping DNA markers are surprisingly low. Extracting DNA costs about $5 per subject, which means that the one-time cost for extracting DNA in a study of 500 individuals would be about $2,500. Obtaining DNA would seem to be an investment well worth while for any valuable sample because it puts the researcher in a position to analyze any relevant genes as soon as they are identified. If a commercial company is used, these costs could be ten times higher; however, collaboration with a molecular genetics colleague, for whom such assays are routine, could reduce the costs considerably.

The message is that, although few personality researchers will join the hunt for genes, it is crucial that the field be prepared to use genes as they are found. How can personality researchers use DNA in their research once genes are found to be associated with behavior? For molecular geneticists, the agenda is clear: Find genes, clone them, and then characterize how they work at a molecular level of analysis. For personality researchers, DNA associated with personality can be used to investigate psychological levels of analysis. The simple answer is that personality researchers can incorporate a relevant gene into whatever topic they are already studying. For example, regardless of whether a personality researcher is studying the factorial structure of personality, the relationship between personality and psychopathology, or attribution theory, the research can be extended in an exciting new direction simply by asking whether the gene is associated with the phenomenon of interest.

In addition to producing even more compelling evidence of genetic influence on personality, the identification of QTLs will revolutionize genetic research on personality by providing measured genotypes for tracking the developmental course of genetic effects, for investigating genetic links between personality and psychopathology and between personality and biological mechanisms, and for identifying interactions and correlations between genotype and environment (Plomin & Caspi, 1998).

Developmental Questions

A developmental approach to the study of individual differences seeks to answer questions about the origins of personality differences as well about change and continuity in personality over time. QTLs are clearly relevant to questions about the origins of personality traits in that they specify genetic etiology. In addition, QTLs for personality are important for studying developmental continuities. Traditionally, in most longitudinal research, psychologists have studied homotypic continuities—the continuity of similar behaviors or phenotypic attributes over time. One of the most obvious developmental questions for a QTL association is the earliest age at which the association can be found for homotypic phenotypes. For example, how early in development does DRD4 relate to Novelty-Seeking behaviors? But development is more complex because personality traits may change their expression over time and situations. As such, it is important to enlarge the definition of continuity to include heterotypic continuity—the continuity of diverse behaviors that are presumed to belong to the same equivalence class. However, it is difficult to identify heterotypic continuity because we have few clues as to what unites diverse behaviors over time. Although genetic effects may change over time, QTLs provide a compass to explore heterotypic continuity. Using DRD4 as an example, is there heterotypic continuity in development in the sense that DRD4 is associated with different behaviors at different points in development? For instance, does DRD4 relate to irritability and low soothability in infancy, or with low behavioral inhibition in early childhood, or with sexual adventurousness in adolescence? In this way, QTLs can be used to expand developmental theories that have, for the most part, only focused on homotypic continuities.

Multivariate Questions

The category of multivariate questions is huge, including such topics as relations between and within personality traits, relations between personality traits and biological processes, and relations between personality and psychopathology. These are multivariate questions in the sense that they focus on covariance among traits rather than on the variance of a single trait.

Relations between and within Personality Traits

The etiology of relations between and within traits can be investigated using measured genotypes. For example, DRD4 may be more strongly associated with certain facets of Novelty Seeking than others—disinhibition, thrill seeking, experience seeking, or boredom susceptibility (Zuckerman, 1994). In relation to hyperactivity, DRD4 may be primarily associated with a Novelty-Seeking component rather than the traditional components of attention or hyperactivity.

The possibility that such research will demonstrate genetic heterogeneity is exciting because, in the case of hyperactivity, such results can lead to differential diagnosis and then to differential prevention and treatment. However, the research on DRD4 mentioned earlier points in the opposite direction, toward more diffuse effects. That is, DRD4 has been reported to be associated not just with Novelty Seeking and hyperactivity but also with opioid dependence, panic disorder, Tourette syndrome, and major depressive disorder. This suggests that genetic processes related to dopamine are shared in common across these diverse behaviors, which is supported by recent research that suggests that dopamine is not only involved in signalling pleasure but it is involved in attention in the sense of highlighting significant stimuli.

More generally, the finding that the same genes are associated with different behaviors raises the possibility that correlations between different personality traits, as well as correlations between different psychiatric disorders (i.e., comorbidity), are accounted for by similar genetic effects. In this way, phenotypic structural models of personality, as well as the structure of phenotypic psychopathology, may be refined and elaborated by the discovery of QTLs.

Biological Mechanisms between Genes and Personality

A second multivariate issue involves the biological pathways between genes and personality. These multivariate relations can be viewed in terms of levels of analysis from basic cellular mechanisms through neurotransmitter systems, through global brain functioning. Molecular geneticists work from the gene to cellular mechanisms, to neural systems, and eventually to behavior. Biopsychologists work in the opposite direction, from behavior to brain functioning, to neurotransmitters, and eventually to gene products. Neuroscientists tend to be in the middle, working back toward genes and forward toward behavior. These different levels and directions of analysis will eventually have to connect, as is beginning to happen in cognitive neuroscience. Finding specific genes involved in these complex pathways between genes and personality will provide discrete windows through which everyone will peer.

Links between Personality and Psychopathology

A third multivariate issue is the relation between personality dimensions of normal variation and psychopathology (Krueger, Caspi, Moffitt, Silva, & McGee, 1996). Multivariate quantitative genetic methods have been used to determine the extent to which the etiologies of normal and abnormal variation overlap. For example, one study showed that most of the observed correlation between the personality trait of Neuroticism and the liability to a diagnosis of major depression was attributable to genetic factors involved in both Neuroticism and major depression (Kendler, Neale, Kessler, Heath, & Eaves, 1993a). QTLs can be used to advance such etiological research by testing the hypothesis that QTLs associated with Neuroticism are also associated with major depression.

Questions about Gene–Environment Interplay

A third use of genes associated with personality is to study the interplay between nature and nurture (Rutter et al., 1997). This interplay can be considered under the general categories of interaction and correlation. Although psychologists tend to think of the environment in terms of psychosocial factors, the environment can of course be investigated at many levels, from cells to celestial bodies. Moreover, environmental factors can be considered in terms of constructed perceptions rather than objective events. However, these and many other important issues related to experience are beyond the scope of this paper (Plomin, 1994).

Gene–Environment Interaction

Gene–environment interaction refers to genetic differences in sensitivity to experiences. For example, psychosocial risk may have a greater effect on individuals who are at genetic risk. Using DRD4 and Novelty Seeking as an example, drug-experimenting peers might be a greater risk for drug abuse for individuals who have a long-repeat DRD4 allele. This is the general form of interactions suggested by the diathesis-stress model of psychopathology: Individuals who are at genetic risk (diathesis) are most sensitive to environmental risk (stress), and to environmental opportunities as well, as suggested in the previous example of the possible influences of peers who use drugs. At present, we know a great deal more about person–environment interactions than we do about how specific genes interact with environmental stressors and opportunities to shape behavioral outcomes. QTLs can advance environmental research by providing information about diatheses.

Gene–Environment Correlation

Gene–environment correlation refers to genetic differences in exposure to environments, literally a correlation between genes and environment. That is, genetic dispositions may be correlated with experiential dispositions. For example, individuals with DRD4 long-repeat alleles might select, and be selected by, thrill-seeking peers. The processes by which such gene–environment correlations develop have been categorized as passive, evocative, or active (Plomin, DeFries, & Loehlin, 1977; Scarr & McCartney, 1983). Children with a 7-repeat allele of DRD4 might experience more chaotic family environments because they passively receive both long-repeat alleles and chaotic family environments from their parents, whose own Novelty Seeking leads to a less ordered family life. Children with a 7-repeat allele of DRD4 might also evoke from people within and outside the family reactions that are correlated with the children's Novelty-Seeking propensities. For example, intrepid children with a 7-repeat allele of DRD4 might be allowed to do things, such as flying unaccompanied on an airplane, that parents of more inhibited children would not consider. Finally, and perhaps most importantly, gene–environment correlations can arise by children's active selection, modification, and construction of their environments, as in the example of selecting thrill-seeking peers. Active gene–environment correlation includes constructed realities consistent with the shift in psychology toward cognitive construction of experience, which views "human experience [as] the construction of reality, not a property of a physical world that imparts the same experience to everyone who encounters it" (Scarr, 1992, p. 5). An interesting developmental hypothesis concerning gene–environment correlation is that evocative and active forms of gene–environment correlation become more important as children experience environments outside the family and begin to play a more active role in the selection and construction of their experiences (Scarr & McCartney, 1983). Based on this hypothesis, DRD4 might be expected to be associated with passive aspects of experience in early childhood, but, later in development, DRD4 might be increasingly associated with active experience.

The topic of gene–environment correlation goes beyond describing and explaining a correlation between genotype and environment. The larger issue involves the environmental mechanisms by which gene–behavior associations develop (Rutter et al., 1997). In terms of the distinction between moderators and mediators (Baron & Kenny, 1986), the association between DRD4 and Novelty Seeking can be mediated by experience in the sense that long-repeat alleles of DRD4 increase exposure to experiences that in turn increase the likelihood of Novelty Seeking.

We predict that tracing the developmental pathways between specific genes and personality through environmental mechanisms is likely to be one of the most important advances that emerges from applications of specific genes associated with personality. Moreover, even personality researchers who are strictly interested in socialization in the family, for example, will profit from genotyping children for specific genes associated with personality in order to control for the effects of those genes, although we also predict that they will be seduced into examining interactions and correlations between family environment and genes.

These three categories of questions—developmental, multivariate, and environmental—serve as a general framework for how personality researchers can use gene–behavior associations once they are found. Many other questions can of course be asked. For example, for any of these categories of questions, additional questions can be asked about group differences. For instance, does the association between DRD4 and Novelty Seeking differ for boys and girls or for different cultures?

Ethical Issues

This new knowledge about specific genes may create new problems as well, such as problems of labeling and ensuing educational and employment discrimination. It also raises fears, such as concerns about using DNA markers prenatally to select "designer babies," and more generally, concerns about free will. However, some of these concerns are based on misunderstandings about genetics (Rutter & Plomin, 1997). For example, QTL associations with complex traits, such as personality, are often confused with the hard-wired genetic determination of single-gene effects in which a single gene is necessary and sufficient. QTL effects are probabilistic and their effect sizes are usually small. Another common confusion is that if genetic effects are found, there is nothing that can be done about it environmentally. The opposite may be the case, as in the classic example of phenylketonuria (PKU), the single-gene cause of a type of mental retardation. When the genetic cause of PKU was understood, an effective environmental intervention—not genetic engineering or eugenics—was designed that prevents the onset of mental retardation. A third confusion is that genetic differences are often thought of in terms of "good" and "bad" genes. DNA differences that make a difference in behavior may be bad for certain behaviors and certain contexts and good for other behaviors and contexts. For example, DRD4 long-repeat alleles may be bad if they increase risk for drug addiction, but they may be good if they contribute to intellectual risk taking that leads to innovation.

Lurking in the shadows is the pervasive fear that genetic differences undermine the foundations of democracy. This confusion comes from thinking that to say that everyone is created equal is the same as saying that people do not differ genetically. The founding fathers of America were not so naive as to think that all people are created *identical*. The essence of a democracy is that all people should have legal equality *despite* their genetic differences. It is not the case that we are all identical genetically except for a few rogue genes that make some of us different. There are millions of DNA sequences that differ in our species; genetic variation is the fundamental natural resource of our species. Recognition of, and respect for, individual differences is essential to the ethic of individual worth.

The benefits of identifying genes seem likely to far outweigh the potential abuses (Rutter & Plomin, 1997). Although the benefits seem to be primarily for basic understanding of the origins of personality and its developmental processes, it holds out the hope that environmental interventions, and especially preventions, can be developed that are especially effective for personality problems. Despite the problems created by such advances in science, it would be a mistake, and futile as well, to try to cut off the flow of knowledge and its benefits in order to avoid having to confront new problems.

CONCLUSIONS

Although molecular genetic attempts to identify specific genes responsible for the heritability of personality are exciting, much remains to be done using more traditional quantitative genetic designs that consider environmental as well as genetic factors. Most notably, behavioral genetic research has scarcely begun to be incorporated in the "New Look" in personality research that emerged after the 1970s, the "decade of doubt" (West, 1983). These include several broad perspectives on personality described in this handbook: evolution (Buss, Chapter 2), psychoanalysis (Westen & Gabbard, Chapter 3), social cognition (Bandura, Chapter 6), interactions (Mischel & Shoda, Chapter 7; Magnusson, Chapter 8), neuroscience (Pickering & Gray, Chapter 10), and social and cultural perspectives (Baumeister, Chapter 14; Cross & Markus, Chapter 15). Most of the specific content chapters other than temperament and emotion, remain untouched by behavioral genetics.

The ratio between what is known and what is not yet known about genetics and personality is very small. One reason for this is that there is so much to be learned from the application of behavioral genetics to personality—a goal of this chapter was to show that behavioral genetics has more to offer the field of personality than heritability estimates. Nonetheless, the past decade has seen some substantial additions to the numerator of this ratio. We predict that in the 21st century, as observers look back on personality research during the 20th century, they will see behavioral genetics as a source of some of the field's most novel and important discoveries.

ACKNOWLEDGMENTS

This work was supported in part by the U.S. National Institute of Child Health (HD35763) and the U.S. National Institute of Mental Health (MH49414). This chapter reviews materials available to us through May 1998.

REFERENCES

Ahern, F. M., Johnson, R. C., Wilson, J. R., McClearn, G. E., & Vandenbergh, S. G. (1982) Family resemblences in personality. *Behavior Genetics, 12,* 261–280.

Allport, G. W. (1937). *Personality: A psychological interpretation.* New York: Holt.

Annas, P. (1997). *Fears, phobias, and the inheritance of learning.* Unpublished manuscript, Department of Psychology, Uppsala University, Uppsaka, Sweden.

Asghari, V., Sanyal, S., Buchwaldt, S., Paterson, A., Jovanovic, V., & Van Tol, H. H. M. (1995). Modulation of intracellular cyclic AMP levels by different human dopamine D4 receptor variants. *Journal of Neurochemistry, 65,* 1157–1165.

Asghari, V., Schoots, O., VanKats, S., Ohara, K., Jovanovic, V., Guan, H. C , Bunzow, J. R., Petronis, A., & Van Tol, H. H. M. (1994). Dopamine D4 receptor repeat: analysis of different native and mutant forms of the human and rat genes. *Molecular Pharmacology, 46,* 364–373.

Asherson, P., Curran, S., Simonoff, E., & Taylor, E. (1997). Candidate gene studies in attention deficit hyperactivity disorder. *American Journal of Medical Genetics (Neuropsychiatric Genetics), 74,* 631.

Bailey, J. N., Palmer, C. G. S., Ramsey, C., Cantwell, D., Kim, K., Woodward, J. A., McGough, J., Asarnow, J. A., Asarnow, R. F., Nelson, S., & Smalley, S. L. (1997). DRD4 gene and susceptibility to attention deficit hyperactivity disorder: Differences in familial and sporadic cases. *American Journal of Medical Genetics (Neuropsychiatric Genetics), 74,* 623.

Ball, D., Hill, L., Freeman, B., Eley, T. C., Strelau, J., Riemann, R., Spinath, F. M., Angleitner, A., & Plomin, R. (1997). The serotonin transporter gene and peer-rated neuroticism. *NeuroReport, 8*(5), 1301–1304.

Baron, R. M., & Kenny, D. A. (1986). The moderator–mediator variable distinction in social psychological research: Conceptual, strategic, and statistical considerations. *Journal of Personality and Social Psychology, 51*(6), 1173–1182.

Beer, J. M., & Rose, R. J. (1995). The five factors of personality [Abstract]. *Behavior Genetics, 25,* 254.

Benjamin, J., Gulman, R., Osher, Y., Segman, R., & Ebstein, R. (1997). Dopamine D4 receptor polymorphism associated with panic disorder [Abstract]. *American Journal of Medical Genetics (Neuropsychiatric Genetics), 74,* 613.

Benjamin, J., Li, L., Patterson, C., Greenburg, B. D., Murphy, D. L., & Hammer, D. H. (1996). Population and familial association between the D4 dopamine receptor gene and measures of novelty seeking. *Nature Genetics, 12,* 81–84.

Bergeman, C. S., Chipuer, H. M., Plomin, R., Pedersen, N. L., McClearn, G. E., Nesselroade, J. R., Costa, P. T., & McCrae, R. R. (1993). Genetic and environmental effects on openness to experience, agreeableness, and conscientiousness: An adoption/twin study. *Journal of Personality, 61,* 159–179.

Bergeman, C. S., Plomin, R., Pedersen, N. L., McClearn, G. E., & Nesselroade, J. R. (1990). Genetic and environmental influences on social support: The Swedish Adoption/Twin Study of Aging. *Journal of Gerontology, 45*(3), 101–106.

Braungart, J. M., Fulker, D. W., & Plomin, R. (1992). Genetic influence of the home environment during infancy: A sibling adoption study of the HOME. *Developmental Psychology, 28,* 1048–1055.

Braungart, J. M., Plomin, R., DeFries, J. C., & Fulker, D. W. (1992). Genetic influence on tester-rated infant temperament as assessed by Bayley's Infant Behavior Record: Nonadoptive and adoptive siblings and twins. *Developmental Psychology, 28,* 40–47.

Brody, N., & Crowley, M. J. (1995). Environmental (and genetic) influences on personality and intelligence. In D. Saklofske & M. Zeidner (Eds.), *International handbook of personality and intelligence* (pp. 59–80). New York: Plenum Press.

Caspi, A. (1998). Personality development across the life course. In W. Damon & N. Eisenberg (Eds.), *Handbook of child psychology: Vol. 3. Social, emotional, and personality development* (pp. 311–388). New York: Wiley.

Caspi, A., Herbener, E. S., & Ozer, D. J. (1992). Shared experiences and the similarities of personalities: A longitudinal study of married couples. *Journal of Personality and Social Psychology, 62* , 281–291.

Castellanos, F. X., Lau, E., Tayebi, N., Lee, P., Long, R. E., Giedd, J. N., Shjarp, W., Marsh, W. L., Rapoport, J. L., & Sidransky, E. (1997). Evidence that a D4DR*7R dopamine receptor polymorphism is not correlated with attention-deficit/hyperactivity disorder. *American Journal of Medical Genetics (Neuropsychiatric Genetics), 74,* 623.

Cattell, R. B. (1982). *The inheritance of personality and ability.* New York: Academic Press.

Cherny, S. S., Fuiles, D. W., Corley, R. P., Plomin, R., & DeFRies, J. C. (1994). Continuity and change in infant shyness from 14 to 20 months. *Behavior Genetics, 24,* 365–379.

Chipuer, H. M., Plomin, R., Pedersen, N. L., McClearn, G. E., & Nesselroade, J. R. (1993). Genetic influence on family environment: The role of personality. *Developmental Psychology, 29,* 110–118.

Cloninger, C. R. (1997). Quantitative trait loci for personality in families of alcoholics [Abstract]. *American Journal of Medical Genetics (Neuropsychiatric Genetics), 74,* 579.

Cloninger, C. R., Adolfsson, R., & Svrakic, D. M. (1996). Mapping genes for human personality. *Nature Genetics, 12,* 3–4.

Cloninger, C. R., Svrakic, D. M., & Przybeck, T. R. (1993). A psychobiological model of temperament and character. *Archives of General Psychiatry, 50,* 975–990.

Cohen, J. (1988). *Statistical power analysis for the behavioral sciences* (2nd ed.). Hillsdale, NJ: Erlbaum.

Compton, P. A., Anglin, M. D., Khalsa-Denison, M. E., & Paredes, A. (1996). The D2 dopamine receptor gene, addiction, and personality: Clinical correlates in cocaine abusers. *Biological Psychiatry, 39,* 302–304.

Corder, E. H., Saunders, A. M., Strittmatter, W. J., Schmechel, D. E., Gaskell, P. C., Small, G. W., RToses, A. D., Haines, J. L., & Pericak Vance, M. A. (1993). Gene dose of apolipoprotein E type 4 allele and the risk of Alzheimer's disease in late onset families. *Science, 261,* 921–923.

Costa, P. T. J., & McCrae, R. R. (1992). *The Revised NEO Personality Inventory (NEO PI-R).* Odessa, FL: Psychological Assessment Resources.

Daniels, D., Dunn, J., Furstenberg, F. F., Jr., & Plomin, R. (1985). Environmental differences within the family and adjustment differences within pairs of adolescent siblings. *Child Development, 56,* 764–774.

Daniels, J., Holmans, P., Williams, N., Turic, D., McGuffin, P., Plimin, R., & Owen, M. J. (1998). A simple method for analysing microsatellite allele image patterns generated from DNA pools and its application to allelic assoication studies. *American Journal of Human Genetics, 62,* 1189–1197.

Dunn, J., & Plomin, R. (1986). Determinants of maternal behavior toward three-year-old siblings. *British Journal of Developmental Psychology, 4,* 127–137.

Dunn, J., & Plomin, R. (1990). *Separate lives: Why siblings are so different.* New York: Basic Books.

Eaves, L. J., Eysenck, H., & Martin, N. G. (1989). *Genes, culture, and personality: An empirical approach.* London: Academic Press.

Ebstein, R. P., & Belmaker, R. H. (1997). Saga of an adventure gene: Novelty Seeking, substance abuse and the dopamine D4 receptor (D4DR) exon III repeat polymorphism. *Molecular Psychiatry, 2,* 381–384.

Ebstein, R. P., Nemanov, L., Klotz, I., Gritsenko, I., & Belmaker, R. H. (1997). Additional evidence for an association beween the dopamine D4 receptor (D4DR) exon III repeat polymorphism and the human personality trait of Novelty Seeking. *Molecular Psychiatry, 2,* 472–477.

Ebstein, R. P., Novick, O., Umansky, R., Priel, B., Osher, Y., Blaine, D., Bennet, E. R., Nemanov, L., Katz, M., & Belmaker, R. H. (1996). Dopamine D4 receptor (D4DR) exon III polymorphism associated with the human personality trait Novelty Seeking. *Nature Genetics, 12,* 78–80.

Ebstein, R. P., Serman, R., Benjamin, J., Osher, Y., Nemanov, L., & Belmaker, R. H. (1997). 5-HT2c (HTR2C) serotonin receptor gene polymorphism associated with the human personality trait of reward dependence: interaction with dopamine 4 receptor (D4DR) and dopamine D3 (D3DR) polymorphisms. *American Journal of Medical Genetics (Neuropsychiatric Genetics), 74,* 65–72.

Emde, R. N., Plomin, R., Robinson, J., Reznick, J. S., Campos, J., Corley, R., DeFries, J. C., Fulker, D. W., Kagan, J., & Zahn Waxler, C. (1992). Temperament, emotion, and cognition at 14 months: The MacArthur Longitudinal Twin Study. *Child Development, 63,* 1437–1445.

Falconer, D. S., & MacKay, T. F. C. (1996). *Introduction to quantitative genetics* (4th ed.). Harlow, UK: Longman.

Finkel, D., & McGue, M. (1997). Sex differences and nonadditivity in heritability of the Multidimensional Personality Questionnaire Scales. *Journal of Personality and Social Psychology, 72*(4), 929–938.

Frankel, W., & Schork, N. J. (1996). Who's afraid of epistasis? *Nature Genetics,* 14, 371–373.

Freeman, B., Ball, D., Powell, J., Craig, I., & Plomin, R. (1997). DNA by mail: The usefulness of cheek scrappings. *Behavior Genetics, 27,* 251–257.

Galton, F. (1865). Heredity talent and character. *Macmillan's Magazine, 12,* 157–166, 318–327.

Ge, X., Conger, R. D., Cadoret, R. J., Neiderhiser, J. M., Yates, W., Troughton, E., & Stewart, M. A. (1996). The developmental interface between nature and nurture: A mutual influence model of child antisocial behaviour and parenting. *Developmental Psychology, 32,* 574–589.

Gebhardt, C., Füreder, Th., Fuchs, K., Urmann, A., Gerhard, E., Heiden, A., STompe, T., Fathi, N., Meszaros, K., Hornik, K., Sieghart, W., Kasper, S., & Aschauer, H. N. (1997, October 19–23). *No evidence for normal personality traits related to dopamine 4 receptor gene polymorphism.* Paper presented at the 1997 World Congress on Psychiatric Genetics, Santa Fe, NM.

Gelernter, J., Kranzler, H., Coccaro, E., Siever, L., New, A., & Mulgrew, C. L. (1997). D4 dopamine-receptor (DRD4) alleles and novelty seeking in substance-dependent, personaltiy disorder, and control subjects. *American Journal of Human Genetics, 61,* 1144–1152.

Goldsmith, H. H. (1983). Genetic inflences on personality from infancy to adulthood. *Child Development, 54,* 331–355.

Goldsmith, H. H. (1993). Nature–nurture and the development of personality: Introduction. In R. Plomin & G. E. McClearn (Eds.), *Nature, nurture, and psychology* (pp. 155–160). Washington, DC: American Psychological Association.

Goldsmith, H. H., Buss, K. A., & Lemery, K. S. (1997). Toddler and childhood temperament: Expanded content, stronger genetic evidence, new evidence for the importance of environment. *Developmental Psychology, 33,* 891–905.

Goldsmith, H. H., & Campos, J. J. (1986). Fundamental issues in the study of early development: The Denver twin temperament study. In M. E. Lamb, A. L. Brown, & B. Rogoff (Eds.), *Advances in developmental psychology* (pp. 231–283). Hillsdale, NJ: Erlbaum.

Goldsmith, H. H., & Gottesman, I. I. (1981). Origins of variation in behavioral style: A longitudinal study of temperament in young twins. *Child Development, 52,* 91–103.

Goldsmith, H. H., Lemery, K. S., Buss, K. A., & Campos, J. (in press). Biometric models of infant temperament. *Behavior Genetics.*

Grice, D. E., Leckman, J. F., Pauls, D. L., Kurlan, R., Kidd, K. K., Pakstis, A. J., Chang, F. M., Buxbaum, J. D., Cohen, D. J., Gelernter, J. (1996). Linkage disequilibrium between an allele at the dopamine D4 receptor locus and Tourette syndrome, by the transmission disequilibrium test. *American Journal of Human Genetics, 59,* 644–652.

Hamer, D. (1997). The search for personality genes: Adventures of a molecular biologist. *Current Directions in Psychological Science,* 6, 111–114.

Hamer, D., & Copeland, P. (1998). *Living with our genes.* New York: Doubleday.

Harris, J. R. (1995). Where is the child's environment? A group socialization theory of development. *Psychological Review, 102,* 458–489.

Heath, A. C., Neale, M. C., Kessler, R. C., Eaves, L. J., & Kendler, K. S. (1992). Evidence for genetic influences on personality from self-reports and informant ratings. *Journal of Social and Personality Psychology, 63,* 85–96.

Hershberger, S. L., Lichtenstein, P., & Knox, S. S. (1994). Genetic and environmental influences on perceptions of organizational climate. *Journal of Applied Psychology, 79,* 24–33.

Hetherington, E. M., & Clingempeel, W. G. (1992). Coping with marital transitions: A family systems perspective. *Monographs of the Society for Research in Child Development, 2* (3, Serial No. 227).

Hetherington, E. M., Reiss, D., & Plomin, R. (1994). *Separate social worlds of siblings: The impact of nonshared environment on development.* Hillsdale, NJ: Erlbaum.

Hoffman, L. W. (1991). The influence of the family environment on personality: Accounting for sibling differences. *Psychological Bulletin, 110,* 187–203.

Jang, K. L., Livesley, W. J., & Vernon, P. A. (1996). Heritability of the Big Five dimensions and their facets: A twin study [Abstract]. *Journal of Personality, 64,* 577–591.

Jönsson, E., Nöthen, M. M. Gustavsson, J. P., Neidt, H., Brené, S., Tylec, A., Propping, P., & Sedvall, G. C. (1997). Lack of evidence for allelic association between personality traits and the dopamine D4 receptor gene polymorphisms. *American Journal of Psychiatry, 154,* 697–699.

Kendler, K. (1977). Social support: A genetic–epidemiological analysis. *American Journal of Psychiatry, 154*(Oct), 1398–1414.

Kendler, K. S. (1996). Parenting: A genetic–epidemiologic perspective. *American Journal of Psychiatry, 153*(1), 11–20.

Kendler, K. S., Neale, M. C., Kessler, R. C., Heath, A. C., & Eaves, L. J. (1992). Childhood parental loss and adult psychopathology in women: A twin study perspective. *Archives of General Psychiatry, 49*(2), 109–116.

Kendler, K. S., Neale, M. C., Kessler, R. C., Heath, A. C., & Eaves, L. J. (1993a). A longitudinal twin study of personality and major depression in women. *Archives of General Psychiatry, 50,* 853–862.

Kendler, K. S., Neale, M. C., Kessler, R. C., Heath, A. C., & Eaves, L. J. (1993b). A twin study of recent life events and difficulties. *Archives of General Psychiatry, 50,* 789–796.

Kessler, R. C., Kendler, K. S., Heath, A. C., Neale, M. C., & Eaves, L. J. (1992). Social support, depressed mood, and adjustment to stress: A genetic epidemiologic investigation. *Journal of Personality and Social Psychology, 62*(2), 257–272.

Kotler, M., Cohen, H., Serman, R., Gritsenko, I., Nemanov, L., Lerer, B., Kramer, I., Zer-Zion, M., Kletz, I., & Ebstein, R. P. (1997). Excess dopamine D4 receptor (*D4DR*) exon III seven repeat allele in opioid-dependent subjects. *Molecular Psychiatry, 2,* 251–254.

Krueger, R. F., Caspi, A., Moffitt, T. E., Silva, A., & McGee, R. (1996). Personality traits are differentially linked to mental disorders: A multitrait–multidiagnosis study of an adolescent birth cohort. *Journal of Abnormal Psychology, 105,* 299–312.

LaHoste, G. J., Swanson, J. M., Wigal, S. B., Glabe, C., Wigal, T., King, N., & Kennedy, J. L. (1996). Dopamine D4 receptor gene polymorphism is associated with attention deficit hyperactivity disorder. *Molecular Psychiatry, 1,* 121–124.

Lerman, C., Coporaso, N., Main, D., Audrain, J., Boyd, N. R., Bowman, E. D., & Shields, P. G. (1998). Depression and self-medication with nicotine: The modifying influence of the dopamine D4 receptor gene. *Health Psychology, 17*(1), 56–62.

Lesch, K. P., Bengel, D., Heils, A., Sabol, S. Z., Greenburg, B. D., Petri, S., Benjamin, J., Müller, C. R., Hamer, D. H., & Murphy, D. L. (1996). Association of anxiety-related traits with a polymorphism in the serotonin transporter gene regulatory region. *Science, 274,* 1527–1531.

Li, T., Xu, K., Deng, H., Cai, G., Liu, J., Liu, X., Wang, R., Xiang, X., Zhao, J., Murray, R. M., Sham, P. C., & Collier, D. A. (1997). Association analysis of the dopamine D4 gene exon III VNTR and heroin abuse in Chinese subjects. *Molecular Psychiatry, 2,* 413–416.

Livak, K. J., Marmaro, J., & Todd, J. A. (1995). Towards fully automated genome-wide polymorphism screening. *Nature Genetics,* 9, 341–342.

Loehlin, J. C. (1992). *Genes and environment in personality development.* Newbury Park, CA: Sage.

Loehlin, J. C. (1998). *Genes and environment in personality and development.* Newbury Park, CA: Sage.

Loehlin, J. C., Horn, J. M., & Willerman, L. (1981). Personality resemblance in adoptive familes. *Behavior Genetics, 11,* 309–330.

Loehlin, J. C., & Nicholls, J. (1976). *Heredity, environment and personality.* Austin: University of Texas.

Loehlin, J. C., Horn, J. M., & Willerman, L. (1990). Heredity, environment, and personality change: Evidence from the Texas Adoption Study. *Journal of Personality, 58,* 221–243.

Loehlin, J. C., Willerman, L., & Horn, J. M. (1982). Personality resemblances between unwed mothers and their adopted-away offspring. *Journal of Personality and Social Psychology, 42,* 1089–1099.

Losoya, S. H., Callor, S., Rowe, D. C., & Goldsmith, H. H. (1997). Origins of familial similarity in parenting: A study of twins and adoptive siblings. *Developmental Psychology, 33,* 1012–1023.

Lyons, M. J., Goldberg, J., Eisen, S. A., True, W., Tsuang, M. T., Meyer, J. M., & Henderson, W. G. (1993). Do genes influence exposure to trauma: A twin study of combat. *American Journal of Medical Genetics (Neuropsychiatric Genetics), 48,* 22–27.

Lytton, H. (1977). Do parents create or respond to differences in twins? *Developmental Psychology, 13,* 456–459.

Lytton, H. (1980). *Parent–child interaction: The socialization process observed in twin and singleton families.* New York: Plenum Press.

Malhotra, A. K., Virkkunen, M., Rooney, W., Eggert, M., Linnoila, M., & Goldman, D. (1996). The association between the dopamine D4 receptor (*D4DR*) 16 amino acid repeat polymorphism and Novelty Seeking. *Molecular Psychiatry, 1,* 388–391.

Manke, B., McGuire, S., Reiss, D., Hetherington, E. M., & Plomin, R. (1995). Genetic contributions to adolescents' extrafamilial social interactions: Teachers, best friends, and peers. *Social Development, 4*(3), 238–256.

Matheny, A. P., Jr. (1980). Bayley's Infant Behavioral Record: Behavioral components and twin analysis. *Child Development, 51,* 1157–1167.

Matheny, A. P., Jr. (1989). Children's behavioral inhibition over age and across situations: Genetic similarity for a trait during change. *Journal of Personality, 57*(2), 215–235.

McGue, M., Bacon, S., & Lykken, D. T. (1993). Personality stability and change in early adulthood: A behavioral genetic analysis. *Developmental Psychology, 29,* 96–109.

McGue, M., & Lykken, D. T. (1992). Genetic influence on risk of divorce. *Psychological Science, 3,* 368–373.

McGuffin, P., Katz, R., & Rutherford, J. (1991). Nature, nurture and depression: A twin study. *Psychological Medicine, 21*(2), 329–335.

McGuire, S., Dunn, J., & Plomin, R. (1995). Maternal differential treatment of siblings and children's behavioral problems: A longitudinal study. *Development and Psychopathology, 7,* 515–528.

Meehl, P. E. (1986). What social scientists don't understand. In D. W. Fiske & R. A. Shweder (Eds.), *Metatheory in social science* (pp. 315–338). Chicago: University of Chicago Press.

Mel, H., Kramer, I., Gritsenko, I., Kotler, M., & Ebstein, R. P. (1997). *Association between dopamine D4 receptor (D4DR) exon III repeat polymorphism and drug abuse.* Manuscript in preparation.

Moffitt, T. E. (1991). *An approach to organizing the task of selecting measures for longitudinal research (Tech. Rep.).* Madison: University of Wisconsin.

Neale, M. C., & Stevenson, J. (1989). Rater bias in the EASI temperament scales: A twin study. *Journal of Personality and Social Psychology, 56,* 446–455.

Neiderhiser, J. M. (1994). Family environment in early childhood, outcomes in middle childhood, and genetic mediation. In R. Plomin & D. W. Fulker (Eds.), *Nature and nurture in middle childhood* (pp. 249–261). Cambridge, MA: Blackwell.

Nigg, J. T., & Goldsmith, H. H. (1998). Developmental psychopathology, personality, and temperament: Reflections on recent behavior genetic research. *Human Biology, 70,* 387–412.

Noble, E. P. (1996). The gene that rewards alcoholism. *Scientific American (Science and Medicine), 2,* 52–61.

O'Connor, T. G., Hetherington, E. M., Reiss, D., & Plomin, R. (1995). A twin-sibling study of observed parent–adolescent interactions. *Child Development, 66,* 812–829.

Ono, Y., Manki, H., Yoshimura, K., Muramatsu, T., Higuchi, S., Yagi, G., Kanba, S., & Asai, M. (1997). Association between dopamine D4 receptor (D4DR) exon III polymorphism and Novelty Seeking in Japanese subjects. *American Journal of Medical Genetics (Neuropsychiatric Genetics), 74,* 501–503.

Owen, M. J., Holmans, P., & McGuffin, P. (1997). Association studies in psychiatric genetics. *Molecular Psychiatry, 2,* 270–273.

Pedersen, N. L., Plomin, R., McClearn, G. E., & Fribereg, L. (1998). Neuroticism Extraversion, and related traits in adult twins reared apart and reared together. *Journal of Personality and Social Psychology, 55, 950–957.*

Perusse, D., Neale, M. C., Heath, A. C., & Eaves, L. J. (1992). Human parental behavior: Evidence for genetic influence and implications for gene-culture transmission [Abstract]. *Behavior Genetics, 22,* 744–745.

Phillips, K., & Matheny, A. P., Jr. (1995). Quantitative genetic analysis of injury liability in infants and toddlers. *American Journal of Medical Genetics (Neuropsychiatric Genetics), 60,* 64–71.

Pike, A., McGuire, S., Hetherington, E. M., Reiss, D., & Plomin, R. (1996). Family environment and adolescent depressive symptoms and antisocial behavior: A multivariate genetic analysis. *Developmental Psychology, 32*(4), 590–603.

Plomin, R. (1986). *Development, genetics, and psychology.* Hillsdale, NJ: Erlbaum.

Plomin, R. (1987). Developmental behavioral genetics and infancy. In J. Osofsky (Ed.), *Handbook of infant development* (pp. 363–417). New York: Interscience.

Plomin, R. (1994). *Genetics and experience: The interplay between nature and nurture.* Thousand Oaks, CA: Sage.

Plomin, R., & Bergeman, C. S. (1991). The nature of nurture: Genetic influences on "environmental" measures. *Behavioral and Brain Sciences, 14,* 373–427.

Plomin, R., & Caspi, A. (1998). DNA and Personality. *European Journal of Personality, 12,* 387–407.

Plomin, R., Chipuer, H. M., & Neiderhiser, J. M. (1994). Behavioural genetic evidence for the importance of nonshared environment. In E. M. Hetherington, D. Reiss, & R. Plomin (Eds.), *Separate social worlds of siblings: The impact of non-shared environment on development* (pp. 1–31). Hillsdale, NJ: Erlbaum.

Plomin, R., Coon, H., Carey, G., DeFries, J. C., & Fulker, D. W. (1991). Parent–offspring and sibling adoption analyses of parental ratings of temperament in infancy and childhood. *Journal of Personality, 59*(4), 705–732.

Plomin, R., Corley, R., Caspi, A., Fulker, D. W., & DeFries, J. C. (1998). Adoption results for self-reported personality: Not much nature or nurture? *Journal of Personality and Social Psychology, 75,* 211–218.

Plomin, R., & Daniels, D. (1987). Children in the same family are very different, but why? *Behavioral and Brain Sciences, 10*(1), 44–55.

Plomin, R., & DeFries, J. C. (1985). *Origins of individual differences in infancy.* Orlando, FL: Academic Press.

Plomin, R., DeFries, J. C., & Fulker, D. W. (1988). *Nature and nurture during infancy and early childhood.* Cambridge, UK: Cambridge University Press.

Plomin, R., DeFries, J. C., & Loehlin, J. C. (1977). Assortative mating by unwed biological parents of adopted children. *Science, 196,* 499–450.

Plomin, R., DeFries, J. C., McClearn, G. E., & Rutter, M. (1997). *Behavioral Genetics* (3rd ed.). New York: W. H. Freeman.

Plomin, R., Emde, R. N., Braungart, J. M., Campos, J., Corley, R., Fulker, D., Kagan, J., Rexnick, J. S., Robinson, J., Zahn Waxler, C., & DeFries, J. C. (1993). Genetic change and continuity from fourteen to twenty months: The MacArthur Longitudinal Twin Study. *Child Development, 64,* 1354–1376.

Plomin, R., & Foch, T. T. (1980). A twin study of objectively assessed personality in childhood. *Journal of Personality and Social Psychology, 38,* 680–688.

Plomin, R., Foch, T. T., & Rowe, D. C. (1981). Bobo clown aggression in childhood: Environment not genes. *Journal of Research in Personality, 14,* 331–342.

Plomin, R., Lichtenstein, P., Pedersen, N. L., McClearn, G. E., & Nesselroade, J. R. (1990). Genetic influence on life events during the last half of the life span. *Psychology and Aging, 5*(1), 25–30.

Plomin, R., Loehlin, J. C., & DeFries, J. C. (1985). Genetic and environmental components of "environmental" influences. *Developmental Psychology, 21,* 391–402.

Plomin, R., McClearn, G. E., Pedersen, N. L., Nesselroade, J. R., & Bergeman, C. S. (1988). Genetic influence on childhood family environment perceived retrospectively from the last half of the life span. *Developmental Psychology, 24,* 738–745.

Plomin, R., McClearn, G. E., Pedersen, N. L., Nesselroade, J. R., & Bergeman, C. S. (1989). Genetic influence on adults' ratings of their current family environment. *Journal of Marriage and the Family, 51,* 791–803.

Plomin, R., & Nesselroade, J. R. (1990). Behavioral genetics and personality change. *Journal of Personality, 58,* 191–220.

Plomin, R., Owen, M. J., & McGuffin, P. (1994). The genetic basis of complex human behaviors. *Science, 264*(5166), 1733–1739.

Pogue-Geile, M., Ferrell, R., Deka, R., Debski, T., & Manuck, S. (1998). Human Novelty Seeking personality traits and dopamine D4 receptor polmorphisms: A twin and genetic association study. *Neuropsychiatric Genetics,* 81, 44–48.

Pogue-Geile, M. F., & Rose, R. J. (1985). Developmental genetic studies of adult personality. *Developmental Psychology, 21,* 547–557.

Reiss, D. (1997). Mechanisms linking genetic and social influences in adolescent development: Beginning a collaborative search. *Current Directions in Psychological Science, 6,* 100–105.

Reiss, D., et al. (1995). Genetic questions for environmental studies: Differential parenting and psychopathology in adolescence. *Archives of General Psychiatry, 52,* 925–936.

Reiss, D., Neiderhiser, J. M., Hetherington, E. M., & Plomin, R. (in press). *The relationship code: Genetic and social analyses of adolescent development.* Cambridge, MA: Harvard University Press.

Reitsma-Street, M., Offord, D. R., & Finch, T. (1985). Pairs of same-sexed siblings discordant for antisocial behaviour. *British Journal of Psychiatry, 146,* 415–423.

Rende, R. D., Slomkowski, C. L., Stocker, C., Fulker, D. W., & Plomin, R. (1992). Genetic and environmental influences on maternal and sibling interaction in middle childhood: A sibling adoption study. *Developmental Psychology, 28,* 484–490.

Ricketts, M. H., Feng, F., Amsterdam, J., Escobar, J. I., Hamer, R. M., Manowitz, P., Menza, M. A., & Sage, J. I. (1997). Association of the serotonin transporter gene promoter polymorphism (5-HTTLPR) and harm avoidance behavior [Abstyract]. *American Journal of Medical Genetics (Neuropsychiatric Genetics), 74,* 621.

Riemann, R., Angleitner, A., & Strelau, J. (1997). Genetic and environmental influences on personality: A study of twins reared together using the self- and peer report NEO-FFI scales. *Journal of Personality, 65,* 449–476.

Riese, M. L. (1990). Neonatal temperament in monozygotic and dizygotic twin pairs. *Child Development, 61*(4), 1230–1237.

Robinson, J. L., Kagan, J., Reznick, J. S., & Corley, R. (1992). The heritability of inhibited and uninhibited behavior: A twin study. *Developmental Psychology, 28,* 1030–1037.

Rodgers, J. L., Rowe, D. C., & Li, C. (1994). Beyond nature versus nurture: DF analysis of nonshared influences on problem behaviors. *Developmental Psychology, 30,* 374–384.

Rosenthal, R. (1980). Summarizing signitificance levels. *New Directions for Methodology of Social and Behavioural Science, 5,* 33–46.

Rowe, D. C. (1981). Environmental and genetic influences on dimensions of perceived parenting: A twin study. *Developmental Psychology, 17,* 203–208.

Rowe, D. C. (1983a). A biometrical analysis of perceptions of family environment: A study of twin and singleton sibling relationships. *Child Development, 54,* 416–423.

Rowe, D. C. (1983b). Biometrical genetic models of self-reported delinquent behavior: A twin study. *Behavior Genetics, 13*(5), 473–489.

Rowe, D. C. (1986). Genetic and environmental components of antisocial pairs: A study of 275 twin pairs. *Criminology, 24,* 513–532.

Rowe, D. C. (1994). *The limits of family influence: Genes experience, and behaviour.* New York: Guilford Press.

Rowe, D. C., & Plomin, R. (1981). The importance of nonshared (E1) environmental influences in behavioural development. *Developmental Psychology, 17,* 517–531.

Rowe, D. C., Rodgers, J. L., & Meseck Bushey, S. (1992). Sibling delinquency and the family environment: Shared and unshared influences. *Child Development, 63*(1), 59–67.

Rutter, M., Dunn, J., Plomin, R., Simonoff, E., Pickles, A., Maughan, B., Ormel, H., Meyer, J., & Eaves, L. (1997). Integrating nature and nurture: Implications of person–environment correlations and interactions for developmental psychopathology. *Development and Psychopathology, 9,* 335–364.

Rutter, M., & Plomin, R. (1997). Opportunities for psychiatry from genetic findings. *British Journal of Psychiatry, 171,* 209–219.

Saudino, K. J. (1997). Moving beyond the heritability question: New directions in behavioral genetic studies of personality. *Current Directions in Psychological Science6,* 86–90.

Saudino, K. J., & Cherny, S. S. (in press-a). Parent ratings of temperament in twins. In R. N. Emde (Ed.), *The transition from infancy to early childhood: Genetic and environmental influences in the MacArthur Longitudinal Twin Study.* Cambridge, UK: Cambridge University Press.

Saudino, K. J., & Cherny, S. S. (in press-b). Sources of continuity and change in observed temperament. In R. N. Emde (Ed.), *The transition from infancy to early childhood: Genetic and environmental influences in the MacArthur Longitudinal Twin Study.* Cambridge, UK: Cambridge University Press.

Saudino, K. J., & Eaton, W. O. (1991). Infant temperament and genetics: An objective twin study of motor activity level. *Child Development, 62,* 1167–1174.

Saudino, K. J., McGuire, S., Reiss, D., Hetherington, E. M., & Plomin, R. (1995). Parent rating of EAS temperaments in twins, full siblings, half siblings, and step siblings. *Journal of Personality and Social Psychology, 68,* 723–733.

Saudino, K. J., Pedersen, N. L., Lichtenstein, P., McClearn, G. E., & Plomin, R. (1997). Can personality explain genetic influences on life events? *Journal of Personality and Social Psychology, 72,* 196–206.

Saudino, K. J., & Plomin, R. (1997). Cognitive and temperamental mediators of genetic contributions to the home environment during infancy. *Merrill-Palmer Quarterly, 43,* 1–23.

Saudino, K. J., Plomin, R., & DeFries, J. C. (1996). Tester-rated temperament at 14, 20, and 24 months: Environmental change and genetic continuity. *British Journal of Developmental Psychology, 14,* 129–144.

Scarr, S. (1992). Developmental theories for the 1990s: Development and individual differences. *Child Development, 63,* 1–19.

Scarr, S., & McCartney, K. (1983). How people make their own environments: A theory of genotype → environmental effects. *Child Development, 54,* 424–435.

Scarr, S., Webber, P. I., Weinberg, R. A., & Wittig, M. A. (1981). Personality resemblance among adolescents and their parents in biologically related and adoptive families. *Journal of Personality and Social Psychology, 40,* 885–898.

Schmitz, S., Saudino, K. J., Plomin, R., Fulker, D. W., & DeFries, J. C. (1996). Genetic and environmental influences on temperament in middle childhood: Analyses of teacher and tester ratings. *Child Development, 67,* 409–422.

Serretti, A., Bertelli, S., Verga, M., Macciardi, F., Nobile, M., Novelli, E., Catalano, M., & Smeraldi, E. (1996). Positive association of DRD4 exon 1 and 3 variants with major psychoses [Abstract]. *Psychiatric Genetics, 6,* 144.

Shakespeare, W. (1974). The Tempest. In G. B. Evans (Ed.), *The Riverside Shakespeare* (pp. 1606–1638). Boston: Houghton Mifflin (Original work performed 1611.)

Sulloway, F. J. (1996). *Born to Rebel: Family conflict and radical genius.* New York: Pantheon.

Sunohara, G., Barr, C. L., Jin, U., Schachar, R., Roberts, W., Tannock, R., Malone, M., & Kennedy, J. L. (1997). Is the dopamine D4 receptor gene associated with children and adults with attention-deficit/hyperactivity disorder? [Abstract]. *American Journal of Medical Genetics (Neuropsychiatric Genetics), 59,* A238.

Sunohara, G., Swanson, J., LaHoste, G., Wigal, S., King, N., Sam, F., Fourie, O., & Kennedy, J. L. (1996). Association of dopamine genes in Attention Deficit Hyperactivity Disorder [Abstract]. *American Journal of Human Genetics, 59,* A238.

Swanson, J. M., Sunohara, G., Kennedy, J. L., Regino, R., Fineberg, E., Wigal, T., Lerner, M., Williams, L., LaHoste, G., & Wigal, S. (1998). Association of the dopamine receptor D4 (DRD4) gene with a refined phenotype of attention deficit hyperactivity disorder (ADHD): A family based approach. *Molucular Psychiatry, 3,* 38–41.

Tellegen, A., Lykken, D. T., Bouchard, T.J., Wilcox, K., Segal, N., & Rich, A. (1988). Personality similarity in twins reared together and apart. *Journal of Personality and Social Psychology, 54,* 1031–1039.

Tsuang, M. T., Lyons, M. J., Eisen, S. A., True, W. T., Goldberg, J., & Henderson, W. (1992). A twin study of drug exposure and initiation of use [Abstract]. *Behavior Genetics, 22,* 756.

Vandenbergh, D. J., Zonderman, A. B., Wang, J., Uhl, G. R., & Costa, P. T. (1997). No association between Novelty Seeking and dopamine D4 receptor (D4DR) exon III seven repeat alleles in Baltimore Longitudinal Study of Aging participants. *Molecular Psychiatry, 2,* 417–419.

Vernon, P. A., Jang, K. L., Harris, J. A., & McCarthy, J. M. (1997). Environmental predictors of personality differences: A twin and sibling study. *Journal of Personality and Social Psychology, 72,* 177–183.

Waller, N. G., & Shaver, P. R. (1994). The importance of nongenetic influence on romantic love styles: A twin-family study. *Psychological Science, 5,* 268–274.

West, S. G. (1983). Personality and prediction: An introduction. *Journal of Personality, 51,* 275–285.

Wilson, R. S., & Matheny, A. P., Jr. (1986). Behavior genetics research in infant temperament: The Louisville Twin Study. In R. Plomin & J. Dunn (Eds.), *The study of temperament: Changes, continuities, and challenges* (pp. 81–97). Hillsdale, NJ: Erlbaum.

Zuckerman, M. (1979). *Sensation seeking: Beyond the optimal level of arousal.* Hillsdale, NJ: Erlbaum.

Zuckerman, M. (1994). *Behavioral expression and biosocial bases of sensation seeking.* New York: Cambridge University Press.

Zuroff, D. C. (1986). Was Gordon Allport a trait theorist? *Journal of Personality and Social Psychology, 51,* 993–1000.

Chapter 10

The Neuroscience of Personality

Alan D. Pickering and Jeffrey A. Gray
University of London

THE SCIENTIFIC STATUS OF PERSONALITY RESEARCH

Personality occupies a peculiar position within the disciplines of modern psychology. The prevalence of "trait" terminology in everyday language shows how frequently the topic of personality crops up in conversation, and the plethora of do-it-yourself "personality" inventories in popular magazines confirms the well-established place that personality occupies in popular thinking and culture. By contrast, it is our perception that personality research is often accorded a low scientific status by some experimental psychologists and is somewhat underrepresented in top-ranking journals. Much of the responsibility for the status quo must lie with personality research itself. In addition to the inevitable correlational nature of personality studies, the discipline has several other features that tend to cause disdain amongst card-carrying experimentalists. These include the central role of subjective instruments (e.g., self-report measures); the historical tendency to describe personality structure rather than to attempt reductionist explanations; and the strong links between personality and learning theory in the information-processing era. In this chapter we will try to illustrate that technical developments in neuroscience over the last 15 years or so may offer a window of opportunity for personality research to undergo a scientific makeover.

Despite the above difficulties, relating to the scientific status of personality research, there have been several theorists, such as Pavlov and H. J. Eysenck, who have attempted to understand personality—and its psychobiological substrates—via the usual methods of natural science. Now, modern versions of these theories are being given fresh impetus by our abilities to carry out functional imaging studies of the brain, to conduct investigations into the molecular genetics of variations in human neurotransmission, and to interpret these findings in relation to neurally inspired computational models of the relevant processing operations and/or brain systems. One goal of the present chapter is to indicate some of the ways one might try to build a modern, integrated neuroscience of personality.

It is also important to point out that those who have advanced the neuropsychology of human personality have been motivated by an additional desire to cast light on human psychopathology. The fundamental assumption underlying the personality–psychopathology linkage, and one that underpins our own research, is of "normal" personality variation lying on a continuum with certain clinical states. The most obvious example is that of anxiety. Healthy individuals vary in trait anxiety, which is simply the degree to which an individual is generally disposed toward anxious cognitions and behavior. In this specific example, the continuum model supposes that certain clinical anxiety disorders are found in individuals who lie at the high pole of the "normal" trait anxiety dimension. It has also long been argued that other disorders (e.g., psychopathy; Lykken, 1957) may occur in individuals who lie at the extreme low end of trait anxiety.

Armed with this continuum view of psychopathology there are distinct advantages to investigating possible psychobiological models of specific psychopathologies through the testbed of studies exploring related personality trait variation within healthy subjects. For example, Patterson and Newman (1993) advance the case for the study of extraversion as a means of elucidating the mechanism of disinhibition, which they believe underpins psychopathy and related disorders. In addition to obvious advantages of subject availability and compliance they note that: "the behavior of extraverts is the least distorted by negative life events and comorbidities (e.g., substance abuse) . . . [and] . . . their social disinhibition and impulsivity or spontaneity are often esteemed or adaptive. . . . In contrast, psychopaths' often troubled childhoods . . . might modify their expression of the diathesis. Most extraverted college students have not experienced the untoward effects of an antisocial lifestyle" (p. 718). Claridge (1987) has made analogous arguments for the study of schizophrenic deficits through the lens of schizotypal personality trait variation in healthy subjects.

In this chapter we will not attempt a comprehensive review of recent neuroscientific findings and theories concerning a range of major personality dimensions. Instead, we will illustrate the use of neuroscience to understand personality better by concentrating largely on the major cluster of personality traits that can be referred to as impulsive sensation seeking (ISS). In this chapter we will propose a neurobiological model of these traits by drawing together differing kinds of neuroscientific findings. A well-known neuroscientific account of another major personality dimension—anxiety—has been presented by one of us previously (Gray, 1982), and this has been recently updated (Gray & McNaughton, 1996, in press).

IMPULSIVE SENSATION SEEKING AND THE REINFORCEMENT SENSITIVITY THEORY OF PERSONALITY

The personality trait of Impulsiveness (or Impulsivity), in its narrow sense, is usually defined as a tendency to act rapidly without deliberation or consideration. However, this trait covaries with a broader set of characteristics known as Sensation Seeking, Novelty Seeking, or venturesomeness. Sensation Seeking individuals tend to engage in behaviors that increase the amount of stimulation that they experience. Such behaviors (e.g., participation in dangerous sports, drug use, etc.) involve seeking out thrills, danger, and arousal. In this chapter we shall refer to the whole cluster of related traits as impulsive sensation seeking (ISS).

ISS traits are typically measured via various standard self-report questionnaires. Examples include the IVE (S. G. B. Eysenck, Pearson, Easting, & Allsopp, 1985), especially its "Impulsiveness" and "Venturesomeness" subscales; "Positive Emotionality" from the Multidimensional Personality Questionnaire (Tellegen & Waller, 1996); various versions of Zuckerman's Sensation Seeking Scales (e.g., Zuckerman, 1979) and associated subscales; and the Novelty-Seeking subscale from the Tridimensional Personality Questionnaire (Cloninger, 1989).

From a theoretical perspective, it has been argued that *Impulsivity,* along with *Anxiety,* represent fundamental dimensions of temperament (Gray, 1970, 1981, 1982, 1987). Individual differences along these dimensions are argued to reflect variation in the reactivity, or sensitivity, of two basic brain systems to their specific classes of input stimuli. These systems—the "behavioral inhibition system" (BIS; for anxiety) and "behavioral activation system" (BAS; for impulsivity)—respond to differing kinds of secondary reinforcing stimuli: the BIS is activated by novel stimuli and by conditioned stimuli signaling punishment or frustrative nonreward; the BAS is activated by conditioned stimuli signaling reward or relief from punishment. We therefore refer to this account of personality as reinforcement sensitivity theory (RST).

The personality trait label of "Impulsivity," when used in relation to the reactivity of a person's BAS, is really a shorthand for impulsive sensation seeking. An individual with a highly reactive BAS is proposed to have high scores on typical ISS inventories, including those listed above. RST specifically proposes that subjects with high ISS scores (henceforth referred to as "high ISS" subjects) will show very strong responses to those stimuli that activate the BAS (cues for reward or relief from punishment). Gray (1970) argued that the BAS personality dimension was situated in the Extraversion × Neuroticism (E × N) plane of Eysenck's personality system with high ISS subjects being neurotic extraverts and low ISS subjects being stable introverts. In subsequent revisions of the Eysenck scales (e.g., EPQ; H. J. Eysenck & Eysenck, 1975) the Impulsivity content is found largely in the EPQ-P scale rather than EPQ-E (Rocklin & Revelle, 1981); and, in male subjects, EPQ-P (partial R^2 = .2) explained more variance in IVE-Impulsiveness than did EPQ-E (partial R^2 = .09; Díaz & Pickering, 1993). The ISS trait reflecting BAS reactivity seems likely to be indexed at least as strongly by EPQ-P as by any other EPQ scale. Depue & Collins (in press) show that ISS trait measures (which incorporate positive affect) are located on the diagonal between two orthogonal axes, which they labelled Extraversion and Constraint (after Tellegen, 1982). High ISS subjects are characterised by high Extraversion and low Constraint. Given that the low pole of Constraint is anchored by EPQ-P, Depue and Collins' analysis implies that personality trait variation related to BAS reactivity lies along the diagonal between EPQ-E and EPQ-P (not EPQ-E and EPQ-N as originally suggested).

In addition to standard personality measures designed to capture variation in Impulsivity and sensation seeking, Carver & White (1994) have recently developed a set of scales that was intended specifically to index the personality trait variation associated with BAS reactivity. They did this by using items directly related to the psychological effects of rewards and reward cues, along with more general items concerning goal directedness and appetitive motivation. These scales complement the existing published scales similarly designed to index BIS-related personality variation (MacAndrew & Steele, 1991; Torrubia & Tobeña, 1984).

The BAS and the BIS compete with one another for control over behavior (Gray & Smith, 1969; Pickering, 1997). When activated, the BAS can be characterized as a "go" system that activates ongoing approach behavior. By contrast, the BIS is a "stop" system that inhibits ongoing behavior and allows further information processing of the environment. These responses are appropriate under BIS-activating conditions in which signals of punishments and/or loss of rewards warn of impending negative consequences. BIS activation is also accompanied by an arousal output that ensures that any actions that are eventually executed (including fight or flight) are carried out with increased force and vigor.

From the perspective of RST, the decision to engage in the dangerous but pleasurable behaviors characteristic of high ISS subjects is viewed in terms of an approach–avoidance conflict, which is resolved by the interactions between BAS and BIS. In a highly BAS reactive (high ISS) subject, the BAS-controlled approach component will tend to predominate, and so these subjects will exhibit a lot of risky, sensation-seeking behaviors. In anxious subjects, with high levels of BIS reactivity, the avoidance component will tend to hold sway, and such subjects will habitually avoid danger and risk.

At this point, we should briefly note some of the psychopathological states that have been related to extremes of the ISS personality dimension. Quay (1988) has hypothesized that childhood behavioral disorders, such as attention deficit disorder with hyperactivity, and conduct disorder, are in part the result of a dysfunctional (overactive) BAS. Impulsivity is a cardinal feature of these childhood disorders. Corresponding disinhibited psychopathologies in adulthood have been similarly ascribed to an overactive BAS (Gorenstein & Newman, 1980) or to difficulties in interrupting or modulating BAS-controlled behavior (Patterson & Newman, 1993).

Finally, we note that RST has mainly been investigated by exploring the behavioral and psychophysiological responses to reward and punishment cues in individuals with different personality trait scores. Subjects' performance on a task is assessed under a control condition in which reinforcements are neither anticipated nor received. This is compared with performance in a condition in which subjects know that their responses will attract explicit reinforcement (usually gains or losses of small sums of money). Despite the existence of many studies, Pickering, Corr, Powell, Kumari, Thornton, & Gray (1997) argued that the theory has not been adequately tested in most, if not all, of the published investigations. It was also pointed out that, within the limitations of the studies, many patterns of findings—from clear supporting evidence through nonsignificant results to clear contradictory evidence—have been reported. Post hoc arguments have often been used to accommodate awkward results. Pickering and his colleagues suggest that the evidence as a whole points to strong links between personality traits and sensitivity to reinforcement, but they argue that it is unclear how well RST describes those links.

RELATED THEORETICAL ACCOUNTS

Influential accounts of personality by Cloninger (Cloninger, Svrakic, & Przybeck, 1993), Zuckerman (1991), and Depue (Depue & Collins, in press) resemble RST in proposing a basic dimension of personality that shares features with the BAS-related ISS dimension hypothesized by RST.

In Cloninger's theory there are four strongly biologically determined temperament dimensions and three more environmentally determined character dimensions. One of the temperament dimensions—Harm Avoidance—is closely akin to the Anxiety dimension of RST. By exploring the correlations between Cloninger's temperament dimensions and those from the EPQ, Corr, Pickering & Gray (1995) outlined possible links between BAS function and two of Cloninger's other temperament dimensions: Novelty Seeking and Reward Dependence. Novelty Seeking showed the positive associations with both EPQ-E and EPQ-P that Depue and Collins (in press) have shown to be a consistent feature of ISS traits. These results were confirmed in a larger study by Zuckerman and Cloninger (1996).

Subjects with high Novelty Seeking scores are characterized in a similar way to subjects with a highly reactive BAS. They are impulsive, exploratory, fickle, excitable, quick-tempered, and extravagant. Of particular importance for the present chapter is Cloninger's proposal that Novelty Seeking involves genetic differences in dopaminergic neurotransmission; as discussed below, there is now direct evidence in support of this suggestion.

Depue and Collins's (in press) recent account differs from those of Cloninger, Zuckerman, and RST in suggesting that the axes of causal neurobiological influence lie jointly with Extraversion and Constraint, rather than on the ISS diagonal between these dimensions. Depue and Collins suggest that ISS traits are emergent from interactions between the fundamental Extraversion and Constraint dimensions and, as such, would be expected to have heterogeneous neurobiological sources of influence. As a result they expect that research attempting to find neurobiological correlates of ISS traits would tend to produce weak and inconsistent results. They argue specifically that evidence for individual differences in dopaminergic functioning should be more consistently aligned with Extraversion than with ISS traits. In their review of some of the pertinent evidence Depue and Collins concede that the data are pretty indecisive. Depue's own studies of prolactin and eye blink indices of D2 dopamine receptor effects (Depue, 1995, 1996; Depue, Luciana, Arbisi, Collins, & Leon, 1994), replicated by another group (Netter, Henning, & Roed, 1996), provide the clearest evidence of strong associations with Extraversion in the absence of the significant relationships with ISS traits or constraint. These findings must be set against the evidence, reviewed below, which finds associations between dopaminergic effects and ISS or Constraint-like traits, rather than associations involving Extraversion.

A final related body of research and theory stems from Newman and his colleagues (Arnett, Smith, & Newman, 1997; Gorenstein & Newman, 1980; Patterson & Newman, 1993). These authors have been less concerned with constructing a theory of personality than with building models of disinhibited pathologies such as psychopathy. As the earlier quotation from their work indicates, these authors have felt that the study of extraverts offers clear insights on their central question.

The remainder of this chapter will build from an analysis of the work of Newman and his colleagues, which will be considered in some detail. We will interpret their information-processing model of disinhibition, and some associated empirical findings, in terms of interactions between the BAS and the BIS. As we have advocated elsewhere (Gray, 1972), this step will lead to the development of a conceptual nervous system architecture for the systems involved. Pickering (1997) has suggested that conceptual nervous system models are naturally implemented as computational neural networks, and so we will use our knowledge of neural network systems to help understand the way in which our conceptual nervous system might function. In particular we will consider the effects of systematically varying network parameters to model personality trait variation.

The next step will be to look at a range of evidence, from varying neuroscience modalities, which may provide clues as to where our conceptual nervous system may reside in the brain. Evidence from cell recording studies, work with motivationally disturbed clinical populations, plus developments in neuroimaging and molecular genetics will implicate the mesolimbic dopamine system in BAS function and in ISS personality traits. Next we will try to map the various inputs to, and outputs from, the striatal target cells of the mesolimbic dopamine pathways, onto the conceptual nervous system architecture that we have suggested. By doing this we can construct a more constrained neural model that we hope will be of use in understanding the complex relationships between ISS personality traits and behavior on experimental tasks. We hope, too, that our general approach, illustrated in this chapter, might be an effective framework that could be employed to help integrate the neuroscience data related to other personality traits.

THE PATTERSON AND NEWMAN DISINHIBITION MODEL

Patterson and Newman (1993) outline a process through which disinhibited individuals (such as extraverts and psychopaths) may exhibit their characteristic impulsive behavioral style. The first stage of this process is the acquisition of a dominant response set for approach behaviors. A very strong approach response set may lead to excessive focus on the behavioral goal, restricting information gathering and consideration of response alternatives, producing perseverative reward-seeking behavior even after environmental contingencies have changed. Patterson and Newman suggest that there are basic differences in the ease with which individuals form approach response sets and the intensity with which the activation of such sets is maintained. They argue that exaggerated responsiveness to reward, of this kind, is responsible for disinhibited behavior. As already noted, they suggest that the relevant individual differences variable is Extraversion.

The second stage of the route to disinhibition occurs when the approach response set is disrupted by an (aversive) event that stalls or prevents further action. Patterson and Newman emphasize the orienting of attention toward the unexpected event and the accompanying increase in arousal. These outcomes are precisely the output functions of the BIS in RST. Furthermore, Patterson and Newman suggest that the key individual differences variable for this processing stage is Neuroticism; Neuroticism is close to the anxiety dimension that RST aligns with BIS reactivity. (It should be noted that although RST has always emphasised the relative closeness of Neuroticism to the anxiety dimension of RST—see Gray, 1970—the issue has been confused somewhat by the simplifying explanatory device of presenting the anxiety dimension as lying on the 45° diagonal between Neuroticism and Extraversion; see Pickering, Corr, & Gray, 1999, for further discussion.)

The third stage of processing according to Patterson and Newman follows immediately after the unexpected disruption of approach behavior. Nondisinhibited individuals use the arousal increment following disruption to make an effortful switch from automatic processing under the reward expectancy to controlled processing of the circumstances surrounding the unexpected interruption. Once again, this precisely resembles the functional account of behavioral inhibition that we have offered (for example, see Pickering, 1997). Patterson and Newman propose that disinhibited individuals often fail to make the automatic-to-controlled processing switch and so show weak modulation of their overt goal-directed behavior and the underlying response set. From the perspective of RST, disinhibited individuals display functionally impaired behavioral inhibition. Patterson and Newman refer to the individual differences at this stage as being differences in "response modulation bias" and relate this bias to Extraversion. It seems likely that failures of response modulation (Stage 3) in extraverts might be responsible for their proposed tendency strongly to maintain the activation of an approach response set (Stage 1), although the acquisition of a response set might logically be distinguishable from modulatory processes involved in its maintenance.

The fourth element of Patterson and Newman's account describes an associative deficit that usually follows disinhibition of appetitive behavior. They suggest that weak response modulation often leads to a failure to pause and process the cues that, through learning, could serve as early warnings signs of the originally unexpected interruptions of reward-seeking behavior. Disinhibited individuals therefore typically show reduced reflectivity following punishments, and the resulting impairment of learning skews response repertoires toward active, goal-directed behavior. Interestingly, Patterson, Kosson, &

Newman (1987) have shown that extraverts do learn from their mistakes when they are forced to pause after corrective feedback, presumably because this allows them time for the kind of reflective processing described above, time that their habitual behavioral style does not usually allow.

A CONCEPTUAL NERVOUS SYSTEM MODEL OF BAS–BIS INTERACTIONS

We have pointed out the close similarities between parts of the above account and the central ideas of RST, similarities that Newman and his colleagues explicitly acknowledge. Following Arnett, Smith, and Newman (1997), we find it helpful to relate the disinhibition model to RST using a diagram; see Figure 10.1. This figure is based on the original diagram from Gray and Smith (1969) and shows multiple outputs from both the BAS and the BIS. Each system responds to its characteristic motivational inputs by producing a modulation output (which inhibits the other system) and an output that has a functionally excitatory effect on a general arousal system. The third output of each system affects response selection and control mechanisms: the BAS output activates and the BIS output inhibits any response habits elicited by other stimuli in the environment.

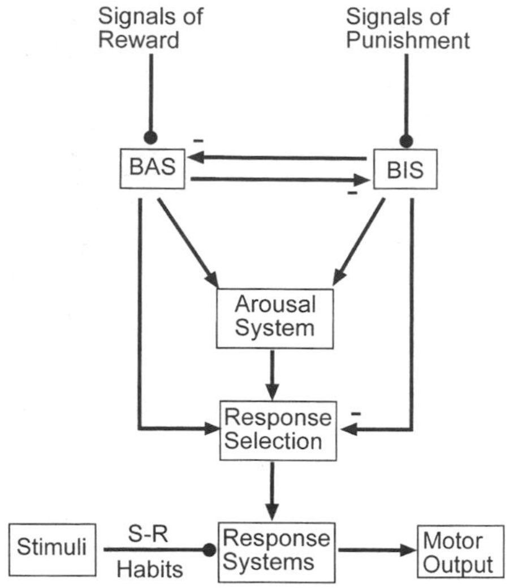

FIGURE 10.1. A schematic representation of the inputs to and outputs from the behavioral activation system (BAS) and behavioral inhibition system (BIS). The arousal system is depicted as affecting response selection mechanisms, but it is likely to have a direct effect on the response systems. Pathways are functionally excitatory except where minus signs denote functionally inhibitory effects. Learned inputs are denoted by pathways ending in rounded arrowheads. In this chapter we argue that inhibition of the BIS by the BAS may be insignificant.

Figure 10.1 represents a simple conceptual nervous system architecture for the BAS and BIS, and their associated personality traits. Next, we need to understand how such an architecture might function. As already noted, this process may be facilitated by interpreting Figure 10.1 as if it were the architecture of a neural network. The simplest version of RST would propose that, in response to a learned cue signaling reward, each of the outputs from the BAS would be stronger for a high ISS subject than for a low ISS subject. (Analogous statements could be made for the BIS and Anxiety.) If one were to construct a neural network model with the basic architecture of Figure 10.1, the simplest version of RST would model ISS traits by allowing the threshold function controlling the output from BAS "cells" to vary across individuals (high BAS reactivity = high ISS = low BAS output threshold). Similarly, trait Anxiety would be modeled by varying the threshold controlling BIS output. It would logically be possible to model variations in the sensitivity of the BAS or BIS to their respective input stimuli in terms of variations in the synaptic efficiency (or weights) of the input pathways to each system. Indeed, Pickering (1997) used this method as a computational convenience. However, for reasons made clear below, we do not advocate this possibility here.

According to RST, Extraversion is a personality dimension that emerges from the interplay between BAS and BIS. The personality traits associated with BAS and BIS reactivity (ISS and Anxiety, respectively) are therefore argued to be causally and biologically more fundamental than Extraversion. As a result, one would not seek to model Extraversion by varying one specific feature within a framework like that in Figure 10.1. Instead, Extraversion would be modeled by simultaneous variations in features of both BAS and BIS. In RST, extraverts are considered to be relatively high in Impulsivity (high BAS output) and also relatively low in Anxiety (low BIS output). We (Pickering, 1997) have previously used a neural network to explore the equilibrium state of the mutually inhibitory BAS and BIS systems when both receive inputs. For an extravert, under the simple version of RST, our previous simulations showed that the outputs from the BAS would be active while the outputs from the BIS would be inactive. This type of model does generate an approach (BAS) dominated behavioral style, consistent with the actions of disinhibited individuals, but it does not fit easily with a number of empirical findings from Newman's laboratory.

The problem for our neural net implementation of BAS–BIS interactions occurs when a punishment cue is experienced during appetitively motivated behavior (stage 2 of Patterson and Newman's disinhibition model). For the BAS-reactive, BIS-unreactive (extravert) subject, the neural net model predicts that there will be no significant BIS outputs and thus little observable response to the punishment cue. The neural net model also predicts that the behavior of the BIS-reactive, BAS-unreactive (introvert) subject, by contrast, will be affected by the combined effects of the inhibition and arousal outputs of the BIS. However, we have pointed out (see Pickering, Díaz, & Gray, 1995) that it might be hard to determine what the combined effects of these opposing outputs would be. These predictions are at odds with the findings (Nichols & Newman, 1986; Patterson et al., 1987) that show that extraverts' response times (RTs) are facilitated following punishment relative to RTs following reward, with the opposite pattern being obtained for introverts. This punishment-related facilitation of RTs in extraverts implies the existence of an active output from the BIS, in response to the punishment cue, even for an extraverted subject who is viewed as being BIS-unreactive.

In order to explain extraverts' RT facilitation following punishment, within the context of Figure 10.1, it is necessary that the BIS can remain activated even when the BAS is activated more strongly. Such a state of affairs will not arise with the strong competitive interactions between BAS and BIS that we have previously employed (Pickering, 1997). It could occur, however, if there were no (modulation) output from the BAS that acted on the BIS directly. In this case activation of the BAS (and thus the level of each BAS output) would be a function of the activating inputs and the inhibitory modulation received from the BIS, whereas BIS activation (and outputs) would be solely determined by its activating inputs. BIS activation would therefore not be driven to zero by inhibitory modulation from the BAS even under conditions that activate the BAS more strongly than the BIS.

How would this revised model explain facilitation of RT in extraverts following punishment cues? The net effect of the BIS-activating cue would result from the facilitatory effects of the BIS arousal output opposed both by the reduction in BAS activation produced by the BIS modulation output and the direct effect of the BIS inhibition output on response selection, acting in opposition to the effects of the BAS activation output. In an extravert or high ISS subject there is some degree of BIS reactivity. Under RST, Neuroticism is aligned much more closely with BIS reactivity than Extraversion, and ISS traits are hypothetically orthogonal to the BIS dimension of anxiety. Therefore, in Extravert or high ISS subjects, a BIS-activating cue will produce a degree of BIS activation. In the modified account of RST, just given, this BIS activation will not be suppressed by the much stronger BAS activation (for extraverts or high ISS subjects) produced by any concurrent BAS-activating cues. The resulting modest BIS modulation output will not have much effect on BAS activation, and the modest BIS inhibition output will not have much success in opposing the effects of the strong BAS activation output on response selection. However, the modest BIS arousal output will be able to express its effects on responses directly and unopposed, leading to an increase in response speed. By comparison, introverted or anxious subjects will have much greater BIS reactivities (as well as reduced BAS reactivities), and so the BIS modulation and inhibition outputs may achieve a marked interference with any ongoing BAS-mediated effects. The overall effect of a punishment cue on appetitively motivated behavior will be determined by these BAS-opposing effects in combination with the effects of the BIS arousal output. An increase in RT may therefore be observed in introverts in response to a punishment cue.

We have now completed our conceptual nervous system analysis of a possible gross neural architecture for the BAS, the BIS, and their interaction. We have seen that an understanding of mutually inhibitory, competitive dynamics between systems, gathered from experience with neural network models, has led to a reformulation of RST to accommodate the findings of Newman and colleagues. In terms of Figure 10.1 we make a simple modification: to drop the arrow denoting direct inhibition of the BIS by the BAS. This reformulation also represents a more detailed specification of the response modulation account of disinhibition suggested by Patterson and Newman. We now turn to evidence relating to the neurobiology of the BAS more directly. By exploring real neural networks in the brain, and how they function under appetitive motivation, we may be able to map the abstract representations of Figure 10.1 onto actual wetware in order to construct a more constrained and realistic model.

THE NEUROBIOLOGY OF THE BAS

Evidence for Dopaminergic Involvement in Appetitive Motivation

We have previously given a thumbnail sketch of the neurobiology of the BAS (Gray, 1987). A central role for dopaminergic neurotransmission in BAS function is mandated given the strong evidence implicating mesolimbic and mesocortical dopaminergic pathways in reward-directed behavior (Bozarth & Wise, 1981; Robbins & Everitt, 1996). This is not to argue that dopaminergic neurotransmission in mesolimbic pathways is exclusively linked to positive incentive motivational effects, as we have emphazed elsewhere (Gray, in press; Gray, Kumari, Lawrence, & Young, in press). It is clear, for example, that aversive stimuli increase mesolimbic dopaminergic neurotransmission (see Salomone, 1994, for a review). It may therefore be more complete to argue that the common denominator underlying the capacity of a stimulus to elicit dopamine release in mesolimbic pathways is its salience (see Gray et al., in press). Nonetheless, we argue here that one type of salience (and hence one route to mesolimbic dopamine release) is a product of the action of the BAS. A major goal of this chapter is to highlight the possible input and output pathways of this system.

A particularly pertinent series of studies has been summarized by Schultz, Romo, Ljungberg, Mirenowicz, Hollerman, & Dickinson (1995). They report cell recordings from monkey dopamine neurons in the substantia nigra (SN) and ventral tegmental area (VTA) that reveal that dopaminergic activity increases in response to primary rewards. After training, however, the cells respond to conditioned stimuli (CSs) that predict the primary reward rather than to the primary reward itself. Such CSs, according to RST, represent one of the classes of stimuli that activate the BAS.

Houk, Adams, and Barto (1995) offer an interpretation of the results described by Schultz et al. that is entirely consistent with RST. In the schematic neural architecture of Figure 10.2, an appetitive unconditioned stimulus (US) leads to increased firing of SN or VTA dopaminergic neurons. Dopamine release at the striatal target cells (S in Figure 10.2) of these dopaminergic neurons is argued to be an additional, critical factor involved in a special form of long-term potentiation (LTP). This LTP is the basis of conditioning in the glutamatergic cortical afferents carrying information about CSs to the striatal cells. After conditioning, a CS is able to elicit robust firing of the striatal neurons in the absence of the US. The outputs from the striatal cells send feedback signals that control the dopaminergic output from the SN/VTA neurons. A CS can produce two types of striatal feedback signal: one indirectly leads to a functional excitation of dopaminergic firing (by inhibition of the inhibitory inputs from various nuclei to the SN/VTA neurons); Houk et al. (1995) argue that there is also a much slower, direct signal (not shown in Figure 10.2) that inhibits dopaminergic firing and so opposes the increase produced by the ensuing US. In this chapter we are going to emphasize the indirect pathways. The other cells receiving dopaminergic input include the prefrontal cortex (PFC in Figure 10.2). These regions are involved in selection and control of such behavioral outputs as learned stimulus–response (S-R) habits. As well as a possible role in modulating learning in these pathways, dopaminergic transmission may also play a direct role in selection of the stimulus inputs that undergo learning (Schultz et al., 1995) and in the psychomotor activation of the selected behavioral outputs (Wickens, 1993).

In terms of RST, the outputs from the striatal cells, elicited in response to an appropriate CS, correspond to the outputs of the BAS. Impulsive sensation seeking subjects, whom RST supposes to have a reactive BAS, should therefore produce strong striatal feedback signals in response to a CS that has previously been associated with reward. We noted earlier that RST suggests that this increased BAS output results from a lowered output threshold of the cells concerned. The Houk et al. model, summarized in Figure 10.2, describes a form of classical conditioning in corticostriatal pathways by which initially neutral CSs can become a secondary positive reinforcer and elicit conditioned dopaminergic cell firing

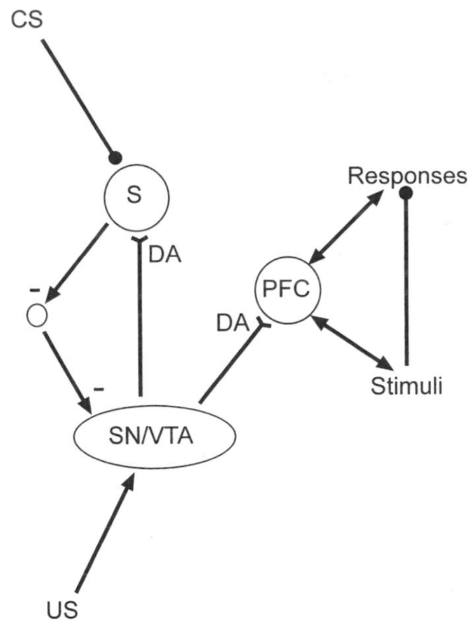

FIGURE 10.2. Outline sketch of part of a neural architecture for the behavioral activation system (BAS). Pathways are excitatory except where minus signs denote inhibitory connections or Y-shaped connections (also marked DA) denote modulatory dopaminergic synapses. Round-headed arrows denote modifiable synapses; double-headed arrows indicate reciprocal connections. Some connections have been omitted for clarity. The indirect pathways from striatal neurons to SN/VTA travel via pallidal and subthalamic neurons, which are left blank in the figure. S, medium spiny striatal neurons; SN/VTA, dopaminergic cells in the substantia nigra or ventral tegmental area; PFC, prefrontal cortex; US, appetitive unconditioned stimulus; CS, conditioned stimulus.

(and hence striatal dopamine release) after pairing with an appetitive US. RST has argued that variations in BAS reactivity are not a function of the ease with which such CSs acquire their secondary reinforcing properties (see Zinbarg & Mohlman, 1998, for an excellent discussion). Hence, there should be no relationship between ISS (BAS-related) personality traits and the strength of the corticostriatal synapses, formed in the way described by Houk et al. A link between ISS traits and the output threshold of the striatal cells is much more in keeping with RST's emphasis on the behavioral effects of *established* secondary reinforcers.

From the foregoing account, a CS previously associated with reward will, via the indirect striatal output routes, initially elicit high levels of dopaminergic firing in an impulsive subject. Below we will develop a more detailed neural model of the BAS, building on the ideas sketched to date. We will suggest that these striatal output signals, and their associated increase in dopaminergic firing, can produce the behavioral activation effects ascribed by RST to the BAS. We will also make a specific suggestion for a possible neurochemical basis for the increased striatal outputs of an impulsive sensation seeking subject. At this point we should also reiterate our earlier statement: namely, that other kinds of stimuli can elicit dopamine release in striatal cells. In the more complete model, presented below, we will briefly suggest how aversive and other events can elicit dopamine release in the ventral striatum. Some of these effects will be interpreted as resulting from the interaction of BIS outputs with BAS processing. Emphasizing this point is important so that the reader does not mistakenly infer any simple equivalence between dopamine release and appetitive motivation. We have stated elsewhere that such a view is at odds with a great deal of evidence (Gray et al., in press).

Other evidence for DA involvement in BAS function comes from studies of patients with clinical abnormalities of appetitive motivation. Powell and her colleagues have developed a simple experimental measure of reward motivation, the CARROT (Card Arranging Reward Responsiveness Objective Test), suitable for use with clinical groups. The CARROT is a repeated-measures test in which subjects are required to perform a very simple card sorting task as quickly as possible on four separate consecutive trials (T1–T4). On one trial (T3) the subjects are offered a financial incentive for fast sorting (10 pence for every five cards sorted); and their sorting rate on this rewarded trial is compared with their sorting rate in nonrewarded trials conducted either side of the rewarded trial (T2 and T4) to yield a "reward responsiveness" index.

These researchers administered the CARROT to 54 patients with organic brain injury, some of whom were characterized by clinically significant impairments of appetitive motivation (Al-Adawi, Powell, & Greenwood, 1998). The reward responsiveness index correlated strongly with independent clinical ratings of motivation during therapy sessions ($r = .64$, $p < .001$), and this reflected neither a general effect of motor slowing (speed in the nonrewarded trials was uncorrelated with motivation) nor generalized intellectual deterioration. In a parallel study (Powell, Al-Adawi, Morgan, & Greenwood, 1996), 11 of the patients with severe motivational impairment were treated with a D2 dopamine agonist, bromocriptine, after they had been stable over two repeated baseline (i.e., drug-free) assessments. There were highly significant improvements at low doses of the drug, both in clinically rated motivation and in the reward responsiveness scores from the CARROT. The effect of bromocriptine was specific to the reward responsiveness index as there were no effects on sorting speed on nonrewarded trials. The CARROT therefore appears to be a simple measure of the effects of reward cues that shows both ecological validity and dependence on dopaminergic neurotransmission.

The next study used the CARROT to test Muslim smokers abstaining from cigarettes during daylight hours throughout Ramadhan (Al-Adawi & Powell, 1997). The subjects were given the CARROT after several hours' abstinence and then again shortly after smoking in the evening, and the smokers compared with nonsmoking Muslim controls. When abstaining the smokers showed virtually no reward responsiveness on the CARROT, but they showed supranormal effects when tested immediately after one cigarette. The controls' levels of reward responsiveness were higher on the first testing occasion and did not change at the second testing point. As with the brain-injured patients, the effect on reward responsiveness was independent of speed in the nonrewarded trials. Because nicotine is thought to stimulate dopamine release in the brain directly, via nicotinic receptors on dopaminergic neurons, and because withdrawal from various addictive drugs has been shown to be associated with abnormal functioning in dopaminergic brain circuitry (see Al-Adawi & Powell, 1997, for references), the results are again consistent with appetitive motivational effects in the CARROT task being mediated by brain dopaminergic activity.

Evidence for Dopaminergic Contributions to Impulsive Behavior and ISS Personality Traits

We shall consider three kinds of evidence implicating brain dopamine systems in impulsive behavior and ISS personality traits: indirect evidence from clinical populations; data from functional neuroimaging investigations; and findings from molecular genetic association studies.

Indirect Evidence

There are clinical conditions in which alterations in the frequency of Impulsive and Sensation Seeking behaviors are observed and in which there is evidence of altered dopamine function. These conditions provide indirect evidence linking ISS personality traits with dopaminergic neurotransmission. Attention deficit disorder with hyperactivity in children is one of the major behavioral disorders of childhood and is characterized, inter alia, by impulsiveness. The most commonly prescribed medication for this condition in the US is methylphenidate (Kwasman, Tinsley, & Lepper, 1995). Methylphenidate acts by inhibiting the dopamine transporter to which it binds specifically (Ding, Fowler, Volkow, Logan, Gatley, & Sagano, 1995). In addition, we have already noted that Quay (1988) has characterized attention deficit disorder and conduct disorder in terms of a disturbance to the functioning of the BAS and its interaction with the BIS. In a general review of the genetics of childhood psychopathology, Alsobrook and Pauls (1998) note the evidence linking Gilles de la Tourette's syndrome—which is also characterized by marked deficits of impulse control—to D2 and D4 dopamine receptor functioning.

In adults, clinicians have anecdotally observed an association between Parkinson's disease and personality characteristics at the low pole of the ISS dimension (i.e., stoicism, industriousness, and inflexibility), both premorbidly and after the onset of symptoms. Menza and colleagues (Menza, Forman, Goldstein, & Golbe, 1990; Menza, Golbe, Cody & Forman, 1993) have documented low levels of Cloninger's Novelty Seeking in Parkinson's disease patients and have argued that damage to the mesolimbic dopaminergic system in Parkinson's disease is responsible for the patients' characteristic (low ISS) personality profile.

Neuroimaging Investigations

There have been relatively few studies that have attempted to use functional neuroimaging to study personality traits. Our own single photon emission tomography (SPET) study in a small group of healthy volunteers (N. S. Gray, Pickering, & Gray, 1994) used a specific radioligand for dopamine D2 receptors ([^{123}I]IBZM). We correlated the left and right hemisphere measures of ligand binding in the basal ganglia with scores on the EPQ. We found significant negative correlations between the P scale from the EPQ with the D2 binding index in each hemisphere, but no significant associations with other personality measures from the EPQ. The binding index, lower in subjects with high EPQ-P scores, is an index of D2 receptor density. There are some noteworthy aspects to these findings.

First, in this chapter we have emphasized the widely held view that EPQ-P is an index of antisocial ISS personality traits and does not satisfy Eysenck's original intention that this scale should index Psychoticism (i.e., a general tendency to psychotic-like thoughts and behaviors). Our earlier analysis of the recent review by Depue and Collins (in press) was that ISS personality traits are usually located along the diagonal running from high EPQ-P and high EPQ-E (high ISS) to low EPQ-P and low EPQ-E (low ISS). The current scanning findings are consistent with this analysis if one assumes that the causal (biological) personality axis, related to variations in dopaminergic neurotransmission, lies along the ISS diagonal rather than with EPQ-E or EPQ-P. Either of these latter dimensions may then act as a proxy for the fundamental ISS traits, with which they are correlated, and reveal associations with dopaminergic indices (such as SPET binding). As Depue and Collins point out, these indirect associations will be weaker, and more inconsistent across studies, than associations with personality measures that tap into the causally significant dimension directly. This expectation of weak and inconsistent effects can explain why there were no EPQ-E correlations in our scanning study, and at the same time why Depue's studies of psychophysiological dopaminergic markers (see above) were associated selectively with Extraversion and not Constraint (a dimension that is approximately the inverse of EPQ-P). By contrast, Depue and Collins's claim that Extraversion is the true dopaminergic personality dimension cannot explain the results obtained by N. S. Gray et al. (1994).

Second, a research group in Sweden (Farde, Gustavsson, & Jönsson, 1997) has independently reported on the personality correlates of D2 receptor binding in a larger group of healthy volunteers. Receptor density (in right and left striatum combined) was measured using positron emission tomography (PET) with a different radioligand, and personality was assessed via the Karolinska Scales of Personality (KSP). Significant negative correlations were obtained for the dimensions of Detachment and Irritability, which index some of the same personality facets as EPQ-P. The correlations with other scales from the KSP were insignificant and were not reported; in particular it would have been interesting to know the relationships with the Impulsiveness and Monotony Avoidance scales, which more directly tap into the hypothetically critical ISS traits.

Finally, a further PET study in a small group of Parkinson's disease patients (Menza, Mark, Burn, & Brooks, 1995) looked at the relationship between Cloninger's Novelty Seeking and striatal uptake of [^{18}F]dopa. Uptake of the ligand in the left caudate, but not other measured regions, was significantly correlated with Novelty Seeking. These workers related these findings to their earlier studies (Menza et al., 1990, 1993) which had shown low levels of Novelty Seeking in Parkinson's disease patients.

Molecular Genetic Association Studies

Recent reports have provided the first evidence, in human personality research, of an association between scores on a specific personality inventory and structural variations in the subjects' DNA. This research is germane to the present chapter as the inventory concerned (Cloninger's Novelty Seeking) measures aspects of ISS personality and the gene codes for the dopamine D4 receptor (Benjamin et al., 1996; Ebstein et al., 1996). This research is described in more detail in Chapter 9 by Plomin and Caspi and so will be only briefly summarized here.

The dopamine D4 receptor (DRD4) marker consists of alleles with from 2 to 8 repeats of a 48 base-pair sequence in exon III of the gene on chromosome 11 that codes for the dopamine D4 receptor. The number of repeats changes the length of the third cytoplasmic loop of the receptor. Various in vitro studies (e.g., Asghari et al., 1994) have shown that the shorter alleles (2 to 5 repeats) code for a receptor that is more efficient in binding dopamine than the larger alleles (6 to 8 repeats). For this reason, DRD4 genotypes have usually been analyzed by comparing individuals who have two short alleles (about two-thirds of genotypes) versus one or two long alleles (one-third of genotypes).

In the original studies individuals with at least one long-repeat DRD4 allele showed significantly higher Novelty Seeking scores than individuals without a long-repeat allele. The other three Cloninger temperament scales (Reward Dependence, Persistence, Harm Avoidance) showed no significant differences between the two groups. These findings have been subsequently replicated (Ebstein et al., 1997; Ono et al., 1997). The positive findings must be considered in light of four studies that failed to find significant associations. However, two of these negative studies showed trends in the expected direction (Jönsson et al., 1997; Vandenbergh, Zonderman, Wang, Uhl, & Costa, 1997). Two other studies showed no association (Malhotra et al., 1996; Pogue-Geile, Ferrell, Deka, Debski, & Manuck, 1998).

The nature of the possible links between these molecular genetic findings and RST poses some interesting questions. The subject characterized by RST as reacting strongly to reward cues might tend to possess the long D4DR allele associated with higher Novelty Seeking scores. This possibility would be consistent with the similarities in personality profile of a BAS-reactive subject (according to RST) and a subject scoring highly on Cloninger's Novelty Seeking. Earlier in this chapter we suggested that high levels of BAS reactivity would lead to increased dopaminergic firing in response to CSs associated with reward. These ideas must be considered in relation to the in vitro findings that suggest that the long D4DR alleles may be associated with less efficient dopaminergic transmission. These latter findings are consistent with the idea that subjects with the long D4DR alleles seek out high levels of the kinds of environmental stimulation likely to increase dopaminergic activity, in order to compensate for their naturally hypofunctioning system. Given the action of opiates on the mesolimbic dopamine pathways in the brain (Di Chiara, Acquas, & Carboni, 1992), this account could explain the findings of three studies that have found high frequencies of long D4DR alleles among heroin addicts (e.g., Li et al., 1997). There is, however, some tension between suggesting that impulsive sensation seeking subjects have increased dopaminergic firing in response to reward cues and at the same time noting evidence possibly indicating that some of their receptors do not bind dopamine very effectively.

The most straightforward resolution to this paradox is to note that the D4 dopamine receptor is part of the "D2-like" family of dopamine receptors (Jaber, Robinson, Missale, & Caron, 1996). D2 dopamine receptors act to inhibit the depolarizing effects of cortical signals on striatal neurons by a presynaptic action on the corticostriatal terminals (e.g., Hsu, Huang, Yang, & Gean, 1995). In the earlier discussion of Figure 10.2 it was suggested that the high ISS subject would have a lowered threshold for output from the striatal cells receiving cortical inputs from CSs associated with reward. It is therefore a natural step to conceive of the inhibitory D2-like dopamine receptors as setting this threshold for striatal output in response to cortical stimulation. Assuming a similar mode of action for D4 and D2 receptors, it follows that when D4 receptors are less efficient a lower striatal output threshold should result. In this way, the long D4DR allele might be associated with the hypothesized higher striatal output of high ISS subjects. This in turn would lead to greater firing of the dopaminergic cells in the VTA/SN. These cells, particularly those of the VTA, have very diffuse projections to many important neural structures, including prefrontal cortex and amygdala. It will be suggested below that greater excitatory dopaminergic effects at these other target sites (perhaps mediated by D1-like receptors) may be partially responsible for the high levels of behavioral activation characteristic of high ISS subjects.

This speculative account is consistent with a recent study (Tarazi, Campbell, Yeghiayan, & Baldessarini, 1998) that concluded that D4, but not D1 or D2, receptors are found on presynaptic corticostriatal afferents. However, there is evidence from in situ hybridisation studies that D4 receptor mRNA expression is very low in striatal regions (see Jaber et al., 1996) and some studies with D4-selective radioligands have revealed no high affinity binding in human striatum (Primus et al., 1997). The suggestion that an inhibitory D2-like mechanism determines the striatal output threshold also fits with our own SPET data reviewed earlier. The high ISS subjects were found to have lower D2 binding in the striatum. This might indicate lower D2 receptor density, which might in turn be expected to result in reduced dopaminergic inhibition and hence greater striatal output.

In addition to the D4DR marker, just discussed, polymorphisms in a number of other genes may have a role in ISS personality traits. Examples include polymorphisms of the dopamine D2 receptor and dopamine transporter genes. The former has been linked to personality in cocaine addicts (Compton, Anglin, Khalsa-Dension, & Paredes, 1996); the latter has been linked to attention deficit disorder (Alsobrook & Pauls, 1998), a condition that we have already noted is characterized by impulsivity.

Some New Data

The evidence reviewed earlier suggests that (1) the CARROT task is a simple measure of the appetitive motivational processes related to BAS functioning; (2) it has successfully revealed deficits in the responses to reward cues of patients with altered motivational processes (brain injured; smokers); and (3) performance on the task may be responsive to changes in brain dopaminergic transmission (bromocriptine study). We (Pickering et al., submitted) therefore set out to explore the relationship between performance on the CARROT task and the ISS personality traits hypothesized (under RST) to be especially sensitive to reward cues. We then carried out a subsequent study addressing the possible associations between CARROT performance and genetic variations at the DRD4 locus.

CARROT performance was measured in 167 young (mostly undergraduate) subjects. Several significant relationships with CARROT performance were found with subscales from each of the ISS questionnaires that we used: Extraversion from H. J. Eysenck and Eysenck's (1975) EPQ; Zuckerman's (1979) Sensation Seeking Scale; S. B. G. Eysenck, Pearson, Easting, and Allsopp's (1985) IVE scales; plus Carver and White's (1994) BIS/BAS scales. On the first (baseline) CARROT trial and/or the second (nonrewarded) trial, subjects scoring high on the above questionnaires showed a significantly higher rate of card-sorting. Card-sorting rate increased significantly between the first and second trial, but this was not associated with any of the personality measures. Subjects who scored *low* on the personality measures, relative to those with high scores, had significantly greater increases in card-sorting rate from the second to third (rewarded) trial, and significantly greater decreases from the third to the fourth (nonrewarded) trial. The data are shown in the upper panel of Figure 10.3 (see next page) with the sample subdivided about the median of the Impulsiveness subscale of the IVE (S. G. B. Eysenck et al., 1985).

In a subsequent study with 47 subjects we also looked at CARROT performance as a function of DRD4 allele length. Long-allele subjects (N = 13) sorted cards significantly faster in both the first and second CARROT trials. They also showed a significantly smaller increase in sorting rate on the third rewarded trial relative to the second trial. The results are depicted in the lower panel of Figure 10.3 where the similarities to the findings for personality measures are obvious. Although the gene–personality associations discussed earlier are being intensely researched, these pilot results are the first to link a specific experimental measure of human behavior to variations in genetic structure. It may be noteworthy that these results were obtained in a sample smaller than those used in gene–personality association studies. This might imply that genetic markers (such as the D4DR alleles) have a stronger influence on specific behaviors or processes than on broad personality traits, such as Novelty Seeking. Broad traits are thought to reflect the influence of a collection of processes, only some of which would relate to any one specific genetic marker.

In both these studies, it appears that the ISS (or long allele) subjects, whom RST would predict to be the most sensitive to reward cues, actually showed the smallest response to the reward cues present during the third trial. However, this aspect of these studies appears to be difficult to interpret unequivocally. There seems to be a ceiling on card-sorting rate at about 1.25 cards/second. As subjects become more practised at the task across several trials, they all tend to increase their card-sorting rate. Hence subjects who start at a faster rate, for whatever reason, tend to reach the performance ceiling in fewer trials. It seems likely that subjects with high scores on ISS personality traits and/or long D4DR alleles (who show clear evidence of faster initial sorting rates) may be approaching the performance ceiling after the second trial and are therefore able to show little improvement on trial 3, which coincidentally happens to be the rewarded trial. Subjects with low ISS trait scores and/or short D4DR alleles (who have slower initial sorting rates) are able to show improvements on trial 3 that are less affected by any ceiling effect.

We are still left with the important observation of baseline differences in sorting-rate. It is possible that they have nothing to do with the processes with which this chapter has been concerned (responses to reward cues and associated dopaminergic neurotransmission). A more interesting possibility, suggested by Pickering (1997), is that the initially faster rate of card-sorting itself may reflect differences in responsiveness to reward cues. The argument rests on the sugges-

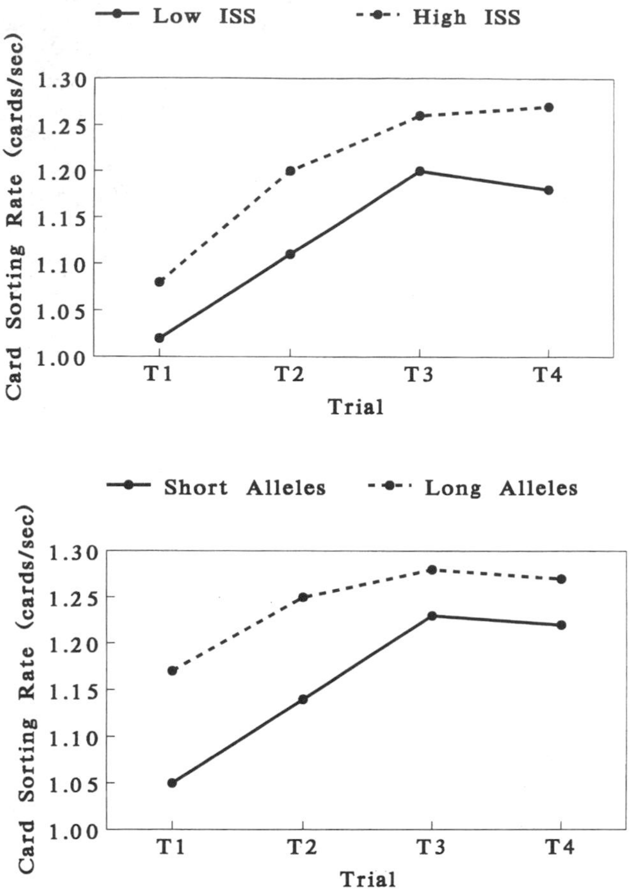

FIGURE 10.3. Mean card-sorting rates during the four trials (T1–T4) of the CARROT task. *Upper panel:* subjects subdivided according to scores on the Impulsiveness subscale from the IVE (S. G. B. Eysenck et al., 1985). *Lower panel:* subjects subdivided according to the presence of at least one long allele (7 or 8 base-pair repeats) in the D4 dopamine receptor gene.

tion that, even in the baseline trial, covert cues of possible rewards are present (e.g., there is the prospect of the subject gaining social reinforcement from the experimenter for performing the task well). If this is accepted then it would be those subjects with a reactive BAS (i.e., high ISS subjects) who would display behavioral activation effects in response to these covert reward cues. Their card-sorting performance would thus be expected to start at a faster level.

To address these interpretations we carried out a third CARROT study in 60 undergraduate subjects to whom we had also given Cloninger's Tridimensional Personality Questionnaire. The Novelty Seeking (NS) score from this scale provided a measure of ISS personality. The CARROT task was modified so that the financial incentives were given on the second trial. It was hoped that this would allow us to see the effect of the reward cues, in relation to NS, uncomplicated by ceiling effects. There was a nonsignificant positive correlation between NS and baseline sorting rate. However, there was a significant positive correlation between NS and the increase in sorting rate between the baseline and the rewarded trial. This finding is in accordance with the predictions of RST (high ISS subjects should show the greatest behavioral activation in response to reward cues). Furthermore, it lends weight to the idea that the differences in baseline sorting rate between high ISS (long D4DR allele) and low ISS (short D4DR allele) subjects may reflect differential responses to covert reward cues present on the baseline trial.

DEVELOPING AND ELABORATING THE NEURAL MODEL OF THE BAS

In Figure 10.1 we sketched a conceptual nervous system architecture for the BAS, the BIS and the interactions between the two systems. We suggested that, in order to accommodate findings by Newman and colleagues, the modulation output from the BAS (i.e., the output that inhibits BIS activity) should be omitted. In Figure 10.2 we began to fill in details of a possible neural network that might form the substrate of the BAS. We suggested that the output threshold of striatal cells might vary systematically as a function of ISS personality traits. Specifically, a low threshold would be characteristic of a subject with high levels of ISS traits, and this would generate a greater degree of BAS output for a given BAS input (such as a secondary positive reinforcer). In this way the high ISS subject would have a highly sensitive/reactive BAS, in keeping with the account offered by RST. Finally, we suggested that the low output threshold from the striatum might be a function of inefficient inhibitory (D2-like) dopaminergic synapses on striatal neurons. The functional properties of these dopaminergic synapses might in part be coded for by genetic variations, such as the polymorphisms that affect the structure of the D4DR and which appear to be related to ISS traits.

In order to develop our model, we must elaborate the neural architecture of Figure 10.2 to locate the sites at which the BAS outputs affect behavior and to locate the neural pathways for BAS–BIS interactions. Thus far we have not differentiated between the dorsal (caudate–putamen) and ventral (nucleus accumbens) parts of the striatum. This was because the cell recording studies summarized by Schultz et al. (1995) revealed no differences when recording from dopaminergic cells in the SN (which project to caudate–putamen) or the VTA (which project to nucleus accumbens, NAcc). It is clear, however, that NAcc (and in particular the shell subregion of NAcc) has the appropriate kinds of connections to underpin the BAS functions and BAS–BIS interactions of Figure 10.1 (see Depue & Collins, in press).

Drawing on the work of Swerdlow and Koob (1987), we have previously emphasized the outputs from NAcc via the ventral pallidum in controlling the execution of motor programs (Gray, Feldon, Rawlins, Hemsley, & Smith, 1991). As described by Schultz et al. (1995; see above), NAcc output may be triggered by conditioned stimuli associated with reward (denoted "BAS input" in Figure 10.4). We have argued that greater output from NAcc (resulting from weaker dopaminergic inhibition) is related to high scores on BAS-reactive ISS personality traits. As shown in Figure 10.4, the outputs from NAcc are inhibitory in nature (mediated by the neurotransmitter γ-aminobutyric acid, GABA). The NAcc output produced by a BAS input stimulus would therefore lead to reduced activity in the ventral pallidum (VP). In turn this would produce reductions in the inhibitory (again GABAergic) outputs from VP. For our present purposes there are two important effects of reduced VP output: The firing rate of the dopaminergic cells of the VTA would increase, and the reverbatory feedback between prefrontal cortex (PFC) and the dorsomedial nucleus of the thalamus (DMNT) would be facilitated. All these effects, in the chain of neural events triggered by a BAS activating input, are expected to be larger in subjects with high ISS trait scores relative to subjects with low ISS scores.

The PFC–DMNT loops are involved in response selection and control, directing the execution of the specific steps in a selected response sequence, and these specific sensorimotor steps are themselves encoded in corticostriatal pathways within the caudate motor system. (The caudate motor system is centered on the dopaminergic pathway from SN to caudate–putamen; see Gray et al., 1991.) The PFC–DMNT loop is represented schematically in Figure 10.4 in terms of competitive interactions between neurons controlling different response outputs (R_1, R_2 etc.). When a conditioned stimulus associated with reward elicits output from NAcc, we have noted that this will give rise to an increase in dopaminergic firing in the VTA. This will subsequently lead to an increase in the dopaminergic inhibition of NAcc firing. This increased inhibition at NAcc therefore acts to provide a natural temporal limit on the NAcc response to BAS input stimuli. A BAS activating stimulus is therefore expected to exert a phasic burst of behavioral activation.

In Figure 10.4, the only activation output from the BAS that is depicted is the projection

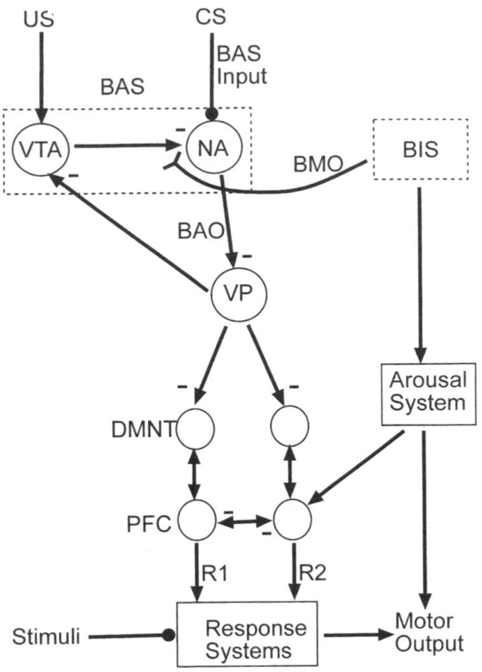

FIGURE 10.4. A schematic neural architecture for the behavioral activation system (BAS) and its interactions with the behavioral inhibition system (BIS). A BAS output to the arousal system and the BIS inhibition output are not shown. The critical neural loci are as follows: the ascending dopaminergic projections from the ventral tegmental area (VTA) to nucleus accumbens (NAcc); the ventral pallidum (VP); the dorsomedial nucleus of the thalamus (DMNT); and the prefrontal cortex (PFC) response control system, which selects between available responses (R1, R2 etc.). The BIS outputs may derive from amygdala, entorhinal cortex, and subiculum. Pathways are excitatory except where minus signs denote inhibitory connections. Rounded arrowheads indicate modifiable synapses; double-headed arrows indicate reciprocal connections. The BIS modulation output (BMO) is depicted by a modulatory synapse to reflect its influence on the inhibitory dopaminergic effects of the VTA–NAcc pathway (see text for details). US, appetitive unconditioned stimulus; CS, conditioned stimulus associated with US; BAO, BAS activation output.

from NAcc to VP. However, the VTA also sends dopaminergic projections to the PFC. This projection may serve as an additional BAS activation output pathway. One might speculatively hypothesize various mechanisms by which this could occur. For example, excitatory dopaminergic mechanisms may activate the outputs from PFC to the response systems after a particular response has been selected via the competitive interactions within PFC. Another BAS activation output can be suggested. The NAcc sends an inhibitory projection to the substantia nigra (SN). The SN provides ascending dopaminergic modulation of the caudate motor system (Gray et al., 1991). Weiner (1991) offers a clear suggestion of how NAcc output would therefore reduce dopaminergic inhibition of the caudate–putamen (CP), facilitating the execution of ongoing motor programs encoded in the corticostriatal pathways from sensorimotor cortex to CP. In each of these BAS activation scenarios (NAcc–VP–DMNT–PFC; NAcc–VP–VTA–PFC; NAcc–SN–CP), we are suggesting that high ISS subjects would tend to produce stronger output from NAcc, with the ultimate effect of facilitating ongoing behavioral responses.

We have focused on the effects of the BAS in motivating and energizing learned motor programs. However, before moving on to consider how the BIS might modulate BAS activity within this scheme, we should briefly discuss how the BAS might affect learning processes. Two important learning processes should be distinguished: operant mechanisms which relate to the acquisition of the stimulus–response habits that comprise the motor programs; and classical conditioning mechanisms, by which a previously neutral stimulus can acquire BAS-activating properties.

As noted earlier, Houk et al. (1995) emphasized a particular form of dopamine-dependent LTP that they argued is responsible for reinforcement learning in corticostriatal pathways. We have suggested that this learning process may be the means by which neutral CSs become associated with reward and thereby are able to act as BAS input stimuli, activating NAcc neurons. In keeping with the traditional framing of RST we suggested that this learning process should be independent of the mechanisms responsible for the greater BAS reactivity of high ISS subjects. Houk et al. argue that the reinforcing properties of dopamine are mediated by D1-like receptors; we have suggested that the variations in BAS output threshold (which affect NAcc output and are the hypothesized substrate of ISS trait variation) are mediated by D2-like receptors. The extent to which D1-like and D2-like receptors are segregated from one another in the brain is a controversial topic (see Jaber et al., 1996), but our account makes it possible that individual differences in the acquisition of secondary reinforcing properties by a stimulus, and individual differences in that stimulus's subsequent motivating effects, could be largely independent.

Despite the arguments just raised, it is possible that the greater VTA dopaminergic firing in high ISS subjects, in response to a BAS input stimulus, might increase the efficiency of their learning mechanisms in corticostriatal pathways relative to those of their low ISS counterparts. In addition, one might speculate that the corticostriatal learning in pathways to the NAcc might encode the acquired motivational properties of the stimulus, whereas corticostriatal learning in pathways to the caudate–putamen (dorsal striatum) might also represent some of the operant learning processes responsible for the formation of stimulus–response habits. If these speculations are correct, then both the acquisition of motivational significance for a BAS input stimulus and the acquisition of stimulus–response habits under appetitive reinforcement could be related to ISS personality traits.

The NAcc-shell also receives projections from various limbic system structures including a subicular output from the hippocampus, plus projections from the entorhinal cortex and amygdala. These outputs to NAcc might correspond to the modulation outputs from the BIS that act to inhibit BAS activity. The amygdala output might be active in the presence of conditioned fear stimuli (LeDoux, 1996); the hippocampal output might signal an associative mismatch (when a particular stimulus is not predicted by preceding stimuli; Honey, Watt, & Good, 1998); and the output from entorhinal and adjacent cortices might signal that a stimulus is unfamiliar (Aggleton & Brown, in press). The BIS is argued to respond to each of these kinds of signal (Gray, 1982). These projections to NAcc are thought to involve the excitatory neurotransmitter glutamate; this is not a serious problem for the current proposal because there is evidence that glutamate can act to potentiate dopaminergic release and thus reduce striatal output (Imperato, Honore, & Jensen, 1990; Wang, 1991). These potential BIS modulation outputs to NAcc could therefore oppose the effects of BAS inputs (i.e., BIS modulation outputs reduce, and BAS inputs increase, NAcc output).

In the above sketch we have not proposed details for the arousal outputs from BIS or BAS, or a route by which a BIS output might directly inhibit response selection. The neurobiology of the BIS arousal output is discussed elsewhere (Gray & McNaughton, in press). Although we saw earlier that the arousal output from the BIS was critical in explaining the results obtained by Newman and his colleagues, it is possible that the other outputs omitted from Figure 10.4 may not be needed for the systems to function in the fashion described by RST. For example, the effects of an output from the BAS to an arousal system would be very difficult to distinguish from the direct behaviorally activating effects of the BAS itself. Similarly, the direct inhibitory effects of the BIS might be hard to distinguish from BIS modulation effects that act on the BAS and thereby interfere with BAS-mediated behavior. Indeed, Gray & McNaughton (in press) argue that BIS outputs affect motor systems via the subicular projection to NAcc. In the framework of the current chapter this pathway corresponds to the BIS modulation output.

HOW THE MODEL MIGHT BE TESTED

The value of the current model will, as always, be judged by its ability to stimulate research and predict experimental findings. We are currently developing a computational neural network version of the theory to aid in this process. We have begun by building a neural net based directly on striatal neurobiology (Salum, Roque da Silva, & Pickering, in press). As a complement to this bottom-up approach we have also been involved in developing a neural network, from the top down, which can simulate important learning phenomena (Schmajuk, Gray, & Lam, 1996). This model was not constrained by any particular neural architecture, but, by identifying one particular component of the model with dopaminergic neurotransmission in the VTA–NAcc pathway, we have been able to simulate specific behavioral effects of amphetamine very closely (Schmajuk, Catalin, & Gray, in press). Modelling individual differences within networks like these will involve allowing parameters of interest (such as those reflecting dopamine receptor binding, for example) to vary and seeing whether this can capture the observed personality task correlations. To close this chapter we will describe another way in which we have begun to explore our account of ISS traits.

Those who are familiar with our account of the neuropsychology of schizophrenia (Gray et al., 1991) will note that the neural architecture and neurochemical mechanisms proposed in that context overlap closely with the circuitry discussed here. Indeed, we related the positive psychotic symptoms (hallucinations, delusions, etc.) of schizophrenia to *increases* in (inhibitory, D2-like) dopaminergic effects at NAcc. As we have noted elsewhere (Gray, in press; Gray et al., in press) the link between schizophrenia and models of ISS personality traits needs careful consideration.

In this chapter, we have suggested that subjects with high scores on ISS personality traits will show increased output from NAcc neurons in response to stimuli associated with reward. We propose that this occurs because of *reductions* in (inhibitory, D2-like) dopaminergic effects at NAcc. The increased NAcc output is responsible for increased behavioral activation effects of reward cues in high ISS subjects and also leads to increased firing of VTA dopamine neurons that project to NAcc. Increased VTA firing might, in turn, contribute further behavioral activation effects. Based on the current model, one might therefore expect the link between schizophrenia and ISS traits to be complex.

To illustrate this, suppose one hypothesized for schizophrenics that increases in dopaminergic effects at NAcc were the result of increased VTA neuron firing (for a more plausible account see Grace, 1991). Suppose also that one had a behavioral task that was selectively influenced by VTA neuronal responses to stimulus cues. Then one might expect schizophrenic patients and subjects with high ISS trait scores to show similar behavior on such a task, and their behavior should be in the direction associated with greater VTA firing responses. By contrast, if one had another task, which was selectively influenced by the responses of GABAergic neurons in NAcc, then one might expect the behavior of high ISS subjects to reflect increased NAcc output and the behavior of schizophrenics to reflect decreased NAcc output. Despite the likely complexity of the results, we feel research that explicitly explores the relationship between ISS traits and schizophrenia will prove highly informative.

As we explain below, the relationship between ISS traits and schizophrenia may be conveniently explored by investigating the effects of ISS and schizotypal personality traits, ideally in the same sample of subjects. Healthy individuals vary in their propensities to experience mild versions of psychotic-like experiences (mild hallucinations and disorganised thinking), to hold unusual beliefs (mild delusions) and to behave in odd ways (with restricted emotions and social interactions). Many questionnaire measures have been developed to measure these aspects of schizotypal personality in healthy individuals. Several large-scale studies, using multivariate statistical techniques, have revealed a strong degree of convergence on the structure of schizotypal personality. Generally, three or four schizotypal personality factors emerge, and these factors bear a close resemblance in content to the clusters that have been found in schizophrenic symptoms (Vollema & van den Bosch, 1995).

Two schizotypal personality factors are particularly relevant for our present arguments. In all studies a major factor of positive schizotypy emerges that reflects propensities to unusual perceptual experiences and beliefs. This clearly relates closely to the positive symptoms of schizophrenia. In most studies, there is a more minor factor related to impulsive, nonconformist, and antisocial behaviors. (Vollema & van den Bosch refer to this as Nonconformity, although the impulsive component has been emphasized in the name adopted by other authors.) This factor is quite close to the kind of ISS personality trait on which this chapter has focused and indeed scales like EPQ-P load heavily on this factor. Impulsive nonconformity does not resemble any features of schizophrenia, but is similar in content to the behaviors of individuals with particular kinds of personality disorder.

As argued at the start of this chapter we adhere to a continuum view of the relationship between personality traits in the healthy population and related clinical states (which are taken to reflect extremes on the personality continuum). By adopting the continuum assumption, we can use schizotypal personality variation as a means to study the processes relevant to the Gray et al. (1991) model of positive schizophrenic symptoms in healthy subjects. One can therefore compare the effects of positive schizotypy and ISS personality traits on relevant tasks and thereby more tightly constrain any model of the biological bases of these traits.

For some tasks, positive schizotypy and ISS traits appear to affect behavior in similar fashion. Negative priming is a much-studied attentional phenomenon that is reliably impaired in schizophrenics and in subjects with high scores on positive schizotypy (e.g., Peters, Pickering, & Hemsley, 1994). Negative priming has also been found to be reduced by high levels of social impulsivity in children (Visser, Das-Smaal, & Kwakman, 1996).

If the biological basis of ISS traits is related to striatal dopaminergic functioning, as we propose, then finding a relationship between an experimental measure of selective attention (negative priming) and impulsivity is also consistent with a role for dopaminergic neurotransmission in NAcc that encompasses more than incentive motivational processes. There is other evidence, too, for the effects of ISS personality traits on selective attention tasks (Martin, 1985). In recent work (Pickering et al., 1999) we have looked at the effect of ISS and schizotypal personality traits on a further attentional phenomenon: filtration category learning.

Filtration learning (see Kruschke, 1993) refers to a situation in which one has to classify multidimensional stimuli but only one of the dimensions on which the stimuli vary is relevant for category membership. (In our task we used visual stimuli based on a rectangular box with an internal line segment; the height of the box and the lateral position of the line segment could vary but only one of these stimulus dimensions was associated with category membership.) Thus, the subject has to learn to attend to salient stimulus features and ignore irrelevant ones: These are precisely the kind of attentional processes relevant to the Gray et al. (1991) model of schizophrenia (see also Gray et al., in press). Schizophrenics with positive symptoms would be expected to be poor at this type of learning task because the disturbance to their mesolimbic dopamine system renders them unable to learn relevance/salience normally.

In a preliminary study using only male subjects we found that subjects with high scores on Cloninger's Novelty Seeking were significantly faster at learning our filtration task than low scoring subjects. In a subsequent study we measured positive schizotypy using Mason, Claridge, and Jackson's (1995) Unusual Experiences scale and ISS personality via EPQ-P. Based on the first study a positive correlation between learning and EPQ-P scores was expected. For the whole sample there was only a nonsignificant trend ($r = .22$, $p = .065$), but the correlation did reach significance in the male subjects (r=.35). In the same subjects, the correlation between learning and Unusual Experiences scores was negative as predicted, although nonsignificant. However, the correlation was significant in female subjects ($r = -.38$, $p < .05$). Taken together with the negative priming findings, the filtration learning results suggest that schizotypal and ISS personality traits may sometimes have opposing, and sometimes similar, effects on behavior. This was exactly the kind of complex relationship that we anticipated above.

For the moment, these data serve to show that there is plenty of work to be done in order to disentangle the complex relationships between schizotypal and ISS personality traits. Such findings, if they prove reliable, will present a considerable challenge to our attempts to model personality traits via biologically constrained neural networks.

The effects of ISS traits on filtration category learning extend earlier findings by Ball and Zuckerman (1990), who showed that subjects with high scores on the Sensation Seeking scale (Zuckerman, 1979) learned a complex concept formation task faster than subjects with low Sensation Seeking scores. The concept formation task, like our filtration paradigm, involved distinguishing relevant from irrelevant stimulus attributes, and the personality effect was found whether or not successful performance was rewarded with money. Finally, in light of the relationship between ISS traits and Parkinson's disease, reviewed earlier, it is interesting to note the findings of Knowlton, Mangels, and Squire (1996). Knowlton et al. found that Parkinson's disease patients showed poor category learning (forecasting the weather by learning the associations with probabilistic visual geometric cues presented on a computer screen), despite having normal episodic memory for details of the category task (e.g., screen layout etc.). Once again, this task involved learning which stimulus attributes were relevant in predicting outcome.

This set of experimental outcomes may once again illustrate that the influence of the dopaminergic substrate of ISS personality traits can be seen in behavioral contexts other than those controlled by explicit appetitive incentives. This is in keeping with our view that the mesolimbic dopamine system responds to a wider range of stimuli than those which transmit appetitive incentive information.

CONCLUDING OBSERVATIONS

We presented the model developed in this chapter to show that it is now possible to use an integrated neuroscience approach to the study of personality. We hope that this kind of approach will improve the status of personality research in the eyes of the psychology and neuroscience communities. We feel that, by drawing together data from a wide range of research areas, we have been able to sketch a reasonably specific, and we hope persuasive, account of the neuroscience of ISS personality traits. This type of personality theory can also be tested by the usual methods of natural science.

We chose to focus on ISS traits in part because there is a degree of consensus in this area among the major biologically oriented personality theorists, and our model resembles other proposals, especially the recent account of Depue and Collins (in press). Depue and Collins argue that there is a dopaminergic substrate to Extraversion that is weakly and inconsistently reflected in correlations between ISS traits and dopamine-sensitive measures. In our version, by contrast, it is ISS traits themselves that are closely aligned with the fundamental biological axis of personality, and Extraversion that correlates with dopamine-sensitive measures by proxy.

The current model relates ISS traits to variations in dopaminergic transmission in the mesolimbic pathways from VTA to NAcc and suggests that NAcc is a vital part of a behavioral activation system (BAS) concerned with appetive motivational effects on behavior. However, we have repeatedly emphasized that one should not align dopaminergic release in NAcc exclusively with appetitive motivation. In the current model, other kinds of signal, reflecting other ways in which a particular stimulus might be salient (because it is unfamiliar, unpredicted by preceding stimuli, or because it signals an upcoming aversive event), also have the capability to stimulate dopamine release in NAcc. We view these other signals as being generated in one of a number of neural loci. We describe these other loci collectively as forming a Behavioral Inhibition System (BIS) that functions to inhibit ongoing behavior, in part through opposing the effects of the BAS. Elsewhere we have related individual differences in the strength of the output signals from the BIS to variations in trait anxiety (Gray & McNaughton, 1996, in press).

REFERENCES

Aggleton, J. P., & Brown, M. W. (in press). Episodic memory, amnesia, and the hippoccampal–anterior thalamic axis. *Behavioral and Brain Sciences.*

Al-Adawi S., Powell, J., & Greenwood, R. J. (1998). Motivational deficits after brain injury: A neuropsychological approach using new assessment measures. *Neuropsychology, 12,* 115–124.

Al-Adawi S., & Powell, J. (1997). The influence of smoking on reward responsiveness and cognitive functions: A natural experiment. *Addiction, 92,* 1773–1782.

Alsobrook, J. P. II, & Pauls, D. L. (1998). Molecular approaches to child psychopathology. *Human Biology, 70,* 413–432.

Arnett, P. A., Smith, S. S., & Newman, J. P. (1997). Approach and avoidance motivation in psychopathic criminal offenders during passive avoidance. *Journal of Personality and Social Psychology, 72,* 1413–1428.

Asghari, V., Schoots, O., VanKats, S., Ohara, K., Jovanocic, V., Guan, H. C., Bunzow, J. R., Petronis, A., & Van Tol, H. H. M. (1994). Dopamine D4 receptor repeat: Analysis of different native and mutant forms of the human and rat genes. *Molecular Pharmacology, 46,* 364–373.

Ball, S. A., & Zuckerman, M. (1990). Sensation seeking, Eysenck's personality dimensions and reinforcement sensitivity in concept formation. *Personality and Individual Differences, 11,* 343–353.

Benjamin, J., Li, L., Patterson, C., Greenberg, B. D., Murphy, D. L., & Hamer, D. H. (1996). Population of familial association between the D4 dopamine receptor gene and measures of novelty seeking. *Nature Genetics, 12,* 81–84.

Bozarth, M. S., & Wise, R. A. (1981). Involvement of the ventral tegmental dopamine system in opioid and psychomotor stimulant reinforcement. *Life Sciences, 28,* 551–555.

Carver, C. S., & White, T. L. (1994). Behavioral inhibition, behavioral activation, and affective responses to impending reward and punishment: The BIS/BAS scales. *Journal of Personality and Social Psychology, 67,* 319–333.

Claridge, G. S. (1987). 'The schizophrenias as nervous types' revisited. *British Journal of Psychiatry, 151,* 735–743.

Cloninger, C. R. (1989). *The Tridimensional Personality Questionnaire.* Department of Psychiatry and Genetics. St. Louis, MO: Washington University School of Medicine.

Cloninger, C. R., Svrakic, D. M., & Przybeck, T. R. (1993). A psychobiological model of temperament and character. *Archives of General Psychiatry, 50,* 975–990.

Compton, P. A., Anglin, M. D., Khalsa-Dension, M. E., & Paredes, A. (1996). The D2 dopamine receptor gene, addiction, and personality: Clinical correlates in cocaine abusers. *Biological Psychiatry, 39,* 302–304.

Corr, P. J., Pickering, A. D., & Gray, J. A. (1995). Personality and reinforcement in associative and instrumental learning. *Personality and Individual Differences, 19,* 47–71.

Depue, R. (1995). Neurobiological factors in personality and depression. *European Journal of Personality, 9,* 413–439.

Depue, R. (1996). Neurobiology and the structure of personality: Implications for the personality disorders. In J. Clarkin & M. Lenzenweger (Eds.), *Major theories of personality disorders.* New York: Guilford Press.

Depue, R. A., & Collins, P. F. (in press). Neurobiology of the structure of personality: Dopamine, facilitation of incentive motivation, and extraversion. *Behavioral and Brain Sciences.*

Depue, R., Luciana, M., Arbisi, P., Collins, P., & Leon, A. (1994). Dopamine and the structure of personality: Relation of agonist-induced dopamine activity to positive emotionally. *Journal of Personality and Social Psychology, 67,* 485–498.

Di Chiara, G., Acquas, E., & Carboni, E. (1992). Drug motivation and abuse: A neurobiological perspective. *Annals of the New York Academy of Sciences, 654,* 207–219.

Díaz, A., & Pickering, A. D. (1993). The relationship between Gray's and Eysenck's personality spaces. *Personality and Individual Differences, 15,* 297–305.

Ding, Y. S., Fowler, J. S., Volkow, N. D., Logan, J., Gatley, S. J., & Sugano, Y. (1995). Carbon-11-d-threo-methylphenidate binding to dopamine transporter in baboon brain. *Journal of Nuclear Medicine, 36,* 2298–2305.

Ebstein, R. P., Novick, O., Umansky, R., Priel, B., Osher, Y., Blaine, D., Bennett, E. R., Nemanov, L., Katz, M., & Belmaker, R. H., (1996). Dopamine D4 receptor (D4DR) exon III polymorphism associated with the human personality trait of Novelty Seeking. *Nature Genetics, 12,* 78–80.

Ebstein, R. P., Segman, R., Benjamin, J., Osher, Y., Nemanov, L., & Belmaker, R. H. (1997). 5-HT2c (HTR2C) serotonin receptor gene polymorphism associated with the human personality trait of Reward Dependence: Interaction with dopamine 4 receptor (D4DR) and dopamine D3 (D3DR) polymorphisms. *American Journal of Medical Genetics (Neuropsychiatric Genetics), 74,* 65–72.

Eysenck, H. J., & Eysenck, S. B. G. (1975). *Manual of the Eysenck Personality Questionnaire (Adults).* London: Hodder & Stoughton.

Eysenck, S. B. G., Pearson, P. R., Easting, G., & Allsopp, J. F. (1985). Age norms for impulsiveness, venturesomeness and empathy in adults. *Personality and Individual Differences, 6,* 613–619.

Farde, L., Gustavsson, J. P., & Jönsson, E. (1997). D2 dopamine receptors and personality traits. *Nature, 385,* 590.

Gorenstein, E. E., & Newman, J. P. (1980). Disinhibitory psychopathology: A new perspective and a model for research. *Psychological Review, 87,* 301–315.

Grace, A. A. (1991). Phasic versus tonic dopmaine release and the modulation of dopamine system responsivity: A hypothesis for the etiology of schizophrenia. *Neuroscience, 41,* 1–24.

Gray, J. A. (1970). The psychophysiological basis of introversion–extraversion. *Behaviour Research and Therapy, 8,* 249–266.

Gray, J. A. (1972). Learning theory, the conceptual nervous system and personality. In V. D. Nebylitsyn & J. A. Gray (Eds), *The biological bases of individual behavior* (pp. 372–399). London: Academic Press.

Gray, J. A. (1981). A critque of Eysenck's theory of personality. In H. J. Eysenck (Ed.), *A model for personality* (pp. 246–276). Berlin: Springer-Verlag.

Gray, J. A. (1982). *The neuropsychology of anxiety: An enquiry into the functions of the septo-hippocampal system.* Oxford, UK: Oxford University Press.

Gray, J. A. (1987). The neuropsychology of emotion and personality. In S. M. Stahl, S. D. Iversen, E. C. Goodman (Eds.), *Cognitive neurochemistry* (pp. 171–190). Oxford, UK: Oxford University Press.

Gray, J. A. (in press). But the schizophrenia connection . . . *Behavioral and Brain Sciences.*

Gray, J. A., Feldon, J., Rawlins, J. N. P., Hemsley, D. R., & Smith, A. D. (1991). The neuropsychology of schizophrenia. *Behavioral and Brain Sciences, 14,* 1–20.

Gray, J. A., Kumari, V., Lawrence, N., & Young, A. J. (in press). Functions of the dopaminergic innervation of nucleus accumbens. *Psychobiology.*

Gray, J. A., & McNaughton, N. (1996). The neuropsychology of anxiety: Reprise. In D. A. Hope (Ed.), *Nebraska symposium on motivation: Vol. 43. Perspectives on anxiety, panic and fear* (pp. 61–134). Lincoln: University of Nebraska Press.

Gray, J. A., & McNaughton, N. (in press). *The neuropsychology of anxiety* (2nd ed.). Oxford, UK: Oxford University Press.

Gray, J. A., & Smith, P. T. (1969). An arousal-decision model for partial reinforcement and discrimination learning. In R. Gilbert & N. S. Sutherland (Eds), *Animal discrimination learning* (pp. 243–272). London: Academic Press.

Gray, N. S., Pickering, A. D., & Gray, J. A. (1994). Psychoticism and dopamine D2 binding in the basal ganglia using single photon emission tomography. *Personality and Individual Differences, 17,* 413–434.

Honey, R. C., Watt, W., & Good, M. (1998). Hippocampal lesions disrupt an associative mismatch process. *Journal of Neuroscience, 18,* 2226–2230.

Houk, J. C., Adams, J. L., & Barto, A. G. (1995). A model of how the basal ganglia generate and use neural signals that predict reinforcement. In J. C. Houk, J. L. Davis, & D. G. Beiser (Eds.), *Models of information processing in the basal ganglia* (pp. 233–248). London: MIT Press.

Hsu, K.-S., Huang, C.-C., Yang, C.-H., & Gean, P.-W. (1995). Presynaptic D2 dopaminergic receptors mediate inhibition of excitatory synaptic transmission in rat neostriatum. *Brain Research, 690,* 264–268.

Imperato, A., Honore, T. & Jensen, L. H. (1990). Dopamine release in the nucleus caudatus and in the nucleus accumbens is under glutamatergic control through non-NMDA receptors: A study in freely moving rats. *Brain Research, 530,* 223–228.

Jaber, M., Robinson, S. W., Missale, C., & Caron, M. G. (1996). Dopamine receptors and brain function. *Neuropharmacology, 35,* 1503–1519.

Jönsson, E. G., Nöthen, M. M., Gustavsson, J. P. Neidt, H., Brené, S., Tylec, A., Propping, P., & Sedvall, G. C. (1997). Lack of evidence for allelic association between personality traits and the dopamine D4 receptor gene polymorphisms. *American Journal of Psychiatry, 154,* 697–699.

Knowlton, B. J., Mangels, J. A., & Squire, L. R. (1996). A neostriatal habit learning system in humans. *Science, 273,* 1399–1402.

Kruschke, J. K. (1993). Human category learning: Implications for backpropagation models. *Connection Science, 5,* 3–36.

Kwasman, A., Tinsley, B. J., & Lepper, H. S. (1995). Pediatricians' knowledge and attitudes concerning diagnosis and treatment of attention deficit and hyperactivity disorders: A national survey approach. *Archives of Pediatrics and Adolescent Medicine, 149,* 1211–1216.

LeDoux, J. (1996). *The emotional brain.* New York: Simon & Schuster.

Li, T., Xu, K., Deng, H., Cai, G., Liu, J., Liu, X., Wang, R., Xiang, X., Zhao, J., Murray, R. M., Sham, P. C., & Collier, D. A. (1997). Association analysis of the dopamine D4 gene exon III VNTR and heroin abuse in Chinese subjects. *Molecular Psychiatry, 2,* 413–416.

Lykken, D. T. (1957). A study of anxiety in the sociopathic personality. *Journal of Abnormal and Social Psychology, 55,* 6–10.

MacAndrew, C., & Steele, T. (1991). Gray's behavioral inhibition system: A psychometric examination. *Personality and Individual Differences, 12,* 157–171.

Malhotra, A. K., Virkkunen, M., Rooney, W., Eggert, M., Linnoila, M., & Goldman, D. (1996). The association between the dopamine D4 receptor (D4DR) 16 amino acid repeat polymorphism and Novelty Seeking. *Molecular Psychiatry, 1,* 388–391.

Martin, M. (1985). Individual differences in sensation seeking and attentional ability. *Personality and Individual Differences, 6,* 637–639.

Mason, O., Claridge, G. & Jackson, M. (1995). New scales for the assessment of schizotypy. *Personality and Individual Differences, 18,* 7–13.

Menza, M. A., Forman, N. E., Goldstein, H. S., & Golbe, L. I. (1990). Parkinson's disease, personality, and dopamine. *Journal of Neuropsychiatry and Clinical Neuroscience, 2,* 282–287.

Menza, M. A., Golbe, L. I., Cody, R. A., & Forman, N. E. (1993). Dopamine-related personality traits in Parkinson's disease. *Neurology, 43,* 505–508.

Menza, M. A., Mark, M. H., Burn, D. J., & Brooks, D. J. (1995). Personality correlates of [18F]dopa striatal uptake: Results of positron-emission tomography in Parkinson's disease. *Journal of Neuropsychiatry and Clinical Neurosciences, 7,* 176–179.

Netter, P., Hennig, J., & Roed, I. (1996). Serotonin and dopamine as mediators of sensation seeking behavior. *Neuropsychobiology, 34,* 155–165.

Nichols, S. L., & Newman, J. P. (1986). Effects of punishment on response latency in extraverts. *Journal of Personality and Social Psychology, 50,* 624–630.

Ono, Y., Manki, H., Yoshimura, K., Muramatsu, T., Higuchi, S., Yagi, G., Kanba, S., & Asai, M. (1997). Association between dopamine D4 receptor (D4DR) exon III polymorphism and Novelty Seeking in Japanese subjects. *American Journal of Medical Genetics (Neuropsychiatric Genetics), 74,* 501–503.

Patterson, C. M., Kosson, D. S., & Newman, J. P. (1987). Reaction to punishment, reflectivity and passive avoidance learning in extraverts. *Journal of Personality and Social Psychology, 52,* 565–575.

Patterson, C. M., & Newman, J. P. (1993). Reflectivity and learning from aversive events: Toward a psychological mechanism for the syndromes of disinhibition. *Psychological Review, 100,* 716–736.

Peters, E. R., Pickering, A. D., & Hemsley, D. R. (1994). "Cognitive inhibition" and positive symptomatology in schizotypy. *British Journal of Clinical Psychology, 33,* 33–48.

Pickering, A. D. (1997). The conceptual nervous system and personality: From Pavlov to neural networks. *European Psychologist, 2,* 139–163.

Pickering, A. D., Corr, P. J., & Gray, J. A. (1999). Interactions and reinforcement sensitivity theory: A theoretical analysis of Rusting and Larsen (1997). *Personality and Individual Differences, 26,* 357–365.

Pickering, A. D., Corr, P. J., Powell, J. H., Kumari, V., Thornton, J. C., & Gray, J. A. (1997). Individual differences in reactions to reinforcing stimuli are neither black nor white: To what extent are they Gray? In H. Nyborg (Ed.), *The scientific study of human nature: Tribute to Hans J. Eysenck at eighty* (pp. 36–67). London: Elsevier Science.

Pickering, A. D., Díaz, A., & Gray, J. A. (1995). Personality and reinforcement: An exploration using a maze-learning task. *Personality and Individual Differences, 18,* 541–558.

Pogue-Geile, M., Ferrell, R., Deka, R., Debski, T., & Manuck, S. (1998). Human novelty seeking personality traits and dopamine D4 receptor polmorphisms: A twin and genetic association study. *American Journal of Medical Genetics, 81,* 44–48.

Powell, J. H., Al-Adawi, S., Morgan, J., & Greenwood, R. J. (1996). Motivational deficits after brain injury: Effects of bromocriptine in 11 patients. *Journal of Neurology, Neurosurgery, and Psychiatry, 60,* 416–421.

Primus, R. J., Thurkauf, A., Xu, J., Yevich, E., McInerney, S., Shaw, K., Tallman, J. F., & Gallagher, D. W. (1997). Localisation and characterisation of dopamine D-4 binding sites in rat and human brain by use of the novel, D-4 receptor-selective ligand [^{3}H]NGD 94–1. *Journal of Pharmacology and Experimental Therapeutics, 282,* 1020–1027.

Quay, H. C. (1988). The behavioral reward and inhibition system in childhood behavior disorders. In L. M. Bloomingdale (Ed.), *Attention deficit disorder* (Vol. 3, pp. 176–186). New York: Pergamon.

Robbins T. W., & Everitt B. J. (1996). Neurobehavioral mechanisms of reward and motivation. *Current Opinion in Neurobiology, 6,* 228–236.

Rocklin, T., & Revelle, W. (1981). The measurement of Extraversion: A comparison of the Eysenck Personality Inventory and the Eysenck Personality Questionnaire. *British Journal of Social Psychology, 20,* 279–281.

Salamone, J. (1994). The involvement of nucleus accumbens dopamine in appetitive and aversive motivation. *Behavioural Brain Research, 61,* 117–133.

Salum, C., Roque da Silva, A., & Pickering, A. (in press). Striatal dopamine in attentional learning: A computational model. *Neurocomputing.*

Schmajuk, N. A., Catalin, V. B., & Gray, J. A. (in press). The psychopharmacology of latent inhibition: A neural network approach. *Behavioural Pharmacology.*

Schmajuk, N. A., Gray, J. A., & Lam, Y. W. (1996). Latent inhibition: A neural network approach. *Journal of Experimental Psychology: Animal Behavior Processes, 22,* 321–349.

Schultz, W., Romo, R., Ljungberg, T., Mirenowicz, J., Hollerman, J. R., & Dickinson, A. (1995). Reward-related signals carried by dopamine neurons. In J. C. Houk, J. L. Davis, D. G. Beiser (Eds.), *Models of information processing in the basal ganglia* (pp. 233–248). London: MIT Press.

Swerdlow, N. R., & Koob, G. F. (1987). Dopamine, schizophrenia, mania and depression: Toward a unified hypothesis of cortico-striato-pallidothalamic function. *Behavioral and Brain Sciences, 10,* 197–245.

Tarazi, F. I., Campbell, A., Yeghiayan, S. K., & Baldessarini, R. J. (1998). Localization of dopamine receptor subtypes in corpus striatum and nucleus accumbens septi of rat brain: Comparison of D-1-, D-2-, and D-4-like receptors. *Neuroscience, 83,* 169–176.

Tellegen, A. (1982). *Multidimensional Personality Questionnaire manual.* Minneapolis: University of Minnesota Press.

Tellegen, A., & Waller, N. G. (1996). Exploring personality through test construction: Development of the multidimensional personality questionnaire. In S. Briggs & J. Cheek (Eds.), *Personality measures: Development and evaluation* (Vol. 1). Greenwich, CT: JAI Press.

Torrubia, R., & Tobeña, A. (1984). A scale for the assessment of "susceptibility to punishment" as a measure of anxiety: Preliminary results. *Personality and Individual Differences, 5,* 371–375.

Vandenbergh, D. J., Zonderman, A. B., Wang, J., Uhl, G. R., & Costa, P. T. (1997). No association between Novelty Seeking and dopamine D4 receptor (D4DR) exon III seven repeat alleles in Baltimore Longitudinal Study of Ageing participants. *Molecular Psychiatry, 2,* 417–419.

Visser, M., Das-Smaal, E., & Kwakman, H. (1996). Impulsivity and negative priming: Evidence for diminished cognitive inhibition in impulsive children. *British Journal of Clinical Psychology, 87,* 131–140.

Vollema, M. G., & van den Bosch, R. J. (1995). The multidimensionality of schizotypy. *Schizophrenia Bulletin, 21,* 19–31.

Wang, J. K. T. (1991). Presynaptic glutamate receptors modulate dopamine release from striatal synaptosomes. *Journal of Neurochemistry, 57,* 819–822.

Weiner, I. (1991). The accumbens–substantia nigra pathway, mismatch and amphetamine. *Behavioral and Brain Sciences, 14,* 54–55.

Wickens, J. R. (1993). *A theory of the striatum.* New York: Pergamon.

Zinbarg, R. E., & Mohlman, J. (1998). Individual differences in the acquisition of affectively valenced associations. *Journal of Personality and Social Psychology, 74,* 1024–1040.

Zuckerman, M. (1979). *Sensation-seeking: Beyond the optimal level of arousal.* Hillsdale, NJ: Erlbaum.

Zuckerman, M. (1991). *Psychobiology of personality.* Cambridge, UK: Cambridge University Press.

Zuckerman, M., & Cloninger, C. R. (1996). Relationships between Cloninger's, Zuckerman's, and Eysenck's dimensions of personality. *Personality and Individual Differences, 21,* 283–285.

Chapter 11

Personality Continuity and Change across the Life Course

Avshalom Caspi
Institute of Psychiatry, University of London
University of Wisconsin–Madison

Brent W. Roberts
University of Tulsa

Longitudinal studies are uniquely suited to answer five questions about personality development across the life course. The goal of this chapter is to review the answers to these questions. First, we evaluate evidence about the early origins of personality. Second, we examine the types of continuity and change that are observed across the life course. Third, we review the factors that moderate continuity and change. Finally, we turn to the dual task of developmental research on continuity and change and seek to describe the processes and mechanisms that promote or transform the continuity of personality across the life course.

THE ORIGINS OF PERSONALITY

How Early Can We Tell?

Differences between children's behavioral styles—or temperamental qualities—are already apparent very early in life. But are these evanescent qualities or do they presage the life patterns to follow? Although many psychological theories subscribe to the view that what is past is prologue, this conjecture has been surprisingly difficult to substantiate empirically because it requires costly and time-consuming longitudinal studies that track people over time and across multiple developmental settings. As such, scientists, clinicians, and parents continue to wonder: Is the child really the father to the man?

The largest study to tackle this question explored links between behavioral styles at age 3 and self-reports of personality traits at age 18 in a longitudinal study of 1,000 children. When the children were 3 years old, they were observed by examiners in a 90-minute testing situation that involved a set of cognitive and motor tasks. Following the testing session, the examiners rated each child on a set of behavioral characteristics, and on the basis of these ratings the children were reliably classified into one of five distinct groups. At age 18, these same children completed the Multidimensional Personality Questionnaire (Tellegen et al., 1988), which measures one of the best known contemporary structural models of personality traits. The longitudinal results underscored the preservation of individual differences from early childhood to young adulthood (Caspi & Silva, 1995).

"Undercontrolled" children at age 3 were impulsive, restless, distractible, and labile in their emotional responses. At age 18, they scored low on traits indexing Constraint and high on traits indexing Negative Emotionality. They were reckless and careless (low Self-Control), favored dangerous and exciting activities (low Harm Avoidance), enjoyed causing discomfort to other persons (high Aggression), yet also felt mistreated, deceived, and betrayed by others (high Alienation). "Inhibited" children at age 3 were socially reticent, fearful, and easily upset by strangers. At age 18 these children scored high on traits indexing Constraint and low on traits indexing Positive Emotionality. They reported being cautious rather than impulsive (high Self-Control), preferred safe activities over dangerous ones (high Harm Avoidance), refrained from trying to take advantage of others and were unlikely to favor aggressive behavior (low Aggression). Finally, they were lacking in social potency—they were submissive, not fond of leadership roles, and had little desire to influence others (low Social Potency). The three remaining groups of children at age 3 also showed continuity, but less striking patterns. The Confident children at age 3 were zealous, eager to explore the testing materials, and adjusted to the testing situation quickly. The Reserved type were timid and somewhat uncomfortable in the testing session; however, unlike "Inhibited" children, their response disposition was not extreme and their caution did not interfere with their task orientation. Finally, the Well-Adjusted type included children who were capable of self-control when it was demanded of them, were adequately self-confident, and did not become unduly upset when confronting new people and situations; their style of approach and response to the testing session was regarded as expectable by the examiners and made for smooth testing. This style was still discernible at age 18: Statistically, well-adjusted children defined normal, average young adults. Confident and Reserved children resembled Well-Adjusted children in most respects, with the exception that Confident children were significantly more reckless and careless (low Self-Control) and Reserved children were significantly more submissive (low Social Potency).

The strength of associations between temperamental characteristics in early childhood and personality differences was weak to moderate. However, the fact that it is possible to chart connections from the first few of years of life—as early as age 3—to young adulthood is a significant achievement, for this was a contested point two decades ago (Kagan, 1980).

The second year of life may be the crucial dividing line for predicting later personality differences because of the intercorrelated cognitive–emotional changes that take place during this period. During the second year of life, perceptual and cognitive changes enable children to master object permanence and engage in symbolic play (Kagan, 1981). Self-conscious emotions, such as embarrassment and shame, also begin to appear at this time (Astington, 1993). These capacities may be necessary for children to form mental representations of their social world and to develop beliefs and expectations that are then affirmed by an expanding and reactive social environment (Kagan, 1984). It is possible that continuity or predictability may not emerge until infants experience these major developmental reorganizations during the second year of life.

There are other reasons to doubt the feasibility of prediction prior to the second year of life. It is possible that much of the observed variation in infant behavior is due to transient conditions, such as temporary allergies. As these conditions disappear with growth, so may their associated behavioral tendencies (Kagan, 1984). It is also possible that predictability may not emerge until a later age because early psychological differences are especially likely to be modified by the child's subsequent experiences with the environment (Chess & Thomas, 1987). Temperamental dimensions in infancy are the entire "personality" of the newborn, but whether they show continuity may depend on the degree of "fit" between the child's temperamental characteristics and the socialization context (Wachs, 1994).

But before giving up on predicting later personality from infant temperament, consider the parallel case of predicting IQ. For many years, psychologists argued that intellectual performance scores obtained in the earliest years of life correlated poorly with IQ scores at later age, implying that infancy and toddlerhood may be especially plastic developmental periods for intellectual status. But new evidence is challenging this claim, as studies have shown that assessments of habituation and recognition memory in the first year of life predict later IQ quite well (McCall & Carriger, 1993). What implications do these findings have for the prediction of personality? According to Asendorpf (1992a), these findings highlight the distinction between the stability of individual differences and the continuity of psychological constructs. Correlations across time may be low either because the rank order of individuals has changed over time or because the construct "intelligence" is indexed by different behaviors at different ages. Thus, it may be that, relative to previous measures of infant intelligence, habituation and recognition paradigms tap an information-processing mechanism that is more similar to those skills tapped by later IQ tests. With regard to the prediction of personality differences, it may be that behavioral indicators in early childhood and those in adulthood have unequal validity coefficients; that is, they do not adequately reflect the behavioral expression of the same personality construct. Further advances in prediction will be made only if we are able to operationalize the same trait construct at different ages.

When Is Personality Fully Developed?

The answer to this question is critical for both psychologists and society. It pertains directly to whether we choose to rehabilitate individuals or subject people to long-term, palliative care. For example, if personality becomes fixed at age 20, then psychologists would approach interventions differently if faced with a sociopath at age 15 or a sociopath at 40. Likewise, it may shift the action of a business owner from trying to shape a supervisor's authoritarian management style to simply firing the person. Despite its obvious importance, the question of when in the life course personality stabilizes has received little direct attention. Most often the answer to this question is implicit in theory and practice rather than explicit. For example, personality disorders are not diagnosed for persons under age 18 (American Psychiatric Association, 1994). This age could not have been selected on an empirical data base, because none exists on the changeability of personality disorders, nor is it clear what theoretical model was used to justify this decision. In this section we review several theories on when personality is fully developed and some empirical data supporting or disconfirming each position.

Psychodynamic theorists and researchers believed that personality structure was set in childhood. Sapir (1934) claimed that personality was formed by the age of 2 or 3, mostly through child training practices. Freud argued that by the time the Oedipal complex was resolved, sometime around age 5, all of the basic structures of personality, the id, ego, and superego, were fully developed. Socialization pressures could bring about minor changes in how these structures were expressed, but the basic tendencies of an individual's personality were set in childhood. Subsequent neo-Freudian theories still located personality development in childhood and essentially ignored development beyond adolescence (e.g., Fenichel, 1945). Anna Freud (1936) alluded to the continued development of defense mechanisms past childhood but refused to describe an explicit chronology. Some ego psychologists broke with Freud, in part because they believed personality continued to develop later in life (e.g., Erikson, 1950; Loevinger, 1966).

Although opinions shifted away from the idea that personality was fixed in childhood as psychodynamic models of development became less popular, these shifts were not predicated on data from empirical tests of these theories. One of the few longitudinal studies to explore psychodynamic constructs and to follow participants from childhood to adulthood is the Block Longitudinal Project (Block & Block, 1980). Among numerous topics examined in this ongoing project, these authors studied the longitudinal consistency of the psychodynamically inspired constructs of ego-control and ego-resiliency. Ego-control reflects an individual's ability and propensity to control impulses and delay gratification. Ego-resiliency reflects an individual's ability to modulate the use of ego-control. That is, it reflects the ability to be controlled when it is desirable and to relax controls and be impulsive when it is appropriate. In the period from childhood (age 3) to young adulthood (age 23) both constructs were moderately to highly consistent and appeared to increase in consistency with age (Block, 1993). Yet the consistency of ego-resiliency and ego-control in adolescence, though moderately high, did not reach unity. This study would appear to disconfirm the notion that deep personality structures stop changing after age 5. Further evidence that psychodynamic constructs continue to develop well into adulthood was provided by Vaillant (1976), who showed that defense mechanisms continued to mature well into middle age. For example, he found that men doubled the use of mature defenses, such as altruism and sublimation, between ages 20 and 35.

Several post-Freudian theories of personality development retained the perspective that the majority of growth occurred in childhood, but stretched the developmental window into adolescence. For example, Bloom (1964) placed the age of full personality development sometime in late adolescence. He argued that there was "rapid personality development in the early years of infancy and childhood, the possibility of marked changes in the adolescent period, and the likelihood of small change during adulthood and maturity" (Bloom, 1964, pp. 132–133). Bloom speculated that personality traits, such as impulse control, reach their highest level of stability somewhere around age 20. Based on his empirical review of 10 studies, Bloom found that personality did not stabilize by age 20. He was unable to draw a more definitive conclusion because at the time of his research only one longitudinal study of personality had followed people beyond the college years (e.g., Kelly, 1955).

Sanford (1962), another psychodynamically influenced theorist, described a fully developed person as one characterized by high degrees of both differentiation and integration. Specifically, the fully developed person had a rich and varied impulse life, a broad and refined conscience, a strong sense of individuality, and a balance of control and expression of needs. As for when most people reach this stage, Sanford argued that most development occurred in childhood and adolescence, but that personality continued to develop into young adulthood depending on the characteristic one focused on and what experiences an individual had been exposed to in adolescence. For example, Sanford placed the development of impulse control in adolescence and the development of ego, or the controlling function of personality (e.g., maturity), in adulthood. In both cases, Sanford did not presuppose that personality ever stopped changing: "the structure is not fixed once and for all, nor is the consistency of behavior absolute: the highly developed individual is always open to new experience, and capable of further learning." Anticipating Neugarten's (1968) theory that age was in part a social–historical construction and that concepts such as adolescence can correspond to different ages in different historical epochs, Sanford refused to pin specific ages on his stages of adolescence, adulthood, and old age. Rather, personality would be fully developed in adulthood, and the age at which adulthood was defined would be specific to each culture's historical and social context.

More recent theoretical positions on personality development are consistent with Sanford's claim that it happens in "adulthood." Costa and McCrae (1988; McCrae & Costa, 1994) put forward the hypothesis that personality is fully developed by age 30, which according to current and historical perspectives is a reasonable estimate of when individuals can be considered adults (Modell, 1989). Their inspiration, in part, comes from William James, who claimed that personality is set like plaster by age 30 (James, 1890). Based on an examination of the rank-order consistency of the Big Five personality dimensions over 3- and 6-year periods, Costa and McCrae (1988) concluded that "in general, it appears that personality is about equally stable for men and women over age 30" (p. 861). Additional evidence was provided through several nonempirical overviews of recent longitudinal research (McCrae & Costa, 1990, 1994; Costa & McCrae, 1997). Based on these reviews, McCrae and Costa (1994) concluded that individual differences in personality traits are "fixed" by age 30.

Several theorists are in agreement that personality becomes increasingly stable in adulthood but are equivocal about when and whether personality ever stops changing. Glenn (1980) claimed that as people get older, their "attitudes, values, and beliefs tend to stabilize and to become less likely to change" (p. 602). He did not claim that people could not change later in life, just that the probability of change decreased with age. Glenn (1980) proposed two reasons for increasing stability. First, early in life there was a dense spacing of life events, many of which were novel or for which a person had yet to learn how to cope. The rapid succession of new experiences challenges existing schema, attitudes, and adaptation patterns and thus leads to change. The second reason for increasing stability was the likelihood that individuals would become crystallized in their self-perceptions over time. The longer people hold beliefs, the more likely it is that experiences that contradict one's beliefs will be ignored or discounted. Several longitudinal studies of attitude change support the aging stability hypothesis (Alwin, Cohen, & Newcomb, 1991). Studies by Nunn, Crockett, and Williams (1978) and Cutler and Kaufman (1975) showed that the magnitude of attitude change was twice as large in young adults as it was in older adults.

Similar to Glenn's Aging Stability Theory, life-span development theories hold that psychological functioning is not fixed at a certain age (Baltes, 1987). Rather, "during development, and at all stages of the life span, both continuous (cumulative) and discontinuous (innovative) processes are at work" (Baltes, 1987, p. 613). Despite the open nature of personality and other components of psychological architecture that develop with time, the effects of psychological, social, and cultural factors are thought to diminish with age (Baltes, 1997). Thus, the range of changeability declines as people grow older. The increasing stability of ontogeny results from a shift in the allocation of resources at different times in the life course (Baltes, 1994). "In childhood, the primary allocation is directed toward growth; during adulthood, the predominant allocation is toward maintenance and recovery (resilience). In old age, more and more resources are directed toward regulation or management of loss" (Baltes, 1997, p. 370). Life span theories do not specify the age at which personality or other psychological constructs stop developing. Rather, they put forward the notion that as we age we become more consistent, yet we retain the potential for change. Empirical research tends to support the life-span theories of personality development. A quantitative review of the longitudinal consistency of personality found that with age people become less likely to change but that change is still possible in midlife and even in old age (Roberts & Friend-DelVicchio, in press). For example, Helson and Wink (1992) found increases in measures of Responsibility, Self-Control, and Masculinity in a longitudinal study of women between the ages of 43 and 52; Roberts (1997) found that occupational experiences, such as working in more prestigious occupations, were associated with changes in measures of Extraversion and Conscientiousness in midlife; Field and Millsap (1991) showed that the Big Five trait of Agreeableness increased significantly in a sample of older individuals (69 to 83).

In sum, evidence indicates that personality does not stop developing in childhood, adolescence, or early adulthood. Rather, personality appears to grow increasingly consistent with age and to reach a plateau later in life than originally thought (e.g., age 50). Furthermore, life experiences appear to be related to individual differences in personality change well into the fourth decade of life. The weakness of the empirical database on personality development lies in the passive nature of the majority of studies in these areas. The questions that remain are whether personality can be changed through proactive means, such as therapy or training, how much we can change personality, and what we must we do to maintain change.

TYPES OF CONTINUITY OBSERVED IN LONGITUDINAL RESEARCH

The assertion that an individual's personality has changed or remained the same over time is ambiguous. The boy who has daily temper tantrums when he is 2 but weekly tantrums when he is 9 has increased his level of emotional control; he has changed in absolute terms. But if he ranks first in temper tantrums among his peers at both ages, he has not changed in relative terms. Further ambiguity arises if the form of the behavior changes. If this boy emerges into adulthood as a man who is irritable and moody, we may grant that the phenotype has changed but claim that the underlying genotype has not. A final ambiguity arises when a claim of continuity rests on observations not of an individual but of a sample of individuals. The continuity of an attribute at the group level may be masking large but mutually canceling changes at the individual level. There are, in short, several meanings denoted by the term "continuity." The purpose of this section is to disentangle those meanings.

Differential Continuity

Differential continuity refers to the consistency of individual differences within a sample of individuals over time, to the retention of an individual's relative placement in a group. This most common definition of continuity is typically indexed by a correlation coefficient.

Evidence about differential continuity has been marshaled using different self-report personality inventories (e.g., Carmichael & McGue, 1994; Costa, McCrae, & Arenberg, 1980; Finn, 1986; Helson & Moane, 1987; McCrae & Costa, 1990; Lubinski, Schmidt, & Benbow, 1996; McGue, Bacon, & Lykken, 1993; Siegler, George, & Okun, 1979; Stevens & Truss, 1985). Personality ratings by clinicians, acquaintances, and spouses reveal significant differential continuities as well (e.g., Block, 1971; Conley, 1985; Costa & McCrae, 1988). Although these conclusions hold for most psychological variables, there is some evidence that different types of variables may exhibit different degrees of differential continuity. Measures of intellectual performance show the strongest continuities; personality variables such as the Big Five are next; and political attitudes and measures of self-opinions (e.g., self-esteem, life satisfaction) are last (Conley, 1984a). What accounts for this hierarchy of continuity? It is unlikely that these differences are simply a function of the differential reliability of the three kinds of variables because this hierarchy obtains even when the measures are corrected for unreliability. However, a related methodological consideration is that ability tests demand maximal performance, whereas personality and attitude questionnaires assess representative, typical performance; the former test format may yield evidence of greater continuity (Ackerman, 1997). It is also possible that consistencies in social behavior require environmental supports, whereas cognitive activities may be supported more by internal feedback systems (Cairns, 1979). This interpretation may account for the relatively lower continuities observed among attitudes, which may be especially susceptible to changes in sociocultural context (Alwin, 1994). Finally, it is noteworthy that this hierarchy of continuity roughly parallels the size of the heritability coefficients for the three kinds of variables, suggesting that genetic and gene–environment correlations may be contributing to continuity. Consistent with this hypothesis, Tesser (1993) showed that, even within the domain of attitudes, those with higher heritabilities are more resistant to change than attitudes with lower heritability.

Absolute Continuity

Absolute continuity refers to constancy in the quantity or amount of an attribute over time. Conceptually, it connotes the continuity of an attribute within a single individual, but it is typically assessed empirically by examining group means in repeated measures analyses of variance (e.g., Conley, 1985). Increasingly, researchers are also making use of growth curve analyses to model mean level changes over time and to examine interindividual differences in intraindividual change (e.g., Jones & Meredith, 1996).

Costa and McCrae (1988) reported that there is little consistent evidence for age changes in mean-levels of personality traits during adulthood. They gathered data about the Big Five personality traits on two occasions, 6 years apart, from 983 participants who ranged in age from 21 to 96. They conducted three different types of analyses: cross-sectional analyses in which individuals of different age were compared to each other; longitudinal analyses in which the same individuals were retested over time; and cross- and time-sequential analyses in which individuals of the same birth cohort (cross-sequential) or of the same age (time-sequential) were compared at different times of measurement. They also gathered spouse reports for a subset of their sample to try to replicate the cross-sectional and longitudinal analyses with different data sources. The results of these various analyses pointed to few consistent age-related personality changes in adulthood. In fact, the lack of convergence among the cross-sectional, longitudinal, and sequential approaches—and the failure to replicate evidence of change using different data sources—led McCrae and Costa (1990) to conclude that sampling differences, practice effects, time of measurement artifacts, and selective mortality may well render spurious many aging effects.

Personality changes have been noted when study participants are first tested as adolescents and young adults (e.g., Carmichael & McGue, 1994; Haan, Millsap, & Hartka, 1986; Helson & Moane, 1987; McGue et al., 1993; Mortimer, Finch, & Kumka, 1982; Stein, Newcomb, & Bentler, 1986; Stevens & Truss, 1985). In general, the evidence points to normative age-related decreases on personality traits related to Neuroticism or Negative Emotionality and to increases on personality traits related to Conscientiousness or Constraint. From late adolescence and through early adulthood, most people become less emotionally labile, more responsible, and more cautious.

In discussing absolute continuity, we have focused on objective indices of personality. But there is also research that examines subjective continuity and change (Heckhausen, Dixon, & Baltes, 1989; Ryff, 1984). For example, Woodruff and Birren (1972) retested a sample of middle-aged adults 25 years after they had originally completed a personality test. In addition to describing their current selves, the sample members were asked to complete the same test as they thought they had answered it in adolescence. Although there were, in fact, very few age changes over the 25-year span, study participants perceived many such changes. The differences between actual continuities and perceived discontinuities suggest that the flow of psychological time (subjective age) may be relatively independent of calendar time and may exert an effect on behavior that is also independent of chronological age (Settersten & Mayer, 1997).

Structural Continuity

Structural continuity refers to the persistence of correlational patterns among a set of variables across time. Typically, such continuity is assessed by examining the similarity of covariation patterns among item and factor relations across repeated measurements. The technical work involved in testing whether a factor structure is invariant across age and in determining whether variables have equivalent measurement properties at different ages can be accomplished with structural equation models (Bollen, 1989).

Structural change may indicate a developmental transformation. For example, factor analyses of mental test items in infancy and early childhood suggest that there are qualitative changes in the nature of intelligence (McCall, Eichorn, & Hogarty, 1977). Some developmental psychologists believe that structural invariance should always be established before investigating other kinds of stability (Baltes, Reese, & Nesselroade, 1977). This strategy has been adopted by several groups of researchers investigating the development of individual differences in temperament and personality (e.g., Pedlow, Sanson, Prior, & Oberklaid, 1993).

Although there do not appear to be qualitative structural shifts beyond adolescence in the personality traits examined in most studies (Costa & McCrae, 1992), there may be qualitative shifts in other psychosocial domains, such as in "theories of oneself" (Brim, 1976). Research employing spontaneously generated descriptions of the self points to qualitative changes in adolescents' self-conceptions (Damon & Hart, 1986). As in the example of the differentiation of abilities cited earlier, it is possible that the self-concept of young children, which is relatively undifferentiated, may evolve to become more complex later in childhood both because of cognitive changes and, increasingly throughout adolescence and adulthood, because the person acquires a larger set of roles and corresponding identities (Harter, 1997).

Ipsative Continuity

Absolute, differential, and structural continuities are indexed by statistics that characterize a sample of individuals. However, continuity at the group level may not mirror continuity at the individual level. For this reason, some researchers examine ipsative continuity, which explicitly refers to continuity at the individual level. Ipsative continuity denotes continuity in the configuration of variables within an individual across time. Ipsative continuity could also be called morphogenic (Allport, 1962) or person-centered continuity. The latter term derives from Block's (1971) distinction between a variable-centered approach to personality, which is concerned with the relative standing of persons across variables, and a person-centered approach, which is concerned with the salience and configuration of variables within the person. An ipsative approach to the study of development seeks to discover continuities in personality functioning across development by identifying each person's salient attributes and their intraindividual organization.

Very little longitudinal research has been conducted from an ipsative point of view. An exception is Block's *Lives through Time* (1971), in which he employed the Q-sort technique of personality description to analyze continuity and change. Continuity and change were indexed by computing correlations across the set of attributes in an individual's Q-sort profiles from different measurement occasions (Q-correlations); the higher the correlation, the more the configuration of attributes within the individual remained stable across time. Block's analysis showed that aggregate indices of continuity mask large individual differences in personality continuity. For example, the average Q-correlations between early and late adolescence exceeded .70 and those between late adolescence and adulthood exceeded .50, but the intraindividual Q-correlations ranged from moderately negative to the maximum imposed by measurement error. Other studies of personality continuity and change between childhood and adolescence report average Q-correlations ranging from .43 to .71, with considerable variability in the distribution of these scores (from –.44 to .92), indicating that from childhood to adolescence people vary widely in how much continuity or change they exhibited (Asendorpf & van Aken, 1991; Ozer & Gjerde, 1989).

The advantage of these Q-sort indices of continuity is that they reference the continuity of each individual within the sample. Unlike assessments of continuity in traditional variable-centered research, these indices do not require reference to other sample members to derive their meaning. The disadvantage of these indices is that they do not yield information about the continuity of individuals along any single attribute (Buss, 1985). Continuity is thus regarded as a general quality of personality only with respect to a set of complex characteristics (Cronbach & Gleser, 1953). This definition is problematic: It can be assumed that people show personality continuity only if the original measurement covered a large proportion of the significant dimensions of personality. To overcome these limitations, Asendorpf (1992b) proposed a technique for deriving measures of each individual's continuity with respect to specific personality dimensions.

Coherence

The kinds of continuity discussed so far refer to "homotypic" continuity—continuity of similar behaviors or phenotypic attributes over time. The concept of coherence enlarges the definition of continuity to include "heterotypic continuity"—continuity of an inferred genotypic attribute presumed to underlie diverse phenotypic behaviors. Moss and Susman (1980) suggested that specific behaviors in childhood may not predict phenotypically similar behavior later in adulthood, but may still be associated with behaviors that are conceptually consistent with the earlier behavior (Livson & Peskin, 1980). Kagan (1969) noted that heterotypic continuities are most likely to be found from the earlier years of life, when children go through numerous rapid changes. In contrast, homotypic continuities are more likely to be found after puberty, when psychological organization nears completion.

Examples of heterotypic continuities were reported by Ryder (1967), who reexamined the data from Kagan and Moss's (1962) longitudinal study *Birth to Maturity*. Childhood task persistence was related to adult achievement orientation. Similarly, childhood aggression, sociability, physical adventurousness, and nonconformity were related to adult sexual behavior. Another example of coherence is provided in a 22-year follow-up study of men and women who had been rated as aggressive by their peers in late childhood (Huesmann, Eron, Lefkowitz, & Walder, 1984). As adults, the men were likely to commit serious criminal acts, abuse their spouses, and drive while intoxicated, whereas the women were likely to punish their offspring severely. Other examples of personality coherence include the findings that shy children leave their parental home at an older age and delay their assumption of adult social roles, such as marriage and work (Caspi, Elder, & Bem, 1988; Gest, 1997).

It is important to emphasize that coherence and heterotypic continuity refer to conceptual rather than a literal continuity among behaviors. Accordingly, the investigator who claims to have discovered coherence must have a theory—no matter how rudimentary or implicit—that specifies the "genotype" or provides the basis on which the diverse behaviors and attributes can be said to belong to the same equivalence class. In what sense is adult sexual behavior a "derivative" of childhood physical adventurousness? In what way is driving while intoxicated the "same thing" as pushing and shoving other children?

As these examples illustrate, the "theories" behind claims of coherence often amount to appeals to the reader's intuition. Often they are post hoc interpretations of empirical relations discovered in large correlation matrices (Moss & Susman, 1980). With the notable exception of the psychoanalytic theory of psychosexual stages and their adult sequelae, most personality theories do not specify links between personality variables at different developmental periods, a topic to which we now turn.

To study the coherence of personality development it is necessary to trace personality variables through social–developmental changes while tracking their continuities and to include both temporal and contextual dimensions in the measurement of personality differences (Conley, 1984b). According to Ozer (1986, p. 52), "the notion of coherence refers to a pattern of findings where a construct, measured by several different methods, retains its psychological meaning as revealed in relationships to a variety of other measures" across time and in different contexts.

Below we review three conceptual approaches to the problem of studying personality coherence across the life course. Each of these social–

developmental approaches provides a framework for understanding coherence by focusing on the distinctive ways in which individuals organize their behavior to meet new environmental demands and developmental challenges.

An Organizational–Adaptational Perspective

Sroufe and his colleagues (Sroufe, Carlson, & Shulman, 1993) have used Anna Freud's concept of "developmental lines" as a heuristic device for the study of personality coherence. By outlining the tasks and milestones that can be expected in the course of development, from infancy through adolescence, they have designed assessment procedures that capture the organization of behavior in different developmental periods. Longitudinal data show that continuity across development can be discerned in children's adaptational profiles with respect to the challenges they face at each developmental phase. This general approach enables Sroufe and his colleagues to confer conceptual coherency on their findings that individuals who are securely attached as infants later explore their environments as toddlers (Matas, Arend, & Sroufe, 1978), are less dependent on their teachers in the preschool years (Sroufe, Fox, & Pancake, 1983), attain higher sociometric status and display greater competence in peer relations in late childhood (Urban, Carlson, Egeland, & Sroufe, 1991), and appear to establish appropriate cross-sex relationships in adolescence (Sroufe et al., 1993). Invariant behavior patterns do not emerge in these findings. Instead, we see a predictable and meaningful way of relating to the environment in different social settings at different ages. The continuities of personality are thus expressed not through the constancy of behavior across time and in diverse circumstances, but through the consistency over time in the ways persons characteristically modify their changing contexts as a function of their behavior.

A Sociological Perspective

Beyond childhood the search for coherence becomes more complicated, and it may be that a purely psychological approach is insufficient for the analysis of personality continuity and change as the individual increasingly negotiates social roles defined by the culture. Indeed, some researchers have found it useful to adopt a sociocultural perspective and to conceive of the life course as a sequence of culturally defined, age-graded roles that the individual enacts over time (Caspi, 1987; Helson, Mitchell, & Moane, 1984).

Helson introduced the concept of a "social clock project" as a framework for studying lifespan development. The concept of a social clock focuses attention on the age-related life schedules of individuals in particular cultures and cohorts and organizes the study of lives in terms of patterned movements into, along, and out of multiple role-paths, such as education, work, marriage, and parenthood. In this fashion, the life course can be charted as a sequence of social roles that are enacted over time, and personality coherence can be explored by investigating consistencies in the ways different persons select and perform different social–cultural roles.

In her 30-year longitudinal study of female college seniors, who were first studied in 1958–1960, Helson examined the personality antecedents and consequences of adherence to a Feminine Social Clock (FSC) and a Masculine Occupational Clock (MOC). For example, women who adhered to the FSC were earlier in life characterized by a desire to do well and by a need for structure; women in this birth cohort who adhered to an MOC were earlier in life more rebellious and less sensitive to social norms. Helson et al. (1984, p. 1079) were thus able to identify "culturally salient need-press configurations through time" and to show predictable and meaningful relations between personality and behavior in different social settings at different ages.

An Evolutionary Psychology Perspective

Bouchard (1995) argued that a purely sociocultural perspective on the life course "ignores the fact that life-histories themselves are complex evolved adaptations." An evolutionary perspective complements the sociocultural perspective by exploring how personality variation is related to those adaptively important problems with which human beings have had to repeatedly contend. Evolutionary psychology thus focuses attention on the coherence of behavioral strategies that people use in, for example, mate selection, mate retention, reproduction, parental care, kin investment, status attainment, and coalition building (see Buss, Chapter 2, this volume). It focuses research on the genetically influenced strategies and tactics that individuals use for survival and reproduction.

An evolutionary perspective on the life course offers a fusion of concerns in evolutionary theory, behavior genetics, and demography (Stearns, 1992). For example, using the evolutionary perspective, Draper and Belsky (1990) and Gangestad and Simpson (1990) have offered hypotheses about personality characteristics and reproductive strategies that facilitate adaptations in different environments at different ages. Although these and other specific models have not yet been tested in the context of longitudinal–developmental studies, they show the promise of evolutionary psychology for organizing longitudinal–developmental data on personality coherence.

MEDIATORS AND MODERATORS OF CONTINUITY AND CHANGE

Age, Time Span, and Method of Assessment

Roberts and Friend-DelVecchio (in press) conducted the most extensive quantitative review of the rank-order consistency of personality to date. To be included in the meta-analysis, each study had to meet three criteria. First, the study focused on variables assumed to be dispositional in nature. Second, the study had to include a longitudinal interval greater than 1 year, to minimize potential test–retest carry-over effects. Third, the sample studied needed to be nonclinical. The 150 identified studies were based on 122 samples, with a total number of 49,968 participants, yielding a total of 3,091 rank-order personality consistency coefficients. The average study in the database had a time interval of 6.7 years.

The meta-analysis confirmed two major conclusions about age and time: Stability coefficients tend to increase as the age of the subjects increases, and they tend to decrease as the time interval between observations increases. The meta-analysis also revealed new evidence about the nature of personality consistency by determining the age at which the rank-order consistency of personality dispositions stabilizes. The results showed that unadjusted (for unreliability) estimates of personality consistency increased from .32 in childhood, to .55 at age 30, and then reached a plateau around .75 between ages 50 and 70. The data do not support the argument that personality becomes fixed at ages 5, 20, or 30. Rather, the data support the conclusion that rank-order consistency peaks at age 50.

To test whether trait domain affects rank-order consistency, Roberts and Friend-DelVecchio (in press) used the five-factor model to categorize the diverse measures used in previous studies of personality consistency. Previous research found that scales assessing Extraversion were the most consistent, but these studies did not assess the full spectrum of the Big Five. The results of this meta-analysis showed that the type of trait measured had minimal effects on personality consistency: The unadjusted correlations were .54 for Extraversion, .55 for Agreeableness, .52 for Conscientiousness, .51 for Neuroticism, and .51 for Openness to Experience. Additional analyses showed that gender had minimal effects on personality consistency. Men and women showed the same patterns of personality consistency across the life course and across trait domains.

The contribution of method of assessment to personality consistency proved difficult to evaluate because method of assessment is frequently confounded with the age of the population studied. Studies of younger populations tend to rely on behavioral observations, whereas studies of older age groups tend to rely on self- and observer-ratings. Debates about the relative merits of these different assessment methods often miss the point that stability and predictive utility are not the only reasons for favoring particular kinds of data. Different kinds of data are differentially suited to answering different questions about continuity and change (Moskowitz, 1986). Ratings may show great consistency in part because they tend to eliminate situational sources of variance. But such assessments are not the method of choice if one is interested in examining the functional relations between an individual's behaviors and other ongoing events in the situation. Despite their lesser individual-difference stability, observational assessments that preserve the precise actions of individuals are well suited for analyzing how social behavior patterns are maintained or changed over time (Cairns & Green, 1979). The study of continuity and change must include both year-to-year assessments of individual differences and minute-to-minute assessments of social interaction. Each provides crucial and complementary information to understanding personality development.

Biosocial Transitions

In the previous section we considered the effects of the passage of time on personality continuity and change. But "age itself is an empty variable, for it is not merely the passage of time, but the various biological and social events that occur with the passage of time that have relevance for personality change" (Neugarten, 1977, p. 633). A life-course perspective invokes two concepts that are useful for thinking about how age-related biosocial events influence personality development (Elder, Modell, & Parke, 1994). Trajectories are long-term pathways of development. Transitions are embedded in trajectories and evolve over shorter times span.

The traditional view is that biosocial transitions (e.g., puberty, marriage, a first job) cause personality change. However, it is important to be explicit about the type of change that is involved. Absolute changes in self-conceptions have been observed when individuals cross important life course transitions, such as becoming parents, but the rank-order of individual differences remains high across this life event (Cowan & Cowan, 1992). Other life-course accounts recognize that the same transition event may not have the same effect on all persons. For example, the age-graded theory of informal social control emphasizes adult social bonds to employment and to partners as "turning points" from crime that can lead some persons to overcome previously established "pathways" into adult crime (Sampson & Laub, 1993). But why do some people change and others do not? Laub and Sampson (1993) suggest three possibilities. First, change involves chance. Second, change comes about as a result of both individual and social–structural characteristics. Third, there may be predictable individual differences in who responds to change-potentiating life events.

It is also important to bear in mind that some life-course transitions are age-graded and expectable, whereas others, even when loosely correlated with age, are unexpected and off-time. Caspi and Moffitt (1993) have proposed that the former may help to bring about change, especially when highly scripted, whereas the latter may accentuate personality differences. This has been called a paradoxical theory because the expectation, according to traditional perspectives on personality change, is that "external life changes are a major catalyst for personality change" (Stewart, Sokol, Healy & Chester, 1986). According to the accentuation hypothesis, just the opposite occurs. Biosocial discontinuities often accentuate preexisting differences between individuals. Rather than change in new and unfamiliar situations, people bring their most characteristic response dispositions to bear on the way they approach and respond to new environmental discontinuities.

Historical Factors

A limitation of most longitudinal studies is their historical specificity. This is because simple longitudinal studies assess members of a single birth cohort. Accordingly, it is unknown to what extent knowledge about personality development is historically specific. This is, of course, a problem in the social sciences generally, but it typically remains unacknowledged; both data and theory are presented as if they were transhistorically valid. Social scientists who deal with longitudinal data have been somewhat more sensitive to the issue and have articulated three responses to this problem.

The Metatheoretical Response

The metatheoretical response has been articulated by social psychologists who question whether psychology is science or history (Gergen, 1982). According to this view, all theory and "findings" are historically conditioned and socially constructed. However, social constructivism as a philosophical perspective negates the possibility of basing applied social practices on scientific findings (Smith, 1994).

The Methodological Response

The methodological response has been led by developmental psychologists who have observed that simple longitudinal designs confound three types of effects: age, cohort (year of birth), and period (time of measurement) (Baltes, Cornelius, & Nesselroade, 1979). Schaie (1965) proposed a general developmental model that addressed the task of estimating the three effects in relation to psychological functioning. This model has clarified ambiguities emerging from cross-sectional and single-cohort longitudinal designs, but for other purposes the model's prescription for performing multiple longitudinal studies of different birth cohorts is unfeasible (McCall, 1977). There are alternatives, however. Gough, who in the early 1950s developed the California Psychological Inventory (CPI), introduced one such alternative. Every year since 1950, the CPI has been administered to thousands of people, many of them students. In order to understand how responses to the CPI had changed over 35 years from 1950 to 1985,

Gough (1991) computed endorsement frequencies for each true–false item on the CPI for successive samples of students from 1950 to 1985. He then correlated the endorsement frequency of each item with the year of testing. The items that correlated significantly with time were combined in an index labeled Secular Trends. Effectively, Gough created an index that reflected historical trends in responses to the CPI over a 35-year period. One interpretation of this index is that it captures, in part, changes in culture or climate that occurred in the United States between 1950 and 1985, such as greater psychological sophistication (Reich, 1970), increases in individualistic and self-centered attitudes (Bellah, Madsen, Sullivan, Swidler, & Tipton, 1985; Lasch, 1979), and decreases in adherence to social norms (Veroff, Douvan, & Kulka, 1981).

The Secular Trends Index is one of the few examples we have found of a quantitative description of change in culture across historical periods. This quantitative index affords two improvements over the cross-sequential time-series approach to understanding the effects of history. The first advantage is that a quantifiable scale permits more detailed inferences to be drawn about how historical changes are registered in psychological functioning. The second advantage is that the Secular Trends Index can be used in single-cohort longitudinal studies to test the effects of historical change on patterns of development. Thus, it affords the opportunity to explore the effect of history within one longitudinal study. For example, change on the Secular Trends Index within a longitudinal study can be compared to the changes demonstrated in the successive cohorts from whom the index was derived. Roberts and Helson (1997) did exactly this by exploring the antecedents and consequences of change on the Gough's Secular Trends Index in the Mills Longitudinal Study (Helson & Wink, 1992), in which the CPI had been administered four times from 1958 through 1989. They found that the women in the Mills Longitudinal study changed on the Secular Trends Index in a fashion similar to the change in cross-sectional samples of students. They also showed that changes on the Secular Trends Index in the longitudinal study were associated with increases in Narcissism and decreases in Social Responsibility. That is, the women of the Mills study changed in the same ways that social critiques described the U.S. culture changing over that same period.

The Secular Trends Index should not be seen as a scale so much as a technique. This new technique could be applied to any personality questionnaire that has been administered widely for a decade or more. Researchers could compute secular trend indices for specific historical periods and over a variety of instruments. Obvious candidates for study would be such personality instruments as the MMPI, Cattell's 16PF, Costa and McCrae's NEO-PI, and Jackson's PRF.

The Sociohistorical Response

The sociohistorical response to transhistorical validity has been led by life-course sociologists who have sought to sketch the flow of influence from macrohistorical developments to the world of the individual and to relate social changes directly to personality development (Elder et al., 1994). Elder's (1979) examination of two birth cohorts who lived through the Great Depression and World War II exemplifies this approach by showing the differential developmental effects of encountering historical events at different points in one's life. However, at least one historian has argued that the coupling of developmental psychology and history represents a "dangerous liaison" because it is unclear whether psychologists are willing to abandon their quest for lawlike predictions (Zuckerman, 1993). Indeed, analyses like Elder's raise a more general epistemological question: How is it possible to move from historically specific findings to a more general understanding of life course processes?

Sometimes it is easy to extract the general finding behind relatively superficial historical differences. For example, a study of men born in the 1920s found that low ego control in adolescence predicted midlife drinking problems (Jones, 1981). A more recent study of children born in the late 1960s found that low ego control in early childhood predicted adolescent marijuana use (Block, Block, & Keyes, 1988). Clearly, the historical change in the drug of choice is trivial; the general finding is obvious. Sometimes the general finding is more obscure. For example, among women the correlation between tested intelligence and the number of children they bear has tended to be negative throughout the 20th century. The exception to this pattern occurred during the postwar baby boom. As Livson and Day (1977) note, these historically specific findings are interesting "only if they are interpreted not as direct if-then relationships, but as providing an understanding of the intrapsychic and interpersonal characteristics that mediate one's child-bearing responses to a social context prevailing during the period in which fertility decisions are made" (p. 321). Sometimes psychological processes remain general even when the psychological content is historically specific. For example, research on political socialization suggests that although the attitudes of different cohorts may differ, the acquisition of these attitudes takes place during adolescence and young adulthood for all cohorts (Schuman & Scott, 1989). As these examples illustrate, research on personality development that is conducted without a sense of history, without recognition that phenotypic expressions represent a point of articulation between biological, social, and historical processes, may miss the point. Ironically, psychologists may have to be historically specific to grasp the more general essence of the phenomena examined in the study of personality development.

HOW IS CONTINUITY ACHIEVED?: MECHANISMS OF CONTINUITY ACROSS THE LIFE COURSE

An extensive database of research attests to personality continuities across the life course. In this section, we examine how environmental, genetic, and transactional processes contribute to personality continuities.

Environmental Influences

One continuity-promoting mechanism is so mundane that it is often overlooked: Personality characteristics may show continuity across the life course because the environment remains stable. To the extent that parental demands, teacher expectancies, and peer and partner influences remain stable over time, we could expect such environmental stability to promote personality continuity (Cairns & Hood, 1983). Sameroff (1995) has coined the term "environtype" to underscore that, like genotypes, stable environmental factors can shape and influence the course of phenotypic expressions over time.

Several longitudinal studies have shown that there is a good deal of continuity in the "psychological press" of children's and adults' socialization environments; significant continuities have been found in observational studies as well as in parents' reports of child-rearing practices from childhood to adolescence (e.g., Hanson, 1975; McNally, Eisenberg, & Harris, 1991; Patterson & Bank, 1989; Pianta, Sroufe, & Egeland, 1989; Roberts, Block, & Block, 1984). In addition, the socioenvironmental conditions of adult life that impinge on material, physical, and psychological well-being also show remarkable intragenerational persistence (Warren & Hauser, 1997). These longitudinal "environmental correlations" are about the same magnitude as longitudinal "personality correlations." If the environments that people inhabit are as stable as these data suggest, then continuities observed in personality measures may simply reflect the cumulative and continuing continuities of those environments (Sameroff, Seifer, Baldwin, & Baldwin, 1993). What is needed is a formal test of the possibility that environmental continuities actually account for observed personality continuities.

It is also unclear from the available studies whether environmental continuity is the product or the cause of stable individual differences. It is possible that features of the environment may reflect the characteristics of individuals who make up the environment. Plomin and Bergeman (1991) showed that measures commonly used by psychologists and sociologists to assess socialization environments both in childhood and adulthood (e.g., parental warmth, social support, social class) may be saturated with genetic variation. What appear to be stable and enduring features of the environment may be a reflection of stable, enduring, and partially heritable individual differences. This may come about through two processes (Plomin, 1994). First, individuals may actively seek out trait-matched environmental experiences for themselves. Second, environmental experiences may reflect social reactions to trait-based individual differences.

Genetic Influences

Quantitative methods that are used to estimate genetic and environmental components of phenotypic variance at a given point in time can be extended to estimate genetic contributions to continuity and change across time (see Plomin & Caspi, Chapter 9, this volume). Genetic factors can contribute both to personality change between measurement occasions and to personality continuity across measurement occasions. Genetic influences on personality change may be explored in twin studies by analyzing within-person change scores; for example, genetic influences on change would be implied by the finding that monozygotic (MZ) twins are more likely to change in concert than dizygotic (DZ) twins. Genetic influences on personality continuity may be explored in twin studies by analyzing cross-twin correlations, that is, by fitting behavior–genetic models to the correlation between twin *A*'s score at t_1 and twin *B*'s score at t_2.

Both of these analytic approaches have been used to analyze longitudinal behavior–genetic studies. Unfortunately, there are only a few such studies, and these are difficult to compare because of wide differences in the age of study participants and in the measures used.

Age-to-Age Change

Some of the earliest studies of genetic influences on change were performed with children in the Louisville Twin Study. Even though assessments of temperament across 6, 12, 18, 24, and 30 months of age showed low to modest stabilities, within-pair analyses revealed that MZ twins were more likely to change in concert than were DZ twins (Matheny, 1983, 1989). These results suggest that changes in childhood temperament may be under some genetic influence, a finding that has been partially replicated in the MacArthur Longitudinal Twin Study (Cherny et al., 1994; Plomin et al., 1993; Saudino, Plomin, & DeFries, 1996).

Turning to adolescence and adulthood, the picture looks different. One study examined twins who completed personality inventories at age 16 and again at age 28 (Dworkin, Burke, Maher, & Gottesman, 1976, 1977). The results showed that changes in trait levels from adolescence to adulthood were influenced by genetic similarity. However, subsequent and larger studies yield mixed evidence about this point. At least two short-term longitudinal studies, as well as one adoption study, did not find evidence for genetic influences on age-to-age personality changes (Eaves & Eysenck, 1976; Loehlin, Horn, & Willerman, 1990; Pogue-Geile & Rose, 1985). It appears that there may be genetic contributions to temperament and personality change in childhood but only slight, if any, genetic contributions to personality change in adulthood. In fact, most of the personality change observed in late adolescence and adulthood appears to be due to unique individual experiences, that is, to nonshared environmental influences (McCartney, Harris, & Bernieri, 1990).

Age-to-Age Continuity

Even fewer studies have explored genetic contributions to temporal continuity by analyzing cross-twin correlations. A notable exception is the MacArthur Longitudinal Twin Study. Analyses of both observational measures and parental reports of infant temperament suggest that a significant portion of the phenotypic stability of temperament may be accounted for by genetic factors (Plomin et al., 1993).

Turning to adulthood, at least one longitudinal study has examined the genetic and environmental etiology of age-to-age continuity. McGue et al. (1993) administered the Multidimensional Personality Questionnaire to a sample of twins on two occasions 10 years apart. The results showed that the MZ cross-twin correlations were consistently and significantly larger than the DZ cross-twin correlations. The authors estimate that approximately 80% of phenotypic stability may be associated with genetic factors.

Although the data suggest that genetic factors can influence the continuity of personality, they do not address the mechanisms by which they do so. One possibility is to examine physiological mechanisms. This is illustrated by research on shyness or "inhibition to the unfamiliar." Individual differences in behavioral inhibition are heritable and stable, and, at least in early childhood, their phenotypic stability appears to be influenced by genetic factors (Plomin et al., 1993). Kagan (1997) has suggested that inherited variations in threshold of arousal in selected limbic sites may contribute to longitudinal consistencies in this behavioral style. Another possibility is that genetic factors exert their influence on phenotypic stability through gene–environment correlations; thus, personality continuity across the life course may be the result of transactional processes that are, in part, genetically influenced.

Person–Environment Transactions across the Life Course

There are many kinds of transactions, but three play particularly important roles both in promoting the continuity of personality across the life course and in controlling the trajectory of the life course itself (cf. Buss, 1987; Plomin, DeFries, & Loehlin, 1977; Scarr & McCartney,

1983). Reactive transactions occur when different individuals exposed to the same environment experience it, interpret it, and react to it differently. Evocative transactions occur when an individual's personality evokes distinctive responses from others. Proactive transactions occur when individuals select or create environments of their own. (We deliberately use the term "person–environment transaction" rather than "interaction" or "correlation" because the former term is methodologically neutral whereas the latter terms have specific statistical and data-analytic connotations; see Rutter, 1983; Wachs & Plomin, 1991. We also deliberately speak of "person–environment" rather than "gene–environment" transactions because we do not presuppose knowledge of the origins of the "person" variance in the equation.)

Reactive Person–Environment Transactions

Each individual extracts a subjective psychological environment from the objective surroundings, and it is that subjective environment that shapes subsequent personality development. This is the basic tenet of the phenomenological approach historically favored by social psychology and embodied in the famous dictum that if people "define situations as real, they are real in their consequences" (Thomas & Thomas, 1928). It is also the assumption connecting several prominent theories of personality development: Epstein's (1991) writings on the development of self-theories of reality; Tomkins's (1979) description of scripts about the self and interpersonal interactions; and Bowlby's (1973) analysis of working models.

All three theories assert that people continually revise their "self-theories," "scripts," and "working models" as a function of experience. But if these function as filters for social information, the question is also raised about how much revision actually occurs (Gurin & Brim, 1984). The answer is provided, in part, by cognitive social psychologists whose research suggests that once self-schemata—psychological constructs of the self—become well organized, a host of cognitive processes makes individuals selectively responsive to information that is congruent with their expectations and self-views (Fiske & Taylor, 1991). Persistent ways of perceiving, thinking, and behaving are preserved, in part, by features of the cognitive system, and because of these features the course of personality is likely to be quite conservative and resistant to change (Westen, 1991).

The role of cognitive factors in promoting the continuity of individual differences in personality and psychopathology has been detailed by Crick and Dodge (1994), whose social information-processing model of children's social adjustment includes five steps: (1) to encode information about the event; (2) to interpret the cues and arrive at some decision about their meaning and significance; (3) to search for possible responses to the situation; (4) to consider the consequences of each potential response and to select a response from the generated alternatives; and (5) to carry out the selected response. Research has identified individual differences in processing social information at all of these steps (Quiggle, Garber, Panak, & Dodge, 1992).

A basic assumption of this and other social information-processing models is that early temperamental characteristics in combination with early social experiences can set up anticipatory attitudes that lead the individual to project particular interpretations onto new social relationships and situations (Rusting, 1998). This is accomplished through a variety of informational processes in which the person interprets new events in a manner that is consistent with his or her experientially established understanding of self and others. Individuals are thus hypothesized to elicit and selectively attend to information that confirms rather than disconfirms their self-conceptions (Snyder & Ickes, 1985). This promotes the stability of the self-concept, which, in turn, promotes the continuity of behavioral patterns that are congruent with that self-concept (Graziano, Jensen-Campell, & Hair, 1996).

Individual differences in social information processing may also reflect unconscious mental processes; individual differences play a more important role in automatic rather than in controlled processing of social information (e.g., Rabiner, Lenhart, & Lochman, 1990). Indeed, psychoanalytic concepts (e.g., transference) are implicit in cognitive perspectives on personality development. For example, methodologically sophisticated $N = 1$ studies and experimental studies using the tools of research in social cognition have shown how recurring emotional states organize experience and how individuals transfer affective responses developed in the context of previous relationships to new relationships (e.g., Andersen & Baum, 1994; Horowitz et al.,

1994). However, persistent ways of perceiving, thinking, and behaving are not preserved simply by psychic forces, nor are they entirely attributable to features of the cognitive system; they are also maintained by the consequences of everyday action (Trachtenberg & Viken, 1994).

Evocative Person–Environment Transactions

Individuals evoke distinctive reactions from others on the basis of their unique personality characteristics. The person acts, the environment reacts, and the person reacts back in mutually interlocking evocative transaction. Such transactions continue throughout the life course and promote the continuity of personality.

Already very early in life children evoke consistent responses from their social environment that affect their subsequent interactions with adults and peers (Bell & Chapman, 1986). It is also through evocative transactions that phenomenological interpretations of situations—the products of reactive interaction—are transformed into situations that are "real in their consequences." Expectations can lead an individual to project particular interpretations onto new situations and relationships and thence to behave in ways that corroborate those expectations (Wachtel, 1994).

The process through which evocative person–environment transactions can sustain individual differences has been explored in social–interactional and experimental analyses of aggressive behavior where children's coercive behaviors have been shown to shape the responses of adults to them (Lytton, 1990; Patterson & Bank, 1989). This is not, however, to merely substitute one "main effects" model (parental influence) with another such model (child influence). A transactional model recognizes that partners react back and forth in mutually interlocking evocative transactions and contribute to the continuity of dispositional characteristics by evoking congruent responses from each other. Increasingly, behavioral genetic designs may help to untangle whether evocative effects are the product of genetic differences or represent true environmental effects (O'Connor, Deater-Deckard, Fulker, Rutter, & Plomin, 1998), and new statistical techniques for analyzing interaction data may help to decompose how different individuals and relationships in the family conspire to maintain behavioral continuity (Cook, Kenny, & Goldstein, 1991).

Individuals also manifest their personalities in expressive behavior (Borkenau & Liebler, 1995). Facial expressions of emotion are especially important in evocative person–environment transactional processes for they convey information to others about what the individual is feeling and about how the individual is likely to act. The finding that personality traits are registered in facial expressions suggests that personality-related expressions of emotion may influence the course of social development by evoking congruent and reciprocal responses from other persons in the social environment (Keltner, 1996).

Proactive Person–Environment Transactions

The most consequential environments for personality development are interpersonal environments, and the personality-sustaining effects of proactive transactions are most apparent in friendship formation and mate selection (Asendorpf & Wilpers, 1998; Kandel, Davies, & Baydar, 1990). Personality effects on social relationships serve to maintain and elaborate initial personality differences between people and proactive transactions may account for the age-related increase in the magnitude of stability coefficients across the life span.

Friends tend to resemble each other in physical characteristics, values, attitudes, and behaviors (e.g., Dishion, Patterson, Stoolmiller, & Skinner, 1991). Whereas popular wisdom holds that members of peer groups are similar because peers influence their friends to behave in similar ways, empirical studies suggest that members of peer groups are similar because individuals selectively choose to affiliate with similar others (e.g., Ennett & Bauman, 1994). Cairns and Cairns (1994) suggest that affiliations with similar others may serve as guides for norm formation and the consolidation of behavior patterns over time. Continuities in social networks may thus contribute to behavioral continuity because the demands of the social environment remain relatively stable over time. Moreover, consistency in how members of the social network relate to the individual may contribute to behavioral continuity because it affects how individuals view and define themselves.

Research on marriage similarly indicates that partners tend to resemble each other in physical characteristics, cognitive abilities, values and attitudes, and personality traits (Epstein & Guttman, 1984). Assortative mating has known genetic and social consequences, and it may also have implications for the course of personality development because similarities between spouses create an environment that reinforces initial tendencies (Buss, 1984). This proactive transactional process is documented in a 50-year longitudinal study of political attitudes. The political liberalism acquired by women while in college in the 1930s was sustained across their life course in part because they selected liberal friends and husbands who continued to support their politically liberal attitudes (Alwin et al., 1991). In a 10-year longitudinal study of couples, Caspi and Herbener (1990) found that persons who married a partner similar to themselves were subsequently more likely to show personality continuity over time. It may be that through assortative mating individuals set in motion processes of social interchange that help to sustain their dispositions, for in selecting marriage partners individuals also select the environments they will inhabit and the reinforcements to which they will be subject for many years (Buss, 1987).

HOW DOES CHANGE COME ABOUT?: MECHANISMS OF CHANGE ACROSS THE LIFE COURSE

With the flood of research demonstrating longitudinal stability, the focus of recent theory has been on processes that contribute to personality continuity. An analogous focus on the processes that result in personality change is lacking. Interestingly, most of the theoretical writings on what causes personality change come from nonpsychological domains (e.g., sociology) or rely on behavioral models or role theories that have not been updated in relation to personality development in over 30 years. In reviewing the disparate literatures on personality change, we identified four primary processes of change: responding to contingencies, watching oneself, watching others, and listening to others. We review each of these in turn.

Responding to Contingencies

One of the most simplistic yet powerful theories of change is the notion that people respond to reinforcers and punishers and that by doing so they change their behavior. As long as these environmental contingencies are in place, then new behaviors are thought to be maintained. The contingencies that people respond to can be either explicit or implicit. Explicit contingencies come in the form of concrete contingencies applied to a person's behavior where that person is aware of the change agenda. Implicit contingencies are more subtle and come in the form of unspoken expectations and demands that often come with the acquisition of new social roles (Sarbin, 1964).

The most direct form of explicit contingency is a parent's attempt to shape a child's behavior. For example, Kagan's (1994) work on behavioral inhibition demonstrates the interplay between parental attempts to shape a child's personality and the child's biologically and genetically based temperament. Behaviorally inhibited children experience greater levels of distress at lower thresholds when confronted with novel situations. Although childhood behavioral inhibition has been related to possessing traits of Shyness, Introversion, and Neuroticism in adulthood, not all inhibited children become shy adults. Several parental interventions on the part of inhibited children can shape whether an inhibited child becomes an introverted adult. Parents who expose their inhibited children to novelty and provide firm and consistent limits and do not overprotect their children from novel situations may help children overcome behavioral inhibition (Kagan, 1994). In contrast, many parents respond to their child's distress in novel situations by rewarding the child for avoiding these situations in the future. The reinforcement of these avoidance behaviors inadvertently promotes continued behavioral inhibition (Gerlsma, Emmelkamp, and Arrindell, 1990) and may increase the likelihood that the child grows up to become an inhibited adult. Likewise, different parenting socialization practices interact with childhood temperament in the development of Conscientiousness (Kochanska, 1991). Fearful children are more likely to internalize regulators of conduct when mothers use subtle, gentle, psychological discipline. Fearless children, in contrast, do not respond well to increased socialization pressures; rather, they tend to develop stronger internalization in response to a mutually positive and cooperative orientation between themselves and their parents (Kochanska, 1997).

Implicit contingencies are often communicated through the acquisition of roles or positions in a group, community, or society. Implicit contingencies are thought to shape behavior, and thus personality, by defining the appropriate way to play a role (Sarbin, 1964). Roles such as being a leader or follower come with specific expectations and demands for appropriate behavior that are known to the person assuming the role and to the people watching that person. For example, Sarbin and Jones (1955) asked respondents to describe their expectations for the manager role. Across several groups the respondents agreed that managers should act industrious, serious, stable, intelligent, fair-minded, tactful, and reasonable. Thus, a person who is impulsive by nature would be expected to set aside his or her predilection to make snap decisions if he or she assumes the role of manager in an organization. Exposure to these implicit role demands over a long period of time may be one factor contributing to personality change (e.g., Roberts, 1997).

Obviously, behaviorist notions of shaping personality directly through parenting styles or role pressures can be overly simplistic. Nonetheless, behavioral models of change are still the most elegant and powerful factors that influence change in a person's behavior and subsequent change in personality. The factors most often missing from behaviorally derived socialization models have to do with the cognitive and volitional aspects of personality. A discussion of these factors follows.

Watching Oneself

In addition to the press of the environment on behavior, one of the critical moderators of change is whether people have the opportunity to reflect on their own actions. For example, many efforts aimed at changing patients in a therapeutic situation focus on promoting insight into maladaptive behaviors. Psychodynamically oriented therapists establish a level of transference in which the patient's unconscious proclivities then arise. Once the maladaptive unconscious drives are identified, a therapist may then attempt to make the patient aware of these patterns in order to strengthen the ego's capacity for more adaptive alternatives. Likewise, cognitively oriented therapists attempt to identify problematic thoughts and replace them through cognitive re-education with more adaptive schemas, scripts, or interpretations of day-to-day events (see Messer & Warren, 1990, for a review). In essence, much of what goes on in therapy is an attempt to shift people's focus to watch themselves more closely in their daily lives. By gaining insight into their behavior, clients can then direct their efforts toward acting differently in future situations.

Change is also thought to come about through watching oneself act differently in new situations or in response to new contingencies. Thus, change comes about through a combination of environmental contingencies and self-insight. The most intensively studied model consistent with this position is Kohn and Schooler's (1983) learning-generalization model. Like the socialization models, the first key position of the learning-generalization model is that one's psychological makeup changes in response to the specific pressures and demands of roles, such as work and parenting. Where thc learning-generalization approach goes beyond behaviorism is in detailing the process through which contingencies are shaped by cognition. Personality is thought to be shaped by role experiences through the internalization of role demands into one's self-concept (Deci & Ryan 1990). This introjection process is facilitated when people draw conclusions about themselves by watching their own actions. For example, if taking on a supervisory role entails less personal connection to coworkers and subordinates, then supervisors may see themselves acting less friendly with subordinates, which they then interpret as a lack of interpersonal connection and diminished sociability (Howard & Bray, 1989).

Invariably the experiences that one watches oneself go through in specific contexts during the internalization process will then be generalized to other domains of life. For example, if a woman becomes more self-directed at work, she will become more self-directed in her marriage and her leisure activities. Kohn and Schooler (1983) report evidence to support the generalization effect, showing that men in intellectually demanding careers increased their engagement in intellectually stimulating leisure time activities.

Watching Others

Another significant source of information and learning comes through watching others, such as parents, teachers, coaches, and mentors. This approach to change is consistent with a social learning perspective that multiple information-processing mechanisms are involved in the acquisition of new behavior (Bandura, 1986). Bandura's (1965) Bobo doll experiments constitute some of the most elegant studies illustrating the human capacity to acquire behavioral potential through simply watching others, especially role models, and further illustrate the importance of combining observation with implicit or explicit reward structures for the behavior to be expressed (see also Bandura, 1986).

The most likely sources of observational learning are parents and significant role models. For example, the child's opportunity to watch their parent's work and how they approach their job may influence the child's own choice of career. Research on vocational interests appears to support this claim, showing that a child's vocational interests are related to the values that parents hold (Holland, 1962). Fathers who value curiosity in their sons have sons who peak on the Investigative and Artistic scales of Holland's Vocational Model (Holland, 1996). Of course, these covariations between parent and child values could be explained in part by the heritability of vocational interests (Bouchard, 1995).

In work contexts, observational learning is afforded through relationships with mentors (Chao, 1997). Mentorship reflects an intense work relationship between senior and junior members of an organization (Kram, 1985). One of the major functions of mentors is to demonstrate role appropriate behaviors and how to behave effectively in the organizational setting. Although there are few longitudinal studies showing that change comes about because of the mentor relationship, outcome studies that compare mentored versus nonmentored workers show some of the potential socializing effects of observing a role model. Riley and Wrench (1985) found that mentored women reported higher levels of career success and satisfaction than nonmentored women. Chao, Walz, and Gardner (1992) found that mentored engineers and managers experienced more job satisfaction, greater understanding of organizational norms and goals, and higher salaries.

Listening to Others

A critical source of information about ourselves, and subsequently a potential source of change, are the people with whom we interact and the feedback they provide to us. This is the primary thesis of symbolic interactionism (Blumer, 1969) and identity theory (Stryker, 1987). Symbolic interactionism emphasizes the meanings that individuals attribute to experience. These meanings are thought to be derived primarily through social interaction (Blumer, 1969).

Identity theory translates the sociological system of symbolic interactionism from the level of society to the level of the individual. According to identity theory, people develop meanings about themselves through receiving feedback from other individuals (Stryker & Statham, 1985). This feedback, described as reflected appraisals, can be either congruent or incongruent with a person's self-perceptions (Kiecolt, 1994). Burke (1991) proposed that when reflected appraisals are incongruent with people's self-perceptions they change their behavior in order to change the reflected appraisals. Thus, when people receive new feedback concerning their personality, either through the changes in their friends' or spouses' opinions or through exposure to new social groups, people will be more likely to change.

Unfortunately, the empirical database showing that listening to others contributes to change is lacking. Rather, the most provocative research in this area, provided by Swann (1987), shows that people tend not to listen to others if it means changing their self-perceptions. In an ingenious series of studies, Swann has shown that (1) people search out feedback that confirms their preexisting self-perceptions, (2) people prefer to associate with others who confirm their self-perceptions, and (3) this process is relatively independent of the evaluative nature of the feedback. That is, people with negative self-perceptions prefer to hear from others that they are seen as neurotic and depressed than hear that they are seen as happy and upbeat (see also Swann, Stein-Seroussi, & McNulty, 1992). Most of Swann's research has been cross-sectional. We still do not know the long term effects of being given feedback by significant people in our lives, such as spouses or respected coworkers, that contradicts our closely held self-views. It may be that persistence on the part of spouses, friends, and coworkers may lead to some personality change.

CONCLUSION

We set out to answer five questions about personality continuity and change across the life course. From the answers provided in this chapter, we now derive several working hypotheses and suggestions for future research.

First, in contrast to earlier reviews that emphasized the discontinuity of personality development during the early years of life, recent evidence indicates that there is modest continuity from childhood to adulthood. As researchers begin to take seriously the temperamental basis for personality, and as more participants in ongoing longitudinal studies "come of age," better estimates of continuity from the first 3 of years of life onward will become more widely available. The next step will be to link this emerging body of predictive evidence with explanatory accounts of how these long-term predictions come about.

Our second working hypothesis appears to contradict the first. While discontinuity has been the major theme of research on childhood personality development, extreme continuity has been the theme of research on adult personality development. Although the evidence does not support the conclusion that personality traits become fixed at a certain age in adulthood, the evidence is consistent with working definitions of personality traits as "relatively enduring."

The third topic addressed in the chapter dealt with the balance between continuity and change across the life course, and the evidence here favors a cumulative continuity model. With time and age people become more adept at interacting with their environment in ways that promote the consistency of personality. Personality becomes more consistent with age, reaching a peak of consistency in the fifth or sixth decade of life. This is not to downplay the importance of environmental factors in adulthood or to argue that change does not occur throughout midlife. Ample evidence shows that social contexts, role experiences, and changing historical and cultural norms affect personality development. But when pitted against one another, the forces of consistency outweigh the forces of change, and with time and experience the battle between change and consistency is won out by the forces of continuity.

Our final hypothesis is that mechanisms of continuity and change are not simply the flip side of the same coin. Rather, these are separate mechanisms that can work at any time to engender continuity and change. For example, people often attempt to select environments deemed suitable to their personality and by doing so reinforce continuity. Inevitably, these new environments may also bring with them some role demands that may force a person to change, even in subtle ways. Restated, it is not likely that new environments—even when proactively selected—will fit perfectly, and the imperfections may be manifest in role demands that lead to personality change.

Our working hypotheses lead to three recommendations that we hope will make easier the job of those who prepare the next edition of this chapter. First, researchers must be explicit about the types of continuity and change they study. We identified five types of continuity and change, each of which assesses somewhat different perspectives on personality development: differential, absolute, structural, ipsative, and coherence. Much of the confusion over the changeability of personality in adulthood is attributable to the imprecise use of the terms continuity and change. Second, we need active longitudinal research programs. To date, most research on personality change has been either passive and longitudinal or experimental and cross-sectional. We now need studies that couple interventionist strategies with longitudinal approaches in order to understand whether active attempts to change personality stick. For example, it is common practice in business to subject managers to extensive training in an effort to make them more effective leaders. How well do these interventions work? If a derailed manager is successfully rehabilitated, what types of changes have occurred? Do they go beyond simple behaviors to more substantive dimensions of personality? The same approach could be taken within clinical psychology. It would be informative to track changes not only in clinically relevant constructs, such as depression and anxiety, but also in personality traits related to these dimensions of psychopathology. Finally, longitudinal studies must be more inclusive and track the development of personality dimensions other than traits. Although the five-factor model has captured the longitudinal imagination, the constructs associated with evolutionary psychology, as well as "middle-level constructs" such as personal goals and motives, need to be integrated into longitudinal research programs to more fully map the course of personality development across the life course.

ACKNOWLEDGMENTS

Preparation of this chapter was supported by Grant No. MH49414 from the National Institute of Mental Health.

REFERENCES

Ackerman, P. L. (1997). Personality, self concept, interests and intelligence: Which construct doesn't fit? *Journal of Personality, 65,* 171–204.

Allport, G. W. (1962). The general and the unique in psychological science. *Journal of Personality, 30,* 405–422.

Alwin, D. F. (1994). Aging personality and social change: The stability of individual differences over the adult life span. In D. L. Featherman, R. M. Lerner, & M. Perlmutter (Eds.), *Lifespan development and behavior* (Vol. 14, pp. 135–185). Hillsdale, NJ: Erlbaum.

Alwin, D. F., Cohen, R. L., & Newcomb, T. M. (1991). *Political attitudes over the life span: The Bennington women after fifty years.* Madison: University of Wisconsin Press.

American Psychiatric Association. (1994). *Diagnostic and statistical manual of mental disorders* (4th ed.). Washington, DC: Author.

Andersen, S. M., & Baum, A. (1994). Transference in interpersonal relations: Inferences and affect based on significant-other representations. *Journal of Personality, 62,* 459–497.

Asendorpf, J. B. (1992a). Beyond stability: Predicting inter-individual differences in intraindividual change. *European Journal of Personality, 6,* 103–117.

Asendorpf, J. B. (1992b). Continuity and stability of personality traits and personality patterns. In J. B. Asendorpf & J. Valsiner (Eds.), *Stability and change in development: A study of methodological reasoning* (pp. 116–154). Newbury Park, CA: Sage.

Asendorpf, J. B., & van Aken, M. A. G. (1991). Correlates of the temporal consistency of personality patterns in childhood. *Journal of Personality, 59,* 689–703.

Asendorpf, J. B., & Wilpers, S. (1998). Personality effects on social relationships. *Journal of Personality and Social Psychology, 74,* 1531–1544.

Astington, J. W. (1993). *The child's discovery of the mind.* Cambridge, MA: Harvard University Press.

Baltes, P. B. (1987). Theoretical propositions of life-span developmental psychology: On the dynamics between growth and decline. *Developmental Psychology, 3,* 611–626.

Baltes, P. B. (1994). *On the overall landscape of human development.* Invited address at the 102nd Annual Convention of the American Psychological Association, Los Angeles.

Baltes, P. B. (1997). On the incomplete architecture of human ontogeny. *American Psychologist, 52,* 366–380.

Baltes, P. B., Cornelius, S. W., & Nesselroade, J. R. (1979). Cohort effects in developmental psychology. In J. R. Nesselroade & P. B. Baltes (Eds.), *Longitudinal research in the study of behavior and development* (pp. 61–87). New York: Academic Press.

Baltes, P. B., Reese, H. W., & Nesselroade, J. R. (1977). *Life-span developmental psychology: Introduction to research methods.* Monterey, CA: Brooks/Cole.

Bandura, A. (1965). Influence of models' reinforcement contingencies on the acquisition of imitative response. *Journal of Personality and Social Psychology, 1,* 589–595.

Bandura, A. (1986). *Social foundations of thought and action.* Englewood Cliffs, NJ: Prentice Hall.

Bell, R. Q., & Chapman, M. (1986). Child effects in studies using experimental or brief longitudinal approaches to socialization. *Developmental Psychology, 22,* 595–603.

Bellah, R. N., Madsen, R., Sullivan, W. M., Swidler, A., & Tipton, S. M. (1985). *Habits of the heart.* New York: Harper & Row.

Block, J. (1971). *Lives through time.* Berkeley, CA: Bancroft.

Block, J. (1993). Studying personality the long way. In D. Funder, R. D. Parke, C. Tomlinson-Keasy, & K. Widaman (Eds.), *Studying lives through time: Personality and development* (pp. 9–41). Washington DC: American Psychological Association.

Block, J., & Block, J. H. (1980). *The California Q-Set.* Palo Alto, CA: Consulting Psychologists Press.

Block, J., Block, J. H., & Keyes, S. (1988). Longitudinally foretelling drug usage in adolescence: Early childhood personality and environmental precursors. *Child Development, 59,* 336–355.

Bloom, B. S. (1964). *Stability and change in human characteristics.* New York: Wiley.

Blumer, H. (1969). *Symbolic interactionism: Perspective and method* (pp. 282–299). Englewood Cliffs, NJ: Prentice Hall.

Bollen, K. A. (1989). *Structural equations with latent variables.* New York: Wiley.

Borkenau, P., & Liebler, A. (1995). Observable attributes as manifestations and cues of personality and intelligence. *Journal of Personality, 63,* 1–25.

Bouchard, T. J., Jr. (1995). Longitudinal studies of personality and intelligence: A behavior genetic and evolutionary psychology perspective. In D. Saklofske & M. Zaidner (Eds.), *International handbook of personality and intelligence.* New York: Plenum Press.

Bowlby, J. (1973). *Attachment and Loss.* New York: Basic Books.

Brim, O. G., Jr. (1976). Life span development of the theory of oneself: Implications for child development. In H. W. Reese (Ed.), *Advances in child development and behavior* (pp. 242–253). New York: Academic Press.

Burke, P. J. (1991). Identity processes and social stress. *American Sociological Review, 56,* 836–849.

Buss, D. M. (1984). Toward a psychology of person–environment correspondence: The role of spouse selection. *Journal of Personality and Social Psychology, 47,* 361–377.

Buss, D. M. (1985). The temporal stability of acts, trends, and patterns. In C. D. Spielberger & J. N. Butcher (Eds.), *Advances in personality assessment* (pp. 165–196). Hillsdale, NJ: Erlbaum.

Buss, D. M. (1987). Selection, evocation, and manipulation. *Journal of Personality and Social Psychology, 53,* 1214–1221.

Cairns, R. B. (1979). *Social development.* San Francisco: Freeman.

Cairns, R. B., & Cairns, B. D. (1994). *Lifelines and risks: Pathways of youth in our time.* Cambridge, UK: Cambridge University Press.

Cairns, R. B., & Green, J. A. (1979). How to assess personality and social patterns: Observations or ratings? In R. B. Cairns (Ed.), *Analysis of social interaction.* Hillsdale, NJ: Erlbaum.

Cairns, R. B., & Hood, K. E. (1983). Continuity in social development: A comparative perspective on individual difference prediction. In P. B. Baltes & O. G. Brim, Jr. (Eds.), *Life-span development and behavior* (Vol. 5, pp. 301–358). New York: Academic Press.

Carmichael, C. M., & McGue, M. (1994). A longitudinal family study of personality change and stability. *Journal of Personality, 62,* 1–20.

Caspi, A. (1987). Personality in the life course. *Journal of Personality and Social Psychology, 53,* 1203–1213.

Caspi, A., Elder, G. H., Jr., & Bem, D. J. (1988). Moving away from the world: Life-course patterns of shy children. *Developmental Psychology, 24,* 824–831.

Caspi, A., & Herbener, E. S. (1990). Continuity and change: Assortative marriage and the consistency of personality in adulthood. *Journal of Personality and Social Psychology, 58,* 250–258.

Caspi, A., & Moffitt, T. E. (1993). When do individual differences matter? A paradoxical theory of personality coherence. *Psychological Inquiry, 4,* 247–271.

Caspi, A., & Silva, P. A. (1995). Temperamental qualities at age 3 predict personality traits in young adulthood: Longitudinal evidence from a birth cohort. *Child Development, 66,* 486–498.

Chao, G. T. (1997). Organizational socialization: Mentoring phases and outcomes. *Journal of Vocational Behavior, 51,* 15–28.

Chao, G. T., Walz, M., & Gardner, D. (1992). Formal and informal mentorships: A comparison on mentoring functions and contrast with non-mentored counterparts. *Personnel Psychology, 45,* 619–636.

Cherny, S. S., Fulker, D. W., Emde, R. N., Robinson, J., Corley, R., Reznick, J. S., Plomin, R., & DeFries, J. C. (1994). Continuity and change in infant shyness from 14 to 20 months. *Behavioral Genetics, 24,* 365–379.

Chess, S., & Thomas, A. (1987). *Origins and evolution of behavior disorders: From infancy to early adult life.* Cambridge, MA: Harvard University Press.

Conley, J. J. (1984a). The hierarchy of consistency: A review and model of longitudinal findings of adult individual differences in intelligence, personality, and self-opinion. *Personality and Individual Differences, 5,* 11–25.

Conley, J. J. (1984b). Relation of temporal stability and cross-situational consistency in personality: Comment of the Mischel–Epstein debate. *Psychological Review, 91,* 491–496.

Conley, J. J. (1985). Longitudinal stability of personality traits: A multitrait–multidimensional–multioccasion analysis. *Journal of Personality and Social Psychology, 49,* 1266–1282.

Cook, W. L., Kenny, D. A., & Goldstein, M. J. (1991). Parental affective style risk and the family system: A social relations model analysis. *Journal of Abnormal Psychology, 100,* 492–501.

Costa, P. T., & McCrae, R. R. (1988). Personality in adulthood: A six year longitudinal study of self-reports and spouse ratings of the NEO personality inventory. *Journal of Personality and Social Psychology, 54,* 853–863.

Costa, P. T., & McCrae, R. R. (1992). Trait psychology comes of age. In T. B. Sonderegger (Ed.), *Nebraska Symposium on Motivation 1991: Vol. 39. Psychology and aging: Current theory and research in motivation.* Lincoln, NE: University of Nebraska Press.

Costa, P. T., & McCrae, R. R. (1997). Longitudinal stability of adult personality. In R. Hogan, J. Johnson, & S. Briggs (Eds.), *Handbook of personality psychology* (pp. 269–292). San Diego, CA: Academic Press.

Costa, P. T., McCrae, R. R., & Arenberg, D. (1980). Enduring dispositions in adult males. *Journal of Personality and Social Psychology, 38,* 793–800.

Cowan, P. A., & Cowan, C. P. (1992). *When partners become parents.* New York: Basic Books.

Crick, N. R., & Dodge, K. A. (1994). A review and reformulation of social information-processing mechanisms in children's social adjustment. *Psychological Bulletin, 115,* 74–101.

Cronbach, L. J., & Gleser, G. C. (1953). Assessing the similarity between profiles. *Psychological Bulletin, 50,* 456–473.

Cutler, S. J., & Kaufman, R. L. (1975). Cohort changes in political attitudes: Tolerance of ideological nonconformity. *Public Opinion Quarterly, 39,* 69–81.

Damon, W., & Hart, D. (1986). Stability and change in children's self-understanding. *Social Cognition, 4,* 102–118.

Deci, E. L., & Ryan, R. M. (1990). A motivational approach to self: Integration in personality. In R. A. Dienstbier (Ed.), *Perspectives on motivation: Nebraska Symposium on Motivation* (Vol. 38, pp. 237–288). Lincoln, NE: University of Nebraska Press.

Dishion, T. J., Patterson, G. R., Stoolmiller, M., & Skinner, M. L. (1991). Family, school, and behavioral antecedents to early adolescent involvement with antisocial peers. *Developmental Psychology, 27,* 172–180.

Draper, P., & Belsky, J. (1990). Personality development in evolutionary perspective. *Journal of Personality, 58,* 141–161.

Dworkin, R. H., Burke, B. W., Maher, B. A., & Gottesman, I. I. (1976). A longitudinal study of the genetics of personality. *Journal of Personality and Social Psychology, 34,* 510–518.

Dworkin, R. H., Burke, B. W., Maher, B. A., & Gottesman, I. I. (1977). Genetic influences on the organization and development of personality. *Developmental Psychology, 13,* 164–165.

Eaves, L., & Eysenck, H. (1976). Genetic and environmental components of inconsistency and unrepeatability in twins' responses to a neuroticism questionnaire. *Behavior Genetics, 6,* 145–160.

Elder, G. H., Jr. (1979). Historical change in life patterns and personality. In P. B. Baltes & O. G. Brim,

Jr. (Eds.), *Life-span development and behavior* (Vol. 2, pp. 117–159). New York: Academic Press.

Elder, G. H., Jr. (1998). *Children of the Great Depression: Social change in life experience* (25th anniversary ed.). Boulder, CO: Westview Press.

Elder, G. H., Jr., Modell, J., & Parke, R. D. (1994). *Children in time and place: Development and historical insights.* New York: Cambridge University Press.

Ennett, S. T., & Bauman, K. E. (1994). The contribution of influence and selection to adolescent peer group homogeneity: The case of adolescent cigarette smoking. *Journal of Personality and Social Psychology, 67,* 653–663.

Epstein, E., & Guttman, R. (1984). Mate selection in man: Evidence, theory and outcome. *Social Biology, 31,* 243–278.

Epstein, S. (1991). Cognitive-experiential self theory: Implications for developmental psychology. In M. R. Gunnar & L. A. Sroufe (Eds.), *Self processes and development: The Minnesota Symposia on Child Development* (pp. 79–123). Hillsdale, NJ: Erlbaum.

Erikson, E. (1950). *Childhood and society.* New York: Norton.

Fenichel, O. (1945). *The psychoanalytic theory of neurosis.* New York: Norton.

Field, D., & Millsap, R. E. (1991). Personality in advanced old age: Continuity or change? *Journal of Gerontology, 46,* 299–308.

Finn, S. E. (1986). Stability of personality self-ratings over 30 years: Evidence for an age–cohort interaction. *Journal of Personality and Social Psychology, 50,* 813–818.

Fiske, S. T., & Taylor, S. (1991). *Social cognition.* New York: McGraw-Hill.

Freud, A. (1936). *The writings of Anna Freud* (Vol. 2). New York: International Universities Press.

Gangestad, S. W., & Simpson, J. A. (1990). Toward an evolutionary history of female sociosexual variation. *Journal of Personality, 58,* 69–96.

Gergen, K. J. (1982). *Toward transformation in social knowledge.* New York: Springer.

Gerlsma, C., Emmelkamp, P. M., & Arrindell, W. A. (1990). Anxiety, depression, and perception of early parenting: A meta-analysis. *Clinical Psychology Review, 10,* 251–277.

Gest, S. D. (1997). Behavioral inhibition: Stability and associations with adaptation from childhood to early adulthood. *Journal of Personality and Social Psychology, 72,* 467–475.

Glenn, N. D. (1980). Values, attitudes, and beliefs. In O. G. Brim, Jr. & J. Kagan (Eds.), *Constancy and change in human development* (pp. 596–640). Cambridge, MA: Harvard University Press.

Gough, H. (1991). *Scales and combinations of scales: What do they tell us, what do they mean?* Invited address, Division of Evaluation and Measurement, American Psychological Association meetings, San Francisco, CA.

Graziano, W. G., Jensen-Campell, L. A., & Hair, E. C. (1996). Perceiving interpersonal conflict and reacting to it: The case for agreeableness. *Journal of Personality and Social Psychology, 70,* 820–835.

Gurin, P., & Brim, O. G. (1984). Change in self in adulthood: The example of sense of control. In P. B. Baltes & O. G. Brim (Eds.), *Life span development and behavior* (Vol. 6, pp. 282–334). New York: Academic Press.

Haan, N., Millsap, R., & Hartka, E. (1986). As time goes by: Change and stability in personality over fifty years. *Psychology and Aging, 1,* 220–232.

Hammen, C. (1991). Generation of stress in the cause of unipolar depression. *Journal of Abnormal Psychology, 100,* 555–561.

Hanson, R. A. (1975). Consistency and stability of home environmental measures related to IQ. *Child Development, 46,* 470–480.

Harter, S. (1997). The development of self representations. In W. Damon & N. Eisenberg (Eds.), *Handbook of child psychology* (Vol. 3, pp. 553–618). New York: Wiley.

Heckhausen, J., Dixon, R. A., & Baltes, P. B. (1989). Gains and losses in development throughout adulthood as perceived by different adulthood age groups. *Developmental Psychology, 25,* 109–121.

Helson, R., Mitchell, V., & Moane, G. (1984). Personality and patterns of adherence and nonadherence to the social clock. *Journal of Personality and Social Psychology, 46,* 1079–1096.

Helson, R., & Moane, G. (1987). Personality change in women from college to midlife. *Journal of Personality and Social Psychology, 53,* 176–186.

Helson, R., & Wink, P. (1992). Personality change in women from the early 40s to the early 50s. *Psychology and Aging, 7,* 46–55.

Holland, J. L. (1962). Some explorations of a theory of vocational choice: I. One- and two-year longitudinal studies. *Psychological Monographs, 76*(26).

Holland, J. L. (1996). *Making vocational choices.* Odessa, FL: PAR.

Horowitz, M. J., Milbrath, C., Jordan, D. S., Stinson, C. H., Ewert, M., Redington, D. J., Fridhandler, B., Reidbord, S. P., & Hartley, D. (1994). Expressive and defensive behavior during discourse on unresolved topics: A single case study of pathological grief. *Journal of Personality, 62,* 527–563.

Howard, A., & Bray, D. (1989). *Managerial lives in transition.* New York: Guilford Press.

Huesmann, L. R., Eron, L. D., Lefkowitz, M. M., & Walder, L. O. (1984). Stability of aggression over time and generations. *Developmental Psychology, 20,* 1120–1134.

James, W. (1890). *The principles of psychology.* New York: Dover.

Jones, C. J., & Meredith, W. (1996). Patterns of personality change across the life course. *Psychology and Aging, 11,* 57–65.

Jones, M. C. (1981). Midlife drinking patterns: Correlates and antecedents. In D. Eichorn, J. A. Clausen, N. Haan, M. P. Honzik, & P. H. Mussen (Eds.), *Past and present in middle life* (pp. 223–242). New York: Academic Press.

Kagan, J. (1969). The three faces of continuity in human development. In D. A. Goslin (Ed.), *Handbook of socialization theory and research* (pp. 983–1002). Chicago, IL: Rand McNally.

Kagan, J. (1980). Perspectives on continuity. In O. G. Brim, Jr. & J. Kagan (Eds.), *Constancy and change in human development* (pp. 26–74). Cambridge, MA: Harvard University Press.

Kagan, J. (1981). *The second year.* Cambridge, MA: Harvard University Press.

Kagan, J. (1984). *The nature of the child.* Cambridge, MA: Harvard University Press.

Kagan, J. (1994). *Galen's prophecy: Temperament in human nature.* New York: Basic Books.

Kagan, J. (1997). Biology and the child. In W. Damon & N. Eisenberg (Eds.), *Handbook of child psychology* (Vol. 3, pp. 177–236). New York: Wiley.

Kagan, J., & Moss, H. A. (1962). *Birth to maturity.* New York: Wiley.

Kandel, D. B., Davies, M., & Baydar, N. (1990). The creation of interpersonal contexts: Homophily in dyadic relationships in adolescence and young adulthood. In L. N. Robins & M. R. Rutter (Eds.), *Straight and devious pathways to adulthood* (pp. 221–241). New York: Cambridge University Press.

Kelly, E. L. (1955). Consistency of adult personality. *American Psychologist, 10,* 659–681.

Keltner, D. (1996). Facial expressions of emotion and personality. In C. Magai & S. H. McFadden (Eds.), *Handbook of emotion, adult development, and aging* (pp. 385–401). San Diego, CA: Academic Press.

Kiecolt, K. J. (1994). Stress and the decision to change oneself: A theoretical model. *Social Psychology Quarterly, 57,* 49–63.

Kochanska, G. (1991). Socialization and temperament in the development of guilt and conscience. *Child Development, 62,* 1379–1392.

Kochanska, G. (1997). Multiple pathways to conscience for children with different temperaments: From toddlerhood to age 5. *Developmental Psychology, 33,* 228–240.

Kohn, M. L., & Schooler, C. (1983). *Work and personality: An inquiry into social stratification.* Norwood, NJ: Ablex.

Kram, K. E. (1985). Mentoring alternatives: The role of peer relationships in career development. *Academy of Management Journal, 28,* 110–132.

Lasch, C. (1979). *The culture of narcissism: American life in an age of diminishing expectations.* New York: Norton.

Laub, J. H., & Sampson, R. J. (1993). Turning points in the life course: Why change matters to the study of crime. *Criminology, 31,* 301–325.

Livson, N., & Day, D. (1977). Adolescent personality antecedents of completed family size. *Journal of Youth and Adolescence, 6,* 311–324.

Livson, N., & Peskin, H. (1980). Perspectives on adolescence from longitudinal research. In J. Adelson (Ed.), *Handbook of adolescent psychology* (pp. 47–98). New York: Wiley.

Loehlin, J. C., Horn, J. M., & Willerman, L. (1990). Heredity, environment and personality change: Evidence from the Texas Adoption Project. *Journal of Personality, 58,* 221–243.

Loevinger, J. (1966). The meaning and measurement of ego development. *American Psychologist, 21,* 195–206.

Lubinski, D., Schmidt, D. B., & Benbow, C. P. (1996). A 20 year stability analysis of the study of values for intellectually gifted individuals from adolescence to adulthood. *Journal of Applied Psychology, 81,* 443–451.

Lytton, H. (1990). Child and parent effects in boys' conduct disorder: A reinterpretation. *Developmental Psychology, 26,* 683–697.

Matas, L., Arend, R., & Sroufe, L. A. (1978). Continuity of adaptation in the second year: The relationship between quality of attachment and later competence. *Child Development, 49,* 547–556.

Matheny, A. P., Jr. (1983). A longitudinal study of stability of components from Bayley's Infant Behavior Record. *Child Development, 54,* 356–360.

Matheny, A. P., Jr. (1989). Children's behavioral inhibition over age and across situations: Genetic similarity for a trait during change. *Journal of Personality, 57,* 215–235.

McCall, R. B. (1977). Challenges to a science of developmental psychology. *Child Development, 48,* 333–344.

McCall, R. B., & Carriger, M. S. (1993). A meta-analysis of infant habituation and recognition memory performance as predictors of later IQ. *Child Development, 64,* 57–79.

McCall, R. B., Eichorn, D. H., & Hogarty, P. S. (1977). Developmental changes in mental performance. *Monographs of the Society for Research in Child Development, 38*(3, Serial No. 171).

McCartney, K., Harris, M., & Bernieri, F. (1990). Growing up and growing apart: A developmental meta-analysis of twin studies. *Psychological Bulletin, 107,* 226–237.

McCrae, R. R., & Costa, P. T., Jr. (1990). *Personality in adulthood.* New York: Guilford Press.

McCrae, R. R., & Costa, P. T., Jr. (1994). The stability of personality: Observation and evaluations. *Current Directions in Psychological Science, 3,* 173–175.

McGue, M., Bacon, S., & Lykken, D. T. (1993). Personality stability and change in early adulthood: A behavioral genetic analysis. *Developmental Psychology, 29,* 96–109.

McNally, S., Eisenberg, N., & Harris, J. D. (1991). Consistency and change in maternal child-rearing practices and values: A longitudinal study. *Child Development, 620,* 190–198.

Messer, S. B., & Warren, S. (1990). Personality change and psychotherapy. In L. Pervin (Ed.), *Handbook of personality: Theory and research* (pp. 371–398). New York: Guilford Press.

Modell, J. (1989). *Into one's own: From youth to adulthood in the United States 1920–1975*. Berkeley: University of California Press.

Mortimer, J. T., Finch, M. D., & Kumka, D. S. (1982). Persistence and change in development: The multidimensional self concept. In P. B. Baltes & O. G. Brim, Jr. (Eds.), *Life-span development and behavior* (Vol. 4, pp. 164–310). New York: Academic Press.

Moskowitz, D. S. (1986). Comparison of self-reports, reports by knowledgeable informants, and behavioral observations data. *Journal of Personality, 54,* 294–317.

Moss, H. A., & Susman, E. J. (1980). Longitudinal study of personality development. In O. G. Brim, Jr., & J. Kagan (Eds.), *Constancy and change in human development.* (pp. 530–595). Cambridge, MA: Harvard University Press.

Neugarten, B. L. (1968). Age norms, age constraints, and adult socialization. In B. L. Neugarten (Ed.), *Middle age and aging: A reader in social psychology*. Chicago: University of Chicago Press.

Neugarten, B. L. (1977). Personality and aging. In J. E. Birren & K. W. Schaie (Eds.), *Handbook of the psychology of aging* (pp. 626–649). New York: Van Nostrand Rienhold.

Nunn, C. Z., Crockett, H. J., Jr., & Williams, J. A., Jr. (1978). *Tolerance for conformity.* San Francisco: Josey-Bass.

O'Connor, T. G., Deater-Deckard, K., Fulker, D., Rutter, M., & Plomin, R. (1998). Genotype–environment correlations in late childhood and early adolescence: Antisocial behavioral problems and coercive parenting. *Developmental Psychology, 34,* 970–981.

Ozer, D. J. (1986). *Consistency in personality: A methodological framework*. New York: Springer.

Ozer, D. J., & Gjerde, P. F. (1989). Patterns of personality consistency and change from childhood through adolescence. *Journal of Personality, 57,* 483–507.

Patterson, G. R., & Bank, L. (1989). Some amplifying mechanisms for pathologic processes in families. In M. R. Gunnar & E. Thelen (Eds.), *Systems and development: The Minnesota Symposia on Child Psychology* (Vol. 22, p. 167–209). Hillsdale, NJ: Erlbaum.

Pedlow, R., Sanson, A., Prior, M., & Oberklaid, F. (1993). Stability of maternally reported temperament from infancy to 8 years. *Developmental Psychology, 29,* 998–1007.

Pianta, R. C., Sroufe, L. A., & Egeland, B. (1989). Continuity and discontinuity in maternal sensitivity at 6, 24, and 42 months in a high risk sample. *Child Development, 60,* 481–487.

Plomin, R. (1994). *Genetics and experience: The interplay between nature and nurture*. Thousand Oaks, CA: Sage.

Plomin, R., & Bergeman, C. S. (1991). The nature of nurture: Genetic influence on "environmental" measures. *Behavioral and Brain Sciences, 14,* 373–386.

Plomin, R., DeFries, J. C., & Loehlin, J. C. (1977). Genotype–environment interaction and correlation in the analysis of human behavior. *Psychological Bulletin, 84,* 309–322.

Plomin, R., Kagan, J., Emde, R. N., Reznick, J. S., Braugart, J. M., Robinson, J., Campos, J., Zahn-Waxler, C., Corley, R., Fulker, D. W., & DeFries, J. C. (1993). Genetic change and continuity from fourteen to twenty months: The MacArthur Longitudinal Twin Study. *Child Development, 64,* 1354–1376.

Pogue-Geile, M., & Rose, R. J. (1985). Developmental genetic studies of adult personality. *Developmental Psychology, 21,* 547–557.

Quiggle, N. L., Garber, J., Panak, W. F., & Dodge, K. A. (1992). Social information processing in aggressive and depressed children. *Child Development, 63,* 1305–1320.

Rabiner, D. L., Lenhart, L., & Lochman, J. E. (1990). Automatic versus reflective social problem solving in relation to children's sociometric status. *Developmental Psychology, 26,* 1010–1016.

Reich, C. A. (1970). *The greening of America: How the youth revolution is trying to make America livable.* New York: Random House.

Riley, S., & Wrench, D. (1985). Mentoring among women lawyers. *Journal of Applied Social Psychology, 15,* 374–386.

Roberts, B. W. (1997). Plaster or plasticity: Are work experiences associated with personality change in women. *Journal of Personality, 65,* 205–232.

Roberts, B. W., & Friend-DelVecchio, W. (in press). Consistency of personality traits from childhood to old age: A quantitative review of longitudinal studies. *Psychological Bulletin.*

Roberts, B. W., & Helson, R. (1997). Changes in culture, changes in personality: The influence of individualism in a longitudinal study of women. *Journal of Personality and Social Psychology, 72,* 641–651.

Roberts, G. C., Block, J. H., & Block, J. (1984). Continuity and change in parents' child rearing practices. *Child Development, 55,* 586–597.

Rusting, C. L. (1998). Personality, mood, and cognitive processing of emotional information: Three conceptual frameworks. *Psychological Bulletin, 124,* 165–196.

Rutter, M. (1983). Statistical and personal interactions: Facets and perspectives. In D. Magnusson & V. I. Allen (Eds.), *Human development: An international perspective* (pp. 295–319). New York: Academic Press.

Ryder, R. G. (1967). Birth to maturity revisited: A canonical analysis. *Journal of Personality and Social Psychology, 1,* 168–172.

Ryff, C. D. (1984). Personality development from the inside: The subjective experience of change in adulthood and aging. In P. B. Baltes & O. G. Brim, Jr. (Eds.), *Life-span development and behavior* (Vol. 6, pp. 244–278). Orlando, FL: Academic Press.

Sameroff, A. J. (1995). General systems theories and developmental psychopathology. In D. Cicchetti & D. J. Cohen (Eds.), *Developmental psychopathology* (pp. 659–695). New York: Wiley.

Sameroff, A. J., Seifer, R., Baldwin, A., & Baldwin, C. (1993). Stability of intelligence from preschool to adolescence: The influence of social and family risk factors. *Child Development, 64,* 80–97.

Sampson, R. J., & Laub, J. H. (1993). *Crime in the making.* Cambridge, MA: Harvard University Press.

Sanford, R. N. (1962). *The American college.* New York: Wiley.

Sapir, E. (1934). Personality. *Encyclopedia of the Social Sciences, 12,* 85–88.

Sarbin, T. R. (1964). Role theoretical interpretation of psychological change. In P. Worchel & D. Byrne (Eds.), *Personality change* (pp. 176–219). New York: Wiley.

Sarbin, T. R., & Jones, D. S. (1955). The assessment of role expectations in the selection of supervisory personnel. *Educational and Psychological Measurement, 15,* 236–239.

Saudino, K. J., Plomin, R., & DeFries, J. C. (1996). Tester-rated temperament at 14, 20, and 24 months: Environmental change and genetic continuity. *British Journal of Developmental Psychology, 14,* 129–144.

Scarr, S., & McCartney, K. (1983). How people make their own environments: A theory of genotype to environment effects. *Child Development, 54,* 424–435.

Schaie, K. W. (1965). A general model for the study of developmental problems. *Psychological Bulletin, 64,* 843–861.

Schuman, H., & Scott, J. (1989). Generations and collective memories. *American Sociological Review, 54,* 359–381.

Settersten, R. A., Jr., & Mayer, K. U. (1997). The measurement of age, age structuring, and the life course. *Annual Review of Sociology, 23,* 233–261.

Siegler, I. C., George, L. K., & Okun, M. A. (1979). A cross-sequential analysis of adult personality. *Developmental Psychology, 15,* 350–352.

Smith, M. B. (1994). Selfhood at risk: Postmodern perils and the perils of postmodernism. *American Psychologist, 49,* 405–411.

Snyder, M., & Ickes, W. (1985). Personality and social behavior. In E. Aronson & G. Lindzey (Eds.), *Handbook of social psychology* (pp. 248–305). New York: Random House.

Sroufe, L. A., Carlson, E., & Shulman, S. (1993). Individuals in relationships: Development from infancy through adolescence. In D. C. Funder, R. D. Parke, C. Tomlinson-Keasey, & K. Widaman (Eds.), *Studying lives through time* (pp. 315–342). Washington, DC: American Psychological Association.

Sroufe, L. A., Fox, N., & Pancake, V. (1983). Attachment and dependency in developmental perspective. *Child Development, 54,* 1615–1627.

Stearns, S. C. (1992). *The evolution of life histories.* New York: Oxford University Press.

Stein, J. A., Newcomb, M. D., & Bentler, P. M. (1986). Stability and change in personality: A longitudinal study from early adolescence to young adulthood. *Journal of Research in Personality, 20,* 276–291.

Stevens, D. P., & Truss, C. V. (1985). Stability and change in adult personality over 12 and 20 years. *Developmental Psychology, 21,* 568–584.

Stewart, A. J., Sokol, M., Healy, J. M., & Chester, N. L. (1986). Longitudinal studies of psychological consequences of life changes in children and adults. *Journal of Personality and Social Psychology, 50,* 143–151.

Stryker, S. (1987). Identity theory: Developments and extensions. In K. Yardley & T. Honess (Eds.), *Self and identity: Psychosocial perspectives* (pp. 89–103). Chichester, UK: Wiley.

Stryker, S., & Statham, A. (1985). Symbolic interaction role theory. In G. Lindzey & E. Aronson (Eds.), *Handbook of social psychology* (pp. 311–378). Hillsdale, NJ: Erlbaum.

Swann, W. B., Jr. (1987). Identity negotiation: Where two roads meet. *Journal of Personality and Social Psychology, 53,* 1038–1051.

Swann, W. B., Stein-Seroussi, A., & McNulty, S. E. (1992). Outcasts in a white-lie society: The enigmatic worlds of people with negative self-conceptions. *Journal of Personality and Social Psychology, 62,* 618–624.

Tellegen, A., Lykken, D. T., Bouchard, T. J., Wilcox, K. J., Segal, N. L., & Rich, S. (1988). Personality similarity in twins reared apart and together. *Journal of Personality and Social Psychology, 6,* 1031–1039.

Tesser, A. (1993). The importance of heritability in psychological research: The case of attitudes. *Psychological Review, 100,* 129–142.

Thomas, W. I., & Thomas, D. (1928). *The child in America.* New York: Knopf.

Tomkins, S. S. (1979). Script theory: Differential magnification of affects. In H. E. Howe, Jr., & R. A. Dienstbier (Eds.), *Nebraska Symposium on Motivation* (Vol. 26, pp. 201–236). Lincoln: University of Nebraska Press.

Trachtenberg, S., & Viken, R. J. (1994). Aggressive boys in the classroom: Biased attributions or shared perceptions? *Child Development, 65,* 829–835.

Urban, J., Carlson, E., Egeland, B., & Sroufe, L. A. (1991). Patterns of individual adaptation across childhood. *Development and Psychopathology, 3,* 445–460.

Vaillant, G. E. (1976). Natural history of male psychological health: V. The relation of choice of ego mechanisms of defense to adult adjustment. *Archives of General Psychiatry, 33,* 535–545.

Vallerand, R. J., Bissonnette, R. (1992). Intrinsic, extrinsic, and motivational styles as predictors of behavior: A prospective study. *Journal of Personality, 60,* 599–620.

Veroff, J., Douvan, E., & Kulka, R. A. (1981). *The inner American: A self-portrait from 1957–1976.* New York: Basic Books.

Wachs, T. D. (1994). Fit, context, and the transition between temperament and personality. In C. F. Halverson, Jr., G. A. Kohnstamm, & R. P. Martin (Eds.), *The developing structure of temperament and personality from infancy to adulthood* (pp. 209–220). Hillsdale, NJ: Erlbaum.

Wachs, T. D., & Plomin, R. (1991). *Conceptualization and measurement of organism–environment interaction.* Washington, DC: American Psychological Association.

Wachtel, P. L. (1994). Cyclical processes in personality and psychopathology. *Journal of Abnormal Psychology, 103,* 51–54.

Warren, J. R., & Hauser, R. M. (1997). Social stratification across three generations: New evidence from the Wisconsin Longitudinal Study. *American Sociological Review, 62,* 561–572.

Westen, D. (1991). Social cognition and object relations. *Psychological Bulletin, 109,* 429–455.

Woodruff, D. S., & Birren, J. E. (1972). Age changes and cohort differences in personality. *Developmental Psychology, 6,* 252–259.

Zuckerman, M. (1993). History and developmental psychology, a dangerous liaison: A historian's perspective. In G. H. Elder, J. Modell, & R. D. Parke (Eds.), *Children in time and place: Developmental and historical insights* (pp. 230–240). New York: Cambridge University Press.

Chapter 12

On the Development of Personality

Michael Lewis
Institute for the Study of Child Development

Studying development, whether it be the development of cognition, personality, or psychopathology has many inherent difficulties. In this chapter, some of these difficulties are considered, in light of the added problem that the *nature* of adult personality is still unclear. The very idea of personality presupposes a set of enduring individual characteristics that are stable and that are consistent across place, tasks, and people's interactions. Given that much of the present volume is concerned with considering these issues, someone interested in the study of personality development—that is the consistency over time—must by necessity find the task difficult.

This chapter approaches this problem from the point of view of the nature of development and how to understand the processes that should impact on personality formation. This requires that we first present an example of our problem by considering the results of a study conducted on early childhood sequelae to school age problems. In this study of depression, we examined who reports on the child's depression and observed the developmental factors that influence individual differences. I chose this topic rather than a more traditional personality variable since my work has focused here and because what we found will provide an example that will set the stage for our further discussion. Following the presentation of this short longitudinal study, I will discuss the various models of development, trying to point out that our theories of personality development derive mostly either from a genetic disposition model or through a process of development called the organismic model. This model holds that development is a unidirectional bounded process of change leading to some outcome called here mature personality, where earlier events are held to be related to later events, and, therefore, later events or personality characteristics can be predicted from them. Moreover, such a theory holds that the developmental process is lawful and regular and that its rules apply to all members of the species regardless of culture.

In the final section, taking data from another longitudinal study, this one of attachment development—a personality characteristic—I will argue that the most fruitful course of study of the development of personality can be found in a contextual framework, where personality is best understood as a dynamic system influenced mostly by the current context and by the personal narratives that we construct around ourselves, others, and goals (Lewis, 1997).

WHO SAYS I'M DEPRESSED AND WHY?

Typically, children themselves do not determine that they are depressed. Rather, a parent or teacher identifies signs of depression and refers the child to a clinician (Lewis, 1990a). An examination of childhood depression must include parents' and teachers' perceptions of the child as well as the child's own perceptions. However, studies of child depression and pathology show that different people's assessments of the same child do not agree (Herjanic & Reich, 1982; Jensen, Salzberg, Richters, & Watanabe, 1993; Kazdin, French, Unis, & Esveldt-Dawson, 1983; Stavrakaki, Vargo, Roberts, & Boodoosingh, 1987). Patterns of agreement are no more consistent when outside raters, such as clinicians, teachers, or peers, are employed. Kazdin et al. (1983) found that parents and clinicians were in stronger agreement than children and clinicians, but Moretti, Fine, Haley, and Marriage (1985), Poznanski, Mokros, Grossman, and Freeman (1985), and Stavrakaki et al. (1987) reported the opposite. Research examining agreement between teachers and children also shows low levels of agreement (Achenbach, 1991; Jacobsen, Lahey, & Strauss, 1983; McConaughy, Stanger, & Achenbach, 1992; Saylor, Finch, Baskin, Furey, & Kelly, 1984). Peer ratings sometimes correlate with the children's self-reported depression (Jacobson et al., 1983; Lefkowitz & Tesiny, 1984; Saylor et al., 1984), but only in normal samples. This raises the general issue of whether the assessment of the child's characteristics may not be consistent across raters or different measures. If this is so, then which factors impact on individual differences may vary depending on the outcome measured.

Raters may disagree about the same child for a number of reasons. First, different instruments are usually used to obtain ratings from different people, and the instruments might not be compatible. When raters complete the same instrument (e.g., parent, child, and teacher versions of the Child Behavior Checklist (CBCL; Achenbach, 1991), agreement is often higher than when different instruments are completed by multiple raters (Angold et al., 1987; Fendrich, Weissman, & Warner, 1991; Weissman, Wickramaratne, et al., 1987). Although using three versions of the CBCL, Achenbach and colleagues (Achenbach, 1991; McConaughy et al., 1992; Stanger, McConaughy, & Achenbach, 1992) found some agreement among parents, children, and their teachers. However, other studies using the CBCL instruments reveal lower levels of agreement between raters' assessments of children's depression and pathology (Stanger & Lewis, 1993).

Low rates of agreement about child depression also may be due to the fact that some raters might not know the child well enough to draw clinical conclusions. This is particularly important for such syndromes as depression, which may reflect a child's "inner state." Without knowing the inner state of the child, an observer might not be able to determine that a child is displaying symptoms of depression. A third reason for low rates of agreement may be due to the rater's own problems. For example, mothers who are more depressed perceive their children as more depressed (Richters, 1992).

Finally, it is likely that people's perceptions are based on the child's behavior in different situations. Teachers and parents experience the child in different circumstances that require different coping skills. The fact that children are seen in different situations that elicit different behaviors is likely to be an important factor. Situationally determined behavior has been well documented (Snyder & Ickes, 1985). There is evidence that different observers base their judgments on different characteristics of the child (Routh, 1990). For example, Kazdin, Moser, Colbus, and Bell (1985) showed that parents and children emphasize different facets of the child's functioning. Children focused on internal feelings and expectancies for the future, whereas parents focused on the child's overt social behavior and outward manifestations of affect. Mischel (1990) has suggested that although behavior differs across situations, it may be consistent within situations. Although parents, teachers, and children may disagree about the child, they may provide accurate assessments *within particular contexts*.

We pursued this question looking at depression in a normal sample of 76 children when they were 9 years old. Ratings of children's psychopathology were provided from multiple raters. Children completed the Children's Depression Inventory (CDI; Kovacs, 1983). Children who scored 13 or above were grouped as depressed; those who scored below as nondepressed (Kovacs, 1983). Mothers completed the Child Behavior Checklist (CBCL; Achenbach, 1978), and we used the internalizing scale as a measure of the mothers' perceptions of their children's depression. Finally, teachers completed the Classroom Behavior Inventory (CBI; Schaefer, Edgerton, & Aaronson, 1979), a measure of children's school adjustment, which generated a depression score (Kohn, 1977).

Do Children, Mothers, and Teachers Agree about Child Pathology?

In order to look at agreement between raters, continuous scores for the three raters were correlated. Correlations between continuous scores were low and not significant. Agreement between raters about depressed and nondepressed groups was observed. Rates of agreement were almost the same regardless of gender. For all three pairs of raters, kappa coefficients were computed, and there was little agreement between children, mothers, and teachers. Multiple tests of agreement among raters revealed that children, mothers, and teachers do not agree with each other regarding children's depression. This suggests that different people may focus on different aspects of the child's behavior in different contexts in order to make their ratings.

Although this example of the difficulty of finding a relation between different ratings of the same construct is restricted to depression, it is clear that similar disagreements in ratings exist for variables that usually fall into the domain more commonly considered personality variables. Thus, for example, in the study of temperament in children, the ratings of individual parents also are only moderately correlated. Moreover, looking at actual behavior of children rather than ratings reveals that across different situations individual differences show little consistency. In a study of fearfulness, there was little individual consistency between fear shown to a visual cliff as opposed to the fear shown at the approach of a stranger (Goldsmith & Campos, 1982). Even when we turn to personality variables such as the Big Five, we again find that the coherence of different measures of the same construct across different people or even across different situations reveals at best moderate relations (see Caspi, 1998).

Findings such as these over the last 25 years has raised a particular challenge for personality theorists, because what characterizes personality is the idea of consistency across time, place, and context. If our data on personality characteristics (regardless of the measure) do not adhere to that standard or at least account for considerable variance, what we mean by personality needs to be questioned.[1] Thus, whether we are studying developmental psychopathology or the development of personality or particular competencies, we are confronted with an inescapable fact that these competencies, although of theoretical importance, are not readily measured. When they are measured, they do not give rise to a high degree of concordance either across different types of measures or different people's rating. This may well represent a measurement error problem. Measurement error, however, is not the only cause of error. Rather, a theoretical alternative has been provided in the idea of either rejecting the traditional concept of personality or moving toward a personality characteristic by situation analysis. From a developmental point of view, it certainly creates difficulty when the variable one seeks to measure, representing the construct under study, varies by observer or varies by tasks. It is quite clear from the fear literature in early childhood that individual differences in fearfulness, while of interest theoretically, is not readily measured across different contexts.

What Predicts, or Are the Antecedents of, Depression?

In this study we looked at three possible precursors of 9-year-old children's depression. These variables included type of attachment, amount of stressful events, and the social network of the children. Theory and research concerning infant–parent attachment, social network, life stress, and maternal depression suggest that each of these factors is related to risk of childhood depression. Bowlby (1973, 1982) argued that a poor quality attachment relationship early in life puts the child at-risk for depression and maladjustment. Although some studies do show that securely attached infants are better adjusted as children (Frankel & Bates, 1990; Matas, Arend, & Sroufe, 1978; Pastor, 1981; Waters, Wippman, & Sroufe, 1979), such relations are not always revealed, particularly when other contextual factors are considered, when children are followed for longer periods of time, or when multiple raters are used (Bates, Maslin, & Frankel, 1985; Lewis, Feiring, McGuffog, & Jaskir, 1984). Nevertheless, developmental psychopathology theory agues that insecure attachment is an important precursor of pathology.

The negative effect of stress on emotional health also is well documented (see Brown & Harris, 1978, and Garmezy & Rutter, 1983, for reviews). Children's reports of negative life events are associated with their concurrent ratings of depression (Dubow, Tisak, Causey, Hryshko, & Reid, 1991; Mullins, Siegel, & Hodges, 1985). These findings suggest that stressful events throughout life relate to the severity of depressive symptomatology. The extent of a child's social network is also an important factor in adjustment. Children who experience more social support from peers also are friendlier, more sociable, and better adjusted than children who experience low levels of peer support (Hartup, 1983). Children with less social support have more adjustment problems in school (Cassidy & Asher, 1992; Dubow et al., 1991) and are lonelier (Renshaw & Brown, 1993).

Maternal depression has been shown to be a risk factor for child depression and psychopathology (Beardslee, Bemporad, Keller, & Klerman, 1983; McKnew, Cytryn, Efran, Gershon, & Bunney, 1979; Orvaschel, Weissman, Padian, & Lowe, 1981; Politano, Stapleton, & Correll, 1992; Weissman, Gammon, et al., 1987; Welner, Welner, McCrary, & Leonard, 1977) that affects the child's behavior quite early in life (Miller, Birnbaum, & Durbin, 1990). Children raised by depressed parents experience more negative parenting, more family conflict, and less family cohesion, expressiveness, and organization (Billings & Moos, 1983; Lovejoy, 1991).

Although there is little consistency between child's, mother's, and teacher's report of the child's depression, it might be the case that these early sets of variables—attachment, stress, and peer network—are likely related to one outcome more than another. Thus, coherence over time might be the method by which to settle the question posed by the lack of coherence at a given time between observers and measures. Although the teacher, the child, and the mother might have different opinions of the child's characteristics, it might be the case that only one of these ratings was related to the early theoretically interesting variables. If such a finding occurred, we would be spared the embarrassment of low agreement among the three raters and choose that rater whose coherence to the past is greatest. Thus, coherence over time would become the criterion for choosing whose outcome is more important. Such a strategy seems reasonable and certainly should have important results for any theory of personality development. Conversely, should we believe that each rater is characterizing the child in their particular situation or context, we would have little reason to believe that coherence over time would be stronger for one situation or rater than another.

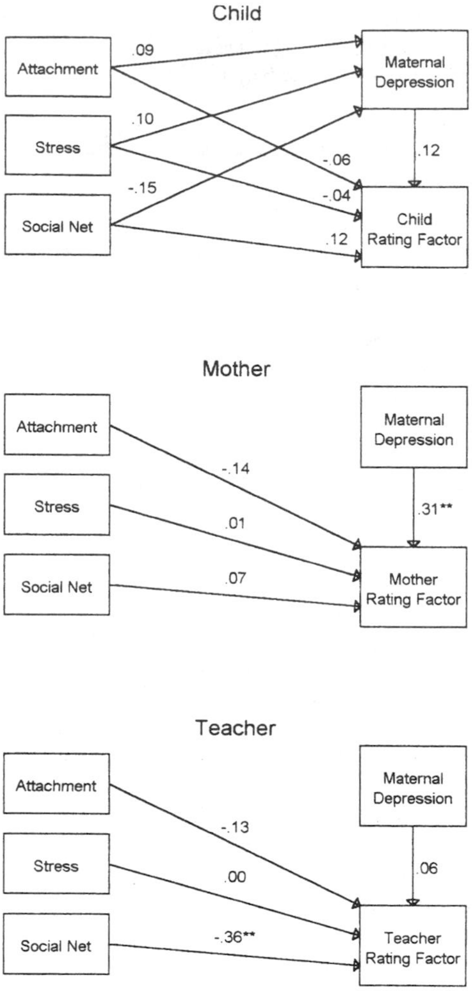

FIGURE 12.1. Predicting child, mother, and teacher ratings of depression.

Figure 12.1 shows the relation between three potentially interesting variables in early childhood as they relate to the ratings of the child's depression at age 9. The figure presents data on developmental paths when the child's rating, the mother's rating, and the teacher's rating of psychopathology represent the outcome variable. Attachment classification was obtained when the children were 1 year old in a standard attachment paradigm, and stress and social networks of the children were obtained from the mothers when the children were 3 and 6 years old. Maternal depression scores were obtained when the children were 3 years old.

Observation of the path analysis reveals that different outcomes have different paths. There are no variables that predict the child's own rating of itself as depressed. The best predictor of the maternal rating of the child's depression is the mother's rating of her own depression. Finally, the teacher's rating is predicted by the size of the peer network the child had when younger, such that children from small peer networks are reported to be more depressed by their teachers than children from larger networks.

These examples support two ideas that need attention in any study of personality development. The first idea is that of an individual having characteristics that are enduring across situations and time. In general, although there may be some consistency across raters or scales and situations, the variance accounted for remains rather low considering the power of the idea of personality transcending situation, context, and others. The second idea is that from a developmental point of view, the idea of predicting individual differences in personality characteristics over time may not be rewarding. Although such a venture receives a considerable amount of focus in the developmental social literature, the data is weak, with the variance accounted for low even though at times significant (see Caspi, 1998). Studies such as the one reported above, although they may be questioned on a variety of grounds, including measurement and methodological issues, raise important questions; individual differences on one measurement system may not be the same as in another and the prediction over time of such a state of affairs requires multiple measures. Even then, the problem of finding coherence over time is dependent upon the idea of the particular developmental model that one espouses. In the next section this idea is considered.

MODELS OF DEVELOPMENT

Organismic Model

Although many different models of development have been suggested, and many are in current use, one in particular underlies our idea of development; it is called the *organismic model* because the processes of development are for the most part located in each person. Most of us have come to accept that our early relationship with our parents—our mothers in particular—is one of the most determining forces in our lives. This force resides in us and is a part of us—a trait, an enduring property that constitutes what some have called personality (Pervin, 1990). Some traits—or dispositions—characterize how we think; others, how we feel and how we are apt to behave in particular situations. Traits vary in how easily they can be altered and in how long they last. Some dispositions may exist in our DNA or in the neural network of our brains, whereas others, learned, can be unlearned; for example, a child's dislike for green peppers, which disappears in adolescence after the child tastes a just-picked pepper from a friend's garden (Jung, 1963; Plomin, 1983). We believe that traits formed by our relationship with our parents survive for a lifetime and that the past influences our present state and is likely to affect our future.

The general proposition, "Things past can affect the present," requires that we believe in history—that there was a real past, that it affected us, and that it still affects us or that there was a real past that did affect us but its effect is no more. If we believe that our past affects our present, we have to believe that there are forces that survive over time, continuing to act in the present. What is the nature of these forces? If biological, they could continue to act in some virus-like fashion. Or they could be patterns of behavior learned earlier and are now firmly part of how we act—automatic, like walking. A third choice is that how we think about the past is likely to affect us in the present. For example, if you think that you were not pretty as a child, you may act "ugly" even though you are now an attractive adult.

We can understand why people behave as they do if the outcome is positive, but none of these alternatives explains why people persist in behaving in a certain way even when doing so causes them pain. Allport (1937) suggested that behaviors learned earlier can become "functionally autonomous," they continue despite the fact that the forces that originally produced them are no longer causing them. Such a theory only confirms our observation that it is possible to behave in a way that is not a result of the initial force. We still do not really know why or whether things such as behavior, feelings, and even desires are sustained over time.

Freud talked about neurotic repetition of behavior, suggesting that there are advantages of maintaining dysfunctional patterns, the major one being familiarity. We would rather know that something will not work out well than try to change it and experience the unknown, even though the unknown may be better (Greenberg & Mitchell, 1983). Others have theorized that we become fixated at certain stages. Erikson (1950) believed that if we do not solve an earlier set of problems, we cannot go on to other, more advanced problems. His life stages are a series of problems that need to be solved if we are to successfully meet the next set. Others (Lewis & Lee-Painter, 1974; Lewis & Rosenblum, 1977; Pervin & Lewis, 1978), in contrast, consider the disposition or behavioral pattern to be located in the interactions between people, sustained through the different forms of interaction that the individual maintains. The disposition to behave thus is supported by the nature of the interaction, or the context. Masters, Johnson, and Kolodny (1977), in studying sexual dysfunction, suggested that the ability to rid oneself of sexual dysfunction requires changing not only one's own habits but also the habits of others who interact with the old patterns.

Another aspect of the organismic model is the belief in primacy versus recency. Memories of yesterday's meal are usually clearer than memories of a meal eaten 10 years ago, so we might expect recent events to exert more power over our behavior than those that happened long ago. The effect of recency is indeed known to play a powerful role in behavior. Yet the organismic model holds that an event that comes first has the greater impact on subsequent behavior than do later events. The theory of critical periods is a good example of this. A critical period is a time-bound interval having a discrete onset and offset. Before and after the period, the theory states, environmental events do not impact on future behavior; between onset and offset, effects of environmental events are profound. In humans, it has been suggested that there are critical periods for the development of perceptual capacities and for language development.

But how is subsequent behavior affected by what happens during critical periods? It is believed that earlier events, when occurring during a critical time, produce or alter particular biologically based structures located in the person. But the theory that structures are changed or created to become biologically supported traits may have been applied too broadly. Hoffman (1974), working with birds, has shown that imprinting does not alter or produce structures or traits but simply causes the baby bird to be friendly to the type of bird it follows and to be fearful of all other types. Because the bird is fearful, it will follow only those birds it has been imprinted on, and thus the imprinting period—the time the bird establishes its identity—appears to have a discrete onset and offset. Hoffman was able to show that when he reduced the fear of the unfamiliar, the baby birds would follow new types and become imprinted on them after the critical period. In other words, imprinting is not an example of a critical period; it is only an example of how early experiences can impact on later experiences and yet not be the cause of that later experience.

A simpler explanation than the critical period idea can account for the phenomenon that earlier events appear to cause later ones. Consider that a young child who learns behavior *A* then has more difficulty learning behavior *B*, not because of *A*'s direct effect on *B* but because the child must first unlearn *A*. In our culture it takes children longer to learn bowel control (using a toilet) because they are first taught to defecate in their diapers and have to unlearn that behavior before they can learn to use the toilet. In cultures that never teach children to use diapers, they gain bowel control much earlier (Largo, Molinari, von Siebenthal, & Wolfensberger, 1996).

In general, the idea of a critical period in human or animal development has not held up against the evidence (Bornstein, 1987). Nevertheless, the concept of primacy is so ingrained that it lingers in the form of so-called sensitive periods. Although appealing in its biological simplicity, there is only little support for the existence of these periods.

The formal properties of the organismic model of development are enumerated below. The last is most relevant to socioemotional development.

1. Development is change with a direction and therefore has an end point.
2. Earlier events are connected to later ones.
3. Change is gradual, a slowly cumulative progression.
4. Events that occur in the first few years of our lives produce the most long-lasting and powerful effects.
5. Mothers are the most important element in the child's environment and are more likely than all others to affect our socioemotional well-being, both in childhood and throughout our lives.

The first and second assumptions follow from a deceptively simple and widely held idea, namely, that current psychological problems are a direct consequence of what occurred earlier in life. We also believe that the process of development is made up of small accretion. Whether these accretions are gradual or sudden, continuous or discontinuous, depends on how we choose to think about the process itself. In Piaget's model, the most popular of developmental models, larva to caterpillar to butterfly (the examples often given when talking about change) is a way of thinking about discrete changes in function, structure, and capacity (Piaget, 1952). Whether we perceive continuity or discontinuity in the world, however, may depend largely on our other ideas about how the world operates. Western scholars have focused their attention on the smooth, accumulative transition around change, whereas Eastern scholars have been more impressed with the fact that, in nature, living systems always are changing and that these systems and this course of change are not necessarily dependent on what occurred previously. The idea of linearity is rejected because time is not viewed as moving in a direction. Reincarnation or repeated return as a property of life, the great circle, characterizes this view.

The Western idea of continuity embraces constancy, uniformity, seriation, and progress and, because of this, is associated with a conservative ideology. Discontinuity is linked with social and political challenge or with political radicalism. That change occurs cannot be questioned. It is the models that describe it that are open to debate: "The essential model issue . . . is whether successive behavioral forms are reducible (i.e., are continuous) or irreducible, here meaning discontinuous, to prior forms" (Reese & Overton, 1970, p. 141). The ideas of slow, gradual accumulation as well as discrete and radical change reside in ideology rather than in the data themselves (see Alvarez, 1982; Eldredge & Gould, 1972, for the challenge to this idea in evolutionary biology).

The three major developmental models that derive from this idea are accretional, transformational, and additive. According to the accretional model, also described as accumulative, the original process remains active. For example, physical growth continues in the same way across a person's entire developmental range. The transformational model relies on the idea that a second developmental process completely replaces the first, the way the butterfly appears to replace the caterpillar. In an additive model, the first process remains active while a second process emerges, resulting in the coexistence of both. The first two models are organismic, whereas the last approaches a contextual model, one that will be taken up later.

The Accretional Model

The accretional or incremental model states that a particular function, structure, or skill exists in its adult form (that is, it will not change) at the beginning of development. The process of development, therefore, involves an increase in amount rather than a change in type, though many variations on the theme are possible. The shape of the growth curve is one possibility. The form can grow rapidly in early life and then level off near maturity, as is the case with a child's physical growth. The form also may grow slowly at first and then suddenly take off before leveling off again. Either way, the structure that exists at the beginning increases or decreases as a function of this process. Because the structure already exists and changes only in amount, it is possible to view this model as continuous. However, not all skills exist in their form at birth; they may appear at different points in the lifetime of an individual. The start up and increase in hormonal activity specifically related to puberty and adolescence constitute prime examples of developmental processes that start later in life. At a certain point after birth, on the average of 12 years or so, new functions "kick in," to be followed by growth and development.

A Transformational Model

A transformational model differs from an accretional model in several ways, the primary feature being that successive behavior forms are irreducible to prior forms. Such models also have been called *stage* models of development. In these models, forms are transformed through their interaction with the world. Transformational models, made most popular by Piaget, are not continuous, but most often they adhere to the view that earlier events are connected to later ones. Why else call development transformational? So, Piaget's model, where the caterpillar became a butterfly, which becomes a larva, involves a change in structure and function. The development of intelligence is viewed as a series of transformations wherein sensorimotor ability is replaced by formal logical operations (Piaget, 1952). In a similar fashion, the psychoanalytic model proposed by Freud (1905/1953) contains transformational processes. More recently, the object relation theorists have used a transformational model to explain how a child's early attachment relationship with his mother becomes peer friendships and then adult romantic relationships (Bowlby, 1988). Each of these examples can be characterized by metamorphosis and change, where earlier behaviors change and ultimately assume adult forms. Even though they are transformed into entities of different form or structure, they can be connected. Thus, this model features what I consider a connected process, where there is a sequence with an order and where early events are related to later ones.

The transformational model represents the prevailing view of development today, yet its underlying assumptions have been criticized. One concern is that the transformational model is directional. Transformations follow a particular order and direction, moving from *A* through *B,* then *C,* and *D.* Even though transformations may require the child to interact with the environment, the transformations themselves and their order appear to be relatively fixed. Yet not all children go through the same sequence. For example, although most children crawl after sitting up and before walking, not all children who walk, crawl.

Second, a feature of transformation is its irreversibility. *A,* in becoming *B,* ceases to exist. This requirement implies that *A,* what occurred earlier, affects or causes *B,* what occurred later. The metaphor of the larva becoming the caterpillar implies explicitly that the larva ceases to exist when the caterpillar emerges and that there is no chance of reversibility. This idea presents problems for the possibility of regression to earlier levels, a phenomenon that is often observed, especially under stress. Of even more concern is that once a level emerges, only this single highest level is available for use in interaction with the environment, regardless of the task or problem at hand. The earlier levels, having been transformed, are no longer present.

Finally, the transformation of *A* into *B* requires that something be added to *A* for it to become *B. B* is different from *A* and, as such, is a different form. Again, this requirement is necessary if we wish to argue that *A* and *B* are different but that *A* and *B* are related and that *B* is derived from *A.* Such a view fails to satisfy logical requirements. Flanagan (1991), in analyzing the problem inherent in this view of development and of Piaget in particular, states, "If the story Piaget tells about cognitive development is right, he needs to explain how the mind builds richer and richer systems of cognitive structures." What we have is a constructivist problem: "One cannot build new and richer hypotheses out of less rich conceptual resources *simpliciter*" (pp. 135, 139). If development is transformational, it is not clear how *A* becomes *B. A* and *B* are different essences, and one cannot be derived from the other (Pascual-Leone, 1990; Sugarman, 1987).

The requirements of a transformational model that insists on these principles violate much of what we know about children. One solution to this dilemma is to suggest that *A* and *B* are unconnected and unrelated. Although *A* may participate in and be necessary for the creation of *B, A* is not itself transformed or lost; *A* is maintained as *B* develops—it is what I call an *additive model.*

An Additive Model: The Move toward Contextualism

There are major differences between transformational and additive models of development. Like the transformational model, the additive model has directionality; it moves from *A* through *B* and *C* to *D.* Also as in the transformational model, development in the additive model takes place in interaction with the environment. Indeed, the environment is a very important aspect of the model. The most significant difference between the two is that in the additive model development does not occur through transformations. *B* may be only partially, or not at all, related to *A.* It may need *A* to come into existence, but it is not made up of *A,* or it may come into existence without *A* ever being present. *B* can arise as a consequence of some environmental interaction. In this case, as the environment changes, *B* comes into existence. Again, *B* follows *A* but is neither of *A* nor caused by it (Mounoud, 1990). *B,* like *A,* may develop further once it emerges, but transformations are not as we might have envisioned them to be. It is more like the addition of new skills and the accretion of those skills that have already emerged, for example, $A \Rightarrow A_1$, $B \Rightarrow B_1$, etc. This model represents radical discontinuities and gradual changes. Such a model now exists as the best estimate of biological evolutionary change; it is called *stasis and sudden change.*

In the additive model there is no single end point, *D*, but rather the coexistence of all earlier abilities and skills. This allows for reversibility or regression; under stress a child who has passed the thumb-sucking stage can and does suck her thumb. It also allows for multiple use; a child who has learned to walk can still crawl if he so desires.

The existence of multiple levels allows for a set of capacities and abilities that can be employed selectively when confronted with a task; that is, the organism can choose which level to employ for which particular task. The choice of ability cannot be a function of the limitation of choice; it must be a function of some other phenomenon. Such choices are probably based on socialization factors or on a program available to the organism to choose which level to employ.

Individual "programming" may also account for which level is used to solve a task. If we think of these levels as involving different processes, we can recognize some levels employing different brain structures. We might suppose that people would use one level for emotional and others for nonemotional tasks (LeDoux, 1990). As we can see, the availability of choice means that the additive model must be more contextually determined than the transformational model and that the developmental process itself cannot be understood without determining the nature of the environment and how it changes.

Contextual Model

The traditional developmental models, although using social interaction to generate individual characteristics, does not need the context to enforce their expression or to change their nature once formed. Thus, the organismic model of development traps us in our past. Freud's theory claimed that particular early experiences determine our future, except, of course, if we are psychoanalyzed. Freud believed that even though early events affected our future, our destiny can be altered by later events. Thus, the theory had it both ways: a theory relating earlier to later events in a deterministic way and a therapy that could alter the impact of earlier events. Why is it that only a psychoanalyst could alter the past? Why not a lifetime of experiences?

The organismic model of development, most often viewed as a causally related chain of events, allows for prediction. There lies its appeal. Our belief in the ability to predict over relatively large spans of time has captured our interest. Given the strength of that model, ample evidence that what happens earlier affects what happens later should have been accumulated. Yet most short- and long-term longitudinal studies have failed to find much relation between earlier and later events. Even when a significant relationship between variables is found over time, 85 to 90% of the association between these variables is not accounted for. Even more disappointing is that as the time between events increases, the relation between them decreases, a common finding called a *simplex pattern.* It is as if we have the power to predict the next 5 minutes and little beyond.

Based on the collective evidence to date—in a multitude of domains, including cognitive, social, emotional, and psychopathological—the best that can be said is that there sometimes is very limited support for the belief that earlier events are connected to later ones. Given that there is very little empirical evidence to support the organismic model, our strong belief rests on belief rather than fact.

I will present the strong alternative, hoping to attract attention to other ways of studying development, especially personality development. James (1975) described a position that is called *pragmatism,* expanded by Pepper's (1942) *contextualism.* Contextualism, for our developmental point of view, argues that to understand meaning we have to understand it as embedded in events occurring now. Contextualism is not historical; events in the past are not related to events now. James (1975) arrived at this position because for him there was no way of knowing if events in the past were related to events now. He said, in discussing the characteristics of the mind, "The mind may change its states and its meanings at different times; may drop one conception and take up another, but the dropped conception can in no intelligible sense be said to change into its successor" (p. 462). For James, these thoughts or properties of mind occurred in the context of the moment. As the context changed, so, too, did the thought. His pragmatic position, in which contextualism played a central role, did not utilize the concept of progress toward an end point; nor did it need the idea of a linear causal relation where earlier events are likely to cause later ones. In regard to progress and causal sequential relations, James's position is best seen as a belief that history is simply a collection of facts that are not necessarily related to one another. Such a view also questions the idea that there is an order or a sequence as an objective reality; that is, that there is something that exists independent of us, toward which we move.

This contextual view is from that of the organismic model because it holds that development is a sequence of causally related changes—that is, development as a historical theme—but is a sequence with a goal, whose order is fixed, with the child coming to this order through basic processes located in the genotype. Thus, although the environment is needed for the child to acquire intelligence, the sequence of acquisition and the nature of intelligence are fixed properties, independent of the child.

Because James did not accept a historical perspective or, therefore, the idea of progress, he also did not believe in an end point in the developmental process. What James did have was an interest in the self and a belief in the self as an active, constructing agent. Because of this, he proposed a type of teleological theory of mind. For him, the mind lent substance to our existence and was determined by our purpose. Our goals, desires, and wishes created mind, and in turn our minds created these goals, desires, and wishes. For James, then, a developmental theory would have several important features:

1. An active self exists, one capable of thinking, planning, and having goals and desires.
2. These goals and desires are best understood within a meaning system occurring now; thus, the emphasis on contextualism.
3. Earlier events need not necessarily determine later events; thus, there is no need to think of development as a unidirectional, bounded process.
4. Finally, there is no need to postulate progress as an essential feature of the developmental process. In other words, there is no end point in the developmental process, no final state to be achieved.

More recent views (Ford & Lerner, 1992) capture the ideas that humans have selves that play a central role in their lives and in their development. The importance of the self forces the idea of history as past events acting on the present to yield to the idea that the present reconstructs the past. That is, it suggests that our pasts are not real but a construction. In the construction, little need remain of that which led to the construction. Even more important is the idea that it is impossible ever to determine what the real thing in the past was.

This antihistorical argument has a parallel in how we now think of memory. Most of us viewed memory as a photograph, an accurate representation that captured in detail all of what occurred. If our memory was so accurate, then history, too, had to be real; it had to be possible to capture the past. More recent views, however, suggest that memory is a construction that may or may not bear a strong resemblance to what occurred. Perhaps even more important, the constructed memory can, over time, undergo elaborate change and transformation. If we reject the memory-as-photograph model, we need to do the same for historicism, the argument that there really is something back there in time that can be measured and that determines what occurs in the future.

Instead, memory may be based on our current needs, either what we anticipate needing for the future or what we know we need now. In other words, memory is contextual and pragmatic as James argued; memory or history has to do with the goals and desires we have at the point of memory. Notice that the point of memory can be either the now when you first experience the event or any now when you remember it in the future. So, if memory depends on the meaning needed at a particular time, memory should have the capacity to change, depending on the context at that point. James's proposed teleology of the mind thus makes sense; minds—or, in this case, memories—are constructed around needs, and the needs that arise are functions of our minds.

A contextual world view also alters our sense of time. According to James, order is not inherent in nature; we create it to understand the world through science and logic. Pepper (1942) picks up on this point as well: "For the contextualist, the dimension 'time' of mechanism [the Newtonian theory of an orderly clock] is a conceptual scheme useful for the control and ordering of events, but not categorical or, in that sense, real" (p. 462). The idea that time is relative allows us to consider an important possibility in understanding both memory and development: that history may represent not the past acting on the present but the present reconstructing the past. If we view history not as what actually occurred in the past but as a construction of what we believe occurred, we allow for the possibility that our *actual* histories have relatively little bearing on our development. Rather, current behavior is influenced by what we think our histories were. Human beings have the capacity to alter the past in light of the present.

As we can see, this backward construction of reality does not agree with our temporal sense of development as being unidirectional, going from earlier to more recent events. Essential to such a view is an active mind, a self with feelings, thoughts, and memories—the important features in determining a life course (Lewis, 1990). In the organismic or passive view, events act in a unidirectional manner on people. In this contextualist view, people act on and create their own lives, including their memories and their futures, through the formation in the present of future goals, desires, and needs. As Bruner (1990) has suggested, we construct a story not only to explain our past but also to explain who we are now. This story contains pieces of smaller stories, or events, that we have chosen selectively from a larger set of recollections to create the desired narrative. The events may or may not be historically correct. The narrative explains our selves as what we are, what we wish we were, or what we want to be in the future. "It is an account given by a narrator in the here and now about a protagonist bearing his (her) name who existed in the there and then" (Bruner, 1990, p. 21). This view, expounded in social psychology by Gergen (1973), also found a voice earlier in time. I am reminded of Kierkegaard's (1846) idea of existential contingency. For him, fear was produced when the past did not provide meaning for the present or the future. It was the present that provided meaning to the past. A meaningful life was one in which the present was sufficient to explain the past. In other words, health, for Kierkegaard, depended on the ability to use the present to explain what we were. This demand on the present for meaning produced trembling, whereas what would be in the future produced fear. Kierkegaard may have been correct; we are caught between the two dilemmas.

Ross (1989) reviewed the mechanisms that underlie the relations of personal histories. He suggested that the first step in constructing our past involves people noting their present status; they ask themselves what they are like now and use this information to make a determination about the past. Ross (1989) argued that people do this because "the present is generally more salient and available than a person's earlier standing" (p. 342). The second step in this process of reconstruction involved deciding about the likely stability of one's current self. Paying attention to one's present self was necessitated by its salience, a proposition that seems quite reasonable. The ideas embedded in this theory have much in common with my propositions that memory is a construct that may or may not reflect what actually happened if we could measure it, which we cannot, and that what we construct about our past is related to our present. Ross's data also implied that a bias in recall may contribute to the maintenance of the exaggerated beliefs. If this is true, we have, in effect, a measure of James's idea of mind; namely, that the mind, or memory, functions to lend substance to our existence, which itself is determined by our purpose. In other words, our belief about our current condition influences our current belief about the past, and our belief about the past in turn gives us meaning about the present.

These studies from the social psychology literature support the idea that what we believe in the present affects our memories of what happened in the past. Although the study of people's recollections or memories has received relatively little scientific attention, the general finding appears to be that there is limited agreement between what happened and the recall of what happened. More important, however, is the finding that the present status impacts on the recall of what was. Perhaps most relevant to our focus on development is a study done by Yarrow, Campbell, and Burton (1970) of both the mother's and the child's recollections of their relationship in the past. In this study they gathered what they called the "baseline data," which were derived when the children were young. Through observations, tests, ratings, and reports, information on the mother–child relationship gathered years before was evaluated. Yarrow and her colleagues found that there was little overall relation between children's recollection of their relationship with their mothers and their actual relationships. Mothers' recall of the earlier relationship was no better. As Yarrow and her colleagues stated (Yarrow et al., 1970), "Mothers who have had pleasant and rewarding experiences in rearing their children, mothers who feel hostile to their children, and mothers who have had especially stressful life situations may not be equally able to report on their own rearing behavior or on the behavior of their children" (p. 41). Even more important to this discussion, however, was that Yarrow et al. found maternal and child recall of their earlier relationship depended on the current relationship. The degree of warmth or coolness in the *current* relationship shifted the *recollection* of the past in the direction of the current status. "For groups in which the relationships were rated as 'cold,' shifts in recall tended to be in an unfavorable direction; and for groups in which the relationships were rated as 'warm,' shifts in recall tended to increase the felicity of earlier times" (Yarrow et al., 1970, p. 48).

Mothers' recollections of the preschool personalities of their children were structured so as to conform to their perceptions of the children's present personalities. For example, if the children were now seen as shy, mothers tended to recall them as being shier in early childhood relative to the actual data collected. If, on the other hand, children were described as outgoing now, they were rated as more outgoing earlier. These occurred not only for the dimensions of shy or outgoing but also for the dimensions of children's response to authority and of their independence. The same was true of the children. If they rated themselves shier now, they also rated themselves as shier when they were younger.

These findings have important implications for longitudinal studies. In such studies we gather data and then try to relate those data to something in the future. The coherence among past, present, and future is most often minimal, perhaps because in predicting the future, past events are less important than our beliefs about those events. If this is the case, then it is important to study not only what occurred in the past but also what people now believe occurred in the past. Obtaining measures on maternal behavior toward children may not, for example, enable us to predict whether or not good mothering affects a child's subsequent development unless we also know what the children think about their past experiences.

John Bowlby (1980), in trying to understand the relation between children's early interaction with their parents and subsequent development, raised the intriguing possibility that children carry with them a working model, or a memory, of the relationship with their mother. He believed that this working model of the relationship should have a correspondence with what occurred in the past but that it might be altered by subsequent experiences. This idea obviously has much in common with the new view of memory. In addition, said Bowlby, this working model affects subsequent relationships; that is, a person's model of her relationship with her mother determines her future social life. For example, a mother who has a working model of a secure attachment with her own mother is likely to behave in such ways as to establish a secure attachment with her own child.

Subsequent experiences can affect memory and past events. This is a heated debate topic in regard to sexual abuse. Although all the information is not yet complete, it appears that subsequent events, in this case how the child is asked about possible sexual abuse, affects whether the child "remembers" the event. A study by Clarke-Stewart and her colleagues (Goodman & Clarke-Stewart, 1991) serves as a good example of this process. In an experimental situation, a child is placed in a room and after a few moments sees a man enter and watches as he dusts the objects in a room, including a doll. After a few minutes, he leaves. Next, an experimenter enters and asks the child a series of questions about what just occurred, such as "What did the man do?" The child has no difficulty responding to such a question. Next comes a series of direct questions, such as "Did the man pick up and kiss the doll?" The child most often remembers correctly and answers, "No, he did not." The experimenter leaves, and another experimenter enters. This experimenter asks the child, "Did the man pick up and kiss the doll?" Surprisingly, a large number of children now report, "Yes." As more and more experimenters ask the child the same question, it becomes more and more likely that the child will answer "Yes." Such studies, along with Ross's analysis, lead us away from an organismic model with a *real* past acting on the individual.

CONTEXUALISM AND ORGANISMIC APPROACHES TO DEVELOPMENT: A CASE STUDY OF ATTACHMENT

James addresses this idea and argues that truth is not a static property of something but rather happens to an idea: it becomes true; it is made true by events. History's role is to create truths. These, rather than earlier events, are likely to cause later events. People remember their pasts in the present to find and maintain their own truth. Elsewhere I have likened this truth to the idea of identity; the idea of me (Lewis, 1990b).

The best way to compare the usefulness of contextualism is to apply it to a problem in development. Consider this example. A child is being raised by a mother who is depressed. The child's condition at one year of age is influenced by her mother's psychopathology. As in most studies, we can ask, "What will that child be like when she is of school age?" Assuming that the child showed poor school adjustment, we could argue that the child's earlier adjustment pattern influenced her later development. The organismic model assumes that, in a trait-like way, the events that occurred earlier produced in the child a quality that impacted on her behavior years later. If we look at the same problem using a contextual model, we can argue that the context in which the child was raised at one year of age affected her current adjustment because there was an interaction between the child and her environment. This is a contextual finding because the child's behavior can be understood in terms of her adaptation to her depressed mother at one year. The prediction of what the child's behavior will be like at age 6 is not based on her current adjustment. What is needed is to study the context of the child at 6 years in terms of her current relationship with the depressed mother. If the child shows poor adjustment earlier because she is adapting to the context of poor mothering, why should the child not remain in trouble if the poor mothering environment continues? The contextual model states that the child's status at *any point will be affected by the environment at that point.*

In other words, an organismic model requires us to assume that the trait of maladjustment is located in the child and that it is this trait, established earlier, that produces the later maladjusted school-age behavior. What if the mother was no longer depressed when the child was school age? In such a case the current context would have changed, and it is likely that the child will not show maladjustment at 6 years. As the context changes, so does adaptation. In the few studies that have supplied data by which alternative models can be considered, the findings support the idea that current status is just as important as, if not more important than, earlier conditions (Lewis & Feiring, 1991). In other words, developmental continuity, which we believe is located in the child, may be located in the context to which the child adapts. This can be seen in a recent longitudinal study of attachment characteristics of children from infancy to late teens.

Attachment: Trait or Idea

We studied attachment because it seeks to explain, in part, the origins of social and emotional behavior. Attachment has been considered both as a set of overt behaviors (e.g., Ainsworth, Blehar, Waters, & Wall, 1978; Belsky, Rovine, & Taylor, 1984) as well as a representation or model of close relationships (e.g., Bowlby, 1973). Early formulations of attachment emphasized a connection between infants' early overt behaviors and later responsiveness. Bowlby (1973) argued for a link between early attachment behaviors and later representations: "The varied expectations of the accessibility and responsibleness of attachment figures that different individuals develop during the years of immaturity are tolerably accurate reflections of the experiences those individuals have actually had" (p. 202). This idea has been held by most (see Main, 1990; Main, Kaplan, & Cassidy, 1985; Sroufe, 1983). The child's model of the attachment relationship is viewed as organized around the history of the caregiver's responses to the infant's actions. Thus, the construct of attachment as measured by mental representations is believed to be formed around early parent–infant experiences. Differences in early mother–infant interactions produce individual differences at one year of age in sets of overt behaviors (Ainsworth et al., 1978; Belsky et al., 1984; Lewis & Feiring, 1989). The differences in types (A, B, C, D), reflecting the quality of the attachment relationship, are seen as predicting subsequent representations (Bretherton, 1985).

Studies used to support this supposition have linked overt attachment behaviors in infancy to later social competence and psychopathology (e.g., Elicker, Englund, & Sroufe, 1992; Lewis et al.,1984; Londerville & Main, 1981; Matas et al., 1978; Pastor, 1981; Sroufe, 1983; Sroufe, Egeland, & Kreutzer, 1990; Sroufe & Fleeson, 1986). The relations between early attachment behaviors and later competencies are assumed to reflect the ongoing impact of a stable attachment construct. Although these studies show associations between early overt attachment behaviors and subsequent competence, they do not examine continuity in attachment behaviors with later representations, therefore not providing support for the idea that infant attachment is a prototype for later attachment. By assuming that attachment remains stable, these studies and their interpretation mistakingly promote the view that infant attachment status is a trait-like attribute of an individual throughout development. As Waters, Posada, Crowell, and Lay (1993) have pointed out, "attachment theorists often referred to infant attachment status as if it were a trait-like characteristic that an individual carried throughout life. This has stood both as dogma and doctrine based on empirical research. Indeed, attachment theorists are often criticized for offering an 'inoculation' theory of development. Secure attachment in infancy inoculates a child from adverse outcomes throughout development. Conversely, early attachment difficulties place the child at risk or even cause subsequent problems" (p. 217). The adolescent literature also has treated attachment as a stable individual characteristic related to competence and psychopathology (e.g., Cole-Detke & Kobak, 1996; Kobak & Sceery, 1988; Kobak, Sudler, & Gamble, 1991; Rosenstein & Horowitz, 1996; Sroufe et al., 1990; Sroufe, Schork, Moffi, Laworsky, & LaFreniere, 1984). Attachment quality is assumed to be stable and therefore continues to have a significant impact on intimate relationships and other competencies into adulthood (e.g., Hazan & Shaver, 1987).

Several possibilities exist. In the first, the current adult representation is solely dependent upon the current environment, with the previous representation having little effect on the current one—a contextual model. Second, early representations form a trait (a set of representatives in whatever form we like), and this trait lasts over time—an organismic model. A third model, the interactional one, holds that the current environment interacts with the past representation to produce a current representation.

For either contextual or interactional models, it is necessary to take the nature of the environment into account. In the attachment literature, there already exists data to show that in early childhood when the caregiving environment changes, the quality of attachment changes as well (Belsky, Campbell, Cohn, & Moore, 1996; Thompson & Lamb, 1983a, 1983b). For example, Vaughn, Egeland, Sroufe, and Waters (1979) found that early attachment classification changes if maternal behaviors change, in this case as a function of stressful life events. In order to relate early to later attachment, it is necessary to measure the environment and its change over time (Bronfenbrenner & Crouter, 1983; Dunn, 1993; Lewis, 1984, Suomi, 1979; Waters Trebors, Crowell, Merrick, & Albersheim, 1993).

In the longitudinal study we looked at a particular environmental factor, divorce, because it captures many aspects of the caregiving environment, directly affecting parents, children, and the emotional and social experiences in the family (Davies & Cummings, 1994; Fauber, Forehand, Thomas, & Wierson, 1990; Grych & Fincham, 1993). As an index of disruption in family life, economic hardship, and decreased availability of caregivers, divorce provides the type of environment that could have an impact on early childhood attachments as well as effecting change in representation.

In the longitudinal study, we examined the consistency of attachment classification from 1 to 18 years using divorce as a measure of the caregiving environment (Lewis, Feiring, & Rosenthal, in press). Eighty-four infants and their mothers were seen at 1 year in a modified Strange Situation Procedure (see Waters et al., 1979). At 18 years, participants were interviewed following the protocol developed by George, Kaplan, and Main (1985) and Kobak, Cole, Ferenz-Gillies, Fleming, and Gamble (1993). Thus, at both ages attachment classification on these children as well as divorce status was obtained.

The results indicated that 1-year attachment was not related to 18-year attachment. Of the insecure 1-year-olds, only 38% (9/24) were insecurely attached at 18 years of age, whereas for the secure 1-year-olds, 43% (26/60) were insecurely attached. Out of 84 families, 14 had experienced a family divorce by the time they were 18 years of age. There was no relation between attachment at one year and subsequent divorce. However, when the teens were 18 years old, attachment classification and divorce are significantly related. Those adolescents whose parents were divorced were more likely to be classified as insecure, whereas those classified as secure were more likely to be from intact families. Because the time of divorce varied, there might be a relation between early or later divorce and 18-year attachment. When the time of the divorce was compared to the 18-year-old attachment classification, no relation was found. Timing of divorce was not related to any of the other measures.

Because of our interest in individual trajectories of attachment coherence and relations with divorce, we followed an analytic strategy that allowed us to examine individual children's paths over time. We determined the path each individual followed in terms of attachment and divorce. As already mentioned, attachment at 18 years is related to divorce status but not to attachment in infancy; thus, there is no support for an organismic model. How about an interactional model? Were there any interactions between attachment in infancy and family divorce as they affect attachment at 18 years? Our findings indicate no interactional effects; secure attachment at 1 year does not buffer children from developing insecure attachments at 18 years if they are from divorced families. If attachment at 1 year and divorce interact in their contributions to attachment at 18 years, one would expect that adolescents who were insecure at 1 year and come from divorced families would have been more likely to be insecure at 18 than adolescents who were secure at 1 year and come from divorced families. This was not the case.

Our findings reveal a lack of continuity between overt attachment behaviors at 1 year of age and representations in adolescence. Others also have found a lack of continuity from infancy, both for predicting attachment behaviors in childhood (Belsky, Spritz, & Crnic, 1996; Thompson & Lamb, 1983a, 1983b) and for predicting representations in adolescence (Zimmerman, Fremmer-Bombik, Spangler, & Grossman, 1997). Even when consistency is found, there exists significant numbers who change their attachment status over time (Main et al., 1985; Waters, 1995). This suggests that continuity in attachment may be influenced by contextual factors, a finding suggested by others (Egeland & Farber, 1984; Lamb, Thompson, Gardner, & Charnov, 1985; Sroufe, 1997; Waters et al., 1995).

The data are coherent. Attachment at 1 year of age as measured by overt behaviors does not show continuity with attachment at 18 years of age as measured by representations. However, concurrent attachment, regardless of the age or method, is related to the nature of the caregiving environment. At 18 years, attachment classification is related to concurrent familial environment. Adult attachment is related to concurrent parenting behaviors (Ainsworth & Eichberg, 1991; Main et al., 1985; Posada, Waters, Crowell, & Lay, 1995; van IJzendoorn, 1995; van IJzendoorn, Kranenburg, Zwart-Woudstra, van Bussbach, & Lambermon, 1991). Together, these findings suggest that although the attachment representation is not stable over time, current representations are related to important indicators of current functioning.

The early studies of attachment did not present any data on the environment at the time when outcome measures were obtained. Without such data, we cannot address whether consistency of the environment or a characteristic of the child accounts for continuity. The few studies that include some indicators of the caregiving environment (Vaughn et al., 1979; Waters et al., 1995) reveal that continuity in attachment is affected by environmental factors.

The data presented in this study support a contextual rather than an organismic model. Stated simply, what is happening concurrently in the child's environment, at least through adolescence, exerts powerful effects on the child's attachment behaviors and representations. The degree to which environment factors remain consistent represents the degree to which the individual's attachment remains consistent. Moreover, a contextual model emphasizes concurrent adaptation as the single most important process in understanding children's emotional and social development. Such a view is supported by the developmental literature (Lerner, 1986; Lewis, 1997).

Unlike an organismic model, a contextual model argues that should the context change, earlier events may have little impact on subsequent behavior. The question, then, is not how a person progresses but how the context in which an organism adapts changes over time. Rather than an orderly progression on the basis of some internally derived imperative driving the person toward an end point, it may be that contexts alter and change, sometimes in an orderly fashion, often disorderly or chaotic. It is these changing contexts that effect change in the child.

The contextual approach also requires that we understand that behavior is produced to aid in the person's current adaptation. Such an approach reflects the pragmatic task of the person—to adapt to the current challenge. It does not rely on the past and so allows for our ability to alter our developmental trajectory. The ability to think about the future, the use of our consciousness to make plans and alter past mistakes, and the occurrence of chance events in the sequence of development are not isolated happenings but the fabric of our lives (Lewis, 1990b). They are, as James said, a collection of unordered facts. These factors suggest that continuity and prediction, even at a group level, are difficult and may be even more so for the individual (Elder, 1986). Without an appreciation of the role of these factors in development, we will remain disappointed by our level of understanding. Bandura (1982), touching on chance encounters, has written, "Developmental theory . . . must specify [the] factors that set and alter particular life courses if it is to provide an adequate explanation of human behavior" (pp. 747–755). This issue, together with the work in physics and evolutionary biology, suggests that developmental theory resting on the assumption that what occurs earlier in time has a direct relation to what occurs later cannot readily be supported.

Thus, besides a Jamesian view of pragmatics, a Kantian view also is required, one that introduces the idea that people have conceptions of what they want and should do to reach the goals they have chosen. Each of these ideas, desires, actions, and goals can be changed. The choices are, in part, the environments that people create. Events that we like to call basic realities are occasions when "indeterminate possibilities are transformed into determinant actualities" (Whitehead, 1978, p. 233), a basic premise of quantum mechanics that needs to be applied to human life as well. A contextual approach allows us to reconstruct how life progresses but does not allow us to predict. Like historians or evolutionary theorists, our strength may be more in how we construct our narratives and less in how such narratives are related over time. Personality development requires we consider such alternatives.

NOTE

1. The variant of course is the standard idea that within context situation, consistency of behavior representing a personality variable can be found. Such an idea is appealing but certainly does not provide the basis for being overwhelmingly confident that a simple structure of personality can be obtained. Thus, even if the Big Five personality variables, or traits, were to emerge as highly salient, the fact that they might each differ across a dozen situations and that each might differ under different situations gives rise to a combinatorial figure beyond the simple idea of five variables as explanatory device.

REFERENCES

Achenbach, T. M. (1978). The child behavior profile: I. Boys aged 6–11. *Journal of Consulting and Clinical Psychology, 46,* 478–488.

Achenbach, T. M. (1991). *Manual for the Child Behavior Checklist and 1991 Child Behavior Profile.* Burlington: University of Vermont, Department of Psychiatry.

Ainsworth, M. D. S., Blehar, M. C., Waters, E., & Wall, S. (1978). *Patterns of attachment: A psychological study of the strange situation.* Hillsdale, NJ: Erlbaum.

Ainsworth, M. D. S., & Eichberg, C. G. (1991). Effects on infant–mother attachment of mother's unresolved loss of an attachment figure or other traumatic experience. In C. M. Parkes, J. Stevenson-Hinde, & P. Marris (Eds.), *Attachment across the life cycle* (pp. 160–183). New York & London: Tavistock/Routledge.

Allport, G. W. (1937). *Personality: A psychological interpretation.* New York: Holt, Rinehart & Winston.

Alvarez, L. W. (1982). Experimental evidence that an asteroid impact led to the extinction of many species 65 million years ago. *Proceedings of the National Academy of Sciences, 80,* 627–642.

Angold, A., Weissman, M., John, K., Merikangas, K. R., Prusoll, B. A., Wickramaratne, P., Gammon, G. D., & Warner, V. (1987). Parent and child reports of depressive symptoms in children at low and high risk of depression. *Journal of Child Psychology and Psychiatry, 28,* 901–915.

Bandura, A. (1982). The psychology of chance encounters and life paths. *American Psychologist, 37,* 747–755.

Bates, J. E., Maslin, C. A., & Frankel, K. A. (1985). Attachment security, mother–child interaction and temperament as predictors of behavior problem ratings at age three years. In I. Bretherton & E. Waters (Eds.), Growing points of attachment theory and research. Monographs of the Society for Research in *Child Development, 50*(1–2, Serial No. 209), 167–193.

Beardslee, W. R., Bemporad, J., Keller, M. B., & Klerman, G. L. (1983). Children of parents with major affective disorder: A review. *American Journal of Psychiatry, 140,* 825–832.

Belsky, J., Campbell, S. B., Cohn, J. F., & Moore, G. (1996). Instability of infant–parent attachment security. *Developmental Psychology, 32,* 921–924.

Belsky, J., Rovine, M., & Taylor, D. G. (1984). The origins of individual differences in infant–mother attachment: Maternal and infant contributions (The Pennsylvania Infant and Family Development Project). *Child Development, 55,* 718–728.

Belsky, J., Spritz, B., & Crnic, K. (1996). Infant attachment security and affective–cognitive information processing at age 3. *Psychological Science, 7,* 111–114.

Billings, A. G., & Moos, R. H. (1983). Comparisons of children of depressed and nondepressed parents: A social–environmental perspective. *Journal of Abnormal Child Psychology, 11,* 463–486.

Bornstein, M. (Ed.). (1987). *Sensitive periods in development: Interdisciplinary perspectives.* Hillsdale, NJ: Erlbaum.

Bowlby, J. (1973). *Attachment and loss: Vol. 2. Separation.* New York: Basic Books.

Bowlby, J. (1980). *Attachment and loss: Loss, sadness, and depression.* New York: Basic Books.

Bowlby, J. (1982). Attachment and loss: Retrospect and prospect. *American Journal of Orthopsychiatry, 52,* 664–678.

Bowlby, J. (1988). *A secure base: Parent–child attachment and healthy human development.* New York: Basic Books.

Bretherton, I. (1985). Attachment theory: Retrospect and prospect. In I. Bretherton & E. Waters (Eds.),

Growing points of attachment theory and research. *Monographs of the Society for Research in Child Development, 50*(1–2, Serial No. 209), 3–35.
Bronfenbrenner, U., & Crouter, A. C. (1983). The evolution of environmental models in developmental research. In W. Kessen & P. H. Mussen (Eds.), *Handbook of child psychology: Vol. 1. History, theory, and methods* (pp. 357–414). New York: Wiley.
Brown, G. W., & Harris, T. O. (1978). *Social origins of depression.* New York: Free Press.
Bruner, J. (1990). *Acts of meaning.* Cambridge, MA: Harvard University Press.
Caspi, A. (1998). Personality development across the life course. In W. Damon (Series Ed.) & N. Eisenberg (Vol. Ed.), *Handbook of child psychology: Vol. 3. Social, emotional, and personality development* (5th ed., pp. 311–388). New York: Wiley.
Cassidy, J., & Asher, S. R. (1992). Loneliness and peer relations in young children. *Child Development, 63,* 350–365.
Cole-Detke, H., & Kobak, R. (1996). Attachment processes in eating disorder and depression. *Journal of Consulting and Clinical Psychology, 64,* 282–290.
Davies, P. T., & Cummings, E. M. (1994). Marital conflict and child adjustment: An emotional security hypothesis. *Psychological Bulletin, 116,* 387–411.
Dubow, E. F., Tisak, J., Causey, D., Hryshko, A., & Reid, G. (1991). A two-year longitudinal study of stressful life events, social support, and social problem-solving skills: Contributions to children's behavioral and academic adjustment. *Child Development, 62,* 583–599.
Dunn, J. (1993). *Young children's close relationships: Beyond attachment.* Newbury Park, CA: Sage.
Egeland, B., & Farber, E. A. (1984). Infant–mother attachment: Factors related to its development and changes over time. *Child Development, 55,* 753–771.
Elder, G. H., Jr. (1986). Military times and turning points in men's lives. *Developmental Psychology, 22,* 233–245.
Eldredge, N., & Gould, S. J. (1972). Punctuated equilibria: An alternative to phyletic gradualism. In T. J. M. Schopf (Ed.), *Models in paleobiology* (pp. 85–115). San Francisco, CA: Freeman, Cooper.
Elicker, J., Englund, M., & Sroufe, L. A. (1992). Predicting peer competence and peer relationships in childhood from early parent–child relationships. In R. Parke & G. Ladd (Eds.), *Family–peer relationships: Modes of linkage* (pp. 77–106). Hillsdale, NJ: Erlbaum.
Erikson, E. (1950). *Childhood and society.* New York: Norton.
Fauber, R., Forehand, R., Thomas, A. M., & Wierson, M. (1990). A mediational model of the impact of marital conflict on adolescent adjustment in intact and divorced families: The role of disrupted parenting. *Child Development, 61,* 1112–1123.
Fendrich, M., Weissman, M. M., & Warner, V. (1991). Longitudinal assessment of major depression and anxiety disorders in children. *Journal of the American Academy of Child and Adolescent Psychiatry, 30,* 38–42.
Flanagan, O. (1991). *The science of the mind.* Cambridge, MA: Bradford, MIT Press.
Ford, D. H., & Lerner, R. M. (1992). *Developmental systems theory: An integrative approach.* Newbury Park, CA: Sage.
Frankel, K. A., & Bates, J. E. (1990). Mother–toddler problem solving: Antecedents in attachment, home behavior, and temperament. *Child Development, 61,* 810–819.
Freud, S. (1953). Three essays on the theory of sexuality. In J. Strachey (Ed. & Trans.), in collaboration with A. Freud, *The standard edition of the complete psychological works of Sigmund Freud* (Vol. 7, pp. 123–243). London: Hogarth Press and the Institute of Psychoanalysis. (Original work published 1905)
Garmezy, N., & Rutter, M. (1983). *Stress, coping and development in children.* New York: McGraw-Hill.
George, C., Kaplan, N., & Main, M. (1985). *The attachment interview for adults.* Unpublished manuscript, University of California–Berkeley, Department of Psychology.
Gergen, K. J. (1973). Social psychology as history. *Journal of Personality and Social Psychology, 26,* 309–320.
Goldsmith, H., & Campos, J. (1982). Toward a theory of infant temperament. In R. Emde & R. Harmon (Eds.), *The development of attachment and affiliative systems* (pp. 161–193). New York: Plenum Press.
Goodman, G. S., & Clarke-Stewart, A. (1991). Suggestibility in children's testimony: Implications for sexual abuse investigations. In J. Doreis (Ed.), *The suggestibility of children's recollections: Implications for eyewitness testimony* (pp. 92–105). Washington, DC: American Psychological Association.
Greenberg, J. R., & Mitchell, S. A. (1983). *Object relations in psychoanalytic theory.* Cambridge, MA: Harvard University Press.
Grych, J. H., & Fincham, F. D. (1993). Children's appraisals of marital conflict: Initial investigation of the cognitive contextual framework. *Child Development, 64,* 215–230.
Hartup, W. (1983). Peer relationships. In E. M. Hetherington (Ed.), *Handbook of child psychology: Vol. 4. Socialization, personality, and social development* (pp. 103–196). New York: Wiley.
Hazan, C., & Shaver, P. (1987). Conceptualizing romantic love as an attachment process. *Journal of Personality and Social Psychology, 52,* 511–524.
Herjanic, B., & Reich, W. (1982). Development of a structured interview for children: Agreement between children and parents on individual symptoms. *Journal of Abnormal Child Psychology, 10,* 307–324.
Hoffman, H. S. (1974). Fear mediated processes in the context of imprinting. In M. Lewis & L. A. Rosenblum (Eds.), *The origins of fear: Vol. 2. The origins of behavior* (pp. 25–48). New York: Wiley.
Jacobsen, R. H., Lahey, B. B., & Strauss, C. C. (1983). Correlates of depressed mood in normal children. *Journal of Abnormal Child Psychology, 11,* 29–40.

James, W. (1975). *Pragmatism* (F. Bowers, Text Ed.). Cambridge, MA: Harvard University Press.

Jensen, P. S., Salzberg, A. D., Richters, J. E., & Watanabe, H. K. (1993). Scales, diagnoses, and child psychopathology: I. CBCL and DISC Relationships. *Journal of the American Academy of Child and Adolescent Psychiatry, 32,* 397–406.

Jung, C. (1963). *Psychology of the unconscious: A study of the transformations and symbolisms of the libido* (B. M. Hinkle, Trans.). New York: Dodd-Mead. (Original work published 1916)

Kazdin, A. E., French, N. H., Unis, A. S., & Esveldt-Dawson, K. (1983). Assessment of childhood depression: Correspondence of child and parent ratings. *Journal of the American Academy of Child Psychiatry, 22,* 157–164.

Kazdin, A. E., Moser, J., Colbus, D., & Bell, R. (1985). Depressive symptoms among physically abused and psychiatrically disturbed children. *Journal of Abnormal Psychology, 94,* 298–307.

Kierkegaard, S. (1846). *The present age* (A. Duc, Trans.). New York: Harper & Row.

Kobak, R. R., Cole, H. E., Ferenz-Gillies, R., Fleming, W. S., & Gamble, W. (1993). Attachment and emotion regulation during mother–teen problem solving: A control theory analysis. *Child Development, 64,* 231–245.

Kobak, R., & Sceery, A. (1988). Attachment in late adolescence: Working models, affect regulation, and representations of self and others. *Child Development, 59,* 135–146.

Kobak, R. R., Sudler, N., & Gamble, W. (1991). Attachment and depressive symptoms during adolescence: A developmental pathways analysis. *Development and Psychopathology, 3,* 461–474.

Kohn, M. (1977). *Social competence, symptoms, and underachievement in childhood: A longitudinal perspective.* New York: Wiley.

Kovacs, M. (1983). *The Children's Depression Inventory: A self-rated depression scale for school-aged youngsters.* Unpublished manuscript, University of Pittsburgh School of Medicine, Pittsburgh, PA.

Lamb, M. E., Thompson, R., Gardner, W., & Charnov, E. (1985). *Infant–mother attachment: The origins and developmental significance of individual differences in strange situation behavior.* Hillsdale, NJ: Erlbaum.

Largo, R. H., Molinari, L., Von Siebenthal, K., & Wolfensburger, U. (1996). Does a profound change in toilet-training affect development of bowel and bladder control? *Developmental Medicine and Child Neurology, 38,* 1106–1116.

LeDoux, J. (1990). Cognitive and emotional interactions in the brain. *Cognition and Emotions, 3,* 265–289.

Lefkowitz, M. M., & Tesiny, E. P. (1984). Rejection and depression: Prospective and contemporaneous analyses. *Developmental Psychology, 20,* 776–785.

Lerner, R. M. (1986). *Concepts and theories of human development* (2nd ed.). New York: Random House.

Lewis, M. (1984). Social influences on development: An overview. In M. Lewis (Ed.), *Beyond the dyad* (pp. 1–12). New York: Plenum Press.

Lewis, M. (1990a). Models of developmental psychopathology. In M. Lewis & S. Miller (Eds.), *Handbook of developmental psychopathology* (pp. 15–28). New York: Plenum Press.

Lewis, M. (1990b). Self knowledge and social development in early life. In L. Pervin (Ed.), *Handbook of personality: Theory and research* (pp. 277–300). New York: Guilford Press.

Lewis, M. (1997). *Altering fate: Why the past does not predict the future.* New York: Guilford Press.

Lewis, M., & Feiring, C. (1989). Infant, mother, and mother-infant interaction behavior and subsequent attachment. *Child Development, 60,* 831–837.

Lewis, M., & Feiring, C. (1991). Attachment as personal characteristic or a measure of the environment. In J. L. Gewirtz & W. M. Kurtines (Eds.), *Intersections with attachment* (pp. 3–22). Hillsdale, NJ: Erlbaum.

Lewis, M., Feiring, C., McGuffog, C., & Jaskir, J. (1984). Predicting psychopathology in six-year-olds from early social relations. *Child Development, 55,* 123–136.

Lewis, M., Feiring, C., & Rosenthal, S. (in press). Attachment over time. *Child Development.*

Lewis, M., & Lee-Painter, S. (1974). An interactional approach to the mother–infant dyad. In M. Lewis & L. A. Rosenblum (Eds.), *The effect of the infant on the care giver: The origins of behavior* (Vol. 1, pp. 21–48). New York: Wiley.

Lewis, M., & Rosenblum, L. A. (Eds.). (1977). *Interaction, conversation, and the development of language: Vol. 5. The origins of behavior.* New York: Wiley.

Londerville, S., & Main, M. (1981). Security of attachment, compliance, and maternal training methods in the second year of life. *Developmental Psychology, 17,* 298–299.

Lovejoy, C. M. (1991). Maternal depression: Effects on social cognition and behavior in parent–child interactions. *Journal of Abnormal Child Psychology, 19,* 693–706.

Main, M. (1990). Cross-cultural studies of attachment organization: Recent studies, changing methodologies, and the concept of conditional strategies. *Human Development, 33,* 48–61.

Main, M., Kaplan, N., & Cassidy, J. (1985). Security in infancy, childhood, and adulthood: A move to the level of representation. In I. Bretherton & E. Waters (Eds.), Growing points of attachment theory and research. *Monographs of the Society for Research in Child Development, 50*(1–2, Serial No. 209), 66–104.

Masters, W. H., Johnson, W. E., & Kolodny, R. C. (Eds.). (1977). *Ethical issues in sex therapy and research.* Boston: Little, Brown.

Matas, L., Arend, R. A., & Sroufe, L. A. (1978). Continuity of adaptation in the second year: The relationship between quality of attachment and later competence. *Child Development, 49,* 547–556.

McConaughy, S. H., Stanger, C., & Achenbach, T. M. (1992). Three-year course of behavioral/emotional problems in a national sample of 4- to 16-year-olds: I. Agreement among informants. *Journal of the American Academy of Child and Adolescent Psychiatry, 31,* 932–940.

McKnew, D. H., Cytryn, L., Efron, A. M., Gershon, E. S., & Bunney, W. E. (1979). Offspring of patients with affective disorders. *British Journal of Psychiatry, 134,* 148–152.

Miller, S. M., Birnbaum, A., & Durbin, D. (1990). Etiologic perspectives on depression in childhood. In S. M. Miller & M. Lewis (Eds.), *Handbook of developmental psychopathology: Perspectives in developmental psychology* (pp. 311–325). New York: Plenum Press.

Mischel, W. (1990). Personality dispositions revisited and revised: A view after three decades. In L. Pervin (Ed.), *Handbook of personality: Theory and research* (pp. 111–134). New York: Guilford Press.

Moretti, M. M., Fine, S., Haley, G., & Marriage, K. (1985). Childhood and adolescent depression: Child-report vs. Parent-report information. *Journal of the American Academy of Child Psychiatry, 24,* 298–302.

Mounoud, P. (1990). Consciousness as a necessary transitional phenomenon in cognitive development. *Psychological Inquiry, 1,* 253–258.

Mullins, L. L., Siegel, L. J., & Hodges, K. (1985). Cognitive problem-solving and life event correlates of depressive symptoms in children. *Journal of Abnormal Child Psychology, 13,* 305–314.

Orvaschel, H., Weissman, M. M., Padian, N., & Lowe, T. L. (1981). Assessing psychopathology in children of psychiatrically disturbed parents: A pilot study. *Journal of the American Academy of Child Psychiatry, 20,* 112–122.

Pascual-Leone, J. (1990). Intension, intention, and early precursors of will: Constructive epistemological remarks on Lewis's research paradigm. *Psychological Inquiry, 1,* 258–260.

Pastor, D. L. (1981). The quality of mother–infant attachment and its relationship to toddlers' initial sociability with peers. *Developmental Psychology, 17,* 326–335.

Pepper, S. C. (1942). *World hypotheses.* Berkeley: University of California Press.

Pervin, L. A. (Ed.). (1990). *Handbook of personality: Theory and research.* New York: Guilford Press.

Pervin, L. A., & Lewis, M. (Eds.). (1978). *Perspectives in interactional psychology.* New York: Plenum Press.

Piaget, J. (1952). *The origins of intelligence in children.* New York: International Universities Press.

Plomin, R. (1983). Childhood temperament. In B. Lahey & A. Kazdin (Eds.), *Advances in clinical child psychology* (Vol. 6, pp. 45–92). New York: Plenum Press.

Politano, P. M., Stapleton, L. A., & Correll, J. A. (1992). Differences between children of depressed and non-depressed mothers: Locus of control, anxiety and self-esteem: A research note. *Journal of Child Psychology and Psychiatry and Allied Disciplines, 33,* 451–455.

Posada, G., Waters, E., Crowell, J. A., & Lay, K. (1995). Is it easier to use a secure mother as a secure base? Attachment Q-Sort correlates of the adult attachment interview. *Monographs of the Society for Research in Child Development, 60*(2–3, Serial No. 244).

Poznanski, E., Mokros, H. B., Grossman, J., & Freeman, L. N. (1985). Diagnostic criteria in childhood depression. *American Journal of Psychiatry, 142,* 1168–1173.

Reese, H. W., & Overton, W. F. (1970). Models of development and theories of development. In L. R. Goulet & P. B. Baltes (Eds.), *Life-span developmental psychology: Research and theory* (pp. 115–145). New York: Academic Press.

Renshaw, P. D., & Brown, P. J. (1993). Loneliness in middle childhood: Concurrent and longitudinal predictors. *Child Development, 64,* 1271–1284.

Richters, J. E. (1992). Depressed mothers as informants about their children: A critical review of the evidence for distortion. *Psychological Bulletin, 112,* 485–499.

Rosenstein, D. S., & Horowitz, H. A. (1996). Adolescent attachment and psychopathology. *Journal of Consulting and Clinical Psychology, 64,* 244–253.

Ross, M. (1989). Relation of implicit theories of the construction of personal histories. *Psychological Review, 96,* 341–357.

Routh, D. K. (1990). Taxonomy in developmental psychopathology: Consider the source. In M. Lewis & S. M. Miller (Eds.), *Handbook of developmental psychopathology* (pp. 53–62). New York: Plenum Press.

Saylor, C. F., Finch, A. J., Baskin, C. H., Furey, W., & Kelly, M. (1984). Construct validity for measures of childhood depression: Application of a multitrait–multimethod methodology. *Journal of Consulting and Clinical Psychology, 52,* 977–985.

Schaefer, E. S., Edgerton, M., & Aaronson, M. (1979). *Classroom Behavior Inventory: A teacher behavior checklist.* Chapel Hill, NC: Frank Porter Graham Child Development Center.

Snyder, M., & Ickes, W. (1985). Personality and social behavior. In G. Lindzey & E. Aronson (Eds.), *Handbook of social psychology: Vol. 2. Special fields and applications* (pp. 883–947). New York: Random House.

Sroufe, L. A. (1983). Infant–caregiver attachment and patterns of adaptation in preschool: The roots of maladaptation and competence. In M. Perlmutter (Ed.), *The Minnesota Symposia on Child Psychology: Vol. 16. Development and policy concerning children with special needs* (pp. 41–83). Hillsdale, NJ: Erlbaum.

Sroufe, L. A. (1997). Psychopathology as an outcome of development. *Development and Psychopathology, 9,* 251–268.

Sroufe, L. A., Egeland, B., & Kreutzer, T. (1990). The fate of early experience following developmental change: Longitudinal approaches to individual adaptation in childhood. *Child Development, 61,* 1363–1373.

Sroufe, L. A., & Fleeson, J. (1986). Attachment and the construction of relationships. In W. Hartup & Z. Rubin (Eds.), *Relationships and development* (pp. 239–252). Hillsdale, NJ: Erlbaum.

Sroufe, L. A., Schork, E., Moffi, E., Laworsky, N., & LaFreniere, P. (1984). The role of affect in social competence. In C. Izard, J. Kagan, & R. Zajonc (Eds.), *Emotion, cognition, and behavior.* New York: Plenum Press.

Stanger, C., & Lewis, M. (1993). Agreement among parents, teachers, and children on internalizing and externalizing behavior problems. *Journal of Clinical Child Psychology, 22,* 107–115.

Stanger, C., McConaughy, S. H., & Achenbach, T. M. (1992). Three-year course of behavioral/emotional problems in a national sample of 4–16 year olds. II: Predictors of syndromes. *Journal of the American Academy of Child and Adolescent Psychiatry, 31,* 941–950.

Stavrakaki, C., Vargo., B., Roberts, N., & Boodoosingh, L. (1987). Concordance among sources of information for ratings of anxiety and depression in children. *Journal of the American Academy of Child and Adolescent Psychiatry, 26,* 733–737.

Sugarman, S. (1987). *Piaget's construction of the child's reality.* Cambridge, MA: Cambridge University Press.

Suomi, S. J. (1979). Differential development of various social relationships by Rhesus monkey infants. In M. Lewis & L. Rosenblum (Eds.), *The child and its family: The genesis of behavior* (Vol. 2, pp. 219–244). New York: Plenum Press.

Thompson, R. A., & Lamb, M. E. (1983a). Individual differences in dimensions of socioemotional development in infancy. In R. Plutchik & H. Kellerman (Eds.), *Emotion: Theory, research, and experience: Vol. 2. Emotions in early development.* New York: Academic Press.

Thompson, R. A., & Lamb, M. (1983b). Security and attachment and stranger sociability in infancy. *Developmental Psychology, 19,* 184–191.

van IJzendoorn, M. H. (1995). Adult attachment representations, parental responsiveness, and infant attachment: A meta-analysis on the predictive validity of the Adult Attachment Interview. *Psychological Bulletin, 117,* 387–403.

van IJzendoorn, M. H., Kranenburg, M. J., Zwart-Woudstra, H. A., van Bussbach, A. M., & Lambermon, M. W. (1991). Parental attachment and children's socio-emotional development: Some findings on the validity of the Adult Attachment Interview in the Netherlands. *International Journal of Behavioral Development, 14,* 375–394.

Vaughn, B., Egeland, B., Sroufe, L. A., & Waters, E. (1979). Individual differences in infant–mother attachment at 12 and 18 months: Stability and change in families under stress. *Child Development, 50,* 971–975.

Waters, E., Posada, G., Crowell, J., & Lay, K. (1993). Is attachment theory ready to contribute to our understanding of disruptive behavior problems? *Development and Psychopathology, 54,* 215–224.

Waters, E., Trebous, D., Crowell, J., Merrick, S., & Albersheim, L. (1995, April). *From the strange situation to the Adult Attachment Interview: A 20-year longitudinal study of attachment security in infancy and early adulthood.* Poster presented at the biennial meeting of the Society for Research in Child Development, Indianapolis, IN.

Waters, E., Wippman, J., & Sroufe, L. A. (1979). Attachment, positive affect, and competence in the peer group: Two studies in construct validation. *Child Development, 50,* 821–829.

Weissman, M. M., Gammon, G. D., John, K., Merikangas, K. R., Warner, V., Prusoff, B. A., & Sholomska, D. (1987). Children of depressed parents: Increased psychopathology and early onset of major depression. *Archives of General Psychiatry, 44,* 847–853.

Weissman, M. M., Wickramaratne, P., Warner, V., John, K., Prusoff, B. A., Merikangas, K. R., & Gammon, G. D. (1987). Assessing psychiatric disorders in children: Discrepancies between mothers' and children's reports. *Archives of General Psychiatry, 44,* 747–753.

Welner, Z., Welner, A., McCrary, M. D., & Leonard, M. (1977). Psychopathology in children of inpatients with depression: A controlled study. *Journal of Nervous and Mental Disease, 164,* 408–413.

Whitehead, A. N. (1978). *Process and reality: An essay in cosmology.* New York: Free Press. (Original work published 1929)

Yarrow, M. R., Campbell, J. D., & Burton, R. V. (1970). Recollections of childhood: A study of the retrospective method. *Monographs of the Society for Research in Child Development, 35*(5).

Zimmerman, P., Fremmer-Bombik, E., Spangler, G., & Grossman, K. E. (1997). Attachment in adolescence: A longitudinal perspective. In W. Koops, J. B. Hoeksema, & D. C. vandenBoom (Eds.), *Development of interaction and attachment: Traditional and non-traditional approaches* (pp. 281–291). Amsterdam, Netherlands: North-Holland.

Chapter 13

Personality and Psychopathology

Thomas A. Widiger
University of Kentucky

Roel Verheul and Wim van den Brink
University of Amsterdam

The importance of personality to psychopathology has been recognized since the beginnings of medicine. Hippocrates (in the fourth century B.C.) distinguished between four fundamental dispositions (i.e., sanguine, melancholic, phlegmatic, and choleric) that were thought to provide a vulnerability to a variety of physical and psychological disorders (Maher & Maher, 1994). Much has been learned since his time, including a healthy appreciation for how little is in fact known. The interplay of personality and psychopathology continues to be a clinically significant yet challenging focus of investigation (Watson & Clark, 1994). Personality and psychopathology influence the presentation or appearance of one another, they can share a common, underlying etiology, and they often contribute to the development or etiology of one another (Klein, Wonderlich, & Shea, 1993). Each of these relationships has significant theoretical and clinical implications, and each will be considered in turn.

PATHOPLASTIC RELATIONSHIPS

The influence of personality and psychopathology on the presentation of one another is typically characterized as a pathoplastic relationship (Klein et al., 1993). This pathoplastic relationship is bidirectional, as psychopathology will vary in its appearance depending upon a person's premorbid personality traits, and the appearance or presentation of personality will likewise be affected by the presence of a comorbid mental disorder. Both directions of relationship will be considered in turn.

Pathoplastic Effects of Personality on Psychopathology

Personality is the characteristic manner in which one thinks, feels, behaves, and relates to others. Mental disorders are clinically significant impairments in one or more areas of psychological functioning, including (but not limited to) one's thinking, feeling, eating, sleeping, and other important components of psychological functioning (American Psychiatric Association [APA], 1994). It would be surprising for the presentation, course, or treatment of an impairment in a psychologically important component of thinking or feeling not to be significantly affected by a person's characteristic manner of thinking and feeling. Mental disorders occur within the context of a premorbid personality structure that will often have a profound effect on the presentation and course of the disorder (Klein et al., 1993; Millon & Davis, 1996).

Appearance and Presentation of a Disorder

The substantial heterogeneity in symptomatology among persons with the same mental disorder is a significant problem for diagnosis and treatment (Clark, Watson, & Reynolds, 1995). An important contribution to this heterogeneity is variation in personality structure. Premorbid personality structure can have a profound effect on the manner in which a mental disorder is manifested or experienced. For example, depression is likely to be experienced differently depending upon a person's vulnerabilities and sources for self-esteem. Depression within a dependent (sociotropic) person will be characterized in particular by feelings of deprivation, loss, loneliness, and unlikeability; depression within a narcissistic (autonomous, self-critical) person will be characterized in particular by feelings of defeat, failure, withdrawal, and self-blame (Robins, Hayes, Block, Kramer, & Villena, 1995).

Substance use disorder research has identified two fundamental differences in the craving for alcohol and other drugs. One motivation for drug usage is perhaps to suppress or minimize negative affects (e.g., anxiety, anger, or depression), whereas another is to induce positive affects. The negative and positive reinforcing properties of alcohol appear to be anatomically and functionally distinct and may be closely associated with fundamental personality dispositions toward Negative Affectivity and Positive Affectivity (Powell, Bradley, & Gray, 1992; McCusker & Brown, 1991). Dyscontrolled drug usage within a person characterized by high levels of Negative Affectivity (Neuroticism) may serve primarily to suppress negative affects, whereas dyscontrolled usage within persons characterized by high levels of Positive Affectivity may be primarily for stimulation and arousal.

Central to both anorexia nervosa and bulimia nervosa (the two fundamental forms of eating disorder) is a preoccupation with body shape, weight, or appearance for one's self-esteem (APA, 1994). Persons with these eating disorders desire intensely to lose weight. Their thoughts and concerns throughout the day will be devoted to this goal. Persons with anorexia are pathologically successful in the effort to maintain a low body weight (i.e., are grossly underweight) whereas persons with bulimia nervosa are relatively unsuccessful due in part to their binge eating and inadequate (but still excessive) compensatory behaviors. "The assumption that dissimilar premorbid traits must account for the divergence of similarly weight-preoccupied individuals into anorexia or bulimia has shaped much of the field's contemporary interest in personality variables" (Vitousek & Manke, 1994, p. 137).

Whether a person who emphasizes body weight for adequate self-esteem becomes anorexic may reflect, at least in part, his or her premorbid level of Conscientiousness. Persons who are high in Conscientiousness will have the discipline, dedication, and devotion to succeed in dieting, as well as in many other endeavors (McCrae & Costa, 1990), whereas those low in Conscientiousness will tend to be unsuccessful, perhaps even impulsive, disinhibited, and dyscontrolled. Anorexia nervosa is not due to excessive Conscientiousness, but the presence of a pathologic preoccupation with losing weight in a person with high conscientiousness may result in the development of excessive weight loss.

Treatment and Course of a Disorder

An additional way in which personality traits can have a pathoplastic effect on psychopathology is the manner or degree to which the person responds to a treatment. It is routine in clinical practice to conduct a personality assessment at the beginning of treatment, because the personality of a patient can have a significant impact on treatment responsivity. "The last 40 years of individual differences research require the inclusion of personality trait assessment for the construction and implementation of any treatment plan that would lay claim to scientific status" (Harkness & Lilienfeld, 1997, p. 349). Reanalyses of the data obtained by the NIMH Treatment of Depression Collaborative Research Program has indicated the importance of pretreatment levels of perfectionism across all forms of treatment, including pharmacologic (Blatt, Quinlan, Pilkonis, & Shea, 1995). "Patients with higher pretreatment levels of perfectionism were more likely to complete treatment but to have less improvement" (Blatt, Zuroff, Quinlan, & Pilkonis, 1996, p. 168).

Personality assessment may itself be incorporated into a treatment, facilitating a patient's development of an active participation and a realistic understanding of the disorder's etiology and development. Harkness and Lilienfield (1997), for example, described how the treatment of a woman's failed relationships were facilitated by "an integrative understanding of how the cyclical pattern of initial attraction and eventual disappointment flows from her personality" (p. 357). Clinicians have long recognized the value of self-reflection and insight regarding the origin and impact of one's personality structure. "As the inscription over the oracle at Delphi instructed, it is important to 'know thyself'" (Finn & Tonsager, 1997, p. 286). The research by Finn and Tonsager (1997), Moffett, Steinberg, and Rohde (1996), Newman and Greenway (1997), and others regarding the value of early feedback "suggest just how valuable and beneficial such knowledge can be" (Finn & Tonsager, 1997, p. 286).

Maladaptive personality traits are given a special status within the American Psychiatric Association's (APA) *Diagnostic and Statistical Manual of Mental Disorders* (DSM-IV; APA, 1994) by being placed on a separate "axis" that requires that clinicians assess for the presence of a personality disorder in virtually every patient. "DSM-III [APA, 1980] provides separate axes—Axis I for all other clinical syndromes and Axis II for personality disorders—to ensure that the personality disorders not be overlooked" (Frances, 1980, p. 1050). "This concern arises from accumulating evidence that the quality and quantity of preexisting personality disturbance may indeed influence the predisposition, manifestation, course, and response to treatment of various Axis I conditions" (Frances, 1980, p. 1050).

Research has focused in particular on the downside of personality, or the extent to which particular personality traits undermine treatment. The predominant understanding is that the presence of a DSM-IV personality disorder (e.g., antisocial, paranoid, or borderline) hinders the treatment of other mental disorders. Simply the presence of a personality disorder (e.g., antisocial) may itself constitute a reason for excluding or dismissing a person from some treatment programs.

There is indeed empirical support for these negative expectations (Brink, 1995; Reich & Vasile, 1993; Shea, Widiger, & Klein, 1992), although the findings have at times been exaggerated or misunderstood (Verheul, Ball, & Brink, 1997). One qualification to the expectation of poor treatment responsivity of a DSM-IV personality disorder is the substantial heterogeneity in relevant personality traits among persons sharing the same diagnosis (Widiger & Sanderson, 1995b). Patients need not have all of the features of a respective personality disorder to be given its diagnosis, and they will often have many additional personality traits not considered in the APA diagnostic nomenclature that could be highly relevant to treatment decisions. For example, one need only have three of the seven features of an antisocial personality disorder to be given its diagnosis (APA, 1994), none of which may be particularly relevant to treatment responsivity (Cacciola, Rutherford, Alterman, & Snider, 1994). Many antisocial persons will indeed improve during clinical treatment (Cacciola, Alterman, Rutherford, & Snider, 1995).

The failure to consider all relevant traits in clinical assessments is due in part to the confinement of the APA (1994) nomenclature to maladaptive functioning. Clinicians are encouraged to assess for personality disorders but not for adaptive personality traits. The five-factor model (FFM) of personality, consisting of the broad domains of Neuroticism, Extraversion, Openness, Conscientiousness, and Agreeableness (McCrae & Costa, 1990), provides perhaps the most comprehensive classification of personality (Saucier & Goldberg, 1996). The DSM-IV personality disorders relate closely to four of these domains (Neuroticism, Extraversion, Conscientiousness, and Agreeableness), whereas a number of studies have indicated a relatively weaker relationship for Openness (versus Closedness) to Experience (Widiger & Costa, 1994). The absence of a consistently strong relationship with Openness has at times been a basis for criticism of the FFM. However, it is perhaps ironic to criticize the FFM for including an important domain of personality functioning that may not be adequately recognized by the APA (McCrae, 1996). Indeed, persons characterized by moderate levels of Openness might be relatively more receptive to psychotherapeutic interventions, self-exploration, and change, whereas persons characterized by a Closedness to Experience would be more resistant, stubborn, and rigid (Miller, 1991; MacKenzie, 1994).

Pathoplastic Effects of Psychopathology on Personality

One of the more heavily researched and well-documented relationships between personality and psychopathology are the effects of episodes of psychopathology on the appearance, presentation, or perception of personality (Widiger, 1993). Clinicians will typically assess a patient's personality during an initial intake procedure, yet this is perhaps the worst time to do so (Widiger & Sanderson, 1995a). Persons who are very anxious, depressed, angry, or distraught will often fail to provide an accurate description of their usual way of thinking, feeling, behaving, and relating to others. Low self-esteem and negativism are central features of a depressive mood disorder (APA, 1994). Persons who are depressed will describe themselves as being more dependent, introverted, self-conscious, vulnerable, or pessimistic than is in fact the case (Widiger, 1993).

Self-report inventories are especially vulnerable to the artifactual distortions in self-descriptions secondary to mood states (e.g., Bagby, Joffe, Parker, Kalemba, & Harkness, 1995; Verheul, Hartgers, Brink, & Koeter, 1998). There is, however, surprisingly little effort by authors of self-report inventories to address this problem. Most self-report inventories do not even include an instruction to the respondents to describe their long-standing, characteristic manner of functioning (Verheul et al., 1998). The Minnesota Multiphasic Personality Inventory (MMPI-2), for example, only instructs a person to indicate "whether [the item] is true as applied to you or false as applied to you" (Hathaway et al., 1989, p. 1). It is not surprising that some self-report inventories fail to adequately distinguish mood states from personality traits, when virtually no effort is being made in the instructions to make any such distinction. Most self-report inventories do include scales to identify and potentially correct for distortions in self-presentation, but the effectiveness of these scales with respect to mood state distortions appears to be limited (Widiger & Sanderson, 1995a; Zimmerman, 1994). In fact, the same items are used in some self-report inventories to assess both personality traits and Axis I mental disorders. For example, the Millon Clinical Multiaxial Inventory–III (MCMI-III; Millon, Millon, & Davis, 1994) items, "I have tried to commit suicide" and "I have given serious thought recently to doing away with myself" (Millon et al., 1994, p. 99), are included in scales to assess Axis II borderline personality and Axis I major depression. It is apparent that these MCMI-III items are readily interpreted by respondents to refer to a recently experienced mood disorder rather than to a long-standing, characteristic manner of thinking or feeling, and they are in fact coded as such by the test authors.

Semistructured interviews might be relatively more successful in distinguishing personality from Axis I psychopathology. Loranger and colleagues (1991), for example, compared the assessments provided at admission by the Personality Disorder Examination (PDE; Loranger, 1988) with assessments obtained 1 week to 6 months later. Changes in scores were not associated with depression or anxiety, and Loranger and colleagues (1991) therefore concluded that the "study provides generally encouraging results regarding the apparent ability of a particular semistructured interview, the PDE, to circumvent trait-state artifacts in diagnosing personality disorders in symptomatic patients" (p. 727). The success of semistructured interviews, relative to self-report inventories, to avoid distortion secondary to Axis I psychopathology is due in part to the fact that all of the items within these interviews are confined to the assessment of personality traits, that explicit instructions are provided to respondents to describe long-standing personality traits as opposed to recently experienced mental disorders, and that interviewers often use the option of follow-up inquiry to ensure that an effort at a distinction is in fact being made. The attention given to the differentiation of personality traits from Axis I mental disorders is a major reason that most personality disorder researchers place more importance and reliance upon the findings obtained from semistructured interviews than from self-report inventories (Coyne & Whiffen, 1995; Widiger & Sanderson, 1995a; Zimmerman, 1994).

Semistructured interviews, however, are not immune to pathoplastic distortions (e.g., Johnson et al., 1997; Peselow, Sanfilipo, & Fieve, 1994), and they do vary substantially in the manner and extent to which they address this issue (Verheul et al., 1997). For example, the DSM-IV requires that the personality disorder diagnostic criteria be evident since late adolescence or young adulthood (APA, 1994), but the PDE only requires that one diagnostic criterion be present since the age of 25. All of the other diagnostic criteria can be present only within the past few years (Loranger, 1988). A 45-year-old adult with a mood disorder might then receive a dependent, borderline, or comparable personality disorder diagnosis by the PDE if just one of the diagnostic criteria was evident since the age of 25. Loranger and colleagues (1991) acknowledged in their study that all but two of the 10 PDE personality disorder scale scores decreased significantly during a brief inpatient hospitalization. This reduction is unlikely to reflect actual, sustained changes in personality functioning.

SPECTRUM RELATIONSHIPS

The identification and differentiation of pathoplastic and etiological relationships between personality and psychopathology is complicated in part by the possibility that personality and psychopathology at times fail to be distinct conditions. Many of the Axis II personality disorders may represent simply extreme and/or maladaptive variants of common personality traits, and some personality traits and personality disorders may also represent characterologic variants of Axis I mental disorders. Each of these variants of spectrum relationships will be discussed in turn.

Personality on a Spectrum with Personality Disorders

The most obvious spectrum relationship is that between personality and personality disorders (Widiger & Costa, 1994). Many prominent personality disorder theorists argue that disorders of personality are qualitatively distinct from normal personality functioning (e.g., Gunderson, Links, & Reich, 1991; Meehl, 1995; Siever & Davis, 1991). To the extent that they are distinct, it would be meaningful to research and describe the interaction of normal personality traits and personality disorders. Some personality traits might provide a disposition or vulnerability to the development of a personality disorder. Just as Introversion can contribute to the development of depression, perhaps Introversion may also contribute to the development of a schizoid personality disorder. However, to the extent that the DSM-IV personality disorders are simply manifestations of extreme variants of normal personality traits, it would be as meaningful to say that Neuroticism contributes to the development of a borderline personality disorder as it is to say that Introversion contributes to the development of extreme Introversion. Borderline personality disorder may represent simply an extreme variant of Neuroticism, and schizoid personality disorder may represent simply an extreme variant of Introversion.

Widiger, Trull, Clarkin, Sanderson, and Costa (1994) suggested that the DSM-IV personality disorders can be understood as maladaptive and/or extreme variants of common (normal) personality traits. They indicated how the diagnostic criteria for the DSM-IV personality disorders (APA, 1994) resemble closely various facets of the FFM. For example, the facets of Negative Affectivity, or Neuroticism, as described by Costa and McCrae (1992), include angry hostility, impulsivity, vulnerability, anxiousness, and depression. Many of the fundamental borderline personality disorder diagnostic criteria clearly involve angry hostility (e.g., borderline inappropriate, intense anger), anxious and depressed Negative Affectivity (e.g., borderline affective instability), vulnerability (e.g., borderline frantic efforts to avoid abandonment), and impulsivity (e.g., borderline impulsivity). DSM-IV obsessive–compulsive personality disorder also clearly resembles extreme Conscientiousness. Persons high in conscientiousness will be organized, disciplined, hard-working, deliberate, ordered, and dutiful (Costa & McCrae, 1992). Persons who are excessive in these traits would manifest the DSM-IV symptoms of an obsessive-compulsive personality disorder, such as overconscientousness, perfectionism, preoccupation with order, organization, and rules, and excessive devotion to work (APA, 1994). The correspondence of the DSM-IV personality disorders with the FFM as described by McCrae and Costa (1990) is particularly remarkable given the development of the FFM within normal personality research, independent of any consideration or even recognition of the APA (1994) personality disorders.

There is also empirical support for the FFM interpretation of the DSM-IV personality disorders (Widiger & Costa, 1994). Personality disorders do not appear to be conditions that are qualitatively distinct from normal personality functioning (Clark, Livesley, Schroeder, & Irish, 1996; Livesley, Schroeder, Jackson, & Jang, 1994; Widiger & Sanderson, 1995b), and a number of studies, using a variety of methodologies, have indicated a close relationship of the personality disorders to the domains and facets of the FFM (e.g., Axelrod, Widiger, Trull, & Corbitt, 1997; Ball, Tennen, Poling, Kranzler, & Rounsaville, 1997; Clark & Livesley, 1994;

O'Connor & Dyce, 1998; Trull, 1992). The exceptions to the predicted relationships appear to be relatively minor and may be due in large part to methodological limitations in the instruments assessing the FFM and/or the personality disorders (Widiger & Costa, 1994).

Personality on a Spectrum with Axis I Mental Disorders

A spectrum relationship may also exist for personality and Axis I mental disorders. For example, the schizotypal personality disorder could be said to provide a disposition toward the development of schizophrenia, as the presence of these maladaptive personality traits increases the likelihood of the development of schizophrenia. However, this might not have the same meaning as dependency providing a disposition toward the development of depression. Schizotypal personality disorder is considered by most theorists to be a characterologic variant of a schizophrenic pathology (Siever & Davis, 1991). The development of schizophrenia after a history of schizotypal personality disorder might not be one disorder that has occurred in part due to the presence of another, different disorder, but simply one disorder that has changed in its manifestation across time. It is for this reason that clinicians are discouraged in DSM-IV from continuing the diagnosis of schizotypal personality once a person has developed schizophrenia (APA, 1994; Widiger, Mangine, Corbitt, Ellis, & Thomas, 1995). The features of schizotypal personality disorder are almost identical to the prodromal phase of schizophrenia (APA, 1994). Once a person has developed schizophrenia, it might be more accurate to say that the schizotypal features were the prodromal symptoms of schizophrenia rather than the symptoms of a distinct, premorbid personality disorder. The *International Classification of Diseases* (ICD-10; World Health Organization, 1992) does not even consider schizotypal personality disorder to be a personality disorder, classifying it instead as a form of schizophrenia.

Such spectrum relationships may exist for other DSM-IV personality disorders. Siever and Davis (1991) proposed that most of the DSM-IV personality disorders are characterologic variants of various Axis I mental disorders (e.g., borderline personality disorder as a characterologic variant of impulse dyscontrol and affective disregulation, depressive personality disorder as a characterologic variant of mood disorder, and avoidant personality disorder as a characterologic variant of anxiety disorder). They suggested that the personality and Axis I mental disorders exist along a common, underlying spectrum of pathology and, as pathological conditions, are qualitatively distinct from normal personality functioning. Schizoid personality disorder, from this perspective, is not a maladaptively extreme variant of normal Introversion. It is qualitatively different from normal Introversion, and is instead a characterologic variant of a broad spectrum of schizophrenic pathology.

One of the more difficult and controversial Axis II versus Axis I differentiations is avoidant personality disorder versus generalized social phobia (Widiger et al., 1995). Social phobia was a narrowly defined condition in DSM-III (APA, 1980), consistent with the definition of a phobia as being an "irrational fear of a specific object, activity, or situation" (APA, 1994, p. 770). However, many of the persons seeking treatment for social phobia displayed a pervasive and chronic social inhibition (Spitzer & Williams, 1985). A generalized subtype of social phobia was therefore included in DSM-III-R (APA, 1987), but the symptomatology for generalized social phobia is almost identical to the symptomatology for avoidant personality disorder (central to both are feelings of timidity, inhibition, insecurity, anxiousness, and shyness). Most persons who meet the diagnostic criteria for one of the two disorders will meet the criteria for the other. Anxiety disorder specialists, however, have argued that it is most accurate to consider persons meeting the diagnostic criteria for avoidant personality disorder as having an anxiety disorder because the symptoms do lessen in response to pharmacologic interventions commonly used to treat anxiety disorders. "One may have to rethink what the personality disorder concept means in an instance where 6 weeks of phenelzine therapy begins to reverse long-standing interpersonal hypersensitivity as well as discomfort in socializing" (Liebowitz, 1992, p. 251). However, beginning to reverse a condition is not actually curing a pathology, and being this mildly responsive to neurochemical interventions is not inconsistent with the presence of a personality trait (Widiger et al., 1995). In any case, given the lack of clarity regarding the differentiation of avoidant personality disorder from generalized social phobia, it might not be meaningful to consider or research the contribution of avoidant traits to the development of this mental disorder.

Even some normal personality traits might be considered on a spectrum with Axis I mental disorders. Two of the facets of the Neuroticism domain of normal personality functioning identified by McCrae and Costa (1990) are depression and anxiety. NEO-PI-R depression "measures normal individual differences in the tendency to experience depressive affect" (Costa & McCrae, 1992, p. 16). However, "high scorers are prone to feelings of guilt, sadness, hopelessness, and loneliness" (Costa & McCrae, 1992, p. 16), many of whom might be diagnosed with the mood disorder of early onset dysthymia in DSM-IV (APA, 1994, pp. 349, 718). Dysthymia was originally considered in DSM-III to be a time-limited condition (APA, 1980), but it was expanded in DSM-III-R (APA, 1987) to include a chronic subtype with an "early and insidious onset" (APA, 1994, p. 347), subsuming what had traditionally been diagnosed as a depressive personality disorder (Phillips, Gunderson, Hirschfeld, & Smith, 1990). As noted in DSM-IV, "it remains controversial whether the distinction between depressive personality disorder and dysthymic disorder is useful" (APA, 1994, p. 732).

An alternative conceptualization of FFM Neuroticism is Negative Affectivity, which is conceptualized as the disposition to experience negative (aversive) emotional states, including anxiety and depression (Clark, Watson, & Mineka, 1994). Clark and colleagues (1994) documented well how "negative affectivity (or Neuroticism) appears to be a vulnerability factor for the development of anxiety and depression" (p. 103). However, the term "vulnerability" can be ambiguous in its meaning. As indicated above, schizotypal personality traits can be said to provide a vulnerability to the development of schizophrenia, but perhaps only in a manner comparable to the vulnerability for an acute psychotic episode provided by the presence of the prodromal phase of schizophrenia. The prodromal and acute phases of schizophrenia are considered by most theorists to be different manifestations of a common pathology (Pinals & Breier, 1997). The acute psychotic phase occurs after the prodromal phase (just as the depressive phase of a bipolar mood disorder might follow a manic phase), but both are considered to be the result of a single, common etiology and pathology. Similarly, depression following a history of depressive Negative Affectivity might represent different phases of the single mood disorder of "double depression" (Gruenberg & Goldstein, 1997) rather than the contribution of personality traits to the development of a mood disorder (Clark et al., 1994).

The distinction between a prodromal phase and a premorbid vulnerability is unclear, at best. Schizotypal personality traits and Negative Affectivity provide a vulnerability for, but are not themselves equivalent to, the neurochemical dysregulation that results in the respective psychotic and mood disorder symptomatology. Not all persons with schizotypal traits and Negative Affectivity develop the respective Axis I disorders (nor does the prodromal phase of schizophrenia always result in the acute psychotic phase, as suggested by the diagnosis of simple schizophrenia; Pinals & Breier, 1997), and many persons with these Axis I disorders will lack the premorbid personality dispositions. Nevertheless, some instances of Negative Affectivity (and schizotypal personality traits) are perhaps appropriately conceptualized as a subthreshold mood disorder (or subthreshold schizophrenic pathology) rather than as a premorbid personality disposition.

ETIOLOGICAL RELATIONSHIPS

One's characteristic way of thinking, feeling, behaving, and relating to others can at times result in or contribute to the development of a mental disorder. And, a severe or chronic mental disorder might in turn contribute to fundamental changes to one's personality (Triebwasser & Shea, 1996). Each of these causal relationships will be discussed in turn.

Causal Effects of Psychopathology on Personality

Personality can change (Heatherton & Weinberger, 1994), for the better and for the worse, and it is conceivable that the experience of having suffered from a severe mental disorder, such as a psychosis or a major depression, might have a fundamental and lasting effect on one's characteristic manner of thinking, feeling, and relating to others. This alteration to personality functioning, often referred to as a "scar" of the Axis I disorder, would not represent simply a direct and continued manifestation of the Axis I pathology (e.g., a residual phase of schizophrenia resulting in schizotypal personality traits) but rather an interaction of the personality traits with the occurrence or experience of the psychopathology (e.g., dependent personality traits resulting from an experience of recurrent panic attacks or psychotic episodes).

The ICD-10 (World Health Organization, 1992) includes a number of mental disorder diagnoses that recognize maladaptive changes to personality functioning, including enduring personality change secondary to a catastrophic experience, personality change resulting from another mental disorder, and personality change secondary to a physical disorder. However, only the latter diagnosis is recognized by the American Psychiatric Association within DSM-IV (APA, 1994). The APA recognizes the occurrence of changes to personality secondary to a brain injury or a physical disease and even identifies specific variants of such change (i.e., labile, disinhibited, aggressive, apathetic, and paranoid; APA, 1994), but the APA does not recognize changes to personality secondary to severe or sustained psychosocial experiences, including prolonged torture, confinement, or victimization (Shea, 1996) or changes to personality secondary to psychopathology (Triebwasser & Shea, 1996).

The reluctance of the American Psychiatric Association to recognize the potential existence of changes to personality resulting from experiences of psychopathology is perhaps understandable, as there is little empirical research to document the reliability or validity of such personality change (e.g., Rohde, Lewinsohn, & Seeley, 1990; Surtees & Wainwright, 1996). For example, it would be difficult, if not impossible, to distinguish meaningfully between a postmorbid schizotypal personality disorder from a residual phase of schizophrenia or to distinguish between dependent personality traits from the agoraphobic sequelae of panic disorder (Widiger et al., 1995).

Shea and colleagues (1996) attempted to document the occurrence of lasting personality changes resulting from episodes of major depression using a subset of the data provided by the longitudinal National Institute of Mental Health (NIMH) Collaborative Program on the Psychobiology of Depression. Their pool of subjects were 556 persons who had no prior or current mental disorder at the time of intake into the study and who were subsequently reassessed 6 years later. Twenty-eight of these persons suffered their first episodes of major depression during the 6-year period. However, "none of the scales for which negative change would be predicted by the scar hypothesis (increased neuroticism, emotional reliance, and lack of social self-confidence; decreased ascendance/dominance, sociability, and extroversion) showed such change" (Shea et al., 1996, p. 1409). The personality scale scores remained largely stable across the 6 years. These findings are in one sense good news for the validity of personality assessment, as they document the stability of test scores across a substantial period of time and across episodes of a severe mental disorder, but they were perhaps bad news for the scar hypothesis.

Shea and colleagues (1996) did indicate that premorbid personality differences were obtained between persons who did or did not eventually become depressed. "Subjects with an episode of major depression during the interval had higher levels of thoughtfulness and, particularly, neuroticism than those remaining well during the interval" (p. 1409). Shea and colleagues concluded that the "the findings overall are more consistent with the vulnerability hypothesis, i.e., that such personality traits may be a risk factor for onset of major depression" (p. 1409). This conclusion is somewhat ironic because, as we will indicate below, these researchers were largely unsuccessful in confirming the vulnerability hypothesis when they analyzed these data with this hypothesis in mind.

Causal Effects of Personality on Psychopathology

> Why do some people collapse under life stresses while others seem unscathed by traumatic circumstances such as severe illness, the death of loved ones, and extreme poverty, or even by major catastrophes such as natural disasters and war? Surprisingly large numbers of people mature into normal, successful adults despite stressful, disadvantaged, or even abusive childhoods. Yet other people are so emotionally vulnerable that seemingly minor losses and rebuffs can be devastating—sometimes even precipitating severe mental disorder. (Basic Behavioral Science Task Force of the National Advisory Mental Health Council, 1996, p. 22)

The contribution of personality to the development of psychopathology has always been of central theoretical and clinical importance (Maher & Maher, 1994). There is little doubt that one's characteristic manner of thinking, feeling, behaving, and relating to others can contribute to the development of a variety of mental disorders. Dependent personality traits can contribute to episodes of major depression (Bowlby, 1980; Bornstein, 1993), Neuroticism to the development of a somatoform disorder (Kirmayer, Robbins, & Paris, 1994), antisocial traits to the development of substance use disorders (Brink, 1995; Sher & Trull, 1994; Verheul et al., 1997), absorption to the development of dissociative disorders (Kihlstrom, Glisky, & Angiulo, 1994), and borderline personality traits to the development of a wide variety of Axis I mental disorders, including eating, mood, impulse dyscontrol, dissociative, and mood disorders (Widiger & Trull, 1993).

Neuroticism is a broad domain of personality functioning that provides an important although nonspecific contribution to the development of a wide variety of Axis I mental disorders. Neuroticism is a person's characteristic level of emotional instability. Persons who are high in Neuroticism will feel self-conscious, anxious, depressed, and vulnerable across a wide variety of stressful and even unstressful situations (Costa & McCrae, 1992). They are prone to develop, and are often stricken with, painful and troubling feelings of guilt, remorse, fear, sadness, anger, or embarrassment (Clark et al., 1994). They lack the emotional strength to simply ignore the hassles of everyday life, and the emotional resilience to overcome the more severe traumas that are perhaps inevitable at some point within most persons' lives (Roberts & Monroe, 1994). Which particular mental disorder they develop may be due in part to other contributing variables (e.g., gender, social–cultural context, childhood experiences, genetic vulnerabilities, and additional personality traits) that either direct the person toward a preferred method of coping (e.g., bulimic, dissociative, or substance use behavior) or reflect an additional vulnerability (e.g., for a sexual dysfunction, sleep, or somatoform disorder).

One might also observe as a clinician instances in which a specific constellation of personality traits appears to play a central role in the development of a mental disorder, either through the creation of, or the inability to respond adequately to, stressful life events (Wachtel, 1994). For example, a major depressive disorder will at times be due in large part to maladaptive dependent personality traits (Bowlby, 1980; Bornstein, 1993). The self-esteem of a person with a dependent personality disorder will depend substantially on the maintenance of a supportive and nurturant relationship (Hamilton & Jensvold, 1992), but the intense needs for reassurance can also have the paradoxical effect of driving the needed person away. The dependent person's worst fears are then realized (i.e., he or she is abandoned and alone), and his or her sense of self-worth, meaning, or value will be further injured, perhaps even crushed by the rejection. The dependent person might then indiscriminately select a readily available but unreliable, undependable, and perhaps even abusive person simply to be with someone. This partner would again reaffirm the worst fears through the abuse, derogation, and denigration (i.e., conveying to the dependent person that he or she is indeed undesirable and unlovable and that the relationship is indeed tenuous).

However, documenting empirically the contribution of personality to the development of psychopathology has been difficult, to say the least. The contribution of personality to the development of psychopathology is neither certain nor specific. Many dependent persons will fail to develop a major depression, most instances of major depression will be independent of dependent personality traits, and many instances of major depression in persons with dependent personality traits will even fail to be due primarily to these traits. Very few, if any, of the Axis I mental disorders may have any specific etiology. The development of psychopathology in most cases appears to be multifactorial and interactive over time, with maladaptive personality traits providing only one possible (but nevertheless at times important) contribution.

Illustrative Negative Research Findings

There have been many failures to confirm empirically expectations regarding the contribution of personality traits to the development of psychopathology (e.g., Schuckit, Klein, Twitchell, & Smith, 1994). One of the fundamental problems has at times been a difficulty documenting even the presence of a trait disposition in the absence of the disorder, or at least its predictive validity in the absence of a concurrent psychopathology (Coyne & Gotlib, 1986; Roberts & Monroe, 1994; Widiger, 1993). One response to this failure has been to argue that the traits are state-dependent, lying dormant until they are primed or triggered by a stressor or a depressed mood (e.g., Miranda, Persons, & Byers, 1990; Teasdale, 1988). However, this might be a somewhat weak or vulnerable response to the negative findings. Personality traits need not be evident across all situations, but perhaps they should be evident independently of the mood states for which they are purportedly etiologic. Such latent personality traits are comparable to suggesting that there is a personality disorder that contributes to the etiology of a mood disorder, but it's evident only after the mood disorder has developed.

Some of the failures to document the etiological significance of personality traits can be attributed to specific methodological limitations of a particular study (e.g., small sample sizes and weakly relevant constructs, as in Schuckit et al., 1994). However, any researcher considering the implementation of a research program on personality and psychopathology should consider the programmatic efforts of Hirschfeld and his colleagues to identify personality traits that may predispose a person to depression (i.e., Hirschfeld & Klerman, 1979; Hirschfeld, Klerman, Andreasen, Clayton, & Keller, 1986a; Hirschfeld, Klerman, Clayton, & Keller, 1983a; Hirschfeld, Klerman, Clayton, Keller, McDonald-Scott, & Larkin, 1983b; Hirschfeld, Klerman, Keller, Andreasen, & Clayton, 1986b; Hirschfeld, Klerman, Lavori, Keller, Griffith, & Coryell, 1989). The reader may find the methodological details regarding this series of studies to be laborious, but it is in the details that the important ambiguities of this research are to be understood and appreciated.

In their first study, Hirschfeld and Klerman (1979) administered self-report personality inventories to 119 depressed inpatients near the time of their hospital discharge. To control for pathoplastic mood state distortions, the patients were instructed explicitly to disregard their current state and to answer the questions according to their usual self. The patients' scores were significantly higher than the published norms on the Neuroticism, Introversion, and Obsessionality scales. To further address possible pathoplastic effects, Hirschfeld and Klerman readministered the scales 2 years later to all of the persons who were by then asymptomatic. The personality inventory scores had changed but not to a degree that was statistically significant. Hirschfeld and Klerman (1979) concluded that "there are abnormalities in the personalities of patients with affective disorders" (p. 69) and, more specifically, that "the depressive is introverted, lacking in self-confidence, unassertive, dependent, pessimistic, and perceives himself or herself as inadequate" (p. 70). However, it was perhaps noteworthy that only 15 persons qualified for the subsequent retesting two years later, providing not only perhaps inadequate statistical power to identify changes in test scores but also suggesting that most of the original 119 subjects had in fact been depressed at the time of the original personality assessments.

Hirschfeld and colleauges (1983a) next compared (1) 23 female patients who had fully recovered from a major depression for at least two weeks, (2) 134 female relatives who had experienced a major depressive episode but had now fully recovered, and (3) 272 female relatives with no history of any (assessed) mental disorder (i.e., never-ill). The Neuroticism scores for the two recovered groups were (1) significantly higher than the scores for the never-ill relatives and (2) comparable to published norms. Hirschfeld and colleagues concluded that these findings were consistent with prior studies that indicated that Neuroticism scores of recovered patients tend to be within normal limits, suggesting perhaps that the elevated Neuroticism scores reported previously by Hirschfeld and Klerman (1979) may have been a pathoplastic artifact of a depressed mood. However, the recovered patients did obtain significantly higher scores than the published norms and the never-ill relatives on the self-report measures of Introversion and Dependency. Hirschfeld and colleagues (1983a) therefore concluded that "social introversion [is] the most powerful personality characteristic associated with primary nonbipolar depression. Increased interpersonal dependency is a modest second factor" (p. 997).

However, Hirschfeld and colleagues (1983b) compared in that same year the self-report test results of 88 patients who were suffering from a major depression at the time of the original assessment with their scores at 1-year follow-up, either fully recovered ($N = 40$) or unrecovered ($N = 48$). Neuroticism, Dependency, and Introversion scores decreased for the recovered patients but not for the unrecovered. Hirschfeld and colleagues (1983b) therefore concluded that "assessments of emotional strength and interpersonal dependency reflect the clinical state of depression rather than enduring personality traits" (p. 698).

Hirschfeld and colleagues (1986a) subsequently compared personality scale scores for 19 pairs of chronic and recovered depressed patients matched on age, sex, prior duration of episode, and primary versus secondary status of depression. The chronic group had been depressed throughout a 2-year period, whereas the recovered had recovered fully within the first year and had remained recovered for the duration of a second year. The chronic group obtained significantly higher Neuroticism scores than the recovered; no differences were obtained for Dependency or Introversion. Hirschfeld and colleagues concluded that premorbid Neuroticism traits contribute to the chronicity of a subsequent depressive episode (i.e., pathoplastic effect of personality on the chronicity of a mental disorder). However, they acknowledged that the findings could reflect instead pathoplastic effects of the chronic depression on personality (or at least its self-description), or "perhaps the personality differences between the two groups . . . are exaggerations of pre-morbid differences" (p. 652).

Hirschfeld and colleagues (1986b) also compared during that year the personality trait scores of 45 recovered bipolar mood disorder patients, 78 recovered unipolar depressives, 1,172 never-ill family members, and population norms. The recovered subjects were considered to be fully recovered, exhibiting no symptoms of an affective disorder for at least 8 weeks. The recovered groups obtained Neuroticism scores that were comparable to published norms but were also significantly higher than those obtained by the never-ill group, consistent with the prior findings of Hirschfeld and colleagues (1983a). However, this time Hirschfeld and colleagues (1986b) concluded that the lower scores obtained by the never-ill group (which in both studies were significantly lower than the published norms) reflected a protective factor. In other words, being statistically normal in Neuroticism does not necessarily mean being psychologically healthy. Never-ill groups are perhaps more psychologically normal (i.e., healthy or without psychopathology) than statistically normal (i.e., normal or average but unhealthy). Hirschfeld and colleagues (1986b) concluded that both the unipolar and bipolar "groups are less emotionally strong, more introverted, and more interpersonally dependent than people who have never been mentally ill" (p. 88).

However, Hirschfeld and colleagues (1989) were subsequently able to report the results of a follow-up study of 399 initially never-ill subjects, 29 of whom experienced an episode of major depression within 6 years after the initial personality assessments. The initial personality scale scores of these 29 first-onset subjects were not significantly different from the scores obtained by the other never-ill subjects on the Introversion or Dependency scales. In addition, the scores for the never-ill and first-onset groups were significantly lower than the scores the authors had obtained in their prior studies of fully recovered patients. "When we began our investigations on personality and depression, we believed that personality assessments would be performed that would accurately reflect premorbid levels. We were mistaken" (p. 350). They now suggested that the elevated scores on measures of Introversion and Dependency that they had previously obtained were the etiological result of the experience of depression. "Our results strongly suggest that the experience of depression does adversely affect personality. The recovered patients in general were much less emotionally strong, were more neurotic, were more interpersonally dependent, were more introverted, and were less active" (p. 350).

However, the first-onset subjects did obtain significantly higher scores on measures of Neuroticism. Hirschfeld and colleagues (1989) therefore concluded that "the personality features most predictive of first onset were those indicating decreased emotional strength, such as emotional stability and less ability to react to stressful situations" (p. 348). Nevertheless, they were disappointed to find that they were unable to confirm their prior conclusions (Hirschfeld et al., 1983a) that Introversion and Dependency were more specifically predictive of an onset of depression than Neuroticism, and they were not particularly enamored by the findings for Neuroticism. "The personality features found to be predictive of first onset major depression do not have well-established theoretical relevance to depression. . . . Rather, they appear to serve as nonspecific vulnerability factors" (p. 348). They even questioned whether the elevated scores on the Neuroticism scales represented premorbid dispositions. "Some of them may in fact reflect subsyndromal affective states in the process of becoming syndromal" (p. 350). In other words, the elevated scores on Neuroticism in persons who eventually became depressed may reflect a spectrum relationship rather than a causal relationship.

> This raises the difficult question of what premorbidity really means. Since subsyndromal states are likely to be long-lasting, how can these states be separated conceptually and operationally from abnormalities of personality? Do individuals have abnormal personality features (personality disorders, perhaps) or do they have chronic (subsyndromal)

affective states? Does it make any difference? At this point we have no answer to these vexing problems. (Hirschfeld et al., 1989, p. 350)

The findings of the Hirschfeld research program to identify a premorbid personality vulnerability are generally disappointing, although there were perhaps fundamental limitations to their prodigious effort. For example, Hirschfeld and colleagues (1989) were attempting to predict the onset of a major depressive episode in biological relatives of persons with major depression who had not previously suffered from a depressive episode. The potential effects of this restriction in sampling are unclear, but it is possible that the sampling weighted the study in favor of identifying depressive episodes with a substantial biogenetic rather than psychosocial etiology (Widiger & Trull, 1992). Sampling persons with a history of major depressive episodes can have the effect of confusing the results with chronic or residual effects of depression, but excluding these persons may also confine the study precisely to persons who are unlikely to have premorbid personality vulnerabilities. Simply because a person has a history of major depressive episodes does not necessarily mean that everything of psychological significance that occurs thereafter is a residual effect of the mood disorder(s). A history of major depressive episodes does increase the likelihood of lasting scars and pathoplastic contaminations, but excluding persons with a history of depressive episodes may also eliminate from the study the very persons who are vulnerable to episodes of depression due to their personality dispositions. It is perhaps contradictory to attempt to identify a vulnerability only in never-ill persons who share the one feature of having so far repeatedly failed to demonstrate this vulnerability. As indicated by Hirschfeld and colleagues (1986b), never-ill persons tend to be low in Neuroticism and other maladaptive personality traits. When they do become depressed, their depression is perhaps then less likely to be secondary to maladaptive personality traits.

Illustrative Positive Research Findings

There have also been many studies that have obtained findings consistent with the hypothesis that maladaptive personality traits provide a vulnerability to the development of psychopathology. Trull and Sher (1994) assessed the relationship of the five broad domains of the FFM with a wide variety of Axis I mental disorders in a nonclinical sample of 468 young adults. This was "the first study to employ a comprehensive assessment of personality and a [relatively more] comprehensive assessment of mental disorders" (Krueger, Caspi, Moffitt, Silva, & McGee, 1996, p. 299). Lifetime rates of substance use disorders (alcohol, drug, and nicotine), anxiety disorder (simple phobia, social phobia, posttraumatic stress, agoraphobia, generalized anxiety, and panic disorder) and major depression were considered. The five domains of the FFM were asssessed by the NEO-Five Factor Inventory (NEO-FFI; Costa & McCrae, 1992). "NEO-FFI scores provided a significant increment in model fit over and above that provided by gender and by the 10 BSI symptom scales . . . in all cases except simple phobia" (p. 357). Neuroticism was especially predictive of a history of any anxiety disorder (particularly posttraumatic stress disorder), whereas "neuroticism and [introversion] scale scores were significantly more sensitive to the social phobia diagnosis" (p. 358). Canonical correlation analyses indicated that "low neuroticism, low agreeableness, low conscientiousness, and high extraversion scores [i.e., the FFM description of psychopathy; Widiger & Lynam, 1998] characterize a nondepressed substance use dimension" (p. 358).

Trull and Sher (1994) acknowledged that "because our study is cross-sectional in nature, cause–effect inferences regarding personality and Axis I psychopathology are not possible" (p. 359). This was partly addressed in a subsequent study by Krueger and colleagues (1996). Krueger and colleagues assessed Axis I disorders in approximately 1,000 persons at ages 15, 18, and 21. These individuals had been given a self-report personality questionnaire at age 18. Multiple regression analyses, in which all of the personality scales were used to predict Axis I symptoms at ages 15, 18, and 21 indicated substantial consistency in postdictive, concurrent, and predictive validity. For example, "specifically, and in concert with Trull and Sher's (1994) findings . . . our participants with substance dependence disorder were higher on Stress Reaction and Aggression, and lower on Control, Traditionalism, and Communion" (Krueger et al., 1996, pp. 309–310). Krueger and colleagues also controlled for the substantial comorbidity among Axis I disorders. "When those with pure substance dependency were examined relative to controls, their higher Alienation and Aggression and their lower Control and Traditionalism could be seen clearly" (p. 310). The higher negative emotionality of the persons with substance use disorder appeared to be due primarily to comorbid anxiety and depressive disorders. Substance use disorder, by itself, was more specifically related to a constellation of personality traits "parallel to empirical accounts of the criminal [psychopathic] personality" (p. 310).

Johnson and colleagues (1996) provided the results of a 3-year, prospective longitudinal study of the physical and psychological functioning of 107 HIV-seropositive and HIV-seronegative homosexual men. Baseline assessments included personality disorder symptomatology (assessed with a semistructured interview), current and lifetime Axis I symptomatology, and overall level of functioning. The personality disorder symptomatology of these men was predominated by the avoidant, obsessive–compulsive, and self-defeating personality disorders. They were periodically reassessed for Axis I symptoms every 6 months. Johnson and colleagues (1996) reported that the presence of a personality disorder predicted the onset of a future Axis I disorder and future psychological impairment even after controlling for HIV status and a history of Axis I disorders. "These [were] the first published findings to demonstrate that persons in the community with personality disorders are at risk of onset of future Axis I disorders and serious impairment, whether or not they have had prior Axis I disorders" (Johnson et al., 1996, p. 355). Johnson and colleagues suggested that the results argued for systematic public health attention to the presence of maladaptive personality traits, given their substantial prevalence within the community and their contribution to the development of additional psychopathology.

Alnaes and Torgersen (1997) reported the results of a 6-year, prospective follow-up study of 284 psychiatric outpatients diagnosed at intake with both self-report inventories and semistructured interviews. The assessments included all of the DSM-III personality disorders (APA, 1980) and many additional personality traits. "Borderline personality disorders [which relate closely to FFM neuroticism; Widiger & Costa, 1994] and dependency personality traits predicted relapses of major depression" (Alnaes & Torgersen, 1997, p. 340), and "both borderline and avoidant personality disorder predicted the development of new cases of major depression" (p. 341). Alnaes and Torgersen compared the predictive validity of the borderline personality disorder diagnosis to a history of major depression and indicated "that the existence of a borderline personality disorder is a better predictor of future major depression than major depression itself" (p. 341). They suggested that "the existence of personality disorders may lead to negative life events which in turn contribute to the development of depression [in] individuals with personality disorders [due to their] unfavorable coping style" (p. 341).

Trull, Useda, Conforti, and Doan (1997) reported the initial results of a longitudinal study of forme fruste cases of borderline personality disorder. Trull and colleagues identified from a sample of 1,700 college students persons who presented with a sufficient number of borderline personality traits (i.e., B+ cases) to consider them to represent potentially premorbid cases. "These initial studies . . . mark an important step in identifying young adults with significant levels of borderline features who may go on to experience significant dysfunction in later years" (Trull et al., 1997, p. 308). The 35 B+ cases did indeed report a wide range of dysfunction over the 2-year follow-up period, even after controlling for such mediating variables as gender and history of Axis I disorder. The diversity of negative outcomes (e.g., dysphoria, substance use, and academic difficulties) was again consistent with the FFM conceptualization of borderline traits as being extreme Neuroticism. Trull and colleagues (1997) concluded that borderline personality traits "are associated with more negative outcome even among nonclinical young adults" (p. 313).

Kendler, Neale, Kessler, Heath, and Eaves (1993) assessed the contribution of personality to the onset of major depression in women within a longitudinal twin study. Participants included 2,035 female twins who completed personality tests at two times, separated by 12 months. The authors observed substantial pathoplastic and scar effects on the personality trait assessments but addressed these confounds through a statistical modeling that took advantage of the twin and longitudinal structure of the data. "We found that controlling for a twin's current or lifetime history of major depression, her level of neuroticism was strongly predicted by her cotwin's history of major depression" (p. 860). The authors suggested that Neuroticism did provide a disposition toward the development of a major depressive episode but it reflected an underlying liability shared with the eventual depression. "In women, the relationship between neuroticism and the liability to major depression is substantial" (p. 853). However, "the causal effect of neuroticism on the liability to major depression is entirely mediated through the genetic and environmental risk factors common to both traits" (p. 861). This spectrum relationship is perhaps not surprising, given the phenomenology of Neuroticism (Clark et al., 1994) and its nonspecific contribution to psychopathology. However, the findings of Kendler and colleagues might also be qualified by the confinement of the vulnerability to major depression within only a 1-year duration in persons with no history of major depression.

Two of the more heavily researched personality dispositions for depressive episodes are sociotropy (or dependency) and self-criticism (or narcissistic autonomy) in response to congruent stressors (Beck, 1983; Blatt & Zuroff, 1992; Clark et al., 1994). Sociotropic (dependent) individuals are predicted to become depressed in response to relationship failures (e.g., separation or loss), whereas self-critical persons become depressed in response to achievement failures. The sociotropy and self-criticism hypotheses are intriguing in their effort to align different personality dispositions with different environmental stressors, although the findings have not always been supportive (Coyne & Whiffen, 1995) and their predictive validity may involve whatever common variance they share with the global vulnerabilities of Neuroticism (Mongrain, 1993; Zuroff, 1994).

Hammen and colleagues (1995) obtained 6-month and 12-month follow-up assessments of 129 high school senior women. They conducted multiple regression analyses to predict depression on the basis of dependency cognitions, prior interpersonal stress, and the interaction between them, controlling for initial levels of depression. All of the young women experienced stressful life events during this period of their lives, including moving away from home, separation from an important relationship, and loss of a romantic partner, but most of them did not become depressed. "It was the women with cognitions about relationships representing concerns about rejection or untrustworthiness of others who were especially challenged by normative changes" (p. 441). Hammen and colleagues concluded that "overall, the results suggest that dysfunctional attachment cognitions contribute to both onset and severity of symptomatology" (p. 441).

Segal, Shaw, and Katz (1992) reported findings from a longitudinal study of 59 remitted depressed patients. Approximately half of these patients suffered a relapse within 6 months of the remission. Segal and colleagues indicated that the interaction between the number of negative achievement events and autonomy/self-criticism scores was predictive of this relapse. "Even when the number of prior depressive episodes was first allowed to capture variance in predicting relapse, the interaction between self-critical characteristics and achievement events significantly augmented the amount of variance accounted for" (Segal et al., 1992, p. 32). They indicated that "the inclusion of a competing predictor variable allowed for a more rigorous demonstration that psychological factors can yield an increment in knowledge about depression vulnerability, beyond the established psychiatric markers such as past history, age of onset, family history, and so forth" (p. 32).

Pathoplastic and spectrum relationships, however, have also been problematic to the sociotropy and self-criticism research (Clark et al., 1994). A particularly thorough critique of this research was provided by Coyne and Whiffen (1995). One of their more intriguing concerns was that the personality dispositions may reflect chronic situational stressors. They noted how some self-report measures of personality traits included items that concerned recent or ongoing situations or relationships in which the person was functioning. "Intimate relationships that are insecure or have an uncertain future may engender dependency and reassurance seeking" (Coyne & Whiffen, 1995, p. 367). Women tend to obtain higher scores than males on dependency scales, and Coyne and Whiffen suggest that their feelings of insecurity may say less about themselves than the males with whom they are involved. "Men and women may differ in what they seek from relationships, but they may also differ in what they provide to each other" (p. 368). In other words, women might appear (and be) less dependent if they weren't involved with such undependable men.

The emphasis given to situational contexts by Coyne and Whiffen (1995), however, is somewhat ironic, given that it was Coyne (1976) who was one of the first researchers to indicate that it was an excessive neediness and dependency of persons that often provoked the feared rejection. Depressed and dependent women will indeed at times contribute to the occurrence and perpetuation of stressful life events (Hammen, 1992). "Dysfunctional interpersonal beliefs may lead not only to emotional reactions, but also to maladaptive behaviors—potentially contributing to a self-fulfilling or self-perpetuating process" (Hammen et al., 1995, p. 442).

The final series of studies, by Roberts and his colleagues, is particularly useful in illustrating difficulties in distinguishing an affectivity spectrum from a personality disposition. Roberts and Monroe (1992) administered a measure of self-esteem to 192 college students 3 days a week for 3 weeks. They found that trait-level self-esteem (aggregated across the nine assessments) did not predict depressive reactions following a stressor that occurred 1 week after the final assessment. However, variability (lability) in self-esteem was a significant predictor, particularly in persons who were initially asymptomatic. Roberts and Moore suggested that it is the uncertainty or instability in self-image or self-worth that makes a person vulnerable to threats to self-esteem. Persons who are characteristically low in self-esteem might be as unresponsive to threats to self-esteem as persons who are characteristically high in self-esteem. Their findings were replicated subsequently by Butler, Hokanson, and Flynn (1994) and Roberts and Gotlib (1997).

Roberts and colleagues rejected the suggestion that they were simply assessing affective instability that at times increases in intensity during periods of stress because instability in mood was not as predictive of reactions to stress as instability in self-esteem. "Difficulties in maintaining a stable self-view from day to day, rather than moodiness, are associated with risk for developing depressive symptoms among nonclinical women" (Roberts & Gotlib, 1997, p. 527). Nevertheless, variability in self-esteem was correlated with variability in mood (Roberts & Gotlib, 1997), and the predictive validity of variability in self-esteem was particularly evident in persons with a prior history of severe episodes of depression (Butler et al., 1994; Roberts & Gotlib, 1997). Roberts and Gotlib (1997), however, argued that the prior history of severe depressions was problematic only for the construct of affective lability, which they suggested was simply a complication or scar of the prior history of depression: "Affective variability [does] not appear to increase the risk for developing future depressive symptomatology; instead, [it seems] to result in part from the experience of previous episodes" (p. 527).

Affective instability, however, has itself been conceptualized as a personality construct. One of the DSM-IV diagnostic criteria for borderline personality disorder is "affective instability due to a marked reactivity of mood (i.e., intense episodic dysphoria, irritability, or anxiety usually lasting a few hours and only rarely more than a few days)" (APA, 1994, p. 654), along with the "unstable self-image or sense of sense" (APA, 1994, p. 654) studied by Roberts and Gotlib (1997). A classic description of borderline personality is a stability (consistency) of the instability in identity, mood, and relationships. Roberts and Gotlib have perhaps provided an operational measure of and validity for this instability in self-image.

Borderline personality disorder is also closely related to the personality constructs of Negative Affectivity (Clark, 1994) and Neuroticism (Widiger et al., 1994). Nevertheless, Roberts and Gotlib (1997) also distinguished instability in self-image from Negative Affectivity and Neuroticism: "Because neuroticism and variability in [depressive affect and negative affect] were not found to be prospective predictors of depressive symptoms, our data are more consistent with the possibility that these factors are consequences, or 'scars,' of previous episodes rather than vulnerability factors for future depressive symptoms" (p. 527). Roberts and Gotlib may have been arguing for the incremental or specific predictive validity of instability in self-esteem, but they also appear to be suggesting that this instability in self-esteem is neither an affective nor a personality construct.

CONCLUSIONS

One basic observation of the research on the relationship of personality and psychopathology is its vibrancy. All aspects of the various relationships between personality and psychopathology (pathoplastic, spectrum, and causal) are the focus of a number of highly productive, sophisticated, and informed research programs. Disentangling the forms of relationship from one another, however, has proven to be a formidable task. Cross-sectional studies can and do provide quite informative results (e.g., Ball et al., 1997; Nestadt, Romanski, Samuels, Folstein, & McHugh, 1992; Trull & Sher, 1994), but it is also evident that the most telling findings will be obtained from longitudinal studies. Personality and psychopathology affect and alter one another over time in a complex, unfolding interaction (Wachtel, 1994). Of particular interest will be prospective studies of persons with a particular personality disposition that begin at the time of the onset of the disposition (e.g., Hammen et al., 1995; Roberts & Gotlib, 1997; Trull et al., 1997). Many vulnerability studies have used samples of convenience (e.g., persons already in treatment for the respective disorder) for which the differentiation among pathoplastic, spectrum, and causal relationships may be impossible to disentangle. Entrance into the causal sequence after a significant amount of time has passed and a significant amount of interaction between personality, psychopathology, and life events has already occurred, does appear to complicate substantially the interpretation of a study's findings, particularly if the persons have already had a history of suffering from the pathologies of interest. One approach to addressing this problem has been to exclude persons with any history of the respective pathology, but this exclusion can eliminate the very persons for whom the personality disposition would be most relevant.

It may also be important to track closely the unfolding interaction of the personality traits, events, and pathologies. Minute-by-minute studies would clearly be an overkill, but year-by-year and perhaps even month-by-month prospective studies may at times become essentially retrospective studies as the researchers attempt to disentangle the interactions that occurred sometime during the past 6 or 12 months. A substantial amount of interaction and influence between a personality trait, a life event, and an episode of psychopathology can occur even within just 1 day. Their interactive influence upon one another will become increasingly difficult to understand and disentangle as each day passes. The contribution of personality to mood and environment, and the contribution of mood and environment to personality, will interact and accumulate over time, perhaps to the point in some cases that it may no longer be particularly meaningful to distinguish between them. Any particular cross-sectional period of time may only represent an arbitrary and unrepresentative slice along a continuously interacting and mutually reaffirming sequence of events.

REFERENCES

Alnaes, R., & Torgersen, S. (1997). Personality and personality disorders predict development and relapses of major depression. *Acta Psychiatrica Scandinavica, 95,* 336–342.

American Psychiatric Association. (1980). *Diagnostic and statistical manual of mental disorders* (3rd ed.). Washington, DC: Author.

American Psychiatric Association. (1987). *Diagnostic and statistical manual of mental disorders* (3rd ed., rev.). Washington, DC: Author.

American Psychiatric Association. (1994). *Diagnostic and statistical manual of mental disorders* (4th ed.). Washington, DC: Author.

Axelrod, S. R., Widiger, T. A., Trull, T. J., & Corbitt, E. M. (1997). Relationships of five-factor model antagonism facets with personality disorder symptomatology. *Journal of Personality Assessment, 67,* 297–313.

Bagby, R. M., Joffe, R. T., Parker, J. D. A., Kalemba, V., & Harkness, K. L. (1995). Major depression and the five-factor model of personality. *Journal of Personality Disorders, 9,* 224–234.

Ball, S. A., Tennen, H., Poling, J. C., Kranzler, H. R., & Rounsaville, B. J. (1997). Personality, temperament, and character dimensions and the DSM-IV personality disorders in substance abusers. *Journal of Abnormal Psychology, 106,* 545–553.

Basic Behavioral Science Task Force of the National Advisory Mental Health Council. (1996). Basic behavioral science research for mental health: Vulnerability and resilience. *American Psychologist, 51,* 22–28.

Beck, A. T. (1983). Cognitive therapy of depression: New perspectives. In P. J. Clayton & J. E. Barrett (Eds.), *Treatment of depression: Old controversies and new approaches* (pp. 265–290). NY: Raven Press.

Blatt, S. J., Quinlan, D. M., Pilkonis, P. A., & Shea, M. T. (1995). Impact of perfectionism and need for approval on the brief treatment of depression: The National Institute of Mental Health Treatment of Depression Collaborative Research Program revisited. *Journal of Consulting and Clinical Psychology, 63,* 125–132.

Blatt, S. J., & Zuroff, D. (1992). Interpersonal relatedness and self-definition: Two prototypes for depression. *Clinical Psychology Review, 12,* 527–562.

Blatt, S. J., Zuroff, D. C., Quinlan, D. M., & Pilkonis, P. A. (1996). Interpersonal factors in brief treatment of depression: Further analyses of the National Institute of Mental Health Treatment of Depression Collaborative Research Program. *Journal of Consulting and Clinical Psychology, 64,* 162–171.

Bornstein, R. F. (1993). *The dependent personality.* New York: Guilford Press.

Bowlby, J. (1980). *Attachment and loss: Vol. 3. Sadness and depression.* Harmondsworth, UK: Penguin.

Brink, W. van den. (1995). Personality and addiction. *European Journal of Addiction Research, 1,* 172–176.

Butler, A. C., Hokanson, J. E., & Flynn, H. A. (1994). A comparison of self-esteem lability and low trait self-esteem as vulnerability factors for depression. *Journal of Personality and Social Psychology, 66,* 166–177.

Cacciola, J. S., Alterman, A. I., Rutherford, M. J., & Snider, E. C. (1995). Treatment response of antisocial substance abusers. *Journal of Nervous and Mental Disease, 183,* 166–171.

Cacciola, J. S., Rutherford, M. J., Alterman, A. I., & Snider, E. C. (1994). An examination of the diagnostic criteria for antisocial personality disorder in substance abusers. *Journal of Nervous and Mental Disease, 182,* 517–523.

Clark, L. A. (1994). *SNAP. Schedule for Nonadaptive and Adaptive Personality: Manual for administration, scoring, and interpretation.* Minneapolis, MN: University of Minnesota Press.

Clark, L. A., & Livesley, W. J. (1994). Two approaches to identifying the dimensions of personality disorder: Convergence on the five-factor model. In P. T. Costa & T. A. Widiger (Eds.), *Personality disorders and the five-factor model of personality* (pp. 261–278). Washington, DC: American Psychological Association.

Clark, L. A., Livesley, W. J., Schroeder, M. L., & Irish, S. L. (1996). Convergence of two systems for assessing specific traits of personality disorder. *Psychological Assessment, 8,* 294–303.

Clark, L. A., Watson, D., & Mineka, S. (1994). Temperament, personality, and the mood and anxiety disorders. *Journal of Abnormal Psychology, 103,* 103–116.

Clark, L. A., Watson, D., & Reynolds, S. (1995). Diagnosis and classification of psychopathology: Challenges to the current system and future directions. *Annual Review of Psychology, 46,* 121–153.

Costa, P. T., & McCrae, R. R. (1992). *Revised NEO Personality Inventory (NEO-PI-R) and NEO Five-Factor Inventory (NEO-FFI): Professional manual.* Odessa, FL: Psychological Assessment Resources.

Coyne, J. C. (1976). Toward an interactional description of depression. *Psychiatry, 39,* 28–40.

Coyne, J. C., & Gotlib, I. H. (1986). Studying the role of cognition in depression: Well-trodden paths and cul-de-sacs. *Cognitive Therapy and Research, 10,* 695–705.

Coyne, J. C., & Whiffen, V. E. (1995). Issues in personality as diathesis for depression: The case of sociotropy–dependency and autonomy–self-criticism. *Psychological Bulletin, 118,* 358–378.

Finn, S. E., & Tonsager, M. E. (1997). Therapeutic effects of providing MMPI-2 test feedback to college students awaiting therapy. *Psychological Assessment, 4,* 278–287.

Frances, A. J. (1980). The DSM-III personality disorders sections: A commentary. *American Journal of Psychiatry, 137,* 1050–1054.

Gruenberg, A. M., & Goldstein, R. D. (1997). Depressive disorders. In A. Tasman, J. Kay, & J. A. Lieberman (Eds.), *Psychiatry* (Vol. 2, 990–1019). Philadelphia: Saunders.

Gunderson, J. G., Links, P. S., & Reich, J. (1991). Competing models of personality disorders. *Journal of Personality Disorders, 5,* 60–68.

Hamilton, J. A., & Jensvold, M. (1992). Personality, psychopathology, and depressions in women. In L. S. Brown & M. Ballou (Eds.), *Personality and psychopathology: Feminist reappraisals* (pp. 116–143). New York: Guilford Press.

Hammen, C. L. (1992). Cognitions and depression: Some thoughts about new directions. *Psychological Inquiry, 3,* 247–250.

Hammen, C. L., Burge, D., Daley, S. E., Davila, J., Paley, B., & Rudolph, K. D. (1995). Interpersonal attachment cognitions and predictions of symptomatic responses to interpersonal stress. *Journal of Abnormal Psychology, 104,* 436–443.

Harkness, A. R., & Lilienfeld, S. O. (1997). Individual differences science for treatment planning: Personality traits. *Psychological Assessment, 9,* 349–360.

Hathaway, S. R., McKinley, J. C., Butcher, J. N., Dahstrom, W. G., Graham, J. R., & Tellegen, A. (1989). *Minnesota Multiphasic Personality Inventory–2 test booklet.* Minneapolis, MN: University of Minnesota Press.

Heatherton, T. F., & Weinberger, J. L. (Eds.). (1994). *Can personality change?* Washington, DC: American Psychological Association.

Hirschfeld, R., & Klerman, G. (1979). Personality attributes and affective disorders. *American Journal of Psychiatry, 136,* 67–70.

Hirschfeld, R., Klerman, G., Andreasen, N., Clayton, P., & Keller, M. (1986a). Psycho-social predictors of chronicity in depressed patients. *British Journal of Psychiatry, 148,* 648–654.

Hirschfeld, R., Klerman, G., Clayton, P., & Keller, M. (1983a). Personality and depression. Empirical findings. *Archives of General Psychiatry, 40,* 993–998.

Hirschfeld, R., Klerman, G., Clayton, P., Keller, M., McDonald-Scott, P., & Larkin, B. (1983b). Assessing personality: Effects of the depressive state on trait measurement. *American Journal of Psychiatry, 140,* 695–699.

Hirschfeld, R., Klerman, G., Keller, M., Andreasen, N., & Clayton, P. (1986b). Personality of recovered patients with bipolar affective disorder. *Journal of Affective Disorders, 11,* 81–89.

Hirschfeld, R., Klerman, G., Lavori, P., Keller, M., Griffith, P., & Coryell, W. (1989). Premorbid personality assessments of first onset of major depression. *Archives of General Psychiatry, 46,* 345–350.

Johnson, J. G., Williams, J. B. W., Goetz, R. R., Rabkin, J. G., Lipsitz, J. D., & Remien, R. H. (1997). Stability and change in personality disorder symptomatology: Findings from a longitudinal study of HIV+ and HIV– men. *Journal of Abnormal Psychology, 106,* 154–158.

Johnson, J. G., Williams, J. B. W., Goetz, R. R., Rabkin, J. G., Remien, R. H., Lipsitz, J. D., & Gorman, J. M. (1996). Personality disorders predict onset of Axis I disorders and impaired functioning among homosexual men with and at risk of HIV infection. *Archives of General Psychiatry, 53,* 350–357.

Kendler, K. S., Neale, M. C., Kessler, R. C., Heath, A. C., & Eaves, L. J. (1993). A longitudinal twin study of personality and major depression in women. *Archives of General Psychiatry, 50,* 853–862.

Kihlstrom, J. F., Glisky, M. L., & Angiulo, M. J. (1994). Dissociative tendencies and dissociative disorders. *Journal of Abnormal Psychology, 103,* 117–124.

Kirmayer, L. J., Robbins, J. M., & Paris, J. (1994). Somatoform disorders: Personality and the social matrix of somatic distress. *Journal of Abnormal Psychology, 103,* 125–136.

Klein, M. H., Wonderlich, S., & Shea, M. T. (1993). Models of relationship between personality and depression: Toward a framework for theory and research. In M. H. Klein, D. J. Kupfer, & M. T. Shea (Eds.), *Personality and depression* (pp. 1–54). New York: Guilford Press.

Krueger, R. F., Caspi, A., Moffitt, T. E., Silva, P. A., & McGee, R. (1996). Personality traits are differentially linked to mental disorders: A multitrait–multidiagnosis study of an adolescent birth cohort. *Journal of Abnormal Psychology, 105,* 299–312.

Liebowitz, M. R. (1992). Diagnostic issues in anxiety disorders. In A. Tasman & M. B. Riba (Eds.), *Review of psychiatry* (Vol. 11, pp. 247–259). Washington, DC: American Psychiatric Press.

Livesley, W. J., Schroeder, M. L., Jackson, D. N., & Jang, K. L. (1994). Categorical distinctions in the study of personality disorder: Implications for classification. *Journal of Abnormal Psychology, 103,* 6–17.

Loranger, A. W. (1988). *The Personality Disorder Examination (PDE) manual.* Yonkers, NY: DV Communications.

Loranger, A. W., Lenzenweger, M. F., Gartner, A. F., Susman, V., Herzig, J., Zammit, G. K., Gartner, J. D., Abrams, R. C., & Young, R. C. (1991). Trait-state artifacts and the diagnosis of personality disorders. *Archives of General Psychiatry, 48,* 720–729.

MacKenzie, K. R. (1994). Using personality measurement in clinical practice. In P. T. Costa & T. A. Widiger (Eds.), *Personality disorders and the five-factor model of personality* (pp. 237–250). Washington, DC: American Psychological Association.

Maher, B. A., & Maher, W. B. (1994). Personality and psychopathology: A historical perspective. *Journal of Abnormal Psychology, 103,* 72–77.

McCrae, R. R. (1996). Social consequences of experiential openness. *Psychological Bulletin, 120,* 323–337.

McCrae, R. R., & Costa, P. T. (1990). *Personality in adulthood.* New York: Guilford Press.

McCusker, C. G., & Brown, K. (1991). The cue-responsivity phenomenon in dependent drinkers: "Personality" vulnerability and anxiety as intervening variables. *British Journal of Addiction, 86,* 905–912.

Meehl, P. E. (1995). Bootstraps taxometrics: Solving the classification problem in psychopathology. *American Psychologist, 50,* 266–275.

Miller, T. R. (1991). The psychotherapeutic utility of the five-factor model of personality: A clinician's experience. *Journal of Personality Assessment, 57,* 415–433.

Millon, T., & Davis, R. (1996). *Disorders of personality: DSM-IV and beyond* (2nd ed.). New York: Wiley.

Millon, T., Millon, C., & Davis, R. (1994). *MCMI-III manual.* Minneapolis, MN: National Computer Systems.

Miranda, J., Persons, J., & Byers, C. (1990). Endorsement of dysfunctional beliefs depends on current mood state. *Journal of Abnormal Psychology, 99,* 237–241.

Moffett, L. A., Steinberg, S. L., & Rohde, P. (1996). Personality assessment of substance-dependent patients in a therapeutic community. *Journal of Substance Abuse Treatment, 13,* 127–134.

Mongrain, M. (1993). Dependency and self-criticism located within the five-factor model of personality. *Personality and Individual Differences, 15,* 455–462.

Nestadt, G., Romanoski, A. J., Samuels, J. F., Folstein, M. F., & McHugh, P. R. (1992). The relationship between personality and DSM-III Axis I disorders in the population: Results from an epidemiological survey. *American Journal of Psychiatry, 149,* 1228–1233.

Newman, M. L., & Greenway, P. (1997). Therapeutic effects of providing feedback to clients at a university counseling service: A collaborative approach. *Psychological Assessment, 9,* 122–131.

O'Connor, B. P., & Dyce, J. A. (1998). A test of models of personality disorder configuration. *Journal of Abnormal Psychology, 107,* 3–16.

Peselow, E. D., Sanfilipo, M. P., & Fieve, R. R. (1994). Patients' and informants' reports of personality traits during and after major depression. *Journal of Abnormal Psychology, 103,* 819–824.

Phillips, K. A., Gunderson, J. G., Hirschfeld, R. M., & Smith, L. (1990). A review of the depressive personality. *American Journal of Psychiatry, 147,* 830–837.

Pinals, D. A., & Breier, A. (1997). Schizophrenia. In A. Tasman, J. Kay, & J. A. Lieberman (Eds.), *Psychiatry* (Vol. 2, pp. 927–965). Philadelphia: Saunders.

Powell, J., Bradley, B., & Gray, J. (1992). Classical conditioning and cognitive determinants of subjective craving for opiates: An investigation of their relative contributions. *British Journal of Psychiatry, 87,* 1133–1137.

Reich, J. H., & Vasile, R. G. (1993). Effect of personality disorders on the treatment outcome of Axis I conditions. An update. *Journal of Nervous and Mental Disease, 181,* 475–484.

Roberts, J. E., & Gotlib, I. H. (1997). Temporal variability in global self-esteem and specific self-evaluation as prospective predictors of emotional distress: Specificity in predictors and outcome. *Journal of Abnormal Psychology, 106,* 521–529.

Roberts, J. E., & Monroe, S. M. (1992). Vulnerable self-esteem and depressive symptoms: prospective findings comparing three alternative conceptualizations. *Journal of Personality and Social Psychology, 62,* 804–812.

Roberts, J. E., & Monroe, S. M. (1994). A multidimensional model of self-esteem in depression. *Clinical Psychology Review, 14,* 161–181.

Robins, C. J., Hayes, A. H., Block, P., Kramer, R. J., & Villena, M. (1995). Interpersonal and achievement concerns and the depressive vulnerability and symptom specificity hypothesis: A prospective study. *Cognitive Therapy and Research, 19,* 1–20.

Rohde, P., Lewinsohn, P. M., & Seeley, J. R. (1990). Are people changed by the experience of having an episode of depression? A further test of the scar hypothesis. *Journal of Abnormal Psychology, 99,* 264–271.

Saucier, G., & Goldberg, L. R. (1996). The language of personality: Lexical perspectives on the five-factor model. In J. S. Wiggins (Ed.), *The five-factor model of personality: Theoretical perspectives* (pp. 21–50). New York: Guilford Press.

Schuckit, M. A., Klein, J., Twitchell, G., & Smith, T. (1994). Personality test scores as predictors of alcoholism almost a decade later. *American Journal of Psychiatry, 151,* 1038–1042.

Segal, Z., Shaw, B., Vella, D., & Katz, R. (1992). Cognitive and life stress predictors of relapse in remitted unipolar depressed patients: Test of the congruency hypothesis. *Journal of Abnormal Psychology, 101,* 26–36.

Shea, M. T. (1996). Enduring personality change after catastrophic experience. In T. A. Widiger, A. J. Frances, H. A Pincus, R. Ross, M. B. First, & W. W. Davis (Eds.), *DSM-IV sourcebook* (Vol. 2, pp. 849–860). Washington, DC: American Psychiatric Association.

Shea, M. T., Leon, A. C., Mueller, T. I., Solomon, D. A., Warshaw, M. G., & Keller, M. B. (1996). Does major depression result in lasting personality change? *American Journal of Psychiatry, 153,* 1404–1410.

Shea, M. T., Widiger, T. A., & Klein, M. H. (1992). Comorbidity of personality disorders and depression: Implications for treatment. *Journal of Consulting and Clinical Psychology, 60,* 857–868.

Sher, K. J., & Trull, T. J. (1994). Personality and disinhibitory psychopathology: Alcoholism and antisocial personality disorder. *Journal of Abnormal Psychology, 103,* 92–102.

Siever, L., & Davis, K. (1991). A psychobiologic perspective on the personality disorders. *American Journal of Psychiatry, 148,* 1647–1658.

Spitzer, R. L., & Williams, J. B. W. (1985). Proposed revisions in the DSM-III classification of anxiety disorders based on research and clinical experience. In A. H. Tuma & J. Maser (Eds.), *Anxiety and the anxiety disorders* (pp. 759–773). Hillsdale, NJ: Erlbaum.

Surtees, P. G., & Wainwright, N. W. J. (1996). Fragile states of mind: Neuroticism, vulnerability and long-term outcome in depression. *British Journal of Psychiatry, 169,* 338–347.

Teasdale, J. D. (1988). Cognitive vulnerability to persistent depression. *Cognition and Emotion, 2,* 247–274.

Triebwasser, J., & Shea, M. T. (1996). Personality change resulting from another mental disorder. In T. A. Widiger, A. J. Frances, H. A. Pincus, R. Ross, M. B. First, & W. W. Davis (Eds.), *DSM-IV sourcebook* (Vol. 2, pp. 861–868). Washington, DC: American Psychiatric Association.

Trull, T. J. (1992). DSM-III-R personality disorders and the five-factor model of personality: An empirical comparison. *Journal of Abnormal Psychology, 101,* 553–560.

Trull, T. J., & Sher, K. J. (1994). Relationship between the five-factor model of personality and Axis I disorders in a nonclinical sample. *Journal of Abnormal Psychology, 103,* 350–360.

Trull, T. J., Useda, D., Conforti, K., & Doan, B-T. (1997). Borderline personality disorder features in nonclinical young adults: 2. Two-year outcome. *Journal of Abnormal Psychology, 106,* 307–314.

Verheul, R., Ball, S. A., & Brink, W. van den (1997). Substance abuse and personality disorders. In H. R. Kranzler & B. J. Rounsaville (Eds.), *Dual diagnosis and treatment: Substance abuse and comorbid medical and psychiatric disorders* (pp. 317–363). New York: Marcel Dekker Press.

Verheul, R., Hartgers, C., Brink, W. van den, & Koeter, M. W. J. (1998). The effect of sampling, diagnostic criteria, and assessment procedures on the observed prevalence of personality disorders among treated alcoholics. *Journal of Studies on Alcohol, 59,* 227–236.

Vitousek, K., & Manke, F. (1994). Personality variables and disorders in anorexia nervosa and bulimia nervosa. *Journal of Abnormal Psychology, 103,* 137–147.

Wachtel, P. L. (1994). Cyclical processes in personality and psychopathology. *Journal of Abnormal Psychology, 103,* 51–54.

Watson, D., & Clark, L. A. (1994). Introduction to the special series on personality and psychopathology. *Journal of Abnormal Psychology, 103,* 3–5.

Widiger, T. A. (1993). Personality and depression: Assessment issues. In M. H. Klein, D. J. Kupfer, & M. T. Shea (Eds.), *Personality and depression: A current view* (pp. 77–118). New York: Guilford Press.

Widiger, T. A., & Costa, P. T. (1994). Personality and personality disorders. *Journal of Abnormal Psychology, 103,* 78–91.

Widiger, T. A., & Lynam, D. R. (1998). Psychopathy and the five-factor model of personality. In T. Millon, E. Simonsen, & M. Birket-Smith (Eds.), *Psychopathy: Antisocial, criminal, and violent behavior* (pp. 171–187). New York: Guilford Press.

Widiger, T. A., Mangine, S., Corbitt, E. M., Ellis, C. G., & Thomas, G. V. (1995). *Personality Disorder Interview–IV. A semistructured interview for the assessment of personality disorders.* Odessa, FL: Psychological Assessment Resources.

Widiger, T. A., & Sanderson, C. J. (1995a). Assessing personality disorders. In J. N. Butcher (Ed.), *Clinical personality assessment: Practical approaches* (pp. 380–394). New York: Oxford University Press.

Widiger, T. A., & Sanderson, C. J. (1995b). Towards a dimensional model of personality disorder in DSM-IV and DSM-V. In W. J. Livesley (Ed.), *The DSM-IV personality disorders* (pp. 433-458). New York: Guilford Press.

Widiger, T. A., & Trull, T. S. (1992). Personality and psychopathology: An application of the five-factor model. *Journal of Personality, 60,* 363–393.

Widiger, T. A., & Trull, T. S. (1993). Borderline and narcissistic personality disorders. In P. B. Sutker & H. E. Adams (Eds.), *Comprehensive handbook of psy-*

chopathology (2nd ed., pp. 371–394). New York: Plenum Press.

Widiger, T. A., Trull, T. S., Clarkin, J. F., Sanderson, C., & Costa, P. T. (1994). A description of the DSM-III-R and DSM-IV personality disorders with the five-factor model of personality. In P. T. Costa & T. A. Widiger (Eds.), *Personality disorders and the five-factor model of personality* (pp. 41–56). Washington, DC: American Psychological Association.

World Health Organization. (1992). *International classification of diseases* (10th ed.). Geneva, Switzerland: Author.

Zimmerman, M. (1994). Diagnosing personality disorders. A review of issues and research methods. *Archives of General Psychiatry, 51,* 225–245.

Zuroff, D. C. (1994). Depressive personality styles and the five-factor model of personality. *Journal of Personality Assessment, 63,* 453–472.

Chapter 14

On the Interface between Personality and Social Psychology

Roy F. Baumeister
Case Western Reserve University

In principle, personality and social psychology are natural allies and natural competitors. The tension between alliance and competition has shaped much of the interface for decades. The basis for both alliance and competition is that the two fields approach the same target from different angles. The target is human behavior, broadly defined to include subjective experience and objective action. In principle, social psychologists examine how external, situational causes operate, using mainly experimental methods, whereas personality psychologists study how people's inner traits and processes operate, relying heavily on correlations and other methods.

The alliance is natural because, as is obvious to nearly everyone, human behavior is a product of both the person and the environment. Both the situationist and the dispositionist views are clearly inadequate. People are not all the same, with behavior directed by situational factors, and so even the most diehard social psychologist must acknowledge that individual differences in personality exist. Neither is behavior purely a product of inner forces and traits, independent of situational context, and so staunch believers in the power of personality must acknowledge the decisive role of external, situational factors. The person by situation interaction is the only defensible model of human behavior.

Moreover, many of the topics that currently preoccupy researchers are inherently part of the social–personality interface. Motivation, for example, draws attention to the roots of personality, but it also responds to situational stimuli. The self and self-regulation reflect inner, stable aspects of operation but also connect to external, situational causes and opportunities. Relationships flourish or fail because of the inner traits of the individuals as well as under the influence of external stresses, opportunities, and forces. Attitudes may change because of external factors (persuasion, conformity pressure) or inner ones (authoritarianism, persuasibility).

Thus it would seem natural that personality and social psychology would join forces and work together to explain behavior. Yet there is another side to the complementarity of the two approaches, which is that in a sense the two are in competition. One way of putting this is that there is only so much human behavior to go around, and the more that can be explained by one approach, the less is left for the other.

This natural competition is what made a political football out of Mischel's (1968) landmark critique of research on individual differences. Mischel noted that most research studies find correlations no higher than about .3 between trait scales and behavioral measures. The reigning mode of thought at the time was to square the correlation coefficient to determine what percent of the variance was explained. If personality could do no better than .3, then only 9% of the variance could be attributed to traits. Social psychologists leapt forward to lay claim to the other 91%. In their view, Mischel's conclusions constituted empirical evidence that social psychology was approximately 10 times more important than personality psychology.

Of course the battering of personality psychology was unfair (see Craik, 1986; West, 1983, 1986). The .3 correlations reflected, among other things, the difficulty of predicting one-shot behaviors from broad trait scales and the simple fact of measurement error. Better measures and aggregated behaviors permitted much higher correlations to be found (e.g., Epstein, 1979a, 1979b, 1980). The inference that a .3 correlation meant only 9% of the behavior has been questioned, and Ozer (1985) proposed that the unsquared correlation may often be a better estimate of the proportion of variance (so that a .3 correlation signifies 30% of the variance). More generally, the view that social psychology is 10 times more important than personality in predicting behavior is not defensible. When Funder and Ozer (1983) examined the effect sizes for several classic experiments in social psychology, these turned out to have almost precisely the same magnitude as those of the personality studies Mischel (1968) had criticized. Situation and disposition are about equally effective at predicting behavior.

Still, considerable damage had been done. Moreover, the timing of that controversy could scarcely have been worse for personality psychology. From the late 1960s through the middle 1970s, psychology departments all over North America were expanding rapidly, partly because college enrollments were rising across the board and partly because psychology was discovered as a relevant, fascinating field that appealed to a broad range of students. New professorships were created left and right, and tenure sometimes had to be granted even to marginal candidates simply because the demand for teachers was rising fast. With personality psychology struggling under a heavy cloud of intellectual doubt, it missed out on the boom, and the additional faculty positions went to social psychology instead.

Social psychology had its own problems, and indeed in the late 1970s it was common to speak of the "crisis in social psychology," which apparently was focused on disaffection with seemingly artificial and ethically questionable research methods as well as a seemingly pervasive superficiality of many theories. By this time, however, the brief phase of departmental expansion was largely over, and moreover there were already a great many social psychologists around who were quite vocal at insisting that their field was doing fine.

The timing problem also had an impact on research funding. I am still amazed to hear senior colleagues speak of the 1960s, in which (they claim) the government agencies used to go looking for researchers to whom they could give money. Even if those memories are exaggerated, there is no doubt that research funds were far easier to get than they are now. The booming economy of the 1960s, coupled with the federal priority for funding institutions of higher learning (with research grants being one mechanism) spread money readily. When the economy turned downward in the early 1970s, federal research budgets gradually became much tighter. The review boards and panels that were in place by the mid-1970s had some chance to continue to fight for dwindling funds, but the opportunities for new initiatives and new fields to claim a piece of the shrinking pie were likely to be slim. Personality psychology never found a place at the National Science Foundation, and its slice of other research funds remained far smaller than what social psychology had.

Hence in terms of institutional growth, social psychology suffered far less from its crisis than personality psychology did from its. There is no questioning the relative size of the two fields today: There are far more social than personality psychologists. Yet there is no a priori reason that that should be true. As far as I can tell, the difference in size is the result of a historical accident.

I have a long-standing and affectionate identification with both social and personality psychology, and so I hope my judgment is not biased or provincial in this regard. My sense is that social psychology is thriving now, whereas personality psychology is struggling. Probably these developments are partly the result of the political and institutional developments during the crucial years of the 1960s and 1970s.

What is the basis for this assessment? For one thing, I have spent the last decade as the newsletter editor for the Society for Personality and Social Psychology. In countless meetings, I have heard the field's leading figures plan for the future, and almost invariably the wish to incorporate more personality psychology goes begging. Whether the discussion concerns finding associate editors for the journals, finding candidates for the executive committee, finding topics for special issues, lining up symposia for the conventions, or even attracting manuscript submissions to the journals, the yield from personality psychology is frequently disappointed and disappointing. One hears periodically that one or another personality psychologist grumbles that the lack of personality psychology in these venues indicates some organizational prejudice against personality, but that is not an adequate explanation. If anything, there has often been a prejudice in favor of accommodating personality. It is difficult to resist the interpretation that personality psychology, as a field, is underachieving—except perhaps if one acknowledges that its vastly smaller size, relative to social psychology, makes this inevitable.

The small size of personality, along with the intellectual need to incorporate personality issues into current theorizing, has resulted in a new movement along the interface. In a sense, social psychologists have begun to "colonize" personality. The editorships and review boards of personality journals are increasingly staffed with people who are in some official sense social psychologists. The topic areas of personality psychology are studied by social psychologists. Social psychologists even teach many of the university courses in personality.

ALL IS INTERFACE

My own view is that it is becoming obsolete to speak of the "interface" as if personality and social psychology were two separate fields with a small area of overlap. Instead, it appears to me, there is mostly overlap, and only relatively small areas of the two fields lack contact with each other.

One of the main reasons for this progressive blurring and overlap is that the cognitive revolution meant that the study of intraindividual, inner processes became vital to social psychology. Personality had nominally claimed inner processes, except perhaps for attitude change. But what differentiates a "personality process" from the inner interplay of cognitive, motivational, and motivational processes that social psychologists now study with such zeal?

The "colonization" process I mentioned is likely to increase this sense that everything is interface. If the domain of personality psychology is increasingly occupied by social psychologists, it will not be surprising if they gradually come to view personality as an extension or wing of social psychology.

Probably there are some exceptions; that is, there are some topics that remain exclusively the province of either personality or social psychologists who may remain indifferent to the other field. Intergroup relations is perhaps an area where individual personality differences and processes play little role. Conversely, personality measurement (assessment) remains the province of personality psychologists who do not need to pay much attention to social psychology. Even in such examples, however, the likelihood of the interface becoming important seems high. Intergroup issues focus on factors such as aggression and self-esteem, and these are not likely to remain impervious to effects of personality factors of group members. And social processes do affect measurement.

The Big Five may be one of the few major developments of recent years to come from personality psychologists who have little contact with social psychology, but this lack of contact is not likely to last. If the Big Five idea is to flourish, it must help predict differences in social behavior, which means that an understanding of social psychology and situational factors will become vital.

Still, there are progressively ever fewer topics that can be classified as belonging entirely in personality and not in social psychology, or in social psychology and not in personality. The lay public (including students in introductory psychology) probably still believes that personality psychology will study inner processes that take place inside the individual whereas social psychology will be concerned with outward behavior occurring between people. This inner–outer form of the distinction is utterly untenable as a description of what is currently going on in the two fields. Personality psychologists have extensive interest in what occurs between people, and social psychologists are concerned, if not obsessed, with inner processes.

THE OTHER INTERFACES: CLINICAL AND DEVELOPMENTAL

Discussion of the interface between social and personality psychology should recognize that these fields have long had productive interfaces with other areas too. Ironically, it appears that social psychology has taken over the lead from personality psychology in interacting with other fields.

In the first half of the 20th century, personality psychology flourished amid strong ties to both clinical and developmental psychology. Most of the major personality theories produced up into the 1960s came from psychologists with a strong clinical background—Freud, Jung, Adler, Horney, Murray, Sullivan, Rogers, and others. Even more recent thinkers, such as Bandura, Mischel, Pervin, Kelly, Rotter, and Epstein, had clinical training. Ideas flowed freely between personality and clinical fields. In fact, my own initial interest in psychology pointed me toward clinical study, not because I had any interest in healing the mentally ill (I didn't) but because I was guided by Freud's career, which seemed to prove that the best route to drawing general conclusions about human nature was to study people with mental illnesses and psychological problems. Still, clinical psychology gradually moved away from its close reliance on personality. The rise of behavioral treatments and behavior therapy was one factor that reduced the ties between personality and clinical, because behavioral approaches suggested that studying deep personality dynamics and childhood roots was not necessary for treating many problems and illnesses.

By the same token, personality psychologists maintained a long hold over developmental psychology. Even today, courses on personality psychology devote a great deal of time to describing child development, starting usually with Freud's oral and anal stages and the Oedipus complex. Somehow it seemed to be generally accepted that part of the task of personality psychology was to explain how the newborn infant developed into an adult human being.

Apart from individual differences in depression, however, today's personality psychology does not maintain those strong links with either clinical or developmental psychology. Instead, social psychology has slowly taken over the role as the mainstream field of normal, adult psychology that swaps ideas with those two. The social–clinical interface has been a productive source of ideas for both fields, and indeed there is a thriving journal (the *Journal of Social and Clinical Psychology*) that is devoted to that interface.

Meanwhile, developmental psychology continues to borrow heavily from social psychology, as the patterns shown for adults are examined by developmental psychologists to ascertain at what ages and in what fashion children acquire them. Social development is a familiar term for an active, busy subdiscipline; the term personality development is heard much less often. To be sure, the field of social development appears to me to be suffering some difficulties, possibly attributable to the lack of overarching theory and the lack or weakness of empirical methods. One sign of this backwardness is the one-way nature of its interface with social psychology: Developmental psychology borrows far more from social psychology than it gives back, and in fact I would be hard put to identify any major theory in social psychology that originated in developmental psychology. Still, this may be a temporary state of affairs, and it is quite possible that developmental psychology will soon have much more to offer social psychology. In any case, developmental psychology has stronger ties to social than to personality psychology at present.

What this suggests is that there has been a change in the constellation of subdisciplines in psychology—and one in which personality and social psychology have been centrally involved. Personality psychology was for a time the central subdiscipline in all of psychology and maintained interfaces with other fields (including social) that were highly productive and mutually influential. Social psychology was then just another of these more peripheral disciplines. Now, the two have seemingly reversed positions. Social psychology has become the central subdiscipline, having developed interfaces with many other fields, such as clinical and developmental (not to mention cognitive and physiological). Personality has moved away from the center.

Thus, in an important sense, the interface between social and personality has endured despite a rotation of everything else.

WHO'S AT THE CENTER?

The exchange of positions of personality and social psychology has broader implications that seem likely to shape the interface between those fields in the coming decades. As I suggested in the preceding section, and as I have argued more thoroughly elsewhere (Baumeister & Tice, 1996), personality psychology was for several decades arguably the intellectual center of all the social sciences. Freud's ideas were used actively in multiple disciplines, including anthropology and history (not to mention some of the humanities, such as literary criticism), and other personality theorists were read and discussed in these fields too. For the first half of the 20th century, it would be hard to find any other subdiscipline in the social sciences whose influence was as broad as that of personality psychology.

The influence was partly based on a bidirectional exchange of ideas. It was not only that the theories of personality psychologists were adopted by researchers in other fields. Personality psychologists were themselves intellectually broad, and they readily incorporated material from other fields into their work.

In contrast to the broad influence of personality psychology, social psychology was for many decades a minor player in the big leagues of interdisciplinary social science. Modern social psychology took shape in the 1950s as an aggressively experimental discipline with deliberately narrow focus. Reacting against the broad theorizing that personality psychologists had done in the preceding decades, social psychologists made a virtue of staying close to their data and tackling small, well-defined problems. For many years, the most popular and influential theory was that of cognitive dissonance, which held only that people generally want to avoid being inconsistent. Attribution theory evolved out of impression formation and addressed simple questions such as "Why did I fail at this task?" and "Why did John laugh at the comedian?"

In any case, it was hardly surprising that the broader intellectual world took relatively little note of social psychology. Behaviorism reigned, and social psychologists took pride in eschewing all discussion of mental events, such as thoughts, feelings, and other inner processes. This is part of what made social psychology look so vacuous to the other social sciences: What kind of psychologist refuses to acknowledge inner thoughts and feelings? The other social sciences want psychology to give them something akin to Freud's theories: complex inner dynamics of motivation, emotion, conscious and unconscious processes, and so forth. The word "consciousness" was taboo in social psychology, and that and similar facts made the whole field seem absurd to outsiders.

I recall having dinner during graduate school with a professor in another department. As we discussed social psychology, I said I thought that many of our experiments and findings were quite clever, but I admitted that the field's overall conceptual structures were quite primitive and, I believe I used the word, "terrible." The man looked at me with an expression of such astonishment that I asked him whether he disagreed. He said no, and in fact he said that that judgment was the consensus held by everyone he knew outside of social psychology. He said he was merely astonished that I knew that the conceptual structures were so bad. Apparently he assumed that social psychologists had all persuaded themselves that they were being profound.

It is therefore ironic that social psychology has grown into an intellectually lively discipline with strong ties to multiple fields, whereas personality psychology has grown far more insular and narrow. I doubt any knowledgeable person would claim today that personality psychology is the intellectual center of the social sciences, in practice. Meanwhile, to accord that label to social psychology may be a bit premature, but I think things are moving in that direction, and social psychology's candidacy for that role is stronger than most.

What happened? For one thing, the discipline of the data came rather late to personality psychology, and when it was accepted in earnest, the grandiose theorizing of earlier generations came to seem something of an embarrassment. The ambitious models of the complete structure of the human psyche, the listing of fundamental motivations and instincts, and the confident analyses of just what had shaped the peculiar psychological profile of the modern Western individual were seen as far beyond what could be proven. Conflicting views could not be resolved.

Instead of carrying on those profound but unresolvable discussions, the new generation of personality psychologists concentrated on two things they could do well. One was to develop scales for measuring personality traits. The other was examining specific individual differences in specific behaviors (often with laboratory methods quite similar to those social psychologists were using). These conclusions were far more solid and reliable, but far less interesting to other social scientists, than the big ideas of the early theorists. Freud's theories about the superego, or projection, or the aggressive instinct could be adapted by many researchers in many fields to tackle many of the problems that social science addresses. Newer findings about how locus of control predicted individuals' choice of task after initial failure had far narrower appeal. And of course the wonderfully crafted new scales for measuring particular traits were of little use to historians, sociologists, political scientists, anthropologists, and others. We can apply psychoanalytic theories to the case history information of Hitler and Napoleon in retrospect, but we cannot give dead people the latest trait scale.

Personality psychologists were not of course going to remain narrow and insular forever. One attempt to return to broader thinking was the emergence of the Big Five personality traits. In this view, all personality traits can be analyzed as variations on five major dimensions of personality. This idea emerged from factor analyses of trait terms and perceptions of other people. It has suffered from some conflicts and controversies, such as how exactly to name and conceptualize the five dimensions, but these issues are to be expected. More seriously, the way the Big Five emerged from theoretical bootstrapping has thus far prevented it from being a modern successor to the full-fledged personality theories of previous decades. That is, why are there only five dimensions? Why these five specifically? Is it true that all personalities must be composed of these five and no others, and why should that be true?

My point is simply that the Big Five, although a valuable contribution of potentially great theoretical and practical importance, is not yet ready to be useful to researchers in other fields. Even if they accepted that the Big Five constitute the ultimate way to classify individual differences, the lack of causal or process theory would diminish their explanatory value. It is possible that this will be remedied in coming decades. For now, however, the Big Five account of personality is not going to restore personality psychology to the centrally influential position it once held vis-à-vis the other social sciences.

Meanwhile, social psychology underwent a dramatic expansion of scope and theory. The reasons for this intellectual broadening are difficult to fathom, let alone verify. It has always seemed to me that the generation of social psychologists entering the field in the late 1970s and early 1980s somehow managed to be intellectually broader, yet that is hardly a satisfactory explanation. Rather, it seems that something forced the field to abandon its theoretical and methodological provincialism.

A pair of important trends in social psychology in the late 1970s and early 1980s may have been responsible for the broadening of the field. One was the rise of social cognition. The other was the study of close relationships. Either of these alone might simply have replaced one narrow focus with another, but together they may have forced social psychology to open up its horizons. Let me explain.

Social cognition meant the death knell of behaviorism. In the early 1970s, many social psychologists boasted of their behavioristic rigor and accepted the discipline (which might be called asceticism) of refusing to speak in mentalistic terms. This position became untenable after the cognitive revolution. As Fiske (1995) has noted, "unabashed mentalism" was a prominent feature of social cognition research from early on. Even attribution researchers could still claim that they were studying behavior, as in the behavior of checking a point on a scale to indicate whether self or situation was responsible for an outcome, but social cognition research no longer bothered with such apologies.

Behind the theoretical leap was methodological progress. Most behaviorists had not really believed that people had no thoughts or feelings. They simply had thought that studying them was necessarily unscientific because such inner states could not be measured. The great methodological creativity of social cognition research (borrowing, to be sure, from methodological advances in cognitive psychology) enabled people to begin rigorous scientific study of these inner states. Once the methods were in place, the taboo on theorizing about them was unnecessary and obsolete. Rigorous methods permitted rigorous theorizing, and even the most skeptical observers gradually had to concede that social cognition research offered substantial advances in the understanding of social psychology. Thus, one set of intellectual barriers was suddenly demolished.

The growth of research on relationships pushed things in another direction. This growth owed much less than social cognition's rise to the emergence of new methods. In fact, the study of relationships had probably lagged behind that of other social processes precisely because of methodological difficulties. The one-session laboratory experiment reigned in the 1970s as the premier method of studying social psychology—but how can long-term relationships, such as marriage, be simulated in a one-session experiment?

What proved decisive, however, was the inability to ignore human relationships. Social psychologists might do a fine job of studying attitude change and impression formation, but if social psychology were to maintain its claim to be interested in all human interaction, there was no way to go on ignoring long-term relationships. Most of social life takes place between people with whom the individual has past and future connections. To study only interactions among strangers is therefore to ignore most of human social life.

The dilemma, then, was whether to relax methodological standards and study relationships, or to hold to experimental rigor but end up failing to understand the field's ostensible subject matter. Gradually, more and more social psychologists realized that it was better to have some data on relationships, even if these studies did not match the rigor of work on other topics. Survey methods, longitudinal studies, and other methods came into popularity as social psychologists accepted the challenge of understanding long-term relationships. The work turned out to be surprisingly good in many instances, and valuable findings and ideas emerged.

Thus, in a relatively short period of time, social psychology expanded into several previously taboo areas, and a slew of new methods accompanied and facilitated this expansion. One expansion was marked by new technology (e.g., desktop computers that could easily administer subliminal primes, adjust stimuli based on previous responses, and measure response latencies to tiny fractions of seconds) that made previously inaccessible phenomena capable of being studied with high degrees of rigor. The other was marked by a relaxation of standards to accommodate the importance of the topic. That pair of developments persuaded many social psychologists that other topics too could be studied, either by developing rigorous new methods or by doing the best one could with existing methods. Journal reviewers implicitly and sometimes explicitly adopted a double standard: For a familiar, well-studied topic (e.g., cognitive dissonance), new research had to be extremely rigorous and thorough, but for a first attempt to study a new topic with new ideas, one could tolerate weaker methods. It was better to study every relevant topic than to study only those amenable to the strictest methods. Errors would be corrected in the long run as better methods became available.

The sheer size of social psychology contributed to its diversity. It was no longer possible for a handful of Ivy League experts to control the field and dictate its intellectual directions. I recall spending part of a sabbatical reading every abstract in the *Journal of Personality and Social Psychology* during the decade of the 1980s. The diversity of contributors amazed me as much as the diversity of topics. True, many articles were contributed by the regular, familiar names in the field, the people with flourishing careers and whom one encountered at every conference. Yet there were also many contributions by people whom I had never seen at the major social psychology conventions, people who might have had only one article in that journal during the entire decade. I recall trying to guess whether the total contribution by the regulars was greater than the total contribution by the one-shot authors, and the answer was not clear. That unclarity is a sign of how much the field owed to its one-time contributors—which in turn is a sign of how open the field (and its leading journal) had become to a broad assortment of authors.

The combination of these patterns produced an intellectual breadth and flowering in social psychology that surprised me. It seemed as if suddenly the field transformed from a narrow-minded focus on a few easy topics into a broad, open undertaking where nothing was off-limits. With broad and vigorous activity compiling an account of all the principles of normal adult human behavior, social psychology has become a reasonable candidate for one of the major intellectual centers of the social sciences, even as personality psychology abdicated that role.

IF IT'S AN INDEPENDENT VARIABLE, IT MUST BE PERSONALITY

A little-discussed aspect of the social–personality interface involves complementarity in research design. To be sure, most research designs and hypotheses involve both independent and dependent variables, at least in the minds of the researchers. But there is a difference of emphasis between the two fields.

Social psychology usually defines its topics by dependent variables. To scan the titles of the chapters in social psychology textbooks is by and large to read a list of dependent variables: attraction, attitude change, attributions, aggression, conformity, helping. Individual social psychologists typically define their own areas of interest in terms of the dependent variables. This is more than a style of speaking: It reflects the way they think about what they do, and indeed it affects how they do it. Social psychologists typically choose a target behavior or outcome and seek to explore the causes of it. Over the course of a career, they will typically look at multiple different causes of this target behavior. In research design terms, they define their interests by dependent variables, and they explore various independent variables that contribute to causing them.

Personality research, however, is organized along the lines of independent variables. A given personality researcher may identify a personality trait of interest and will either choose an existing trait scale or develop one. The career then involves showing various behaviors that are predicted, and at the theoretical level caused, by this trait. For a personality researcher interested in self-esteem, for example, a career may involve studying how self-esteem predicts task persistence, interpersonal behavior, and health-related outcomes. In research design terms, they define their interest by the independent variables, and they explore various dependent variables that may be predicted by them.

For example, even in the large and complex field of study of the self, social and personality psychologists have different emphases. Social psychologists easily and comfortably study the self as a dependent variable, such as in self-attributions, but when the goal is to study the self as an independent variable, suddenly the focus shifts to personality traits (e.g., self-monitoring, self-esteem) or motivations (e.g., self-verification). Self-awareness was one of the few topic areas in social psychology to emerge defined by an independent variable (see Wicklund & Duval, 1971), but before long there was a trait scale for it (Fenigstein, Scheier, & Buss, 1975).

This dichotomy is far from absolute, but it is undoubtedly what researchers would call a significant difference. Moreover, there are familiar patterns that seem to reflect this style of thinking.

In particular, when some social psychologists do finally define a topic area by an independent variable, it is a good bet that there will soon be a trait scale. It is as if social psychologists believe that topics based on independent variables belong in the personality category, and so when social psychology produces such an area it converts it into a personality trait. Many examples can be listed, from self-awareness, to control, to attachment style.

Undoubtedly there are deeper and more profound reasons for this difference than mere stereotyping. The conceptual structure and theoretical goals of the field differ along the same lines. To simplify recklessly, social psychology aims to explain the causes of the full range of social behaviors, and so the set of dependent variables is in a sense the target that needs explaining. Meanwhile, personality psychology aims to identify the dimensions and structure of personality, and so the roster of traits—the independent variables—is the target domain that is to be elucidated.

This different emphasis has implications for the personality–social interface. It depicts the two fields less as rivals than as complementary. Social psychologists, with their elaborate conceptual structure of dependent variables (and ways to measure them), offer a great deal to the personality psychologists, who are holding well-defined independent variables and looking for things to predict with them, and vice versa.

The danger in this arrangement, however, is that not all independent variables are or should be thought of as traits. It should be possible for social psychologists to identify topics of study in terms of situational independent variables. The lack of a well-articulated theory of situational structure is due in part to this reticence on the part of social psychologists to organize information (other than individual differences) by independent variables (cf. Baumeister & Tice, 1985). Social psychologists might learn from personality psychologists how to construct broad integrative theories from independent variables. The eventual theory of situational structure may well end up resembling the Big Five personality traits: a set of major dimensions that in principle contain all the specific, narrowly defined variables that have been studied. It is certainly no accident that the Big Five emerged in personality long before social psychologists have anything comparable to offer for situation structure.

GETTING TENURE AFTER THE UNIVERSALS ARE DONE

The scientific evolution of psychology depends not only on methods, ideas, and the gradually emerging truth of phenomena: It depends also on career politics. Individual researchers have to build their careers by publishing new findings. My thesis is that these pressures will bind personality and social psychology ever closer together in the coming decades.

My prediction of increasing integration depends on the assumption that the range of interesting potential findings is finite. If there is an unlimited supply of discoveries to be made, then there is no reason to predict that the march of progress will throw personality and social psychologists into each other's arms, for each group could go on indefinitely pursuing its own independent work, heedless of the other.

Let us assume, however, that there is a finite amount of truth to be discovered about the human psyche—or, at least, that there is a finite quantity of general principles that can be discovered and rendered interesting to the intellectual community. This quantity might be quite large, but it is limited and will eventually be exhausted.

The likely course of scientific progress is that early researchers will identify the broadest, most important, and general principles. Dramatic major breakthroughs may occur with some regularity early in a field's history. As the field matures, however, many basic questions are settled, and later researchers are left with much less sensational material to discover. Their careers are more likely to be spent looking for smaller effects, more narrowly defined phenomena, and refinements or subtle elaborations on the general principles already laid down.

This view of the development of a scientific field seems consistent with what has happened in the older sciences, although I confess to being far from an expert in the history and philosophy of science. It seems unlikely to me that biology will see another thinker as important and influential as Darwin, or that physics will see many more breakthroughs comparable to Newtonian mechanics or quantum theory. Today, many cutting-edge researchers in the hard sciences are seeking to find breakthroughs at the intersections of fields, such as biophysics and biochemistry, but these too will gradually be used up.

For social psychology, one implication is that many of the major principles have already been identified. The phenomena of maintaining cognitive consistency, actor–observer and self-serving attributional biases, need to belong, similarity and attraction, and the like may be broad principles that are true for everyone, but as time goes by there will be fewer and fewer undiscovered principles that apply to all people. At present it still seems quite plausible that several more major principles, of the magnitude of cognitive dissonance, remain undiscovered because of having escaped the intuitions (or methodological capabilities) of social psychologists—although frankly it would not surprise me if that were false and most of the big ideas have at least been proposed already. But even if it is true now that some big principles remain unsuspected, I doubt that claim will still be plausible a century from now. Assuming that social psychologists continues to produce research at the present rate, it is hard to imagine anything as important as cognitive dissonance escaping discovery for another century.

Once the big general principles have been discovered, how are future social psychologists to make their careers? One response is to look at smaller, more subtle effects. To some extent, this is already happening. When I was in graduate school, the standard experiment involved a 2×2 design with 10 subjects in each cell. Nowadays the graduate students working with me routinely expect to run 15 or 20 subjects per cell (plus they often include extra cells). Increasing the number of subjects per cell increases statistical power—which is precisely what one has to do to detect weaker effects. Social psychology's recent rise in interest in effect sizes is in part based on this enduring concern that the journals are filling up with small effects. To be sure, there are complex interpretive issues surrounding the meaning of effect sizes in experimental studies, and I do not wish to take that detour here. The relevant point is that as the field matures, one should expect the big effects to be discovered early, and future researchers will have to content themselves with smaller and smaller effects.

The other response to the gradual depletion of undiscovered phenomena, however, is to abandon the insistence on finding principles that are true for everybody and focus instead on principles that are true for some people only. This is where personality psychology may prove extremely useful to social psychologists, for personality can help identify subpopulations among which certain principles may hold even if these same laws do not apply across the full spectrum. People who share a certain trait may well think, act, and feel in similar ways, and future researchers can concentrate on identifying these patterns.

Already there are some trends in that direction. Depressed people have certain styles of interpretive response and interpersonal behavior that nondepressed people do not have. Other traits have similar implications. By identifying a well-defined, homogeneous group, researchers can make plenty of discoveries that would be impossible without restricting the focus to that particular group. Hence social psychologists will need to make increasing use of personality factors.

Meanwhile, the evolution of personality is also likely to borrow increasingly from social psychology. Future personality psychologists will face the same pressure to publish in order to earn tenure and advance their careers. What will they do? Undoubtedly some can continue to generate new trait scales, but again it is difficult to imagine that a hundred years from now there will still be important personality traits that lack valid, reliable measures.

Hence the career pressure will take the form of using the traits to predict behavior. If the roster of traits is finite, then career success will depend on finding new behaviors to predict with them. And that is where social psychology becomes useful, because it has the dependent variables to offer (including the procedures for measuring them).

In short, the interface between personality and social psychology will increasingly be where the action is—not (just) because the ultimate truth depends on the interactive interplay of trait and situation, but because career pressures will push researchers to look to the interface to find the novel combinations of variables that will enable them to continue to make new discoveries.

ULTIMATE BASIC THINGS

In the final analysis, psychology always seems to come down to motivation and cognition. The history of psychology can be described as a series of pendulum swings between emphases on motivation and cognition, and certainly personality and social psychology have seen these two factors rotate in and out of fashion. At present, most observers would probably agree that the fields are coming off a heavily cognitive phase and rediscovering motivation. In fact, some writers are describing "motivated cognition" as if it were an entirely new concept and breakthrough, seemingly heedless of the fact that Freud's theory of defense mechanisms offered a provocative account of motivated cognition nearly a century ago.

I have already said that the cognitive revolution in social psychology made the inner–outer distinction between personality and social psychology obsolete and untenable. If the field is now shifting toward a more motivational phase, what will that spell for the social–personality interface?

The two fields have historically handled motivation differently, and in that sense a rise of motivational thinking could push them apart in the near future. In the past, personality has approached motivation in terms of individual differences. The literature on achievement, affiliation, intimacy, and power motivations, for example, were characterized by attempting to compare the acts of people who had high versus low levels of those motivations. In contrast, social psychology has preferred to think in terms of universal motivations. The desire for cognitive consistency, the wish to be liked by others, and the urge to sustain a favorable self-image are examples of motives that social psychologists rely on. Because presumably no one is immune to those concerns, they can be invoked whenever a relevant finding about social behavior needs a motivational interpretation.

On closer inspection the two fields are receptive to the alternative approach. Some personality theories, after all, postulated instincts as basic patterns of universal motivation, and the precise configuration of a particular personality depended on how the person had managed to pattern and satisfy those basic motives (again, Freud, Adler, and Sullivan serve as excellent examples of this approach). Meanwhile, social psychologists have often relied on situational manipulations to increase or decrease particular motivations, so they recognize that the general applicability of these motives is at least contingent on situational factors.

Perhaps the past is not a reliable guide to the future on the issue of motivation, however. For one thing, it seems difficult to imagine that the next pendulum swing will carry things so far in the motivational direction that all the advances of the cognitive phase will be abandoned and certainly not to the extent that the previous motivational phase's love affair with drive theory was eclipsed during the cognitive craze of the 1980s. Hence we may be in for a phase of relatively sophisticated integration.

Moreover, I have to assume that in the long run the truth will exert ever greater pressure on the field's development, thereby constraining the power of intellectual fads and fashions. And the truth is likely to force social and personality psychologists to work together again. Social psychology cannot probably get by for long with simply invoking universal motivations. Individual differences in motivation will have to be recognized, if only because they will help young social psychologists generate significant findings and advance their careers.

Conversely, personality psychologists will probably have to recognize the power of situational factors in developing further motivational theories. It was fine for Freud to propose sex and aggression as universal, fundamental motivations that arise from deep inside the psyche and are always there. But future work cannot afford to ignore the fact that people become sexual and aggressive in highly specific, well-demarcated situations and not in others. Moreover, the dependent variables associated with particular motivations are likely to be drawn increasingly from social psychology, and so again some integration of the two fields is likely.

Thus far, motivation does not have the power that cognition has to blur the distinctions between personality and social psychology so thoroughly. Hence it is possible that a phase of motivational theorizing will permit conceptual distinctions between the two fields to survive. But we do not yet know what form the next motivational paradigm will take. My hunch is that it will end up integrating personality and social psychology too—because it will be inadequate on conceptual grounds and will lack theoretical rigor if it fails to do so.

CONCLUSION

The interface between personality and social psychology is institutionalized in the field's main journals as well as in some organizations. Although the two fields have moved apart and back together repeatedly over the past decades, the interface endures because they are inextricably linked. The complementarity of the two fields is not going to disappear, even if some psychologists might wish it would. Rather, my forecast is that the coming decades will see ever more thorough integration and a progressive blurring of the distinctions between them.

The persistence of the link does not entail that things have remained static. On the contrary, I have suggested that in some respects the two fields have exchanged places. Early in the history of psychology, personality was a central and dominant field, and the link to social psychology was only one of the many productive interfaces that personality psychology enjoyed. Social psychology, meanwhile, struggled along on the margins of the field. Todays students still read and study the contributions of early personality psychologists, and the most current journals continue to cite the work of these pioneers; however the social psychology of the early decades of the 20th century is all but forgotten. The outlook today is quite different. Personality has become a small field and its interface with social psychology is undoubtedly its most important and productive disciplinary bond, whereas social psychology maintains thriving ties to a multitude of other areas both within and outside of psychology.

REFERENCES

Baumeister, R. F., & Tice, D. M. (1985) Toward a theory of situational structure. *Environment and Behavior, 17,* 147–192.

Baumeister, R. F., & Tice, D. M. (1996). Rethinking and reclaiming the interdisciplinary role of personality psychology: The science of human nature should be the center of the social sciences and humanities. *Journal of Research in Personality, 30,* 363–373.

Craik, K. H. (1986). Personality research methods: An historical perspective. *Journal of Personality, 54,* 18–51.

Epstein, S. (1979a). The stability of behavior : I. On predicting most of the people much of the time. *Journal of Personality and Social Psychology, 37,* 1097–1126.

Epstein, S. (1979b). The stability of behavior: II. Implications for psychological research. *American Psychologist, 35,* 790–806.

Fenigstein, A., Scheier, M. F., & Buss, A. H. (1975). Public and private self-consciousness: Assessment and theory. *Journal of Consulting and Clinical Psychology, 43,* 522–527.

Fiske, S. T. (1995). Social cognition. In A. Tesser (Ed.), *Advanced social psychology* (pp. 149–193). New York: McGraw-Hill.

Funder, D. C., & Ozer, D. J. (1983). Behavior as a function of the situation. *Journal of Personality and Social Psychology, 44,* 107–112.

Mischel, W. (1968). *Personality and assessment.* New York: Wiley.

Ozer, D. J. (1985). Correlation and the coefficient of determination. *Psychological Bulletin, 97,* 307–315.

West, S. G. (1983). Personality and prediction: An introduction. *Journal of Personality, 51,* 275–285.

West, S. G. (1986). Methodological developments in personality research: An introduction. *Journal of Personality, 54,* 1–17.

Wicklund, R. A., & Duval, S. (1971). Opinion change and performance facilitation as a result of objective self-awareness. *Journal of Experimental Social Psychology, 7,* 319–342.

Chapter 15

The Cultural Constitution of Personality

Susan E. Cross
Iowa State University

Hazel R. Markus
Stanford University

From the *India Tribune:*

> Gujarati Vaishnav parents invite correspondence from never married Gujariti well settled, preferably green card holder from respectable family for green card holder daughter 29 years, 5′4″, good looking, doing CPA.

> Gujarati Brahmin family invites correspondence from a well cultured, beautiful Gujarati girl for 29 years, 5′8″, 145 lbs. handsome looking, well-settled boy.

> Patel parents invite professional for their U.S.-raised daughter 26 (computer science) and son 24 (civil engineer), family owns construction firm.

From the *San Francisco Chronicle:*

> 28, SWM, 6′1″, 160 lbs. handsome, artistic, ambitious, seeks attractive WF, 24–29, for friendship, romance, and permanent partnership.

> Very attractive, independent SWF, 29, 5′6″, 110 lbs., loves fine dining, the theater, gardening and quiet evenings at home. In search of handsome SWM 28–34 with similar interests.

> Where shall I kiss thee? Across Sierra shoulder, skiing. Between acts of Aida, sharing? Forthright, funny, fiery, fit, seeking perceptive, profound permanent partner.

These personal ads seeking relationships appeared in California newspapers on the same day. The ads focus on adults of similar ages apparently interested in marriage or long-term relationships. Four of the six ads note that the target person is handsome, good-looking, or attractive. Beyond these similarities, however, the ads are striking for their differences. What counts as "personal" information seems to differ in the Indian American ad, and it is the parents of the person requiring a relationship that are inviting the contact; in the European American ad, it is the individuals themselves. Moreover, in the Indian American ad the sociocultural positioning of the family is clearly specified. Gujarati refers to a state of India; Vaishnav and Brahmin refers to castes. Patel refers to the last name of

Gujarati family. Someone who is a green card holder has permanent residence in the United States but cannot vote. In the European American ad, beyond identifying the sex of the person seeking a relationship, the only sociocultural positioning information provided is that of race and marital status.

In the Indian American ad, knowing about the person seems to require knowing about how the family is located in social space and also about the qualities of the family (e.g., respectable, owns construction firm). In the European American ad, it is the attributes of the individual who will engage in the relationship that are most salient (e.g., ambitious, independent, artistic) and that comprise the majority of the ad. Moreover, the European American ads include references to preferences and ways of spending one's time (loves fine dining and gardening) and seem written to draw attention to what is unique and special (Where shall I kiss thee, across Sierra shoulder, skiing?) about the individual. Finally, the ads diverge in what counts as a desirable partner. For the Indian Americans, the potential partner should be well settled, well cultured, educated, and a green card holder. For the European Americans, the ad-writer seeks another person with matching traits and preferences. We learn nothing of any distinguishing individual characteristics from the Indian American papers; and conversely, we learn nothing of the roles or positions in society of the European Americans—Do these people work, what is their education level, do they have families, and where did they grow up? All of this remains a mystery or at least in the background at the point of first contact.

Another example illustrating a similar cultural difference comes from a study that compares preschool practices in the United States, China, and Japan. This study by Tobin (1989) involves teachers from each of these cultural contexts commenting on the pedagogical practices of the other two contexts. In a video that accompanies the study, a Japanese boy, Hiroki, is being obviously disruptive to the class, standing on the table, throwing cards, telling jokes, singing, and disturbing other kids during a session where the teacher is giving a lesson. The American teachers are disturbed by the boy's behavior but particularly concerned about the teacher's response, and they wonder out loud why the Japanese preschool teacher does not intervene to stop him. They suggest that Hiroki is obviously very intelligent and must be bored by the dull lesson and should be given some special attention or instruction. The Japanese teacher is most surprised by this characterization of Hiroki and although agreeing that he disrupts the class, questions how he could possibly be "intelligent" if he doesn't even know how to behave toward his peers in class.

A third example comes from studies of Chinese organizational behavior. From these studies it is evident that people are selected not on the basis of scores on diagnostic tests or on interviews but most commonly on the basis of the applicants' ties to current employees (Redding & Wong, 1986).

Practices of seeking relationships, responding to students, and hiring employees in contexts other than the well-known European American ones are small moments of culture that can pose a set of challenging questions for the study of personality. To the extent that these examples are surprising it is because they appear to be at odds with a number of basic assumptions inherent in most analyses of personality. These largely implicit assumptions include (1) that social behavior is rooted in and determined by underlying dispositions or traits; (2) that the person's behavior can and should be understood apart from the person's particular social experiences and roles in society, and (3) that positively distinctive or nonnormative behavior is particularly diagnostic and "good" in the sense of valued. Most research in personality assumes a consensual understanding of what is included in the personological signature of an individual and consensual answers to questions such as "What or where is the person?", "What is critical or significant for defining a person?", and "What is individual behavior and how do we categorize it?" Yet such questions can result in different answers depending on the cultural context in which they are asked.

European American understandings and generalizations, both lay and scientific, for example, locate the essentials of personhood, the source of the action, the agency, squarely within or inside the autonomous individual—in a set of attributes, emotions, and motives. In many Asian cultural contexts, the source of individual action and behavior is distributed throughout the configuration of one's relations to others; it can be found in the net of expectations and role obligations that binds one to a particular set of others. Where the individual is assumed to be in control of behavior and the primary source of most behavior, it is likely that individual differences among people in behavior will be emphasized and valued, and as a consequence personality (i.e., an individual's characteristic pattern of thoughts, feelings, and actions) will be particularly important in the analysis of behavior. Without such marking and fostering of individual variation in behavior, it would be hard to support the idea that the source of behavior is in the individual. In contexts where behavior is assumed to result primarily from the person being responsive to the requirements of others and the obligations and demands of roles and situations, the individual's contribution to behavior may not, as the introductory examples suggest, be as salient, and as a consequence, personality or the individual's characteristic role in behavior will not receive the same kind of emphasis or be accorded the same kind of role in organizing social life that it is given in more individualistic contexts.

A personality, or way of being a person, is not an obvious or natural category but depends on what a person is thought to be and on culture-specific models of what a person is and what the person's role is in giving direction or coherence to behavior or, more broadly, to life. The qualities and characteristics of being a person are thus fully interdependent with the meanings and practices that characterize particular sociocultural contexts. People develop personalities over time. Being a person is then a social and cultural achievement; it requires incorporating and becoming attuned to a set of cultural understandings of human nature and participation in the creation and maintenance of a social world that is organized in a way that fosters these ideas. These models of the person are not applied after behavior has occurred; instead they are fully active in the definition, categorization, and constitution of behavior. Consequently, where cultural theories and practices of the person diverge, personalities will diverge.

A cultural approach is useful because it raises many questions and issues that are often overlooked by researchers schooled in Western personality psychology. For example, how have Western assumptions about the nature of the person shaped contemporary theories of personality, and what are alternative assumptions? Given alternative models of the person, how might agency be framed differently? What is the basis of a sense of personal coherence in other cultures? What are the basic units of personality? In the remainder of this chapter we explore some of the available answers to these and other questions raised by viewing personality through the lens of culture.

WHY EXAMINE PERSONALITY IN LIGHT OF CULTURE?

A cultural approach is like a device that will allow us to image the various social worlds—sets of culture-specific meanings and practices—that continually afford and maintain individual behavior. In some respects, it is like an MRI, which allows us to image brain activity, something that had been previously hidden. Likewise, a cultural approach can illuminate what has also been hidden, at least within an individualist culture; it makes visible the systems of meanings and practices—the language, the collective representations, the metaphors, the social scripts, the social structures, the policies, the institutions, the artifacts—within which people come to think and feel and act.

Without the tools provided by cultural approaches, a monocultural personality psychology will fall short of a comprehensive understanding of human behavior. Introducing cultural psychology, much like the introduction of the MRI, brings to light dimensions of a phenomenon that were previously obscured or overlooked. It makes visible previously invisible aspects of the person and the situation, allowing more careful construction of theories and research into the fundamentals of personality.

One of the starting points for a comprehensive science of personality is the comparison of findings from one culture with that of other cultures. These cross-cultural comparisons are necessary for the testing of the generalizability of findings produced in one culture. For example, cross-cultural comparisons have shown that Western theories of attribution processes (Miller, 1984; Morris & Peng, 1995) do not apply well to non-Western populations, but distinctions between the sexes appear to be cultural universals (Brown, 1991). During much of the history of cross-cultural comparison, the direction of this "transport and test" process (so named by Berry, Poortinga, Segall, & Dasen, 1992) was one-way: research based on Western theories was tested in non-Western cultures. Unfortunately, this approach yields a distorted picture of human nature, particularly of the non-Western society. Much of this research yielded inconsistent results and failed to shed much light on the psychological realities of the non-Western society (Sinha & Kao, 1997). As Azuma (1984) notes, "When a psychologist looks at a non-Western culture through Western glasses, he may fail to notice important aspects of the non-Western culture since the scheme for recognizing them are not provided by his culture." (p. 49). The articulation of a truly universal understanding of human nature and personality therefore also requires the development of theories of behavior originating in the indigenous psychologies of Asian, Latin American, African, and other non-Western societies.

These indigenous approaches can bring to light a wider variety of aspects of the human experience than is afforded by monocultural research. "What is taken for granted, purposely discounted, or inadvertently ignored in the social behavior of one's own culture may be focal and objectified in another, and these foreign insights may be relevant and useful in the analysis and understanding of the social behavior of one's own culture" (Markus, Kitayama, & Heiman, 1996, p. 862.) For example, the self system was long assumed to take a single form—as independent, autonomous, and separate from the social context. Two decades of research on self-related processes assumed this basic structure. Cross-cultural research has shown that for many individuals, others are included in the self and the self system is much more interdependent, contextualized, or situation-specific than had previously been considered. These conceptions of an interdependent self-construal are now being used to more fully understand variation in the self system of members of Western societies, especially women (Cross & Madson, 1997). Similarly, theories of self-esteem that have previously assumed an autonomous individual are being challenged by theories that take into account the influence of collectives and social groups (Leary, Tambor, Terdal, & Downs, 1995).

The cultural approach also allows more careful specification of the ways that personality processes and mechanisms are created and maintained by engagement in particular interpersonal and collective processes and milieus (Markus et al., 1996). In other words, the cultural approach allows one to focus more critically on the situations and contexts that generate and maintain or support particular personality processes. For the most part, social and personality research has been restricted to a relatively homogenous range of cultural and situational contexts and to groups of people who are extremely similar with respect to their sociocultural positions (e.g., young, white, middle-class college student samples). When personality is considered cross-culturally, the variety of situations and contexts that shape and channel personality is enlarged. In monocultural research, because there is relatively little variation in the situational contexts, individuals become foreground. However, with a cultural perspective, there is much more variation in the situations and contexts that shape behavior; therefore, the interdependence between personality and particular conditions or cultures can be more carefully scrutinized. In addition, a cultural approach allows us to disentangle personality from the particulars of American life. For example, Eriksonian theorists have argued that identity development requires an active questioning of one's roles and identities, followed by an active commitment to preferred identities (Marcia, 1966). Individuals who fail in this task are given negative labels such as "diffused" or "foreclosed." But to what extent is this process predicated on a particularly American phenomenon of late adolescence and the existence of opportunities for varied roles and identities? What are the foundations of identity (in fact, how important are personal identities?) in cultures in which roles are given by one's place in the family, one's caste or status, or one's gender, and few opportunities for exploration of identities are available? A cultural approach can highlight the assumptions of universality that underlie many culture-specific processes.

Most importantly, a cultural perspective magnifies the mutual constitution of culture and the person (Shweder, 1991; Shweder & Sullivan, 1990). In this perspective, culture is not an independent "influence" or factor that somehow acts on an set of processes that we label "personality," but instead what might be thought of as personality is a cultural product. Indeed, individual processes are very often inseparable from cultural processes, in that the ways that situations are framed and experienced and the factors that a person brings to a situation are cultural products (Markus, et al., 1996). From a global perspective, the discipline of personality psychology is itself a cultural product, developed and maintained based on Western assumptions and beliefs about the nature of the person (Markus & Kitayama, 1998; Triandis, 1997). Contemporary personality psychology is primarily a Western-European and American phenomenon, and has been shaped by specific beliefs about human nature as independent and separate from social contexts, by Judeo-Christian beliefs about the "good" or moral person, and by particular assumptions of the internal causes of behavior (Guisinger & Blatt, 1994; Sampson, 1989).

Consequently, the current literature on personality may be thought of as an "indigenous psychology" of Western Europeans and North Americans, rather than a universal psychology of human behavior. The most recent three-volume *Handbook of Cross-Cultural Psychology* (Berry et al., 1997) omitted a chapter on personality, and many recent textbooks in the area give it scant attention. If a goal of personality psychology is to understand all of human behavior—to construct a universal theory of personality—a cultural perspective is necessary. Even if one's goal is not so grand—perhaps the primary concern is with delineating a culture-specific theory of personality—cultural psychology raises questions that can aid in the development and refinement of that theory.

WHAT IS PERSONALITY?

An examination of definitions of personality is a useful starting point for a cultural appraisal of the field. Personality has been defined as "The complex organization of cognitions, affects, and behaviors that gives direction and pattern (coherence) to the person's life" (Pervin, 1996, p. 414). Similarly, "personality refers to an individual's characteristic patterns of thought, emotion, and behavior, together with the psychological mechanisms—hidden or not—behind those patterns" (Funder, 1997, p. 1). Although these definitions appear to be universally applicable, research deriving from them has often framed how these issues are addressed in quite culture - specific ways. For example, a central focus in much of personality psychology is all the ways that individuals differ from one another (Funder, 1997, p. 6). This practice is based on a cultural model of the person as separate, unique, and distinct from others – a model that is valued in North American culture but may not be valued in other societies. As a result, researchers have at times focused on topics (such as individuation, identity development, self-enhancement, self-monitoring, self-consciousness, self-verification, or self-affirmation) that may not be similarly relevant in other societies. In addition, Western personality research has assumed that the mechanisms behind characteristic patterns of thought, emotion, and behavior are "inside" the person. In other communities and societies, the causes of behavior are often viewed as lying "outside" the person, in networks of relationships, roles, and obligations (Miller, 1997). This narrowing of the definition of personality to primarily intra-psychic processes may be one reason why researchers in other cultures have tended not to focus on personality.

What Is a Person?

The examples presented at the beginning of the chapter suggest significant cultural diversity in implicit theories or understandings of what is a person. The ads seeking relationships presumably reflect the local conventions around writing such an ad, but they may also point to some shared understanding of the essential or most important aspects of a person. For the European Americans, the essential features are the familiar ones—a somewhat distinctive configuration of traits and preferences. For the Indian Americans, the prominent descriptors are the person's sociocultural coordinates—now and in the past—and of what is likely to be—the potential social trajectory. The adjectives of choice—respectable, well-cultured, well-settled—reveal a focal concern with others' views, with status, and with reputation, and also mark the nature of the person's current social participation and how the person is attuned to, or incorporated into, society (e.g., well-settled). Ignoring the other differences in the two sets of ads, one could argue that well-cultured means "artistic," and "well-settled" means "independent," and that the differences are just semantic, but we suggest that these differences are semantic and also much more. They reveal differences in observations and understandings of the sources and nature of individual behavior and of patterns and coherence in this behavior.

For the most part personality psychology has been rooted in an individualist model of the person where a separate, bounded individual is seen as the fact of first order (Pervin, 1994; Markus & Kitayama, 1998). In this model, priority is accorded to the separate, essentially nonsocial individual who is considered to secondarily enter into social relations by mutual consent with other similar individuals (Taylor, 1989). This ontological context reinforces the obvious separation between mind and social world, between self and society, or between person and culture. The assumption of the person as a self-contained individual on-guard against the influence of others is a key idea of Western personality psychology and of lay understanding of personality. In the earlier example, through American eyes, Hiroki, the boy who is acting out in class, is seen as resisting the strictures of the classroom and railing against the coercive and boring expectations of others. Such nonnormative, out-of-role, or distinctive behavior is thought to reveal the "real" individual, the person unconstrained by situation, his quintessential traits—in this case, intelligence (Kelley, 1967). For the Japanese teachers, his actions reveal that he has yet to become proficient in the all-important skills of being a group member.

The fact that the science of personality has incorporated the individualist ontology into its theories and models is hardly surprising. The model of the person as an autonomous, independent "free" entity is the model of most of the social sciences, including psychology, sociology, and economics, and biology as well. This model builds on a philosophical legacy that includes Hobbs in the 17th century, Bentham in the 19th, and Dawkins in the late 20th (Schwartz, 1986). Moreover, this model of the person has been objectified and made real through the practices and institutions that have been structured according to these understandings.

Individualism is typically analyzed as the critical element of Western society (e.g., Carrithers, Collins, & Lukes, 1987; Guisinger & Blatt, 1994; Triandis, Bontempo, Villareal, Asai, & Lucca, 1988). Many theorists contend that the Enlightenment gave rise to the notion of the Kantian individual and the importance of individual reason and free will. Others suggest that individualism in its current form shows the stamp of the late industrial capitalism. Lebra (1992) further contends that individualism is a function of a Cartesian categorization system that draws a sharp distinction between the self and others.

The study of personality then has not been value-free but has tacitly championed and promoted a particular model of the person in much of its theorizing. It is not, however, the only model of how to be a person or the only answer to "What is a person?" Another model of the person suggests that persons are not independent, autonomous entities but are instead fundamentally interdependent with one another. The person is not, and cannot be, separated from others and the surrounding social context. Thus providing information about one's uniqueness or positive difference from others is not emphasized or rewarded, and one's internal dispositions are not accorded the same importance in understanding social behavior, whether it is school performance, marriage, or a job. Instead, as the ads in the beginning example suggest, it is better to reveal the ways in which the person is situated and connected in the social world. Such a view appears to be generally characteristic of Japan, China, Korea, Southeast Asia, and much of South America and Africa (Geertz, 1975; Markus & Kityama, 1991, Marsella, DeVos, & Hsu, 1985; Miller, 1984).

In this model, instead of describing personality in terms of essences that are inside the body and that significantly organize behavior, the interdependent model of the person gives priority to social structures and interpersonal frameworks, such as families, work groups, social roles, positions, or relationships, in defining the person (for more detailed analyses of this ontological view see Fiske, Kitayama, Markus, & Nisbett, 1998; Markus et al., 1996). Accordingly, coherence in behavior is a function of the specific model of the person that is invoked. Social contexts frame the meanings of individual behavior and afford characteristic patterns to behavior.

In this alternative model of the person, it is important not to become separate from others but instead to fit with others, to fulfill and create obligation, and in general to become part of various interpersonal relationships. Persons are made meaningful in reference to those relationships of which they are a part (Ames, Dissanayake, & Kasulis, 1994). And people will feel good and experience well-being when they maintain such social embeddedness. It is one's willingness to incur social obligation that gives meaning to existence—being "part of it" with multiple ties and social entailments is the basis of being a person. For example, Sinha and Sinha (1997), in describing Western and American views of the person and society note that in the West, the relation between person and society is expressed as "man and society" or perhaps "man in society," whereas in India the expression "man–society" is most appropriate; it captures a symbiotic relationship between the two and implies that the two cannot be separated. When a person is understood as separated and independent from others and made up of traits or dispositions, responsibilities to others or connections to others are framed as volitional and as a consequence of individual preferences or desires. Responding to the needs or requirements of others can be seen as sacrificing one's individual control. When, for example, Americans are thanked for something that they have done for others, it is common to hear "Oh I like to do these kinds of things" or "It was my pleasure," implying it was an autonomous act revealing one's altruistic and prosocial dispositions.

Further, in cultural contexts that reflect and promote an interdependent understanding of the person, consistency and distinctiveness are not moral obligations in the sense that they are not key to being a "good" or "appropriate" cultural participant. In fact, consistency or distinctiveness in a person's behavior may indicate inappropriate behavior or moral failing; they can suggest that a person is being too self-concerned, inflexible, and insufficiently responsive to the requirements of others in the situation. Moreover, given the relatively tight organization of social life (Triandis, 1995) in cultural contexts with an interdependent view of the person, many social activities are heavily scripted and a person's actions are highly prescribed—what to wear, what gift to bring, what and when to eat, who to address and how, when to arrive, when to leave, what to say, what not to say. Given knowledge of the social situation, predicting individual behavior is likely to be a more straightforward endeavor, and knowledge of the distinctive features or tendencies of the individual may not be particularly helpful.

The view of the person as interdependent has a variety of philosophical origins. In East Asian contexts, the core cultural idea of the cultivation of the individual into a social person through virtuous actions is anchored in the writing of Confucius and Mencius and finds expression in an array of economic, political, and social institutions. From a Confucian perspective, for example, groups are not separate from individuals. Individuals must work through others—that is their nature. To reveal themselves, they must be part of groups, such as families, communities, and nations (Lebra, 1976; Tu, 1994). Being receptive to others or influenced by them and their often competing requirements is not a sign of inauthenticity, waffling, or hypocrisy but rather a sign of self-control and maturity.

WHAT IS HUMAN AGENCY?

Cultural perspectives on personality raise such questions as "What is the source of agency?" or "How is agency and control represented and construed?" and reveal that conceptions of agency or control are also based on culture-specific theories of personhood. In North American perspectives, personal agency is anchored in the fundamental assumption that the self is autonomous and separate from others and situations and that individual choice is opposed to social influence. In the Western conception of the self as independent and separate from others, one's own wishes, desires, interests, and abilities are the chief constituents of selfhood. To be a person—to demonstrate selfhood—one must express and develop these wishes, desires, abilities, and interests; one must make individual choices at every point and not be influenced by the situation or by others. Not to do so is to be less than one's complete or self-actualized self; constraints on one's total expression of wishes, desires, abilities, or interests are self-limiting and viewed as opposed to being a fully functioning human. Identities are not given (or are not believed to be given) by ethnicity, gender, status, or family conditions; instead, the person is expected to explore the multiplicity of possibilities available, to match those possibilities to his or her abilities and interests, and to "choose" the option that best maximizes this match. This Western view of the person is summed up by one contemporary theorist who wrote, "We are not what we are but what we make of ourselves" (Giddens, 1991, p. 75). In this view of the person, "because one wants to" is the most basic element of self-determination, and freedom, unconstrained choice, and personal desire are the purest forces in directing behavior (Lillard, 1998). When behavior is not based on freedom, choice, and autonomy, it is viewed as inauthentic, incomplete, or immature.

In this Western view, agency is located entirely within the person and the person's intentions, thoughts, wishes, or goals are fundamental in understanding behavior. Indeed, intentionality is such a basic assumption that one observer commented that it becomes almost impossible for North Americans to conceptualize a situation in which choice or intention is not implicated in efforts to understand another person's behavior (Rosen, 1995). He elaborated with this example: "When Bismarck said, upon hearing of the death of the czar, 'I wonder what he could have meant by that?' he showed just how far our explanatory scheme may have carried us" (Rosen, 1995, p. 7). Not only do North Americans impute intentionality to events that are outside a person's control, but they also tend to impute intentionality to inanimate objects. For example, it would not be uncommon to hear a person who is having trouble budging a tight screw complain, "It doesn't want to come loose." Such statements, though illogical, express the individualist's concern with and presumptions concerning intention as the basis of motivation and agency.

Consequently, Western theories of agency and motivation have tended to view personal choice as the ultimate good; research with Western populations often supports the view that decisions based on personal choice (rather than the influence of others, rewards, or situational pressures) are the most potent in directing behavior, in providing satisfaction, and in channeling motivation (Batson, 1991; Lepper, Greene, & Nisbett, 1973). Duties, obligations, or roles are viewed as constraints on the "true self" that lies behind and is prior to social roles and relationships.

For example, Deci and Ryan's (1991) motivational theory is based on the view that the more autonomous or self-determined a person's reasons for engaging in a behavior, the more positive are the outcomes and attitudes associated with it. When a person's reasons for a behavior are influenced by outside factors (such as social norms, expectations of others, or expectations of reward), the outcomes and attitudes associated with it will be less positive. They suggest that the "true self" is represented fully in completely self-determined behavior; behavior that is controlled by outside forces is not representative of the true self or true agency. Research based on this theory shows that individuals who pursue autonomous or self-determined goals report higher levels of self-actualization, vitality, and well-being than those who pursue goals that were controlled or influenced by others (Kasser & Ryan, 1996).

Research in Asian cultures presents a somewhat different view of agency and motivation. For example, in contrast to North Americans, who report feeling less satisfaction and desire to help when helping is given in response to social expectations or reciprocity than when it is freely given, Hindu Indians report equal degrees of satisfaction and liking to help in these two types of situations (Miller & Bersoff, 1994). Contrary to the North American view that good marriages are a consequence of personal choices based on romantic love, attraction, and similarity, Hindu Indians whose marriages were arranged by their families reported more intense love for their partners after several years of marriage than did similar couples in marriages based on love (Gupta & Singh, 1982). Similarly, Chinese American and Japanese American children report higher levels of interest in a task when their mothers have chosen the activity than when the activity was self-selected (Sethi & Lepper, 1997).

As these examples indicate, individualistic theories of human agency and control may not fully account for behavior when the self is based on social relationships. A central premise in the interdependent model of the self is the belief that self-development or human nature is based on cultivating close bonds through empathy and sensitivity to the others with whom one is related; behaviors predicated upon wishes, needs, or conditions of significant others are not understood as distinct from or in opposition to the individual's wishes and desires (Tu, 1994). In fact, in many cultural constructions, such as among Hindu Indians, acting in response to duty, obligation, or social expectations is viewed as a sign of maturity and as "emanating from one's nature—one can't help doing it" (O'Flaherty and Derritt, 1978; quoted in Miller & Bersoff, 1994). Given this perspective, there is no necessary conflict between self-determined action and social obligations. In cultures such as India or Japan, personal agency may not be located entirely in the individual but may instead be located in the network of relationships among people or in the social obligations that affirm and express the self.

Recognition of these divergent understandings of the self requires reconsideration of what it means to be self-directed, self-determined, and agentic. If the self is understood in terms of internal essences, then self-determined, self-directed behavior requires expression of these essences. But if the self is understood as socially constructed and interdependent with others, then the notions of self-direction or self-determination take on a different cast. In this view, agentic behavior is not free from influence by others or the social context, but rather is quite often indistinguishable from social norms, social obligations, or the expectations of others. Describing the Japanese notion of *sunao* (or cooperativeness), White and LeVine (1986) observe that "a child that is *sunao* . . . has not yielded his or her personal autonomy for the sake of cooperation: cooperation does not suggest giving up the self, as it may in the West: it implies that working with others is the appropriate way of expressing and enhancing the self" (p. 58).

Given the interdependent model of the self, expressing one's internal attributes through choices is not as important as fitting in with others and behaving appropriately in one's social interactions. This lack of emphasis on personal choice is reflected in the core Japanese cultural concept of *enryo,* which represents avoidance of expressing personal desires, preferences, or wishes. To show *enryo* one is expected not only to refrain from expressing one's opinions but also to "sidestep choices when they are offered" (Smith, 1983, p. 87). In fact, choices are less often offered in Japan than in the United States (Wierzbicka, 1997). American guests are offered a multitude of options by their hosts, which reflects the cultural belief in the individual as composed of unique wishes and desires that require expression (Doi, 1981; Markus & Kitayama, 1991). This can overwhelm Japanese visitors, who are accustomed to hosts who attempt to anticipate the wishes and preferences of a guest and to provide the experiences or foods that they believe the guest will enjoy. It is then the guest's obligation to partake of what is offered so that he does not give offense to the host by suggesting that he has made poor decisions (Smith, 1983). So *enyro* also reflects the motivation not to hurt, inconvenience, or embarrass others, or, in some cases, the self (Wierzbicka, 1997).

Choice, then, can be expected to play a reduced role in directing motivation among Japanese and other Asians relative to its prominence in theories of motivation in the West. It can in fact be viewed as a burden. This effect is most salient in cross-cultural studies of cognitive dissonance. Briefly, most cognitive dissonance paradigms require that participants perceive themselves to have acted "freely" in a situation in which they anticipated a negative consequence of their behavior. However, some attempts to replicate cognitive dissonance studies cross-culturally have failed (see Heine & Lehman, 1997b, for a review). For example, Heine and Lehman (1997b) found that Japanese students displayed less dissonance reduction in a forced-choice study than did Canadian students. In the forced choice paradigm, participants are asked to select one of two options that they have previously designated as similarly desirable. Dissonance is created as a result of postdecisional regret ("Did I make the right choice?"). After making the choice, they are asked to rerate the desirability of these two options. Repeatedly, studies with American participants show that they reduce dissonance by exaggerating the differences between the chosen and nonchosen options (relative to their initial ratings). Japanese participants, however, did not show this pattern of spreading the alternatives. Heine and Lehman suggest that because internal wishes, preferences, and other attributes are not as indicative of the true self as are roles, relationships, and group memberships for the Japanese, the possibility of making a bad choice is not a strong threat to the interdependent self and would not cause distress or dissonance.

It is unclear whether previous studies of cognitive dissonance with Asian populations have employed paradigms that might be threatening to the interdependent self. In a situation in which one's status as a good group member or relationship partner is threatened, individuals with interdependent self-construals may experience dissonance. The route to recovery from dissonance, however, may be very different for individuals who define themselves interdependently than for those with an independent self-construal. The former may be more likely to seek to repair the potentially damaged relationship or to seek forgiveness from others in the situation rather than seek to affirm an independent view of themselves as competent and effective decision makers. Along these lines, Japanese have a much greater likelihood of offering apologies in situations, even when they are not at fault (see Heine, Lehman, Kitayama, & Markus, 1998, for a review).

Culture and Self-Enhancement

Other self-related motivations may engage different processes when the self is construed as interdependent or relational compared to the independent self. In the United States, where the cultural criteria of selfhood are to be unique, to be different, and to express a core self, individuals routinely display self-serving biases, illusions of invulnerability, and other forms of self-enhancement. Self-enhancement, in this case, may be defined as efforts to view oneself as above average on domains that are important to self-definition. These self-enhancing efforts are generally related to self-esteem and well-being in Western populations (Taylor & Brown, 1988). Studies of self-enhancement and its consequences in collectivist cultures are more mixed. Although some studies have revealed that Asian respondents engage in self-enhancement (e.g. Falbo, Poston, Triscari, & Zhang, 1997), others have shown that members of Asian cultures are less likely to self-enhance than are their North American counterparts (Yik, Bond, & Paulhus, 1998; Heine & Lehman, 1997a). One might expect that an interdependent person, although not self-enhancing on attributes indicative of the independent self (as is typical in studies of self-enhancement) might be more likely to self-enhance in domains relevant to the interdependent self-construal. Some evidence supports this suggestion; for example, Heine and Lehman (1997a) found that Japanese showed more favorability biases when asked to evaluate a close family member than when asked to evaluate themselves (see also Endo, Heine, & Lehman, 1998).

Self-enhancing biases and illusions serve quite nicely as a means of demonstrating one's attainment of the Western cultural ideal—of being an independent, unique, autonomous individual. But very different processes and behaviors are required to demonstrate the Eastern cultural ideal—of fitting into and being interdependent with others. One achieves the cultural task of fitting into and mutual participation in a relationship or situation by identifying first the consensual standards of excellence for that relationship or situation and then by identifying the ways in which one falls short of these standards (Kitayama, Markus, Matsumoto, & Norasakkunkit, 1997). As a result, individuals are encouraged and afforded opportunities to examine their shortcomings, problems, and deficits and to identify ways in which they can improve (Lewis, 1995). Children in Japanese elementary school, for example, are taught to reflect on the day's activities and their part in them and on what problems can be identified, and then they are encouraged to think about what can be improved in the coming day. Such practices of self-reflection and self-criticism are pervasive in Japanese society. This apparently negative orientation, however, is unrelated to general self-esteem for the Japanese (Kitayama et al., 1997). In other words, Japanese who engage in a self-critical orientation do not feel particularly badly about themselves as a person. Kitayama and his colleagues conclude that among Japanese, feelings of well-being or satisfaction may not depend on positive appraisals of the self (see also Suh, Diener, Oishi, & Triandis, 1998).

Japanese cultural practices and Japanese situations that emphasize a self-critical orientation may be so pervasive as to influence sojourners from other cultures. Heine and Lehman (1998) found that American teachers working in Japan for the first time experienced decreases in self-esteem over a several-month period. Conversely, newly arrived Japanese students in Canada experienced increases in esteem over time, presumably as a result of the culture's emphasis on attention to positive aspects of the self. In short, the underlying purpose of standing out and being unique in the West and of self-criticism among Japanese may be similar—to demonstrate one's selfhood and adequacy as a member of society. But these findings point out the underlying individualistic assumptions in current theories of self-esteem and demonstrate the need for new conceptualizations of self-esteem in sociocultural contexts that emphasize fitting in, playing one's proper role, and being part of a network of relationships (see also Wierzbicka, 1996).

Theories of Control and Ephemeral Forces

Many East Asian and other collectivist cultures also locate agency or causes in a third factor—supernatural or ephemeral forces. Among some groups, dead ancestors, ghosts, or other sorts of spirits are believed to direct individuals' lives either completely or periodically (Fajans, 1985; Fortes, 1987; Lutz, 1985; Mageo & Howard, 1996). Among other cultural groups, fate, destiny, or concepts like the Chinese notion of *yuan* are important causes of situations and people's actions. *Yuan,* translated as "fate" or "destiny," particularly influences interpersonal relationships. The Chinese believe that many relationships are predestined and *yuan* determines whether a relationship is good or bad. The wise person, then, accepts the relationship as it is and need not take responsibility for whether it is good or bad. Consequently, attributing a bad relationship to *yuan* "makes a life fraught with misery in interpersonal relationships more bearable, because *yuan* is an external factor over which one has no control, and it therefore strengthens the durability of interpersonal relationships (especially close ones in the family or clan) regardless of how unhappy they may be" (Yang, 1997, p. 255). In situations in which marriages have been arranged by families, attributing a bad relationship to *yuan* makes the person less likely to blame others and thus able to avoid interpersonal conflict. Likewise, recognition of *yuan* reduces the likelihood of others' jealousy and promotes social harmony with others who have not been so fortunate (Yang, 1997).

Recognition of the importance of beliefs in fate, destiny or chance highlights cultural differences in beliefs about personal control. When fate, chance, the gods, or other ephemeral forces have some control over one's life, the degree of personal control that is expected or encouraged from the individual is necessarily diminished. In the West, individuals are viewed as having control over most domains of their lives. The implicit assumption, which is often made explicit, is "If you don't like something (about yourself, your life, your situation), then change it!" One consequence of this assumption is the well-documented illusion of control; numerous studies of Americans show that they tend to assume more control over chance or uncontrollable events than is warranted (see Taylor & Brown, 1988). In contrast, in many collectivist cultures, the individual's realm of control is viewed as much more limited. For example, Japanese students report feeling much less control over both positive and negative events than do North American students (Heine & Lehman, 1995). Similarly, Crandall & Martinez (1996) found that Mexicans viewed others' weight as much less controllable than did students in the United States, and were consequently less likely to blame overweight individuals for their size.

When the causes of behavior are multiply determined, then efforts to locate a single or primary cause and to modify it may prove futile. Consequently, notions of personal control and efficacy in East Asian cultures may be more complex, contextual, or situation-specific than those in the West. In Japan, as noted by Weisz, Rothbaum, and Blackburn (1984), attempts to change a situation to fit one's own desires (what they have termed "primary control") are often not as valued or effective as efforts to achieve harmony in the situation and to adjust to it (termed "secondary control"). This valuing of fitting in, accepting, and accommodating to a situation may be very effective when the causes of a situation are multiple, interrelated, or uncontrollable and so not amenable to personal attempts to change. Concern with adapting to or fitting into one's situation is reflected in the Japanese cultural ideal *akirame,* which may be defined as being "at peace with what fate has given" (Weisz, Eastman, & McCarty, 1996). For the Japanese, the mature person is the one who can restrain his or her own wishes and desires so as to fit into and work together with others. Similarly, in some Hindu Indian traditions, voluntarily giving up control and detaching oneself from the vicissitudes of life is seen as having positive consequences for mental health (Berry et al., 1992). These perspectives contrast sharply with Western interpretations of such behavior as passive, helpless, and related to depression (Alloy & Abramson, 1988; Peterson & Seligman, 1984).

In summary, the cultural psychology of personality should incorporate the fact that there is cultural divergence in the very meanings and understandings of the terms "person," "behavior," and "agency"—terms upon which a theory of personality rests. Table 15.1 briefly summarizes a few of the differences in cultural understandings we have addressed. Although the number of answers that can be given to the questions posed here are not infinite, it should be clear there are a variety of ways that each can be answered and the answer given will have significant consequences for a theory and science of personality. Table 15.1 illustrates this variability by giving two examples for each question.

In addition, a cultural approach suggests that members of Western cultures who frame the self as relational or interdependent may be motivated differently than those who adopt an independent view of the self. Even among those with an independent self-construal, there may be times and situations in which self-criticism, secondary control, or other-directed behavior is adaptive and supportive of well-being. For example, many Americans include specific close relationships (e.g., one's spouse or mother) within the self (Aron, Aron, Tudor, & Nelson, 1991). In some of these relationships, efforts to harmonize with one's relationship partner may be more adaptive and conducive to well-being than attempts to change the person or the relationship (Van Lange, Rusbult, & Drigotas, 1997). Similarly, research on the self-improvement motive lags behind research on other self-related motives (e.g., self-enhancement, self-verification, and self-assessment; Sedikides & Strube, 1997). Western researchers may find it helpful to look to their Asian colleagues for insight into this process and effective means of investigating it. Cultural psychology promotes a more global view of the origins and processes underlying human agency as well as a richer understanding of possible variations within cultures.

WHAT DOES A CULTURAL APPROACH SUGGEST ABOUT TRAIT THEORIES OF PERSONALITY?

This cultural examination of the causes of behavior and the basis of agency brings us to the question of the role of traits in personality theory. Much of Western academic personality theory has focused on traits and their interrela-

TABLE 15.1. Two Approaches to Questions Raised by a Cultural Analysis of Personality

Question	Independent view of self	Interdependent view of self
What is a person?	• An autonomous, "free" entity • "Possesses" distinctive attributes or processes	• An interdependent entity • Fundamentally connected to others • Part of encompassing social relationships
What are the sources of behavior?	• Behavior results from the operation or expression of internal attributes—traits, preferences, attitudes, goals, motives	• Behavior results from adjusting to or being responsive to the others with whom one is interdependent; and from restraining or controlling individual desires, tendencies
What is the basis of individual coherence in behavior?	• The operation of traits, dispositions, internal attributes	• Fulfilling consensual roles; meeting expectations, obligations; conforming to norms
Where is individual agency?	• In "choosing" goals; in "making" plans; in "doing what one wants"; in "controlling," mastering, or changing the social world from which one is independent	• In "adjusting to" and "attuning with" the standards, expectations, or duties that define one's encompassing relationships and thus the person; in fitting or harmonizing with the social world with which one is interdependent

tions as the fundamental basis of understanding the person. As described above, causes of behavior are assumed to be "inside" the person and based on the individual's unique assemblage of attributes, abilities, attitudes, and beliefs. Yet our brief overview of perspectives on causality and control suggests that internal causes of behavior, such as traits, may not be as central in understanding behavior in non-Western cultures.

Our goal in this section is not to exhaustively review the evidence for and against the universality of traits (or any particular model of traits), but rather to bring to light some issues that become more apparent through the lens of cultural psychology. (For recent reviews of the existing cross-cultural literature on traits, see Church & Lonner, 1998; de Raad, Perugini, Hrebickova, & Szarota, 1998; McCrae, Costa, del Pilar, Rolland, & Parker, 1998). To keep this section relatively brief, we confine our comments to three primary questions:

1. How significant are traits for understanding the personality structure of members of non-Western cultures?
2. How adequate are Western approaches or models for capturing personality structure in other cultures?
3. How do personality traits relate to culturally appropriate behavioral outcomes?

Other issues, such as methodological concerns in cross-cultural research on traits, are important as well, and the interested reader is directed to other treatments of this issue (see Berry, Poortinga, Segall, & Dasen, 1992; Church & Lonner, 1998; Geisinger, 1994). Shweder and Sullivan (1990) also critique the dualistic assumptions underlying the trait approach to personality. Much of the discussion that follows is focused on the five-factor model (FFM) of personality, yet we hasten to add that the FFM is not the only model of personality or particularly the most widely accepted model in the West. There are certainly other approaches and programs of research that have made important contributions to understanding personality structure and function. Cross-cultural research on the FFM has boomed in the past two decades and thus is used here as an example for addressing trait theories in general.

How Significant Are Traits for Understanding the Personality Structure of Members of Non-Western Cultures?

Overhead among a group of young people on the street in Tokyo: "He's much too particular and inflexible for me—a typical blood type A. I'm looking for an ambitious and romantic type O." In China, a similar group of young people may discuss balances between yin and yang or hot and cold factors as explanations for their own and others' behavior. As these examples suggest, Japanese, Chinese, and indeed members of most cultures mark and delineate individual differences in characteristics or attributes. Mounting evidence, however, indicates that these factors are not accorded the weight or importance that traits and similar terms are given in the West. In many Asian cultures, traits and dispositions are used less often to explain behavior than are situations and relationships. For example, when asked to describe why a person committed a highly publicized murder, Chinese participants explained the situation in terms of failed relationships, societal pressures, and situational factors, whereas U.S. participants tended to explain the murders in terms of personality traits, attitudes, or psychological problems (Morris & Peng, 1995). Likewise, Hindu Indians are less likely to attribute behavior to dispositional causes than are North Americans (Miller, 1988). When asked to describe themselves, Japanese and Chinese respondents use far fewer trait terms than do American respondents (Bochner, 1994; Kanagawa, Cross, & Markus, 1998; Rhee, Uleman, Lee, & Roman, 1995; Shweder & Bourne, 1984). Japanese students' self-descriptions are also more likely to be influenced by situational factors than are North American student's self-descriptions, indicating that the Western idea of a stable set of attributes that underlie the individual's self-concept is not fully shared by the Japanese (Kanagawa et al., 1998).

One purpose of a focus on traits as a central means of understanding the person may be to provide a sense of individual coherence. As we described earlier, coherence and continuity in many Asian cultures is defined by one's place in the family, in one's community, or in the social structure. In contemporary Western society, traditional markers of identity (e.g., one's occupation, marital status, age, or gender) do not provide clear directives as to how one should behave or who one is—they no longer define the person. Thus, the coherence and predictability of an individual's behavior is not anchored in external referents (such as roles or statuses), so the individual must establish an internal basis for coherence and continuity (Camilleri & Melewska-Peyre, 1997). The tools provided by Western culture for this project are traits, attributes, goals, abilities, and other internal characteristics. So for members of these cultures, a sense of coherence and predictability in understanding oneself and others derives from identifying internal characteristics that are assumed to be stable and enduring. In contrast, in Asian cultures, coherence and predictability lie in one's roles, relationships, obligations, and social ties, which are viewed as stable and enduring.

If traits and similar individual differences are not the foundation of personal coherence and consistency in Asian cultures, they may be less powerful in predicting behavior in those cultures than in Western societies. As Triandis (1995) suggests, members of many collectivist cultures may be less "traited"; proportionally less of the life space of the individual can be represented in terms of traits. Although trait terms and other conceptions of internal attributes may be used to characterize the self and others in these various cultures, the relationships between measures of personality traits and behavioral measures may be lower in these cultures than in Western cultures (Church & Lonner, 1998). More useful measurement of personality traits may need to take into account the situational specificity of many behaviors in collectivist cultures or the dynamic interplay between personal characteristics and roles or situations in behavior.

How Adequate Are Western Approaches or Models for Capturing Personality Structure in Other Cultures?

Critics from among Western personality psychologists have often argued that the trait approach, and the five-factor approach it has spawned, is atheoretical. The FFM is largely a product of factor analysis rather than a theoretical development (Block, 1995). As such, it draws particular scrutiny from non-Western psychologists, who question whether a theory based on North American folk beliefs and the English language should apply to other cultures who may not share Western ideologies and conceptions of the person. Yet advocates of the approach point to mounting evidence for the replicability of the five-factor model in a wide range of cultures (Bond, 1994; Church & Lonner, 1998; McCrae & Costa, 1997). There is, however, also mounting evidence of its inadequacies as a universal model. Much of the existing support for the FFM comes from research based on translated instruments developed in North America (such as the NEO-PI; McCrae & Costa, 1997), which, when administered in other societies, often reveal factor structures very similar to existing findings based on North American samples. Critics of this approach argue that studies that take concepts and measures created with respect to one culture and import them into another culture (termed "imposed etic") are especially likely to reveal evidence of cross-cultural comparability and are unlikely to identify culture-specific constructs (Church & Lonner, 1998). As a result, these studies will likely only map a portion of the life space that can be characterized by traits.

The remainder of the trait-based life space may be captured by terms for salient individual differences represented in the local lexicon. Several studies have used a lexical approach, examining the structure of personality terms derived from dictionaries of the natural language (see for example, De Raad et al., 1998). This approach (labeled "emic," meaning culture-specific) often reveal dimensions that are very similar to dimensions of the FFM, but just as often they reveal culturally specific dimensions as well (see Church & Lonner, 1998, for a review). For example, research among Chinese populations (Cheung & Leung, 1998) and in the Philippines (Guanzon-Lapena, Church, Carlota, & Katigbak, 1998) has identified culturally unique personality attributes that do not clearly map onto the FFM (see also Diaz-Guerro & Diaz-Loving, 1994, for a Latin American example). Among the Chinese, the dimension Chinese Tradition has been shown to be an important component of Chinese personality structure that is not represented by the FFM (Zhang & Bond, 1998).

How Do Personality Traits Relate to Culturally Appropriate Behavioral Outcomes?

Much of the cross-cultural research with the five-factor model has focused on identifying similar factor structures across cultures. Less often has cross-cultural research on Western models of personality focused on the relation between these dimensions and important aspects of well-being or behavior. This leaves unanswered the critical question of the utility of these measures in the task of predicting and explaining human behavior or promoting well-being. Among the Fulani people of Burkino Faso, attributes such as optimism or a tendency toward depression are viewed as aspects of personality, but "the Fulani, contrary to ourselves, do not in the least see the personality as affecting one's eventual success or failure in life" (Riesman, 1992, p. 165).

Other empirical evidence that Western trait measures may not adequately predict behavior in other cultures comes from studies of Chinese populations. In comparative studies that included measures of the Big Five, the Chinese Tradition factor was positively related to life satisfaction and negatively related to antisocial behavior (Cheung & Leung, 1998). In addition, it predicted unique variance in an important Chinese characteristic, filial piety, over that predicted by the FFM dimensions (Zhang & Bond, 1998). Zhang & Bond (1998) concluded that indigenous constructs were better predictors of filial piety than universal constructs, and that Western models of personality are often unable to adequately explain phenomena that are uniquely important to non-Westerners. In short, even though the factor structure of the FFM can be more or less replicated in many cultures, this finding, in and of itself, says nothing about whether that structure or those dimensions adequately represent the lived experience of other peoples (Markus & Kitayama, 1998).

These findings suggest that Western models have ignored potentially important components of personality structure, particularly those that reflect interpersonal relationships and social interaction. Perhaps more importantly, these imported Western approaches may *conceive* of personality very differently from their East Asian counterparts. The prevailing view in much of North American psychology is that traits are relatively stable, enduring aspects of the person (Allport & Odbert, 1936). In contrast, a central concept in Confucian perspectives is that personality is a *process* of self-realization rather than a relatively fixed state. In the words of one scholar, "Confucians do not believe in fixed personalities. While they regard personalities as accomplishments, they insist that the strength of one's personality lies not in its past glories but in its future promises. Real personalities are always evolving" (Tu, 1994, p. 183). As Pervin (1994) has noted, Western researchers have tended to focus on the stability of personality and have slighted evidence for its change and development with shifting contexts and life stages.

In addition, Chinese perspectives on personality often include the notion of an "ideal" toward which one should strive. One of the central doctrines of Confucian ideology is the doctrine of the Mean. It dictates that the individual should strive to avoid one-sidedness and extremity in personality development and should instead seek to possess all the valued attributes in moderation (Yang, 1997). In Japanese culture, many descriptions of persons include references to a prototypical ideal for the particular roles the person inhabits (termed *rashii*) (see Markus & Kitayama, 1998, for a full description). The young person whose characteristics are very similar to the ideal student is described as "student-*rashii*." Likewise, a father who fits the ideal prototype is described as "father-*rashii*." Few Western theories of personality include this conception of an ideal and the implications for personality theory that derive from it. Furthermore, models of personality such as the FFM seldom articulate the processes involved in personality development across the life span. A truly universal theory of personality must account for different basic dimensions of personality as well as cultural variation in conceptualizations of the nature and goal of personality itself.

This dynamic view of personality as situated in contexts and social environments can be found in North American personality theory. It is most clearly expressed in the work of Mischel and his colleagues (Mischel, 1990; Mischel & Shoda, 1995) and Cantor and her colleagues (Cantor, 1990, 1994; Cantor & Kihlstrom, 1987). In Cantor's work, personality is the social knowledge that individuals use in working on important life tasks. From this perspective, personality is adaptive and domain specific; it is the sum of one's efforts toward solving particular life problems and fitting into the social niches one inhabits. Personality is not represented as a stable constant that drives behavior, but it is contingent, responsive to the social world, and calibrated to the situation and particular task at hand—much like the interdependent view of behavior. Indeed, Cantor recognizes that "we too often act as if individuals 'have' personalities, forgetting that what people 'do' or try to do, and with whom they do it, can define and redefine who they are and who they will become" (quoted in Pervin, 1996, p. 267).

Mischel (1990) also focuses on dynamic interplay between aspects of the person and characteristics of the situation in understanding personality. In contrast to the search for cross-situational consistency that has characterized much of personality research, Mischel and Shoda (1995) recommend a "process" conception of personality, in which an "explicit focus on the relationships between psychological features of situations and the individual's patterns of behavior variation across situations, rather than undermining the existence of personality, needs to become part of the conception of personality" (p. 250). In this perspective, the goal of personality researchers is not only to understand stable individual differences between people but also to understand stable intraindividual patterns of variability across situations, or distinctive "if . . . then . . . situation–behavior profiles" (Mischel & Shoda, p. 255). This conception of the dynamics of personality takes into account the social requirements and constraints of situations, as well as idiosyncratic or situation-specific construals of the self.

In short, these perspectives on personality articulated by Cantor and Mischel and Shoda align with Asian views of the person and personality. Their similarities include a focus on understanding individual variations as defined by social situations, and thus they acknowledge that different social situations, roles, and expectations encourage and afford different behavioral patterns. They also share the assumption of the person as an explicitly social being. The notion of "social" employed in these perspectives, however, may be very different from the predominant view in Western personality theory, in which the autonomous, self-contained individual *inhabits* a world of other autonomous, self-contained individuals. In contrast, the Asian interdependent personality model and the Mischel–Cantor–Shoda perspective represent the social as *constituting* the person. Sociocultural worlds, both local (as in the school camp studied by Mischel and Shoda) and extensive (as in the broad cultural system of Japan) create, foster, and promote certain characteristic modes of behavior, thinking, and feeling. These modes are consolidated and continued within the structure of the practices and institutions of everyday life.

In conclusion, viewing personality as defined, constituted, and enlivened by culture results in new answers to the questions "What is a person?", "Where is individual agency?", and even "What is personality?" The understandings gleaned when examining these questions cross-culturally not only challenge prevailing theories and paradigms in Western psychology but also provide new tools and concepts for expanding and enhancing those theories. Just as the exploration of the moon and beyond has yielded innumerable benefits for contemporary society, so also the exploration of psychology from a cultural perspective is likely to yield multiple benefits for the discipline of personality. Because the task of identifying the diversity of answers to these and other basic questions about personality and human behavior has only recently begun, today's researchers are uniquely poised to articulate the agenda and goals of a cultural psychology of personality for the 21st century.

REFERENCES

Alloy, L. B., & Abramson, L. Y. (1988). Depressive realism: Four theoretical perspectives. In L. B. Alloy (Ed.), *Cognitive processes in depression* (pp. 223–265). New York: Guilford Press.

Allport, G. W., & Odbert, H. S. (1936). Trait-names: A psycho-lexical study. *Psychological Monographs, 47* (211).

Ames, R. T., Dissanayake, W., & Kasulis, T. P. (1994). *Self as person in Asian theory and practice.* Albany, NY: State University of New York Press.

Aron, A., Aron, E. N., Tudor, M., & Nelson, G. (1991). Close relationships as including other in the self. *Journal of Personality and Social Psychology, 60,* 241–253.

Azuma, H. (1984). Secondary control as a heterogeneous category. *American Psychologist, 39,* 970–971

Batson, C. D. (1991). *The altruism question: Toward a social–psychological answer.* Hillsdale, NJ: Erlbaum.

Berry, J. W., Poortinga, Y. H., Panday, J. , Dasen, P. R., Saraswathi, T. S., Segall, M. H., & Kagitcibasi, C. (1997). *Handbook of cross-cultural psychology* (2nd ed.). Boston: Allyn and Bacon.

Berry, J. W., Poortinga, Y. H., Segall, M. H. & Dasen, P. R. (1992). *Cross-cultural psychology: Research and applications.* Cambridge: Cambridge University Press.

Block, J. (1995). A contrarian view of the five-factor approach to personality description. *Psychological Bulletin, 117,* 187–215.

Bochner, S. (1994). Cross-cultural differences in the self-concept: A test of Hofstede's individualism/collectivism distinction. *Journal of Cross-Cultural Psychology, 25,* 273–283.

Bond, M. H. (1994). Trait theory and cross-cultural studies of person perception. *Psychological Inquiry, 5,* 114–168.

Brown, D. E. (1991). *Human universals.* New York: McGraw-Hill.

Camilleri, C., & Malewska-Peyre, H. (1997). Socialization and identity strategies. In J. W. Berry, P. R. Dasen, & T. S. Saraswathi (Eds.), *Handbook of cross-cultural psychology: Vol. 2. Basic processes and human development* (pp. 41–67). Boston: Allyn & Bacon.

Cantor, N. (1990). From thought to behavior: "Having" and "doing" in the study of personality and cognition. *American Psychologist, 45,* 735–750.

Cantor, N. (1994). Life task problem solving: Situational affordances and personal needs. *Personality and Social Psychology Bulletin, 20,* 235–243.

Cantor, N., & Kihlstrom, J. F. (1987). *Personality and social intelligence.* Englewood Cliffs: Prentice Hall.

Carrithers, M., Collins, S., & Lukes, S. (1987). *The category of the person: Anthropology, philosophy, history.* Cambridge, UK: Cambridge University Press.

Cheung, F. M. & Leung, K. (1998). Indigenous personality measures—Chinese examples. *Journal of Cross-Cultural Psychology, 29,* 233–248.

Church, A. T., & Lonner, W. J. (1998). The cross-cultural perspective in the study of personality: Rationale and current research. *Journal of Cross-Cultural Psychology, 29,* 32–62.

Crandall, C. S., & Martinez, R. (1996). Culture, ideology, and antifat attitudes. *Personality and Social Psychology Bulletin, 22,* 1165–1176.

Cross, S. E., & Madson, L. (1997). Models of the self: Self-construals and gender. *Psychological Bulletin, 122,* 5–37.

Deci, E. L., & Ryan, R. M. (1991). A motivation approach to self: Integration in personality. In R. A. Dienstbier (Ed.), *Perspectives on motivation, Nebraska Symposium on Motivation, 1990* (pp. 237–288). Lincoln, NE University of Nebraska Press.

De Raad, B., Perugini, M., Hrebickova, M., & Szarota, P. (1998). Lingua franca of personality—taxonomies and structures based on the psycholexical approach. *Journal of Cross-Cultural Psychology, 29,* 212–232.

Diaz-Guerro, R, & Diaz-Loving, R. (1994). Personality across cultures. In L. L. Adler & U. P. Gielen (Eds.), *Cross-cultural topics in psychology* (pp. 125–138). Westport, CT: Praeger.

Doi, T. (1981). *The anatomy of dependence.* Tokyo: Kodansha.

Endo, Y., Heine, S. J., & Lehman, D. R. (1998). *Culture and positive illusions in close relationships: How my friendship is better than yours.* Unpublished manuscript, Nara University, Nara, Japan.

Fajans, J. (1985). The person in social context: The social character of Baining "psychology." In G. M. White & J. Kirkpatrick (Eds.), *Person, self, and experience* (pp. 367–400). Berkeley: University of California Press.

Falbo, T., Poston, D. L., Jr., Triscari, R. S., & Zhang, X. (1997). Self-enhancing illusions among Chinese schoolchildren. *Journal of Cross-Cultural Psychology, 28,* 172–191.

Fiske, A. P., Kitayama, S., Markus, H. R., & Nisbett, R. E. (1998). The cultural matrix of social psychology. In D. Gilbert, S. Fiske, & G. Lindzey (Eds.), *Handbook of social psychology* (pp. 915–981). New York: McGraw-Hill.

Fortes, M. (1987). *Religion, morality, and the person: Essays on Tallensi religion.* Cambridge, UK: Cambridge University Press.

Funder, D. C. (1997). *The personalty puzzle.* New York: Norton.

Geertz, C. (1973). *The interpretation of cultures.* New York: Basic Books.

Geertz, C. (1975). On the nature of anthropological understanding. *American Scientist, 63,* 47–53.

Geisinger, K. F. (1994). Cross-cultural normative assessment: Translation and adaptation issues influencing the normative interpretation of assessment instruments. *Psychological Assessment, 6,* 304–312.

Giddens, A. (1991). *Modernity and self-identity: Self and society in the late modern age.* Cambridge, UK: Polity Press.

Guanzon-Lapena, M. A. , Church, A. T., Carlota, A. J., & Katigbak, M. S. (1998). Indigenous personality measures—Philippine examples. *Journal of Cross-Cultural Psychology, 29,* 249–270.

Guisinger, S., & Blatt, S. J. (1994). Individuality and relatedness: Evolution of a fundamental dialect. *American Psychologist, 49,* 104–111.

Gupta, U., & Singh, P. (1982). Exploratory studies in love and liking and types of marriages. *Indian Journal of Applied Psychology, 19,* 92–97.

Heine, S. J., & Lehman, D. R. (1995). Cultural variation in unrealistic optimism: Does the West feel more invulnerable than the East? *Journal of Personality and Social Psychology, 68,* 595–607.

Heine, S. J., & Lehman, D. R. (1997a). The cultural construction of self-enhancement: An examination of group-serving biases. *Journal of Personality and Social Psychology, 72,* 1268–1283.

Heine, S. J. & Lehman, D. R. (1997b). Culture, dissonance, and self-affirmation. *Personality and Social Psychology Bulletin, 23,* 389–400.

Heine, S. J. & Lehman, D. R. (1998). *Acculturation and self-esteem change: Evidence for a Western cultural foundation in the construct of self-esteem.* Unpublished manuscript, University of Pennsylvania, Philadelphia, Pennsylvania.

Heine, S. J., Lehman, D. R., Kitayama, S., & Markus, H. R. (1998). *Culture and the need for positive self-regard.* Manuscript in preparation, University of Pennsylvania, Philadelphia, Pennsylvania.

Kanagawa, C., Cross, S. E., & Markus, H. R. (1998). *Who Am I: The cultural psychology of the conceptual self.* Unpublished manuscript.

Kasser, T., & Ryan, R. M. (1996). Further examining the American dream: Differential correlates of intrinsic and extrinsic goals. *Personality and Social Psychology Bulletin, 22,* 280–287.

Kelley, H. H. (1967). Attribution theory in social psychology. In D. Levine (Ed.), *Nebraska symposium on motivation* (Vol. 15, pp. 192–240). Lincoln, NE: University of Nebraska Press.

Kitayama, S., Markus, H. R., Matsumoto, H., & Norasakkunkit,V. (1997). Individual and collective processes in the construction of the self: Self-enhancement in the United States and self-criticism in Japan. *Journal of Personality and Social Psychology, 72,* 1245–1267.

Leary, M. R., Tambor, E. S. Terdal, S. K., & Downs, D. L. (1995). Self-esteem as an interpersonal social monitor: The sociometer hypothesis. *Journal of Personality and Social Psychology, 68,* 518–530.

Lebra, T. S. (1976). *Japanese patterns of behavior.* Honolulu: University of Hawaii Press.

Lebra, T. S. (1992). *Culture, self and communication.* Unpublished manuscript, University of Michigan, Ann Arbor, Michigan.

Lepper, M., Greene, D. & Nisbett, R. E. (1973). Undermining children's intrinsic interest with extrinsic reward: A test of the overjustification hypothesis. *Journal of Personality and Social Psychology, 28,* 129–137.

Lewis, C. C. (1995). *Educating hearts and minds: Reflections on Japanese preschool and elementary school.* New York: Cambridge University Press.

Lillard, A. (1998). Ethnopsychologies: Cultural variations in theories of mind. *Psychological Bulletin, 123,* 3–32.

Lutz, C. (1985). Ethnopsychology compared to what? Explaining behavior and consciousness among the Ifaluk. In G. M. White & J. Kirkpatrick (Eds.), *Person, self, and experience* (pp. 35–79). Berkeley: University of California Press.

Mageo, J., & Howard, A. (Eds.). (1996). *Spirits in culture, history, and mind.* New York: Routledge.

Marcia, J. E. (1966). Development and validation of ego-identity status. *Journal of Personality and Social Psychology, 5,* 551–558.

Markus, H., & Kitayama, S. (1991). Culture and the self: Implications for cognition, emotion, and motivation. *Psychological Review, 98,* 224–253.

Markus, H. R. & Kitayama, S. (1998). The cultural psychology of personality. *Journal of Cross-Cultural Psychology, 29,* 63–87.

Markus, H. R., Kitayama, S., & Heiman, R. J. (1996). Culture and "basic" psychological principles. In E. T. Higgins & A. W. Kruglanski (Eds.), *Social psychology: Handbook of basic principles* (pp. 857–913). New York: Guilford Press.

Marsella, A. J., DeVos, G., & Hsu, F. L. (Eds.). (1985). *Culture and self: Asian and Western perspectives.* New York: Tavistock.

McCrae, R. R., & Costa, P. T., Jr. (1997). Personality trait structure as a human universal. *American Psychologist, 52,* 509–516.

McCrae, R. R., Costa, P. T., Jr., del Pilar, G. H., Rolland, J.-P., & Parker, W. D. (1998). Cross-cultural assessment of the five-factor model—The revised NEO personality inventory. *Journal of Cross-Cultural Psychology, 29,* 171–188.

McCrae, R. R., Costa, P. T., & Yik, M. S. (1996). Universal aspects of Chinese personality structure. In M. H. Bond (Ed.), *The Handbook of Chinese Psychology* (pp. 189–207). Hong Kong: Oxford University Press.

Miller, J. G. (1984). Culture and the development of everyday social explanation. *Journal of Personality and Social Psychology, 46,* 961–978.

Miller, J. G. (1988). Bridging the content-structure dichotomy: Culture and the self. In M. H. Bond, *The cross-cultural challenge to social psychology* (pp. 266–281). Newbury Park, CA: Sage.

Miller, J. G. (1997). Agency and context in cultural psychology: Implications for moral theory. *New Directions for Child Development, 76,* 69–85.

Miller, J. G., & Bersoff, D. M. (1994). Cultural influences on the moral status of reciprocity and the discounting of endogenous motivation. *Personality and Social Psychology Bulletin, 20,* 592–602.

Mischel, W. (1990). Personality dispositions revisited and revised: A view after three decades. In L. A. Pervin (Ed.), *Handbook of personality: Theory and research,* (pp. 111–134). New York: Guilford Press.

Mischel, W., & Shoda, Y. (1995). A cognitive–affective system theory of personality: Reconceptualizing the invariances in personality and the role of situations. *Psychological Review, 102,* 246–268.

Morris, M. W. & Peng, K. (1995). Culture and cause: American and Chinese attributions for social and physical events. *Journal of Personality and Social Psychology, 67,* 949–971.

Pervin, L. A. (1994). A critical analysis of current trait theory. *Psychological Inquiry, 5,* 103–113.

Pervin, L. A. (1996). *The science of personality.* New York: Wiley.

Peterson, C., & Seligman, M. E. P. (1984). Causal explanations as a risk factor for depression: Theory and evidence. *Psychological Review, 91,* 347–374.

Redding, S. G., & Wong, G. Y. Y. (1986). The psychology of Chinese organizational behavior. In M. H. Bond (Ed.), *The psychology of the Chinese people* (pp. 267–295). Oxford, UK: Oxford University Press.

Rhee, E., Uleman, J. S., Lee, H. K., & Roman, R. J. (1995). Spontaneous self-descriptions and ethnic identities in individualistic and collectivistic cultures. *Journal of Personality and Social Psychology, 69,* 142–152.

Riesman, P. (1992). *First find your child a good mother.* New Brusnwick, NJ: Rutgers University Press.

Rosen, L. (1995). Introduction. In L. Rosen (Ed.), *Other intentions: Cultural contexts and the attribution of inner states* (pp. 1–11). Santa Fe, NM: School of American Research.

Sampson, E. E. (1989). The challenge of social change for psychology: Globalization and psychology's theory of the person. *American Psychologist, 44,* 914–921.

Schwartz, B. (1986). *The battle for human nature.* New York: Norton.

Sedikides, C., & Strube, M. J. (1997). Self-evaluation: To thine own self be good, to thine own self be sure, to thine own self be true, and to thine own self be better. *Advances in Experimental Social Psychology, 29,* 209–269.

Sethi, S., & Lepper, M. (1997). *Rethinking the role of choice in intrinsic motivation.* Unpublished manuscript, Stanford University, Stanford, California.

Shweder, R. A. (1991). *Thinking through cultures: Expeditions in cultural psychology.* Cambridge, MA: Harvard University Press.

Shweder, R. A. & Bourne, E.J. (1984). Does the concept of the person vary cross-culturally? In R. A. Shweder & R. A. LeVine (Eds.), *Culture theory: Essays on mind, self, and emotion* (pp. 158–199). New York: Cambridge University Press.

Shweder, R. A., & Sullivan, M. A., (1990). The semiotic subject of cultural psychology. In L. A. Pervin (Ed.), *Handbook of personality: Research and theory* (pp. 399–416). New York: Guilford Press.

Sinha, D. & Kao, H. S. R. (1997). The journey to the East: An introduction. In H. S. R. Kao & D. Sinha (Eds.), *Asian perspectives on psychology* (pp. 9–22). New Delhi: Sage.

Sinha, D., & Sinha, M. (1997). Orientations to psychology: Asian and Western. In H. S. R. Kao & D. Sinha (Eds.), *Asian perspectives on psychology* (pp. 25–39). New Delhi: Sage.

Smith, R. J. (1983). *Japanese society: Tradition, self and the social order.* Cambridge, UK: Cambridge University Press.

Suh, E-K., Diener, E., Oishi, S., & Triandis, H. C. (1998). The shifting basis of life satisfaction judgements across cultures: Emotions vs. norms. *Journal of Personality and Social Psychology, 52,* 881–889.

Taylor, C. (1989). *Sources of the self: The making of the modern identity.* Cambridge, MA: Harvard University Press.

Taylor, S., & Brown, J. (1988). Illusion and well-being: A social psychological perspective on mental health. *Psychological Bulletin, 103,* 193–210.

Tobin, J. J. (1989). *Preschool in three cultures: Japan, China, and the United States.* New Haven: Yale University Press.

Triandis, H. C. (1995). *Individualism and collectivism.* Boulder, CO: Westview Press.

Triandis, H. C. (1997). Cross-cultural perspectives on personality. In R. Hogan, J. Johnson, & S. Briggs (Eds.), *Handbook of personality psychology* (pp. 439–465). San Diego, CA: Academic Press.

Triandis, H. C., Bontempo, R., Villareal, M. J., Asai, M., & Lucca, N. (1988). Individualism and collectivism: Cross-cultural perspectives on self-in-group relationships. *Journal of Personality and Social Psychology, 54,* 323–338.

Tu, W. (1994). Embodying the universe: A note on Confucian self-realization. In R. T. Ames, W. Dissanayake, & T. P. Kasulis (Eds.), *Self as person in Asian theory and practice* (pp. 177–186). Albany, NY: State University of New York Press.

Van Lange, P. A. M., Rusbult, C. E., Drigotas, S. M. (1997). Willingness to sacrifice in close relationships. *Journal of Personality and Social Psychology, 72,* 1373–1395.

Weisz, J. R., Eastman, K. L., & McCarty, C. A. (1996). Primary and secondary control in East Asia: Comments on Oerter et al. (1996). *Culture and Psychology, 2,* 63–76.

Weisz, J. R., Rothbaum, R. M., & Blackburn, T. C. (1984). Standing out and standing in: The psychology of control in America and Japan. *American Psychologist, 39,* 955–969.

White, M., & LeVine, R. A. (1986). What is an Ii Ko (good child)? In H. Stevenson, H. Azuma, & K. Hakuta (Eds.), *Child development and education in Japan* (pp. 55–62). New York: Freeman.

Wierzbicka, A. (1996). Japanese cultural scripts: Cultural psychology and "cultural grammar." *Ethos, 24,* 527–555.

Wierzbicka, A. (1997). *Understanding cultures through their key words: English, Russian, Polish, German, & Japanese.* New York: Oxford University Press.

Yang, K. S. (1997). Theories and research in Chinese personality: An indigenous approach. In H. S. R. Kao & D. Sinha (Eds.) *Asian perspectives on psychology* (pp. 236–262). New Delhi: Sage.

Yik, M. S. M., Bond, M. H., & Paulhus, D. L. (1998). Do Chinese self-enhance or self-efface? It's a matter of domain. *Personality and Social Psychology Bulletin, 24,* 399–406.

Zhang, J. & Bond, M. H. (1998). Personality and filial piety among college students in two Chinese societies. *Journal of Cross-Cultural Psychology, 29,* 402–417.

PART FOUR
CONTENT AREAS

Chapter 16

Temperament: A New Paradigm for Trait Psychology

Lee Anna Clark and David Watson

University of Iowa

ANCIENT HISTORY

Temperament is an ancient concept. As early as the fifth century B.C.E., Greek physicians believed that health depended on a harmonious blend of the four "humors." Extending this view, Galen (second century C.E.) proposed that predominance of one of the humors resulted in a characteristic emotional style or temperament that formed the core, respectively, of four basic personality types (indeed, the word "temperament" derives from the Latin "to blend," so that differences in the blend of humors were equated with differences in temperament; Digman, 1994). The "sanguine" or cheerful, active temperament reflected an excess of blood; the "melancholic" or gloomy temperament reflected an excess of black bile; "choleric" or angry, violent types had an excess of yellow bile; and an excess of phlegm was associated with the "phlegmatic" or calm, passive temperament.

Two aspects of this ancient formulation remain alive in current theories of temperament: (1) biological factors underlie observable characteristics and (2) emotions are core and defining features of temperament. As is so often the case with personality-related constructs, Allport (1937) provided a definition that captures the essential features.

> Temperament refers to the characteristic phenomena of an individual's emotional nature, including his susceptibility to emotional stimulation, his customary strength and speed of response, the quality of his prevailing mood, and all peculiarities of fluctuation and intensity of mood; these phenomena being regarded as dependent on constitutional makeup and therefore largely hereditary in origin. (p. 54)

As we discuss later, researchers today investigate serotonin deficits, the noradrenergic system, or mesolimbic dopaminergic pathways rather than imbalances among the humors, but the recognition that behavior is—in part—a function of physical characteristics was a remarkable insight. Moreover, while there is still debate on a precise definition of temperament and its distinction from personality (which we will not resolve in this chapter), following Allport, there is now widespread agreement that emotional experience and emotional regulation are intrinsic to these concepts (see Digman, 1994, for a brief history of the concept of temperament and further discussion of definitions).

A third aspect of the Greek model is humbling to admit. The observation that there were four main temperaments maps remarkably well onto the four quadrants that emerge from crossing the two primary personality dimensions, Neuroticism (or Emotional Stability) and Extraversion, of the modern theorist Hans Eysenck. Thus, the stable extravert is sanguine, the unstable extravert is choleric, the unstable introvert is melancholic, and the stable introvert is phlegmatic (Eysenck & Eysenck, 1975). Although there remains controversy regarding "What lies beyond E and N?" (Zuckerman, Kuhlman, & Camac, 1988), these two dimensions are found in all major models of temperament and personality.

A BRIEF MODERN HISTORY OF TEMPERAMENT RESEARCH

In addition to the notion that temperament reflects biologically based individual differences in emotional responding, modern temperament theories also incorporate Allport's idea that these biological differences are innate and form the foundation upon which mature personality develops. Space limitations prohibit comprehensive consideration of the variety of temperament models and measures that have been proposed, but a brief review is instructive. Since the late 1960s or so, research in childhood temperament has been dominated by the nine-dimensional structure proposed by Thomas, Chess, and Birch (1968; Thomas & Chess, 1977). Numerous spin-off measures have been developed, spanning the developmental range from birth (Medoff-Cooper, Carey, & McDevitt, 1993) through adolescence (Windle & Lerner, 1986).

Gradually accumulating research has indicated significant limitations of the model, such as the unreliability of some dimensions and, correspondingly, the replication of a smaller number of dimensions (five or perhaps seven) using factor analysis (Martin, Wisenbaker, & Huttunen, 1994). As a result, the model appears to be giving way to newer structures (e.g., Rothbart, Ahadi, & Hershey, 1994; Rothbart, Derryberry, & Posner, 1994); nevertheless, it succeeded in promoting the important view that childhood behavior was structured, measurable, and systematically related to later personality development. In addition to advances in measurement, a strength of current work in this area is the attempt to understand the phenotypic dimensions of infant and childhood temperament in terms of their underlying biological bases and also to consider their continuity and development from infancy to adult personality. In particular, considerations of infant and child data in light of Gray's (1982, 1987) and Eysenck's (1967, 1997) work has illuminated both of these efforts (e.g., Rothbart, Derryberry, & Posner, 1994).

Several researchers of adult temperament, most notably Eysenck and Strelau, derived their models from Pavlov's theory of central nervous system (CNS) properties. Not widely known in the United States, Strelau's model (1983; Strelau, Angleitner, & Ruch, 1990; Ruch, Angleitner, & Strelau, 1991; Strelau & Zawadzki, 1995) has been quite influential among European temperament researchers, and both models have spawned numerous learning-based experimental studies. The general notion of both theories is that individual differences in CNS properties (e.g., strength of excitation, arousability) influence personality, and that this linkage can be tested by observing how various conditioning parameters differ as a function of personality. Although these theories were instrumental in helping to link biological variables with dimensions of temperament, it now seems likely that they will be superseded by more sophisticated and complex models emerging in the newly developing fields of cognitive and affective neuroscience.

Gray (1982, 1987) also has offered a biological model of temperament that has notable points of overlap with Eysenck's work. Based to a large extent on pharmacological studies with animals, Gray's work has strongly influenced theorizing about dimensions of adult personality or temperament. It is noteworthy, however, that with the exception of studies of psychopathy, relatively little direct testing of his model has been carried out in people, perhaps due to difficulties in assessing the hypothesized neuropsychological systems. By contrast, Buss and Plomin (1975) articulated a temperament model that has had relatively little theoretical impact but that has been widely used in research, owing to the EASI Temperament Survey, which they developed to measure their four proposed dimensions of Emotionality, Activity, Sociability, and Impulsivity. As with other seminal work in these fields, both of these models are gradually being superseded by more recent investigations.

THE STRUCTURAL "TRAIT" APPROACH

In contrast to developmentalists and European temperament researchers, American personologists showed relatively little interest in the study of temperament as a biologically based concept through much of the 20th century. Rather, trait psychologists focused their attention on structural analyses, with the goal of creating comprehensive descriptive taxonomies of personality traits, and tended to ignore the etiology of the dimensions that they identified. This emphasis on structure led to a widespread criticism that trait psychology offered only a sterile, static description of behavior, not a true explanation for it (see Liebert & Spiegler, 1982; Mischel, 1968, 1990; Pervin, 1994). This criticism escalated with the ascendance of behaviorism during the middle part of the 20th century. Led by B. F. Skinner, behavioral theorists argued that inferred mental constructs (such as traits, habits, and instincts) were uninteresting pseudoexplanations that actually represented redundant descriptions of behavior. Skinner (1953), for instance, argued that "When we say that a man eats because he is hungry, smokes a great deal because he has the tobacco habit, fights because he has the instinct of pugnacity, behaves brilliantly because of his intelligence, or plays the piano well because of his musical ability, we seem to be referring to causes. But on analysis, these phrases prove to be merely redundant descriptions" (p. 31).

Mischel (1968) fanned the fires further when he presented evidence suggesting that trait concepts accounted for relatively little variance in—and failed to provide even a useful summary description of—behavior. Mischel's attack ignited the long-standing "person–situation debate" that continued well into the 1980s (Epstein & O'Brien, 1985; Kenrick & Funder, 1988; Mischel & Peake, 1982). Although a diversity of issues eventually was incorporated into this debate, the core controversy revolved around two central questions: First, are traits "real" in some basic psychological sense or, alternatively, do they simply reflect cognitive constructions that people impose on reality to satisfy their need for predictability and control? Second, are trait concepts useful predictors of important real-world criteria? Although critics of trait theory may remain unconvinced (e.g., Pervin, 1994), after nearly 20 years of theoretical and empirical debate, trait psychologists eventually mustered sufficient evidence to establish that the answer to both questions was "yes": Traits represent real entities that can be used to make important real-world predictions.

CONVERGENCE OF TEMPERAMENT AND STRUCTURAL APPROACHES

A key element in the resolution of the debate was the growing recognition that the major traits of personality represent basic *psychobiological* dimensions of temperament (e.g., Eysenck, 1992, 1997; Tellegen, 1985; Watson & Clark, 1993). The emergence of this recognition undoubtedly reflects several factors, three of which we highlight here. First, an explosion of research demonstrated that most personality traits have a substantial genetic component (e.g., Eysenck, 1990b; Loehlin, 1992; McCartney, Harris, & Bernieri, 1990; Plomin & Daniels, 1987; Tellegen et al., 1988); we summarize this evidence in a later section. These data indicated that underlying phenotypic descriptions of traits were more satisfying genotypic explanations of behavior.

Second, rapidly accumulating evidence in the 1980s and early 1990s established that major dimensions of personality—especially Neuroticism and Extraversion—were strongly associated with individual differences in affective experience (e.g., Meyer & Shack, 1989; Tellegen, 1985; Watson & Clark, 1984, 1992b, 1997; Watson, Wiese, Vaidya, & Tellegen, in press). This evidence provided systematic links both to the rich literature on the neurobiological basis of mood and emotion and to temperament research, as temperament had long been considered to have an emotional basis. This development thus held out promise for integrating research in the three fields of personality, mood and emotion, and temperament. Thus, the extensive data regarding the genetic and biological etiology of individual differences in each of these domains helped to establish that traits are real and represent true causes of behavior, rather than mere descriptive summaries.

Third, after decades of seemingly indifferent progress, structural research finally began to bear fruit, as researchers converged on a consensual phenotypic taxonomy of personality traits, which we describe subsequently (see also Goldberg, 1993; Watson, Clark, & Harkness, 1994). This development enabled researchers to focus more intensively on a relatively small number of consensually recognized traits, incorporating them into more complex and sophisticated conceptual schemes and generating more detailed, systematic hypotheses, which helped to clarify the real-world correlates of these traits (e.g., Watson & Clark, 1984, 1993, 1997). Thus, the emergence of a temperament-based paradigm elevated trait psychology to the status of a more mature science, which—for the first time—shows the promise of offering a comprehensive explanation of human individual differences.

Having said this, it is noteworthy that many writers continue to offer the criticism that traits represent atheoretical descriptions of behavior (see Liebert & Spiegler, 1982; Liebert & Liebert, 1998). For instance, Westen (1996) argues that "traits are simply descriptive and provide little insight into the how and why of personality. . . . They may describe and even predict behavior, but they cannot explain it" (p. 478). Similarly, Baron (1998) argues that "the trait approach . . . seeks to describe the key dimensions of personality but does not attempt to determine *how* various traits develop or *how* they influence behavior" (p. 488; emphasis in original). Although these may be accurate characterizations of the older trait literature, they fail to recognize the extraordinary developments of the past decade. With the emergence of a temperament-based paradigm, traits now can provide legitimate causal explanations for behavior, rather than mere descriptions of it.

A STRUCTURAL MODEL FOR STUDYING TEMPERAMENT

The "Big Three" as a Structural Framework

We have noted that personologists recently converged on a consensual, phenotypic taxonomy of personality traits. One factor that facilitated this consensus was the recognition that personality traits are ordered hierarchically, so that there is no fundamental incompatibility between models emphasizing a few general "superfactors" and those that include a much larger number of narrower traits (see Digman, 1997; Jang, McCrae, Angleitner, Riemann, & Livesley, 1998; John, 1990; Watson et al., 1994). At the apex of this hierarchy are the "big" traits—such as Neuroticism and Extraversion—that comprise the superfactor models. At the next lower level of the hierarchy, these very broad dispositions can be decomposed into several distinct yet empirically correlated traits. For instance, the general trait of Extraversion can be subdivided into the more specific facets of assertiveness, gregariousness, cheerfulness, and energy (Depue & Collins, in press; Watson & Clark, 1997). These facets, in turn, can be further decomposed into even more specific constructs, including very narrow traits (e.g., talkativeness) and behavioral habits (Digman, 1997).

Of course, all these levels need to be considered in a comprehensive assessment of personality. We focus primarily on the broad higher-order superfactors, because the available data are most extensive at this level of the hierarchy. For instance, there is much more evidence regarding the genetic basis of Extraversion and Neuroticism than for any other traits (Loehlin, 1992; Viken, Rose, Kaprio, & Koskenvuo, 1994). Similarly, the biological substrates of these general traits have been studied more intensively than those of the lower-order facets (e.g., Depue, 1996; Depue & Collins, in press; Eysenck, 1997; Tellegen, 1985). Consequently, we will use these superfactors as our basic organizing framework, but will consider data related to the lower-order facets when relevant.

What are the basic superfactors that comprise the apex of this hierarchy? On this point the consensus is less than complete, because the field is divided between proponents of two distinct—but closely related—models: the Big Three (e.g., Eysenck & Eysenck, 1975; Gough, 1987; Tellegen, 1985; Watson & Clark, 1993) and the Big Five (e.g., Digman, 1990, 1997; Goldberg, 1993; John, 1990; McCrae & Costa, 1987, 1997).[1] We will center our discussion around the Big Three model for two related reasons. First, this model has long guided our thinking in this area and eventually led us to develop our own Big Three instrument, the General Temperament Survey (GTS; Clark & Watson, 1990). Second, researchers within this tradition have placed a much greater value on explicating the underlying neurobiological substrates of these superfactors (e.g., Eysenck, 1992, 1997; Tellegen, 1985); in contrast, proponents of the Big Five have focused more on the phenotypic description of personality. It must be acknowledged, however, that this gap is rapidly narrowing, as Big Five researchers recently have demonstrated great interest in the biological etiology of these dimensions (e.g., Jang, Livesley, & Vernon, 1996; Jang et al., 1998; McCrae & Costa, 1996; Riemann, Angleitner, & Strelau, 1997).

As its name suggests, the Big Three model is based on the argument that three broad superfactors—which we will call Neuroticism/Negative Emotionality (N/NE), Extraversion/Positive Emotionality (E/PE), and Disinhibition versus Constraint (DvC)—are necessary to describe the highest level of the personality hierarchy. Briefly, N/NE reflects individual differences in the extent to which a person perceives the world as threatening, problematic, and distressing. High scorers experience elevated levels of negative emotions and report a broad array of problems; whereas those low on the trait are calm, emotionally stable, and self-satisfied. E/PE involves an individual's willingness to engage the environment. High scorers (i.e., extraverts) approach life actively, with energy, enthusiasm, cheerfulness, and confidence; as part of this general approach tendency, they seek out and enjoy the company of others and are facile and persuasive in interpersonal settings. In contrast, those low on the dimension (i.e., introverts) tend to be reserved and socially aloof, and they report lower levels of energy and confidence. Finally, DvC reflects individual differences in the tendency to behave in an undercontrolled versus overcontrolled manner. Disinhibited individuals are impulsive and somewhat reckless and are oriented primarily toward the feelings and sensations of the immediate moment; conversely, constrained individuals plan carefully, avoid risk or danger, and are controlled more strongly by the longer-term implications of their behavior (see Watson & Clark, 1993; Watson et al., 1994).

This model arose from the pioneering work of Eysenck and colleagues (e.g., Eysenck, 1967, 1992, 1997; Eysenck & Eysenck, 1975). As noted earlier, Eysenck originally created a widely influential two-factor model consisting of the broad traits of Neuroticism (versus emotional stability) and Extraversion (versus introversion) which, when crossed, yielded the four Greek temperaments. Subsequent analyses of expanded pools of questionnaire items later led to the identification of a third broad dimension, labeled Psychoticism (which, despite its name, is better viewed as a measure of psychopathy or disinhibition; see Digman, 1990; Watson & Clark, 1993). A scale assessing this third superfactor was included in the Eysenck Personality Questionnaire (EPQ; Eysenck & Eysenck, 1975).

Other theorists since have postulated very similar three-factor models. Tellegen (1985) proposed a scheme consisting of Negative Emotionality (cf. Neuroticism), Positive Emotionality (cf. Extraversion), and Constraint (which has a strong negative correlation with Psychoticism). We (Watson & Clark, 1993) subsequently articulated a highly similar model, with factors named Negative Temperament, Positive Temperament, and Disinhibition (versus Constraint), respectively. Furthermore, in his reformulation of the California Psychological Inventory (CPI), Gough (1987) introduced three higher-order "vectors" of Self-Realization, Internality, and Norm-Favoring, which reflect the low ends of Neuroticism, Extraversion, and Psychoticism, respectively.

Finally, Cloninger (1987) also formulated a three-dimensional model—consisting of Harm Avoidance, Reward Dependence and Novelty Seeking—that resembled these other schemes in important respects. However, the scales comprising Cloninger's Tridimensional Personality Questionnaire (TPQ; Cloninger, 1987) do not show an impressive level of convergence with the dimensions articulated by the other theorists (e.g., Heath, Cloninger, & Martin, 1994; Waller, Lilienfeld, Tellegen, & Lykken, 1991). Moreover, analyses revealed that Reward Dependence actually subsumed two unrelated factors. As a result, Cloninger (Cloninger, Svrakic, & Przybeck, 1993) revised his instrument to include four temperament factors but has not yet clearly articulated a revised theory to account for it.

With the exception of Cloninger's scheme, therefore, all of these models appear to define a single common structure. For example, Tellegen (1985) demonstrated a high degree of convergence between his factors and those of both Eysenck and Gough. Similarly, we have obtained strong correlations between our factors and those of Eysenck and Tellegen (Watson & Clark, 1993, 1997). Finally, Gough (1987) reported substantial correlations between his higher-order vectors and Eysenck's scales. To document this important point further, we administered three purported Big Three instruments—the EPQ, the CPI, and our own GTS—to a sample of 250 University of Iowa undergraduates. We then subjected the nine higher-order scales from these instruments—three for each superfactor—to a principal factor analysis (squared multiple correlations in the diagonal). As expected, three factors clearly emerged and were rotated using varimax.

The resulting factor loadings (shown in Table 16.1) clearly establish that these instruments define a common three-dimensional structure. The three factors—each of which is strongly defined by a scale from all three instruments—are easily

TABLE 16.1. Varimax-Rotated Factor Loadings of the Higher-Order Scales from the EPQ, CPI, and GTS

Scale	Factor 1	Factor 2	Factor 3
EPQ Extraversion	**.84**	–.09	–.06
GTS Positive Temperament	**.71**	–.13	–.25
CPI Internality	**–.73**	.06	–.13
GTS Negative Temperament	–.09	**.84**	.09
EPQ Neuroticism	–.16	**.81**	.07
CPI Self-Realization	.02	**–.66**	–.16
GTS Disinhibition	.19	.20	**.73**
EPQ Psychoticism	–.05	.09	**.64**
CPI Norm-Favoring	.29	–.05	**–.61**

Note. N = 250. Loadings of |.40| or greater are shown in **boldface.** EPQ, Eysenck Personality Questionnaire; CPI, California Psychological Inventory; GTS, General Temperament Survey.

identifiable as E/PE, N/NE, and DvC, respectively. It should be noted, however, that consistent with earlier studies in this area (e.g., Watson & Clark, 1993), the markers of the DvC dimension generally showed the weakest level of convergence. In addition, the GTS and EPQ scales showed the strongest convergence and consistently emerged as the best markers of the underlying dimensions.

Relating the Big Three to the Big Five

As noted earlier, the Big Three and Big Five models actually define similar trait structures. Although we are using the Big Three as our primary structural framework, we also can take advantage of the enormous amounts of data that have been collected using various Big Five measures. To integrate these findings into our framework, however, we need to consider the relation between these two taxonomies.

The Big Five model originally developed out of a series of attempts to understand the natural language of trait descriptors (see Block, 1995; Digman, 1990; Goldberg, 1993; John, 1990). Extensive structural analyses of these descriptors consistently revealed five broad factors: Neuroticism (versus Emotional Stability), Extraversion (or Surgency), Conscientiousness (or Dependability), Agreeableness (versus Antagonism), and Openness to Experience (or Imagination, Intellect, or Culture). This structure has proven to be remarkably robust, with the same five factors emerging in both self- and peer ratings (e.g., McCrae & Costa, 1987), in analyses of both children and adults (Digman, 1990, 1994), and across a wide variety of languages and cultures (e.g., Ahadi, Rothbert, & Ye, 1993; Jang et al., 1998; McCrae & Costa, 1997).

In brief, the available data indicate that these five factors represent an expanded and more differentiated version of the Big Three. Most notably, it now is clear that the Neuroticism and Extraversion factors of the Big Five essentially are equivalent to the N/NE and E/PE dimensions, respectively, of the Big Three (e.g., McCrae & Costa, 1985; Watson & Clark, 1992b, 1993; Watson, Clark, & Harkness, 1994). Thus, these taxonomic schemes share a common "Big Two" of N/NE and E/PE.

Furthermore, the DvC dimension of the Big Three has been shown to be a complex combination of (low) Conscientiousness and Agreeableness; that is, disinhibited individuals tend to be impulsive, carefree, reckless (low Conscientiousness), uncooperative, deceitful, and manipulative (low Agreeableness) (e.g., Digman, 1997; Eysenck, 1997; John, 1990; Watson et al., 1994). Finally, Openness appears to be largely unrelated to all of the Big Three dimensions (McCrae & Costa, 1985; Watson et al., 1994). Taken together, these data suggest that one can transform the Big Three into the Big Five by (1) decomposing the DvC dimension into component traits of Conscientiousness and Agreeableness and (2) including the additional dimension of Openness.

To clarify these relations further, we assessed 327 undergraduates (185 from Southern Methodist University [SMU], 142 from the University of Iowa; note that preliminary analyses of the SMU data were reported by Watson et al., 1994) on the GTS, the EPQ, and two Big Five instruments: the Revised NEO Personality Inventory (NEO-PI-R; Costa & McCrae, 1992a) and the Big Five Inventory (BFI; John, Donahue, & Kentle, 1991). We first subjected the higher-order EPQ and GTS scales to a principal factor analysis; three factors were clearly identifiable and were rotated using varimax. We then computed regression-based scores to assess each respondent's standing on these three dimensions. Next, we repeated this process using the BFI and NEO-PI-R domain scales; in this case, we calculated factor scores representing each of the Big

TABLE 16.2. **Correlations between the Big Three and Big Five Factor Scores**

Big Five score	Big Three score		
	N/NE	E/PE	DvC
Neuroticism	**.83**	–.14	–.08
Extraversion	–.10	**.78**	.09
Conscientiousness	–.08	.19	**–.54**
Agreeableness	–.17	.09	**–.50**
Openness	.03	.21	.04

Note: $N = 327$. Correlations of |.40| or greater are shown in **boldface.** Correlations of |.14| and greater are significant at $p < .05$, two-tailed. N/NE, Neuroticism/Negative Emotionality; E/PE, Extraversion/Positive Emotionality; DvC, Disinhibition versus Constraint.

Five traits. Finally, we computed correlations between these Big Three and Big Five factor scores.

The results are shown in Table 16.2. These data again clearly demonstrate that the two structural schemes share a common "Big Two" of N/NE and E/PE. In addition, the DvC dimension combines strong elements of both Conscientiousness and Agreeableness; indeed, taken together, these Big Five traits account for slightly more than half of the total variance in the DvC factor score. Finally, Openness was only weakly correlated (.21) with E/PE and was completely unrelated to the other Big Three superfactors.

These data regarding Conscientiousness, Agreeableness, and DvC have provoked an ongoing controversy (e.g., Digman, 1997; Eysenck, 1997; Goldberg, 1993). At one extreme, proponents of the Big Five have argued that the DvC dimension is an artificial "shotgun marriage" of two distinct and relatively independent traits. At the other extreme, Eysenck (1997) has asserted that Conscientiousness and Agreeableness represent lower-order components of the DvC superfactor. Although a comprehensive discussion of this issue is beyond the scope of our chapter, we must emphasize that neither of these extreme views offers a fully satisfactory account of the data.

The problem with Eysenck's argument is that it is impossible to subsume all of the content related to Conscientiousness and Agreeableness within a single higher-order dimension. For instance, we subjected the Agreeableness and Conscientiousness facets of the NEO-PI-R to a principal factor analysis and found no evidence of a single general factor; in fact, the Modesty and Tender-Mindedness scales both had loadings below .20 on the first unrotated factor. Furthermore, although the DvC factor score showed moderately strong negative associations with most of the facets of both Conscientiousness (e.g., $r = –.52$ with Dutifulness, –.52 with Deliberation, –.45 with Self-Discipline, –.43 with Achievement Striving) and Agreeableness (e.g., $r = –.53$ with Straightforwardness, –.40 with Altruism, –.36 with Compliance), it correlated only –.15 with Tender-Mindedness. Thus, existing measures of Conscientiousness and Agreeableness (particularly the latter) contain content that cannot easily be subsumed within the DvC dimension.

On the other hand, we have found no evidence to suggest that the DvC dimension represents an artificial, heterogeneous "shotgun marriage" of distinct elements related to Agreeableness and Conscientiousness. To examine this issue in greater detail, we subjected the 35 GTS Disinhibition items to a principal factor analysis in a very large sample ($N = 2,454$) of SMU undergraduates. This analysis confirmed that these items define a general factor that accounted for 73% of the common variance. Nevertheless, we also found evidence of two meaningful subfactors: The first appeared to be strongly related to (low) Conscientiousness, whereas the second seemed more relevant to (low) Agreeableness. We therefore created subscales consisting of items that were significant markers of each subfactor: The Carefree Orientation scale consists of seven positively keyed (e.g., "I don't pay much attention to where my money goes," "When I am having a good time, I don't worry about the consequences") and six negatively keyed (e.g., "I am a cautious person," "Before making a decision, I carefully consider all sides of the issue") items; whereas Antisocial Behavior includes nine positively keyed statements (e.g., "Lying comes easily to me," "I really enjoy beating the system," "The way I behave gets me into trouble").

On the basis of their content, one would expect that the Carefree Orientation and Antisocial Behavior subscales would be strongly correlated with (low) Conscientiousness and Agreeableness, respectively. We confirmed this expectation in our combined undergraduate sample. Specifically, Carefree Orientation correlated –.67 with the Conscientiousness factor score and only –.20 with the Agreeableness factor score; conversely, Antisocial Behavior correlated –.50 with Agreeableness and only –.32 with Conscientiousness (the correlations within each pair differed significantly from one another at $p < .01$, two-tailed). These results again demonstrate that the DvC dimension subsumes content relevant to both of these Big Five traits.

More importantly, our data also demonstrate that this integration of the two domains is systematic and meaningful, rather than artificial. Specifically, the correlation between the Carefree Orientation and Antisocial Behavior subscales was .47 in the original SMU derivation sample and .50 in the combined undergraduate sample. Moreover, we found significant positive correlations between many of the NEO-PI-R Agreeableness and Conscientiousness facets in the latter sample. Indeed, by creating reduced four-facet domain scales for Agreeableness (Trust, Straightforwardness, Altruism, Compliance) and Conscientiousness (Competence, Dutifulness, Self-Discipline, Deliberation), we obtained a moderate correlation of .32 between these traits. Finally, it is noteworthy that Digman (1997) found that Agreeableness and Conscientiousness consistently combine to form a higher-order $\propto$ metatrait (with N/NE defining the other pole) in analyses of Big Five scales (Extraversion and Openness formed a second metatrait). These data indicate that Eysenck's (1997) argument is not without merit, and that some (though not all) content relevant to both Conscientiousness and Agreeableness can be subsumed within an even broader superfactor.

BEYOND STRUCTURAL VALIDITY

Development of a clear structural model is an important first step in the articulation of scientific concepts, but we argued earlier that trait models had begun to transcend structuralism to provide authentic explanations for human behavior. In the following sections, we present a portion of these data as illustrative offerings. The first section draws largely from our own research and presents—in overview—a systematic array of correlates for each of the Big Three. We begin by documenting the relation between mood and temperament; thereafter, we deliberately avoid data on variables whose correlations with temperament may be explained—directly or in large part—by a shared mood component (e.g., the voluminous literature on life and job satisfaction). Subsequent sections summarize (1) accumulated genetic evidence that supports the existence of these traits, (2) recent structural–functional biological models, (3) factors that affect trait stability and change, and (4) relations with psychopathology.

Correlates of the Big Three Traits

Mood

As mentioned earlier, a great deal of data link N/NE and E/PE with individual differences in affective experience, to the point that affectivity may be viewed as a core—if not *the* core—of these two dimensions. More specifically, mood also has been shown to have two major dimensions, commonly labeled negative and positive affect, respectively (see Watson & Tellegen, 1985). Negative Affect (NA) is a general dimension of subjective distress, encompassing a number of specific negative emotional states, including fear, sadness, anger, guilt, contempt, and disgust. Positive Affect (PA), by contrast, reflects the co-occurrence among a wide variety of positive mood states, including joy, interest, attentiveness, excitement, enthusiasm, and pride.

Despite the conceptual distinctiveness of these various specific negative (or positive) mood states, it is quite well established that they substantially co-occur both within and across individuals to form general (i.e., higher-order) negative (or positive) affect dimensions (Diener, Smith, & Fujita, 1995; Watson & Clark, 1992a, 1992b). These two highly robust mood dimensions have been recovered from mood ratings of widely ranging terms, formats, and time frames (e.g., from momentary mood to average mood over the past year) (Watson, 1988), as well as in diverse cultures and languages (e.g., Balatsky & Diener, 1993; Watson, Clark, & Tellegen, 1984). It is important to stress that, despite their opposite-sounding labels, these dimensions are largely orthogonal; that is, they represent independent biopsychosocial dimensions that are under the influence of different external variables (Clark & Watson, 1988, 1991) and distinct internal biological systems (Clark, Watson, & Leeka, 1989; Depue, 1996; Depue & Collins, in press).

Individuals high in N/NE report higher levels of NA in virtually any situation, from baseline conditions to highly stressful circumstances (e.g., Watson & Clark, 1984). Conversely, high E/PE individuals are more likely to report higher levels of PA across a wide variety of situations (Watson & Clark, 1992b, 1997). Indeed, as stated earlier, the propensity to experience NA (or PA) more frequently and intensely can be considered a core feature of the N/NE (or E/PE) dimension (Tellegen, 1985; Watson & Clark, 1984, 1992b; Watson et al., in press). Although these relations have been well established in various ways by the studies cited (and many others as well), we cannot resist the temptation to present additional data to document the point using yet another method.

The data in Table 16.3 are from four longitudinal studies of college students who completed mood and activity forms repeatedly over varying lengths of time. Mood ratings were obtained using the 20-item Positive and Negative Affect Schedule (PANAS; Watson, Clark, & Tellegen, 1988). Respondents rated the extent to which they had experienced each mood term (10 each for NA and PA) on a five-point scale (*very slightly or not at all* to *very much*). The mood ratings in Table 16.3 represent respondents' mood "today" (Samples 1 and 2), "over the past few days" (Sample 3), or "over the past week" (Sample 4). In each sample, the data for each participant were averaged across the entire rating period to yield overall mean NA and PA scores. The Big Three scores are from the GTS (Studies 1 and 3) or represent factor scores calculated from the GTS and EPQ combined (Sample 2) or from the GTS, EPQ, and CPI (Sample 4). The data in Table 16.3 demonstrate that, regardless of the time frame over which it is measured or the manner in which the Big Three scores are derived, NA is strongly and consistently related to N/NE, largely unrelated to E/PE, and slightly related to DvC. Conversely, PA is strongly and consistently related to E/PE and largely unrelated to either N/NE or DvC. Clearly and simply, N/NE and E/PE define the prototype for dimensions of temperament as individual differences in affectivity.

TABLE 16.3. Correlations between the Big Three and Aggregated Mood Ratings in Four Studies

Sample	N/NE	E/PE	DvC
		Negative Affect	
1	**.41**	–.02	.19
2	**.41**	.05	.23
3	**.60**	–.26	.18
4	**.54**	–.10	.29
		Positive Affect	
1	–.14	**.35**	–.03
2	–.12	**.44**	–.09
3	–.24	**.49**	–.06
4	.01	**.44**	.12

Note. Correlations of |.30| or greater are shown in **boldface**. N/NE, Neuroticism/Negative Emotionality; E/PE, Extraversion/Positive Emotionality; DvC, Disinhibition versus Constraint. Sample 1, N = 379; mood measured daily for an average of 44 days (range = 30 to 55); Sample 2, N = 136; mood measured daily for an average of 48 days (range = 21 to 54). Sample 3, N = 61; mood measured over a minimum of 42 two-day periods (range = 39 to 45). Sample 4, N = 115; mood measured over an average of 13 weekly periods (range = 7 to 14). Temperament was measured using the GTS (Studies 1 and 3) or factor scores computed from the GTS, EPQ, and CPI (Studies 2 and 4).

Social Behavior

Social engagement is a primary defining characteristic of the E/PE dimension. Indeed, it seems tautological to present data demonstrating that extraverts have a higher level of social involvement than introverts. Rather, it is important to establish that social activity is associated with the Positive Emotionality component of E/PE as well as the Extraversion component. We have written extensively this topic elsewhere (e.g., Watson & Clark, 1997) and so only summarize these data here. In a series of studies, indices of social behavior were first shown to be correlated with measures of state positive affect (e.g., Clark & Watson, 1988). Second, social behavior was shown to be as highly correlated with measures of trait positive affect (e.g., the PANAS PA scale) as with more "pure" measures of Extraversion (e.g., EPQ-E). For example, number of hours spent with friends (measured daily for approximately 6 weeks) was equally correlated (approximately .30) with measures of positive temperament and social dominance. Similarly, a 15-item scale of social activity completed weekly for 13 weeks correlated equally (again, approximately .30) with the PANAS PA scale and with EPQ-E. In both cases, social activity was unrelated to either N/NE or DvC. More specific measures of social behavior, such as number of leadership roles, number of close friends or dating partners, and frequency of partying versus percent of weekend nights spend alone, showed similar patterns (see Watson & Clark, 1997). Although these nonaggregated indices of social behavior showed somewhat lower correlations with both types of E/PE measures (approximately .20), they again were virtually uncorrelated with the other two Big Three dimensions. These types of data demonstrate that positive emotionality and social engagement are specific to, and integral parts of, the E/PE dimension.

Lifestyle: Daily Rhythms and Sleep

Biologically based diurnal and seasonal rhythms are observed in many important behaviors of plants and animals; human behavior is no exception. For example, there is strong and consistent diurnal variation in mood: PA (but not NA) shows a roughly sinusoidal curve that tracks with other bodily cycles, such as body temperature (Clark, Watson, & Leeka, 1989; Thayer, 1989). Given that mood is a core feature of temperament, it is plausible that individual differences in daily behavior might reflect underlying variations in temperament. Research examining variation in diurnal mood cycles due to temperament, however, has been quite inconsistent, suggesting that there is no simple relation between temperament and daily mood rhythms (e.g., Clark et al., 1989). However, to investigate whether temperament might influence other aspects of daily behavior, we had students in Sample 2 record the number of hours they slept each day, whereas students in Sample 4 kept a daily log of their rising and retiring times, from which we computed total hours of sleep. The Sample 4 students also completed a revised version (Smith, Reily, & Midkiff, 1989) of the Horne and Ostberg (1977) Morningness–Eveningness Questionnaire.

There was no relation between hours of sleep and either N/NE or E/PE in either study; this nonfinding is consistent with the prior literature, which has found few simple or straightforward relations between diurnal rhythms and general affective temperament. In Sample 2, amount of sleep correlated modestly with DvC ($r = .27$, $p < .01$), with those high in disinhibition sleeping longer. In Sample 4, however, when actual rising and retiring times were recorded, so that we calculated the students' sleep time rather than having them estimate it themselves, this relation disappeared.

It is noteworthy, however, that although there was no clear relation with total sleep amount, there were significant associations between temperament and *when* students slept. First, disinhibited individuals both retired later at night and arose later in the morning ($rs = .33$ and $.36$, respectively; $p < .001$). Moreover, this effect was due significantly more to the DvC Carefree Orientation subscale ($rs = .39$ and $.43$, respectively) than to Antisocial Behavior ($rs = .19$, $p < .05$ and $.14$, ns). Similarly, disinhibited individuals displayed a more characteristic "night owl" orientation on the MEQ than did those low in disinhibition ($r = -.27$), with a much stronger relation observed for Carefree Orientation ($r = -.34$) than Antisocial Behavior ($r = -.08$).

Conversely, individuals high in E/PE were more likely to be "morning larks" (MEQ $r = .34$, $p < .01$)and to record both earlier rising ($r = -.17$, $p < .07$) and retiring times ($r = -.21$, $p < .03$, respectively). Further analysis of these data using the two GTS Positive Temperament subscales yielded interesting results. The 12-item Energy subscale reflects the more purely physical aspects of the dimension that likely are tied more directly to biological parameters (e.g., "Most days I have a lot of 'pep' or vigor" and "I can work hard, and for a long time, without feeling tired"). The Positive Affectivity subscale items, by contrast, are more laden with cognitive content (e.g., "I lead a very interesting life" and "I can make a game out of some things that others consider work"). The subscales are substantially related ($r = .57$), so strongly differential correlates are relatively rare; nevertheless, both earlier rising time ($rs = -.19$ vs. $-.06$) and MEQ scores ($rs = .33$ vs. $.23$) related significantly more to the Energy than to the Positive Affectivity subscale. (Curiously, however, retiring time was equally related to Energy and Positive Affectivity.) Although these relations are not strong and the differences are not huge, they clearly suggest that sleep behavior is tied more closely to the physical, biological aspects of positive temperament.

Lifestyle: Substance Use, Sexuality, and Spirituality

We and others have previously documented the strong relation between DvC and substance use, as well as the striking *lack* of relation of substance use with both N/NE and E/PE. For example, in a large ($N = 901$) sample of college students, alcohol use correlated .44 with DvC, but −.04 with N/NE, and .05 with E/PE (Watson & Clark, 1993, Table 23.4). Correlations with use of marijuana, cigarettes, psychedelics, and caffeine pills ranged from .23 to .33 for DvC, but were all less than $|.10|$ for both N/NE and E/PE.

Two additional large-sample replications of these data are reported in Table 16.4, along with data from two other samples. Samples 1 and 2 used a slightly modified version of the inventory described by Watson and Clark (1993); the substance-use variables from this inventory are aggregations of multiple items that assess both frequency and quantity of use. Sample 3 participants completed an abbreviated version of the survey in which all substances other than alcohol were assessed with single items. Sample 4 is the same Sample 4 whose prospective, longitudinal data are presented in Table 16.3. The alcohol use variable is the percentage of days on which students reported drinking alcohol. Only correlations with DvC and its subscales, Carefree Orientation and Antisocial Behavior, are shown in Table 16.4, because all correlations with N/NE and E/PE hover around zero.

In the college student population, it appears that use of alcohol—which is quite widespread despite its general illegality in this age group (Wechsler, Davenport, Dowdall, Moeykens, & Castilllo, 1994)—is associated more strongly with a carefree than an antisocial lifestyle (in Big Five terms, with low Conscientiousness more than low Agreeableness). This relation emerges most clearly when the usage variable represents pure frequency of use (Sample 4). College students who "just want to have fun" turn to drink on many occasions. Similarly, cigarette use (which itself is correlated with alcohol use) is nonsignificantly more related to a carefree than an antisocial lifestyle. By contrast, use of substances that are illegal regardless of age (e.g., marijuana, psychedelics, or "any nonalcohol substance" [Sample 3]), as well as substance use–related problems, are somewhat more indicative of an antisocial lifestyle. Although few of these differences were statistically significant, the consistency of the pattern is noteworthy. However, it is unclear whether this pattern will generalize to samples that include a significant proportion of individuals with serious, chronic alcohol use, in which case stronger correlations with antisocial behavior might be expected.

Promiscuous sexual behavior has also been shown to be related to DvC (e.g., Watson & Clark, 1993; Zuckerman, Tushup, & Finner, 1976). For example, in the Watson and Clark (1993) data set, sexual behavior (e.g., number of sex partners in past year) was correlated with DvC (r = .37) but not with either N/NE or E/PE (r = –.02 and –.01, respectively). Additional data—again, only for DvC and its subscales—are reported in Table 16.5. Samples 1 through 3 are the same as those reported in Table 16.4; Sample 4 (Haig, 1997) is another large (N = 408) college sample who completed a modified version of the behavioral inventory used by Watson and Clark (1993). Once again, the pattern is clear: Disinhibited individuals have more positive attitudes toward casual sex and, concomitantly, engage more freely in a variety of sexual behaviors, including those associated with some risk. Moreover, this appears to reflect an antisocial more than simply a carefree lifestyle, which is consistent with the inclusion

TABLE 16.4. Correlations of Disinhibition and Its Subscales with Substance Use

Sample	DvC	CO	AB
		Alcohol	
1	.46	**.44**	.35
2	.44	**.40**	.33
3	.43	**.41**	.29
4	.35	**.40**	.13
		Cigarettes	
1	.25	**.24**	.21
2	.30	**.26**	.25
		Marijuana	
1	.40	.34	.34
2	.36	.26	**.38**
		Psychedelics	
1	.32	.24	**.31**
2	.25	.18	**.27**
		Any nonalcohol substance	
3	.24	.19	**.27**
		Substance use-related problems	
1	.36	.31	**.35**
2	.38	.27	**.34**

Note. DvC, Disinhibition versus Constraint; CO, Carefree Orientation; AB, Antisocial Behavior. Sample 1, N = 638. Sample 2, N = 827. Sample 3, N = 197. See Watson and Clark (1993) for details regarding method, which were identical for Studies 1 and 2 and slightly modified for Sample 3. Sample 4, N = 115; see text for details. The larger of the two subscale correlations is in **boldface**; if the difference between them is significant, it is also underlined.

TABLE 16.5. Correlations of Disinhibition and Its Subscales with Sexual Behavior

Sample	DvC	CO	AB
	Number of sexual partners in the past year		
1	.30	.19	**.34**
2	.30	.19	**.31**
4	.22	.14	**.20**
	Positive attitudes toward casual sex[a]		
3	.45	.28	**.45**
4	.43	.26	**.45**
	Variety of sexual partners (seven-item scale)		
3	.32	.20	**.33**
	Risky sexual behavior (four-item scale)		
3	.32	.22	**.33**

Note. DvC, Disinhibition versus Constraint; CO, Carefree Orientation; AB, Antisocial Behavior. Sample 1, N = 638. Sample 2, N = 827. Sample 3, N = 197. See Watson and Clark (1993) for details regarding method, which were identical for Studies 1 and 2 and slightly modified for Sample 3. Sample 4 (Haig, 1997), N = 408; see text for details. The larger of the two subscale correlations is in **boldface**; if the difference between them is significant, it is also underlined.

[a]Eight-item scale in Sample 3; three-item scale in Sample 4.

of "promiscuous sexual behavior" among the criteria for psychopathy (Cleckley, 1964; Hare, 1991).

Watson and Clark (1993) also reported that "perceived spirituality" was related positively to E/PE and negatively to DvC. To examine this further, Samples 3 and 4 provided additional data on religious beliefs and behaviors, shown in Table 16.6. Scores from all Big Three factors are shown, because of the established relations of these behaviors to E/PE as well as DvC. Replicating the Watson and Clark (1993) finding, all measures relating to religious behaviors or beliefs were related to both E/PE and DvC, with some mild indication that nonreligiosity reflects a more antisocial than simply a carefree lifestyle. That religious people should be more behaviorally constrained comes as no great surprise, although it might be interesting to test the generalizability of these relations in cultures with a less puritanical streak than the United States. The extent to which the relation with E/PE may be due to the social aspects of religious behavior is unknown, but is an issue that is worthy of further investigation.

TABLE 16.6. Correlations of the Big Three and DvC Subscales with Selected Lifestyle Variables

	Big Three			DvC	
Variable (No. of items)	N/NE	E/PE	DvC	CO	AB
Sample 3					
Religious behavior (10)	–.03	.14	–.32	–.28	–.27
Conservative religious beliefs (11)	–.01	.23	–.15	–.12	–.13
Sample 4					
Religious service attendance (1)	.06	.15	–.19	–.12	**–.22**
Importance of religion (1)	.02	.17	–.23	–.15	**–.25**
Reckless driving (4)	–.02	.01	.40	.26	**.36**
Thrill seeking behaviors (17)	–.14	.24	.24	.15	**.17**
Sample 5					
High school GPA	.01	.03	–.22	**–.25**	–.13
College GPA	.06	-.02	–.27	**–.30**	–.17

Note. DvC, Disinhibition versus Constraint; CO, Carefree Orientation; AB, Antisocial Behavior; GPA, grade point average. Sample 3, N = 197. See Watson and Clark (1993) for details regarding method, which were slightly modified for this study. Correlations $\geq |.15|, p < .05$; $r \geq |.19|, p < .01$. Sample 4 (Haig, 1997), N = 408; see text for details. Correlations $\geq |.10|, p < .05$; $r \geq |.13|\ p < .01$. Sample 5, N = 716 for high school GPA; N = 831 for college GPA. The larger of the two DvC subscale correlations is in **boldface**; if the difference between them is significant, it is also underlined.

Work and Achievement

At the other end of the spectrum, a number of work- and achievement-related behaviors have been shown to have opposite associations with temperament (e.g., Barrick & Mount, 1991; Digman, 1972). For example, in Barrick and Mount's (1991) meta-analysis, Conscientiousness emerged as a significant predictor of all job performance criteria for all occupational groups, whereas E/PE was a valid predictor for two occupations involving social interaction. Watson and Clark (1993) reported that DvC scores were a stronger predictor of both first and second semester college grades than were SAT scores, even after controlling for the latter or for high school grades (the best overall predictor). In order to determine whether academic performance was differentially related to the DvC subscales, we replicated this study using a much larger sample. The results, presented at the bottom of Table 16.6, indicate that college performance is unrelated to either N/NE or E/PE but can be predicted by DvC, especially by Carefree Orientation. Thus, again not surprisingly, poor grades early in college are more likely to be obtained by those who lack discipline and prefer to live day to day rather than plan carefully for the future. The lower relation with Antisocial Behavior suggests that some students high on this dimension actually may succeed in "beating the system" whereas others do not.

Putting all of these data together, we obtain a picture that is consistent with theoretical models positing that the DvC dimension is related more to the style of affective regulation rather than the overall affective level (which is more the case with N/NE and E/PE). Disinhibited individuals experience greater reinforcement from positive stimuli and simultaneously are capable of diverting attention away from negative stimuli. This leads them to focus more strongly on the rewards than the risks of behavior and thus to engage in a wide range of pleasurable behaviors. Nonetheless, they are not immune to the negative consequences of these behaviors and so also report a greater number of behavior-related problems. The end result is a zero balance in terms of overall affective level (i.e., no strong correlation of either DvC or these various behaviors with N/NE or E/PE), but a broader range of affective experience. We return to these ideas when we discuss biological theories of the DvC dimension.

Genetic and Environmental Contributions to the Big Three Traits

We have postulated that the major traits of personality represent basic biobehavioral dimensions of temperament. We now consider data supporting this assertion. That temperament is biologically based implies that observed individual differences are substantially heritable and that they are—at least in latent form—present at birth (e.g., Buss & Plomin, 1975; Digman, 1994). That is, while biological parameters may be changed by life experiences (cf. stress reactions), our basic biological makeup is innate. Therefore, one crucial line of evidence concerns the possible hereditary basis of thesc traits.

After decades of neglect, the genetic basis of personality began to be researched systematically approximately 20 years ago, starting with the seminal contribution of Loehlin and Nichols (1976). Interest in this topic accelerated in the latter half of the 1980s (e.g., Plomin & Daniels, 1987; Tellegen et al., 1988) and has continued unabated. Consequently, we now have sufficient data to permit several basic conclusions. First, it is quite clear that all of the Big Three dimensions—and, indeed, virtually every trait that has ever been examined—has a substantial genetic component. Heritability estimates based on twin studies generally fall in the .40 to .60 range, with a median value of approximately .50 (Eysenck, 1990b; Finkel & McGue, 1997; Loehlin, 1992; Plomin & Daniels, 1987). Adoption studies tend to yield somewhat lower heritability estimates, but this may be due largely to their failure to assess nonadditive genetic variance (Plomin, Corley, Caspi, Fulker, & DeFries, 1998).

As stated earlier, the data are particularly extensive for N/NE and E/PE, and it is noteworthy that virtually identical findings have emerged across a wide variety of instruments, including the EPQ (e.g., Eysenck, 1990b; Viken et al., 1994), the CPI (Loehlin & Gough, 1990), the Multidimensional Personality Questionnaire (MPQ; Finkel & McGue, 1997; McGue, Bacon & Lykken, 1993; Tellegen et al., 1988), the Minnesota Multiphasic Personality Inventory (MMPI; Beer, Arnold, & Loehlin, 1998), and the NEO-PI-R (Jang et al., 1996, 1998). The data for the DvC dimension also have been quite consistent, with the exception of the unusually low heritability estimate (.18) for the CPI Norm-Favoring vector scale that was reported by Loehlin and Gough (1990). However, the existing data are inconsistent regarding the extent to which the genetic variance is additive versus nonadditive. Nevertheless, it is noteworthy that nonadditive dominance effects are found much more frequently for the E/PE dimension than for the other superfactors (Eysenck, 1990b; Heath et al., 1994; McGue et al., 1993).

Second, the evidence overwhelmingly suggests that the common rearing environment (i.e., the effects of living together in the same household) exerts virtually no effect on personality development (e.g., Beer et al., 1998; Eysenck, 1990b; Goldsmith, Buss, & Lemery, 1997; Plomin & Daniels, 1987; Tellegen et al., 1988). This finding was unanticipated and initially was met with some skepticism, but it has emerged so consistently that it now must be acknowledged as a necessary component in any model of personality development. Indeed, virtually the only supportive evidence comes from analyses of the E/PE factor; here, three different studies have reported significant shared environment effects (Beer et al., 1998; Goldsmith et al., 1997; Tellegen et al., 1988). However, this positive evidence must be weighed against a much larger number of studies that have found no effects due to the common rearing environment (e.g., Eysenck, 1990b; Finkel & McGue, 1997; Jang et al., 1996, 1998). We therefore see no reason to dispute Beer and colleagues' (1998) conclusion that "shared familial environmental variation is an unimportant source of individual differences in personality and interests" (p. 818).

In contrast, researchers consistently have reported substantial effects due to the unshared environment (i.e., idiosyncratic environmental stimuli that are experienced by a single individual but not by his or her biological relatives). A commonplace finding is that roughly half of the variance is attributable to hereditary, with the other half attributable to unique aspects of the environment (see Loehlin, 1992; Plomin & Daniels, 1987; Tellegen et al., 1988). However, this neat symmetry almost certainly represents a substantial overestimate of the unshared environmental variance. The problem—which has been frequently noted by investigators in this area (e.g., Eysenck, 1990b; Riemann et al., 1997; Tellegen et al., 1988)—is that the traditional method of estimating the unshared environment actually confounds (1) true environmental variance with (2) measurement error. In this regard, it is noteworthy that Riemann and colleagues (1997) were able to separate out these two effects by conducting combined analyses of both self- and peer ratings. Using this expanded approach, they found that nearly 70% of the variance in both N/NE and E/PE was due to genetic factors, with only roughly 30% attributable to the unshared environment.

Researchers also have become quite interested in examining how genetic and environmental influences may vary as a function of demographic variables such as sex and age. The data regarding sex have been markedly inconsistent, although several investigators have reported higher heritabilities for women than for men (for a review, see Finkel & McGue, 1997). The evidence regarding age is much more systematic, as several studies now have found that heritability estimates for both N/NE and E/PE are significantly lower in older respondents (McCartney et al., 1990; McGue et al., 1993; Pedersen, 1993; Viken et al., 1994). The causes of these age-related declines have not yet been clearly established, but it appears that they may differ across these two dimensions. Specifically, McGue et al. (1993) found that whereas the lower value for N/NE was due to a true decline in heritability, that for E/PE was attributable to the increased influence of the unshared environment (coupled with a stable genetic component).

Finally, this recent explosion of genetics research has yielded valuable evidence regarding the interesting issue of assortative mating; that is, whether or not people are attracted to—and ultimately marry—individuals who are phenotypically (and, therefore, genotypically) similar to themselves. In other words, do "birds of a feather flock together" or do "opposites attract"? Assortative mating is of keen interest to behavior geneticists because if it occurs, people actually will be more genetically similar to their first-degree relatives than the 50% that traditionally is assumed in the classic models. Generally speaking, however, there appears to be little or no assortative mating on any of the Big Three superfactors (e.g., Beer et al., 1998; Eysenck, 1990b; Finkel & McGue, 1997). Indeed, based on his review of the earlier literature, Eysenck (1990b) concluded that "mating is essentially random for personality differences" (p. 252). It is unclear whether this is because temperament is irrelevant in mating or because both axioms are true to some extent and their effects cancel out. There is evidence supporting assortative mating for more attitudinal aspects of personality (e.g., McCrae, 1996), but this is beyond our scope.

Biological Models of Temperament

Eysenck (1967) and Gray (1982, 1987) provided the seminal modern work on the biological bases of temperament and Eysenck (1990a) has continued to develop his ideas. Recent work has built on their "remarkably insightful ideas" (Depue, 1996; p. 348), incorporating the tremendous progress that has been made in the neurosciences in recent decades. Depue (1996; Depue & Collins, in press) has developed a comprehensive theory of the biological bases of the Big Three; Siever and Davis (1991) offered a strikingly similar psychobiological model arising from a psychiatric perspective on personality disorder. The major dimensions that underlie the various behavioral manifestations of personality disorder according to Siever and Davis (1991) are Anxiety/Inhibition, Affective Instability, Impulsivity/Aggression, and Cognitive/Perceptual Organization. The first three dimensions map onto N/NE, dysregulation in E/PE, and DvC in a remarkably straightforward way (see Clark, in press); their fourth dimension may prove to be related to the Big Five dimension of Openness, or perhaps the Peculiarity factor discussed by Berenbaum and Fujita (1994) in their review of personality dimensions in schizophrenia. We focus here on Depue's model and refer the interested reader to Siever and Davis (1991) and Clark (in press) for a discussion of their parallel schemes.

Depue has concentrated most on the dimension of E/PE, so we begin with a discussion of that dimension, followed by presentations of DvC and N/NE. First, however, we outline the basic characteristics of general "neurobehavior-emotional systems" (abbreviated here as NBE systems) according to Depue. This overview is necessarily oversimplified and, with a few exceptions, we do not reference each point with original citations. Rather, we base our description on Depue (1996) and Depue and Collins (in press) and refer the interested reader to those papers for detailed references.

Similar to the overt, phenotypic systems they underlie, general NBE systems are hierarchical. At lower levels are goal-specific systems—behavior patterns that are tied to a particular stimulus context. At intermediate levels are processes (e.g., motivational, emotional, cognitive) that operate jointly in the various specific contexts and provide a general modulating influence on behavior across changing environmental contexts. Finally, the system at its most general level is the coordination of these various processes. What distinguishes one general NBE system from another are the distinctive (1) broad classes of activating stimuli, (2) "driving" motivations and emotions, (3) facilitative cognitive processes, (4) resultant behavioral patterns, and (5) neurotransmitter systems that underlie them. What distinguishes individuals from one another in this domain (i.e., what constitutes temperament) is the strength (both absolute and relative) of their sensitivity to the particular classes of stimuli that activate each of the general NBE systems.

Extraversion/Positive Emotionality

Depue suggests that positive incentive stimuli—or signals of reward—activate the neurobiological system underlying E/PE. At the most basic level, these would include such unconditioned stimuli as food, a potential mate, and safety. With increasing environmental, social, and cognitive complexity, the stimuli that signal reward also become more complex and may include conditioned stimuli such as social interaction, hobbies, or opportunities for leadership. The motivation associated with E/PE is, accordingly, positive incentive and, as we have seen, the associated emotion is positive affect. Activation of the incentive motivation thus primes the organism to seek potential rewards with positive anticipation, feelings that might be labeled excitement, desire, or hope. The most general behavioral pattern associated with E/PE is, accordingly, approach, "forward locomotion and search behavior as a means of satisfying an animal's need for food, a sex partner, social interaction, a nesting place" (Depue, 1996, p. 350). Moreover, active goal seeking increases interaction with the environment and, therefore, increases the needs (1) to evaluate what is encountered in terms of its relevance to the target goal and (2) to develop adaptive strategies in response. Thus, the cognitive processes component of the BFS supports evaluation and behavioral flexibility.

The term "temperament" typically is centered on the motivational/emotional and behavioral components of NBE systems, but it is important to recognize their integrated nature. That is, the prototypic behavior of the high E/PE individual does not occur in a contextual vacuum. Rather, that a particular class of stimuli activates incentive motivation differentially across individuals is just as important a defining characteristic of this complex temperamental system as the resulting "extraverted" behavior.

Depue (1996) further argues that two major ascending dopamine (DA) projection systems—mesolimbic and mesocortical—underlie the facilitation of incentive motivation and, by extension, E/PE behavior. The mesolimbic system arises from the ventral tegmental area (VTA) and projects to limbic structures (amygdala, hippocampus, and nucleus accumbens [NAS]). Animal research has demonstrated that increases of DA activity in this system increase motor activity, exploratory and aggressive behavior, as well as the variety of behavior strategies employed; moreover, such increases facilitate the acquisition and maintenance of both approach and active avoidance behaviors. Conversely, lesions in this system produce major deficits in the initiation and facilitation of behavior specifically associated with incentive motivation such as sexual behavior, food hoarding, nursing, social interaction, and exploration of novel environments. The notion of "incentive motivation" is key in this regard because rote motor behaviors and nonvolitional behaviors (e.g., escape) are unaffected by such lesions.

The mesocortical system, which also originates in the VTA but projects to all areas of the cerebral cortex, modulates cognitive functions needed for behavioral flexibility and approach, and hence may be associated with E/PE. Perturbation of environmental conditions that require adaptive responding is associated with enhanced DA utilization by neurons in this system. Moreover, this system appears to play a role in spatial working memory, which would facilitate evaluation of novel environments. In summary, these DA systems working together activate the emotional response system that initiates those motor behaviors necessary for goal acquisition, and facilitates the cognitive processes that support goal acquisition by increased evaluation of the environment. Individual differences in the sensitivity of this biological system to the signals of reward that activate, in succession, incentive motivation and positive affect, approach behavior, and supportive cognitive processes, form the basis of the E/PE dimension of temperament.

Disinhibition versus Constraint

The DvC dimension is conceptualized by Depue as "reflecting the ease with which behavior is elicited by controlling stimuli" (1996, p. 360; see also Depue & Collins, in press). Thus, DvC is itself a nonaffective dimension (which is consistent with its lack of strong correlations with mood levels), but it will interact with the affective dimensions of N/NE and E/PE by affecting the links between stimulus and response. For example, individuals who are similarly sensitive to reward stimuli may still differ in their level of approach behavior because of differences on DvC. Individuals who act readily in response to stimuli are, by definition, impulsive; moreover, actions taken before full cognitive processing of information regarding the level of risk in the environment may be either reckless (danger is present) or maladaptive (e.g., fleeing from a potential reward when no true danger is present). Thus, this view of DvC is consonant with our earlier description of the dimension as reflecting individual differences in the tendency to behave in an undercontrolled versus overcontrolled manner.

In Depue's model (1996; Depue & Collins, in press), the biological basis of DvC is functional activity in CNS serotonin (5-HT) projections. The 5-HT signal exerts a tonic inhibitory influence on information flow, regardless of the type of information being conveyed. For example, both DA-mediated effects on the initiation of exploratory activity and N/NE-based warning signals are subject to its inhibitory influence. Individuals low in 5-HT are hypersensitive to sensory input so that even low-intensity stimuli may elicit a response. Consequently, each new input serves as one emotion-eliciting stimulus after another in such individuals, which is manifest as emotional lability. Moreover, chronic buffeting by stimulation is aversive and results in a tonic level of irritability, which may be the basis for the low moderate (*rs* = .20 to .30) correlation with NA. Another effect of this stimulus sensitivity is the greater influence of current, relative to future, signals of both reward and punishment. With reward signals, behavior is thus more strongly motivated by short-term than by long-term goals (e.g., fun at tonight's party rather than doing well on tomorrow's test), whereas with signals of punishment, active avoidance behavior patterns (e.g., fleeing a potentially dangerous situation or quitting a job at the first sign of difficulty) may be readily initiated rather than delaying action pending further situational assessment (e.g., that the danger is trivial or that the problems can be solved). Both of these behavior patterns describe impulsive behavior.

In addition, there is an increased magnitude of response, because negative feedback mechanisms are engaged more slowly. When DA is administered in the context of low 5-HT activity, for example, affective aggression—that is, an "attack" program that resembles incentive-reward oriented behavior—is enhanced. Similarly, in humans, low 5-HT activity is strongly associated with impulsive aggression, including arson, homicide, and suicidal behavior (Coccaro et al., 1989). Finally, low 5-HT activity is associated with increased use—and, not surprisingly, abuse—of DA-activating drugs, including alcohol, whose initial effects include increased DA release. This may seem to contradict our earlier statement about the aversiveness of chronic stimulation, but it makes sense if we assume that there also is enhancement of DA-related emotional rewards (i.e., positive affect) in low 5-HT conditions. Relatedly, primary (i.e., early onset, chronic-course, poor-outcome) alcoholism is associated with reduced 5-HT functioning.

Neuroticism/Negative Emotionality

Ironically, whereas N/NE may be the best described of the Big Three dimensions phenotypically, the least is known about its underlying neurobiology, especially in people. Thus, the formulation offered is here is speculative. Depue's neurobiological model builds on Tellegen's (1985) view that N/NE is a warning system activated under conditions of uncertainty that produce a diffuse state of NA, which motivates the organism to direct attention to scanning the environment for danger. Behavior is initially inhibited but, at the same time, the organism is prepared physiologically to deal with the danger (Cannon's [1929] fight–flight response). If uncertainty is reduced by signals of safety, NA decreases, inhibition is lifted and, if incentive conditions are present, exploratory behavior resumes.

Depue's (1996) hypothesis is that norepinephrine (NE) activity in the locus ceruleus (LC) modulates the N/NE system. In contrast to the regular firing of the 5-HT system, the LC system is more phasic, such that discharge rates are correlated with changes in vigilance and alertness, with large increases seen when threat or unexpected stimuli (and also potentially rewarding stimuli under conditions of uncertainty) are encountered. Further, peripheral (somatosensory and autonomic) stimuli provide information about the relevance of the external environment; in response to this peripheral input, LC activity increases in two ways. First, through ascending projections from the LC to the forebrain and neocortex, vigilance and scanning are activated or enhanced. Second, descending projections to the spinal cord send inhibitory signals to the autonomic nervous system, thereby modulating autonomic arousal.

It is important to note that this system does not appear to be activated by clear, unconditioned aversive signals (e.g., shock), when increased scanning would not serve an adaptive function. Rather, its critical role is in signaling the presence of stimuli that require investigation because their meaning is uncertain. Concomitantly, NE may be involved in aversive conditioning. Specifically, it has been shown that during associative learning, NE activity serves to increase the salience of relevant to irrelevant stimuli, which may work through a two-fold mechanism: NE reduces the spontaneous firing rate, which makes chance responding to irrelevant stimulus less likely and also increases the response to stronger, relevant stimuli. The net consequence is reduced uncertainty with regards to future incoming stimuli, because the distinction between relevant and irrelevant stimuli is thereby enhanced. However, if NE activity is *reduced* during the conditioning process, then the distinction between relevant and irrelevant stimuli is poorly learned and, as a consequence, the meaning of future stimuli remains highly uncertain. This creates the paradox that *low* NE activity during conditioning produces a situation in which the organism is more likely to experience frequent uncertainty, which leads, in turn, to *increased* NE activity because the LC NE system is activated by uncertainty.

Ironically, therefore, Depue (1996) has speculated that although increases in NE activity are associated with the activation of negative affect, vigilance, and scanning, it is actually more trait-like *low* NE activity that leads to the chronic uncertainty and resulting sense of apprehension that define the N/NE temperament dimension. As mentioned earlier, however, the extent to which manifest levels of N/NE "are associated with central NE reactivity is, unfortunately, completely untested" (Depue, 1996, p. 372).

The Temporal Stability of Personality

We now consider the stability of personality over time. To some readers, this discussion may seem superfluous in light of our earlier review of the heritability evidence. Indeed, a popular misconception is that because we are born with a full complement of genes, their influence necessarily must be stable and invariant throughout the life span; this, in turn, implies that there should be a direct, positive correlation between the heritability of a trait and its temporal stability (for discussions of this point, see Pedersen, 1993; Viken et al., 1994). In actuality, however, genes can be a source of both stability and change in personality. Indeed, age-specific genes (e.g., a gene that influences temperament during adolescence but is quiescent during adulthood) generally can be expected to lead to instability in individual differences over time (McGue et al., 1993; Pedersen, 1993). Conversely, unchanging aspects of the environment (e.g., a long-term career or marriage) may well play an important role in maintaining the stability of temperament. Consequently, there is no necessary correlation between stability and heritability.

Having said that, however, we also must acknowledge that the available evidence suggests that this popular view is reasonably accurate after all: Genes do appear to be the major source of the observed stability in temperament, whereas environmental factors are primarily responsible for change (McGue et al., 1993; Pedersen, 1993; Viken et al., 1994). For instance, McGue and colleagues (1993) estimated the heritability of the stable component to be .71, .89, and .89 for N/NE, E/PE, and DvC, respectively. Note that although these values demonstrate that genetic factors are overwhelmingly responsible for phenotypic stability, they also indicate that the unshared environment has a nontrivial influence on the observed continuity of temperament. Conversely, McGue et al. (1993) found that although the unshared environment was primarily responsible for observed changes on these traits, genetic factors also played a moderate role in the instability of N/NE and DvC, and a more modest role in producing changes on E/PE. McGue et al. (1993) suggested these genetic sources of instability may well be linked to the observed declines in heritability that were discussed earlier. For example, age-specific genes may exert a significant influence on N/NE in adolescence, but then decline in importance during adulthood; this would lead to both lower heritabilities and phenotypic instability in N/NE over time.

These data establish that genes are primarily responsible for stability, but they do not address the issue of stability itself. How stable are the major dimensions of temperament over time? In discussing this issue, it is useful to distinguish three different types of stability: mean-level stability, rank-order stability, and structural stability (see Pedersen, 1993). We consider first the issue of mean-level stability, that is, whether or not average levels of a trait change systematically with age. For example, do people generally become more cautious and constrained as they grow older?

Unfortunately, most of the available data are cross-sectional, rather than longitudinal; moreover, the existing evidence is not entirely consistent. Still, the data permit some tentative conclusions. First, it is clear that N/NE scores show a significant decline with age, starting in late adolescence and continuing at least into middle adulthood (Aldwin & Levenson, 1994; Helson & Klohnen, 1998; McGue et al., 1993; Viken et al., 1994; Watson & Walker, 1996). Watson and Walker (1996), for example, reported a significant decline in N/NE scores in individuals who initially were assessed in the early years of college and then were retested 6 to 7 years later (when they were, on average, approximately 25 years old). McGue et al. (1993) reported a significant decrease in participants who were roughly 20 years old at the initial assessment and approximately 30 years old at retest. Helson and Klohnen (1998) extended these findings by demonstrating a significant decrease in N/NE between the ages of 27 and 43. After that, the evidence is less clear, but it appears that N/NE scores eventually may stabilize and show little further change (Costa & McCrae, 1992b; Helson & Klohnen, 1998). Helson & Klohnen (1998), for instance, found no further decline in N/NE between the ages of 43 and 52.

Similarly, DvC scores also decline with age (e.g., Eysenck & Eysenck, 1975; Helson & Klohnen, 1998; McGue et al., 1993). Again, most of this evidence is cross-sectional, but two recent longitudinal studies have reached the same conclusion. Specifically, McGue et al. (1993) reported a significant decline in DvC across the ages of 20 to 30, whereas Helson and Klohnen (1998) found a corresponding decrease from 27 to 43. Consistent with their findings for N/NE, however, Helson and Klohnen (1998) found no evidence of significant change between the ages of 43 and 52.

Finally, the findings regarding E/PE are markedly inconsistent and permit no clear conclusion. Cross-sectional data generally show a modest negative correlation between E/PE scores and age, suggesting a slight decline across the life span (e.g., Costa & McCrae, 1992a; Eysenck & Eysenck, 1975); furthermore, analyses of the NEO-PI-R indicate that this effect is much stronger for the Excitement Seeking facet than for other components of the trait. Unfortunately, the longitudinal evidence paints a very different—and confusing—picture. Consistent with the cross-sectional evidence, Viken et al. (1994) reported a significant decline in E/PE from the early to middle 20s. In contrast, however, McGue et al. (1993) and Watson and Walker (1996) both found that E/PE scores did not change significantly across a similar age span. Finally, Helson and Klohnen (1998) reported a significant *increase* in E/PE scores between the ages of 27 and 43.

We turn now to the issue of rank-order stability, that is, the extent to which individuals maintain their relative position on the trait continuum over time. Here, the data are quite consistent and permit some firm conclusions. The clearest and best-replicated finding is that starting sometime around the age of 25 to 30, most personality traits show an impressive level of stability, even over lengthy time spans. Costa and McCrae (1992b), for instance, reported 24-year retest stabilities ranging from .61 to .71 (median = .65) on the 10 scales comprising the Guilford–Zimmerman Temperament Survey (Guilford, Zimmerman, & Guilford, 1976). Helson and Klohnen (1998) obtained very similar results in an examination of the Big Three. Specifically, they assessed women at the ages of 27 and 52 (i.e., a span of 25 years) and reported stability coefficients of .65 (N/NE), .62 (E/PE), and .51 (DvC). Not surprisingly, even higher stability estimates—generally falling in the .65 to .80 range—are obtained across shorter retest intervals of 6 to 12 years (see Costa & McCrae, 1988, 1992b; Viken et al., 1994). Thus, it now seems clear that individual differences become strongly stable and invariant after the age of 30.

But how stable are these temperamental characteristics *prior* to the age of 30? The available evidence indicates that lower—but still impressive—levels of stability can be observed on the Big Three traits starting around the age of 20. McGue et al. (1993) retested twins between the ages of 20 and 30 (i.e., a 10-year time span) and obtained stability coefficients of .60 (N/NE), .59 (E/PE), and .59 (DvC). Similarly, Viken et al. (1994) computed 6-year retest correlations on measures of N/NE and E/PE using two age-based twin cohorts (aged 18–23 and 24–29 at Time 1). Analyses of the younger cohort yielded moderate to strong stability correlations ranging from .48 to .60; not surprisingly, those for the older cohort were even higher, ranging from .56 to .69. Thus, strongly stable individual differences in temperament can be observed as early as late adolescence.

Finally, what about the stability of temperament in childhood and early adolescence? A thorough review of this large and complex literature is beyond the scope of our chapter. Briefly put, however, studies within this age range generally report significant rank-order stabilities that are substantially lower than those seen in adults (for discussions, see Caspi & Silva, 1995; Gest, 1997; Morison & Masten, 1991; Rubin, Hymel, & Mills, 1989). These lower stabilities likely reflect both (1) true developmental effects (i.e., temperamental characteristics actually are more fluid during this period) and (2) assessment problems (e.g., insufficient aggregation; the difficulties inherent in attempting to identify valid trait indicators at different stages of development). In this regard, it is noteworthy that Gest (1997) obtained extensive observational data relevant to the trait of behavioral inhibition (which, despite its name, appears to be a better marker of E/PE than DvC) at ages 10 and 20 (i.e., a 10-year time span). After aggregating both sets of data to produce highly reliable measures, he obtained evidence of strong stability (r = .57) across this extended time interval. These data indicate that it is possible to observe substantial stability even starting in childhood.

Next, we consider the issue of structural stability, that is, the extent to which the phenotypic structure of temperament is invariant across the life span. An extensive body of evidence—based on measures of both the Big Three and the Big Five—has established that essentially identical structures can be identified in high school student, college student, normal adult, and older adult samples (e.g., Costa & McCrae, 1992a; Digman, 1990; Eysenck & Eysenck, 1975; John, 1990; Mackinnon et al., 1995; McCrae, Costa, & Arenberg, 1980). Thus, personality structure shows impressive stability from adolescence through old age.

Fewer data exist for the pre-high school period, but the available evidence indicates that structures closely paralleling the Big Three and Big Five emerge at an early age. For instance, Digman and associates have replicated the Big Five structure in a series of studies in which teachers rated the characteristics of elementary school children (Digman, 1997; Digman & Inouye, 1986). Similarly, several studies have examined the factor structure of the Children's Behavior Questionnaire (CBQ; Rothbart & Ahadi, 1994; Rothbart et al., 1994), a parent-report instrument that assesses temperament in children ages 3 to 8 years. These analyses consistently have identified three higher-order factors that closely resemble the Big Three: Surgency/Extraversion (i.e., E/PE), Negative Affectivity (i.e., N/NE), and Effortful Control (i.e., DvC) (see Ahadi et al., 1993; Goldsmith et al., 1997; Rothbart & Ahadi, 1994; Rothbart et al., 1994). Coupled with evidence demonstrating the broad cross-cultural robustness of these models (e.g., Ahadi et al., 1993; Jang et al., 1998), these data support McCrae and Costa's (1997) claim that "personality structure is a human universal" (p. 514).

Temperament and Psychopathology

A prominent theme of this chapter is that the emergence of a theoretical model of temperament has led to widespread progress in the field. Like any good theory, this model not only explains a range of existing data but also suggests avenues for further exploration; moreover, it has the power to change in fundamental ways how certain phenomena are conceptualized. The domain of psychopathology is one that the emerging temperamental paradigm has the potential to transform. For decades, research in personality and psychopathology developed independently, with little cross-fertilization. Eventually, however, investigators in each of these fields began to take notice of the work in the other, to note parallelisms between findings, and to ask how personality and psychopathology might be interrelated: Does personality act as a vulnerability factor for the development of psychopathology? Is personality changed by the experience of mental disorder? Does personality affect the way in which psychopathology is manifested? Widiger, Verhuel, and van den Brink (Chapter 13, this volume) ably explore many of these questions and plumb research conducted to answer them.

The paradigm we have been discussing points in particular to one of the possibilities that Widiger and associates discuss, which they label "spectrum relationships." They note that "personality and psychopathology at times fail to be distinct conditions" (p. 351) and they use the example of personality disorder (perhaps the clearest example of the identity of personality and psychopathology) as an illustration, pointing out that it may be no more "meaningful to say that Neuroticism contributes to the development of a borderline personality disorder [than] to say that Introversion contributes to the development of extreme Introversion" (p. 351). In these cases, perhaps we may invoke Occam's razor and dispense with the notion that there is a *relationship* between personality and psychopathology, which treats them as if they were separate entities in independent domains. Rather, given that associations between N/NE and a wide range of psychopathology are now quite well established (Mineka, Watson, & Clark, 1998; Watson et al., 1994; Watson & Clark, 1994), it may be most parsimonious simply to consider N/NE an inherent component of many types of psychopathology, and to recognize that what we call personality in one context shares a common origin (not only a genetic diathesis but perhaps environmental or learning-based etiologies as well) with what we call psychopathology in another.

Similarly, extensive data point to the importance of the E/PE dimension in various types of psychopathology including, for example, bipolar and unipolar depression (e.g., Clark et al., 1989; Clark, Watson, & Mineka, 1994; Depue, 1995), schizophrenia (Fowles, 1992), and eating disorder (Vitousek & Manke, 1994). Likewise, the DvC dimension has been linked with psychopathy/antisocial personality disorder and substance abuse (Sher & Trull, 1994) and eating disorder (Vitousek & Manke, 1994). Again, it may be more parsimonious to consider the temperament dimension as a component of these disorders rather than as a separable personality factor that stands in relation to them.

Adopting this view of temperament in relation to psychopathology has far-ranging implications. First, extensive comorbidity among psychological disorders has been acknowledged as a major challenge to categorical systems of diagnosis. In community-based studies, more than half of all individuals who meet criteria for one diagnosis also have at least one additional comorbid disorder (Clark, Watson, & Reynolds, 1995). In clinical samples, the rates are considerably higher, and it is very difficult to explain these data if diagnoses are conceived as distinct entities. However, if one adopts the view that a few basic temperament dimensions underlie psychopathology, the phenomenon of comorbidity is easily understood: If a person is high on N/NE, which is a component in multiple psychological disorders, they are at increased risk for developing a broad range of disorders. Thus, the likelihood that they will develop more than one of these disorders is likewise increased. Similarly, if DvC is a major component of psychopathy and primary alcoholism, the probability that an individual will manifest neither, one, or both disorders will increase relative to an individual's level on the DvC dimension.

This analysis raises the question of the most appropriate way to conceptualize diagnoses. Clearly, it is untenable to argue that the DSM disorders represent distinct independent entities in the way that chicken pox is independent of measles. Given what appears to be a universal penchant for categorization, it is unlikely that diagnostic taxonomies will be replaced with purely dimensional systems for classifying disorders. However, it is not improbable that a systematic ordering of diagnoses could emerge from a temperament-based taxonomy, with disorders grouped into classes based in part on the primary dimensions that comprise them. Thus, for example, disorders in which a high level of N/NE is a major component (e.g., anxiety and depressive disorders, certain personality disorders) might form a higher-order category of "distress disorders" (Clark et al., 1994). Similarly, substance abuse and antisocial personality disorder might be part of a cluster of "disinhibitory psychopathology" (Sher & Trull, 1994). Finally, disorders of E/PE dysregulation might include bipolar disorder and borderline personality disorder.

The issue of diagnostic severity is a second major challenge to categorical systems of diagnosis that is addressed by adopting a temperament-based approach. Under the current system, a certain threshold of severity must be passed for an individual to receive any given diagnosis. However, in many domains of psychopathology, subclinical cases have been shown not only to exist with high prevalence but, more importantly, to represent a serious public health problem in terms of personal suffering, increased psychosocial dysfunction, and economic consequences such as unemployment, increased sick days, and lower productivity (e.g., Kessler, Zhao, Blazer, & Swartz, 1997; Klein, Lewinsohn, & Seeley, 1996; Martin, Blum, Beach, & Roman, 1996). Thus, the distinction between above-threshold and subclinical cases appears to be arbitrary and not to represent a true, natural boundary between disorder and nondisorder. This observed lack of a distinctive boundary is predicted, of course, from a temperament dimensional perspective.

In sum, the temperament-based model of personality that has emerged recently from the study of trait psychology is a powerful tool that has been fruitful in integrating diverse findings regarding personality structure and processes, the neurobiology of personality, child development, and related domains. It also has far-ranging implications for the study of psychopathology. As the recent work of Depue and Collins (in press) illustrates, full specification of this theory will prove to be extraordinarily complex. Nonetheless, we are optimistic that the broad outlines of a temperament-based paradigm have been mapped out, and that pursuing understanding the details of these temperamental systems will carry us well into the 21st century.

ACKNOWLEDGMENTS

We thank Richard Depue for his comments on a draft of this chapter.

NOTE

1. Digman (1997) has argued that the Big Five represent a *second* tier with two "metatraits" at an even higher level. We consider aspects of his argument subsequently.

REFERENCES

Ahadi, S. A., Rothbart, M. K., & Ye, R. (1993). Child temperament in the U.S. and China: Similarities and differences. *European Journal of Personality, 7,* 359–378.

Aldwin, C. M., & Levenson, M. R. (1994). Aging and personality assessment. In M. P. Lawton & J. A. Teresi (Eds.), *Annual review of gerontology and geriatrics* (Vol. 14, pp. 182–209). New York: Springer.

Allport, G. W. (1937). *Personality: A psychological interpretation.* New York: Holt.

Balatsky, G., & Diener, E. (1993). Subjective well-being among Russian students. *Social Indicators Research, 28,* 21–39.

Baron, R. A. (1998). *Psychology* (4th ed.). Boston: Allyn & Bacon.

Barrick, M. R., & Mount, M. K. (1991). The Big Five personality dimensions and job performance: A meta-analysis. *Personnel Psychology, 44,* 1–26.

Beer, J. M., Arnold, R. D., & Loehlin, J. C. (1998). Genetic and environmental influences on MMPI factor scales: Joint model fitting to twin and adoption data. *Journal of Personality and Social Psychology, 74,* 818–827.

Berenbaum, H., & Fujita, R. (1994). Schizophrenia and personality: Exploring the boundaries and connections between vulnerability and outcome. *Journal of Abnormal Psychology, 103,* 148–158.

Block, J. (1995). A contrarian view of the five-factor approach to personality description. *Psychological Bulletin, 117,* 187–215.

Buss, A., & Plomin, R. (1975). *A temperament theory of personality development.* New York: Wiley-Interscience.

Cannon, W. B. (1929) *Bodily changes in pain, hunger, fear and rage.* Boston: Branford.

Caspi, A., & Silva, P. A. (1995). Temperamental qualities at age three predict personality traits in young adulthood: Longitudinal evidence from a birth cohort. *Child Development, 66,* 486–498.

Clark, L. A. (in press). Mood, personality, and personality disorder. In R. Davidson (Ed.), *Emotion and psychopathology.* New York: Oxford University Press.

Clark, L. A., & Watson, D. (1991). Affective dispositions and their relation to psychological and physical health. In C. R. Snyder & D. R. Forsyth (Eds.), *Handbook of social and clinical psychology* (pp. 221–245). Elmsford, NY: Pergamon Press.

Clark, L. A., & Watson, D. (1988). Mood and the mundane: Relations between daily life events and self-reported mood. *Journal of Personality and Social Psychology, 54,* 296–308.

Clark, L. A., & Watson, D. (1990). *The General Temperament Survey.* Unpublished manuscript, University of Iowa, Iowa City, IA.

Clark, L. A., Watson, D., & Leeka, J. (1989). Diurnal variation in the positive affects. *Motivation and Emotion, 13,* 205–234.

Clark, L. A., Watson, D., & Mineka, S. (1994). Temperament, personality, and the mood and anxiety disorders. *Journal of Abnormal Psychology, 103,* 103–116.

Clark, L. A., Watson, D., & Reynolds, S. (1995). Diagnosis and classification in psychopathology: Challenges to the current system and future directions. *Annual Review of Psychology, 46,* 121–153.

Cleckley, H. (1964). *The mask of sanity* (4th ed.). St. Louis, MO: Mosby.

Cloninger, C. R. (1987). Neurogenetic adaptive mechanisms in alcoholism. *Science, 236,* 410–416.

Cloninger, C. R., Svrakic, D. M., & Przybeck, T. R. (1993). A psychobiological model of temperament and character. *Archives of General Psychiatry, 50,* 975–990.

Coccaro, E., Siever, L., Klar, H., Maurer, G., Cochrane, K., Cooper, T., Mohs, R., & David, K. (1989). Serotonergic studies in patients with affective and personality disorders. *Archives of General Psychiatry, 46,* 587–599.

Costa, P. T., Jr., & McCrae, R. R. (1988). Personality in adulthood: A six-year longitudinal study of self-reports and spouse ratings on the NEO Personality Inventory. *Journal of Personality and Social Psychology, 54,* 853–863.

Costa, P. T., Jr., & McCrae, R. R. (1992a). *Revised NEO Personality Inventory (NEO-PI-R) and NEO Five-Factor Inventory (NEO-FFI) professional manual.* Odessa, FL: Psychological Assessment Resources.

Costa, P. T., Jr., & McCrae, R. R. (1992b). Trait psychology comes of age. In T. B. Sonderegger (Ed.), *Nebraska symposium on motivation: Psychology and aging* (pp. 169–204). Lincoln, NE: University of Nebraska Press.

Depue, R. (1995). Neurobiological factors in personality and depression. *European Journal of Personality, 9,* 413–439.

Depue, R. (1996). A neurobiological framework for the structure of personality and emotion: Implications for personality disorders. In J. F. Clarkin & M. F. Lenzenweger (Eds.), *Major theories of personality disorder* (pp. 347–390). New York: Guilford Press.

Depue, R., & Collins, P. F. (in press). Neurobiology of the structure of personality: Dopamine, facilitation of incentive motivation, and extraversion. *Behavioral and Brain Sciences.*

Diener, E., Smith, H., & Fujita, F. (1995). The personality structure of affect. *Journal of Personality and Social Psychology, 69,* 130–141.

Digman, J. M. (1972). High school academic achievement as seen in the context of a longitudinal study of personality. *Proceedings of the Annual Convention of the American Psychological Association, 7,* 19–20.

Digman, J. M. (1990). Personality structure: Emergence of the five-factor model. *Annual Review of Psychology, 41,* 417–440.

Digman, J. M. (1994). Child personality and temperament: Does the five-factor model embrace both domains? In C. F. Halverson, G. A. Kohnstamm, & R. P. Martin (Eds.), *The developing structure of temperament and personality from infancy to adulthood* (pp. 323–338). Hillsdale, NJ: Erlbaum.

Digman, J. M. (1997). Higher-order factors of the Big Five. *Journal of Personality and Social Psychology, 73,* 1246–1256.

Digman, J. M., & Inouye, J. (1986). Further specification of the five robust factors of personality. *Journal of Personality and Social Psychology, 50,* 116–123.

Epstein, S., & O'Brien, E. J. (1985). The person-situation debate in historical and current perspective. *Psychological Bulletin, 98,* 513–537.

Eysenck, H. J. (1967). *The biological bases of personality.* Baltimore, MD: University Park Press.

Eysenck, H. J. (1990a). Biological dimensions of personality. In L. A. Pervin (Ed.), *Handbook of personality: Theory and research* (pp. 244–276). New York: Guilford Press.

Eysenck, H. J. (1990b). Genetic and environmental contributions to individual differences: The three major dimensions of personality. *Journal of Personality, 58,* 245–261.

Eysenck, H. J. (1992). Four ways five factors are not basic. *Personality and Individual Differences, 13,* 667–673.

Eysenck, H. J. (1997). Personality and experimental psychology: The unification of psychology and the possibility of a paradigm. *Journal of Personality and Social Psychology, 73,* 1224–1237.

Eysenck, H. J., & Eysenck, S. B. G. (1975). *Manual of the Eysenck Personality Questionnaire.* San Diego, CA: Educational and Industrial Testing Service.

Finkel, D., & McGue, M. (1997). Sex differences and nonadditivity in heritability of the Multidimensional Personality Questionnaire scales. *Journal of Personality and Social Psychology, 72,* 929–938.

Fowles, D. C. (1992). Schizophrenia: Diathesis–stress revisited. *Annual Review of Psychology, 43,* 303–336.

Gest, S. D. (1997). Behavioral inhibition: Stability and associations with adaptation from childhood to early adulthood. *Journal of Personality and Social Psychology, 72,* 467–475.

Goldberg, L. R. (1993). The structure of phenotypic personality traits. *American Psychologist, 48,* 26–34.

Goldsmith, H. H., Buss, K. A., & Lemery, K. S. (1997). Toddler and childhood temperament: Expanded content, stronger genetic evidence, new evidence for the importance of environment. *Developmental Psychology, 33,* 891–905.

Gough, H. G. (1987). *California Psychological Inventory* [Administrator's guide]. Palo Alto, CA: Consulting Psychologists Press.

Gray, J. A. (1982). *The neuropsychology of anxiety: An enquiry into the functions of the septa-hippocampal system.* Oxford, U.K.: Clarendon Press.

Gray, J. A. (1987). *The psychology of fear and stress* (2nd ed.). Cambridge, U.K.: Cambridge University Press.

Guilford, J. S., Zimmerman, W. S., & Guilford, J. P. (1976). *The Guilford–Zimmerman Temperament Survey Handbook: Twenty-five years of research and application.* San Diego, CA: EdITS Publishers.

Haig, J. (1997). *Sexual expectations and sexual behavior.* Unpublished manuscript, University of Iowa.

Hare, R. D. (1991). *The Hare Psychopathy Checklist—Revised manual.* North Tonawanda, NY: Multi-Health Systems.

Heath, A. C., Cloninger, C. R., & Martin, N. G. (1994). Testing a model for the genetic structure of personality: A comparison of the personality systems of Cloninger and Eysenck. *Journal of Personality and Social Psychology, 66,* 762–775.

Helson, R., & Klohnen, E. C. (1998). Affective coloring of personality from young adulthood to midlife. *Personality and Social Psychology Bulletin, 24,* 241–252.

Horne, J. A., & Ostberg, O. (1977). A self-assessment questionnaire to determine morningness-eveningness in human circadian rhythms. *International Journal of Chronobiology, 4,* 97–110.

Jang, K. L., Livesley, W. J., & Vernon, P. A. (1996). Heritability of the Big Five personality dimensions and their facets: A twin study. *Journal of Personality, 64,* 575–591.

Jang, K. L., McCrae, R. R., Angleitner, A., Riemann, R., & Livesley, W. J. (1998). Heritability of facet-level traits in a cross-cultural twin sample: Support for a hierarchical model of personality. *Journal of Personality and Social Psychology, 74,* 1556–1565.

John, O. P. (1990). The "Big Five" factor taxonomy: Dimensions of personality in the natural language and in questionnaires. In L. A. Pervin (Ed.), *Handbook of personality: Theory and research* (pp. 66–100). New York: Guilford Press.

John, O. P., Donahue, E. M., & Kentle, R. L. (1991). *The Big Five Inventory—Versions 4a and 54.* (Technical report), Institute of Personality and Social Research, University of California, Berkeley, CA.

Kenrick, D. T., & Funder, D. C. (1988). Profiting from controversy: Lessons from the person–situation debate. *American Psychologist, 43,* 23–34.

Kessler, R. C., Zhao, S., Blazer, D. G., & Swartz, M. (1997). Prevalence, correlates, and course of minor depression and major depression in the national comorbidity survey. *Journal of Affective Disorders, 45,* 19–30.

Klein, D. N., Lewinsohn, P. M., & Seeley, J. R. (1996). Hypomanic personality traits in a community sample of adolescents. *Journal of Affective Disorders, 38,* 135–143.

Liebert, R. M., & Liebert, L. L. (1998). *Personality: Strategies and issues* (8th ed.). Pacific Grove, CA: Brooks/Cole.

Liebert, R. M., & Spiegler, M. D. (1982). *Personality: Strategies and issues* (4th ed.). Pacific Grove, CA: Brooks/Cole.

Loehlin, J. C. (1992). *Genes and environment in personality development.* Newbury Park, CA: Sage.

Loehlin, J. C., & Gough, H. G. (1990). Genetic and environmental variation on the California Psychological Inventory vector scales. *Journal of Personality Assessment, 54,* 463–468.

Loehlin, J. C., & Nichols, R. C. (1976). *Heredity, environment, and personality.* Austin, TX: University of Texas Press.

Mackinnon, A., Jorm, A. F., Christensen, H., Scott, L. R., Henderson, A. S., & Korten, A. E. (1995). A latent trait analysis of the Eysenck Personality Questionnaire in an elderly community sample. *Personality and Individual Differences, 18,* 739–747.

Martin, J. K., Blum, T. C., Beach, S. R. H., & Roman, P. M. (1996). Subclinical depression and performance at work. *Social Psychiatry, 31,* 3–9.

Martin, R. P., Wisenbaker, J., & Huttunen, M. (1994). Review of factor analytic studies of temperament measures based on the Thomas–Chess structural model: Implications for the Big Five. In C. F. Halverson, G. A. Kohnstamm, & R. P. Martin (Eds.), *The developing structure of temperament and personality from infancy to adulthood* (pp. 157–172). Hillsdale, NJ: Erlbaum.

McCartney, K., Harris, M. J., & Bernieri, F. (1990). Growing up and growing apart: A developmental meta-analysis of twin studies. *Psychological Bulletin, 107,* 226–237.

McCrae, R. R. (1996). Social consequences of experiential openness. *Psychological Bulletin, 120,* 323–337.

McCrae, R. R., & Costa, P. T., Jr. (1985). Comparison of EPI and psychoticism scales with measures of the five-factor model of personality. *Personality and Individual Differences, 6,* 587–597.

McCrae, R. R., & Costa, P. T., Jr. (1987). Validation of a five-factor model of personality across instruments and observers. *Journal of Personality and Social Psychology, 52,* 81–90.

McCrae, R. R., & Costa, P. T., Jr. (1996). Toward a new generation of personality theories: Theoretical contexts for the five-factor model. In J. S. Wiggins (Ed.), *The five-factor model of personality: Theoretical perspectives* (pp. 51–87). New York: Guilford Press.

McCrae, R. R., & Costa, P. T., Jr. (1997). Personality trait structure as a human universal. *American Psychologist, 52,* 509–516.

McCrae, R. R., Costa, P. T., Jr., & Arenberg, D. (1980). Constancy of adult personality structure in males: Longitudinal, cross-sectional and times-of-measurement analyses. *Journal of Gerontology, 35,* 877–883.

McGue, M., Bacon, S., & Lykken, D. T. (1993). Personality stability and change in early adulthood: A behavioral genetic analysis. *Developmental Psychology, 29,* 96–109.

Medoff-Cooper, B., Carey, W. B., & McDevitt, S. C. (1993). Early Infancy Temperament Questionnaire. *Journal of Developmental and Behavioral Pediatrics, 14,* 230–235.

Meyer, G. J., & Shack, J. R. (1989). Structural convergence of mood and personality: Evidence for old and new directions. *Journal of Personality and Social Psychology, 57,* 691–706.

Mineka, S., Watson, D. B., & Clark, L. A. (1998). Psychopathology: Comorbidity of anxiety and unipolar mood disorders. *Annual Review of Psychology, 49,* 377–412.

Mischel, W. (1968). *Personality and assessment.* New York: Wiley.

Mischel, W. (1990). Personality dispositions revisited and revised: A view after three decades. In L. A. Pervin (Ed.), *Handbook of personality: Theory and research* (pp. 111–134). New York: Guilford Press.

Mischel, W., & Peake, P. K. (1982). Beyond *déjà vu* in the search for cross-situational consistency. *Psychological Review, 89,* 730–755.

Morison, P., & Masten, A. S. (1991). Peer reputation in middle childhood as a predictor of adaptation in adolescence: A seven-year follow-up. *Child Development, 62,* 991–1007.

Pedersen, N. L. (1993). Genetic and environmental continuity and change in personality. In T. J. Bouchard Jr. & P. Propping (Eds.), *Twins as a tool of behavioral genetics* (pp. 147–162). New York: Wiley.

Pervin, L. A. (1994). A critical analysis of current trait theory. *Psychological Inquiry, 5,* 103–113.

Plomin, R., Corley, R., Caspi, A., Fulker, D. W., & DeFries, J. (1998). Adoption results for self-reported personality: Evidence for nonadditive genetic effects? *Journal of Personality and Social Psychology, 75,* 211–218.

Plomin, R., & Daniels, D. (1987). Why are children in the same family so different from one another? *Behavioral and Brain Sciences, 10,* 1–16.

Riemann, R., Angleitner, A., & Strelau, J. (1997). Genetic and environmental influences on personality: A study of twins reared together using the self- and peer report NEO-FFI scales. *Journal of Personality, 65,* 449–475.

Rothbart, M. K., & Ahadi, S. A. (1994). Temperament and the development of personality. *Journal of Abnormal Psychology, 103,* 55–66.

Rothbart, M. K., Ahadi, S. A., & Hershey, K. L. (1994). Temperament and social behavior in childhood. *Merrill-Palmer Quarterly, 40,* 21–39.

Rothbart, M. K., Derryberry, D., & Posner, M. I. (1994). A psychobiological approach to the development of temperament. In J. E. Bates & T. D. Wachs (Eds.), *Temperament: Individual differences at the interface of biology and behavior* (pp. 83–116). Washington, DC: American Psychological Association.

Rubin, K. B., Hymel, S., & Mills, R. S. L. (1989). Sociability and social withdrawal in childhood: Stability and outcomes. *Journal of Personality, 57,* 237–255.

Ruch, W., Angleitner, A., & Strelau, J. (1991). The Strelau Temperament Inventory—Revised (STI-R): Validity studies. *European Journal of Personality, 5,* 287–308.

Siever, L. J., & Davis, K. L. (1991). A psychobiological perspective on the personality disorders. *American Journal Psychiatry, 148,* 1647–1658.

Sher, K. J., & Trull, T. J. (1994). Personality and disinhibitory psychopathology: Alcoholism and antisocial personality disorder. *Journal of Abnormal Psychology, 103,* 92–102.

Skinner, B. F. (1953). *Science and human behavior.* New York: Macmillan.

Smith, C. S., Reily, C., & Midkiff, K. (1989). Evaluation of three circadian rhythm questionnaires with suggestions for an improved measure of morningness. *Journal of Applied Psychology, 74,* 728–738.

Strelau, J. (1983). *Temperament–personality–activity.* London: Academic Press.

Strelau, J., Angleitner, A., & Ruch, W. (1990). Strelau Temperament Inventory (STI): General review and studies based on German samples. In J. N. Butcher & C. D. Spielberger (Eds.), *Advances in personality assessment* (Vol. 8, pp. 187–242). Hillsdale, NJ: Erlbaum.

Strelau, J., & Zawadzki, B. (1995). The Formal Characteristics of Behavior—Temperament Inventory (FCB-TI): Validity studies. *European Journal of Personality, 9,* 207–229.

Tellegen, A. (1985). Structures of mood and personality and their relevance to assessing anxiety, with an emphasis on self-report. In A. H. Tuma & J. D. Maser (Eds.), *Anxiety and the anxiety disorders* (pp. 681–706). Hillsdale, NJ: Erlbaum.

Tellegen, A., Lykken, D. T., Bouchard, T. J., Jr., Wilcox, K. J., Segal, N. L., & Rich, S. (1988). Personality

similarity in twins reared apart and together. *Journal of Personality and Social Psychology, 54,* 1031–1039.
Thayer, R. E. (1989). *The biopsychology of mood and arousal.* New York: Oxford University Press.
Thomas, A., Chess, S., & Birch, H. (1968). *Temperament and behavior: Disorders in children.* New York: New York University Press.
Thomas, A., & Chess, S. (1977). *Temperament and development.* New York: Brunner/Mazel.
Viken, R. J., Rose, R. J., Kaprio, J., & Koskenvuo, M. (1994). A developmental genetic analysis of adult personality: Extraversion and neuroticism from 18 to 59 years of age. *Journal of Personality and Social Psychology, 66,* 722–730.
Vitousek, K., & Manke, F. (1994). Personality variables and disorders in anorexia nervosa and bulimia nervosa. *Journal of Abnormal Psychology, 103,* 137–147.
Waller, N. G., Lilienfeld, S. O., Tellegen, A., & Lykken, D. T. (1991). The Tridimensional Personality Questionnaire: Structural validity and comparison with the Multidimensional Personality Questionnaire. *Multivariate Behavioral Research, 26,* 1–23.
Watson, D. (1988). The vicissitudes of mood measurement: Effects of varying descriptors, time frames, and response formats on measures of Positive and Negative Affect. *Journal of Personality and Social Psychology, 55,* 128–141.
Watson, D., & Clark, L. A. (1984). Negative affectivity: The disposition to experience aversive emotional states. *Psychological Bulletin, 96,* 465–490.
Watson, D., & Clark, L. A. (1992a). Affects separable and inseparable: A hierarchical model of the negative affects. *Journal of Personality and Social Psychology, 62,* 489–505.
Watson, D., & Clark, L. A. (1992b). On traits and temperament: General and specific factors of emotional experience and their relation to the five-factor model. *Journal of Personality, 60,* 441–476.
Watson, D., & Clark, L. A. (1993). Behavioral disinhibition versus constraint: A dispositional perspective. In D. M. Wegner & J. W. Pennebaker (Eds.), *Handbook of mental control* (pp. 506–527). Upper Saddle River, NJ: Prentice Hall.
Watson, D., & Clark, L. A. (Eds.). (1994). Personality and psychopathology [Special issue]. *Journal of Abnormal Psychology, 103*(1).
Watson, D., & Clark, L. A. (1997). Extraversion and its positive emotional core. In R. Hogan, J. Johnson, & S. Briggs (Eds.), *Handbook of personality psychology* (pp. 767–793). San Diego, CA: Academic Press.
Watson, D., Clark, L. A., & Harkness, A. R. (1994). Structures of personality and their relevance to psychopathology. *Journal of Abnormal Psychology, 103,* 18–31.
Watson, D., Clark, L. A., & Tellegen, A. (1984). Cross-cultural convergence in the structure of mood: A Japanese replication and comparison with U. S. findings. *Journal of Personality and Social Psychology, 47,* 127–144.
Watson, D., Clark, L. A., & Tellegen, A. (1988). Development and validation of brief measures of Positive and Negative Affect: The PANAS Scales. *Journal of Personality and Social Psychology, 54,* 1063–1070.
Watson, D., & Tellegen, A. (1985). Toward a consensual structure of mood. *Psychological Bulletin, 98,* 219–235.
Watson, D., & Walker, L. M. (1996). The long-term stability and predictive validity of trait measures of affect. *Journal of Personality and Social Psychology, 70,* 567–577.
Watson, D., Wiese, D., Vaidya, J., & Tellegen, A. (in press). The two general activation systems of affect: Structural findings, evolutionary considerations, and psychobiological evidence. *Journal of Personality and Social Psychology.*
Wechsler, J., Davenport, A., Dowdall, G., Moeykens, B., & Castillo, S. (1994). Health and behavioral consequences of binge drinking in college: A national survey of students in 140 campuses. *Journal of the American Medical Association, 272,* 1672–1677.
Westen, D. (1996). *Psychology: Mind, brain, and culture.* New York: Wiley.
Windle, M., & Lerner, R. M. (1986). Reassessing the dimensions of temperamental individuality across the life span: The Revised Dimensions of Temperament Survey (DOTS-R). *Journal of Adolescent Research, 1,* 213–229.
Zuckerman, M., Kuhlman, D. M., & Camac, C. (1988). What lies beyond E and N? Factor analyses of scales believed to measures basic dimensions of personality. *Journal of Personality and Social Psychology, 57,* 96–107.
Zuckerman, M., Tushup, R., & Finner, S. (1976). Sexual attitudes and experience: Attitude and personality correlates and changes produced by a course in sexuality. *Journal of Consulting and Clinical Psychology, 44,* 7–19.

Chapter 17

The Psychological Unconscious

John F. Kihlstrom
University of California, Berkeley

The doctrine of mentalism, which lies at the heart of psychology, states that mental states are to actions as causes are to effects. As psychology developed as an empirical science, and especially after the cognitive revolution overthrew behaviorism in the 1960s, research focused on those mental states that were accessible to consciousness. However, even the 19th-century psychologists recognized that consciousness is not all there is to the mind.

HISTORICAL PERSPECTIVES

Based on his observations of hysterical patients, and his analysis of such phenomena as dreams, errors, and jokes, Freud (1900/1953, Chap. 7) initially proposed a topographical division of the mind into three mental compartments, or "systems," which he called CsT, PCS, and Ucs. The system Cs, or conscious mind, contained those thoughts, feelings, motives, and actions of which we are phenomenally aware at the moment. Consciousness was explicitly likened to a sensory organ capable of perceiving other mental contents. The system PCS, by contrast, contained mental contents not currently in conscious awareness, but which were available to consciousness, and which could be brought into awareness under certain conditions. Finally, the system Ucs contained mental contents that are unavailable to consciousness—that could not enter awareness under any circumstances.

Freud maintained this account of the vicissitudes of consciousness for approximately two decades (Freud, 1915–1917/1962, 1963), but then introduced a wholesale revision of his view, shifting from a topographical to a functional analysis of the mind (Freud, 1940/1964). Rather than three different storage structures, this new account postulated three different types of mental activity, the id, ego, and superego. The id was described as the seat of the instincts, which were expressed through either the automatic discharge of reflex action, or the hallucinatory wish-fulfillment of primary process thought. The ego is concerned with the external physical environment, and discovers reality by means of the logical operations of secondary process thought. The superego, similarly, is concerned with the constraints on instinctual expression imposed by the moral values of the external social environment.

The problem of reconciling the two different divisions of the mind, topographic and functional, was not solved by Freud before he died.

Nevertheless, his assignment of some nonconscious mental functions to the ego, in both its defensive and nondefensive spheres, initiated an important research tradition within post-Freudian psychoanalysis. Beginning with the work of Anna Freud, and especially in the hands of Heinz Hartmann, David Rapaport, and George Klein, psychoanalytic ego psychology focused on the nondefensive, reality-oriented tasks of the ego. The tradition of psychoanalytic ego psychology was linked most closely with mainstream experimental psychology by the work of Bruner, Klein, and others on the "New Look" in perception and attendant research on such topics as subliminal perception, perceptual defense and vigilance, and repression-sensitization.

Dissociation and Neodissociation

Whereas Freud described the mechanism of the dynamic unconscious as one of repression, his intellectual rival Pierre Janet (1889, 1907) described the process as one of dissociation or "desagregation" (Ellenberger, 1970). Janet's theoretical work was predicated on Claude Bernard's paradigm of analysis followed by synthesis: the study of elementary psychological functions taken separately, and then the reconstruction of the whole mind based on knowledge of these parts. The elementary mental functions were labeled psychological automatisms: Far from the elementary sensations, images, and feelings of the structuralists, they were construed as complex intelligent acts, adjusted to their circumstances, and accompanied by a rudimentary consciousness. Each automatism unites cognition, emotion, and motivation with action.

Janet held that under normal circumstances, all psychological automatisms were bound together into a single stream of consciousness—each accessible to introspection, and each susceptible to voluntary control. However, the occurrence of mental trauma, especially in a vulnerable individual, could result in the splitting off of one or more psychological automatisms from conscious monitoring and control. Under these circumstances, there would exist two or more streams of mental functioning, each processing inputs and outputs, but only one of which is accessible to phenomenal awareness and voluntary control. The dissociated automatisms constitute fixed ideas (*idée fixe*), which possess some degree of autonomy with respect to their development and effects on ongoing experience, thought, and action. The operation of these dissociated (as opposed to integrated or synthesized) psychological automatisms provides the mechanism for the major symptoms of hysteria: They produce the ideas, images, and behaviors that intrude, unbidden, on the stream of conscious thought and action; and their capacity to process information is responsible for the paradoxical ability of the hysterically blind or deaf to negotiate their environments successfully. Janet described these dissociated automatisms as *sub*conscious as opposed to *un*conscious, and considered repression as just one possible mechanism for dissociation.

Janet's ideas were championed by the American psychologist Morton Prince (1906), and more recently by E. R. Hilgard (1977b), who proposed a "neodissociation" theory of divided consciousness (see also Kihlstrom, 1992a). Whether in its original or updated forms, dissociation theory provides a rather different view of nonconscious mental functioning than does psychoanalytic theory. In the first place, dissociation theory holds that nonconscious mental contents are not necessarily restricted to primitive sexual and aggressive ideas and impulses, nor are nonconscious mental processes necessarily irrational, imagistic, or in any other way qualitatively different from conscious ones; they are simply not consciously accessible. In the second place, dissociation theory holds that the restriction of awareness need not be motivated by purposes of defense, nor need it necessarily have the effect of reducing conflict and anxiety; rather, it can occur simply as a consequence of particular psychological operations. Although largely compatible with the principles of contemporary cognitive psychology, dissociation theory also offers a somewhat different perspective on the cognitive unconscious. Thus, nonconscious mental processes are not restricted to unconscious procedural knowledge, and nonconscious mental contents are not limited to unattended or degraded percepts and memories. These differences suggest that dissociative processes deserve more attention by both cognitive and clinical psychologists than they have received in the recent past.

The Psychological Unconscious in Cognitive Theory

Within 19th-century academic psychology, perhaps the most forceful advocate of nonconscious mental life was William James (1890/1980), who held that mental states could be unconscious in at least two different senses. First, a mental event can be excluded from attention or consciousness. These unattended, unconscious feelings are themselves mental states. Second, and more important, James drew on the clinical observations of cases of hysteria and multiple personality—some made by others, some by himself (Taylor, 1996)—to argue for a division of consciousness into primary and secondary (and, for that matter, tertiary and more) "consciousnesses," only one of which is accessible to phenomenal awareness at any point in time. To avoid possible oxymoron in the negation of consciousness, which was what really bothered him, James preferred to speak of "co-conscious" or "subconscious" mental states, rather than "unconscious" ones.

The radical behaviorists were no more interested in nonconscious than in conscious mental life, so empirical interest in the kinds of problems that interested Helmholtz and James, not to mention Freud, declined precipitously in the years after World War I. Serious theoretical interest in nonconscious mental life had to wait the triumph of the cognitive revolution (Hilgard, 1977a, 1980a, 1987). For example, the classic multistore model of information processing implicitly makes consciousness coterminous with attention and primary (short-term, working) memory. In this way, the model seems to identify nonconscious mental life with early, "preattentive" mental processes such as feature detection and pattern recognition, that occur prior to the formation of a mental representation of an event in primary memory. The idea that complex mental states and processes could influence experience, thought, and action despite being inaccessible to phenomenal awareness and voluntary control required a wholesale revision of our concepts of attention and memory, as represented by research on automatic and implicit memory.

THE COGNITIVE UNCONSCIOUS

Most research on unconscious mental life has focused on the cognitive unconscious (Kihlstrom, 1984, 1987, 1999a). The rediscovery of the unconscious began with comparisons between automatic and effortful mental processes and between explicit and implicit memory, and it has continued with the extension of the explicit–implicit distinction into the domains of perception, learning, and thought. More recent developments, to be treated in later sections, have involved the extension of the explicit–implicit distinction further, to the domains of motivation and emotion.

Automatic and Unconscious Processing

The earliest information-processing theories of attention were based, to one degree or another, on the metaphor of the filter (for reviews, see Kahneman & Treisman, 1984; Logan, 1997; Pashler, 1997). Information that made it past the filter was available for "higher" information-processing activities, but information that did not make it past the filter was not. Later, the notion of an attentional filter was replaced by the notion of attentional capacity. The capacity view, in turn, led to a distinction between "automatic" and "controlled" processes (e.g., LaBerge & Samuels, 1974; Posner & Snyder, 1975; Schneider & Shiffrin, 1977). Automatic processes are inevitably engaged by the presentation of specific stimulus inputs, regardless of any intention on the part of the subject. Some automatic processes are innate, whereas others have been automatized through extensive practice. In either case, automatic processes are unconscious in the strict sense that they are inaccessible to phenomenal awareness under any circumstances.

The defining feature of an automatic process is that it is executed automatically in response to appropriate stimulus inputs. In this way, the notion of an automatic processes is tacitly modeled after the reflexes, taxes, and instincts (fixed action patterns) familiar from physiology and ethology, as well as the conditioned responses familiar from traditional learning theory (whether Pavlovian or Skinnerian). Of course, such a definition of automatic is circular. Thus a second criterion, that automatic processes consume no attentional resources, seems to have been adopted in part to escape tautology, and perhaps because of anticipated difficulties in objectively measuring or controlling subjects' intentions. But it should be noted that, at base, the concept of automatic does not *require* anything other than independence from intention. It is certainly possible to conceive of automatic processes that, once invoked by appropriate stimulus conditions, consume attentional resources—just as a room heater, automatically activated by a thermostat, consumes electricity. Hasher and Zacks (1979, 1984) offered additional criteria for defining a process as automatic, such as age-invariance or independence of individual differences. However, it seems advisable to decouple these additional criteria from the concept of automatic, and treat the effects of such factors as empirical questions, as opposed to a priori assumptions.

The concept of automatic has played an increasingly powerful role in social psychology and personality (e.g., Bargh, 1984, 1997; Bargh & Barndollar, 1996; Devine, 1989; Fazio, Sanbonmatsu, Powell, & Kardes, 1986; Newman & Uleman, 1989; Pratto, 1994; Smith, 1994; Taylor & Fiske, 1978; Uleman, Newman, & Moskowitz, 1996; Wegner & Bargh, 1998; Wegner & Smart, 1997). The general argument is that some of the processes involved in social cognition, and some of the processes by which social cognitions are translated into social behavior, are executed automatically. Thus, it is generally accepted that attitudes, impressions, and other social judgments, as well as aggression, compliance, prejudice, and other social behaviors, are often mediated by automatic processes that operate outside phenomenal awareness and voluntary control.

To some extent, what might be called the "automatic juggernaut" within personality and social psychology seems to represent a reaction to a cognitive view of social interaction which seems, to some, to inappropriately emphasize conscious, rational, cognitive processes, at the expense of the unconscious, irrational, emotive, and conative. After all, the concept of automatic is, at least tacitly, modeled on innate stimulus–response (S-R) connections such as reflexes, taxes, and instincts (fixed action patterns), as well as on those S-R connections acquired through the processes of classical and instrumental or operant conditioning. James (1890/1980), after all, discussed automatic in relation to habit. Thus, in some respects, invocation of the concept of automatic represents a reversion to earlier situationist views within social psychology (Berkowitz & Devine, 1995).

This regressive situation has been clearly articulated by Bargh (1997): "As Skinner argued so pointedly, the more we know about the situational causes of psychological phenomena, the less need we have for postulating internal conscious mediating processes to explain those phenomena" (p. 1). Bargh goes on to argue that most social behavior is indeed automatic in nature. In his view, social behavior occurs largely in response to environmental triggers, independent of the person's conscious intentions, beliefs, and choices; and it is preattentive, independent of the person's deployment of attention. Bargh's position is not classically Skinnerian, because he shares the central dogma of cognitive social psychology—that social behavior is caused by the actor's internal mental representation of the situation, rather than the situation as it might be described objectively. But Bargh goes on to argue that this internal mental representation is itself constructed automatically and preconsciously. Thus, Bargh is able to maintain a superficial allegiance with cognitivism while at the same time harkening back to radical situationism. If the cognitive processes underlying social cognition and social behavior are largely automatic, then—to put it bluntly—not too much thought has gone into them.

At the same time, however, and somewhat ironically, the most recent developments in attention theory have been to undermine even the seemingly fundamental assumptions that automatic processes are independent of intention and of attentional capacity (Logan, 1997; Pashler, 1997). Although the concept of automatic is intuitively appealing, and has proved extremely attractive to both cognitive and social psychologists, the empirical evidence generally fails to support the primary claims about automatic processes: that they are executed involuntarily and consume no cognitive resources. Of course, it is possible that alternative conceptualizations of automatic will prove more viable than the those based on resource theories of attention (Anderson, 1992; Logan, 1997).

Implicit Memory

Although procedural knowledge structures may be unconscious, the declarative knowledge structures on which they operate are ordinarily thought to be available to conscious awareness. We generally assume that people consciously perceive and remember the events that influence their experience, thought, and action. On the other hand, an increasingly large literature from both patient and nonpatient populations indicates that people can display priming effects, savings in relearning, and other memory-based phenomena without having any conscious recollection of the events that form the experiential bases of the effects. On the basis of results such as these, Schacter (1987) has drawn a distinction between explicit and implicit memory. Explicit memory involves the conscious reexperiencing of some aspect of the past, whereas implicit memory is revealed by a change in task performance that is attributable to information acquired during a prior episode. Implicit memory is, in effect, unconscious memory: Mental representations of past events influence current experience, thought, and action in the absence of, or independent of, conscious recollection of those events.

Because the literature on implicit memory is so large, and has been reviewed in many places (Graf & Masson, 1993; Roediger & McDermott, 1993; Schacter, Chiu, & Ochser, 1993), this chapter will not attempt a full-scale review of the field. For present purposes, it is enough to catalog some of the out-of-the-way domains in which dissociations between explicit and implicit memory have been observed: posthypnotic amnesia (Kihlstrom, 1980, 1985); dissociative disorders such as psychogenic amnesia, psychogenic fugue, and multiple personality (Kihlstrom, 1999b; Kihlstrom & Schacter, 1995; Schacter & Kihlstrom, 1999); general anesthesia (for reviews, see Cork, Couture, & Kihlstrom, 1997; Merikle & Daneman, 1996); and conscious sedation (Polster, 1993). Somewhat surprisingly, despite early hints to the contrary (Eich, 1990), implicit memory appears to be impaired by sleep (Wood, Bootzin, Kihlstrom, & Schacter, 1992)—an apparent contradiction that will be resolved only by further research.

Implicit Perception

Effects analogous to implicit memory may be observed in perception (Kihlstrom, 1996a; Kihlstrom, Barnhardt, & Tataryn, 1992). Ever since the first demonstration of subliminal perception, by Peirce and Jastrow (1884), however, a variety of methodological critiques have sought to demonstrate that events cannot be analyzed for meaning unless they have been consciously identified and attended to (e.g., Erickson, 1960). Recently, however, a number of compelling demonstrations of preconscious semantic processing have appeared in the literature (e.g., Marcel, 1983). Despite persisting methodological critiques (e.g., Holender, 1986; Shanks & St. John, 1994), the available literature clearly supports the proposition that certain aspects of semantic processing can occur in the absence of conscious awareness (Draine & Greenwald, 1998; Greenwald, Klinger, & Liu, 1989; Greenwald & Draine, 1998). At the same time, there appear to be strict limits to the processing of subliminal and preattentive events (Greenwald, 1992; Merikle & Reingold, 1992).

In subliminal perception, the stimulus is degraded by means of tachistoscopic presentation, or masking. In other instances, the stimulus, although not strictly subliminal, is degraded by virtue of presentation outside of the focus of attention—in parafoveal segments of the visual field, for example, or over the unattended channel in dichotic listening experiments. However, there are other circumstances in which perception without awareness occurs even though the environmental stimulus is not degraded in any sense. For example, Weiskrantz (1986, 1997) and his colleagues have reported a patient who had extensive damage to the striate cortex of the occipital lobes. Although the patient reported an inability to see, he was nonetheless able to respond appropriately to some visual stimuli—a phenomenon called "blindsight" (for a review see Campion, Latto, & Smith, 1983, and commentaries). Similarly, patients with bilateral lesions to the mesial portions of the occipital and temporal cortex are unable to consciously recognize previously encountered faces as familiar—a condition known as prosopagnosia. Nevertheless, there are now several reports indicating that prosopagnosic patients show differential behavioral responses to old and new faces (e.g., deHaan, Young, & Newcombe, 1987; Tranel & Damasio, 1985)—a dissociation similar to the implicit memory seen in the amnesic syndrome. Similar phenomena have been observed in the visual neglect syndromes resulting from damage to the temporoparietal areas of the cerebral cortex (Bisiach, 1993; Rafal, 1998). Further evidence that implicit perception goes beyond the subliminal and the preattentive are studies of the conversion disorders, once labeled "conversion hysteria" and in the phenomena of hypnotic suggestion (for reviews, see Hilgard, 1977b; Kihlstrom, 1992b, 1999b; Kihlstrom et al., 1992).

Because perception without awareness extends to cases beyond stimuli that are subliminal or unattended, Kihlstrom et al. (1992; see also Kihlstrom, 1996a) have argued for a distinction between explicit and implicit perception, paralleling the distinction between explicit and implicit memory. Explicit perception entails the subject's conscious perception of some object in the current environment, or the environment of the very recent past, as reflected in his or her ability to report the presence, location, form, identity, and/or activity of that object. Implicit memory refers to any change in the person's experience, thought, or action attributable to such an event, in the absence of (or independent of) conscious perception of that event. Explicit and implicit perception can be dissociated, just as explicit and implicit memory can be. The term "implicit perception" captures a broader domain than is covered by the term "subliminal perception," because it covers the processing, outside of conscious awareness, of stimulus events that are clearly perceptible in terms of intensity, duration, and other characteristics. It also has the extra advantage of skirting the difficult psychophysical concept of the *limen*.

Implicit perception effects are conceptually similar to subliminal memory effects, in that both reveal the impact on experience, thought, and action of events that are not accessible to conscious awareness. However, in contrast to implicit perception, the events contributing to implicit memory effects are clearly detectable by the subject at the time they occurred, attention was devoted to them, and they were at least momentarily represented in phenomenal awareness. Arguably, implicit memory should be reserved for those situations in which a consciously perceived event is subsequently lost to conscious recollection, leaving implicit perception for instances (including, in principle, sleep and general anesthesia) in which the stimulus was not consciously perceived in the first place. Because memory is the residual trace of perceptual activity, it stands to reason that implicit percepts can reveal themselves in memory— even if it should turn out that implicit percepts produce only implicit memories. However, evidence for implicit perception and memory should not be taken as grounds for concluding that *all* current and past events, regardless of whether they are consciously attended, are encoded in memory and influence ongoing experience, thought, and action—as implied, for example, by the specter of subliminal advertising (Moore, 1988), or subliminal persuasion (Greenwald, Spangenberg, Pratkanis, & Eskenazi, 1991; Merikle, 1988; Merikle & Skanes, 1992; Moore, 1995).

Implicit Thought

Implicit perception and memory do not exhaust the domain of the psychological unconscious. Although the evidence is somewhat sparse, it appears we can also have implicit *thought* (Dorfman, Shames, & Kihlstrom, 1996; Kihlstrom, Shames, & Dorfman, 1996). Implicit thought is somewhat hard to define, but it is illustrated by some studies of problem solving by Bowers and his associates (Bowers, 1984, 1987; Bowers, Farvolden, & Marmigis, 1995; Bowers, Regehr, Balthazard, & Parker, 1990). In some of these experiments, subjects were presented with word triads patterned after those of the Remote Associates Test (RAT; Mednick, 1962), and instructed to think of a word that all three words had in common. Some of the triads were soluble, but others were not. Bowers and colleagues found that subjects could distinguish between soluble and insoluble triads, even if they were unaware of the solution to the soluble one—an effect conceptually similar to the "feeling of knowing" analogous to that observed in metamemory tasks (Reder, 1996). Unsolved RAT solutions produce unconscious priming effects analogous to those observed in studies of implicit perception and memory (Shames, 1994; see also Dorfman et al., 1996; Kihlstrom et al., 1996).

The kinds of effects observed by Bowers et al. (1990, 1995) and Shames (1994) seem relevant to the phenomena of intuition, incubation, and insight in problem solving (Dorfman et al., 1996; Kihlstrom et al., 1996). These phenomena have proven difficult to study under controlled laboratory conditions, and intuition has acquired an especially bad reputation as a source of error in human judgment. On the contrary, Bowers (1984, 1987) has argued that intuitions represent our tendency, as intelligent problem solvers, to go beyond the information given by a problem or a retrieval cue. As the way out of the closed cognitive loop of induction and deduction, intuitions are important elements in the creative process. In the present context, intuitions should be reconstrued as implicit thoughts—gut feelings that we are correct, without knowing why, or even whether, we are right. Perhaps these implicit thoughts come into awareness through the process of incubation, culminating in insight—the moment in which the solution to a problem, or some other thought, appears in conscious awareness.

Implicit Learning

Despite persisting questions, implicit perception and memory illustrate the cognitive unconscious, by showing perception and memory outside of phenomenal awareness. A rather different line of research has sought to document the conceptually related phenomenon of implicit *learning*—as demonstrated by subjects' ability to use rules acquired through experience, in the absence of awareness of the rules themselves. In some ways, implicit learning is exemplified by language acquisition, in which speakers acquire the ability to distinguish grammatical from ungrammatical utterances, even though they cannot articulate the grammatical rules underlying the judgments. Reber (1993) has attempted to model this process in the laboratory by developing artificial grammars whose rules control the construction of well-formed strings of letters. In Reber's procedure, subjects are asked to memorize a set of (perhaps) 20 grammatical letter strings (e.g., PVPXVPS or PTTTVPS). They are then tested with a number of new strings, some of which (e.g., PTTTTVPS) conform to the rule, while others (e.g., PTVPXVSP) do not. Reber has found that subjects are able to distinguish grammatical from nongrammatical letter strings at better than chance levels, even though none of them are able to give a full and accurate account of the grammatical rule they have clearly induced from the study set.

Other investigators have produced similar sorts of demonstrations (for comprehensive reviews, see Berry & Dienes, 1993; Lewicki, 1986; Seger, 1994). However, it should be noted that the interpretation of implicit learning in terms of the unconscious acquisition of knowledge remains somewhat controversial (Dulany, 1997; Shanks & St. John, 1994). In the first place, the subjects are by no means unconscious in the sense of being asleep or anesthetized. Nor is the learning experience inaccessible to conscious awareness in the same sense that the events implicated in implicit perception and implicit memory are. Even the claim that subjects are unaware of what they have learned is controversial. In the artificial grammar experiments, for example, the mere fact that subjects cannot articulate the Markov process by which grammatical strings were generated does not mean that they are unaware of what they have learned. Above-chance classification performance could well result from partial knowledge which is consciously accessible. The best that can be said, for now, is that the subjects in artificial grammar and sequence learning experiments experience themselves as behaving randomly, without an awareness of what they are doing.

THE EMOTIONAL UNCONSCIOUS

As psychology shrugged off radical behaviorism in the 1960s, its renewed interest in conscious (and then unconscious) mental life was focused on cognition, and it treated cognition as cold and hard, conscious and deliberate. As the cognitive revolution developed, however, two trends emerged. On the one hand, as discussed above, cognitive psychology increasingly made room for the cognitive unconscious, as reflected in the rise of research on automaticity and on implicit memory. On the other hand, largely under the influence of personality, social, and clinical psychology, the study of cognition expanded to include the hot and the wet—reflected in increased interest in emotional and motivational influences on memory and other cognitive processes. This second trend seems to have eventuated in an "affective revolution," in which emotional life is studied in its own right, and not merely as a byproduct of cognitive processing. But this affective revolution, epitomized by the emergence of an interdisciplinary "affective science" (Ekman & Davidson, 1994) or "affective neuroscience" (Panskepp, 1991) modeled on cognitive science and cognitive neuroscience, seems to be focused on conscious feeling states. If we are ready to accept the notion of a cognitive unconscious, perhaps we are also ready to accept the notion of an emotional unconscious as well (Kihlstrom, Mulvaney, Tobias, & Tobis, 1999).

Of course, the idea of an emotional unconscious is not new. As we all know, Sigmund Freud argued that our conscious experience, thought, and action is shaped by emotional and motivational states of which we are unaware. All the classic Freudian defense mechanisms were designed to render us unaware of our true emotional states. However, in order to talk about the emotional unconscious we need not embrace the whole conceptual panoply of classical, or even neo-Freudian, psychoanalysis—we don't need the division of the mind into id, ego, and superego, the theory of infantile sexuality, the stages of psychosexual development, repression, or any of the rest of it. Modern research on cognition and the cognitive unconscious owes nothing whatsoever to Freud, and that is also the case with modern research on emotion and the emotional unconscious.

Emotion as an Expression of Implicit Perception and Memory

With respect to the emotional unconscious, the first thing to be noted is that conscious emotional responses can serve as expressions of implicit memory and perception, and perhaps implicit learning and thought as well. In both cases, the people in question are consciously aware of their feeling state, but are unconscious of the source of those emotions in their past or current experience.

On the memory side, brain-damaged, amnesic patients can acquire new emotional responses through experience, even though they cannot consciously remember the experiences themselves. For example, a study by Johnson and her colleagues exposed alcoholic Korsakoff syndrome patients, who suffer an anterograde amnesia as a result of bilateral damage to the diencephalon, to unfamiliar Korean melodies (Johnson, Kim, & Risse, 1985). Some melodies were played only once during the study phase, whereas others were played 5 or 10 times. Later, the patients were played these same melodies, along with other Korean melodies that were entirely new, and asked to indicate which they preferred. Both amnesic patients and control subjects preferred the old over the new melodies, reflecting what Zajonc (1968) has called the "mere exposure effect" (for a review, see Bornstein, 1989). However, the patients, being amnesic, showed greatly impaired levels of recognition: They liked what they heard, but they didn't know why.

With respect to perception, we now know that intact subjects can show mere exposure effects on preference judgments even though the exposures were so degraded as to be consciously imperceptible. A case in point is a study by Kunst-Wilson and Zajonc (1980), involving tachistoscopic presentations of drawings of irregular polygons. The subjects in this case were neurologically intact, but the exposures were so brief that they were not consciously perceived by the subjects, as confirmed by a later recognition test. Nevertheless, the subjects showed the mere exposure effect: the more subliminal presentations the stimuli received, the more the subjects liked them (see also Bornstein, 1992). The subjects liked what they saw, but they didn't know why.

Bornstein and his colleagues have extended the subliminal mere exposure effect found with neutral stimuli to faces: Not only did subjects show more positive attitudes toward people depicted in tachistoscopically presented photographs, but they also interacted more positively with these same individuals when they later encountered them in a contrived social interaction (Bornstein, Leone, & Galley, 1987). Zajonc (1980) has used these results to claim that affective responses are independent of, and perhaps even prior to, cognitive processing. However, Mandler and his colleagues showed that mere exposure, outside of awareness, also increased ratings of brightness, darkness, and *dis*liking (Mandler, Nakamura, & Van Zandt, 1987). This finding suggests that the preference effect of Kunst-Wilson and Zajonc (1980) seems to be a specific instantiation of a more general principle that activation of an internal representation of an object affects judgment about any relevant dimension that object (Mandler et al., 1987), and does not support specific claims concerning the priority of affect. On the other hand, Seamon and his colleagues have recently reported subliminal exposure effects on liking and disliking judgments, but not on judgments of lightness and darkness (Seamon, McKenna, & Binder, 1998). This discrepancy in the literature remains to be resolved.

Nevertheless, unconscious effects on preference judgments, and other emotional responses, set the stage for other analyses of unconscious influences on personality and social interaction. Some early research along these lines was reported by Nisbett and Wilson (1977), who argued that people largely lack introspective access to the actual determinants of their judgments and other behaviors. More recently, research by Lewicki (1986) has shown that presumably affect-laden information about the features of social stimuli (and the covariations among them) can be acquired through implicit learning, and influence behavior even though it is stored in a form that is inaccessible to conscious awareness.

This much is pretty clear from the available research, although more needs to be done in both arenas. In particular, the acquisition of emotional responses by amnesic patients has not been studied much since Johnson and colleagues' (1985) original work. However, in view of the ongoing debate over recovered memories of trauma, it is important to enter a strong cautionary note. The recovered memory literature frequently distinguishes between a conscious "recall memory" and an unconscious "feeling memory," the latter term referring to an emotional response to a current situation that is triggered by an unconscious memory of past trauma (e.g., Frederickson, 1993). The notion of a feeling memory is a throwback to the prepsychoanalytic notion of Breuer and Freud (1893–1895/1955, p. 7) that "hysterics suffer . . . from reminiscences," and finds some support in experimental demonstrations of emotion as an expression of implicit memory. But there is an important difference: The experimental literature provides independent corroboration of the past emotion-eliciting event—information that may be rarely available in clinical practice. Nevertheless, clinicians who embrace the concept of recovered memory may inappropriately infer a history of prior trauma from the patient's current emotional state, in the absence of any independent corroborative evidence. This is, of course, a mistake—the logical mistake of "affirming the consequent"—a mistake that may lead patients to reconstruct distorted or false memories of their past (Kihlstrom, 1996b, 1998). Although there is no question that implicit memories of trauma can, in principle, affect a person's current experience, thought, and action, in the absence of independent, objective, corroboration, there is no scientific basis for inferring the past from current emotional symptoms (Kihlstrom, 1997b).

Implicit Emotion

Another side of the emotional unconscious concerns the proposition that there is a formal distinction between two expressions of emotion—explicit and implicit. Paralleling the usage of these descriptors in the domain of the cognitive unconscious, "explicit emotion" refers to the person's conscious awareness of an emotion, feeling, or mood state; "implicit emotion," by contrast, refers to changes in experience, thought, or action that are attributable to one's emotional state, independent of his or her conscious awareness of that state. In terms of measurement, explicit emotion tasks require the subject to reflect on, and report, his or her conscious feeling states; implicit emotion tasks do not.

The inspiration for this idea comes from Lang's (1968) multiple-systems theory of emotion. According to Lang, every emotional response consists of three components: verbal-cognitive, corresponding to a subjective feeling state such as fear; overt motor, corresponding to a behavioral response such as escape or avoidance; and covert physiological, corresponding to a change in some autonomic index such as skin conductance or heart rate. Although we usually construe these three components or systems as varying together, Lang has proposed that these three systems are partially independent, so that under some conditions they can move in quite different directions. Rachman and Hodgson (1974; Hodgson & Rachman, 1974) picked up on Lang's theme and applied the term "desynchrony" to cases in which one component of emotional response is dissociated from the others (for critical reviews of desynchrony, see Hugdahl, 1981; Turpin, 1991; Zinbarg, 1998).

Apparently, dissociations between emotional awareness and physiology are found quite commonly in the anxiety disorders. For example, cardiology clinics frequently encounter patients who complain of tachycardia but have no other signs of coronary arrest. It turns out that these patients are not having heart attacks at all. Instead, they are having *panic* attacks, even though they experience no subjective fear (aside from distress over the heart symptom itself). This syndrome even has a name: fearless panic attacks (Beitman, Mukerji, Russell, & Grafing, 1993). The patient is showing all the physiological signs of fear, but doesn't experience fear itself. The emotional deficits associated with schizophrenia also have a flavor of desynchrony. Thus, "flat affect" refers to a deficit in the behavioral expression or display of emotion, which may not extend to subjective experience or physiology. Anhedonia, another feature of schizophrenia (and a dimension of normal personality as well; see Chapman, Chapman, & Raulin, 1976) is a deficit in the conscious experience of positive emotion that leaves the behavioral or physiological expressions of emotion unimpaired. A whole host of individual differences in emotional experience and expression may involve just this form of desynchrony: repressive style (Weinberger, 1997; Weinberger, Schwartz, & Davidson, 1979); alexithymia (Lane, Ahern, Schwartz, & Kaszniak, 1997), and level of emotional awareness (e.g., Lane & Schwartz, 1987).

Turning from personality to social psychology, Greenwald and Banaji (1995) have recently applied the explicit–implicit distinction to the concept of "attitude." This is interesting because, as Thurstone noted long ago, emotion is central to social attitudes: They are affective dispositions to favor or oppose certain individuals, groups, or policies, and they are measured on dimensions that have affective connotations: pro and anti, like and dislike, positive and negative, and so on. Classical social psychology assumes that people are aware of their attitudes, which is why attitudes are typically assessed by self-report scales. However, Greenwald and Banaji have suggested that people may possess positive and negative *implicit attitudes* about themselves and other people, which can affect ongoing social behavior outside of conscious awareness.

An experimental demonstration of implicit attitudes is provided by a series of studies of the "false fame" effect by Banaji and Greenwald (1995). However, it is one thing to demonstrate the implicit effect of attitudes on tasks that do not require conscious awareness of those attitudes, and something else to demonstrate that explicit and implicit attitudes are actually dissociable. Wittenbrink, Judd, and Park (1997) found that the magnitude of the race-specific priming effect was correlated with scores on a questionnaire measure of racial prejudice. Implicit measures may be very useful in studies of attitudes and prejudice, but researchers need to actually test for explicit–implicit dissociations before we accept implicit attitudes as evidence of an emotional unconscious whose contents are different from those that are accessible to phenomenal awareness.

In light of the earlier discussion of "feeling memories," more should be said at this point about the logic of inferring unconscious emotions. We recognize priming effects as evidence of implicit memory because we can trace them to specific objectively observable events, and we can objectively trace the relationship between the prime and the target. Put another way, we can identify an implicit expression of memory because we know what happened to the subject in the past. But by the same logic, in order to identify an implicit expression of emotion, we have to know what emotional state the subject *should* be experiencing—which emotional state is being represented, and expressed, outside of conscious awareness.

Still and all, at least in principle, the emotional unconscious has two different aspects. On the one hand, we may be unaware of the percepts, memories, and thoughts that give rise to our emotional feelings. In this case, emotion serves as an implicit expression of perception, memory, and thought. On the other hand, we may be aware of what we are perceiving, remembering, or thinking, but unaware of the emotions instigated by these cognitions. In this case, behavioral and physiological changes serve as implicit expressions of emotion.

Interestingly, both aspects of the emotional unconscious are anticipated in the neuropsychological model of fear recently offered by LeDoux (1996). The fact that a powerful neuropsychological model of emotion can produce both aspects of the emotional unconscious is, in my view, warrant to pursue the matter further. Still, it must be remembered that LeDoux's model is based almost entirely on animal research on fear. It would be useful to know more about dissociable neural systems for emotions other than fear, and to have positive evidence of implicit emotion in humans, who can talk to us about their conscious experiences. For the present, the experimental and clinical evidence for a dissociation between explicit and implicit emotion is not yet convincing, and the methodological requirements for such demonstrations have not yet been fully met. But while the hypothesis of unconscious emotional states has not yet garnered convincing support, it can no longer be rejected out of hand. If we are willing to speak of implicit percepts, memories, and thoughts that are dissociated from their explicit counterparts, then we must be willing to speak of implicit emotions in the same terms.

THE MOTIVATIONAL UNCONSCIOUS

If we are willing to speak of implicit emotions, we must also be prepared to speak of implicit motives. Although Emmanuel Kant asserted that feeling and desire (along with knowledge) were irreducible faculties of mind (Hilgard, 1980b), emotion and motivation are often closely linked. Often one of these terms is defined, at least in part, by the other. Thus the motivational states that energize, direct, and select behavior often have a hedonic quality of pleasure or unpleasure to them, whereas emotions can have the same drive or incentive functions traditionally ascribed to motives. Buck (1985) defined emotion as the mechanism by which we read out information concerning motivational systems. Viewed from this perspective, emotions might be construed are consciously accessible while motives may be unconscious. But we have already determined that, at least in principle, emotions can be unconscious too; and certainly, many of our motivational states are accessible to phenomenal awareness. Thus we are returned to the question: Can motivational states be unconscious?

Put more precisely, can we observe dissociations between explicit and implicit expressions of motivation? In parallel with the cognitive and emotional cases, we must entertain a formal distinction between two expressions of motivation—explicit and implicit. "Explicit motivation" can be defined as the conscious representation of a conative state, or the desire to engage in some particular activity, as represented by craving for food, yearning for love, and the like. By contrast, "implicit motivation" refers to changes in experience, thought, or action that are attributable to one's motivational state, independent of one's conscious awareness of that state. In terms of measurement, explicit motivation tasks require the subject to reflect on, and report, his or her conscious desires; implicit motivation tasks do not. Closing the parallel with emotion, we might hypothesize that behavioral or physiological signs of motivation can be dissociated from conscious desires.

Implicit Motives

In the recent history of psychology, the notion of implicit motivation was first articulated by McClelland, Koestner, and Weinberger (1989) —interestingly, without any reference to the already-emerging concept of explicit memory (Schacter, 1987). For McClelland and colleagues, explicit motives are self-attributed: The person is aware of the motive, can reflect on it, and report it in interviews or on personality questionnaires. Implicit motives, by contrast, are inferred from the person's performance on exercises such as the Thematic Apperception Test (TAT). As such, the distinction between explicit and implicit motives is an extension of McClelland's (1980) earlier distinction between respondent and operant motive measures.

Of course, it has long been known that motives as assessed by "projective" instruments such as the TAT, even when investigators employ reliable coding schemes, do not correlate with nominally the same motives as assessed by "objective" instruments such as the Personality Research Form (PRF; Jackson, 1974). Rather than taking such empirical findings as a reason for abandoning picture-story and other projective measurements, McClelland and colleagues (1989) conclude that implicit and self-attributed motives influence different classes of behavior, and that they respond to different types of influence (e.g., Bornstein, 1998). Implicit motives are more strongly related to long-term behavioral trends, whereas self-attributed motives are more strongly related to immediate choices. Self-attributed motives are more strongly linked to normative goals than are their implicit counterparts. Self-attributed motives are aroused by extrinsic social demands, whereas implicit motives are aroused by intrinsic task incentives.

In other words, McClelland and colleagues postulate two dissociable motive systems, one explicit and the other implicit, just as Schacter (1987) and Squire (Squire & Knowlton, 1995) postulate two dissociable memory systems or Lang (1968) postulates multiple, dissociable, components of emotion. The low correlations between TAT and PRF motive scores, far from reflecting the poor psychometric properties of the TAT (or, for that matter, the PRF), instead reflect the dissociability of the underlying motivational systems that these measures respectively tap. One of these motive systems is accessible to conscious awareness; the other is not, and influences the individual's experience, thought, and action unconsciously. By virtue of implicit motives, people engage in goal-oriented behavior without being aware of what their motives or goals are. Or, at least, that is the hypothesis.

Automatic Motives

A rather different perspective on the motivational unconscious is offered by Bargh (1997; Bargh & Barndollar, 1996), as part of his general embrace of the concept of automaticity. According to the traditional, folk-psychological model of motivation, the person consciously selects some intended behavior in order to achieve some goal, and then deliberately executes that behavior. Although it is commonly accepted that some skilled, goal-directed behaviors are executed automatically and unconsciously, much like a concert pianist plays an arpeggio, Bargh also automates the process of goal-selection—the selection of the music, not just the touch of fingers to keys. According to this "auto-motive model," by virtue of having been frequently and consistently chosen in particular situations, goals and motives (these terms are essentially interchangeable) themselves can be automatically and unconsciously invoked by environmental events. Once activated, goal-oriented behaviors can be executed outside of awareness as well.

It should be noted, however, that whereas the implicit motives discussed by McClelland and colleagues (1989) are themselves inaccessible to conscious awareness (at least on hypothesis), Bargh's (1997) auto-motive model asserts only that the person's motives are selected automatically, in the absence of conscious intention or choice. It does not necessarily follow that the person is not aware of the motives themselves. Thus, it may very well be that achievement or affiliation goals may be primed by events in the current or past environment (Bargh, 1997); but these goals themselves may well be represented in the person's conscious awareness. In the absence of evidence that the motives themselves are inaccessible to phenomenal awareness, the automatically activated motives envisioned by Bargh are probably better construed as motivational expressions of implicit perception or memory, rather than as implicit motives.

THIS IS NOT YOUR PSYCHOANALYST'S UNCONSCIOUS

The wide variety of clinical and experimental studies summarized here, conducted in a wide variety of domains and with many different types of subjects, provide evidence for several different aspects of the psychological unconscious. In the first place, there is ample evidence that certain mental procedures, if not strictly automatic, operate unconsciously in the sense that we have no direct introspective awareness of them: They can be known only indirectly, by inference. With respect to the cognitive contents on which these processes operate, there is also ample evidence for implicit memories and implicit percepts, which influence experience, thought, and action independent of, and even in the absence of, conscious perception or recollection. There is also more tentative evidence for implicit thoughts, supporting the experience of intuition in creative problem solving, and for implicit learning processes. There is evidence that emotional responses, in the form of consciously experienced feeling states, can occur as expressions of implicit perception and memory, if not as products of implicit learning and thought as well. Similarly, motivational states can be activated automatically; further research may establish that motives, like emotions, can serve as expressions of implicit cognition. Moreover, setting the cognitive unconscious aside, there are good theoretical reasons to suspect that implicit emotional and motivational states can themselves affect expressive and goal-directed behavior outside of conscious awareness.

Lately, there has been some tendency to claim that these findings prove that Freud was right after all. For example, Westen (1998a, 1998b) after performing a review not unlike this one, has concluded that "the notion of unconscious processes is not psychoanalytic voodoo, and it is not the fantasy of muddle-headed clinicians. It is not only clinically indispensable, but it is good science" (p. 35). True enough, so far as it goes, but Westen ignores the fact that none of the literature he has reviewed bears on the particular view of unconscious mental life offered by Freud. The fact that amnesic patients show priming effects on word-stem completion tasks, and can acquire positive and negative emotional responses to other people, without having any conscious recollection of the experiences responsible for these effects, cannot be offered in support of a theory that attributes conscious behavior to repressed sexual and aggressive urges. None of the experiments reviewed involve sexual or aggressive contents, none of their results imply defensive acts of repression, and none of their results support hermeneutic methods of interpreting manifest contents in terms of latent contents. To say that this body of research supports psychoanalytic theory is to make what the philosopher Gilbert Ryle called a category mistake.

It is true, as noted earlier, that the notion of a psychological unconscious, which long predated Freud (Ellenberger, 1970), was conserved by scientific and clinical psychoanalysts throughout the dark days of behaviorism, and into the early days of the cognitive revolution, when cognitive psychologists were preoccupied by manifestations of conscious mental life, such as attention, short-term memory, and mental imagery. However, the revival of research on the psychological unconscious, in the late 1970s and early 1980s, was essentially independent of psychoanalysis. With the possible exception of Silverman's (1976) work on subliminal symbiotic stimulation, modern laboratory research provides no support for the psychoanalytic view of unconscious mental life. That line of research, in turn, directly contradicts the overwhelming conclusion from carefully controlled empirical research that subliminal and other forms of preattentive processing is analytically limited—too limited to permit the analysis of symbiotic stimuli.

One response to this state of affairs is to argue that psychoanalytic theory itself has evolved since Freud, and that it is therefore unfair to bind psychoanalysis so tightly to the Freudian vision of repressed infantile sexual and aggressive urges, symbolically represented in dreams, errors, and symptoms, and revealed on the couch through free association. Westen (1998b) himself recently attempted this gambit, arguing that critics of psychoanalysis attack an archaic, obsolete version of psychodynamic theory, and ignore more recent developments such as ego psychology and object relations theory. But, to borrow the language of the Vietnam War, this destroys the village in order to save it. Culturally, the 20th century has been the century of Sigmund Freud, not the century of Heinz Kohut or Melanie Klein. Freud's legacy is not to be assessed in terms of ideas that emerged since Freud died, but rather in terms of the ideas propounded by Freud himself through the 24 volumes of his collected works. Chief among these, as Bornstein and Masling (1998) note at the very beginning of their book, is a particular view of unconscious mental life—a view that, to date, has found little or no support in empirical science.

A TAXONOMY OF THE PSYCHOLOGICAL UNCONSCIOUS

More positively, the studies reviewed here indicate that consciousness is not to be identified with any particular perceptual-cognitive functions such as discriminative response to stimulation, perception, memory, or the higher mental processes involved in judgment or problem solving. All of these functions can proceed outside of phenomenal awareness. Rather, consciousness is an experiential quality that may accompany any of these functions. The fact of conscious awareness may have particular consequences for psychological function—it seems necessary for voluntary control, for example, as well as communicating one's mental states to others, and for sponsored teaching. But it is not necessary for many forms of complex psychological functioning. Moreover, these findings suggest a taxonomy of nonconscious mental structures and processes constituting the domain of the psychological unconscious.

There are, within the domain of procedural knowledge, a number of complex processes that are *unconscious* in the proper sense—unavailable to introspection, in principle, under any circumstances. By virtue of routinization (or perhaps because they are innate), such procedures operate on declarative knowledge without either conscious intent or conscious awareness, in order to construct the person's ongoing experience, thought, and action. Execution of these mental processes, which can be known only indirectly through inference, is inevitable and consumes no attentional capacity. They may be described as unconscious in the strict sense of that term—in short, they comprise the *unconscious proper*.

In principle, declarative knowledge is available to phenomenal awareness, and can be known directly through introspection or retrospection. However, it is now clear that procedural knowledge can interact with, and utilize, declarative knowledge that is not itself accessible to conscious awareness. Many phenomena of implicit perception, memory, and thought, especially those associated with degraded stimulus processing, suggest a category of *preconscious* declarative knowledge structures. Unlike truly unconscious procedural knowledge, these aspects of declarative knowledge would be available to awareness under ordinary circumstances. Although activated to some degree by current or prior perceptual-cognitive activity, and thus able to influence ongoing experience, thought, and action, they do not cross the threshold required for representation in working memory, and thus for conscious awareness. These representations, which underlie the phenomena of implicit perception and memory, reside on the fringes of consciousness and changed circumstances could render them consciously accessible—at least in principle.

Finally, the phenomena of hypnosis, hysteria, and related states seem to exemplify a category of *subconscious* declarative knowledge. These mental representations, fully activated by perceptual inputs or acts of thought, above the threshold ordinarily required for representation in working memory, and available to introspection and retrospection under some circumstances, seem nevertheless dissociated from phenomenal awareness (Hilgard, 1977b). Dissociative phenomena are of theoretical interest because they do not comfortably classify as either unconscious or preconscious. They are not limited to innate or routinized procedural knowledge; their execution is not automatic in the traditional sense, because it is sensitive to context and consumes cognitive capacity. The stimulus input has not been degraded in any way, and the resulting memory traces are fully encoded and available for explicit retrieval. From the point of view of activation notions of consciousness, these phenomena are theoretically interesting because they indicate that high levels of activation, supported by the active deployment of attention and complex mental processing, while presumably necessary for residence in working memory, are not sufficient for conscious awareness.

CONSCIOUSNESS, THE PSYCHOLOGICAL UNCONSCIOUS, AND THE SELF

What is required in order to achieve conscious awareness? At a psychological level of analysis, it seems that conscious awareness requires that a mental representation of an event be connected with some mental representation of the self as agent or experiencer of that event (Kihlstrom, 1997a). In his discussion of the stream of consciousness, James (1890/1980) wrote that "the first fact for . . . psychologists is that thinking of some sort goes on" (p. 219). He also wrote, immediately thereafter, that "thought tends to personal form" (p. 220)—that is, every thought (by which James meant every conscious mental state) is part of a personal consciousness: "The universal conscious fact is not 'feelings exist' or 'thoughts exist' but '*I* think' and '*I* feel' " (p. 221, emphasis added). In other words, an episode of ongoing experience, thought, and action becomes conscious if, and only if, a link is made between the mental representation of the event itself and some mental representation of the self as the agent or experiencer of that event.

This mental representation of self (Kihlstrom & Klein, 1994, 1997), including one's internal cognitive, affective, and conative environment, resides in working memory, as a memory structure, along with coexisting representations of the current external environment (Anderson, 1983). Both self and context representations are necessary for the construction of a full-fledged conscious perception—which, following James, always seems to take the following form: "I *see* [or hear, smell, taste, etc.] *this, now*." And since memory is the residual trace of perceptual activity, these elements are necessary for the reconstruction of a full-fledged conscious recollections as well.

Within a generic associative network theory of knowledge representation (e.g., Anderson, 1983), an episode of experience is represented by one node connecting three others: an event node, containing a raw description of an event; a context node, specifying the spatial and temporal (and perhaps emotional and motivational) context in which the event occurred; and a self node, indicating the person as the agent or the experiencer of the event. Conscious recollection of such an event occurs only when the representation of the self is retrieved along with some other information about the event. The inability to retrieve the links among all three types of propositions accounts for some of the peculiarities in conscious memory (Kihlstrom, 1997a). What unites the various phenomena of the cognitive unconscious—unconscious procedural knowledge and the various forms of implicit perception, memory, and thought comprising preconscious or subsconscious declarative knowledge—is that the link to self either does not get forged in the first place, or else it is subsequently lost. Thus, Claparède (1911/1951; see also Kihlstrom, 1995a) wrote of the amnesic syndrome: "If one examines the behavior of such a patient, one finds that everything happens as though the various events of life, however well associated with each *other* in the mind, were incapable of integration with the *me* itself" (p. 71, emphasis in original).

TOWARD A NEW CENTURY OF RESEARCH

As the 19th century turned into the 20th, the psychological unconscious was much in the air, but little was known about its nature and limits. When James said to Freud, "The future of psychology belongs to your work," he was referring to unconscious mental life in general, rather than Freud's particular conception of it. That work was suspended during the heyday of behaviorism, but it is in full swing again as the 20th century turns into the 21st. The success and vigor of research on unconscious mental life is clear to almost everyone. Of course, some doubters and sceptics remain—egged on no doubt by the excessive claims of some theorists, and some clinicians, who retain a romantic view of the unconscious as all-powerful and all-knowing. This work promises much to the personality and social psychologists of the future. A full century since the publication of Janet's (1889) *Psychological Automatisms,* and James (1890) *Principles,* and six decades since the death of Freud, and 50 years since the birth of the New Look, the study of nonconscious life has been completely revolutionized. For the first time, contemporary cognitive psychology has begun to offer a clear theoretical framework for studying the relations between conscious and nonconscious mental life. Along with the development of a new class of psychological theories has come a new set of observations, derived from sophisticated new experimental paradigms, including research in cognitive neuropsychology. Thus far, this body of research has revealed a view of nonconscious mental life that is more extensive than the unconscious inference of Helmholtz, but also quite different—kinder, gentler, and more rational—from the seething unconscious of Freud.

Still and all, it should be recognized that almost all of the work to date has been done within the confines of cognitive psychology and cognitive neuropsychology, with relatively little attention paid to unconscious emotional and motivational life, or to the role of unconscious processes in personality and social interaction. Thus, it would seem that an important agenda item over the near term would be the deliberate adoption by personality and social psychologists of the concepts and principles that have served their cognitive colleagues so well, and the systematic extension of research on the psychological unconscious beyond words and polygons to people and actions, and beyond implicit cognition to implicit emotion and implicit motivation.

ACKNOWLEDGMENTS

The point of view represented herein is based in part on research supported by Grant Nos. MH-35856 and MH-44739 from the National Institute of Mental Health. I thank Jennifer Beer, Michael Kim, Andres Martinez, Lillian Park, Katherine Shobe, and Heidi Wenk for their comments at various stages in the preparation of this chapter.

REFERENCES

Anderson, J. R. (1983). The architecture of cognition. Cambridge, MA: Harvard University Press.

Anderson, J. R. (1992). Automaticity and the ACT* theory. *American Journal of Psychology, 105,* 165–180.

Banaji, M. R., & Greenwald, A. G. (1995). Implicit gender stereotyping in judgments of fame. *Journal of Personality and Social Psychology, 68,* 181–198.

Bargh, J. A. (1984). Automatic and conscious processing of social information. In R. S. Wyer & T. K. Srull (Eds.), *Handbook of social cognition* (Vol. 3, pp. 1–43). Hillsdale, NJ: Erlbaum.

Bargh, J. A. (1997). The automaticity of everyday life. In R. S. Wyer (Ed.), *Advances in social cognition* (Vol. 10, pp. 1–61). Mahwah, NJ: Erlbaum.

Bargh, J. A., & Barndollar, K. (1996). Automaticity in action: The unconscious as a repository of chronic goals and motives. In P. M. Gollwitzer & J. A. Bargh (Eds.), *The psychology of action* (pp. 457–481). New York: Guilford Press.

Beitman, B. D., Mukerji, V., Russell, J. L., & Grafing, M. (1993). Panic disorder in cardiology patients: A review of the Missouri Panic/Cardiology Project. *Journal of Psychiatric Research, 27,* 35–46.

Berkowitz, L., & Devine, P. G. (1995). Has social psychology always been cognitive? What is "cognitive" anyhow? *Personality and Social Psychology Bulletin, 21,* 696–703.

Berry, D. C., & Dienes, Z. (1993). *Implicit learning: Theoretical and empirical issues.* Hove, UK: Erlbaum.

Bisiach, E. (1993). Mental representation in unilateral neglect and related disorders. *Quarterly Journal of Experimental Psychology, 46A,* 435–462.

Bornstein, R. F. (1989). Exposure and affect: Overview and meta-analysis of research, 1968–1987. *Psychological Bulletin, 106,* 265–289.

Bornstein, R. F. (1992). Subliminal mere exposure effects. In R. F. Bornstein & T. S. Pittman (Eds.), *Perception without awareness: Cognitive, clinical, and social perspectives* (pp. 191–210). New York: Guilford Press.

Bornstein, R. F. (1998). Implicit and self-attributed dependency strivings: Differential relationships to laboratory and field measures of help seeking. *Journal of Personality and Social Psychology, 75,* 778–787.

Bornstein, R. F., Leone, D. R., & Galley, D. J. (1987). The generalizability of subliminal mere exposure effects: Influence of stimuli perceived without awareness on social behavior. *Journal of Personality and Social Psychology, 53,* 1070–1079.

Bornstein, R. F., & Masling, J. M. (1998). *Empirical perspectives on the psychoanalytic unconscious.* Washington, DC: American Psychological Association.

Bowers, K. S. (1984). On being unconsciously influenced and informed. In K. S. Bowers & D. Meichenbaum (Eds.), *The unconscious reconsidered.* New York: Wiley-Interscience.

Bowers, K. S. (1987). Revisioning the unconscious. Canadian Psychology, *28,* 93–104.

Bowers, K. S., Farvolden, P., & Mermigis, L. (1995). Intuitive antecedents of insight. In S. M. Smith, T. M. Ward, & R. A. Finke (Eds.), *The creative cognition approach* (pp. 27–52). Cambridge, MA: MIT Press.

Bowers, K. S., Regehr, G., Balthazard, C., & Parker, K. (1990). Intuition in the context of discovery. Cognitive Psychology, *22,* 72–110.

Breuer, J., & Freud, S. (1955). Studies on hysteria. In J. Strachey (Ed.), *The standard edition of the complete psychological works of Sigmund Freud* (Vol. 2). London: Hogarth Press. (Original work published 1893–1895)

Buck, R. (1985). Prime theory: An integrated view of motivation and emotion. *Psychological Review, 92,* 389–413.

Campion, J., Latto, R., & Smith, Y. M. (1983). Is blindsight an effect of scattered light, spared cortex, and near-threshold vision? *Behavioral and Brain Sciences, 6,* 423–486.

Chapman, L. J., Chapman, J. P., & Raulin, M. L. (1976). Scales for physical and social anhedonia. *Journal of Abnormal Psychology, 85,* 374–382.

Claparède, E. (1951). [Recognition and "me-ness."] In D. Rapaport (Ed.), *Organization and pathology of thought.* New York: Columbia University Press. (Original work published 1911)

Cork, R. L., Couture, L. J., & Kihlstrom, J. F. (1997). Memory and recall. In T. L. Yaksh, C. Lynch, W. M. Zapol, M. Maze, J. F. Biebuyck, & L. J. Saidman, (Eds.), *Anesthesia: Biologic foundations* (pp. 451–467). New York: Lippincott-Raven.

deHaan, E. H. F., Young, A., & Newcombe, F. (1987). Face recognition without awareness. Cognitive Neuropsychology, *4,* 385–415.

Devine, P. G. (1989). Stereotypes and prejudice: Their automatic and controlled components. *Journal of Personality and Social Psychology, 56,* 680–690.

Dorfman, J., Shames, V. A., & Kihlstrom, J. F. (1996). Intuition, incubation, and insight: Implicit cognition in problem-solving. In G. Underwood (Ed.), *Implicit cognition* (pp. 257–296). Oxford, UK: Oxford University Press.

Draine, S. C., & Greenwald, A. G. (1998). Replicable unconscious semantic priming. *Journal of Experimental Psychology: General, 127,* 286–303.

Dulany, D. (1997). Consciousness in the explicit (deliberative) and implicit (evocative). In J. D. Cohen & J. W. Schooler (Eds.), *Scientific studies of consciousness* (pp. 179–212). Mahwah, NJ: Erlbaum.

Eich, E. (1990). Learning during sleep. In R. R. Bootzin, J. F. Kihlstrom, & D. L. Schacter (Eds.), *Sleep and cognition* (pp. 88–108). Washington, DC: American Psychological Association.

Ekman, P., & Davidson, R. J. (1994). Affective science: A research agenda. In P. Ekman & R. J. Davidson (Eds.), *The nature of emotion: Fundamental questions* (pp. 411–430). New York: Oxford University Press.

Ellenberger, H. F. (1970). *The discovery of the unconscious: The history and evolution of dynamic psychiatry.* New York: Basic Books.

Erickson, C. W. (1960). Discrimination and learning without awareness: A methodological survey and evaluation. *Psychological Review, 67,* 279–300.

Fazio, R. H., Sanbonmatsu, D. M., Powell, M. C., & Kardes, F. R. (1986). On the automatic activation of attitudes. *Journal of Personality and Social Psychology, 69,* 1013–1027.

Frederickson, R. (1993). *Repressed memories: A journey to recovery from sexual abuse.* New York: Simon & Schuster.

Freud, S. (1953). The interpretation of dreams. In J. Strachey (Ed.), *The standard edition of the complete psychological works of Sigmund Freud* (Vols. 4–5). London: Hogarth Press. (Original work published 1900)

Freud, S. (1961, 1963). Introductory lectures on psychoanalysis. In J. Strachey (Ed.), *The standard edition of the complete psychological works of Sigmund Freud* (Vols. 15–16). London: Hogarth Press. (Original work published 1915–1917)

Graf, P., & Masson, M. E. J. (1993). *Implicit memory: New directions in cognition, development, and neuropsychology.* Hillsdale, NJ: Erlbaum.

Greenwald, A. G. (1992). New Look 3: Unconscious cognition reclaimed. *American Psychologist, 47,* 766–779.

Greenwald, A. G., & Banaji, M. R. (1995). Implicit social cognition: Attitudes, self-esteem, and stereotypes. *Psychological* Review, *102,* 4–27.

Greenwald, A. G., & Draine, S. C. (1998). Distinguishing unconscious from conscious cognition—Reasonable assumptions and replicable findings: Reply to Merikle & Reingold (1998) and Dosher (1998). *Journal of Experimental Psychology: General, 127,* 320–324.

Greenwald, A. G., Klinger, M. R., & Liu, T. J. (1989). Unconscious processing of dichoptically masked words. *Memory and Cognition, 17,* 35–47.

Greenwald, A. G., Spangenberg, E. R., Pratkanis, A. R., & Eskenazi, J. (1991). Double-blind tests of sbliminal self-help audiotapes. *Psychological Science, 2,* 119–122.

Hasher, L., & Zacks, R. T. (1979). Automatic and effortful processes in memory. *Journal of Experimental Psychology: General, 108,* 356–388.

Hasher, L., & Zacks, R. T. (1984). Automatic processing of fundamental information: The case of frequency of occurrence. *American Psychologist, 39,* 1372–1388.

Hilgard, E. R. (1977a). Controversies over consciousness and the rise of cognitive psychology. *Australian Psychologist, 12,* 7–26.

Hilgard, E. R. (1977b). *Divided consciousness: Multiple controls in human thought and action.* New York: Wiley-Interscience.

Hilgard, E. R. (1980a). Consciousness in contemporary psychology. *Annual Review of Psychology, 31,* 1–26.

Hilgard, E. R. (1980b). The trilogy of mind: Cognition, affection, and conation. *Journal of the History of the Behavioral Sciences, 16,* 107–117.

Hilgard, E. R. (1987). *Psychology in America: A historical survey.* San Diego: Harcourt Brace Jovanovich.

Hodgson, R., & Rachman, S. (1974). II. Desynchrony in measures of fear. *Behaviour Research and Therapy, 12,* 319–326.

Holender, D. (1986). Semantic activation without conscious identification in dichotic listening, parafoveal vision, and visual masking: A survey and appraisal. *Behavioral and Brain Sciences, 9,* 1–66.

Hugdahl, K. (1981). The three-system model of fear and emotion—A critical examination. *Behaviour Research and Therapy, 19,* 75–85.

Jackson, D. N. (1974). *Manual for the Personality Research Form.* Goshen, NY: Research Psychology Press.

James, W. (1890/1980). *Principles of psychology.* Cambridge, MA: Harvard University Press. (Original work published 1880)

Janet, P. (1889). [*Psychological automatisms.*] Paris: Alcan.

Janet, P. (1907). *The major symptoms of hysteria.* New York: Macmillan.

Johnson, M. K., Kim, J. K., & Risse, G. (1985). Do alcoholic Korsakoff's syndrome patients acquire affective reactions? *Journal of Experimental Psychology: Learning, Memory, and Cognition, 11,* 27–36.

Kahneman, D., & Treisman, A. (1984). Changing views of attention and automaticity. In R. Parasuraman & D. R. Davies (Eds.), *Varieties of attention* (pp. 29–61). New York: Academic Press.

Kihlstrom, J. F. (1980). Posthypnotic amnesia for recently learned material: Interactions with "episodic" and "semantic" memory. *Cognitive Psychology, 12,* 227–251.

Kihlstrom, J. F. (1984). Conscious, subconscious, unconscious: A cognitive view. In K. S. Bowers & D.

Meichenbaum (Eds.), *The unconscious reconsidered* (pp. 149–211). New York: Wiley-Interscience.
Kihlstrom, J. F. (1985). Posthypnotic amnesia and the dissociation of memory. In G. H. Bower (Ed.), *The psychology of learning and motivation* (Vol. 19, pp. 131–178). New York: Academic Press.
Kihlstrom, J. F. (1987). The cognitive unconscious. *Science, 237,* 1445–1452.
Kihlstrom, J. F. (1992a). Dissociation and dissociations: A comment on consciousness and cognition. *Consciousness and Cognition, 1,* 47–53.
Kihlstrom, J. F. (1992b). Dissociative and conversion disorders. In D. J. Stein & J. Young (Eds.), *Cognitive science and clinical disorders* (pp. 247–270). San Diego: Academic Press.
Kihlstrom, J. F. (1995a). Memory and consciousness: An appreciation of Claparède and his "Recognition et Moiïtè." *Consciousness and Cognition, 4,* 379–386.
Kihlstrom, J. F. (1996a). Perception without awareness of what is perceived, learning without awareness of what is learned. In M. Velmans (Ed.), *The science of consciousness: Psychological, neuropsychological, and clinical reviews* (pp. 23–46). London: Routledge.
Kihlstrom, J. F. (1996b). The trauma-memory argument and recovered memory therapy. In K. Pezdek & W. P. Banks (Eds.), *The recovered memory/false memory debate* (pp. 297–311). San Diego: Academic Press.
Kihlstrom, J. F. (1997a). Consciousness and me-ness. In J. Cohen & J. Schooler (Eds.), *Scientific approaches to the question of consciousness* (pp. 451–468). Mahwah, NJ: Erlbaum.
Kihlstrom, J. F. (1997b). Suffering from reminiscences: Exhumed memory, implicit memory, and the return of the repressed. In M. A. Conway (Ed.), *Recovered memories and false memories* (pp. 100–117). Oxford, UK: Oxford University Press.
Kihlstrom, J. F. (1998). Exhumed memory. In S. J. Lynn & K. M. McConkey (Eds.), *Truth in memory* (pp. 3–31). New York: Guilford Press.
Kihlstrom, J. F. (1999a). Conscious versus unconscious cognition. In R. J. Sternberg (Ed.), *The concept of cognition* (pp. 173–204). Cambridge, MA: MIT Press.
Kihlstrom, J. F. (1999b). Dissociative disorders. In H. E. Adams & P. B. Sutker (Eds.), *Comprehensive handbook of psychopathology* (2nd ed.). New York: Plenum Press.
Kihlstrom, J. F., Barnhardt, T. M., & Tataryn, D. J. (1992). Implicit perception. In R. F. Bornstein & T. S. Pittman (Eds.), *Perception without awareness: Cognitive, clinical, and social perspectives* (pp. 17–54). New York: Guilford Press.
Kihlstrom, J. F., & Klein, S. B. (1994). The self as a knowledge structure. In R. S. Wyer & T. K. Srull (Eds.), *Handbook of social cognition* (2nd ed., Vol. 1, pp. 153–208). Hillsdale, NJ: Erlbaum.
Kihlstrom, J. F., & Klein, S. B. (1997). Self-knowledge and self-awareness. In J. G. Snodgrass & R. L. Thompson (Eds.), The self across psychology: Self-recognition, self-awareness, and the self-concept. *Annals of the New York Academy of Sciences, 818,* 5–17.
Kihlstrom, J. F., Mulvaney, S., Tobias, B. A., & Tobis, I. P. (1999). The emotional unconscious. In E. Eich, J. F. Kihlstrom, G. H. Bower, J. P. Forgas, & P. M. Niedenthal, *Counterpoints: Cognition and emotion.* New York: Oxford University Press.
Kihlstrom, J. F., & Schacter, D. L. (1995). Functional disorders of autobiographical memory. In A. Baddeley, B. A. Wilson, & F. Watts (Eds.), *Handbook of memory disorders* (pp. 337–364). London: Wiley.
Kihlstrom, J. F., Shames, V. A., & Dorfman, J. (1996). Intimations of memory and thought. In L. Reder (Ed.), *Implicit memory and metacognition* (pp. 1–23). Mahwah, NJ: Erlbaum.
Kunst-Wilson, W. R., & Zajonc, R. B. (1980). Affective discrimination of stimuli that cannot be recognized. *Science, 207,* 557–558.
LaBerge, D., & Samuels, S. J. (1974). Toward a theory of automatic information processing in reading. *Cognitive Psychology, 6,* 293–323.
Lane, R. D., Ahern, G. L., Schwartz, G. E., & Kaszniak, A. W. (1997). Is alexithymia the emotional equivalent of blindsight? *Biological Psychiatry, 42,* 834–844.
Lane, R. D., & Schwartz, G. E. (1987). Levels of emotional awareness: A cognitive-developmental theory and its application to psychopathology. *American Journal of Psychiatry, 144,* 133–143.
Lang, P. J. (1968). Fear reduction and fear behavior: Problems in treating a construct. In J. M. Schlein (Ed.), *Research in psychotherapy* (Vol. 3, pp. 90–103). Washington, DC: American Psychological Association.
LeDoux, J. (1996). *The emotional brain: The mysterious underpinnings of emotional life.* New York: Simon & Schuster.
Lewicki, P. (1986). *Nonconscious social information processing.* New York: Academic Press.
Logan, G. D. (1997). The automaticity of academic life: Unconscious applications of an implicit theory. In R. S. Wyer (Ed.), *Advances in social cognition* (Vol. 10, pp. 157–179). Mahwah, NJ: Erlbaum.
Mandler, G., Nakamura, Y., & Van Zandt, B. J. S. (1987). Nonspecific effects of exposure on stimuli that cannot be recognized. *Journal of Experimental Psychology: Learning, Memory, and Cognition, 13,* 646–648.
Marcel, A. (1983). Conscious and unconscious perception: Experiments on visual masking and word recognition. *Cognitive Psychology, 15,* 197–237.
McClelland, D. C. (1980). Motive dispositions: The merits of operant and respondent measures. In L. Wheeler (Ed.), *Review of personality and social psychology* (Vol. 1, pp. 10–41). Beverly Hills, CA: Sage.
McClelland, D. C., Koestner, R., & Weinberger, J. (1989). How do self-attributed and implicit motives differ? *Psychological Review, 96,* 690–702.
Mednick, S. A. (1962). The associative basis of the creative process. *Psychological Review, 69,* 220–232.
Merikle, P. M. (1988). Subliminal auditory messages: An evaluation. *Psychology and Marketing, 5,* 355–372.

Merikle, P. M., & Daneman, M. (1996). Memory for events during anaesthesia: A meta-analysis. In B. Bonke, J. G. Bovill, & N. Moerman (Eds.), *Memory and awareness in anaesthesia 3* (pp. 108–121). Assen, The Netherlands: Van Gorcum.

Merikle, P. M., & Skanes, H. E. (1992). Subliminal self-help audiotapes: A search for placebo effects. *Journal of Applied Psychology, 77,* 772–776.

Merikle, P. M., & Reingold, E. M. (1992). Measuring unconscious processes. In R. F. Bornstein & T. S. Pittman (Eds.), *Perception without awareness: Cognitive, clinical, and social perspectives* (pp. 55–80). New York: Guilford Press.

Moore, T. E. (1988). The case against subliminal manipulation. *Psychology and Marketing, 5,* 297–316.

Moore, T. E. (1995). Subliminal self-help auditory tapes: An empirical test of perceptual consequences. *Canadian Journal of Behavioural Science, 27,* 9–20.

Newman, L. S., & Uleman, J. S. (1989). Spontaneous trait inference. In J. S. Uleman & J. A. Bargh (Eds.), *Unintended thought* (pp. 155–188). New York: Guilford Press.

Nisbett, R., & Wilson, T. D. (1977). Telling more than we can know: Verbal reports on mental processes. *Psychological Review, 84,* 231–259.

Panskepp, J. (1991). Affective neuroscience: A conceptual framework for the neurobiological study of emotions. In K. Strongman (Ed.), *International reviews of studies in emotions* (Vol. 1, pp. 59–99). Chichester, UK: Wiley.

Pashler, H. E. (1997). *The psychology of attention.* Cambridge, MA: MIT Press.

Peirce, C. S., & Jastrow, J. (1884). On small differences of sensation. Memorials of the National Academy of Sciences, *3,* 73–83.

Polster, M. R. (1993). Drug-induced amnesia: Implications for cognitive neuropsychological investigations of memory. *Psychological Bulletin, 114,* 477–493.

Posner, M. I., & Snyder, C. R. R. (1975). Attention and cognitive control. In R. L. Solso (Ed.), *Information processing and cognition: The Loyola symposium* (pp. 55–85). Hillsdale, NJ: Erlbaum.

Pratto, F. (1994). Consciousness and automatic evaluation. In P. M. Niedenthal & S. Kitayama (Eds.), *The heart's eye: Emotional influences in perception and attention* (pp. 115–143). San Diego: Academic Press.

Prince, M. (1906). *The dissociation of a personality.* New York: Longmans, Green.

Rachman, S., & Hodgson, R. (1974). I. Synchrony and desynchrony in measures of fear. *Behaviour Research and Therapy, 12,* 311–318.

Rafal, R. D. (1998). Neglect. In R. Parasuraman (Ed.), *The attentive brain* (pp. 489–525). Cambridge, MA: MIT Press.

Reber, A. R. (1993). *Implicit learning and tacit knowledge: An essay on the cognitive unconscious.* New York: Oxford University Press.

Reder, L. M. (Ed.). (1996). *Implicit memory and metacognition.* Mahwah, NJ: Erlbaum.

Roediger, H. A., & McDermott, K. B. (1993). Implicit memory in normal human subjects. In F. Boller & J. Grafman (Eds.)., *Handbook of neuropsychology* (Vol. 8, pp. 63–131). Amsterdam: Elsevier Science.

Schacter, D. L. (1987). Implicit memory: History and current status. *Journal of Experimental Psychology: Learning, Memory, and Cognition, 13,* 501–518.

Schacter, D. L., Chiu, C. -Y. P., & Ochser, K. N. (1993). Implicit memory: A selective review. *Annual Review of Neuroscience, 16,* 159–182.

Schacter, D. L., & Kihlstrom, J. F. (1999). Functional amnesia. In F. Boller & J. Graffman (Eds.), *Handbook of neuropsychology* (2nd ed.). Amsterdam: Elsevier.

Schneider, W., & Shiffrin, R. M. (1977). Controlled and automatic human information processing: I. Detection, search, and attention. *Psychological Review, 84,* 1–66.

Seamon, J. G., McKenna, P. A., & Binder, N. (1998). The mere exposure effect is differentially sensitive to different judgment tasks. *Consciousness & Cognition, 7,* 85–102.

Seger, C. A. (1994). Implicit learning. *Psychological Bulletin, 115,* 163–196.

Shames, V. A. (1994). *Is there such a thing as implicit problem solving?* Unpublished doctoral dissertation, University of Arizona, Tucson, Arizona.

Shanks, D. R., & St. John, M. F. (1994). Characteristics of dissociable learning systems. *Behavioral and Brain Sciences, 17,* 367–447.

Silverman, L. H. (1976). Psychoanalytic theory: "The reports of my death are greatly exaggerated." *American Psychologist, 31,* 621–637.

Smith, E. R. (1994). Procedural knowledge and processing strategies in social cognition. In R. S. Wyer & T. K. Srull (Eds.), *Handbook of social cognition* (2nd ed., Vol. 1, pp. 99–152). Hillsdale, NJ: Erlbaum.

Squire, L. R., & Knowlton, B. J. (1995). Memory, hippocampus, and brain systems. In M. Gazzaniga (Ed.), *The cognitive neurosciences* (pp. 825–837). Cambridge, MA: MIT Press.

Taylor, E. (1996). *William James on consciousness beyond the margin.* Princeton, NJ: Princeton University Press.

Taylor, S. E., & Fiske, S. T. (1978). Salience, attention, and attribution: Top of the head phenomena. In L. Berkowitz (Ed.), *Advances in experimental social psychology* (Vol. 11, pp. 249–288). New York: Academic Press.

Tranel, D., & Damasio, A. R. (1985). Knowledge without awareness: An autonomic index of facial recognition by prosopagnosics. *Science, 228,* 1453–1454.

Turpin, G. (1991). The psychophysiological assessment of anxiety disorders: Three-systems measurement and beyond. *Psychological Assessment, 3,* 365–375.

Uleman, J. S., Newman, L., & Moskowitz, G. B. (1996). People as flexible interpreters: Evidence and issues from spontaneous trait inference. In M. Zanna (Ed.), *Advances in experimental social psychol-*

ogy (Vol. 28, pp. 211–280). San Diego: Academic Press.

Wegner, D. M., & Bargh, J. A. (1998). Control and automaticity in social life. In D. T. Gilbert, S. T. Fiske, G. Lindzey (Eds.), *Handbook of social psychology,* 4th ed. (Vol. 2, pp. 446–496). Boston: McGraw-Hill.

Wegner, D. M., & Smart, L. (1997). Deep cognitive activation: A new approach to the unconscious. *Journal of Consulting and Clinical Psychology, 65,* 984–995.

Weinberger, D. A. (1997). Distress and self-restraint as measures of adjustment across the life span: Confirmatory factor analyses in clinical and nonclinical samples. *Psychological Assessment, 9,* 132–135.

Weinberger, D. A., Schwartz, G. E., & Davidson, R. J. (1979). Low-anxious, high-anxious, and repressive coping styles: Psychometric patterns and behavioral and physiological responses to stress. *Journal of Abnormal Psychology, 88,* 369–380.

Weiskrantz, L. (1986). *Blindsight: A case study and implications.* Oxford, UK: Oxford University Press.

Weiskrantz, L. (1997). *Consciousness lost and found.* Oxford, UK: Oxford University Press.

Westen, D. (1998a). The scientific legacy of Sigmund Freud: Toward a psychodynamically informed psychological science. *Psychological Bulletin, 124,* 333–371.

Westen, D. (1998b). Unconscious thought, feeling, and motivation: The end of a century-long debate. In R. F. Bornstein & J. M. Masling (Eds.), *Empirical perspectives on the psychoanalytic unconscious* (pp. 1–44). Washington, DC: American Psychological Association.

Wittenbrink, B., Judd, C. M., & Park, B. (1997). Evidence for racial prejudice at the implicit level and its relationship with questionnaire measures. *Journal of Personality and Social Psychology, 72,* 262–274.

Wood, J. M., Bootzin, R. R., Kihlstrom, J. F., & Schacter, D. L. (1992). Implicit and explicit memory for verbal information presented during sleep. *Psychological Science, 3,* 236–239.

Zajonc, R. B. (1968). The attitudinal effects of mere exposure. *Journal of Personality and Social Psychology* (monograph supplement) *9*(2, Pt. 2).

Zajonc, R. B. (1980). Feeling and thinking: Preferences need no inferences. *American Psychologist, 35,* 151–175.

Zinbarg, R. E. (1998). Concordance and synchrony in measures of anxiety and panic reconsidered: A hierarchical model of anxiety and panic. *Behavior Therapy, 29,* 301–323.

Chapter 18

Naturalizing the Self

Richard W. Robins
University of California, Davis

Julie K. Norem and Jonathan M. Cheek
Wellesley College

Late in his life, Michelangelo began carving what many art historians consider his most mature and provocative piece of sculpture, the Florentine Pietà, an enormous 8-foot statue he intended to place at the top of his own tomb. After working intensely for a decade on this monumental project, the artist entered his studio one day and took a sledgehammer to it. He broke away the hands and legs and nearly shattered the work before his servants dragged him away. Why did Michelangelo attempt to destroy one of his greatest creations, a statue that has been described as among the finest works of the Renaissance?

How would a personality psychologist answer this question? A trait researcher might say that Michelangelo was highly neurotic and lacked conscientiousness. A biologically oriented researcher might speculate that he had elevated levels of testosterone and low levels of serotonin. A motivational researcher might assume that Michelangelo's personal projects shifted and the Florentine Pietà came into conflict with another important goal. Yet clearly none of these explanations provides a completely satisfactory account of Michelangelo's seemingly irrational act. It is only through a consideration of self-processes—identity, self-esteem, and self-regulation—that one can begin to understand Michelangelo's behavior. An analysis of Michelangelo's "self" allows us to formulate hypotheses concerning a breakdown in self-regulation, a heightened sense of perfectionism and shame in the achievement domain, a failure to live up to his own expectations, and an identity crisis due to his impending death.

Many aspects of human behavior seem inexplicable without the notion that people have a self. It is our contention that an understanding of the self is necessary for a complete understanding of personality processes—the processes that generate and regulate thoughts, feelings, and behaviors. An understanding of the self helps explain not only exceptional behaviors such as Michelangelo's destructive act but also many aspects of everyday social life: Why do some individuals feel shy in social circumstances whereas others do not? Why are some individuals boastful in some situations but insecure in others? Why are some individuals preoccupied by achievement concerns whereas others crave intimacy?

PSYCHOLOGY'S MOST PUZZLING PUZZLE

In *Principles of Psychology*, William James (1890) referred to the self as psychology's "most puzzling puzzle" (p. 330). For the past century, psychologists have debated whether it is a puzzle worth puzzling about. In an article titled "Is the Concept of Self Necessary?," Gordon Allport (1955) raised the possibility that the self is "an impediment in the path of psychological progress" (p. 25). B. F. Skinner (1990) argued that "there is no place in a scientific analysis of behavior for a mind or self" (p. 1209). John Searle (1992) claimed that an understanding of consciousness and subjective experience is beyond the reach of objective science. Steven Pinker (1997) described self-awareness as an intractable problem that we as a species are not sufficiently evolved to grasp. Indeed, to many psychologists, research on the self seems like the "blooming, buzzing confusion" James (1890) believed characterized infancy. Faced with this daunting level of pessimism, we propose the perhaps overly optimistic thesis that a scientific understanding of the self is not only possible but is in fact fundamental to a science of personality.

The complexities of the self-concept literature reflect the intrinsic complexity of the self as a construct. This complexity exists because self-processes operate at multiple levels, and different research camps have emerged to address the role of the self at different levels. Thus, there are researchers studying how the self relates to conscious and unconscious mental processes, motives and goals, emotions, memory and judgment, neural activity, interpersonal processes, situational factors, cultural factors, and so on. In this research, the self is sometimes an independent variable, sometimes a dependent variable, and sometimes a mediator, moderator, or confound.

HISTORY OF THE SELF AS A CENTRAL CONSTRUCT IN PERSONALITY THEORY

In the early days of scientific psychology, the self was an integral part of many general theories of the person. Indeed, many "classic" readings on the self come from the writings of the most influential theorists of the first half of the century: James (1890), Baldwin (1897), Cooley (1902), Mead (1934), McDougall (1923, 1963), Murphy (1947), Hilgard (1949), and Allport (1955). Three basic themes recur in these broad conceptions of the person. First, the self was seen as fundamental to social behavior and personality, and many early theorists attempted to link self processes to other basic psychological processes; thus, the self was seen as an executive body coordinating the thoughts, feelings, and behavior of a highly complex, dynamic organism. Second, many of these perspectives emphasized the interplay between biological and social forces—the self is constructed out of the raw materials endowed by nature and shaped by nurture. Third, the self was conceptualized from an evolutionary and functionalist perspective. The early theorists were working in the immediate aftermath of Darwin, and many drew heavily on evolutionary thinking. In particular, James (1890) was committed to a *naturalistic* explanation of the origin and present function of consciousness and self, assuming that conscious mental life "emerged by way of natural selection because it gave our species certain survival, and therefore reproductive, advantages" (p. 52).

Contemporary research on the self has moved away from the three themes emphasized in early personality theories, and researchers have generally shifted from a naturalist position to a view of the self as a social and cultural construction. This shift occurred in part because general personality theories that incorporated the self were not particularly amenable to empirical inquiry. They included conceptually ambiguous concepts that were difficult, if not impossible, to operationalize. As a result, self researchers moved toward midlevel models and concepts that could be studied empirically, including self-esteem, self-attribution, expectations, social comparisons, reactions to feedback, and so on. Moreover, in contrast to traditional personality theories, the vast majority of contemporary theories and models of the self address a specific process or structure and do not attempt to integrate the

TABLE 18.1. **Self-Concept Theories**

- Action identification theory (Vallacher & Wegner, 1987)
- Cognitive adaptation theory (Aspinwall & Taylor, 1992)
- Cognitive-experiential self theory (Epstein, 1990)
- Cybernetic theory of self-regulation (Carver & Scheier, 1981, 1998)
- Defensive pessimism theory (Norem & Cantor, 1986)
- Hierarchy of selves (Kihlstrom & Cantor, 1984)
- Implicit self theory (Dweck, Chiu, & Hong 1995)
- Impression management (Schlenker, 1980)
- Objective self-awareness theory (Duval & Wicklund, 1972)
- Object relations/narcissism theory (Freud, 1914/1953; Kohut, 1971)
- Optimal distinctiveness theory (Brewer, 1993)
- Possible selves (Markus & Nurius, 1986)
- Role theory (Sarbin & Allen, 1968)
- Schema-based models (Markus, 1977)
- Self-affirmation theory (Steele, 1988)
- Self- assessment model (Trope, 1980, 1986)
- Self-categorization theory (Turner et al., 1987; Turner & Onorato, 1999)
- Self-complexity theory (Linville, 1987)
- Self-consciousness theory (Buss, 1980)
- Self-consistency theory (Lecky, 1945)
- Self-deception theory (Gur & Sackeim, 1979; Lockard & Paulhus, 1988)
- Self-determination theory (Deci & Ryan, 1985)
- Self-discrepancy theory (Higgins, 1987)
- Self-efficacy theory (Bandura, 1982)
- Self-enhancement theory (Taylor & Brown, 1988)
- Self-evaluation maintenance theory (Tesser, 1988)
- Self-handicapping models (Jones & Berglas, 1978; Snyder 1990)
- Self-monitoring theory (Snyder, 1974, 1987)
- Self-perception theory (Bem, 1972)
- Self-presentation theory (Baumeister, 1982; Goffman, 1959; Jones & Pittman, 1982)
- Self-verification theory (Swann, 1996b, 1997)
- Social comparison theory (Festinger, 1954)
- Social identity theory (Tajfel & Turner, 1986)
- Socioanalytic theory (Hogan, 1982)
- Symbolic self-completion theory (Wicklund & Gollwitzer, 1982)
- Symbolic interactionism/looking glass self (Cooley, 1902; Mead, 1934)
- Terror management theory (Solomon, Greenberg, & Pyszczynski, 1991)

self into a broader conception of psychological functioning (for exceptions, see Carver & Scheier, 1981, 1998; Higgins, 1987; Singer, 1995). These limited-domain theories and models have proliferated rapidly over the past few decades.

Table 18.1 shows a list of self theories proposed over the last several decades. These theories have generated a considerable amount of research and empirical findings that have advanced our understanding of the structure and content of the self and the processes involved in self-perception. Yet most self researchers are frustrated by the plethora of theories and models that have resisted attempts at broader integration (e.g., Robins & John, 1997b; Swann, 1996a).

RETURNING TO A NATURALIST VIEW OF THE SELF

Recently, there has been renewed interest in the role of the self in general theories of the person, but, interestingly, this shift has *not* been spearheaded by personality and social psychologists. Instead, the battle to understand psychology's most puzzling puzzle has been taken up by scientists from many different areas who share an interest in understanding how the mind works. Gazzaniga (1995, 1998), Crick (1994), and other neuroscientists are studying the neural bases of consciousness and subjective experience, and speculating about how a sense of self emerges from the activity of the brain. Emotion researchers including LeDoux (1996) and Davidson (1994) are searching for the neural bases of affective experience and discovering basic facts about how the brain is wired that have profound implications for self researchers. Memory researchers such as Tulving (1993b) are discussing how various forms of memory (e.g., episodic, semantic) relate to the conscious experience of self, and this work is being used in some highly innovative research on self-knowledge in amnesics (Klein, Loftus, & Kihlstrom, 1996; Klein & Kihlstrom, 1998). Psychiatrists such as Peter Kramer (1993) are discussing how neurophysiological changes associated with psychoactive drugs such as Prozac can radically alter one's sense of self; psychiatrist Kay Jamison (1995) describes her manic depression as an "outside force that was at war with my natural self" (p. 15). Molecular geneticist Dean Hamer (Hamer & Copeland, 1998) believes that recent research linking specific genes to personality traits has implications for the search for self-knowledge. Philosophers continue to debate the Cartesian mind–body duality, and Daniel Dennett (1991) argues that the self is an illusion generated by the physical activity of the brain. Steven Pinker (1997) and other evolutionary psychologists are discussing how the self evolved and what its adaptive functions might be. Neurologist Oliver Sacks (1995) describes case studies that vividly illustrate how neurological disorders can profoundly disrupt self and identity. Developmental researchers interested in theory of mind are studying how our understanding of self and others develops (e.g., Wellman, 1990), and psychiatrist Simon Baron-Cohen's research on autism provides insights into where the theory of mind module might reside in the brain (e.g., Baron-Cohen, 1995; Stone, Baron-Cohen, & Knight, 1998). Thus, basic issues about the self are being grappled with from a wide range of perspectives outside of the traditional boundaries of personality and social psychology.

What unites many of these perspectives is a naturalist view of the self—a belief that the self can be studied in the same way as any other natural phenomenon. One goal of this chapter is to help self research recover its roots by reconnecting it with broader scientific concerns. In this chapter, we return to a set of foundational issues that preoccupied William James when he formulated his naturalist perspective of the mind.

OVERVIEW OF CHAPTER

The literature on the self is enormous. A search of the Psychinfo database for the keyword "self" identified more than 153,000 articles! Even restricting the search to the past 30 years and to a single journal—the *Journal of Personality and Social Psychology (JPSP)*—yielded nearly 2,000 articles with the keyword "self." To examine how interest in the self has changed over time, we charted trends in the *proportion* of *JPSP* articles with the keyword "self" from 1969–1998 (see Figure 18.1).[1] The results revealed a surge of interest in the 1970s, reaching a high plateau around 35% to 40% in the 1980s and 1990s. The increase in self research during the 1970s probably reflects the widespread rise of the cognitive perspective in psychology as a whole (Robins, Gosling, & Craik, 1999), which produced a renewed interest in mental events including self-perception (Bem, 1972), self-awareness (e.g., Duval & Wicklund, 1972; Buss, 1980), self-schemas (Markus, 1977), self-presen-

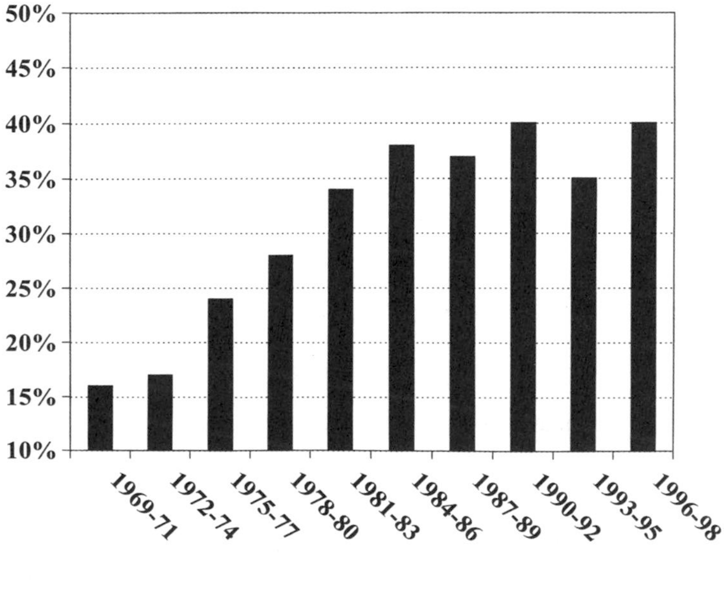

FIGURE 18.1. Percentage of articles in *JPSP* with "self" as a keyword.

tation concerns (e.g., Snyder, 1974), and other aspects of subjective experience.

In this chapter, we do *not* attempt to provide a comprehensive review of the voluminous social-personality literature on the self. Several recent books and chapters provide such reviews: see Brown (1998) and Baumeister (1998) for general overviews of self research; Harter (1998) for a review of research on self-concept development; Cross and Markus (Chapter 15, this volume) for a cultural perspective on the self; Sedikides and Strube (1997) and Robins and John (1997b) for discussions of motives in the self-perception process; Byrne (1996) for an overview of self-concept measures. Instead, our goal is to step back and reflect on some broader questions about the self. We will review the current state of the field with regard to these fundamental issues, in the hope of promoting better integration of self research into the personality literature. We will address a number of basic questions about the self that are abiding concerns of psychologists in general and personality theorists in particular: What is the self? What is the structure of the self? How stable is the self? Is the self distinctive to humans? How and where is the self realized in the brain? How did the self evolve and what are its adaptive functions? These questions return us to James's initial set of issues when he first formulated a naturalist perspective on self and consciousness.

BASIC QUESTIONS ABOUT THE SELF

What Is the Self? Definitional and Conceptual Issues

The question—what is the self?—has been an abiding concern of philosophers, writers, scientists, and laypeople. Although self-concept theorists have offered many definitions, there is no consensual framework for conceptualizing the various aspects of the self. Thus, many of the models and theories presented in Table 18.1 adopt their own definitions and labels, often with little attention to previous usage. Although some researchers embrace the theoretical richness of the field, others bemoan its conceptual muddiness.

One source of confusion is that the "self" does not refer to a single entity but rather to myriad structures and processes. Consider the example of happiness. One aspect of the self is the feeling or experience of happiness itself. This is what philosophers refer to as *qualia* or *sentience*. A second aspect is the conscious recognition that my feeling of happiness belongs to me—it is I who feels happy. As Flanagan (1991) observed, "thoughts, feelings, and the like do not sit around disembodied. All thoughts and feelings are 'owned,' that is, all thoughts and feelings occur to someone" (p. 31). A third aspect refers to attentional focus—I can be aware or not aware of my current state of happiness. For example, I could be feeling happy but not pay attention to this because I am focused on skiing down the mountain. Finally, I can have a stable representation of myself as happy—that is, I can think of myself as a generally happy person or have the belief that "I always feel happy when I am skiing." These four aspects of the self are just a sampling of the many ways the self has been defined and discussed in the literature.

In our view, however, all of the definitions boil down to two basic classes of phenomena: (1) an ongoing sense of self-awareness and (2) stable mental representations (cf. Hart & Karmel, 1996). These two aspects of the self correspond to the classic distinction between the self-as-perceiver (the "I") and the self-as-object of perception (the "Me").

Table 18.2 shows some of the phenomena that relate to these two aspects of the self. What unites the different conceptions listed in Table 18.2 under "ongoing sense of self-awareness" is a view of the self as an active agent that processes information and regulates behavior. Our ongoing sense of awareness and agency is the one psychological phenomenon for which we seem to have direct and irrefutable evidence—we all know how consciousness feels from the inside. As Farthing (1993) notes, "casual introspection seems to reveal a self: the unique entity that is the perceiver of our perceptions, the thinker of our thoughts, the feeler of our emotions and desires, and the agent of our actions . . . the concept of self seems inseparable from the concept of consciousness" (p. 139). Self-awareness refers to a particular form of consciousness in which the object is the self, as a public or private object (Buss, 1980; Carver & Scheier, 1981). Thus, I can be conscious that I am seeing a colorful painting, but my consciousness becomes self-consciousness when I become aware that I think the picture is beautiful, or when I begin to worry that others are evaluating my appreciation of the painting. Thus, to be self-aware means more than simply focusing attention on the self; it also

TABLE 18.2. Two Classes of Self Phenomena

Ongoing sense of self-awareness	Stable self-representations
"I"	"Me"
Self as subject	Self as object
Self as perceiver	Self as perceived
Sentience Qualia	Personal (episodic) memories
Phenomenology Subjective experience	Self-knowledge (semantic memory)
Agent/homunculus	Linguistic/symbolic self
Self-awareness	Self-concept
Self-consciousness	Self-representation
	Self-theories
	Ideal/ought/possible selves

means identification with the object of self-awareness, that is, with one's self (Hart & Karmel, 1996). Pinker (1997) refers to two aspects of self-awareness—sentience and access to information. Sentience, or phenomenal awareness, refers to being physically conscious, as opposed to being unconscious (e.g., asleep or "knocked out"). Access to information refers to the ability to report on the contents of the mind, including thoughts, feelings, and intentions. It relates to the Freudian concept of repression, as well as to recent research on the "cognitive unconscious" showing that information may be out of awareness yet still shaping our behaviors and perceptions (Kihlstrom, Chapter 17, this volume).

A second class of self-phenomena involve "stable mental representations" (see Table 18.2). The self as mental representation is a product of reflexive activity ("Me"), rather than the reflexive activity itself ("I"). According to Mead (1934), "the essential problem of self-hood" is for the individual to "get outside himself (experientially) in such a way as to become an object to himself" (p. 138). Mental representations can be of the person as a physical, social, psychological, or moral being in the past, present, or future. This is what contemporary researchers mean by a self-concept, and what Epstein (1973) meant by the self as a "theory of the person." It is also related to what Sedikides and Skowronski (1997) referred to as the linguistic/symbolic self, and what Pinker (1997) referred to as self-knowledge, that is, "building an internal model of the world that contains the self" (p. 134).

The cognitive contents of self-representations take three forms, ranging from very specific to global (Hart & Karmel, 1996). At the most specific level are personal or autobiographical memories, which are related to episodic memory. For example, "I remember feeling shy last time I was with this person." At the next level are semantic representations or generalized knowledge about the self. For example, "I am a shy person." Finally, at the most abstract or conceptual level, are theories about the self. For example, Dweck and Leggett's (1988) notion of implicit self theories suggests that some people hold the belief that "my shyness is fixed and I will always be shy" whereas others believe that "I can overcome my shyness if I really try."

Both self-awareness ("I") and self-representations ("Me") have been conceptualized as personality variables. People can be more or less chronically self-aware; they can focus more or less attention on their public and private selves; and their self-representations can vary in content, structure, stability, clarity, and complexity. Thus, there are meaningful individual differences in both aspects of the self; although, as we will argue, the basic capacity for self-awareness and self-representation is common to all humans.

Another important definitional issue concerns self-esteem. In our ongoing sense of self-awareness we are continually evaluating ourselves (the "I" evaluates the "Me"). At the same time, we also form stable mental representations that have an evaluative component. The former can be thought of as the self-evaluation process (e.g., feeling competent while working on a task) whereas the latter can be thought of as self-esteem (e.g., stable representation of the self as competent or likable). This raises the question of what is the "Me" that is being evaluated? From our perspective it is largely (but not exclusively) one's personality, that is, one's tendency to think, feel, and act in certain ways. However, our self-representations may or may not accurately reflect our personality characteristics (Robins & John, 1997b).

Finally, it is important to note that some self theorists would object to a wholly "individualistic" conceptualization of the self. In particular, "social-self" researchers would question several assumptions presented above (e.g., Scheibe, 1995; Tyler, Kramer, & John, 1999). First, they would question the assumption that the self is a representation of the individual person. From a social-self perspective, we have selves reflecting our group memberships and collective identities; that is, the self is the intersection of all the social groups to which an individual belongs (e.g., Turner & Onorato, 1999). McGuire, McGuire, and Cheever (1986), for example, argue that modern society enmeshes the individual in multiple specific social contexts, each imposing a role that confers a distinctive sense of self. Second, social-self theorists would question the assumption that the self is a unique psychological structure and a unique property of the perceiver. From a social-self perspective, self-identity is shared and not unique—the self is a social reflection, not a personal reflection (e.g., Gergen, 1991; Sampson, 1985; Turner & Onorato, 1999), and we therefore have normative social identities (e.g., stereotypes). Third, social-self theorists would question the assumption that the contents of the self come from personal experience (private self) or even from the interpersonal context (i.e., internalized reflected appraisals). According to Turner (e.g., Turner & Onorato, 1999), a person's self derives from self-categorizations in multiple social groups. Finally, social-self researchers would question the assumption that the self is an enduring cognitive structure. Instead, they view the self as inherently fluid, context specific, and constructed on-line within social contexts (Gergen, 1991; Scheibe, 1995). Overall, the social-self perspective emphasizes that the self is a fluid and context-specific entity constructed through social interaction. Of course, some of these differences are more apparent than real, reflecting different emphases on the unique versus shared aspects of the self. As McDougall (1963) observed, the self is inherently social and a comprehensive conception of self "implies constant reference to others and to society in general, and is, in fact, not merely a conception of self, but always of one's self in relation to other selves" (p. 155).

What Are the Structural Components of the Self?

In answering the question "Who am I?", people come up with a vast array of responses (e.g., Gordon, 1968). Our representations of who we are encompass everything from our beliefs about our private thoughts and feelings to our place in the larger nexus of relationships, social roles, and cultural institutions (Cheek, 1989). The self is correspondingly a highly complex mental structure that represents years of transactions between the individual and the culture. Because the self does not achieve an ideal unity, discussions of "the self" in terms of various structural aspects must address the "multiple selves" that each individual is assumed to possess (James, 1890). Indeed, as Murphy (1947) emphasized, the extent to which both psychologists and the individuals they study consider the self to be an abstract, integrated, and important entity varies considerably across cultures and, within a culture, among groups of individuals (Cross & Markus, Chapter 15, this volume). For example, Donahue, Robins, Roberts, and John (1993) measured the degree to which people have differentiated versus integrated selves and found that greater consistency of self-representations across social roles (e.g., with friends, at work, at school, with parents, with romantic partners) was associated with better psychological adjustment.

Over the past century, psychologists have been refining and improving the model proposed by William James for dividing the self into its constituent parts and processes. The most general distinction is between private and public aspects of the self—the perception of one's inner or subjective processes versus the recognition one receives from other people (Buss, 1980; Carver & Scheier, 1981; Cheek, 1989). A summary table classifying divisions within the self first appeared in James's *The Principles of Psychology* (1890, p. 329), and recently this table has gone through a number of revisions and expansions (cf., Brewer & Gardner, 1996, p. 84; Brown, 1998, p. 39; Greenwald & Breckler, 1985, p. 134).

Table 18.3 shows our own interpretation of the levels and structures of the self. The first row shows the *personal* or individual self, which reflects people's beliefs about their private self, including their traits, values, and abilities. The second row shows the *relational* self, which reflects how people see themselves in the context of intimate relationships. The third row shows the *social* self, which reflects how people see themselves in more general interpersonal contexts, including their social roles and reputation. The fourth row shows the *collective* self, which reflects people's identities concerning their various reference groups, such as their religion, ethnicity, and nationality. Some aspects of identity, such as gender, permeate all levels of the self from the personal (e.g., perceptions of feminine characteristics) to the collective (e.g., identity as a "feminist").

People derive self-regard differently depending on which level of the self they are representing.

TABLE 18.3. Layers and Structures of the Self

Levels/locus of audience	Orientation	Description	Example	Basis of self-regard	Cultural differences	Individual differences
Personal	Private	Traits, values, and abilities	"I am a sensitive person."	Personal aspirations and standards	Independent/ individualistic	Personal Identity Orientation Rosenberg Self-Esteem Scale Private Self-Consciousness Individualism Scale
Relational	Intimate	Other people with whom we have direct personal contact	"I am Amy's close friend."	Mutual regard; pride in and validation from intimate others	↕	Inclusion of Other in Self Scale Mutuality Scale Interdependent Self-Construal Scale Internal Working Models
Social	Interpersonal	Social roles and reputation	"I am a popular professor."	Public recognition; praise from others		Social Identity Orientation Public Self-Consciousness Scale Social Self-Confidence (vs. Shyness)
Collective	Communal	Social categories to which we belong	"I am Irish."	Ethnic pride; pride in one's social groups	Interdependent/ collectivistic	Collective Identity Orientation Collective Self-Esteem Scale Inclusion of Other in Group Scale Collectivism Scale

For example, when an individual is focused on the personal self, self-esteem is rooted in meeting personal aspirations and achievements are gauged relative to personal standards of success. In contrast, when an individual is focused on the collective self, self-esteem is rooted in the accomplishments and prestige of the collective group to which the person belongs (Rubin & Hewstone, 1998). This is related to Cialdini and colleagues' (1976) idea of basking in reflected glory, in which people derive self-esteem from the accomplishments of others with whom they feel connected.

A great deal of recent research has demonstrated cross-cultural differences in the degree of emphasis on these various levels of the self (e.g., Triandis, 1997). Viewed in terms of broad generalizations, Western cultures (e.g., United States, Canada, Western European countries) tend to be more individualistic and focused on the personal self, whereas Eastern cultures (e.g., Japan, China, India) tend to be more collectivistic and focused on the collective self. Markus and Kitayama (1991) have characterized this difference in terms of independent versus interdependent self-construals. On the other hand, Wink (1997) cautions personality psychologists to avoid overemphasizing cultural and ethnic group differences while underemphasizing both individual differences within groups and other variables that can cut across cultures, such as religion and gender. For example, even within Western cultures, women tend to have relatively interdependent selves, whereas men tend to have relatively independent selves (Josephs, Markus, & Tafarodi, 1992).

Each of the levels of the self can be conceptualized in terms of individual differences. For example, the Aspects of Identity Questionnaire (Cheek, Tropp, Chen, & Underwood, 1994) measures the importance people attach to their personal, social, and collective identities. Similarly, Aron, Aron, and Smollan's (1992) Inclusion of Other in Self scale assesses the degree to which people see their own self as connected to, or enmeshed with, their close relationship partners; Tropp and Wright (1995) modified this scale to assess the degree to which people see their own self as connected to the collective groups to which they belong. Interestingly, research suggests that information about the personal self (e.g., "altruistic") may be represented in memory separately (and thus encoded and retrieved separately) from information about the social and collective self (e.g., "peace activist") (Trafimow, Triandix, & Goto, 1991; but see Reid & Deaux, 1996).

Is the structure of the self the same as the structure of personality? For example, is the five-factor model (FFM; John & Srivastava, Chapter 4, this volume) an appropriate way to describe the structure of the self-concept? Few self researchers would agree with this. Clearly our mental representations of ourselves include far more than just beliefs about personality traits. The FFM was not intended as a complete model of personality, but rather as a model of personality traits (John & Robins, 1994b). Thus, relational, social, and collective aspects of the self were not included in the research that led to the discovery of the FFM; for example, following Allport and Odbert (1936) and Norman (1967), most lexical studies of personality structure have explicitly excluded social roles and relationships. Indeed, the FFM represents only a subset of the attributes that self researchers would include even in the personal self. That is, self-schemas about traits, such as dependence–independence (Markus, 1977), do not exhaust the content of the personal self; as John (1989) has shown, there are a number of additional personal self-schemas, including personal-value schemas, which reflect beliefs about appropriate behavior and standards in various contexts. Thus, responses to the "Who am I?" measure show a wide range of nontrait characteristics, including references to aspects of relational, social, and collective identities. A self-concept structure that includes only aspects of *personal* identity necessarily fails to capture the full content of the self. Moreover, many aspects of the structure of the self do not refer to content domains such as the Big Five but rather to how the content of the self is organized, including the degree of differentiation, complexity, and compartmentalization (e.g., Donahue et al., 1993; Linville, 1987; Showers & Kling, 1996). It is important to note, however, that when the content of the personal self is studied and restricted to personality traits, the resulting structure can be described by the five broad dimensions that constitute the FFM.

How Stable Is the Self over Time?

Our beliefs about ourselves seem to be relatively enduring. When we wake up in the morning we have the sense that we are the same person we were the previous day. Similarly, our self-representations do not go through radical changes. It is unlikely that a person will think he is shy and introverted one day and socially bold and extraverted the next. As James (1890) noted, "My name and profession and relations to the world are identical, my face, my faculties and store of memories are practically indistinguishable, now and then. Moreover, the Me of now and the Me of then are *continuous:* the alterations were gradual and never affected the whole of me at once" (p. 186).

The study of self-esteem and self-concept change has been addressed from two different perspectives—life history and systemic. The "life history" perspective assumes that the self is a stable mental structure that shows continuity over time and across situations. As with personality traits, however, the self is assumed to show some changes over the life course as a function of developmental period, as well as life experiences and transitions. Life history research on the self aims to document the degree to which aspects of the self (e.g., self-esteem) show stability and change.

The "systemic" perspective adopts a process orientation and emphasizes experimental studies of self-evaluation. This perspective views the self as a cognitive–affective system that includes motives such as self-enhancement and self-verification, self-regulatory mechanisms, implicit and explicit beliefs and expectations, and a host of other mechanisms. Systemic research on the self aims to understand the workings of this system, and by doing so better understand the factors that contribute to change in self-evaluation. In contrast to the life history perspective, this perspective views self-evaluations and self-conceptions as repeatedly constructed "on-line" during social interactions, emerging out of a constantly changing and highly malleable system (e.g., Gergen, 1981; Markus & Nurius, 1986).

Researchers from the life history and systemic camps have generally worked independent of each other, and research on long-term changes in the self rarely informs or is informed by experimental research on self processes. These perspectives mirror the two sides of the "can personality change?" debate (Heatherton & Weinberger, 1994), in which one side emphasizes the stability of the structures of personality and the other side emphasizes the personality processes that promote change. In the self literature, however, it is more difficult to reach conclusions about stability and change because there is relatively little empirical research on people's self-views across the life course. Although numerous studies have documented that personality is highly stable (Caspi & Roberts, Chapter 11, this volume), few studies have directly assessed the stability of the self over long periods of time.

Most research on the stability of the self has focused on the development of self-esteem in childhood and adolescence (Demo, 1992). One trend that emerges across studies is that self-esteem is relatively high during early childhood but then declines as children move through elementary school (e.g., Harter, 1982; Marsh, Byrne, & Shavelson, 1992; Ruble, Eisenberg, & Higgins, 1994). This decline has been attributed to greater reliance on social comparison information and external feedback, which leads to more realistic self-appraisals (Harter, 1998). Several studies suggest a second drop in self-esteem during the transition to adolescence (Piers & Harris, 1964; Rosenberg, 1986; Simmons, Rosenberg, & Rosenberg, 1973; but see Hirsch & Rapkin, 1987; Simmons, Blyth, Van Cleave, & Bush, 1979). This decline in self-esteem has been attributed to maturational changes associated with puberty, cognitive changes associated with the emergence of formal operational thinking, and social-contextual changes associated with the transition from grade school to junior high school.

The extant literature does not provide a clear picture of how self-esteem develops during adolescence and the transition to adulthood. Some studies report a gradual rise in self-esteem (Marsh, 1989; McCarthy & Hoge, 1982; Mullis, Mullis, & Normandin, 1992; O'Malley & Bachman, 1983; Prawat, Jones, & Hampton, 1979; Roeser & Eccles, 1998); others report no change (e.g., Chubb, Fertman, & Ross, 1997; Dusek & Flaherty, 1981); and still others report declines in self-esteem (e.g., Keltikangas-Jarvinen, 1990; Monge, 1973; Zimmerman, Copeland, Shope, & Dielman, 1997). Part of the complexity may lie in gender differences. Boys and girls do not respond to the cultural press of adolescence in the same way, and the two sexes often show different patterns of change during adolescence. For example, using data from a longitudinal study, Block and Robins (1993) found that males tend to increase in self-esteem whereas females tend to decrease from age 14 to 23. This gender divergence during adolescence was also found in a large cross-sectional study (AAUW, 1991). Similarly, Alsaker and Olweus (1993) reported that females, but not males, show a drop in self-esteem after beginning seventh grade. Finally, a recent meta-analysis found that a gender difference in self-esteem first emerges in early adolescence (Major, Barr, Zubek, & Babey, 1999).

Research on adulthood, although minimal, has produced more consistent findings. Several studies have reported gradual improvements in self-esteem and an increase in positive self-conceptions over the course of adulthood (Gove, Ortega, & Style, 1989; Helson & Wink, 1992; Morganti, Nehrke, Hulicka, & Cataldo, 1988; Nehrke, Hulicka, & Morganti, 1980). For example, Roberts and Bengtson (1996) reported an increase in self-esteem over a 20-year period from early adulthood to middle adulthood. However, this rosy picture of normative increases in self-esteem during adulthood may not hold into old age; Jaquish and Ripple (1981) found that positive self-conceptions increase until middle adulthood but then decline in late adulthood (over age 60).

In addition to normative change in self-esteem, researchers have also examined the stability of individual differences in self-esteem. Stability correlations are comparable in magnitude to those found for personality traits, such as the Big Five (Caspi & Roberts, Chapter 11, this volume; John & Srivastava, Chapter 4, this volume). For example, using data from a longitudinal study of college students, Robins and Hendin (1999) reported correlations averaging in the .60s over 1 to 4 year intervals. Even over longer time periods, the stability correlations are moderate in size. Block and Robins (1993) found correlations of .65 (girls) and .36 (boys) from age 14 to 23. In their longitudinal study spanning early to middle adulthood, Roberts and Bengtson (1996) found correlations of .38 over a 17-year period, .30 over a 20-year period, and .75 over a 3-year period during middle adulthood. Developmentally, stability generally increases over the life span, with lower stability found in childhood and higher stability in adulthood (Roberts & DelVecchio, in press). Nonetheless, even in adulthood, stability is far from perfect, particularly over long periods of time. Thus, a central issue confronting self-concept researchers is to better understand the factors—both psychological and social-contextual—that promote change across the life span.

In our view, the best way to understand self-esteem change is to understand the self-evaluative mechanisms that drive the self system; that is, the processes presumed to play a role in how self-evaluations are formed, maintained, and changed. Although experimental research has linked a number of self-evaluative processes to short-term changes in self-evaluation (e.g., Brown & Mankowski, 1993; Gergen, 1981; Heatherton & Polivy, 1991; Jones, Rhodewalt, Berglas, & Skelton, 1981; Kernis, 1993; Markus & Kunda, 1986; Tesser, 1988), we know little about the influence of such processes on self-esteem change over longer periods of time and in real-world contexts. Life history research on the self can draw on this body of research to develop hypotheses about long-term change in self-esteem. This approach, which integrates the systemic and life history approaches, explores how self-evaluative processes documented in the lab play out in a real-world context. In our research, we have explored how three self-evaluative factors impact self-esteem change: implicit self-theories, positive illusions, and defensive pessimism. All three have been linked to motivational and self-regulatory processes involved in self-evaluation and are presumed to play a role in the development and maintenance of self-esteem. In all three studies, we used a multiwave longitudinal design that allowed us to examine self-esteem growth curve trajectories (rather than the more commonly used difference scores, which have serious methodological problems).

According to Dweck's cognitive-motivational model of implicit theories, individuals who hold an Entity theory about their intelligence (i.e., believe their intelligence is a fixed quantity) are prone to show a helpless response to academic failure whereas individuals who hold an Incremental theory (i.e., believe their intelligence can change) show a mastery-oriented pattern (Dweck, Chiu, & Hong, 1995; Dweck & Leggett, 1988). Dweck argues that people's implicit self-views influence how they derive self-worth: Entity theorists derive self-esteem from proving their ability level is adequate, whereas Incremental theorists derive self-esteem from pursuing and mastering challenging tasks. In college, where failure experiences are likely, Entity theorists' self-esteem should be particularly vulnerable because they attribute their failures to lack of ability. Consistent with this prediction, we found that Entity theorists generally had lower self-esteem than did incremental theorists, and this disparity widened over 4 years of college (Robins & Pals, 1999). Thus, the college experience adversely impacted the self-esteem of Entity theorists but bolstered the self-esteem of Incremental theorists.

Taylor and Brown (1988) postulate that positive illusions promote self-esteem by buffering people against the consequences of failure. Consistent with this, we found that students who entered college with positive illusions about their academic ability reported higher self-esteem during college than individuals with more accurate or overly negative self-views (Robins & Beer, 1999). However, despite their higher average level of self-esteem, individuals with positive illusions were on a downward trajectory relative to non–self-enhancing individuals. Thus, college adversely impacted the self-esteem of individuals with positive illusions, whereas individuals without such illusions were better able to maintain their self-esteem during college.

Norem (1997) found that different self-regulatory strategies were associated with different patterns of self-esteem change. During their first four years in college, women who used optimism as a self-regulatory strategy showed consistently high self-esteem and little change over time. Defensive pessimists showed significant positive change in self-esteem over the same period, fitting with the prediction that their strategy allowed them to identify negative aspects of themselves and work productively to change them. In contrast, women who didn't use defensive pessimism and who felt like impostors (Clance & Imes, 1978) showed significant decreases in self-esteem during their first year in college, a subsequent return to baseline, but no net increase across their college years.

Together, these three examples illustrate how the systemic and life history approaches to self-evaluation and self-esteem can be integrated. Individuals show different patterns of self-esteem change over time, and these differences may be obscured in research that examines only average trends and ignores individual trajectories. Thus, we need to understand the motives and beliefs that regulate self-evaluative processes and ultimately contribute to developmental changes in global self-esteem.

A final question of interest to personality psychologists concerns the relation between self-perceived change in personality and actual change in scores on a personality measure. We recently examined this question in a longitudinal study that tracked a sample of students throughout college (Robins, Fraley, Roberts, & Trzesniewski, 1999). At the end of college, we asked the students how they thought their personality and self-esteem had changed over the 4 years. Perceived change in self-esteem correlated .29 with actual change in self-esteem (measured by individual growth curve trajectories over 4 years of college), suggesting that the students in our sample had some insight into the degree to which their self-esteem had increased or decreased during college. Similarly, perceived change in personality showed some convergence with actual changes in NEO-FFI scores over four years of college (*r*s ranged from .15 to .34). In contrast, Costa and McCrae (1989) did not find a relation between perceived change and change in NEO scores over a 6-year period, raising the possibility that our findings are specific to the college context—college is, after all, a time when people are acutely focused on how they are changing. The question of how people's beliefs about their personality converge with actual changes in personality lies at the center of the connection between self and personality and is a topic worthy of further study.

Is the Self Distinctive to Humans? Do Nonhuman Animals Have the Same Kind of Self as Humans?

If omniscient beings from another planet were to study the inhabitants of the earth, what would stand out about the human species? Our use of tools? Our leisure time and range of creative endeavors? Our complex social organization and interactions? Certainly all of these. But what would be perhaps most salient about the human species would be our inner world—the richness of our mental life. Tapping into the inner life of other species is unlikely to reveal the same rich stream of thoughts, feelings, intentions, and so on.

The capacity for self-awareness and self-representations seems to be a universal characteristic of humans. In all cultures, people have an awareness of their own thoughts and feelings and have relatively stable mental representations of themselves. The universality of these basic aspects of the self is a striking and highly significant fact that is often overlooked in light of the substantial individual and cross-cultural variability that exists in the way the self is manifested (Cross & Markus, Chapter 15, this volume; Kashima, 1995; Markus & Kitayama, 1991; Roland, 1997).[2]

Whenever universal (i.e., species-typical) characteristics are found, scientists generally proceed to comparative, cross-species studies. The self may be part of human nature, but is it unique to humans? In some sense, this is clearly *not* true. Virtually all animals have an aspect of self-awareness—they can distinguish self from nonself, and consequently do not eat themselves when they get hungry. Moreover, comparative researchers have provided evidence of relatively advanced forms of self-awareness in a number of species (for reviews, see Gallup, 1982; Hart & Karmel, 1996; Parker, Mitchell, & Boccia, 1994; Povinelli, Rulf, Landau, & Bierschwale, 1993; Tomasello, 1998). This research is complicated by the fact that nonhuman animals cannot communicate what they are thinking and feeling so researchers need to infer the presence of a self from overt behavioral markers. Hart and Karmel (1996) cited three classes of evidence for the existence of a sense of self: linguistic markers, cognitive-behavioral markers, and emotional markers.

"Linguistic markers" include self-referencing (e.g., use of personal pronouns), narrative language use (e.g., reference to events of personal significance that happened in the past), and declarative labeling speech. Language-trained great apes (chimps, gorillas, orangutans) show all three forms of linguistic markers. Koko the gorilla, for example, displayed the capacity for reflexive self-referencing and narrative language use when she signed "me love happy Koko there" after being shown a picture of herself at a birthday party (Patterson & Linden, 1981, p. 86). As Koko's statement suggests, gorillas might also have personal memories that serve as the basis for some forms of linguistic self-referencing. Monkeys and other nonprimates do not show any of these linguistic markers.

"Cognitive-behavioral markers" include mirror self-recognition, imitation, and role-taking. In a series of seminal studies, Gallup (1970) showed that chimpanzees can develop the ability to recognize themselves in a mirror. Gallup allowed chimps to view themselves in front a mirror for a few days and then, while they were anesthetized, marked their faces with dye. The dye is odorless and nonirritating, and cannot be seen without the aid of a mirror. Upon seeing their image in the mirror, the chimps frequently touched the marks on their face and then smelled and looked at their fingers. Mirror self-recognition has been interpreted as evidence for objective self-awareness, subjective self-awareness, and self-representation.[3] When an animal sees its image with an unexpected mark on it, the animal needs to focus attention on and identify itself in the mirror and become aware that the current image differs from some stable representation of its typical appearance. Based on these findings, Gallup (1977) concluded that "contrary to popular opinion and preconceived ideas, man may not have a monopoly on the self-concept. Man may not be evolution's only experiment in self-awareness" (p. 14).

In subsequent research dozens of animal species have been subject to the mark test, but only chimpanzees (Gallup, 1970), orangutans (Suarez & Gallup, 1981), gorillas (Parker, 1994; Patterson & Cohn, 1994), dolphins (Hart & Whitlow, 1995), and killer whales (Delfour & Marten, 1997) have demonstrated the capacity for self-recognition.[4] Interestingly, the first reactions to mirrors by both infant chimps and infant humans are social in nature—smiling, kissing, and vocalizing to their mirror image (Scheel, Gardner, & Gardner, 1998). Gallup (1977) found that chimpanzees reared without social contact (in complete isolation from other chimps) do not show mirror self-recognition. This finding is consistent with Cooley (1902) and Mead's (1934) theory that the self develops through social interaction and the experience of seeing oneself from the perspective of others. Importantly, self-recognition seems to be rooted in the capacity to adopt the psychological perspective of the other, not the physical perspective; Priel and de Schonen (1986) found that Bedouin children without previous exposure to mirrors showed mirror self-recognition at the same age and to the same extent as a control group of children with habitual mirror familiarity. The other two cognitive-behavioral markers—imitation and role-taking—are present in humans by 2 years of age but are extremely rare in other primates. Nonetheless they have been observed in a few cases, which suggests that chimps, orangutans, gorillas, and possibly monkeys have at least some capacity for imitation and role-taking.

"Emotional markers" include self-conscious emotions and empathy. According to Lewis (1992), self-conscious emotions such as shame, pride, guilt, and embarrassment require a sense of self. Pride, for example, reflects a match between the person's accomplishments and the person's goals. Russon and Galdikas (1993) reported an incident that suggests orangutans can experience pride. Supinah, an orangutan, was observed attempting the difficult task of hanging a hammock from two trees, apparently in imitation of humans. After successfully hanging the hammock, Supinah "sat up and then threw herself back in the hammock" with apparent joy and "hugged herself with both arms" (Hayes, 1951, p. 188). In the primate literature, anecdotal evidence of self-conscious emotions abounds, but more controlled studies are needed. Similarly, the evidence for empathy in primates is also mostly anecdotal. Nonhuman primates clearly show helping behaviors. For example, it is not uncommon for a wounded chimp to be attended to—fed, groomed, and protected—by other members of the social group. Dominant adult males even chase away playing infants or noisy group members to keep them from disturbing the injured chimp (Boesch, 1992). However, there is no clear evidence for genuine empathy, in which the individual recognizes that another individual is experiencing an emotion and then vicariously experiences the same emotion.

Based on their review of the literature, Hart and Karmel (1996) concluded that monkeys do not have a self in the same way that humans do: "The lack of evidence reflects a genuine deficit: monkeys probably do not have much of a sense of self" (p. 342). However, as Gardner and Gardner (1996) cautioned, "comparative psychologists cherish the dictum that absence of evidence is never evidence of absence" (p. 683).

In contrast to monkeys and most other species of nonprimates, chimpanzees and orangutans differ quantitatively, not qualitatively, from humans. Like other aspects of human psychology—personality, memory, attachment—we show the same capacities as our phylogenetic cousins, but we differ in the complexity and frequency with which we display these capacities. Interestingly, several studies suggest that the more human the environment to which great apes are exposed, the more sophisticated their response to human artifacts such as mirrors (Parker, Mitchell, & Boccia, 1994).

The findings of cross-species research on the self have several implications. First, they illustrate the value of a comparative perspective in personality and social psychology (Gosling, 1999). As Hart and Karmel (1996) put it, "discovering what great apes think about themselves sheds light not only on these species' cognitive abilities and experiences, but also on our understanding of ourselves" (p. 343). Comparative research helps identify which aspects of the self are uniquely human and which are common across species. More generally, comparative research provides a framework for understanding individual differences within a phylogenetic context, and how individual variability may reflect the influence of social environments on the development of evolved capacities (Snowden, 1995).

Second, the finding that other species share certain aspects of the human self implies that self-awareness and self-recognition may be evolved capacities. Any capacity that is common to several species of primates is probably not crucially dependent on any species-specific factors, such as culture or language. Yet clearly there are some unique aspects of the human self, which raises the question of whether these aspects are newly evolved differences or purely the product of human culture. Moreover, the comparative perspective shows what our conscious mental life may have been like at an early period in our evolutionary history; that is, our evolutionary ancestors may have had the same level of self-awareness as chimps. A phylogenetic perspective suggests that the self may have evolved from the most basic form of self-awareness (distinguishing self and nonself) to more complex forms of self-awareness seen in nonhuman primates (e.g., self-recognition) to the most complex forms of human self-representations (e.g., identity).

Finally, the existence of cross-species differences suggests one route to understanding the neuroanatomical basis of the self. Can we identify brain regions that are distinctive to animals that show evidence of having a sense of self? For example, are there ways in which our brains are similar to chimpanzees but different from monkeys?

Where Is the Self?: A Neuroscience Agenda for Self Research

The self is clearly dependent in some way on the brain. If we did not have a brain we would not have a self. But, as Hofstadter and Dennett (1981) pondered, "Who, or what, is the you that has the brain?" (p. 5). At the heart of the mind–body debate is the puzzle of how a mass of tissue and the firing of brain cells can possibly produce a mind that is aware of itself and that can experience the color orange, the feeling of pride, and a sense of agency.

Historically, the primary philosophical stance was to accept the mind–body distinction and assume that the self is not a physical entity but rather arises from a soul or spirit. For example, Anton van Leeuwenhoek (1632–1723) believed that the brain contained a special vital animal spirit or fluid that embodied consciousness, and the writer Goethe argued that the brain contained an active life force—an animating energy that turned its tissue into something living and dynamic.

Most scientists, however, have rejected dualism and generally champion some form of materialism. Francis Crick (1994), codiscoverer of the molecular structure of DNA in 1953, illustrates this position: "You, your joys and your sorrows, your memories and your ambitions, your sense of personal identity and free will, are in fact no more than the behavior of a vast assembly of nerve cells and their associated molecules" (p. 3).

Recent attempts to understand exactly how the brain builds a sense of self have not been particularly successful, and speculative accounts abound (Hameroff, Kaszniak, & Scott, 1996). For example, echoing Darwin's notion that the brain "secretes" the mind, philosopher John Searle (1992) argued that intentionality and consciousness are caused by the "physico-chemical" properties of the human brain, but he never says what those properties are. Two Nobel laureates—Francis Crick (1994, 1996) and Gerald Edelman (1989; Tononi & Edelman, 1998)—have each provided accounts of the neural substrates of consciousness, but unfortunately the two accounts do not look much alike. Another position is that conscious mental activity takes place at a quantum level, and cannot be described simply in terms of chemical and electrical processes as we currently understand them (e.g. Penrose, 1994). In contrast, some researchers believe that eventually it will be possible to say that activity in a particular combination of neurons means that a person is having a particular thought or feeling. Consciousness emerges as different groups of neurons—dealing with vision, memory, or touch—are activated. From this perspective, "there is no seat of consciousness, no internal theater where consciousness is a permanent spectator. Instead, what we experience as consciousness is this constant procession of waxing and waning of neuronal groupings" (Greenfield, 1996, p. 159).

Those adopting a computational view of the mind believe that at least some aspects of the self can be explained by neural information processing: "Computation has finally demystified mentalist terms. Beliefs are inscriptions in memory, desires are goal inscriptions, thinking is computation, perceptions are inscriptions triggered by sensors, trying is executing operations triggered by a goal" (Pinker, 1997 p. 78). Thus, our understanding of how the brain processes information applies to self-referential information, just as it does to information about the world and others. Similarly, Maddox (1998) argued that "the eventual explanation of consciousness will be qualitatively no different from the explanation of a single behavioral choice by a cat's brain" (p. 307), it will simply involve information processing by more complex neuronal circuitry. Also adopting a computational view, artificial intelligence pioneer Marvin Minsky (1985) describes the mind as a "society of agents"—the agents of the brain are organized hierarchically into nested subroutines with a set of master decision rules. Although it may seem as though there is an agent running the "society," in fact it is just the collective action of neural information processing in multiple parts of the brain. Finally, some adopt a materialist stance in principle, but assume that science may never unravel the mystery of consciousness and that this is a puzzle perhaps best left to philosophers.

Clearly, our current understanding of the neural mechanisms underlying the self is woefully inadequate. If we accept the materialist position and search for the proximate neural mechanisms involved in self processes, we need to go further than grand speculation about a "society of agents" or "physicochemical" properties. We need to approach the problem of how the brain produces a sense of self using the full array of methods used by cognitive neuroscientists. Below we discuss several specific neuroscientific methods that can be used to study the self and self-related phenomena (see Klein & Kihlstrom, 1998, for a review of neuropsychological research relevant to social–personality psychology).

Electrical Stimulation of the Brain

In their pioneering work applying small levels of electrical current to the brain's cortex, Penfield and Jasper (1954) discovered that electrical stimulation of the temporal lobe can elicit memories. In some sense, activating an episodic memory through neural stimulation is activating an aspect of the self and altering the content of self-awareness. The implications of this research are unclear, however, because it is not yet known whether patients recall actual experiences or just construct fictions about people and events that are familiar to them.

Single-Cell Recording

This method examines how a particular stimulus pattern or behavioral response affects the activity of individual neurons, and thus provides a way to locate which areas of the brain are active when an animal becomes self-focused or accesses self-relevant information. At this point, single-cell recording requires intrusive procedures and cannot be done on humans. Nonetheless, researchers could examine, for example, whether mirror self-recognition in nonhuman primates is associated with the activity of neurons in a particular cortical region.

Neuroanatomical Studies

An understanding of the gross anatomy of the brain can help us to better understand cross-species comparisons. For example, what distinguishes the brain of a human from the brain of a nonhuman primate? What distinguishes the brain of a chimp (which show evidence of self-recognition) from the brain of a monkey (which do not)? Which neuroanatomical areas are common to animals that show the capacity for mirror self-recognition, or linguistic self-referencing, or self-conscious emotions? One clue is that humans begin to show evidence of mirror self-recognition around 18 to 24 months of age, which is when the prefrontal cortex begins to mature in structure and function.

Neuroanatomical studies can also help by exploring how behavioral, cognitive, and affective deficits associated with neurological disorders map onto damage to particular brain regions. Patients with cerebellar damage show problems with subtle cognitive functions such as planning, as well as flat affect. Interestingly, these findings converge with research showing that children with autism—a disorder that many consider characterized by an abnormal sense of self—have smaller cerebellums and fewer cerebellar neurons. Some researchers have hypothesized that the cerebellum, initially viewed as a motor center, may now be utilized by higher-level perceptual and cognitive systems to filter and integrate the stream of incoming sensory information (Courchesne & Allen, 1997). Consistent with this, the neocerebellum has undergone tremendous expansion in primate evolution and is now closely connected with the frontal cortex. Moreover, a particular region of the cerebellum—the neodentate—is present only in humans, and thus is a plausible candidate to account for unique aspects of the human self.

Brain Lesioning and Functional Neurosurgery

As with other intrusive techniques, the intentional lesioning of a particular brain region cannot be done on humans. However, researchers could lesion nonhuman primates to determine whether damage to a particular area eliminates the capacity for mirror self-recognition and other markers of a sense of self. One kind of brain lesioning that is done on humans is functional neurosurgery. The earliest example is frontal lobotomies of individuals with severe psychoses. The dramatically altered behavior of lobotomized individuals shows how removing brain tissue can destroy what we normally think of as a person's self. Another example is split-brain (commisurotomized) patients in which the corpus collosum has been severed. Research on such patients has demonstrated a host of cognitive deficits (Gazzaniga, 1970) but has not systematically explored whether there are deficits related to self processes. More recently, neurologists have conducted research on the surgical addition of neural tissue to the brains of Parkinson's patients. It will be interesting to see whether the addition of neural tissue, which has proven effective in treating the physical symptoms of Parkinson's, will also prove effective in treating the socioemotional symptoms that seem linked to self processes (e.g., a distorted sense of identity and personal history).

Research on Neurological Disorders and Damage

Some of the most fascinating avenues for understanding the self have come from the experimental study of neurological patients in whom brain damage has produced cognitive, affective, and behavioral deficits. New advances in structural imaging techniques have allowed researchers to more precisely pinpoint the location of neurological damage. According to neurologist Oliver Sacks (1995), the complete loss of a sense of self is extremely rare, but many neurological disorders, including autism, Alzheimer's, Parkinson's, and epilepsy, produce profound changes in the self. There are also a host of neurological disorders characterized by bizarre distortions in body self-schemas, including macropsia and micropsia (an Alice in Wonderland-like feeling in which one feels as though one has either grown incredibly large or incredibly small in size), asomatognosia (e.g., denial that the left side of one's body is part of one's self and assertions that any actions by one's left side were caused by someone else), and exosomesthesia (a pathological extension of the body image in which touches to the self are experienced as touches to nearby physical objects and vice versa.) Finally, the presence of soft neurologic signs among persons with personality disorders (e.g., borderline personality; dissociation) raises the possibilities that the disturbances of the self (e.g., "splitting") associated with these disorders may reflect subtly damaged or deficient neural mechanisms (e.g., Gardner, Lucas, & Cowdry, 1987; Quitkin, Rifkin, & Klein, 1976).

Studies of patients with neurological damage due to strokes or accidents suggest that the frontal lobes are involved in self-regulation. For example, Pinker (1997) describes the case of a 15-year-old boy with frontal lobe damage who would stay in the shower for hours at a time, unable to decide whether to get out. Phineas Gage, who had frontal lobe damage, showed a diminished capacity to self-regulate as well as dramatic personality changes (he became more irreverent, obstinate, and impatient, and less persistent and focused); according to one of his friends, "Gage was no longer Gage" (Gazzaniga, Ivry, & Mangun, 1998, p. 424). In general, patients suffering from frontal lobe damage show deficits in the capacity to monitor and reflect on their own mental states (Damasio, 1985), suggesting that aspects of the self related to self-awareness (or the "I") may be located in the frontal lobes. Interestingly, Baron-Cohen and colleagues (1994) found that the frontal lobes are activated when individuals make inferences about mental states, suggesting a link between self-awareness and awareness of the mind's of others.

Another provocative set of studies has examined impairments in self-awareness and self-representations in patients with amnesia. Tulving (1993a) relates the story of K.C., an amnesic patient who lost the capacity to form new episodic memories. K.C. has a sense of self-awareness but not autonoetic awareness (autobiograpical remembering, or the feeling that one "owns" one's memories)—K.C. is conscious in a similar way that a dog is probably conscious but not in the same way as individuals without neurological damage. Surprisingly, K.C. seems to have the capacity to revise his self-representations even without episodic memories of his specific behaviors and experiences: K.C.'s self-descriptions converge with his mother's descriptions of his current personality more closely than with her descriptions of his pre-amnesic personality (Tulving, 1993a). Similarly, Klein, Loftus, and Kihlstrom (1996) found evidence that another amnesic patient, W.J., showed stable and seemingly accurate self-ratings of personality over a period of time during which she lacked the capacity to remember any personally experienced events. Klein and Kihlstrom (1998) concluded that "neurally impaired individuals who have lost the ability to recall personal experience show no obvious impairment in the ability to make accurate personality judgments about themselves" (p. 231). This conclusion, if supported by further research, has important implications for research on the personality judgment process. In particular, it suggests that trait judgments about the self reflect different cognitive and neural mechanisms than do judgments about specific behaviors or acts performed by the self (Gosling, John, Craik, & Robins, 1998; Klein & Loftus, 1993).

Studies of Neural Functioning in Healthy Individuals

Recent advances in the neuroimaging techniques, including methods based on electrical signals (EEG, ERP, MEG) and those based on functional imaging (PET, fMRI), permit more precise measurement of the structure and function of the brain. For example, functional MRI (fMRI) provides a way to map brain activity and allows researchers to see which part of the brain "lights up" when someone performs a cognitive, affective, or behavioral task. Researchers have used these methods to image the brains of healthy individuals, as well as those with neurological damage.

Recently, personality and social psychologists have begun to adopt such methods. Cacioppo, Crites, and Gardner (1996) have used event-related brain potentials (ERPs) to examine brain activity during attitude formation. Carter and others (e.g., Carter, Lederhendler, & Kirkpatrick, 1997; Fisher, 1998) have studied the neural substrates of attachment, affiliation, and related social behaviors. Davidson (1994) has examined how asymmetries in the prefrontal region of the brain relate to the behavioral approach and inhibition systems, and he has begun to use a host of neuroscience methods (fMRI, PET, EEG) to explore the neural correlates of reactions to emotionally charged stimuli and more generally individual differences in affective style. Davidson's research is particularly interesting in light of recent research suggesting that the ability to reflect on one's mental states, as well as those of others, might reflect evolved changes in the prefrontal cortex (Povinelli & Preuss, 1995).

Although cognitive neuroscience research on social phenomena is very much in its infancy, we see many avenues for future research. For example, we already know that semantic memory (which serves as the basis for self-representations) and episodic memory (which serves as the basis for autobiographical memories) have separate neural bases, with only episodic memory fully dependent on the hippocampus (Vargha-Khadem et al., 1997). Semantic retrieval activates the left frontal lobe whereas episodic retrieval activates the right medial temporal lobe (including the hippocampus). One could envision future self researchers exploring whether responding to the question "Are you shy?" activates the left frontal lobe region because trait knowledge is stored in semantic memory, whereas responding to the question "How did you feel when you met the stranger?" activates the right medial-temporal lobe because it involves episodic retrieval.[5] Similarly, retrieval of self-defining memories (Singer & Salovey, 1993), which presumably have both episodic and semantic content, might activate both regions (perhaps in a sequence of activating the right region and then the left).

Together, these examples illustrate various ways in which the brain can affect self processes, as well as personality functioning more generally. The ultimate goal of neuroscience research on the self is to understand how the brain generates self-awareness and self-representations. This goal is complicated because, like other higher-order mental functions, self processes probably emerge out of a complex interplay among multiple brain regions. Moreover, there is a crucial issue of disentangling the causal relations among neural activity, self-reflection, and behavior; for example, does conscious self-reflection cause behavior or is behavior initiated through unconscious cerebral processes and then the conscious mind watches and reflects (Libet, 1985)? Despite these complexities, it is not too early to pursue this promising line of research and begin to integrate a neuroscience perspective into areas of psychology, such as the self, that have traditionally shied away from research on neural mechanisms (Klein & Kihlstrom, 1998; Robins et al., 1999). Although we still have a way to go before we truly understand the neural correlates of different forms of subjective experience and self-representation, new neuroimaging methods that allow us to delve into the mind have opened up a new frontier for self researchers.

In What Sense Is the Self a Product of Evolution?

The eminent geneticist Theodosius Dobzhansky (1964) remarked that the self is the chief evolutionary novelty possessed by humans. If the self is a consequence of evolutionary processes, then scientific theories of the self need to incorporate an evolutionary perspective.[6] From an evolutionary perspective, there are four possible stances one could take toward the self. First, the self may be "genetic junk"—a trait that neither contributes to nor detracts from an organism's fitness but is nonetheless carried along and passed down to succeeding generations. A second possibility is that the self is a functionless by-product of an adaptation that does not solve any adaptive problems but is carried along with some characteristic that is functional. For example, the self has been described as an incidental by-product of high-level intelligence and complex sensory processing associated with large brains.

However, it is difficult to write off the self as an evolutionary accident or a functionless by-product. The self seems to fulfill the criteria of an adaptive design outlined by Williams (1966)—it is universal, complex, reliably developing, well-engineered, and reproduction-promoting. Clearly the self is a universal (i.e., species-typical) characteristic—although there is individual variability in self-awareness and self-representations, all humans have both capacities. The self is also clearly complex, reliably developing, and, as we will argue subsequently, promotes survival and reproduction.

Yet, even if we accept that the self meets the criteria of adaptive design, it may not be an adaptation in the technical sense of the word. Instead, in the third possible stance, the self may be an exaptation—"a feature, now useful to an organism, that did not arise as an adaptation for its present role, but was subsequently co-opted for its current function" (Gould, 1991); for example, a fly's wings were originally selected for thermoregulation but were later used for flying. Thus it may be difficult to identify the evolutionary history of a mechanism by focusing on its current utility. "The fact that humans can use fingers to type does not mean that the function of fingers is to type. Typing is an evolutionary novel use of fingers, not the functional basis for which fingers evolved" (Buss & Kenrick, 1998, p. 989). However, it seems unlikely that the self is an exaptation because the characteristics of our ancestral environment believed to have created selection pressures for a self (e.g., complex social interaction) continue to exist in the current environment.

Finally, the self may be a full-fledged adaptation. Simply stated, adaptations are evolved solutions to the problems of survival and reproduction. As Pinker (1997) noted, "If consciousness is useless—if a creature without it could negotiate the world as well as a creature with it—why would natural selection have favored the conscious one?" (p. 132). The self has been described as an evolved capacity that is hardwired into the brain. Just as the brain has evolved a module governing language acquisition, humans may also have a module governing aspects of the self such as self-awareness and self-deception (Pinker, 1997). According to the modularity approach to the mind, the mind is organized into modules, each with a specialized design that makes it particularly suited to one arena of interaction with the world. A more moderate position is that people have a genetic blueprint for the basic parts of the self, but then the self is assembled through interaction with the current environment (Caporael, 1998). From this perspective, we all have a neurologically rudimentary self that comes with our genetic programming, but the parts are now assembled in a complex way because of the social and cultural environment in which we currently live. It is possible that we share with other great apes the same neurologically rudimentary self, but through language development and complex social interaction, we simply do more with the raw materials we have. This position nicely integrates universalist and cultural relativist positions on the self.

The assumption that the self is an adaptation leads to the question: What function does it serve? What reproductive or survival advantage is conferred by the capacity to reflect on one's internal states and form stable self-representations?

Why Do We Have a Self? What Are Its Adaptive Functions?

Self theorists and researchers have always been functionally oriented, but they have not always been guided and constrained by evolutionary theory. In contrast to more proximal functional approaches, evolutionary theory provides a coherent metatheory and a way of integrating findings within a larger scientific body of cumulative knowledge (Bock & Cardew, 1997; Buss & Kenrick, 1998). From an evolutionary perspective, the central functionalist question is: How did the self facilitate the goals of survival and reproduction during the evolutionary history of the species? Sedikides and Skowronski (1997) discuss in depth the ecological and social selection pressures that might have led to the evolution of the self. They concluded that the symbolic self (the capacity for complex linguistic self-representations) was an adaptive solution to complex social problems faced by our ancestors when they began living in large, flexibly structured social groups. Survival and reproduction depended on overcoming numerous complex social problems, including "dyadic, triadic, or group-level cooperation, smooth group functioning; cheating; detection of cheaters; intragroup (and, particularly, intrasexual) competition, and intergroup competition" (p. 92).

How does the self help an individual solve these adaptive problems? Sedikides and Skowronski (1997) focus on the role of the self in regulating cognitive, affective, motivational, and behavioral processes, and describe the many ways in which the self shapes information processing, emotional responses and experience, and goal-directed behavior. Below we build on the ideas presented by Sedikides and Skowronski and provide a more general overview of the specialized functions of the self that might have served to enhance survival and reproduction over the course of our evolutionary history.

In our view, the various functions of the self can be subsumed within four general categories: self-regulation, information-processing filter, understanding others, and identity processes. Each adaptive function requires the ability to form stable self-representations and to reflect on one's own mental processes. Below we describe the four categories of psychological functions and discuss how they might be linked to adaptive outcomes.

Self-Regulation

The self serves an executive function. It helps control, regulate, and organize the mind, and in so doing, it guides our behaviors, our emotions, our thoughts, and our goals. Povinelli (1998) speculated that self-awareness evolved in part to help us plan and execute complicated movements in an arboreal environment; after falling flat on their faces for several thousand years, our tree-dwelling ancestors eventually learned how to regulate their behavior, a capacity that was facilitated by self-awareness and a high level self-representational system (which Povinelli refers to as a kinesthetic self-concept). Eventually this self-regulatory capacity was used to help our ancestors regulate their behaviors, thoughts, and feelings in a complex social environment. According to Klinger (1998), the human brain is wired for purposeful living; Klinger believes that self-regulation and goal striving are fundamental to all living organisms and that goals serve as the "linchpin of psychological organization" (p. 44).

Brown (1998) outlines three aspects of the self-regulation process: goal selection, preparation for action (including rehearsing action), and the cybernetic cycle of comparing present states with desired states and assessing progress. Both self-awareness and stable self-representations are fundamental throughout ongoing self-regulatory efforts. Self-awareness provides a sense of volition and agency that facilitates goal-directed behavior, and makes possible evaluation of goal-relevant outcomes. Stable self-representations function as both goals to be pursued and standards against which outcomes are measured. The self prioritizes and organizes goal-directed behavior, amidst a complex and multiply-nested structure of goals and subgoals. Carver and Scheier's (1981, 1998) control theory of self-regulation provides one model of how the self compares current states with desired states, the emotional and motivational consequences of different outcomes of those comparisons, and the effects of different levels of self-awareness on the process.

Higgins's (1987) self-discrepancy theory also assumes that one's actual state is compared to desired end states, and proposes two "self-guides" that represent different desired end-states. "Ideal" self-guides represent attributes people would ideally like to possess and their wishes and aspirations; becoming aware of actual–ideal self-discrepancies results in dejection-related emotions such as sadness. "Ought" self-guides represent morals, values and norms, or how we believe we ought to be; actual–ought discrepancies lead to agitation-related emotions such as guilt and anxiety (Higgins, Bond, Klein, & Strauman, 1986). The relative strength of different self-guides serves to prioritize goal-directed behavior.

Markus and her colleagues have focused on both desired and undesired goals represented in self-knowledge (Markus & Nurius, 1986; see also Ogilvie, 1987), and have also considered the potential motivational and affective significance of "future" self representations. Our representations of what we believe is possible for ourselves in the future may motivate behaviors that increase the likelihood of desirable possible future selves, and decrease the likelihood of undesirable future selves thus influencing development and change over time.

Recently, Higgins (1997, 1998) has considered the role of undesirable outcomes in self-regulation by connecting different kinds of self-discrepancy and their affective outcomes with a motivational theory of "regulatory focus." He argues that self-regulation may have a prevention focus or a promotion focus, with the former stemming from experience with basic survival needs related to security, and the latter developing from experience with nurturance needs. A prevention focus is associated with strong ought self-guides, a sensitivity toward negative outcomes, and avoidance strategies; whereas a promotion focus is associated with strong ideal self-guides, sensitivity toward positive outcomes, and approach strategies. Higgins's work on self-regulatory focus illustrates some of the important links between the adaptive functions of the self, self structure, and personality in ways that go beyond self-esteem. Although his work primarily considers situational influences on regulatory focus, there are clearly chronic individual differences in regulatory focus: trait anxiety is likely to reinforce a prevention focus, for example.

Clearly the potential and capacity for self-regulation does not guarantee problem-free and effective pursuit of goals. Humans often engage in self-defeating and maladaptive behaviors (e.g., Baumeister & Scher, 1988; Curtis, 1989). Apparent failures of self-regulation may tell us a great deal about how the self system functions, as in the case of self-handicapping (Jones et al., 1981), in which individuals set themselves up for failure in a way that somewhat paradoxically protects self-esteem. Problems in self-regulation and goal pursuit may relate to particular constellations of self-knowledge or conflicts between private self-awareness and self-presentations. Those who feel like impostors, for example, tend to face considerable difficulty in resolving conflict among their goals, because they lack a reference to a stable "real" self that could apply across situations, and because they have mutually conflicting ideal and ought selves (Norem, 1996; Worcel & Norem, 1996). These examples illustrate an important point: An adequate understanding of adaptive and maladaptive self-regulation requires consideration of other aspects of personality, just as an understanding of personality processes would be enhanced by more systematic consideration of the structure and content of the self.

Information-Processing Filter

In a complex social environment, it is inefficient to attend to and encode all of the information bombarding the individual. The self serves as a filter or lens through which the world is experienced. Just as individuals do not process all the visual information in their environment, individuals selectively process self-relevant information and organize it according to certain priorities. In general, information about the self is organized and processed differently from information about others, particularly non-intimate (e.g., nonkin) others. Our self-representations consist of cognitive structures, or schemas, that organize and direct processing of information about the self. Thus, the self serves as a top-down information filter that is guided by a set of heuristics. In particular, the self operates in the service of four basic motives: accuracy, consistency, popularity (i.e., social status and approval), and positivity. These motives influence what the self attends to, encodes, retrieves, and acts on. We have described these motivational orientations in terms of four basic metaphors: the Scientist, the Consistency Seeker, the Politician, and the Egoist (Robins & John, 1997b; for alternative conceptions of self-concept motives, see Sedikides & Strube, 1997; Swann & Schroeder, 1995; Wayment & Taylor, 1995).

The Scientist (Accuracy Motive)

The basic assumption guiding the Scientist metaphor is that individuals are driven to understand themselves and the world, and seek out information in a dispassionate search for truth. This metaphor has its roots in George Kelly's personal construct theory and in the early attribution theories of Fritz Heider and Harold Kelley. George Kelly (1955) argued that just as the scientist develops empirically based theories, the layperson uses facts and observations to develop "personal constructs," or theories about the self and the world. As with scientific theories, these constructs allow people to interpret and predict behavior. Several theories of the self also incorporate the notion that people act, at least in part, like scientists (e.g., Bem, 1972; Festinger, 1954; Trope, 1980, 1986). In short, the Scientist metaphor suggests that people are data-driven and engage in a dispassionate search for accurate self-knowledge. Clearly accurate self-representations can serve an adaptive function, helping us to formulate realistic goals and act in accordance with our actual social status, mate value, and so on. However, as Pinker (1997) notes, "our brains were shaped for fitness, not for truth. Sometimes the truth is adaptive and sometimes it is not" (p. 305). Consequently, we sometimes adopt information-processing strategies that do not promote accurate self-representations.

The Consistency Seeker (Consistency Motive)

The Consistency Seeker metaphor assumes that individuals strive to see themselves in a consistent manner, and to confirm their preexisting self-views with little regard for reality. Its origins can be traced to self-consistency theory (e.g., Lecky, 1945), balance theory (e.g., Heider, 1958) and cognitive dissonance theory (e.g., Festinger, 1957). More recently, Swann and his colleagues (e.g., 1996b, 1997; Swann, Stein-Seroussi, & Giesler, 1992) have amassed considerable evidence that people actively seek out and create contexts in which their self-views will be confirmed, even when their self-views are negative. For example, people with negative self-views would prefer to interact with individuals who have a negative rather than a favorable impression of them. Another way in which people verify their self-conceptions is through cognitive distortions (e.g., selective attention). When individuals process information about themselves they are biased by their existing self-conceptions, and may fail to attend to valid information if it is incongruent with their self-schemas (e.g., Higgins & Bargh, 1987; Markus & Wurf, 1987). Similarly, research on autobiographical memories suggests that people selectively remember life events that are consistent with how they see themselves currently; that is, they reconstruct their past to fit their current self-views (Ross, 1989). Although consistency seeking may lead to information-processing errors, it can be a useful and efficient heuristic in a highly chaotic social environment. As Swann, Pelham, and Krull (1989) noted, "stable self-conceptions act like the rudder of a ship, bolstering people's confidence in their ability to navigate through the sometimes murky seas of everyday social life" (p. 783). Consistency also serves an interpersonal function, ensuring that people will honor the identities they negotiated in previous social interactions and act similarly over time.

The Politician (Social Approval and Status Motive)

The Politician metaphor assumes that people strive to present themselves in ways that create the most favorable impressions on others. This metaphor represents a fusion of ideas from symbolic interactionism, role theory, and impression management theory, as well as more recent elaborations of these theories (e.g., Hogan, 1982; Schlenker, 1980; Snyder, 1987; Tetlock, 1992). These theories emphasize the reciprocal nature of social interaction: Social reality is constructed and negotiated through interactions with others. In these interactions, people's behaviors represent public performances that "present images of the self for the social world to see and evaluate" (Schlenker, 1985, p. 21). The primary goals of these self-presentations are to *get along* (i.e., gain approval from others) and to *get ahead* (i.e., attain social status and power) (Hogan, Jones, & Cheek, 1985). Like politicians, people are accountable to different audiences (or constituencies), which place multiple and often conflicting demands and expectations on them. The person-as-politician seeks to "maintain the positive regard of important constituencies to whom he or she feels accountable" (Tetlock, 1992, p. 332), which should increase status, reduce conflict, and facilitate coalition building.

The Egoist (Self-Enhancement Motive)

The Egoists metaphor assumes that people narcissistically distort information to enhance their self-worth. Virtually every self theory posits some variant of the motive to protect and enhance self-worth (e.g., Allport, 1937; Epstein, 1990; Greenwald, 1980; James, 1890; Rogers, 1959). Allport (1937) referred to the defense of the ego as "nature's eldest law," and believed that ego-enhancement is a fundamental human motive tied to the need for survival. Many contemporary models of self-perception have been infused with ideas from the Egoist metaphor. Most notably, a large body of research emerged in the 1980s aimed specifically at documenting positivity biases in self-perception in a wide range of contexts, including self-conceptions of personality attributes, self-attributions of success and failure, perceptions of control, responses to feedback, and beliefs about the likelihood of future events. In a review of this literature, Taylor and Brown (1988; 1994) argued that self-perceptions exhibit pervasive and enduring positive distortions, presumably stemming from the basic motive toward self-enhancement (John & Robins, 1994a; Lockard & Paulhus, 1988). Research suggests that the self-enhancement may reflect an automatic process that is accentuated under high cognitive load (Paulhus, Graf, & Van Selst, 1989; Paulhus & Levitt, 1987). The automaticity of the process suggests that it may be an evolved mechanism. Self-enhancement bias, or more generally positive illusions about the self, may facilitate goal striving, emotional well-being, mate attraction, and other adaptive behaviors (e.g., Robins & Beer, 1999; Taylor & Brown, 1988; see Krebs & Denton, 1997; Nesse & Lloyd, 1992, for discussions of the adaptive benefits of positive illusions and defense mechanisms). For example, in terms of mate selection, evolutionary psychologists see the self-concept as a way of gauging our value to prospective partners (e.g., our mate value). Individuals with higher self-perceived mate value may demand more in a partner and consequently pair up with partners who have higher mate value.

Together the four motives that drive processing of self-relevant information—accuracy, consistency, social approval and status, and enhancement—provide a flexible arsenal of tools that help us (and presumably our evolutionary ancestors) adapt to a complex, multistructured social environment. As Pinker (1997) points out, "the mind has many parts, some designed for virtue, some designed for reason, some clever enough to outwit the parts that are neither. One self may deceive another, but every now and then a third self sees the truth" (p. 424). In general, then, the ideal mind from an evolutionary perspective would be able to convince itself that it is better, smarter, and faster than it really is when this facilitates survival and reproduction, but switch to reality mode when this increases fitness. Consistent with this, Swann and Schroeder (1995) proposed that the various self-evaluative motives can be organized into a hierarchical system in which different motives are prioritized at different stages of processing depending on the resources available to the individual; specifically, self-relevant evaluations may proceed through a series of cognitive operations, with positivity or enhancement driving the first stage of self-evaluative processing, consistency driving the second stage, and more deliberate and effortful cost–benefit analyses driving self-evaluations in a third stage. This possibility makes sense from an evolutionary perspective and shows how processing of information about the self may indeed reflect the workings of a specialized adaptive design.

Understanding Others' Minds

In many ways the self serves as a reference point for understanding others. We explain other people's behavior by their intentions, beliefs, and desires because our introspection tells us that our own behavior is driven by our intentions, beliefs, and desires. More specifically, people assume that the way they act in a particular situation is the way that others will act in the same situation. Thus, self-awareness, or self-insight, can facilitate insight into others. This sentiment is seen in a line from *Pelleas and Melisande* (Debussy, 1862–1918), Act 1: "I have never for one instant seen clearly within myself; how then would you have me judge the deeds of others?" In a complex social environment, survival and reproduction depend in part on the ability to explain, predict, and manipulate others. The capacity for self-awareness facilitates introspectively based social strategies such as empathy, sympathy, gratitude, deception, and pretense.

Some theorists have even argued that subjective awareness evolved for the specific purpose of helping us to understand others (e.g., Humphrey, 1990); that is, we are wired for projection. In developmental psychology, proponents of simulation theory suggest that children learn to understand others by reflecting on their own internal states, feelings, and intentions, and simulating what might be happening in the mind of others (Goldman, 1992; Harris, 1992). Consistent with this, autistic children show an inability to understand what other people know, want, or feel, and correspondingly they have dramatically diminished social interaction skills (Baron-Cohen, 1995).

The capacity to reflect on our internal states and feelings and project them onto others contributes to one other capacity: the experience of empathy and self-conscious emotions. As Pinker (1997) noted, "The body is the ultimate barrier to empathy. Your toothache simply does not hurt me the way it hurts you . . . [But] love, compassion, and empathy are invisible fibers that connect genes in different bodies. They are the closest we will ever come to feeling someone else's toothache" (p. 401). Several theorists have proposed that empathy emerged with the evolution of mammals and the extended caregiving and long-term pairbonding characterizing the human family unit (Hoffman, 1975; MacLean, 1985). Trivers (1971) has a similar view of the social or "moralistic" emotions (liking, anger, gratitude, sympathy, guilt, shame) but sees them as adaptive strategies in the reciprocity game (reciprocal altruism) that characterizes human interaction: We have some ability to discriminate between real and sham emotions in part because we realize that if we can fake emotions so can others. More generally, self-conscious emotions such as embarrassment, shame, and pride serve to regulate social behavior and promote adaptive behaviors in complex social interactions (Lewis, 1997; Miller & Leary, 1992); for example, embarrassment serves as an appeasement signal to indicate to others the recognition that a norm has been violated (Keltner & Buswell, 1997).[7]

Although self-conscious emotions can be linked to adaptive social behaviors they can also be maladaptive. For example, the tendency to become anxiously preoccupied in social situations and excessive worries about being negatively evaluated by others can contribute to decreased social competence in the form of shyness. Yet despite the potential for shyness to produce maladaptive interpersonal behaviors, shyness also seems to have a number of adaptive consequences. Social anxiety is functional when it motivates preparation and rehearsal for important interpersonal events, such as planning ahead for the first day of teaching at a new school (Thyer, 1987). As a social emotion, shyness also helps to facilitate cooperative group living by inhibiting individual behavior that is socially unacceptable (Ford, 1987). A moderate amount of wariness regarding strangers and unfamiliar or unpredictable situations has considerable adaptive value (Izard & Hyson, 1986); for example, Wilson, Coleman, Clark, and Biederman (1993) argue for an adaptive mix of shyness and boldness within a species based on research with pumpkinseed sunfish.

The self-conscious emotion of pride also seems to be adaptive in some contexts and maladaptive in others. In the Greek myth, Narcissus ultimately dies from his excessive pride. From an evolutionary perspective, Narcissus acted in a particularly maladaptive manner because he spent all of his time gazing at his own reflection and ignored the nymph who was in love with him and who presumably could have produced offspring. Yet, research on positive illusions suggests that narcissistic pride can have adaptive as well as maladaptive consequences (e.g., Robins & Beer, 1999; Taylor & Brown, 1988; 1994).[8]

The examples of shyness and narcissism illustrate the complexities of the evolutionary perspective—certain aspects of the self may be maladaptive in some ways and adaptive in others. These opposing selection pressures lead to individual differences. Consistent with this, there is considerable variability in the degree to which individuals show self-enhancement, with shy individuals showing relatively low levels of self-enhancement and even self-deprecation (Cheek & Melchoir, 1990) and highly narcissistic individuals showing very high levels of self-enhancement (John & Robins, 1994; Robins & John, 1997a). Shyness and narcissism may be two ways of approaching the conflict between the dominant social goals of getting along and getting ahead—shy individuals have chosen to focus on getting along and seeking approval whereas narcissistic individuals have focused on getting ahead (Roberts & Robins, 1998). Each may be a viable strategy from an evolutionary perspective.

Identity Processes

Human social life may be viewed as a series of games—the rules are reflected in cultural norms and the parts that individuals play are defined by their social roles (Hogan, 1982). Winning this game requires that humans form dyadic and group coalitions and generally navigate within a social structure that, more so than with any other species, has complex layers of multiple, overlapping, and sometimes non-transitive social hierarchies (e.g., the highest status hunters were not always the highest status warriors). To survive and reproduce, our evolutionary ancestors needed to figure out who was their friend and who was their foe, who could be trusted to reciprocate and who was likely to cheat, who held them in high esteem and who did not, and so on. In other words, the ancestral environment in which the self evolved was much like contemporary social life. Imagine living in such a complex social environment without a self—that is, without any stable awareness of your position in the social structure and the roles you play in different contexts and with different interaction partners.

As discussed earlier, people's self-representations consist of multiple identities—personal, relational, social, and collective. According to some theories of identity, the content and organization of the self reflects the content and organization of society (Hewitt, 1976). From this perspective, identities are internalized social roles that reflect a person's position within the social structure (e.g., teacher, parent, daughter). These role identities prescribe specific values and role-appropriate behaviors, which we are compelled to enact during social interactions. We also have identities at a more relational level. These identities are negotiated and constructed in ongoing social interactions. Our identities, therefore, are flexible and can vary from situation to situation and from one interaction partner to another.

All forms of identity allow us to differentiate ourselves from others, provide a sense of continuity and unity over time, and help us adapt to and navigate within complex social structures and hierarchies. Social identities also facilitate identification with the social group to which a person belongs. In any social group, the young, low-status members are tempted to defect to other groups. A sense of identity, and associated in-group biases and out-group derogation, may help keep individuals from leaving their social group and disrupting their kinship network.

Stable identities are also efficient. It is more adaptive to have social interactions that are predictable, structured, and even ritualized, and to have identities internalizing the rules of each social context so that individuals do not have to relearn their social roles each day. Scheibe (1995) argues that people's survival quite literally depends on their ability to locate themselves successfully within their various social ecologies and role systems. Drawing from research on the social organization of primates, he suggests that "one may begin to see some respectable evolutionary anchorage for such a phrase as the 'need for stable identification with a social collectivity'" (p. 131). By placing the need for social identity at a level as fundamental as the biological sex drive, Scheibe presents a provocative challenge to contemporary evolutionary psychology, which until recently has tended to focus on sexuality. An evolutionary perspective on the relation between self-concept and social roles is needed for a completely biosocial model of human behavior (Hogan, 1976; Mead, 1934; Murphy, 1947). The self provides a bridge between the individual (and his/her personality characteristics) and the collective (and its associated social roles).

In summary, we are proposing that the two aspects of the self—self-awareness and self-representations—are evolved mechanisms that serve four adaptive functions: self-regulation, information-processing filter, understanding others, and identity formation. It seems plausible that these four functions helped our evolutionary ancestors to survive and reproduce in a complex social environment characterized by long-term kinship relationships. Yet one may question what an evolutionary perspective, with its emphasis on ultimate function, can contribute beyond more proximate functional accounts. Thus, one challenge facing researchers working toward a naturalist account of the self is to provide more precise empirical demonstrations of how the specific functions of the self enhance reproductive success.

WHY SHOULD PERSONALITY PSYCHOLOGISTS CARE ABOUT THE SELF?

We hope that this review of theory and research on the self has demonstrated that our understanding of many personality processes would be impoverished without the concept of self. Personality psychology is an unusually broad field because it covers a wide spectrum of phenomena and levels of analysis, from genetic markers of behavioral traits to neural mechanisms underlying emotions to lexical studies of trait adjectives to motives in personal life stories to sociocultural perspectives on the formation of values. What provides coherence to these diverse themes is an emphasis on understanding consistencies in people's thoughts, feelings, and behaviors, and the mechanisms that underlie these consistencies. The self ties together these various personality processes and, as Allport (1960) aptly put it, "makes the system cohere in any one person" (p. 308).

There are several reasons personality psychologists should pay attention to the self (Brown, 1998; McCrae & Costa, 1988). First, people's consistent patterns of thoughts, feelings, and behavior—that is, personality—influence how people *think* about themselves. What we think we are like is linked—albeit imperfectly—to what we are really like. A large body of research demonstrates that self-representations show some degree of correspondence with non-self-report measures of personality (Funder & Colvin,1997; Robins & John, 1997b).

Second, personality shapes how people *feel* about themselves. Basic temperamental characteristics, rooted largely in genetic differences, influence our feelings about what kind of person we are. Not surprisingly, individuals with a low threshold for the experience of negative affect also tend to feel negatively about themselves (Watson & Clark, 1984). Moreover, self-esteem is moderately heritable, with about 30% of the variance due to genetic differences (Kendler, Gardner, & Prescott, 1998).

Third, the self plays a critical role in personality processes. Research over the past few decades has documented many ways in which the self influences how people act, think, and feel in particular situations, the goals they pursue in life, and the ways they cope with and adapt to new environments. The self is a regulator of behavior and experience—it serves an executive function much like the driver of a car. The driver interprets the street signs (i.e., situational factors), and consequently an individual with a "race car driver" self-concept may go through a red light, regardless of whether he/she is driving a BMW or a Dodge Dart. Thus, to explain many aspects of human behavior we often assume people have the capacity for self-awareness, self-representation, and self-regulation. Our interpretations of a particular action would be quite different if exhibited by an animal without a human sense of self. Consider, for example, the possibility that Michelangelo's dog knocked over the Pietà statue and broke it to pieces. Our interpretation of this act would be quite different than for Michelangelo's destruction of the statue. Many currently prominent areas of personality research assume a central role for the self, including the study of self-conscious emotions such as shame and embarrassment (e.g., Miller & Leary, 1992; Tangney & Fischer, 1995), work on traits such as shyness (e.g., Cheek & Melchoir, 1990) and narcissism (e.g., John & Robins, 1994a; Robins & John, 1997a), the study of internal working models in the context of attachment in close relationships (e.g, Shaver, Collins, & Clark, 1996), and research on the personality judgment process (e.g., Funder & Colvin, 1997; John & Robins, 1993; Robins & John, 1996), self-defining memories (e.g., Singer & Salovey, 1993; Pals & Robins, 1999), implicit personal memories (e.g., Ross, 1989), and goals and motivation (e.g., Carver & Scheier, 1998; Singer, 1995).

Fourth, personality is often assessed by self-reports, including personality questionnaires.

Many claims about personality—how it is shaped by nature and nurture, how it changes over the life course, how it relates to important life outcomes—are based on research using self-report questionnaires. The validity of using self-report scales depends on the degree to which people can (and do) report accurately on their cognitive, affective, and behavioral tendencies. A better understanding of the self-perception process and the factors that influence accuracy and bias will improve our psychological understanding of the self-report method for assessing personality.

Finally, the capacity for complex forms of self-awareness and self-representation is a distinctive aspect of our species and perhaps a few others. Clearly from an evolutionary perspective the self is likely to be important to social behavior and therefore to personality functioning.

TOWARD A NATURALIST APPROACH TO UNDERSTANDING THE SELF

In this chapter we have attempted to outline a naturalist approach to the self. We have reviewed the current state of the field with regard to several fundamental questions concerning the structure, development, and function of the self. Our review of the literature was guided by a particular stance toward the self. In particular, we believe that research on the self should be: (1) central to any theory of personality; (2) informed by an evolutionary perspective and organized around functionalist explanations; (3) informed by comparative, cross-species research; and (4) linked to basic psychological processes such as attention, memory, and emotion, and their associated neural mechanisms. Although the self continues to be "puzzling puzzle," we believe that progress is being made in the field and that a scientific understanding of the self is fundamental to a science of personality.

The psychology of the self has an important role to play in the integration of evolutionary biology and neuroscience into personality psychology. The self sits in a privileged position, encompassing and integrating all levels of the person from the biological to the social. This privileged position is fundamentally an inclusionary one: There is ample room, and indeed serious need, for a variety of approaches to understanding the structure and function of the self and its relation to other psychological processes.

Self-awareness and self-representation are species-typical characteristics that have been studied in terms of both phylogenesis and ontogenesis. An evolutionary perspective on the self-concept was central to the theories of personality and social behavior developed in the early days of the field, and it must be considered a central issue for contemporary personality theories. The naturalist agenda outlined by James (1890) remains a worthwhile path for the next century of research on the science of the self. By naturalizing the self, we move the field of personality toward a truly biosocial perspective.

ACKNOWLEDGMENTS

Preparation of this chapter was supported by a Faculty Research Grant (University of California, Davis). We thank Jack Block, Robert Emmons, Chris Fraley, Dan Hart, Holly Hendin, Robert Hogan, Oliver John, Stan Klein, Jennifer Pals, Del Paulhus, Larry Pervin, Joanna Scheib, Sanjay Srivastava, Bill Swann, Kali Trzesniewski, and Drew Westen for comments on an earlier version of this chapter.

NOTES

1. The keyword "self" is clearly overinclusive and will detect articles examining psychological phenomena beyond the scope of research on the self. However, any other keyword (e.g., self-esteem, self-concept, self-awareness) is necessarily underinclusive and would fail to detect important aspects of the self literature.

2. We see a parallel here between research on the self and research on emotions. In each case, there is evidence of both universality and cultural specificity. As with emotions, the universal aspects of the self exist at the core of considerable cultural shaping of the way the self is experienced and expressed in everyday life. For example, individuals from some cultures may be more chronically self-focused, derive self-esteem from different sources, and have more complex self-representations than individuals from other cultures. But in all cultures, individuals working in a performance context will reflect on how they are doing, evaluate their behavior relative to some (often culture specific) internalized standard, and form stable beliefs about their overall competence.

3. This interpretation of mirror self-recognition has been questioned (e.g., Fox, 1982; Parker, Mitchell, & Boccia, 1994; see Gallup, 1998, and Povinelli, 1998, for a debate about the implications of mirror self-recognition).

4. Some researchers dispute that mirror self-recognition has been demonstrated in any species other than humans, chimpanzees, and organutans (e.g., Gallup, 1998).

5. Consistent with this hypothesis, Craik et al. (1999) found left frontal activation when participants judged trait adjectives for self-descriptiveness.

6. Some theorists reject the notion that the self evolved. Julian Jaynes (1976) has argued that a sense of self only developed about 3,000 years ago. Before that, he claims, the left and right hemispheres of the brain were not integrated.

7. Importantly, the development of mirror self-recognition precedes the development of self-conscious emotions such as embarrassment, as well as empathy and an understanding of others' mental states.

8. Narcissistic behavior also seems to be present and in some cases adaptive in non-human animals. Sapolsky (1997) describes an orangutan named Hobbes—the "cocky son of a high-ranking female" (p. 83)—who immediately began acting like the alpha male after migrating to a new troop. To Sapolsky's surprise, Hobbes was quickly treated by others as a high-status animal, despite his initial low status in the group. Although we clearly do not know whether Hobbes had an overly positive self-representation, his narcissistic behavior does seem to have served the adaptive function of helping him attain social status and consequently mates. Similar benefits may accrue to humans who believe they are more brilliant and powerful than they really are. An interesting point relevant to the positive illusions debate is that Hobbes had unusually high cortisol levels; as Sapolsky pointed out, "it doesn't come cheap to be a bastard twelve hours a day—a couple of months of this sort of thing is likely to exert a physiological toll" (p. 86).

REFERENCES

Allport, G. W. (1937). *Personality: A psychological interpretation.* New York: Holt.

Allport, G. W. (1955). Is the concept of self necessary? In *Becoming: Basic considerations for a psychology of personality.* New Haven, CT: Yale University Press.

Allport, G. W. (1960). The open system in personality theory. *Journal of Abnormal and Social Psychology, 61,* 301–310.

Allport, G. W., & Odbert, H. S. (1936). Trait names. A psycho-lexical study. *Psychological Monographs, 47* (1, No. 211).

Alsaker, F. D., & Olweus, D. (1993). Global self-evaluations and perceived instability of self in early adolescence: A cohort longitudinal study. *Scandinavian Journal of Psychology, 34,* 47–63.

American Association of University Women. (1991). *Shortchanging girls, shortchanging America: A call to action.* Washington, DC: American Association of University Women.

Aron, A., Aron, E. N., & Smollan, D. (1992). Inclusion of Other in Self scale and the structure of interpersonal closeness. *Journal of Personality and Social Psychology, 63,* 596–612.

Aspinwall, L. G., & Taylor, S. E. (1992). Modeling cognitive adaptation: A longitudinal investigation of the impact of individual differences and coping on college adjustment and performance. *Journal of Personality and Social Psychology, 63,* 989–1003.

Baldwin, J. M. (1897). *Social and ethical interpretations in mental development.* New York: Macmillan.

Bandura, A. (1982). Self-efficacy mechanism in human agency. *American Psychologist, 37,* 122–147.

Baron-Cohen, S. (1995). *Mindblindness: An essay on autism and theory of mind.* Cambridge, MA: MIT Press.

Baron-Cohen, S., Ring, H., Moriarty, J., Schmitz, B., Costa, D., & Ell, P. (1994). Recognition of mental state terms: Clinical findings in children with autism and a functional neuroimaging study in normal adults. *British Journal of Psychiatry, 165,* 640–649.

Baumeister, R. F. (1982). A self-presentational view of social phenomena. *Psychological Bulletin, 91,* 3–26.

Baumeister, R. F. (1998). The self. In D. T. Gilbert, S. T. Fiske, & G. Lindzey (Eds), *The handbook of social psychology* (4th ed., Vol. 2, pp. 680–740). Boston: McGraw-Hill.

Baumeister, R. F. & Scher, S. J. (1988). Self-defeating behavior patterns among normal individuals. *Psychological Bulletin, 194,* 3–22.

Bem, D. J. (1972). Self-perception theory. In L. Berkowitz (Ed.), *Advances in experimental social psychology* (Vol. 6, pp. 1–62). New York: Academic Press.

Block, J., & Robins, R. W. (1993). A longitudinal study of consistency and change in self-esteem from early adolescence to early adulthood. *Child Development, 64,* 909–923.

Bock, G. R., & Cardew, G. (1997). (Eds). *Characterizing human psychological adaptations.* Chichester, UK: Wiley.

Boesch, C. (1992). New elements of a theory of mind in wild chimpanzees. *Behavioral and Brain Sciences, 15,* 149–150.

Brewer, M. B. (1993). The role of distinctiveness in social identity and group behaviour. In M. A. Hogg & D. Abrams (Eds.), *Group motivation: Social psychological perspectives* (pp. 1–16). London: Harvester Wheatsheaf.

Brewer, M. B., & Gardner, W. (1996). Who is this "we"? Levels of collective identity and self representations. *Journal of Personality and Social Psychology, 71,* 83–93.

Brown, J. D. (1998). *The self.* New York: McGraw-Hill.

Brown, J. D., & Mankowski, T. A. (1993). Self-esteem, mood, and self-evaluation: Changes in mood and the way you see you. *Journal of Personality and Social Psychology, 64,* 421–430.

Buss, A. H. (1980). *Self-consciousness and social anxiety.* San Francisco: Freeman.

Buss, D. M., & Kenrick, D. T. (1998). Evolutionary social psychology. In D. T. Gilbert, S. T. Fiske, & G. Lindzey (Eds), *The handbook of social psychology,* (4th ed., Vol. 2, pp. 982–1026). Boston: McGraw-Hill.

Byrne, B. M. (1996). *Measuring self-concept across the life span: Issues and instrumentation.* Washington, DC: American Psychological Association.

Cacioppo, J. T., Crites, S. L., & Gardner, W. L. (1996). Attitudes to the right: Evaluative processing is associated with lateralized late positive event-related brain potentials. *Personality and Social Psychology Bulletin, 22,* 1205–1219.

Caporael, L. R. (1998). The evolution of truly social cognition: The core configurations model. *Personality and Social Psychology Review, 1,* 276–298.

Carter, C. S., Lederhendler, I. I., & Kirkpatrick, B. (Eds.). (1997). *The integrative neurobiology of affiliation.* New York: New York Academy of Sciences.

Carver, C. S., & Scheier, M. F. (1981). *Attention and self-regulation: A control theory approach to human behavior.* New York: Spinger-Verlag.

Carver, C. S., & Scheier, M. F. (1998). *On the self-regulation of behavior.* New York: Cambridge University Press.

Cheek, J. M. (1989). Identity orientations and self-interpretation. In D. M. Buss & N. Cantor (Eds.), *Personality psychology: Recent trends and emerging directions* (pp. 275–285). New York: Springer-Verlag.

Cheek, J. M., & Melchoir, L. A. (1990). Shyness, self-esteem, and self-consciousness. In H. Leitenberg (Ed.), *Handbook of social and evaluation anxiety* (pp. 47–82). New York: Plenum Press.

Cheek, J. M., Tropp, L. R., Chen, L. C., & Underwood, M. K. (1994, August). *Identity orientations: Personal, social, and collective aspects of identity.* Paper presented at the annual meeting of the American Psychological Association, Los Angeles.

Chubb, N. H., Fertman, C. I., & Ross, J. L. (1997). Adolescent self-esteem and locus of control: A longitudinal study of gender and age differences. *Adolescence, 32,* 113–129.

Cialdini, R. B., Borden, R. J., Thorne, A., Walker, M. R., Freeman, S., & Sloan, L. R. (1976). Basking in reflected glory: Three (football) field studies. *Journal of Personality and Social Psychology, 34,* 366–375.

Clance, P. R., & Imes, S. A. (1978). The impostor phenomenon in high achieving women: Dynamics and therapeutic intervention. *Psychotherapy: Theory, Research and Practice, 15,* 241–247.

Cooley, C. H. (1902). *Human nature and the social order.* New York: Scribner's.

Costa, P. T., Jr., & McCrae, R. R. (1989). Personality continuity and the changes of adult life. In M. Storandt & G. VandenBos (Eds.), *The adult years: Continuity and change* (pp. 45–77). Washington, DC: American Psychological Association.

Courchesne, E., & Allen, G. (1997). Prediction and preparation, fundamental functions of the cerebellum. *Learning and Memory, 4,* 1–35.

Craik, F. I. M., Moroz, T. M., Moscovitch, M., Stuss, D. T., Winocur, G., Tulving, E., & Kapur, S. (1999). In search of the self: A Positron Emission Tomography study. *Psychological Science, 10,* 26–34.

Crick, F. H. C. (1994). *The astonishing hypothesis: The scientific search for the soul.* New York: Scribner's.

Crick, F. H. C. (1996). Visual perception: Rivalry and consciousness. *Nature, 379,* 485–486.

Curtis, R. C. (Ed.). (1989). *Self-defeating behaviors: Experimental research, clinical impressions, and practical implications.* New York: Plenum Press.

Damasio, A. R. (1985). The frontal lobes. In K. M. Heilman & E. Valenstein (Eds.), *Clinical neuropsychology* (pp. 339–375). New York: Oxford University Press.

Davidson, R. J. (1994). Temperament, affective style, and frontal lobe asymmetry. In G. Dawson & K. W. Fischer (Eds.), *Human behavior and the developing brain* (pp. 518–536). New York: Guilford Press.

Debussy, C. (1862–1918). *Pelleas and Melisande,* lyric drama in five acts, taken from the play by M. Maiterlinck. English version by Charles Alfred Byrne. New York: C.E. Burden, c1907.

Deci, E. L., & Ryan, R. M. (1985). *Intrinsic motivation and self-determination in human behavior.* New York: Plenum Press.

Delfour, F. & Marten, K. (1997). Self-recognition in dolphins (*Tursiops truncatus*) and killer whales (*Orcinus orca*): An interspecific comparison. In M. Taborsky & B. Taborsky (Eds.), *Advances in ethology* (Vol. 32). Berlin: Blackwell Wissenschafts-Verlag.

Demo, D. H. (1992). The self-concept over time: Research issues and directions. *Annual Review of Sociology, 18,* 303–326.

Dennett, D. C. (1991). *Consciousness explained.* Boston: Little, Brown.

Dobzhansky, T. (1964). *Heredity and the nature of man.* New York: New American Library.

Donahue, E. M., Robins, R. W., Roberts, B. W., & John, O. P. (1993). The divided self: Concurrent and longitudinal effects of psychological adjustment and social roles on self-concept differentiation. *Journal of Personality and Social Psychology, 64,* 834–846.

Dusek, J. B., & Flaherty, J. F. (1981). The development of the self-concept during the adolescent years. *Monographs of the Society for Research in Child Development, 46,* 1–61.

Duval, S., & Wicklund, R. A. (1972). *A theory of objective self awareness.* New York: Academic Press.

Dweck, C. S., Chiu, C., & Hong, Y. (1995). Implicit theories and their role in judgments and reactions: A world from two perspectives. *Psychological Inquiry, 6,* 267–285.

Dweck, C. S., & Leggett, E. L. (1988). A social-cognitive approach to motivation and personality. *Psychological Review, 25,* 109–116.

Edelman, G. M. (1989). *The remembered present: A biological theory of consciousness.* New York: Basic Books.

Epstein, S. (1973). The self-concept revisited or a theory of a theory. *American Psychologist, 28,* 405–416.

Epstein, S. (1990). Cognitive experiential self-theory. In L. A. Pervin (Ed.), *Handbook of personality: Theory and research* (pp. 165–192). New York: Guilford Press.

Farthing, G. W. (1993). The self paradox in cognitive psychology and Buddhism: Review of "The embodied mind: Cognitive science and human experience." *Contemporary Psychology, 38,* 139–140. Cambridge, MA: MIT Press.

Festinger, L. (1954). Motivation leading to social behavior. In M. R. Jones (Ed.), *Nebraska Symposium on Motivation* (Vol. 2, pp. 191–218). Lincoln, NE: University of Nebraska.

Festinger, L. (1957). *A theory of cognitive dissonance.* Palo Alto, CA: Stanford University Press.

Fisher, H. E. (1998). Lust, attraction, and attachment in mammalian reproduction. *Human Nature, 9,* 23–52.

Flanagan, O. J. (1991). *The science of the mind.* Cambridge, MA: MIT Press.

Ford, D. H. (1987). *Humans as self-constructing living systems.* Hillsdale, NJ: Erlbaum.

Fox, M. W. (1982). Are most animals "mindless automatons"? A reply to Gordon G. Gallup Jr., *American Journal of Primatology, 3,* 341–343.

Freud, S. (1953). On narcissism: An introduction. In J. Strachey (Ed.), *The standard edition of the complete psychological works* (Vol. 14, pp. 69–102). London: Hogarth Press. (Original work published 1914)

Funder, D. C., & Colvin, C. R. (1997). Congruence of self and others' judgments of personality. In R. Hogan, J. A. Johnson, & S. R. Briggs (Eds.), *Handbook of personality psychology.* New York: Academic Press.

Gallup, G. G. (1970). Chimpanzees: Self-recognition. *Science, 167,* 86–87.

Gallup, G. G. (1977). Self-recognition in primates: A comparative approach to the bidirectional properties of consciousness. *American Psychologist,* 32, 329–338.

Gallup, G. G. (1982). Self-awareness and the emergence of mind in primates. *American Journal of Primatology, 2,* 237–248.

Gallup, G. G. (1998, November). Can animals emphathize?—Yes. *Scientific American.* www.sclam.com/1998/1198intelligence/1198debate.html.

Gardner, D., Lucas, P. B., & Cowdry, R. W. (1987). Soft sign neurological abnormalities in borderline personality disorder and control subjects. *Journal of Nervous and Mental Disease, 175,* 177–180.

Gardner, R. A., & Gardner, B. T. (1996). On the side of angels: Review of "Self-awareness in animals and humans: Developmental perspectives." *Contemporary Psychology,* 41, 682–684.

Gazzaniga, M. S. (1970). *The bisected brain.* New York: Appleton-Century-Crofts.

Gazzaniga, M. S. (1995). Consciousness and the cerebral hemispheres. In M. S. Gazzaniga (Ed.), *The cognitive neurosciences* (pp. 1391–1399). Cambridge, MA: MIT Press.

Gazzaniga, M. S. (1998). *The mind's past.* Berkeley, CA: University of California Press.

Gazzaniga, M. S., Ivry, R. B., & Mangun, G. R. (1998). *Cognitive neuroscience: The biology of the mind.* New York: Norton.

Gergen, K. J. (1981). The functions and foibles of negotiating self-conceptions. In M. D. Lynch, A. A. Norem-Hebeisen, & K. J. Gergen (Eds.), *Self-concept: Advances in theory and research.* Cambridge, MA: Ballinger.

Gergen, K. J. (1991). *The saturated self.* New York: Basic Books.

Goffman, E. (1959). *The presentation of self in everyday life.* New York: Doubleday.

Goldman, A. I. (1992). In defense of simulation theory. Special Issue: Mental simulation: Philosophical and psychological essays. *Mind and Language, 7,* 104–119.

Gordon, C. (1968). Self-conceptions: Configurations of content. In C. Gordon & K. J. Gergen (Eds.), *The self in social interaction* (pp. 115–136). New York: Wiley.

Gosling, S. D. (1999). *From mice to men: What can animal personality research tell us about personality?* Manuscript under review. Department of Psychology, University of California, Berkeley.

Gosling, S. D., John, O. P., Craik, K. H., & Robins, R. W. (1998). Do people know how they behave? Self-reported act frequencies compared with on-line codings by observers. *Journal of Personality and Social Psychology,* 74, 1337–1449.

Gove, W. R., Ortega, S. T., & Style, C. B. (1989). The maturational and role perspectives on aging and self through the adult years: An empirical evaluation. *American Journal of Sociology, 94,* 1117–1145.

Gould, S. J. (1991). Exaptation: A crucial tool for evolutionary psychology. *Journal of Social Issues, 47,* 43–65.

Gur, R. C., & Sackeim, H. A. (1979). Self-deception: A concept in search of a phenomenon. *Journal of Personality and Social Psychology,* 37, 147–169.

Greenfield, S. A. (Ed.). (1996). *The human mind explained.* New York: Holt.

Greenwald, A. G. (1980). The totalitarian ego: Fabrication and revision of personal history. *American Psychologist,* 35, 603–618.

Greenwald, A.G., & Breckler, S.J. (1985). To whom is the self presented? In B. R. Schlenker (Ed.), *The self and social life* (pp. 126–145). New York: McGraw-Hill.

Hamer, D., & Copeland, P. (1998). *Living with our genes: Why they matter more than you think.* New York: Doubleday.

Hameroff, S. R., Kaszniak, A. W., & Scott, A. C. (Eds.). (1996). *Toward a science of consciousness: The first Tucson discussions and debates.* Cambridge, MA: MIT Press.

Harris, P. L. (1992). From simulation to folk psychology: The case for development. Special Issue: Mental simulation: Philosophical and psychological essays. *Mind and Language, 7,* 120–144.

Hart, D., & Karmel, M. P. (1996). Self-awareness and self-knowledge in humans, apes, and monkeys. In A. E. Russon, K. A. Bard, S. T. Parker (Eds.), *Reaching into thought: The minds of the great apes* (pp. 325–347). Cambridge, UK: Cambridge University Press,

Hart, D., & Whitlow, J. W. (1995). The experience of self in the bottlenose dolphin. *Consciousness and Cognition: An International Journal, 4,* 244–247.

Harter, S. (1982). The Perceived Competence Scale for Children. *Child Development, 53,* 87–97.

Harter, S. (1998). The development of self-representations. In W. Damon (Ed.) and N. Eisenberg (Volume Ed.), *Handbook of child psychology: Vol. 3. Social, emotional, and personality development.* (5th ed., pp. 553–617). New York: Wiley.

Hayes, C. (1951). *The ape in our house.* New York: Harper and Brothers.

Heatherton, T. F., & Polivy, J. (1991). Development and validation of a scale for measuring state self-esteem. *Journal of Personality and Social Psychology, 60,* 895–910.

Heatherton, T. F., & Weinberger, J. L. (Eds). (1994). *Can personality change?* Washington, DC: American Psychological Association.

Heider, F. (1958). *The psychology of interpersonal relations.* New York: Wiley.

Helson, R., & Wink, P. (1992). Personality change in women from the early 40s to the early 50s. *Psychology and Aging, 7,* 46–55.

Hewitt, J. P. (1976). *Self and society: A symbolic interactionist social psychology.* Boston, MA: Allyn & Bacon.

Higgins, E. T. (1987). Self-discrepancy: A theory relating self and affect. *Psychological Review, 94,* 319–340.

Higgins, E. T. (1997). Beyond pleasure and pain. *American Psychologist, 52,* 1280–1300.

Higgins, E. T. (1998). Promotion and prevention: Regulatory focus as a motivational principle. *Advances in Experimental Social Psychology, 30,* 1–46.

Higgins, E. T., & Bargh, J. A. (1987). Social cognition and social perception. In M. R. Rosenzweig & L. Porter (Eds.), *Annual review of psychology* (Vol. 38, pp. 369–425). Palo Alto, CA: Annual Reviews.

Higgins, E. T., Bond, R. N., Klein, R., & Strauman, T. (1986). Self-discrepancies and emotional vulnerability: How magnitude, accessibility and type of discrepancy influence affect. *Journal of Personality and Social Psychology, 51,* 5–15.

Hilgard, E. R. (1949). Human motives and the concept of the self. *American Psychologist, 4,* 374–382.

Hirsch, B. J., & Rapkin, B. D. (1987). The transition to junior high school: A longitudinal study of self-esteem, psychological symptomatology, school life, and social support. Special Issue: Schools and development. *Child Development, 58,* 1235–1243.

Hoffman, M. L. (1975). Developmental synthesis of affect and cognition and its interplay for altruistic motivation. *Developmental Psychology, 11,* 607–622.

Hofstadter, D. R. & Dennett, D. C. (1981). *Introduction. The mind's I.* New York: Bantam.

Hogan, R. (1976). *Personality theory: The personological tradition.* Englewood Cliffs, NJ: Prentice Hall.

Hogan, R. (1982). A socioanalytic theory of personality. In M. M. Page (Ed.), *Nebraska Symposium on Motivation* (Vol. 29, pp. 55–89). Lincoln, NE: University of Nebraska Press.

Hogan, R., Jones, W. H., & Cheek, J. M. (1985). Socioanalytic theory: An alternative to armadillo psychology. In B. R. Schlenker (Ed.), *The self and social life* (pp. 175–198).

Humphrey, N. (1990). The uses of consciousness. In J. Brockman (Ed.), *Speculations: The reality club* (pp. 67–84). New York: Prentice Hall.

Izard, C. E., & Hyson, M. C. (1986). Shyness as a discrete emotion. In W. H. Jones, J. M. Cheek, & S. R. Briggs (Eds.), *Shyness: Perspectives on research and treatment* (pp. 147–160). New York: Plenum Press.

James, W. (1890). *The principles of psychology.* Cambridge, MA: Harvard University.

Jamison, K. R. (1995). *An unquiet mind: A memoir of moods and madness.* New York: Vintage.

Jaquish, G. A., & Ripple, R. E. (1981). Cognitive creative abilities and self-esteem across the adult lifespan. *Human Development, 24,* 110–119.

Jaynes, J. (1976). *The origin of consciousness in the breakdown of the bicameral mind.* Boston: Houghton Mifflin.

John, O. P. (1989). Toward a taxonomy of personality descriptors. In D. M. Buss & N. Cantor (Eds.), *Personality psychology: Recent trends and emerging directions* (pp. 261–271). New York: Springer-Verlag.

John, O. P., & Robins, R. W. (1993). Determinants of interjudge agreement on personality traits: The Big Five domains, observability, evaluativeness, and the unique perspective of the self. *Journal of Personality, 61,* 521–551.

John, O. P., & Robins, R. W. (1994a). Accuracy and bias in self-perception: Individual differences in self-enhancement and the role of narcissism. *Journal of Personality and Social Psychology, 66,* 206–219.

John, O. P., & Robins, R. W. (1994b). Traits and types, dynamics and development: No doors should be closed in the study of personality. *Psychological Inquiry, 5,* 137–142.

Jones, E. E., & Berglas, S. (1978). Control of attributions about the self through self-handicapping strategies: The appeal of alcohol and the role of under-achievement. *Personality and Social Psychology Bulletin, 4,* 200–206.

Jones, E. E., & Pitman, T. S. (1982). Toward a general theory of strategic self-presentation. In J. Suls (Ed.), *Psychological perspectives on the self* (Vol. 1, pp. 231–262). Hillsdale, NJ: Erlbaum.

Jones, E. E., Rhodewalt, F., Berglas, S., & Skelton, J. A. (1981). Effects of strategic self-presentation on subsequent self-esteem. *Journal of Personality and Social Psychology, 41,* 407–421.

Josephs, R. A., Markus, H. R., & Tafarodi, R. W. (1992). Gender and self-esteem. *Journal of Personality and Social Psychology, 63,* 391–402.

Kashima, Y. (1995). Introduction to the special section on culture and self. *Journal of Cross-Cultural Psychology, 26,* 698–713.

Kelly, G. A. (1955). *The psychology of personal constructs.* New York: Norton.

Keltikangas-Jarvinen, L. (1990). The stability of self-concept during adolescence and early adulthood: A six-year follow-up study. *Journal of General Psychology, 117,* 361–368.

Keltner, D., & Buswell, B. N. (1997). Embarrassment: Its distinct form and appeasement functions. *Pyschological Bulletin, 122,* 250–270.

Kendler, K. S., Gardner, C. O., & Prescott, C. A. (1998). A population-based twin study of self-esteem and gender. *Psychological Medicine, 28,* 1403–1409.

Kernis, M. H. (1993). The role of stability and level of self-esteem in psychological functioning. In R. F. Baumeister (Ed.), *Self-esteem: The puzzle of low self-regard* (pp. 167–182). New York: Plenum Press.

Kihlstrom, J. F., & Cantor, N. (1984). Mental representations of the self. In L. Berkowitz (Ed.), *Advances in experimental social psychology* (Vol. 17, pp. 1–47). New York: Academic Press.

Klein, S. B., & Kihlstrom, J. F. (1998). On bridging the gap between social-personality psychology and neuropsychology. *Personality and Social Psychology Review, 2,* 228–242.

Klein, S. B., & Loftus, J. (1993). The mental representation of trait and autobiographical knowledge about the self. In T. K. Srull, & R. S. Wyer Jr. (Eds.), *The mental representation of trait and autobiographical knowledge about the self. Advances in social cognition* (Vol. 5, pp. 1–49). Hillsdale, NJ: Erlbaum.

Klein, S. B., Loftus, J., & Kihlstrom, J. F. (1996). Self-knowledge of an amnesic patient: Toward a neuropsychology of personality and social psychology. *Journal of Experimental Psychology: General, 125,* 250–260.

Klinger, E. (1998). The search for meaning in evolutionary perspective and its clinical implications. In P. T. P. Wong & P. S. Fry (Eds.), *The human quest for meaning: A handbook of psychological research and clinical applications* (pp. 27–50). Mahwah, NJ: Erlbaum.

Kohut, H. K. (1971). *The analysis of the self.* Madison, WI: International University Press.

Kramer, P. D. (1993). *Listening to Prozac.* New York: Penguin.

Krebs, D. L., & Denton, K. (1997). Social illusions and self-deception: The evolution of biases in person perception. In J. A. Simpson and D. T. Kenrick (Eds.), *Evolutionary social psychology* (p. 21–48). Mahwah, NJ: Erlbaum.

Lecky, P. (1945). *Self-consistency: A theory of personality.* New York: Island Press.

LeDoux, J. E. (1996). *The emotional brain: The mysterious underpinnings of emotional life.* New York: Simon & Schuster.

Lewis, M. (1992). *Shame: The exposed self.* New York: Free Press.

Lewis, M. (1997). The self in self-conscious emotions. In J. G. Snodgrass & R. L. Thompson (Eds.), The self across psychology: Self-recognition, self-awareness, and the self concept. *Annals of the New York Academy of Sciences, 818,* 119–142.

Libet, B. (1985). Unconscious cerebral initiative and the role of conscious will in voluntary action. *Behavioral and Brain Sciences, 8,* 529–566.

Linville, P. W. (1987). Self-complexity as a cognitive buffer against stress-related illness and depression. *Journal of Personality and Social Psychology, 52,* 663–676.

Lockard, J. S., & Paulhus, D. L. (1988). *Self-deception: An adaptive mechanism?* Englewood Cliffs, NJ: Prentice Hall.

MacLean, P. D. (1985). Brain evolution relating to family, play, and the separation call. *Archives of General Psychiatry, 42,* 405–417.

Maddox, J. (1998). *What remains to be discovered.* New York: Free Press.

Major, B., Barr, L., Zubek, J., & Babey, S. H. (1999). Gender and self-esteem: A meta-analysis. In W. B. Swann, J. H. Langlois, L. A. Gilbert (Eds.), *Sexism and stereotypes in modern society: The gender science of Janet Taylor Spence* (pp. 223–253). Washington, DC: American Psychological Association.

Markus, H. (1977). Self-schemata and processing of information about the self. *Journal of Personality and Social Psychology, 35,* 63–78.

Markus, H. R., & Kitayama, S. (1991). Culture and the self: Implications for cognition, emotion, and motivation. *Psychological Review, 98,* 224–253.

Markus, H., & Kunda, Z. (1986). Stability and malleability of the self-concept. *Journal of Personality and Social Psychology, 51,* 858–866.

Markus, H., & Nurius, P. (1986). Possible selves. *American Psychologist, 41,* 954–969.

Markus, H., & Wurf, E. (1987). The dynamic self-concept: A social psychological perspective. In M. R. Rosenweig & L. W. Porter (Eds)., *Annual Review of Psychology, 38,* 299–337.

Marsh, H. W. (1989). Age and sex effects in multiple dimensions of self-concept: Preadolescence to early adulthood. *Journal of Educational Psychology, 81,* 417–430.

Marsh, H. W., Byrne, B. M., & Shavelson, R. J. (1992). A multidimensional, hierarchical self-concept. In R. P. L. E. Thomas M. Brinthaupt (Ed.), *The self: Definitional and methodological issues. SUNY series, studying the self* (pp. 44–95). Albany, NY: State University of New York Press.

McCarthy, J. D., & Hoge, D. R. (1982). Analysis of age effects in longitudinal studies of adolescent self-esteem. *Developmental Psychology, 18,* 372–379.

McCrae, R. R., & Costa, P. T. (1988). Age, personality, and the spontaneous self-concept. *Journal of Gerontology, 43,* 177–185.

McDougall, W. (1923). *Outline of psychology.* New York: Scribner's.

McDougall, W. (1963) *An introduction to social psychology* (31st ed.). London: Methuen. (Original work published 1908)

McGuire, W. J., McGuire, C. V., & Cheever, J. (1986). The self in society: Effects of social contexts on the sense of self. Special Issue: The individual–society interface. *British Journal of Social Psychology, 25,* 259–270.

Mead, G. H. (1934). *Mind, self, and society from the standpoint of a social behaviorist.* Chicago: University of Chicago Press.

Miller, R. S., & Leary, M. R. (1992). Social sources and interactive functions of emotion: The case of embarrassment. In M. S. Clark (Ed.), *Emotion and social behavior. Review of personality and social psychology* (Vol. 14, pp. 202–221). Newbury Park, CA: Sage.

Minsky, M. (1985). *The society of mind.* New York: Simon & Schuster.

Monge, R. H. (1973). Developmental trends in factors of adolescent self-concept. *Developmental Psychology, 8,* 382–393.

Morganti, J. B., Nehrke, M. F., Hulicka, I. M., & Cataldo, J. F. (1988). Life-span differences in life satisfaction, self-concept, and locus of control. *International Journal of Aging and Human Development, 26,* 45–56.

Mullis, A. K., Mullis, R. L., & Normandin, D. (1992). Cross-sectional and longitudinal comparisons of adolescent self-esteem. *Adolescence, 27,* 51–61.

Murphy, G. (1947). *Personality: A biosocial approach to origins and structure.* New York: Harper.

Nehrke, M. F., Hulicka, I. M., & Morganti, J. B. (1980). Age differences in life satisfaction, locus of control, and self-concept. *International Journal of Aging and Human Development, 11,* 25–33.

Nesse, R. M., & Lloyd, A. T. (1992). The evolution of psychodynamic mechanisms. In J. H. Barkow, L. Cosmides, & J. Tooby (Eds.), *The adapted mind: Evolutionary psychology and the generation of culture* (pp. 601–624). New York: Oxford University Press.

Norem, J. K. (1996, June). *There is no such thing as an average situation.* Invited paper presented in the symposium on *Motivated Individuals in Situations* at the Society for Personality and Social Psychology Conference on "Lewin Revisited," San Francisco.

Norem, J. K. (1997, August). Plus ça change, plus c'est . . . ? Different patterns of change as a function of cognitive strategies. In B. Roberts & R. Robins (Chairs), *Patterns and processes of personality and self-concept change.* Symposium presented at the meeting of the American Psychological Association, Chicago.

Norem, J. K., & Cantor, N. (1986). Defensive pessimism: Harnessing anxiety as motivation. *Journal of Personality and Social Psychology, 51,* 1208–1217.

Norman, W. T. (1967). *2800 personality trait descriptors: Normative operating characteristics for a university population.* Ann Arbor, MI: University of Michigan, Department of Psychology.

Ogilvie, D. M. (1987). The undesired self: A neglected variable in personality research. *Journal of Personality and Social Psychology, 52,* 379–385.

O'Malley, P. M., & Bachman, J. G. (1983). Self-esteem: Change and stability between ages 13 and 23. *Developmental Psychology, 19,* 257–268.

Pals, J. S., & Robins, R. W. (1999). *Self-defining memories in a longitudinal study of the college experience.* Unpublished manuscript, Department of Psychology, University of California, Davis.

Parker, S. T. (1994). Incipient mirror self-recognition in zoo gorillas and chimpanzees. In S. T. Parker, R. W. Mitchell, M. L. Boccia (Eds.), *Self-awareness in animals and humans: Developmental perspectives* (pp. 301–307). New York: Cambridge University Press.

Parker, S. T., Mitchell, R. W., & Boccia, M. L. (Eds.). (1994). *Self-awareness in animals and humans.* New York: Cambridge University Press.

Patterson, F. G. P., & Cohn, R. H. (1994). Self-recognition and self-awareness in lowland gorillas. In S. T. Parker, R. W. Mitchell, M. L. Boccia (Eds.), *Self-awareness in animals and humans: Developmental perspectives* (pp. 273–290). New York: Cambridge University Press.

Patterson, F., & Linden, E. (1981). *The education of Koko.* New York: Holt, Rinehart, & Winston.

Paulhus, D. L., Graf, P., & Van Selst, M. (1989). Attentional load increases the positivity of self-presentation. *Social Cognition, 7,* 389–400.

Paulhus, D. L., & Levitt, K. (1987). Desirable responding triggered by affect: Automatic egotism? *Journal of Personality and Social Psychology, 52,* 245–259.

Penfield, W., & Jasper, H. (1954). *Epilepsy and the functional anatomy of the human brain.* Boston: Little, Brown.

Penrose, R. (1994). *Shadows of the mind: A search for the missing science of consciousness.* New York: Oxford University Press.

Piers, E. V., & Harris, D. B. (1964). Age and other correlates of self-concept in children. *Journal of Educational Psychology, 55,* 91–95.

Pinker, S. (1997). *How the mind works.* New York: Norton.

Povinelli, D. J. (1998, November). Can animals emphathize?—No. *Scientific American.* www.sclam.com/1998/1198intelligence/1198debate.html.

Povinelli, D. J., & Preuss, T. M. (1995). Theory of mind: Evolutionary history of cognitive specialization. Special issue: Evolution and development of the cerebral cortex. *Trends in Neurosciences, 18,* 418–424.

Povinelli, D. J., Rulf, A. B., Landau, K. R., & Bierschwale, D. T. (1993). Self-recognition in chimpanzees (Pan troglodytes): Distribution, ontogeny, and patterns of emergence. *Journal of Comparative Psychology, 107,* 347–372.

Prawat, R. S., Jones, H., & Hampton, J. (1979). Longitudinal study of attitude development in pre-, early, and later adolescent samples. *Journal of Educational Psychology, 71,* 363–369.

Priel, B., & de Schonen, S. (1986). Self-recognition: A study of a population without mirrors. *Journal of Experimental Child Psychology, 41,* 237–250.

Quitkin, F., Rifkin, A., & Klein, D. F. (1976). Neurologic soft signs in schizophrenia and character disorders. *Archives of General Psychiatry, 33,* 845–853.

Reid, A., & Deaux, K. (1996). Relationship between social and personal identities: Segregation or integration? *Journal of Personality and Social Psychology, 71,* 1084–1091.

Roberts, B. W., & DelVecchio, W. (in press). The rank-order consistency of personality traits: A quantitative review of longitudinal studies. *Psychological Bulletin.*

Roberts, B. W., & Robins, R. W. (1998). *Broad dispositions, broad aspirations: The intersection of personality and major life goals.* Manuscript under review. Department of Psychology, University of Tulsa, Oklahoma.

Roberts, R. E. L., & Bengtson, V. L. (1996). Affective ties to parents in early adulthood and self-esteem across 20 years. *Social Psychology Quarterly, 59,* 96–106.

Robins, R. W., & Beer, J. S. (1999). *Positive illusions about the self: Their correlates and consequences.* Manuscript under review. Department of Psychology, University of California, Davis.

Robins, R. W., Fraley, C. R., Roberts, B. W., & Trzesniewski, K. (1999). *A longitudinal study of personality change in young adulthood.* Manuscript under review. Department of Psychology, University of California, Davis.

Robins, R. W., Gosling, S. D., & Craik, K. H. (1999). An empirical analysis of trends in psychology. *American Psychologist, 54,* 117–128.

Robins, R. W., & Hendin, H. M. (1999). *Measuring self-esteem: Construct validation of a single-item measure and the Rosenberg Self-Esteem Scale.* Manuscript under review. Department of Psychology, University of California, Davis.

Robins, R. W., & John, O. P. (1996). Toward a broader agenda for research on self and other perception: Comments on Kenny's manifesto. *Psychological Inquiry, 7,* 279–287.

Robins, R. W., & John, O. P. (1997a). Effects of visual perspective and narcissism on self-perception: Is seeing believing? *Psychological Science, 8,* 37–42.

Robins, R. W., & John, O. P. (1997b). The quest for self-insight: Theory and research on accuracy and bias in self-perception. In R. Hogan, J. Johnson, and S. Briggs (Eds.), *Handbook of personality psychology* (pp. 649–679). New York: Academic Press.

Robins, R. W., & Pals, J. L. (1999). *Implicit self-theories in the academic domain: Implications for goal orientation, attributions, affect, and self-esteem change.* Manuscript under review. Department of Psychology, University of California, Davis.

Roeser, R. W., & Eccles, J. S. (1998). Adolescents' perceptions of middle school: Relation to longitudinal changes in academic and psychological adjustment. *Journal of Research on Adolescence, 8,* 123–158.

Rogers, C. R. (1959). A theory of therapy, personality, and interpersonal relations, developed in the client-centered framework. In S. Koch (Ed.), *Psychology: A study of a science* (Vol. 3, pp. 185–256). New York: McGraw-Hill.

Roland, A. (1997). How universal is psychoanalysis? The self in India, Japan, and the United States. In D. Allen & A. Malhotra (Eds.), *Culture and self: Philosophical and religious perspectives, East and West* (pp. 27–39). Boulder, CO: Westview Press.

Rosenberg, M. (1986). Self-concept from middle childhood to adolescence. In J. Suls & A. G. Greenwald (Eds.), *Psychological perspectives on the self* (Vol. 3, pp. 107–135). New York: Academic Press.

Ross, M. (1989). Relation of implicit theories to the construction of personal histories. *Psychological Review, 96,* 341–357.

Rubin, M., & Hewstone, M. (1998). Social identity theory's self-esteem hypothesis: A review and some suggestions for clarification. *Personality and Social Psychology Review, 2,* 40–62.

Ruble, D. N., Eisenberg, R., & Higgins, E. T. (1994). Developmental changes in achievement evaluation: Motivational implications of self–other differences. *Child Development, 65,* 1095–1110.

Russon, A. E., & Galdikas, B. M. (1993). Imitation in free-ranging rehabilitant orangutans (Pongo pygmaeus). *Journal of Comparative Psychology, 107,* 147–161.

Sacks, O. (1995). *An anthropologist on Mars: Seven paradoxical tales.* New York: Knopf.

Sampson, E. E. (1985). The decentralization of identity: Towards a revised concept of personal and social order. *American Psychologist, 40,* 1203–1211.

Sapolsky, R. M. (1997). *The trouble with testosterone: And other essays on the biology of the human predicament.* New York: Scribner's.

Sarbin, T. R., & Allen, V. L. (1968). Role theory. In G. Lindzey & E. Aronson (Eds.), *The handbook of social psychology* (2nd ed., Vol. 1, pp. 488–567). Reading, MA: Addison-Wesley.

Scheel, M. H., Gardner, B. T., & Gardner, R. A. (1998, July). *Development of mirror interactions in cross-fostered chimpanzees.* Presented at the 10th Annual Meeting of the Human Behavior and Evolution Society, Davis, California.

Scheibe, K. E. (1995). *Self studies: The psychology of self and identity.* Westport, CT: Praeger.

Schlenker, B. (1980). *Impression management: The self-concept, social identity, and interpersonal relations.* Monterey, CA: Brooks/Cole.

Schlenker, B. R. (1985). Introduction: Foundations of the self in social life. In B. R. Schlenker (Ed.), *The self and social life.* New York: McGraw-Hill.
Searle, J. (1992). *The rediscovery of the mind.* Cambridge, MA: MIT Press.
Sedikides, C., & Skowronski, J. J. (1997). The symbolic self in evolutionary context. *Personality and Social Psychology Review, 1,* 80–102.
Sedikides, C., & Strube, M. J. (1997). Self-evaluations: To thine own self be good, to thine own self be sure, to thine own self be true, and to thine own self be better. In M. P. Zanna (Ed.), *Advances in experimental social psychology* (Vol. 29, pp. 209–269). New York: Academic Press.
Shaver, P. R., Collins, N., & Clark, C. L. (1996). Attachment styles and internal working models of self and relationship partners. In G. J. O. Fletcher & J. Fitness (Eds.), *Knowledge structures in close relationships: A social psychological approach* (pp. 25–61). Mahwah, NJ: Erlbaum.
Showers, C. J., & Kling, K. C. (1996). The organization of self-knowledge: Implications for mood regulation. In L. L. Martin & A. Tesser (Eds.), *Striving and feeling: Interactions among goals, affect, and self-regulation* (pp. 151–173). Mahwah, NJ: Erlbaum.
Simmons, R. G., Blyth, D. A., Van Cleave, E. F., & Bush, D. M. (1979). Entry into early adolescence: The impact of school structure, puberty, and early dating on self-esteem. *American Sociological Review, 44,* 948–967.
Simmons, R. G., Rosenberg, F., & Rosenberg, M. (1973). Disturbance in the self-image at adolescence. *American Sociological Review, 38,* 553–568.
Singer, J. A. (1995). Seeing one's self: Locating narrative memory in a framework of personality. *Journal of Personality, 63,* 429–457.
Singer, J. A., & Salovey, P. (1993). *The remembered self: Emotion and memory in personality.* New York: Free Press.
Skinner, B. F. (1990). Can psychology be a science of the mind? *American Psychologist, 45,* 1206–1210.
Snowden, C. T. (1995). Editorial statement. *Journal of Comparative Psychology, 109,* 3–4.
Snyder, C. R. (1990). Self-handicapping processes and sequelae: On the taking of a psychological dive. In R. L. Higgins (Ed), *Self-handicapping: The paradox that isn't* (pp. 107–150). New York: Plenum Press.
Snyder, M. (1974). Self-monitoring of expressive behavior. *Journal of Personality and Social Psychology, 30,* 526–537.
Snyder, M. (1987). *Public appearances / private realities: The psychology of self-monitoring.* New York: Freeman.
Solomon, S., Greenberg, J., & Pyszczynski, T. (1991). A terror management theory of social behavior: The psychological function of self-esteem and cultural world views. In M. P. Zanna (Ed.), *Advances in experimental social psychology* (Vol. 24, pp. 93–159). San Diego, CA: Academic Press.
Steele, C. M. (1988). The psychology of self-affirmation: Sustaining the integrity of the self. In L. Berkowitz (Ed.), *Advances in experimental social psychology* (pp. 261–302). San Diego, CA: Academic Press.
Stone, V. E., Baron-Cohen, S., & Knight, R. T. (1998). Frontal lobe contributions to theory of mind. *Journal of Cognitive Neuroscience, 10,* 640–656.
Suarez, S. D., & Gallup, G. G. (1981). Self-recognition in chimpanzees and organutans, but not gorillas. *Journal of Human Evolution, 10,* 175–188.
Swann, W. B., Jr. (1996a). *The motivated self.* Paper presented at the Society of Experimental Social Psychologists, Sturbridge, Mass.
Swann, W. B., Jr. (1996b). *Self-traps: The elusive quest for higher self-esteem.* New York: Freeman.
Swann, W. B., Jr. (1997). The trouble with change: Self-verification and allegiance to the self. *Psychological Science, 8,* 177–180.
Swann, W. B., Jr., Pelham, B. W., & Krull, D. S. (1989). Agreeable fancy or disagreeable truth? Reconciling self-enhancement and self-verification. *Journal of Personality and Social Psychology, 57,* 782–791.
Swann, W. B., & Schroeder, D. G. (1995). The search for beauty and truth: A framework for understanding reactions to evaluations. *Personality and Social Psychology Bulletin, 21,* 1307–1318.
Swann, W. B., Jr., Stein-Seroussi, A., & Giesler, R. B. (1992). Why people self-verify. *Journal of Personality and Social Psychology, 62,* 392–401.
Tajfel, H., & Turner, J. C. (1986). The social identity theory of intergroup behavior. In S. Worchel & W. Austin (Eds.), *Psychology of intergroup relations* (pp. 7–24). Chicago: Nelson-Hall.
Tangney, J. P., & Fischer, K. W. (Eds.). (1995). *Self-conscious emotions: The psychology of shame, guilt, embarrassment, and pride.* New York: Guilford Press.
Taylor, S. E., & Brown, J. (1988). Illusion and well-being: A social psychological perspective on mental health. *Pyschological Bulletin, 103,* 193–210.
Taylor, S. E., & Brown, J. (1994). Positive illusions and well-being revisited: Separating fact from fiction. *Pyschological Bulletin, 116,* 21–27.
Tesser, A. (1988). Toward a self-evaluation maintenance model of social behavior. In L. Berkowitz (Ed.), *Advances in experimental social psychology* (Vol. 21, pp. 181–227). New York: Academic Press.
Tetlock, P. E. (1992). The impact of accountability on judgment and choice: Toward a social contingency model. In M. P. Zanna (Ed.), *Advances in experimental social psychology* (Vol. 25, pp. 331–376). New York: Academic Press.
Thyer, B. A. (1987). *Treating anxiety disorders.* Newbury Park, CA: Sage.
Tomasello, M. (1998). Uniquely primate, uniquely human. *Developmental Science, 1,* 1–30.
Tononi, G., & Edelman, G. M. (1998). Consciousness and complexity. *Science, 282,* 1846–1851.

Trafimow, D., Triandix, H. C., & Goto, S. G. (1991). Some tests of the distinction between the private self and collective self. *Journal of Personality and Social Psychology, 60,* 649–655.

Triandis, H. C. (1997). Cross-cultural perspectives on personality. In R. Hogan, J. Johnson, and S. Briggs (Eds.), *Handbook of personality psychology,* (pp. 439–464). New York: Academic Press.

Trivers, R. L. (1971). The evolution of reciprocal altruism. *Quarterly Review of Biology, 46,* 35–57.

Trope, Y. (1980). Self-assessment, self-enhancement, and task performance. *Journal of Experimental Social Psychology, 16,* 116–129.

Trope, Y. (1986). Self-enhancement and self-assessment in achievement behavior. In R. M. Sorrentino, E. T. Higgins (Eds.), *Handbook of motivation and cognition: Foundations of social behavior* (pp. 350–378). New York: Guilford Press.

Tropp, L. R., & Wright, S. C. (1995, June). *Inclusion of in-group in the self: Adapting Aron & Aron's IOS scale.* Paper presented at the American Psychological Society, New York.

Tulving, E. (1993a). Self-knowledge of an amnesic patient is represented abstractly. In T. K. Srull & R. S. Wyer (Eds.), *The mental representation of trait and autobiographical knowledge about the self: Advances in social cognition* (Vol. 5, pp. 147–156). Hillsdale, NJ: Erlbaum.

Tulving, E. (1993b). Varieties of consciousness and levels of awareness in memory. In A. D. Baddeley and L. Weiskrantz (Eds.), *Attention: Selection, awareness, and control* (pp. 283–299). Oxford, UK: Oxford University Press.

Turner, J. C., Hogg, M. A., Oakes, P. J., Reicher, S. D., & Wetherell, M. S. (1987). *Rediscovering the social group: A self-categorization theory.* Oxford, UK: Basil Blackwell.

Turner, J. C., & Onorato, R. S. (1999). Social identity, personality, and the self-concept: A self-categorization perspective. In T. R. Tyler, R. M. Kramer, & O. P. John (Eds.), *The psychology of the social self* (pp. 11–46). Mahwah, NJ: Erlbaum.

Tyler, T. R., Kramer, R. M., & John, O. P. (Eds.). (1999). *The psychology of the social self.* Mahwah, NJ: Erlbaum.

Vallacher, R. R., & Wegner, D. M. (1987). What do people think they're doing? Action identification and human behavior. *Psychological Review, 94,* 3–15.

Vargha-Khadem, F., Gadian, D. G., Watkins, K. E., Connelly, A., and others (1997). Differential effects of early hippocampal pathology on episodic and semantic memory. *Science, 277,* 376–380.

Watson, D., & Clark, L. A. (1984). Negative affectivity: The disposition to experience aversive emotional states. *Pyschological Bulletin, 96,* 465–490.

Wayment, H. A., & Taylor, S. E. (1995). Self-evaluation processes: Motives, information use, and self-esteem. *Journal of Personality, 63,* 729–757.

Wellman, H. M. (1990). *The child's theory of mind.* Cambridge, MA: MIT Press.

Wicklund, R. A., & Gollwitzer, P. M. (1982). *Symbolic self-completion.* Hillsdale, NJ: Erlbaum

Williams, G. C. (1966). *Adaptation and natural selection: A critique of some current evolutionary thought.* Princeton, NJ: Princeton University Press.

Wilson, D. S., Coleman, K., Clark, A. B., & Biederman, L. (1993). Shy–bold continuum in pumpkinseed sunfish (*Lepomis gibbosus*): An ecological study of a psychological trait. *Journal of Comparative Psychology, 107,* 250–260.

Wink, P. (1997). Beyond ethnic differences: Contextualizing the influence of ethnicity on individualism and collectivism. *Journal of Social Issues, 53,* 329–349.

Worcel, S. D. & Norem, J. K. (1996). *The imposter phenomenon: Implications for academic and social adjustment among college women.* Manuscript under review.

Zimmerman, M. A., Copeland, L. A., Shope, J. T., & Dielman, T. E. (1997). A longitudinal study of self-esteem: Implications for adolescent development. *Journal of Youth and Adolescence, 26,* 117–141.

Chapter 19

Personal Narratives and the Life Story

Dan P. McAdams
Northwestern University

Human beings are storytellers by nature. In a multitude of guises, as folktale, legend, myth, fairy tale, history, epic, opera, motion picture, television sit-com, novel, biography, joke, and personal anecdote, the story appears in every known human culture. We expect much of stories. We expect them to entertain, educate, inspire, and persuade; to keep us awake and to put us to sleep; to make us feel joy, sadness, anger, excitement, horror, shame, guilt, and virtually any other emotion we can name; to help us communicate with each other; to explain things that are difficult to understand; to cause us to wonder about things that seem so simple; to clarify and to obfuscate; to make the mundane sacred and the sacred mundane; to help us pass the time; to distract us; to get us focused; to tell us who we are. From the time of Homer to the present day, people have relied on stories to explain everything from the origins of the universe to what will happen to me if I eat the wrong kind of food (Campbell, 1949). Stories can help us tell lies, but they can also convey truth. The idea that certain stories contain or reveal important truths is probably as old as human civilization itself, and it is an idea that has not been lost on psychologists. Freud (1900/1953) mined the manifest content of dream narratives to unearth buried personal truths, whereas Adler (1927) viewed storied accounts of earliest memories as foreshadowings of a person's style of life. Since the time of Murray (1938), personality researchers have coded imaginative stories told in response to picture cues (as in the Thematic Apperception Test [TAT]) to assess individual differences in motivations (McClelland, Atkinson, Clark, & Lowell, 1953) and developmental concerns (Stewart, 1982). We tend to believe that the stories a person tells tell us something about the person.

Since the mid-1980s, personality psychology has witnessed a strong upsurge of interest in personal narratives and life stories. An increasing emphasis on narrative methods and concepts may also be seen in many other branches of psychology, including cognitive (Schank & Abelson, 1995), social (Murray & Holmes, 1994), developmental (McCabe & Peterson, 1991), life-span (Cohler, 1982), clinical (Howard, 1991), counseling (Polkinghorne, 1988), and industrial–organizational (Pondy, Morgan, Frost, & Dandridge, 1983) psychology. In addition, many psychotherapists today, especially those who treat families, practice one form or another of narrative therapy (e.g., White & Epston, 1990). Surveying the proliferation of theories and research programs centered on stories, scripts, myths, autobiographical recollections, and the like, Sarbin (1986) contends that the concept of narrative provides a new "root metaphor" for the field of psychology as a whole.

Outside psychology, many scholars have remarked on a turn toward narrative in the social sciences and the humanities (Gergen, 1992). For example, life-history research methods are enjoying a renaissance in sociology (Denzin & Lincoln, 1994) and in research in education (Casey, 1996). Many historians now view historiography as, in part, the construction of convincing narratives about the past in light of current cultural concerns. Narrative theology has become an extremely influential movement in many Protestant and Catholic seminaries, and in moral philosophy, MacIntyre (1981) argues that human virtue has its essential meaning within the narrative quest that defines an individual life. In an applied vein, religious and moral educators underscore the importance of storytelling in the socialization of virtue and the enhancement of moral development (Vitz, 1990). Scholars of many persuasions speak of contemporary social life in the postindustrial West as akin to a storied text to be interpreted as if it were a literary product, as they debate a wide variety of hermeneutical problems pertaining to authorship, power, and identity in the construction of social texts (Shotter & Gergen, 1989). Josselson and Lieblich (1993) write about the "narrative study of lives" as a wide-ranging and loosely coordinated interdisciplinary effort to write, interpret, and disseminate people's life stories, with special attention paid to the accounts of women, people of color, and representatives of other groups whose lives and whose stories have historically been squelched, marginalized, or ignored (Franz & Stewart, 1994; Heilbrun, 1988; Rosenwald, 1992).

Within personality psychology itself, the upsurge of interest in narrative is reflected both in a proliferation of narrative methodologies, through which psychologists obtain and interpret storied accounts of personal experiences to shed light on personality and social processes (e.g., Baumeister, 1994a; Singer & Salovey, 1993), and in the articulation of several narrative theories of personality (e.g., Hermans & Kempen, 1993; McAdams, 1985). From the standpoint of new narrative theories of personality, the life story is itself a "construct"—a psychological phenomenon in its own right that functions as an integral component of personality. Thus, a researcher may employ narrative methods (e.g., the TAT, analysis of autobiographical memories, interpretation of diaries) to examine many different things (e.g., motives, emotions, interpersonal relationships). Among those phenomena that may be accessed through narrative methodologies are narrative constructs, that is, aspects of personality and interpersonal functioning that may exist as stories themselves. These include such constructs as the person's representations of nuclear scenes in his or her life (Tomkins, 1987), internalized interpersonal scripts (Thorne, 1995a), and narrative working models of attachment relationships (Main, Kaplan, & Cassidy, 1985), as well as the larger internalized life stories that constitute what Hermans and Kempen (1993) call the dialogical self and what McAdams (1985) views as an adult's ego identity.

This chapter focuses mainly on empirical and theoretical developments in the study of personal narratives and life stories as they affect personality psychology—the scientific study of individual persons. I will begin by considering the nature of narratives and narrative thought and by examining the meanings and uses of stories and storytelling in normal human development. Next, I will discuss the role of narrative in personality theory, with an emphasis on the development of three new personality theories that place life stories at the center of human functioning. Reading across the three theories, I will propose seven integrative principles for the narrative study of human lives. Finally, I will discuss problems and possibilities in empirical research in personality, sampling representative studies that have used narrative methods and concepts to address the issues of personality coherence, personality change, and the question of different life-story types.

THE NARRATIVE MIND

Narrative Thought

Bruner (1986) argues that human beings think about the world and about themselves in two very different ways. In the "paradigmatic" mode of thought, people think in terms of logically deduced and empirically validated propositions. Like good scientists, they articulate principles and theories to explain how the world works, and they present objective data to back up their claims. The paradigmatic mode is ideally suited for explaining cause-and-effect relations in the physical world. Operating in the paradigmatic mode, therefore, the scientist strives to eliminate ambiguity and uncertainty about the world and to arrive at a single, objective theoretical account for a given set of phenomena. Paradigmatic explanations of the same events ultimately compete with each other, the assumption being that only one theory about a particular phenomenon can be true.

In the "narrative" mode of thought, by contrast, people filter and make sense of experience through stories. Like good novelists, they invoke plots, scenes, and characters to explain how and why it is that people do what they do. The narrative mode of thought is the preferred mode for understanding how human intentions and desires get translated into human actions and how those actions play out over time. Thus, stories seek not so much truth in the paradigmatic sense, but rather verisimilitude, or life-likeness (Hermans, 1996). Unlike theories, stories are structured not so much to rule out other possibilities, but rather to open up new possibilities, to widen the horizon of life experience (Bruner, 1990). Unlike theories, stories depend on who tells them—that is, on point of view. The subjectivity of the storyteller cannot be separated from the story, for stories are assumed to incorporate the feelings, goals, needs, and values of the people who create them. Stories are evaluated and understood with respect to their success in conveying the intricate subjectivity of the author.

The distinction between paradigmatic and narrative thought mirrors a number of related dichotomies. Cognitive psychologists routinely distinguish between "semantic" and "episodic" memory, the former referring to abstract and conceptual knowledge and the latter to the recollection of particular events and storied scenes. In life-span cognitive theory, Labouvie-Vief (1990) contrasts the development of "logos" as hypothetico-deductive knowing and "mythos" as the narrative knowing associated with personal experience, human emotions, and interpersonal relationships. In personality theory, Epstein (1994) distinguishes between the "rational" and "experiential" systems, the latter associated with "concrete images, metaphors, and narrative" (p. 711). As with all these distinctions, however, it is important to note that human beings regularly draw on both sides of the ledger in everyday thought and experience. A skilled debater knows that a convincing argument may blend the logic and formal categories of the paradigmatic mode with powerful narrative illustrations. Even scientists regularly draw on anecdotal stories to buttress their points, and some formal scientific theories may evoke implicit narratives or may contain certain structural features that are typically found in good stories (Landau, 1986). Nonetheless, Bruner's two modes of thought ultimately serve very different intellectual agendas, and the masters of each end up producing strikingly different expressions of the mind. One need only contrast Darwin to Dostoyevsky or Einstein to Joyce to see that paradigmatic and narrative knowing are fundamentally different enterprises that accomplish very different ends.

What Is a Story?

A story is a symbolized account of human action organized in time (Sarbin, 1986). Stories structure events in such a way as to demonstrate a connectedness and directional movement of human actions and experiences over time. In most literary traditions, it is expected that a story takes place in a particular spatial and temporal "setting." The setting establishes a frame of meaning for understanding the story; thus, it makes a very big difference if a story is set in ancient Mesopotamia as opposed to "yesterday in Portland, Oregon." Equally critical for framing the meaning of a story is the narrator's point of view. Every story is conveyed by an explicit or implicit narrator, and again it is essential to know if that narrator is, say, a third-person omniscient voice or a first-person protagonist whose own actions are part of the plot. A story must have human or human-like "characters" (Bruner, 1986). Furthermore, something has to happen in the story to make the characters want to do something. In other words, the characters must be endowed with "intention" or will. Stories typically evoke curiosity and suspense in the minds of the listeners (Brewer & Lichtenstein, 1982). What will happen next? How will it all turn out? Once a plot is initiated the action assumes a teleological orientation and the listener comes to expect that he or she will eventually encounter an "ending" that resolves the problems and tensions that got the story going in the first place (Kermode, 1967).

Many investigators underscore the goal-directed quality of narrative action (Applebee, 1978; Mandler, 1984). Stories are typically about characters who have goals, and typically different characters' goals conflict with each other. As Robert Penn Warren once said, "No conflict, no story" (1962, p. 148). Stein and Policastro (1984) argue that goal-based stories typically conform to a set of rules that together constitute a "story grammar." The story grammar yields a six-phase sequence of goal-directed action: setting, initiating event, internal response, the attempt, consequence, reaction. In "Little Red Riding Hood," the (1) setting is once upon a time in a faraway place. The (2) initiating event takes place when mother sends Little Red Riding Hood on a journey to deliver cakes to her grandmother. The girl accedes to her mother's wishes—(3) internal response—and sets off on her (4) attempt to accomplish the goal. Her attempt leads to (5) the consequence, which in this story thickens the plot considerably as she encounters the big bad wolf, whose own intentions—to eat her—remain disguised. Little Red Riding Hood's (6) reaction to her first encounter with the wolf is to divulge the location of her grandmother's cottage, which complicates the plot further, for now her grandmother is also in danger. The cycle of initiating event through reaction repeats again and again, as the story extends forward to future episodes in which the two main characters will face a showdown. Finally, there is an ending, which typically resolves conflicts and tensions in the story and brings the temporal sequence of action to a close.

Although any goal-based sequence of human action can, in principle, be made into a story, people choose to narrate only certain incidents and possibilities. Not all sequences are tellable. Storytelling requires an interested audience that is able to comprehend and appreciate the telling. An audience will not be interested unless the events to be narrated deviate from the canonical order of things. "Good story hinges on a breach or departure from expectation or conventionality," writes Lucariello (1990, p. 131). I may choose to tell you a story about my waking up this morning, taking a shower, shaving, and then eating breakfast, but unless you are starved for entertainment, you will find such an account too boring to hear. However, if I tell you that I woke up this morning, had breakfast, went outside to get the newspaper, and then found a baby lying in a basket at my door, well now we have a story fit to tell. The second account deviates from the canonical morning script. It violates shared expectations about a routine morning. Storytellers of all stripes—from barbers to playwrights—engage their audience's interest by providing accounts that deviate from the canonical patterns of everyday human existence. A favorite strategy for accomplishing this is to infuse the story with the possibility of danger (Bruner, 1990).

The Development of Storytelling

The developmental origins of narrative understanding can probably be traced to the first year of life. Face-to-face play between caregivers and their infants may create the fundamental theatrical context for the performance of stories (Sutton-Smith, 1986, p. 69). In these intricately choreographed interactions, babies learn the rudiments of turn-taking and state-sharing as they perform their feelings in action and witness the reciprocal performances of their partners. As described by Stern (1985), early face-to-face play may assume the form of a story. In a typical play scenario, two characters (caregiver and infant) share emotional states, revealing their intentions to interact through such behaviors as smiling, laughter, and eye contact. The sharing of emotional states in play produces a sequence of goal-directed actions that build to a climax and then slow down toward a resolution. The story-like sequence is enacted through smiling, gazing, touch, laughter, and other nonverbal actions that speak in the languages of rhythm, tempo, intensity, and so on (Stern, 1985). Through experiences like these, infants may develop an implicit sense of narrative patterning, years before they are able to tell stories in words.

Telling stories presupposes a sense of the self as a storyteller. Developmental research suggests that a coherent sense of the self as subject, what William James (1892/1963) deemed the subjective self or the "I," emerges in the second year of life (Harter, 1983). By the age of 18 months or so, children understand themselves to be causal, independent agents in the world. The emergence of the subjective self paves the way for the articulation of a self-concept, or what James referred to as the objective self or "Me." In the 2-year-old's first self-descriptive verbalizations, the I is beginning to fashion a Me. According to Mancuso (1986), children who can conceptualize the self as an agent "promptly set self into the narrative grammar category 'actor,' and then proceed to extend self stories by inserting events and objects which fit the grammar category outcome'" (p. 105). In other words, once the I begins to perceive and construct a Me, the I is ready to assume the guise of storyteller. There are many stories to tell, including those especially self-relevant stories wherein the Me plays the role of main character.

Children can begin to tell stories themselves in the third or fourth year of life when this activity is encouraged by parents or teachers (Sutton-Smith, 1986). Preschoolers show a clear understanding of commonplace familiar events, such as birthday parties, making cookies, going to the store, and eating snacks at school (Nelson, 1993). Before they arrive at kindergarten, furthermore, children are likely to have consolidated a basic "theory of mind" (Wellman, 1993), which entails an understanding that other people have feelings and desires, just as they do, and that people's external actions are thereby motivated by these internal feelings and desires. The storytelling I, therefore, can now create story characters whose intentions can be translated into goal-directed actions. Early stories are, of course, very simple, but they increase in complexity and nuance as children grow older (Applebee, 1978). The move toward complexity reflects cognitive development and changes in self-understanding (Hart, 1988). For example, the stories told by kindergartners may suggest limited perspective-taking and a preoccupation with the physical actions and momentary states of human characters. In the terms of Feldman, Bruner, Renderer, and Spitzer (1990), young children's stories are sketched almost exclusively on a "landscape of action." By contrast, adolescents will articulate more complex plots entailing long-term relationships between characters, and they will endow their characters with traits, motives, and a rich inner life. More experienced storytellers, therefore, may operate as well on the "landscape of consciousness" (Feldman et al, 1990). Stories emplot both actions and consciousness; with greater development, individuals are able to narrate effectively in both realms and to coordinate and juxtapose the two in increasingly interesting ways.

Autobiographical Stories

One of the main things that stories do is to integrate disparate elements of human experience into a more-or-less coherent whole (McAdams, 1985). Stories integrate human action and consciousness in time, providing a sequence of events that specifies beginning, middle, and ending. Ricoeur (1984) writes that "time becomes human time to the extent it is organized after the manner of narrative; narrative in turn is meaningful to the extent it portrays the features of temporal existence" (p. 3). Stories help to organize the chaos of raw experience into a more-or-less followable narrative form. Developmental psychologists have examined the ways in which children tell stories to organize and regulate their emotional experience (Engel, 1995). "Plot structures organize the judgmental and rhetorical acts that make up emotional life," writes Sarbin (1995, p. 218). Sarbin argues that each of us experiences emotions as an actor in a scenario—that is, from the position of a moral agent embedded in a plot. To feel anger is to live out one of a number of socially constructed, morally instantiated plots: I may experience anger by virtue of being demeaned, as a result of an offense (a wrong) against me or mine; I may experience shame by virtue of not living up to a personal standard, or by virtue of having humiliated my people; I am happy by virtue of being embedded in a progressive plot in which I am making steady progress toward my goals (Lazarus & Lazarus, 1994). Emotional life is itself organized by plots; it is a storied experience, socially constructed and rhetorically performed (Gregg, 1991).

The integrative power of narrative is evident in autobiographical recollections. Nelson (1993) has shown that the sharing of personal stories between mothers and preschool children enhances children's memory of events in their lives. Research and theory suggest that autobiographical memory serves the twin purposes of preserving a more-or-less veridical past and interpreting that past in a way that makes sense in the present (Kotre, 1995). To a certain extent, then, autobiographical recollection is an act of imaginative storytelling—the past is selected and reconstructed such that it can be integrated with the perceived present and anticipated future.

People who write formal autobiographies often identify the desire to integrate their lives as a prime motive for their efforts. In one of the first and most famous autobiographies in Western history, Saint Augustine (354–430 C.E.) sought to regroup and recover from what he described as a "shattered" and "disordered" state of mind. By composing the story that became his *Confessions,* Augustine was able to construct a unified view of himself and his place in God's creation and to orient to the envisioned future with direction and purpose. Since Augustine's time, the history of autobiographical writing in the West parallels the rise of individualism and the increasing value that Westerners have placed on the person's private, inner experience (Alasuutari, 1997). Among other things, cultural individualism suggests that every individual life is unique in some way. Every life deviates from convention in some manner, and because deviation from the canonical is a criterion for a tellable story, there is almost always a life story to tell. As the title of one self-help book puts it, "every person's life is worth a novel" (Polster, 1987). Personal narratives and life stories enjoy a privileged status in contemporary Western societies, for they mirror the value those societies place on individualism as well as the struggles people living in those societies perennially have in integrating their lives.

NARRATIVE THEORIES OF PERSONALITY

In surveying the grand theories of personality developed in the first half of the 20th century, one will encounter occasional allusions to the idea that human lives are like stories or that human beings may construct their lives into stories (Barresi & Juckes, 1997; McAdams, 1994). Narrative assumptions are implicit, for example, in the theories offered by Adler (1927), Jung (1936/1969), Murray (1938), and Erikson (1950)—all of whom expressed considerable interest in the temporal nature of human lives, how lives develop over time and how human beings understand that development.

First followers and later rivals of Sigmund Freud, Adler and Jung developed their own comprehensive theories of personality that, in very different ways, construed the human life course in narrative terms. Alfred Adler was preoccupied with story beginnings and endings. From Adler's perspective, the "earliest memory" is an adult's origin myth, presaging a particular style of life, and an adult's "fictional finalism" represents a vision for the future with respect to which the individual understands his or her reconstructed past and perceived present. The fictional finalism functions, therefore, as an anticipated ending toward which the thrust of the life narrative is aimed. Drawing explicitly from world religions and mythology, Carl Jung viewed human development as an intrapsychic adventure story. Over the long and exciting odyssey through the personal and collective unconscious, the heroic self confronts gods, beasts, villains, and a host of other personified "archetypes." For Jung, individuation awaits the man or woman who is bold enough to accept the narrative challenge of exploring the unconscious realm of life. Whereas Adler's more cognitive and rational approach focuses on how people live out their stories in the real world, Jung's archetypal myths are daring journeys through the wilderness within.

Strongly influenced by Jung and Adler, Henry Murray viewed human beings as "time-binding" organisms who find direction and continuity of purpose in their lives by organizing experience into temporal sequences (1938, p. 49). "The history of the organism is the organism," Murray (1938, p. 39) proclaimed, and he sought to capture the storylike quality of lives in time through such theoretical constructs as "proceedings," "durances," "serials," "needs," "press," and "thema." After working with Murray and his colleagues for a short period in the 1930s, Erik Erikson articulated a monumental theory of personality development whose eight psychosocial stages may be viewed as successive chapters in a generic story of human life. Much of what is so compelling in Erikson's theory comes from the power of the story he tells (McAdams, 1997a). It is a story that contains some of the most familiar and beloved plots in mythic literature—the birth in innocence ("trust vs. mistrust"), the expulsion from paradise ("autonomy vs. shame and doubt"), the confrontation with omnipotent authority ("initiative vs. guilt"), the heroic quest to find the self ("identity vs. role confusion"), the passing of one's legacy to the next generation ("generativity vs. stagnation"), and the satisfying ending that brings the hero home in peace to where things ultimately began ("ego integrity vs. despair"). For Erikson, furthermore, not only is the human life course a storied affair, but human beings themselves must adopt a storytelling perspective on their lives if they are to attain psychosocial maturity. In one of his most revealing passages, Erikson describes how becoming an adult involves constructing a narrative understanding of the self and then taking ownership of it:

> To be adult means among other things to see one's own life in continuous perspective, both in retrospect and prospect. By accepting some definition as to who he is, usually on the basis of a function in an economy, a place in the sequence of generations, and a status in the structure of society, the adult is able to selectively reconstruct his past in such a way that, step for step, it seems to have planned him, or better, he seems to have planned *it*. In this sense, psychologically we *do* choose our parents, our family history, and the history of our kings, heroes, and gods. By making them our own, we maneuver ourselves into the inner position of proprietors, of creators. (Erikson, 1958, pp. 111–112)

Certain narrative motifs may also be detected in personality theories offered by the existentialists (e.g., Binswanger, Frankl) and in the writings of Allport and Kelly. But it was not until the late 1970s that narrative assumed a prominent role in personality theorizing. Although Adler, Jung, Murray, Erikson, and a few others hinted at the importance of stories in understanding human individuality, none of these theorists explicitly conceived of human lives and human selves as storied texts. Before the late 1970s, personality theorizing had no language for thinking about the ways in which lives are constructed, conceptualized, and performed as stories. The turn toward narrative in personality theorizing began with Silvan Tomkins (1979) and the development of "script theory." In the 1980s, a growing number of personality psychologists began to incorporate narrative ideas into their work. The most extensively articulated theoretical approaches developed during this time are McAdams' (1985) "life-story model of identity" and Hermans' (1988) "theory of the dialogical self."

Tomkins: Scenes and Scripts

A drama student who wrote plays as a college undergraduate, Tomkins came to psychology as a storywriter. It was through dramatic narrative that Tomkins first wrestled with the question that ultimately served as the underpinnings for his life work: "What do people really want?" (Tomkins, 1981, p. 306). In search of an answer, he entered psychology graduate school in 1930 but soon dropped out because he could find no satisfying approach to the understanding of human motivation. After receiving a PhD in philosophy, he returned to psychology to work with Murray and his colleagues at the Harvard Psychological Clinic. Though Tomkins initially accepted Murray's belief that psychogenic needs are the main forces in human motivation, he soon departed from this view in favor of a theory emphasizing primary *affects*. Tomkins (1962, 1963) proposed that natural selection has endowed human beings with a highly differentiated and specialized system of affects, each of which addresses a set of timeless problems by motivating behavior that is ultimately consonant with adaptive goals.

As developmental psychologists extended and refined Tomkins' seminal ideas on affect (e.g., Izard, 1977), Tomkins moved on to consider how affects fit into a comprehensive theory of personality. He returned to his early fascination with drama to fashion script theory. According to Tomkins (1979, 1987), whereas affect is the supreme motivator in human life, scenes and scripts are the great organizers. Tomkins views the person as a playwright who creates his or her own personal drama from the earliest weeks of life onward. The basic component of the drama is the "scene," the memory of a specific happening or event in one's life that contains at least one affect and one object of the affect. Each scene is "an organized whole that includes persons, place, time, actions, and feelings" (Carlson, 1981, p. 502). Life in time is a series of scenes, one after another, extending from birth to the present. But certain kinds of scenes appear again and again, and certain typical groupings or families of scenes can be discerned. Thus, *scripts* enable people to make sense of the relations among various scenes. A script is a set of rules for interpreting, creating, enhancing, or defending a family of related scenes. Each person implicitly organizes his or her life according to his or her own idiosyncratic scripts.

The process of organizing scenes into scripted narrative families is called "psychological magnification." People often organize affectively positive scenes around "variants," or variations on a common theme. In other words, in remembering good events from the past, people tend to accentuate the differences among them, as if to suggest that there are many different ways to experience joy and excitement. By contrast, people tend to organize affectively negative scenes around "analogs," or the detection of similarities in different events. This strategy confers the feeling of "here we go again" when it comes to experiences of sadness, anger, guilt, and so on. People tend to experience negative scenes, then, as repetitions of the same kind of event again and again, as if to suggest that there are only a few different ways to be miserable in life.

The number of different kinds of scenes and scripts that can be derived from human life would appear to be very large. But Tomkins has identified at least two contrasting types of scripts that seem especially salient in some lives. In a "commitment script," the person binds him- or herself to a life program or goal that promises the reward of intense positive affect. The person may have a vision of the ideal life or society and dedicate his or her life to realizing or accomplishing this vision. According to Tomkins, a "commitment script" begins with an intensely positive early scene or series of scenes from childhood that the individual implicitly seeks to reexperience or re-create in later life. The person whose life is organized around a commitment script strives to accomplish his or her desired paradise with singleness of purpose and steadfast dedication. There is little ambivalence and virtually no conflict around, say, competing goals or ideological doubts. Even in the face of great obstacles and repeated negative-affect experiences, such a person focuses steadily on the object of commitment, laboring under the conviction that "bad things can be overcome" (Carlson, 1988, p. 111).

In sharp contrast to commitment scripts, the "nuclear script" is marked by confusion and ambivalence about life goals. The nuclear script may begin with a nuclear scene, which is the recollection of a childhood event in which a very positive scene goes bad. What begins as joyful and exciting may suddenly turn toward fear, anger, guilt, shame, or sadness. The nuclear script is formed as an attempt to reverse the nuclear scene, to turn the bad scene into a good scene again. The attempt is only partially successful, Tomkins writes, as the protagonist of the nuclear script is typically fated to repeat the good-turns-bad sequence again and again, through subsequent analog scenes. Therefore, while the commitment script suggests a life story in which the protagonist strives to accomplish clear goals that promise the reenactment of positive early scenes, the nuclear script organizes a very different kind of narrative in which the protagonist struggles to achieve a number of conflicting goals in a desperate effort to undo the bad outcomes that came from frustrating and frightening early scenes.

In sum, Tomkins presents the first fully formed personality theory that adopts a narrative framework for understanding human lives. From infancy onward, human beings function as playwrights and protagonists in the dramas they create. Therefore, people actively construct narrative meaning in their lives from the very beginning of life, even as they find themselves to be the unwitting recipients and victims of the powerful influences of family, peers, and societal contexts. The parameters of lifelong scripts for living are laid down in affectively charged early experiences. The quality of childhood scenes helps to determine the kinds of dramas that a person will eventually enact. Tomkins seems to suggest that early experience is both determinative of later experience and subject to some dramatic revision over time. But early experience is very compelling, and Tomkins does not seem to be sanguine about the possibility of attaining substantially greater authorial control over life scripts as one grows older (Barresi & Juckes, 1997). There is an interesting ambiguity and tension in Tomkins script theory concerning the extent to which a person does indeed function as an agential playwright versus the extent to which he or she enacts roles and reads scripts that have been laid down in early experience. Tomkins does not address directly the problematic and multifaceted relation between the storyteller him- or herself and the story he or she tells (and lives). It is, however, that precise relation that serves as a touchstone for a number of other narrative approaches for understanding lives, including the theories offered by McAdams and Hermans.

McAdams: Identity as a Life Story

McAdams (1985, 1990, 1993) begins with James's (1892/1963) distinction between the subjective self as "I" and the objective self as "Me." If the I corresponds to the storyteller, the Me is the story the I tells (and lives). But the I does not adopt a storytelling perspective toward the Me, and the Me itself does not take the form of a life story, until infancy and childhood have passed and the individual faces what Erikson called the challenge of ego *identity*. With respect to storytelling and the stories people tell to make sense of their own lives, therefore, something rather dramatic happens in late adolescence and young adulthood. At that time, the person first confronts the problem of unity and purpose in human life: Who am I? How do I fit into the adult world? How do I construct a unified and purposeful life as an adult? Cognitively, emotionally, and interpersonally, people are not prepared to address these kinds of questions until they are on the brink of adulthood (Breger, 1974). It is at that time, then, that the person begins to construe his or her life in narrative terms with the implicit goal of creating an internalized story of the self that binds together the reconstructed past, perceived present, and anticipated future in such a way as to confer upon adult life a sense of unity and purpose.

Whereas Tomkins traces scripts directly back to the apprehension of affectively charged childhood scenes, McAdams suggests that (1) such scenes are just one kind of raw material that infants and children collect over time and (2) discrete childhood scenes ultimately serve, as do many other experiences and influences in the early years, as grist for the storymaking mill of adolescence and adulthood. Toward the end of the second and beginning of the third decade of life, many people begin to adopt an historical perspective on the self such that they come to select, rearrange, and reconstruct scenes, characters, and plots from the autobiographical past in light of the perceived present and anticipated future to come. Identity is that internalized and evolving story that results from this selective appropriation of past, present, and future. Once a person begins to work on his or her identity, the life storymaking process will continue apace through the healthy adult years and well into old age. During times of significant transition, identity work may move to the front burner of everyday consciousness as the person seeks explicitly to align his or her evolving story with rapidly changing events and self-conceptions. During other periods of marked stability in the life course, however, the person may do no more than occasionally tweak and edit the story. During these quiescent times, little of identity significance may occur. Identity concerns, therefore, wax and wane across the adult life course as a function of various on-time (e.g., graduation, marriage, birth of first child, turning 40, retirement) and off-time (e.g., unexpected job change, new opportunity, sudden death of spouse) events, which themselves can become important scenes in the life story that the adult continues to construct (McAdams, 1996a).

McAdams has focused considerable attention on variability in the structural and content features of the life story. With respect to structure, life stories vary from those containing few characters and simple plots to those manifesting higher levels of "narrative complexity." Up through midlife, life stories may become increasingly complex, but complexity in and of itself is not necessarily associated with greater levels of well-being. With respect to content, life stories differ with respect to the relative salience of "thematic lines" associated with what Bakan (1966) called "agency" and "communion." Agency encompasses themes such as power, achievement, independence, and the expansion of the self; communion encompasses themes such as love, intimacy, attachment, social integration, and other forms of human connectedness. The themes of agency and communion may be expressed through the main characters in the life story, which McAdams calls "imagoes." An imago is a personified and idealized image of the self that functions as a protagonist during particular chapters of the life story. For example, a life story may contain two contrasting imagoes—say, "the caregiver" and "the warrior." Each is a personified idealization of the self, implicitly constructed by the individual (James's "I") to enact particular roles and attributes that are important for the self-concept (the "Me"). By scripting one's life in such a way that different characters or subselves take on different roles and attributes, the I is able to express the multiplicity of selfhood within a single story of the self. In this way, especially integrative life stories solve the perennial identity problem, identified clearly by James (1892/1963), of the self's need to be many things and one thing at the same time (Knowles & Sibicky, 1990; McAdams, 1997b).

Among the other features that may differentiate one life story from another, McAdams has identified "narrative tone." Narrative tone is the overall affective quality of a life story, ranging from boundless optimism (as in the mythic archetypes of comedy and romance) to extreme pessimism (as in tragedy and irony; Frye, 1957). Each life story, furthermore, expresses a unique pattern of "imagery." Imagery refers to the characteristic metaphors, symbols, and pictures that an author draws on to express character and plot. Life stories are typically situated within an "ideological setting." The ideological setting is the backdrop of belief and value that positions the story and the storyteller in a particular religious and ethical context. Erikson argued that ideology and identity are two sides of the same coin. In McAdams' view, the ideological setting is typically consolidated in late adolescence and young adulthood, during which time the individual makes important choices, often implicit, concerning what he or she believes to be true, good, and worthy. Finally, life stories extend into the anticipated future, ultimately suggesting a sense of an ending to life. As adults move into and through midlife, they are increasingly likely to frame their life stories in terms of a "generativity script" that specifies the sense in which they have and will have made some kind of meaningful contribution to the next generation, as in parenting, teaching, mentoring, leadership, and other agentic and communal forms of generating a personal legacy (McAdams & de St. Aubin, 1992). By extending the self's products and outcomes into the next generation and beyond, the generativity script may help to confer upon a life story a meaningful and, in some cases, satisfying sense of an ending, in that while one's own story will eventually come to a close, it may be successful in generating new (and good) stories for the future.

Most recently, McAdams has sought to integrate the life-story model of identity into a larger system for understanding personality as a whole (McAdams, 1996b). If the goal of personality psychology is to provide an account of human individuality, then such an account can be approached from three different perspectives or levels. At Level 1, individuality is conveyed through dispositional traits, such as those encoded in the Big Five factor scheme. Level 1 traits provide a dispositional signature for individuality. At Level 2, individuality is conveyed in more specific and contextualized terms through such characteristic adaptations as personal concerns, values, projects, goals, stages, tasks, strategies, and other motivational, developmental, and strategic concerns that contextualize a person's life in time, place, and/or role. Thus, while Level 1 traits provide an initial outline of human individuality, Level 2 adaptations fill in the conditional details. Neither Level 1 nor Level 2 constructs, however, speak to what a person sees as the overall meaning and purpose of his or her life. At Level 3, therefore, integrative life stories capture that aspect of human individuality concerned with identity and purpose. Level 3 life stories are an especially important component of individuality in *modern* societies wherein persons are expected to construct and work on a self that specifies how one is similar to as well as different from others, a self that is coherent amidst diversity and integrated in time (Taylor, 1989). Under conditions of cultural modernity, therefore, "a person's identity is not to be found in behavior, nor—important though this is—in the reactions of others, but in the capacity *to keep a particular narrative going*" (Giddens, 1991, p. 54). In a modern society, therefore, human individuality is conveyed as a patterning of dispositional traits, characteristic adaptations, and integrative life stories.

Hermans: The Dialogical Self

Hermans (1988, 1996; Hermans & Kempen, 1993; Hermans, Kempen, & van Loon, 1992) has articulated a narrative theory of personality that shares similarities with Tomkins and McAdams but departs from their perspectives in a few important ways. Like Tomkins, Hermans pays careful attention to particular scenes and affective experiences in a person's life. Emotionally laden, autobiographical scenes are one of many different kinds of phenomena that Hermans groups under the concept of "valuation." A valuation is "anything that a person finds to be of importance when thinking about his or her life situation" (Hermans, 1988, p. 792). Other sorts of valuations include recurrent dreams, plans for the future, important interpersonal relationships, and so on—all of which may be viewed as basic units of meaning in a person's life. Through self-reflection, people organize their valuations into narratives that situate them in time and space. Valuations themselves can be evaluated in terms of two different motivational trends. "S-motives" concern self-strivings for superiority, expansion, power, control, and other agentic tendencies; "O-motives" are other-oriented strivings for contact, union, intimacy, and other communal goals. Like McAdams, then, Hermans organizes the basic content of life narratives into the superordinate thematic categories of agency and communion. In addition, Hermans classifies valuations in terms of their positive and negative valences, paralleling Tomkins' distinction between positive and negative primary affects and McAdams' distinction between optimistic and pessimistic narrative tone.

The especially distinctive feature of Hermans' conception concerns his understanding of the authorial "I." Whereas McAdams assumes a certain measure of unity in consciousness that gives rise to an integrative storytelling self, Hermans decenters the storytelling I and decomposes it into multiple storytelling voices. In simple terms, McAdams sees one storyteller who tells a story with many different characters (imagoes), whereas Hermans sees many storytellers who each correspond to a character in the story itself. In Hermans' terms, the self is multivoiced; that is, "there is no single 'I' as an agent of self-organization but several, relatively independent 'I' positions that complement and contradict each other in dialogical relationships" (Hermans, Rijks, & Kempen, 1993, p. 61). The self is dialogical in the sense that different storytelling voices engage in imaginal dialogues out of which a complex and multivoiced narrative arises. Drawing from Bakhtin's (1973) literary theory, Hermans analogizes the self to a "polyphonic novel"—a complex story with many voices. Each voice presents its own unified world, as in the great novels of Dostoyevsky wherein different characters develop their own ideologies and world views, which in turn play off against each other:

> In Dostoyevsky's novels there is not one single author, Dostoyevsky himself, but several authors or thinkers (e.g., the characters Raskolnikov, Myshkin, Stavrogin, Ivan Karamazov, and the Grand Inquisitor). Each of these heroes has his own voice ventilating his own view, and each hero is authoritative and independent. A hero is not simply the object of Dostoyevsky's finalizing artistic vision but comes across as the author of its own ideology. According to Bakhtin, there is not a multitude of characters within a unified objective world, illuminated by Dostoyevsky's individual vision, but a plurality of perspectives and worlds: a polyphony of voices. As in a polyphonic composition, the several voices or instruments have different spatial positions and accompany and oppose each other in a dialogical relation. (Hermans et al., 1992, p. 27)

Hermans' conception of the dialogical self captures a number of ideas that are associated with "postmodern" understandings of selfhood (e.g., Gergen, 1992; Sampson, 1989). Gergen (1992) writes that the postmodern condition more generally is marked by a "plurality of voices vying for the right to reality—to be accepted as legitimate expressions of the true and the good" (p. 7). No single authorial voice is dominant, just as no single self-conception can accommodate the flux and the multiplicity of postmodern social life. People change selves, move from one identity to the next, as situations change and life moves on (Lifton, 1993). To put a positive spin on it, the postmodern self is flexible, dynamic, and multifaceted—the I is distributed across different domains and fields. To put a negative spin on it, the postmodern self can be seen as fragmented, rootless, and lacking in commitment. People construct provisional selves, here today and gone tomorrow, through sharing stories in dialogue. Stories, like all texts, are made up of symbols, but symbols have no inherent meanings and can, therefore, be deconstructed to mean, ultimately, anything whatsoever, or nothing at all (Sampson, 1989). Hermans, however, seems to steer clear of the nihilism and the playful irony that pervade much of postmodernist scholarship, and he ultimately argues for the integrative power of life stories. In Hermans' view, some kind of psychic integration and overall personal meaning can emerge amidst the dialogical cacophony. The multivoiced self does not typically degenerate into chaotic fragmentation, as might be the case in multiple personality disorder. Hermans argues instead that people can be very creative and effective in capturing and conveying the richness of their different life experiences through the dialogical, polyphonic novels that they construct and reconstruct, from multiple points of view, over time and across different life roles.

Integrative Themes: Principles of a Narrative Psychology of Personality

Reading across a wide diversity of sources on narrative psychology and the narrative theories of personality offered by Tomkins, McAdams, and Hermans, one can begin to see some common assumptions that many of the authors share. Despite considerable variety in perspective, many approaches that conceive of human lives in storied terms appear to converge on a set of common themes. I have identified seven of these integrative themes, which I propose as seven general principles of a narrative psychology of personality.

1. *Selfhood is storied.* The I apprehends experience in narrative terms, casting the Me as one or more characters in an ongoing sequence of scenes. As a self-conscious, intentional agent, living in time, the person experiences events as narrative episodes with characters and plots, and the person experiences life itself as having an ongoing storylike structure (Barresi & Juckes, 1997; Singer, 1995; Polkinghorne, 1988). Stories are ideally suited to capture how a human character, endowed with consciousness and motivated by intention, enacts desires and strives for goals over time (Bruner, 1990; Ricoeur, 1984).

2. *Life stories organize disparate experience into integrated wholes.* Many theorists underscore the *integrative* function of people's internalized life narratives (Gergen & Gergen, 1993; Josselson, 1995a; Singer, 1997; White & Epston, 1990) and claim that identity itself takes the form of an integrative story of the self (Funkenstein, 1993; McAdams, 1985; Rosenwald & Ochberg, 1992). The formulation of an integrative narrative identity is an especially salient challenge for persons living in modern societies, who often begin in late adolescence to integrate the reconstructed past, perceived present, and anticipated future into an encompassing self-defining story or personal myth (Giddens, 1991; McAdams, 1985, 1996b).

3. *Life stories are cultural texts.* There is a sense in which a life story is jointly authored, both by the person whose story it is and the culture within which the story is embedded. Different

cultures offer different narrative opportunities and constraints. As Rosenwald (1992) puts it, "when people tell life stories, they do so in accordance with the models of intelligibility specific to the culture" (p. 265). Not all stories are tellable in all contexts. For example, Heilbrun (1988) has remarked that many women have been "deprived of the narratives, or the texts, plots, or examples, by which they might assume power over—take control over—their lives" (p. 17). It is clear that life stories echo gender and class constructions in society and reflect, in one way or another, prevailing patterns of hegemony in the economic, political, and cultural contexts wherein human lives are situated (Rosenwald & Ochberg, 1992). Power elites in societies privilege certain life stories over others, and therefore a number of narrative researchers and clinicians seek to give voice and expression to forms of life narrative that have been traditionally suppressed or marginalized (Franz & Stewart, 1994; Gergen & Gergen, 1993; Singer, 1997; White & Epston, 1990).

4. *People tailor their life stories for particular audiences.* A simple but profound truth about stories is that *they are told.* Underscoring the discursive and performative aspects of life storytelling, many scholars argue that any narrative expression of the self cannot be understood outside the context of its assumed listener or audience, with respect to which the story is designed to make a point or produce a desired effect (Alasuutari, 1997; Hermans, 1996; Josselson, 1995a). Audiences are both social and intrapsychic. Internalized life stories may be constructed with certain *private audiences* in mind (Baldwin & Holmes, 1987), such as the internalized representation of a spouse, best friend, religious leader, business colleague, or even God.

5. *A person tells many stories, and those stories change over time.* Narrative psychologists tend to emphasize the multiplicity, contextuality, and malleability of the stories people tell about their lives. For a particular individual at a given point in time, no single story organizes the many disparate elements of a self-conception, and over time the many stories that a person may tell are likely to change substantially as a function of development and changing life circumstances. Narrative theorists differ with respect to the relative emphasis they place on life-story stability versus change. Postmodernists like Gergen (1992) view life narratives as multiple and fleeting, whereas McAdams (1993) tends to emphasize the extent to which a person's multiple smaller stories can get organized into a unifying larger one that helps to provide a life with a sense of overall purpose and unity. Nonetheless, even McAdams leaves considerable room for multiplicity in life stories and views stories as transforming themselves significantly over time and across discursive situations. As such, life stories are considerably less stable and considerably more contingent than, say, personality traits (McAdams, 1996b). Indeed, it is in large part for their ability to capture the contingency and contextuality of human experience that life stories are an indispensable window through which to study human individuality.

6. *Some stories are better than others.* A life story always suggests a moral perspective, in that human characters are intentional, moral agents whose actions can always be construed from the standpoint of what is "good" and what is "bad" (MacIntyre, 1981; Taylor, 1989). Furthermore, stories themselves can be evaluated as relatively good or bad from a psychological standpoint, though these evaluations also suggest moral perspectives and reflect the values and norms of the society within which a story is evaluated (McAdams, 1993). Narrative therapists help clients transform their faulty life narratives into new stories that affirm growth, health, and adaptation (White & Epston, 1990). From this effort alone, it is clear that some stories work better than others for some people at some times. McAdams (1993) has suggested that criteria for a "good" life story in modern societies include coherence, openness, credibility, differentiation, reconciliation, and generative integration. For McAdams, psychosocial maturity in the adult years involves a developmental move toward better and better life-narrative form. In a similar vein, Rosenwald (1992) speaks of "satisfactory" life stories that "help to advance living action" (p. 284)

7. *The sharing of stories builds intimacy and community.* The root meaning of "intimacy" is the sharing of one's inner self with another (McAdams, 1989). If the self is storied, then interpersonal intimacy must entail a good deal of reciprocal storytelling. In emphasizing the dialogical nature of life narrative and the sense in which stories exist to be told or performed in the presence of others (e.g., the audience), narrative psychologists have been especially sensitive to the community-affirming functions of life narrative (Franz & Stewart, 1994; Hermans, 1996; Maruna, 1997). Furthermore, narrative research can be viewed as a vehicle for promoting social

integration and understanding between people. Hearing or seeing another's story may stretch one's powers of empathy. Josselson (1995b) writes that certain forms of narrative research become "a process of overcoming distance rather than creating it, moving what was Other, through our understanding of their independent selfhood and experience, into relation with us" (p. 31).

NARRATIVE RESEARCH: PROBLEMS AND POSSIBILITIES

Research Traditions

Contemporary research on personal narratives and life stories draws from at least four different research traditions in the social sciences: thematic analysis, psychobiography, life history studies, and hermeneutics. Each of the four favors particular methods for collecting and interpreting life-narrative data, and each is premised on a set of epistemological assumptions that determine what the primary aims of narrative inquiry should be. Of the four, only the tradition of thematic analysis has historically enjoyed a favorable status in mainstream, empirically based personality psychology. Nonetheless, influences from all four traditions can be detected in the current ferment of narrative studies within personality psychology and in related fields.

The term "thematic analysis" is used to refer to a wide range of empirical approaches that endeavor to develop, validate, and utilize objective coding schemes for analyzing the structure and content of narratives (e.g., Smith, 1992). These approaches range from coding the structure of personal narratives for the degree of integrative complexity (deVries & Lehman, 1996) to coding TAT stories for the needs for achievement, power, and intimacy. Because these methods usually aim to reduce qualitative data to quantitative scores, they are ready-made for testing hypotheses in nomothetic studies. Researchers who employ these methods typically conform to the conventions of objective scientific inquiry in psychology. Therefore, they endeavor to define coding categories with great precision, to attain high levels of intercoder reliability, and to minimize any sources of interpretive bias. Researchers who employ thematic analysis typically operate out of a post-positivist scientific paradigm (Guba & Lincoln, 1994). They view narrative accounts as approximations of a psychological or social reality that itself cannot be directly observed but that exists nevertheless as an objective phenomenon independent of the subjective viewer.

A second tradition of inquiry that has had some influence on contemporary narrative research is "psychobiography" (Elms, 1994; Runyan, 1982). McAdams (1988) defines psychobiography as the "systematic use of psychological (especially personality) theory to transform a life into a coherent and illuminating story" (p. 2). In psychobiography, the life to be transformed is usually that of a famous, enigmatic, or paradigmatic figure, and the storied rendering of the life is communicated to the public in written form. Thus, while researchers who employ thematic analysis typically collect data in the form of (usually first-person) narrative accounts, psychobiographers seek to organize data into (third-person) explanatory narratives. Most psychobiographies have traditionally adopted some variation on a psychoanalytic frame to interpret their subjects' lives. As such, the kinds of explanatory stories psychobiographers have typically written explain a resultant personality pattern or life outcome in terms of the psychodynamics of early family life. In that they almost always focus on a single subject, psychobiographies take the form of case studies. In recent years, personality psychologists have shown an increasing interest in the application of personality theory to the single case (McAdams & West, 1997). Recent psychobiographical efforts have moved beyond psychoanalytic theories to employ trait and motive theories, Tomkins' script theory, and McAdams' life-story model of identity to the interpretation of the single life (Carlson, 1988; de St. Aubin, 1998; Nasby & Read, 1997; Winter & Carlson, 1988). These efforts typically blend Bruner's paradigmatic and narrative modes of exposition, as authors reconstruct life histories and make causal claims in their efforts to produce a convincing verbal text that accounts for a single life in toto.

Going back to the 1930s, the collection of "life histories" was a well-established and thriving methodology in European psychology and in the disciplines of sociology and anthropology. Working in Vienna, Buhler (1933) and Frenkel (1936) collected written life histories in order to chart general developmental principles common to many disparate lives. In sociology, the symbolic-interactionist school relied heavily on life-historical investigations of such phenomena as "deviance" (Shaw, 1930). In the early years, life histories were typically viewed as more-or-less veridical accounts of the past that charted "the growth of a person in a cultural milieu" (Dollard, 1935, p. 3). After World War II, researchers developed methods for formalizing qualitative analysis of life histories (Denzin & Lincoln, 1994). Especially influential in this regard was the development of "grounded theory" methodology (Glaser & Strauss, 1967), a procedure through which the social scientist systematically reads successive autobiographical texts, categorizing and recategorizing narrative content in a continuously evolving effort to arrive at an inductive portrait of a given social phenomenon. Grounded theory methodology generates new theory that is "grounded" in the data, and as such it has proven to be a useful technique for the generation of theory in both sociology (Bertaux, 1981) and psychology (Merriam, 1980).

Finally, I gather together under the rubric of "hermeneutics" a wide and expanding range of intellectual agendas in the social sciences and humanities that concern themselves with the vexing issues of truth, meaning, power, legitimacy, and the relation between subject and object in the interpretation of storied texts. Informed by structuralist and poststructuralist philosophy, literary deconstructionism, feminist epistemologies, critical Marxist theories, cultural postmodernism, and a number of other late 20th-century intellectual strands, various hermeneutical approaches to narrative studies emphasize some or all of the following:

1. The primacy of the story over the storyteller (what the author "meant" is probably irrelevant, for what really matters is the text itself).
2. Local rather than universal truths (all texts are particular; all interpretations are specific to particular texts, contingent on local contexts).
3. The inseparability of subject and object (textual knowledge is subjective; observer and observed are in a dialectical relationship).
4. The indeterminacy of language and meaning (texts are made of symbols, which themselves have no ultimate meanings but instead refer to other (ambiguous) symbols).
5. The primacy of subjective construals over the (myth of) objective reality (when it comes to social life, there is no meaningful objective reality, only social constructions).
6. Contextuality and contingency in social life (lives, like texts, are deeply embedded in contexts; human agency is diminished).
7. The subjugating influence of power hierarchies and social inequalities in the construction of life narratives (economic and political forces shape texts and lives; gender, race, and social class can be strong hegemonic forces).

Hermeneutical perspectives on personal narratives and life stories adopt critical theory and radical constructivist paradigms of inquiry (Guba & Lincoln, 1994). As such, hermeneutical perspectives strike many empirically minded personality psychologists as strange and vaguely threatening. Nonetheless, there is evidence that some of these ideas may be slowly making their way into personality psychology and the scientific study of lives. Writing from a hermeneutical perspective, Josselson (1995a) argues that empirically minded psychologists need to cultivate "narrative understanding":

> Narrative understanding is based on philosophical hermeneutics, a tradition regnant in Europe but only recently penetrating American intellectual consciousness. Within this epistemology, there is only the text (communicated in language), which is itself about a text, and dialogue within and among these texts. There is no prior place to stand to make truth claims: there are only interpretations made from a particular historical and value-implicated stance. The "hermeneutic circle" describes a process in which understanding requires references to all prior understandings such that knowledge accrues in a circular, dialectical fashion. No knowledge can be independent of context or interpreter. The enterprise of science then becomes conversation from which emerge consensual ideas that constitute ways of perceiving and interpreting future texts. (p. 330)

On the contemporary scene, the traditions of hermeneutics and thematic analysis seem to define two opposite poles on an epistemological continuum for the narrative study of lives. The radical constructivist paradigm for hermeneutics, for example, holds no faith in the objective reality that postpositivists (representing the other end of the continuum) believe must lie behind the narrative approximations to which they apply thematic coding schemes. From the standpoint of traditional thematic analysis, therefore, something as innocent and fundamental as interrater reliability makes no sense in a hermeneutical context, for all knowledge in the hermeneutical tradition comes from particular and unrepeatable subject–object interchanges (Guba & Lincoln, 1994). Although personality psychology continues to find most compatible the postpositivist perspective undergirding research in thematic analysis, future epistemological debates may nonetheless be in the offing. In a thoughtful critique, Smith (1994) addresses some key questions raised by hermeneutical, postmodern views of selfhood (e.g., Gergen, 1992) and tries to stake out a middle ground that accommodates some of the main themes of the hermeneutical tradition without giving up a commitment to science as an "evidential, public, self-critical social enterprise that has successfully sought progressively more adequate and comprehensive understandings of the phenomena in its domain" (p. 408). In a similar vein, McAdams, Diamond, de St. Aubin, and Mansfield (1997) have argued for a position of "psychosocial constructionism" in the narrative study of lives. These researchers adopt some of the standard methods of thematic analysis for coding life stories, but rather than view life stories as approximations of an objective but unknowable reality, they conceive of them as ever-changing constructions whose reality is socially negotiated. Nonetheless, as psychosocial constructions, life stories have enough substantive integrity to sustain systematic (and reliable) scrutiny within a social-scientific culture of shared meanings.

Personality Coherence

A number of researchers have employed personal narratives to demonstrate consistency and coherence in personality. They have argued that narrative accounts of personally significant events illuminate subtle patterns and organizational themes in personality that cannot typically be discerned from the vantage points of self-report inventories, behavioral observations, and other traditional methods of personality measurement (Singer & Salovey, 1993). For example, Thorne (1995a) employed narrative methods to reveal the juxtaposition of conflicting interpersonal scripts in autobiographical memory. Thorne showed how what looks to be a contradiction at the level of traits—high extraversion and high interpersonal avoidance—represents a coherent pattern of interpersonal orientations as revealed in narratives of memorable encounters. In a similar vein, Woike (1995) showed that extrinsic motives (obtained from self-report questionnaires) correlate with motive-related themes in narrative accounts of routine autobiographical events, whereas implicit motives (obtained from fantasy-based measures, such as the TAT) correlate with motive-related themes in accounts of highly memorable and affectively charged autobiographical events. Both Thorne and Woike, then, use personal narratives to show that superficial discordance or inconsistency in personality functioning can sometimes signal a coherent patterning of individuality below the surface.

A common strategy for narrative research on personality coherence involves (1) collecting detailed written or verbal autobiographical accounts of especially significant life episodes, (2) coding the narratives for psychologically meaningful themes, and (3) linking the individual differences in content or structure scores to other aspects of personality functioning that theory suggests should be thematically related. McAdams and his colleagues have done a number of studies showing that the themes of agency and communion as revealed in life-story events are significantly correlated with other personality variables. For example, agentic and communal themes in accounts of peak experiences, important learning experiences, important friendship episodes, life-story turning points, significant religious or spiritual experiences, and other salient life-story scenes are positively correlated with power and intimacy motivation, respectively, as assessed in TAT stories and personal strivings (McAdams, 1982; McAdams, Booth, & Selvik, 1981; McAdams, Hoffman, Mansfield, & Day, 1996). Turning to the structural qualities of personal narratives, McAdams and his colleagues have shown that higher levels of ego development (Loevinger, 1976), as assessed on a sentence-completion test, predict greater levels of life-story complexity, as indexed in the number of different generic plots employed in the narrative (McAdams, 1985) and in the extent to which the narrative accommodates dramatic changes in the protagonist's ideological outlooks (McAdams et al., 1981).

Personality coherence is often displayed at the level of goals and life tasks. Singer (1990) collected narrative accounts of memories related to each of 15 goals, based on Murray's (1938) needs. Participants' ratings of their affective responses to each memory were positively associated with the relevance of the memories to goal attainment. Moffitt and Singer (1994) collected narrative accounts of "self-defining memories" (memories of events that have been instrumental in shaping one's self-conception) and personal strivings. College students who recalled more memories relevant to the attainment of their strivings expressed greater levels of positive affect about their memories. In addition, participants who reported high numbers of avoidance strivings also recalled memories with fewer positive-affect themes. Research on narrative accounts of earliest memories has also documented linkages among goals, memories, and the affective responses people report to goals and memories (e.g., Acklin, Sauer, Alexander, & Dugoni, 1989).

In a methodologically innovative case analysis, Demorest and Siegel (1996) assessed the extent to which individuals have characteristic ways of looking at the world that are revealed both in their life stories and in their professional work. Focusing on the autobiographical and scientific writings of B. F. Skinner, the researchers identified common scripts that link Skinner's self-conception and his approach to scientific research. A blind matching task indicated that the scripts derived from Skinner's scientific work and personal life were more similar than random pairs of scripts, suggesting a coherence in imagery across different domains in a person's life. A similar kind of cross-domain coherence is demonstrated in de St. Aubin's (1996) study of the relation between personal ideology and the emotional quality of personal narratives among 64 adults. Consistent with hypotheses drawn from Tomkins' script theory, de St. Aubin found that adults with a normative ideological perspective (emphasizing rules and norms) tend to narrate autobiographical scenes high in anger, whereas adults with a humanistic ideological perspective (emphasizing individual growth) highlight scenes of joy, distress, fear, and shame. In one of the first longitudinal examinations of life narrative accounts, Thorne, Cutting, and Skaw (in press) collected stories of relationship memories from young adults on two occasions, separated by about six months. The analysis indicated moderate thematic consistency across the two sets of memories. The authors argue that relationship memories tend to illustrate enduring concerns of personality more so than they signal dramatic transformations of outlook.

Personality Change

Narrative theories of personality suggest that life stories are likely to change substantially over time. To date, however, virtually no researchers have undertaken longitudinal studies of life narrative to document patterns of change (for an exception, see Thorne et al., in press). In recent years, however, personality researchers have begun to employ life-narrative methods to explore personality change in general. Two approaches have been used. First, researchers have begun to examine individuals' personal accounts of change to understand better how it is that people believe they have changed over time. Second, researchers have coded personal narratives for developmental themes to test hypotheses about personality change proposed in developmental theories.

Heatherton and Nichols (1994) asked college students to write narrative accounts of successful and failed efforts to change their lives. Stories reporting successful life changes were more likely, compared to those describing failures, to underscore intense emotional experiences, external threats, and pivotal events that often culminated in a crystallization of discontent (see also Baumeister, 1994b). In addition, the successful change stories showed more themes of social support and a sense that life changes were integrated into the self as a whole. By contrast, unsuccessful efforts to change were often described as lapses in will power and failures to break away from the status quo.

Failure in will power is an important theme in Singer's (1997) intensive study of life stories of addiction. Singer's evocative case studies highlight the problems that alcoholics and drug addicts experience in developing coherent life stories that affirm personal agency and interpersonal communion. Maruna (1997) finds a happier story, however, in his analysis of the life narratives created by criminals who eventually desist from crime. Analyzing the published autobiographies of 20 ex-convicts, Maruna identified a prototypical "reform narrative" with which virtually all of the accounts shared remarkable similarities. It is a story in which early scenes of passive victimization lead to a delinquent quest and repeated scenes of "bottoming out." The negative cycle is not broken until the protagonist experiences a "second chance" for agency and/or communion, often through the intervention of a good friend or potential lover. The final life-story chapters consolidate reform through the protagonist's generative efforts to "give something back" to the world as he endeavors to help other actual or would-be criminals develop their own reform stories. Both

Singer and Maruna emphasize the healing power of articulating a coherent life story that emplots the thematic lines of agency and communion while articulating a vision of generativity that expands the storyteller's breadth of care and extends the story into the anticipated future with hope and optimism.

Personal narratives have proven useful for testing developmental hypotheses about personality change among children (Rogers, Brown, & Tappan, 1994), adolescents (Pratt, Arnold, & Hilbers, in press), and adults. Stewart, Franz, and Layton (1988) and Peterson and Stewart (1990) found support for Erikson's (1950) stage model in adulthood by documenting a move from preoccupations with identity in adolescence to preoccupations with intimacy and generativity in middle adulthood in an intensive analysis of autobiographical narratives written by the feminist author Vera Brittain over the course of her life. Thorne (1995b) coded the narrative accounts of childhood and adolescence told by young adults for "developmental truths." Supporting predictions from a number of developmental theories, memories of encounters with parents and about wanting help prevailed in childhood, whereas memories of encounters with close friends and about wanting intimacy prevailed by mid-adolescence. Memories about wanting to help others were sparse in this young-adult sample but, like intimacy themes, increased with age. Moving to developmental issues in middle adulthood, Hermans and Oles (in press) focused on reports of midlife crisis in men. Personal narratives told by men who scored high on a midlife crisis scale showed lower levels of self-enhancement and positive affect and higher levels of negative affect, compared to men who scored low on the midlife crisis scale. The authors interpreted the results as indicating a convergence between a particular kind of life narrative form and particular psychosocial problems that may arise in the midlife years.

Types of Stories

Since the time of Aristotle, scholars have speculated about the extent to which the world of stories might be reduced to a finite number of basic forms. Aristotle distinguished among tragedy, comedy, romance, and satire/irony—a distinction that has been translated into mythic archetypes by Frye (1957) and into psychological theorizing and research about life stories by McAdams (1985), K. Murray (1989), and Crewe (1997). Focusing on the protagonist's developmental movement, Gergen and Gergen (1986) distinguish among stability, progressive, and regressive life narratives. Along with many other authors, they also identify Campbell's (1949) monomyth of the heroic quest as an extremely common narrative form in Western societies, especially for the construction of men's identities. Speaking of gender, Gergen and Gergen (1993) suggest that women's life stories are likely to be less linear and more multiple, ambivalent, recursive, and embodied, compared to men's. Other authors have suggested that the structures of women's stories, as well as those constructed by other disadvantaged groups, remain largely a mystery to psychologists, in that these stories have often been silenced or trivialized in patriarchal societies (Heilbrun, 1988; Stewart, 1994).

Whereas some authors have proposed a priori taxonomies of narrative forms, others have worked from the bottom up by delineating the patterns they observe in life narrative research. And whereas some researchers have examined life stories writ large, others have focused on more circumscribed narrative domains, such as stories of work (Mishler, 1992; Ochberg, 1988) or parenting (Pratt et al., in press). For example, Modell (1992) identified common themes and narrative strategies in the stories told by birthparents about why they gave their children up for adoption; Walkover (1992) found that couples poised on the edge of parenthood imagined the future in overwrought and highly idealized ways, suggesting a subtext of the perfectibility of childhood; Linn (1997) found common themes in Israeli soldiers' narrations of moral resistance; Harding (1992) traced biblical motifs from the ancient stories of Abraham, Job, and Christ through the life story of a contemporary Christian preacher; Gregg (1996) identified a hybrid life narrative that mixes themes of modernity and traditional Islamic faith among contemporary young Moroccans; and Linde (1990) observed that many of her respondents routinely borrowed images and themes from popular psychology in the narrative construction of their lives.

Drawing on ideas from Tomkins' script theory and Colby and Damon's (1992) work on the lives of moral exemplars, McAdams et al. (1997) examined lengthy life-narrative accounts of 40 highly generative adults and 30 matched adults scoring low on external measures of generativity. The highly generative adults were more likely to reconstruct the past and anticipate the future as a variation on a prototypical "commitment story" in which the protagonist (1) enjoys an early family blessing or advantaged, (2) is sensitized to others' suffering at an early age, (3) is guided by a clear and compelling personal ideology that remains stable over time, (4) transforms or redeems bad scenes into good outcomes, and (5) sets goals for the future to benefit society and the next generation. The authors argue that a commitment story sustains and reinforces the modern adult's efforts to contribute in positive ways to the next generation. Although many different life stories may be constructed by highly generative people, the adult who works hard to guide and foster the next generation may make sense of his or her strong commitment in terms of an internalized narrative that suggests that he or she has been "called" or summoned to do good things for others, that such a calling is deeply rooted in childhood, reinforced by a precocious sensitivity to the suffering of others, and bolstered by a clear and convincing ideology that remains steadfast over time. Perceiving one's life in terms of redemption sequences (bad scenes give way to good outcomes), furthermore, provides the hope that hard work today will yield positive dividends for the future, a hope that may sustain generative efforts as private as raising one's child and as public as committing oneself to the advancement of one's own society. Stories in literature, myth, and folklore that celebrate generativity often display the kinds of themes identified as part of the commitment story (McAdams, 1993).

Projecting into the future, one might imagine a wide range of research programs focused on delineating the particular types of life narrative forms associated with particular psychological and social phenomena. Certain kinds of life stories, for example, may be associated with certain age groups and historical cohorts, representatives of certain socioeconomic strata and niches, certain professions, religious and political groups, subcultures, and even personality types defined by a characteristic trait or personal concern. Should this kind of research proliferate in the future, psychologists and other social scientists would begin to catalogue the many prevalent forms of identity constructed by contemporary adults within a given society and across cultures.

CONCLUSION

Although the story is an ancient form of human expression, personality psychologists have only recently focused their attention on it as a serious method for investigation and a powerful metaphor for understanding human lives. The study of personal narratives and life stories is becoming a significant force in the discipline of personality psychology. Increasingly, researchers are employing narrative methodologies that ask participants to describe important personal scenes in their lives and to tell stories about work and careers, friendship and love, parenting, beliefs and values, personal commitments, and many other aspects of human living that hold meaning and significance for individuals. Furthermore, a new generation of personality theories has emerged in which scenes, scripts, and life stories are placed at the center of human individuality. Narrative approaches to the study of lives converge on a set of integrative conceptual themes such as the idea that selfhood itself is storied, that life stories integrate disparate experience, that life stories are cultural texts, that people construct different stories for different internal and external audiences, that some stories work better than do others, and that sharing stories builds intimacy and community between people as it also consolidates identity for individuals and groups.

The study of personal narratives and life stories raises a host of thorny epistemological issues concerning the role of authorship and agency in the construction of psychosocial texts, the multiplicity of textual meanings and interpretations, the relation between the investigator (audience) and the participant (storyteller), and the different senses in which a story or a story's interpretation can be said to be "true." Disagreements among different researchers and different traditions of inquiry concerning these issues are likely to continue into the foreseeable future. Therefore, narrative research will continue to assume a wide variety of forms spread across many different disciplines. Within personality psychology, systematic research on personal narratives and life stories has begun to flourish in the last few years. Personality researchers have begun to make progress in narrative studies of personality coherence, personality change, and the identification of life-story types. As more personality, social, and developmental psychologists become familiar with emerging methods and theories in narrative psychology, narrative research should expand into more and more domains.

In the year 1900, Sigmund Freud published what is arguably the most famous book every written on the interpretation of personal narratives. In *The Interpretation of Dreams,* Freud argued that dreams stories are the royal road to the unconscious. Freud may have promised too much, and he may have placed too much faith on but one kind of story that people tell. But he had it right when he surmised that stories hold psychological truth. Now, at the beginning of the 21st century, personality psychologists appear poised to explore systematically the wide range of stories, about themselves and others, that people create, tell, and enact. The personal narrative may not be the only royal road to understanding human individuality, but it is still a "road less traveled" until now, and one that promises to lead psychologists on a rewarding journey.

ACKNOWLEDGMENTS

I would like to thank Hubert Hermans, Ruthellen Josselson, Avril Thorne, Shadd Maruna, and the editors of this volume for their helpful suggestions concerning an earlier draft of this chapter. Preparation of the chapter was greatly aided by grants from The Spencer Foundation and the Foley Family Foundation.

REFERENCES

Acklin, M. W., Sauer, A., Alexander, G., & Dugoni, B. (1989). Predicting depression using earliest childhood memories. *Journal of Personality Assessment, 53,* 51–59.

Adler, A. (1927). *The practice and theory of individual psychology.* New York: Harcourt Brace World.

Alasuutari, P. (1997). The discursive construction of personality. In A. Lieblich & R. Josselson (Eds.), *The narrative study of lives* (Vol. 5, pp. 1–20). Thousand Oaks, CA: Sage.

Applebee, A. N. (1978). *The child's concept of story.* Chicago: University of Chicago Press.

Bakan, D. (1966). *The duality of human existence: Isolation and communion in Western man.* Boston: Beacon Press.

Bakhtin, M. (1973). *Problems of Dostoyevsky's poetics* (2nd ed.). Ann Arbor, MI: Ardis.

Baldwin, M. W., & Holmes, G. (1987). Salient private audiences and awareness of the self. *Journal of Personality and Social Psychology, 53,* 1087–1098.

Barresi, J., & Juckes, T. J. (1997). Personology and the narrative interpretation of lives. *Journal of Personality, 65,* 693–719.

Baumeister, R. F. (1994a). Introduction to symposium: Samples made of stories. *Personality and Social Psychology Bulletin, 20,* 649.

Baumeister, R. F. (1994b). The crystallization of discontent in the process of major life change. In T. F. Heatherton and J. L. Weinberger (Eds.), *Can personality change?* (pp. 281–298). Washington, DC: American Psychological Association Press.

Bertraux, D. (Ed.). (1981). *Biography and society.* Beverly Hills, CA: Sage.

Breger, L. (1974). *From instinct to identity: The development of personality.* Englewood Cliffs, NJ: Prentice Hall.

Brewer, W. F., & Lichtenstein, E. H. (1982). Stories are to entertain: A structural–affect theory of stories. *Journal of Pragmatics, 6,* 473–486.

Bruner, J. S. (1986). *Actual minds, possible worlds.* Cambridge, MA: Harvard University Press.

Bruner, J. S. (1990). *Acts of meaning.* Cambridge, MA: Harvard University Press.

Bühler, C. (1933). *Der menschliche lebenslauf als psychologisches problem.* Leipzig: S. Hirzel Verlag.

Campbell, J. (1949). *The hero with a thousand faces.* New York: Bollingen Foundation.

Carlson, R. (1981). Studies in script theory: 1. Adult analogs of a childhood nuclear scene. *Journal of Personality and Social Psychology, 40,* 501–510.

Carlson, R. (1988). Exemplary lives: The uses of psychobiography for theory development. *Journal of Personality, 56,* 105–138.

Casey, K. (1996). The new narrative research in education. In M. W. Apple (Ed.), *Review of research in education* (Vol. 21, pp. 211–253). Washington, DC: American Educational Research Association.

Cohler, B. J. (1982). Personal narrative and the life course. In P. Baltes & O. G. Brim, Jr. (Eds.), *Life span development and behavior* (Vol. 4, pp. 205–241). New York: Academic Press.

Colby, A., & Damon, W. (1992). *Some do care: Contemporary lives of moral commitment.* New York: Free Press.

Crewe, N. M. (1997). Life stories of people with long-term spinal cord injury. *Rehabilitation Counseling Bulletin, 41,* 26–42.

Demorest, A. P., & Siegel, P. F. (1996). Personal influences on professional work: An empirical case study of B. F. Skinner. *Journal of Personality, 64,* 243–261.

Denzin, N. K., & Lincoln, Y. S. (1994). Introduction: Entering the field of qualitative research. In N. K. Denzin & Y. S. Lincoln (Eds.), *Handbook of qualitative research* (pp. 1–17). Thousand Oaks, CA: Sage.

de St. Aubin, E. (1996). Personal ideology polarity: Its emotional foundation and its manifestation in individual value systems, religiosity, political orientation, and assumptions concerning human nature. *Journal of Personality and Social Psychology, 71,* 152–165.

de St. Aubin, E. (1998). Truth against the world: A psychobiographical exploration of generativity in the life of Frank Lloyd Wright. In D. P. McAdams & E. de St. Aubin (Eds.), *Generativity and adult develop-*

ment: How and why we care for the next generation (pp. 391–428). Washington, DC: American Psychological Association.

de Vries, B., & Lehman, A. J. (1996). The complexity of personal narratives. In J. E. Birren, G. M. Kenyon, J. E. Ruth, J. J. F. Schroots, & T. Svensson (Eds.), *Aging and biography: Explorations in adult development* (pp. 149–166). New York: Springer.

Dollard, J. (1935). *Criteria for the life history.* New Haven, CT: Yale University Press.

Elms, A. C. (1994). *Uncovering lives: The uneasy alliance of biography and psychology.* New York: Oxford University Press.

Engel, S. (1995). *The stories that children tell.* San Francisco: Freeman.

Epstein, S. (1994). Integration of the cognitive and psychodynamic unconscious. *American Psychologist, 49,* 709–724.

Erikson, E. H. (1950). *Childhood and society.* New York: Norton.

Erikson, E. H. (1958). *Young man Luther: A study in psychoanalysis and history.* New York: Norton.

Feldman, C. F., Bruner, J. S., Renderer, B., & Spitzer, S. (1990). Narrative comprehension. In B. K. Britton & A. D. Pellegini (Eds.), *Narrative thought and narrative language* (pp. 1–79). Hillsdale, NJ: Erlbaum.

Franz, C., & Stewart, A. J. (Eds.). (1994). *Women creating lives: Identities, resilience, and resistance.* Boulder, CO: Westview Press.

Frenkel, E. (1936). Studies in biographical psychology. *Character and Personality, 5,* 1–35.

Freud, S. (1953). *The interpretation of dreams.* In J. Strachey (Ed.), *The standard edition of the complete psychological works of Sigmund Freud* (Vols. 4–5). London: Hogarth Press (Original work published 1900)

Frye, N. (1957). *The anatomy of criticism.* Princeton, NJ: Princeton University Press.

Funkenstein, A. (1993). The incomprehensible catastrophe: Memory and narrative. In R. Josselson & A. Lieblich (Eds.), *The narrative study of lives* (Vol. 1, pp. 21–29). Thousand Oaks, CA: Sage.

Gergen, K. J. (1992). *The saturated self: Dilemmas of identity in contemporary life.* New York: Basic Books.

Gergen, K. J., & Gergen M. M. (1986). Narrative form and the construction of psychological science. In T. R. Sarbin (Ed.), *Narrative psychology* (pp. 22–44). New York: Praeger.

Gergen, M. M., & Gergen, K. J. (1993). Narratives of the gendered body in popular autobiography. In R. Josselson & A. Lieblich (Eds.), *The narrative study of lives* (Vol. 1, pp. 191–218). Thousand Oaks, CA: Sage.

Giddens, A. (1991). *Modernity and self-identity: Self and society in the late modern age.* Stanford, CA: Stanford University Press.

Glaser, B. G., & Strauss, A. L. (1967). *The discovery of grounded theory.* Chicago: Aldine.

Gregg, G. (1991). *Self-representation: Life narrative studies in identity and ideology.* New York: Greenwood Press.

Gregg, G. (1996). Themes of authority in life-histories of young Moroccans. In S. Miller & R. Bourgia (Eds.), *Representations of power in Morocco.* Cambridge, MA: Harvard University Press.

Guba, E. G., & Lincoln, Y. S. (1994). Competing paradigms in qualitative research. In N. K. Denzin & Y. S. Lincoln (Eds.), *Handbook of qualitative research* (pp. 105–117). Thousand Oaks, CA: Sage.

Harding, S. (1992). The afterlife of stories: Genesis of a man of God. In G. Rosenwald & R. L. Ochberg (Eds.), *Storied lives: The cultural politics of self-understanding* (pp. 60–75). New Haven, CT: Yale University Press.

Hart, D. (1988). The adolescent self-concept in social context. In D. K. Lapsley & F. C. Powers (Eds.), *Self, ego, and identity: Integrative approaches* (pp. 71–90). New York: Springer-Verlag.

Harter, S. (1983). Developmental perspectives on the self-system. In P. H. Mussen (Ed.), *Handbook of child psychology: Vol 4. Socialization, personality, and social development* (pp. 275–386). New York: Wiley.

Heatherton, T. F., & Nichols, P. A. (1994). Personal accounts of successful versus failed attempts at life change. *Personality and Social Psychology Bulletin, 20,* 664–675.

Heilbrun, C. G. (1988). *Writing a woman's life.* New York: Norton.

Hermans, H. J. M. (1988). On the integration of nomothetic and idiographic research methods in the study of personal meaning. *Journal of Personality, 56,* 785–812.

Hermans, H. J. M. (1996). Voicing the self: From information processing to dialogical interchange. *Psychological Bulletin, 119,* 31–50.

Hermans, H. J. M., & Kempen, H. J. G. (1993). *The dialogical self: Meaning as movement.* New York: Academic Press.

Hermans, H. J. M., Kempen, H. J. G., & van Loon, R. J. P. (1992). The dialogical self: Beyond individualism and rationalism. *American Psychologist, 47,* 23–33.

Hermans, H. J. M., & Oles, P. K. (in press). Midlife crisis in men: Affective organization of personal meanings. *Human Relations.*

Hermans, H. J. M., Rijks, T. I., & Kempen, H. J. G. (1993). Imaginal dialogues in the self: Theory and method. *Journal of Personality, 61,* 207–236.

Howard, G. S. (1991). Culture tales: A narrative approach to thinking, cross-cultural psychology, and psychotherapy. *American Psychologist, 46,* 187–197.

Izard, C. E. (1977). *Human emotions.* New York: Plenum Press.

James, W. (1963). *Psychology.* Greenwich, CT: Fawcett. (Original work published 1892)

Josselson, R. (1995a). Narrative and psychological understanding. *Psychiatry, 58,* 330–343.

Josselson, R. (1995b). Imagining the real: Empathy, narrative, and the dialogical self. In R. Josselson & A. Lieblich (Eds.), *The narrative study of lives* (Vol. 3, pp. 27–44). Thousand Oaks, CA: Sage.

Josselson, R., & Lieblich, A. (Eds.). (1993). *The narrative study of lives* (Vol. 1). Thousand Oaks, CA: Sage.

Jung, C. G. (1969). The archetypes and the collective unconscious. In *The collected works of C. G. Jung* (Vol. 9). Princeton, NJ: Princeton University Press. (Original work published 1936)

Kermode, F. (1967). *The sense of an ending*. New York: Oxford University Press.

Knowles, E. S., & Sibicky, M. E. (1990). Continuity and diversity in the stream of selves: Metaphorical resolutions of William James's one-in-many-selves paradox. *Personality and Social Psychology Bulletin, 16,* 676–687.

Kotre, J. (1995). *White gloves: How we create ourselves through memory*. New York: Free Press.

Labouvie-Vief, G. (1990). Wisdom as integrated thought: Historical and developmental perspectives. In R. J. Sternberg (Ed.), *Wisdom: Its nature, origins, and development* (pp. 52–83). Cambridge, UK: Cambridge University Press.

Landau, M. (1986). Trespassing in scientific narrative: Grafton Elliot Smith and the Temple of Doom. In T. Sarbin (Ed.), *Narrative psychology: The storied nature of human conduct* (pp. 45–64). New York: Praeger.

Lazarus, R. S., & Lazarus, B. N. (1994). *Passion and reason: Making sense of our emotions*. New York: Oxford University Press.

Lifton, R. J. (1993). *The protean self.* New York: Basic Books.

Linde, C. (1990). *Life stories: The creation of coherence* (Monograph No. IRL90–0001). Palo Alto, CA: Institute for Research in Learning.

Linn, R. (1997). Soldiers' narratives of selective moral resistance: A separate position of the connected self? In A. Lieblich & R. Josselson (Eds.), *The narrative study of lives* (Vol. 5, pp. 94–112). Thousand Oaks, CA: Sage.

Loevinger, J. (1976). *Ego development*. San Francisco: Jossey-Bass.

Lucariello, J. (1990). Canonicality and consciousness in child narrative. In B. K. Britton & A. D. Pellegrini (Eds.), *Narrative thought and narrative language* (pp. 131–149). Hillsdale, NJ: Erlbaum.

MacIntyre, A. (1981). *After virtue*. Notre Dame, IN: University of Notre Dame Press.

Main, M., Kaplan, N., & Cassidy, J. (1985). Security in infancy, childhood, and adulthood: A move to the level of representation. *Monographs of the Society for Research in Child Development, 50*(1 & 2), 66–104.

Mancuso, J. C. (1986). The acquisition and use of narrative grammar structure. In T. Sarbin (Ed.), *Narrative psychology: The storied nature of human conduct* (pp. 91–110). New York: Praeger.

Mandler, J. M. (1984). *Stories, scripts, and scenes: Aspects of schema theory*. Hillsdale, NJ: Erlbaum.

Maruna, S. (1997). Going straight: Desistance from crime and life narratives of reform. In A. Lieblich and R. Josselson (Eds.), *The narrative study of lives* (Vol. 5, pp. 59–93). Thousand Oaks, CA: Sage.

McAdams, D. P. (1982). Experiences of intimacy and power: Relationships between social motives and autobiographical memory. *Journal of Personality and Social Psychology, 42,* 292–302.

McAdams, D. P. (1985). *Power, intimacy, and the life story: Personological inquiries into identity*. New York: Guilford Press.

McAdams, D. P. (1988). Biography, narrative, and lives: An introduction. *Journal of Personality, 56,* 1–18.

McAdams, D. P. (1989). *Intimacy: The need to be close.* New York: Doubleday.

McAdams, D. P. (1990). Unity and purpose in human lives: The emergence of identity as a life story. In A. I. Rabin, R. A. Zucker, R. A. Emmons, & S. Frank (Eds.), *Studying persons and lives* (pp. 148–200). New York: Springer.

McAdams, D. P. (1993). *The stories we live by: Personal myths and the making of the self.* New York: William Morrow.

McAdams, D. P. (1994). *The person: An introduction to personality psychology* (2nd Ed.). Fort Worth, TX: Harcourt Brace.

McAdams, D. P. (1996a). Narrating the self in adulthood. In J. E. Birren, G. M. Kenyon, J. E. Ruth, J. J. F. Schroots, & T. Svensson (Eds.), *Aging and biography: Explorations in adult development* (pp. 131–148). New York: Springer.

McAdams, D. P. (1996b). Personality, modernity, and the storied self: A contemporary framework for studying persons. *Psychological Inquiry, 7,* 295–321.

McAdams, D. P. (1997a). The three voices of Erik Erikson. *Contemporary Psychology, 42,* 575–578.

McAdams, D. P. (1997b). The case for unity in the (post)modern self: A modest proposal. In R. Ashmore & L. Jussim (Eds.), *Self and identity: Fundamental issues* (pp. 46–78). New York: Oxford University Press.

McAdams, D. P., Booth, L., & Selvik, R. (1981). Religious identity among students at a private college: Social motives, ego stage, and development. *Merrill-Palmer Quarterly, 27,* 219–239.

McAdams, D. P., & de St. Aubin, E. (1992). A theory of generativity and its assessment through self-report, behavioral acts, and narrative themes in autobiography. *Journal of Personality and Social Psychology, 62,* 1003–1015.

McAdams, D. P., Diamond, A., de St. Aubin, E., & Mansfield, E. (1997). Stories of commitment: The psychosocial construction of generative lives. *Journal of Personality and Social Psychology, 72,* 678–694.

McAdams, D. P., Hoffman, B. J., Mansfield, E. D., & Day, R. (1996). Themes of agency and communion in significant autobiographical scenes. *Journal of Personality, 64,* 339–378.

McAdams, D. P., & West, S. (1997). Introduction: Personality psychology and the case study. *Journal of Personality, 65,* 757–783.

McCabe, A., & Peterson, C. (Eds.). (1991). *Developing narrative structure*. Hillsdale, NJ: Erlbaum.

McClelland, D. C., Atkinson, J. W., Clark, R. A., & Lowell, E. L. (1953). *The achievement motive*. New York: Appleton-Century-Crofts.

Merriam, S. (1980). *Coping with male mid-life: A systematic analysis using literature as a data source.* Washington, DC: University Press of America.

Mishler, E. (1992). Work, identity, and narrative: An artist-craftsman's story. In G. C. Rosenwald & R. L. Ochberg (Eds.), *Storied lives: The cultural politics of self-understanding* (pp. 21–40). New Haven, CT: Yale University Press.

Modell, J. (1992). How do you introduce yourself as a "childless mother"? Birthparent interpretations of parenthood. In G. C. Rosenwald & R. L. Ochberg (Eds.), *Storied lives: The cultural politics of self-understanding* (pp. 76–94). New Haven, CT: Yale University Press.

Moffitt, K. H., & Singer, J. A. (1994). Continuity in the life story: Self-defining memories, affect, and approach/avoidance personal strivings. *Journal of Personality, 62,* 21–43.

Murray, H. A. (1938). *Explorations in personality.* New York: Oxford University Press.

Murray, K. (1989). The construction of identity in the narratives of romance and comedy. In J. Shotter and K. Gergen (Eds.), *Texts of identity* (pp. 176–205). London: Sage.

Murray, S. L., & Holmes, J. G. (1994). Storytelling in close relationships: The construction of confidence. *Personality and Social Psychology Bulletiin, 20,* 650–663.

Nasby, W., & Read, N. (1997). The life voyage of a solo circumnavigator: Theoretical and methodological perspectives [Special issue]. *Journal of Personality, 65*(4).

Nelson, K. (1993). Events, narratives, memory: What develops? In K. Nelson (Ed.), *The Minnesota Symposium on Child Development: Memory and affect in development,* Vol. 26 (pp. 1–24). Hillsdale, NJ: Erlbaum.

Ochberg, R. L. (1988). Life stories and the psychosocial construction of careers. *Journal of Personality, 56,* 173–204.

Peterson, B. E., & Stewart, A. J. (1990). Using personal and fictional documents to assess psychosocial development: The case study of Vera Brittain's generativity. *Psychology and Aging, 5,* 400–411.

Polkinghorne, D. (1988). *Narrative knowing and the human sciences.* Albany, NY: SUNY Press.

Polster, E. (1987). *Every person's life is worth a novel.* New York: Norton.

Pondy, L. R., Morgan, G., Frost, P. J., & Dandridge, T. C. (Eds.). (1983). *Organizational symbolism.* Greenwich, CT: JAI Press.

Pratt, M. W., Arnold, M. L., & Hilbers, S. M. (in press). A narrative approach to the study of moral orientation in the family: Tales of kindness and care. In E. E. A. Skoe & A. L. von der Lippe (Eds.), *Personality development in adolescence: A cross-national and life-span perspective.* London: Routledge.

Ricoeur, P. (1984). *Time and narrative* (Vol. 1). Chicago: University of Chicago Press.

Rogers, A. G., Brown, L. M., & Tappan, M. B. (1994). Interpreting loss in ego development in girls: Regression or resistance? In A. Lieblich & R. Josselson (Eds.), *Exploring identity and gender: The narrative study of lives* (Vol. 2, pp. 1–35). Thousand Oaks, CA: Sage.

Rosenwald, G. C. (1992). Conclusion: Reflections on narrative self-understanding. In G. C. Rosenwald & R. L. Ochberg (Eds.), *Storied lives: The cultural politics of self-understanding* (pp. 265–289). New Haven, CT: Yale University Press.

Rosenwald, G. C., & Ochberg, R. L. (1992). Introduction: Life stories, cultural politics, and self-understanding. In G. C. Rosenwald & R. L. Ochberg (Eds.), *Storied lives: The cultural politics of self-understanding* (pp. 1–17). New Haven, CT: Yale University Press.

Runyan, W. M. (1982). *Life histories and psychobiography.* New York: Oxford University Press.

Sampson, E. E. (1989). The challenge of social change for psychology: Globalization and psychology's theory of the person. *American Psychologist, 44,* 914–921.

Sarbin, T. (1986). The narrative as root metaphor for psychology. In T. Sarbin (Ed.), *Narrative psychology: The storied nature of human conduct* (pp. 3–21). New York: Praeger.

Sarbin, T. (1995). Emotional life, rhetoric, and roles. *Journal of Narrative and Life History, 5,* 213–220.

Schank, R. C., & Abelson, R. P. (1995). Knowledge and memory: The real story. In R. S. Wyer, Jr. (Ed.), *Advances in social cognition* (Vol. 8, pp. 1–86). Hillsdale, NJ: Erlbaum.

Shaw, C. (1930). *The jack-roller: A delinquent boy's own story.* Chicago: University of Chicago Press.

Shotter, J., & Gergen, K. J. (Eds.). (1989). *Texts of identity.* London: Sage.

Singer, J. A. (1990). Affective responses to autobiographical memories and their relationship to long-term goals. *Journal of Personality, 58,* 535–563.

Singer, J. A. (1995). Seeing one's self: Locating narrative memory in a framework of personality. *Journal of Personality, 63,* 429–457.

Singer, J. A. (1997). *Message in a bottle: Stories of men and addiction.* New York: Free Press.

Singer, J. A., & Salovey, P. (1993). *The remembered self.* New York: Free Press.

Smith, C. P. (Ed.). (1992). *Motivation and personality: Handbook of thematic content analysis.* New York: Cambridge University Press.

Smith, M. B. (1994). Selfhood at risk: Postmodern perils and the perils of postmodernism. *American Psychologist, 49,* 405–411.

Stein, N. L., & Policastro, M. (1984). The concept of a story: A comparison between children's and teachers' viewpoints. In H. Mandl, N. L. Stein, & T. Trabasso (Eds.), *Learning and comprehension of text.* Hillsdale, NJ: Erlbaum.

Stern, D. (1985). *The interpersonal world of the human infant.* New York: Basic Books.

Stewart, A. J. (1982). The course of individual adaptation to life changes. *Journal of Personality and Social Psychology, 42,* 1100–1113.

Stewart, A. J. (1994). Toward a feminist strategy for studying women's lives. In C. Franz & A. J. Stewart (Eds.), *Women creating lives: Identities, resilience, and resistance* (pp. 11–35). Boulder, CO: Westview Press.

Stewart, A. J., Franz, C., & Layton, L. (1988). The changing self: Using personal documents to study lives. *Journal of Personality, 56,* 41–74.

Sutton-Smith, B. (1986). Children's fiction making. In T. Sarbin (Ed.), *Narrative psychology: The storied nature of human conduct* (pp. 67–90). New York: Praeger.

Taylor, C. (1989). *Sources of the self: The making of the modern identity.* Cambridge, MA: Harvard University Press.

Thorne, A. (1995a). Juxtaposed scripts, traits, and the dynamics of personality. *Journal of Personality, 63,* 593–616.

Thorne, A. (1995b). Developmental truths in memories of childhood and adolescence. *Journal of Personality, 63,* 139–163.

Thorne, A., Cutting, L., & Skaw, D. (in press). Young adults' relationship memories and the life story: Examples or essential landmarks? *Narrative Inquiry.*

Tomkins, S. S. (1962). *Affect, imagery, consciousness* (Vol. 1). New York: Springer.

Tomkins, S. S. (1963). *Affect, imagery, consciousness* (Vol. 2). New York: Springer.

Tomkins, S. S. (1979). Script theory. In H. E. Howe, Jr. & R. A. Dienstbier (Eds.), *Nebraska symposium on motivation,* Vol. 26 (pp. 201–236). Lincoln, NE: University of Nebraska Press.

Tomkins, S. S. (1981). The quest for primary motives: Biography and autobiography of an idea. *Journal of Personality and Social Psychology, 41,* 306–329.

Tomkins, S. S. (1987). Script theory. In J. Aronoff, A. I. Rabin, & R. A. Zucker (Eds.), *The emergence of personality* (pp. 147–216). New York: Springer.

Vitz, P. C. (1990). The use of stories in moral development: New psychological reasons for an old education method. *American Psychologist, 45,* 709–720.

Walkover, B. C. (1992). The family as an overwrought object of desire. In G. C. Rosenwald & R. L. Ochberg (Eds.), *Storied lives: The cultural politics of self-understanding* (pp. 178–191). New Haven, CT: Yale University Press.

Warren, R. P. (1962, October 20). Why do we read fiction? *Saturday Evening Post,* pp. 148–158.

Wellman, H. M. (1993). Early understanding of mind: The normal case. In S. Baron-Cohen, H. Tager-Flusberg, & D. J. Cohen (Eds.), *Understanding other minds: Perspectives from autism* (pp. 10–39). New York: Oxford University Press.

White, M., & Epston, D. (1990). *Narrative means to therapeutic ends.* New York: Norton.

Wiersma, J. (1988). The press release: Symbolic communication in life history interviewing. *Journal of Personality, 56,* 205–238.

Winter, D. G., & Carlson, L. A. (1988). Using motive scores in the psychobiographical study of an individual: The case of Richard Nixon. *Journal of Personality, 56,* 75–104.

Woike, B. A. (1995). Most-memorable experiences: Evidence for a link between implicit and explicit motives and social cognitive processes in everyday life. *Journal of Personality and Social Psychology, 68,* 1081–1091.

Chapter 20

Personality and Motivation: Personal Action and the Conative Evolution

Brian R. Little
Carleton University

A fundamental change has been evolving in how personality psychologists think about human motivation. The sources of this change are diverse and its implications are far-reaching. It is an evolution in the constructs deemed central to understanding human lives, the methodological probes through which such constructs are appraised and the practical implications for how we conceive of human flourishing. The shift has been away from seeing either unconscious motives or contextual forces as the overriding influences on motivational life and, more contentiously, away from seeing motivation solely through the prism of a restrictive cognitive theory. The shift has been *toward* the study of intentional personal action. It explores what people are trying to do in their daily pursuits, their engagement in personal projects and life tasks, and the commitments with which they struggle in their lives. In short, we have witnessed a "conative evolution" in personality psychology.[1]

I wish to trace the roots of this change, selectively appraise its empirical yield, and discuss its implications both for personality psychology and for the social and life sciences more broadly. Relative to other treatments of this topic this chapter highlights a crucial but relatively neglected element of the conative evolution: the development of new criteria for fundamental measurement and assessment in personality psychology.

At the outset, I wish to delimit the scope of the chapter and declare my own biases. I believe that the conative evolution is the most significant change that has occurred at the intersection of personality and motivational psychology over the past two decades, but it is clearly not the only change. Also, the conative evolution has not been restricted just to personality psychology. Similar changes can be discerned in developmental, social, and cognitive psychology. Some of the relevant research in these areas will be incorporated selectively into my review.

PERSONAL ACTION AND CONATION: A BRIEF CONCEPTUAL AND HISTORICAL ANALYSIS

Projects in Waiting: Lunchtime at the Schwedische Café

Imagine it is 1927 and we are having lunch at the Schwedische Café across the plaza from the Psychological Institute of the University of Berlin. We are watching Paul, the waiter, who seems rather preoccupied today. As regular customers who just happen to be psychologists, we try to figure out what is going on. Initially we adopt the behaviorist stance that has become popular in America recently and simply note the observable behaviors that he is engaged in: serving customers, speaking to the chef about an overdone steak, blinking frequently, interacting with Kurt and Bluma in the corner, running across the square to an art gallery where he receives an envelope from a woman. What has Paul been up to?

We could speculate on the contingencies that are controlling his behavior and the drives that are being reduced as he completes his various tasks. But as longtime customers, we have a vested interest in understanding Paul's action in a more personal sense. We might make some reasonable guesses about his conduct. Although he has been going through the routine actions of a waiter, he seems rather tense and is now off on a break, perhaps getting information on a potential purchase at the gallery. Beyond that we have little to go on. But assume we see him in the square after lunch and say, "Hey Paul, what's up? How are you doing?," adding that he seemed rather distracted that day. Paul answers that he has been "finishing up my job at the Schwedische Café." He confirms that serving customers was indeed part of his routine activities as a waiter, but he explains that his frequent blinking wasn't a nervous tick but an intentional act. He also tells us that his talking to Kurt and Bluma had been rather exasperating.[2] He did not go to the gallery to purchase a print but to get a cheque from his aunt, the owner of the shop, which would allow him to pay for a boat ticket to America. Now that arrangements had been made, Paul was all set to embark on his life's core project of "being a musician" in New York City.

This imaginary scenario illustrates a number of key aspects of motivation and personality as viewed through the lens of personal action. First, much of Paul's behavior could only be understood by soliciting his own account of the personal action in which he was engaged. His serving of customers was routine activity requiring little by way of explication or subtle motivational analysis. His repeated blinking is more complex. Normally we think of blinking as reflex behavior designed to keep the eye lubricated or, as in this case, as a sign of emotional tension. But upon direct questioning he informs us that his blinking is a rehabilitative task designed by his occupational therapist to stabilize his visual field after an ear fenestration operation.[3] Such behavior constitutes intentional action with personal consequences. In short, Paul's behavior that noon hour makes sense only to the extent that we understand what has been *personally salient* to Paul that lunchtime.

Second, the scenario was played out in a particular restaurant in Berlin during the 1920s. The scene unfolds during the period of the Weimar Republic when many people (including Kurt and some of his students in the corner) were watching with alarm the rise of Nazism and planning the possibilities of emigration. And while the '20s were still very much roaring in New York, economic disaster was looming. Personal action is embedded in such contextual elements.[4] In addition, not all of the projects that Paul was engaged in would necessarily have been communicated and yet would have an impact on his ecosystem. Indeed, he may hesitate to even think about, let alone communicate about the impact of the choices he is making at this point in his life. For example, his project of leaving for America has effectively ended his three-year romantic relationship with Gerda. Clearly not all of the contextual features of personal action can be specified: Considerable winnowing is required. But there can be little doubt that a reasonable understanding of what Paul has been up to requires the most important features of his social ecology to come into view. In short, personal action assessment needs to be *contextually sensitive*.

Third, Paul was not engaged in just one personal action that lunch hour. Depending upon the level of resolution with which one observes his conduct, he was engaged in dozens of personal actions and several key projects. Two projects were of overarching significance and were systemically linked—his leaving Germany and pursuing his musical career in New York. Some of the projects were in conflict: His exchange with Bluma and Kurt had a temporal conflict with getting the cheque from his aunt before the gallery closed. Also, and this is crucial, these personal actions are not independent of his mood, cognitive processing, and overt behavior but rather are a central and pervasive determinant of them. His seeming obliviousness to his longtime customers was, in this scenario, intricately connected to his need to complete his lunchtime projects and his attention was focused on pursuits that were ongoing rather than completed or off in the distance. His general well-being and sense of excitement were directly linked to the fact that he was on the verge of pursuing his lifelong dream. Disparate psychological processes are *systemically integrated* with ongoing personal action.

Fourth, in contrast with perspectives focusing on fixed traits or unconscious motives, a concern with personal action highlights the contingent nature of daily action and the developmental possibilities of people. Paul is at a crossroads in his life and his choices will launch him into new places, new relationships, and new projects. But, in contrast with fixed traits or the "harder" situational forces immediately present in his environment, Paul's personal action has greater potential to be reconstrued, forestalled, redirected, reformulated, abandoned, shelved or sacrificed. The facts of project pursuit take on added significance in the context of the counterfactual possibilities that are foregone. Such concerns illustrate a distinctive feature of personal action units in personality psychology—they are not fixed features of personality but dynamic and potentially *tractable* aspects of agentic conduct. As Paul posts his "For Rent" sign on his apartment door, he feels he can "do no other." Gerda suspects he could, if he cared enough about their relationship. Paul's musicality and general geniality may be relatively hard-wired propensities, but his goal of giving up everything to pursue his vocation is a volitional decision with a ripple effect that extends well beyond his Berlin walls.

Paul and his projects will serve as a sustained reference point throughout the chapter to illustrate some of the emerging issues in conative personality psychology. We will use the New Media concept of "morphing" figures by occasionally stretching Paul into new identities. He will jump from Berlin in the 1920s to Berkeley in the 1950s without aging a day. Paul will become Gauguin. He will emerge as Pauline and his projects will transform radically as she struggles with the same core projects that her conceptual brother is pursuing.

Perspectives on Paul in Motion: Motivational Theory as Moveable Feast

Etymologically, the root term underlying motivation is "movement," and the discernment of the forces impelling such movement is the common goal of motivational theorists, despite differences in the presumed source of such movement. Whether Paul's lunchtime activity is seen as motivated by unconscious forces or conscious choice, by drive reduction or stimulus seeking, by infantile needs or current commitments, depends on the particular theoretical vantage point and historical period in 20th-century motivational theory. To illustrate these issues concisely, not only will we morph Paul into relevant contexts, we will adopt another rather surrealistic (or postmodern) device to help advance the narrative. Using the Schwedische restaurant as a home base, we will have Paul's activities observed by different tables of motivational theorists. This will help us illustrate recurring themes as we proceed through classical, critical, and contemporary perspectives on motivation. Some of the tables seem permanently reserved for succeeding generations of like-minded theorists. Others disappear for a generation and then return.[5] Still others, relegated to the patio for years, simply move their table inside and declare themselves hosts of the feast. This device will also allow us some anachronistic licence in the service of conciseness.

Classical Perspectives: The Roots of Motivation

Consider first a table of psychodynamic theorists. They are deeply interested in the unconscious motivation underlying Paul's action, much of which would have aggressive or sexual roots. They are particularly attuned to detecting the conflict-laden nature of his activities and of the defences he erects against the anxiety caused by such conflict. They are alert to nuances in his conduct that might escape the attention of those viewing him from different vantage points. Through the haze of cigar smoke they pose some distinctive questions.[6] Why did Paul wait so long before securing the financial assistance from his aunt? Is his abandonment of Gerda a reaction to his own feelings of desertion by his parents who were essentially emotional strangers? Is it significant that the few times his parents expressed emotional warmth was when he performed well in his music recitals?[7]

There is a separate Harvard table at the Schwedische Café with a permanent "Reserved" sign prominently displayed in crimson. It is a long table because not only psychologists but anthropologists, sociologists, and various scholars in the humanities are all offering their versions of Paul's pursuits. At the head of the table sits Henry Murray. Their perspective on Paul is similar to the psychodynamic one, although guided more by a wide-angled Jungian lens than a purely Freudian one. But they also invoke "need" constructs so that Paul's frequent interactions with the Berlin Psychology group may be seen as an indication of a need for affiliation (nAff) and his pursuit of a career in music as due to needs for exhibition (nExh) and achievement (nAch). They comment too on the environmental "press" that allows Paul's needs to be facilitated or frustrated. The Murrayans also see temporal factors as crucial in understanding his daily behavior: The explanation of Paul's motivation should take into account the time-binding, long-term "serials" through which his needs are expressed. The pursuit of his dream of being a musician is a natural analytic unit for these theorists, though such analytic units were primarily conceptual and remained unoperationalized for decades (Little, 1983).

Also sitting at the Harvard table, but a bit off to the side, is Gordon Allport, Murray's contemporary at Harvard. Allport was one of the founders of the modern academic study of personality and a theorist who early and frequently raised the key issue of "what units shall we employ" in the study of motivation and personality (Allport, 1958). Allport voices concerns about the Freudian accounts of Paul's conduct, calling attention instead to the enduring traits that distinguish him as well as the extent to which his goal of becoming a musician represents his deepest (propriate) strivings. In addition, he reminds his colleagues that, although Paul's leaving Berlin may have initially been impelled by unconscious forces, his eventual departure may have become functionally autonomous of its original motivation. It would be propitious, suggests Allport, for us to ask Paul himself to explain the motivational concerns that lead him to undertake his trip abroad.

To this last point, vigorous nods of approval would most certainly come from George Kelly, and his personal construct theorists, sitting at what appears to be a patio table moved inside by passing construction workers. Kelly (1955) promoted a credulous approach to personality assessment, one in which the Pauls of this world were assumed to have privileged status with respect to the reasons for their actions. Indeed, Kelly's whole iconoclastic stance was captured at the beginning of his address to the prestigious Nebraska Symposium on Motivation in 1962, in which he declared that he had no use for the concept of motivation whatsoever.[8] His reason was that people are in motion from the very start: Movement is a constituent aspect of the human condition. Paul does not need to be loaded up with either the prods of unconscious stimulations or the seductive incentives of learning theory to get himself to America. He is pursuing a path laid out for him by the personal constructs through which he sees the world and which provide channels for movement. This view stands in direct contrast with those perspectives that see choice distorted by irrational forces. Those at the Kellian table, a surprising number of whom have British accents, see the invoking of either unconscious or externally manipulated forces to "motivate" Paul as setting up smoke screens that obscure a clear picture of human motivation. With respect to explanatory transparency, the Kellians clearly sit in the "No Smoking" section of the Schwedische restaurant.

Two other groups are lurking about. Looking down on the proceedings from the rafters are a group of Barkerian ecological psychologists (Barker, 1968). This perspective, although obscuring the distinctive motivational features of the individuals below, does reveal a powerful source of motivation—the behavior setting itself, which can coerce us to act "restaurant" rather than "rodeo" or "funeral." And to complete the assemblage, we spot a disputatum of analytic philosophers who have been at the feast for centuries and still feel rather proprietary about explanations of human motivation. They are not watching Paul; they are watching us watching Paul. As walking manifestations of the disposition to think otherwise, philosophers need to be listened to and we will invite them over to our table on several occasions in this chapter.

Do You Have Reservations?: The Cognitive Incursion at Midcentury

During the late 1950s, psychology was having major reservations about traditional motivational theory and its emphasis on drive reduction. White (1959), in an influential review, proposed that a more fundamental motivational principle than the seeking of reduced stimulation was competency and its motivational counterpart of "effectance." The demise of drive reduction theory was coterminous with the rise of cognitive psychology as the dominant influence in psychology. Certainly if entry into the restaurant during the 1950s were based on a group's influence on the emerging cognitive psychology of the day, a number of the groups we have been discussing would have found it difficult to get a table. Orthodox psychodynamic theorists, classical learning theorists, and trait theorists would have been turned away. The Kellians, seen by others (but not themselves) as proto-cognitive psychologists, would have been allowed to keep their table, though one senses they were still regarded as "patio people"—interesting folks but a bit far out. One group who would be ushered right in is those following in the Murrayan tradition, particularly McClelland and his colleagues, whose influential program of theoretical and applied research on motivation withstood the cognitive revolution and provided a needed line of continuity between the classical and contemporary periods of motivational theory (Winter, 1996).

In the ensuing decade there was a substantial shift within psychology toward more cognitive, competency-focused perspectives. Some of the traditional perspectives became "cognitivized" during the 1960s and early 1970s. Thus learning theory became cognitive social learning theory; psychodynamic theory accorded greater prominence to Hartmann's earlier concept of a "conflict free" ego sphere and focused increasingly on object relations. Orthodox trait theory was challenged by a dynamic person–environment interactionism (Argyle & Little, 1972; Endler, 1983; Mischel, 1968). The scene was now set for the arrival of a van load of new customers for the café, who quickly took to their tables and began discussing Paul.

Contemporary Perspectives: The Routes of Motivation

Imagine now a contemporary restaurant on virtually the same site as the Schwedische Café.[9] A contemporary group of psychologists has been observing Paul who has been engaging in virtually the same acts as his predecessor. Some of the patrons are direct descendants of the group at the Schwedische Café and have kept their tables reserved for the better part of the century.[10] But there is one group we need to visit with and another with which we will spend the rest of this chapter. The first are trait theorists who have rallied around Big Five units (e.g., John, 1990); the second are conative theorists who study "personal action constructs" (hereafter PAC units) (Little, 1989).

Like their predecessors of seven decades ago, both the trait and the conative psychologists start their explanatory ventures by observing the outward and visible behaviours of Paul and others in the café. However, following the lead of Buss and Craik (1983) we will now refer to these as *acts* rather than behaviors, a subtle but important difference affording a greater possibility for convergence among theoretically disparate positions in personality psychology (Little, 1987). Imagine we are watching Paul deal with the customer who is "sending back his overcooked steak." Buss and Craik (1983) invoked precisely this example in a seminal article that, among other things, clarified the difference between trait and motive accounts of observed acts. The trait psychologist may see this act as a highly prototypical exemplar of a trait of "dominance." Were a large number of such acts, relative to appropriate norms, to be observed, the trait concept of "dominance" could be ascribed to this person. Alternatively, this act could be seen as the means through which the person carries out a personal project of "impressing the boss" (Buss & Craik, 1983). Personal projects are prime examples of PAC units. Such constructs serve as "carrier units" for motivation and are at the heart of the emerging conative perspectives in personality psychology.

PACs have emerged in the past 20 years as viable alternatives to other analytic units in the field of personality psychology. They include such constructs as current concerns (Klinger, 1975), personal projects (Little, 1983, 1993), life tasks (Cantor, 1990), and personal strivings (Emmons, 1986).[11] It is helpful to consider the PAC units along an internal–external spectrum in which some are *primarily* regulated by internal factors and others by external forces. Current concerns and personal strivings are relatively more "internal" PAC units, life tasks are more external, and personal projects lie in the middle of the PAC spectrum (Little, 1998).

Paul's conduct displays examples of each of these analytic units. His preoccupation with his trip to New York and its interference with some of his cognitive activities (such as his inattentiveness) reflects Klinger's (1975) conception of "current concerns." A current concern is a state of having a particular unmet goal. Current concerns sensitize us to cues associated with those personal goals in ways that create the idiosyncratic richness of mental life. As Klinger argues, current concerns create the highly adaptive ability of a person to be distracted. For example, Paul may be distracted from his conversation with Bluma because of the directive influence of his more pressing concern of getting his cheque from his aunt. In contrast with earlier views that would predict that Paul's fantasy life would reflect aggressive and sexual themes, Klinger's research suggests that his dreams, both night and day versions, will reflect the current concerns in which he is still engaged.

Paul's action also exemplifies Emmons's concept of a "personal striving" (Emmons, 1986). Personal strivings are goals or pursuits that individuals are *typically* trying to pursue. Several of Paul's sets of actions might be subsumed under the personal striving of "trying not to be influenced unduly by others." This is not a one-off activity or a singular pursuit but a representation of a relatively enduring idiosyncratic motive that undergirds diverse activities.

Personal projects are conceptually situated at the juncture point between the internal and external ends of the PAC spectrum (Little, 1972, 1983). Personal projects are extended sets of personally salient action. Projects have inner representation as aspirations and goals, but they also have an external manifestation as observable acts that are impacted by and impact upon the social ecology. Projects can leave imprints and residues. Paul's project to "leave for America" serves both as a source of motivation for him and as a source of deep concern for Gerda. Moreover, appraisals of this project in the Berlin of the 1920s in comparison with the 1990s would reveal social ecological differences that are central to explaining motivated action.[12]

That cultural, societal, and other systemic sources of influence may prescribe or proscribe our pursuits is also seen clearly in Cantor's construct of "life tasks" (Cantor, 1990). Cantor sees life tasks as age-graded, normatively shaped pursuits that individuals in particular settings are likely to be engaged in, even though they may pursue these common tasks in idiosyncratic ways. For example, a contemporary Paul may be working at the restaurant part time while also attending the university. And at the university he is expected to be engaging in various tasks that would include "getting independent of parents," "finding a career," "performing well academically," and "forming intimate attachments," tasks that his student counterparts in Bologna and Berkeley are also likely to be engaged in. Paul's actual work at the restaurant may be in the service of remaining relatively independent of his parents' support (though not his aunt's), and his musical vocation may be, at least in part, a key aspect of his resolution of the normatively graded life task of achieving a vocational identity.

Another closely related analytic unit, Markus's concept of "possible selves," can also be seen as a key element of the motivational dynamics of Paul's personal action (Markus & Nurius, 1986). A possible self is a representation of both desired and feared future selves that serve to motivate action and commitments. Both the 1920s Paul and his 1990s counterpart may have had images of themselves in New York, perhaps receiving a standing ovation in Carnegie Hall, and both may have worried that the recurring ear problem may be a warning sign of an incipient fatal disease.

It is important to emphasize that each of these examples of the new generation of motivational units has a dynamic and contingent nature to it compared with traditional motivational units. Concerns and strivings may be accomplished or abandoned; projects and tasks may be reconstrued as meaningless or may provide the ground structure for a life's course. These units, in short, provide access to both the "stasis and flow" of human lives (Pervin, 1983).

Introductions to these units and reviews of the research stimulated by them is now extensive (Cantor & Zirkel, 1990; Emmons, 1998; Little, 1998, in press-b,c,d; Austin & Vancouver, 1996). However, one key aspect of PAC units has received very little attention: the measurement and methodological assumptions underlying PAC unit research. I believe that it is these assumptions that have made a distinctive conative psychology viable and will examine them in detail in this chapter. Because personal projects analysis was among the first systematic methodological frameworks to be developed for conative assessment and because it served as the basis for some of the other PAC units, I will adopt the project language for much of what follows. Where appropriate, however, other PAC units will also be invoked.

FOUNDATIONS OF PAC UNIT ASSESSMENT: METHODOLOGICAL PROCEDURES, MEASUREMENT CRITERIA, AND RESEARCH FRAMEWORK

Methodological Procedures

Studies using PAC units have evolved a general set of methodological procedures that, although not rigidly standardized, have typically involved four basic steps.

1. Individuals generate a set of PACs (goals, projects, strivings, etc.) expressed in their own terms. Both written and oral lists have

been generated, and typically 10 to 15 PACs are elicited.

2. Respondents rate each PAC (or subset of those generated) on appraisal dimensions selected on the basis of theoretical or practical relevance to the particular study.
3. Respondents provide information on where and with whom projects are undertaken and complete modules that locate the elicited PACs within a hierarchy of more superordinate and subordinate constructs. They also complete matrices showing the impact of PACs on each other within the individuals' own system and upon those of other relevant individuals.
4. Issues relating to PAC change are appraised, such as resistance to change, factors currently impeding and facilitating progress, and changes that might be undertaken to improve functioning in the overall system.

These procedural steps, either individually or in combination, bring into focus each of the conceptual issues that we discussed earlier as comprising essential attributes of personal action: personal saliency, ecological sensitivity, systemic integration, and tractability. We can now address these more formally as measurement criteria for PAC assessment.

Measurement Criteria

Personally Salient Units

If we wish to ascribe valid predicates to people about their motivations, it is essential that we give them the chance to provide us with information that is personally salient to them. At the outset PAC assessment adopts the Kellian credulous approach and in this respect differs from other assessment perspectives, such as orthodox trait assessment.

PAC assessment techniques are not unique in providing the opportunity for personally salient information to be conveyed. Open-ended narrative methods, free association, and projective tests also provide an opportunity for individuals to reveal salient information without the constraints of orthodox testing formats. However, PAC methods are distinctive in providing a crucial "winnowing" function in personality methodology. By generating a sampling of the analytic units themselves, phrased in idiosyncratic language, PAC methods maintain subjective saliency, but in manageable "packets" of information that provide natural units for both quantitative and qualitative analysis. From the innumerable set of subjective concerns, discriminated stimuli, construable objects, and quotidian events within which lives are constructed, PAC elicitation procedures ensure that a workable subset of typically a dozen or so salient projects, tasks, goals, or concerns are generated. Just as personal construct theory differed from general cognitive theory by generating a few distinctive constructs that characterized a given person, PAC units allow us to say of a given individual "*here* are her major life tasks" or "*these* are his core personal projects."[13] It is this person-centered aspect of PAC unit assessment that makes it distinctively a form of personality assessment as well as providing the potential for more general motivational assessment.

Ecologically Sensitive Assessment

This criterion requires that the assessment of personal action provide access to important contextual features. PAC units accomplish this by providing information on the spatial and temporal contexts of action and by using modular assessment so that appraisal dimensions of particular significance to people in specific social ecologies can be selectively integrated into the assessment process.

Sensitivity to the spatial contexts of personal action is afforded by several aspects of PAC methodology. Ecological features may emerge in the elicitation phase, when individuals list their ongoing concerns and projects (e.g., "Find a better daycare center for my daughter"). The spatial context can also be framed in terms of the places within which projects are enacted (Little, 1983). Personal projects analysis (PPA), for example, often uses an "open column" that allows individuals to specify the particular places within which each of their projects are primarily enacted, from which various spatial indices can be calculated.[14] In the appraisal matrix it is possible to obtain ratings on the impact of environmental features on individual's pursuits. For example it has been shown that an important determinant of job satisfaction is the extent to which individuals perceive each of their projects as impeded or facilitated by the organizational climate of their workplace (Phillips, Little, & Goodine, 1996, 1997).

Given our assumption that much of human motivation takes the form of sets of action that serve as carrier units for parcels of motivation, we need to be sensitive to the temporal ecology as well as the social ecology that frame and limit their enactment. Early studies examined the ratio of the actual time spent on projects to the time desired (Palys & Little, 1983), and more recent studies have looked at issues such as whether individuals have sufficient time for their projects, the urgency entailed, and the extent to which they procrastinate (Pychyl & Little, 1998). From the beginning of research on personal projects, the elucidation of temporal stages through which they progress (inception, planning, action, and termination) was a defining aspect of the construct (Little, 1983). Indeed, personal projects analysis was developed, in part, to operationalize the temporal units, such as "serials," that were a central tenet of Murrayan theory.[15] In a detailed analysis of the personal projects of doctoral students, Pychyl (1995) found that procrastination and other temporal pressures were pervasive features of student life. Although it is possible to look at procrastinatory tendencies as trait-like dispositions, to directly assess the process of temporizing we need to sample the ongoing, temporally extended (and extended, and extended . . .) sets of activities that people pursue and sometimes never complete.

Modular flexibility in PAC units means that researchers interested in studying personality and motivation in distinctive eco-settings can create new, ecologically representative appraisal dimensions.[16] The modular flexibility also extends to being able to "provide" common projects or tasks that characterize a particular group (e.g., "watching your weight" in a study of eating disorders (Goodine, 1986)).[17] The call for modular flexibility in goal assessment respects the need for ecologically appropriate units and appraisal dimensions and requires ingenuity and sensitivity on behalf of the researcher/assessor. Clearly, as a generalized methodology for the elicitation, appraisal, and systemic measurement of the motivational doings in a person's life, PAC unit appraisal is far more like a MANOVA than an MMPI.

Systemically Integrative Measurement

From its modern inception, personality psychology has had a strong commitment to providing an integrative core to the diverse specialties within psychology. However, this integrative aspiration has often been compromised by the methodological approaches that have dominated the field over the past 6 decades (e.g., Carlson, 1971). PAC methodology attempts to meet the integrative challenge in several ways.

PAC units comprise hierarchically organized personal systems (Little, 1983; Pervin, 1983), and their measurement is most appropriately examined at the individual level of analysis.[18] PAC units are typically viewed as "middle level units" that allow investigators to examine different sets of systemic influence. Within a single person's project system, for example, each project is systemically related to three different contexts. First, each project may be linked tightly or loosely with superordinate and subordinate analytic units (Little, 1983).[19] Second, each project can be linked with the other ongoing projects in that person's system, and we can study the extent to which an individual's system is one of congruent, mutually supportive pursuits or of pervasive internal conflict. This is assessed by cross-impact matrices in which each project is rated in terms of its positive or negative impact on other projects within the system (Little, 1983).[20] Third, project systems do not exist as self-contained individualistic fiefdoms, but impact for better or for worse on the projects and tasks of other individuals. This too can be examined by the use of *joint* cross-impact matrices, where two individuals examine the impact of each others' projects on their own (Little, 1983). Paul, for example, may have a high degree of internal coherence in his own project system, whereas the joint cross-impact analysis with Gerda may reveal major conflicts.[21]

Another way in which PAC assessment is integrative is that it is not restricted to assessing personality in one domain only (e.g., exclusively cognitive).[22] Projects, tasks, and strivings can all be studied in terms of their affective, cognitive, and behavioral aspects by adopting the conative unit as an embarkation point and directly soliciting information in the other domains.

Tractable Units

The analytic units used in conative assessment are tractable in the sense that, unlike fixed traits or the immutable features of our environment, they are dynamic features of personality that have the potential to be modified. Three aspects of this tractability deserve emphasis.

First, the use of tractable units of analysis in personality research affords the opportunity for therapeutic or personal development activities to be centered directly on the units that have been assessed.[23] The problematic core project, life goal, or set of tasks can serve as the direct focus for clinical, counseling, or development activities. It is this practical accessibility and mutability of PAC units that make them particularly attractive to applied fields, such as occupational therapy (see Christiansen, Little, & Backman, 1998) and organizational psychology (Phillips, Little, & Goodine, 1997). Also, influence attempts that are enacted without awareness of the project system within which they must be accommodated are likely to be resisted. Awareness provided by PAC units might help forestall both therapeutic noncompliance and organizational sabotage. They can also be the direct targets of developmental activities in which individuals enhance the meaning and support of their personal projects, particularly their core projects, while being sensitive to the social ecology within which those projects are embedded (Little, 1998).

Second, PAC assessment has been designed from the outset as a methodology for the joint appraisal of both individual level and normative level data (Little, 1983; Krahé, 1992). It is also possible to expand normative level information to allow for interventions at the level of the social ecology. Each of these levels of potential intervention deserves comment. As alluded to above, it is possible to examine the relationship between any set of appraisal dimensions within the single case (e.g., we can run correlations between any two project dimensions, such as stress and control, across each of the 10 personal projects for each individual). But most of the published research using PAC units over the past 20 years has involved normative analyses, in which a column mean on appraised project dimensions (that is, mean level stress and mean level control) are treated as vectors just as we would use trait dimensions.[24]

A key issue, from a measurement perspective, is the extent to which there is isomorphism between individual level project spaces and normative level spaces.[25] In an extensive analysis of this issue, Gee (1998) has provided very strong evidence of convergence between the underlying personal project spaces measured at the individual and joint or normative levels. One practical implication of this finding is that there is relatively strong justification for moving back and forth between individual and normative levels of analyses with PAC units. It also means that the use of case studies (or of invoking figures like Paul) serve more than ornamental purposes.

The question of whether individual or normative levels of measurement deserve primacy in the research strategies of personality psychologists remains contentious (Krahé, 1992). My own view is that both levels are necessary for a comprehensive and integrative personality psychology but that the individual level assessment takes precedence in programmatic research. Individual level assessment provides what philosophers refer to as "thick" rather than "thin" accounts of action—it samples the singular and specific components and contexts of a particular person's action. But the fact that these idiosyncratic motivational "packets" of PAC units can be rendered commensurable by the use of common appraisal dimensions and other indices that provide for normative measurement means that both of our historically important approaches to personality can be preserved. By inductively aggregating individuals showing similar patterns at the individual level into relatively homogeneous clusters, it is possible to make broader generalizations at the normative level.

The third distinctive aspect of PAC methods relates to the status of the information that has been generated and its use beyond ascribing personal predicates to individuals. We have described this as the "social indicator potential" of data gathered with PAC units (Little, 1989). By storing data on the specific content and appraisals of personal projects and associated demographic characteristics of the individuals who are pursuing them, it is possible to shift the interventional focus from the individual person level up to the level of the social ecology within which that individual pursues defining projects.[26] By encouraging the analysis of information gathered at the level of groups or eco-settings, PAC units have been used to address issues in public policy analysis (Phillips, Little, & Goodine, 1996, 1997), epidemiology (Ewart, 1991) and political philosophy (Little, 1998, in press-c). They not only afford us images of the individuals and their contexts but, by being tractable, also allow us to improve the quality of lives by intervention at both the level of the individual and the social ecology (Little, 1996).

A Research Framework for Conative Personality Psychology

Taken together, the foundational measurement criteria provide the base for what has emerged as a research framework within which most of the current conative personality psychology is car-

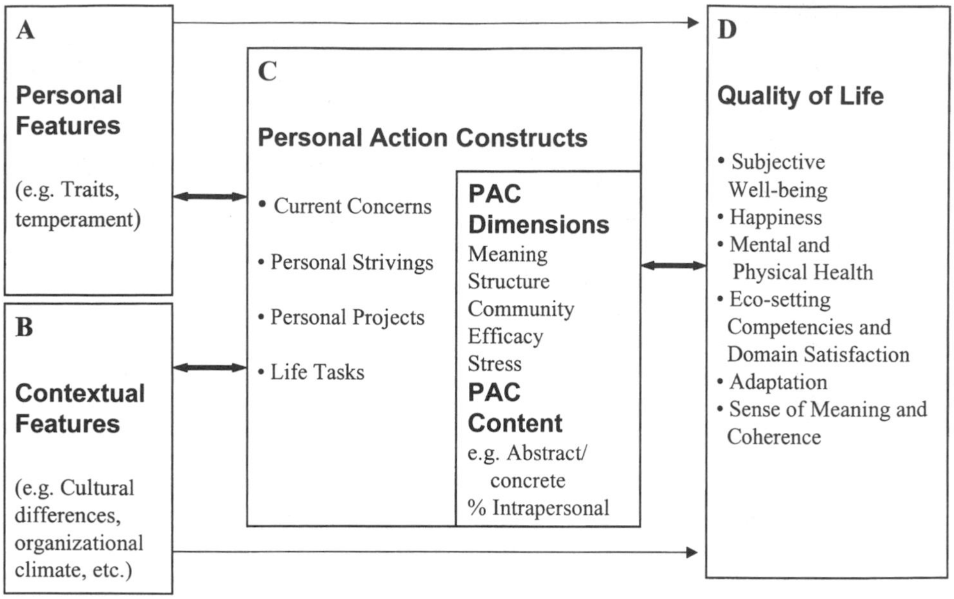

FIGURE 20.1. A social ecological model of personality.

ried out. As depicted in Figure 20.1, there are four major blocks of research variables that constitute this approach to personality. Moving from right to left, Block D represents the major outcome or quasi-dependent variables used in conative personality research related to human adaptation and well-being. Essentially these measures assess well-being broadly defined so as to include measures of subjective well-being (and its affective opposites, such as depression or anxiety), life satisfaction, and ecological competency (Sundberg, 1980), which is the ability to adapt successfully in different eco-settings, such as academia (e.g., as indexed by GPA) or work settings (e.g., as indexed by performance ratings). Increasingly, physical health outcome measures are also being adopted in conative personality psychology (e.g., Ryff & Singer, 1998).

Box C represents the different PAC units that are the focus of this chapter. Typically a vector of scores is derived from these measures involving mean scores calculated across the elicited PACs on dimensions such as importance, enjoyment, perceived control, and stress. These scores can be analyzed either ipsatively or normatively. In addition categorical measures are often used, such as the frequency with which different types of projects, tasks, or strivings are mentioned in the free elicitation phase of the assessment process or the level of molarity or abstraction of goals (e.g., Little, 1987; Emmons, 1992).

Boxes A and B refer to person and environmental/ecological features that can have both direct and indirect (via PAC units) effects on well-being and adaptational measures in Box D. For clarity and simplicity, the effects in the flow model that are of particular importance in this chapter are drawn with bold arrows. Reciprocal effect of PAC unit variables upon well-being and adaptation is a core assumption of the model, as is the reciprocal effect of PAC variables on measures of traits and of environments. There is also considerable research activity going on within the block of PAC variables, particularly relating to the relationship among different dimensions of appraisal, such as commitment and perceived progress or a sense of meaning and control. Some of these will be discussed below.[27]

CONATIVE PERSONALITY PSYCHOLOGY: THEMES AND ISSUES IN CONTEMPORARY RESEARCH

Much of the empirical research in conative personality psychology has been concerned with identifying the relationships between appraisal dimensions of PAC units and their relationship with other blocks of variables in Figure 20.1. We first discuss different stages of project and action pursuit. We then discuss five factors that underlie PAC ratings, with an emphasis on the prediction of well-being. Finally, we examine recent studies pitting PAC unit explanations against alternative theoretical constructs (such as trait and contextual models), which, together, make a strong case for the distinctive strengths of this approach to personality and motivation.

Action Stages and Project Pursuit

In the original article on personal projects, considerable attention was devoted to the temporal stages (and substages) through which projects can proceed en route from the original hint of their possibility to their eventual completion, sustained effectiveness, or demise (Little, 1983). We will use the major stages of inception, planning, action, and termination to help organize a growing literature on action phases and project pursuit. Adopting a temporal perspective allows us to see the unfolding of diverse influences that impact on project pursuit. Even more important, from the perspective of contemporary personality psychology, it allows us to bring into focus motivational issues that have, in recent years, receded in influence within personality psychology because of the demise of motivational features that occurred during the cognitive revolution. The full spectrum of motivational factors can, in theory and increasingly in practice, be brought into common focus by the adoption of PAC units, particularly when viewed in temporal perspective. Because much of this literature overlaps with self-regulatory models discussed elsewhere in this volume (see Carver & Scheier, Chapter 22), I will place particular emphasis upon distinctive issues raised by the integrative potential of PAC units in personality psychology.

Project Inception

The inception phase of personal projects extends from the discernment of the possibility of a course of personal action through to a commitment to undertake it. It is at this stage that the most extensive array of influences occur, ranging from unconscious forces impelling people away from or toward a particular project, through traits that can "attune" them to systemic and ecological constraints and resources.

With respect to unconscious influences, Baldwin, Carrell, and Lopez (1990) have shown that when graduate students are considering how well they are likely to do in their upcoming term's research projects, they appraise them as less likely to succeed if they had been exposed to a tachistoscopic image of the face of a threatening senior professor, in contrast with exposure to the more benign countenance of a postdoctoral fellow. Such priming schema may cause a person to foreclose on a particular project or at least to exclude it from active consideration. Paul may never have embarked on a musical career if an image of his music teacher's pained expression silently suggested he was more appalling than appealing. The growing evidence that these cues may be tacit or unconscious provides a nice line of continuity between the classical psychodynamic theorists of motivation and contemporary conative theorists.

The trait dimension of Openness to Experience (Costa & McCrae, 1992) has an interesting relationship to the inception state of personal projects. It is the only Big Five trait dimension that is consistently related to the tendency to engage in a diversity of personal projects, but it has little relationship with the appraisal of projects once they have passed through into the planing and action stages (Little, Lecci, & Watkinson, 1992).

Social ecological factors influence whether a person will even consider the possibility of pursuing a particular project or task. At different stages of the life cycle, different types of personal project or life task becoming normatively salient (Cantor, 1990). Sanctions, ranging from mild censure to outrage, can ensue from a person undertaking nonnormative tasks and from not engaging in those that are prescribed as appropriate. For example, Helson, Mitchell, and Moane (1984) have described the operation of "social clock projects" in which women, in particular, are expected to entrain their pursuits to a particular socially defined timetable. This was especially so with the cohort of women who came of age during the 1950s, where the social expectations of engaging in educational, marriage, and motherhood projects, in that order, held considerable sway over the types of goals that women would even consider. Their projects were both prescribed and proscribed by their social ecology. In Berlin there was still the remnants of the *Kinder, Kirche, Küche* (children, church and kitchen) constraints upon women, while even in Berkeley, the normative expectations were that bright, well-educated women would end up living lives more like Harriet Nelson (at least her

TV persona) than Harriet Beecher Stowe. Even contemporary women at the most senior levels in public and private sector management show considerably greater sensitivity to contextual influences than do their equally high-status male colleagues. In a study that measured the degree of linkage between personal project appraisals and appraisals of organizational climate, there was a considerably higher degree of project–context linkage for women than for men (Phillips, Little, & Goodine, 1996, 1997).

It will be helpful here if we morph Paul into his conceptual twin, Pauline, and see what the research literature suggests with respect to *her* approach to the inception stage of a personal project to pursue a career as a musician. Unconscious "voices" might have been heard, particularly in the early decades of the 20th century, warning against the unseemly nature of such pursuits for respectable women. In the 1920s, even if Pauline were dispositionally "open" enough to pursue a musical career on another continent, there would be structural features that would have made her task a more onerous venture than that of her brother. She would almost certainly not have had a job as a waitress at that particular café in the 1920s if she were also going to university, though the pictures we have of the contemporary restaurant suggest that there are certainly women servers in that restaurant today. Nor is it likely that her aunt would have offered the financial means to pursue that particular dream when the expectation was that she should be seriously considering settling down and being fecund. Paul, conversely, might be given greater latitude to sow his wild muesli while practising his music. The perils of Pauline's project pursuit would thus entail both the subtle tyrannies of introjected voices and the stony hard constraints of economic opportunity. But the essential aspect of this stage of project pursuit is that these influences are not so much weighed and agonized over, but that they are tacit injunctions about what one can even *consider* undertaking.

Project Planning

If a project survives the first major stage of inception, either by an implicit or explicit statement of commitment to pursue it, *then* the agonizing can begin as the task of planning the project becomes paramount. Unlike the previous stage, where goal pursuit might be precluded before it is ever ruminated over, this stage involves explicit concerns about whether to engage in the pursuit and if so, how it will be implemented. One of the most important programs of research in conative psychology has been undertaken in large part by German scholars on the factors that are operating with respect to the planning of action (e.g., Gollwitzer, 1990).[28] One key distinction here is between different "mindsets" that one might entertain with respect to a given goal or project and that can be studied as experimentally induced sets or as individual differences measures.[29] Gollwitzer distinguishes between deliberative versus implemental mindsets. Deliberative mindsets involve careful weighing of the pros and cons of undertaking a particular project. Gollwitzer has demonstrated that the deliberative mindset is associated with open-minded processing of information and leads to a more realistic appraisal of the likely project path (Gollwitzer, 1990; Taylor & Gollwitzer, 1995). Contrastingly, an implemental mindset is one in which the individual is explicitly focused on the actions necessary to achieve the goal of the project. This set leads individuals to scan cues in a more self-serving way, shields them from information that may distract them from the goal, and fosters illusory optimism about the likelihood of successful completion of the project (Gollwitzer & Brandstätter, in press; Taylor & Gollwitzer, 1995; cf. Norem, 1989).

Consider another Paul, the artist Gauguin, with a similar decision: Should he abandon his family in Paris and pursue his artistic projects in Tahiti? Williams (1981), using a somewhat fictionalized version of Gauguin's story, raises some intriguing questions about the nature of such decisions. Williams's concern is a philosophical one.[30] He invokes the seemingly oxymoronic concept of "moral luck" to indicate the dilemmas of project commitment, particularly commitment to "ground projects" without which our lives may not be seen as worth living. In essence he argues that only to the extent that Gauguin's artistic project turns out successfully could there be any justification for leaving his family. Yet the success of his project was radically contingent upon luck, of fashion, of health, of finances, and all the vagaries that attend our doings in the real world (cf. Bandura, 1982). Contemporary research on motivation and personality add another complexity to Williams's richly textured analysis of project pursuit. At different stages of those pursuits our ability to foresee the likelihood of success realistically may be undermined. It is particularly in the postcommitment stage that both Pauls may view their artistic projects with undue optimism. For one Paul the pursuit of his core project ended up transforming the very nature of modern art, and its impact still radiates to this day. Who knows what will be the downstream impact of our other Paul's pursuits?

Project Action

This stage is where the individual is engaged in the effortful activity necessary to achieve a particular project and the ability to motivate oneself to persist in the project assumes central importance. In terms of Gollwitzer's mindsets, it is clearly the implemental one that will be most adaptive here.[31] Through implemental goggles, distractions are ignored, peripheral discordant cues are not processed, and self-conceptions are distorted in such a way as to increase the motivation necessary to muddle through.

An interesting variant on the desirability of somewhat self-distorting images and the implementation of tasks has been provided by Norem and other researchers using Cantor's construct of "life tasks." These researchers have identified two strategies that can be adopted strategically to help advance a person through the action stage of a task: defensive pessimism and illusory glow optimism (Norem & Cantor, 1986). The defensive pessimist constructs a worse case scenario that motivates through fear of failure. The illusory glow optimist, contrastingly, creates a best case scenario and uses this positive and reinforcing image as a motivational resource. Interestingly, each strategy works equally well. Both serve to keep the action phase of the project or task chugging along, though the evidence suggests that the defensive pessimist may incur some costs in terms of decreasing the supportiveness of others around her.

The successful resolution of the action stage of a personal goal or project requires sustained effort. The influential self-determination theory of Deci and Ryan (1991) provides strong evidence that a central determinant of such effort and persistence in project pursuit is the extent to which the individual feels that the project emanates from internal, autonomous processes rather than being simply compliant with external demands or unwelcomed inner urges. They propose a continuum of internally versus externally motivated pursuits, ranging from freely chosen, self-initiated pursuits to those that are completely externally regulated. Two intermediate categories are "identified" regulation, in which the pursuits, although not being initiated by the individual, are affirmed and valued, and "introjected" regulation, in which there is lack of full identification and the main pressures for continuance are fear and guilt. There is increasing evidence that the more internal the regulatory nature of tasks and long-term goals (i.e., the more internal and identified rather than external or introjected), the greater is persistence and eventual performance effectiveness. In a major prospective study of high school dropouts, for example, Vallerand and his colleagues (Vallerand, 1997; Vallerand, Fortier, & Guay, 1997) have provided strong evidence that individuals most at risk for dropping out are characterized by very low profiles of self-directed autonomy.

There are several excellent examples of recent research demonstrating that PAC units can operationalize and test motivational models related to the management of action (Sheldon & Kasser, 1998; Sheldon & Elliot, 1999; Elliot, Sheldon, & Church, 1997). For example, when PAC units are elicited from students and categorized according to the four-point continuum of internally to externally regulated action, it was found that although high levels of external inducement on personal projects predicted initial effort *intentions,* it did not predict *actual* effort several weeks later. Autonomous goals, on the other hand, were associated both with initial intentions and with actual effort during the later, action stages of their projects (see Sheldon & Elliot, 1999, for a summary and integrative model of these studies).

How might Paul's projects be understood in the light of the research on the action stage of project pursuit? Our scenario suggests that his "musical" project may have been more autonomous than was his "interpersonal" one. The latter may have been sustained more by assuaging guilt than sustaining Gerda. His way of expressing this, were he to have filled out a project listing just before leaving Germany, may have been "try not to hurt Gerda too much." There is compelling evidence that the prevalence of such "avoidance" projects in one's project system may incur physical health costs (Elliot & Sheldon, 1998).[32] Paul's recurring earache may be as integral to the complexities of his project pursuit as is Gerda's heartache.

Project Termination

Some projects never end. Interminable projects, such as "treasuring my children" may take different forms over the years, but as a core defining aspect of self will only perish with that self. Most projects, however, are brought to completion, resulting in feelings of satisfaction ranging from relief to rapture. There is increasing empirical evidence that progress in project pursuit, over time, enhances well-being (Brunstein, 1993; Sheldon & Elliot, 1999). Relative to the other stages, not much research has been done on project completion, though it involves some of the most subtle aspects of daily human motivation. Klinger (1977) provides a compelling picture of some of the motivational issues surrounding disengagement from a goal, or "current concern." He argues that when a valued goal or current concern becomes frustrated or when it begins to lose incentive value, a predictable cycle will ensue. First, there is an invigoration of effort, then a more aggressive and primitive level of responding, then a downswing into depression, and later, an upswing into recovery (Klinger, 1977). Thus when he began to realize that his relationship with Gerda was not intrinsically rewarding for him, he may have engaged in a frenetic attempt to reinvest in the relationship, increasing the time he spent with her and composing and dedicating a piece of music to her (perhaps a fugue?). Subsequently, he might have gone through a period of barely suppressed hostility. Finally, when it is clear that he no longer loves her, Paul is likely to feel apathetic and even depressed. But as he lies in bed mulling over the mess his life is in, his thoughts turn again to New York—his new current concern and core project—and his mood begins to lift.

Personal Action and Well-Being: The Happiness of Pursuit

The rise of a conative personality psychology has been accompanied by increased research interest in subjective well-being, happiness, and perceived quality of life. In contrast with an earlier emphasis in personality psychology on maladaptation and psychopathology, contemporary research is increasingly concerned with factors that underlie human flourishing. For example, much of the early and continuing research with PAC units (Palys & Little, 1983; Emmons, 1986) has focused upon the prediction of subjective well-being (SWB) (Diener, 1984). The central notion underlying current PAC perspectives on well-being is that human happiness and quality of life is intimately related to the content and appraisal of one's ongoing pursuits.

Content Analyses of PAC Units

Content measures are typically taken from the elicitation phase of PAC assessment and involve examination of both the various domains (e.g., interpersonal, health, recreational) that individuals are involved in and theoretically important categorical variables, such as the level of molarity (Little, 1989) or abstractness (Emmons, 1998) of projects and strivings. Consider, for example, "intrapersonal projects," those concerned with changing or exploring aspects of one's personality (e.g., "being less shy," "figure out why I am so excited when Kurt is around"). Several studies have shown that the frequency of such intrapersonal projects in an individual's project system is inversely related to well-being, particularly to measures of depressive affect (Little, 1989; Salmela-Aro, 1992; Salmela-Aro & Nurmi,1996).[33]

PAC Appraisal Dimensions: A Five-Factor Model of Well-Being

The various appraisal dimensions that have been used in PAC research can be theoretically subsumed under five theoretical factors of meaning, structure, community, efficacy, and stress.

The *meaning* dimensions in PAC research address the question of how subjectively worthwhile are the pursuits engaged in by individuals. For example, personal project appraisal dimensions include having people indicate how enjoyable, important, and value congruent their projects are, and how expressive they are of their sense of personal identity (Little, 1989).[34] To the extent that the overall level of meaning in a person's project system is high, we anticipate that well-being will be enhanced; contrastingly, we anticipate that negative affect will be higher in individuals whose projects are essentially meaningless (Little, 1989).

Although having meaningful projects has been consistently associated with higher well-being, it will be shown later that meaningful projects are not sufficient in themselves to ensure high levels of well-being. This is because no matter how worthwhile one's projects might be, they may lack a sense of coherence and therefore be difficult to manage. We address this by including a set of dimensions relating to project *structure*—such as whether an individual initiated her projects, has a sense of control over them, and has sufficient time to devote to the them. There is clear empirical evidence that dimensions such as perceived control over one's projects are significantly related to measures of well-being and health (Little, 1989; Wilson, 1990). The projects most likely to offer a sense of structure are not necessarily those that are meaningful. Indeed, we suggest that people often experience a manageability–meaning trade-off in which they are caught between impossible dreams and achievable inconsequentialities.

A person's pursuits may be personally meaningful and manageable yet be accorded little significance or value by other significant individuals. Given the social origin of many pursuits (e.g., normatively valued life tasks) and the importance of having the larger eco-setting support and facilitate projects, we refer to this as a set of *community* dimensions, using the term in the broad sense of being socially valued and supported. A person's most treasured projects may be blocked by others, forcefully or artfully. Or one may learn at a very early age that there is a whole domain of pursuits that come with the label, "Don't even think about it." Some PAC units, such as life tasks, are of conceptual interest primarily because they are accorded significance as normative expectations within various "social ecologies." Thus, "achieving well academically" is typically a goal shared by students and their families even though the specific aspects of task pursuit for a given student may be subtly sabotaged by well-meaning others. For projects or tasks to be supported, they need to be known by the microcommunity within which they are enacted. But many individuals keep their projects well hidden, and even their most cherished strivings may be known only to themselves. Although well-being appears to be enhanced to the extent that individuals are engaged in projects that are high on visibility, perceived importance to others, and support by others, it is not yet clear whether this influences well-being beyond the effects of project meaning and structure (Ruehlman & Wolchik, 1988).

One of the most important dimensions affecting well-being is the extent to which individuals feel their projects are progressing well and are likely to continue to do so. This is essentially a factor of "efficacy." Even though one may have meaningful, manageable and supported projects, if it is expected that they will fail, well-being will be compromised. The relationship between efficacy of ongoing personal projects and well-being is one of the most robust findings in the PAC literature (Little, 1989; Salmela-Aro & Nurmi, 1996; Wilson, 1990).

The fifth core dimension of PAC units is that of *stress,* and, like efficacy, it has been found to be a consistently strong predictor (inversely) of well-being (Little, 1989). Stress in one's personal projects is related to Neuroticism and is high in both anxious and depressed individuals (Little, Lecci, & Watkinson, 1992; Lecci, Karoly, Briggs, & Kuhn, 1994). Relatedly, conflict within one's personal strivings (arguably a measure of both lack of structure and of stress) prospectively predict health problems (Emmons & King, 1988).

Although dimensions from each of the five major PAC dimensions is associated with well-being, there are interdimensional interactions that need to be explored. An intriguing example is shown in the work of Lydon and Zanna (1990). They found that the demandingness of volunteer projects enhances commitment and hence may have an indirect salutary influence on well-being. However, this effect only held with projects that were value-congruent (one of the meaning dimensions). Thus, although the five-dimension perspective provides some needed taxonomic structure to PAC units and each serve as predictors of well-being, the subtleties of motivation will be captured more effectively by looking at interactions among the component dimensions. Some important new developments in precisely this more finely textured approach to PAC units and well-being can now be discussed.

Recent Developments with PAC Units: Refining the PAC Well-Being Model

In recent years several conceptual and methodological advances have been published in the PAC literature illustrating the distinctive strengths of the conative framework for exploring personality and motivation.

One area needing clarification was the relationship between the meaning dimensions of PAC units and global measures of well-being. An apparent paradox appearing in a meta-analytic review of this area was that, of the five major factors, project meaning (with the exception of enjoyment) was the least strongly linked with measures of well-being (Little, 1998). Efficacy and the absence of stress were consistently better predictors of well-being. Two recent studies help explain the apparent paradox that measures of the meaningfulness of pursuit were not the best predictors of overall well-being.

McGregor and Little (1998) showed that it is important to ensure that global well-being measures include components tapping into a sense of meaning in life in addition to measures of happiness and positive and negative affect (cf. Ryff & Singer, 1998). They showed that efficacy was more associated with the happiness component of well-being, whereas project meaning dimensions were, as originally anticipated, more closely associated with a global sense of living a meaningful life.

A closely related issue has been studied by Sheldon and Kasser (1998; Sheldon & Elliot, 1998) who address the issue of project meaning and efficacy, invoking Deci and Ryan's concept of autonomous action and integrating it with aspects of Rogerian theory about the importance of self-congruence. They show that although efficacy is a significant predictor of well-being, it is particularly so with strivings and projects that are high in autonomous regulation and are self-congruent. Most personal projects generated by individuals are, in an absolute sense, meaningful acts (see Little, 1998, for empirical evidence) and hence autonomously regulated. It makes sense, then, that most of the studies that have examined efficacy or have focused primarily upon efficacy dimensions (e.g., Salmela-Aro, 1992) have found significant links with well-being. However, the fact that project meaning is a significant moderator of this relationship is an important finding.

Issues relating to the longitudinal study of personal projects and well-being have also been studied and provide important information about the likely mechanisms subsuming meaningful goal pursuit and subsequent well-being. Brunstein (1993), with German undergraduates, explored changes in well-being over an academic term. He showed that several project appraisal factors successfully predicted changes in well-being over the term. A particularly crucial role was found for project commitment, a dimension that has also been found to be important in studies of organizational behavior (Phillips, Little, & Goodine, 1996, 1997). Another series of longitudinal studies with Finnish undergraduates (Salmela-Aro, 1992) showed a clear pattern of relationship between project content and appraisal factors and measures of counseling readiness and depressive affect. In a causal path analysis of the relationship between project factors and depressive affect it was shown that there were significant paths from depressive affect to subsequent project appraisal and from project appraisal to depressive affect, though the former effect was notably stronger. This suggest that although dispositional factors may play a key role in influencing the appraisal of our ongoing personal action, there is still evidence of sufficient bidirectionality of influence that intervention studies to enhance well-being are not ruled out.[35]

A final example of the increasing rigor of design in studies of well-being and PAC units is reported by Fleeson and Cantor (1997). In showing the relationship between life task appraisals and daily affect, they examined carefully the possible confounding effect of environmental/contextual features that could be common to the appraisal of both tasks and current mood. They found that PAC effects, above and beyond environmental factors, influence outcome measures. Together with the Sheldon and Elliot results, this strengthens the claim that PAC units are distinct sources of influence on well-being above and beyond their expected relationship with stable aspects of individual differences or environments.

PERSONALITY AND THE INTEGRATIVE CHALLENGE: CONSILIENCE AND CONATION

The central and distinctive contribution of a conative personality psychology is its providing both conceptual and methodological tools for integration within personality psychology (cf. McAdams, 1995). Given personality psychology's commitment to provide the integrative core for psychological science, it is worth emphasizing, by way of review, how the conative evolution advances the integrative aspirations of our field.

We began by showing that Paul's lunchtime pursuits, as examined from an informed but informal perspective, entailed recognition that his personal action was idiosyncratically construed, contextually embedded, systemically linked, and potentially tractable. We developed these four characteristics, more formally, into essential methodological criteria for the elicitation and empirical exploration of personal action constructs (PAC units). We reviewed how the content and appraisal of personal strivings, personal projects, and life tasks allowed us to explore human motivation in a distinctive and, it would appear, increasingly fruitful fashion. PAC units were proposed as occupying a middle ground between stable aspects of persons, stable aspects of situations, and outcome measures relating to well-being and ecological competency. We showed how PAC units have important temporal properties and that the dynamics of motivation shift subtly as a function of the stage of the pursuits to which we are committed. Five core factors underlying PAC units—meaning, structure, community, efficacy, and stress, were shown to relate both to subjective well-being and to other aspects of the conative research model, such as stable traits. More importantly, the case was made that the modular flexibility, temporal sensitivity, and mixed idiographic–nomothetic strengths of PAC methodology allows for increasingly complex and informative studies to be carried out in which conative explanations of human conduct are pitted against theoretically plausible alternative perspectives.

At the very outset it was suggested that the conative evolution has been a shift away from an emphasis on unconscious motives and contextual forces and also a movement away from a restrictive cognitive perspective. These points now need to be clarified in the light of the propositions advanced in the chapter. It should be clear that an emphasis on personal action is not an exclusionary perspective in personality but one that simply places primary emphasis upon extended sets of personally meaningful, contextually embedded action. We acknowledge that unconscious forces may play a vital role in the initiation of tasks and projects and in the difficulties one experiences in managing them. However, we see the assessment and analysis of the high-priority personal actions with which a person is currently engaged to be the key starting point of serious investigation in personality. When such action becomes dangerously disorganized, persistently self-defeating, bizarre, and futile, PAC theorists will want to invoke psychodynamic, evolutionary, or other perspectives to help clarify the incoherence experienced in the lives of our respondents and co-investigators. Similarly, though we argue that environmental factors are not overriding influences on daily motivation, our emphasis on ecologically representative measurement means that our explanatory constructs are more likely to have a contextualist tone than personality theories that are focused exclusively on internalized units of analysis.[36]

I suggested that conative personality psychology goes beyond a "restrictive cognitive theory" and that this will be a more contentious point. This issue turns crucially on the question of whether personal action constructs are simply goal concepts. Much of the research reviewed in the chapter can be described as goal research, and the most frequently used PAC units are often referred to as personal goal units. Is there a difference? I believe there is: Goals are the *inception* point of personal action, and they have played an illustrious and increasingly influential role in the psychology of motivation, from early Lewinian theorizing to the considerable resurgence in personality and social psychology documented in Pervin (1989). But action, particularly personal action, extends further into the domain of impactful behavior than do goals and in that respect open up different domains for integration into the core of personality psychology. It is true that goal researchers can monitor the environmental impact and behavioral consequences of goal pursuit, but, to invoke Kellian terms, such concerns are at the edge of the range of convenience of the goal construct. PAC units, such as tasks and projects, have a rather different and complementary focus of convenience, and it tips the balance of theory, assessment, and research into domains that had been lost sight of during the cognitive revolution. Expressive behavior, for example, the distinctive semiswagger of Paul as he clears the tables, seems more accessible if we are talking about project action than the goal undergirding it, and it seems more natural to talk about the transactional nature of persons in context by invoking PAC units than goal units. The effortful activity put into projects, strivings, and tasks, the sheer *physicality* of volitional pursuit aligns PAC units more easily with recent advances in the psychophysiological basis of human flourishing (Ryff & Singer, 1998).[37] To put it tendentiously, goal units are the culmination of cognitive personology; PAC units are the beginning of a conative personology.

The fact that the constructs are intimately linked, as subtle as the difference between Paul's planning and parting, should not obscure the fact that the small shift in perspective provides different sight lines on matters of enduring concern to the study of personality and motivation. For example, PAC units can access each of the theoretical perspectives represented by the revolving tables and evolving constructs we encountered at the Schwedische Café—from needs as conceived in the Murray–McClelland tradition (Omodei & Wearing, 1990), to classical learning theory (Ogilvie & Rose, 1996).

The conative evolution has not been restricted to personality research. There is increasing evidence of a general conative psychology taking hold in social, developmental, and even cognitive psychology.[38] Certainly the increasing interest in "hot" cognition and the rapid rise of interest in affective processes, emotion, and hedonic psychology (see Chapter 21) suggests that the hegemony of cognition as psychology's central core may be starting to fade.[39] But there is also a subtle difference between affective psychology and conative psychology. The former is concerned with the social, cognitive, and physiological concomitants of emotional experience. But where it is concerned about the nature of "hot" itself, conative psychology is concerned with the question, "Hot about what?"

One of the exciting things about the changes that are occurring in personality and psychology in general as we enter the new millennium is that one detects a sense of convergence, a loosening of exclusionary epistemic sects and a more ecumenical atmosphere among psychological researchers. Indeed, the increasing conciliatory nature of our scientific pursuits has been nicely captured in the titles and messages of two recent publications. Mischel and Shoda (1998) have written about "reconciling" processing dynamic and dispositional views in personality psychology. E. O. Wilson (1998) talks about the increasing sense of "consilience" (literally, a "jumping together") that he detects in the biological sciences. Consilience occurs when findings in one domain are increasingly converging with those in adjacent research domains so that the possibility of a grand synthesis appears more hopeful than ever. More contentiously (as if a Grand Synthesis were not contentious enough!) Wilson argues for consiliency to extend from the life sciences to incorporate the humanities. He is especially hopeful that evolutionary psychology, for example, may provide a viable framework for the study of human ethics (Wilson, 1998).

I suggest that, although evolutionary psychology has considerable claim on our attention both in the sciences and humanities, its focus of convenience, again, is displaced too far away from the "thick" textures of personal action that are the natural foci for a conative psychology. I suspect that the small steps towards interdisciplinary consiliency, particularly in the domains of psychology and ethics, will come through research on the small interdomain linkages that show how individuals pursue their singular projects while respecting those of others. For personality psychology to be part of this integrative effort, it will require concepts, methods, and interventional philosophies capable of bridging the most disparate and potentially conflicting roots of human nature and human conduct. The argument of this chapter has been that such integration will be found in the study of personal action, its volitional dynamics and contextual challenges—in short, in a conative personality psychology.

NOTES

1. Conation derives from the Latin, *conatio* (to try) and historically has been contrasted with cognition and affection.

2. They were asking him if he could recall what each of them had eaten for lunch. He responded that he couldn't because they had already paid half an hour ago and didn't they have better things to do over in the Psychological Institute? Paul (I have been unable to determine his real name) had been, of course, the unwitting instigator of Kurt Lewin and Bluma Zeigarnik's speculations leading to the formulation of the Zeigarnik effect. It held that memory for noncompleted tasks is better than for those completed—a landmark in early motivational research. One of the unintended consequences of his projects in waiting had been that he was committing data.

3. I am indebted to Stephen Toulmin for this example (Toulmin, 1970).

4. Such depictions can be "objective," grounded in consensual judgements about the physical, social, or cultural aspects of a person's context, and they may be viewed from the subjective, idiosyncratic perspective of the individual's *personal context* (Little, in press-a). Personality psychology requires information on both objective and personal contexts or in Murray's terms, alpha and beta press. For more detailed treatment of the ecology of personal action (Little, 1987, in press-b).

5. Compare Craik (1986) who has provided a detailed analysis of the historical trends in methodologies in personality psychology.

6. Sometimes a cigar is merely a metaphor.

7. At this last comment the ears of some of the Behaviorists at the next table perk up and mutterings about it finally being Dollard and Miller time are heard over the clanking of tankards. They are a large and diverse group, conceptually emphatic and noisy. Those arriving early in the century would emphasize that Paul's behavior was explicable in terms of the rewards and punishments operating in the environment and as a result of the power of drive reduction in the maintenance of action. The later arrivals would also suggest that much of Paul's behavior was modeled by his cousin, who had left Germany three years earlier to pursue an academic career in Toronto.

8. He even suggested that they change the name of the symposium to the Nebraska Symposium on What's Next? (Kelly, 1962).

9. This restaurant actually exists as the Opern Cafe unter den Linden and is across from Humboldt University. Thanks to the efforts of Anne Tschida and Will Fleeson, a picture of it can be seen in Winter (1996, p. 36). The theorists I am discussing are just out of sight around the corner but can be glimpsed fleetingly with imaginative peripheral vision.

10. Three of them receive extensive treatment in other chapters of this volume—the cognitive social learning theorists (see Chapters 6 and 7), the Murray–McClelland group (see Chapter 1) and the psychodynamicists (see Chapter 3). We shall pass by their table for now (though we will be revisiting each in later sections). We shall also defer discussion with a voluble table of evolutionary psychologists who clearly have much to say about Paul and the distal provenance of his projects: They too have spirited representation in this handbook (see Chapter 2).

11. These are among the more actively researched PAC units and are useful to focus on as they have similar but subtly different foci of convenience in explaining action. For a more extensive discussion of similar types of construct see Cantor and Zirkel (1990).

12. For example, "leaving for America" from Berlin in the 1920s was a far more onerous and irrevocable commitment than it would likely be today. The barriers to coming and going, the relative costs, and the symbolism it entailed suggests that there were a multitude of idiosyncratic Berlin walls in the motivational agendas of individuals.

13. In this respect PAC methodology can be used as both a person-centered and variable-centered measurement framework and is able to address some of the challenges posed by Carlson (1971) in her critique of orthodox methodologies in personality psychology.

14. For example, it has been shown that anorexic patients are more likely to have personal projects concentrated in a very few places relative to comparison groups, and behavioral geographers have shown that the mean distance between project locations is inversely related to well-being among working women (see Little, 1983).

15. There is an important psychometric implication to the temporal extension and dynamic nature of projects and other PAC units. Unlike the "snapshot" nature of fixed traits, PAC units are conceived of as "moving pictures." This means that there is no expectation of substantial test–retest reliabilities for indices derived from the ratings of projects at two different times: Temporal stability of PAC appraisal units is not a canonical requirement but an open empirical question. Interestingly, when test–retest analyses have been carried out, project system characteristics are notably high, suggesting that there are relatively stable project spaces underlying appraisals of one's current projects (see Gee, 1998).

16. For example, new dimensions have been added to the standard appraisal matrix to study single parents, patients with eating disorders, Indo-Chinese refugees, type A personalities, and senior corporate executives (Little, 1989).

17. A comprehensive and authoritative anthology of over 200 ad hoc dimensions that have been used in research on distinctive social ecologies or to provide local nuance to a standard dimension is available (Chambers, 1997).

18. PAC methodology provides means for rigorous measurement of variables within the single case. This can be illustrated by considering the difference between systemic and discrete measurement of two important personality constructs relating to motivation: a sense of control and perceived stressfulness. Discrete measurement of these two constructs involves the appraisal of each variable separately with a separate measurement tool (e.g., a locus of control scale and a perceived stress scale). The relation between these measures would be a correlation across subjects between the two discrete measures. *Systemic* measurement of control and stress would be carried out very differently. The analytic unit, such as a personal goal, striving, or project, would serve as the common focus for ratings by individuals of their perceived control and perceived stress. The correlations could be carried out either at the individual or the normative level of analysis. In the former case, it is possible that for one individual there will be a negative correlation between stress and control in her particular system, whereas for another subject there may be a positive correlation. Systemic measurement, in short, allows for the study of the interactions among key motivational and personality variables within the personal action systems of the respondents rather than relying on normative, aggregative levels of analysis, which may, theoretically, provide a very different picture of the relationship.

19. The superordinate constructs may be core values or overarching life plans while the subordinate constructs are typically acts or behavioral sequences through which the PAC units are achieved. The molecular units are frequently accessed by the use of sampling techniques using 'beeper technology" (e.g. Klinger, 1984).

20. Sheldon and Kasser (1995) have referred to these two types of linkage as vertical and horizontal integration, respectively.

21. The philosophers in the cafe would tell us that such a datum provides a rich example of the difference between prudential and ethical concerns in human conduct.

22. A similar case emphasizing the need for integrative assessment has been forcefully argued by Craik (1986), who criticizes the guild-like nature of methodologically like-minded researchers in personality psychology. Craik's concern is the promotion of methodological pluralism and the avoidance of sectarian isolation. My concern is equally with the need to avoid sectarian splits, but it takes a somewhat different route to achieving this. As well as having personality researchers achieving integration by wedding insights gleaned from disparate methodologies, I think we also need to have integrative methodologies. The former strategy places the onus for integration on the assessor. The strategy I am advocating sees the assessment instruments themselves as integrative devices for personality psychology.

23. This contrasts with approaches such as trait measurement, which offer more oblique applicability. Trait measurement, for example, helps clinicians match clients with trait-relevant clinical procedures (e.g., group therapy as more appropriate for extraverted clients) (see Costa & McCrae, 1992). But, given the presumed fixity of personality traits, there is little attempt to directly intervene with them as part of a therapeutic plan.

24. When PAC methods are used in this way, the resulting quantitative indices are subject to some, but not all, of the psychometric constraints to which standard normative measures are held accountable (e.g., internal consistency, test–retest reliability etc.) and generally have held up well under such constraints (Little, 1987; Little, Lecci, & Watkinson, 1992).

25. It should be noted that there is no *necessary* mathematical isomorphism between individual and joint level measurement spaces: The ecological fallacy, the individual difference fallacy, and Simpson's paradox all hold that results between variables measured at one level of a system may not necessarily hold at another level (see Gee, 1998).

26. For example, in our own SEAbank (Social Ecological Assessment data bank) we have stored personal project data from thousands of respondents, preserving their idiosyncratic description of the project, their appraisals, and personality, demographic, and other relevant data on individuals generating the data. Such strings of data can be used as social indicators for relevant groups of populations and helps us pose practical questions relating to the quality of life that go beyond individual level analysis.

27. The model (based on Little, 1987, in press-d) is very similar to a recently proposed model of functionalist psychology (e.g., Snyder, 1993). The convergence between conative assessment in personality psychology and similar developments within social psychology is noteworthy. Although there are some subtle differences between the functionalist and conative perspectives in psychology, there is sufficient overlap to suggest that the conative turn is far from a parochial development in personality psychology.

28. A superb review of the motivational literature that gives due weight to these influences is Heckhausen (1991).

29. The study of "sets" and their impact on action has a long history in psychology. One important but infrequently cited work is that of Leff, who has shown how different cognitive sets can influence environmental experience (Leff, 1976). A comprehensive set of "sets" for a conative psychology has been recently proposed by Karoly (1998).

30. Essentially he is criticizing both Kantian and utilitarian views of moral choice and offering a more radically "personalist" (see Trianovsky, 1990) perspective on ethics.

31. At least, so it would seem from the perspective of the *prudential* management of one's personal set of pursuits (see Haslam & Baron, 1994). However, when we begin to take other individuals and their projects into account, and in so doing enter the domain of ethical theory, things become intriguingly complex, particularly with respect to the tension between project pursuit and the well-being of others (Flanagan, 1991; Lomasky, 1984, 1987; Williams, 1981).

32. Higgins' self-discrepancy theory provides an intriguing explanatory framework for understanding Paul's current choices (Higgins, 1987; Higgins, Shah, & Friedman, 1997). Paul's music and interpersonal projects reflect different self-regulatory foci. Music, for Paul, is a "promotional" goal, oriented to achievement of a delight; "Gerda" is a "prevention" goal, oriented toward fulfilling a duty. Failure of the first may lead Paul to depression; failure on the second, to anxiety. Success with the music would be rapturous; success with the interpersonal obligation would be relief. Given his choices, then, we would have to regard Paul as perplexed.

33. However, there is also some evidence that such projects are *also* associated with measures of creativity (Little, 1989), raising interesting questions about how depressogenic and creative intrapersonal projects differ. One possibility is that autonomously regulated intrapersonal projects (in the Deci & Ryan sense) will be associated with creative acts of self-exploration, whereas externally regulated ones will be associated with depression. Thus, for Gerda, the project "figure out why I get involved with unreliable people" may lead to creative self discovery were she to

initiate it. But if it came down as a family injunction, it could end up as ruminative worrying about her inability to sustain intimate relationships (see Nolen-Hoeksema, 1987).

34. There are a large number of PAC appraisal dimensions that are explicitly concerned with the self, and they have received detailed attention elsewhere (Little, 1993; McGregor & Little, 1998). An intriguing self dimension that has been utilized in goal research has been that of self-completion—the extent to which a course of personal action symbolizes the type of person one wishes to be and the compensatory actions that are engaged in if the original goal is frustrated (see Wicklund & Gollwitzer, 1982). This is a research topic, it should be noted, that also had its original inception in the Lewinian group discussions in the Schwedische Café.

35. Relatedly, an important set of longitudinal studies by Sheldon and Elliot (1999) has provided clear evidence not only for the effectiveness of PAC units in the prediction of well-being but also that the effect is not due to the confounding effect of traits such as Neuroticism.

36. Indeed, Figure 20.1 can be augmented by having PAC unit-relevant subregions of both stable traits ("free traits") and environments ("personal contexts") that also meet the four measurement criteria and provide a conative bridge to a transactional psychology (see Little, in press-b,c).

37. Clearly, the line differentiating goal units and PAC units is a fine one. Pervin (1991), for example, has given a persuasive account of the affective significance of goal units in the context of self-regularity failure.

38. I even detect points of common ground between ethology and conative psychology. It is unlikely we could generate personal projects as such with other animals (though I fantasize about getting the whale's view of Melville's masterpiece beginning with: "Call me Moby"). But the study of extended sets of salient activity and the likely goals underlying them are entirely appropriate aspirations.

39. Though I must point out that 30 years ago at Oxford, Patrick Rabbit offered a lecture course entitled "Uncognitive Psychology"—suggesting he was either in denial or way ahead of his time.

REFERENCES

Allport, G. W. (1958). What units shall we employ? In G. Lindzey (Ed.), *Assessment of human motives* (pp. 239–260). New York: Rinehart.

Argyle, M., & Little, B. R. (1972). Do personality traits apply to social behavior? *Journal for the Theory of Social Behavior, 2,* 1–35.

Austin, J. T., & Vancouver, J. B. (1996). Goal constructs in psychology: Structure, process and content. *Psychological Bulletin, 120,* 338–375.

Baldwin, M. W., Carrell, S. E., & Lopez, D. F. (1990). Priming relationship schemas: My advisor and the pope are watching me from the back of my mind. *Journal of Experimental Social Psychology, 26,* 435–454.

Bandura, A. (1982). The psychology of chance encounters and life paths. *American Psychologist, 37,* 747–755.

Barker, R. G. (1968). *Ecological psychology: Concepts and methods for studying the environment of human behavior.* Stanford, CA: Stanford University Press.

Brunstein, J. C. (1993). Personal goals and subjective well-being: A longitudinal study. *Journal of Personality and Social Psychology, 95* , 1061–1070.

Buss, D. M., & Craik, K. H. (1983). The act frequency approach to personality. *Psychological Review, 90,* 105–125.

Cantor, N. (1990). From thought to behavior: "Having" and "doing" in the study of personality and cognition. *American Psychologist, 45,* 735–750.

Cantor, N., & Zirkel, S. (1990). Personality, cognition, and purposive behavior. In L. A. Pervin (Ed.), *Handbook of personality: Theory and research* (pp. 135–164). New York: Guilford Press.

Carlson, R. (1971). Where is the person in personality research? *Psychological Bulletin, 75,* 203–219.

Chambers, N. (1997). *Personal projects analysis: The maturation of a multidimensional methodology.* Unpublished manuscript, Social Ecology Laboratory, Department of Psychology, Carleton University, Ottawa.

Christiansen, C., Little, B. R., & Backman, C. (1998). Personal projects: A useful concept for occupational therapy. *American Journal of Occupational Therapy.*

Costa, P. T., & McCrae, R. R. (1992). Normal personality assessment in clinical practice: The NEO Personality Inventory. *Psychological Assessment, 4,* 5–13.

Craik, K. H. (1986). Personality research methods: An historical perspective. *Journal of Personality, 54,* 18–51.

Deci, E., & Ryan, R. M. (1991). A motivational approach to self: Integration in personality. In R. Dienstbier (Ed.), *Nebraska Symposium on Motivation: Vol. 38. Perspectives on motivation* (pp. 237–288). Lincoln, NE: University of Nebraska Press.

Diener, E. (1984). Subjective well-being. *Psychological Bulletin, 23,* 915–927.

Elliot, A. J., & Sheldon, K. M. (1998). Avoidance personal goals and the personality–illness relationship. *Journal of Personality and Social Psychology, 75,* 1282–1299.

Elliot, A. J., Sheldon, K. M., & Church, M. (1997). Avoidance personal goals and subjective well-being. *Personality and Social Psychology Bulletin, 23,* 915–927.

Emmons, R. A. (1986). Personal strivings: An approach to personality and subjective well-being. *Journal of Personality and Social Psychology, 51,* 1058–1068.

Emmons, R. (1992). Abstract versus concrete goals: Personal goals and subjective well-being. *Journal of Personality and Social Psychology, 62,* 292–300.

Emmons, R. A. (1998). Motives and life goals. In R. Hogan, J. Johnson & S. Briggs (Eds.), *Handbook of personality psychology* (pp. 485–512). San Diego, CA: Academic Press.

Emmons, R. A., & King, L. A. (1988). Conflict among personal strivings: Immediate and long-term implications for psychological and physical well-being. *Journal of Personality and Social Psychology, 54,* 1040–1048.

Endler, N. S. (1983). Interactionism: A personality model, but not yet a theory. In M. M. Page (Ed.), *Nebraska Symposium on Motivation: Vol. 31. Personality: Current theory and research* (pp. 155–200). Lincoln, NE: University of Nebraska Press.

Ewart, C. K. (1991). Social action theory for a public health psychology. *American Psychologist, 46,* 931–946.

Flanagan, O. (1991). *Varieties of moral personality: Ethics and psychological realism.* Cambridge, MA: Harvard University Press.

Fleeson, W., & Cantor, N. (1995). Goal relevance and the affective experience of daily-life: Ruling out situational explanations. *Motivation and Emotion, 19,* 25–27.

Gee, T. L. (1998). *Individual and joint-level properties of personal project matrices: An exploration of the nature of project spaces.* Unpublished doctoral dissertation, Carleton University, Ottawa.

Gollwitzer, P. M. (1990). Action phases and mind-sets. In E. T. Higgins & R. M. Sorrentino (Eds.), *Handbook of motivation and cognition* (Vol. 2, pp. 53–92). New York: Guilford Press.

Gollwitzer, P. M., & Brandstätter, V. (1997). Implementation intentions and effective goal pursuit. *Journal of Personality and Social Psychology, 73,* 186–199.

Goodine, L. A. (1986). *Anorexics, bulimics and highly weight preoccupied women: A comparison of personal project systems and personality factors.* Unpublished master's thesis, Carleton University, Ottawa.

Haslam, N., & Baron, J. (1994). Intelligence, personality, and prudence. In R. J. Sternberg & P. Rusgiz, (Eds.), *Personality and intelligence* (pp. 32–58). Cambridge, UK: Cambridge University Press.

Heckhausen, H. (1991). *Motivation and action.* Berlin: Springer-Verlag.

Helson, R., Mitchell, V., & Moane, G. (1984). Personality and patterns of adherence and nonadherence to the social clock. *Journal of Personality and Social Psychology, 46,* 1079–1095.

Higgins, E. T. (1987). Self-discrepancy: A theory relating self and affect. *Psychological Review, 94,* 319–340.

Higgins, E. T., Shah, J. Y., & Friedman, R. (1997). Emotional responses to goal attainment: Strength of regulatory focus as moderator. *Journal of Personality and Social Psychology, 72,* 515–525.

John, O. P. (1990). The Big Five factor taxonomy: Dimensions of personality in the natural language and in questionnaires. In L. Pervin (Ed.), *Handbook of personality: Theory and research* (pp. 66–100). New York: Guilford Press.

Karoly, P. (1998). *Intentional mindsets: Goal framing in seven dimensions.* Paper presented at American Psychological Society Annual Meeting (May), Washington, DC.

Kelly, G. A. (1955). *The psychology of personal constructs.* New York: Norton.

Kelly, G. A. (1962). Europe's matrix of decision. *Nebraska Symposium on Motivation* (Vol. 10). Lincoln, NE: University of Nebraska Press.

Klinger, E. (1975). Consequences of commitment to and disengagement from incentives. *Psychological Review, 82,* 223–231.

Klinger, E. (1977). *Meaning and void: Inner experience and the incentives in people's lives.* Minneapolis, MN: University of Minnesota Press.

Klinger, E. (1984). A consciousness-sampling analysis of test anxiety and performance. *Journal of Personality and Social Psychology, 47,* 1376–1390.

Krahé, B. (1992). *Personal and social psychology: Toward a synthesis.* London: Sage.

Lecci, L., Karoly, P., Briggs, C., & Kuhn, K. (1994). Specificity and generality of motivational components in depression: a personal projects analysis. *Journal of Abnormal Psychology, 103*(2), 404–408.

Leff, H. L. (1978). *Experience, environment and human potentials.* New York: Oxford University Press.

Little, B. R. (1972). Psychological man as scientist, humanist and specialist. *Journal of Experimental Research in Personality, 6,* 95–118.

Little, B. R. (1983). Personal projects: A rationale and method for investigation. *Environment and Behaviour, 15*(3), 273–309.

Little, B. R. (1987). Personality and the environment. In D. Stokols & I. Altman (Eds.), *Handbook of environmental psychology.* New York: Wiley.

Little, B. R. (1989). Personal projects analysis: Trivial pursuits, magnificent obsessions, and the search for coherence. In D. M. Buss & N. Cantor (Eds.), *Personality psychology: Recent trends and emerging issues* (pp. 15–31). New York: Springer-Verlag.

Little, B. R. (1993). Personal projects and the distributed self: Aspects of a conative psychology. In J. Suls (Ed.), *Psychological perspectives on the self* (Vol. 4, pp. 157–181). Hillsdale, NJ: Erlbaum.

Little, B. R. (1996). Free traits, personal projects and idio-tapes: Three tiers for personality research. *Psychological Inquiry, 8,* 340–344.

Little, B. R. (1998). Personal project pursuit: Dimensions and dynamics of personal meaning. In P. T. P. Wong & P. S. Fry (Eds.), *The human quest for meaning: A handbook of research and clinical applications.* Mahwah, NJ: Erlbaum.

Little, B. R. (in press-a). Free traits and personal contexts: Expanding a social ecological model of well-being. In. W. B. Walsh, K. H. Craik, & R. H. Price (Eds.). *Person–environment psychology: Models and perspectives* (2nd ed.). Hillsdale, NJ: Erlbaum.

Little, B. R. (in press-b). Persons, contexts, and personal projects: Assumptive themes of a methodological transactionalism. In S. Wapner, J. Demick, H. Minami, & T. Yamamoto (Eds.), *Theoretical perspectives in environment–behavior research: Underlying assumptions, research problems and methodologies.* New York: Plenum Press.

Little, B. R. (in press-c). Personal projects and social ecology: Themes and variations across the life span. In J. Brandstädter & R. M. Lerner (Eds.), *Action and self-development: Theory and research through the life-span.* Thousand Oaks, CA: Sage.

Little, B. R. (in press-d). Personality psychology: Havings, doings and beings in context. In S. Davis & J. Halonen (Eds.), *The many faces of psychology in the twenty first century.* Washington, DC: American Psychological Association.

Little, B. R., Lecci, L., & Watkinson, B. (1992). Personality and personal projects: Linking Big Five and PAC units of analysis. *Journal of Personality, 60,* 501–525.

Lomasky, L. E. (1984). Personal projects as the foundation of human rights. *Social Philosophy and Policy, 1,* 35–55.

Lomasky, L. E. (1987). *Persons, rights and the moral community.* New York: Oxford University Press.

Lydon, J. E., & Zanna, M. P. (1990). Commitment in the face of adversity: A value-affirmation approach. *Journal of Personality and Social Psychology, 58,* 1040–1047.

Markus, H. & Nurius, P. (1986). Possible selves. *American Psychologist, 41,* 954–969.

McAdams, D. P. (1995). What do we know when we know a person? *Journal of Personality, 63,* 365–396.

McGregor, I., & Little, B. R. (1998). Personal projects, happiness and meaning: On doing well and being yourself. *Journal of Personality and Social Psychology, 74,* 494–512.

Mischel, W. (1968). *Personality and assessment.* New York: Wiley.

Mischel, W., & Shoda, Y. (1998). Reconciling processing dynamics and personality dispositions. *Annual Review of Psychology, 49,* 229–258.

Murray, H. A. (1938). *Explorations in personality.* New York: Oxford University Press.

Nolen-Hoeksema, S. (1987). Sex differences in uni-polar depression: Evidence and theory. *Psychological Bulletin, 101,* 259–282.

Norem, J. (1989). Cognitive strategies as personality: Effectiveness, specificity, flexibility, and change (pp. 45–60). In D. Buss & N. Cantor (Eds.), *Personality psychology: Recent trends and emerging directions.* New York: Springer-Verlag.

Norem, J. K., & Cantor, N. (1986). Defensive pessimism: "Harnessing" anxiety as motivation. *Journal of Personality and Social Psychology, 51,* 1208–1217.

Ogilvie, M. D., & Rose, K. M. (1996). Self-with-other representations and a taxonomy of motives: Two approaches to studying persons. *Journal of Personality, 63*(3), 633–679.

Omodei, M. M., & Wearing, A. J. (1990). Need satisfaction and involvement in personal projects: Toward an integrative model of subjective well-being. *Journal of Personality and Social Psychology, 59* (4), 762–769.

Palys, T. S., & Little, B. R. (1983). Perceived life satisfaction and the organization of personal projects systems. *Journal of Personality and Social Psychology, 44,* 1221–1230..

Pervin, L. A. (1983). The stasis and flow of behavior: Toward a theory of goals. In M. M. Page (Ed.), *Nebraska Symposium on Motivation* (Vol. 31, pp. 1–53). Lincoln, NE: University of Nebraska Press.

Pervin, L. A. (1985). Personality: Current controversies, issues, and directions. *Annual Review of Psychology, 36,* 83–114.

Pervin, L. A. (Ed.). (1989). *Goal concepts in personality and social psychology.* Hillsdale, NJ: Erlbaum.

Phillips, S. D., Little, B. R., & Goodine, L. A.(1996). *Organizational climate and personal projects: Gender differences in the public service.* Ottawa, ON: Canadian Centre for Management Development.

Phillips, S. D., Little, B. R., & Goodine, L. A. (1997). Reconsidering gender and public administration: Five steps beyond conventional research. *Canadian Public Administration, 40,* 563–581.

Pychyl, T. (1995). *Personal projects, subjective well-being and the lives of doctoral students.* Unpublished doctoral dissertation, Carleton University, Ottawa, Ontario.

Pychyl, T., & Little, B. R. (1998). Dimensional specificity in the prediction of well-being: Personal projects in pursuit of the Ph.D. *Social Indicators Research, 45,* 423–473.

Ruehlman, L. S., & Wolchik, S. A. (1988). Personal goals and interpersonal support and hindrance as factors in psychological distress and well-being. *Journal of Personality and Social Psychology, 55,* 293–301.

Ryff, C. D., & Singer, B. (1998). The contours of positive human health. *Psychological Inquiry, 9,* 1–28.

Salmela-Aro, K. (1992). Struggling with self: The personal projects of students seeking psychological counselling. *Scandinavian Journal of Psychology, 33,* 330–338.

Salmela-Aro, K., & Nurmi, J. (1996). Depressive symptoms and personal project appraisals: A cross-lagged longitudinal study. *Personality and Individual Differences, 21,* 373–381.

Sheldon, K. M., & Elliot, A. (1998). Not all personal goals are personal. Comparing autonomous and controlled reasons for goals as predictors of effort and attainment. *Personality and Social Psychology Bulletin, 24,* 546–557.

Sheldon, K. M., & Elliot, A. J. (1999). Goal striving, need satisfaction, and longitudinal well-being: The self-concordance model. *Journal of Personality and Social Psychology, 76,* 482–497.

Sheldon, K. M., & Kasser, T. (1995). Coherence and congruence: Two aspects of personality integration.

Journal of Personality and Social Psychology, 68, 531–543.

Sheldon, K. M., & Kasser, T. (1998). Pursuing personal goals: Skills enable progress but not all progress is beneficial. *Personality and Social Psychology Bulletin, 24,* 1319–1331.

Snyder, M. (1993). Basic research and practical problems: The promise of a "functional" personality and social psychology. *Personality and Social Psychology Bulletin, 19,* 251–264.

Sundberg, N. D. (1980). Assessment of persons. Englewood Cliffs, NJ: Prentice Hall.

Taylor, S. E., & Gollwitzer, P. M. (1995). Effects of mindset on positive illusions. *Journal of Personality and Social Psychology, 69,* 213–226.

Toulmin, S. (1970). Reasons and causes. In R. Borger & F. Cioffi (Eds.). *Explanation in the behavioural sciences* (pp. 1–26) Cambridge, UK: Cambridge University Press.

Trianosky, G. (1990). Natural affection and responsibility for character: A critique of Kantian views of the virtues. In O. Flanagan & A. O. Rorty (Eds.), *Identity, character, and morality: Essays in moral psychology* (pp. 93–109). Cambridge, MA: MIT Press.

Vallerand, R. (1997). Toward a hierarchical model of intrinsic and extrinsic motivation. In M. Zanna (Ed.), *Advances in experimental social psychology* (pp. 271–360). New York: Academic Press.

Vallerand, R. J., Fortier, M. S., & Guay, F. (1997). Self-determination and persistence in a real-life setting: Toward a motivational model of high-school dropout. *Journal of Personality and Social Psychology, 72,* 1161–1176.

White, R. W. (1959). Motivation reconsidered: The concept of competence. *Psychological Review, 66,* 297–333.

Wicklund, R. A., & Gollwitzer, P. M. (1982). Symbolic self-completion. Hillsdale, NJ: Erlbaum.

Williams, B. (1981). *Moral luck.* Cambridge, UK: Cambridge University Press.

Wilson, D. A. (1990). *Personal project dimensions and perceived life satisfaction: A quantitative synthesis.* Unpublished master's thesis, Department of Psychology, Carleton University, Ottawa, Ontario.

Wilson, E. O. (1998). *Consilience: The unity of knowledge.* New York: Knopf.

Winter, D. G. (1996). *Personality: Analysis and interpretation of lives.* New York: McGraw-Hill.

Chapter 21

Emotion and Emotion Regulation

James J. Gross
Stanford University

Emotions figure so prominently in our lives that it's hard to imagine not having them. We'd feel no love when we saw our children; no sadness when we botched an important job interview; no amusement when a friend regaled us with stories of collegiate misdeeds; and no embarrassment when we used the wrong name in addressing a colleague. Without emotions, "no one portion of the universe would then have importance beyond another; and the whole character of its things and series of its events would be without significance, character, expression, or perspective" (James, 1902, p. 150). Our once-colorful world would be bleached a drab gray. We'd drift along aimlessly, under slack sails, bereft of the impulses that motivate and direct our everyday pursuits.

The idea that emotions are important is far from new. Indeed, just about everyone who has considered the human condition has appreciated the centrality of emotions. Everyone, that is, except psychologists. Psychologists have long considered emotion "one of the most confused and difficult topics in all of psychology" (Plutchik, 1994, p. 1), and for much of the past century, they have made a point of ignoring emotion. Indeed, when psychologists *have* attended to emotion, it typically has been to despair at its complexity or to suggest that the term "emotion" be banned from the psychological lexicon (Duffy, 1941).

Since the 1980s, all this has changed. Psychology has rediscovered emotion. Hand wringing and definitional dodging have given way to a stream of empirical studies and theoretical analyses. Each week brings journals with new findings on emotion, each month brings monographs and edited books on emotion, and each year brings brand new journals that give pride of place to emotion. This outpouring of interest is a welcome change from decades of neglect. At long last, psychologists are acknowledging the centrality of emotion.

This outpouring of interest also poses problems. Emotions are complex multicomponential processes, at once biologically based and socially constituted. As such, emotions have been studied from a variety of home disciplines, including psychology, biology, ethology, anthropology, sociology, psychiatry, philosophy, artificial intelligence, economics, linguistics, and history. Given the newness of the topic to psychology, as well as its interdisciplinary nature, few psychologists have had formal training in the topic. Fewer still have the luxury of keeping abreast of the burgeoning emotion literature. What is to be done when even one of the wisest scholars in the field has concluded that "a global view of research and theory in the field of emotion does not offer a coherent picture" (Zajonc, 1998, p. 594)?

What is needed is a basic framework for organizing the bewildering array of findings. My aim in this chapter is to provide such a framework. My particular goal is to provide a conceptual map and readable introduction useful to researchers interested in personality psychology. In the first section, I orient the reader to an evolutionary perspective by relating instincts, fixed action patterns, and emotions. In the second section, I use a process model of emotion generation to review key findings regarding emotion antecedents and responses. In the third section, I present a coordinated process model of emotion regulation that describes the points in the emotion-generative process at which individuals influence their emotions. Throughout this chapter, my strategy is first to focus on basic emotional processes and then to discuss individual differences in these emotional processes.

INSTINCTS, FIXED ACTION PATTERNS, AND EMOTIONS

Almost 2,000 years ago, the stoics first used the notion of instinct to describe how birds built nests, bees built honeycombs, and spiders built webs (Berkinblit, Feldman, & Fukson, 1986). Darwin (1859/1962) argued that "instincts are as important as corporeal structures for the welfare of each species, under its present conditions of life . . . and if it can be shown that instincts do vary ever so little, then I can see no difficulty in natural selection preserving and continually accumulating variations of instinct to any extent that was profitable" (p. 245). Thus, just as variation in the physical features of an organism can influence its chances of reproduction, so too can variation in its psychological features, such as memory or emotion.

When psychologists came onto the scene, it seemed natural to draw on instinct theory. In his essay "What Is an Emotion?" William James (1884) wrote that

> the nervous system of every living thing is but a bundle of predispositions to react in particular ways upon the contact of particular features of the environment. . . . The neural machinery is but a hyphen between determinate arrangements of matter outside the body and determinate impulses to inhibition or discharge within its organs. . . . Every living creature is in fact a sort of lock, whose wards and springs presuppose special forms of key,—which keys however are not born attached to the locks, but are sure to be found in the world near by as life goes on. (pp. 190–191)

The close relation between emotion and instinct was cemented by McDougal (1923). He asserted that humans have 13 instincts (e.g., parenting, food seeking, repulsion, curiosity, gregariousness), and defined emotion as "a mode of experience which accompanies the working within us of instinctive impulses" (p. 128).

From Instincts to Response Tendencies

The vagueness of the notion of instinct, and the absence of criteria with which to verify the correctness of statements concerning instincts, soon made biologists worry about how the term instinct was being used. To combat "the erroneous belief that one can approach the problem of instinctive behavior patterns with noninductive methods and pronounce upon 'instinct' without defined experiments," Lorenz (1970, p. 259) and other early ethologists used careful observation and rigorous deprivation experiments. Rather than the murky concept of instinct, they spoke of "fixed action patterns" (FAPs). These patterns, as Eibl-Eibesfelt (1975) put it, refer to the fact that "in the behavioral repertoire of an animal one encounters recognizable and therefore 'form-constant' movements that do not have to be learned by the animal and provide, like morphological characteristics, distinguishing features of a species" (p. 16).

It soon became clear, however, that both releasers and responses were more variable than initially thought. Indeed, even the best examples of fixed action patterns seemed to dissolve upon closer examination. For example, Barlow (1968) found that courtship displays of the cichlid fish *Etroplus maculatus,* which involve a quivering of the head from side to side and a flicking of the pelvic fins, showed considerable variability across individuals in the same species. Findings such as these led some to assert that "the term 'FAP' cannot presently be used in effective scientific communication" (Dewsbury, 1978, p. 311), whereas others asked, "is anything fixed in a fixed action pattern?" (Evoy, 1986). Barlow (1977) proposed a new term—modal action pattern—which refers to "a spatiotemporal pattern of coordination movement [in which] the pattern clusters about some mode, making the behavior recognizable" (p. 230). Others suggested restricting the use of the concept of "fixed action pattern" (e.g., Duncan & Hughes, 1984), whereas others still insisted that all the fuss was unnecessary and that methodological problems had blinded scholars to impressive temporal stabilities of fixed action patterns (Pellis, 1985).

Paradoxically, just as the notion of a fixed action pattern was getting an increasingly cool reception in its own home discipline of ethology, psychologists embraced the notion. For example, Tomkins (1962) made explicit use of the notion of an "affect program." Plutchik (1962) described emotions as biologically based adaptive behavior patterns. Ekman (1972) also drew upon the core notion of a fixed action pattern in his "facial affect program," as did Scherer (1984) in his analysis of emotion as a "decoupled reflex."

Over the past few decades, psychologists have moved away from the stereotypy implied by the notion of a fixed action pattern. For example, Frijda (1986) has emphasized that "to the extent that action programs are fixed and rigid, the concept of action tendency loses much of its meaning. . . . To the extent that the program is flexible, however, action tendency, and action readiness generally, become meaningful concepts. Flexible programs are those that are composed of alternative courses of action, that allow for variations in circumstances and for feedback from actions executed" (p. 83). Lazarus (1991a) similarly has stressed response flexibility, arguing that "in more advanced species, especially humans, through evolution, hardwired affect programs have given way to a complex and flexible process" (p. 198).

Today, proponents of an evolutionary perspective (e.g., Johnson-Laird & Oatley, 1992; Tooby & Cosmides, 1990) speak of response *tendencies* and acknowledge the role of social forces in shaping emotion (see Averill, 1980). The functions emotions serve can be described at the level of the individual, species, or culture; they range from preparing for a fight to eliciting a caregiver's attention to enhancing social bonds. Because behaviors do not leave a fossil record of the sort that bones do, it is difficult to verify an evolutionary perspective. Three types of evidence have been used to support the claim that emotions are part of our evolutionary heritage, rather than learned: (1) blind children produce spontaneous emotion-expressive behavior similar to that of normal children (Galati, Scherer, & Ricci-Bitti, 1997); (2) cross-cultural similarities are evident in the antecedents of emotion (Scherer, Wallbott, & Summerfield, 1986) and in emotional responses, including experience (Russell, 1980) and facial behavior (Ekman, 1994); and (3) human emotion expressions such as smiling and laughing have homologues in chimpanzee expressions (Van Hooff, 1972).

Defining Emotion

This discussion of instincts, fixed action patterns, and response tendencies has emphasized the role of behavior in emotional responding. But when it comes to humans, common usage treats *experience* as the essence of emotion. Does emotion refer to behavior or experience? Unfortunately, scholars have had great difficulty deciding just what they mean by emotion. In part, this is because they have aspired to a classical definition that specifies the necessary and sufficient conditions for something to be an emotion. Yet, such an aspiration collides directly with the fact that *emotion* is a heavily freighted term that was lifted from common language, including excess baggage, fuzziness, and all. Furthermore, in American English, at least, "emotion" refers to an astonishing array of happenings, from the mild to the intense, the private to the public, the simple to the complex, and the brief to the extended. Irritation with a recalcitrant doorknob, grief at the death of a child, surprise at a soap opera revelation, anger at grave social injustices, and amusement at a clever turn of phrase all count as emotions.

A growing appreciation of the mismatch between the wish for definitional precision and the ill-bounded subject matter has led to prototype conceptions of emotion (Ekman, 1992; Russell, 1991; Shaver, Schwartz, Kirson, & O'Connor, 1987). Unlike classical conceptions of emotion, a prototype conception emphasizes typical features, which may or may not be evident in any given case, but whose presence makes it more likely that something is an emotion. One advantage of the prototype conception is that it discourages futile debates about what is "really" an emotion (Chaplin, John, & Goldberg, 1988). Three features of the emotion prototype are noteworthy.

First, emotions arise when an individual evaluates a situation as significant (see Clore & Ortony, 1998). The goals, standards, needs, or wishes that underlie this evaluation may be central and enduring (e.g., to be a good father) or peripheral and transient (e.g., to finish reading a comic strip). They may be conscious and highly elaborated (e.g., to maneuver a divided committee to closure) or unconscious and simple (e.g., to get away from a snake). They may be biologically based (e.g., to expel a noxious substance) or culturally derived (e.g., to honor one's elders). They may be widely shared and understood (e.g., to have friends) or idiosyncratic and personal (e.g., to communicate telepathically with aliens). Whatever the source of the situational meaning for the individual, it is this meaning that triggers emotion.

Second, emotions are multifaceted, whole-body processes that involve changes in the domains of subjective experience, behavioral expression, and central and peripheral physiology (Lang, Rice, & Sternbach, 1972). The subjective feeling of emotion is, of course, so intimately bound up with what we mean by emotion that the terms emotion and feeling often are used interchangeably. Given the importance and salience of emotion experience, it is little wonder that the part (feeling) is taken for the whole (emotion). But the whole it is not. Indeed, the behavioral elements of the emotional response are often at least as important as the experiential element. Emotions not only make us feel something, they make us feel like *doing* something. This is reflected in the language we use to describe emotions: We say we were "moved to tears," "fighting mad," or "frozen with fear." Central nervous system changes link stimulus and response tendencies, but peripheral physiological changes are important also. Our impulses to feel and to do are associated with a host of autonomic and neuroendocrine changes. These changes both anticipate the associated behavioral response (thereby providing metabolic support for the action) and follow the response, often as a direct consequence of the motoric activity associated with the emotional response.

Third, emotions may be described either as dimensions or as categories. The dimensional approach uses relatively broad dimensions to describe changes in emotion experience, expression, and physiology. On this approach, emotions are seen as continuously distributed over a few dimensions, such as positive affect and negative affect (Watson, Clark, & Tellegen, 1988), intensity and pleasantness (Larsen & Diener, 1992), or approach and withdrawal (Lang, 1995). The categorical approach focuses on discrete emotions, highlighting the differences among specific emotions, particularly negatively valenced emotions such as anger, fear, and sadness (Ekman, 1992). As they have evolved, dimensional and categorical approaches differ in two ways. First, they differ as to whether emotions are continuous or discrete. Second, they differ as to how many theoretical entities are postulated, with the dimensional approach focusing on a few (typically two) broad dimensions, and the categorical approach focusing on six or more "basic" emotions.

A Consensual Process Model of Emotion

Historically, emotion researchers have emphasized differences among approaches and definitions. This has led to "conceptual and definitional chaos" (Buck, 1990, p. 330). Following Scherer (1984), I use "affect" as the superordinate category for various kinds of valenced states including (1) general *stress responses* to taxing circumstances, (2) *emotions* such as anger and sadness, (3) *emotion episodes* such as a bar-room brawl and delivering bad news to a close friend, and (4) *moods* such as depression and euphoria.[1] My focus here is on emotions (see Gross, 1998b).

Despite the definitional chaos, there are important similarities among approaches to emotion. In Figure 21.1, I present a process model of emotion generation (Gross, 1998b) that distills major points of convergence among researchers concerned with emotion (e.g., Arnold, 1960; Buck, 1985; Ekman, 1972; Frijda, 1986; Izard, 1977; Lazarus, 1991a; Levenson, 1994; Plutchik, 1962; Scherer, 1984; Tomkins, 1962). According to this model, emotion begins with an evaluation of emotion cues. When attended to and evaluated in certain ways, emotion cues trigger a coordinated set of response tendencies that facilitate adaptive responding. These response tendencies involve experiential, behavioral, and physiological systems. Response tendencies from each system may be modulated, and it is this modulation that gives final shape to the manifest emotion.

Individual differences are evident at every step in the emotion-generative process. First, people's day-to-day experiences vary enormously, providing different "inputs" to their emotion programs. Second, these differential inputs may be diminished or magnified by the way they are evaluated. Third, research on temperament suggests that there are important differences in the activation thresholds of emotional response tendencies. Finally, there are clear individual differ-

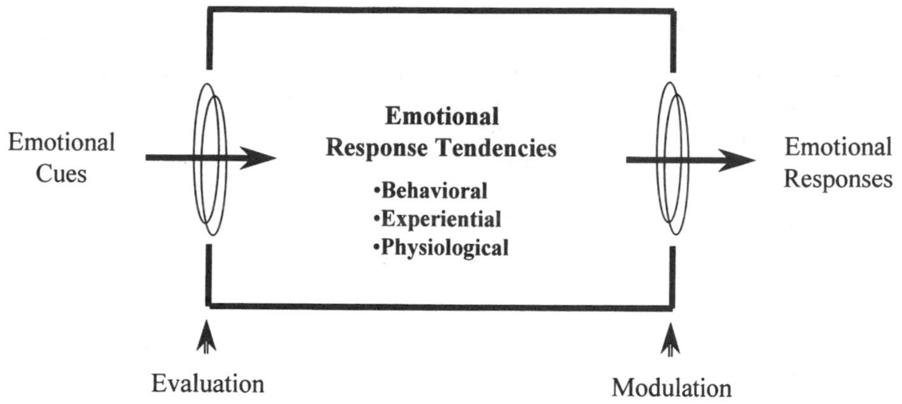

FIGURE 21.1. A consensual process model of emotion generation. Adapted from Gross (1998b). Copyright 1998 by the Educational Publishing Foundation. Adapted by permission.

ences in the modulatory "output filter"—that is, differences in how any given emotional response tendency is translated into a manifest response.

EMOTION: ANTECEDENTS AND RESPONSES

In the following sections, I review the literature on emotion antecedents and responses. My focus in this chapter is on the adult literature (for a review of the developmental literature, see Malatesta, 1990). I organize this review according to the model in Figure 21.1. I begin with emotion antecedents (the input to the system) and then consider the three major classes of emotion responses (the output of the system).

Emotion Antecedents

William James (1884) likened emotional responses to the turning of a key in a lock. This analogy implies that emotions are direct—almost unmediated—responses to certain events. More than a century later, this perspective still has currency. For example, Buck (1985) has argued that internal and external emotion-eliciting stimuli impinge on the emotion systems directly and without cognitive mediation. This "direct view" suggests that it should be possible to provide descriptions of the objective events that lead to particular emotions. In Figure 21.1, these events would correspond with the emotion cues drawn outside the box. More typically, however, theorists have assumed that potentially emotion-eliciting stimuli must be cognitively processed before emotion arises. This "indirect view" suggests that it is not the event or situation that leads to the emotion, but rather the subjective evaluation of the event or situation. If this is so, emotion antecedents must be defined subjectively rather than objectively. In the early 1980s, Zajonc (1980, 1984) and Lazarus (1981, 1984) debated the relative value of the direct and indirect views. Recent neuroanatomic findings suggest that both may have merit: There appear to be two kinds of processing pathways—one relatively automatic that involves relatively little cognitive mediation and a second, slower pathway that is more cognitively elaborated. In the following sections I briefly describe both the direct (objectively defined) and indirect (subjectively defined) approaches to emotion antecedents.

Objectively Defined Emotion Antecedents

Given the flexibility of input–output relations that characterizes human emotions, it is hardly surprising that descriptions of antecedent conditions for specific emotions in everyday life have been largely anecdotal. Lists such as the one offered by Ellsworth (1994) are typical: "loss of support or sense of direction, separation from a mother, sudden intense noises, abrupt movements, caresses, and secondary sexual characteristics" (p. 151). However, as Ellsworth herself admits, "the actual research record is quite thin" (p. 151). To put the study of objectively defined emotion antecedents on firmer ground, Scherer Summerfield, and Wallbott (1983) asked students to recall events that elicited joy, sadness, anger, and fear. Subjects then described these events, and raters coded subjects' descriptions of the antecedents of their emotions. In the initial study, seven general categories were derived inductively. These included news (good or bad), relationships, success/self-esteem, experiences (pleasant or unpleasant), material objects (gain or loss), organic tissue (well-being or damage), and other. News was important to none of the emotions, whereas success/esteem was important to all. Categories that discriminated among emotions included the relationship category (important to all emotions but fear), experiences (important to joy and fear but not sadness or anger), material objects (prominent in anger), and organic tissue (important to fear). When described at this level of abstraction, however, these antecedents are a far cry from the direct emotion triggers called to mind by James's (1884) lock and key analogy.

Subjectively Defined Emotion Antecedents

A second approach to emotion antecedents has focused on the subjective meaning of emotion-eliciting situations. The logic of this approach is captured by Frijda's (1988) law of apparent reality: "Emotions are elicited by events appraised as real, and their intensity corresponds to the degree to which this is the case" (p. 352). Even situations that are patently artificial (e.g., a film or a play) can arouse emotions as long as the individual sees them as meaningful (see Frijda, 1989 for a discussion of aesthetic emotions; see Gross & Levenson, 1995 for film clips that elicit discrete emotions). In terms of Figure 21.1, this approach refers to the filter (labeled "evaluation") that translates a situation into something that has emotional significance. Researchers have explored the subjective meaning of situations by asking individuals how they evaluate emotionally charged situations such as exams. A number of "appraisal" theorists have offered lists of meaning dimensions (including de Rivera, 1977; Frijda, Kuipers, & ter Schure, 1989; Oatley & Johnson-Laird, 1987; Ortony, Clore, & Collins, 1988; Roseman, Spindel, & Jose, 1990; Scherer, 1988; Smith & Ellsworth, 1985; Smith & Lazarus, 1990). For example, Ellsworth (1994) reported six meaning dimensions: novelty (is this relevant?), valence (is this good or bad?), certainty (how sure can I be about novelty or valence?), control (can i handle this?), agency (who or what caused this?), and norm/self-concept compatibility (does this meet my own or the group's goals?).

Individual Differences in Emotion Antecedents

As common sense would have it, some people should be happier than others because they live in better physical, social, and economic conditions. In study after study, however, factors such as income and education explain little of the variance in typical emotional states (Brickman, Coates, & Janoff-Bulman, 1978; Costa & McCrae, 1980; Myers & Diener, 1995). At the extremes, external circumstances clearly matter. It is not likely one will be happy-go-lucky on arriving in prison, or sad immediately after winning a lottery. Yet even in "strong situations" that would seem to determine the emotional response, individuals differ dramatically in emotional responding. If general features of our objective environments have less power to determine our emotions than we might imagine, does this mean that objective emotion antecedents are irrelevant to individual differences in emotion?

One possibility is that global analyses of individuals' environments miss subtle but important processes that would help explain individual differences in emotional responding. In proactive interaction, individuals actively seek out particular environments (Caspi & Bem, 1990). For example, individuals high on Extraversion seek out social situations, which are known to increase positive affect (Clark & Watson, 1988); individuals with aggressive tendencies seek out others similarly inclined, thereby increasing the likelihood of confrontation and the emotions that entails. The second type of person–environment interaction relevant to emotion antecedents is evocative interaction, which refers to the fact that individuals differ in the responses they evoke from others (Caspi & Bem, 1990). In one study, for example, depressed women did not differ from nondepressed individuals in the levels of objective stress and adversity they encountered, but they did differ in the frequency of dependent interpersonal events—stressful interpersonal interactions that were created, at least in part, by the depressed individuals themselves (Hammen, 1991). In a similar vein, Bolger and Schilling (1991) used daily diaries to track stressors in a sample of married subjects. They found that subjects who scored higher in Neuroticism had more arguments with spouses and others than subjects who scored low in Neuroticism. Even within grossly similar environments, then, proactive and evocative interaction patterns lead to importantly different emotion antecedents, and hence individual differences in emotional responding.

Individual differences in emotion antecedents are relevant not just as they pertain to objective features of the environment, but also as they pertain to our interpretations of whatever situation we are in. Reactive interaction refers to individual differences in how the same environment is interpreted and experienced (Caspi & Bem, 1990). In Figure 21.1, this notion moves us from a consideration of objective stimuli to the evaluations we make of these stimuli. Cognitive therapists such as Ellis, Beck, and Seligman have long emphasized the role of such evaluations in creating individual differences in emotional responding. Although their emphasis has been on the extremes of anxiety and depression, the logic of their analysis applies with equal force to normal variation in emotion. For example, aggressive children frequently expect others to be aggressive and may read hostile intent into neutral behaviors of others (Dodge, 1991). At the other extreme, optimists see good news in neutral or ambiguous situations (Scheier & Carver, 1993). Differences in evaluation matter. For example, Aspinwall and Taylor (1992) found that optimistic undergraduates had lower levels of distress during their freshman year than did less optimistic classmates. How we think about an event has a profound effect on the emotions we have, and individual differences in thinking constitute a potent source of individual differences in emotional responding.

Emotion Responses

Once emotion has been triggered, emotion responses run the gamut from tiny twinges of guilt that are noticeable to no one but ourselves, to full-scale outbursts of anger that are replete with rich emotion experience, unmistakable epithet hurling and nonverbal displays, and a whole host of powerful autonomic and neuroendocrine changes. Given this variability, both across emotions and within any one emotion across intensities, there is no one-size-fits-all description of emotion responses. Like many others before me, I find it useful to distinguish among three major response domains: emotion experience, emotion-expressive behavior, and emotion physiology.[2] In the following sections, I review these three domains, which correspond to the output element in Figure 21.1.

Emotion Experience

Contemplating the awesome scope of emotion experience, researchers generally have taken one of two approaches. The first approach has been to examine specific emotions. Proponents of this categorical approach give emotions such as sadness, fear, or anger their own chapter headings, and describe the phenomenology of each (e.g., Lazarus, 1991a). One liability of this approach is that it almost inevitably leads to the question as to how many distinct emotions there are. Common language gives few clues as to how to answer this question. There are over 550 emotion words in English (Averill, 1975), and many more in other languages that cannot be readily translated into English (e.g., *Schadenfreude,* the German word that refers to a sense of pleasure that someone has had his comeuppance). As long as we take a prototype view of emotion, however, I see no reason that a categorical approach to emotion experience must lead to fruitless debates about how many emotions there "really" are.

The second approach has been to examine the dimensionality of emotion experience by having respondents rate their experience on various sets of emotion terms. Dimensional studies have differed in which emotions were emphasized as fundamental to the emotion space and in whether ratings of emotion experience were made by many individuals at one time, or by one individual at many different times. Despite these variations in research designs, the results have been remarkably consistent. Two dimensions emerge reliably, with emotions arrayed along the circle formed by these two dimensions. How best to conceptualize these two dimensions defining the circle has been somewhat more controversial, because there are no a priori principles to help ascertain which dimensions reflect the causal processes that produce the emotion space. Russell (1980, 1983), Larsen & Diener (1992), and Feldman Barrett (1998) have labeled these two dimensions pleasantness and activation, depicted by the solid lines in Figure 21.2. Tellegen, Watson and colleagues (e.g., Tellegen, 1985; Watson & Tellegen, 1985) have proposed a 45° rotation of the two axes in Figure 21.2, and labeled the two dimensions positive affect and

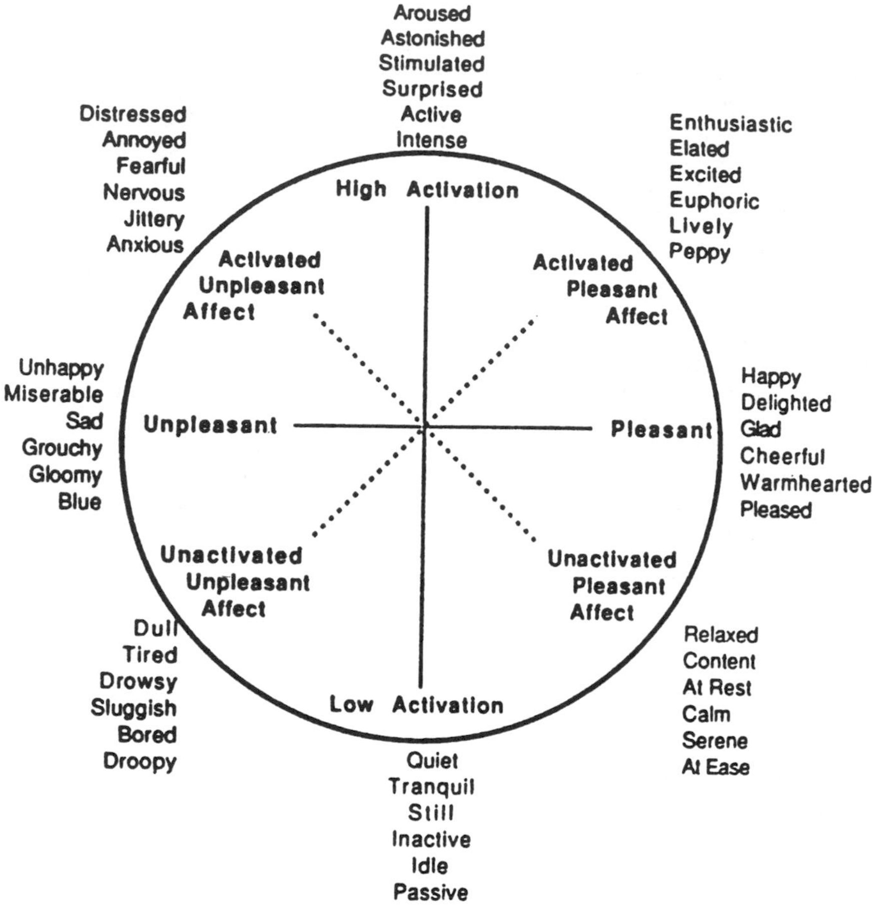

FIGURE 21.2. The structure of emotion experience. From Larsen and Diener (1992). Copyright 1992 by Sage Publications. Reprinted by permission.

negative affect or, more recently, positive and negative activation (Watson, Wiese, Vaidya, & Tellegen, 1999). These dimensions are depicted by the dotted lines in Figure 21.2. There is considerable debate as to which of these rotational schemes is preferable, and a special section of the *Journal of Personality and Social Psychology* (Vol. 76, 1999) was devoted to this topic.

One puzzle is how to reconcile the two apparently incompatible approaches to conceptualizing emotion experience. Is emotion experience discrete, as suggested by the categorical approach? Or does emotion experience vary along two orthogonal dimensions, as suggested by the dimensional approach? In the 1990s, several groups of researchers suggested that the debate may be resolved by conceptualizing emotion experience in hierarchical terms (Diener, Smith, & Fujita, 1995; Russell & Feldman Barrett, 1999; Watson & Clark, 1992). For example, in Diener and colleagues' (1995) study of long-term emotion experience, they found evidence for a hierarchical model in which positive and negative affect were the superordinate dimensions, and within each, the more specific emotions of love, joy, shame, fear, sadness, and anger took their place. According to hierarchical models such as this, both categorical and dimensional approaches are "right" (Tellegen, Watson, & Clark, in press). Which level of analysis is most useful depends on the explanatory and predictive goals of the research.

Individual Differences in Emotion Experience

It is a mark of our common humanity that we each experience emotions. Yet these emotions are by no means evenly distributed among us. Some individuals are more prone to experiencing particular emotions than other individuals. Personality psychologists have examined individual differences in emotion experience from both categorical and dimensional perspectives.

From a categorical perspective, there are a number of questionnaires that assess individual differences in the experience of specific emotions such as anxiety (Taylor, 1953) and anger (Spielberger & Sydeman, 1994). There are also omnibus inventories designed to assess multiple emotions, such as the Differential Emotions Scale (Izard, Libero, Putnam, & Haynes, 1993), the Multiple Affect Adjective Checklist (Zuckerman & Lubin, 1985), and the Profile of Mood States (McNair, Lorr, & Droppleman, 1971). Researchers have used these measures to document stable individual differences in the experience of specific emotions. Another approach has been to assess individual differences not in the experience of any particular emotion, but rather in the nature of emotion experience itself. Lane and colleagues have measured individual differences in the ability to verbally represent a given emotional state using the Levels of Emotional Awareness Scale (Lane, Quinlan, Schwartz, Walker, & Zeitlin, 1990). At the one extreme are alexithymics (Taylor, Bagby, & Parker, 1997), who have little capacity to identify and describe feelings. At the other extreme are individuals who show high levels of emotional awareness, as evidenced by their capacity to appreciate and describe complex blends of emotion.

From a dimensional perspective, Watson and colleagues' Positive and Negative Affect Schedule (PANAS; Watson, Clark, & Tellegen, 1988) assesses individual differences in positive and negative activated affect. Larsen's (1984) Affective Intensity Measure (AIM) assesses individual differences in the intensity of emotional experience. The PANAS and the AIM both define emotion as high activation states; they differ, however, in their assumptions about the structure of emotion experience. Another approach has been to examine the relative weight that individuals give to each dimension of emotion experience when describing their experience. Feldman (1995) has explored individual differences in the use of the dimensions of pleasantness and activation in describing emotion experience. Virtually all subjects used the pleasantness dimension, but they differed in the degree to which they used the activation dimension. For some individuals, emotion experience was essentially the difference between "good" and "bad" (a flattened version of the circle presented in Figure 21.2). Others made more fine-grained distinctions among their emotion experiences (a fully developed version of the emotion circumplex, as in Figure 21.2).

One advantage of the dimensional perspective on emotion experience is that this perspective brings into focus the structural similarities between emotion and personality (Meyer & Shack, 1989). In particular, the dimensional perspective suggests a mapping between the dimension of negative emotion and Neuroticism, and between the dimension of positive emotion and Extraversion. These links have been born out in several studies (e.g., Emmons & Diener, 1985; Tellegen, 1985; Watson & Clark, 1984, 1992; Watson et al., 1999; for a discrete emotions perspective, see Izard et al., 1993). For example, Costa and McCrae (1980) found that Neuroticism predicted negative affect in everyday life, whereas Extraversion predicted positive affect; these relations held even over a 10–year period. On the basis of these relations, McCrae and Costa (1991) have proposed that Neuroticism and Extraversion represent temperamental personality dimensions that predispose individuals to negative and positive emotions.

However, as Larsen and Ketelaar (1991) observed, correlations between emotion in everyday life and personality traits do not provide a rigorous test of the temperamental view. This is because different personalities may generate different environments, as described above in the section on emotion antecedents. If this is so, any observed relations between personality and emotion could be the result of these instrumentally generated circumstances, rather than differences in predispositions to respond to events with negative or positive emotion per se (see Caspi, Bem, & Elder, 1989; McCrae & Costa, 1991). A more direct evaluation of the temperamental view is possible by taking an experimental approach in which all individuals are presented with the same standardized stimuli in a laboratory setting. For example, Larsen and Ketelaar (1991) found that Neuroticism was related to negative emotion experience when imagining an unpleasant situation (e.g., having a close friend die from a painful disease), whereas extraversion was related to positive emotion experience when imagining a pleasant situation (e.g., winning $50,000 in a lottery and then taking a vacation).

Based upon these results, it might seem reasonable to conclude that individuals high in Neuroticism have stronger negative emotional reactions to unpleasant stimuli than those low in Neuroticism, and individuals high in Extraversion have stronger positive emotional reactions to pleasant stimuli than those low in Extraversion. However, even these experiments do not establish that heightened emotional *reactivity* is the most appropriate interpretation of these personality–emotion relations.

Because personality and emotion have been shown to be related across a broad range of everyday situations (e.g., Bolger & Schilling, 1991), it is necessary to distinguish two views of the link between personality traits and emotional experience. The first is the level view, which holds that personality predicts emotion experience at any given point in time. The second is the reactivity view, which holds that personality predicts how much emotion increases or decreases from one time point to the next. To experimentally separate these two views, Gross, Sutton, and Ketelaar (1998) measured emotion experience before and after subjects watched films designed to elicit amusement, fear, sadness, or disgust. They found support for both the level view and the reactivity view. For example, Neuroticism predicted how sad subjects felt during the baseline period and during the sadness-inducing film, which is consistent with the level view. However, Neuroticism also predicted the increase in sadness experience from baseline to the sadness-inducing film, which is consistent with the reactivity view. These findings indicate that a full appreciation of individual differences in emotion experience will require an understanding of how personality shapes not only emotional reactivity but also tonic levels of emotion (Tellegen, 1991).

Emotion-Expressive Behavior

When we feel emotion, we often show how we feel through our verbal and nonverbal behavior. Despite the commonness of emotional expressions, little research has been done to link spontaneous emotional experience to particular patterns of expressive behavior. In part, this is due to the difficulty of measuring spontaneous emotional behavior. In part, too, this is due to the profound effects of context on expressive behavior. In some circumstances, indeed, the context may be a more potent determinant of "emotion-expressive" behavior than the emotion experience itself. Because research on emotion–expressive behavior has focused on the face, I do the same. I focus first on the neural bases of facial behavior, and then on how facial expressive behavior is measured. Finally, I consider nonfacial emotional behavior.

Facial Expressive Behavior. Emotion-expressive facial behavior results from the contractions of facial muscles that move the overlying skin and connective tissue (Rinn, 1984).[3] Eighteen of the 22 pairs of facial muscles are involved in emotion-expressive behavior; the other four pairs are involved in chewing. What makes the facial muscles move? As shown in Figure 21.3, volitional movements of the facial muscles originate in the primary motor cortex in each hemisphere, and then travel along the upper motor neurons (UMNs) that extend from the cortex via the corticobulbar tract to the motor nuclei of the 7th cranial nerve (the facial motor nuclei) deep in the brainstem. Emotional movements, by contrast, originate in as-yet-undetermined subcortical regions in each hemisphere far from the cortical motor strip, and from there make their way to the facial motor nuclei. The cell clusters that generate emotional impulses are not shown in Figure 21.3 because they have not yet been identified. Whether volitional or emotional, action impulses that reach the facial motor nucleus travel along the lower motor neurons (LMNs) in each hemisphere to the 18 pairs of facial muscles. The course taken by the LMNs from the facial motor nucleus (or the facial nerve) varies across individuals. As shown in Figure 21.3, there typically are five major branches: (1) temporal, (2) zygomatic, (3) buccal, (4) mandibular, and (5) cervical.

Four lines of evidence support the distinction between volitional and emotional facial movements. First, patients with lesions of the cortical motor strip are unable to move one half of the face, yet they continue to exhibit normal emotional behavior using exactly the same muscles. Second, patients with lesions to subcortical nuclei, such as in Parkinson's disease, which affects the basal ganglia, show no spontaneous emotion-expressive behavior, but are nonetheless able to move muscles on command. These first two lines of evidence clearly document a double dissociation between volitional and emotion-

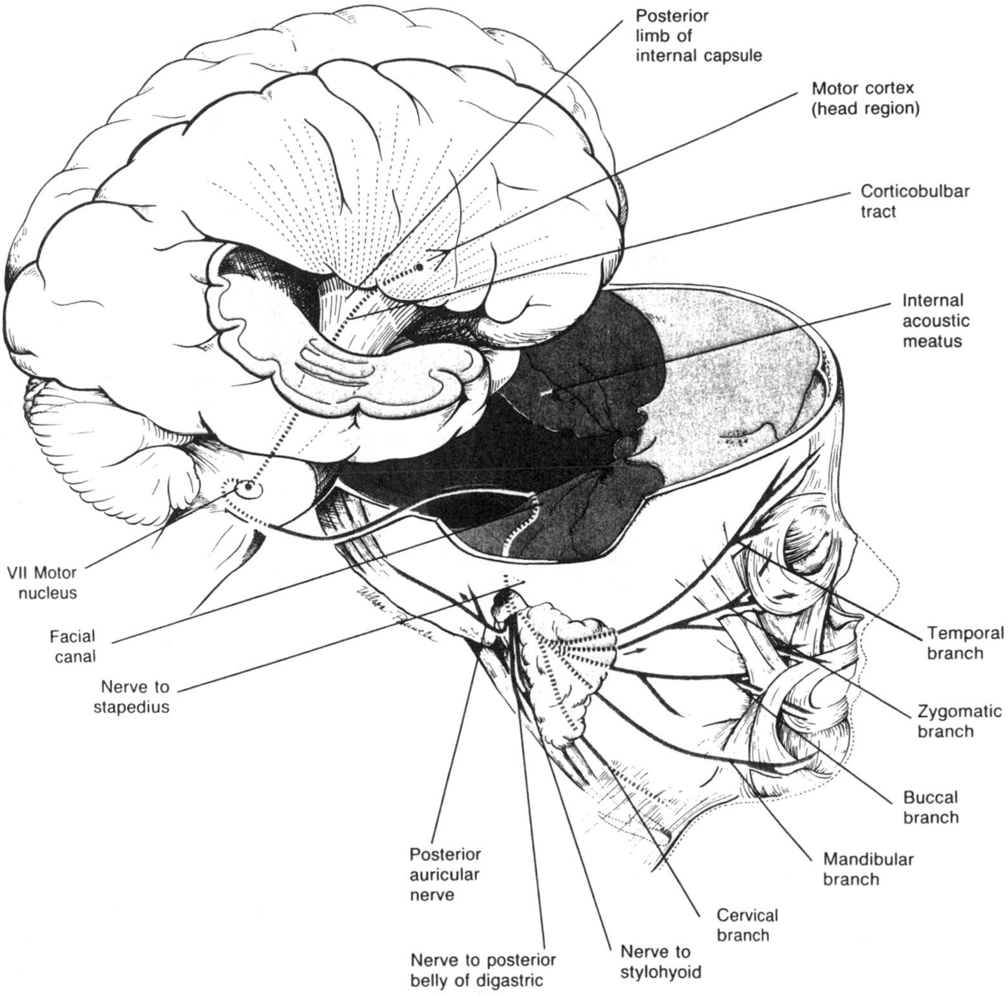

FIGURE 21.3. The innervation of the muscles of facial expression: Five branches of the facial nerve. From Wilson-Pauwels, Akesson, and Stewart (1988). Copyright 1988 by B. C. Decker. Reprinted by permission.

expressive behavior, thereby providing powerful evidence that the neural generators in each case must differ. Third, when patients have a lesion of the facial nerve, it is possible to reanimate the damaged facial nerve using fibers from another cranial nerve. Interestingly, although these patients learn to voluntarily control their facial muscles, they do not regain spontaneous emotion expression on the affected side, suggesting that the emotional impulses are still being sent to the facial motor nucleus and are not plastic enough to be rerouted. Finally, patients with pseudobulbar palsy, which involves lesions of the pathways from the cortical motor strip, show voluntary motor paralysis and involuntary laughing or crying that is not accompanied by any experience of amusement or sadness. It seems likely these uncontrolled outbursts are due to an incapacity to inhibit episodic bursts of activity in the subcortical generators of spontaneous emotion-expressive behavior.

Whatever its neural generators may be, emotion-expressive behavior must be quantified if it is to be analyzed. One approach to quantifying expressive behavior has been to use global ratings, either of specific emotions (e.g., amusement, disgust) or broad dimensions (e.g., pleasantness, intensity). With a modest amount of training, coders reliably make such global judgments (e.g., Gross & Levenson, 1993; Kring, Smith, & Neale, 1994). To allow greater precision in describing facial expressive behavior, Ekman and Friesen (1978) developed the Facial Action Coding System (FACS). This anatomically based coding system specifies 44 distinct facial movements ("action units"). For example, action unit 1 (AU1) refers to raising the inner eyebrows, AU4 to drawing the brows down and together. Research findings using FACS have accumulated steadily since the 1980s (Ekman & Rosenberg, 1997). For example, Keltner (1995) has documented the expressive signs of embarrassment. Frank, Ekman, and Friesen (1993) have distinguished felt smiles (associated with happiness) from false smiles (not associated with happiness) on the basis of their precise morphology: Felt smiles more often involve "crows feet" by the eyes, due to the lifting of the cheek muscles. A third approach to quantifying facial behavior has been to measure facial behavior using facial electromyography (EMG; e.g., Cacioppo, Martzke, Petty, & Tassinary, 1988). This approach has the advantage of continuous measurement. EMG sensors also can register activity that is too weak to produce visible movements of facial muscles. EMG has several important disadvantages, however. Attaching EMG sensors may draw attention to expressive behavior and heighten self-consciousness; moreover, EMG can sample only a subset of facial muscle groups, providing a narrow window onto behavior.

Other Nonverbal and Verbal Behavior. There is more to emotion-expressive behavior than facial movements. Indeed, changes in the likelihood of large-motor activity are probably one of the most important (but least well understood) aspects of the emotional response (e.g., slumping in dejection, sitting upright in pride; Stepper & Strack, 1993). Such changes are not just reactive. Emotions anticipate, as well as react to, situations as they unfold. Often, verbal behavior accompanies nonverbal emotion-expressive behavior (Averill, 1997). Verbal behavior most obviously includes what we say when we are angry, as when we hurl epithets. Some of the speech content involves descriptions of feeling states ("I'm angry"). Other speech content taps into shared metaphors commonly used to describe emotional states (Lakoff, 1987), including heat ("He's hot-headed") and explosions ("I'm so angry I could explode"). In addition to semantic content, verbal behavior also includes *how* we say what we say (e.g., loudly versus softly). Research has shown that alterations in fundamental frequency (F0) are one dimension of vocal responding (Scherer, 1986); the voice also appears to contain information about specific emotions (Scherer & Wallbott, 1994).

Individual Differences in Emotion-Expressive Behavior

Personality psychologists have long been concerned with general differences in expressive behavior, and early conceptions of expressivity encompassed a broad range of behaviors. For example, Allport and Vernon (1933) defined expressivity as all "aspects of movement which are distinctive enough to differentiate one individual from another" (p. vii), and argued that an analysis of consistencies in expressive behavior was a necessary first step in understanding personality. Expressivity included all manner of expressive behaviors, ranging from handwriting to handgrip to emotional expressivity, and Allport and Vernon (1933) saw "the direct study of expression [as] the most natural possible approach to the study of personality" (p. v). However, their pioneering experimental study found little evidence for a general expressivity factor; they concluded that it was necessary to understand more specific aspects of expressivity (see Allport, 1937).

After a lull, research on individual differences in expressivity resumed in the early 1970s (e.g., Buck, Savin, Miller, & Caul, 1972; Snyder, 1974). This was also the time when exciting new research on facial expression of emotion was underway (e.g., Ekman, Friesen, & Ellsworth, 1972; Izard, 1971). This confluence led to an increased interest in one specific type of expressivity, namely *emotional* expressivity. Initial conceptions broadly emphasized "individual differences in the extent to which individuals can and do monitor their self-presentation, expressive behavior, and nonverbal affective display" (Snyder, 1974, pp. 526–527), and even included potential consequences of expressiveness, such as "a strong element of interpersonal success" (Friedman, Prince, Riggio, & DiMatteo, 1980, p. 348). More recently, conceptions of expressivity have become more focused. Kring et al. (1994) focused on individual differences in the extent to which people "outwardly display their emotions" (p. 934), and Gross and John (1995) defined emotional expressivity as the behavioral (e.g., facial, postural) changes that typically accompany emotion, such as smiling, frowning, crying, or storming out of the room.

Many of these conceptions of expressivity are unidimensional (e.g., Friedman et al., 1980; Kring et al., 1994). By contrast, I have emphasized the multifaceted nature of emotional expressivity (Gross & John, 1997, 1998), and found that three correlated facets consistently emerge in both self-reports and peer-ratings of expressivity, namely Positive Expressivity, Negative Expressivity, and Impulse Strength (conceptualized as the strength of the emotional impulses). These facets differentially predict criterion measures such as emotion-expressive behavior measured in the laboratory. Positive Expressivity predicts amusement expressions such as laughing (but not sadness expressions), and Negative Expressivity predicts sadness expressions such as crying (but not amusement expressions). These findings suggest the need for a hierarchical model, in which specific expressivity facets are subsumed under a more general expressivity factor (Gross & John, 1997).

Emotion Physiology

Discussing the physiology of emotion is akin to discussing the physiology of living. Virtually every system is implicated in one way or another. Early conceptions of physiological responding in emotion emphasized the unitary nature of bodily changes in emotion. In its classic form, arousal theory postulated a unidimensional continuum of whole-organism activation ranging from quiescence to states of great agitation and excitement (Duffy, 1962; Malmo, 1959). Heightened arousal was thought to involve sympathetic and endocrine activation, energized behavior, and electroencephalogram (EEG) activation. General arousal theory was a very powerful conceptual scheme because it allowed researchers to plot an organism's behavior with respect to intensity (varying states of general arousal) as well as direction (approach or withdrawal). In the data-rich but theory-poor field of psychophysiology, this overarching unidimensional continuum of arousal appeared to organize a wide range of findings.

Questions about the unitary nature of arousal began to gather with growing urgency in the 1960s. Lacey's (1967) critique of arousal theory was a particularly important catalyst. In this critique, Lacey elaborated on the notion of directional fractionation, which referred to the fact that at times one physiological response system showed a change in one direction, while another response system showed either no change, or a change in another direction. Imagine a night watchman who hears a noise. He freezes—still as can be—and his heart rate slows as he stares intently into the dark. At the same time, he begins to sweat profusely, and he shows EEG changes consistent with heightened activation. A unitary conception of arousal has great difficulty accounting for these changes, and after 30 years of research, the notion of generalized arousal is no longer tenable in its classical form. Instead, the field has moved toward analyzing specific response systems.

Peripheral Systems. When we are emotional, our bodies respond: We sweat, our hearts pound, and we breathe more quickly. In William James's famous thought experiment regarding emotion, he suggested, "If we fancy some strong emotion, and then try to abstract from our consciousness of it all the feelings of its characteristic bodily symptoms, we find we have nothing left behind, no 'mind-stuff' out of which the emotion can be constituted, and that a cold and neutral state of intellectual perception is all that remains" (James, 1884, p. 193). James proposed that the patterned autonomic and somatic changes that occurred in emotion were what gave rise to the subjective experience of emotion. This perspective accords well with common sense. When we are angry, it seems quite clear that our body is reacting very differently from when we are happy, sad, or in a relatively neutral state.

Two research traditions have pursued questions about peripheral physiological responding in emotion. The first is the stress physiology tradition. Historically, stress physiologists have emphasized the common features of an organism's central, somatic, autonomic, and neuroendocrine responses to a wide range of challenges (the "stress response") (Sapolsky, 1994). However, both animal and human literatures suggest that at least two kinds of stress response can be distinguished. The animal literature refers to this as the distinction between the defense reaction and the vigilance reaction (Fisher, 1991). Both reactions involve increased physiological activation. However, the defense reaction (also known as the fight-or-flight response) leads to increased arterial pressure, heart rate, and cardiac output, with little change in total peripheral resistance. By contrast, the vigilance reaction (also known as the freezing response) leads to increased arterial pressure and total peripheral resistance, along with decreased heart rate and cardiac output. In the human literature, Tomaka, Blascovich, Kelsey, and Leitten (1993) have proposed a similar distinction to defense and vigilance, which they call challenge and threat.

The second research tradition is the emotion-specificity tradition. This tradition draws inspiration from William James, and from the widely shared belief that emotions have different physiological signatures. Researchers have tried to document distinct autonomic emotion profiles. Generally, these attempts have met with less success than our intuitions would predict. Levenson (1992) concluded that there was evidence for (1) heart rate acceleration during anger, (2) heart rate acceleration during fear, (3) heart rate acceleration during sadness, (4) heart rate deceleration during disgust, and (5) greater peripheral vasoconstriction in fear than anger. Cacioppo, Klein, Bernston, and Hatfield (1993) found that "the cumulative evidence for emotion-specific autonomic patterns remains inconclusive" (p. 132). Gray (1994) has argued that the autonomic and endocrine systems are "the *wrong* places to look" for emotion specificity because these systems are concerned with housekeeping functions that bear no clear relation to any particular metabolic demands (p. 243). All that may be evident in peripheral systems, he suggests, is a dimension of activation.[4]

Central Systems. If peripheral systems are the wrong place to look for emotion specificity, where should we look? The answer for many has been the brain. More than 60 years ago, Papez (1937) proposed that emotions arose in a circuit that involved the hypothalamus, anterior thalamus, cingulate, and hippocampus. Over the next few decades, Maclean (1949, 1975, 1990) added additional brain regions to the Papez model, including the amygdala, prefrontal cortex, and septal nuclei. MacLean called this phylogenetically old circuit the limbic system, and this term has gained wide popularity. However, because there are no clear criteria for deciding what is part of this system, the list of brain regions associated with the limbic system has continued to grow without an end in sight. This uncontrolled growth has led to the consensus that "the concept suffers from imprecision at both the structural and functional levels" (LeDoux, 1993, p. 109), and hence may have outlived its usefulness.

To increase precision in the analysis of brain regions subserving emotion, neuroscience tools developed for research on cognitive processes recently have been used to study emotion. This has led to the emergence of the field of affective neuroscience (Davidson & Sutton, 1995; Panksepp, 1991). Based largely on animal models, affective neuroscientists have argued that emotions arise not in one but in multiple neural circuits (e.g., Gray, 1994; Panksepp, 1998). As Panksepp (1991) put it, "The brain appears to contain a number of functionally and anatomically distinct emotional circuits" for emotions such as separation distress, fear, rage, curiosity, and play (p. 63). The fear circuit is the most clearly defined of these postulated circuits because it has relatively clearly demarcated inputs and outputs.

Using the rat as a model, LeDoux has traced the circuitry that underlies fear conditioning. In Figure 21.4, LeDoux (1995) summarizes almost two decades of work, showing how auditory information passes first to the sensory thalamus, and then on to higher and higher brain centers (sensory cortex, perirhinal cortex, and hippocampus). Of particular interest is the direct pathway from the sensory thalamus to the amygdala (marked "1" on the figure). LeDoux (1993) interprets this pathway by suggesting that "subcortical sensory inputs to the amygdala may represent an evolutionarily primitive system passed on from early vertebrates that lacked well-developed neocortices. . . . However, these pathways continue to function as an early warning system, allowing the amygdala to be activated by simple stimulus features that may serve as emotional triggers" (p. 112). The sensory and cognitive inputs to the amygdala (see figure, areas marked 1–4) converge on the lateral nucleus, which routes impulses to the central nucleus. The central nucleus in turn relays the impulses to the central gray (which controls freezing), to the lateral hypothalamus and rostral ventral lateral medulla (which controls sympathetic nervous system responses), and to the bed nucleus of the stria terminalis and paraventricular nucleus (which controls the pituitary–adrenal axis).

Given the obvious ethical constraints on experiments with humans, our understanding of the neural bases of human emotion draws heavily on clinical findings. More than a century ago, clinical reports of the railworker Phineas Gage documented the role of the frontal lobes in emotional responding. Gage was injured in a freak accident when a tamping iron tore through the front of his skull. The iron not only damaged his brain (most likely the ventromedial region of both frontal lobes), but also his personality, and

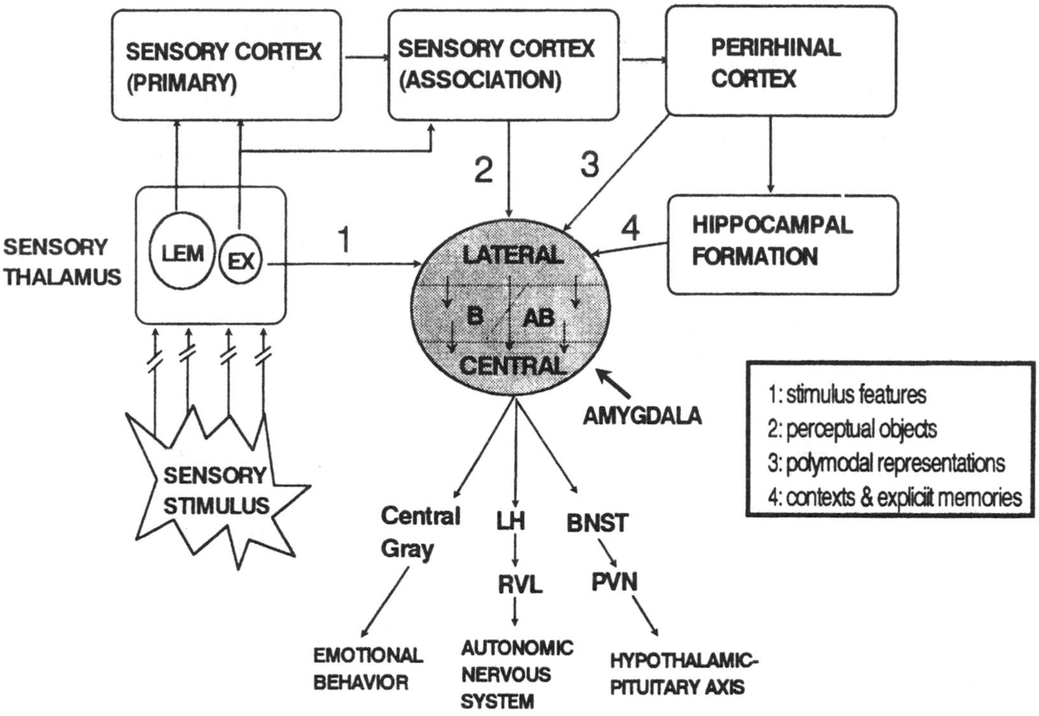

FIGURE 21.4. The role of the amygdala in emotion generation. From LeDoux (1995). With permission from the *Annual Review of Psychology,* Volume 46. Copyright 1995 by Annual Reviews.

this conscientious, well-liked man suddenly became an uncouth, ill-controlled, and thoroughly unpleasant character (Damasio, Grabowski, Frank, Galaburda, & Damasio, 1994). Since that time, clinical reports have accumulated suggesting that damage to the frontal lobes alters emotional responding (Damasio, 1994), and that the two hemispheres play quite different roles in the generation and regulation of emotion (Kolb & Taylor, 1990).

Experimental evidence has begun to corroborate both the clinical findings and the findings from animal work. For example, Davidson, Ekman, Saron, Senulis, and Friesen (1990) used EEG recording techniques to examine neural bases of emotion. They presented adult subjects with short film clips that elicited comparable intensities of happiness, amusement, and disgust. Disgust was associated with greater right-sided action than was happiness, whereas happiness was associated with greater left-sided activation than was disgust. Recently, newer assessment methodologies such as positron emission tomography (PET) and functional magnetic resonance imaging (fMRI) have also been used. These techniques have poorer temporal resolution than does EEG but vastly superior spatial resolution.

Studies using PET have shown left amygdala activation in sadness (Schneider et al., 1997). Adopting a dimensional perspective, Lane and colleagues (1997) used slides to elicit emotions and found brain activation that distinguished affective from neutral slides. More specifically, they found greater activation in the medial prefrontal cortex, thalamus, hypothalamus, and midbrain during affective slides. Unpleasant affect was distinguished from neutral and pleasant affect by bilateral activation in occipito-temporal cortex and cerebellum and left hippocampus and amygdala. Studies using fMRI have shown that the left amygdala is activated in sadness and happiness (Schneider et al., 1995) as well as fear (Birbaumer et al., 1998). If different emotions have different neural circuits, as has frequently been claimed, one puzzle is why several emotions all involve the amygdala. One possibility is that different subregions of the amygdala are active in different emotions. Another possibility is that neural specificity is lent to emotion not by the amygdala but some other brain structure. Affective neuroscience is currently an extremely active research area, and I suspect that in the next decade much progress will be made in mapping the brain regions associated with emotion.

Individual Differences in Physiological Responding

We are accustomed to thinking about individual differences in outer appearance. Small wonder: such differences stare us in the face every day. Some of us have blond hair, others brown or black. Some are tall and others short, and so forth. We typically give less thought to individual differences that are buried deep in the nervous system. Yet differences there are, and anatomists tell us that individual differences in the organs inside us are at least as substantial as the differences that are evident on the outside. Which of these many differences might be relevant to an understanding of emotion?

Historically, this question was addressed by examining individual differences in autonomic nervous system responding. Eppinger and Hess (1910) proposed that individuals differed in autonomic balance, that is, the degree to which they showed preferential sympathetic or parasympathetic nervous system activation. Vagotonics were individuals who showed large responses to drugs that activated the parasympathetic nervous system, and sympathicotonics were particularly responsive to drugs that activated the sympathetic nervous system. Wenger (1941) derived measures of autonomic balance and reported that sympathetic dominance was related to greater incidence of physical and psychological disorders. A variant on this approach was individual response (IR) stereotypy, which referred to the notion that individuals showed stable differences in the degree to which their various organ systems were activated across situations (Engel, 1972; Lacey, Kagan, Lacey, & Moss, 1963). Thus, some individuals were thought to be "heart responders" and others were "stomach responders." Differences in IR stereotypy were noteworthy because they were thought to predict psychosomatic disorders (Engel & Moos, 1967). However, the constructs of autonomic balance and IR stereotypy fell from favor as it became clear that sympathetic and parasympathetic systems do not operate in a simple reciprocal manner (Cacioppo, 1994), and that IR stereotypy showed limited stability (Sternbach, 1966). One related individual difference variable that continues to receive considerable attention is vagal tone (Porges, 1997). Vagal tone refers to the degree of activation of the parasympathetic branch of the autonomic nervous system, typically indexed by the degree to which respiratory changes influence heart rate (the greater the vagal tone, the greater the linkage between respiratory and cardiovascular systems). Individuals high rather than low in vagal tone are thought to be more effective at self-regulation.

Individual differences are also evident in the central nervous systems involved in emotional responding. One obvious starting point is the primarily subcortical amygdala-related circuits traced by LeDoux and others. Do differences in the thresholds of these fear-related circuits reveal themselves in individual differences in emotional responding? Kagan and Snidman (1991) have championed the notion that individual differences in the amygdala circuit give rise to individual differences in inhibition—which they operationalize as fear proneness and a hesitation to approach novel stimuli. As they put it: "One of our major assumptions is that inhibited children, and by inference high-motor–high-cry infants, have a low threshold of reactivity in the central nucleus of the amygdala and its projections to the hypothalamus, sympathetic chain, and cardiovascular system" (p. 859). Recent imaging and pharmacologic studies have tested this assumption. Using the local anesthetic procaine, Ketter et al. (1996) have shown that left amygdala activation correlated positively with subjective reports of fear and negatively with subjective reports of euphoria. Servan-Schreiber and Perlstein (1997) showed that procaine-induced bilateral activation of the anterior limbic network, along with experiential and autonomic changes consistent with an emotional state. Importantly, subjects varied considerably in how they responded to this injection. This variability in response suggests that pharmacologic challenges may be helpful in assessing individual differences in subcortical emotional circuitry, shedding new light on individual differences in emotion.

To assess individual differences in two of the subcortical response systems thought to be important to emotional responding, Carver and White (1994) developed scales for the Behavioral Inhibition System (BIS) and the Behavioral Activation System (BAS). The BIS scale measures individual differences in the tendency to experience negative affect and withdrawal tendencies in the context of threats (e.g., "If I think something unpleasant is going to happen I usually get pretty 'worked up'"). The BAS scale measures individual differences in the tendency to experience positive affect and approach tendencies in the context of reward contexts (e.g., "When I get something I want, I feel excited and energized"). Using these scales, Sutton and Davidson (1997) demonstrated that the strength of the BAS relative to the BIS was related to midfrontal EEG asymmetry. Individuals who reported greater relative approach tendencies showed greater left-frontal EEG activation during a baseline period. Interestingly, individual differences in the relative activation of left and right frontal regions predict the intensity of emotion experience during pleasant and unpleasant films (Wheeler, Davidson, & Tomarken, 1993) and even mood disorders (Henriques & Davidson, 1991). One puzzle is that Gray (1994) has emphasized subcortical substrates of the BIS and BAS systems in his work with rats, whereas Davidson's findings suggest cortical activation. It may be that there are important individual differences in both cortical and subcortical activation patterns, and future behavioral and imaging work will be needed to more completely describe the neural bases of emotional responding.

EMOTION REGULATION

From an evolutionary perspective, emotions represent the "wisdom of the ages" (Lazarus, 1991b, p. 820), prompting us to respond in ways that have been proven advantageous over the millennia. This scheme is correct so far as it goes. However, it is also incomplete. This is because emotions do not just wash over us like a powerful tide that is beyond our control. We also influence our emotions.

Given the impact of our emotions on a wide range of mental processes (e.g., memory, decision making) and manifest behaviors (e.g., helping behavior, drug use), emotion regulatory processes are fundamental to personality functioning and represent an important source of individual differences (e.g., she stays cool under pressure; he's a volcano). Emotion regulation also figures prominently in psychological and physical health. Over half of the Axis I disorders and all of the Axis II personality disorders involve some form of emotion dysregulation (Gross & Levenson, 1997). Thus, major depressive disorder is characterized by a deficit of positive emotion and/or a surplus of negative emotion; and histrionic personality disorder by excessive emotionality. In the physical health arena, chronic hostility and anger inhibition are associated with hypertension and coronary heart disease (e.g., e.g., Julkunen, Salonen, Kaplan, Chesney, & Salonen, 1994). Emotion inhibition may also exacerbate minor ailments (Pennebaker, 1990) and may even accelerate cancer progression (Fawzy et al., 1993; Gross, 1989).

In the following sections, I consider why we might want to regulate our emotions. I then return to the process model of emotion that I used previously to structure my discussion of emotion research. This time, however, I point to key places in the emotion generative process where other regulatory structures can influence emotional responding. Whenever possible, I relate these emotion regulatory processes to individual difference constructs.

Why Regulate Emotions?

One apparent embarrassment for the evolutionary perspective is the degree to which emotions seem be *un*helpful in our everyday efforts to meet the challenges posed by the world around us. With alarming regularity, it seems, we have to ignore or even override our emotions in order to perform well during a challenging test or avoid a nasty blowup with a colleague. How can we account for the tension between a functionalist, evolutionary perspective on emotion on the one hand, and the obvious need to influence our emotions on the other hand?

Contemporary environments differ in dramatic ways from the environments that forged our emotions, and responses that once were useful are often ill suited to modern exigencies. In part, this mismatch is due to technological advances that have greatly magnified the consequences that our emotional responses have for ourselves and others. Thus, a moment of dejection that once would have passed without a trace now leads to a suicidal drug overdose. A moment of exuberance that once would have led to a laughable boast now leads a ruinous bet. An angry impulse that once would have bruised now kills. From an evolutionary perspective, then, emotion regulation is necessary because some parts of our brain (the highly conserved emotion centers) incline us to do one thing in a particular situation, whereas other parts of our brain (the newer cortical centers) appreciate that this emotional impulse may not be well matched to our current situation, and thus incline us to do something else (or nothing at all).

This perspective helps us make sense of why emotion regulation is often so difficult, involving as it does a house divided against itself. One classic illustration of the difficulty of regulating emotions may be found in Darwin (1872/1998), who described his failed efforts to control his fearful retreat from a caged snake:

> I put my face close to the thick glass-plate in front of a puff-adder in the Zoological Gardens, with the firm determination of not starting back if the snake struck at me; but, as soon as the blow was struck, my resolution went for nothing, and I jumped a yard or two backwards with astonishing rapidity. My will and reason were powerless against the imagination of a danger which had never been experienced. (pp. 43–44)

It may be objected that this is an unfair example, in that this fear response is so tightly bound up with the more primitive withdrawal reflex that it is particularly difficult to control. However, similar failures of control occur in other more complex emotions. A college student gave this response when asked to describe a time when she tried to alter her emotions:

> This past week I have tried to feel "romantically" about a friend of mine, who apparently is in love with me. I had previously only thought of this person as my friend and one of the nicest guys I have ever met, but never sexually. Well he confessed his true emotions to me and I, since I like him so much as a friend, wanted to feel the same way about him; to make him happy. So I tried and tried and tried to think of him that way, but I just couldn't. I tried to think of how sweet he was and what a great relationship it would be, and how good he would be to me, but it just didn't "turn me on." I would try to view him in a sexual light and find things that appealed to me sexually, but these things were just the components of my good friend, and not of a future partner.

These examples suggest that emotion regulation may involve either increasing or decreasing emotion, and may involve positive as well as negative emotions. Regulation that involves *decreasing* or *stopping* emotions occurs when (1) emotions arise from an overly simple appraisal of the situation, such as mistaking a stick for a snake; (2) emotions prompt behavioral responses that are no longer useful, such as physically attacking an irritating subordinate; and (3) emotion response tendencies conflict with other goals, such as when saving one's skin by fleeing a fight conflicts with saving face by standing one's ground. Regulation that involves *initiating* or *increasing* emotions occurs when (1) emotion response tendencies are lacking because one's attention is elsewhere, but one wishes to muster an appropriate response, such as enthusiasm at another's good news, or (2) one desires to replace one emotion with another, such as when one is feeling down, yet wants to summon a more positive emotional state before calling on friends. As we consider these possibilities, it appears that far from being an embarrassment to the evolutionary perspective, the capacity to influence our emotions may be testament to the flexibility of the emotion-generative process.

Surveying the many ways individuals may influence their emotions, we may define emotion regulation as the ways individuals influence which emotions they have, when they have them, and how they experience or express these emotions (Gross, 1998b). Such regulation may be automatic or controlled, and may be conscious or unconscious. Because emotions are multicomponential processes that unfold over time, emotion regulation involves changes in the latency, rise time, magnitude, duration, and offset of responses in behavioral, experiential, or physiological domains. Emotion regulation may be distinguished from several related constructs. Paralleling the distinctions drawn above among members of the affective family, I see emotion regulation as subordinate to the broader construct of affect regulation. Under this broad heading fall all manner of efforts to influence our valenced feelings (Westen, 1994). Affect regulation includes (among other things): (1) coping, (2) emotion regulation, and (3) mood regulation. My focus here is on emotion regulation (see Gross, 1998b).

Emotion Regulatory Processes

There are many different ways of regulating emotions, but no obvious way of organizing them. Take a simple example—that of a couple planning an evening out. Before they go out, one partner, aware of her shyness, vetoes several possible ways of spending the evening (e.g., a large party and a football game) because these settings would engender negative emotion. They decide to have dinner at a restaurant that is usually quiet. They are seated near a boisterous group who have been drinking for some time. Knowing that sitting this close to a loud group would frustrate their plans for a quiet conversation, they ask to be reseated. Once reseated, they relax into dinner and conversation. Each partner chooses to attend to one thought or another and to pursue one topic or another, in part due to the desire to experience certain emotions and not others. Toward the end of the evening, one partner remarks how rare it is for them to have such a nice evening out. Although this comment can be read either as a compliment or a criticism, the other partner interprets it as a compliment, and responds in kind, saying how much fun the evening had been. The first partner then makes the criticism explicit—they really haven't been going out enough. Although hurt by this comment, the recipient does not want to spoil the happy evening, so does not show any sign of feeling hurt.

How should we conceptualize the diverse processes involved in regulating emotion throughout an evening such as the one described above? The emotion model presented in Figure 21.1 suggests a process-oriented organization of the emotion regulatory domain. The most obvious distinction is between antecedent-focused emotion regulation, which occurs before any emotion is generated, and response-focused emotion regulation, which occurs after the emotion is generated (Gross & Munoz, 1995). Even this basic distinction sheds light on the divergent consequences of different forms of emotion regulation. Antecedent-focused emotion regulation, such as construing a potentially upsetting situation in nonemotional terms, decreases both emotion experience and expression (Gross, 1998a). By contrast, response-focused emotion regulation, such as suppressing one's emotion-expressive behavior, produces little or no change in emotion experience, and comes at the physiological price of increased sympathetic nervous system activation (Gross, 1998a; Gross & Levenson, 1993, 1997).

The distinction between antecedent- and response-focused emotion regulation is clearly a simplification. What more can be done to distinguish among emotion regulatory processes? As shown in Figure 21.1, emotion generation involves an encounter with an emotion cue that is attended to and then evaluated in a particular way. This gives rise to emotion response tendencies that may be experienced or expressed. In Figure 21.5 (see next page), I have redrawn this model, highlighting five points in the emotion-generative process at which individuals might regulate their emotions: situation selection, situation modification, attentional deployment, cognitive change, and response modulation (Gross, 1998b).

Before turning to each of these five regulatory processes, I touch on the important issue of individual differences in emotion regulation. Because the field of emotion regulation is new, the study of individual differences in emotion regulation is less well developed than the study of individual differences in emotion antecedents and responses. However, one can imagine (at least) three important domains of individual difference. The first has to do with an individual's emotion regulatory goals. What does the individual believe constitutes appropriate emotion experience, expression, and physiological responding in a given situation? The second domain has to do with how frequently an individual attempts to regulate emotions in each of a variety of ways. How often does an individual use a particular strategy to achieve a given emotion regulatory goal? The third has to do with what an individual is capable of. Whereas traits refer to what an individual *typically* does, capabilities refer to the range of emotion regulatory behaviors an individual is *capable* of performing.

Eventually, we need constructs that distinguish among the three individual difference domains of goals, strategies, and capabilities for each of the major forms of emotion regulation. At this point, we are far from that goal. Instead, we have a number of constructs that are specified at a broader level of abstraction. For example, ego control refers to the "degree of impulse control and modulation" an individual has and can be measured by items such as "I like to stop and think things over before I do them" (Block & Block, 1980, p. 41). Other personality constructs are broader still. For example, emotional intelligence includes "the verbal and nonverbal appraisal and expression of emotion, the regulation of emotion in the self and others, and the utilization of emotional context in problem solving" (Mayer & Salovey, 1993, p. 433). Other constructs are narrower and more clearly focused on specific processes. In the following sections, I mention several of these more specific individual difference constructs as I describe the five emotion regulatory processes I have identified.

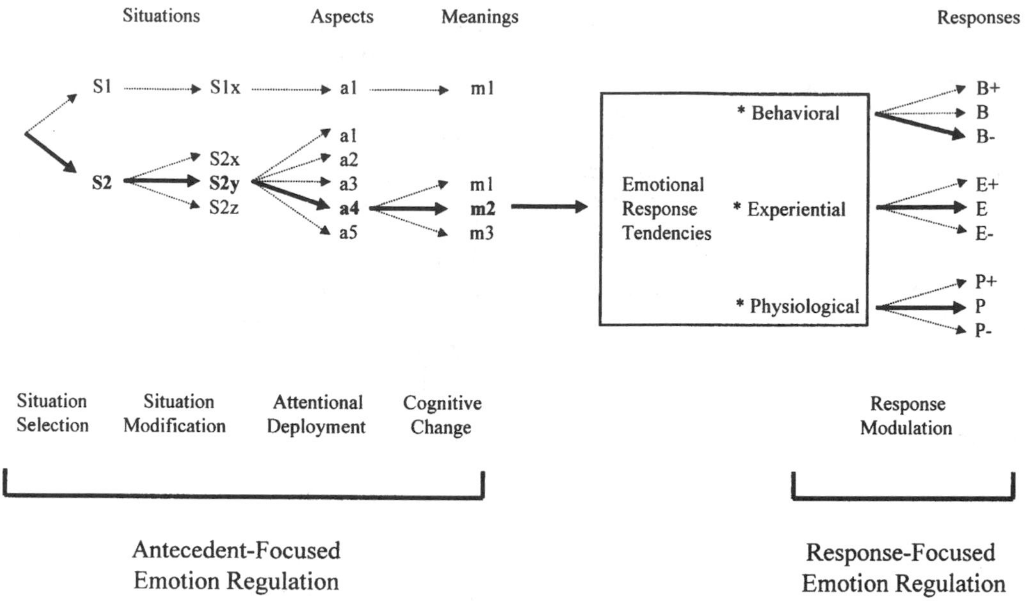

FIGURE 21.5. A process model of emotion regulation. From Gross (1998). Copyright 1998 by the Educational Publishing Foundation. Reprinted by permission.

Situation Selection

Situation selection refers to approaching or avoiding certain people, places, or objects in order to influence one's emotions. Situation selection is illustrated in Figure 21.5 by the solid line toward situation two (S2) rather than situation one (S1). In the previous example of a couple going out for the evening, situation selection refers to choosing how and where to spend the evening so as to maximize pleasant feelings. Other examples include taking a different route to the store to avoid a neighbor who tells offensive jokes or seeking out a friend with whom one can have a good cry. Individuals seek out situations consistent with their dispositions (Caspi & Roberts, Chapter 11, this volume). Thus, extraverts seek out social situations that provide opportunities for fun and enjoyment, influencing the emotions they experience. Individuals high in Sensation Seeking search out challenges and risky situations because they enjoy the thrill and excitement that these situations provide (Zuckerman, 1979).

Situation Modification

Potentially emotion-eliciting situations—whether a flat tire on the way to an important appointment or loud music next door at 3:00 A.M.—do not ineluctably call forth emotions. We can convert a meeting into a phone conference, convince a neighbor to tone down a raucous party, or—in the previous example—ask for a quiet table at a restaurant. Active efforts to directly modify the situation so as to alter its emotional impact constitute an important form of emotion regulation. As shown in Figure 21.5, situations differ in terms of how much they may be modified, ranging from a hypothetical limiting case of a situation with no room for change (denoted by S1x) to a situation with modest potential for change (S2x, S2y, S2z). Individual differences in situation modification have largely been studied in the context of problem-focused coping (Lazarus & Folkman, 1984). The personality trait of dominance or assertiveness also involves situation modification. Instead of sitting at home and fuming at a loud party next door, an assertive individual asks to have the music turned down.

Attentional Deployment

Situations vary in complexity, ranging from the limiting case of a situation with one aspect (a1) to a situation with multiple aspects (a1, a2, a3, a4, a5). As shown in Figure 21.5, attentional deployment is used to select which aspect of a situation is focused upon. In the previous example, attentional deployment refers to attentional shifts in the conversation that are aimed at fostering certain emotions rather than others. Specific forms of attentional deployment include distraction, concentration, and rumination. In distraction, an individual refocuses attention on nonemotional aspects of the situation or moves attention away from the immediate situation altogether. Through concentration, an individual can create a self-sustaining transcendent state that Csikszentmihalyi (1975) calls "flow." Rumination involves attentional focus on feelings and their consequences; in cases of depression, this leads to longer and more severe symptoms (Just & Alloy, 1997). Several individual difference constructs involve attentional deployment. Repressive copers deflect attention away from potentially threatening stimuli (Boden & Baumeister, 1997; Krohne, 1996). Ruminators attend to (and stew over) painful feelings and situations (Nolen-Hoeksema, 1987). Monitors turn attention toward threatening stimuli, whereas blunters turn away from threatening stimuli (Miller, 1987). Finally, compared with those low in Neuroticism, individuals high in Neuroticism are less able to shift attention from motivationally relevant stimuli when doing so is desirable (Wallace & Newman, 1997).

Cognitive Change

Emotion requires that individuals imbue percepts with meaning (Clore & Ortony, 1998), and evaluate their capacity to manage the situation (e.g., Bandura, 1997; Lazarus & Folkman, 1984). As shown in Figure 21.5, cognitive change refers to selecting which of the many possible meanings (m1, m2, m3) that a situation affords will be attached to the situation. In the example above, cognitive change refers to how a person chooses to construe the meaning of an event, such as a comment about how rarely the couple has such nice evenings out. Cognitive change may decrease emotional responding, as when one imagines that graphic news footage has been faked, or increase emotional responding, as when one reinterprets a joke as a thinly veiled insult. In terms of subjective experience, cognitive change decreases negative emotion experience (Cantor & Wilson, 1984; Gross, 1998a; Lazarus & Alfert, 1964). Physiologically, results have been mixed. In the context of graphic films, there is no decrease in physiological responding (e.g., Gross, 1998a; Steptoe & Vogele, 1986), whereas in the context of more cognitively complex situations such as verbal harassment, decreases in physiological responding have been documented (Stemmler, 1997). Related individual difference constructs include optimism (Scheier & Carver, 1985), attributional style (Peterson 1991), constructive thinking (Epstein & Meier, 1989), and psychological defenses such as denial, isolation, and intellectualization.

Response Modulation

In contrast with other emotion regulatory processes, response modulation occurs late in the emotion generative process, after response tendencies have been initiated. Response modulation refers to directly influencing behavioral, physiological, or experiential responding. In Figure 21.5, response modulation is illustrated by decreasing behavioral response tendencies (B– rather than B), one of the more common forms of emotion regulation (Gross, Feldman Barrett, & Richards, 1999). In the example above, response modulation refers to deciding to hide hurt feelings at the end of the evening. Predictably, increasing emotion-expressive behavior seems to increase other aspects of the emotional response. Rather more interestingly, decreasing emotion-expressive behavior seems to have mixed effects on emotion experience (decreasing positive emotion experience but not negative emotion experience) and actually increases sympathetic activation (Gross, 1998a; Gross & Levenson, 1993, 1997). Drugs (e.g., beta blockers) and relaxation techniques are effective means of decreasing autonomic nervous system responses; physiological down-regulation appears to decrease other aspects of the emotional response (Wolpe, 1958). Finally, as is widely appreciated, alcohol and recreational drugs (e.g., Pervin, 1988) may be used to enhance or diminish emotion experience. Individual difference measures relevant to response modulation abound, particularly for the response components of expressive behavior and subjective experience. Watson and Greer's (1983) Coutauld Emotional Control Scale and Roger and Najarian's (1989) Emotion Control Scale assess differences in typical behavior inhibition. For emotion experience, Catanzaro and Mearns's (1990) measure of negative mood regulation assesses individual differences in the ability to influence emotion experience; Salovey and colleagues' (1995) Trait Meta-Mood Scale similarly concerns individual differences in attempts to maintain positive moods or repair negative ones.

CONCLUDING COMMENT

The primary function of the nervous system is "the transforming of sensory patterns into patterns of motor coordination" (Sperry, 1952, p. 297). Emotions represent a key element in this transformation. They offer nature's best guess as to how to anticipate and respond to many of the vitally significant situations we face in everyday life. To examine how emotions help us match action with circumstance, I have taken an evolutionary perspective on emotion. In the first section, I traced the origins of contemporary emotion theory from instincts through fixed action patterns to response tendencies. In the second section, I used a process-oriented model of emotion generation to organize research on emotion antecedents and on experiential, behavioral, and physiological responses. In the third section, I argued that individuals exert considerable influence over which emotions they have (antecedent-focused emotion regulation) and how these emotions are expressed (response-focused emotion regulation). More specifically, I distinguished five points in the emotion generative process at which regulation may occur: (1) selection of the situation, (2) modification of the situation, (3) deployment of attention, (4) change of cognitions, and (5) modulation of responses. Surveying the major personality theories, "none presents a well-articulated theory of the specific affects and their relation to other aspects of personality functioning" (Pervin, 1993, p. 309). This chapter has taken a step toward such a theory by elaborating a process conception of emotion generation that addresses basic emotion processes as well as individual differences in emotion and emotion regulation.

ACKNOWLEDGMENTS

Preparation of this chapter was supported by Grant No. MH53859 from the National Institute of Mental Health and by Grant No. SBR-9728989 from the National Science Foundation to James J. Gross. I would like to thank Lisa Feldman Barrett, Russ Fernald, Mark Lepper, Auke Tellegen, and David Watson for commenting on an earlier draft of this chapter.

NOTES

1. Like other animals, humans must meet a number of adaptive challenges if they are to survive. These challenges include avoiding bodily harm, obtaining food, and exploring the environment. Affects constitute one important mechanism for meeting these challenges. Three other mechanisms are reflexes, motives, and cognitions (see Smith & Lazarus, 1990; Zajonc, 1998).

2. These distinctions have heuristic value but should not be reified given the highly permeable boundaries among categories. For example, some facial expressions (e.g., blushing, crying) have clear autonomic bases, and emotion experience has been associated with activity of the anterior cingulate cortex (Lane, Fink, Chau, & Dolan, 1997). At present, however, the three-way distinction among emotion experience, expression, and physiology remains a useful way of organizing research on emotion.

3. The following section draws on Rinn's (1984) excellent review.

4. Proponents of autonomic specificity reply that methodological problems have played an important role in the inconsistent reports of autonomic differences among emotions (Levenson, 1988). For example, (a) comparable emotional states are not always elicited across subjects (in both intensity and kind), (b) "baseline" states are not always provided to have a comparison standard for the emotional responses, and (c) measures are typically intrusive and thus interfere with the emotional response of interest. However, even careful studies with relatively unobtrusive measures have not gone far beyond a few basic distinctions among emotions. One puzzle is why something as phenomenologically obvious as bodily differences among emotions has been so empirically elusive.

REFERENCES

Allport, G. W. (1937). *Personality: A psychological interpretation.* New York: Holt.

Allport, G. W., & Vernon, P. E. (1933). *Studies in expressive movement.* New York: Macmillan.

Arnold, M. (1960). *Emotion and personality.* New York: Columbia University Press.

Aspinwall, L. G., & Taylor, S. E. (1992). Modeling cognitive adaptation: A longitudinal investigation of the impact of individual differences and coping on college adjustment and performance. *Journal of Personality and Social Psychology, 63,* 989–1003.

Averill, J. R. (1975). A semantic atlas of emotional concepts. *JSAS Catalog of Selected Documents in Psychology, 5,* 330 (Ms. No. 421).

Averill, J. R. (1980). A constructivist view of emotion. In R. Plutchik & H. Kellerman (Eds.), *Emotion:*

Theory, research, and experience (pp. 305–339). Orlando, FL: Academic Press.

Averill, J. R. (1997). The emotions: An integrative approach. In R. Hogan, J. Johnson, & S. Briggs (Eds.), *Handbook of personality psychology* (pp. 513–541). San Diego, CA: Academic Press.

Bandura, A. (1997). *Self-efficacy: The exercise of control.* New York: Freeman.

Barlow, G. W. (1968). Ethological units of behavior. In D. Ingle (Ed.), *The central nervous system and fish behavior* (pp. 217–232). Chicago: University of Chicago Press.

Barlow, G. (1977). Modal action patterns. In T. A. Sebeok (Ed.), *How animals communicate* (pp. 98–134). Bloomington, IN: Indiana University Press.

Berkinblit, M. B., Feldman, A. G.,& Fukson, O. I. (1986). Adaptability of innate motor patterns and motor control mechanisms. *Behavioral and Brain Sciences, 9,* 585–638.

Birbaumer, N., Grodd, W., Diedrich, O., Klose, U., Erb, M., Lotze, M., Schneider, F., Weiss, U., & Flor, H. (1998). fMRI reveals amygdala activation to human faces in social phobics. *Neuroreport, 9,* 1223–1226.

Block, J. H., & Block, J. (1980). The role of ego-control and ego-resiliency in the organization of behavior. In W. A. Collins (Ed.), *Development of cognition, affect, and social relations: The Minnesota symposia on child psychology* (Vol. 13, pp. 39–51). Hillsdale, NJ: Erlbaum.

Boden, J. M., & Baumeister, R. F. (1997). Repressive coping: Distraction using pleasant thoughts and memories. *Journal of Personality and Social Psychology, 73,* 45–62.

Bolger, N., & Schilling, E. A. (1991). Personality and the problems of everyday life: The role of neuroticism in exposure and reactivity to daily stressors. *Journal of Personality, 59,* 355–386.

Brickman, P., Coates, D., & Janoff-Bulman, R. (1978). Lottery winners and accident victims: Is happiness relative? *Journal of Personality and Social Psychology, 36,* 917–927.

Buck, R. (1985). Prime theory: An integrated view of motivation and emotion. *Psychological Review, 92,* 389–413.

Buck, R. (1990). Mood and emotion: A comparison of five contemporary views. *Psychological Inquiry, 1,* 330–336.

Buck, R. W., Savin, V. J., Miller, R. E., & Caul, W. F. (1972). Communication of affect through facial expressions in humans. *Journal of Personality and Social Psychology, 23,* 362–371.

Cacioppo, J. T. (1994). Social neuroscience: Autonomic, neuroendocrine, and immune responses to stress. *Psychophysiology, 31,* 113–128.

Cacioppo, J. T., Klein, D. J., Berntson, G. G., & Hatfield, E. (1993). The psychophysiology of emotion. In M. Lewis & J. M. Haviland (Eds.), *Handbook of emotions* (pp. 119–142). New York: Guilford Press.

Cacioppo, J. T., Martzke, J. S., Petty, R. S., & Tassinary, L. G. (1988). Specific forms of facial EMG response index emotions during an interview: From Darwin to the continuous flow hypothesis of affect laden information processing. *Journal of Personality and Social Psychology, 54,* 592–604.

Cantor, J., & Wilson, B. J. (1984). Modifying fear responses to mass media in preschool and elementary school children. *Journal of Broadcasting, 28,* 431–433.

Carver, C. S., & White, T. L. (1994). Behavioral inhibition, behavioral activation, and affective responses to impending reward and punishment: The BIS/BAS Scales. *Journal of Personality and Social Psychology, 67,* 319–333.

Caspi, A., & Bem, D. J. (1990). Personality continuity and change across the life course. In L. A. Pervin (Ed.), *Handbook of personality: Theory and research* (pp. 549–575). New York: Guilford Press.

Caspi, A., Bem, D., & Elder, G. H., Jr. (1989). Continuities and consequences of interaction styles across the life course. *Journal of Personality, 57,* 375–406.

Catanzaro, S. J., & Mearns, J. (1990). Measuring generalized expectancies for negative mood regulation: Initial scale development and implications. *Journal of Personality Assessment, 54,* 546–563

Chaplin, W. F., John, O. P., & Goldberg, L. R. (1988). Conceptions of states and traits: Dimensional attributes with ideals as prototypes. *Journal of Personality and Social Psychology, 54,* 541–557.

Clark., L. A., & Watson, D. (1988). Mood and the mundane: Relations between daily life events and self-reported mood. *Journal of Personality and Social Psychology, 54,* 296–308.

Clore, G. L., & Ortony, A. (1998). Cognition in emotion: Always, sometimes, or never? In L. Nadel & R. Lane (Eds.), *The cognitive neuroscience of emotion.* New York: Oxford University Press.

Costa, P. T., & McCrae, R. R. (1980). Influence of extraversion and neuroticism on subjective well-being. *Journal of Personality and Social Psychology, 38,* 668–678.

Csikszentmihalyi, M. (1975). *Beyond boredom and anxiety: The experience of play in work and games.* San Francisco: Jossey-Bass.

Damasio, A. R. (1994). *Descartes' error: Emotion, reason, and the human brain.* New York: Grossett/Putnam.

Damasio, H., Grabowski, T., Frank, R., Galaburda, A. M., & Damasio, A. R. (1994). The return of Phineas Gage: Clues about the brain from the skull of a famous patient. *Science, 264,* 1102–1105.

Darwin, C. (1859/1962). *The origin of species by means of natural selection or the preservation of favoured races in the struggle for life.* New York: Collier.

Darwin, C. (1872/1998). *The expression of emotions in man and animals* (3rd ed.). New York: Oxford University Press.

Davidson, R. J., Ekman, P., Saron, C. D., Senulis, J. A., & Friesen, W. V. (1990). Approach–withdrawal and cerebral asymmetry: Emotional expression and brain physiology I. *Journal of Personality and Social Psychology, 58,* 330–341.

Davidson, R. J., & Sutton, S. K. (1995). Affective neuroscience: The emergence of a discipline. *Current Opinion in Neurobiology, 5,* 217–224.

de Rivera, J. (1977). *Psychological issues: A structural theory of the emotions, 10,* 9–169. New York: International Universities Press.

Dewsbury, D. A. (1978). What is (was?) the "Fixed Action Pattern"? *Animal Behaviour, 26,* 310–311.

Diener, E., Smith, H., & Fujita, F. (1995). The personality structure of affect. *Journal of Personality and Social Psychology, 69,* 130–141.

Dodge, K. A. (1991). Emotion and social information processing. In J. Garber & K. A. Dodge (Eds.), *The development of emotion regulation and dysregulation* (pp. 159–182). New York: Cambridge University Press.

Duffy, E. (1941). The conceptual categories of psychology: A suggestion for revision. *Psychological Review, 48,* 177–203.

Duffy, E. (1962). *Activation and behavior.* New York: Wiley.

Duncan, I. J. H., & Hughes, B. O. (1984). Behaviour patterns. *Applied Animal Behaviour Science, 13,* 163–166.

Eibl-Eibesfeldt, I. (1975). *Ethology: The biology of behavior.* New York: Holt, Rinehart & Winston.

Ekman, P. (1972). Universals and cultural differences in facial expression of emotion. In J. Cole (Ed.), *Nebraska symposium on motivation* (pp. 207–283). Lincoln, NE: University of Nebraska Press.

Ekman, P. (1992). An argument for basic emotions. *Cognition and Emotion, 6,* 169–200.

Ekman, P. (1994). Strong evidence for universals in facial expressions: A reply to Russell's mistaken critique. *Psychological Bulletin, 115,* 268–287.

Ekman, P., & Friesen, W. V. (1978). *Facial Action Coding System.* Palo Alto, CA: Consulting Psychologists Press.

Ekman, P., Friesen, W. V., & Ellsworth, P. (1972). *Emotion in the human face: Guidelines for research and an integration of findings.* Elmsford, NY: Pergamon Press.

Ekman, P., & Rosenberg, E. L. (1997). *What the face reveals: Basic and applied studies of spontaneous expression using the Facial Action Coding System (FACS).* New York: Oxford University Press.

Ellsworth, P. C. (1994). Some reasons to expect universal antecedents of emotion. In P. Ekman & R. J. Davidson (Eds.), *The nature of emotion: Fundamental questions* (pp. 150–154). New York: Oxford University Press.

Emmons, R. A., & Diener, E. (1985). Personality correlates of subjective well-being. *Personality and Social Psychology Bulletin, 11,* 89–97.

Engel, B. T. (1972). Response specificity. In N. J. Greenfield & R. A. Sternbach (Eds.), *Handbook of psychophysiology* (pp. 571–576). New York: Holt, Rinehart & Winston.

Engel, B. T., & Moos, R. H. (1967). The generality of specificity. *Archives of General Psychiatry, 16,* 575–581.

Eppinger, H., & Hess, L. (1910). *Vagatonia.* New York: Nervous and Mental Disease Pub. Co.

Epstein, S., & Meier, P. (1989). Constructive thinking: A broad coping variable with specific components. *Journal of Personality and Social Psychology, 57,* 332–350.

Evoy, W. H. (1986). Is anything fixed in an action pattern? *Behavioral and Brain Sciences, 9,* 603–604.

Fawzy, F., Fawzy, N., Hyun, C., Elashoff, R., Guthrie, D., Fahey, J., & Morton, D. (1993). Malignant melanoma: Effects of an early structured psychiatric intervention, coping, and affective state on recurrence and survival 6 years later. *Archives of General Psychiatry, 50,* 681–689.

Feldman, L. A. (1995). Valence focus and arousal focus: Individual differences in the structure of affective experience. *Journal of Personality and Social Psychology, 69,* 153–166.

Feldman Barrett, L. (1998). Discrete emotions or dimensions? The role of valence focus and arousal focus. *Cognition and Emotion, 12,* 579–599.

Fisher, L. (1991). Stress and cardiovascular physiology in animals. In M. R. Brown, G. F. Koob, & C. Rivier (Eds.), *Stress: Neurobiology and neuroendocrinology* (pp. 463–474). New York: Dekker.

Frank, M., Ekman, P., & Friesen, W. (1993). Behavioral markers and recognizability of the smile of enjoyment. *Journal of Personality and Social Psychology, 64,* 83–93.

Friedman, H. S., Prince, L. M., Riggio, R. E., & DiMatteo, M. R. (1980). Understanding and assessing nonverbal expressiveness: The affective communication test. *Journal of Personality and Social Psychology, 39,* 333–351.

Frijda, N. H. (1986). *The emotions.* Cambridge, UK: Cambridge University Press.

Frijda, N. H. (1988). The laws of emotion. *American Psychologist, 43,* 349–358.

Frijda, N. H. (1989). Aesthetic emotions and reality. *American Psychologist, 44,* 1546–1547.

Frijda, N. H., Kuipers, P., & ter Schure, E. (1989). Relations among emotion, appraisal, and emotional action readiness. *Journal of Personality and Social Psychology, 57,* 212–228.

Galati, D., Scherer, K. R., & Ricci-Bitti, P. E. (1997). Voluntary facial expression of emotion: Comparing congenitally blind with normally sighted encoders. *Journal of Personality and Social Psychology, 73,* 1363–1379

Gray, J. A. (1994). Three fundamental emotion systems. In P. Ekman & R. J. Davidson (Eds.), *The nature of emotion: Fundamental questions* (pp. 243–247). New York: Oxford University Press.

Gross, J. (1989). Emotional expression in cancer onset and progression. *Social Science and Medicine, 28,* 1239–1248.

Gross, J. J. (1998a). Antecedent- and response-focused emotion regulation: Divergent consequences for experience, expression, and physiology. *Journal of Personality and Social Psychology, 74,* 224–237

Gross, J. J. (1998b). The emerging field of emotion regulation: An integrative review. *Review of General Psychology, 2,* 271–299.

Gross, J. J., Feldman Barrett, L., & Richards, J. M. (1999). *Emotion regulation in everyday life.* Manuscript in preparation.

Gross, J. J., & John, O. P. (1995). Facets of emotional expressivity: Three self-report factors and their correlates. *Personality and Individual Differences, 19,* 555–568.

Gross, J. J., & John, O. P. (1997). Revealing feelings: Facets of emotional expressivity in self-reports, peer ratings, and behavior. *Journal of Personality and Social Psychology, 72,* 435–448.

Gross, J. J., & John, O. P. (1998). Mapping the domain of emotional expressivity: Multi-method evidence for a hierarchical model. *Journal of Personality and Social Psychology, 74,* 170–191

Gross, J. J., & Levenson, R. W. (1993). Emotional suppression: Physiology, self-report, and expressive behavior. *Journal of Personality and Social Psychology, 64,* 970–986.

Gross, J. J., & Levenson, R. W. (1995). Emotion elicitation using films. *Cognition and Emotion, 9,* 87–108.

Gross, J. J., & Levenson, R. W. (1997). Hiding feelings: The acute effects of inhibiting positive and negative emotions. *Journal of Abnormal Psychology, 106,* 95–103.

Gross, J. J., & Munoz, R. F. (1995). Emotion regulation and mental health. *Clinical Psychology: Science and Practice, 2,* 151–164.

Gross, J. J., Sutton, S. K., & Ketelaar, T. V. (1998). Relations between affect and personality: Support for the affect-level and affective-reactivity views. *Personality and Social Psychology Bulletin, 24,* 279–288.

Hammen, C. (1991). Generation of stress in the course of unipolar depression. *Journal of Abnormal Psychology, 100,* 555–561.

Henriques, J. B., & Davidson, R. J. (1990). Regional brain electrical asymmetries discriminate between previously depressed and healthy control subjects. *Journal of Abnormal Psychology, 99,* 22–31.

Izard, C. E. (1971). *The face of emotion.* New York: Appleton-Century-Crofts.

Izard, C. E. (1977). *Human emotions.* New York: Plenum Press.

Izard, C. E., Libero, D. Z., Putnam, P., & Haynes, O. M. (1993). Stability of emotion experiences and their relations to traits of personality. *Journal of Personality and Social Psychology, 64,* 847–860.

James, W. (1884). What is an emotion? *Mind, 9,* 188–205.

James, W. (1890). *The principles of psychology.* New York: Holt.

James, W. (1902). *Varieties of religious experience: A study in human nature.* New York: Longman.

Johnson-Laird, P. N., & Oatley, K. (1992). Basic emotions, rationality, and folk theory. *Cognition and Emotion, 6,* 201–223.

Julkunen, J., Salonen, R., Kaplan, G. A., Chesney, M. A., & Salonen, J. T. (1994). Hostility and the progression of carotid atherosclerosis. *Psychosomatic Medicine, 56,* 519–525.

Just, N., & Alloy, L. B. (1997). The response styles theory of depression: Tests and an extension of the theory. *Journal of Abnormal Psychology, 106,* 221–229.

Kagan, J., & Snidman, N. (1991). Temperamental factors in human development. *American Psychologist, 46,* 856–862.

Keltner, D. (1995). Signs of appeasement: Evidence for the distinct displays of embarrassment, amusement, and shame. *Journal of Personality and Social Psychology, 68,* 441–454.

Ketter, T. A., Andreason, P. J., George, M. S., Lee, C., Gill, D. S., Parekh, P. I., Willis, M. W., Herscovitch, P., & Post, R. M. (1996). Anterior paralimbic mediation of Procaine-induced emotional and psychosensory experiences. *Archives of General Psychiatry, 53,* 59–69.

Kolb, B., & Taylor, L. (1990). Neocortical substrates of emotional behavior. In N. Stein & B. Leventhal (Eds.), *Psychological and biological approaches to emotion* (pp. 115–144). Hillsdale, NJ: Erlbaum.

Kring, A. M., Smith, D. A., & Neale, J. M. (1994). Individual differences in dispositional expressiveness: Development and validation of the Emotional Expressivity Scale. *Journal of Personality and Social Psychology, 66,* 934–949.

Krohne, H. W. (1996). Individual differences in coping. In M. Zeidner & N. S. Endler (Eds.), *Handbook of coping: Theory, research, applications* (pp. 381–409). New York: Wiley.

Lacey, J. I. (1967). Somatic response patterning and stress: Some revisions of activation theory. In M. H. Appley & R. Trumbull (Eds.), *Psychological stress: Issues in research* (pp. 14–37). Englewood Cliffs, NJ: Prentice Hall.

Lacey, J. I., Kagan, J., Lacey, B. C., & Moss, H. A. (1963). The visceral level: Situational determinants and behavioral correlates of autonomic response patterns. In P. H. Knapp (Ed.), *Expression of emotion in man* (pp. 161–196). New York: International Universities Press.

Lakoff, G. (1987). *Women, fire, and dangerous things.* Chicago: University of Chicago Press.

Lane, R. D., Fink, G. R., Chau, P. M., & Dolan, R. J. (1997). Neural activation during selective attention to subjective emotional responses. *Neuroreport, 8,* 3969–3972.

Lane, R. D., Quinlan, D. M., Schwartz, G. E., Walker, P. A., & Zeitlin, S. B. (1990). The levels of emotional awareness scale: A cognitive-developmental measure of emotion. *Journal of Personality Assessment, 55,* 124–134.

Lang, P. J. (1995). The emotion probe: Studies of motivation and attention. *American Psychologist, 50,* 372–385.

Lang, P. J., Rice, D. G., & Sternbach, R. A. (1972). The psychophysiology of emotion. In N. J. Greenfield & R. A. Sternbach (Eds.), *Handbook of psychophysiology* (pp. 623–643). New York: Holt, Rinehart & Winston.

Larsen, R. J. (1984). Theory and measurement of affect intensity as an individual difference characteristic. *Dissertation Abstracts International, 45,* 07B (University microfilm no. AAG8422112).

Larsen, R. J., & Diener, E. (1992). Promises and problems with the circumplex model of emotion. In M. S. Clark (Ed.), *Emotion. Review of personality and social psychology* (Vol. 13, pp. 25–59). Newbury Park, CA: Sage.

Larsen, R. J., & Ketelaar, T. (1991). Personality and susceptibility to positive and negative emotional states. *Journal of Personality and Social Psychology, 61,* 132–140.

Lazarus, R. S. (1981). A cognitivist's reply to Zajonc on emotion and cognition. *American Psychologist, 36,* 222–223.

Lazarus, R. S. (1984). On the primacy of cognition. *American Psychologist, 39,* 124–129.

Lazarus, R. S. (1991a). *Emotion and adaptation.* Oxford: Oxford University Press.

Lazarus, R. S. (1991b). Progress on a cognitive-motivational-relational theory of emotion. *American Psychologist, 46,* 819–834.

Lazarus, R. S., & Alfert, E. (1964). Short-circuiting of threat by experimentally altering cognitive appraisal. *Journal of Abnormal and Social Psychology, 69,* 195–205.

Lazarus, R. S., & Folkman, S. (1984). *Stress, appraisal and coping.* New York: Springer.

LeDoux, J. E. (1993). Emotional networks in the brain. In M. Lewis & J. M. Haviland (Eds.), *Handbook of emotions* (pp. 109–118). New York: Guilford Press.

LeDoux, J. E. (1995). Emotion: Clues from the brain. *Annual Review of Psychology, 46,* 209–235.

Levenson, R. W. (1988). Emotion and the autonomic nervous system: A prospectus for research on autonomic specificity. In H. L. Wagner (Ed.), *Social psychophysiology and emotion: Theory and clinical applications* (pp. 17–41). London: Wiley.

Levenson, R. W. (1992). Autonomic nervous system differences among emotions. *Psychological Science, 3,* 23–27.

Levenson, R. W. (1994). Human emotions: A functional view. In P. Ekman & R. J. Davidson (Eds.), *The nature of emotion: Fundamental questions* (pp. 123–126). New York: Oxford University Press.

Lorenz, K. (1970). *Studies in animal and human behaviour: Vol. 1. The establishment of the instinct concept* (pp. 259–315). (Robert Martin, trans.). London: Methuen & Co. (Original work published 1937)

MacLean, P. D. (1949). Psychosomatic disease and the "visceral brain." *Psychosomatic Medicine, 11,* 338–353.

MacLean, P. D. (1975). Sensory and perceptual factors in emotional functions of the triune brain. In L. Levi (Ed.), *Emotions—Their parameters and measurement* (pp. 71–92). New York: Raven Press.

MacLean, P. D. (1990). *The triune brain in evolution: Role in paleocerebral functions.* New York: Plenum Press.

Malatesta, C. Z. (1990). The role of emotions in the development and organization of personality, *Nebraska symposium on motivation, 1988: Socioemotional development* (pp. 1–56). Lincoln, NE: University of Nebraska Press.

Malmo, R. B. (1959). Activation: A neuropsychological dimension. *Psychological Review, 66,* 367–386.

Mayer, J. D., & Salovey, P. (1993). The intelligence of emotional intelligence. *Intelligence, 17,* 433–442.

McCrae, R. R., & Costa, P. T. (1991). Adding *liebe und arbeit*: The full five-factor model and well-being. *Personality and Social Psychology Bulletin, 17*(2), 227–232.

McDougal, W. (1923). *Outline of psychology.* New York: Scribner's.

McNair, D. M., Lorr, M., & Droppleman, L. F. (1971). *Manual: Profile of Mood States.* San Diego, CA: Educational and Industrial Testing Service.

Meyer, G. J., & Shack, J. R. (1989). Structural convergence of mood and personality: Evidence for old and new directions. *Journal of Personality and Social Psychology, 57,* 691–706.

Miller, S. M. (1987). Monitoring and blunting: Validation of a questionnaire to assess styles of information seeking under threat. *Journal of Personality and Social Psychology, 52,* 345–353.

Myers, D. G., & Diener, E. (1995). Who is happy? *Psychological Science, 6,* 10–19.

Nolen-Hoeksema, S. (1987). Sex differences in unipolar depression: Evidence and theory. *Psychological Bulletin, 101,* 259–282.

Oatley, K., & Johnson-Laird, P. N. (1987). Towards a cognitive theory of emotions. *Cognition and Emotion, 1,* 29–50.

Ortony, A., Clore, G. L., & Collins, A. (1988). *The cognitive structure of emotions.* New York: Cambridge University Press.

Panksepp, J. (1991). Affective neuroscience: A conceptual framework for the neurobiological study of emotions. In K. T. Strongman (Ed.), *International review of studies of emotion* (pp. 53–99). Chichester, UK: Wiley.

Panksepp, J. (1998). *Affective neuroscience: The foundations of human and animal emotions.* Oxford: Oxford University Press.

Papez, J. W. (1937). A proposed mechanism of emotion. *Archives of Neurology and Psychiatry, 38,* 725–743.

Pellis, S. M. (1985). What is 'fixed' in a fixed action pattern? A problem of methodology. *Bird Behaviour, 6,* 10–15.

Pennebaker, J. (1990). *Opening up: The healing powers of confiding in others.* New York: William Morrow.
Pervin, L. A. (1988). Affect and addiction. *Addictive Behaviors, 13,* 83–86.
Pervin, L. A. (1993). Affect and personality. In M. Lewis & J. M. Haviland (Eds.), *Handbook of emotions.* New York: Guilford Press.
Peterson, C. (1991). The meaning and measurement of explanatory style. *Psychological Inquiry, 2,* 1–10.
Plutchik, R. (1962). *The emotions: Facts, theories, and a new model.* New York: Random House.
Plutchik, R. (1994). *The psychology and biology of emotion.* New York: HarperCollins.
Porges, S. W. (1997). Emotion: An evolutionary by-product of the neural regulation of the autonomic nervous system. In C. S. Carter, I. I. Lederhendler, & B. Kirkpatrick (Eds.), The integrative neurobiology of affiliation. *Annals of the New York Academy of Sciences, 807,* 62–77.
Rinn, W. E. (1984). The neuropsychology of facial expression: A review of the neurological and psychological mechanisms for producing facial expressions. *Psychological Bulletin, 95,* 52–77.
Roger, D., & Najarian, B. (1989). The construction and validation of a new scale for measuring emotion control. *Personality and Individual Differences, 10,* 845–853.
Roseman, I. J., Spindel, M. S., & Jose, P. E. (1990). Appraisals of emotion-eliciting events: Testing a theory of discrete emotions. *Journal of Personality and Social Psychology, 59,* 899–915.
Russell, J. A. (1980). A circumplex model of affect. *Journal of Personality and Social Psychology, 39,* 1161–1178.
Russell, J. A. (1983). Pancultural aspects of human conceptual organization of emotions. *Journal of Personality and Social Psychology, 45,* 1281–1288.
Russell, J. A. (1991). In defense of a prototype approach to emotion concepts. *Journal of Personality and Social Psychology, 60,* 37–47.
Russell, J. A., & Feldman Barrett, L. (1999). Core affect, prototypical emotional episodes, and other things called emotion: Dissecting the elephant. *Journal of Personality and Social Psychology, 76,* 805–819.
Salovey, P., Mayer, J. D., Golman, S. L., Turvey, C., & Palfai, T. P. (1995). Emotional attention, clarity, and repair: Exploring emotional intelligence using the trait meta-mood scale. In J. W. Pennebaker (Ed.), *Emotion, disclosure, and health* (pp. 125–154). Washington, DC: American Psychological Association.
Sapolsky, R. M. (1994). *Why zebras don't get ulcers: A guide to stress, stress-related diseases, and coping.* New York: Freeman.
Scheier, M. F., & Carver, C. S. (1985). Optimism, coping, and health: Assessment and implications of generalized outcome expectancies. *Health Psychology, 4,* 219–247.
Scheier, M. F., & Carver, C. S. (1993). On the power of positive thinking: The benefits of being optimistic. *Current Directions in Psychological Science, 2,* 26–30.
Scherer, K. R. (1984). On the nature and function of emotion: A component process approach. In K. R. Scherer & P. E. Ekman (Eds.), *Approaches to emotion* (pp. 293–317). Hillsdale, NJ: Erlbaum.
Scherer, K. R. (1986). Vocal affect expression: A review and a model for future research. *Psychological Bulletin, 99,* 143–165.
Scherer, K. R. (1988). Cognitive antecedents of emotion. In V. Hamilton, G. H. Bower, & N. H. Frijda (Eds.), *Cognitive perspectives on emotion and motivation* (pp. 89–126). Dordrecht, The Netherlands: Martinus Nijhoff.
Scherer, K. R., Summerfield, A. B., & Wallbott, H. G. (1983). Cross-national research on antecedents and components of emotion: A progress report. *Social Science Information, 22,* 355–385.
Scherer, K. R., & Wallbott, H. G. (1994). Evidence for universality and cultural variation of differential emotion response patterning. *Journal of Personality and Social Psychology, 66,* 310–328.
Scherer, K. R., Wallbott, H. G., & Summerfield, A. B. E. (1986). *Experiencing emotion: A cross-cultural study.* Cambridge, UK: Cambridge University Press.
Schneider, F., Grodd, W., Weiss, U., Klose, U., Mayer, K. R., Nagele, T., & Gur, R. (1997). Functional MRI reveals left amygdala activation during emotion. *Psychiatry Research, 76,* 75–82.
Schneider, F., Gur, R. E., Mozley, L. H., Smith, R. J., Mozley, P. D., Censits, D. M., Alavi, A., & Gur, R. C. (1995). Mood effects on limbic blood flow correlate with emotional self-rating: A PET study with oxygen-15 labeled water. *Psychiatry Research: Neuroimaging, 61,* 265–283.
Servan-Schreiber, D., & Perlstein W. M. (1997). Pharmacologic activation of limbic structures and neuroimaging studies of emotions. *Journal of Clinical Psychiatry, 58,* 13–15.
Shaver, P., Schwartz, J., Kirson, D., & O'Connor, C. (1987). Emotion knowledge: Further exploration of a prototype approach. *Journal of Personality and Social Psychology, 52,* 1061–1086.
Smith, C. A., & Ellsworth, P. C. (1985). Patterns of cognitive appraisal in emotion. *Journal of Personality and Social Psychology, 48,* 813–838.
Smith, C. A., & Lazarus, R. S. (1990). Emotion and adaptation. In L. A. Pervin (Ed.), *Handbook of personality: Theory and research* (pp. 609–637). New York: Guilford Press.
Snyder, M. (1974). Self-monitoring of expressive behavior. *Journal of Personality and Social Psychology, 30,* 526–537.
Sperry, R. W. (1952). Neurology and the mind-brain problem. In A. M. Child (Ed.), *American scientist* (Vol. 40, pp. 291–312). New Haven: The Society of the Sigma Xi.

Spielberger, C. D., & Sydeman, S. J. (1994). State-Trait Anger Inventory and State–Trait Anger Expression Inventory. In M. E. Maruish (Ed.), *The use of psychological testing for treatment planning and outcome assessment* (pp. 292–321). Hillsdale, NJ: Erlbaum.

Stemmler, G. (1997). Selective activation of traits: Boundary conditions for the activation of anger. *Personality and Individual Differences, 22,* 213–233.

Stepper, S., & Strack, F. (1993). Proprioceptive determinants of emotional and nonemotional feelings. *Journal of Personality and Social Psychology, 64,* 211–220.

Steptoe, A., & Vogele, C. (1986). Are stress responses influenced by cognitive appraisal? An experimental comparison of coping strategies. *British Journal of Psychology, 77,* 243–255.

Sternbach, R. A. (1966). *Principles of psychophysiology.* New York: Academic Press.

Sutton, S. K., & Davidson, R. J. (1997). Prefrontal brain asymmetry: A biological substrate of the behavioral approach and inhibition systems. *Psychological Science, 8,* 204–210.

Taylor, G. J., Bagby, R. M., & Parker, J. D. A. (1997). *Disorders of affect regulation: Alexithymia in medical and psychiatric illness.* Cambridge, UK: Cambridge University Press.

Taylor, J. A. (1953). A personality scale of manifest anxiety. *The Journal of Abnormal and Social Psychology, 48,* 285–290.

Tellegen, A. (1985). Structures of mood and personality and their relevance to assessing anxiety, with an emphasis on self-report. In A. H. Tuma & J. D. Maser (Eds.), *Anxiety and the anxiety disorders* (pp. 681–706). Hillsdale, NJ: Erlbaum.

Tellegen, A. (1991). Personality traits: Issues of definition, evidence, and assessment. In W. M. Grove & D. Cicchetti (Eds.), *Thinking clearly about psychology* (Vol. 2, pp. 10–35). Minneapolis: University of Minnesota Press.

Tellegen, A., Watson, D., & Clark, L. A. (in press). On the dimensional and hierarchical structure of affect. *Psychological Science.*

Tomaka, J., Blascovich, J., Kelsey, R. M., & Leitten, C. L. (1993). Subjective, physiological, and behavioral effects of threat and challenge appraisal. *Journal of Personality and Social Psycholgy, 65,* 248–260.

Tomkins, S. S. (1962). *Affect, imagery, consciousness: The positive affects* (Vol. 1). New York: Springer.

Tooby, J., & Cosmides, L. (1990). The past explains the present: Emotional adaptations and the structure of ancestral environments. *Ethology and Sociobiology, 11,* 375–424.

Van Hoof, J. A. R. A. M. (1972). A comparative approach to the phylogeny of laughter and smiling. In R. A. Hinde (Ed.), *Non-verbal communication* (pp. 209–237). Cambridge, UK: Cambridge University Press.

Wallace, J. F., & Newman, J. P. (1997). Neuroticism and the attentional mediation of dysregulatory psychopathology. *Cognitive Therapy and Research, 21,* 135–156.

Watson, D., & Clark, L. A. (1984). Negative affectivity: The disposition to experience aversive emotional states. *Psychological Bulletin, 96,* 465–490.

Watson, D., & Clark, L. A. (1992). Affects separable and inseparable: On the hierarchical arrangement of the negative affects. *Journal of Personality and Social Psychology, 62,* 489–505.

Watson, D., Clark, L. A., & Tellegen, A. (1988). Development and validation of brief measures of positive and negative affect: The PANAS scales. *Journal of Personality and Social Psychology, 54,* 1063–1070.

Watson, D., & Tellegen, A. (1985). Toward a consensual structure of mood. *Psychological Bulletin, 98,* 219–235.

Watson, D., Wiese, D., Vaidya, J., & Tellegen, A. (1999). The two general activation systems of affect: Structural findings, evolutionary considerations, and psychobiological evidence. *Journal of Personality and Social Psychology, 76,* 820–838.

Watson, M., & Greer, S. (1983). Development of a questionnaire measure of emotional control. *Journal of Psychosomatic Research, 27,* 299–305.

Wenger, M. A. (1941). The measurement of individual differences in autonomic balance. *Psychosomatic Medicine, 3,* 427–434.

Westen, D. (1994). Toward an integrative model of affect regulation: Applications to social-psychological research. *Journal of Personality, 62,* 641–667.

Wheeler, R. E., Davidson, R. J., & Tomarken, A. J. (1993). Frontal brain asymmetry and emotional reactivity: A biological substrate of affective style. *Psychophysiology, 30,* 82–89.

Wilson-Pauwels, L., Akesson, E. J., & Stewart, P. A. (1988). *Cranial nerves: Anatomy and clinical comments.* Toronto: B. C. Decker.

Wolpe, J. (1958). *Psychotherapy by reciprocal inhibition.* Stanford: Stanford University Press.

Zajonc, R. B. (1980). Feeling and thinking: Preferences need no inferences. *American Psychologist, 35,* 151–175.

Zajonc, R. B. (1984). On the primacy of affect. *American Psychologist, 39,* 117–123.

Zajonc, R. B. (1998). Emotions. In D. Gilbert, S. T. Fiske, & G. Lindzey (Eds.), *Handbook of social psychology* (4th ed., Vol. 1, pp. 591–632). New York: McGraw-Hill.

Zuckerman, M. (1979). *Sensation seeking: Beyond the optimal level of arousal.* Hillsdale, NJ: Erlbaum.

Zuckerman, M., & Lubin, B. (1985). *Manual for the MAACL-R: The Multiple Affect Adjective Checklist Revised.* San Diego, CA: Educational and Industrial Testing Service.

Chapter 22

Stress, Coping, and Self-Regulatory Processes

Charles S. Carver
University of Miami

Michael F. Scheier
Carnegie Mellon University

This chapter considers three topics—stress, coping, and self-regulation. The topics of stress and coping typically go hand-in-hand. It's less common to see them discussed jointly with self-regulation, however. What exactly do self-regulatory activities have to do with stress and coping? A great deal, we think. Indeed, we think coping essentially constitutes efforts at self-regulation in times of duress.

At their core, self-regulatory models of action and experience are organized around people's efforts to create and maintain desired conditions in their lives. These desired conditions can be relatively stable (e.g., a house set up the way you want it, a stable sense of how relationships work, good health, a coherent picture of a just—or at least predictable—world). They can also be much more dynamic. Examples of dynamic desired conditions include developing a professional career, fostering a child's growth into a responsible adult, and taking an interesting and revitalizing vacation trip. Whether the person's goal is to maintain a stable picture of reality or to make something happen, the process by which the goal is realized is a process of self-regulation.

Self-regulatory efforts often run smoothly, unimpeded by external impediments or personal shortcomings. Sometimes, however, people encounter difficulties in doing what they want to do, being what they want to be, or keeping their reality ordered the way they want it. Self-regulatory models also address what happens in these situations.

In this chapter we explore what self-regulation models tell us about the experience of stress and the processes of coping. We begin by describing a set of orienting assumptions and principles embedded in models of self-regulation. In so doing, we focus on constructs we have found useful in our own work. After presenting orienting principles, we move to a more explicit consideration of how the principles relate to models of stress and coping, and then how stress arises from the experiences of life. The final section of the chapter turns to data, and describes some findings that have emerged from the attempt to integrate the literatures on stress, coping, and self-regulation.

BEHAVIORAL SELF-REGULATION

The Central Role of Goals

A common view among contemporary personality theorists is that human behavior is organized around the pursuit of goals (Austin & Vancouver, 1996; Elliott & Dweck, 1988; Miller & Read, 1987; Pervin, 1982, 1989; see also Bandura, Chapter 6, this volume; Little, Chapter 20, this volume). Because of differences in emphasis, theorists use different terms to refer to goals. Klinger (1975, 1977), for example, uses the phrase "current concerns" to characterize goals the person is actively pursuing. The sense of goal engagement is also conveyed by terms such as "personal projects" (Little, 1983, 1989), "personal strivings" (Emmons, 1986), and "life tasks" (Cantor & Kihlstrom, 1987).

Two additional goal constructs are the "possible self" (Markus & Nurius, 1986) and the "self-guide" (Higgins, 1987, 1996). These constructs were developed to bring a more dynamic quality to thinking about the nature of the self-concept. They reflect more explicitly than did older views of the self-concept the fact that a self-concept is more than a self-definition. The elements of the self-concept function to influence what actions people engage in and what they become. Consistent with this picture of an active, evolving self, possible selves are explicitly future-oriented. They concern how people think about their as-yet-unrealized potential, the kind of person they might be. Self-guides similarly reflect dynamic aspects of the self-concept.

Although these various goal constructs differ among themselves in ways that are far from trivial (for broader discussions see Austin & Vancouver, 1996; Carver & Scheier, 1998, in press-d), what's more important at present is their similarities. All include the idea that goals energize and direct activities (Pervin, 1982). These views implicitly (and sometimes explicitly) convey the sense that goals give meaning to people's lives (Baumeister, 1989; Scheier & Carver, in press). In each approach there is an emphasis on the idea that understanding the person means understanding the person's goals. Indeed, in the view represented by these theories, it is often implicit that the self consists partly of the person's goals and the organization among them.

We should also reiterate that although some goals have a static quality, others are quite dynamic. The goal of taking a vacation isn't to be sitting in your driveway at the end of the two weeks, but to experience the events planned for the vacation. The goal of developing a career isn't just the goal of finally being "established." It's the pathway of steps involved in getting there.

Feedback Processes

Clearly, there are important links between people's goals and their actions. But how exactly are goals used in acting? Most people discuss this question in terms of the decomposition of goals into subgoals. Although this is part of the answer, it's not the whole answer. Another part of the story is that goals serve as reference values for feedback processes. A feedback loop is made of four elements in a particular organization (cf. Miller, Galanter, & Pribram, 1960). The elements are an input function, a reference value, a comparator, and an output function (Figure 22.1).

An input function is a sensor, a source of information about what exists. For present purposes this input function is equivalent to perception. The reference value is a second source of information (i.e., in addition to the input function). In the kinds of feedback loops we will be discussing, reference values are equivalent to goals. The comparator is a device that makes comparisons between input and reference value. The comparison yields one of two outcomes: either the values being compared are discriminably different from one another or they're not. The comparator can vary in sensitivity, however, meaning that it may be able to detect very small discrepancies, or it may detect only much larger ones.

Following the comparison is an output function. For present purposes, this is equivalent to behavior, though sometimes the behavior is internal. If the comparison yields a "no difference," the output function remains whatever it was. This may mean no output, or it may mean that the ongoing output continues at its current level. If the comparison yields "discrepancy," however, the output function changes.

There are two kinds of feedback loops, corresponding to two kinds of goals (Carver & Scheier, 1998, in press-d). In a discrepancy reducing loop, the output function is aimed at diminishing any discrepancy detected between input and reference value (Figure 22.2). The conformity of input to reference is seen in attempts to approach or attain valued or desired goals.

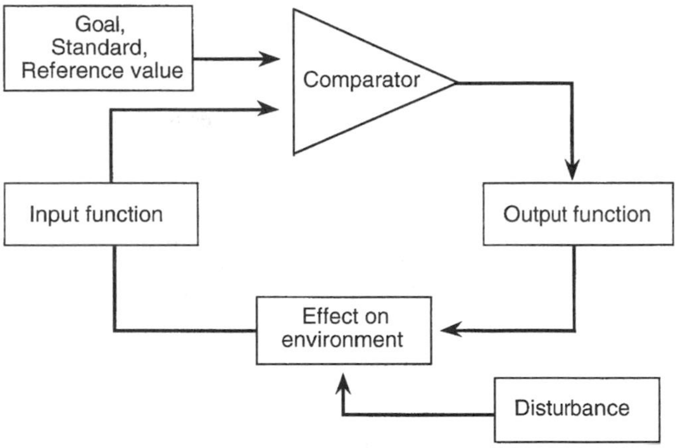

FIGURE 22.1. Schematic depiction of a feedback loop. In such a loop a sensed value is compared to a reference value or standard, and adjustments are made in an output function (if necessary) to shift the sensed value in the direction of the standard.

Keep in mind that this isn't behavior for the sake of behavior, but behavior in the service of creating and maintaining desired conformity of input to a standard. That is, the value sensed by the input function depends on more than the output (Figure 22.1). Disturbances from outside can change present conditions, either adversely (increasing a discrepancy) or favorably (diminishing a discrepancy). In the first case, the recognition of a discrepancy prompts a change in output, as always. In the second case, though, the disturbance *preempts* the need for an adjustment in output. Because the system sees no discrepancy, there's no need for a change in output.

The second kind of feedback loop is a discrepancy enlarging loop (Figure 22.2). The value here isn't one to approach, but one to avoid. It may be simpler to think of it as an "anti-goal." Examples include being fired from your job, getting a speeding ticket, and experiencing a humiliating interpersonal rejection. A discrepancy enlarging loop senses present conditions, compares them to the anti-goal, and tries to enlarge the discrepancy between the two. For example, the Cuban American in Miami who wants to avoid any appearance of sympathy with Castro compares her opinions with the positions of Castro's government, and tries to make her opin-

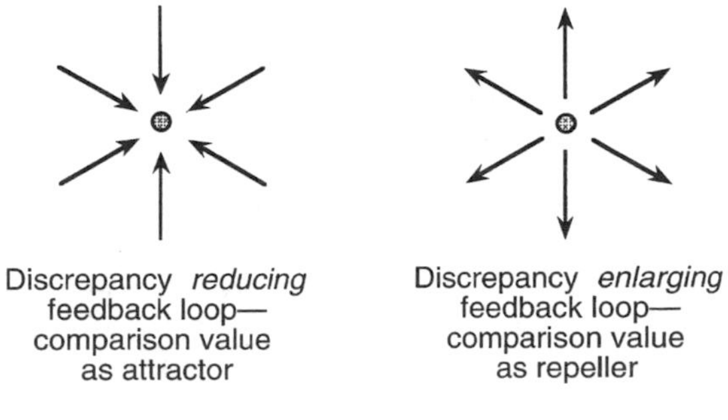

FIGURE 22.2. Discrepancy reducing feedback loops cause sensed qualities to shift *toward* positively valenced reference points. Discrepancy enlarging feedback loops cause sensed qualities to shift *away from* negatively valenced reference points.

ions as different from those positions as she can (Carver & Humphries, 1981).

The action of discrepancy enlarging processes in living systems is typically constrained in some way by discrepancy reducing loops (see Carver & Scheier, 1998, in press-b). To put it differently, avoidance behaviors often lead into approach behaviors. An avoidance loop creates an attempt to increase distance from the anti-goal. Movement away occurs until the behavior comes within the sphere of influence of some approach loop. This loop then serves to pull the activity into its orbit. For example, the woman who wants to avoid the appearance of sympathizing with Castro may become active in an anti-Castro organization.

Hierarchical Organization among Goals

Goals differ among themselves in many ways. As just noted, some are approach goals, others are avoidance goals (anti-goals). An additional way in which goals differ is in their level of abstraction (for broader treatment of this issue, see Carver & Scheier, 1998).

The notion that goals differ in their level of abstraction is easy to illustrate. A man might have the goal, at a high level of abstraction, of being a good father. He may also have the goal, at a lower level of abstraction, of taking his son to his soccer game. The first goal is to be a particular kind of *person,* the second concerns completing particular kinds of *action.* You can also imagine goals that are even more concrete than the latter ones, such as the goal of turning left to park the car. Such goals are closer to specifications of individual acts than were the second, which was more a summary statement about the desired outcome of intended action patterns.

You may have noticed that our example of concrete goals link directly to our example of an abstract goal. This helps us point out that goals can be interconnected in a hierarchical manner. In 1973, William Powers argued that self-regulation of behavior occurs via a hierarchical organization of feedback loops. Because feedback loops imply goals, his argument also created a model of hierarchical structuring among the goals involved in creating action.

His line of thinking ran as follows: In a hierarchical organization of feedback systems, the output of a high-level system consists of resetting reference values at the next lower level. To put it differently, higher-order systems "behave" by providing goals to the systems just below them. The reference values are more concrete and restricted as one moves from higher to lower levels. Control at each level regulates a quality that contributes to the quality controlled at the next higher level. Each level monitors input at the level of abstraction of its own functioning, and each level adjusts output to minimize its discrepancies. One processor is not presumed to handle functions at various levels of abstraction (cf. Greene, 1972, 1982). Rather, structures at various levels handle their concerns simultaneously.

Powers focused on low levels of abstraction. He said much less about the levels of most interest to personality psychologists, except to suggest labels for several levels whose existence makes intuitive sense. "Programs" are activities involving conscious decisions at various points (what Schank & Abelson, 1977, called "scripts"). "Sequences," the next level down, are sets of acts that run off directly once cued. The level above programs is "principles," qualities that are abstracted from (or implemented by) programs. These are the kinds of qualities represented by trait terms. Powers gave the name "system concepts" to the highest level he considered. Goal representations there include the idealized overall sense of self, of a close relationship, or of a group identity.

Figure 22.3 shows a simple portrayal of this hierarchy. This diagram omits the loops of feedback processes, using lines to indicate only the links among goal values. The lines imply that moving toward a particular lower goal contributes to the attainment of a higher goal (or even several at once). Multiple lines to a given goal indicates that several lower-level action qualities can contribute to its attainment. As indicated previously, there are goals to "be" a particular way and goals to "do" certain things (and at lower levels, goals to create physical movement).

A similar notion of hierarchicality in behavior is embedded in Vallacher and Wegner's (1985, 1987) theory of action identification theory. Although the Vallacher and Wegner model is framed in terms of how people think about the actions they're taking, how people think about their actions is also informative about the goals by which the actions are guided. Work done within the framework of action identification theory has developed considerable support for the idea that there is a hierarchicality within the flow of behavior.

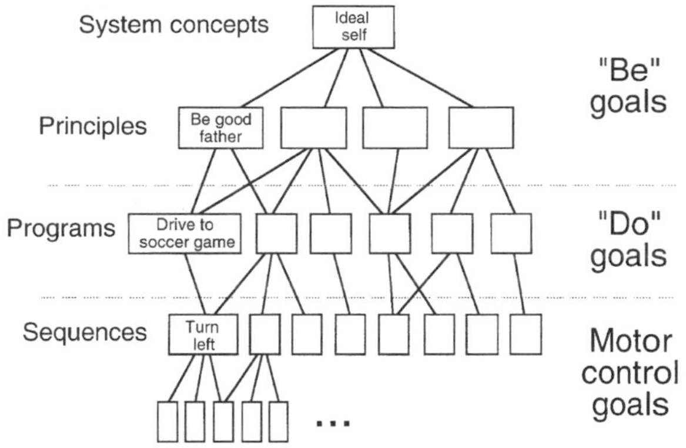

FIGURE 22.3. A hierarchy of goals (or feedback loops). Lines indicate the contribution of lower-level goals to specific higher-level goals. They can also be read in the opposite direction, indicating that a given higher-order goal specifies more-concrete goals at the next lower level. The hierarchy described in text involves goals of "being" particular ways, which are attained by "doing" particular actions. Adapted from Carver and Scheier (1998). Copyright 1998 by Cambridge University Press. Adapted and reproduced with permission of publisher and authors.

Hierarchicality and Behavioral Complexity

Although this hierarchy is in some ways simple, it has implications for several issues in thinking about behavior (see Carver & Scheier, 1998). It is implicit here that goals at any given level often can be achieved by a variety of means at lower levels. This permits one to address the fact that people sometimes shift radically the manner in which they try to reach a goal, when the goal itself has not changed. This is common when the quality that constitutes the higher-order goal is implied by several different kinds of lower-order activities. For example, you can be kind (fulfilling an abstract goal) by helping a child who has fallen off her bicycle, by picking up trash that's blown into a neighbor's yard, by telling a hostess that a not-particularly good meal was great, or by putting an injured animal out of its misery.

Just as a given goal can be obtained via multiple pathways, so can a specific act be performed in the service of diverse goals. For example, there are many reasons to buy someone a gift—to make him feel good, to repay a kindness, to put him in your debt, to satisfy a perceived holiday-season role, or to prevent other people from thinking you stingy. Thus, a given act can have strikingly different meanings, depending on the purpose it's intended to serve. This is an important subtheme of a self-regulation view on action: Behavior can be understood only by identifying the goals to which behavior is addressed.

Some conceptions of hierarchicality assume no cross-linking such that two midlevel elements can work through the same lower-level element. This is not what we have in mind here (see also Gallistel's [1980] discussion of what he calls "lattice hierarchies"). We assume that the act of stretching out one's arm can involve the same loops at concrete levels of abstraction (taking the same actions) whether the reaching is ultimately aimed at helping someone up a steep hill, reaching for a cup of coffee, or reaching out to steal a wallet (for more detail see Chap. 6 of Carver & Scheier, 1998).

A related point made by the notion of hierarchical organization concerns the fact that goals are not equal in importance (see Carver & Scheier, 1998). The higher you go in the organization, the more fundamental to the overriding sense of self are the qualities encountered. Thus, goal qualities at higher levels would tend to be more important, by virtue of their closer links to the core sense of self, than those at lower levels.

Even two goals at a lower level aren't necessarily equivalent in importance, though. In a hierarchical system there are two ways for importance to accrue to a lower-level goal (Figure 22.4). First, the more directly the attainment of a concrete goal contributes to the attainment of a valued abstract goal, the more important is the

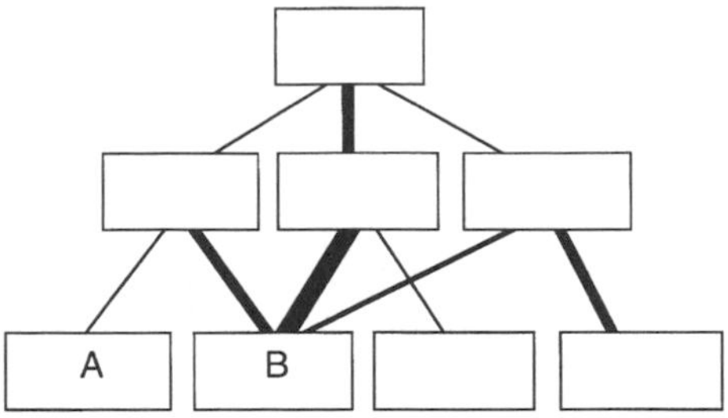

FIGURE 22.4. Importance accrues to a given concrete action goal in either of two ways: (1) The action can contribute in a major way to the attainment of a higher-order goal (indicated here by a thicker line), or (2) the action can contribute to several higher-order goals at once (indicated here by a larger number of upward projections). On both of these criteria, concrete action goal *A* is relatively unimportant, whereas *B* is more important.

concrete goal. Second, a concrete act that contributes to attaining several higher-level goals at once is more important than an act that contributes to the attainment of only one such goal. With respect to the significance of a person's goals, then, importance tends to accrue (1) as one considers goals higher in the hierarchy, (2) as a concrete goal relates more directly to the attainment of a higher-level goal, or (3) as a concrete goal represents a step toward multiple higher-order goals simultaneously (see also Carver & Scheier, in press-c).

Feelings

Thus far we've addressed only control of action. People also experience feelings during their actions. Some self-regulatory models also address feelings. We think affect arises through the operation of a second feedback process (Carver, Lawrence, & Scheier, 1996; Carver & Scheier, 1990, 1998). This second process operates simultaneously with the behavior-guiding system and in parallel to it. One way to characterize what it does is to say it's continuously checking on how well the behavior system is doing at carrying out its job. Thus, the perceptual input for the affect-creating loop is a representation of the *rate of discrepancy reduction in the action system over time.*

We find an analogy useful here. Because action implies change between behavioral states, consider behavior as analogous to distance (change from one physical position to another). If the action loop deals with distance, and if the affect loop assesses the *progress* of the action loop over time, then the affect loop is dealing with the psychological equivalent of velocity (change in physical distance over time).

We don't believe the "velocity" input creates affect by itself, because a given rate of progress has different affective consequences under different circumstances. As in any feedback system, this input is compared against a reference value (cf. Frijda, 1986, 1988): an acceptable or desired rate of behavioral discrepancy reduction. As in other feedback loops, the comparison checks for a deviation from the standard. We suggest that the result of the comparison process at the heart of this loop (the error signal from the comparator) is manifest phenomenologically as a hazy and nonverbal sense of confidence or doubt, and as affect—a sense of positiveness or negativeness. Several studies have yielded evidence that tends to support this view of the source of affect (e.g., Brunstein, 1993; Guy & Lord, 1998; Hsee & Abelson, 1991; Lawrence, Carver, & Scheier, 1997; for a more thorough discussion, see Carver & Scheier, 1998).

Although success in goal attainment often yields positive affect, this view suggests that the context in which goal attainment occurs can have a large influence on whether or not positive affect is experienced. For example, in some cases people experience a slowdown before goal attainment, which can make the attainment itself feel anticlimactic. As another example, sometimes the attainment of a goal brings on a dead end, leaving nothing to pursue in that domain. Such an attainment can feel hollow and empty. We believe that success is most likely to lead to sustained positive feelings when the attainment of one goal slides smoothly into a sense of progress toward other goals.

Earlier we said that goals and anti-goals promote approach and avoidance tendencies, respectively. If there are systems that regulate behavior with respect to both goals and anti-goals, some questions follow. Should there be an affect system for each type of goal? If so, do they differ? The view we just described rests on the idea that positive feelings arise when an action system is doing well at *doing what it's organized to do.* Approach systems are organized to reduce discrepancies. When approach systems are making good progress toward desired goals, positive affect is experienced. When satisfactory progress isn't being made, affect turns more negative. Avoidance systems function to enlarge discrepancies. If avoidance systems are doing well at what they're organized to do—distancing the person from anti-goals—positive affect should result. If they are doing poorly at what they're organized to do, the affective experience should be negative.

This much seems the same across the two types of systems. On the other hand, we do see a difference in the specific affects that are involved (Carver & Scheier, 1998). For both approach and avoidance systems there's a positive pole and a negative pole, but the positives aren't quite the same, nor are the negatives. Following in part the lead of Higgins (1987, 1996) and colleagues, we suggest that the affect dimension relating to discrepancy reducing loops (in its purest form) runs from depression to elation. The affect dimension that relates to discrepancy enlarging loops (in its purest form) runs from anxiety to relief or contentment.

As Higgins and his colleagues note, these two dimensions capture the core qualities behind dejection-related and agitation-related affects. The link between specific affect quality and type of system is compatible not just with the Higgins model, but with others. For example, Roseman (1984, p. 31) has argued that joy and sadness are related to appetitive (moving-toward) motives, whereas relief and distress are related to aversive (moving-away-from) motives. Davidson (1992, 1995) has argued that the left frontal cerebral cortex is part of the neural substrate for approach and for feelings of eagerness and depression, and that the right frontal cortex serves as part of the neural substrate for avoidance and for feelings of anxiety and relief.

Interface between Affect and Action

We characterized the affect system as working simultaneously with and in parallel to the system guiding action. How do the two systems interface? Put differently, how does affect influence action? The answers to these questions lie in the nature of the mechanism behind the generation of affect. That is, we argued that affect is the error signal of a feedback loop. What's the *output function* of this loop? If the input function is a perception of rate of progress, then the output function must be an *adjustment* in rate of progress.

Some adjustments are straightforward—go faster. Some adjustments are less obvious. The rates of many "behaviors" (higher-order activities) aren't defined by the literal pace of physical action. Rather, they're defined in terms of choices among potential actions, or even potential *programs* of action. For example, increasing your rate of progress on a reading assignment may mean choosing to spend a weekend working rather than playing. Increasing your rate of kindness means choosing to do an action that reflects that value. Thus, adjustment in rate must often be translated into other terms, such as concentration, or reallocation of time and effort.

It should be apparent, however, that the action system and the rate system work in concert with one another. Both are involved in the flow of action. They influence different *aspects* of the action, but both are always involved (for more extensive treatment see Carver & Scheier, 1998).

It's of interest that the functions we've just been describing are roughly comparable to two functions typically ascribed to motivation. The action loop handles most of what's sometimes called the "directional" aspect of motivation (the choice of an action from among many options, keeping an action on the track intended); the affect loop handles the "intensity" aspect of motivation (the vigor, enthusiasm, effort, concentration, or thoroughness with which the action is pursued).

Confidence and Doubt

In describing the processes behind affect, we suggested that one mechanism yields two subjective readouts: affect, and a hazy sense of confidence versus doubt. We turned first to affect, describing different qualities of affect and the way in which affect relates to behavior. However, the affect and expectancies generated "on-line" as behavior unfolds are intertwined. Thus, what we've said about affect applies equally well to the vague sense of confidence and doubt that also emerges along with ongoing action.

This hazy sense of confidence and doubt does not operate in a psychological vacuum. We've often suggested that when people experience adversity in trying to move toward their goals, they periodically interrupt their efforts, to assess in a more deliberative way the likelihood of a successful outcome (e.g., Carver & Scheier, 1981, 1990, 1998). In effect, people suspend the behavioral stream, step outside it, and evaluate the possibility of success in a more thoughtful way than occurs while acting (Figure 22.5). This may happen once, or often. It may be brief or prolonged. In this assessment people presumably

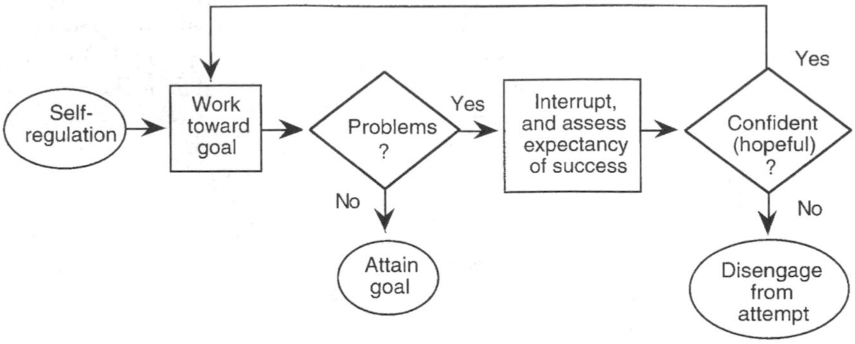

FIGURE 22.5. Flow-chart depiction of self-regulatory possibilities, indicating that action sometimes continues unimpeded toward goal attainment, that obstacles to goal attainment sometimes induce a sequence of evaluation and decision making, and that if expectancies for eventual success are sufficiently unfavorable the person may disengage from further effort. From Carver and Scheier (1998). Copyright 1998 by Cambridge University Press. Reproduced with permission of publisher and authors.

depend heavily on memories of prior outcomes in similar situations, and consider such things as additional resources they might bring to bear (cf. Lazarus, 1966; MacNair & Elliott, 1992) or alternative approaches to the problem. People also use social comparison information (e.g., Wills, 1981; Wood, 1989; Wood, Taylor, & Lichtmann, 1985) and attributional analyses of prior events (Pittman & Pittman, 1980; Wong & Weiner, 1981).

How do these thoughts influence the expectancies that result? In some cases, when people retrieve "chronic" expectancies from memory, the information already *is* expectancies, summaries of products of previous behavior. These chronic expectancies may simply substitute for those that were derived from immediate experience, or they may blend with and color those immediate expectancies to a greater or lesser degree.

In some cases, however, people think more expansively about possibilities for the situation's potential evolution. For these possibilities to influence expectancies, their consequences must be evaluated. They probably are briefly played through mentally as behavioral scenarios (cf. Taylor & Pham, 1996), leading to conclusions that influence the expectancy. ("If I try approaching it this way instead of that way, it should work better." "This is the only thing I can see to do, and it will just make the situation worse.")

It seems reasonable that this mental simulation engages the same mechanism as creates the sense of affect and confidence during actual behavior. When your progress is temporarily stalled, playing through a scenario that leads to a positive outcome yields faster perceived progress. The confidence loop thus yields a more optimistic outcome assessment than is being derived from current action. If the scenario is negative and hopeless, it indicates a further loss of progress, and the confidence loop yields further doubt.

What determines whether the simulation leads to positive or negative assessments? Taylor, Pham, Rivkin, and Armor (1998) have argued that effective mental scenarios emphasize explicit processes needed for reaching a goal, the concrete steps that must be enacted in order to get there (see also Cameron & Nicholls, 1998). Simply imagining the goal as attained is not good enough to facilitate self-regulatory activities, and it can even be detrimental (Oettingen, 1996).

How does imagining the process of goal-attainment foster positive assessments? At least three possibilities suggest themselves. First, actively considering the steps involved in reaching the goal necessarily provides the person with information suggesting that the goal can be reached. This in itself is grounds for greater optimism. Second, the person running the mental simulation can speed up the mental tape when considering the simple parts of the goal-attainment process. If this enhances the subjective sense of forward progress, the result will also be greater confidence. Third, perhaps mental simulation of the concrete unfolding of events more closely resembles the information used to process real behavior on-line, compared to other simulation formats. If so, these mental simulations may produce a more robust readout from the affect-generating system than scenarios in which such information is lacking.

Efforts and Giving Up

Whatever their source, the expectancies that result have an influence on behavior. If expectations for the desired outcome are sufficiently favorable, the person renews effort to work toward the goal. If doubts are strong enough, the result is an impetus to disengage from further effort, and even from the goal itself. Sometimes the disengagement that follows from doubt is overt. Sometimes disengagement takes the form of mental disengagement—off-task thinking, daydreaming, wishful thinking, and so on. Often mental disengagement can't be sustained, as situational cues force the person to reconfront the difficulty in question. In such cases, the result is a phenomenology of repetitive negative rumination, which often focuses on self-doubt and perceptions of inadequacy. This cycle is both unpleasant and performance-impairing.

In thinking about responses to adversity, we have long argued that these two general classes of responses form a "psychological watershed" (Carver & Scheier, 1981, 1998). That is, one set of responses consists of continued comparisons between present state and goal, and continued efforts at movement toward desired goals. The other set consists of disengagement from comparisons, and quitting (see also Klinger, 1975; Kukla, 1972; Wortman & Brehm, 1975). Just as rainwater falling on a mountain ridge ultimately flows to one side of the ridge or the other, so do behaviors ultimately flow to one of these classes or the other. This theme—divergence in cognitive and behavioral response as a function of expectancies—is an important one, applying to a surprisingly broad range of literatures (Carver & Scheier, 1998, in press-d).

Expectancies Vary in Their Specificity

The fact that goals vary in specificity—from very general, to those pertaining to a particular domain of life, to very concrete and specific—suggests that people have a comparable range of variations in expectancies (Armor & Taylor, 1998; Carver & Scheier, 1998). To put it more concretely, you can be confident or doubtful about having an interesting life, about avoiding boring people, about being able to speak clearly in public, or about buttoning your shirt.

Which of these sorts of expectancies matter? Probably all of them. Expectancy-based theories often hold that behavior is predicted best when the specificity of the expectancy matches that of the behavior. Sometimes it's argued that prediction is best when taking into account several levels of specificity. But many outcomes in life have multiple causes, people often face situations they've never experienced before, and situations unfold and change over time. It's been suggested that in circumstances such as these, generalized expectations are particularly useful in predicting behavior and emotions (Scheier & Carver, 1985).

The same principles that apply to focused confidence also apply to the generalized sense of optimism and pessimism. When researchers talk about variables such as optimism and pessimism, the sense of confidence that's at issue is simply more diffuse and broader in scope. Thus, when confronting a challenge (presumably any type of challenge), optimists should tend to take a posture of confidence and persistence, assuming the adversity can be handled successfully in one way or another. Pessimists should be more doubtful and hesitant, more ready to anticipate disaster.

Scaling Back Goals as Limited Disengagement

Sometimes when people give up trying to reach a goal, they quit and that's the end of it. Sometimes, however, something else happens. In some cases when things are going poorly, expectancies of success are dim, and people want to quit, but don't quit altogether. Rather, they trade the threatened goal for a less demanding one. This is a kind of limited disengagement. They've given up on the first goal at the same time as they're adopting a lesser one. This limited disengagement has an important positive consequence: By doing this, people remain engaged in the general domain they'd wanted to quit (or felt the need to quit). By scaling back (giving up in a small way), they keep trying to move ahead (thus *not* giving up, in a larger way).

As an example, a student who wants an A in a course, but who's struggling ineffectually to attain high exam scores, may decide that an A is out of the question and lower his sights to a B or C. Given the change in goal, exam scores in the

B or C range will represent better progress than they would have represented toward the initial goal. The result is that the student keeps plugging along, completes the course adequately instead of dropping it, and may feel satisfied with a C.

Another example comes from research on couples in which one partner is becoming ill and dying from AIDS (Moskowtiz, Folkman, Collette, & Vittinghoff, 1996). Some healthy subjects have the goal of overcoming their partners' illness and continuing to have active lives together. As the illness progresses, however, and it becomes apparent that this goal won't be met, the healthy partners often scale back their aspirations. Now the goal is to do more limited activities during the course of a day, for example. Choosing a goal that's more limited and manageable ensures it will be possible to move successfully toward it. The result is that even in these difficult circumstances, the person experiences more positive feeling than would otherwise be the case and stays engaged behaviorally with efforts to move forward with this aspect of life.

We believe this principle of scaling back—partial disengagement without complete abandonment of the goal domain—is a very important one. As we indicate later on, by keeping the person engaged in goal pursuits in particular domains, it keeps the person engaged in living.

SELF-REGULATION AND STRESS MODELS

The model of self-regulation sketched in the preceding pages was intended to characterize the structure and processes of normal everyday behavior. Although many examples used to illustrate the ideas were taken from achievement- or task-related contexts, the conceptualization is not one of achievement behavior, or even of "task" behavior. Rather, the principles are applicable to human behavior in general. Some human goals are highly valued and subjectively very important to the people who hold them. Other goals are mundane, even trivial, specifications of the maintenance activities of daily life (e.g., doing laundry, brushing your teeth). Some goals concern professional achievement, others concern the maintenance and nourishment of human relationships. We believe, however, that the behaviors that are linked to these disparate goals have a common structure, and that the structure is moderately well captured by the principles outlined above.

This approach to understanding the human experience is about all of behavior, rather than just stress and coping. Yet we believe that it provides an interesting window on the experiences of stress and coping. From the self-regulatory viewpoint, stress is a particular class of experiences and coping is the responses that follow from these experiences (Carver, Scheier, & Pozo, 1992). In particular, from this viewpoint stress occurs when people encounter impediments to attaining desired goals or avoiding anti-goals. Coping is efforts to create conditions that permit one to continue moving toward desired goals (or away from anti-goals), or efforts to disengage from goals that are seen as no longer attainable.

Although it may not be completely apparent, this line of thought has resemblances to several conceptual analyses that were devised explicitly to address stress and coping per se (for a broad overview of issues pertaining to stress and coping see Zeidner & Endler, 1996). In this section we briefly consider three of those approaches and their relations to these principles of self-regulation.

Stress and Coping: Lazarus and Folkman

Most contemporary views of stress and coping trace in one way or another to the work of Lazarus and Folkman and their colleagues (e.g., Lazarus, 1966; Lazarus & Folkman, 1984). That work incorporates several themes. One theme is that stress entails the perception of threat, loss, or challenge (though challenge has held up less well in this respect than the other two perceptions). Threat is the perception of the impending occurrence of something bad or harmful. Loss is the perception that something bad or harmful has already happened.

In both of these cases, impediments to desired conditions are either looming or already in place. Although work in the Lazarus and Folkman tradition has not always emphasized this point, threats and losses are conditions that either prevent or impede maintenance or attainment of desired goal values. Loss prevents the continued existence of a desired state of affairs (e.g., the death of a spouse prevents the continued relationship). Threat suggests imminent interference with continued pursuit of desired activities, goals, or conditions (e.g., a serious illness threatens one's life goals, one's golf game, and one's perception of reality).

We framed this statement in terms of interference with desired goals. It should be obvious, however, that the principles apply just as well to the avoidance of anti-goals. Conditions that imply the imminent occurrence of an anti-goal condition, or suggest the inability to escape from such a condition, will be experienced as stressful.

Another point of similarity between self-regulation models and the Lazarus–Folkman model concerns the dynamic, continuous evaluation of the situation and one's responses to it. In the Lazarus–Folkman model, people don't always respond to stressful encounters in a reflexive, automatic way. Rather, they often weigh various options and consider the consequences of those options before acting. Decisions about how to cope depend in part on implicit confidence or doubt about the usefulness of a particular strategy of responding. Thus, issues of confidence and doubt, as well as the disruption of intended courses of behavior, are embedded in this theoretical model.

Conservation of Resources: Hobfoll

Another view on the experience of stress has been suggested by Hobfoll (1989). He holds that people have an accumulation of resources that they try to protect, defend, and conserve. These resources can be physical (e.g., a house, car, clothing), they can be conditions of one's current life (e.g., friends and relatives, stable employment, sound marriage), they can be personal qualities (e.g., a positive view of the world, work skills, social prowess), or they can be energy resources (e.g., money, credit, or knowledge). Resources are anything the person values.

This theory holds that people try to sustain the resources that they have and acquire further resources. From this viewpoint, stress occurs when resources are threatened or lost, or when people invest their resources and don't receive an adequate return on the investment. Hobfoll (1989) argues that loss is the central experience in stress (see also Hobfoll, Freedy, Green, & Solomon, 1996). Threat is an impending loss. One might think of the failure to receive an adequate return on investment of resources as the loss of an anticipated new resource.

Hobfoll (1989) has argued that this theory differs in important ways from other models of stress (and he has generated hypotheses that might not be as readily derived from other models). However, we want to emphasize here not uniquenesses but resemblances. This stress theory uses an economic metaphor for human experience. People acquire resources, defend them, and use them to acquire more resources. Stress occurs when the market has a downturn in the value of your resources or when an event of some sort wipes out part of your resource base.

We would argue that it's important to step back from a consideration of those resources and ask what their usefulness is. In our view (and nothing about this view intrinsically contradicts Hobfoll's position), these resources matter to people inasmuch as they facilitate the person's movement toward desired goals (or avoidance of anti-goals). What use is a car? It can take you places and it can make an impression on other people. What use are friends? They can help you feel better when you're upset, and you can do interesting things of mutual enjoyment with them. What use is a positive life view? It keeps you moving toward a variety of goals. Work skills permit you to complete projects, achieve things, and hold a job that fosters continued movement toward goals. Money and influence are means to a variety of ends.

In short, for most people, resources are intimately bound up in the continuing pursuit of goals. Thus, any attempt to conserve resources occurs in the implicit service of eventual continued goal attainment. A loss of resources represents a threat to that continued goal attainment. Once again, there is a strong implicit connection to principles of self-regulation.

Bereavement: M. Stroebe and W. Stroebe

Another view on stress to which we would like to devote some attention is that of M. Stroebe, W. Stroebe, and their colleagues (e.g., Stroebe, Stroebe, & Hansson, 1993). Their work has been conducted within the context of grieving over loss—particularly bereavement. The theoretical perspective they put forward assumes two focuses on the part of the bereaved. The first focus is on the person who has been lost and the relationship of the bereaved with that person. The second focus is on potential relationships with other persons.

Traditionally, many approaches to bereavement have held that the task of the bereaved is to disengage from the lost relationship and move on to new attachments (e.g., Worden, 1991). This sequence is not unlike that described more generally in self-regulatory models as a disengagement of commitment to one incentive to take up another incentive (Klinger, 1975). From this view, the key to successful adaptation for the bereaved person is finalizing the past well enough to make a start toward a future of involvement with others.

There's no question that movement forward is important. M. Stroebe (1994) reviewed the literature on bereavement and mortality, and found that people who die after bereavement tend to lack contact with others during the bereavement period, compared to those who survive the bereavement process. Those vulnerable to dying do not remarry, they don't have people to talk to on the phone, they live alone, and they feel isolated. The general picture of those at risk that Stroebe uncovered is one of loneliness and little integration with other people.

The Stroebes and their colleagues have argued, however, that the optimal solution is not to completely disengage psychologically from the person who's been lost (cf. Bowlby, 1980). Rather, they argue that it's better to reconfigure the psychological bond with that person into something different than it was, something that remains positive but is more restricted than it was. Thus the person can continue to draw on that connection psychologically, in smaller ways than was once the case, but in ways that provide benefits to the person (for broader treatment see Klass, Silverman, & Nickman, 1996).

This reconfiguration of the sense of the lost relationship resembles the scaling back process of the self-regulation model. By letting go and disengaging from attempts to reach the unreachable (a continuation of life as it was), the bereaved person becomes free for potential attachments to others. By disengaging only partly, the person retains a sense of connection with the disrupted relationship. To the extent that the positive value of the disrupted relationship can be encapsulated and used by the bereaved as a psychological resource, the residual sense of attachment might help the bereaved person return to activities and connections with other people. If the limited disengagement did *not* return the person to an active life, the resolution would not be adaptive.

THREAT, LOSS, DISRUPTION, AND LIFE PROCESSES

In the first portion of this chapter we outlined a set of principles as a model of self-regulation. In the second section we indicated some broad similarities between that model and three views on the coping process. We now turn to a different point.

Although it is certainly possible to think of stress and coping in terms of such events as natural disasters, life-threatening illnesses, and human-inflicted cruelties, not all stress has the character of being so distinct from the normal flow of behavior. Much of the stress in life arises from being boxed into corners or experiencing conflict within oneself. These experiences have the same structure as we earlier argued underlies stress in general. That is, in each case an impediment exists to forward movement toward desired goals or away from threatening anti-goals.

As a way of illustrating the breadth of applicability of this idea, in this section we consider several sorts of impediments that originate fairly readily within the flow of ordinary behavior. We do so within the framework of self-regulation outlined earlier (for broader discussion see Carver & Scheier, 1998; for related views see Baumeister & Heatherton, 1996; Baumeister, Heatherton, & Tice, 1994; Hamilton, Greenberg, Pyszczynski, & Cather, 1993; Kirschenbaum, 1987).

Misregulation

People self-regulate by sensing current states, comparing that perception to some reference value, and making adjustments to move the input closer to the reference value. To regulate effectively, all components of the loop must be functioning properly. If there's no sensing, there can be no self-regulation. If there's no reference value, there can be no self-regulation. If any component of the loop fails to function, self-regulation cannot occur.

Sometimes, however, people think they are self-regulating appropriately when they are not. We've used the term misregulation to refer to such cases (Carver & Scheier, 1981). This occurs when people use feedback that's irrelevant to the goal. If the proper input isn't used, you may not be producing the effect you intend. Even if you keep very close track of an input channel, if the channel you're monitoring is irrelevant, self-regulation will be faulty.

An example comes from the domain of health psychology. For some time, theorists within this area have construed people as active "health care systems," rather than as passive recepients of treatment (e.g., Leventhal, 1981; Leventhal, Meyer, & Nerenz, 1980; Rodin, 1985; Schwartz, 1977, 1979a, 1979b). In this view, people act so as to keep themselves in a healthy state. When an injury or illness occurs, the person monitors relevant symptoms and takes action with the goal of reducing the symptoms and returning to a healthier status (e.g., Kovatchev, Cox, Gonder-Frederick, Schlundt, & Clarke, 1998).

But this monitoring and adjustment process can go awry. For example, hypertension has no reliable symptoms. Yet people who enter treatment for it quickly conclude they can tell when their blood pressure is up (Meyer, Leventhal, & Gutmann, 1985; Baumann & Leventhal, 1985). More than 90% of people in treatment for more than 3 months claim to be able to tell (Meyer et al., 1985). Can they? Generally, no (Baumann & Leventhal, 1985). However, because they're monitoring the symptom, they use it to decide whether to take their medication. If they think their blood pressure isn't up (because there's no symptom), they stop the medication. If there's no symptom over time, they may stop treatment altogether. This can lead to serious medical problems—all because they're relying on irrelevant feedback information to guide their actions.

Misregulation per se doesn't constitute stress, but it permits situations to evolve in ways that ultimately yield stress. Stress arises only when the person becomes aware that misregulation has taken place. At that point the person realizes there's a gap—sometimes a big gap—between the actual and the intended. Someone whose untreated hypertension has led to serious medical complications has suddenly realized that a large discrepancy with respect to health has existed for some time. At that point, there is stress.

Similarly, the man who habitually reads his wife's mind about how she's feeling, instead of asking her how she's feeling, may feel good about the regulation of his marriage, only to discover at some point that there's been a big discrepancy between his goal and the existing situation. His wife actually may have been unhappy for some time, but he hasn't realized it. His misregulation isn't stressful for him as long as he doesn't realize it's happening. If an event occurs to make him aware of the situation as it exists, however, there's a sudden burst of stress.

Problems as Conflicts among Goals

Another way in which stress can arise derives from the fact that the goal structures that people hold often contain the potential for conflict. Conflict occurs when a person is committed to two or more goals that can't be attained easily at the same time (e.g., being a successful physician while being an involved wife and mother; having a close relationship while being emotionally independent). The bind here resembles that of role conflict. You can't do two mutually exclusive things at once. The very act of devoting strong efforts to attaining one goal can constitute an impediment to attaining the other goal. Given this imediment, the person experiences stress.

There's evidence that conflict among goals does create stress. Emmons and King (1988) had subjects report the personal strivings that motivate their lives and then make some further ratings about those strivings. These included ratings of the extent to which success in one striving tended to create problems for another one. The researchers found that conflicts between personal strivings were tied to psychological distress and physical symptoms. In contrast, people who value their strivings and see them as important express greater satisfaction with their lives (Emmons, 1986; see also Lecci, Okun, & Karoly, 1994).

Given the distress produced by goal conflict, people might try to engage in tactics to avoid its occurrence. One strategy is to alternate between the conflicting goals, addressing first one then the other. Jumping back and forth can be exhausting, however. It's also hard to keep the conflict from reemerging. Another solution is to decide that one goal matters more to your higher-order values than the other, and to reorganize or reweight your hierarchy accordingly. But this isn't easy to do either. The self as an organization of values is relatively stable (Greenwald, 1980). Still, although reorganization of the self is difficult and painful (and thus resisted), it does sometimes happen (cf. Crocker & Major, 1989; Heatherton & Nichols, 1994; Kling, Ryff, & Essex, 1997).

Automatic Doubts

Another source of stress in people's lives is the residue of doubt that can build up in people's minds over extended experiences of adverse outcomes in some domain. As we noted earlier in the chapter, encountering difficulty while acting induces a hazy sense of doubt, which may promote a more conscious deliberation on the likelihood of success. If the person has had a lot of experience in some domain, memories from those experiences are encoded with a great deal of redundancy. When things get difficult in that domain, people often rely heavily on those memories to inform them about the likely outcome of what's happening now.

Although this sometimes works to people's advantage (for people whose memories are mostly successes), all too often the residual sense is one of doubt or inadequacy. If that residual sense is strong enough, or redundantly encoded enough, the person will experience the impulse to give up at the first signs of adversity. When doubts are deeply ingrained, you may not even attend well to what's *going on* in the current situation. Being convinced that the situation will end badly, you fail to realize that the difficulty you're experiencing is minor and easily resolved. You give up trying and the doubt strengthens further. This can eventuate in a tendency to "catastrophize," which is a particularly problematic response among pain patients (Turk & Rudy, 1992).

This automatic overreliance on heavily encoded doubts might be viewed as a case in which people bring "stress-readiness" to the situation. There are many situations in life in which real-but-minor impediments arise along the way. The person who brings this heavy burden of doubt into the situation is creating further impediments that needn't be there. These further impediments constitute a source of stress for some people in situations that aren't stressful for others.

Premature Disengagement of Effort

Let's consider further the consequences of doubt. Doubt can cause people to scale back on goals or to give up on goals entirely. It can be bad for this to happen too readily. A person who gives up whenever things get difficult will have trouble reaching any goal in life. Disengaging too fast keeps you from trying your best, and it short-circuits potential successes. Sometimes the result is a repetitive pattern of quitting and going on to something else. Such a lack of persistence, moving the person endlessly from goal to goal, is a potentially serious problem. It's not clear that it involves great stress, however. If people really can put the failures behind them and move on, the stress of failure should be short-lived. Only if the recurring lack of commitment serves as a source of problems in and of itself will the stress be maintained (e.g., if it results in dissatisfaction with oneself).

There's also a more subtle pattern associated with premature disengagement. It involves disengagement of *effort,* but a continued commitment to the goal. This person is no longer trying, but hasn't gotten the goal out of mind. This combination may be reflected in several ways, including rumination, efforts at self-distraction, off-task thinking, temporarily leaving the scene of the behavior, or cognitive interference (Sarason, Pierce, & Sarason, 1996). Despite these goal-irrelevant activities, the goal hasn't been abandoned. But any attempt to move toward it is sporadic, disrupted repeatedly by withdrawal of effort and off-task thinking.

The process seems to go like this: Difficulty leads to an interruption, and the person's doubts prompt disengagement, which is deflected into mental disengagement. This can't be maintained, because the person hasn't given up the goal and eventually must reconfront it. The reconfrontation leads to a re-engagement of effort, which may quickly lead to re-evoking of doubts and a renewal of the impulse to disengage (cf. Carver, 1996; McIntosh & Martin, 1992; Wine, 1971, 1980). Because there's continued commitment to the goal but no movement toward it, the person also experiences distress (Carver & Scheier, 1990, 1998; Klinger, 1975; Pyszczynski & Greenberg, 1992).

Premature disengagement of effort represents another case in which there's an impediment to movement toward a goal. The impediment in this case is the lack of effort, which stems from doubt. This situation could be made less stressful either by renewing effort, or by abandoning the goal or scaling it back to something more attainable.

Struggling Too Long toward Unattainable Goals

If there are drawbacks to withdrawing effort too quickly from goals that might be attained, it's also bad to keep struggling toward goals that are unattainable. Giving up is an indispensable part of self-regulation, because people need to be able to retrace their steps, back out of corners, free themselves to go elsewhere. Continued commitment to a goal that's truly unattainable wastes resources in futile efforts. If those futile efforts are extensive, so is the waste of resources.

Continued commitment to a goal that's unattainable shares two consequences with the case just considered—that is, with premature disengagement of effort while retaining commitment. In both instances, the person is prevented from taking up new, viable goals, because the person is prevented from noticing, recognizing, or responding to new opportunities (cf. Baumeister & Scher, 1988; Feather, 1989; Janoff-Bulman & Brickman, 1982). Both also cause distress. The person who's unable to move forward but is unable to let go is condemned to suffer. These consequences suggest how important it can be to accept the reality of a permanent change in one's situation (Carver et al., 1993; Scheier & Carver, in press).

Pursuit of the unattainable is another situation in which there is an impediment to forward movement. The impediment in this case is real, because the goal is truly out of reach. Thus, stress can arise both from lack of effort (stemming from doubt) or from commitment to a goal that's impossible to attain. What's different is that in the former case there are two ways to reduce the stress, in the latter only one. That is, if the goal is attainable, stress can potentially be reduced either by renewing one's effort to attain the goal or by disengaging from the goal (either completely or by scaling back the goal to something that is more attainable). In contrast, renewed effort won't be effective in reducing stress if the goal is truly unattainable. For unattainable goals, the only way to reduce stress is to disengage in some fashion.

Hierarchicality and Importance Can Impede Disengagement

There is one important qualification on the goal disengagement process, however. Put simply, sometimes goal disengagement is difficult. There are many reasons this might be the case. One prominent cause stems from the idea that goals are hierarchically arranged. Recall that goals are more important and central to the self as one moves from lower to higher levels of a person's goal hierarachy. Also recall that lower-order goals vary in the number of links that they have to higher-order goals and in the strength of those connections (Figure 22.4). Some lower-order goals connect to only a few higher-order goals; other lower-order goals connect to many higher-order goals. Some lower goals connect intimately to higher goals; other lower goals connect only weakly to the higher goals to which they project.

Presumably, disengaging from higher-order goals is always troublesome. Disengaging from a higher-order goal means giving up on a core element of the self, which people resist (Greenwald, 1980). Less obvious is the fact that disengagement from concrete goals is also difficult if those concrete goals are closely linked to higher-order goals. Under such circumstances, giving up on a lower-order goal means more than simply abandoning the concrete behavior in question. It also means creating a problem regarding the higher-order goals to which the lower goal is linked. As a result, disengagment from the concrete goal is much more difficult.

Thus, the emergence of stress in people's lives is determined partly by the nature of the organization among the person's goals and values. It can be easy to step away from a particular unattained goal, in and of itself. But sometimes the relationship of that goal to core values of the self make it harder to do so. The attempt to give up and step away then *induces* stress, because it creates an impediment to the attainment or maintenance of the higher value.

When Is Disengagement the Correct Response?

It will be apparent from the foregoing that a critical question in life is when to keep trying and when to give up, when it's right to keep "hanging on" and when "letting go" is the right response (Pyszczynski & Greenberg, 1992). On the one hand, disengagement (at some level, at least) is a necessity. Disengagement is a natural and indispensable part of self-regulation. If we are ever to turn away from efforts at unattainable goals, if we're ever to back out of blind alleys, we must be able to disengage, to give up and start over somewhere else.

The importance of disengagement is particularly obvious regarding concrete, low-level goals: People must be able to remove themselves from literal blind alleys and wrong streets, give up plans that have been disrupted by unexpected events. The tendency is also important, however, with regard to some higher-level goals. A vast literature attests to the importance of moving on with life after the loss of close relationships, even if the moving on doesn't imply a complete putting aside of the old (e.g., Cleiren, 1993; Orbuch, 1992; Stroebe et al., 1993). People sometimes must even be willing to give up values that are deeply embedded in the self, if those values create too much conflict and distress in their lives. Remaining stuck in the past instead of moving on has been found to create problems for people who've experienced a variety of life traumas (Holman & Silver, 1998).

Giving up is a functional and adaptive response *when it leads to the taking up of other goals,*

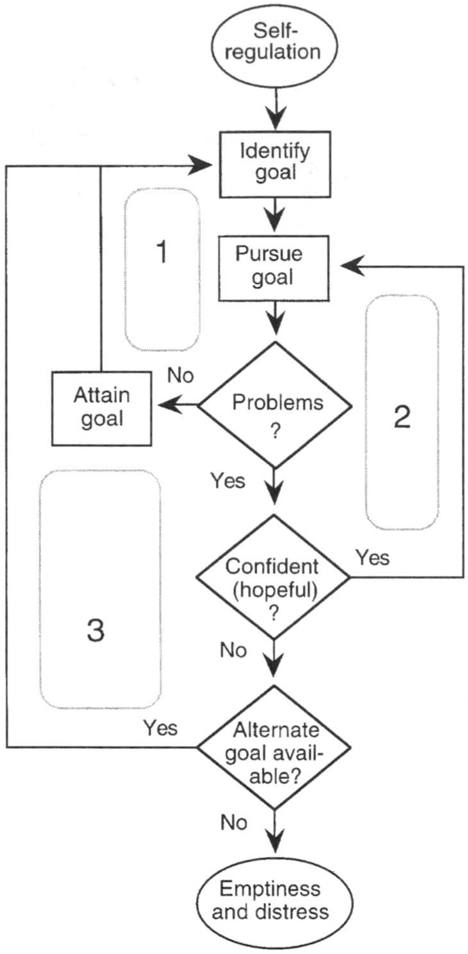

FIGURE 22.6. Successful self-regulation is a continuing process of identifying goals, pursuing them, attaining them, and identifying further ones (Loop 1). Given adversity, another step is added (Loop 2), involving evaluating chances of success, but sufficient confidence places the person back into the first loop. If confidence is low enough, the person may seek an alternate goal (Loop 3). If one is available, it returns the person to goal pursuit and attainment. If no alternative is available, however, the person may feel empty and experience considerable distress. From Carver and Scheier (1998). Copyright 1998 by Cambridge University Press. Reproduced with permission of publisher and authors.

whether substitutes for the lost goal or simply new goals in a different domain. By providing the context for the pursuit of alternative goals, giving up provides the opportunity to re-engage and move ahead again (Carver & Scheier, 1998; Scheier & Carver, in press). In such cases, giving up occurs in service to the broader function of returning the person to an engagement with life. This appears to apply to goal values and doubts that extend fairly deeply into the sense of self. People need multiple paths to such values (cf. Linville, 1985, 1987; Showers & Ryff, 1996; Wicklund & Gollwitzer, 1982). If one path is barricaded, people need to be able to jump to another one.

It seems likely that substituting a new path for an obstructed one is made easier by having clearly specified goals at a more abstract level. For example, if a person who has valued a sense of connectedness in a close marriage relationship loses his or her spouse, the sense of connection can be experienced in different ways. A person in this situation who understands that his or her core desire is to *experience closeness* can more readily recognize that there are many ways to do this than can someone who's less clear about the nature of the higher-level goal. Similarly, it seems likely that a person who already recognizes the multiple paths that exist to a given goal will be better prepared to make such shifts, as necessary.

In any case, it seems apparent that the ability to shift to a new goal, or a new path to a continuing goal, is a very important part of remaining goal-engaged. What happens if there's no alternative to take up? In such a case disengagement from an unattainable goal is not accompanied by a shift, because there's nothing to shift to (see Figure 22.6). This is the worst situation, in which there is nothing to pursue, nothing to take the place of what's seen as unattainable (cf. Moskowitz et al., 1996). If commitment to the unattainable goal remains, the result is considerable distress. If the commitment wanes, the result is emptiness. There is reason to suspect that such a state might also be implicated in premature death (Carver & Scheier, 1998).

SELF-REGULATORY PRINCIPLES AND RESEARCH ON COPING

An important theme that we have developed in discussing self-regulatory activities is that expectations play a pivotal role in people's responses to adversity. When impediments are encountered (and the experience of stress commences), what happens next depends on whether the person feels the obstacles can be overcome, the problems solved or circumvented. When people expect to succeed (given the opportunity for further effort), they keep trying and even enhance their efforts. When people believe success is out of reach, they withdraw effort, even give up completely on the attempt to reach the goal.

These self-regulatory principles have important implications for conceptualizing coping as a set of responses and for thinking about individual differences in coping. Indeed, the disjunction between effort and giving up is embodied in current views on the nature of coping responses. It is common to refer to three classes of coping: Problem-focused coping consists of attempts to remove the obstacle or to minimize its impact. Emotion-focused coping consists of attempts to reduce the distress emotions caused by the obstacle (which can entail either reappraisal of the obstacle or management of the emotion per se—Gross, 1998). Avoidance coping cuts across the problem–emotion distinction. It's a class of responses that appear to be aimed either at avoiding any acknowledgement that the problem exists (via self-distraction, denial, substance use, wishful thinking, etc.) or at giving up the attempt to do anything about the problem (by substance use, giving up goals that are being interfered with, etc.).

With respect to individual differences, it follows from our emphasis on expectancies as an influence on self-regulation that use of these classes of coping responses should differ as a function of people's expectancies. There is considerable evidence that this is so. The part of the evidence on which we focus here comes from research in which expectancies were operationalized in terms of generalized optimism versus pessimism.

Optimism, Pessimism, and Coping

Differences in coping methods used by optimists and pessimists have been found in a number of studies (for a review, see Carver & Scheier, in press-a, or Scheier & Carver, 1992). One early project (Scheier, Weintraub, & Carver, 1986) asked undergraduates to recall the most stressful event of the previous month and rate a list of coping responses with respect to that event. Optimism related positively to problem-focused coping, especially when the stressful situation was seen as controllable. Optimism also related to the use of positive reframing and, when the situation was seen as uncontrollable, with the tendency to accept the reality of the situation. In contrast, optimism related negatively to the use of denial and the attempt to distance oneself from the problem.

The fact that optimists and pessimists differed in their use of problem-focused coping is entirely consistent with the self-regulation model. Not directly predicted, however, was the fact that optimists and pessimists also differed on a variety of other responses, including accepting the reality of difficult situations and putting the situations in the best possible light. In retrospect, however, the findings make sense within the self-regulation framework. That is, it may be easier to accept the reality of a negative situation if one is confident of favorable eventual outcomes.

This general pattern of effects has continued to emerge in work on coping and optimism. For example, in research on dispositional coping styles (Carver, Scheier, & Weintraub, 1989; Fontaine, Manstead, & Wagner, 1993), optimists reported a tendency to rely on active, problem-focused coping, and to be planful when confronting stressful events. Pessimism related to the tendency to disengage from the goals with which the stressor is interfering. Optimists also reported accepting the reality of stressful events, and trying to see the best in bad situations and to learn something from them. In contrast, pessimists reported tendencies toward overt denial and substance abuse—strategies that lessen their awareness of the problem.

Other projects have studied relationships between optimism and coping strategies in specific contexts. For example, Strutton and Lumpkin (1992) studied coping in the work environment. They found that optimists used problem-focused coping (such as directed problem solving) more than pessimists. Pessimism was related to the use of avoidant coping (self-indulgent escapism including sleeping, eating, and drinking). Another study (Long, Kahn, & Schutz, 1992), focusing on managerial women, found that optimists appraised, evaluated, and reacted to problems at work differently than did pessimists. Compared to pessimistic women, optimistic managers perceived problems at work to be less threatening to the attainment of their goals. Optimistic women were also more likely to use active, problem-focused coping strategies in dealing with their problems, and less likely to use disengagement coping. Finally, optimistic women were more likely than pessimistic women to rely on the general use of preventive coping strategies in their lives (i.e., strategies that might help promote personal well-being and reduce the likelihood of potential problems).

Coping and Emotional Outcomes

The foregoing studies establish that optimists cope differently than do pessimists. Other work has linked these differences in coping to differences in emotional outcomes. One study followed women undergoing breast biopsy (Stanton & Snider, 1993). Optimism, coping, and mood were assessed the day before biopsy; women who received a cancer diagnosis were reassessed 24 hours before surgery and 3 weeks after surgery. Women with a benign diagnosis completed a second assessment that corresponded to either the second or the third assessment of the cancer group. Pessimists used more cognitive avoidance in coping with the upcoming diagnostic procedure than did optimists. This contributed significantly to distress prior to biopsy, and also predicted postbiopsy distress among women with positive diagnoses.

Another study of cancer patients examined how women cope with treatment for early stage breast cancer across the first year after treatment (Carver et al., 1993). Optimism, coping (with the diagnosis of cancer), and mood were assessed the day before surgery, 10 days postsurgery, and at three follow-up points. Both before and after surgery, optimism was associated with a pattern of coping tactics that revolved around accepting the reality of the situation, placing as positive a light on it as possible, trying to relieve the situation with humor, and (at presurgery only) taking active steps to do whatever there was to be done. Pessimism was associated with denial and behavioral disengagement (giving up) at each measurement point.

These coping tactics also related strongly to subjects' distress. Positive reframing, acceptance, and the use of humor all related inversely to distress, both before surgery and after. Denial and behavioral disengagment related positively to distress at all measurement points. Not unexpectedly, given the pattern of the correlations, the effect of optimism on distress was largely indirect through coping, particularly at postsurgery.

Other studies have also found that coping mediates the relationship between optimism and well-being. For example, Aspinwall and Taylor (1992) tracked adjustment among undergraduates as they settled into college. Optimism, self-esteem, and other variables were assessed when the students arrived on campus. Measures of coping, psychological well-being, and physical well-being were obtained at entry into the study and again at the end of the semester. Initial optimism predicted lower levels of psychological distress at the end of the semester (independent of other personality factors and baseline mood). Optimists were also more likely than pessimists to use active coping and less likely to use avoidance coping. Avoidance coping related to poorer adjustment, and active coping (separately) related to better adjustment. Finally, the beneficial effects of optimism seemed to operate at least partly through the coping differences.

A similar point is made by a study by Park et al. (1997) concerning adjustment to pregnancy. Optimistic women in this study were more likely than pessimistic women to engage in constructive thinking (the tendency to think about and solve daily problems in an effective way). Optimism and constructive thinking also related negatively to later anxiety and postively to later positive states of mind. Additional analyses showed that the association between optimism and emotional adjustment was mediated through the tendency of optimists to engage in constructive thinking.

In sum, these various studies indicate that optimists differ from pessimists in their stable coping tendencies and in the kinds of coping responses they generate when confronting stressful situations. In general, findings from this research suggest that optimists tend to use more problem-focused coping strategies than pessimists do. When problem-focused coping is not a possibility, optimists turn to adaptive emotion-focused coping strategies such as acceptance, use of humor, and positive reframing. These are strategies that keep them engaged with the effort to move forward with their lives. Pessimists tend to cope through overt denial and by disengaging from the goals with which the stressor is interfering. Moreover, these differences in coping responses appear to be at least partially responsible for differences between optimists and pessimists in the emotional well-being they experience. Findings of this sort serve to link elements of self-regulation models of behavior with the literature of coping responses and their consequences.

It is particularly noteworthy to us that optimists turn in part toward acceptance in uncontrollable situations, whereas pessimists tend toward the use of denial. Denial and acceptance differ in important ways. Denial (the refusal to accept the reality of the stressful situation) means attempting to adhere to a worldview that is no longer valid. In contrast, acceptance implies a restructuring of one's experience to come to grips with the reality of the situation that one confronts. Acceptance thus may involve a deeper set of processes, in which the person actively works through the experience, attempting to integrate it into an evolving worldview.

The attempt to come to terms with the existence of problems may confer special benefit to acceptance as a coping response. We should be very clear, however, about what we mean. The acceptance we have in mind is a willingness to admit that a problem exists or that an event has happened—even an event that may irrevocably alter the fabric of the person's life. We are *not* talking about a stoic resignation, a fatalistic acceptance of the negative consequences to which the problem event might lead, no matter how likely those consequences might be. The latter response doesn't confer a benefit and may even be detrimental (Greer, Morris, & Pettingale, 1979; Greer, Morris, Pettingale, Haybittle,1990; Pettingale, Morris, & Greer, 1985; Reed, Kemeny, Taylor et al., 1994; for further discussion of this issue, see Scheier & Carver, in press)

CONCLUDING COMMENT

In this chapter we have tried to point to links between a model of the self-regulation of action and the experiences of stress and coping. This effort was far from exhaustive. Our intent was simply to provide a series of illustrations of how the concepts can be integrated. In the preceding sections we pointed to conceptual links between the elements of the self-regulation model and three other conceptualizations of various aspects of stress; to a series of ways in which stress can arise in the course of ordinary behavior; to distinctions among aspects of coping that seem to flow readily from the self-regulation model; and to a few findings that reveal both the divergent self-regulatory functions involved in coping (effort and disengagement) and individual differences in the manner in which people cope with adverse circumstances. Although space constraints prevent a deeper discussion of the stress literature, we believe many more aspects of that literature also fit this picture (see Zeidner & Endler, 1996).

In closing, we would like to make one last point about the link between stress, coping, and self-regulation. This point is surely not unique to the perspective we've take here, but it seems to be implied with particular clarity by it. The point is that stress is not an all-or-none phenomenon, and that coping is not fundamentally different in kind from other behavior. Disruptions in life fall along a continuum, ranging from minor frustrations to devastating losses. All disruptions raise issues that need to be resolved by the people involved. The approach taken here suggests that the underlying structure of those issues is the same regardless of whether the disruption is due to some minor frustration or a devasting loss. This is not to say that the way in which the issues are resolved is the same for such disparate cases, only that the decision points are the same. Thus, the confrontation with adversity (regardless of its source) can be seen as the origin of stress, whether mild or severe. The person's effort to dissolve the adversity, to dampen its subjective impact, or to accommodate to the new life situation that the adversity brings with it, are the essence of coping—and of self-regulation.

ACKNOWLEDGMENTS

Preparation of this chapter was facilitated by support from the National Cancer Institute (Grants No. CA64710 and No. CA62711). We would also like to thank Michael Bridges for reading and commenting on a preliminary draft of the chapter.

REFERENCES

Armor, D. A., & Taylor, S. E. (1998). Situated optimism: Specific outcome expectancies and self-regulation. In M. Zanna (Ed.), *Advances in experimental social psychology* (Vol. 29, pp. 309–379). San Diego: Academic Press.

Aspinwall, L. G., & Taylor, S. E. (1992). Modeling cognitive adaptation: A longitudinal investigation of the impact of individual differences and coping on college adjustment and performance. *Journal of Personality and Social Psychology, 61,* 755–765.

Austin, J. T., & Vancouver, J. B. (1996). Goal constructs in psychology: Structure, process, and content. *Psychological Bulletin, 120,* 338–375.

Baumann, L. J., & Leventhal, H. (1985). "I can tell when my blood pressure is up, can't I?" *Health Psychology, 4,* 203–218.

Baumeister, R. F. (1989). The problem of life's meaning. In D. M. Buss & N. Cantor (Eds.), *Personality psychology: Recent trends and emerging directions* (pp. 138–148). New York: Springer-Verlag.

Baumeister, R. F., & Heatherton, T. F. (1996). Self-regulation failure: An overview. *Psychological Inquiry, 7,* 1–15.

Baumeister, R. F., Heatherton, T. F., & Tice, D. M. (1994). *Losing control: Why people fail at self-regulation.* San Diego: Academic Press.

Baumeister, R. F., & Scher, S. J. (1988). Self-defeating behavior patterns among normal individuals: Review and analysis of common self-destructive tendencies. *Psychological Bulletin, 104,* 3–22.

Bowlby, W. J. (1980). *Attachment and loss: Vol. 3. Loss: Sadness and depression.* London: Hogarth.

Brunstein, J. C. (1993). Personal goals and subjective well-being: A longitudinal study. *Journal of Personality and Social Psychology, 65,* 1061–1070.

Cameron, L. D., & Nicholls, G. (1998). Expression of stressful experiences through writing: Effects of a self-regulation manipulation for pessimists and optimists. *Health Psychology, 17,* 84–92.

Cantor, N., & Kihlstrom, J. F. (1987). *Personality and social intelligence.* Englewood Cliffs, NJ: Prentice Hall.

Carver, C. S. (1996). Goal engagement and the human experience. In R. S. Wyer Jr. (Ed.), *Advances in social cognition* (Vol. 9, pp. 49–61). Mahwah, NJ: Erlbaum.

Carver, C. S., & Humphries, C. (1981). Havana daydreaming: A study of self-consciousness and the negative reference group among Cuban Americans. *Journal of Personality and Social Psychology, 40,* 545–552.

Carver, C. S., Lawrence, J. W., & Scheier, M. F. (1996). A control-process perspective on the origins of affect. In L. L. Martin & A. Tesser (Eds.), *Striving and feeling: Interactions between goals and affect* (pp. 11–52). Hillsdale, NJ: Erlbaum.

Carver, C. S., Pozo, C., Harris, S. D., Noriega, V., Scheier, M. F., Robinson, D. S., Ketcham, A. S., Moffat, F. L., Jr., & Clark, K. C. (1993). How coping mediates the effect of optimism on distress: A study of women with early stage breast cancer. *Journal of Personality and Social Psychology, 65,* 375–390.

Carver, C. S., & Scheier, M. F. (1981). *Attention and self-regulation: A control-theory approach to human behavior.* New York: Springer Verlag.

Carver, C. S., & Scheier, M. F. (1990). Origins and functions of positive and negative affect: A control-process view. *Psychological Review, 97,* 19–35.

Carver, C. S., & Scheier, M. F. (1998). *On the self-regulation of behavior.* New York: Cambridge University Press.

Carver, C. S., & Scheier, M. F. (in press-a). Optimism. In C. R. Snyder (Ed.), *Coping: The psychology of what works.* New York: Oxford University Press.

Carver, C. S., & Scheier, M. F. (in press-b). Self-discrepancies and affect: Incorporating the role of the feared self. *Personality and Social Psychology Bulletin.*

Carver, C. S., & Scheier, M. F. (in press-c). Several more themes, a lot more issues: Commentary on the commentaries. In R. S. Wyer Jr. (Ed.), *Advances in social cognition* (Vol. 12). Mahwah, NJ: Erlbaum.

Carver, C. S., & Scheier, M. F. (in press-d). Themes and issues in the self-regulation of behavior. In R. S. Wyer Jr. (Ed.), *Advances in social cognition* (Vol. 12). Mahwah, NJ: Erlbaum.

Carver, C. S., Scheier, M. F., & Pozo, C. (1992). Conceptualizing the process of coping with health problems. In H. S. Friedman (Ed.), *Hostility, coping, and health* (pp. 167–199). Washington, DC: American Psychological Association.

Carver, C. S., Scheier, M. F., & Weintraub, J. K. (1989). Assessing coping strategies: A theoretically based approach. *Journal of Personality and Social Psychology, 56,* 267–283.

Cleiren, M. (1993). *Bereavement and adaptation: A comparative study of the aftermath of death.* Washington, DC: Hemisphere.

Crocker, J., & Major, B. (1989). Social stigma and self-esteem: The self-protective properties of stigma. *Psychological Review, 96,* 608–630.

Davidson, R. J. (1992). Anterior cerebral asymmetry and the nature of emotion. *Brain and Cognition, 20,* 125–151.

Davidson, R. J. (1995). Cerebral asymmetry, emotion, and affective style. In R. J. Davidson & K. Hugdahl (Eds.), *Brain asymmetry* (pp. 361–387). Cambridge, MA: MIT Press.

Elliott, E. S., & Dweck, C. S. (1988). Goals: An approach to motivation and achievement. *Journal of Personality and Social Psychology, 54,* 5–12.

Emmons, R. A. (1986). Personal strivings: An approach to personality and subjective well being. *Journal of Personality and Social Psychology, 51,* 1058–1068.

Emmons, R. A., & King, L.A. (1988). Conflict among personal strivings: Immediate and long-term implications for psychological and physical well-being. *Journal of Personality and Social Psychology, 54,* 1040–1048.

Feather, N. T. (1989). Trying and giving up: Persistence and lack of persistence in failure situations. In R. C. Curtis (Ed.), *Self-defeating behaviors: Experimental research, clinical impressions, and practical implications* (pp. 67–95). New York: Plenum Press.

Fontaine, K. R., Manstead, A. S. R., & Wagner, H. (1993). Optimism, perceived control over stress, and coping. *European Journal of Personality, 7,* 267–281.

Frijda, N. H. (1986). *The emotions.* Cambridge, UK: Cambridge University Press.

Frijda, N. H. (1988). The laws of emotion. *American Psychologist, 43,* 349–358.

Gallistel, C. R. (1980). *The organization of action: A new synthesis.* Hillsdale, NJ: Erlbaum.

Greene, P. H. (1972). Problems of organization of motor systems. In R. Rosen & F. M. Snell (Eds.), *Progress in theoretical biology* (Vol. 2, pp. 303–338). New York: Academic Press.

Greene, P. H. (1982). Why is it easy to control your arms? *Journal of Motor Behavior, 14,* 260–286.

Greenwald, A. G. (1980). The totalitarian ego: Fabrication and revision of personal history. *American Psychologist, 35,* 603–618.

Greer, S., Morris, T., & Pettingale, K. W. (1979). Psychological response to breast cancer: Effect on outcome. *Lancet, 2,* 785–787.

Greer, S., Morris, T., Pettingale, K. W., & Haybittle, J. L. (1990). Psychological response to breast cancer and 15-year outcome. *Lancet, 1,* 49–50.

Gross, J. J. (1998). Antecedent- and response-focused emotion regulation: Divergent consequences for experience, expression, and physiology. *Journal of Personality and Social Psychology, 74,* 224–237.

Guy, J. L., & Lord, R. G. (1998, May). *The effects of perceived velocity on job satisfaction: An expansion of current theory.* Paper presented and the 10th Annual Conference of the American Psychological Society, Washington, DC.

Hamilton, J. C., Greenberg, J., Pyszczynski, T., & Cather, C. (1993). A self-regulatory perspective on psychopathology and psychotherapy. *Journal of Psychotherapy Integration, 3,* 205–248.

Heatherton, T. F., & Nichols, P. A. (1994). Personal accounts of successful versus failed attempts at life change. *Personality and Social Psychology Bulletin, 20,* 664–675.

Higgins, E. T. (1987). Self-discrepancy: A theory relating self and affect. *Psychological Review, 94,* 319–340.

Higgins, E. T. (1996). Ideals, oughts, and regulatory focus: Affect and motivation from distinct pains and pleasures. In P. M. Gollwitzer & J. A. Bargh (Eds.), *The psychology of action: Linking cognition and motivation to behavior* (pp. 91–114). New York: Guilford Press.

Hobfoll, S. E. (1989). Conservation of resources: A new attempt at conceptualizing stress. *American Psychologist, 44,* 513–524.

Hobfoll, S. E., Freedy, J. R., Green, B. L., & Solomon, S. D. (1996). Coping in reaction to extreme stress: The roles of resource loss and resource availability. In M. Zeidner & N. S. Endler (Eds.), *Handbook of coping: Theory, research, applications* (pp. 322–349). New York: Wiley.

Holman, E. A., & Silver, R. C. (1998). Getting "stuck" in the past: Temporal orientation and coping with trauma. *Journal of Personality and Social Psychology, 74,* 1146–1163.

Hsee, C. K., & Abelson, R. P. (1991). Velocity relation: Satisfaction as a function of the first derivative of outcome over time. *Journal of Personality and Social Psychology, 60,* 341–347.

Janoff-Bulman, R., & Brickman, P. (1982). Expectations and what people learn from failure. In N. T. Feather (Ed.), *Expectations and actions: Expectancy-value models in psychology* (pp. 207–237). Hillsdale, NJ: Erlbaum.

Kirschenbaum, D. S. (1987). Self-regulatory failure: A review with clinical implications. *Clinical Psychology Review, 7,* 77–104.

Klass, D., Silverman, P. R., & Nickman, S. L. (Eds.) (1996) *Continuing bonds: New understandings of grief.* Washington, DC: Taylor and Francis.

Kling, K. C., Ryff, C., & Essex, M. J. (1997). Adaptive changes in the self-concept during a life transition. *Personality and Social Psychology Bulletin, 23,* 981–990.

Klinger, E. (1975). Consequences of commitment to and disengagement from incentives. *Psychological Review, 82,* 1–25.

Klinger, E. (1977). *Meaning and void: Inner experience and the incentives in people's lives.* Minneapolis: University of Minnesota Press.

Kovatchev, B., Cox, D., Gonder-Frederick, L., Schlundt, D., & Clarke, W. (1998). Stochastic model of self-regulation decision making exemplified by decisions concerning hypoglycemia. *Health Psychology, 17,* 277–284.

Kukla, A. (1972). Foundations of an attributional theory of performance. *Psychological Review, 79,* 454–470.

Lawrence, J. W., Carver, C. S., & Scheier, M. F. (1997). *Velocity and affect in immediate personal experience.* Unpulished manuscript.

Lazarus, R. S. (1966). *Psychological stress and the coping process.* New York: McGraw-Hill.

Lazarus, R. S., & Folkman, S. (1984). *Stress, appraisal, and coping.* New York: Springer.

Lecci, L., Okun, M. A., & Karoly, P. (1994). Life regrets and current goals as predictors of psychological adjustment. *Journal of Personality and Social Psychology, 66,* 731–741.

Leventhal, H. (1981). Toward a comprehensive theory of emotion. In L. Berkowitz (Ed.), *Advances in experimental social psychology* (Vol. 13, pp. 140–194). New York: Academic Press.

Leventhal, H., Meyer, D., & Nerenz, D. (1980). The common sense representation of illness danger. In S. Rachman (Ed.), *Contributions to medical psychology* (Vol. 2, pp. 7–30). New York: Pergamon Press.

Linville, P. (1985). Self-complexity and affective extremity: Don't put all of your eggs in one cognitive basket. *Social Cognition, 3,* 94–120.

Linville, P. (1987). Self-complexity as a cognitive buffer against stress-related illness and depression. *Journal of Personality and Social Psychology, 52,* 663–676.

Little, B. R. (1983). Personal projects: A rationale and methods for investigation. *Environment and Behavior, 15,* 273–309.

Little, B. R. (1989). Personal projects analysis: Trivial pursuits, magnificant obsessions, and the search for coherence. In D. M. Buss & N. Cantor (Eds.), *Personality psychology: Recent trends and emerging directions* (pp. 15–31). New York: Springer-Verlag.

Long, B. C., Kahn, S. E., & Schutz, R. W. (1992). Causal model of stress and coping: Women in management. *Journal of Counseling Psychology, 39,* 227–239.

MacNair, R. R., & Elliott, T. R. (1992). Self-perceived problem-solving ability, stress appraisal, and coping over time. *Journal of Research in Personality, 26,* 150–164.

Markus, H., & Nurius, P. (1986). Possible selves. *American Psychologist, 41,* 954–969.

McIntosh, W. D., & Martin, L. L. (1992). The cybernetics of happiness: The relation of goal attainment, rumination, and affect. In M. S. Clark (Ed.), *Review of personality and social psychology: Vol. 14. Emotion and social behavior* (pp. 222–246). Newbury Park, CA: Sage.

Meyer, D., Leventhal, H., & Gutmann, M. (1985). Common-sense models of illness: The example of hypertension. *Health Psychology, 4,* 115–135.

Miller, G. A., Galanter, E., & Pribram, K. H. (1960). *Plans and the structure of behavior.* New York: Holt, Rinehart & Winston.

Miller, L. C., & Read, S. J. (1987). Why am I telling you this? Self-disclosure in a goal-based model of personality. In V. J. Derlega & J. Berg (Eds.), *Self-disclosure: Theory, research, and therapy* (pp. 35–58). New York: Plenum Press.

Moskowitz, J. T., Folkman, S., Collette, L., & Vittinghoff, E. (1996). Coping and mood during AIDS-related caregiving and bereavement. *Annals of Behavioral Medicine, 18,* 49–57.

Oettingen, G. (1996). Positive fantasy and motivation. In P. M. Gollwitzer & J. A. Bargh (Eds.), *The psychology of action: Linking cognition and motivation to behavior* (pp. 219–235). New York: Guilford Press.

Orbuch, T. L. (Ed.). (1992). *Close relationship loss: Theoretical approaches.* New York: Springer-Verlag.

Park, C. L., Moore, P. J., Turner, R. A., & Adler, N. E. (1997). The roles of constructive thinking and optimism in psychological and behavioral adjustment during pregnancy. *Journal of Personality and Social Psychology, 73,* 584–592.

Pervin, L. A. (1982). The stasis and flow of behavior: Toward a theory of goals. In M. M. Page & R. Dienstbier (Eds.), *Nebraska symposium on motivation* (Vol. 30, pp. 1–53). Lincoln, NE: University of Nebraska Press.

Pervin, L. A. (Ed.). (1989). *Goal concepts in personality and social psychology.* Hillsdale, NJ: Erlbaum.

Pettingale, K. W., Morris, T., & Greer, S. (1985). Mental attitudes to cancer: An additional prognostic factor. *Lancet, 1,* 750.

Pittman, T. S., & Pittman, N. L. (1980). Deprivation of control and the attribution process. *Journal of Personality and Social Psychology, 39,* 377–389.

Powers, W. T. (1973). *Behavior: The control of perception.* Chicago: Aldine.

Pyszczynski, T., & Greenberg, J. (1992). *Hanging on and letting go: Understanding the onset, progression, and remission of depression.* New York: Springer-Verlag.

Reed, G. M., Kemeny, M. E., Taylor, S. E., et al. (1994). "Realistic acceptance" as a predictor of decreased survival time in gay men with AIDS. *Health Psychology, 13,* 299–307.

Rodin, J. (1985). Insulin levels, hunger, and food intake: An example of feedback loops in the body weight regulation. *Health Psychology, 4,* 1–24.

Roseman, I. J. (1984). Cognitive determinants of emotions: A structural theory. In P. Shaver (Ed.), *Review of personality and social psychology* (Vol. 5, pp. 11–36). Beverly Hills, CA: Sage.

Sarason, I. G., Pierce, G. R., & Sarason, B. R. (Eds.). (1996). *Cognitive interference: Theories, methods, and findings.* Hillsdale, NJ: Erlbaum.

Schank, R. C., & Abelson, R. P. (1977). *Scripts, plans, goals, and understanding.* Hillsdale, NJ: Erlbaum

Scheier, M. F., & Carver, C. S. (1985). Optimism, coping and health: Assessment and implications of generalized outcome expectancies. *Health Psychology, 4,* 219–247.

Scheier, M. F., & Carver, C. S. (1992). Effects of optimism on psychological and physical well-being: Theoretical overview and empirical update. *Cognitive Therapy and Research, 16,* 201–228.

Scheier, M. F., & Carver, C. S. (in press). Adapting to cancer: The importance of hope and purpose. In A. Baum & B. L. Andersen (Eds.), *Psychosocial interventions for cancer.* Washington, DC: American Psychological Association.

Scheier, M. F., Weintraub, J. K., & Carver, C. S. (1986). Coping with stress: Divergent strategies of optimists and pessimists. *Journal of Personality and Social Psychology, 51,* 1257–1264.

Schwartz, G. E. (1977). Biofeedback and the self-management of disregulation disorders. In R. B. Stuart (Ed.), *Behavioral self-management: Strategies, techniques, and outcome* (pp. 49–70). New York: Brunner/Mazel.

Schwartz, G. E. (1979a). Disregulation and systems theory: A biobehavioral framework for biofeedback and behavioral medicine. In N. Birbaumer & H. D. Kimmel (Eds.), *Biofeedback and self-regulation* (pp. 19–48). Hillsdale, NJ: Erlbaum.

Schwartz, G. E. (1979b). The brain as a health care system. In G. D. Stone, F. Cohen, & N. E. Adler (Eds.), *Health psychology—A handbook* (pp. 549–571). San Francisco: Jossey-Bass.

Showers, C. J., & Ryff, C. D. (1996). Self-differentiation and well-being in a life transition. *Personality and Social Psychology Bulletin, 22,* 448–460.

Stanton, A. L., & Snider, P. R. (1993). Coping with breast cancer diagnosis: A prospective study. *Health Psychology, 12,* 16–23.

Stroebe, M. S. (1994). The broken heart phenomenon: An examination of the mortality of bereavement. *Journal of Community and Applied Social Psychology, 4,* 47–61.

Stroebe, M. S., Stroebe, W., & Hansson, R. O. (Eds.). (1993). *Handbook of bereavement: Theory, research, and intervention.* Cambridge, UK: Cambridge University Press.

Strutton, D., & Lumpkin, J. (1992). Relationship between optimism and coping strategies in the work environment. *Psychology Reports, 71,* 1179–1186.

Taylor, S. E., & Pham, L. B. (1996). Mental stimulation, motivation, and action. In P. M. Gollwitzer & J. A. Bargh (Eds.), *The psychology of action: Linking cognition and motivation to behavior* (pp. 219–235). New York: Guilford Press.

Taylor, S. E., Pham, L. B., Rivkin, I. D., & Armor, D. A. (1998). Harnessing the imagination: Mental simulation, self-regulation, and coping. *American Psychologist, 53,* 429–439.

Turk, D. C., & Rudy, T. E. (1992). Cognitive factors and persistent pain: A glimpse into Pandora's box. *Cognitive Therapy and Research, 16,* 99–122.

Vallacher, R. R., & Wegner, D. M. (1985). *A theory of action identification.* Hillsdale, NJ: Erlbaum.

Vallacher, R. R., & Wegner, D. M. (1987). What do people think they're doing? Action identification and human behavior. *Psychological Review, 94,* 3–15.

Wicklund, R. A., & Gollwitzer, P. M. (1982). *Symbolic self-completion.* Hillsdale, NJ: Erlbaum.

Wills, T. A. (1981). Downward comparison principles in social psychology. *Psychological Bulletin, 90,* 245–271.

Wine, J. D. (1971). Test anxiety and direction of attention. *Psychological Bulletin, 76,* 92–104.

Wine, J. D. (1980). Cognitive-attentional theory of test anxiety. In I. G. Sarason (Ed.), *Test anxiety: Theory, research, and application* (pp. 349–378). Hillsdale, NJ: Erlbaum.

Wong, P. T. P., & Weiner, B. (1981). When people ask "why" questions, and the heuristics of attributional search. *Journal of Personality and Social Psychology, 40,* 650–663.

Wood, J. V. (1989). Theory and research concerning social comparisons of personal attributes. *Psychological Bulletin, 106,* 231–248.

Wood, J. V., Taylor, S. E., & Lichtman, R. R. (1985). Social comparison in adjustment to breast cancer. *Journal of Personality and Social Psychology, 49,* 1169–1183.

Worden, W. J. (1991). *Grief counseling and grief therapy: A handbook for the mental health practitioner* (2nd ed.). New York: Springer-Verlag.

Wortman, C. B., & Brehm, J. W. (1975). Responses to uncontrollable outcomes: An integration of reactance theory and the learned helplessness model. In L. Berkowitz (Ed.), *Advances in experimental social psychology* (Vol. 8, pp. 277–336). New York: Academic Press.

Zeidner, M., & Endler, N. S. (Eds.). (1996). *Handbook of coping: Theory, research, applications.* New York: Wiley.

Chapter 23

Personality and Health: Dispositions and Processes in Disease Susceptibility and Adaptation to Illness

Richard J. Contrada, Corinne Cather, and Ann O'Leary
Rutgers—The State University of New Jersey

A subject of speculation for over 2,000 years, the relationship between personality and health is currently a topic of considerable scientific interest. Major questions about personality and health have persisted since the prescientific era: Can personality cause or protect against disease? Which personality factors are most important in this regard? How can relationships between personality and health be explained? Continuity also may be found in some answers to these questions. For example, aspects of personality that involve the determinants and physiological correlates of emotions figure prominently both in ancient writings and in the current scientific literature. Of course, there are many new questions and some new answers as well. In this chapter, we review recent developments in research and theory concerning the relationship between personality and health and discuss the prospects for further advances in this area.

APPRAISAL OF RECENT ADVANCES

Since 1990, when Contrada, Leventhal, and O'Leary addressed this topic in the first edition of this handbook, research on personality and health has displayed two prominent trends: A large volume of work has been published, and much of it shows increasing methodological sophistication. Indications of these trends may be found in recent reviews of evidence linking personality to physical disease (e.g., Jorgensen, Johnson, Kolodziej, & Schreer, 1996; T. Q. Miller, Smith, Turner, Guijarro, & Hallet, 1996; Suls, Wan, & Costa, 1995) and to markers for processes that may promote disease (Lyness, 1993; Suls & Wan, 1993). These reviews covered large numbers of studies and examined measurement, research design, and other methodological factors in relation to the strength and consistency of empirical findings. With quantitative reviews of an ever-growing body of literature framed around critical methodological factors, it has been possible to achieve increasingly fine-grained assessments of the status of hypotheses linking personality to health.

In addition to improvements in the fundamentals of measurement and research design, there have been some interesting innovations in these areas. Collection of "real time" psychological data in naturalistic settings has seen several applications, such as Affleck et al.'s (1998) examination of personal goals in relation to the pain and fatigue associated with fibromyalgia, and Bolger and Schilling's (1991) study of personality Neuroticism in relation to the process of coping with daily stress. Similarly, techniques for acquiring psychophysiological data outside the laboratory have been used to examine the relationship of anger-related attributes to cardiovascular responses produced by social interactions (e.g., Guyll & Contrada, 1998), and to episodes of myocardial ischemia precipitated by everyday activities (e.g., Helmers et al., 1995). Another set of methodological advances is the application of sophisticated statistical techniques such as clustering analysis (Jorgenson, Gelling, & Kliner, 1992), multilevel regression analysis (Schwartz & Stone, 1998), and structural equation modeling (Bolger, Foster, Vinokur, & Ng, 1996).

We agree with others whose assessment is that theoretical progress has lagged behind empirical and methodological advances (Ouellette & DiPlacido, in press; Scheier & Bridges, 1995; Wiebe & Smith, 1997). This may be attributable, in part, to the empirical emphasis in health science. Among health researchers, theoretical interest in psychological aspects of a personality factor is likely to be limited until an empirical link to physical disease is established. Moreover, measurement tools reflecting theoretical innovations must be subject to an expensive and time-consuming research program to demonstrate their utility for predicting disease. This has been circumvented in "retroprospective" research (T. Q. Miller et al., 1996), in which archival data has been used to examine longitudinal associations between personality and health. However, personality measures available in such data sets rarely will be optimal for capturing current theoretical perspectives.

Practical impediments notwithstanding, there have been some theoretical advances. Broad conceptual frameworks have been used to model the relationship between personality and health, including a transactional perspective that highlights the reciprocal influence of person and environment (Bolger & Zuckerman, 1995; Smith, 1994), self-regulation models that emphasize goal constructs (Scheier & Bridges, 1995), and a framework that integrates health-related person factors within a cognitive-social perspective (S. M. Miller, Shoda, & Hurley, 1996). Other developments involve specific personality constructs that are newly applied to the study of physical disease, several of which will be discussed in this chapter. It also should be pointed out that research on personality has contributed to the development of theory concerning biological processes that promote physical disorders (e.g., Krantz & Manuck, 1984). Perhaps because this work has a biological focus, and is mainly concerned with consequences of personality rather than its causes and expression, it is not always given due consideration in evaluations of theoretical developments in the study of personality and physical health.

CHAPTER CONTENT AND ORGANIZATION

We begin with a discussion of basic principles, issues, and strategies in the investigation of personality and physical disease. This is followed by a review of research on two personality factors that we selected because they have received so much recent attention: Type A behaviors, with a particular focus on Hostility, and Dispositional Optimism. We then discuss work involving constructs that are relatively new to the study of personality and health or are, in some respects, outside the mainstream of research in this area. First we consider the role of goal constructs in the development of illness and experience of physical symptoms. Then we discuss the health consequences of two sets of concepts drawn from the study of self and identity: evaluative selves and social identity. The third topic, disclosure of traumatic events, is a process construct that has implications for understanding the physical health correlates of individual differences in Emotional Expressiveness. In the final section of this chapter, we address a set of conceptual issues that emerge from the discussion of specific constructs and have general relevance for the study of personality in relation to physical health and disease.

THE PERSONALITY–DISEASE INTERFACE

To characterize the difficulties encountered in attempting to establish connections between personality and physical disease, Contrada and colleagues (1990) used a metaphor involving the construction of a transcontinental railway with building crews starting at each coast: Without a map of the territory and adequate instruments to define the two crews' locations, the two ends can never meet. In retrospect, this image now seems too static, coastal cities too stable and monolithic to represent personality or health, and a connecting railway too stationary, unidimensional, and linear to represent personality–health linkages. It also fails to capture temporal considerations involved in relating personality, which is stable in some respects and changing in others, to diseases, which have their own temporal dynamics. Perhaps the metaphor works better if it is imagined that the building is not to be done on Earth, but on another planet, where boundaries separating atmosphere, land masses, and bodies of water are less definite, conditions less stable, and knowledge of those conditions and their temporal variations less direct and certain.

General Considerations from the Perspective of Physical Health/Disease

Chronic diseases have become the major sources of morbidity and mortality in the United States, a consequence of significant advances in public health practices and biomedical science since the early 1900s, when acute, infectious conditions were the dominant health problems. Rather than reflecting exposure to a single, infectious agent, chronic conditions—such as cardiovascular disease, stroke, cancers, and diabetes—are multiply determined. In many cases, they are also slowly developing, persisting, and/or degenerative. A salient departure from the gradual ascendance of chronic versus infectious conditions—the sudden emergence of acquired immune deficiency syndrome (AIDS)—is in some respects not an exception. Although caused by an infection, AIDS susceptibility is determined by lifestyle patterns not readily altered by public health measures that are currently feasible from a social and political standpoint. Such is also the case for most chronic disorders. Another similarity with major chronic disorders is that an AIDS diagnosis often is followed by a significant period of time in which a person can expect to live with disease and disease-management as major facts of life.

The domain of physical health and disease allows at least three major points of entry for personality and other psychological factors. Personality can be studied in relation to physical disorders, processes that culminate in physical disorders, or factors that influence health care utilization and its outcome. Although research separately addressing health in each of these ways can and has generated important findings regarding the role of personality, coordinated examination of all three is required to construct a coherent and unified view of the personality–health interface.

Table 23.1 outlines some aspects of physical disease and its treatment that pose difficulties for determining psychological and behavioral causes. These include definitional and technical problems that impede the performance and interpretation of medical diagnosis. They also include the challenge of unraveling the web of multiple, interacting determinants to isolate the independent contribution to disease of any one factor. Also noted are confounding effects of disease and treatment on psychological functioning and measurement in medical patients. Still other factors threaten the generalizability of health-related research to the general population. Taken together, the study of physical disease faces conceptual and practical barriers that constitute serious impediments even for state-of-the-art research involving appropriate subject populations, so-called "hard" or objective indices of physical functioning, and optimal research designs.

Despite these and other difficulties, it has been possible to conduct epidemiologic work that implicates personality as a potential cause of physical health problems. Epidemiological research seeks to characterize the distribution of diseases in the population and to identify variables, such as personality attributes, that operate as risk factors (disease predictors). Identification of risk factors requires evidence based on (1) objective verification of disease; (2) prospective research, that is, research in which risk factors are measured prior to the development of disease; (3) representative study samples; (4) statistical adjustments for other, better-established risk factors; (5) associations of nontrivial magnitude; and (6) data patterns that are consistent across multiple studies.

Although research addressing the foregoing points is fundamental to establishing personality as a determinant of physical disease, it is subject to several limiting conditions. One is that an association between personality (or any risk factor) and disease that satisfies these criteria can be spurious in the sense of reflecting the operation of a third variable that influences both personality and disease. Another is that the requirement of an association that is independent of better-established risk factors may obscure processes whereby personality operates as a distal cause of disease by increasing levels of risk factors more proximal to disease-promoting processes. A third consideration is that major prospective studies of personality and health are too expensive to be

TABLE 23.1. Obstacles to Personality–Health Research That Stem from the Nature of Disease/Treatment

Features of disease	Implications for understanding the role of personality
Diagnostic imprecision	Medical diagnoses are susceptible to all the sources of bias and error that can affect human judgment.
	Multiple bases for diagnoses vary in reliability and may yield conflicting conclusions.
	More definitive diagnostic techniques are often risky and therefore performed only in individuals likely to test positively who are not representative of the larger population.
Multiple determination	Most chronic disorders reflect multiple, often interacting determinants, making it difficult, even artificial, to isolate the independent contribution of any individual cause.
Symptom heterogeneity	Variations in presenting symptoms may reflect differences in etiology or undetected comorbidity.
	Symptoms may affect personality or its measurement.
	Absence of symptoms also may influence personality measurement in patient populations.
Natural history	Even prospective associations between personality and disease may reflect effects of (preclinical) disease on personality measures.
	The developmental course of a disease may influence symptomatology.
	Factors that cause disease to progress, including personality, may vary in their importance over time.
Treatment	Medication and surgical treatments that influence disease also may affect personality measurement.
	Interactions with the health care system may affect personality measurement.
	Factors that influence treatment-seeking or affect access to treatment reduce generalizability of research involving patients in treatment.

undertaken without a sound basis for believing that there is an association to be detected. For these reasons, risk factor status established on the basis of epidemiologic research is, at best, merely a starting point for analyzing the potential causal effect of a personality factor on physical health.

To some degree, limitations of resting entirely on disease-focused research can be addressed in research that focuses on causal mechanisms that culminate in or exacerbate physical disorders. Evidence linking personality to such mechanisms encourages epidemiologic investigations of previously unexamined associations between the personality factor in question and physical disease. Mechanism-oriented work also can probe hypotheses to explain personality–disease relationships already suspected or established—a necessary step if it is to be demonstrated that personality exerts a causal effect on physical health. One type of mechanism-focused research that can strengthen causal inference employs experimental manipulation of psychological/emotional states that can be taken as analogs, in the short term, of processes associated with personality in longer time frames. Examples of this strategy include the experimental manipulation of interpersonal conflict to explore effects of anger (hostility) on cardiovascular processes, or of trauma disclosure to examine effects of emotional expression (expressiveness) on immune function (both described below).

Disease-promoting mechanisms are defined in terms of the final link in the causal chain leading to disease (Krantz, Glass, Contrada, & Miller, 1981). They fall into two broad categories: psychophysiological and behavioral. Psychophysiological mechanisms involve effects of psychological events on physiological, neuroendocrine, and metabolic processes. They are closely identified with processes involved in psychological stress and emotion. It has long been established that stressful events and conditions activate the sympathetic–adrenomedullary (SAM) and pituitary–adrenocortical (PAC) systems (Mason, 1972), whose physiologic and metabolic effects are plausibly involved in the initiation and progression of many forms of physical disorder. The effects of stress and emotion on cardiovascular functioning are also well documented (Obrist, 1981). By contrast, accumulation of evidence that the immune system is responsive to social and psychological events and emotional states is a more recent development (Herbert & Cohen, 1993a, 1993b). Although linkages between stress/emotion and these biological processes are well established, implications of such associations for understanding human health and illness are less clear, and vary depending upon the particular biological system (for example, see Cohen, & Herbert, 1996, with regard to the immune system; and Manuck, Marsland, Kaplan, & Williams, 1995, with regard to the cardiovascular system).

Behavioral mechanisms contributing to physical health/disease involve overt actions and inactions that influence exposure to pathogenic agents. Examples include cigarette smoking, dietary practices, and unprotected sexual intercourse. As in the case of physiologic processes, health-damaging behaviors may plausibly be involved in disease initiation, disease progression, or both. Behavioral factors play a major role in infectious diseases, including HIV/AIDS (Kalichman, 1995), as well as in major chronic disorders such as cardiovascular disease (Ockene & Ockene, 1992) and various cancers (Doll, 1996). Despite the importance of behavioral risk factors for physical disorders, and the role of personality as a determinant of behavior, the study of personality and physical health has placed greater emphasis on psychophysiological than on behavioral causation of disease. Accordingly, we will emphasize psychophysiological pathways to disease in this chapter. However, it should be borne in mind that overt behaviors may play a greater role in mediating the disease-producing effects of personality than is currently appreciated. Moreover, health-related behaviors must be viewed as potential confounds of personality–disease associations that are interpreted in terms of direct psychophysiological processes. This is particularly true in light of evidence that psychological stress and emotion contribute to certain health-damaging behavior patterns in addition to directly affecting physiologic functioning (e.g., Wills & Hirky, 1996).

Personality also can influence physical well-being by influencing the use and effectiveness of formal and informal means of detecting and treating health problems. In this role, personality may not contribute directly to the initiation or progression of disease but, nonetheless, may alter its course and outcome. As with the behavioral causation of disease, the explanation of psychological reactions to health threats, physical illness, and its treatment has not been a dominant goal of research on personality and health. However, the potential area of contact between personality and these processes is quite extensive. It begins with utilization of disease screening and surveillance methods involving either self-examination or biomedical technology. It also includes cognitive and affective reactions to symptoms and signs of illness that may initiate, delay, or promote avoidance of health-care seeking and self-treatment (Croyle, 1992). Subsequently, personality may play a role throughout the natural history of a physical disorder, influencing aspects of illness management that center around monitoring and treating the disease and minimizing its effects on psychological well-being, physical activity, and social role functioning (Nicassio & Smith, 1995).

General Considerations from the Perspective of Personality

Conceptual and methodological issues that arise in the scientific analysis of personality are no less thorny than those associated with the study of physical disease. However, because these issues are given detailed examination throughout this handbook, our discussion will focus instead on those elements of the personality construct that form a basis for expecting connections with physical disease (see Table 23.2). Efforts to detect and explain relationships between personality and physical health involve a number of diverse subproblems that, at least when taken separately, do not require a single view of personality. For example, Contrada and colleagues (1990) noted that epidemiologic research is highly compatible with a dispositional approach to personality, and mechanism-focused research, with a process approach. Ultimately, however, it will be necessary to forsake the comfort afforded by these compatibilities to create a more complete picture of the personality–disease interface.

Table 23.2 starts with the observation that the role of personality in adaptation—both at the level of the individual and the species—sets the stage for potential influences on physical health. Physical well-being is, in part, a product of cognitions and actions that foster adaptation and survival. Thus, a basis for linkages between per-

TABLE 23.2. Personality–Disease Interface: General Principles from the Standpoint of Personality

Features of personality	Implications for understanding physical disease
Relevance to adaptation	Personality is related both to individual adaptation and to processes reflecting evolutionary adaptations, which provides a basis for linkages to various health-related processes.
Patterning in behavior	
Temporal stability	Compatible with disease-related processes that unfold gradually over time.
Cross-situational consistency	Compatible with disease-related processes that involve exposure to risks in diverse settings.
Situation–behavior profiles	Compatible with disease-related processes that involve particular responses to particular situations.
Personality structure	Cognitive-affective structures underlying disease-promoting behavior patterns may cause disease. Neurobiological structures may be causal factors in both personality and disease.
Personality organization	
Pervasiveness	Relevance of personality to cognitive, affective, and biological systems affords multiple possible linkages to disease-related processes.
Hierarchical form	Associations with disease at one level of personality organization may reflect factors operating at other levels of personality.
Process	
• Personality development, expression, change • Regulation of behavior • Interplay of person and environment	The role of personality in organizing, directing, energizing, and maintaining behavior affords multiple possible linkages to disease-related processes.
• Selection into situations • Construction/alteration of situations • Responses to situations • Evaluation of impact on situation • Duration of situational exposure	Personality affects physical health largely through the processes whereby personality shapes, and in turn is shaped by, person–environment interactions.

sonality and processes that affect physical health lies in the functional importance that personality assumes through its effects on goal-directed behavior (Carver & Scheier, Chapter 22, this volume), decision making (Pinkerton & Abramson, 1995) identification and control of environmental hazards (Myers, Henderson-King, & Henderson-King, 1997) and resources (Russell, Booth, Reed, & Laughlin, 1997), appraisal of stressors (Hemenover & Dienstbier, 1996), selection of coping strategies (Costa, Somerfield, & McCrae, 1996) and, more generally, the successful negotiation of life's demands, constraints, and opportunities. One implication of this view is that the full range of personality variation is relevant to understanding physical disease, by contrast with simpler views emphasizing the presence or absence of psychopathology or of some exceptional, health-damaging (or health-promoting) attribute.

In addition to its relevance for understanding the area of overlap between individual adaptation and health-promoting processes, personality may be related to evolutionary adaptations that affect physical health and disease. Linkages of this sort might be reflected in evidence of the heritability of personality that has been obtained in research employing traditional twin and family study methodologies. Small but reliable heritability coefficients have been found for measures of personality Hostility, which has been a focus of much health research (Cates, Houston, Vavak, Crawford, & Uttley, 1993). There is also evidence of a genetic basis for Dispositional Optimism, another potentially health-related personality attribute (Plomin, Scheier, Bergeman,

Pedersen, & Nesselroade, 1992). Measures of dispositions of more general interest to personality researchers, such as traits of the five-factor model (Loehlin, 1992), are associated with substantial heritability coefficients that may ultimately be found to have implications for disease susceptibility.

Evidence of heritability, by itself, does not provide an evolutionary account of a personality attribute, regardless of whether its effects on health are damaging or protective. However, there may be a specific evolutionary basis for physiological responses to psychological stress that appear to link personality to health problems. These responses, to which genetic factors seem to contribute (Rose, 1992), involve neuroendocrine adjustments that are conventionally seen as by-products of adaptations favoring the mobilization of energy stores that support vigorous motor activity (i.e., "fight or flight") (Sapolsky, 1992). They are recruited by emotions, which themselves represent evolutionary adaptations (Lazarus, 1991). Physiological concomitants of stress and emotion presumably have become damaging to life as a consequence of modern lifestyles (e.g., high-fat diets) that alter their metabolic effects, and social-cultural conventions that favor coping responses in which impulses to retaliate physically or to flee stressful situations are inhibited. Recently, in a somewhat different view, Maier and Watkins (1998) suggested that cognitive, emotional, behavioral, and physiological changes associated with stress in humans may reflect neurobiological mechanisms that initially evolved as an adaptation to sickness rather than as a stress response. These mechanisms were only later incorporated into the stress response, and now underlie patterns of adaptive, recuperative adjustments to both sickness and to stress that include certain forms of depression and helplessness. The possibility that depression and helplessness reflect an adaptation of this sort may provide a new perspective for research in which they are examined as elements or consequences of health-damaging personality attributes.

Whatever its functional significance, behavior patterning is of central importance to personality. It is patterning that distinguishes personality from temporally and situationally limited states of cognition, emotion, and behavior, whose relationship to personality in any given instance is an open empirical question. Of the three forms of behavioral patterning listed in Table 23.2, the first two—temporal and cross-situational consistency—are defining features of personality in most theoretical approaches. It is noteworthy, therefore, that each meets a requirement of certain disease-promoting processes. Temporal stability in personality increases its plausibility as a factor in slowly developing etiological processes such as atherogenesis and the growth of certain cancers. Similarly, cross-situational consistency provides a basis for conceptualizing personality as a facilitator of health-damaging processes that reflect multiple exposures to risky environments or conditions, such as those associated with stress, or with the performance of unhealthy behaviors. By the same token, health-protective practices also may reflect patterns of activity that extend over time and setting, such as physical exercise and the maintenance of supportive social relationships.

The third form of behavioral patterning involves consistency in behavioral variation across different situations. Mischel and Shoda (1998) discussed situation–behavior profiles displayed by children who were observed systematically at a summer camp. For example, some children consistently displayed more verbal aggression in response to being approached or teased by peers than when warned or punished by an adult. These variations appear to be stable, meaningful expressions of personality, but would not be detected in more conventional, trait approaches, which emphasize consistency in behavior that is aggregated across situations. There are health-related processes that may reflect the influence of behavioral consistencies that take this form. For example, whether or not a person expresses anger may have physiologic benefits or costs depending upon situational constraints (Engebretson, Matthews, & Scheier, 1989). In addition, coping may be less effective when the same strategy is used in an inflexible manner across different stressors (Lester, Smart, & Baum, 1994; Schwartz, Peng, Lester, Daltroy, & Goldberger, 1998). Thus, coping effectiveness may depend not so much on a person's overall tendency to cope in one manner or another in response to various stressful situations, but on coping patterns that take the form of the situation–behavior profiles described by Mischel and Shoda (1998).

Personality structure refers to real neurobiological and/or psychological entities that exist, literally, under the skin. Personality structures cause the consistent patterning in behavior that defines personality at the descriptive level. Initially, this view may entail circularity because the causal structure often is first inferred solely on the basis of its observable consequences. This circularity can only be overcome with the development of conceptually divergent and procedurally independent methods to operationalize personality structure and behavioral patterning. Research of this sort may reveal that personality and physical health outcomes are related because they reflect shared or interacting neurobiological structures. An example of a model that posits such an arrangement was proposed by Dienstbier (1989), who discussed the health-protective effects of "physiological toughness." Physiological toughness is characterized biologically by high levels of catecholamine availability. Tough individuals are thought to exhibit low levels of depression and its physiological correlates (e.g., corticosteroids), as a consequence of central catecholaminergic activity, and rapid and ample mobilization of effort and energy under challenge, reflecting peripheral catecholaminergic effects associated with SAM activation. To reconcile this positive perspective on SAM activity with its long-standing association with pathogenic processes, Dienstbier points to the importance of distinguishing between SAM activity occurring in conjunction with PAC activation, versus that occurring in a more pure state, a distinction seldom made in the human stress literature.

It is more typically the case that, despite involving neurobiological phenomena, personality structures can be characterized only in psychological language (in this connection, see Turkheimer, 1998, for a discussion of strong and weak conceptions of biological explanation). Constructs that refer to psychological personality structures include mental representations that encode beliefs, affects, action plans, self-concept, worldview, goals, motives, or social relationships (Cantor & Zirkel, 1990). These structures are viewed as participants in the processes whereby experience is organized and given meaning and value, and through which personality enters into the generation, maintenance, and alteration of behavior. Thus, they provide a basis for explanations of observable forms of behavioral patterning described earlier, and potentially for the health consequences of such behavioral patterning.

Personality organization has several different meanings. In one sense, it refers to the idea that personality involves the whole person, coordinating activity across different response domains. Thus, personality dispositions often are conceptualized in terms of individual differences in cognition, emotion, action, and even biological functioning. Specific models of personality organization have been described in terms of the form of personality-related behavior patterns. For example, the classic hierarchical trait model (e.g., Eysenck, 1967) identifies a vertical arrangement of behavior patterns, with situation-specific habits lying at the lowest level of organization, their intercorrelations reflecting broader dispositions (traits) located at a higher level, and their intercorrelations, in turn, forming still more general behavior patterns (types) at the highest level of abstraction. Models of this sort are often thought of as depictions of personality structure. However, "structure" here is statistical, rather than real, though statistical structure may reveal underlying cognitive–affective and neurobiological structures. In trait approaches, higher-level statistical structures are often imbued with explanatory value. Cervone (1997) recently described how an alternative, social-cognitive approaches seeks the determinants of behavioral consistency at lower levels, closer to situation-specific causal processes, in what he referred to as a "bottom-up" strategy. Consideration of personality organization, like temporal and cross-situational consistency, may provide clues regarding potential relevance to physical health, but there is no general rule. For example, it might be argued that the more pervasive the influence of a personality attribute (e.g., the higher its position in a hierarchical model), the greater the probability (all other things equal) that its manifestations and effects include health-promoting or health-protecting processes. On the other hand, more circumscribed personality attributes may lie closer to situation-specific processes that affect physical health.

Process constructs are critical to developing a rationale for personality effects on physical health. The etiology, pathophysiology, course, and outcome of a physical disorder reflect multiple processes operating at and across social, psychological, and biological levels of analysis, as do the detection, cure, and management of disease (Engel, 1977). In considering psychological processes related to personality that contribute to physical wellness or disease, those that shape person–environment interactions appear most critical. Dubos (1965) characterized sickness as a fact of life that reflects our imperfect adaptation to a changing environment that inevitably puts us in contact with an ever-increasing array of physical and psychological pathogens.

More positive perspectives, in which physical well-being is viewed as potentially controllable by psychological sources of disease resistance and health enhancement, also emphasize person–environment transactions such as purposeful activity, connections to others, and mastery (Ryff & Singer, 1998). Even the expression of genetic factors, whether health-promoting or health-damaging, may be extensively dependent upon environmental activation (Gottlieb, 1998). Table 23.2 indicates that personality may influence a person's contact with health-damaging (or health-protecting) environments through its effects on selection into situations, the construction or alteration of situations, responses to situations, the evaluation of one's impact on a situation, and duration of situational exposure (see Contrada & Guyll, in press, for a discussion of these processes).

Thus, to establish the role of personality in physical health, it is necessary to conceptualize *how* personality is linked to disease. This requires theory involving the three pathways to disease described earlier, namely, psychophysiologic and behavioral mechanisms that promote disease, and psychological processes that shape reactions to disease and its treatment. We turn now to an examination of specific personality constructs that have been implicated as contributing to physical health or disease through one or more of these pathways.

PERSONALITY CONSTRUCTS AND PHYSICAL HEALTH AND ILLNESS

Type A Behavior and Hostility: Evolving Constructs

The Type A behavior pattern and its constituent elements have been defined in a number of different ways. Table 23.3 presents some of the major approaches to defining Type A behaviors generally, and Hostility in particular. As reflected in upper portion of Table 23.3, conceptualizations of Type A behavior have evolved by showing an increasing emphasis on cognitive factors. Originally conceived as an "action–emotion" complex, belief content and information-generating processes lie at the core of the more recent models. Another way definitions of Type A have evolved is in the increasing importance they have come to place on constructs that involve mental representations of self. Contrada and colleagues (1990) noted that all the major theoretical perspectives on Type A behavior have either explicitly involved a person's conception or evaluation of self, or can readily be reconceptualized in terms of self-constructs. For example, Glass's (1977) controllability model can be seen as implying a self-evaluative standard according to which Type A individuals believe they ought to maintain control over environmental events and internal states. Price's (1982) model directly implicates contingencies of self-esteem (e.g., self-worth depends on accomplishment) and self-esteem maintenance as bases for Type A behavior, and Strube's (1987) model implicates a self-knowledge motive. Other models not described in Table 23.3 have variously invoked self-evaluation, self-involvement, and self-perceptual processes as factors responsible for the generation and maintenance of Type A behavior (see Contrada et al., 1990).

The shift in focus away from the broad Type A pattern, and toward hostility and other anger-related attributes, was primarily empirically driven. It was stimulated by findings suggesting that anger-related responses displayed during a structured interview, including hostility directed at the interviewer captured in a rating of the subject's Potential for Hostility, account for much of the association between the more global Type A construct and coronary disease (e.g., Matthews, Glass, Rosenman, & Bortner, 1977). At first, this shift highlighted the importance of behavioral and, especially, emotional aspects of anger and hostility. However, current conceptualizations have come to emphasize their cognitive elements, as reflected in the definitions presented in the lower half of Table 23.3.

As in the transition from the broad Type A pattern to the domain of anger and hostility, the increasing cognitive emphasis within the latter domain was empirically based. It arose in large part from examination of the item content of the Cook and Medley (1954) Hostility scale (Ho), after it was found to measure coronary-prone attributes when archival databases containing MMPI and health data were reanalyzed. Conceptualizations of Ho item content emphasize attitudes, attributions, and other cognitive factors, with less emphasis on emotion and behavior (Barefoot, Dodge, Peterson, Dahlstrom, & Williams, 1989), though it is recognized that the cognitive structures involved in hostility have emotional and behavioral correlates.

In another parallel with the more global Type A construct, hostility too has come to be viewed in terms of self-referent constructs. Although several Ho items refer to anger and to aggressive

TABLE 23.3. Conceptualizations of Type A Behavior and Hostility

Type A behavior
Original definition (Friedman & Rosenman (1974)
"... an action–emotion complex that can be observed in any person who is aggressively involved in a chronic, incessant struggle to achieve more and more in less and less time, and if required to do so, against the opposing efforts of other things or other persons." (p. 67)
Uncontrollability model (Glass, 1977)
"... Type A's work hard to succeed, suppress subjective states (like fatigue) that might interfere with task performance, exhibit rapid pacing of their activities, show little tolerance for interruption, and express hostility after being harassed in their efforts at task completion ... in the interests of asserting control over environmental demands and requirements." (p. 72)
Cognitive social learning model (Price, 1982)
"Three of the personal beliefs that form the core of the Type A pattern...[are] the belief that one must constantly prove himself... [t]he belief that no universal moral principle exists [and] [t]he belief that resources are scarce." (Price, 1982, pp. 66–70)
Self-appraisal model (Strube, 1987)
"... when Type A's are confronted with uncertainty about their abilities, they respond with behaviors that are intended to generate diagnostic information." (pp. 212–213)
Hostility
Potential for hostility (Dembroski & Czajkowski, 1989)
"... the relatively stable tendency to react to a broad range of frustration-inducing events with responses indicative of anger, irritation, disgust, contempt, resentment, and the like, and/or actually to express antagonism, criticalness, uncooperativeness, and other disagreeable behaviors in similar situations." (p. 30)
Hostility (Smith, 1992)
"... a view of others as frequent and likely sources of mistreatment, frustration, and provocation and, as a result, a belief that others are generally unworthy and not to be trusted." (p. 139)
Hostility (Smith, 1994)
"... a devaluation of the worth and motives of others, an expectation that others are likely sources of wrongdoing, a relational view of being in opposition toward others, and a desire to inflict harm or see others harmed." (p. 26)

behavioral tendencies, for the most part, endorsement of Ho items indicates a generally cynical view of the world and negative, untrusting beliefs about others and their motives. As captured in Smith's (1994) more recent definition of hostility (see Table 23.3), these beliefs and attitudes can be seen as reflecting a mental representation of self that is defined in terms of its oppositional relationship with a world in which most people are unfair, deceitful, and manipulative. Houston and Vavak (1991) discussed the similarity of this view to the notion in attachment theory of internal working models (Bowlby, 1973) that comprise beliefs about the self, others, and the social world, and are thought to influence close relationships and other aspects of social behavior.

Associations with Physical Disease

A series of meta-analyses (Booth-Kewley & Friedman, 1987; Matthews, 1988; T. Q. Miller et al., 1996) has provided updates on the status of Type A behavior and Hostility as risk factors for coronary heart disease. The review by Booth-Kewley and Friedman (1987) supported the risk factor status of both the global Type A construct and Hostility, and suggested that a broader conception of coronary-prone personality factors was required to accommodate findings implicating other attributes, such as anxiety and depression. By contrast, Matthews's (1988) meta-analysis, which covered findings not available to Booth-Kewley and Friedman and differed both methodologically and with regard to how studies were selected and their results aggregated, came to different conclusions. It showed a significant association with coronary heart disease when Type A behavior was measured in initially healthy individuals, but not in high-risk individuals, that is, those with pre-existing coronary disease or who were selected for their high levels of traditional risk factors. It also showed that associations with disease were significant when Type A was assessed using a structured interview that emphasizes Hostility, but not for Type A behaviors measured by questionnaires that do not emphasize Hostility. Matthews also found that results for interview- and questionnaire-based measures that specifically target Hostility yielded a significant association with coronary heart disease.

The recent meta-analysis of T. Q. Miller and colleagues (1996), which focused on Hostility, was based on a much larger number of studies than was available to Booth-Kewley and Friedman (1987) or Matthews (1988). It also addressed several conceptual and methodological issues concerning the relationship between Hostility and disease. Overall, this review found support for the hypothesis that Hostility and other anger-related attributes increase risk for coronary heart disease. Support was strongest for Hostility ratings based on a structured interview, which identifies the behavioral expression of anger as a disease-producing attribute. The Ho yielded evidence of a consistent, but smaller association with CHD, which identifies cognitive aspects of Hostility as disease-producing. Self-report measures of anger experience, which have been used less frequently than the structured interview and Ho, did not appear consistently associated with CHD.

As in the meta-analysis reported by Matthews (1988), T. Q. Miller and colleagues (1996) found that associations between Type A behavior/Hostility and coronary disease were weaker in studies of high-risk individuals. In contrast to the findings for initially healthy individuals, results of high-risk studies are much less consistent, yielding positive (e.g., Brackett & Powell, 1988), inverse (e.g., Ragland & Brand, 1988), and no relationship (e.g., Case et al., 1985) to health outcomes. One factor that appears to contribute to inconsistencies across populations in the association between personality and heart disease is a range restriction problem. Strategies for selecting subjects in these studies produce samples with little representation of individuals devoid of coronary disease, limiting the range of both disease and Type A behavior. T. Q. Miller and colleagues (1996) showed that effect sizes have generally been lower in studies subject to this selection factor. Age also may explain some of the inconsistencies, with stronger associations often found in younger compared with older participants (e.g., Dembroski, MacDougall, Costa, & Grandits, 1989).

Pathways to Physical Disease

Type A behavior, Hostility, and related attributes may contribute to coronary disease through pathways involving psychophysiologic processes, health-damaging behaviors, and reactions to illness. However, psychophysiologic processes have received the greatest amount of attention, as reflected in a large volume of research that has made use of both laboratory and field methods, both human and infrahuman species, and sophisticated paradigms for the measurement of potentially pathogenic correlates of Type A behavior and Hostility. Meta-analyses indicate reliable associations between global Type A behavior and cardiovascular responses to laboratory stressors and challenges (Lyness, 1993; but see Myrtek, 1995), and between Hostility and blood pressure responses to laboratory-experimental provocations containing elements likely to produce anger (Suls & Wan, 1993). The cardiovascular and neuroendocrine measures used in this research reflect activation of the sympathetic–adrenomedullary system, which is thought to contribute to the initiation and progression of coronary disease and its clinical manifestations through a number of physiological and metabolic mechanisms (Krantz & Manuck, 1984). A reduction in parasympathetic activity, which can modulate the cardiovascular effects of sympathetic activation, also may be involved (Kamada, Miyake, Kumashiro, Monou, & Inoue, 1992). Additional stress-related physiologic mechanisms that have been investigated as possible explanations for associations linking Type A behavior and Hostility to coronary disease and other health problems include the secretion of hormones such as cortisol and testosterone (Suarez, Kuhn, Schanberg, Williams, & Zimmerman, 1998), activity of blood platelets that may be involved in atherogenesis and thrombosis (Markovitz, Matthews, Kiss, & Smitherman, 1996), and episodes of myocardial ischemia in coronary patients (Helmers et al., 1995). The hypothesis that physiologic correlates of Type A behavior and Hostility reflect causal mechanisms culminating in coronary disease is supported by research linking stress-induced cardiovascular reactivity to measures of disease in humans (Kamarck et al., 1997), and by findings generated by a well-developed animal model of psychosocial stress, behavior patterns, and cardiovascular reactivity (Manuck et al., 1995).

Both Type A behavior and Hostility also appear correlated with health-damaging behaviors and reactions to illness that may permit physical health problems to worsen (for recent reviews, see Contrada & Guyll, in press; Smith, 1992). For example, Type A behavior is associated with delay in health care seeking in the early stages of a suspected myocardial infarction (Matthews, Siegel, Kuller, Thompson, & Varat, 1983), and Hostility has been linked to cigarette smoking (Siegler, 1994), poor sleep (Koskenvou et al., 1988), and greater alcohol use (Houston & Vavak, 1991; Koskenvou et al., 1988). Glass's (1977) uncontrollability model has been used to derive the prediction that Type A's will show poor adherence to medical regimens because they arouse psychological reactance (e.g., Rhodewalt & Fairfield, 1990; but see Lynch et al., 1992). It is important to note that health-related behaviors do not appear to explain away the relationship between Hostility and coronary disease in epidemiological studies (T. Q. Miller et al., 1996). Thus, the breadth of the correlational networks surrounding Type A and Hostility permits points of contact with multiple pathways to disease.

Dispositional Optimism

"Dispositional Optimism" refers to a stable dimension of individual differences in generalized expectations for favorable versus unfavorable outcomes (Carver & Scheier, in press; Scheier & Carver, 1985). In other words, Optimism involves generally having positive expectations for the future and Pessimism, generally negative expectations, with most individuals falling somewhere in between. Optimism is most frequently measured using the Life Orientation Test (LOT), a brief self-report measure (Scheier & Carver, 1985; Scheier, Carver, & Bridges, 1994). As with Type A behavior and Hostility, personality attributes resembling Optimism have long been suspected as determinants of physical well-being (e.g., compare Hippocrates's notion of a sanguine temperament). However, unlike Type A/Hostility, scientific interest in Optimism did not begin with an interest in its possible contribution to degree of risk for a particular physical disorder, nor has it been examined extensively in prospective epidemiologic studies of any disease. Instead, Optimism was introduced as possibly having positive effects on physical health through its hypothesized role in maintaining a person's efforts to attain valued goals (Scheier & Carver, 1985).

Relationship to the Coping Process

The role of Optimism in goal-directed activity forms part of a self-regulation model that draws upon cybernetic control-systems theory (Scheier & Carver, 1985). The model emphasizes the importance of goals in directing and energizing human behavior and in making life meaningful. Optimism is thought to promote active engagement in the pursuit of life goals because optimists expect to achieve their goals and they persist in their efforts when confronted by obstacles to goal attainment. This provides a basis for linkages between Optimism and the process of coping with psychological stress and negative emotions, which has been conceptualized in terms of goal constructs (Lazarus, 1991; Lazarus & Folkman, 1984), a topic to which we will return later in this chapter. Consistent with this perspective are findings indicating that Optimism is associated with greater use of coping responses that reflect active engagement with stressors, such as planfulness and taking direct action, and less use of coping responses that reflect disengagement, such as denial and avoidance (e.g., Scheier, Weintraub, & Carver, 1986). Research has also generated evidence indicating that coping strategies employed by optimists confronting adverse conditions are associated with lower levels of emotional distress and more positive states of mind (for reviews, see Carver & Scheier, in press, and Chapter 22, this volume).

Pathways to Physical Disease

To the degree that coping strategies associated with Optimism are effective in reducing psychological stress, Optimism might be expected to protect against physiologic responses to stressors that may contribute to the development of physical disease. Evidence to support this hypothesis recently was reported by Räikkönen, Matthews, Flory, Owens, and Gump (1999). An important feature of this study was that Optimism and Pessimism were examined as related but separable dimensions, rather than as opposite poles of the same continuum. Study participants were healthy, middle-aged men and women who underwent ambulatory blood pressure and mood monitoring during the course of their usual activities for three days. Pessimists had higher overall blood pressure levels than optimists, especially when Pessimism was assessed as low scores on Optimism (rather than high scores for Pessimism). These findings are in general agreement with previous research on Optimism involving the use of laboratory stressors to provoke cardiovascular reactivity (e.g., Williams, Riels, & Roper, 1990).

A recent study sought to determine whether Optimism is related to immune changes produced by psychological stress (Segerstrom, Taylor, Kemeny, & Fahey, 1998). Subjects were students attending their first semester at law school. Dispositional Optimism was associated with significantly less avoidant coping, and significantly less emotional disturbance, as in research reviewed earlier. Dispositional Optimism also was associated with higher scores on immune parameters thought to be beneficial for physical health, but those associations did not achieve statistical significance. However, a measure of *situational* Optimism, which reflected participants' ratings of their expectations for success during the first semester of law school and was moderately correlated with Dispositional Optimism, was significantly related to better immunity.

There is evidence to suggest that Optimism may promote physical well-being through pathways that involve health-related behaviors. Carver and Scheier (in press) reviewed evidence indicating that, in a sample of HIV-negative gay men, Optimism was associated with having fewer anonymous sexual partners. Carver and Scheier also cited evidence that optimistic cardiac patients make more positive behavioral changes than do their pessimistic counterparts, such as adjusting their dietary intake of fat and enrolling in a cardiac rehabilitation program. There is also evidence that Optimism was associated with a lower probability of dropout from an aftercare program in a sample of men with alcohol dependence (Strack, Carver, & Blaney, 1987), and with less substance abuse in a sample of pregnant women (Park, Moore, Turner, & Adler, 1997).

Adjustment and Survival in Serious Medical Conditions

The role of Optimism in maintaining active engagement in the coping process may facilitate adjustment to medical problems, both by reducing distress and by promoting physical functioning (e.g., Carver et al., 1993; Scheier et al., 1989; Taylor et al., 1992). Recent evidence also indicates that Optimism may protect against negative health outcomes in patients with serious medical conditions. In a study of patients undergoing open heart surgery, Scheier et al. (in press) found that Optimism was associated with a lower rate of complications following heart surgery. In a sample of patients with advanced cancer, Schulz, Bookwala, Knapp, Scheier, and Williamson (1996) studied Optimism in relation to mortality. As in the Räikkönen et al. (1999) study, Optimism and Pessimism were examined independently. Results indicated that Pessimism scores interacted with age, such that high Pessimism scores were associated with shorter survival times for patients aged 30 to 59, but not for older patients. By contrast, Optimism scores were unrelated to mortality in patients of all ages.

Personal Goals

Although it is hypothesized to have consequences for goal-related psychological processes, Dispositional Optimism is itself a generalized expectancy construct, rather than a goal construct per se. By contrast, several personality factors are more directly conceptualized in terms of goals (Pervin, 1989). These concepts share an emphasis on mental representations of desired states of being and activities that may be instrumental in achieving those desired states: cognitive-motivational structures and processes that direct and sustain a person's purposeful engagement in activities of living. As discussed earlier in connection with Dispositional Optimism, goal constructs provide a potential means of integrating health-related personality factors with general models of self-regulation that draw from cybernetic control-systems theory (e.g., Bandura, 1986; Scheier & Carver, 1985). This places goal constructs in contact with processes involved both in the production of physical disease and in adaptation to the impact of illness on the person.

Personal Strivings and Physical Well-Being

Emmons (1989) examined personal strivings as a possible determinant of physical health problems. He defined "personal strivings" as coherent patterns of goal-directed activity that specify what a person currently is trying to do, for example, "trying to appear attractive to the opposite sex," or "trying to be better than others." This places personal strivings at a level of personality organization that is more specific than that of major motivational dispositions, such as intimacy or achievement, yet more general than particular concerns, projects, and tasks (e.g., "lose weight," "improve grades"). Emmons has found that attributes a person associates with personal strivings—such as their value, importance, past fulfillment, and probability of success—are related to emotional well-being and life satisfaction (Emmons, 1989). More germane to this chapter are the findings of Emmons and King (1988, Studies 1 and 2), which indicate that conflict between two personal strivings—the perception that succeeding at one may work against succeeding at the other—is associated with self-report measures of physical health problems. Additional findings suggest that this association might reflect the effects of conflict on goal-related rumination and inhibition of goal-directed activity (Emmons & King, 1988, Study 3). This line of work was recently extended by Sheldon and Kasser (1995), who found that measures reflecting the congruence or coherence of personal strivings were positively associated with health and well-being.

Emmons (1992) examined personal striving *level* in relation to physical health. This parameter of personal strivings refers to the distinction between high-level goals, which are broad, abstract, and expansive (e.g., "be totally honest," "compete against myself rather than others"), and low-level goals, which are concrete, specific, and more superficial (e.g., "look physically conditioned and physically fit," "relaxing tomorrow after an examination"). It was found that subjects who reported high-level strivings experienced more psychological distress and less physical illness, whereas the opposite pattern was seen in those reporting low-level strivings. In discussing possible explanations for these results, Emmons hypothesized that low-level thinking (including that pertaining to personal strivings) may reflect an avoidant response to the threat inherent in being asked about one's goals in life. Avoidant coping, in turn might be associated with illness-producing processes (Contrada, Czarnecki, & Pan, 1997; Suls & Fletcher, 1985).

Personal Goals and the Experience of Illness Symptoms

The term "quality of life" is used to refer to broad domains of social, psychological, and behavioral functioning that are increasingly being examined as outcomes of disease and its treatment (Spilker, 1996). Affleck et al. (1998) employed the concept of personal goals in a psychological approach to quality of life in women with fibromyalgia, a pain syndrome accompanied by sleep disturbance, fatigue, psychological distress, and limitations in routine activities of living. At the study's inception, patients were asked to identify current, medium-range, personal goals. Most of the women provided either a fitness–health-related goal, or a social relationship-related goal. Then, each night for 30 consecutive nights, the women were asked to complete a diary that contained measures of goal-related effort, disease-related goal hindrance, and goal progress. In addition, the women were given hand-held computers, also for 30 consecutive days, that prompted them at randomly selected times during the morning, afternoon, and evening to provide information on their sleeping, pain, fatigue, and mood.

The numerous data points generated in this study were analyzed on a prospective, within-subjects basis, using a multilevel random-effects model. Results included several interesting findings. It was found that progress toward health and fitness-related goals appeared to be regulated by the quality of the previous night's sleep, whereas progress toward social relationship goals appeared regulated by changes in the course of pain during the day. It also was found that goal variables predicted mood independently of symptoms. For example, the perception that daily progress toward health–fitness goals was impeded by that day's pain and fatigue predicted decreases in mood from morning to evening independently of changes in that day's reported pain and fatigue. Similarly, the perception of progress toward social relationship goals predicted improvement in positive mood during the day independently of physical symptoms.

Personal goals also form the basis of a measure of quality of life described by Rapkin et al. (1994) that was developed using data collected from a sample of AIDS patients. Patients' personal goals were obtained in response to interview questions asking them about what they hoped to accomplish, problems they wanted to solve, outcomes they wanted to prevent or avoid, changes they did not want to take place, and commitments they wanted to relinquish. Variables assessed in relation to patients' goals included goal-related activities and the difficulty level, amount of help received, and need for help associated with each. Among the findings were associations between scores on conventional quality of life questionnaires, and goal-related measures, such as the number of goals not pursued due to health problems, the number of activities that had become more difficult in the past month, the number of painful activities, and difficulty of goal attainment. Other data suggested that goal-related measures predicted various physical health indicators, including physical symptoms, use of home care, and practitioner-rated physical functioning, after controlling statistically for scores on more conventional quality of life measures.

Evaluative Selves

The concept of "self," which has been with psychology from the time of its inception (e.g., James, 1890), defies simple definition. Numerous definitions of self and self-related constructs have been suggested in psychology as well as in other social sciences (for historical and conceptual overviews, see Ashmore & Jussim, 1997). These generally emphasize either process and executive function (James's "I" or "self as knower"), or content and structure (James's "Me" or "self as known"). Among the latter set of self concepts are evaluative selves, which are mental representations of the self that a person would like to be or feels he or she should be (Higgins, 1987). Self-evaluative concepts have long been studied in relation to psychological well-being, and this topic has received increased attention in the 1990s as part of a general reinvigoration of self and identity research (Ashmore & Jussim, 1997; Baumeister, 1998). The role of evaluative self-representations in determining well-being provides a theoretical basis for at least two ways they might increase understanding of physical health: (1) as a determinant of physiological processes involved in the development or exacerbation of disease, and (2) as a factor influencing adjustment to serious physical conditions. Two recent studies illustrate each of these applications.

Strauman, Lemieux, and Coe (1993) used a priming paradigm to assess the effects of activating negative self-evaluations on measures of immunity. As expected on the basis of self-discrepancy theory (Higgins, 1987), dysphoric subjects scored highest on a measure of actual self–ideal self discrepancy, and anxious subjects scored highest on a measure of actual self–ought self discrepancy. More important from a physical health perspective were data for natural killer (NK) cell activity, a measure of immunity thought to play a role in combating viral infections, tumor surveillance, and the regulation of antibody production by other cells of the immune system. When primed by being asked to write about attributes involved in their self-discrepancies, significantly lower NK activity was found in anxious subjects (though not for dysphoric subjects), and individual differences in combined anxious and dysphoric content were significantly correlated with lower NK cell activity for both groups.

Heidrich, Forsthoff, and Ward (1994) were interested in the role of self-evaluation in adjustment to cancer. A sample of patients with various cancer diagnoses completed a measure in which they provided ratings of the degree to which they experienced an actual self–ideal self discrepancy across 20 life domains (e.g., "my physical health," "coping with change," "pursuing my leisure interests and hobbies"). Higher levels of self-discrepancy were found to be inversely correlated with measures of psychological well-being (purpose in life, personal growth, positive relations) and positively correlated with a measure of depressive symptoms. They also were inversely associated with scores on a set of measures reflecting subjective assessments of physical health (e.g., overall health rating, symptoms, and capacity to perform activities of daily living). Further statistical analysis suggested that effects of physical health perceptions on psychological adjustment were mediated by scores on the measure of evaluative self-discrepancy.

Social Identity

The concept of "identity," as with "self," has had a long history and has recently experienced a resurgence in psychology and other social and behavioral sciences (Ashmore & Jussim, 1997).

These two constructs share a number of similarities; indeed, in some usages, the two terms are synonymous. In this section, we describe recent research in which concepts related to *social* identity have been applied to problems of physical health. By "social identity," we refer broadly to mental representations of self that involve socially meaningful categories defined by social roles, social attributes, or group memberships (Thoits & Virshup, 1997). Here we consider recent health research involving constructs related to gender identity and homosexual identity.

Sex and gender have been conceptualized in a number of different ways in social and behavioral research. Although some approaches explicitly examine sex and gender as elements of a person's mental representation of self or identity, the dominant strategy has involved trait constructs (Ashmore, 1990). Among these are Agency and Communion. "Agency" refers to active, instrumental aspects of masculinity and involves a focus on the self and attributes such as independence, competitiveness, and self-confidence. "Communion" refers to interpersonal, expressive aspects of femininity and involves a focus on others and attributes such as cooperativeness, connectedness, and warmth (Bakan, 1966). Helgeson (1994) suggested that both Agency and Communion may promote well-being, except in their extreme ("unmitigated") forms, in which one exists in the absence of the other. Unmitigated Agency involves a focus on self to the exclusion of others, and unmitigated Communion involves a focus on others to the exclusion of self (Spence, Helmreich, & Holahan, 1979). Evidence to support Helgeson's suggestion as it pertains to unmitigated Agency was obtained in a study of 70 male and 20 female heart disease patients, in which unmitigated Agency was associated with length of delay in health care seeking, and severity of myocardial infarction (Helgeson, 1990). More recently, Helgeson and Lepore (1997) reported that unmitigated Agency was associated with poorer quality of life in a sample of men with prostate cancer. Regarding the physical health consequences of unmitigated Communion in women, Helgeson and Fritz (in press) reviewed recent evidence indicating associations with poor adjustment to chronic illnesses, failure to adhere to physicians' instructions, and neglect of physical symptoms.

Related to a person's gender-related traits and self-representations are social identities that involve sexuality and sexual orientation (Brooks-Gunn & Graber, in press). Sexuality and sexual orientation per se have obvious connections to physical health problems associated with specific sexual behaviors, such as sexually transmitted infections, but have received very limited attention as aspects of social identity that might be seen as relevant to the study of personality and health. However, an exception can be found in the work of Cole and colleagues examining homosexual identity in relation to physical health outcomes in gay men (Cole, Kemeny, & Taylor, 1997; Cole, Kemeny, Taylor, & Visscher, 1996; Cole, Kemeny, Taylor, Visscher, & Fahey, 1996). Their initial research showed that concealment of homosexual identity—being "in the closet"—appeared to be health-damaging in gay men, whether they were HIV seropositive (Cole, Kemeny, Taylor, Visscher, & Fahey, 1996) or HIV seronegative (Cole, Kemeny, Taylor, & Visscher, 1996). However, a more recent study suggests a somewhat more complex picture (Cole et al., 1997).

Cole and colleagues (1997) examined concealment of homosexual identity in initially healthy, HIV-seropositive homosexual men, in relation to the construct of Social Rejection Sensitivity. Social Rejection Sensitivity refers to the degree to which subjects indicated that they would expect to feel discomfort if they were to enact their homosexual identity in various social situations (e.g., attending a family function with a partner, buying a book about homosexuality). Results over a 9-year follow-up period indicated that, among men who did not conceal their homosexual identity, Social Rejection Sensitivity in relation to unfamiliar others predicted significant acceleration in the progression of HIV disease. Accelerated HIV progression was not seen in rejection-sensitive subjects who concealed their homosexual identity. Thus, concealment of homosexual identity may be health-protective for gay men high in Rejection Sensitivity, and health-damaging in those low in Rejection Sensitivity. It is noteworthy that these findings were independent of a set of other potentially health-related psychosocial factors that included Negative and Positive Affectivity, depressive symptoms, and the Repressive Coping style.

Emotional Expressiveness and Trauma Disclosure

Personality attributes that involve a tendency toward emotional inexpressiveness have long been studied in relation to physical health (for reviews, see Jorgensen et al., 1996; Scheier &

Bridges, 1995). Of these, the idea of a "cancer-prone," or "Type C" personality that influences the development and course of cancer has the longest history (examined from a psychobiological perspective by Contrada et al., 1990). Conceptual difficulties and measurement problems entailed in separating experiential and expressive aspects of emotion, together with the usual limitations of correlational research, have greatly hindered progress in this area (Contrada & Guyll, in press). For example, it is unclear whether Expressiveness should be measured with reference to particular emotions (e.g., anger, anxiety), or to Negative Affect in general. In addition, expressive styles have variously been conceptualized as involving repression, as in the classic, ego-defensive process; suppression, in the sense of conscious, deliberate efforts to inhibit the experience and/or expression of emotion; and the tendency not to discuss feelings with others, among the many possible orientations toward emotion.

A recently burgeoning body of experimental research may have important implications for understanding health-related aspects of personality that involve emotion expression. This work has evaluated the health effects of an intervention that requires participants to write or talk privately about traumatic events. In a now-classic study (Pennebaker & Beall, 1986), 46 undergraduate students were randomly assigned to an experimental condition in which they were instructed to write about personally traumatic events, or about trivial topics, for sessions on each of four consecutive days. Those in the trauma disclosure condition were encouraged to write about traumatic experiences that they had not discussed with others. Although subjects in the trauma disclosure group experienced higher blood pressure and greater distress, they made significantly fewer visits to the student health center during the ensuing 6 months. This study was followed by several efforts to replicate, extend, and explain the basic findings. A recent meta-analysis conducted by Smyth (1998) indicates that the health-promoting effects of trauma disclosure appear reliable.

It is not clear to what degree trauma disclosure provides a suitable experimental analog for personality attributes involving emotional expressiveness. But this work has generated findings that are highly relevant from a personality perspective. Some of these come from studies in which trauma disclosure has been used to generate a measure of individual differences in Disclosiveness. In one study (Pennebaker, Barger, & Tiebout, 1989), 33 Holocaust survivors described their experiences in concentration camps; thus everyone received a disclosure "intervention." Health was monitored for 14 months after the interview. Those whose narratives were rated by judges as disclosing more traumatic events exhibited fewer health problems during the follow-up period.

A number of studies have sought to explore the psychological mediators of trauma disclosure effects. In one, the text of the traumatic passages was analyzed to identify linguistic predictors of health effects (Pennebaker & Francis, 1996). Participants whose protocols showed increased use of words that seem to reflect insightful thinking experienced the greatest reduction in health center visits. Number of positive affect words also predicted fewer visits. These data suggest that integration of cognitive and affective processes may serve a mediating role in disclosure effects. It is also possible that putting feelings into words illustrates their "shareability" with others (Freyd, 1983), thereby rendering them less threatening to the individual. Another study (Cameron & Nicholls, 1998) tested the effect of instructing subjects to develop coping strategies. The addition of the coping strategy task to the writing instructions did, indeed, lead to a greater reduction in health center visits, though this effect was moderated by Dispositional Optimism (added benefits were seen only among optimists), and the experimental design did not include a condition in which coping instructions were delivered without trauma disclosure. Nonetheless, this study suggests that, at least for some participants, the spontaneous development of coping strategies during the course of writing might mediate the effects of trauma disclosure.

Recently, Pennebaker and Keough (in press) employed self/identity constructs to conceptualize the effects of trauma, emotional inhibition, and disclosure. They began with the premise that traumas produce stress, at least in part, because they threaten central aspects of self-definition (Janoff-Bulman, 1989). The underlying assumption is that, when a person copes with trauma by inhibiting the expression of trauma-related thoughts and experiences, the trauma cannot be assigned meaning and assimilated into the person's self-definition. By contrast, actively confronting trauma may help the person to understand the event and, ultimately, to reappraise it in such a way that it can be assimilated into the self (Harber & Pennebaker, 1992). This process may, in turn, mediate positive psychological and physical health outcomes of trauma disclosure.

Biological factors have been examined as possible mediators of the health effects of trauma disclosure. Early studies examined electrodermal activity because it was thought to provide an index of neurophysiological processes underlying behavioral inhibition (e.g., Pennebaker, Hughes, & O'Heeron, 1987). Potentially of greater relevance for explaining physical health changes are more recent findings involving measures of immunity. Pennebaker, Kiecolt-Glaser, and Glaser (1988) demonstrated that trauma disclosure enhances a parameter of immunity involving proliferative responses of lymphocytes to PHA mitogen, although only among participants whose essays reflected higher Disclosiveness. Other studies have linked individual differences in Disclosiveness (Esterling, Antoni, Kumar, & Schneiderman, 1990), and randomization to a trauma disclosure intervention (Esterling, Antoni, Fletcher, Margulies, & Schneiderman, 1994), to immunological control of latent herpes virus. Immunity to hepatitis B has also been enhanced by written emotional disclosure (Petrie, Booth, Pennebaker, Davison, & Thomas, 1995). Results obtained by Christensen and colleagues (1996) suggest that immune enhancement associated with trauma disclosure may be moderated by Hostility. Following trauma disclosure, there was a significantly greater increment in NK cell activity in high-Hostile students compared to low-Hostile students.

GENERAL CONCEPTUAL THEMES AND ISSUES

Work described in the previous sections attests to the diversity of conceptual and methodological approaches represented in research on personality and health. It also shows that this area of inquiry is still at an early stage of development. Even the study of Type A and Hostility, which is associated with the greatest volume of work and is most advanced from an epidemiologic standpoint, is subject to basic questions about construct definition, risk factor status, and mechanisms of influence on health. In the following sections, we discuss three conceptual issues that have emerged in the study of one or more of the constructs discussed above. These issues have general relevance for the broad range of research and theory concerned with the relationship between personality and health, and involve matters that must be addressed if work in this area is to show progress and integration. They have to do with hierarchical organization in personality, the relationship between personality and stress, and the notions of self, identity, and self-regulation.

Hierarchical Organization

In at least three different ways, recent research on Dispositional Optimism has raised issues involving personality organization and the breadth of personality units that were touched upon earlier in this chapter (see Table 23.2). Perhaps most pertinent are findings such as those of Smith, Pope, Rhodewalt, and Poulton (1989), who found that low scores on Optimism reflect high levels of Neuroticism (or "Negative Affectivity"), and that Neuroticism accounted for the relationship between Optimism and measures of physical symptoms and coping. Also germane are results of the Segerstrom et al. (1998) study, described earlier, in which a measure of Optimism with regard to academic success was significantly associated with better immune functioning in first year law students, whereas Dispositional Optimism was not (for conceptually similar findings involving health outcomes associated with HIV/AIDS, see Reed, Kemeny, Taylor, & Visscher, in press; Reed, Kemeny, Taylor, Wang, & Visscher, 1994). Still another set of relevant observations comes from studies described earlier in which separate scores reflecting Optimism and Pessimism yielded different associations with health-related outcomes (e.g., Räikkönen et al., 1999; Schulz et al. 1996). These results are consistent with factor-analytic findings indicating that Optimism and Pessimism items of the Life Orientation Test often form correlated but separable dimensions rather than opposite poles of the same broad continuum, as originally was expected (e.g., Scheier et al., 1994).

A concern raised by the findings of Smith and colleagues (1989) is that some associations between Dispositional Optimism and physical health indicators may be spurious, reflecting a contaminating relationship between Neuroticism and both predictor and outcome. This process is thought to involve the biasing effects on responses to self-report instruments of the neurotic individual's tendencies toward self-focus and/or negativity—tendencies that may underlie associations linking a number of personality measures to self-report indicators of physical illness (Watson & Pennebaker, 1989). Note, however, that contamination of this sort is less capable of explaining relationships between Optimism and objective (non–self-report) outcomes such as cardiovascular activity (Räikkönen et al., in press) or mortality (Schulz et al., 1996). Nor can it account for data in which statistical control for markers of Neuroticism does not eliminate relationships between Optimism and measures reflecting physical health problems (e.g., Scheier et al., in press).

Whereas the potential contaminating influence of Neuroticism is an important methodological issue, findings such as those of Smith and colleagues (1989) can be seen as raising larger questions about personality theory and research strategy. Even in the case of objective physical health indicators that cannot be confounded by Neuroticism at the measurement level, it is not clear how to interpret the overlapping predictive contributions of Optimism and Neuroticism. This state of affairs may not be confined to Neuroticism: Questions also have been raised about the independence of Dispositional Optimism from other personality factors, such as Self-Esteem and Self-Mastery (Cozzarelli, 1993; but see Scheier et al., 1994). In addition, a similar issue might be raised regarding behavioral correlates of Optimism. In a classic trait interpretation, the engaged coping responses of individuals with high Dispositional Optimism, and the optimistic beliefs that define Optimism at the measurement level, might be seen as behavioral and cognitive manifestations of the very same trait. If so, establishing associations between Optimism and coping would amount to mapping the surface manifestation of a single underlying source trait.

The question of how Optimism is related to Neuroticism and other broad dimensions of personality can be seen as part of the same issue raised by findings such as those of Segerstrom and colleagues (1998) and Reed and colleagues (1994, in press) regarding the relative predictive value of Dispositional and Situational Optimism, and by findings indicating separable dimensions of Optimism and Pessimism: At what level of personality organization should associations with physical disease be sought? Further, what inferences are to be drawn if statistical controls for factors at a high level of abstraction (e.g., Neuroticism) reduce or eliminate associations with health outcomes observed at a lower levels (e.g., Dispositional or Situational Optimism)? Alternatively, what if lower-level factors do predict health independently of higher-level ones? Finally, at any level of abstraction, how should differential results for separate measures of Optimism and Pessimism be explained?

In discussing these issues, Scheier and colleagues (1994) suggest that because a low level of Optimism can be seen as a facet of Neuroticism, it may be misleading to think of Neuroticism as a more basic explanatory factor in research concerned with the health effects of Optimism. In this view, Optimism warrants consideration as a *component* of (low) Neuroticism that may have important effects on physical well-being. Other facets of Neuroticism, such as Emotional Lability, may show a different pattern of associations with adaptive outcomes. Regarding the issue of dimensionality, Robinson-Whelen, Kim, MacCallum, and Kiecolt-Glaser (1997) make a strong case for the distinctiveness of Optimism and Pessimism, at least among middle-aged and older individuals, with Pessimism potentially more important for predicting health outcomes.

There are some parallels here with the progression from interest in the health-damaging effects of a multifaceted, global Type A construct to a focus on Hostility. The trend in the literature is toward increasingly more circumscribed elements (*Neuroticism → Dispositional Optimism → Situational Optimism,* and *global Optimism–Pessimism → Distinctive Optimism and Pessimism constructs*), and those elements are construed in terms of cognitions. One difference is that the Hostility focus that emerged from the study of Type A behavior reflected epidemiologic findings that presented a changing picture of the relationship between Type A/Hostility and coronary heart disease. This might suggest that a focus on Hostility (versus the more global Type A construct) is better justified than that involving Optimism (versus the more global Neuroticism construct). However, as indicated by the T. Q. Miller et al. (1996) review, even at its moderately well-developed stage, the literature on various Hostility-related constructs does not permit rigorous tests of the relative importance of these attributes in promoting physical disease.

The clear implication would seem to be that research on personality and health would benefit from joint consideration of personality units drawn from different levels of organization or abstraction. This begs the question of what model of personality organization to use to guide this research. Marshall, Wortman, Vickers, Kusulas, and Hervig (1994) and Smith and Williams (1992) showed how the five-factor model can be used to represent personality organization in health-related research. More recently, Ouellette (in press) suggested that the study of personality and health might profit by utilizing a three-level model of personality organization described by McAdams (1996). This model utilizes nontrait personality constructs to complement a trait approach. McAdams places traits such as those comprised by the five-factor model at one level of organization, constructs involving personal goals and possible selves at a second ("personal concerns") level of organization, and personal narratives at the third ("identity as a life story") level. Whatever model of personality organization is employed, it will be useful to go beyond analytic methods in which multiple personality predictors simply compete for their shared variance in accounting for health outcomes. Statistical models such as these are useful for research purposes that require the identification of *individual units of personality* that are independent predictors of physical disease. By contrast, methods for simultaneous statistical modeling of multiple levels of personality (e.g., Li, Duncan, Harmer, Acock, & Stoolmiller, 1998) might provide a useful means of representing the relationship between *personality organization* and physical health.

The Personality–Stress Relationship

Not all effects of personality on health involve physiological or behavioral responses to psychological stress, but many do. It is in the nature of the stress and personality constructs that each provides a way of elaborating and explaining the other's role in shaping human adaptation. Research guided by models of the relationship between these two conceptual domains is therefore more likely to foster a comprehensive understanding of psychosocial influences on physical health than is work in which one of these constructs is used to the exclusion of the other.

Much work in the area of personality and health is either implicitly or explicitly guided by a model in which personality interacts with stress. In most applications of this approach, personality is thought to influence health by increasing (or by attenuating) physiologic manifestations of stress. This model is well illustrated by psychophysiologic research on Type A behaviors described earlier in this chapter. However, disease-promoting mechanisms that involve health-damaging behaviors, and the detection and control of physical illness, also may reflect stress-related processes. For example, use of tobacco and alcohol can reflect strategies for coping with life stress (Wills & Hirky, 1996), and psychological responses to symptoms (Matthews et al., 1983) and adaptation to serious illness (Scheier et al., 1989) can be conceptualized as coping responses initiated by health threats.

This model has several distinct, but non–mutually exclusive variants, major elements of which are depicted in Figure 23.1 (see next page). All have been discussed in relation to Type A behaviors/hostility (Contrada et al., 1990; Smith, 1992; Smith & Frohm, 1985; T. Q. Miller et al., 1996; Wiebe & Smith, 1997). However, they have implications for understanding the personality–stress relationship in general, and more broadly, for conceptualizing processes of interplay between person and environment (see Table 23.2). In a "trait–situation interaction model," individuals possessing the personality attribute in question are more (or less) likely to respond with health-damaging physiological or behavioral responses when exposed to stressors. Variations of this model may specify linkages between the personality attribute and particular classes of stressors, as in the notion of the Type A individual's responsivity to threatened loss of control (Glass, 1977), or the idea that hostile individuals are especially responsive to interpersonal threats and challenges (Suarez et al., 1998). These models also may propose specific pathways of interaction between personality and stressors. The latter include the cognitive appraisal of stressors, which may reflect the influence of personality attributes such as Hardiness (Ouellette, in press), and the selection and execution of coping responses, as in the example of Optimism reviewed earlier in this chapter. A third possibility that has received less attention is that personality may influence the evaluation of coping efforts. Through the rose-tinted glasses of Optimism, engaged coping may appear more effective than is actually the case (or than it does to pessimists), and a similar process may influence the hostile person's assessment of the impact of his or her antagonistic interpersonal style. Thus, it may be partly through effects on the evaluation of coping outcomes that personality sustains biases in stressor appraisal and preferences for particular coping strategies (Contrada & Guyll, in press).

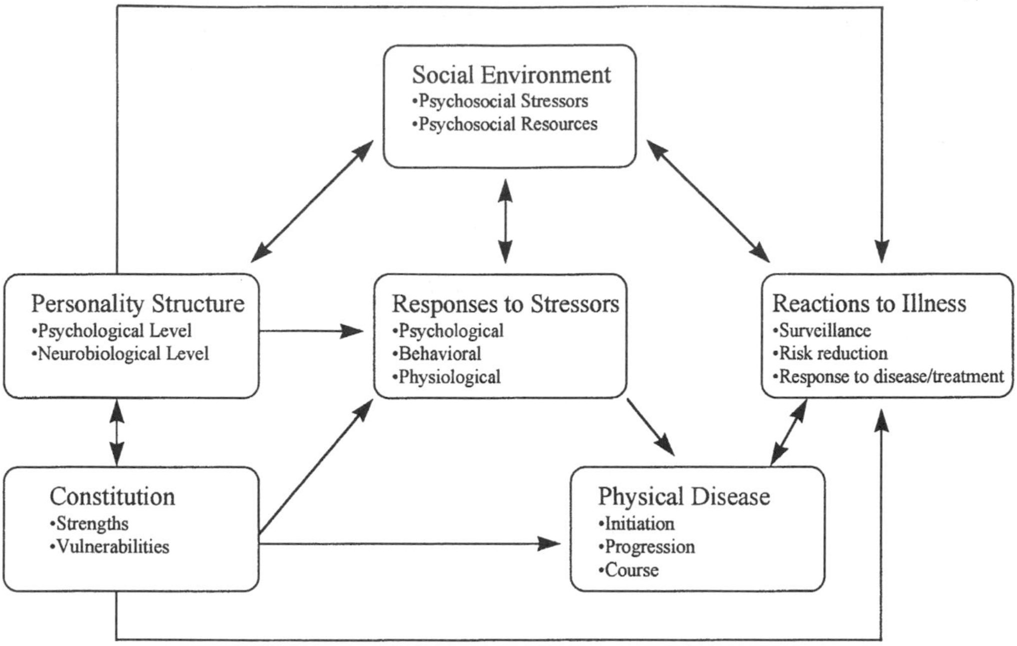

FIGURE 23.1. Some elements of models in which personality influences effects of psychological stress on disease. The bidirectional arrow between personality and social–environmental factors reflects the transactional perspective, which incorporates the simpler trait interaction and psychosocial vulnerability models. The bidirectional arrow between constitution and personality represents the constitutional vulnerability model. Responses to stress and reactions to illness represent processes that explain associations linking personality and stress to physical health outcomes.

A second view of the relationship between personality and stress, the "psychosocial vulnerability model," emphasizes the role of psychosocial factors constributing to the development of health-related personality attributes. For example, in the case of Type A/Hostility, relevant environmental factors may include a low level of social support and a high level of interpersonal stress (Smith, 1992). To the degree that these features of the social context are stable, they would be expected to increase the frequency of occasions in which stressors will provoke health-damaging physiologic and behavioral responses in hostile individuals. Similarly, environmental factors may play a role in determining the frequency with which health-promoting (or health-damaging) processes are activated in individuals characterized by other health-related personality attributes. Unlike the trait–situation interaction model, the psychosocial vulnerability model does not require that personality account for individual differences in psychological or physiological responses to stressors. It would be consistent with the psychosocial vulnerability model if personality interacts with stress solely through its effects on the frequency of occurrence of stressful events.

The trait–situation interaction and psychosocial vulnerability models have been integrated and elaborated into a "transactional model," described by Smith (1989) with reference to Type A/Hostility. In this model, the overt display of antagonism and aggressiveness associated with Type A behavior and Hostility, and their cognitive underpinnings, are viewed as determinants of interpersonal conflict and as factors that undermine social support. These effects of personality on the environment, in turn, increase exposure to stressful conditions and associated bouts of physiologic reactivity and displays of health-damaging coping responses. They also diminish the availability of resources for coping effectively with stress. Over time, this sort of personality–environment transaction may complete a self-fulfilling prophecy by confirming and reinforcing the cynical attitudes that maintain antagonistic and aggressive behavior. As with the trait–situation interaction and psychosocial vulnerability models, the transactional model would seem to have broad relevance for understanding processes linking personality and physical health.

In a manner that parallels the psychosocial vulnerability model, a "constitutional vulnerability model" emphasizes genetic and/or early environmental factors associated with the development of health-related personality attributes. One possible example is physiological toughness, which was mentioned earlier in this chapter. Krantz and Durel (1983) provided another, hypothesizing that a constitutional factor that contributes to individual differences in physiological reactivity to stressors may underlie Type A behaviors. Constitutionally based reactivity may increase coronary risk and, through a somato-psychic process, interact with cognitive structures and situational cues to initiate, promote, and sustain hostile and aggressive behavior. In this model, Type A and Hostility need not be causally linked to disease-promoting processes. The association with disease could be spurious, reflecting the effects of a temperamentally based hyperreactivity of the sympathetic–adrenomedullary system on both behavioral patterns and health. This type of model is particularly relevant for personality attributes with reliable heritability coefficients, whose relationship to health may reflect underlying neurobiological processes involved in the physiologic stress response.

In summary, psychological stress is of central importance to many formulations of the relationship between personality and health. Interaction, transaction, and vulnerability models provide several ways to conceptualize the personality–stress relationship. They all warrant more explicit and deliberate application in the study of personality attributes that have been implicated as contributing to (or protecting against) physical disease. It is unfortunate how little epidemiologic literature has explicitly examined these hypotheses, even in the fairly well-developed, Type A/Hostility area. A similar state of affairs exists in research linking personality to health-related behaviors and reactions to health threats. Stress-related models have been examined in work concerned with physiologic processes linking personality to disease, but virtually all of that work has been confined to the simplest trait–situation interaction model. Moreover, this research has emphasized the demonstration, rather than explanation, of personality by stressor interactions. For example, it remains an open question as to whether psychophysiologic correlates of Type A/Hostility reflect cognitive appraisal, coping, or some other process activated by stressful provocations.

Self, Identity, and Self-Regulation

Consideration of personality organization and the personality–stress interface leads to questions about useful ways to model the relationship between the two. In the absence of an explicit model, research findings can only generate rather barren propositions involving monolithic personality units and a generic notion of psychological stress. For example, the same "Type A" designation has been used to refer both to the cause and to the outcome of a stressful person–situation interaction. To apply even the simple, trait–situation interaction model as an explanatory device, it is necessary to draw connections between units of personality residing at appropriate levels of organization, and specific processes underlying psychological, behavioral, and biological responses to environmental demands. Application of more complex and dynamic conceptions, such as the vulnerability and transaction models, are more challenging. Multiple levels of personality organization need to be represented (e.g., broad traits, narrower cognitive–affective units, dimensions of temperament), and isolated from their environmental correlates (e.g., life stress, unsupportive social networks). In addition to processes involved in responses to stressors, it is necessary to delineate processes whereby stressful environmental situations and conditions are selected, altered, created, and maintained. Because these models entail reciprocal causality between person and environment, measurement strategies and research designs are required that are capable of demonstrating both that personality acts as input to person–environment transactions and that those transactions sustain or modify personality.

The study of personality organization in relation to psychological stress might be facilitated by work guided explicitly by principles of self-regulation and concepts of self and identity. By self-regulation, we refer to theory regarding the evaluation and control of behavior by factors within the person (Bandura, 1986; Scheier & Carver 1985), salient among which are goal constructs such as were discussed earlier in this chapter. Self and identity, also discussed earlier, involve a person's mental representations of self, including but not limited to self-concept, evaluative selves, and social identities (Ashmore & Jussim, 1997; Baumeister, 1998). Although not without exception (e.g., Baumeister, 1997; Higgins, 1997), the study of self/identity constructs such as these, and the study of self-regulation, have largely been pursued separately in health-related research.

It was noted earlier that the role of goals in self-regulation provides a specific basis for conceptualizing relationships between personality and the concepts of cognitive appraisal and coping that are central to psychological stress theory (Lazarus, 1991; Lazarus & Folkman, 1984). In cognitive appraisal, the initiating process in stress and emotion, a person evaluates the implications that environmental demands and constraints hold for personal goals and concerns. The process of coping can be construed as goal-directed cognitive and behavioral activity, aimed, at a general level of analysis, at the goal of altering circumstances giving rise to the initiating appraisal (problem-focused coping), or of ameliorating emotional distress and other subjective concomitants of stress (emotion-focused coping). Coping activity is evaluated through an assessment of the impact of coping responses in relation to coping goals, which may provide feedback that alters the person's perception of the stressor (reappraisal) or leads to an alternative coping strategy. Thus, personality attributes thought to operate as stress moderators might be examined in relation to the content and structure of specific goals that are threatened by life stressors and that initiate, direct, and terminate subsequent coping activity. This approach flows directly from theory surrounding Dispositional Optimism (Carver & Scheier, in press) and, in part, it would involve extending the work of Affleck and colleagues (1998) and Rapkin and colleagues (1994), discussed earlier, to stressors other than physical illness. It might be pursued by investigating trait-like constructs, such as Optimism and Hostility, in relation to goal constructs, such as personal strivings (Emmons, 1989), where the latter are defined and measured in relation to stressful life events and conditions.

Self and identity constructs also may facilitate the development of more detailed conceptual linkages between personality organization and the stress process. Goals involved in the generation of stress may take the form of self-representations, as in that subset of "possible selves" (Markus & Nurius, 1986) that involve desired future states of being, or the self-evaluative standards examined in the Strauman et al. (1993) study described earlier. More generally, life events may be appraised as stressors when they challenge self-definition. This process may operate not only in trauma, as discussed by Pennebaker and Keough (in press), but also when more commonly occurring events—such as divorces, professional set-backs, and medical diagnoses—lead to identity change (e.g., becoming a divorcee, unemployed person, or AIDS patient) and lowered self-regard (Baumeister, 1997; Deaux, 1992; Thoits, 1993). It follows that coping activity, while at some level either problem- or emotion-focused, also may be *self*-focused; that is, directed at repairing, replacing, or reaffirming threatened aspects of self-definition and at bolstering self-esteem (Deaux, 1992).

Self/identity and goal concepts may also guide efforts to move beyond a generic stress construct and toward a more differentiated view of specific emotions in health-related personality processes. Lazarus (1991) described a theoretical perspective in which the implications of events for a person's perception of self/identity, and for valued goals, contribute to the production of qualitatively distinct emotional responses. Strauman and colleagues (1993) showed that distinctive patterns of self-evaluation may be responsible for physiologic changes associated with dysphoria and anxiety. Direct examination of self-representations and goals of individuals characterized by health-related traits such as Optimism/Pessimism, and unmitigated forms of Communion or Agency, might reveal linkages to specific patterns of emotional response. This approach also might shed light on the cognitive underpinnings of coronary-prone behaviors, which appear closely associated with a tendency to experience anger (Contrada et al., 1990). To the degree that self/identity and goal-related cognitions color the subjective quality of specific emotional states provoked by stressful events, and regulate associated coping responses, their examination may allow a more fine-grained understanding of processes whereby particular personality factors contribute to diseases.

As even this brief discussion makes clear, the use of self/identity and self-regulation concepts to examine personality organization in relation to stress requires research that is multivariate, experimental or quasi-experimental, and longitudinal. Multivariate methods are needed to represent multiple units of personality organization, such as traits, self/identity concepts, and situationally referent goals. Experimental and quasi-experimental approaches are required to study stressful events and experimental interventions. Longitudinal designs are needed to capture processes that unfold over time, including psychological and biological responses to stressors, coping, and health-related effects of experimental treatments. With regard to the latter, work on trauma disclosure illustrates how an intervention that requires research participants to confront trauma and emotion may serve both as an experimental probe and as a means of assessing individual differences in disclosiveness. It cannot be assumed that experimental treatments reflect the same psychological processes that are involved in seemingly similar aspects of personality. However, careful appraisal of their value as experimental analogs offers an important opportunity for causal analysis. Experimental interventions also can be used to alter beliefs and coping preferences associated with health-damaging personality attributes, as in work aimed at modifying aspects of Type A behavior to reduce coronary risk (e.g., Bracke & Thoreson, 1996).

CONCLUSION

Personality has become an active and enduring focus of research concerned with psychological aspects of physical health. There have been significant empirical and methodological advances in this area, as well as somewhat more modest conceptual developments. Personality may influence risk for serious health problems, and it appears involved in adaptation to physical disease. Detailed models have been proposed to describe biological, psychological, and behavioral processes that explain relationships between personality and health. Promising strategies for future work include the examination of personality in relation to the biologic correlates of particular cognitions, emotions, and events through "real-time" measurement of psychological and physiological activity. This may make it possible to proceed "upward," from psychological activity most proximal to biologic processes affecting health, to identify the optimal level of abstraction of health-related personality units. In addition to contributing to the understanding, prevention, and control of disease, research along these lines may provide a valuable opportunity to advance and to integrate process and disposition approaches to personality.

ACKNOWLEDGMENTS

We thank Elliott Coups for his helpful comments on an earlier draft of this chapter. Preparation of this chapter was supported by Grant No. AG15160 from the National Institute on Aging.

REFERENCES

Affleck, G., Tennen, H., Urrows, S., Higgins, P., Abeles, M., Hall, C., Karoly, P., & Newton, C. (1998). Fibromyalgia and women's pursuit of personal goals: A daily process analysis. *Health Psychology, 17,* 40–47.

Ashmore, R. D. (1990). Sex, gender, and the individual. In L. A. Pervin (Ed.), *Handbook of personality: Theory and research* (pp. 486–526). New York: Guilford Press.

Ashmore, R. D., & Jussim, L. (1997). Toward a second century of the scientific analysis of self and identity. In R. D. Ashmore & L. Jussim (Eds.), *Self and identity: Fundamental issues* (Vol. 1, pp. 3–19). New York: Oxford University Press.

Bakan, D. (1966). *The duality of human existence.* Chicago: Rand McNally.

Bandura, A. (1986). *Social foundations of thought and action: A social cognitive theory.* Englewood Cliffs, NJ: Prentice Hall.

Barefoot, J., Dodge, K., Peterson, B., Dahlstrom, G., & Williams, R. (1989). The Cook–Medley Hostility Scale: Item content and ability to predict survival. *Psychosomatic Medicine, 51,* 46–57.

Baumeister, R. F. (1997). Esteem threat, self-regulatory breakdown, and emotional distress as factors in self-defeating behavior. *Review of General Psychology, 1,* 145–174.

Baumeister, R. F. (1998). The self. In D. T. Gilbert, S. T. Fiske, & G. Lindzey (Eds.), *The handbook of social psychology* (4th ed., Vol. 2, pp. 680–740). New York: McGraw-Hill.

Bolger, N., Foster, M., Vinokur, A. D., Ng, R. (1996). Close relationships and adjustments to a life crisis: The case of breast cancer. *Journal of Personality and Social Psychology, 70,* 283–294.

Bolger, N., & Schilling, E. A. (1991). Personality and the problems of everyday life: The role of Neuroticism in exposure and reactivity to daily stressors. *Journal of Personality, 59,* 525–537.

Bolger, N., & Zuckerman, A. (1995). A framework for studying personality in the stress process. *Journal of Personality and Social Psychology, 69,* 890–902.

Booth-Kewley, S., & Friedman, H. S. (1987). Psychological predictors of heart disease: A quantitative review. *Psychological Bulletin, 101,* 343–362.

Bowlby, J. (1973). *Attachment and loss: Vol. 2. Separation.* New York: Basic Books.

Bracke, P. E., & Thoreson, C. E. (1996). Reducing Type A behavior patterns: A structured-group approach. In R. Allan & S. Scheidt (Eds.), *Heart and mind: The practice of cardiac psychology* (pp. 255–

290). Washington, DC: American Psychological Association.
Brackett, C. D. & Powell, L. H. (1988). Psychosocial and physiological predictors of sudden cardiac death after healing of acute myocardial infarction. *American Journal of Cardiology, 61,* 979–983.
Brooks-Gunn, J., & Graber, J. A. (in press). What's sex got to do with it? The development of sexual identity during the adolescent years. In R. J. Contrada & R. D. Ashmore (Eds.), *Self, social identity, and physical health: Interdisciplinary explorations.* New York: Oxford University Press.
Cameron, L. D., & Nicholls, G. (1998). Expression of stressful experiences through writing: Effects of a self-regulation manipulation for pessimists and optimists. *Health Psychology, 17,* 84–92.
Cantor, N., & Zirkel, S. (1990). Personality, cognition, and purposive behavior. In L. A. Pervin (Ed.), *Handbook of personality: Theory and research* (pp. 135–164). New York: Guilford Press.
Carver, C. S., Pozo, C., Harris, S. D., Noriega, V., Scheier, M. F., Robinson, D. S., Ketcham, A. S., Moffat, F. L., Jr., & Clark, K. C. (1993). How coping mediates the effect of Optimism on distress: A study of women with early stage breast cancer. *Journal of Personality and Social Psychology, 65,* 375–390.
Carver, C. S., & Scheier, M. F. (in press). Optimism. In C. R. Snyder (Ed.), *Coping: The psychology of what works.* New York: Oxford University Press.
Case, R. B., Heller, S. S., Case, N. B., Moss, A. J., & The Multicenter Post-Infarction Research Group. (1985). Type A behavior and survival after acute myocardial infarction. *New England Journal of Medicine, 312,* 737–741.
Cates, D. S., Houston, B. K., Vavak, C. R., Crawford, M. H., & Uttley, M. (1993). Heritability of hostility-related emotions, attitudes, and behaviors. *Journal of Behavioral Medicine, 16,* 237–256.
Cervone, D. (1997). Social-cognitive mechanisms and personality coherence: Self-knowledge, situational beliefs, and cross-situational coherence in perceived self-efficacy. *Psychological Science, 8,* 43–50.
Christensen, A. J., Edwards, D. L., Wiebe, J. S., Benotsch, E. G., McKelvey, L., Andrews, M., & Lubaroff, D. M. (1996). Effect of self-disclosure on natural killer cell activity: Moderating influence of cynical hostility. *Psychosomatic Medicine, 58,* 150–155.
Cohen, S. B., & Herbert, T. B. (1996). Health psychology: Physiological factors and physical disease from the perspective of human psychoneuroimmunology. *Annual Review of Psychology, 47,* 113–142.
Cole, S. W., Kemeny, M. E., & Taylor, S. E. (1997). Social identity and physical health: Accelerated HIV progression in rejection-sensitive gay men. *Journal of Personality and Social Psychology, 72,* 320–335.
Cole, S. W., Kemeny, M. E., Taylor, S. E., & Visscher, B. R. (1996). Elevated physical health risk among gay men who conceal their homosexuality. *Health Psychology, 15,* 243–251.
Cole, S. W., Kemeny, M. E., Taylor, S. E., Visscher, B. R., & Fahey, J. L. (1996). Accelerated course of human immunodeficiency virus infection in gay men who conceal their homosexual identity. *Psychosomatic Medicine, 58,* 219–231.
Contrada, R. J., Czarnecki, E. M., Pan, R. L-C. (1997). Health-damaging personality traits and verbal-autonomic dissociation: The role of self-control and environmental control. *Health Psychology, 16,* 451–457.
Contrada, R. J., & Guyll, M. (in press). *On who gets sick and why: The role of personality and stress.* To appear in A. Baum, T. A. Revenson, & J. E. Singer (Eds.), *Handbook of health psychology.* Hillsdale, NJ: Erlbaum.
Contrada, R. J., Leventhal, H., & O'Leary, A. (1990). Personality and health. In L. A. Pervin (Ed.), *Handbook of personality: Theory and research* (pp. 638–669). New York: Guilford Press.
Cook, W., & Medley, D. (1954). Proposed hostility and pharisaic-virtue scales for the MMPI. *Journal of Applied Psychology, 38,* 414–418.
Costa, P. T., Somerfield, M. R.., & McCrae, R. R. (1996). Personality and coping: A reconceptualization. In M. Zeidner & N. S. Endler (Eds.), *Handbook coping: Theory, research, applications* (pp. 44–61). New York: Wiley.
Cozzarelli, C. (1993). Personality and self-efficacy as predictors of coping with abortion. *Journal of Personality and Social Psychology, 65,* 1224–1236.
Croyle, R. T. (1992). Appraisal of health threats: Cognition, motivation, and social comparison. *Cognitive Therapy and Research, 16,* 165–182.
Deaux, K. (1992). Focusing on the self: Challenges to self-definition and their consequences for mental health. In D. N. Ruble, P. R. Costanzo, & M. E. Oliveri (Eds.), *The social psychology of mental health: Basic mechanisms and applications* (pp. 301–327). New York: Guilford Press.
Dembroski, T. M., & Czajkowski, S. M. (1989). Historical and current developments in coronary-prone behavior. In A. W. Siegman & T. M. Dembroski (Eds.), *In search of coronary-prone behavior: Beyond Type A* (pp. 21–39). Hillsdale, NJ: Erlbaum.
Dembroski, T. M., MacDougall, J. M., Costa, P. T., Jr., & Grandits, G. A. (1989). Components of hostility as predictors of sudden death and myocardial infarction in the Multiple Risk Factor Intervention Trial. *Psychosomatic Medicine, 51,* 514–522.
Dienstbier, R. A. (1989). Arousal and physiological toughness: Implications for physical and mental health. *Psychological Review, 96,* 84–100.
Doll, R. (1996). Nature and nurture: Possibilities for cancer control. *Carcinogenesis, 17,* 177–184.
Dubos, R. (1965). *Man adapting.* New Haven, CT: Yale University Press.
Emmons, R. A. (1989). The personal striving approach to personality. In L. A. Pervin (Ed.), *Goal concepts in personality and social psychology* (pp. 87–126). Hillsdale, NJ: Erlbaum.

Emmons, R. A. (1992). Abstract versus concrete goals: Personal striving level, physical illness, and psychological well-being. *Journal of Personality and Social Psychology, 62,* 292–300.

Emmons, R. A., & King, L. A. (1988). Conflict among personal strivings: Immediate and long-term implications for psychological and physical well-being. *Journal of Personality and Social Psychology, 54,* 1040–1048.

Engebretson, T. O., Matthews, K. A., & Scheier, M. F. (1989). Relations between anger expression and cardiovascular reactivity: Reconciling inconsistent findings through a matching hypothesis. *Journal of Personality and Social Psychology, 57,* 513–521.

Engel, G. L. (1977). The need for a new medical model: A challenge for biomedicine. *Science, 196,* 129–136.

Esterling, B. A., Antoni, M. H., Fletcher, M. A., Margulies, S., & Schneiderman, N. (1994). Emotional disclosure through writing or speaking modulates latent Epstein–Barr virus antibody titers. *Journal of Consulting and Clinical Psychology, 62,* 130–140.

Esterling, B. A., Antoni, M. H., Kumar, M., & Schneiderman, N. (1990). Emotional repression, stress disclosure responses, and Epstein-Barr viral capsid antigen titers. *Psychosomatic Medicine, 52,* 397–410.

Eysenck, H. J. (1967). *The biological bases of personality.* Springfield, IL: Charles C. Thomas.

Freyd, J. J. (1983). Shareability: The social psychology of epistemology. *Cognitive Science, 7,* 191–210.

Friedman, M., & Rosenman, R. H. (1974). *Type A behavior and your heart.* New York: Knopf.

Glass, D. C. (1977). *Behavior patterns, stress, and coronary disease.* Hillsdale, NJ: Erlbaum.

Gottlieb, G. (1998). Normally occurring environmental and behavioral influences on gene activity: From central dogma to probabilistic epigenesis. *Psychological Review,* 105, 792–802.

Guyll, M., & Contrada, R. J. (1998). Trait hostility and ambulatory cardiovascular activity in males and females. *Health Psychology, 17,* 30–39.

Harber, K. D., & Pennebaker, J. W. (1992). Overcoming traumatic memories. In S. Christianson (Ed.), *The handbook of emotion and memory research and theory* (pp. 359–387). Hillsdale, NJ: Erlbaum.

Heidrich, S. M., Forsthoff, C. A., & Ward, S. E. (1994). Psychological adjustment in adults with cancer: The self as mediator. *Health Psychology, 13,* 346–353.

Helgeson, V. S. (1990). The role of masculinity in a prognostic predictor of heart attack severity. *Sex Roles, 22,* 755–774.

Helgeson, V. S. (1994). Relation of agency and communion to well-being: Evidence and potential explanations. *Psychological Bulletin, 116,* 412–428.

Helgeson, V. S., & Fritz, H. L. (in press). A theory of unmitigated communion. *Personality and Social Psychology Review.*

Helgeson, V. S., & Lepore, S. J. (1997). Men's adjustment to prostate cancer: The role of Agency and unmitigated Agency. *Sex Roles, 37,* 251–267.

Helmers, K. F., Krantz, D. S., Bairey Merz, C. N., Klein, J., Kop, W. J., Gottdiener, J. S., & Rozanski, A. (1995). Defensive hostility: Relationship to multiple markers of cardiac ischemia in patients with coronary disease. *Health Psychology, 14,* 202–209.

Hemenover, S. H., & Dienstbier, R. A. (1996). The effects of an appraisal manipulation: Affect, intrusive cognitions, and performance for two cognitive tasks. *Motivation and Emotion, 20,* 319–340.

Herbert, T. B., & Cohen, S. (1993a). Depression and immunity: A meta-analytic review. *Psychological Bulletin, 113,* 472–486.

Herbert, T. B., & Cohen, S. (1993b). Stress and immunity in humans: A meta-analytic review. *Psychosomatic Medicine, 55,* 364–379.

Higgins, E. T. (1987). Self-discrepancy: A theory relating self and affect. *Psychological Review, 94,* 319–340.

Higgins, E. T. (1997). Beyond pleasure and pain. *American Psychologist, 52,* 1280–1300.

Houston, B. K., & Vavak, C. R. (1991). Hostility: Developmental factors, psychosocial correlates, and health behaviors. *Health Psychology, 10,* 9–17.

James, W. (1890). *Principles of psychology.* New York: Holt.

Janoff-Bulman, R. (1989). Assumptive worlds and the stress of traumatic events: Applications of the schema construct. *Social Cognition, 7,* 113–136.

Jorgensen, R. S., Gelling, P. D., Kliner, L. (1992). Patterns of social desirability and anger in young men with a parental history of hypertension: Association with cardiovascular activity. *Health Psychology, 11,* 403–412.

Jorgensen, R. S., Johnson, B. T., Kolodziej, M. E., Schreer, G. E. (1996). Elevated blood pressure and personality: A meta-analytic review. *Psychological Bulletin, 120,* 293–320.

Kalichman, S. (1995). *Understanding AIDS.* Washington, DC: American Psychological Association.

Kamada, T., Miyake, S., Kumashiro, M., Monou, H., & Inoue, K. (1992). Power spectral analysis of heart rate variability in Type As and Type Bs during mental workload. *Psychosomatic Medicine, 54,* 462–470.

Kamarck, T. W., Everson, S. A., Kaplan, G. A., Manuck, S. B., Jennings, J. R., Salonen, R., & Salonen, J. T. (1997). Exaggerated blood pressure responses during mental stress are associated with enhanced carotid atherosclerosis in middle-aged Finnish men: Findings from the Kuopio Ischemic Heart Disease Study. *Circulation, 96,* 3842–3848.

Koskenvou, M., Kapiro, J., Rose, R. J., Kesnaiemi, A., Sarnaa, S., Heikkila, K., & Langinvanio, H. (1988). Hostility as a risk factor for mortality and ischemic heart disease in men. *Psychosomatic Medicine, 50,* 330–340.

Krantz, D. S., & Durel, L. A. (1983). Psychobiological substrates of the Type A behavior pattern. *Health Psychology, 2,* 393–411.

Krantz, D. S., Glass, D. C., Contrada, R. J., and Miller, N. E. (1981). Behavior and health. In National Science Foundation, *Five year outlook on science and technology: 1981 Source materials* (Vol. 2, pp. 561–

588). Washington, DC: U.S. Government Printing Office.

Krantz, D. S., & Manuck, S. B. (1984). Acute psychophysiologic reactivity and risk of cardiovascular disease: A review and methodological critique. *Psychological Bulletin, 96,* 435–464.

Lazarus, R. S. (1991). *Emotion and adaptation.* New York: Oxford University Press.

Lazarus, R. S., & Folkman, S. (1984). *Stress, appraisal, and coping.* New York: Springer.

Lester, N., Smart, L., & Baum, A. (1994). Measuring coping flexibility. *Psychology and Health, 9,* 409–424.

Li, F., Duncan, T. E., Harmer, P., Acock, A., Stoolmiller, M. (1998). Analyzing measurement models of latent variables through multilevel confirmatory factor analysis and hierarchical linear modeling approaches. *Structural Equation Modeling, 5,* 294–306.

Loehlin, J. C. (1992). *Genes and environment in personality development.* Newbury Park, CA: Sage.

Lynch, D. J., Birk, T. J., Weaver, M. T., Gohara, A. F., Leighton, R. F., Eppka, F. J., & Walsh, M. E. (1992). Adherence to exercise interventions in the treatment of hypercholesterolemia. *Journal of Behavioral Medicine, 15,* 365–377.

Lyness, S. A. (1993). Predictors of differences between Type A and B individuals in heart rate and blood pressure reactivity. *Psychological Bulletin, 114,* 266–295.

Maier, S. F., & Watkins, L. R. (1998). Cytokines for psychologists: Implications of bidirectional immune-to-brain communication for understanding behavior, mood, and cognition. *Psychological Review, 105,* 83–107.

Manuck, S. B., Marsland, A. L., Kaplan, J. R., & Williams, J. K. (1995). The pathogenicity of behavior and its neuroendocrine mediation: An example from coronary artery disease. *Psychosomatic Medicine, 57,* 275–283.

Markovitz, J. H., Matthews, K. A., Kiss, J., & Smitherman, T. C. (1996). Effects of hostility on platelet reactivity to psychological stress in coronary heart disease patients and in healthy controls. *Psychosomatic Medicine, 58,* 143–149.

Markus, H., & Nurius, P. (1986). Possible selves. *American Psychologist, 41,* 954–969.

Marshall, G. N., Wortman, C. B., Vickers, R. R., Kusulas, J. W., & Hervig, L. K. (1994). The five-factor model of personality as a framework for personality-health research. *Journal of Personality and Social Psychology, 67,* 278–286.

Mason, J. W. (1972). Organization of psychoendocrine mechanisms. In N. S. Greenfield and R. A. Sternbach (Eds.), *Handbook of psychophysiology* (pp. 3–121). New York: Holt, Rinehart & Winston.

Matthews, K. A. (1988). CHD and Type A behaviors: Update on and alternative to the Booth-Kewley and Friedman quantitative review. *Psychological Bulletin, 104,* 373–380.

Matthews, K. A., Glass, D. C., Rosenman, R. H., & Bortner, R. W. (1977). Competitive drive, Pattern A, and coronary heart disease: A further analysis of some data from the Western Collaborative Group Study. *Journal of Chronic Diseases, 30,* 489–498.

Matthews, K. A, Siegel, J. M., Kuller, L. H., Thompson, M., & Varat, M. (1983). Determinants of decisions to seek medical treatment by patients with acute myocardial infarction symptoms. *Journal of Personality and Social Psychology, 44,* 1144–1156.

McAdams, D. P. (1996). Personality, modernity, and the storied self: A contemporary framework for studying persons. *Psychological Inquiry, 7,* 295–321.

Miller, S. M., Shoda, Y., & Hurley, K. (1996). Applying cognitive-social theory to health-protective behavior: Breast self-examination in cancer screening. *Psychological Bulletin, 119,* 70–94.

Miller, T. Q., Smith, T. W., Turner, C. W., Guijarro, M. L., & Hallet, A. J. (1996). A meta-analytic review of research on hostility and physical health. *Psychological Bulletin, 119,* 322–348.

Mischel, W. & Shoda, Y. (1998). Reconciling processing dynamics and personality dispositions. *Annual Review of Psychology, 49,* 229–258.

Myers, J. R, Henderson-King, D. H., & Henderson-King, E. I. (1997). Facing technological risks: The importance of individual differences. *Journal of Research in Personality, 31,* 1–20.

Myrtek, M. (1995). Type A behavior pattern, personality factors, disease, and physiological reactivity: A meta-analytic update. *Personality and Individual Differences, 18,* 491–502.

Nicassio, P. M., & Smith, T. W. (Eds.) (1995). *Managing chronic illness: A biopsychosocial perspective.* Washington, DC: American Psychological Association.

Obrist, P. A. (1981). *Cardiovascular psychophysiology: A perspective.* New York: Plenum Press.

Ockene, I. S., & Ockene, J. K. (1992). *Prevention of coronary heart disease.* Boston: Little, Brown.

Ouellette, S. C. (in press). The relationship between personality and health: What self and identity have to do with it. In R. J. Contrada & R. D. Ashmore (Eds.), *Self, social identity, and physical health: Interdisciplinary explorations.* New York: Oxford University Press.

Ouellette, S. C., & DiPlacido, J. (in press). Personality's role in the protection and enhancement of health: Where the research has been, where it is stuck, how might it move. In A. Baum, T. A. Revenson, & J. E. Singer (Eds.), *Handbook of health psychology.* Hillsdale, NJ: Erlbaum.

Park, C. L., Moore, P. J., Turner, R. A., & Adler, N. E. (1997). The roles of constructive thinking and Optimism in psychological and behavioral adjustment during pregnancy. *Journal of Personality and Social Psychology, 73,* 584–592.

Pennebaker, J. W., Barger, S. D., & Tiebout, J. (1989). Disclosure of traumas and health among Holocaust survivors. *Psychosomatic Medicine, 51,* 577–589.

Pennebaker, J. W., & Beall, S. K. (1986). Confronting a traumatic event: Toward an understanding of inhibition and disease. *Journal of Abnormal Psychology, 95,* 274–281.

Pennebaker, J. W., & Francis, M. E. (1996). Cognitive, emotional, and language processes in disclosure. *Cognition and Emotion, 10,* 601–626.

Pennebaker, J. W., Hughes, C. F., & O'Heeron, R. C. (1987). The psychophysiology of confession: Linking inhibitory and psychosomatic processes. *Journal of Personality and Social Psychology, 52,* 781–793.

Pennebaker, J. W., and Keough, K. A. (in press). Revealing, organizing, and reorganizing the self in response to stress and emotion. In R. J. Contrada & R. D. Ashmore (Eds.), *Self, social identity, and physical health: Interdisciplinary explorations.* New York: Oxford University Press.

Pennebakcr, J. W., Kiecolt-Glaser, J. K., & Glaser, R. (1988). Disclosure of traumas and immune function: Health implications for psychotherapy. *Journal of Consulting and Clinical Psychology, 56,* 239–245.

Pervin, L. A. (Ed.). (1989). *Goal concepts in personality and social psychology.* Hillsdale, NJ: Erlbaum.

Petrie, K. J, Booth, R. J., Pennebaker, J. W, Davison, K. P., & Thomas, M. G. (1995). Disclosure of trauma and immune response to a hepatitis B vaccination program. *Journal of Consulting and Clinical Psychology, 63,* 787–792.

Pinkerton, S. D., & Abramson, P. R. (1995). Decision making and personality factors in sexual risk-taking for HIV/AIDS: A theoretical integration. *Personality and Individual Differences, 19,* 713–723.

Plomin, R. Scheier, M. F., Bergeman, C. S., Pedersen, N. L., & Nesselroade, J. R. (1992). Optimism, Pessimism and mental health: A twin/adoption analysis. *Personality and Individual Differences, 13,* 921–930.

Price, V. A. (1982). *Type A behavior pattern: A model for research and practice.* New York: Academic Press.

Ragland, D. R., & Brand, R. J. (1988). Type A behavior and mortality from coronary heart disease. *The New England Journal of Medicine, 318,* 65–69.

Räikkönen, K., Matthews, K. A., Flory, J. D., Owens, J. F., & Gump, B. (1999). Effects of Optimism, Pessimism, and trait anxiety on ambulatory blood pressure and mood during everyday life using experiential sampling method. *Journal of Personality and Social Psychology, 76,* 104–113.

Rapkin, B. D., Smith, M. Y., Dumont, K., Correa, A., Palmer, S., & Cohen, S. (1994). Development of the idiographic functional status assessment: A measure of the personal goals and goal attainment activities of people with AIDS. *Psychology and Health, 9,* 111–129.

Reed, G. M., Kemeny, M. E., Taylor, S. E., & Visscher, B. R. (in press). Negative HIV-specific expectancies and AIDS-related bereavement as predictors of symptom onset in asymptomatic HIV-positive gay men. *Health Psychology.*

Reed, G. M., Kemeny, M. E., Taylor, S. E., Wang, H-Y, J., & Visscher, B. R. (1994). Realistic acceptance as a predictor of decreased survival time in gay men with AIDS. *Health Psychology, 13,* 299–307.

Rhodewalt, F., & Fairfield, M. (1990). An alternative approach to Type A behavior and health: Reactance and medical noncompliance. *Journal of Social Behavior and Personality, 5,* 323–342.

Robinson-Whelen, S., Kim, C., MacCallum, R. C., & Kiecolt-Glaser, J. K. (1997). Distinguishing Optimism from Pessimism in older adults: Is it more important to be optimistic or not to be pessimistic? *Journal of Personality and Social Psychology, 73,* 1345–1353.

Rose, R. J. (1992). Genes, stress, and cardiovascular reactivity. In R. J. Turner, A. Sherwood, & K. C. Light (Eds.), *Individual differences in cardiovascular response to stress* (pp. 87–102). New York: Plenum Press.

Russell, D. W., Booth, B., Reed, D., & Laughlin, P. R. (1997). Personality, social networks, and perceived social support among alcoholics: A structural equation analysis. *Journal of Personality, 65,* 649–692.

Ryff, C. D., & Singer, B. (1998). The contours of positive human health. *Psychological Inquiry, 9,* 1–28.

Sapolsky, R. M. (1992). *Stress: The aging brain and the mechanisms of neuron death.* Cambridge, MA: MIT Press.

Scheier, M. F., & Bridges, M. W. (1995). Person variables and health: Personality predispositions and acute psychological states as shared determinants for disease. *Psychosomatic Medicine, 57,* 255–268.

Scheier, M. F., & Carver, C. S. (1985). Optimism, coping, and health: Assessment and implications of generalized outcome expectancies. *Health Psychology, 4,* 219–247.

Scheier, M. F., Carver, C. S., & Bridges, M. W. (1994). Distinguishing Optimism from Neuroticism (and trait anxiety, self-mastery, and self-esteem): A reevaluation of the Life Orientation Test. *Journal of Personality and Social Psychology, 67,* 1063–1078.

Scheier, M. F., Matthews, K. A., Owens, J. F., Magovern, G. J., Lefebvre, R. C., Abott, R. A., & Carver, C. S. (1989). Dispositional Optimism and recovery from coronary artery bypass surgery: The beneficial effects on physical and psychological well-being. *Journal of Personality and Social Psychology, 57,* 1024–1040.

Scheier, M. F., Matthews, K. A., Owens, J. F., Schulz, R., Bridges, M. W., Magovern, G. J., & Carver, C. S. (in press). Optimism and rehospitalization following coronary artery bypass graft surgery. *Archives of Internal Medicine.*

Scheier, M. F., Weintraub, J. K., & Carver, C. S. (1986). Coping with stress: Divergent strategies of optimists and pessimists. *Journal of Personality and Social Psychology, 51,* 1257–1264.

Schulz, R., Bookwala, J., Knapp, J. E., Scheier, M. F., Williamson, G. M. (1996). Pessimism, age, and cancer mortality. *Psychology and Aging, 11,* 304–309.

Schwartz, C. E., Peng, C-K, Lester, N., & Daltroy, L., & Goldberger, A. L. (1998). Self-reported coping behavior in health and disease: Assessment with card sort game. *Behavioral Medicine, 24,* 41–44.

Schwartz, J. E, & Stone, A. A. (1998). Strategies for analyzing ecological momentary assessment data. *Health Psychology, 17,* 6–16.

Segerstrom, S. C., Taylor, S. E., Kemeny, M. E., & Fahey, J. L. (1998). Optimism is associated with mood, coping and immune change in response to stress. *Journal of Personality and Social Psychology, 74,* 1646–1655.

Sheldon, K. M., & Kasser, T. (1995). Coherence and congruence: Two aspects of personality integration. *Journal of Personality and Social Psychology, 68,* 531–543.

Siegler, I. C. (1994). Hostility and risk: Demographic and lifestyle variables. In A. W. Siegman & T. W. Smith (Eds.), *Anger, hostility, and the heart* (pp. 199–214). Hillsdale, NJ: Erlbaum.

Smith, T. W. (1989). Interactions, transactions, and the Type A pattern: Additional avenues in the search for coronary-prone behavior. In A. W. Siegman & T. M. Dembroski (Eds.), *In search of coronary-prone behavior* (pp. 91–116). Hillsdale, NJ: Erlbaum.

Smith, T. W. (1992). Hostility and health: Current status of a psychosomatic hypothesis. *Health Psychology, 11,* 139–150.

Smith, T. W. (1994). Concepts and methods in the study of anger, hostility, and health. In A. W. Siegman & T. W. Smith (Eds.), *Anger, hostility and the heart* (pp. 23–42). Hillsdale, NJ: Erlbaum.

Smith, T. W., & Frohm, K. D. (1985). What's so unhealthy about Hostility? Construct validity and psychosocial correlates of the Cook and Medley Ho scale. *Health Psychology, 4,* 503–520.

Smith, T. W., Pope, M. K., Rhodewalt, F., Poulton, J. L. (1989). Optimism, Neuroticism, coping, and symptom reports: An alternative interpretation of the Life Orientation Test. *Journal of Personality and Social Psychology, 56,* 640–648.

Smith, T. W., & Williams, P. G. (1992). Personality and health: Advantages and limitations of the five-factor model. *Journal of Personality, 60,* 395–423.

Smyth, J. M. (1998). Written emotional expression: Effect sizes, outcome types, and moderating variables. *Journal of Consulting and Clinical Psychology, 66,* 174–184.

Spence, J. T., Helmreich, R. L., & Holahan, C. K. (1979). Negative and positive components of psychological masculinity and femininity and their relationship to self-reports of neurotic and acting out behaviors. *Journal of Personality and Social Psychology, 37,* 1673–1682.

Spilker, B. (Ed.). (1996). *Quality of life and pharmacoeconomics in clinical trials.* Philadelphia: Lippincott-Raven.

Strack, S., Carver, C. S., & Blaney, P. H. (1987). Predicting successful completion of an aftercare program following treatment for alcoholism: The role of Dispositional Optimism. *Journal of Personality and Social Psychology, 53,* 579–584.

Strauman, T. J., Lemieux, A. M., & Coe, C. L. (1993). Self-discrepancy and natural killer cell activity: Immunological consequences of negative self-evaluation. *Journal of Personality and Social Psychology, 64,* 1042–1052.

Strube, M. J. (1987). A self-appraisal model of the Type A behavior pattern. In R. Hogan & W. H. Jones (Eds.), *Perspectives in personality: Theory, measurement and interpersonal dynamics* (pp. 201–250). Greenwich, CT: JAI press.

Suarez, E. C., Kuhn, C. M., Schanberg, S. M., Williams, R. B., Jr., & Zimmermann, E. A. (1998). Neuroendocrine, cardiovascular, and emotional responses of hostile men: The role of interpersonal challenge. *Psychosomatic Medicine, 60,* 78–88.

Suls, J., & Fletcher, B. (1985). The relative efficacy of avoidant and nonavoidant coping strategies: A meta-analysis. *Health Psychology, 4,* 249–288.

Suls, J. & Wan, C. K. (1993). The relationship between trait hostility and cardiovascular reactivity: A quantitative review and analysis. *Psychophysiology, 30,* 615–626.

Suls, J., Wan, C. K., & Costa, P. T. (1995). Relationship of trait anger to resting blood pressure: A meta-analysis. *Health Psychology, 14,* 444–456.

Taylor, S. E., Kemeny, M. E., Aspinwall, L. G., Schneider, S. G., Rodriguez, R., & Herbert, M. (1992). Optimism, coping, psychological distress, and high-risk sexual behavior among men at risk for acquired immunodeficiency syndrome (AIDS). *Journal of Personality and Social Psychology, 63,* 460–473.

Thoits, P. A. (1993). On merging identity theory and stress research. *Social Psychology Quarterly, 54,* 101–112.

Thoits, P. A., & Virshup, L. K. (1997). Me's and we's: Forms and functions of social identities. In R. D. Ashmore & L. Jussim (Eds.), *Self and identity: Fundamental issues* (Vol. 1, pp. 106–133). New York: Oxford University Press.

Turkheimer, E. (1998). Heritability and biological explanation. *Psychological Review, 105,* 782–791.

Watson, D., & Pennebaker, J. W. (1989). Health complaints, stress, and distress: Exploring the central role of negative affectivity. *Psychological Review, 96,* 234–254.

Wiebe, D. J., & Smith, T. W. (1997). Personality and health: Progress and problems in psychosomatics. In R. Hogan, J. Johnson, & S. Briggs (Eds.), *Handbook of personality psychology* (pp. 891–918). New York: Academic Press.

Williams, R. D., Riels, A. G., Roper, K. A. (1990). Optimism and distractibility in cardiovascular reactivity. *Psychological Record, 40,* 451–457.

Wills, T. A., & Hirky, A. E. (1996). Coping and substance abuse: A theoretical model and review of the evidence. In M. Zeidner & N. S. Endler (Eds.), *Handbook of coping: Theory, research, applications* (pp. 279–302). New York: Wiley.

Chapter 24

Attribution in Personality Psychology

Bernard Weiner and Sandra Graham
University of California, Los Angeles

Attribution theory is concerned with causal inferences, or the perceived reason(s) an event has occurred. Thus, attribution theorists attempt to resolve how individuals answer questions such as: "Why has Mary rejected my proposal?" or "Has Bill intentionally harmed me?" and so forth. The originator of this conceptual approach, Fritz Heider, and subsequent key contributors, including Edward Jones and Harold Kelley, are social psychologists. Their primary interests in interpersonal relations and social behavior were greatly illuminated when they took into account the replies to the queries posed above. However, causal issues are as much a concern to personality psychologists as to social psychologists. For instance, answers to a question such as "Why have I failed?" surely can affect self-esteem (consider the consequences of the answer "I am stupid"). In addition, self-esteem is likely to influence the answer to that question. In this example, the intersection of attribution theory and personality psychology is evident. Our task in this chapter is to document that attributional analyses have contributed much to the understanding of problems that lie at the very heart of personality psychology. Indeed, it could readily be argued that attribution theory is as central to personality psychology as it is to social psychology.

To accomplish our goal, it is helpful to employ a distinction invoked by Kelley and Michela (1980) in their review of the attribution literature. They state that the linkage between antecedents and causal inferences, a stimulus–organism (S–O) connection, be labeled "the attribution process," and that the relation between causal inferences and the organism's responses to those constructions (O–R) be called "the attributional process." The attribution process pertains to how causal inferences are reached—that is, how one knows. As such, the attribution process relates to epistemology. Attributional processes, on the other hand, refer to "So what?" That is, given a causal inference, what are its implications for future thought and action? Attributional processes thus relate to function. Attribution theory, which includes both attribution and attributional processes, therefore may be considered a cognitive functionalism. Guided by the S–O versus O–R distinction, this chapter is divided into two main sections. The first section considers the attribution process; the second section examines the attributional process. Three topics of interest to personality psychologists are addressed in the first section:

1. The effects of self-involvement on causal inferences. Inasmuch as the self may be perceived as a causal agent, biases are possible, and causal attributions become linked with mechanisms of defense.
2. The effects of the perspective of the person (actor or observer) on causal inferences. This issue has implications for the perceived normativeness of behavior and for conceptions of traits. The trait versus state distinction in personality theory also finds correspondence and empirical support in attribution language.
3. The existence of individual differences in both the process and content of causal inferences. It has been contended that there are enduring tendencies or inclinations toward particular causal perceptions. If so, then attributional predispositions may be considered cognitive traits.

The functional consequences of causal ascriptions are considered in the second section. It will be seen that behavioral dynamics are guided to a surprising extent by causal ascriptions. Behavioral dynamics are one of the main subthemes (along with structure and development) of the field of personality, so that any theory shedding light on the dynamics of behavior is also in part a theory of personality. The topics examined in the second section include:

1. The role of attributions in self-esteem maintenance.
2. Attribution–affect linkages and attributional approaches to emotion.
3. The mediating influence of causal ascriptions on the dynamics of prosocial and antisocial behavior.

In sum, attribution theorists have addressed a daunting array of topics that are pertinent to personality psychology. Because one of our aims in this chapter is breadth of coverage, each theme is examined, but in less depth than the cited authors would consider sufficient.

THE ATTRIBUTION PROCESS: DETERMINANTS OF CAUSAL PERCEPTIONS

One of the very early issues of concern to researchers in social cognition generally, and to attribution theorists more specifically, was whether the perception of people obeys the same rules as the perception of objects. Heider (1958), for example, contended that "many of the principles underlying social perception have parallels in the field of nonsocial or thing perception" (p. 21). However, he and others certainly acknowledged some differences in perceptual rules, given that people but not objects are interactive with the perceiver, evaluate the perceiver, express emotions, and so on. In a similar vein, questions were raised about the similarity of the rules of other-perception and self-perception. Again, there was recognition of both differences and congruence, with differences of particular interest to personality psychologists, and similarities of greater concern to social psychologists.

The most influential and enduring conceptual approach to the formation of causal ascriptions has been offered by Kelley (1967, 1971). As a social psychologist, he is more concerned with general rules than with possible differences when judging the self as opposed to judging others. Kelley, like others before him, presumes that covariation is the foundation of the attribution process, and he likens the ascription of causality to the more formal statistical procedures employed by scientists.

Assume, for example, that an individual enjoys a movie. A question then raised is whether the enjoyment is to be attributed to the person (e.g., he or she is easily pleased) or to the perceived properties of the entity (it is a good movie). Kelley (1967) reasons that the responsible factor is primarily determined by examining the covariation of the effect and the causal factors over (1) entities (movies), (2) persons (other viewers of the movie), and (3) time (the same person on repeated exposures). Attribution of enjoyment to the entity rather than to the person (or self) is more likely if the individual responds differentially to movies, if the response to this movie is consistent over time, and if the response agrees with the social consensus of others. Thus, the probability of attribution to the movie is maximized when the individual enjoys only that movie, he or she enjoys it on repeated occasions, and others also like the movie. On the other hand, if the individual likes all movies (i.e., his or her response to the entity is not distinctive), and if no one else likes this particular movie (i.e., there is low consensus), then enjoyment would be attributed to characteristics of the viewer (e.g., he or she is a movie cultist). Another way of describing this process is to propose that the causal factor is different or not part of the generalization being made. Hence, if only Person *X* likes a movie, or if Person *X* likes all movies except Film *Y*, then the perceived causal factors are the person and the movie, respectively (see Hewstone & Jaspars, 1987; Hilton & Slugoski, 1986). These patterns have been for the most part empirically substantiated in many investigations (see Kelley & Michela, 1980). However, complex issues remain about how and under what circumstances people actually use covariation principles, and what information is needed to reach causal judgments, although these issues may be of more concern to cognitive psychology than to personality or social psychology (see, e.g., Hilton, Smith, & Kim, 1995; Cheng & Novick, 1990; Van Overwalle, 1998).

In other early formulations related to the attribution process (say, during the 1970–1980 decade), the study of differences between self- and other-perception was dominant. The labels of two of the most popular topics stressing disparities are the "hedonic bias" and the "actor versus observer perspective."

The Hedonic Bias

The hedonic bias (or error) also is known as the "self-serving attribution bias," "ego enhancement," "ego defensiveness," and "beneffectance." The concept refers to the tendency to take credit for success and/or to attribute failure to factors external to the self (e.g., "I succeeded because I am smart but failed because the teacher is biased," or "I succeeded because I worked hard but failed because the economy is bad"). It is presumed that this pattern of ascriptions maximizes the pleasure linked with success and minimizes the pain generated by failure. Hence, the hedonic bias is one manifestation of the underlying pleasure–pain principle of personality and motivation most often associated with Freudian thinking and philosophers such as Jeremy Bentham. Other hedonic attribution patterns also are possible, such as ascribing success to permanent (stable) factors and failure to temporary or unstable causes. However, differences in the perceived locus of causality (internal or external to the actor) have been the focus of attention in examinations of hedonic or motivational influences on perceived causality. Many personality theorists have contended that we are motivated to see ourselves in a positive light. However, Heider (1958) first applied this principle to the formation of causal ascriptions, suggesting that the perceived reasons for an event or outcome tend to "fit the wishes" of the person. In opposition to the cognitive antecedents outlined by Kelley and the presumed rationality of the attribution process, the hedonic bias intimates that causal beliefs also are determined by "irrational" forces, or by rationalization as well as rationality. Dynamically oriented psychologists have embraced the idea of a self-serving bias, and a large experimental literature has emerged examining this phenomenon.

The vast majority of self-serving bias investigations has taken place in achievement-related contexts, in which success and failure can be manipulated or readily ascertained. The data convincingly document the existence of the proposed bias (see reviews by Bradley, 1978; Mullen & Riordan, 1988; Zuckerman, 1979). For example, prototypical studies in achievement-related contexts have revealed that in athletic settings, players in a competitive game attribute their wins to skill and effort and their losses to bad luck (Snyder, Stephan, & Rosenfield, 1976); in school environments, teachers ascribe improved performance of students to good teaching, but lack of improvement to students' low ability and/or lack of effort (Beckman, 1970; Johnson, Feigenbaum, & Weiby, 1964; McAllister, 1996); and in gambling situations, following a loss but not a win, gamblers search for possible external reasons (Gilovich, 1983). Similar findings also have been observed in the political arena. For example, politicians ascribe victories to personal characteristics but losses to party label (Kingdon, 1967). So prevalent is this bias that at an earlier date, one of us suggested that mere documentation may not be of great value: "In the face of overwhelming evidence that behavior is a function of both the id and the ego (wishes and reality), it seems impossible that motivated inferential errors do not exist. And everyday observations often reveal instances of mass personal delusion!" (Weiner, 1980, p. 297).

Implications for Personality

The hedonic bias, when mediated by motivational processes, has the function of maintaining a positive affective state for the individual. It has been proposed that a positive view of the self and a positive mood state are necessary for adaptation and for persistence toward goals (see Taylor & Brown, 1988). Thus, this is a very central ego mechanism, deserving more study within the larger framework of other possible self-enhancing and self-protective mechanisms.

However, as with other defenses, the possibility of maladaptive use exists, so that the organism ultimately is more harmed than benefited from hedonic biasing. For example, individuals may engage in self-defeating (self-handicapping) behavior to avoid attributions for failure to low ability (e.g., Jones & Berglass, 1978; Arkin & Oleson, 1998). We will return to the hedonic bias phenomenon and its relationship to defense mechanisms later in this chapter as part of our discussion of attributional consequences.

The Actor–Observer Perspective

The presumed contrast between the causal perceptions of actors and observers is traceable to an insight of Heider (1958), as are so many other hypotheses about attribution processes. Heider stated, "The person tends to attribute his own reactions to the object world, and [the reactions] of another . . . to personal characteristics [of that other]" (p. 157). This assumption was elaborated and formalized by Jones and Nisbett (1971). Their frequently cited contention is as follows: "There is a pervasive tendency for actors to attribute their actions to situational requirements, whereas observers tend to attribute the action to stable dispositions" (p. 80). Both the actor and the observer are therefore presumed to be engaged in the same attributional endeavor—attempting to explain some observed behavior. The answers to the "why" question, however, are assumed to differ as a function of the perspective of the perceiver: Actors see the situation as causal (e.g., "I did it because I was provoked"), whereas observers perceive the person as causal (e.g., "He did it because he is aggressive").

Following the Jones and Nisbett (1971) publication, a plethora of studies were conducted in an attempt to verify the suggested actor–observer attributional disparity. Unfortunately, the earlier results were not always replicable (see review in Monson & Snyder, 1977; also see Robins, Spranca, & Mendelsohn, 1996). Monson and Snyder conclude that "in a variety of circumstances, actors attribute to themselves more responsibility for their own behaviors and the consequences of their actions than do observers" (p. 92). Furthermore, at times it is difficult to distinguish a person from a situation attribution, so that some reported findings regarding actor–observer differences are ambiguous (e.g., Lewis, 1995; Robins et al., 1996). For example, choosing a girlfriend because she is tall implies a situation (entity) attribution, yet this is perhaps indistinguishable from an ascription "I like tall girls," which is a person attribution.

Implications for Personality

Let us assume that there are differences between actors and observers in the tendency to make person versus situation attributions, even though this may occur only on some occasions in some settings. What consequences does this have for personal functioning and for issues germane to personality psychology? If actors perceive that behavior is situationally determined, then others may be expected to behave in the same way as the actor when in those situations. To use Kelley's terms once more, situation–behavior covariation is anticipated, and causal attributions are to external (situation) factors. One's own behavior therefore would be perceived as normative. This has implications for underrecognition of personal pathology as well as the uniqueness and distinctiveness of the self (see Lopez, 1989). Evidence supporting this deduction emerges from work related to the so-called "false consensus effect." For example, Ross, Greene, and House (1977) report that students overestimate the commonness of their own responses; that is, they perceive that their own behavior is typical of what other students think and do (see Marks & Miller, 1987, Mullen et al., 1985). On the other hand, if observers perceive that behavior is person-determined, then situational determinants of behavior may be discounted. That is, there is perceived person–behavior covariation, which results in internal ascriptions. The tendency to overattribute behavior to the person and underestimate the influence of the environment is labeled "the fundamental attribution error" (Ross, 1977).

In sum, actor–observer differences imply that actors subscribe to a theory of personality akin to that espoused by contingency reinforcement theorists; that is, they believe that behavior is altered to fit the situation and the demands of the environment. On the other hand, the perspective hypothesis also implies that observers entertain naive theories of personality that are more consistent with the beliefs of "pure" trait theorists. The existence of these biases in causal thinking has been suggested to be one reason personality psychologists have pursued the discovery of traits. Some attribution theorists have contended that traits may exist more in the minds of perceivers, including perceiving psychologists, than in the actions of the actor. This error could be enhanced because trait ascriptions provide a mechanism to make predictions about actors across a variety of settings, including environments in which the person has not been observed. Further implications of attribution theory for trait inferences are evident in the analysis of the trait–state distinction, which follows.

Trait–State Concepts from an Attribution Perspective

An important distinction made by personality psychologists contrasts traits and states, a distinction that can be examined using some of the attributional constructs introduced thus far. To investigate some of the differential features discriminating traits and states, Chaplin, John, and Goldberg (1988) had subjects rate a series of acknowledged traits and states on a variety of characteristics, including stability, consistency over situations, source of causality, duration, intensity, and controllability. It was found that stability, consistency, and internal causality were linked with traits; whereas instability, inconsistency, and external causality were associated with states. As already discussed, consistency over time and lack of distinctiveness have been identified by Kelley (1967) as criteria for personal causality. On the other hand, inconsistency over time and distinctive responding are criteria for entity causality. In sum, the trait–state distinction finds correspondence in the analysis of causal attributions, and particularly with the distinction between internal and external causality.

Chaplin and colleagues (1988) also discuss the function or utility of the trait–state distinction. They reason,

> We have suggested that traits and states serve people's needs to predict, explain, and control social behavior. The easiest way to accomplish this would be to have only two kinds of person characteristics. The first kind would include those that enable people to predict behavior reliably over time and situations and thus lead to social actions based on the person (e.g., to seek out or to avoid people with that characteristic). The second kind of characteristic, being unstable over time, cannot be predicted from past experience with the person, but may be controlled by manipulating the situation. (p. 555)

Chaplin and colleagues conclude that the trait–state distinction therefore "organizes the layperson's understanding of human action" (p. 555). This statement certainly is in accord with the presumptions of attribution theorists.

Individual Differences in Causal Perceptions

For some psychologists, the actor–observer literature suggests that traits are not inherent in persons, but rather are causal inferences about others. Furthermore, these inferences are quite likely to be biased, inasmuch as they are derived from limited observations and information. The position of most personality psychologists, on the other hand, is that traits are intrinsic or essential components of what it means to be a "person." These enduring structures are then manifested in a variety of situational contexts. One endeavor of attribution theorists consistent with this position has been the search for individual differences in causal perceptions.

Although one can conceive of many potential individual difference tendencies that capture causal perceptions, in general the literature has uncovered two types of attributional "traits." Some individual difference measures relate to the process of causal thinking and assess how people vary in the likelihood that they will engage in causal thinking as well as their preference for such thinking. Included among these process variables are attributional uncertainty and attributional complexity. These individual difference measures have only recently been proposed and have not (yet) spawned a large supporting literature. The more dominant individual difference approach in attribution theory pertains to the content of causal ascriptions, or the tendency to perceive that particular causes or types of causes will have or have had an effect. Here we review constructs that have a long history in personality psychology, such as locus of control and explanatory style, as well as more recently proposed causal constructs, such as political ideology and theories of intelligence.

Individual Differences in Causal Processes

Attributional Uncertainty. Both Heider (1958) and Kelley (1971) maintained that the need to reduce uncertainty about the social world is a primary motivation for people to engage in attributional activity. Recognizing that people vary in their propensity to engage in causal search, Weary and Edwards (1994) proposed the construct of causal uncertainty as a stable individual difference variable. Causal uncertainty is defined as individuals' beliefs about their ability to understand cause–effect relations in the social world (Weary & Edwards, 1994). This trait is measured on the 14-item Causal Uncertainty scale (CUS), in which respondents report their agreement with statements such as, "When I receive poor grades, I usually do not understand why I did so poorly" and "I often feel like I don't have enough information to come to a conclusion about why things happen to other people" (Edwards, Weary, & Reich, 1998). Thus the scale measures causal uncertainty about both one's own and other people's outcomes. Individuals who are high in causal uncertainty not only believe that they have inadequate knowledge of cause–effect relations, they also feel that they lack a more general understanding of the consistencies and regularities in social experiences—what Heider (1958) called the "dispositional properties of the world."

The causal uncertainty construct was formulated by Weary and her colleagues largely as part of their efforts to understand the social information processing correlates of depression. It has been documented that mildly and moderately depressed individuals are high on causal uncertainty, which would be consistent with their general perception of response–outcome noncontigency (Weary & Edwards, 1994). Uncertainty also has been associated with high Neuroticism on the Big Five Personality Factors scale (Edwards et al., 1998). Finally, there is evidence that heightened causal uncertainty can be reduced by strategic seeking of diagnostic information (Weary & Jacobson, 1997). Thus the construct bears some resemblance to other cognitive personality traits—such as need for cognition (Cacioppo & Petty, 1982), desire for control (Burger, 1992), and need for closure (Webster & Kruglanski, 1994)—that explore how and under what conditions individuals engage in effortful social information processing.

Attributional Complexity. Whereas attributional uncertainty concerns people's confidence about whether they *can* understand the causes of behavior, attributional complexity measures whether they *want* to engage in such causal search. Fletcher and his colleagues view the motivation to seek causal information as an individual difference variable, which they measure with an instrument labeled the Attributional Complexity scale (ACS; Fletcher, Danilovics, Fernandez, Peterson, & Reeder, 1986). The ACS is a 28-item scale that employs an agree–disagree response format. The instrument measures constructs such as an individual's intrinsic motivation to explain behavior (e.g., "I really enjoy analyzing the reasons or causes for people's behavior"); preference for complex explanations or those that involve multiple causes (e.g., "I have found that the causes for people's behavior are usually complex rather than simple"); metacognitive awareness, or thoughts about the process of causal thinking (e.g., "When the reasons I give for my own behavior are different from someone else's, this often makes me think about the thinking processes that lead to my explanations"); and use of a temporal dimension of causality (e.g., "When I analyze a person's behavior, I often find the causes form a chain that goes back in time, sometimes for years"). Thus, the scale taps more than motivation to engage in attributional activity.

As with causal uncertainty, much of the interest in attributional compexity grew out of a concern with understanding the attributional underpinnings of depression. It has been documented, for example, that mildly and moderately depressed individuals are more attributionally complex than their severely depressed or nondepressed counterparts in that they prefer multiple to single cause explanations as well as causes that invoke both personal and environmental factors. Attributional complexity also has been linked to adaptive mental health outcomes in that individuals who prefer complex causal explanations have greater self-insight (Reeves, Watson, Ramsey, & Morris, 1995) and are less prone to become easily bored (Polly, Vodanovick, Watt, & Blanchard, 1993).

Individual Difference in Causal Content

The literature on causal content has focused less on how people vary in the endorsement of particular attributions than on individual differences in the underlying dimensions or properties of the causes that they endorse. We have already made reference to some of these dimensions in the prior sections, but here we define them more formally. By "causal dimensions" we mean certain second-order concepts that can be used to distinguish among causes. Three such causal properties have been identified with much certainty in attribution research (see reviews in Weiner, 1986, 1995). These are (1) locus, or whether a cause is internal or external to the individual; (2) stability, which designates a cause as constant or varying over time; and (3) controllability, which refers to whether a cause is subject to volitional influence. Among the dominant perceived causes, ability and effort are perceived as internal because they reflect on the person, whereas luck (chance) and objective task difficulty are perceived as environmental determinants of success and failure. Causes such as effort and luck are typically unstable because they fluctuate from situation to situation, whereas aptitude (ability) and objective task difficulty tend to be judged as relatively unchanging. Finally, low aptitude as a cause for failure tends to be perceived as uncontrollable; this is in contrast to lack of effort because people generally have control over how much effort they are willing to expend. Five constructs are reviewed below that measure individual differences in causal content, drawing on one or more of these causal dimensions.

Locus of Control. As its name implies, locus of control is theoretically linked to the locus dimension of causality. Locus of control and the measurement instruments devised by Julian Rotter and others have fostered a voluminous psychological literature (see Lefcourt, 1992). Perhaps what we can best do in this context is to provide some historical background that often is overlooked and to offer one interpretation of the empirical and theoretical legacy of this approach. Rotter is identified with social learning and, as a clinician, wanted to create a conceptual system that would be useful in dealing with clinical problems while remaining true to the logical positivism represented in social learning theory. He also accepted expectancy-value theory, contending that the strength of motivation to perform an action is in part determined by the expectancy of attaining the desired goal. Clinical difficulties were anticipated when expectancies of success were nonveridical and when there was a low expectancy for a highly valued goal. Hence, one of Rotter's central quests was to identify the determinants of expectancy of success.

In a series of experimental studies, Rotter and his colleagues (e.g., James & Rotter, 1958) documented that performance at skill tasks results in different changes in expectancy of success than does performance at chance tasks. For example, following a loss at a skill task, expectancy of future success frequently drops, whereas it remains the same or may even increase after a loss at a chance task (the "gambler's fallacy"). This laboratory experimental research suggested to Rotter that some individuals may perceive the world as if it were composed of skill tasks, whereas others perceive life outcomes as chance-determined. That is, he contended that there are individual differences in causal beliefs about the self determination of outcomes; these, in turn, result in disparate subjective likelihoods of success and failure across a variety of situations.

The measure of locus of control, or the I–E scale, was constructed to assess individual differences in personal constructions of the world as skill-related (internal) or chance-related (external) (Rotter, 1966). To the best of our knowledge, however, the scale never has been successfully reported to relate to expectancy of success or to expectancy change. Rather, the I–E scale took on a life of its own, divorced from expectancy-value theory and from social learning. Indeed it was a very active life. Scores on the scale were related to literally hundreds of different variables. There was also a strong impulse to consider the scores as evaluative: It was "good" to be an "internal," inasmuch as internality was thought to be associated with information processing, openness to experience, positive mental health, and so on (Rotter, 1975). Correspondingly, it was "bad" to be an "external." Even during the heyday of the I–E scale (say, from 1967 to 1982), there were concerns about the breadth of personality traits, or their cross-situational generality. Such doubts also were raised about locus of control. In response to this uncertainty, and to enhance predictive validity, specific locus of control scales began to be developed. For example, Lefcourt, von Baeyer, Ware, and Cox (1979) distinguished between locus for affiliative and achievement outcomes in their control scale. Further, health locus of control scales were constructed to examine whether individuals consider health-related outcomes as subject to personal or environmental control (e.g., Lau & Ware, 1981; Wallston & Wallston, 1981). The connection of internal locus of control with physical well-being further promoted the linkage between perceived personal control and positive adaptation and coping.

In sum, studies of individual differences in causal attributions began with the search by Rotter to understand the determinants of expectancy of success. This led to the study of skill and chance tasks and to the conception that individuals differentially perceive the world as skill- or chance-governed. The I–E scale did not shed light on subjective expectancies; there is little theoretical legacy in this research, nor any solutions to the generality of this predisposition. However, there is an empirical heritage: Perceiving control over life events is an important correlate of physical and mental health. This principle has been demonstrated in a variety of contexts including schools, nursing homes, work environments, and other situations in which there is a trend toward fostering personal freedom and responsibility.

Entity versus Incremental Theories of Intelligence and Traits. A relative newcomer to the individual differences literature focuses on the stability dimension of causality and distinguishes people according to whether they view intelligence (aptitude) and various personality traits as chronic versus amenable to change. In the achievement domain, in which this line of research first surfaced, Dweck and her colleagues have proposed a distinction between individuals who hold entity versus incremental theories of intelligence (Dweck & Leggett , 1988; Dweck, Chiu, & Hong, 1995). According to Dweck, children and adults hold one of two implicit theories about intelligence. Some individuals are what Dweck labels "entity" theorists: They believe that intelligence is basically fixed and unmalleable, as when they endorse statements such as "You can learn new things, but you can't really change your basic intelligence" (Dweck et al., 1995, p. 925). In contrast, other individuals appear to be "incremental" theorists: They believe that intelligence is modifiable and are more likely to agree with statements such as "Smartness is something you can increase as much as you want to" (Dweck & Leggett, 1988, p. 273). These implicit theories have been related to a variety of achievement-related cognitions and behaviors. For example, children who subscribe to the incremental conception of intelligence prefer challenging tasks so that they can both increase their ability and achieve greater mastery. Entity theorists, on the other hand, often avoid challenge because their primary concern is with the adequacy of their presumedly fixed ability. Recently there have been efforts to broaden the generality of the entity–incremental distinction to include perceptions of the malleability of moral traits (e.g., honesty, conscientiousness) and the general social order (Dweck et al., 1995; Chiu, Dweck, Tong, & Fu, 1997).

Political Ideology. Political ideology also can be conceptualized as an individual difference variable that bears on attributions. What especially distinguishes a conservative from a liberal political orientation are beliefs about the controllability of causes of personal outcomes. Conservatives, for example, tend to attribute poverty to causes such as self-indulgence and laziness, whereas liberals are more likely to place causality within the social structure and view the poor as victims of society (see, for example, Skitka & Tetlock, 1993; Zucker & Weiner, 1993). Furthermore, for any given cause of a situation or a condition, conservatives tend to perceive that cause as more controllable by individuals than do liberals, thereby ascribing greater responsibility to the person in need (Zucker & Weiner, 1993). These attributional inferences are more fundamentally rooted in beliefs about individualism and the Protestant work ethic. The Protestant ethic is an ideology including the conviction that individual hard work leads to success and that lack of success is the result of moral failings of self-indulgence and lack of discipline. This belief system is manifested differentially in specific political ideologies.

Each individual difference measure briefly reviewed thus far focuses primarily on one dimension of causality. That is, locus of control is concerned with preferences for internal versus external causes; the entity–incremental distinction classifies people on their endorsement of stable versus unstable causes; and political ideology can be conceptualized as a preference for attributions primarily to controllable causes (conservatives) versus uncontrollable causes (liberals). The next two attributional traits examine individual differences in causal perceptions that vary on multiple dimensions.

Characterological versus Behavioral Self-Blame. A distinction that has been useful for understanding coping with victimization contrasts characterological and behavioral self-blame. In studies of reactions to rape, Janoff-Bulman (1979) describes these two types of self-blame as follows:

> Behavioral self-blame is control related, involves attributions to a modifiable source (one's behavior), and is associated with a belief in the future avoidability of a negative outcome. Characterological self-blame is esteem related, involves attributions to a relatively nonmodifiable source (one's character), and is associated with a belief in personal deservingness for past outcomes. (p. 1798)

In a causal dimension framework, behavioral self-blame is internal, unstable, and controllable (akin to lack of effort for achievement failure); whereas characterological self-blame is internal, stable, and uncontrollable (akin to low aptitude). Hence this distinction captures individual differences in causal perceptions that vary on both the stability and controllability dimensions.

In adult research guided by this framework, it has been documented that individuals who make characterological attributions for negative outcomes cope more poorly, feel worse about themselves, and are more depressed than individuals who make behavioral self-attributions (see reviews in Anderson, Miller, Riger, Dill, & Sedikides, 1994; Janoff-Bulman, 1992). Recent findings with early adolescents reveal that characterological self-blaming attributions for academic and social failure result in heightened depression (Cole, Peeke, & Ingold, 1996). Similarly, young adolescents who make characterological attributions for chronic peer victimization are lonelier, more anxious, and lower in self-esteem than those who blame their victim status on their behavior (Graham & Juvonen, 1998). Although there is some diasgreement in the literature as to whether behavioral self-blame is consistently adaptive (e.g., Frazier & Schauben, 1994; Meyer & Taylor, 1986), it is apparent that poor coping is associated with the perception of traumatic events as due to relatively stable personal attributes over which the person has little control.

Explanatory Style. Explanatory style, also known as attributional style, emerged in the late 1970s as part of early efforts to understand the role of attributions in learned helplessness and depression. Abramson, Seligman, and Teasdale (1978) gave attributions a central role in this analysis: "We argue that when a person finds that he is helpless, he asks *why* he is helpless. The causal attrbution he makes then determines the generality and chronicity of helplessness deficits as well as his later self-esteem" (p. 50). Abramson and colleagues suggested that attributing failure to the self is dysfunctional, inasmuch as this results in low self-esteem. In addition, attributions of failure to causes that do not change over time (causal stability) and to causes that appear in a variety of settings (causal globality) are also maladaptive. On the other hand, ascriptions of failure that are external, unstable, and specific are considered adaptive. This thinking resulted in the development of a measure of attributional style that was designed to assess individual differences in the way people habitually explain both the good and bad events that happen to them (Peterson, Semmel, von Baeyer, Abramson, Metalsky, & Seligman, 1982). Over the years, the labeling of this instrument has shifted from "attributional" to "explanatory" style as it has been applied to contexts other than helplessness and depression.

In broad individual difference terms, explanatory style classifies respondents as pessimists versus optimists. People who explain negative outcomes as internal ("it's me"), stable ("things will always be this way"), and global ("it affects many areas of my life") are judged to have a pessimistic explanatory style. In contrast, those who typically attribute negative events to external, unstable, and specific causes are considered to have an optimistic explanatory style. Attributions for good events also can be considered as pessimistic (external, unstable, specific) or optimistic (internal, stable, global). Thus explanatory style incorporates two dimensions of causality from attribution theory (locus and stability) as well as a third dimension (globality) that has been more closely associated with the helplessness literature (Abramson et al., 1978). The typical way to measure explanatory style is to present individuals with a series of hypothetical positive or negative outcomes (e.g., "You go to a party and do not meet new friends") (see Peterson, 1991). Respondents then generate a causal explanation for each event and rate that cause on the dimensions of locus, stability, and globality. Dimension ratings are then summed across events and aggregated to create overall scores, although this method has been criticized on psychometric grounds (Cutrona, Russell, & Jones, 1985; Carver, 1989). Explanatory style also has been measured by content analysis of written and spoken material such as diaries, speeches, interviews, and even Thematic Apperception Test (TAT) protocols (Peterson & Ulrey, 1994).

Research on explanatory style has generated a large empirical literature that spans the clinical, academic, interpersonal, athletic, health, and work domains (see review in Peterson, Maier, & Seligman, 1993). We return to its clinical impact in a later section on attributional approaches to depression. Among nonclinical populations, it has been hypothesized that people with an optimistic as opposed to pessimistic explanatory style do better in school (e.g., Peterson & Barrett, 1987), have greater work productivity (e.g., Seligman & Schulman, 1986), enjoy more financial gain (Lee & Seligman, 1997), are more successful in gaining political office (Zullow & Seligman, 1990), and have a better prognosis for long-term health (e.g., Peterson, Seligman, & Valliant, 1988). Although the broad and sweeping claims of some explanatory style proponents are probably unwarranted (see Anderson, Jennings, & Arnoult, 1988 for a critique), it also is true that when measured at the appropriate level of specificity, how people explain good and bad events may be moderately related to (predictive of) their subsequent outcomes.

Summary

There are individual differences that influence both the process and the content of causal thinking. To date, the content effects have been more far reaching and have generated a much larger literature than has the study of how individuals vary in causal process. Indeed, the fact that studies of locus of control, entity versus incremental theories of traits, political ideology, characterological versus behavioral self-blame, and explanatory style all bear upon causal inference is rather mind-boggling in terms of the number of investigations that are included under these rubrics. Clearly, then, personality as a causal antecedent should be more fully recognized as a core topic in the field of personality.

THE ATTRIBUTIONAL PROCESS: CONSEQUENCES OF CAUSAL PERCEPTIONS

We now turn to the effects of causal ascriptions on the dynamics of behavior. This topic has not been totally neglected in the prior pages: The hedonic bias relates to experienced positive and negative affect; the actor–observer difference has implications for perceived normality and deviance; and all of the individual difference constructs have been associated with a variety of processes and states. Nonetheless, these consequences have up to this point been secondary to the issue of attributional selection or choice of causal ascriptions. That is, biases, perspectives, and individual differences have all been considered to be determinants or antecedents of causal ascriptions.

The discussion of attributional process is organized around the three dimensions of causality that were introduced earlier, for each of these dimensions has distinct psychological consequences that are relevant to personality (see review in Weiner, 1985, 1986). The locus dimension of causality is related to self-esteem, and we review research on self-handicapping, attributions of the stigmatized, and excuse tactics as illustrations of how individuals implicitly make use of this relation. The stability dimension influences subjective expectancy about future outcomes. This linkage is the organizing construct for reviewing research on goal expectancy, attributional change programs, and hopelessness theories of depression. As the third dimension of causality, controllability is related to a variety of complex human emotions, including shame, guilt, pity, and anger. Here we describe a general attributional approach to emotion as well as specific research on the controllability-related emotions listed above. It will be seen that attributions of controllability and emotional reactions of pity versus anger have been related to prosocial and antisocial behavior, two core topics in the study of personality dynamics. The section therefore concludes with a discussion of attributional approaches to altruism and aggression.

It should be evident from this overview of the second part of the chapter that the linkages between locus–self-esteem, stability–expectancy, and controllability–emotions have been extended to account for a vast array of psychological phenomena relevant to personality. Many (but not all) of the phenomena are associated with large empirical literatures, so that these topics already have been the subject of comprehensive reviews. Our task is therefore not one of detailed research summaries. Rather, our goal is to point out the relational fertility and theoretical breadth of the consequences associated with the dimensions of causal thinking. Although we have no illusions that any of the topics is solely explained by a causal dimension analysis, we believe that the range of application to personality psychology is compelling.

Locus of Causality and Self-Esteem

Locus of causality, the causal dimension first introduced by Rotter to distinguish internal from external causes, influences self-esteem and self-worth. More specifically, successful outcomes that are ascribed to the self (e.g., personality, ability, effort) result in greater self-esteem and pride than does success that is externally attributed (e.g., task ease, good luck). As Isenberg (1980) stated, "The definition of pride, then, has three parts. There is (1) a quality which (2) is approved and (3) is judged to belong to oneself" (p. 357). This quality is exemplified in self-statements such as "I succeeded because I [am smart, worked hard, etc.]."

The relation between internality and high self-esteem is directly relevant to the hedonic bias, examined in the first section of this chapter. Indeed, the basic premise of hedonic bias research is that internal attributions for goal attainment, and external attributions for nonattainment of a goal, enhance and protect self-esteem. Thus, documenting the self-serving attributional bias can also be considered as evidence supporting the relation between locus of causality and self-esteem.

Self-Handicapping

Other than hedonic bias, it is possible that individuals might engage in various strategies, some of which may be quite dysfunctional, to avoid self-ascriptions for failure to low ability. Jones and Berglas (1978) first described a phenomenon, labeled "self-handicapping," in which people create situations that make failure more likely, but where presumably that failure is nondiagnostic of their abilities. For example, a student may avoid effort by partying all night before an important exam, so that poor performance on the exam can be attributed to factors other than his or her ability. Jones and Berglas (1978) also reason that self-destructive behaviors such as alcoholism may in some instances be instigated by a self-handicapping strategy. In both of these examples, lack of effort and drunkenness can provide attributions that reduce low ability beliefs. It is also possible that pride and positive self-esteem can be enhanced if success is achieved despite the handicap (i.e., the person must have very high ability to succeed in spite of lack of effort or drinking too much).

Self-handicapping is a construct with considerable intuitive appeal that has found its niche in research on defensive self-attributions (see reviews in Arkin & Baumgardner, 1985; Arkin & Oleson, 1998). There also appears to be a growing interest in studying the phenomenon in school-aged children who encounter academic difficulty (Midgley, Arunkumar, & Urdan, 1996; Urdan, Midgely, & Anderman, 1998). However, the supporting literature is not extensive and it is unclear whether the tactics to discount low ability attributions reflect private beliefs or public self-presentation strategies. One also wonders about the pervasiveness of self-handicapping—after all, most individuals prefer success to failure.

Self-Esteem Maintenance in Stigmatized Groups

A second area of research that can be incorporated within the locus–esteem linkage focuses on self-perceptions of the stigmatized. By stigmatized we mean those groups or individuals who are perceived to possess characteristics or social identities that are devalued in certain contexts—for example, ethnic minorities, women, and people who are obese, facially disfigured, learning disabled, mentally ill, homosexual, or criminally delinquent. There are many reasons to believe that such stigmatized individuals will have low self-esteem because feelings of worth are partly determined by how one's primary social group is evaluated (see Cartwright, 1950). However, this hypothesis has not been supported. As summarized by Crocker and Major (1989), "Prejudice against members of stigmatized or oppressed groups generally does *not* result in lowered self-esteem for members of those groups" (p. 60). These authors go on to suggest a number of mechanisms that might contribute to the maintenance of high self-esteem among the stigmatized (Crocker & Major, 1989; Major & Crocker, 1993).

One such esteem-protecting mechanism is to attribute negative feedback or poor outcomes to external factors, particularly to the prejudiced attitudes of others. For example, in one representative study (Crocker, Voelkl, Testa, & Major, 1991, Experiment 2) African American college students who were seen by a white evaluator were more likely to attribute negative feedback to prejudice than were other African Americans not seen by their evaluator. Furthermore, African American students' self-esteem actually increased following negative feedback from an evaluator who was aware of their race—presumably due to the attribution of evaluator prejudice. Ascribing failure to others' prejudice as a tactic for protecting self-esteem is fully consistent with the locus–esteem linkage; failure attributed to external causes is less likely to undermine positive self-esteem than is failure attributed to internal causes.

The notion of self-protective mechanisms in stigmatized groups has been quite popular because it provides a compelling theoretical account for what appears to be a paradoxical finding in personality research (i.e., high self-esteem in low-status groups) and it has implications for a number of broader social issues surrounding marginalized status and opportunity in contemporary society (see Crocker, Major, & Steele, 1998). However, empirical support for the esteem-protecting function of attributions to prejudice is limited. For example, studies by Ruggiero and Taylor (1995, 1997) reveal that women and minority groups (Asians and African Americans) actually minimize attributions for achievement failure to evaluator prejudice unless the biased beliefs of the evaluator are made very salient. Moreover, when stigmatized individuals do make such external attributions, their feelings of personal control and acceptance by others (what the authors label social self-esteem) are dampened. These findings suggest that an attribution to prejudice may have uncertain placement along the locus dimension inasmuch as perceived discrimination implicates one's personal attributes as well as the characteristics of external agents. Finally, stigmatized individuals are unlikely to attribute negative outcomes to external factors including prejudice when their stigmatizing condition is perceived to be personally controllable, as in the case of obesity (Crocker, Cornwell, & Major, 1993). A fuller understanding of how particular types of attributions influence self-esteem among stigmatized groups needs to incorporate the causal dimension of controllability in addition to locus.

Communicating Excuses

As one type of account for social transgressions, excuses also implicate a relation between causal locus and self-esteem. In their review, Snyder and Higgins (1988) define excuses as

> the motivated process of shifting causal attributions for negative personal outcomes from sources that are relatively more central to the person's sense of self to sources that are relatively less central, thereby resulting in perceived benefits to the person's image. . . . A primary assumption in the literature on excuse-making is that excuses are designed to protect the person from self-esteem threats. (pp. 23–24)

In more recent formulations (Sigmon & Snyder, 1993; Snyder & Higgins, 1997), excuses have been conceptualized as core features of a reality negotiation process whereby individuals constantly engage in tactics to both privately and publicly present themselves in a favorable light. Given these broad definitons, the hedonic bias, self-handicapping, and attributions to prejudice, as well as a vast array of mechanisms reviewed by Snyder and Higgins including psychological defenses, all could be conceptualized as excuses. Each is, in part, guided by a locus–esteem relation in which the goal is to alter causality for failure from internal to external.

One of us (Weiner, Figueroa-Munoz, & Kakihara, 1991) subsequently offered a more circumscribed definition of excues as "the conscious supplanting of one cause by another . . . producing a discrepancy between the privately known 'true' cause . . . and the imparted cause which is false . . . with the goal of manipulating the thoughts, feelings, and actions of others" (p. 5). Among the goals of excuses identified by Weiner and colleagues (1991) was to protect the self-esteem of another (as well as oneself). For example, Folkes (1982) asked female college students to assume that they had refused a dating request. The real reasons were provided by the experimenter, some being internal to the rejected person (e.g., "His face and body type are not attractive"), whereas others were external to him (e.g., "You have the flu"). The female participants reported that they would honestly communicate the causes external to the requestor, but that they would lie (provide a false reason or excuse) when the cause of rejection was internal to the requestor. Other data revealed that this was a benevolent strategy, used to protect the self-esteem of the rejected other. Baumeister and his colleagues proposed a similarly benevolent goal on the part of rejectors in their research on unrequited love (Baumeister, Wotman, & Stillwell, 1993). Rejectors often communicated mixed or false messages about the reasons for the breakup of the relationship in order minimize the hurt feelings of their would-be lovers. In sum, several types of excuses or false accounts for interpersonal dilemmas are governed by awareness of the linkage between causal locus and self-esteem.

Summary

Locating the self as the cause of an outcome, such as achievement-related failure or affiliative rejection, influences self-appraisal, which, in turn, has affective consequences. Because views of the self and self-esteem play such an important role in coping and adjustment, the locus–esteem connection and its psychological consequences intersect with a number of topics in personality research.

Causal Stability and Expectancy of Success

Earlier we stated that causal stability, or the perceived duration of a cause, is related to expectancy for success. For example, when achievement failure is attributed to a stable cause such as low aptitude or poverty, one is more likely to expect the same outcome to occur again than when the cause is perceived as an unstable factor such as lack of effort or bad luck. The logic of this argument is that if conditions (i.e., the presence or absence of causes) are anticipated to remain the same, then the outcome experienced on the prior occasion will be expected to occur again. Thus a success under these circumstances would produce relatively large gains in the anticipation of future success, and a failure would strengthen the belief that there will be subsequent failure. Whether future expectations of success increase, decrease, or remain unchanged depends, therefore, on the initial expectancy, the outcome, and the stability of the attributed cause for the outcome. In the following sections we apply this analysis to research on goal expectancies, achievement change programs, and attributional approaches to depression.

Goal Expectancy and Persistence

It is evident that some themes throughout the study of personality dynamics are considered more important or central than others and constantly reappear. One such focus is goal expectancy. A number of major theorists, including Atkinson, Lewin, and Rotter, include the expectancy of success among the determinants of aspiration level (goal selection). In criticizing the approach of psychoanalytic theory to goal seeking, Rotter and Hochreich (1975) stated:

> Simply knowing how much an individual wants to reach a certain goal is not sufficient information for predicting his behavior. A student may want very badly to finish school and qualify himself for a well-paying job. But his past experiences may have led him to believe that no amount of studying will result in a passing grade. . . . A fellow student may share the same strong goals and, as a result of a different set of past experiences in school, will have a high expectancy that studying will lead to academic success. . . . The goals in these two cases are identical, but the expectancies differ, and as a result, the behavior of the two students is likely to differ. (p. 95)

It has been proposed that the stability of attributions for negative outcomes influences goal expectancies, which in turn affect persistence in the face of failure. One question of interest for personality theory is whether stability attributions are primarily determined by dispositional or situational factors.

Anderson (1983) and Anderson and Jennings (1980) documented that both dispositional and situational determinants of causal stability ascriptions affect persistence at an achievement-related task. They had subjects engage in telephone solicitations to donate blood to the Red Cross. The first call, however, was to a confederate who refused to donate. Prior to this rejection, the subjects were assessed for ability versus effort self-blame with an attributional style questionnaire. In addition, an experimental manipulation varied the perceived cause of possible rejection. The instruction eliciting stable attributions stated that success was determined by a stable personality trait ("Some guys have it, some don't"), whereas the instruction evoking unstable attributions indicated that strategy was the main outcome determinant ("Use different tactics . . . until finding one that works").

In these studies, it was found that both the dispositional tendency and the attributional manipulation influenced how many subsequent phone calls were made after the initial failure. Given no experimental manipulation, those high in effort self-blame persisted longer than subjects classified as high in ability self-blame. But in the experimental conditions, the instructions overrode the individual difference tendencies: Subjects given instructions that elicited unstable ascriptions made more phone calls than those ascribing rejection to a personality trait.

Attributional Therapies

In conjunction with the development of an attributional approach to personality dynamics, there has been a growing field of attributional therapy (see reviews in Forsterling, 1985, 1988; Perry, Hechter, Menec, & Weinberg, 1993). Attributional therapies are guided by the fundamental principle that thoughts (in this case, causal ascriptions) guide behavior. It then follows that a change in thinking should produce a change in action. The goal of attributional therapies, therefore, has been to substitute adaptive causal ascriptions for those that are presumed to be maladaptive.

Attributional therapies have been largely confined to achievement-related contexts. The researchers (change agents) have assumed that dysfunctional attributions have greater impact in situations of failure than of success, and that the most maladaptive causal ascription for achievement failure is lack of ability. This logically follows inasmuch as lack of ability is conceived of as an internal, stable, and uncontrollable cause. In the majority of experimental reports, the adaptive cause that the therapist or researcher has sought to substitute is lack of effort (e.g., Menec, Perry, Struthers, Schonwetter, Hechter, & Eichholz, 1994).

From an attributional perspective, self-ascriptions to lack of effort are adaptive largely because effort is unstable and therefore leads to the expectation that failure need not be repeated in the future. But any self-ascription perceived as unstable theoretically should have the same positive effects as lack of effort. Research by Wilson and Linville (1982, 1985), partially replicated by Van Overwalle, Segebarth, and Goldchstein (1989) and Struthers and Perry (1996), has documented that positive motivational consequences occur when the stability of the cause is manipulated. For example, Wilson and Linville (1982) manipulated stability by telling a group of subjectively failing college freshmen that their grades would improve from the first to the second year; that is, the reasons for poor performance in the freshman year were unstable. Compared to a control group who received no such attributional information, the experimental students had greater expectations for success in their sophomore year and also obtained higher grades.

Less frequently, the designated causal attribution for achievement failure has been bad luck or an overly difficult task. Because these are external causes for failure, self-esteem is maintained. Luck and task difficulty ascriptions do differ, however, in other respects. Luck is perceived as more unstable than is task difficulty, so that expectancies for success should be higher given an ascription to luck rather than characterisitics of the task. It should be noted, therefore, that lack of effort, bad luck, and an overly difficult task are all specified to improve motivation and coping, relative to a low-ability ascription for failure. However, the variables mediating the hypothesized improvement are not identical for the three causal ascriptions. Effort attributions theoretically maintain expectancy while still lowering self-esteem (a performance inhibitor); luck attributions theoretically maintain expectancy of success as well as self-esteem; and task difficulty attributions maintain only positive self-esteem, while lowering expectancy estimates. This analysis reveals some of the insights provided by attribution theory (see Weiner, 1988, for a fuller discussion of attributional therapy).

Hopelessness Theory of Depression

In an earlier section, we briefly considered attributional approaches to learned helplessness and depression in the context of discussing research on explanatory style. A model proposed by Abramson et al. (1978) predicted that depression occurs when negative life events are attributed to internal, stable, and global causes. In a recent revision of the model, the locus dimension (and its associated loss in self-worth) is no longer viewed as central in the etiology of depression. Rather, the combination of stable and global attributions for negative events results in hopelessness, which in turn leads to a particular subtype of depression. Abramson, Metalsky, and Alloy (1989) describe this model as follows:

> According to hopelesssness theory, a proximal sufficient cause of the symptoms of hopelessness depression is an expectation that highly desired outcomes will not occur or that highly aversive outcomes will occur . . . the symptoms of hopelessness depression are more likely to occur when negative life events are attributed to stable (i.e., en-

during) and global (i.e., likely to affect many outcomes) causes . . . than when they are attributed to unstable, specific causes. (pp. 359, 361)

Thus hopelessness is a negative expectancy that follows directly from attributing failure to stable (global) causes. In this sense, the revised hopelessness model is more focused on a particular set of attributional linkages (stability–expectancy) than the earlier helplessness model.

Studies testing the hypotheses of this model of depression have yielded mixed results (see reviews in Abramson, Alloy, & Metalsky, 1995; Joiner & Wagner, 1995). Although stable and global attributions for negative outcomes consistently are linked to depressive symptoms, the causal pathway is not always through reported hopelessness. That is, it is unclear whether hopeless expectations *cause* depression, which the revised theory predicts, or whether hopelessness is a correlate of depressive symptomatology (e.g., Whisman & Pinto, 1997). There is also uncertainty about whether low self-esteem is a symptom of hopelessness depression, which is inconsistent with beliefs that self-esteem is related to the locus dimension, or whether self-esteem functions as a causal antecedent, which would be more consistent with the earlier formulation (e.g., Metalsky, Joiner, Hardin, & Abramson, 1993). In sum, whether the revised hopelessness model will bring greater theoretical clarity to attributional approaches to depression remains to be seen.

Summary

For the personality theorist, the prior discussion intimates that when there is quitting in the face of nonattainment of a goal (task failure, social rejection, etc.), when expectancy of success following failure is low, and when there is hopelessness about the future, then one should be alerted to find stable attributions for past failures. On the other hand, if there is persistence given failure, if expectancy of success remains reasonably high, and if there is optimism about the future, then one should be alerted to find unstable ascriptions for prior goal nonattainments. The reverse conditions characterize ascriptions for success (i.e., stable attributions result in more positive anticipations than do unstable ascriptions). A wide range of antecedents and consequences that involve causal stability and expectancy estimates have already been identified; these are very pertinent for the study of personality.

Causal Controllability and Emotions

The third identified dimension of causality, causal controllability, refers to the capability of the actor or someone else to volitionally alter the cause. The concept of controllability bears a close resemblance to what is meant by personal responsibility, although these are not identical constructs (Weiner, 1995). From an attributional perspective, controllability refers to a property of causes, whereas responsibility is an inference about a person. In the absence of mitigating circumstances, an individual who fails because of not trying usually is held responsible (by self and others), because lack of effort is perceived as a controllable cause of failure. In contrast, if failure is due to lack of aptitude, then one is not held responsible (able to respond), inasmuch as the cause is not subject to volitional control. Other theoretical distinctions between controllability and responsibility and concepts such as fault, intentionality, and blame are not considered in this chapter (see Weiner, 1995).

Causal controllability is related to a set of social emotions that includes shame, guilt, pity, and anger. As background to a discussion of these linkages, it is useful to first provide a brief overview of how attributions have been incorporated in the study of emotions.

Attributional Approaches to Emotion

There have been two quite distinct attributional approaches to emotion. The initial and more encompassing theory was proposed by Schachter and Singer (1962), for whom the concept of "arousal" played a central role in the experience of emotion. Schachter and Singer specify two different ways in which an emotion can be generated. One is the usual, everyday experience; the second is more atypical but has been responsible for a number of oft-cited research studies. In everyday emotional states, external cues trigger physiological processes and serve as a label to which feelings are attached. For example, someone takes out a gun; this is appraised and interpreted as a threat; arousal increases; the arousal is linked with (attributed to) the gun; and an emotion is experienced. The second way in which an emotional state can be initiated is with the perception of "unexplained" arousal. In an experimental setting, this can be created by having the research participants unknowingly ingest an activating drug. The arousal theoretically generates a search to determine the source of arousal, given that an instigating source is not immediately evident. Again, arousal and attribution or inference about the arousal source then produce an emotional state.

The Schachter and Singer (1962) formulation was for a time the most influential cognitive approach to emotions. More recently, however, the theory has met with many criticisms and its influence has markedly declined (see Reisenzein, 1983). There is evidence, for example, that unexplained arousal is in itself a negative affective state; that individuals do not necessarily search the environment for the source of their arousal; and that arousal is not necessary for an emotional experience. That is, "the role of arousal in emotion had been overstated" (Reisenzein, 1983, p. 239).

The second attributional approach to the study of emotion emerges from our own work (see Weiner, Russell, & Lerman, 1978, 1979; Weiner & Graham, 1984). Our basic assumption is that cognitions of increasing complexity enter into the emotion process to further refine and differentiate affective experience. It is proposed that following the outcome of an event, there is initially a generally positive or negative reaction (a "primitive" emotion), based on the perceived success or failure of that outcome (the "primary" appraisal). For example, after receiving an "A" in a course, hitting a home run in a baseball game, or being accepted for a date, an individual will feel "happy." In a similar manner, after receiving an "F" in a course, failing to get a hit, or being rejected, the person will experience sadness. These emotions are labeled "outcome-dependent/attribution-independent," for they are determined by the attainment or nonattainment of a desired goal, and not by the cause of that outcome.

Following the appraisal of the outcome, a causal ascription is sought. A different set of emotions is then generated by the chosen attribution(s) or the dimensions of that attribution. Each dimension of the ascription is in turn uniquely related to a set of feelings. We now turn to the linkages between causal controllability and two other-directed emotions (anger and pity) as well as two complementary self-directed emotions (guilt and shame). Controllability also is related to regret (Zeelenberg, van Dijk, Manstead, & van der Pligt, 1998) and gratitude (Tesser, Gatewood, & Driver, 1968), but space limitations prohibit a discussion of these emotions.

Anger and Pity

Imagine, for example, your feelings when your child is doing poorly in school because of a refusal to do homework, or when an athlete on your favorite team is loafing. Not only are there thoughts about causal controllability and inferences about personal responsibility, but there are feelings of anger as well. You are mad at the rebellious child and at the lackadaisical athlete. Anger is an accusation or a value judgment that follows from the belief that another person "could and should have done otherwise" (see Averill, 1982, 1983; Reisenzein & Hoffman, 1990; Roseman, 1991).

There is an array of research supporting this cognitive appraisal position, where thoughts are necessary and sufficient determinants of feelings. Averill (1983), for example, asked persons to report about recent events that made them angry. In this research, more than 50% of the incidents were considered "voluntary" in that the harmdoer was fully aware of the consequences of the action and the act was not only intentional but perceived by the victim as unjustified. Avoidable harm that was not necessarily intended was the next largest category of acts that give rise to anger. These findings have been replicated many times (see Weiner, 1995).

In contrast to the linkage between controllability and anger, the absence of control and personal responsibility given the plight of another often is associated with sympathy and the related emotions of pity and compassion. Thus, a person confined to a totalitarian state (situational causality), athletic failure because of a physical handicap (internal, uncontrollable causality), and school failure because of the need to care for a sick mother (a mitigating circumstance) are typical predicaments that elicit sympathy inasmuch as the person is not held responsible for his or her negative plight. As summarized by Wispé (1991), "one will sympathize more with a brave sufferer, in a good cause, in which one's afflictions are beyond one's control" (p. 134).

Guilt and Shame

In their review of the guilt literature, Wicker, Payne, and Morgan (1983) concluded: "In general, guilt is said to follow from acts that violate ethical norms . . . or moral values. Guilt is accompanied by feelings of personal responsibility" (p. 26). Similarly, Lindsay-Hartz, de Rivera, and Mascolo (1995) propose that we experience guilt "when there is a violation of the moral order for which we take responsibility with our conviction that we could and should have done otherwise" (p. 278). Thus guilt, like anger, is related to the moral constructs of "ought" and "should." It has even been suggested that guilt is analogous to anger directed inward. Whereas most conceptualizations of guilt focus on its intrapsychic qualities, Baumeister, Stillwell, and Heatherton (1994) also elaborate on the interpersonal nature of guilt. For example, victims sometimes use their own suffering to induce feelings of guilt in their perpetrators, which has the effect of redistributing emotional distress within the dyad. The use of such interpersonal tactics is still guided by an implicit understanding of a responsibility–guilt linkage.

Shame often is indistinguishable from guilt in that both "involve negative self-evaluations that are painful, tense, agitating, real, present, and depressing" (Wicker et al., 1983, p. 33). However, shame and the related affect of humiliation seem to arise from uncontrollable causes, such as lack of aptitude. This is consistent with the conception that shame is generated by appraisals that one has been unable to live up to others' standards, or that one is unworthy or incompetent (see Tangney & Fischer, 1995).

The contrasts between guilt and shame in the emotion literature further illustrate how these emotions are differentially linked to the controllability dimension. For example, Mascolo and Fischer (1995) distinguish the two emotions as follows:

> In guilt one is concerned with a wrongful act, whereas in shame one's entire self seems to be experienced as unworthy. In guilt, one has done something wrong even though one is not really a bad person; in shame one is an unworthy person. Although both guilt and shame can be generated by the same event, shame in these situations involves a focus on one's unworthy self in the eyes of others, whereas guilt involves a focus on one's wrongful act. (p. 68)

These contrasting portrayals are reminiscent of Janoff-Bulman's (1979) distinction between characterological self-blame (attributions to stable, uncontrollable causes) and behavioral self-blame (attributions to unstable, controllable causes). Consistent with findings we reviewed in an earlier section on the maladaptivity of characterological relative to behavioral self-blame, Tangney and her colleagues report a number of studies revealing that shame-proneness is related to adjustment difficulties such as low self-esteem, depression, and anxiety; whereas guilt-proneness is unrelated to these indices of psychopathology (Tangney, Burggraf, & Wagner, 1995).

Each of the four emotions examined above is associated with particular action tendencies, as illustrated in Table 24.1. Anger tends to evoke "retaliation," or, in the words of Karen Horney (1937), "going against others"; pity and guilt tend to elicit "restitution," or "going toward tasks or others." That is, pity and guilt give rise to "repayment," or the tendency to make a situation more equitable and in balance (see Trivers, 1971). Finally, shame tends to produce withdrawal and retreat. To use the vocabulary of Horney once more, a person who feels shame is inclined to go away from others. Note, then, that each of these emotions brings with it a program for action. Thus, emotions summarize the past, providing an overall evaluation for what has occurred, while they also prescribe for the future. Hence, they seem to provide the glue between thinking and acting, or between attributions and behavior.

The analyses outlined in Table 24.1 can be used to explain behavior in a variety of contexts.

TABLE 24.1. Relations among Causal Thinking, Affect, and Action

Causal antecedent	Affect	Action tendency
Personal "failure," controllably caused by others	Anger	Retaliation (going against)
Failure of another, uncontrollable	Pity	Restitution (going toward)
Failure of self or another, controllably casued by actor	Guilt	Restitution (going toward)
Failure of self, uncontrollable	Shame	Retreat (going away from)

Here we elaborate on the linkages involving pity and anger as we briefly consider attributional appproaches to altruism and aggression.

Altruism

The substantiated and supposed determinants of help giving are voluminous, ranging from enduring internal factors, such as genetic dispositions, to temporary external variables, such as temperature or even the clothes that one is wearing (if, for example, someone is asked to help change a tire). An attributional approach to helping presumes that perceptions of the reasons for needing help, and the affects elicited by this causal analysis, are pivotal in understanding why aid might or might not be offered.

It has been suggested that if the cause of a need is under personal control (that is, the person is held responsible), then anger is elicited and help, in turn, is withheld. On the other hand, if the cause of the need is uncontrollable (that is, the person is not judged as responsible), then sympathy is evoked and help is offered. Thus, for example, shy or introverted children in need of school help are aided more by teachers than are hyperactives (Brophy & Rohrkemper, 1981); a person falling in a subway because of illness is aided more than another falling because of drunkenness (Piliavin, Rodin, & Piliavin, 1969), and a student requiring class notes because of eye problems is assisted more than one wanting the notes because "he went to the beach" (Reisenzein, 1986). In a similar manner, the cause of a stigma determines to a great extent whether help is offered or withheld so that, for example, a person with AIDS is more likely to be helped if the disease was due to a blood transfusion rather than due to promiscuous sexual behavior (e.g., Dooley, 1995). Earlier in this chapter it was indicated that the belief in individual responsibility is differentially represented in political party affiliation. For example, conservatives are more likely to ascribe controllability and responsibility to those on welfare than are liberals (e.g., Skitka & Tetlock, 1993). As a consequence, conservatives should be less aid giving than their liberal counterparts, and this is an accepted empirical fact (e.g., Feather, 1995; Kluegel, 1990).

In more recent research, it has been clearly documented with path-analytic techniques that the emotions of anger and pity (and particularly the latter) are the proximal determinants of decisions to aid others, whereas beliefs about controllability and responsibility are distal determinants of behavior, influencing helping through the mediational role of emotions (see Weiner, 1995).

Aggression

The study of aggression has had a very different history and focus than the study of altruism. Among the issues of most concern to aggression researchers is the identification of individual differences that make some people more prone than others to engage in antisocial behavior. In the search for aggressive traits, attributions have played a pivotal role. A robust finding in the developmental aggression literature is that aggressive children display an attributional bias to infer hostile intent on the part of peer provocateurs, particularly in situations in which the causes of the provocation are ambiguous (see reviews in Crick & Dodge, 1994; Coie & Dodge, 1998). For example, imagine a situation in which a youngster experiences a negative outcome instigated by a peer, such as being pushed while waiting in line, and it is unclear whether the peer's behavior was intentional or not. When asked if the push occurred "on purpose" (an index of responsibility), aggressive children are more likely than their nonaggressive counterparts to infer that the behavior was motivated by hostile intent. Attributions to hostile intent are then hypothesized to lead to aggressive retaliation. The aggressive consequences of attributions to hostile intent are not confined to research with children on peer-directed hostility. For example, it is well documented that abusive caregivers frequently overattribute negative intent on the part of their misbeheving children (see review in Milner, 1993), and maritally violent husbands are more likely than their nonviolent counterparts to attribute spousal conflict to hostile intentions on the part of their wives (e.g., Holtzworth-Munroe & Hutchinson, 1993).

What processes mediate inferences about intentions and subsequent aggressive behavior? As in the study of altruism, attributional analyses have uncovered a temporal sequence from cognitions to emotions to behavior. A number of studies now document that feelings of anger mediate the relation between attributions and aggressive behavior (e.g., Betancourt & Blair, 1992; Graham, Hudley, & Williams, 1992). Thus affect is a more proximal determinant of action than cognition, and the temporal sequence is one of perceived responsibility (intentionality) $\rightarrow$ anger $\rightarrow$ aggression.

One of the strengths of this conception is that it has clear implications for intervention. If attributions and inferences about responsibility instigate a set of reactions that lead to aggression, then it might be possible to train aggressive-prone individuals to see provocations as less intended (i.e., the provocateur is not responsible). This should mitigate anger as well the tendency to react with hostility. Note that the theoretical underpinnings of this approach—that a change in cognition can lead to a change in social behavior—is exactly that which guided attributional therapies in the achievement domain that we reviewed earlier. Hudley and Graham (1993) successfully applied attributional analyses in an intervention designed to reduce antisocial behavior among African American boys labeled as aggressive. The school-based intervention taught participants to understand better the meaning of intentionality and to infer nonhostile peer intent following ambiguously caused provocation. Compared to a control group who received no intervention, participants were observed to be less angry and they were rated by their teachers as less aggressive.

Summary

The field of personality has long addressed prosocial and antisocial behavior, outlining both the individual difference tendencies as well as contextual determinants of these disparate types of social conduct. But few theorists have attempted to address these contrasting behaviors within the same theoretical system—as attribution theory has. It is true that a great deal of both altruism and aggression are not subject to a causal analysis. However, prosocial or antisocial behavior that is mediated by causal thinking is substantial and cannot be overlooked by personality psychologists.

GENERAL CONCLUSIONS AND FUTURE THOUGHTS

In the very first paragraph of this chapter we stated that attribution theory is as central to personality psychology as it is to social psychology. We believe that this assertion has been documented in this chapter, which has examined attributions as defense mechanisms, attributions as determinants of trait inferences, individual differences in causal ascriptions, self-esteem maintenance, attributional determinants of expectancy of success, depression, affective experience, the dynamics of altruism and aggression, and behavioral change. We do not think that one can ask for a broader range of relevance from any extant theoretical system.

It is worthwhile to ask, now 40 years after the publication of Heider's (1958) book *The Psychology of Interpersonal Relations,* about the future of attribution theory. Is this *Zeitgeist* over? To answer a question about the future, it is informative to turn back to the past and consider the precursors of attribution theory. Festinger's (1957) theory of cognitive dissonance provided the dominant research paradigm for social psychology in the 1960s. Dissonance theory offered a non-commonsense approach to attitude formation and change, based on the "fit" between cognitive elements. In part because of the intention of social psychologists in the 1950s to progress beyond what was known as "bubba" (grandmother) psychology, the dominance of dissonance is readily understood. But by the end of the 1960s dissonance had run its course. The many studies that were conducted left others to search for new places to leave their personal mark. Of equal importance, however, was that dissonance was linked to drive theory and mechanism; yet the conception of drive already had been discarded by most motivational theorists. Of perhaps greatest importance, dissonance theory was conceptually sparse, so that there were few new directions toward which the theory could turn.

Attribution theory replaced dissonance as the dominant paradigm within social psychology. Unlike dissonance, it grew from naive psychology and relied upon accessible, conscious experience. Unlike dissonance, it was not linked to drive theory, but rather to the emerging cognitive conceptions of action. And unlike dissonance, it was conceptually rich, with systems of interrelated concepts and many directions to explore.

Attribution theory continues to incorporate new concepts and has been responsive to empirical challenges. Hence, we suspect that it still has a future. Attribution theory has become an established part of psychotherapy and it has been applied to areas ranging from sports psychology to consumer behavior; it has successfully addressed issues related to reactions to the stigmatized, excuse giving, and consequences of perceived responsibility; it is established in motivational and educational psychology; and on and on. We see the immediate future as including diversification and entry into still widening areas, each serving as a place for both specific modification and general theoretical development. Certainly, with the ever-increasing interest in self-perception, affective experience, and construals of the environment, personality psychology will remain closely tied to attributional concerns.

REFERENCES

Abramson, L. Y., Alloy, L. B., & Metalsky, G. I. (1995). Hopelessness depression. In G. Buchanan & M. Seligman (Eds.), *Explanatory style* (pp. 113–134). Hillsdale, NJ: Erlbaum.

Abramson, L. Y., Metalsky, G. I., & Alloy, L. B. (1989). Hopelessness depression: A theory-based subtype of depression. *Psychological Review, 96,* 358–372.

Abramson, L. Y., Seligman, M. E. P., & Teasdale, J. (1978). Learned helplessness in humans: Critique and reformulation. *Journal of Abnormal Psychology, 87,* 49–74.

Anderson, C. A. (1983). Motivational and performance deficits in interpersonal settings: The effects of attribution style. *Journal of Personality and Social Psychology, 45,* 1136–1147.

Anderson, C. A., & Jennings, D. L. (1980). When experiences of failure promote expectations of success: The impact of attributing failure to ineffective strategies. *Journal of Personality, 48,* 393–407.

Anderson, C. A., & Jennings, D. L., & Arnoult, L. H. (1988). The validity and utility of attributional style construct at a moderate level of specificity. *Journal of Personality and Social Psychology, 55,* 979–990.

Anderson, C., Miller, R., Riger, A., Dill, J., & Sedikides, C. (1994). Behavioral and characterological attributional styles as predictors of depression and loneliness: Review, refinement, and test. *Journal of Personality and Social Psychology, 66,* 549–558.

Arkin, R. M., & Baumgardner, A. H. (1985). Self-handicapping. In J. H. Harvey & G. Weary (Eds.), *Attribution: Basic issues and applications* (pp. 169–202). New York: Academic Press.

Arkin, R. M., & Oleson, K. C. (1998). Self-handicapping. In J. Darley & J. Cooper (Eds.), *Attribution and social interaction: The legacy of Edward M. Jones.* Washington, DC: American Psychological Association.

Averill, J. R. (1982). *Anger and aggression: An essay on emotion.* New York: Springer-Verlag.

Averill, J. R. (1983). Studies on anger and aggression. *American Psychologist, 38,* 1145–1160.

Baumeister, R., Stillwell, A., & Heatherton, T. (1994). Guilt: An interpersonal approach. *Psychological Bulletin, 115,* 243–267.

Baumeister, R. F., Wotman, S. R., & Stillwell, A. M. (1993). Unrequited love: On heartbreak, guilt, scriptlessness, and humiliation. *Journal of Personality and Social Psychology, 64,* 377–394.

Beckman, L. (1970). Effects of students' performance on teachers' and observers' attribution of causality. *Journal of Educational Psychology, 61,* 76–82.

Betancourt, H., & Blair, I. (1992). A cognition-(attribution)-emotion model of violence in conflict situations. *Personality and Social Psychology Bulletin, 18,* 343–350.

Bradley, G. W. (1978). Self-serving biases in the attribution process: A reexamination of the fact and fiction question. *Journal of Personality and Social Psychology, 36,* 56–71.

Brophy, J., & Rohrkemper, M. (1981). The influence of problem ownership on teachers' perceptions of strategies for coping with problem students. *Journal of Educational Psychology, 73,* 295–311.

Burger, J. M. (1992). *Desire for control.* New York: Plenum Press.

Cacioppo, J., & Petty, R. (1982). The need for cognition. *Journal of Personality and Social Psychology, 42,* 116–131.

Cartwright, D. (1950). Emotional dimensions of group life. In M. L. Raymert (Ed.), *Feelings and emotions* (pp. 439–447). New York: McGraw-Hill.

Carver, C. S. (1989). How should multifaceted personality constructs be tested? Issues illustrated by self-monitoring, attributional style, and hardiness. *Journal of Personality and Social Psychology, 56,* 577–585.

Chaplin, W. F., John, O. P., & Goldberg, L. R. (1988). Conceptions of traits and states: Dimensional attributes with ideals as prototypes. *Journal of Personality and Social Psychology, 54,* 541–557.

Cheng, P., & Novick, L. (1990). A probabilistic contrast model of causal induction. *Journal of Personality and Social Psychology, 58,* 545–567.

Chiu, C., Dweck, C. S., Tong, J., & Fu, J. (1997). Implicit theories and conceptions of morality. *Journal of Personality and Social Psychology, 73,* 923–940.

Coie, J., & Dodge, K. A. (1998). Aggression and antisocial behavior. In N. Eisenberg (Ed.), *Handbook of child psychology* (Vol. 4, pp. 779–862). New York: Wiley.

Cole, D., Peeke, L., & Ingold, C. (1996). Characterological and behavioral self-blame in children: Assessment and developmental considerations. *Development and Psychopathology, 8,* 381–397.

Crick, N., & Dodge, K. A. (1994). A review and reformulation of social information processing mechanisms in children's social adjustment. *Psychological Bulletin, 115,* 74–101.

Crocker, J., Cornwell, B., & Major, B. (1993). The stigma of overweight: Affective consequences of attributional ambiguity. *Journal of Personality and Social Psychology, 64,* 60–70.

Crocker, J., & Major, B. (1989). Social stigma and self-esteem: The self-protective properties of stigma. *Psychological Review, 96,* 608–630.

Crocker, J., Major, B., & Steele, C. (1998). Social stigma. In D. Gilbert & S. Fiske (Eds.), *The handbook of social psychology* (Vol. 2, pp. 504–553). New York: McGraw-Hill.

Crocker, J., Voelkl, K., Testa, M., & Major, B. (1991). Social stigma: The affective consequences of attributional ambiguity. *Journal of Personality and Social Psychology, 60,* 218–228.

Cutrona, C. E., Russell, D., & Jones, R. D. (1985). Cross-situational consistency in causal attributions: Does attributional style exist? *Journal of Personality and Social Psychology, 47,* 1043–1058.

Dooley, P. A. (1995). Perceptions of onset controllability of AIDS and helping judgments: An attributional analysis. *Journal of Applied Social Psychology, 25,* 858–869.

Dweck, C. S., Chiu, C., & Hong, Y. (1995). Implicit theories and their role in judgments and reactions: A world from two perspectives. *Psychological Inquiry, 6,* 267–285.

Dweck, C. S., & Leggett, E. (1988). A social-cognitive approach to motivation and personality. *Psychological Review, 95,* 256–273.

Edwards, J. A., Weary, G., & Reich, D. A. (1998). Causal uncertainty: Factor structure and relation to the Big Five personality factors. *Personality and Social Psychology Bulletin, 24,* 451–462.

Feather, N. (1985). Attitudes, values, and attributions: Explanations for unemployment. *Journal of Personality and Social Psychology, 48,* 876–889.

Festinger, L. (1957). *A theory of cognitive dissonance.* Evanston, IL: Row, Peterson.

Fletcher, G. J. O., Danilovics, P., Fernandez, G., Peterson, D., & Reeder, G. D. (1986). Attributional complexity: An individual difference measure. *Journal of Personality and Social Psychology, 51,* 875–884.

Folkes, V. S. (1982). Communicating the causes of social rejection. *Journal of Experimental Social Psychology, 18,* 235–252.

Forsterling, F. (1985). Attributional training: A review. *Psychological Bulletin, 98,* 495–512.

Forsterling, F. (1988). Attribution theory in clinical psychology. New York: Wiley.

Frazier, P., & Schauben, L. (1994). Causal attributions and recovery from rape and other stressful life events. *Journal of Social and Clinical Psychology, 13,* 1–14.

Gilovich, T. (1983). Biased evaluation and persistence in gambling. *Journal of Personality and Social Psychology, 44,* 1110–1126.

Graham, S., Hudley, C., & Williams, E. (1992). Attributional and emotional determinants of aggression among African American and Latino young adolescents. *Developmental Psychology, 28,* 731–740.

Graham S., & Juvonen, J. (1998). Self-balme and peer victimization in middle school: An attributional analysis. *Developmental Psychology, 34,* 587–599.

Heider, F. (1958). *The psychology of interpersonal relations.* New York: Wiley.

Hewstone, M., & Jaspars, J. (1987). Covariation and causal attribution: A logic model of the intuitive analysis of variance. *Journal of Personality and Social Psychology, 53,* 663–672.

Hilton, D. J., & Slugoski, B. R. (1986). Knowledge based causal attribution: The abnormal conditions focus model. *Psychological Review, 93,* 663–672.

Hilton, D. J., , Smith, R. H., & Kim, S. H. (1995). The process of causal explanation and dispositional attribution. *Journal of Personality and Social Psychology, 68,* 377–387.

Holtzworth-Munroe, A., & Hutchinson, G. (1993). Attributing negative intent to wife behavior: The attributions of maritally violent versus nonviolent men. *Journal of Abnormal Psychology, 102,* 206–211.

Horney, K. (1937). *Neurotic personality of our times.* New York: Norton.

Hudley, C., & Graham, S. (1993). An attributional intervention to reduce peer-directed aggression in African American boys. *Child Development, 64,* 124–138.

Isenberg, A. (1980). Natural pride and natural shame. In A. O. Rorty (Ed.), *Explaining emotions* (pp. 355–384). Berkeley, CA: University of California Press.

James, W., & Rotter, J. B. (1958). Partial and 100% reinforcement under chance and skill conditions. *Journal of Experimental Psychology, 55,* 397–403.

Janoff-Bulman, R. (1979). Characterological versus behavioral self-blame: Inquiries into depression and rape. *Journal of Personality and Social Psychology, 37,* 1798–1809.

Janoff-Bulman, R. (1992). *Shared assumptions: Toward a new psychology of trauma.* New York: Free Press.

Johnson, T. J., Feigenbaum, R., Weiby, M. (1964). Some determinants and consequences of the teachers' perception of causation. *Journal of Educational Psychology, 55,* 237–246.

Joiner, T. E., & Wagner, K. D. (1995). Attributional style and depression in children and adolescents: A meta-analytic review. *Clinical Psychology Review, 15,* 777–798.

Jones, E. E. & Berglas, S. (1978). Control of attributions about the self through self-handicapping strategies: The appeal of alchohol and the role of underachievement. *Personality and Social Psychology Bulletin, 4,* 200–206.

Jones, E. E., & Nisbett, R. E. (1971). The actor and the observer: Divergent perceptions of the causes of behavior. In E. E. Jones , D. E. Kanouse, H. H. Kelley, R. E. Nisbett, S. Valins, & B. Weiner (Eds.), *Attribution: Perceiving the causes of behavior* (pp. 79–94). Morristown, NJ: General Learning Press.

Kelley, H. H. (1967) Attribution theory in social psychology. In D. Levine (Ed.), *Nebraska Symposium on Motivation* (Vol. 15, pp. 192–238). Lincoln, NE: University of Nebraska Press.

Kelley, H. H. (1971). Causal schemata and the attribution process. In E. E. Jones , D. E. Kanouse, H. H. Kelley, R. E. Nisbett, S. Valins, & B. Weiner (Eds.), *Attribution: Perceiving the causes of behavior* (pp. 151–174). Morristown, NJ: General Learning Press.

Kelley, E. E., & Michela, J. L. (1980). Attribution theory and research. *Annual Review of Psychology, 31,* 457–501.

Kingdon, J. W. (1967). Politicians' beliefs about voters. *American Political Science Review, 14,* 137–145.

Kluegel, J. (1990). Trends in whites' explanations of the black–white gap in socioeconomic status, 1977–1989. *American Sociological Review, 55,* 521–525.

Lau, R. R., & Ware, J. W. (1981). The conceptualization and measurement of a multidimensional health-specific locus of control scale. *Medical Care, 19,* 1147–1158.

Lee, Y., & Seligman, M. E. P. (1997). Are Americans more optimisitc than the Chinese? *Personality and Scoial Psychology Bulletin, 23,* 32–40.

Lefcourt, H. (1992). Durability and impact of the locus of control construct. *Psychological Bulletin, 112,* 411–414.

Lefcourt, H. M. & von Baeyer, C. L., Ware, E. E., & Cox, D. J. (1979). The Multidimensional–Multiattributional Causality Scale: The development of a goal specific locus of control scale. *Canadian Journal of Behavioral Science, 11,* 286–304.

Lewis, P. (1995). A naturalistic test of two fundamental propositions: Correspondence bias and the actor–observer hypothesis. *Journal of Personality, 63,* 87–109.

Lindsay-Hartz, J., de Rivera, J., & Mascolo, M. F. (1995). Differentiating guilt and shame and their effects on motivation. In Tangney, J. P., & Fischer, K. W. (Eds.), *Self-conscious emotions* (pp. 274–300). New York: Guilford Press.

Lopez, S. R. (1989). Patient variable biases in clinical judgment: A conceptual overview and some methodological considerations. *Psychological Bulletin, 106,* 184–203.

Major, B., & Crocker, J. (1993). Social stigma: The affective consequences of attributional ambiguity. In D. Mackie & D. Hamilton (Eds.), *Affect, cognition, and stereotyping: Interactive processses in intergroup perception* (pp. 345–370). New York: Academic Press.

Mascolo, M., & Fischer, K. (1995). Developmental transformations in appraisals for pride, shame, and guilt. In J. Tangney & K. Fischer (Eds.), *Self-consious emotions* (pp. 64–113). New York: Guilford Press.

Marks, G., & Miller, N. (1987). Ten years of research on the false-consensus effect: An empirical and theoretical review. *Psychological Bulletin, 102,* 72–90.

McAllister, H. (1996). Self-serving bias in the classroom: Who shows it? Who knows it? *Journal of Educational Psychology, 88,* 123–131.

Menec, V., Perry, R., Struthers, C., Schonwetter, D., Hechter, F., & Eichholz, B. (1994). Assisting at-risk college students with attributional retraining and effective teaching. *Journal of Applied Social Psychology, 24,* 675–701.

Metalsky, G. I., Joiner, T. E., Hardin, T. S., & Abramson, L. Y. (1993). Depressive reactions to failure in a naturalistic setting: A test of the hopelessness and self-esteem theories of depression. *Journal of Abnormal Psychology, 102,* 101–109.

Meyer, C., & Taylor, S. (1986). Adjustment to rape. *Journal of Personality and Social Psycholgy, 50,* 1226–1234.

Midgley, C., Arunkumar, R., & Urdan, T. (1996). "If I don't do well tomorrow, there's a reason": Predictors of adolescents' use of academic self-handicapping strategies. *Journal of Educational Psychology, 88,* 423–434.

Milner, J. S. (1993). Social information processing and physical child abuse. *Clinical Psychology Review, 13,* 275–294.

Monson, T. C., & Snyder, M. (1977). Actors, observers, and the attribution process: Toward a reconceptualization. *Journal of Experimental Social Psychology, 13,* 89–111.

Mullen, B., Atkins, J. L., Champion, D. S., Edwards, C., Hardy, D., Story, J. E., & Vanderklok, M. (1985). The false consensus effect: A meta-analysis of 115 hypothesis tests. *Journal of Experimental Social Psychology, 21,* 262–283.

Mullen, B., & Riordan, C. A. (1988). Self-serving attributions for performance in naturalistic settings: A meta-analytic review. *Journal of Applied Social Psychology, 18,* 3–22.

Perry, R., Hechter, F., Menec, V., & Weinberg, L. (1993). Enhancing achievement motivation and performance in college students: An attributional retraining perspective. *Research in Higher Education, 34,* 164–172.

Peterson, C. (1991). The meaning and measurement of explanatory style. *Psychological Inquiry, 2,* 1–10.

Peterson, C., & Barrett, L. (1987). Explanatory style and academic performance among university freshmen. *Journal of Personality and Social Psychology, 53,* 603–607.

Peterson, C., Maier, S., & Seligman, M. E. P. (1993). *Learned helplessness: A theory for the age of personal control.* New York: Oxford University Press.

Peterson, C., Seligman, M. E. P., & Valliant, G. (1988). Pessimistic explanatory style is a risk factor for physical illness: A thirty-five year longitudinal study. *Journal of Personality and Social Psychology, 55,* 23–27.

Peterson, C., Semmel, A., von Baeyer, C., Abramson, L. Y., Metalsky, G. I., & Seligman, M. E. P. (1982). The Attributional Style Questionnaire. *Congitive Therapy Research, 6,* 287–299.

Peterson, C., & Ulrey, L. (1994). Can explanatory style be scored from TAT protocols? *Personality and Social Psychology Bulletin, 20,* 102–106.

Piliavin, I., Rodin, J., & Piliavin, J. (1969). Good Samaritanism: An underground phenomenon? *Journal of Personality and Social Psychology, 13,* 289–299.

Polly, L., Vodanovick, S., Watt, J. M., & Blanchard, M. (1993). The effects of attributional processes on boredom proneness. *Journal of Social Behavior and Personality, 8,* 123–132.

Reeves, A., Watson, P., Ramsey, A., & Morris, R. (1995). Private self-consciousness factors, need for cognition, and depression. *Journal of Social Behavior and Personality, 10,* 431–443.

Reisenzein, R. (1983). The Schachter theory of emotions: Two decades later. *Psychological Bulletin, 94,* 239–264.

Reisenzein, R. (1986). A structural equation analysis of Weiner's attribution-affect model of helping behavior. *Journal of Personality and Social Psychology, 50,* 1123–1133.

Reisenzein, R., & Hoffman, T. (1990). An investigation of the dimensions of cognitive appraisal in emotion using the repertory grid technique. *Motivation and Emotion, 14,* 1–26.

Robins, R. W., Spranca, M. D., & Mendelsohn, G. (1996). The actor–observer effect revisited: Effects of individual differences and repeated social interactions on actor and observer attributions. *Journal of Personality and Social Psychology, 71,* 375–389.

Roseman, I. (1991). Appraisal determinants of discrete emotions. *Cognition and Emotion, 5,* 161–200.

Ross, L. (1977). The intuitive psychologist and his shortcomings: Distortions in the attribution process. In L. Berkowitz (Ed.), *Advances in experimental social psychology* (Vol. 10, pp. 173–220). New York: Academic Press.

Ross, L., Greene, D., & House, P. (1977). The "False Consensus Effect": An egocentric bias in social perception and attribution process. *Journal of Experimental Social Psychology, 13,* 279–301.

Rotter, J. B. (1966). Generalized expectancies for internal versus external control of reinforcement. *Psychological Monographs, 80*(1, Whole No. 609).

Rotter, J. B. (1975). Some problems and misconceptions related to the construct of internal versus external control of reinforcement. *Journal of Consulting and Clinical Psychology, 43,* 56–67.

Rotter, J. B., & Hochreich, D. J. (1975). *Personality.* Glenview, IL: Scott, Foresman.

Ruggierro, K. M., & Taylor, D. M. (1995). Coping with discrimination: How disadvantaged group members perceive the discrimination that confronts them. *Journal of Personality and Social Psychology, 68,* 826–838.

Ruggiero, K. M., & Taylor, D. M. (1997). Why minority group members perceive or do not perceive the discrimination that confronts them: The role of self-esteem and perceived control. *Journal of Personality and Social Psychology, 72,* 373–389.

Schachter, S., & Singer, J. E. (1962). Cognition, social and psychological determinants of emotional state. *Psychological Review, 69,* 379–399.

Seligman, M. E. P., & Schulman, P. (1986). Explanatory style as a predictor of performance as a life insurance agent. *Journal of Personality and Social Psychology, 50,* 832–838.

Sigmon, S. T., & Snyder, C. R. (1993). Looking at oneself in a rose-colored mirror: The role of excuses in the negotiation of a personal reality. In M. Lewis & C. Saarni (Eds.), *Lying and deception in everyday life* (pp. 146–165). New York: Guilford Press.

Skitka, L. J., & Tetlock, P. E. (1993). Providing public assistance: Cognitive and motivational processes underlying liberal and conservative policy preferences. *Journal of Personality and Social Psychology, 65,* 1205–1223.

Snyder, C. R., & Higgins, R. L. (1997). Reality negotiation: Governing one's self and being governed by others. *Review of General Psychology, 1,* 336–350.

Snyder, C. R., & Higgins, R. L. (1998). Excuses: Their effective role in the negotiation of reality. *Psychological Bulletin, 104,* 23–35.

Snyder, M. L., Stephan, W. G., & Rosenfield, D. (1976). Egotism and attribution. *Journal of Personality and Social Psychology, 35,* 435–441.

Struthers, C. W., & Perry, R. P. (1996). Attributional style, attributional retraining, and innoculation against motivational deficits. *School Psychology of Education, 2,* 171–187.

Tangney, J., Burggraf, S., & Wagner, P. (1995). Shame-proneness, guilt-proneness, and psychological symptoms. In J. Tangney & K. Fischer (Eds.), *Self-conscious emotions* (pp. 343–367). New York: Guilford Press.

Tangney, J., & Fischer, K. (Eds.). (1995). *Self-conscious emotions.* New York: Guilford Press.

Taylor, S. E., & Brown, J. D. (1988). Illusion and well-being: A social psychological perspective on mental health. *Psychological Bulletin, 103,* 193–210.

Tesser, A., Gatewood, R., & Driver, M. (1968). Some determinants of gratitude. *Journal of Personality and Social Psychology, 3,* 233–236.

Trivers, R. L. (1971). The evolution of reciprical altruism. *Quarterly Review of Biology, 46,* 35–57.

Urdan, T., Midgley, C., & Anderman, E. (1998). The role of classroom goal structure in students' use of self-handicapping strategies. *American Educational Research Journal, 35,* 101–122.

Van Overwalle, F. (1998). Causal explanation as constraint satisfaction: A critique and a feedforward connectionist alternative. *Journal of Personality and Social Psychology, 74,* 312–328.

Van Overwalle, F. Segebarth, K., & Goldchstein, M. (1989). Improving performance of freshmen through attributional testimonies from fellow students. *British Journal of Educational Psychology, 59,* 75–85.

Wallston, K. A., & Wallston, B. S. (1981). Health locus of control scales. In H. Lefcourt (Ed.), *Research with the locus of control construct* (pp. 189–243). New York: Academic Press.

Weary, G., & Edwards, J. A. (1994). Individual differences in causal uncertainty. *Journal of Personality and Social Psychology, 67,* 308–318.

Weary, G., & Jacobson, J. (1997). Causal uncertainty beliefs and diagnostic information seeking. *Journal of Personality and Social Psychology, 73,* 839–848.

Webster, D. M., & Kruglanski, A. W. (1994). Individual differences in need for cognitive closure. *Journal of Personality and Social Psychology, 67,* 1049–1062.

Weiner, B. (1980). *Human motivation.* New York: Holt, Rinehart & Winston.

Weiner, B, (1985). An attributional theory of acheivement motivation and emotion. *Psychological Review, 92,* 548–573.

Weiner, B. (1986). *An attributional theory of motivation and emotion.* New York: Springer.

Weiner, B. (1988). Attribution and attributional therapy: Some theoretical observations and suggestions. *British Journal of Clinical Psychology, 27,* 93–104.

Weiner, B. (1995). *Judgments of responsibility: Foundations for a theory of social behavior.* New York: Guilford Press.

Weiner, B., Figueroa-Munoz, A., & Kakihara, C. (1991). The goals of excuses and communication strategies related to causal perceptions. *Personality and Social Psychology Bulletin, 17,* 4–13.

Weiner, B., & Graham, S. (1984). An attributional approach to emotional development. In C. Izard, J. Kagan, & R. Zajonc (Eds.), *Emotions, cognition, and behavior* (pp. 167–191). New York: Cambridge University Press.

Weiner, B., Russell, D., & Lerman, D. (1978). Affective consequences of causal ascriptions. In J. H. Harvey, W. J. Ickes, & R. F. Kidd (Eds.), *New directions in attribution research* (Vol. 2, pp. 59–88). Hillsdale, NJ: Erlbaum.

Weiner, B., Russell, D., & Lerman, D. (1979). The cognition-emotion process in acheivement-related contexts. *Journal of Personality and Social Psychology, 37,* 1211–1220.

Wicker, W. F., Payne, G. C., & Morgan, R. D. (1983). Participant descriptions of guilt and shame. *Motivation and Emotion, 7,* 25–39.

Wilson, T., & Linville, P. (1982). Improving academic performance of college freshmen: Attribution therapy revisited. *Journal of Personality and Social Psychology, 42,* 367–376.

Wilson, T., & Linville, P. (1985). Improving the performance of college freshmen with attributional techniques. *Journal of Personality and Social Psychology, 49,* 287–293.

Wispé, L. (1991). *The psychology of sympathy.* New York: Plenum Press.

Whisman, M. A., & Pinto, A. (1997). Hopelessness depression in depressed inpatient adolescents. *Cognitive Therapy and Research, 21,* 345–358.

Zeelenberg, M., van Dijk, W., Manstead, A., & van der Pligt, J. (1998). The experience of regret and disappointment. *Cognition and Emotion, 12,* 221–230.

Zucker, G., & Weiner, B. (1993). Conservatism and perceptions of poverty: An attributional analysis. *Journal of Applied Social Psychology, 23,* 925–943.

Zuckerman, M. (1979). Attribution of success and failure revisited, or: The motivational bias is alive and well in attribution theory. *Journal of Personality, 47,* 245–287.

Zullow, H., & Seligman, M. E. P. (1990). Pessimistic rumination predicts defeat of presidential candidates, 1900 to 1984. *Psychological Inquiry, 1,* 52–61.

Chapter 25

Creativity and Genius

Dean Keith Simonton
University of California, Davis

Creativity and genius are highly desirable but also rather elusive qualities. Employers in high-tech industries often wish that their workers were more creative, and so creativity workshops that purport to attain that end have proliferated. Parents are usually pleased to learn that they have given birth to a "budding genius," and will often fight hard to get their child enrolled in special problems for the gifted.

Although a person can exhibit creativity without being a genius, and be a genius without being creative, both characteristics can converge in a single personality. Indeed, the creative genius is often viewed as the highest or purest manifestation of both creativity and genius. Isaac Newton, René Descartes, Miguel de Cervantes, Leonardo da Vinci, and Ludwig van Beethoven offer clear examples. Creative genius is so highly valued that special honors are devoted to its recognition—the Nobel Prize perhaps constituting the most conspicuous example. A more recent instance are the special grants awarded by MacArthur Foundation, which the mass media have taken to confer the official title of "genius" upon the recipients (Shekerjian, 1990).

Curiously, of the two attributes, genius has the longer history as an individual-difference variable. The first scientific study was Galton's (1869) book *Hereditary Genius*. Creativity, in contrast, did not come into its own as an independent research topic until nearly a century later. Often this latter development is taken as beginning with Guilford's (1950) Presidential Address before the American Psychological Association. In fact, it was not until the 1960s that research on creativity really exploded. The *Journal of Creative Behavior,* for example, did not begin publication until 1962. Although creativity research got a late start, it quickly overtook research on genius as a topic for personality research. Despite something of a decline in interest in the 1980s, research on creativity has picked up again. This increased activity is evident in the founding of the *Creativity Research Journal* in 1988, and the recent publication of several creativity handbooks and anthologies (e.g., Glover, Ronning, & Reynolds, 1989; Runco, 1997; Sternberg, 1988), and the forthcoming publication of the *Encyclopedia of Creativity* (Runco & Pritzker, 1999). With this upsurge has come an increased interest in genius as well (e.g., Albert, 1992; Eysenck, 1995; Ochse, 1990; Simonton, 1997c).

The main goal of this chapter is to provide an overview of the substantive findings and issues regarding individual differences in creativity and genius, with a special emphasis on the two combined. But before we can begin that task, we first must define our terms.

DEFINITION

What do we mean when we call someone "creative"? How do we know when a person can be considered a "genius"? Because creativity is perhaps the most difficult to define, we will start with the first question.

Creativity

It is not easy to give a universally acceptable definition of creativity. This difficulty holds even though there exists a strong consensus on what creativity entails, at least in the abstract. In particular, most researchers would agree that creativity involves the generation of creative ideas. At least two prerequisites must be met for an idea to be deemed "creative."

First, the idea must represent a relatively uncommon response. This is the criterion of *originality*. An idea that arose from only one person in the history of the human race is considered more original than an idea that emerged from many people. Although many individuals have spontaneously used a sandal or shoe to keep a beach blanket from being carried away by the wind, just one person revolutionized physics by introducing the theory of relativity—Albert Einstein. Of course, originality is not an absolute, all-or-none criterion. Instead, we can speak of degrees of originality.

Second, to count as creative, an original idea must exhibit *adaptiveness*. That is, the idea must provide the solution to some significant problem or achieve some important goal. Without this second criterion, it would be difficult to separate the rambling thoughts of a hebephrenic psychotic from the shocking innovations of an avant-garde artist. Notice that this condition may also admit of degrees. Some solutions may prove superior to others—not every "better mouse trap" will be equally efficient or inexpensive.

A creative idea must simultaneously meet both stipulations. One useful manner of viewing their joint relevance is to conceive creativity in terms of a simple multiplicative model. Let us hypothetically express both originality and adaptiveness as ratio variables, O and A, where $O = 0$ if the idea is utterly unoriginal and $A = 0$ if the idea is completely unworkable. If C is taken to designate the amount of creativity in the idea, then we can say that $C = O \times A$. If the idea is commonplace (e.g., using a coat hanger to open a locked car door), creativity is zero. Likewise, if the idea is impractical (e.g., making a space station out of cinder blocks), creativity will again be zero. Only when originality and adaptiveness are both reasonably high will creativity prove significant.

Although most researchers would agree with this abstract conception of creativity, they will often differ when they turn to the concrete study of the phenomenon. This divergence occurs because there is more than one way to investigate the emergence of creative ideas. These different ways essentially represent contrary levels of psychological analysis. Three viewpoints, in particular, are paramount:

1. Creativity is a mental *process* (or collection of processes) that results in the production of ideas simultaneously original and adaptive. This is the perspective favored by cognitive psychologists who study problem solving and insight using either laboratory experiments (e.g., Smith, Ward, & Finke, 1995; Sternberg & Davidson, 1995) or computer simulations (e.g., Langley, Simon, Bradshaw, & Zythow, 1987; Shrager & Langley, 1990). The cognitive operations under examination may include insight, intuition, imagination, and heuristic search (Hayes, 1989; Newell & Simon, 1972).
2. Creativity is a characteristic of a *product*, such as a discovery, invention, poem, painting, or composition. A product is deemed creative if it satisfies the combined criteria of originality and adaptiveness. The former criterion might specifically entail novelty, surprise, and complexity, whereas the latter criterion might involve truth, beauty, elegance, and virtuosity, the specifics depending on the particular domain of creativity. The study of creative products is the primary occupation of psychologists in experimental aesthetics (e.g., Martindale, 1990; Simonton, 1980b, 1980c, 1989a), albeit some psychologists have also attempted to comprehend better the nature of scientific products (e.g., Shadish, 1989; Simonton, 1979, 1992b; Sternberg & Gordeeva, 1996).
3. Creativity is a trait or personality profile that characterizes a *person*. That is, it is some quality or capacity that some individuals have more than others, and some may not even have at all. For instance, creativity may consist of

some special combination of such individual-difference factors as intelligence, ambition, determination, independence, openness, and originality. Needless to say, this is the perspective adopted by personality psychologists who wish to identify that set of personal attributes that distinguish creative individuals from people who display little if any creativity (e.g., Aguilar-Alonso, 1996; Barron, 1969; Eysenck, 1993; MacKinnon, 1978; Roe, 1952).

These are the process, product, and person definitions of creativity. Of course, the divergence in outlook notwithstanding, these three definitions are not totally independent. At the very least, we might hope that creative products are generated by creative persons using creative processes. It is for this reason that investigators will often combine two or three perspectives in a single inquiry. For example, psychologists might examine cross-sectional variation in cognitive styles, the latter then determining the odds that a person will use the mental operations necessary for the generation of creative ideas (e.g., Sternberg & Lubart, 1995). Other researchers might gauge individual differences in creativity in terms of their comparative output of creative products, and then attempt to predict that variation using cognitive and personality variables (e.g., Feist, 1993; Helmreich, Spence, Beane, Lucker, & Matthews, 1980; Simonton, 1992b). Nonetheless, most investigators tend to concentrate on just one of the three perspectives, the remaining two becoming secondary at best. This is true for the bulk of the personality research, which usually concentrates on the creative person, assigning noticeably less attention to the process and product aspects (but see, e.g., Mendelsohn, 1976; Stavridou & Furnham, 1996).

Genius

The term "genius" has a much longer history than that of "creativity" (Murray, 1989). In fact, the word originates in the times of ancient Rome, when each person was believed to be born with a "guardian angel." This private genius looked out for the individual's fate. As time went on, genius became integrated with the person. First it was extended to encompass those qualities that made an individual unique. This usage is still common in some Romance languages, such as Spanish, in which genius (*genio*) can denote a person's temperament or disposition. Later still, the term acquired a more restrictive usage, namely, the distinctive abilities and attributes that enabled certain individuals to make major contributions to human culture. This signification still retained something of the idiosyncratic significance of the previous meanings, but with a more narrow application. Not everyone had genius.

Beginning with Galton's 1869 *Hereditary Genius,* the term began to find its way into the behavioral sciences. With this incorporation, the word also began to accrue a more objective and quantitative meaning. Eventually, psychologists proposed two rather contrary operational definitions of the construct—the psychometric and the historiometric.

Psychometric Definition

Galton (1869) conceived of genius in terms of the normal distribution of what he called "natural ability," which he saw as a general adaptive capacity or intelligence. Those individuals whose natural ability placed them in the remote upper tail of the bell-shaped distribution were identified as geniuses. Unfortunately, although Galton (1883) attempted to devise instruments that would directly measure individual differences in natural ability, the resulting "anthropometric" methods failed miserably. However, the advent of the intelligence test placed Galton's conception on a much sounder basis. Although these tests were originally designed to help identify children who were below average in intellect, they soon were used to label other children as intellectually gifted. Pioneers such as Lewis Terman (1925) and Leta Hollingworth (1926, 1942) helped to establish the practice of styling a child a "genius" if he or she scored above a certain set level on some standardized IQ test, such as the Stanford-Binet. Later, when adult intelligence tests emerged, this psychometric definition was carried over with minimal modification. A genius was simply a child or adult who scored above some predetermined level.

Often the cutoff was put at IQ 140, a hypothetical threshold that has found its way into many dictionaries and encyclopedias (e.g., *American Heritage,* 1994). Others would relax the criterion somewhat. For instance, the Mensa Society sets the figure at two standard deviations above the population mean, which results in a requirement of around 132 on many tests (Serebriakoff, 1985). Naturally, because scores on IQ tests can be considered interval variables, genius can be also conceived in a more continuous fashion. It is then possible to speak of relative degrees of genius, or grades of genius. Indeed, this very practice has inspired the appearance of additional clubs of even more elite intellects (Storfer, 1990). The Four Sigma Society requires its members to be four standard deviations above the mean (or around IQ 164), whereas the Mega Society stipulates an IQ only obtained by one in a million (or around IQ 176). The highest grade genius, according to the *Guinness Book of World Records* (McFarlan, 1989), is Marilyn Vos Savant, who has a certified IQ of 228.

The psychometric definition of genius has many assets. One important advantage is the impressive reliabilities of the best intelligence tests, which tend to be among the most reliable of all psychometric instruments. Another is the applicability of the definition to any population for which there exists an appropriate IQ test. Hence, the definition is as applicable to children as it is to adults. On the other hand, psychometric genius also encounters problems when it is extended to the domain of creative achievement. As will be discussed later, the association between intelligence and creativity is very weak for both child and adult samples. In fact, the correlation tends to become quite negligible for populations that are above-average in intelligence (Simonton, 1985). Although there is some debate exactly where the association begins to disappear, the figure of IQ 120 is often bandied about in the research literature (Barron & Harrington, 1981). Such a threshold implies that the various grades of intellectual genius do not correspond to the different grades of creative genius.

A concrete illustration of this lack of correspondence may be found in the series of volumes that make up Terman's classic *Genetic Studies of Genius* (see Terman, 1925). Having selected more than 1,500 children on the basis of exceptional IQ scores, Terman conducted a longitudinal study to determine whether these young geniuses would grow up to become highly accomplished adults (Terman & Oden, 1959). Although many attained considerable success, it is fair to say that none achieved the highest levels of acclaim. For example, there were no Nobel laureates among the group. The ironic fact eventually emerged that among those screened in the early 1920s was a child who did earn a Nobel Prize in Physics, William Shockley, the co-inventor of the transistor. Yet Shockley's childhood IQ was not high enough to get him included in Terman's elite sample (Eysenck, 1995).

Historiometric Definition

When Galton wrote his *Hereditary Genius,* there existed no psychometric measures that could be used to define genius. Therefore, Galton introduced a rather different operational definition, the historiometric (Woods, 1909, 1911). According to this alternative, genius is defined in terms of an individual's contributions to a particular domain of human achievement. A genius is then a person whose effects on a domain are so numerous and so distinctive that the domain is appreciably transformed. The most prominent geniuses often make names for themselves by becoming eponyms for discoveries, movements, or events (Hendrickson, 1988). Illustrations include the Copernican revolution, Newtonian physics, Darwinism, Pasteurization, and Freudian slips. Furthermore, as in the psychometric definition, historiometric assessment can be designed to gauge the relative magnitude of genius (Simonton, 1990). The greater the degree of impact, the more prominent is the individual's reputation, and hence the higher the caliber of genius (see, e.g., Cattell, 1903; Ludwig, 1992b; Simonton, 1997c). Thus, according to their comparative impression on the classical repertoire, Mozart can be said to have displayed more genius than Salieri, just as Salieri can be styled a greater genius than Türk (Simonton, 1990; cf. Moles, 1958/1968). Assertions such as this can be based on two distinct kinds of measurements; eminence and productivity.

1. "Eminence" measures gauge the total global impact an individual has made upon a given domain (Simonton, 1984b, 1990). This impression may be defined according to the ratings of peers or experts (e.g., Helson & Crutchfield, 1970; MacKinnon, 1978; Roe, 1952), the receipt of special honors or awards, such as the Nobel Prize (e.g., Cole & Cole, 1973; Rothenberg, 1979, 1990), the frequency of performance, discussion, or citation (e.g., Feist, 1993; Martindale, 1995b; Simonton, 1991b, 1992b), or the amount of space assigned the individuals in encyclopedias, biographical dictionaries, history texts, anthologies, and other reference works (e.g., Cattell, 1903; Cox, 1926; Simonton, 1998a; Zusne & Dailey, 1982).

2. "Productivity" measures assess the number of concrete contributions an individual has made to a given domain (Albert, 1975). These most commonly consist of counts of books, articles, poems, paintings, inventions, compositions, and the like (e.g., Matthews, Helmreich,

Beane, & Lucker, 1980; Simonton, 1977b, 1997a), although occasionally more refined units may be used, such as the number of melodies created by composers (e.g., Simonton, 1991b). These tabulations may include all works generated, regardless of impact (e.g., Dennis 1954a, 1954b, 1955), or they may only include those works that were truly influential, such as determined by citation or performance frequencies (e.g., Simonton, 1977b, 1991a).

Fortunately, because productivity constitutes the single most prominent predictor of differential eminence, these two alternative definitions are, for all practical purposes, equivalent (Albert, 1975; Cole & Cole, 1973; Simonton, 1997a). Beyond this convergence, historiometric definitions have other measurement virtues. First, historiometric measures have clear "face validity," that is, they seem to correspond closely with what most people would consider indicative of creative achievement. If Beethoven, Michelangelo, Shakespeare, or Descartes cannot count as creative genius, it is doubtful that the word could have any meaning whatsoever. Second, research indicates that such measures have highly respectable reliabilities, multiple indicators of eminence or productivity usually displaying coefficient alphas in the upper .80s and .90s (Rushton, 1984; Simonton, 1977b, 1984b, 1991a). Third, research has also shown that such measures display a high degree of cross-cultural invariance (e.g., Simonton, 1991c). For example, the most eminent figures according to the African American minority culture are also the most eminent figures according to the European American majority culture of the United States (Simonton, 1998a). Fourth, historiometric assessments enjoy a high degree of transhistorical stability (Simonton, 1991c). Despite the existence of occasional exceptions—such as Johann Sebastian Bach and Gregor Mendel—those who are most famous in their own time also tend to be the most eminent today (see also Farnsworth, 1969; Over, 1982; Rosengren, 1985). This result is important, because it suggests that whenever psychologists study distinguished contemporaries, it is highly likely that those luminaries will continue to have exceptional posthumous reputations (Simonton, 1998b).

One last feature of the historiometric definition is worth noting. The word genius was first used as a label for those persons who made outstanding creative contributions. However, with time it became applicable to other forms of exceptional achievement. As a result, it is now acceptable to talk of political, military, religions, and entrepreneurial genius. Thus, the historiometric definition can apply to accomplishment in leadership domains as well as that in creativity domains (Simonton, 1990). To be sure, the products of a leader are not the same as those of a creator, and so the productivity definition cannot be utilized. Nonetheless, it is often possible to gauge both creators and leaders on a comparable scale of differential eminence, something first demonstrated by James McKeen Cattell back in 1903. This common denominator has permitted psychologists to examine the similarities and contrasts in the personality profiles of distinguished creators and leaders (e.g., Cox, 1926; Simonton, 1991d; Thorndike, 1950).

Although it is feasible to speak of genius in leadership domains as well as genius in creative domains, the current chapter will concentrate on the latter. There are three reasons for this focus. First, the research literature on the personal characteristics of leaders is so immense that it would easily take up considerable space (Bass, 1990; Simonton, 1995b). The number of investigations on the personality of U.S. presidents alone is quite prodigious (Simonton, 1987d). Second, individual-differences variables appear to play a much less conspicuous role in outstanding leadership than they do in exceptional creativity (Simonton, 1995b). Very often situational factors dominate over individual factors (e.g., Simonton, 1980a, 1984d, 1986b). Even when personal attributes have some role to play, frequently their effects are moderated by contextual variables (e.g., Fiedler, 1967; Simonton, 1987c). Third, although leaders can clearly qualify as geniuses by the historiometric definition, they are rather less likely to do so under the psychometric definition. Not only do leaders often display lower levels of intellectual ability than do creators (e.g., Cox, 1926; Simonton, 1976a), but in addition there is evidence that leadership effectiveness can actually be compromised by a leader's possessing an excessively high intelligence (Simonton, 1995b). Sometimes the relation between leadership and intelligence may be best described by a curvilinear, inverted-U function (Simonton, 1985). This nonmonotonic association contrasts greatly with what is observed for creativity.

Having defined the terms and delineated this chapter's scope, I next wish to provide a general personality sketch of the highly creative individual. After doing so, I will turn to a discussion of some of the key issues in the study of the creative personality.

GENERAL PERSONALITY SKETCH

Since the onset of research on the creative personality, researchers have periodically published reviews of the central research findings (e.g., Stein, 1969; Dellas & Gaier, 1970; Barron & Harrington, 1981; Martindale, 1989). These reviews show that the body of research seems to have reached a fairly strong consensus about the factors associated with cross-sectional variation in creativity. That is, individuals who display high levels of creativity appear to differ from less creative individuals on a large number of cognitive and dispositional characteristics. The most conspicuous overall feature of this distinctive profile is its complexity. The creative genius often has the appearance of being a bundle of highly variable and sometimes even contradictory attributes. To make this point, consider the following six clusters of findings:

1. Creative individuals are almost invariably more intelligent than average, at least by a standard deviation or more (Haensly & Reynolds, 1989; Simonton, 1984b). Yet as pointed out earlier, intelligence appears to operate more as a threshold function (Simonton, 1994). Below a certain minimal intellect, it is improbable that a person can display culturally significant levels of creative behavior. But beyond this threshold level, further increases in intelligence may or may not translate into higher degrees of creative genius. Someone with IQ 200 may not be any more creative than someone with IQ 120, and may even be less so—albeit it is likely that the most creative person with the higher IQ will display more creativity than the most creative person with the lower IQ. Complicating matters still further is the very real possibility that intelligence can assume many different forms besides those captured by the traditional intelligence test. Gardner (1983), for example, has argued for the existence of at least seven distinct intelligences; verbal, logical-mathematical, spatial-visual, bodily-kinesthetic, musical, intrapersonal, and interpersonal. Yet only the first two or three of these intelligences are normally assessed by the typical psychometric instrument. This omission is critical because all of these seven intelligences are associated with major forms of creative genius. According to Gardner's (1993) *Creating Minds,* typical 20th-century representatives of these seven intelligences were, respectively, T. S. Eliot, Albert Einstein, Pablo Picasso, Martha Graham, Igor Stravinsky, Sigmund Freud, and Mahatma Gandhi. Many of these geniuses would not have has their intellectual powers fully and fairly evaluated by most intelligence measures.

2. Besides the diversity of intelligences, creativity seems to entail a cognitive style more than an intellectual ability in the strict sense. In Sternberg's (1985) triarchic theory of intelligence, for example, creativity is set aside as a separate mode of intellectual functioning, as distinct from the analytical and practical forms of intelligence. Likewise in Guilford's (1967) classic "structure of intellect model," intelligence is broken into 120 distinct types, only a subset of which has any direct involvement in creativity (Bachelor & Michael, 1997). Particularly influential was Guilford's distinction between convergent and divergent processes. "Convergent" thought endeavors to identify the single correct response to a given problem situation, whereas "divergent" thought tries to generate many different responses. The latter concept has led to the emergence of a large number of divergent thinking tests that that have had some success in predicting creativity (e.g., Crammond, 1994; Michael & Wright, 1989; Torrance, 1988). In a similar vein, a number of investigations have suggested that creative individuals exhibit the capacity for generating many unusual associative linkages between otherwise diverse concepts or stimuli (Gough, 1976; MacKinnon, 1978; Mednick, 1962; Rothenberg, 1979). The creative mind is thus cognitively rich, with complex semantic networks loosely interlinking various ideas.

3. Paralleling this cognitive richness is the creator's perceptual richness. Creative persons exhibit a tremendous amount of openness to diverse experiences and demonstrate exceptional tolerance of ambiguity (McCrae, 1987; Rogers, 1954). Indeed, they tend to actively seek out novelty and complexity (Barron, 1963; MacKinnon, 1978). Especially fascinating is the ability to engage in "defocused attention," which enables the creator to attend to more than one stimulus and/or cognition at the same time (Martindale, 1995a; Mendelsohn, 1976). Not surprisingly, given these results, creative personalities are more likely to display a wide range of interests and hobbies (e.g., Root-Bernstein, Bernstein, & Garnier, 1995). Consistent with this point is the tendency for creative individuals

to be voracious and omnivorous readers (Chambers, 1964; Goertzel, Goertzel & Goertzel, 1978; Simonton 1984b). This breadth often takes the form of extraordinary versatility that enables creators to make contributions to more than one domain of achievement (Raskin, 1936; Simonton, 1976a; White, 1931).

4. Beyond these more cognitive aspects of the creative disposition are the motivational attributes. Creators deeply love what they do, and thus show exceptional enthusiasm, energy, and commitment to their chosen domain of creative endeavor (e.g., Chambers, 1964; Roe, 1952). So strong is this emotional involvement that creators are often perceived by family and friends as "workaholics"—an attribution that is not without empirical justification (Helmreich, Spence, & Pred, 1988; Matthews et al., 1980). In any case, because of this characteristic, creators are extremely persistent in the face of obstacles and disappointments (e.g., Chambers, 1964; Cox, 1926). They do not give up easily. Yet at the same time, creative individuals tend to be highly flexible, altering strategies and tactics—and even problems—when repeated failure seems to recommend such action. This behavioral flexibility is facilitated by the tendency to work on multiple projects, each at various stages of development (Hargens, 1978; Root-Bernstein, Bernstein, & Garnier 1993; Simon, 1974). Furthermore, these projects are interrelated in complex ways, forming what has been styled a "network of enterprises" (Gruber, 1989). As a consequence, the solution to one problem often provides the needed clue for getting around an impasse in the solution of another problem.

5. The foregoing cognitive and motivational attributes are usually coupled with a characteristic social orientation. Creative individuals are far more likely to be introverted than extroverted (e.g., Eysenck, 1995; Roe, 1952). Indeed, this introversion can reach the level of being rather remote, withdrawn, and even antisocial (Cattell, 1963; Eysenck, 1995). At the same time, creative persons are prone to exhibit a high degree of independence and autonomy, often displaying a pronounced rebellious streak in their categorical refusal to conform to conventional norms (e.g., Crutchfield, 1962; Roe, 1952).

6. As one might surmise from the foregoing aspects of the personality sketch, creative individuals, and especially creative geniuses, seem to show higher than average rates of psychopathology of various kinds (Ellis, 1926; Jamison, 1993; Ludwig, 1995; cf. Rothenberg, 1990). A fine line separates divergent thought and remote association from the production of truly crazy ideas; the dogged and energetic pursuit of ambitious goals can easily veer on a manic disposition; the extreme introverted independence from social niceties and conventions can seem awfully similar to psychopathological withdrawal. These symptoms are often joined by inclinations toward obvious disorders such as suicidal depressions as well as alcoholism or other forms of substance abuse (Goertzel et al., 1978; Ludwig, 1995; Post, 1996). In addition, highly creative personalities will often exhibit elevated scores on psychometric instruments that are indicative of mental disorder or emotional instability, such as the psychoticism scale of the Eysenck Personality Questionnaire (Eysenck, 1995) or the clinical subscales of the Minnesota Multiphasic Personality Inventory (Barron, 1969; MacKinnon, 1978). Yet the surprising thing is that creators appear to have unusual levels of ego strength or other psychological resources that enable to hold these adverse forces in check (Barron, 1969; Cattell & Butcher, 1968).

I hasten to point out that the empirical and theoretical literature is by no means consistent regarding the above personality sketch. Many researchers would delete one or more of the listed attributes, and a few researchers would omit virtually all of them. The points raised in the next section will help us understand some of the reasons this may be the case.

SPECIFIC SUBSTANTIVE ISSUES

We now need to discuss seven critical questions that complicate any attempt to understand the personality of the creative genius. These issues concern everyday versus exceptional achievements, childhood versus adulthood creativity, cognitive versus dispositional attributes, scientific versus artistic creativity, nature versus nurture in creative development, individual versus situational determinants of creativity, and empirical versus theoretical personality profiles.

Everyday versus Exceptional Achievements

The primary focus of the personality sketch was to describe the creative genius. The implicit assumption was the most eminent creators would provide the most typical or characteristic profile of cognitive and dispositional traits. Yet many studies of creative behavior examine more mundane forms of the phenomenon, such as workers in industrial research and development units (Ford & Gioia, 1995; West & Farr, 1990). Indeed, much research in creativity looks at student populations, including children (e.g., Getzels & Jackson, 1962; Wallach & Kogan, 1965). Therefore, to what extent are the personality profiles gathered from the examination of creative geniuses truly indicative of what holds in more everyday creators? There are two main alternative responses to this question (cf. Nicholls, 1972).

On the one hand, we can argue that the creative genius differs only in degree from an individual whose creativity will never earn significant recognition beyond the confines of a rather circumscribed time and place. In other words, there exists some continuum linking the universally recognized genius with the average person on the street. On this continuum may be placed various intermediate grades of creators. All of the traits associated with creativity would then vary according to a person's placement on this latent continuum. Eysenck (1995), for example, argued that psychoticism represented just such a dimension. Low levels of psychoticism predicts the absence of creativity, and increased psychoticism predicts ever elevated creativity. The genius emerges at the exalted level near the dangerous borderline between creativity and madness.

One attractive feature of this continuity hypothesis is the fact that creative behavior itself displays some degree of continuity. This is most obvious when creativity is gauged in terms of the output of creative products. Lifetime creative productivity forms a well-defined ratio scale on which people may vary. In the sciences, for instance, there are those who made no contribution, those who made two, those who made three, and so forth. Furthermore, there already exists ample evidence that the magnitude of creative output can display a monotonic relationship with certain personality traits (e.g., Eysenck, 1995). Hence, continuous variation in creative behavior may be grounded in underlying variation in personality.

On the other hand, we can take the position that there are qualitative differences among the various forms that creativity may take. To appreciate this alternative, consider seven hypothetical levels of creative attainment:

1. Those who made a significant and enduring impact on their chosen domain of creative activity, and who have left a major imprint on general culture. Examples include scientists such as Galileo and Einstein, artists Michelangelo and Van Gogh, and composers Mozart and Stravinsky. Besides producing contributions in their fields, these figures became virtual icons of popular culture. Their images grace T-shirts, their lives become the basis for plays and movies, and their works the subject of television documentaries.

2. Those who have made a significant and enduring impact on their chosen domain of creative activity, but who have left virtually no imprint on general culture. Illustrations might include scientists such as Evangelista Torricelli and Joseph Priestley, artists Masaccio and Juan Gris, and composers Vincent d'Indy and Mikhail Ippolitov-Ivanov. These figures will always have at least a modest place in the encyclopedias and biographical dictionaries, but will probably never become household names.

3. Those who endeavored to make lasting contributions to their chosen domain of creative activity, but failed to do so. Such individuals only enjoyed a transient or local celebrity, but their "15 minutes of fame" have long since elapsed. Their works long forgotten, they have been reduced to mere footnotes in the more esoteric histories of their fields. Examples might include the philosopher Henri du Roy or the painter Henri Bloemaert.

4. Those who attempted to make a lasting contribution, but who never managed to make even the most minimal impression on their colleagues or on audiences or appreciators. These are the scientists who publish journal articles that no one reads or cites, artists whose works appear in local galleries without success, and composers whose works get a one-time performance by an amateur orchestra.

5. Those who never succeed in producing something that went beyond private consumption. These are the inventors who build prototypes in the garage but never patent anything; the Sunday afternoon painter of landscapes and seascapes; the amateur poets who writes volumes but are never published. If these silent creators do seek a larger audience, their work never makes it past the preliminary evaluation of a patent official, selection juror, or journal editor, though it may nevertheless afford the creators great personal pleasure.

6. Those who do not create anything of their own, but do display a profound appreciation of the creativity of others. They may read scientific or literary magazines, attend concerts of new music, or regularly visit art galleries. If they have the resources, such persons may even become patrons of the arts who demonstrate their creativity in their commissions or purchases.

7. Those who don't like new ideas, nor newfangled technologies, and who believe that art, music, and literature are for whimsy pseudo-intellectuals and nerds.

Now it could be that these seven levels are mere points on an underlying personality dimension that provides the basis for creativity. But it may be more likely that qualitative shifts appear at certain places. To begin with, there may be a profound contrast between producing creative ideas and appreciating those ideas. Why are some people satisfied with absorbing another's novel ideas but others feel the compulsion to express themselves through some form of creative expression? Even if we confine our attention to those who are actively generating products for public evaluation, certain discontinuities are possible. For example, might there not be a difference between amateur and professional creators? And even among the professional creators, might there not be a contrast between the successful and unsuccessful ones? Finally, may those creators who attain universal acclaim depart in significant ways from those whose success is confined to a narrow discipline?

To address questions such as these, we must determine whether distinct traits must kick in for a person to cross over from one level to the next. It may also be the case that some of the underlying personality effects are nonlinear or nonmonotonic. An interesting example is a recent result concerning the relation between versatility and eminence in science (Sulloway, 1996). Rather than discover a positive linear function, an intriguing J-curve was found. The most famous scientists are those who make contributions to many different domains of science, whereas the next most famous were those who specialized in a single circumscribed topic. The least eminent were those who were neither highly specialized nor highly versatile. To the extent that versatility reflects some deeper personality disposition, then this curvilinear function implies the existence a peculiar discontinuity in the etiology of creative genius.

Needless to say, if creativity falls into qualitatively distinct types, then there would have to exist more than one "typical" personality profile. Even creative geniuses might feature two or more different profiles.

Childhood versus Adulthood Creativity

So far we have been discussing creativity in adult samples. Yet studies of creativity often focus on creativity in children, including many of the classic investigations in this field (e.g., Getzels & Jackson, 1962; Wallach & Kogan, 1965). In fact, this constitutes an important topic in educational and developmental psychology (Winner, 1996). It is also a question that can have significant practical consequences for the design and evaluation of programs for the education of gifted children (Colangelo & Davis, 1997). Nevertheless, these inquiries have a somewhat ambiguous status from the standpoint of understanding the personality basis of creativity and genius. There are two main difficulties.

First is the matter of identification. How does the researcher decide that a given child is creative? One common approach to make this decision according to performance on some "creativity test," usually some measure of divergent thinking (Runco, 1992). Yet this approach somewhat begs the question. Such assessment is only as good as the instruments are valid. Unfortunately, the divergent and convergent validity of various creativity tests can sometimes be rather low (McNemar, 1964; Michael & Wright, 1989). An alternative approach is to identify creativity according to actual behavioral performance—the generation of genuine creative products. This method is especially useful in the case of children who display precocious talent, such as child prodigies in a particular domain of creativity (e.g., Feldman & Goldsmith, 1986). Nonetheless, this line of attack does not completely remove the validity problem. It is extremely rare for children (and even adolescents) to generate products that satisfy adult standards of creativity (Winner, 1996). The products may reveal a precocious acquisition of specialized skills, and a certain virtuosity in the execution of those skills, but without displaying the originality and adaptiveness necessary to be competitive with the output of mature creators (Runco, 1989). Given these problems of identification, it is not always safe to assume that the personality profile characteristic of youthful creativity is the same as that for adulthood creativity (see, e.g., Parloff, Datta, Kleman, & Handlon, 1968). The selection procedures may not entail sufficiently overlapping criteria.

Second is the matter of continuity. Development from childhood through adolescence and even adulthood is fraught with a great variety of changes in cognitive makeup and personality structure. Besides progressive developmental differentiation of various functions, specific personality traits may wax and wane, with particularly dramatic effects taking place during puberty. Some of these transformations may be exogenous (environmental) and others endogenous (genetic), but in combination they signify the instability of a youth's constitution during the course of their growth and maturation. At various points during the course of development, creativity may undergo spurts and slumps, and may even vanish altogether—for the remainder of a person's life (Albert, 1996; Runco & Charles, 1997). Even in adulthood, creativity may come and go, whether we assess it psychometrically (McCrae, Arenberg, & Costa, 1987) or historiometrically (Dennis, 1956, 1966; Lehman, 1953, 1962; Simonton, 1977a, 1988a, 1989b). These developmental instabilities within individuals holds even though differences in creativity across individuals may be relatively stable over time (Dennis, 1954b; Helmreich, Spence, & Thorbecke, 1981; Simonton, 1997a).

It should be pointed out that these two difficulties are mitigated if not entirely obliterated when we revert to the psychometric definition of genius. That is, if genius is defined as an exceptionally high IQ, then the problem of identification disappears by definitional fiat. Furthermore, such IQ scores are highly stable across childhood, adolescence, and adulthood (Simonton, 1976a; Terman & Oden, 1959). The main source in developmental instability would then probably be concentrated in the personality profiles that characterize highly intelligent persons. However, even if these latter profiles were highly stable across time, that stability would not contribute much to our understanding of the dispositional qualities of the exceptional creator. For both in youth and in maturity, the personality profiles of highly intelligent individuals differs markedly from those of highly creative individuals (Albert, 1994; Getzels & Jackson, 1962; Wallach & Kogan, 1965). The psychometric genius and the historiometric genius are dispositionally different people.

Cognitive versus Dispositional Attributes

Research on individual differences in creativity may be said to have roots in two distinct psychological traditions. The first harks back to the Gestalt psychologists who were the pioneers in research on problem solving and insightful behavior (e.g., Köhler, 1925; Wertheimer, 1945/1982). In line with this tradition, much research on creativity has focused more on the creative process than the person. Some investigators have even gone so far as to suggest that creativity is a mental operation accessible to all, and thus largely unrelated to general individual-difference dimensions (e.g., Weisberg, 1992). Creative geniuses are merely persons who have acquired the necessary expertise in a given domain, but otherwise they employ the same cognitive processes as the rest of us in problem-solving situations. In contrast, other researchers in this cognitive tradition maintain that the person is indeed important, because creative individuals were those who had superior access to certain special mental operations, such as the capacity for remote association (Mednick, 1962) or divergent thought (Guilford, 1967) or intuition (Wescott, 1968). Many psychometric instruments were in fact predicated on the assumption that individual differences in creativity were grounded in certain cognitive abilities (e.g., Mednick, 1962). Also in this class of studies may be placed the work on how creativity relates to cognitive styles, or distinctive patterns of thinking (e.g., Sternberg & Lubart, 1995). Whatever the specifics, this tradition asserts that a complete understanding of the creator requires that we understand the cognitive process behind creativity. If individual differences exist in the capacity for creativity (besides those grounded in domain-specific expertise), then this variation has to do with creative cognition (Finke, Ward, & Smith, 1992).

The second research tradition may be said to have its source in personality and clinical assessment. Here researchers are fascinated with the richness of the human personality, with its complex of differentiating interests and values, emotions and motives, activities and reactions. For investigations in this tradition, the creative genius must be distinguished by a highly distinctive profile of traits that enables a person to exhibit creativity. Some investigators would even argue that this defining cluster of dispositional attributes are far more critical in a creative life than are any putative cognitive differences (e.g., Dellas & Gaier, 1970). Of course, this second tradition implies a whole different manner of constructing "creativity tests." Rather than measure the intellectual capacity for certain cognitive operations, the tests may assess preferences, attitudes, and activities associated with creative behavior (e.g., Davis, 1975, 1989). Standard personality measures may even be used to identify the characteristic profile of the highly creative person (Cattell & Butcher, 1968; Gough, 1979, 1992; MacKinnon, 1978). In such circumstances, the assessment of creativity becomes a manner of scoring performance on a generic inventory rather than the application of a test specifically designed to tap the creative personality.

Although some researchers have taken extreme positions, advocating exclusively either cognitive or dispositional assessment, many recent investigators have argued for the involvement of both intellect and personality in the making of a creative individual (e.g., Eysenck, 1995; Simonton, 1988c; Sternberg & Lubart, 1995). Creativity of the highest order, especially that of the creative genius, may require a special combination of cognitive and dispositional attributes. In fact, it may be the distinctiveness of that combination that renders exceptional creativity so rare. The vast majority of the population may be simply missing one or more essential components.

Scientific versus Artistic Creativity

Researchers often treat creativity as a single, relatively homogeneous phenomenon. Creativity is some generic capacity for generating original and adaptive ideas without regard to the specific domain in which the creativity is to take place. Although this simple view may have some justification when discussing everyday creativity or the creativity displayed by children, it becomes clearly invalid when extended to extraordinary creativity, especially when it attains the level of creative genius. The expected cognitive and dispositional profiles vary conspicuously according to the type of creative achievement. The disciplinary contrast that has attracted the most empirical documentation is that between scientific and artistic creativity (e.g., Cattell & Butcher, 1968; Hudson, 1966; Raskin, 1936; Terman, 1954). Expressed in general terms, creative scientists tend to exhibit traits that fall somewhere between those of the creative artist and those of the average human being (Simonton, 1988c). For example, remote associations and divergent thinking are less prominent, and that which does occur is more restricted to concepts within the scientific specialty—in contrast to artists who seem to have wild ideas about almost everything. The scientific genius also tends to have a more conventional, predictable, and stable personality structure than does the artistic genius. Especially remarkable is the less conspicuous inclination toward psychopathology seen in great scientists, albeit even here this characteristic seems still higher than found in the general population (Ludwig, 1995; Raskin, 1936). The only major attribute on which scientists score more prominently than artists relative to the normal baseline is intelligence (Cox, 1926). On the average, the brightest creative geniuses are those who make major contributions to scientific disciplines. In Cox's (1926) study of 301 geniuses, for example, the estimated IQs for scientists were around a standard deviation higher than those for artists. However, these mean differences may merely reflect the tendency of intelligence to be conceived in terms of the kinds of cognitive skills that are most suitable for exceptional performance in science.

I should point out that the foregoing differentiations represents only the first cut in the laying out of some typology of creative personality. Although scientists are broadly different from artists, neither scientific nor artistic creators form homogeneous groups. In the sciences, for instance, some personality differences separate contributors to the mathematical, physical, biological, and behavioral or social sciences (Chambers, 1964; Roe, 1952; Terman, 1954). Thus, social scientists, as a group, are more extroverted than are most natural scientists. Even within a particular scientific discipline, revolutionary scientists tend to be much more "artistic" in their disposition than are practitioners of what Kuhn (1970) styled "normal science" (Simonton, 1988c). In the arts the variability in empirical profiles is even more remarkable (Cox, 1926; Ludwig, 1992a). This diversity is perhaps most apparent in Ludwig's (1995) recent study of psychopathology in eminent moderns. The incidence rates for various disorders depends very much on the prevalent form of artistic expression. Poets tend to suffer from extremely high rates, for example, whereas architects are more similar to the scientists in their lower susceptibility to psychopathology (see also Martindale, 1972; Post, 1994).

It should now be evident that there are many types of creative personalities, not just one. This is reflected not just in their dispositions, but in their backgrounds besides. For instance, scientific creators, in contrast to artistic creators, hail from backgrounds that tend to favor more conformity, conventionality, and stability (Berry, 1981; Bliss, 1970; Schaefer & Anastasi, 1968). But this fact brings us naturally to the next substantive issue.

Nature versus Nurture in Creative Development

One of the oldest controversies in psychology is the relative importance of nature and nurture in the development of human individuality. Interestingly, this issue was first raised—and christened—with respect to the study of creative genius. The debate began with Galton's 1869 *Hereditary Genius,* in which he attempted to show that genius of all kinds clustered into talented family pedigrees (see also Bramwell, 1948; Simonton, 1983b). Galton explicitly took the position that genius is born rather than made. It was the immediate consequence of the genetic inheritance of extraordinary intelligence, energy, and determination. This extreme stance was soon challenged, most notably by Candolle (1873), who endeavored to show how the appearance of scientific creativity was contingent on a diverse array of the climatological, political, and sociocultural environment. As a result, Galton conceded that both factors may play a role in the emergence of creative genius. This concession was ably made in his 1874 book on *English Men of Science: Their Nature and Nurture*. The subtitle is significant, for it represents the first formal use of the terms nature and nurture to label the debate.

Unfortunately, later research on genius and creativity moved even further away from the position that development was a function of both biological endowment and environmental influences. This movement toward nurture accounts can be partly ascribed to the increased influence of U. S. psychology, which had tended to have a strong emphasis on learning as the central factor in personality development. In addition, the eugenics movement founded by Galton seemed discredited by the genocidal programs of the Nazi regime during World War II. But perhaps most importantly, a great deal of research accumulated that seemed to show that the development of creativity was contingent on a host of environmental factors (Walberg, Rasher, & Parkerson, 1980). For example, Galton (1874) himself pointed to the impact of birth order, a finding replicated by many later researchers (e.g., Albert, 1980; Clark & Rice, 1982; Helson & Crutchfield, 1970; Sulloway, 1996; Terry, 1989). Other apparent influences include early traumatic experiences (Eisenstadt, 1978; Roe, 1952; Silverman, 1974), the familial intellectual environment (Goertzel et al., 1978; Schaefer & Anastasi, 1968; Terman, 1925); formal education and special training (Hudson, 1958; Simonton, 1976a, 1983a; 1986a); geographic, ethnic, religious, or professional marginality (Arieti, 1976; Lehman & Witty, 1931; Simonton, 1977b, 1984c; Stewart, 1986); and the larger political, social, cultural, and economic milieu (e.g., Simonton, 1975, 1988b, 1992a, 1997b). This large inventory of developmental variables seemed to prove that nurture was supreme over nature in the appearance of creative talent and genius (Simonton, 1987a).

However, recently the tide has turned against this extreme environmentalist view, a turnaround due to the advent of modern behavioral genetics (Plomin, 1986), including the sophisticated analysis of monozygotic and dizygotic twins, an approach first introduced by Galton (1883) himself. Therefore, it now appears rather likely that at least a portion of what it takes to display creativity, outstanding or otherwise, arises from our genes (Waller, Bouchard, Lykken, Tellegen, & Blacker, 1993). In fact, research in behavioral genetics suggests that some so-called environmental factors might actually be genetic in their underlying causality (Plomin & Bergeman, 1991; Scarr & McCartney, 1983). There are two main ways this can happen:

1. Offspring obtain their genotypes from the parental genotypes. The parental genotype is also associated with a particular parental phenotype, part of which may leave an imprint on the home environment. For instance, highly intelligent parents will more likely have more intellectual and cultural hobbies and recreational activities. As a consequence, the home may be filled with books, magazines, art prints, and music recordings. This available stimulation may then be improperly given all of the credit for the appearance of a young genius. Yet the apparent connection may be partly or completely spurious from a causal standpoint. It is the shared genotype,

not the home circumstances per se, that may be responsible for the bulk of the developmental effect.

2. Even more dramatically, we must recognize a person's genotype helps shape the environment in which the phenotype must emerge. Children or adolescents are not passive receptacles for events impinging on some tabula rasa, but rather these youths are acting upon their world, trying to make it conform more closely to their abilities and interests. They may ask their parents to provide them with music lessons, to purchase certain books or magazines, to visit science or art museums, and so forth. Indeed, there is ample anecdotal evidence that gifted children often will continue to pursue activities in the face of active parental discouragement. Blaise Pascal continued to study mathematics on his own even after his father deliberately hid books on that subject, believing that his son was slighting classical studies. So Pascal independently invented a large portion of Euclidean geometry (Cox, 1926).

It is crucial to recognize the possibility that genes might affect the environment in a manner that sometimes is extremely subtle, and therefore not easily deciphered. Take, for instance, the research suggesting that creative geniuses exhibit higher rates of orphanhood or parental loss in childhood or adolescence (e.g., Eisenstadt, 1978; Roe, 1952; Silverman, 1974). This might be seen as an obvious case of a nurture effect, and this developmental influence is often so interpreted (e.g., Eisenstadt, Haynal, Rentchnick, & De Senarclens, 1989). Presumably such traumatic experiences can dramatically change the course of personality development. Nevertheless, it can be readily argued that this linkage represents a hidden genetic effect (Simonton, 1994). To provide but one such alternative interpretation (Simonton, 1992c), we know that the parents of geniuses tend to have gotten married later in life and to have had their offspring at later ages than is the norm (e.g., Bowerman, 1947; Ellis, 1926; Galton, 1874; Raskin, 1936; Visher 1947). This may simply reflect the fact that highly intelligent and ambitious people tend to delay family responsibilities until they have fully established their careers. If so, then when all other factors are held constant, it could be that this phenomenon alone might account for the higher incidence of parental loss. The traumatic event itself has no developmental consequence. What does have an effect is that the young genius inherited those qualities, such as intelligence and drive, that enable them to succeed in life

Of course, at present we cannot say with any precision precisely the relative contributions of nature and nurture to creative development. Insofar as creativity depends on intellectual growth, then the genetic contribution should be substantial. After all, intelligence features among the highest heritability coefficients of all individual-difference variables (Plomin & Petrill, 1997). At the same time, the heritability coefficients for motives, dispositions, interests, and values are rather less prominent, genes at best accounting for only half as much variance as they account for in intellectual traits (Bouchard, 1994; Bouchard, Lykken, McGue, Segal, & Tellegen, 1990). Thus, the determination of the comparative impact of nature and nurture for creativity must depend on the determination of the relative importance of the diverse characteristics that enter into the profile of the creative person. If intelligence is the primary factor, then more than half of creativity may be ascribed to genetic influences. But if personality attributes provide the most critical components of the profile, then maybe less than a quarter of the observed individual differences may be attributed to genetic makeup.

Finally, I must point out that this nature–nurture issue is subject to taking a more specific and politically sensitive form: Whether certain human groups exhibit less genius and creativity than do others. Galton (1869) first raised this debate when he proposed to rank races according to the magnitude of intellectual or creative genius they displayed. Although this practice has some modern proponents (e.g., Lynn, 1991; Rushton, 1995), these rankings have provoked considerable controversy as well (e.g., Anderson, 1991; Zuckerman, 1990). As is so often the case, it is extremely difficult to isolate the contributions of cultural heritage from those of biological endowment (Hertz, 1928/1970; Simonton, 1994). This same difficulty attends the debate over whether men and women display the same or different creative capacities. There can be no doubt that there exist substantial genetically based differences between the two genders. It is also quite evident that female genius is far less common than male genius in the annals of history (Ochse, 1991; Simonton, 1996). What is far from clear is whether biological contrasts have any responsibility for the differential representation of men and women among creative geniuses. Some have suggested that women may be inherently less inclined to engage in extraordinary creative activities because they are biologically disposed to exhibit an intellectual and personality profile that militates against such achievement (e.g., Eysenck, 1995). Alternatively, it has been argued from evolutionary theory that men exhibit greater variation on individual-difference variables, especially intelligence, and thus more men than women will be found in the upper tails of the normal curve (Shields, 1975). In contrast, others deny the validity of these arguments, instead affirming that the effects of human culture are so overwhelming that any lowered representation of female genius merely reflects differential sex-role socialization and gender-based discrimination (Eccles, 1985; Ochse, 1991; Simonton, 1992a). Although proponents of this environmentalist position are probably in the majority, we are still far from a conclusive resolution of this debate.

Individual versus Situational Determinants of Creativity

Thus far we have been assuming that creativity has its locus *inside* the person—that it is an individual characteristic or behavior. Not all researchers accept this viewpoint, however (e.g., Csikszentmihály, 1990). Many sociologists and anthropologists, especially, have argued that creativity, even creative genius, is more a sociocultural than an individual phenomenon (e.g., Sorokin, 1937–1941; White, 1949). There are two main arguments for this position, one general and the other specific.

The general argument ensues from the fact that creative genius is not evenly distributed across history and geography. Instead, exceptional creativity tends to cluster into what Kroeber (1944) styled "cultural configurations." Typically, there will exist long periods in the history of any civilization in which creative activity is virtually nil ("dark" ages), punctuated by other periods in which creativity reaches the greatest heights ("golden" and "silver" ages). The Classical Age of Greece or the Italian Renaissance are prime examples. Kroeber (1944) has documented the existence of these configurations in every civilization known to have existed in the world, and so we cannot doubt that this is a very general phenomenon (see also Sorokin & Merton, 1935). Moreover, Kroeber and others argue from this secure fact that the creative genius is basically an epiphenomenon produced by the zeitgeist, or "spirit of the times." At best, the creators are mere spokespersons for the culture in which they live.

The specific argument concerns the curious phenomenon called "multiples" (Merton, 1961). This occurs whenever two or more individuals independently and often simultaneously come up the same scientific discovery or technological invention. Classic examples include the creation of calculus by Newton and Leibnitz, the discovery of Neptune by Adams and Leverrier, the theory of evolution by natural selection by Darwin and Wallace, and the invention of the telephone by Bell and Gray. In fact, some have claimed that the number of such multiple discoveries and inventions easily runs into the hundreds, if not thousands (Merton, 1961). Furthermore, many social scientists have argued that the very occurrence of these events prove that creativity ensues from the sociocultural system, and not from the individual (Brannigan, 1981; Kroeber, 1917; Lamb & Easton, 1984). At a particular moment in the history of any creative domain, certain ideas become absolutely inevitable, and so it really matters not who actually makes the contribution. The new ideas are "in the air" to be picked by anyone. Indeed, some proponents of this social-deterministic account have actually argued that the discoverer or inventor does not even need to possess any special intellectual or dispositional attributes (e.g., White, 1949).

Needless to say, if these arguments are correct, then creativity and genius would no longer become the proper subject of psychological analysis, for creative genius would become a sociocultural process. Nonetheless, scrutiny of both arguments reveal several weaknesses that seriously undermine the thesis of sociocultural determinism (Simonton, 1988c). In the case of cultural configurations, for instance, it has been shown that certain political, economic, cultural, social, and disciplinary circumstances play an important part in creative development, and thus the milieu is operating *through* creative individuals (e.g., Simonton, 1975, 1976b, 1976c). An excellent example is the impact of role models on the early development of the creative genius (Simonton, 1984a, 1988a). In the case of multiples, it is possible to construct theoretical models of the phenomenon that are based on how creativity operates within individual minds (Simonton, 1987b, 1988c). Not only can these psychological models explicate the same phenomenon, but in addition they lead to precise predictions that have so far withstood empirical tests (e.g., Simonton, 1979, 1988c). According to these alternative models, the contribution of the sociocultural milieu is limited to the provision of the necessary (but not sufficient) conditions for the emergence of certain ideas. The creative genius must do the rest.

Although recent research seems to undermine a strong-form sociocultural determinism, that is not tantamount to the claim that creativity and genius are located entirely in the individual. On the contrary, there exists ample empirical evidence that the creative person is open to all sorts of external influences that directly affect the amount and type of creativity displayed (e.g., Doty, Peterson, & Winter, 1991; Hasenfus, Martindale, & Birnbaum, 1983). Furthermore, to some extent, creativity operates as a state rather than trait variable, changing from moment to moment according to the circumstances, social and otherwise (e.g., Amabile, 1985; Isen, Daubman, & Nowicki, 1987; Krampen, 1997; Martindale, 1973; Nemeth & Wachtler, 1983; Rothenberg, 1986; Sobel & Rothenberg, 1980). Indeed, this openness to extrinsic influences are what inspire many researchers to search for environmental stimuli that are most conducive to the manifestation of creative behavior (e.g., Amabile, 1996). Especially crucial are various disciplinary networks, such as collaborative and competitive relationships with colleagues in the same field (Simonton, 1984a, 1992c; cf. Jackson & Padgett, 1982). In fact, it is this social exchange that may be partly responsible for the clustering of creative genius into cultural configurations.

What these data suggest is that creativity is not just a cognitive, developmental, and personological phenomenon, but a social psychological phenomenon besides. Creative behavior is affected by a host of factors that reside outside the individual creator. Making matters all the more complicated, the creative personality, not just creative activity, is also susceptible to external influences. Just as creativity may change according to the circumstances, so may the personality corresponding to that creativity. To appreciate the possible complexity, consider the empirical linkage between literary creativity and substance abuse. The list of alcoholics among greater writers, in particular, is extremely long and frequently tragic (Davis, 1986; Lester, 1991; Post, 1996). However, the causal relation underlying this high incidence rate is more controversial (Ludwig, 1992a). For instance, there is empirical evidence that the following career progression might sometimes obtain: (1) after a period of obscurity, the creator begins to attain a level of recognition that stimulates considerable attention in the mass media; (2) this extensive media coverage begins to produce a high level of self-consciousness in the creator, a self-consciousness not present in the creator's pre-fame career; (3) because self-consciousness is a generally unpleasant psychological state, the creator begins to "self-medicate" with alcohol or drugs; and (4) this addiction may then lead to a decline in creativity, and perhaps even death by suicide (Schaller, 1997). What this progression suggests is that both creativity and personality can be a function of a complex and dynamic interaction between individual characteristics and situational circumstances.

Empirical versus Theoretical Personality Profiles

Much of the research on the personality basis of creativity has been purely empirical in nature. Investigators have been often content with simply subjecting creative individuals to standard assessment techniques in order to determine the personality profiles that correspond with the syndrome. Nevertheless, five theoretical systems or orientations have been put forward as providing a personality basis for the phenomenon: psychoanalytic, humanistic, cognitive, economic, and evolutionary.

Psychoanalytic Theories

Although far from Sigmund Freud's main focus, creativity and genius were of interest to the founder of psychoanalysis. This interest is evident in both his psychobiographical study of Leonardo da Vinci (Freud, 1910/1964) and his theory of creativity, which was rooted in primary-process thought (Freud, 1908/1959). Freud's contributions to this area continue to leave an impression on scholarly inquiry. The psychobiographical analysis of creative geniuses remains an active research area, albeit more popular in the humanities than in the behavioral sciences (see Elms, 1994). The psychoanalytic theory of creativity has been developed in many directions (e.g., Kris, 1952), and still has important adherents in the present day (e.g., Gedo, 1997). Perhaps more significant is the fact that psychoanalysis provided a foundation for many personality measures, such as the Thematic Apperception and Rorschach tests, which have played a prominent role in the assessment of creative individuals of all kinds (e.g., Barron, 1955; Dudek & Hall, 1984; Eiduson, 1962; Roe, 1952). Unfortunately, psychoanalysis may have been far more successful as a theory of cognitive processes than as a theory of personality development. Therefore, most current researchers in the area, while believing that unconscious processes have a major part in the emergence of creative ideas (e.g., Ochse, 1989; Suler, 1990), do not subscribe to the notion that the personality profiles may have a psychoanalytic basis.

Humanistic Theories

Humanistic psychologists have often theorized about the significance of creativity in the constitution of the healthy human being (e.g., May, 1975). Creativity had a special place in Abraham Maslow's (1959, 1972) theory of the self-actualizing person, and several of the self-actualizers whom he studied were creative geniuses of note, including Albert Einstein, William James, Wolfgang von Goethe, John Keats, Camille Pissaro, and Joseph Haydn (Maslow, 1970). However, with the minor exception of Carl Rogers's (1954) theory of creativity (see, e.g., Harrington, Block, & Block, 1987), these humanistic theories have inspired relatively little empirical research in mainstream psychology. Moreover, the proposed linkage between creativity and mental health seems to run counter to the connection between creative genius and psychopathology (but see Eysenck, 1995, for an attempted reconciliation).

Cognitive Theories

For the most part, cognitive psychologists have tended to take little interest in personality factors, no matter what the phenomenon (Gardner, 1987). Creativity, in particular, is often viewed as primarily if not entirely a matter of intellect rather than character (e.g., Weisberg, 1992). Nonetheless, recent researchers have greatly broadened the cognitive perspective, most notably Sternberg and Lubart (1995), who have linked creativity with both cognitive styles and various personality traits. In the reverse direction, personality researcher Eysenck (1995) has attempted to make a direct link between psychoticism and the cognitive processes underlying the creative process. Another fascinating development are attempts to examine creativity from the standpoint of attribution theory and social cognition (Kasof, 1995, and ensuing commentary). To some extent, creativity may be more in the "eyes of the beholder" (cf. Simonton, 1995a). Personality traits may lead to the attribution of creativity without participating directly in the creative process.

Economic Theories

The work of Sternberg and Lubart (1995) is interesting for another reason besides its integration of intellectual and dispositional variables: They have also cast their formulation in economic terms, calling it an investment theory of creativity (Sternberg & Lubart, 1991). Theirs is not the only attempt to comprehend the creative person in economic terms (e.g., Rubenson & Runco, 1992). Although these theories differ in details, economic interpretations tend to view the creative individual as someone who (1) invests in "human capital" pertaining to a particular enterprise, (2) takes exceptional risks to achieve exceptional goals, and (3) possesses the personal resources, including the optimal character, to make the risky investments pay off.

Evolutionary Theories

Darwin's theory of evolution has left a major impression on the behavioral sciences, and research on creativity is no exception. In fact, the first psychologist to discuss the creative individual in Darwinian terms was William James (1880) well over a century ago. Later, Donald Campbell (1960) developed this notion into his blind-variation and selective-retention theory of creativity. Although Campbell's focus was on the creative process, others have expanded the theory to encompass the creative person as well (Eysenck, 1995; Martindale, 1995a; Simonton, 1988c, 1997a). In addition, several researchers have used evolutionary theory to embed both the creative individual and the creative product in the larger sociocultural context (e.g., Eysenck, 1995; Martindale, 1990; Simonton, 1988c). The Darwinian perspective therefore holds great promise as a comprehensive integrative framework for the analysis of creative genius.

Although theorizing has been very active, we are still far from having in hand a universally accepted theory. Until we do so, it will be impossible to know the precise causal connection between personality and creativity—or even whether a causal connection actually exits or which direction the causality is moving. In addition, it will always be precarious using personality inventories to assess the creative potential of individuals until we can establish with some confidence that certain dispositional traits have a necessary theoretical link with the creative process and the generation of creative products.

FUTURE PROSPECTS

It should be apparent from the foregoing discussion that research on creativity and genius has already produced an extremely rich, complex, and controversy-laden literature. It is certainly not a topic for those researchers who wish to investigate a subject in which questions are easily posed and more easily answered. Indeed, it is possible that many psychologists are scared away from the field simply owing to the several methodological and theoretical difficulties it presents. Nonetheless, creativity and genius are human realities too practically important for psychologists to ignore (Sternberg & Lubart, 1996). Whether we are speaking of everyday creativity at home and work or the highly acclaimed accomplishments of creative genius, this a phenomenon that has affected the lives of everyone, and will probably continue to do so for the duration of human civilization. Therefore, it is hardly a topic that eventually is going to languish into oblivion. That does not mean that research activity will not wax and wane as the field progresses. Such oscillations have happened in the past, and they will probably continue to do so in the future. Nevertheless, inquiries into creativity will be continually revived as new developments take place in other fields of psychological study.

I believe that this resurgence will be specifically the case with respect to research on the creative personality. Studies into the dispositional attributes of creators and geniuses have slackened considerably since their heyday in the 1970s (Feist & Runco, 1993). Nonetheless, much of this decline may merely reflect a more pervasive slump in personality research as a whole. Now that personality has recovered its vitality and mission as a substantial subdiscipline of psychology, I foresee increased attention to those personal qualities that enable individuals to exhibit creativity—even creativity that assumes the form of genius.

REFERENCES

Aguilar-Alonso, A. (1996). Personality and creativity. *Personality and Individual Differences, 21,* 959–969.

Albert, R. S. (1975). Toward a behavioral definition of genius. *American Psychologist, 30,* 140–151.

Albert, R. S. (1980). Family positions and the attainment of eminence: A study of special family positions and special family experiences. *Gifted Child Quarterly, 24,* 87–85.

Albert, R. S. (Ed.). (1992). *Genius and eminence* (2nd ed.). Oxford, UK: Pergamon Press.

Albert, R. S. (1994). The achievement of eminence: A longitudinal study of exceptionally gifted boys and their families. In R. F. Subotnik & K. D. Arnold (Eds.), *Beyond Terman: Contemporary longitudinal studies of giftedness and talent* (pp. 282–315). Norwood, NJ: Ablex.

Albert, R. S. (1996). Some reasons why childhood creativity often fails to make it past puberty into the real world. In M. A. Runco (Ed.), *Creativity from childhood through adulthood: The developmental issues* (pp. 43–56). San Francisco: Jossey-Bass.

Amabile, T. M. (1985). Motivation and creativity: Effects of motivation orientation on creative writers. *Journal of Personality and Social Psychology, 48,* 393–399.

Amabile, T. M. (1996). *Creativity in context.* Boulder, CO: Westview.

American heritage electronic dictionary (3rd ed.). (1994). Boston: Houghton Mifflin.

Anderson, J. L. (1991). Rushton's racial comparisons: An ecological critique of theory and method. *Canadian Psychology, 32,* 51–60.

Arieti, S. (1976). *Creativity: The magic synthesis.* New York: Basic Books.

Bachelor, P. A., & Michael, W. B. (1997). The structure-of-intellect model revisited. In M. A. Runco (Ed.), *The creativity research handbook* (Vol. 1, pp. 155–182). Cresskill, NJ: Hampton Press.

Barron, F. X. (1955). The disposition toward originality. *Journal of Abnormal and Social Psychology, 51,* 478–485.

Barron, F. X. (1963). The needs for order and for disorder as motives in creative activity. In C. W. Taylor & F. X. Barron (Eds.), *Scientific creativity: Its recognition and development* (pp. 153–160). New York: Wiley.

Barron, F. X. (1969). *Creative person and creative process.* New York: Holt, Rinehart & Winston.

Barron, F. X., & Harrington, D. M. (1981). Creativity, intelligence, and personality. *Annual Review of Psychology, 32,* 439–476.

Bass, B. M. (1990). *Bass & Stogdill's handbook of leadership: Theory, research, and managerial applications* (3rd ed.). New York: Free Press.

Berry, C. (1981). The Nobel scientists and the origins of scientific achievement. *British Journal of Sociology, 32,* 381–391.

Bliss, W. D. (1970). Birth order of creative writers. *Journal of Individual Psychology, 26,* 200–202.

Bouchard, T. J., Jr. (1994). Genes, environment, and personality. *Science, 264,* 1700–1701.

Bouchard, T. J., Jr., Lykken, D. T., McGue, M., Segal, N. L., & Tellegen, A. (1990). Sources of human psychological differences: The Minnesota study of twins reared apart. *Science, 250,* 223–228.

Bowerman, W. G. (1947). *Studies in genius.* New York: Philosophical Library.

Brannigan, A. (1981). *The social basis of scientific discoveries.* Cambridge, UK: Cambridge University Press.

Bramwell, B. S. (1948). Galton's "Hereditary Genius" and the three following generations since 1869. *Eugenics Review, 39,* 146–153.

Campbell, D. T. (1960). Blind variation and selective retention in creative thought as in other knowledge processes. *Psychological Review, 67,* 380–400.

Candolle, A. de (1873). *Histoire des sciences et des savants depuis deux siècles.* Geneva, Switz.: Georg.

Cattell, J. M. (1903). A statistical study of eminent men. *Popular Science Monthly, 62,* 359–377.

Cattell, R. B. (1963). The personality and motivation of the researcher from measurements of contemporaries and from biography. In C. W. Taylor & F. Barron (Eds.), *Scientific creativity: Its recognition and development* (pp. 119–131). New York: Wiley.

Cattell, R. B., & Butcher, H. J. (1968). *The prediction of achievement and creativity.* Indianapolis: Bobbs-Merrill.

Chambers, J. A. (1964). Relating personality and biographical factors to scientific creativity. *Psychological Monographs: General and Applied, 78*(Whole No. 584), 1–20.

Clark, R. D., & Rice, G. A. (1982). Family constellations and eminence: The birth orders of Nobel Prize winners. *Journal of Psychology, 110,* 281–287.

Colangelo, N., & Davis, G. A. (Eds.). (1997). *Handbook of gifted education* (2nd ed.). Boston: Allyn & Bacon.

Cole, S., & Cole, J. R. (1973). *Social stratification in science.* Chicago: University of Chicago Press.

Cox, C. (1926). *The early mental traits of three hundred geniuses.* Stanford, CA: Stanford University Press.

Crammond, B. (1994). The Torrance Tests of Creative Thinking: From design through establishment of predictive validity. In R. F. Subotnik & K. D. Arnold (Eds.), *Beyond Terman: Contemporary longitudinal studies of giftedness and talent* (pp. 229–254). Norwood, NJ: Ablex.

Crutchfield, R. (1962). Conformity and creative thinking. In H. E. Gruber, G. Terrell, & M. Wertheimer (Eds.), *Contemporary approaches to creative thinking* (pp. 120–140). New York: Atherton Press.

Csikszentmihály, M. (1990). The domain of creativity. In M. A. Runco & R. S. Albert (Eds.), *Theories of creativity* (pp. 190–212). Newbury Park, CA: Sage.

Davis, G. A. (1975). In frumious pursuit of the creative person. *Journal of Creative Behavior, 9,* 75–87.

Davis, G. A. (1989). Testing for creative potential. *Contemporary Educational Psychology, 14,* 257–274.

Davis, W. M. (1986). Premature mortality among prominent American authors noted for alcohol abuse. *Drug and Alcohol Dependence, 18,* 133–138.

Dellas, M., & Gaier, E. L. (1970). Identification of creativity: The individual. *Psychological Bulletin, 73,* 55–73.

Dennis, W. (1954a). Bibliographies of eminent scientists. *Scientific Monthly, 79,* 180–183.

Dennis, W. (1954b). Predicting scientific productivity in later maturity from records of earlier decades. *Journal of Gerontology, 9,* 465–467.

Dennis, W. (1954c). Productivity among American psychologists. *American Psychologist, 9,* 191–194.

Dennis, W. (1955). Variations in productivity among creative workers. *Scientific Monthly, 80,* 277–278.

Dennis, W. (1956). Age and productivity among scientists. *Science, 123,* 724–725.

Dennis, W. (1966). Creative productivity between the ages of 20 and 80 years. *Journal of Gerontology, 21,* 1–8.

Doty, R. M., Peterson, B. E., & Winter, D. G. (1991). Threat and authoritarianism in the United States, 1978–1987. *Journal of Personality and Social Psychology, 61,* 629–640.

Dudek, S. Z., & Hall, W. B. (1984). Some test correlates of high level creativity in architects. *Journal of Personality Assessment, 48,* 351–359.

Eccles, J. S. (1985). Why doesn't Jane run? Sex differences in educational and occupational patterns. In F. D. Horowitz & M. O'Brien (Eds.), *The gifted and talented: Developmental perspectives* (pp. 251–295). Washington, DC: American Psychological Association.

Eiduson, B. T. (1962). *Scientists: Their psychological world.* New York: Basic Books.

Eisenstadt, J. M. (1978). Parental loss and genius. *American Psychologist, 33,* 211–223.

Eisenstadt, J. M., Haynal, A., Rentchnick, P., & De Senarclens, P. (1989). *Parental loss and achievement.* Madison, CT: International Universities Press.

Ellis, H. (1926). *A study of British genius* (rev. ed.). Boston: Houghton Mifflin.

Elms, A. C. (1994). *Uncovering lives: The uneasy alliance of biography and psychology.* New York: Oxford University Press.

Eysenck, H. J. (1993). Creativity and personality: Suggestions for a theory. *Psychological Inquiry, 4,* 147–178.

Eysenck, H. J. (1995). *Genius: The natural history of creativity.* Cambridge, UK: Cambridge University Press.

Farnsworth, P. R. (1969). *The social psychology of music* (2nd ed.). Ames, IA: Iowa State University Press.

Feist, G. J. (1993). A structural model of scientific eminence. *Psychological Science, 4,* 366–371.

Feist, G. J., & Runco, M. A. (1993). Trends in the creativity literature: An analysis of research in the *Journal of Creative Behavior* (1967–1989). *Creativity Research Journal, 6,* 271–286.

Feldman, D. H., with Goldsmith, L. T. (1986). *Nature's gambit: Child prodigies and the development of human potential.* New York: Basic Books.

Fiedler, F. E. (1967). *A theory of leadership effectiveness.* New York: McGraw-Hill.

Finke, R. A., Ward, T. B., & Smith, S. M. (1992). *Creative cognition: Theory, research, applications.* Cambridge, MA: MIT Press.

Ford, C. M., & Gioia, D. A. (Eds.). (1995). *Creative action in organizations: Ivory tower visions and real world voices.* Thousand Oaks, CA: Sage.

Freud, S. (1959). Creative writers and day-dreaming. In J. Strachey (Ed. and Trans.), *The standard edition of the complete psychological works of Sigmund Freud* (Vol. 9, pp. 141–153). London: Hogarth Press. (Original work published 1908)

Freud, S. (1964). *Leonardo da Vinci and a memory of his childhood* (A. Tyson, Trans.). New York: Norton. (Original work published 1910)

Galton, F. (1869). *Hereditary genius: An inquiry into its laws and consequences.* London: Macmillan.

Galton, F. (1874). *English men of science: Their nature and nurture.* London: Macmillan.

Galton, F. (1883). *Inquiries into human faculty and its development.* London: Macmillan.

Gardner, H. (1983). *Frames of mind: A theory of multiple intelligences.* New York: Basic Books.

Gardner, H. (1987). *The mind's new science: A history of the cognitive revolution.* New York: Basic Books.

Gardner, H. (1993). *Creating minds: An anatomy of creativity seen through the lives of Freud, Einstein, Picasso, Stravinsky, Eliot, Graham, and Gandhi.* New York: Basic Books.

Gedo, J. E. (1997). Psychoanalytic theories of creativity. In M. A. Runco (Ed.), *The creativity research handbook* (Vol. 1, pp. 29–39). Cresskill, NJ: Hampton Press.

Getzels, J., & Jackson, P. W. (1962). *Creativity and intelligence: Explorations with gifted students.* New York: Wiley.

Glover, J. A., Ronning, R. R., & Reynolds, C. R. (Eds.). (1989). *Handbook of creativity.* New York: Plenum Press.

Goertzel, M. G., Goertzel, V. & Goertzel, T. G. (1978). *300 eminent personalities: A psychosocial analysis of the famous.* San Francisco: Jossey-Bass.

Gough, H. G. (1976). Studying creativity by means of word association tests. *Journal of Applied Psychology, 61,* 348–353.

Gough, H. G. (1979). A creative personality scale for the Adjective Check List. *Journal of Personality and Social Psychology, 37,* 1398–1405.

Gough, H. G. (1992). Assessment of creative potential in psychology and the development of a Creative Temperament Scale for the CPI. In J. C. Rosen & P. McReynolds (Eds.)., *Advances in psychological assessment* (Vol. 8, pp. 225–257). New York: Plenum Press.

Gruber, H. E. (1989). The evolving systems approach to creative work. In D. B. Wallace & H. E. Gruber (Eds.), *Creative people at work: Twelve cognitive case studies* (pp. 3–24). New York: Oxford University Press.

Guilford, J. P. (1950). Creativity. *American Psychologist, 5,* 444–454.

Guilford, J. P. (1967). *The nature of human intelligence.* New York: McGraw-Hill.

Haensly, P. A., & Reynolds, C. R. (1989). Creativity and intelligence. In J. A. Glover, R. R. Ronning, & C. R. Reynolds (Eds.), *Handbook of creativity* (pp. 111–132). New York: Plenum Press.

Hargens, L. L. (1978). Relations between work habits, research technologies, and eminence in science. *Sociology of Work and Occupations, 5,* 97–112.

Harrington, D. M., Block, J. H., & Block, J. (1987). Testing aspects of Carl Rogers's theory of creative environments: Child-rearing antecedents of creative potential in young adolescents. *Journal of Personality and Social Psychology, 52,* 851–856.

Hasenfus, N., Martindale, C., & Birnbaum, D. (1983). Psychological reality of cross-media artistic styles. *Journal of Experimental Psychology: Human Perception and Performance, 9,* 841–863.

Hayes, J. R. (1989). *The complete problem solver* (2nd. ed.). Hillsdale, NJ: Erlbaum.

Helmreich, R. L., Spence, J. T., & Pred, R. S. (1988). Making it without losing it: Type A, achievement motivation, and scientific attainment revisited. *Personality and Social Psychology Bulletin, 14,* 495–504.

Helmreich, R. L., Spence, J. T., & Thorbecke, W. L. (1981). On the stability of productivity and recognition. *Personality and Social Psychology Bulletin, 7,* 516–522.

Helmreich, R. L., Spence, J. T., Beane, W. E., Lucker, G. W., & Matthews, K. A. (1980). Making it in academic psychology: Demographic and personality correlates of attainment. *Journal of Personality and Social Psychology, 39,* 896–908.

Helson, R., & Crutchfield, R. S. (1970). Mathematicians: The creative researcher and the average Ph.D. *Journal of Consulting and Clinical Psychology, 34,* 250–257.

Hendrickson, R. (1988). *The dictionary of eponyms: Names that became words.* New York: Dorset Press.

Hertz, F. (1970). *Race and civilization* (A. S. Levetus & W. Entz, Trans.). New York: Ktav Publishing House. (Original work published 1928)

Hollingworth, L. S. (1926). *Gifted children: Their nature and nurture.* New York: Macmillan.

Hollingworth, L. S. (1942). *Children beyond 180 IQ: Origin and development.* Yonkers-on-Hudson, NY: World Book.

Hudson, L. (1958). Undergraduate academic record of Fellows of the Royal Society. *Nature, 182,* 1326.

Hudson, L. (1966). *Contrary imaginations.* Baltimore: Penguin.

Isen, A. M., Daubman, K. A., & Nowicki, G. P. (1987). Positive affect facilitates creative problem solving. *Journal of Personality and Social Psychology, 52,* 1122–1131.

Jackson, J. M., & Padgett, V. R. (1982). With a little help from my friend: Social loafing and the Lennon-McCartney songs. *Personality and Social Psychology Bulletin, 8,* 672–677.

James, W. (1880). Great men, great thoughts, and the environment. *Atlantic Monthly, 46,* 441–459.

Jamison, K. R. (1993). *Touched with fire: Manic–depressive illness and the artistic temperment.* New York: Free Press.

Kasof, J. (1995). Explaining creativity: The attributional perspective. *Creativity Research Journal, 8,* 311–366.

Köhler, W. (1925). *The mentality of apes* (E. Winter, Trans.). New York: Harcourt, Brace.

Krampen, G. (1997). Promotion of creativity (divergent productions) and convergent productions by systematic-relaxation exercises: Empirical evidence from five experimental studies with children, young adults, and elderly. *European Journal of Personality, 11,* 83–99.

Kris, E. (1952). *Psychoanalytic explorations in art.* New York: International Universities Press.

Kroeber, A. L. (1917). The superorganic. *American Anthropologist, 19,* 163–214.

Kroeber, A. L. (1944). *Configurations of culture growth.* Berkeley, CA: University of California Press.

Kuhn, T. S. (1970). *The structure of scientific revolutions* (2nd ed.). Chicago: University of Chicago Press.

Lamb, D., & Easton, S. M. (1984). *Multiple discovery.* England: Avebury.

Langley, P., Simon, H. A., Bradshaw, G. L., & Zythow, J. M. (1987). *Scientific discovery.* Cambridge, MA: MIT Press.

Lehman, H. C. (1953). *Age and achievement.* Princeton, NJ: Princeton University Press.

Lehman, H. C. (1962). More about age and achievement. *Gerontologist, 2,* 141–148.

Lehman, H. C., & Witty, P. A. (1931). Scientific eminence and church membership. *Scientific Monthly, 33,* 544–549.

Lester, D. (1991). Premature mortality associated with alcoholism and suicide in American writers. *Perceptual and Motor Skills, 73,* 162.

Ludwig, A. M. (1992a). Creative achievement and psychopathology: Comparison among professions. *American Journal of Psychotherapy, 46,* 330–356.

Ludwig, A. M. (1992b). The Creative Achievement scale. *Creativity Research Journal, 5,* 109–124.

Ludwig, A. M. (1995). *The price of greatness: Resolving the creativity and madness controversy.* New York: Guilford Press.

Lynn, R. (1991). Race differences in intelligence: A global perspective. *Mankind Quarterly, 31,* 254–296.

MacKinnon, D. W. (1978). *In search of human effectiveness.* Buffalo, NJ: Creative Education Foundation.

Martindale, C. (1972). Father absence, psychopathology, and poetic eminence. *Psychological Reports, 31,* 843–847.

Martindale, C. (1973). An experimental simulation of literary change. *Journal of Personality and Social Psychology, 25,* 319–326.

Martindale, C. (1989). Personality, situation, and creativity. In J. A. Glover, R. R. Ronning, & C. R. Reynolds (Eds.), *Handbook of creativity* (pp. 211–232). New York: Plenum Press.

Martindale, C. (1990). *The clockwork muse: The predictability of artistic styles.* New York: Basic Books.

Martindale, C. (1995a). Creativity and connectionism. In S. M. Smith, T. B. Ward, & R. A. Finke (Eds.), *The creative cognition approach* (pp. 249–268). Cambridge, MA: MIT Press.

Martindale, C. (1995b). Fame more fickle than fortune: On the distribution of literary eminence. *Poetics, 23,* 219–234.

Maslow, A. H. (1959). Creativity in self-actualizating people. In H. H. Anderson (Ed.), *Creativity and its cultivation* (pp. 83–95). New York: Harper & Row.

Maslow, A. H. (1970). *Motivation and personality* (2nd ed.). New York: Harper & Row.

Maslow, A. H. (1972). A holistic approach to creativity. In C. W. Taylor (Ed.), *Climate for creativity* (pp. 287–293). New York: Pergamon Press.

Matthews, K. A., Helmreich, R. L., Beane, W. E., & Lucker, G. W. (1980). Pattern A, achievement striving, and scientific merit: Does Pattern A help or hinder? *Journal of Personality and Social Psychology, 39,* 962–967.

May, R. (1975). *The courage to create.* New York: Norton.

McCrae, R. R. (1987). Creativity, divergent thinking, and openness to experience. *Journal of Personality and Social Psychology, 52,* 1258–1265.

McCrae, R. R., Arenberg, D., & Costa, P. T. (1987). Declines in divergent thinking with age: Cross-sectional, longitudinal, and cross-sequential analyses. *Psychology and Aging, 2,* 130–136.

McFarlan, D. (Ed.). (1989). *Guinness book of world records.* New York: Bantam.

McNemar, Q. (1964). Lost: Our intelligence? Why? *American Psychologist, 19,* 871–882.

Mednick, S. A. (1962). The associative basis of the creative process. *Psychological Review, 69,* 220–232.

Mendelsohn, G. A. (1976). Associative and attentional processes in creative performance. *Journal of Personality, 44,* 341–369.

Merton, R. K. (1961). Singletons and multiples in scientific discovery: A chapter in the sociology of science. *Proceedings of the American Philosophical Society, 105,* 470–486.

Michael, W. B., & Wright, C. R. (1989). Psychometric issues in the assessment of creativity. In J. A. Glover, R. R. Ronning, & C. R. Reynolds (Eds.), *Handbook of creativity* (pp. 33–52). New York: Plenum Press.

Moles, A. (1968). *Information theory and esthetic perception* (J. E. Cohen, Trans.). Urbana: University of Illinois Press. (Original work published 1958)

Murray, P. (Ed.). (1989). *Genius: The history of an idea.* Oxford: Blackwell.

Nemeth, C. J., & Wachtler, J. (1983). Creative problem solving as a result of majority vs. minority influence. *European Journal of Social Psychology, 13,* 45–55.

Newell, A., & Simon, H. A. (1972). *Human problem solving.* Englewood Cliffs, NJ: Prentice Hall.
Nicholls, J. G. (1972). Creativity in the person who will never produce anything original and useful: The concept of creativity as a normally distributed trait. *American Psychologist, 27,* 717–727.
Ochse, R. (1989). A new look at primary process thinking and its relation to inspiration. *New Ideas in Psychology, 7,* 315–330.
Ochse, R. (1990). *Before the gates of excellence: Determinants of creative genius.* New York: Cambridge University Press.
Ochse, R. (1991). Why there were relatively few eminent women creators. *Journal of Creative Behavior, 25,* 334–343.
Over, R. (1982). The durability of scientific reputation. *Journal of the History of the Behavioral Sciences, 18,* 53–61.
Parloff, M., Datta, L., Kleman, M., & Handlon, J. (1968). Personality characteristics which differentiate creative male adolescents and adults. *Journal of Personality, 36,* 528–552.
Plomin, R. (1986). Behavior genetic methods. *Journal of Personality, 54,* 226–261.
Plomin, R., & Bergeman, C. S. (1991). The nature of nurture: Genetic influence on environmental measures. *Behavioral and Brain Sciences, 14,* 373–386.
Plomin, R., & Petrill, S. A. (1997). Genetics and intelligence: What's new? *Intelligence, 24,* 53–77.
Post, F. (1996). Verbal creativity, depression and alcoholism: An investigation of one hundred American and British writers. *British Journal of Psychiatry, 168,* 545–555.
Raskin, E. A. (1936). Comparison of scientific and literary ability: A biographical study of eminent scientists and men of letters of the nineteenth century. *Journal of Abnormal and Social Psychology, 31,* 20–35.
Roe, A. (1952). *The making of a scientist.* New York: Dodd, Mead.
Rogers, C. R. (1954). Toward a theory of creativity. *ETC: A Review of General Semantics, 11,* 249–260.
Root-Bernstein, R. S., Bernstein, M., & Garnier, H. (1995). Correlations between avocations, scientific style, work habits, and professional impact of scientists. *Creativity Research Journal, 8,* 115–137.
Root-Bernstein, R. S., Bernstein, M., & Garnier, H. (1993). Identification of scientists making long-term, high-impact contributions, with notes on their methods of working. *Creativity Research Journal, 6,* 329–343.
Rosengren, K. E. (1985). Time and literary fame. *Poetics, 14,* 157–172.
Rothenberg, A. (1979). *The emerging goddess: The creative process in art, science, and other fields.* Chicago: University of Chicago Press.
Rothenberg, A. (1986). Artistic creation as stimulated by superimposed versus combined-composite visual images. *Journal of Personality and Social Psychology, 50,* 370–381.
Rothenberg, A. (1990). *Creativity and madness: New findings and old stereotypes.* Baltimore: Johns Hopkins University Press.
Rubenson, D. L., & Runco, M. A. (1992). The psychoeconomic approach to creativity. *New Ideas in Psychology, 10,* 131–147.
Runco, M. A. (1989). The creativity of children's art. *Child Study Journal, 19,* 177–189.
Runco, M. A. (1992). Children's divergent thinking and creative ideation. *Developmental Review, 12,* 233–264.
Runco, M. (Ed.). (1997). *Handbook of creativity research* (Vol. 1).Cresskill, NJ: Hampton Press.
Runco, M. A., & Charles, R. E. (1997). Developmental trends in creative potential and creative performance. In M. A. Runco (Ed.), *The creativity research handbook* (Vol. 1, pp. 115–152). Cresskill, NJ: Hampton Press.
Runco, M. A., & Pritzker, S. (Eds.). (1999). *Encyclopedia of creativity.* San Diego: Academic Press.
Rushton, J. P. (1984). Evaluating research eminence in psychology: The construct validity of citation counts. *Bulletin of the British Psychological Society, 37,* 33–36.
Rushton, J. P. (1995). *Race, evolution, and behavior: A life history perspective.* New Brunswick, NJ: Transaction Publishers.
Scarr, S., & McCartney, K. (1983). How people make their own environments: A theory of genotype → environmental effects. *Child Development, 54,* 424–435.
Schaefer, C. E., & Anastasi, A. (1968). A biographical inventory for identifying creativity in adolescent boys. *Journal of Applied Psychology, 58,* 42–48.
Schaller, M. (1997). The psychological consequences of fame: Three tests of the self-consciousness hypothesis. *Journal of Personality, 65,* 291–309.
Serebriakoff, V. (1985). *Mensa: The society for the highly intelligent.* London: Constable.
Shadish, W. R., Jr. (1989). The perception and evaluation of quality in science. In B. Gholson, W. R. Shadish, Jr., R. A. Neimeyer, & A. C. Houts (Eds.), *The psychology of science: Contributions to metascience* (pp. 383–426). Cambridge, UK: Cambridge University Press.
Shekerjian, D. (1990). *Uncommon genius: How great ideas are born.* New York: Viking Press.
Shields, S. A. (1975). Functionalism, Darwinism, and the psychology of women: A study in social myth. *American Psychologist, 30,* 739–754.
Shrager, J., & Langley, P. (Eds.). (1990). *Computational models of scientific discovery and theory formation.* San Mateo, CA: Morgan Kaufmann.
Silverman, S. M. (1974). Parental loss and scientists. *Science Studies, 4,* 259–264.
Simon, R. J. (1974). The work habits of eminent scientists. *Sociology of Work and Occupations, 1,* 327–335.
Simonton, D. K. (1975). Sociocultural context of individual creativity: A transhistorical time-series analy-

sis. *Journal of Personality and Social Psychology, 32,* 1119–1133.
Simonton, D. K. (1976a). Biographical determinants of achieved eminence: A multivariate approach to the Cox data. *Journal of Personality and Social Psychology, 33,* 218–226.
Simonton, D. K. (1976b). Philosophical eminence, beliefs, and zeitgeist: An individual–generational analysis. *Journal of Personality and Social Psychology, 34,* 630–640.
Simonton, D. K. (1976c). The sociopolitical context of philosophical beliefs: A transhistorical causal analysis. *Social Forces, 54,* 513–523.
Simonton, D. K. (1977a). Creative productivity, age, and stress: A biographical time-series analysis of 10 classical composers. *Journal of Personality and Social Psychology, 35,* 791–804.
Simonton, D. K. (1977b). Eminence, creativity, and geographic marginality: A recursive structural equation model. *Journal of Personality and Social Psychology, 35,* 805–816.
Simonton, D. K. (1979). Multiple discovery and invention: Zeitgeist, genius, or chance? *Journal of Personality and Social Psychology, 37,* 1603–1616.
Simonton, D. K. (1980a). Land battles, generals, and armies: Individual and situational determinants of victory and casualties. *Journal of Personality and Social Psychology, 38,* 110–119.
Simonton, D. K. (1980b). Thematic fame and melodic originality in classical music: A multivariate computer-content analysis. *Journal of Personality, 48,* 206–219.
Simonton, D. K. (1980c). Thematic fame, melodic originality, and musical zeitgeist: A biographical and transhistorical content analysis. *Journal of Personality and Social Psychology, 38,* 972–983.
Simonton, D. K. (1983a). Formal education, eminence, and dogmatism: The curvilinear relationship. *Journal of Creative Behavior, 17,* 149–162.
Simonton, D. K. (1983b). Intergenerational transfer of individual differences in hereditary monarchs: Genes, role-modeling, cohort, or sociocultural effects? *Journal of Personality and Social Psychology, 44,* 354–364.
Simonton, D. K. (1984a). Artistic creativity and interpersonal relationships across and within generations. *Journal of Personality and Social Psychology, 46,* 1273–1286.
Simonton, D. K. (1984b). *Genius, creativity, and leadership: Historiometric inquiries.* Cambridge, MA: Harvard University Press.
Simonton, D. K. (1984c). Is the marginality effect all that marginal? *Social Studies of Science, 14,* 621–622.
Simonton, D. K. (1984d). Leaders as eponyms: Individual and situational determinants of monarchal eminence. *Journal of Personality, 52,* 1–21.
Simonton, D. K. (1985). Intelligence and personal influence in groups: Four nonlinear models. *Psychological Review, 92,* 532–547.
Simonton, D. K. (1986a). Biographical typicality, eminence, and achievement style. *Journal of Creative Behavior, 20,* 14–22.
Simonton, D. K. (1986b). Presidential personality: Biographical use of the Gough Adjective Check List. *Journal of Personality and Social Psychology, 51,* 149–160.
Simonton, D. K. (1987a). Developmental antecedents of achieved eminence. *Annals of Child Development, 5,* 131–169.
Simonton, D. K. (1987b). Multiples, chance, genius, creativity, and zeitgeist. In D. N. Jackson & J. P. Rushton (Eds.), *Scientific excellence: Origins and assessment* (pp. 98–128). Beverly Hills, CA: Sage.
Simonton, D. K. (1987c). Presidential inflexibility and veto behavior: Two individual-situational interactions. *Journal of Personality, 55,* 1–18.
Simonton, D. K. (1987d). *Why presidents succeed: A political psychology of leadership.* New Haven, CT: Yale University Press.
Simonton, D. K. (1988a). Age and outstanding achievement: What do we know after a century of research? *Psychological Bulletin, 104,* 251–267.
Simonton, D. K. (1988b). Galtonian genius, Kroeberian configurations, and emulation: A generational time-series analysis of Chinese civilization. *Journal of Personality and Social Psychology, 55,* 230–238.
Simonton, D. K. (1988c). *Scientific genius: A psychology of science.* Cambridge, UK: Cambridge University Press.
Simonton, D. K. (1989a). Shakespeare's sonnets: A case of and for single-case historiometry. *Journal of Personality, 57,* 695–721.
Simonton, D. K. (1989b). The swan-song phenomenon: Last-works effects for 172 classical composers. *Psychology and Aging, 4,* 42–47.
Simonton, D. K. (1990). *Psychology, science, and history: An introduction to historiometry.* New Haven, CT: Yale University Press.
Simonton, D. K. (1991a). Career landmarks in science: Individual differences and interdisciplinary contrasts. *Developmental Psychology, 27,* 119–130.
Simonton, D. K. (1991b). Emergence and realization of genius: The lives and works of 120 classical composers. *Journal of Personality and Social Psychology, 61,* 829–840.
Simonton, D. K. (1991c). Latent-variable models of posthumous reputation: A quest for Galton's G. *Journal of Personality and Social Psychology, 60,* 607–619.
Simonton, D. K. (1991d). Personality correlates of exceptional personal influence: A note on Thorndike's (1950) creators and leaders. *Creativity Research Journal, 4,* 67–78.
Simonton, D. K. (1992a). Gender and genius in Japan: Feminine eminence in masculine culture. *Sex Roles, 27,* 101–119.
Simonton, D. K. (1992b). Leaders of American psychology, 1879–1967: Career development, creative out-

put, and professional achievement. *Journal of Personality and Social Psychology, 62,* 5–17.
Simonton, D. K. (1992c). The social context of career success and course for 2,026 scientists and inventors. *Personality and Social Psychology Bulletin, 18,* 452–463.
Simonton, D. K. (1994). *Greatness: Who makes history and why.* New York: Guilford Press.
Simonton, D. K. (1995a). Exceptional personal influence: An integrative paradigm. *Creativity Research Journal, 8,* 371–376.
Simonton, D. K. (1995b). Personality and intellectual predictors of leadership. In D. H. Saklofske & M. Zeidner (Eds.), *International handbook of personality and intelligence* (pp. 739–757). New York: Plenum Press.
Simonton, D. K. (1996). Presidents' wives and First Ladies: On achieving eminence within a traditional gender role. *Sex Roles, 35,* 309–336.
Simonton, D. K. (1997a). Creative productivity: A predictive and explanatory model of career trajectories and landmarks. *Psychological Review, 104,* 66–89.
Simonton, D. K. (1997b). Foreign influence and national achievement: The impact of open milieus on Japanese civilization. *Journal of Personality and Social Psychology, 72,* 86–94.
Simonton, D. K. (1997c). *Genius and creativity: Selected papers.* Greenwich, CT: Ablex.
Simonton, D. K. (1998a). Achieved eminence in minority and majority cultures: Convergence versus divergence in the assessments of 294 African Americans. *Journal of Personality and Social Psychology, 74,* 804–817.
Simonton, D. K. (1998b). Fickle fashion versus immortal fame: Transhistorical assessments of creative products in the opera house. *Journal of Personality and Social Psychology, 75,* 198–210.
Smith, S. M., Ward, T. B., & Finke, R. A. (Eds.). (1995). *The creative cognition approach.* Cambridge, MA: MIT Press.
Sobel, R. S., & Rothenberg, A. (1980). Artistic creation as stimulated by superimposed versus separated visual images. *Journal of Personality and Social Psychology, 39,* 953–961.
Sorokin, P. A. (1937–1941). *Social and cultural dynamics* (4 vols.). New York: American Book.
Sorokin, P. A., & Merton, R. K. (1935). The course of Arabian intellectual development, 700–1300 A.D. *Isis, 22,* 516–524.
Stavridou, A., & Furnham, A. (1996). The relationship between psychoticism, trait-creativity and the attentional mechanism of cognitive inhibition. *Personality and Individual Differences, 21,* 143–153.
Stein, M. I. (1969). Creativity. In E. F. Borgatta & W. W. Lambert (Eds.), *Handbook of personality theory and research* (pp. 900–942). Chicago: Rand McNally.
Sternberg, R. J. (1985). *Beyond IQ: A triarchic theory of human intelligence.* New York: Cambridge University Press.
Sternberg, R. J. (Ed.). (1988). *The nature of creativity: Contemporary psychological perspectives.* New York: Cambridge University Press.
Sternberg, R. J., & Davidson, J. E. (Eds.). (1995). *The nature of insight.* Cambridge, MA: MIT Press.
Sternberg, R. J., & Gordeeva, T. (1996). The anatomy of impact: What makes an article influential? *Psychological Science, 7,* 69–75.
Sternberg, R. J., & Lubart, T. I. (1991). An investment theory of creativity and its development. *Human Development, 34,* 1–31.
Sternberg, R. J., & Lubart, T. I. (1995). *Defying the crowd: Cultivating creativity in a culture of conformity.* New York: Free Press.
Sternberg, R. J., & Lubart, T. I. (1996). Investing in creativity. *American Psychologist, 51,* 677–688.
Stewart, J. A. (1986). Drifting continents and colliding interests: A quantitative application of the interests perspective. *Social Studies of Science, 16,* 261–279.
Storfer, M. D. (1990). *Intelligence and giftedness: The contributions of heredity and early environment.* San Francisco: Jossey-Bass.
Suler, J. R. (1980). Primary process thinking and creativity. *Psychological Bulletin, 88,* 144–165.
Sulloway, F. J. (1996). *Born to rebel: Birth order, family dynamics, and creative lives.* New York: Pantheon.
Terman, L. M. (1925). *Mental and physical traits of a thousand gifted children.* Stanford, CA: Stanford University Press.
Terman, L. M. (1954). Scientists and nonscientists in a group of 800 gifted men. *Psychological Monographs: General and Applied, 68*(Whole No. 378), 1–44.
Terman, L. M., & Oden, M. H. (1959). *The gifted group at mid-life.* Stanford, CA: Stanford University Press.
Terry, W. S. (1989). Birth order and prominence in the history of psychology. *Psychological Record, 39,* 333–337.
Thorndike, E. L. (1950). Traits of personality and their intercorrelations as shown in biography. *Journal of Educational Psychology, 41,* 193–216.
Torrance, E. P. (1988). The nature of creativity as manifest in its testing. In R. Sternberg (Ed.), *The nature of creativity: Contemporary psychological perspectives* (pp. 43–75). New York: Cambridge University Press.
Visher, S. S. (1947). Starred scientists: A study of their ages. *American Scientist, 35,* 543, 570, 572, 574, 576, 578, 580.
Walberg, H. J., Rasher, S. P., & Parkerson, J. (1980). Childhood and eminence. *Journal of Creative Behavior, 13,* 225–231.
Wallach, M. A., & Kogan, N. (1965). *Modes of thinking in young children.* New York: Holt, Rinehart & Winston.
Waller, N. G., Bouchard, T. J., Jr., Lykken, D. T., Tellegen, A., & Blacker, D. M. (1993). Creativity, heritability, familiality: Which word does not belong? *Psychological Inquiry, 4,* 235–237.
Weisberg, R. W. (1992). *Creativity: Beyond the myth of genius.* New York: Freeman.

Wertheimer, M. (1982). *Productive thinking* (M. Wertheimer, Ed.). Chicago: University of Chicago Press. (Original work published 1945)

West, M. A., & Farr, J. L. (Eds.). (1990). *Innovation and creativity at work: Psychological and organizational strategies.* New York: Wiley.

Westcott, M. R. (1968). *Toward a contemporary psychology of intuition.* New York: Holt, Rinehart & Winston.

White, L. (1949). *The science of culture.* New York: Farrar, Straus.

White, R. K. (1931). The versatility of genius. *Journal of Social Psychology, 2,* 460–489.

Winner, E. (1996). *Gifted children: Myths and realities.* New York: Basic Books.

Woods, F. A. (1909). A new name for a new science. *Science, 30,* 703–704.

Woods, F. A. (1911). Historiometry as an exact science. *Science, 33,* 568–574.

Zuckerman, M. (1990). Some dubious premises in research and theory on racial differences: Scientific, social, and ethical issues. *American Psychologist, 45,* 1297–1303.

Zusne, L., & Dailey, D. P. (1982). History of psychology texts as measuring instruments of eminence in psychology. *Revista de Historia de la Psicología, 3,* 7–42.

Chapter 26

The Fields of Interpersonal Behavior

Jerry S. Wiggins and Krista K. Trobst
Gerontology Research Center, National Institute on Aging

In this chapter we provide a historical account of several different approaches to the conceptualization and measurement of interpersonal behavior that were influenced, in differing ways and to differing degrees, by the construct of "field" in physical theory. We contrast the "interactionist" approach, which originated with Kurt Lewin, with the "interpersonalist" approach of Harry Stack Sullivan. Although interactionism was emphasized in the corresponding chapter of the first edition of this volume (Magnusson, 1990), we emphasize interpersonalism in this chapter and stress the extent to which this approach has "come of age" in the ensuing decade.

FIELD THEORY IN THE NATURAL AND SOCIAL SCIENCES

> Such . . . is the respect paid to science that the most absurd opinions may become current, provided they are expressed in language, the sound of which recalls some well-known scientific phrase.
> —JAMES CLERK MAXWELL (1831–1879)

The extent to which the concepts and findings of the natural sciences may have applicability to formulations in the social sciences and humanities has been a contentious issue for more than a century. That the controversy continues is clear from the current "science wars" in which relativists who conduct science and technology studies have suggested that scientific knowledge is a "mere construction" (Pickering, 1997) and from "Sokal's hoax" in which the use of scientific constructs in the social sciences and humanities was brutally parodied (Sokal, 1996). Whether appropriate or not, the origins of present day conceptions of interpersonal behavior may be traced directly to corresponding conceptions in physical science. In this chapter, we will show how the "field" concept in classical physics has influenced formulations of interpersonal behavior in psychology since the early 20th century. In so doing, we are uncomfortably aware that such an enterprise might not have been encouraged by the mathematical physicist who was the originator of physical field theory (quoted above).

FIELD THEORY IN PHYSICS

Faraday's Fields

Michael Faraday (1791–1867) had little formal education, and virtually none in mathematics. However, his talent for performing and conceptualizing experiments in physics was unparalleled. In 1831, he conducted experiments which demonstrated that (1) when a magnet is moved through a coil of wire, it induces an electric current in that wire and (2) a current can be induced in an electrical circuit by changing the current in an adjacent circuit. A changing magnetic field creates an electric current and a changing electric current creates another electric current. These two facts, and Oersted's earlier discovery that a steady current could produce a magnetic field, provided the basis for the eventual unification of electricity and magnetism into one theory.

"Faraday pondered on the idea of action at a distance, and there grew in his mind the idea that, surrounding a magnet or a charged body, there was an invisible, immaterial "sea," an entity that exists in space, rather like the waves that spread out from a stone thrown into a pond" (Silver, 1998, p. 91). This "sea" was visualized by Faraday as consisting of "electromagnetic fields." In attempting to formalize Faraday's fields in mathematical terms, William Tomson (1814–1907) found what he thought was a connection between electromagnetism and light. To test this proposition, Faraday passed a beam of light through a piece of glass in a magnetic field and found such an effect. The possibility of a unified field theory of electricity, magnetism, and light was suggested but the mathematics were formidable.

Maxwell's Equations

James Clerk Maxwell (1831–1879) summarized the existing knowledge concerning electromagnetism in a series of differential equations that provided a quantitative expression of the form of electric and magnetic fields. His theory differed from all preceding theories in being based on an analogy rather than on a physical model capable of being visualized. The significance of Maxwell's findings was little appreciated at the time, but Einstein and Infeld (1938) were later to describe them as "the most important event in physics since Newton's time, not only because of their wealth of content, but also because they form a pattern for a new type of law . . . representing the structure of the field" (p. 143). Maxwell's equations actually turned out to be more successful than Newton's laws because they "survived all the changes introduced by relativity and the quantum theory; they are as valid in the light of present knowledge as they were when they were first introduced a century ago" (Asimov, 1966, p. 238). These equations may be thought of as an idealized experiment performed in imagination in which the experiments of both Oersted and Faraday were repeated, with the magnetic and electric circuits involved being shrunk to a point in an electromagnetic field which was postulated to exist quite independent of magnets or wires. "*It needed great imagination to recognize that it is not the charges nor the particles but the field in the space between the charges and the particles which is essential for the description of physical phenomena*" (Einstein & Infeld, 1938, p. 244; emphasis in original). Maxwell's equations also emphasized that "the field *here* and *now* depends on the field in the *immediate neighborhood* at a time *just past*" (Einstein & Infeld, 1938, pp. 152–153). From these equations, Maxwell predicted in 1856 that electromagnetic waves travel through space at the speed of light (a prediction confirmed by Hertz in 1888) and the rest, so to speak, was history.

Maxwell's equations provided the laws governing electromagnetic fields without reference to matter and with reference to "waves" that travel in a vacuum. Although it was not possible to visualize the subject matter of the laws, this did not deter subsequent generations of physicists from using them. "Maxwell's laws allow us to calculate the strength of the electric and magnetic fields for any system, including light waves. They give the right answers, and it is of no practical importance whether we have a reassuring physical picture of electromagnetic waves. Logical positivism ignores such questions" (Silver, 1998, p. 198).

FIELD THEORY IN PSYCHOLOGY

Within experimental psychology, the field-theoretical approach to understanding human behavior was championed by the influential Gestalt school of thought (Koffka, 1935; Koehler, 1929; Wertheimer, 1912). As Woodworth (1931) observed, "Since the work of Faraday and Maxwell the field and its characteristics are very important in the science of physics. . . . The Gestalt psychologists attempt to apply this physical concept of a dynamic field not only figuratively but literally to the visual field, to the organism, and especially to the cerebral cortex" (pp. 131–132). So great was Koehler's (1920) enthusiasm for Gestalt theory that he attempted to extend it to biology and physics as well.

As is well known, Kurt Lewin (1939/1997b), a member of the original Gestalt group, applied field theory to developmental and social psychology, and launched a brilliant program of research and theorizing that is still recognizable in current research. As is less well known, J. R. Kantor (1924–1926) had earlier founded his school of interbehavioral psychology that was also heavily influenced by the field-theoretical ideas of the physics of his day (Kantor, 1953). The field-theoretical perspective in physics was also highly influential in the theoretical formulations of Harry Stack Sullivan (1940), whose interpersonal theory of psychiatry inspired a substantial body of theory and research in current personality and clinical psychology. In this chapter, we will trace the origins of current work in interpersonal behavior that evolved primarily from the formulations of Lewin and Sullivan, respectively, with an emphasis on the latter theorist whose current influence is not as widely appreciated.

Interactionism and Interpersonalism

A useful distinction may be made between interactionism and interpersonalism in personality psychology. "Interactionism" refers to the manner in which a theory conceptualizes and measures the relation between a person and the environment in which that person is located. "Interpersonalism" refers to the manner in which a theory conceptualizes and measures the interrelation between two people within a common environment. Within the interactionist framework, the relative importance of the person and the situation may be assessed proportionally. Within the interpersonalist framework, interpersonal relationships *are* the situation, which is studied over time and in different contexts.

At the height of the heated debates of the 1970s regarding the importance or even existence of personality traits, Ekehammer (1974) distinguished three heterogeneous and partially overlapping positions on interactionism (as opposed to interpersonalism). Using the terms of Lewin's (1935) famous equation, he expressed these three positions as: personologism [$B = f(P)$], situationism [$B = f(E)$], and interactionism [$B = f(P,E)$] to represent the *relative* emphases placed on person and environment in accounting for behavior within each of these three interactionist positions. Among many possible interpretations of $B = f(P,E)$, Ekehammer emphasized the one that was formulated independently by Kantor and Lewin, which postulated a *reciprocal, bidirectional influence* between person and environment; a view that characterized a number of other theoretical positions at that time (e.g., Bowers, 1973; Endler, 1975; Jessor, 1958; Mischel, 1973; Pervin, 1968; Rotter, 1954).

Ekehammer's (1974) scholarly presentation of the origins of interactionism in personality psychology did much to correct the notion that the spate of papers on this topic that appeared in the 1970s reflected a "New Look" within the field. He traced the origins of interactionist thought back to Aristotle and documented the singular relevance of the early writings of J. R. Kantor to contemporary formulations of interactionism. However, from the hindsight of 25 years, Ekehammer's dismissive treatment of the influence of Harry Stack Sullivan on contemporary personality psychology seems to have been premature. Like Kantor, Sullivan formulated a behavioral version of field theory that emphasized the uniqueness of the *interpersonal* field as a unit of investigation. In so doing, Sullivan provided the conceptual foundation for the extensive literature that is the subject matter of later sections of this chapter.

J. R. Kantor and the Interbehavioral Field

Historically, Kantor (1924–1926) was among the first to apply physical field theory to psychological science. Although his impact on the field of personality was not large, he had a direct influence on Rotter's (1954) interactionist formulations (see Strickland, 1997). In addition, Kantor's radical behaviorism and his recognition of the unique nature of interpersonal adaptations presaged aspects of Sullivan's later interpersonal formulations. As a psychologist, philosopher, and historian of science, Kantor was well aware of the history and significance of the field concept in physics and in psychology. Kantor (1959) stressed that "psychological events are in all respects as natural as chemical reactions, electromagnetic radiation, or gravitational attraction" (p. vii). In accord with this strong naturalistic and behavioristic position, he rejected all dualistic concepts of "mind" and "spirit" that postulated mentalistic events occurring over and above (or under and below) the concrete, observable interbehavior between organisms and stimulus objects.

The interbehavioral field reflects a historical process in which behavior segments become increasingly complex as a function of repeated contacts between organisms and stimulus objects. The "behavior segment" is the basic unit of psychological events that centers around a "response function" (an action of the organism) and a "stimulus" function (an action of the stimulus object). The interbehavior of organisms and objects occurs in a specific "medium of contact" (light, sound). Of particular importance are "setting factors" (the immediate circumstances of the field) that influence which particular behavior segment will occur (Kantor, 1959).

The evolution of behavior segments into psychological fields may be thought of as a process involving different stages or levels of analysis in the interrelation of organism and object. In the prepsychological stage, the organism is considered in terms of biological structures and functions and the object is considered in terms of physiochemical properties and actions. In the early stages of psychological development, the organism responds and builds up response functions and the objects stimulate and develop stimulus functions through a specific contact medium in the presence of limited setting factors. Over time, the organism and objects increase the number of response and stimulus functions through repeated interbehavioral contacts in different settings. Thus, through the development of stimulus and response functions, interbehavioral history consists of the "evolution of acts and traits as responses to objects, conditions, and institutions" (Kantor, 1959, p. 43).

Kantor (1924–1926) considered interpersonal action to be a unique type of psychological behavior because it has adaptational characteristics that distinguish it from other psychological activities. During interpersonal actions,

> the stimulus object is a person endowed with an exceedingly large number of stimulational functions. . . . Essentially, interpersonal reactions are responses occurring in situations in which the individuals concerned have mutual influences upon each other. . . . It must appear clear that interpersonal behavior is always constituted of, or at least is invariably involved with, contingential activity of all sorts. (pp. 290–292)

Kurt Lewin and the Social Field

In formulating behavior as a function of the person and the environment, Lewin emphasized the interdependence of the two. A person's perception of the environment is influenced by the state of the person and the person's state is, in turn, influenced by the environment. Lewin used the term "life space" (Lsp) to refer to the totality of this constellation of person/environment interdependent factors: $B = F(P,E) = F(LSp)$.

> A totality of coexisting facts which are conceived of as mutually interdependent is called a *field* (Einstein, 1933). . . . The concept of the psychological field as a determinant of behavior implies that everything that affects behavior at a given time should be represented in the field existing at that time, and that only those facts can affect behavior which are part of the present field. (Lewin, 1946/1997a, pp. 338–339)

When all objects or events are characterized by the way they affect the situation, "every type of fact is placed on the same level and becomes interrelated to any other fact which affects the situation" (Lewin, 1939/1997b, p. 275). Lewin preferred this characterization to one that would classify objects and events in terms of their similarity or dissimilarity of appearance.

In distinguishing between a person and a group, Lewin tended to emphasize the influence of the latter on the former (e.g., the group touches "central regions" of the person). However, he did discuss dyads, and particularly the marriage group, emphasizing that the smallness of the group increases *interdependence* and *intimacy* (Lewin, 1940/1997c). He listed the factors that make marriage the most interdependent and intimate of all groups and concluded, "Their combined effect produces one of the most closely integrated social units. That means, on the one hand, a high degree of so-called identification with the group and a readiness to stand together; on the other hand, great sensitivity to shortcomings of the partner or of oneself" (p. 71).

In general, Lewin's field theory was meant to be a way of thinking about psychological phenomena rather than a strict reductionist account (Cartwright, 1959; Deutsch, 1968). And although he used mathematical concepts as part of his general logic, such concepts were used descriptively rather than formally (Estes, 1954). Lewin's formulations were meant to be, and decidedly were, *heuristic*; they generated a host of innovative experiments and provided new ways to view persons in situations. Although Lewin should be credited for his emphasis on the person in the life space, at a time when behaviorism dominated the field, "[He] was so little interested in individual differences that personality is not the place to assign his major impact" (Hilgard, 1987, p. 589).

Harry Stack Sullivan and the Interpersonal Field

As a young man, Sullivan showed a very early interest in physics (Perry, 1982), and it is not surprising that he later turned to the concepts of modern physics as the model for a scientific psychiatry. He felt that "scientific psychiatry has to be defined as the study of interpersonal relations, and in this end calls for the use of the kind of conceptual framework that we now call *field theory*" (Sullivan, 1953, p. 368). But the manner in which Sullivan partitioned the variance of person and situation in this field was radically different from preceding accounts.

Radical Interpersonalism

For Sullivan (1940), the basic unit for observing and theorizing about "personality" is: *"the relatively enduring pattern of recurrent interpersonal situations which characterize a human life"* (pp. 110–111). This radical idea does not hold out the hope of identifying a "person" or "persons" who may be considered independent from the complex field (situation) of bidirectional causalities in which they are embedded over time. Sullivan maintained that in this formulation, "personality" is a *hypothetical* and for those who are not convinced by his stimulating, but often opaque, expositions on this topic (e.g., Sullivan, 1948, 1950/1964), he suggested considering what might be gained conceptually from adopting this view:

> No great progress in this field of study can be made until it is realized that the field of observation is what people do with each other, what they can communicate to each other about what they do with each other. When that is done, no such thing as the durable, unique, individual personality is ever clearly justified. For all I know every human being has as many personalities as he has interpersonal relations; and as a great many of our relations are actual operations with imaginary people—that is, in-no-sense-materially-embodied people—and as they may have the same or greater validity and importance in life as have our operations with material-embodied people like the clerks in the corner store, you can see that even though "the illusion of personal individuality" sounds quite lunatic when first heard, there is at least food for thought in it. (Sullivan, 1950/1964, pp. 220–221)

Interpersonal Nature of Needs

Sullivan subscribed to Eldridge's (1925) general biological principle of communal existence: "The living cannot live when separated from what might be described as their necessary environment" (cited in Sullivan, 1953, p. 31) and for the human organism, that environment is culture. Further, since "culture is an abstraction pertaining to people . . . man requires interpersonal relationships or interchange with others" (p. 32). Within this communal context, needs may be thought of as states of disequilibrium created by deficits, the restoration of which results in a state of satisfaction. Associated with each need is a pattern of overt or covert activity that may "achieve, approach, compromise, or suppress action towards the objective" (Sullivan, 1948, p. 4). Most importantly, this pattern of satisfaction-seeking involves the behavior of *other persons* whose cooperation and "complementary" patterns of response are required to satisfy the need involved. Thus, all needs are *interpersonal* in the sense that they depend on complementary patterns of motivation existing in cooperative others. Perhaps the moment of truth for the developing child is the time at which he or she first recognizes that *survival* depends upon "bringing about the appearance, approach, and cooperation of the good mother in connection with the satisfaction of a need" (Sullivan, 1953, p. 92).

Representation of an Interpersonal Situation

Sullivan was the most empirical of the so-called neo-Freudian theorists (Thompson, 1957). He was also "behavioral" in the sense that he focused on the things that people *do* to one another rather than upon the things that people

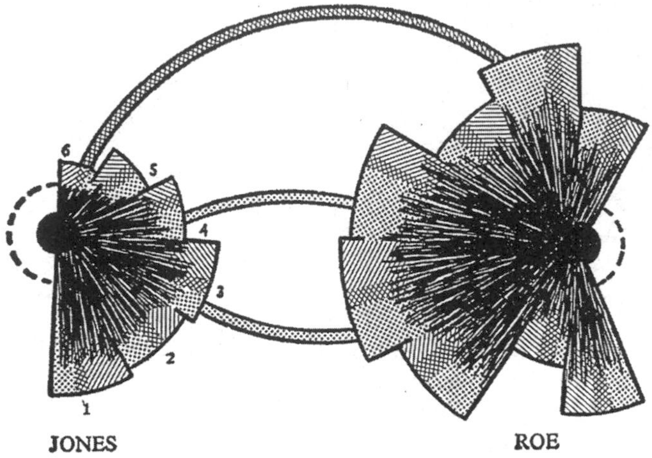

FIGURE 26.1. Interpersonal situation of Johnnie Jones and Richard Roe. From Sullivan (1948, p. 7). Adapted and reproduced by special permission of the publisher, William Alanson White Psychiatric Foundation.

might *have,* such as unconscious drives or instincts. Perhaps for that reason, he was never entirely satisfied with his own attempts to represent the interpersonal situation diagramatically (Perry, 1964). Nevertheless, his representation that appears in Figure 26.1 will be most relevant to our later discussion of contemporary theory and research on interpersonal behavior.

Figure 26.1 is meant to represent the interpersonal situation of two hypothetical "personalities" (Johnnie Jones on the left and Richard Roe on the right) who live in the same boarding house. Roe apparently tried to be friendly with Jones but the relationship miscarried, due in large part to Jones's suspicion that Roe had been trying to poison him. The two circular diagrams represent the "major motivational systems" of the participants. The content of these systems is, with one exception (Sector 6 is heterosexual motivation), not specified by Sullivan. However, one might easily think of these as "circumplex" representations of Murray's needs (Wiggins & Broughton, 1985), as we will explain later. The shadings within these sectors are meant to represent a continuum of awareness from inaccessible experience fraught with anxiety (darker) to experience accessible to awareness (lighter). In the *early* stage of the relationship depicted here, Richard Roe is seen as having a more nearly "well rounded" or more developed personality.

The uppermost (cross-hatched) connection between the two men represents a "disjunctive" field force (anxiety), which keeps them from becoming intimate. The two (dotted) lines below are potentially "conjunctive" field forces which, although not specified, are meant to represent forces that draw the men together (Sectors 3 & 4). Note that in Sector 6 (heterosexual motivation), Jones has a much smaller area than Roe and this sector is linked by Jones's anxiety. Hence, "Johnnie Jones cannot discuss comfortably with his friend, Mr. Roe, matters pertaining to this phase of living. Mr. Roe readily becomes aware of the embarrassment and avoidances that ensue after any remarks which touch upon Jones's deficiencies in this area" (Sullivan, 1948, pp. 7–8).

Sullivan (1948) goes on to consider a later stage in this developing relationship in which both disjunctive and conjunctive forces connect Sector 6 and the topic of heterosexual motivation is permitted a certain amount of "risky" discussion. Also, an additional conjunctive force has developed in Sector 5, which arose exclusively from the "extra-self" areas of awareness of both men's sectors: "Powerful conjunctive forces can arise from congruent motivational systems and exert influence in the interpersonal field wholly exterior to the awareness of the persons concerned" (p. 244). Space does not permit a description of the dramatic changes in the pattern of field forces that takes place following a "schizophrenic episode" in the relationship of Jones with his friend, but the interested clinician may wish to read the account given by one of this century's foremost authorities on schizophrenia (pp. 245–254).

FIELD THEORY IN CONTEMPORARY INTERPERSONAL PSYCHOLOGY

Metaconcepts of Agency and Communion

In a highly influential essay on the nature of human existence, David Bakan (1966) distinguished "two fundamental modalities in the existence of living forms, agency for the existence of an organism as an individual, and communion for the participation of the individual in some larger organism of which the individual is a part" (pp. 14–15). A structural representation of these two modalities is presented in Figure 26.2. At its positive pole, agency (Ag+) involves themes of power, mastery, and assertion; at its negative pole (Ag–) are themes of weakness, failure, and submission. Orthogonal to the agentic dimension is one of communion, which at its positive pole (Co+), involves themes of intimacy, union, and solidarity; and at its negative pole (Co–), themes of remoteness, hostility, and disaffiliation.

Bakan (1966) applied these concepts to a wide range of topics, including religion, science, sexuality, and disease. Subsequently, Wiggins (1991) argued that the "metaconcepts" of agency and communion were propaedeutic to the understanding and measurement of interpersonal behavior and summarized their role in philosophical worldviews from Confucius to Bakan, personality theories from Freud to McAdams, psycholinguistic and historicodevelopmental studies of the language of personality, and conceptions of men and women within a variety of disciplines.

Metaphorically speaking, agency and communion are the axes around which the social

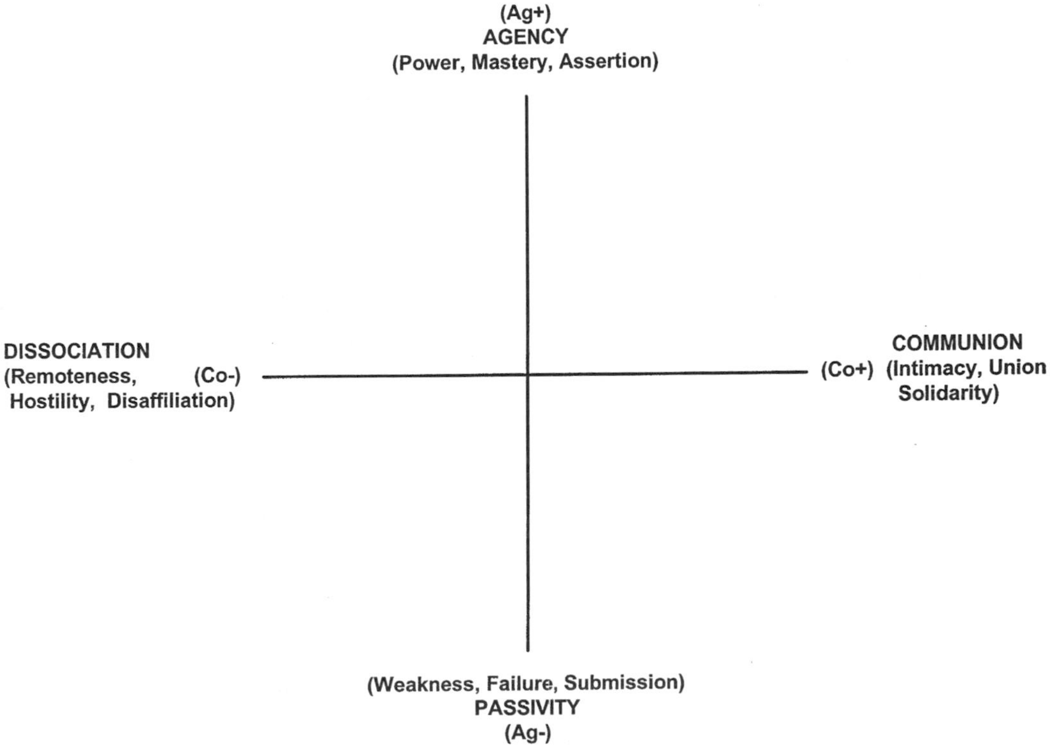

FIGURE 26.2. Structural representation of the metaconcepts of agency and communion. From Wiggins (1991, p. 91). Reproduced by permission of the publisher, University of Minnesota Press.

TABLE 26.1. Conceptions of Agency and Communion within Different Disciplines

Field	Level	Focus	Agency	Communion
Evolutionary psychology (Buss, 1991b)	Species	Solution of reproductive problems	Negotiation of status hierarchies	Formation of reciprocal alliances
Anthropology (Redfield, 1960)	Group life	Common challenges provided by all societies	Getting a living	Living together
Cross-cultural psychology (Triandis, 1995)	Societal structure	Cultural bases of social behavior among societies	Individualistic societies	Collectivist societies
Sociology (Parsons & Bales, 1955)	Social roles	Divisions of labor within societies	Instrumental roles	Communal roles
Narrative life history (McAdams, 1993)	Life histories	Themes in myth, stories, and individual lives	Power	Intimacy
Interpersonal psychology (Kiesler, 1996)	Dynamics of interpersonal behavior	Recurrent interpersonal situations	Status	Love

Note. Adapted from Wiggins and Trapnell (1996, p. 91). Copyright 1997 by The Guilford Press. Adapted by permission.

world revolves. The concepts have been used to characterize everything from the way American children play together (Jones, 1984) to the dynamics of domestic service in India (Tellis-Nayak, 1983), and their importance for general psychological well-being has been thoroughly documented (Helgeson, 1994). It is not surprising therefore that conceptions of agency and communion have appeared in many different guises within the behavioral and social sciences, as is indicated in Table 26.1.

As can be seen from this table, interpersonal psychology and the other social and behavioral sciences analyze behavior on different levels and focus on different issues that are central to their respective disciplines. However, from the examples given in Table 26.1, it can be seen that the different central issues focused upon have all been resolved conceptually with reference to the abstract metaconcepts of agency and communion. For example, evolutionary theory suggests that men's inclusive fitness is ensured by high status (Ag+), which is associated with more resources and better mating opportunities. Women's inclusive fitness is ensured by reciprocal alliances (Co+), which provide greater access to protection and resources.

From an anthropological perspective, the common challenges provided by all societies are those of "getting ahead" (Ag+) and "getting along" (Co+) (Hogan, Jones, & Cheek, 1985). Cross-cultural psychology has emphasized the differences between individualistic cultures (Ag+), which emphasize the pursuit of personal goals, the attainment of which benefits individuals; and collectivist cultures (Co+), which emphasize the pursuit of goals shared with one or more collective, the attainment of which benefits the group. Within a sociological framework, the tasks of getting a living and living together require the enactment of instrumental (Ag+) and expressive (Co+) roles. Within the field of narrative life history, two superordinate content themes are distinguished in myth, stories, and individual lives. Agentic themes emphasize power/achievement (Ag+) and communal themes emphasize intimacy/love (Co+).

Our earlier metaphorical observation that agency and communion are the axes around which the social world revolves may be thought of in field-theoretical terms. Imagine combining the interrelated phenomena from the various levels and foci of observation suggested by Table 26.1 into a grand interdisciplinary "force field," the coordinates of which are agency and communion. Sullivan (1964) might have approved of such speculation because of his commitment to the fusion of psychiatry and social science. However, although there may be a certain intuitive appeal to this "big picture," such a representation is of little value in the absence of demonstrations of the manner in which the postulated societal forces of agency and communion determine the *structure* of a societal force field. A humble beginning in this direction will be described next.

Interpersonal Force Fields

> *Interpersonal theory asserts that each of us continually exudes a force field that pushes others to respond to us with constricted classes of control and affiliation actions; thereby we pull from others complementary responses designed to affirm and validate our chosen style of living and being.* . . . The abnormal individual imposes an extreme and intense force field on his or her interpersonal transactions. (Kiesler, 1996, p. 85, 128; emphasis in original)

In the above quotations, Kiesler provides an exceptionally succinct statement of several interrelated principles concerning the dynamics of interpersonal behavior. Although stated somewhat differently by different interpersonal theorists, the central idea here is that when interacting with Person *B*, Person *A*, perhaps unknowingly, attempts to negotiate her preferred definition of an interpersonal situation with respect to the dimensions of control (agency) and affiliation (communion). To the extent that Person *A* does this rigidly and inflexibly with all partners, the recurrent pattern of interpersonal situations in which she is involved would be considered maladaptive.

Social Exchange

Interpersonal transactions may be thought of as occasions for "exchange" in which participants give or take away social resources from each other. Although such resources may include money, goods, services and information, the resources of *status* (agency) and *love* (communion) are the coins of the realm of *interpersonal* exchange (Foa & Foa, 1974). Table 26.2a (see next page) provides a slight modification of Foa's (1965) facet analysis of interpersonal *variables* in which the facet composition of each variable has been specified with respect to the status (agency) and love (communion) consequences of such behaviors for *both* participants in a dyadic interaction (self and other).

Thus, for example, the "PA" variable (assured–dominant) involves the granting of love and status to self, and the granting of love but *not* status to other. The "BC" variable (arrogant–calculating) involves the granting of love and status to self and the denial of *both* love and status to the other. Similar facet definitions are provided for the remaining variables of "DE" (cold-hearted), "FG" (aloof–introverted), "HI" (unassured–submissive), "JK" (unassuming–ingenuous), "LM" (warm–agreeable), and "NO" (gregarious–extraverted). Note that the facet composition of each variable differs from that of its preceding variable by *one* element. For example, the arrogant–calculating variable differs from the assured–dominant variable in denying love to the other. Note also that the last variable (gregarious–extraverted) differs from the first variable (assured–dominant) by *one* element. Thus, the *postulated* agentic (status) and communal (love) facets are distributed across the eight variables in a circular fashion.

To the extent that the hypothesized values just assigned to these variable are in fact appropriate, the *empirical* intercorrelations among measures of these variables will necessarily form a circumplex (Foa, 1965). Nevertheless, there are a number of different ways of assigning love and status facets to variables that will yield a circumplex structure. Confirmation of the present assignment requires additional research, such as that of Buss (1991a) who demonstrated that both wives and husbands of dominant (PA) spouses complained that their spouses were condescending. This finding supports the notion that PA involves the granting of love and status to self, and the granting of love but *not* status to the other.

Treating the entries in this table as standard scores ($M = 0$; $SD = 1$), the relation between any two variables in Table 26.2a may be obtained by summing the cross-products of their respective row elements. Thus, the relation between PA and BC is:

$$(+1 \times +1) + (+1 \times +1) + (+1 \times -1) + (-1 \times -1) = 2$$

The sums of the cross-products for all combinations of the eight variables are presented in Table 26.2b. Dividing the elements of Table 26.2b by the number of "observations" (i.e., 4) yields the *circulant* correlation matrix (Guttman, 1954) shown in Table 26.2c. Extracting and rotating two principal components from the matrix in Table 26.1c yields the factor matrix presented in Table 26.1d. A factor plot of Table 26.1d would reveal a perfect, evenly spaced circumplex. Figure 26.3 is a plot of the *empirical* circumplex

TABLE 26.2. Derivation of the Interpersonal Circumplex

a. Facet composition of interpersonal variables

	Self		Other	
	Status	Love	Love	Status
PA	+1	+1	+1	−1
BC	+1	+1	−1	−1
DE	+1	−1	−1	−1
FG	−1	−1	−1	−1
HI	−1	−1	−1	+1
JK	−1	−1	+1	+1
LM	−1	+1	+1	+1
NO	+1	+1	+1	+1

b. Sums of cross-products (ΣXY)

	PA	BC	DE	FG	HI	JK	LM	NO
PA	4							
BC	2	4						
DE	0	2	4					
FG	−2	0	2	4				
HI	−4	−2	0	2	4			
JK	−2	−4	−2	0	2	4		
LM	0	−2	−4	−2	0	2	4	
NO	2	0	−2	−4	−2	0	2	4

c. Correlation matrix ($\Sigma XY/N$)

	PA	BC	DE	FG	HI	JK	LM	NO
PA	1.00							
BC	.50	1.00						
DE	.00	.50	1.00					
FG	−.50	.00	.50	1.00				
HI	−1.00	−.50	.00	.50	1.00			
JK	−.50	−1.00	−.50	.00	.50	1.00		
LM	.00	−.50	−1.00	−.50	.00	.50	1.00	
NO	.50	.00	−.50	−1.00	−.50	.00	.50	1.00

d. Rotated factor matrix

	I	II	h^2
PA	.92	.00	.85
BC	.65	−.65	.85
DE	.00	−.92	.85
FG	−.65	−.65	.85
HI	−.92	.00	.85
JK	−.65	.65	.85
LM	.00	.92	.85
NO	.65	.65	.85
% Variance	42.5%	42.5%	85%

Note. Adapted from Wiggins and Trapnell (1996, p. 122). Copyright 1996 by The Guilford Press. Adapted by permission.

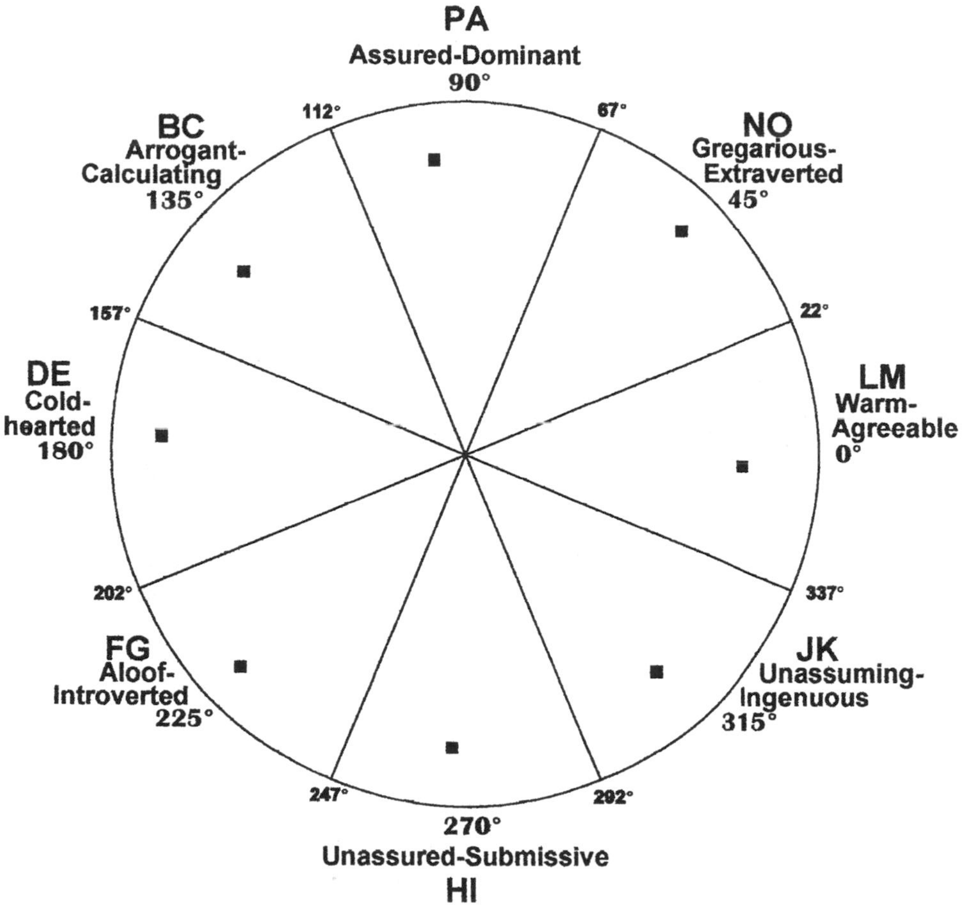

FIGURE 26.3. Circumplex structure of IAS Scales (N = 2,988).

structure of the Interpersonal Adjective Scales (IAS; Wiggins, 1995) in which the black squares indicate the location of the eight variables.

THE INTERPERSONAL CIRCUMPLEX

Origins

The Kaiser Foundation Research Project, in which Timothy Leary (1957) was the preeminent investigator, attempted to operationalize Sullivanian concepts in terms of concrete measurement procedures (Pincus, 1994). An analysis of clinicians' observations of the things that patients did to each other (and to themselves) in group psychotherapy led to a taxonomy of interpersonal behaviors that appeared to be empirically well captured by a circular arrangement of 16 (later 8) interpersonal variables organized around the two bipolar coordinates of dominance (versus submission) and affiliation (versus hostility).

Ten years after the first interpersonal circumplex was reported (Freedman, Leary, Ossorio, & Coffey, 1951), Foa (1961) noted a strong convergence of thinking and results in the work done by several investigators on interpersonal circumplex models. Later, Wiggins (1982) identified at least 20 circumplex models that were independently constructed, all of which employed agentic and communal axes. Most recently, Kiesler (1996) identified 21 different domains or content areas (e.g., parent–child interactions, vocational behavior) in which comparable two-dimensional representations have been reported.

A recent version of an interpersonal circumplex was shown in Figure 26.3. Interpersonal behaviors are assumed to be distributed *continuously* around this circle, although for practical reasons it is desirable to classify them as falling into sectors. The eight sectors illustrated are thought of as different "blends" of the underlying coordinates of dominance and nurturance. Thus, the assured–dominant (PA) sector represents "pure" dominant behaviors, arrogant–calculating (BC) is a "blend" of dominance and hostility, and cold-hearted (DE) is the polar opposite of "pure" nurturance. The centers of each sector are marked by eight approximately equally spaced squares that denote behaviors assumed to be "prototypical" of that sector. It should be emphasized that the circular or "circumplex" structure (Guttman, 1954) shown in Figure 26.3 has been empirically substantiated in a large number of studies (see Plutchik & Conte, 1997 and Kiesler, 1996).

Interpersonal Space

Although the basic geometry of interpersonal space is well established and may be analyzed by a variety of methods (e.g., Browne, 1992; Gurtman, 1994; Wiggins, Steiger, & Gaelick, 1981) the boundary conditions of its applications are less well established (Wiggins & Trobst, 1997b). In measuring interpersonal dispositions ("traits"), for example, the fit between the circumplex model and interpersonal theory is so close that one can hardly distinguish the theory from the model (Wiggins, Phillips, & Trapnell, 1989). But the precise relations between interpersonal dispositional space and the many circumplex structures obtained for other "spaces" such as interpersonal problems (Alden, Wiggins, & Pincus, 1990), covert reaction tendencies (Kiesler & Schmidt, 1993) and emotions (e.g., Plutchik, 1980), has yet to be determined.

Conceptually, it might be helpful here to think of multiple interpersonal "fields", as we did earlier, but the mathematical and empirical work still remains to be done.[1] A recent comparison of two different circumplex spaces suggests that much can be learned from such comparisons. For example, in a recent study of "social support" behaviors, Trobst (in press) examined the relations between interpersonal dispositional space [as measured by the Interpersonal Adjective Scales (IAS) discussed in the next section] and her newly constructed circumplex of social support space (Support Actions Scale–Circumplex; SAS-C). When scales from either of these two measures were projected onto the space of the other, the dominance axis of the projected measure "collapsed." This structural finding suggests that whereas dispositional nurturance (IAS) and nurturant social support style (SAS-C) are closely related, dispositional dominance and dominant social support style are largely unrelated. Additional analyses demonstrated that, in comparison with other personality "types," dispositionally nurturant individuals reported performing more of all potentially helpful behaviors (including relatively dominant actions such as giving advice). In contrast, dispositionally non-nurturant (i.e., cold) individuals reported performing more of all potentially unhelpful behaviors. Metaphorically speaking, the "force field" of a social support "context" appears to perturb the usual structure of a dispositional "field."

Representative Assessment Instruments

Interpersonal Adjective Scales

The Interpersonal Adjective Scales (IAS; Wiggins, 1995) evolved from a psychological taxonomy of trait-descriptive terms that was developed within the framework of a larger program of collaborative research on language and personality (Goldberg, 1977). Within a representative pool of trait-descriptive adjectives selected from an unabridged dictionary, an "interpersonal domain" was distinguished from other domains, such as temperamental, characterological, and cognitive (Wiggins, 1979).[2] Approximately 800 interpersonal adjectives were assigned to the original categories of the interpersonal circumplex (Leary, 1957) on both conceptual and empirical grounds. Using computer-based multivariate procedures it was found that scales based on the original categories failed to meet certain circumplex criteria that could be better met with scales based on the revised categories that now constitute the IAS (Wiggins, 1995). The IAS consists of 64 adjectives that respondents rate for self-descriptive accuracy on an eight-place Likert scale ranging from "extremely inaccurate" to "extremely accurate." Eight scales, or "octants," of eight items each, assess the interpersonal dispositions listed in the second column of Table 26.3. The PA octant, for example, includes items such as "dominant," "forceful," and "assertive."

TABLE 26.3. Interpersonal Assessment Instruments

Octant	IAS (Interpersonal Adjective Scales)	IIP (Inventory of Interpersonal Problems)	IMI (Impact Message Inventory)
PA	Assured–Dominant	Domineering	Dominant
BC	Arrogant–Calculating	Vindictive	Hostile–Dominant
DE	Cold-hearted	Cold	Hostile
FG	Aloof–Introverted	Socially-Avoidant	Hostile–Submissive
HI	Unassured–Submissive	Nonassertive	Submissive
JK	Unassuming–Ingenuous	Exploitable	Friendly–Submissive
LM	Warm–Agreeable	Overly nurturant	Friendly
NO	Gregarious–Extraverted	Intrusive	Friendly–Dominant

Inventory of Interpersonal Problems

Horowitz (1979) transcribed statements of interpersonal problems expressed by psychiatric outpatients in the course of videotaped intake interviews and employed these statements as items in the construction of the Inventory of Interpersonal Problems (IIP) in which respondents are required to indicate the extent to which each of 127 statements is problematic on a five-place Likert scale ranging from "not at all" to "extremely" (Horowitz, Rosenberg, Baer, Ureno, & Villasenor, 1988). Subsequently, Alden, Wiggins, and Pincus (1990) developed a circumplex version of this inventory (IIP-C) that consists of eight scales, of eight items each, that assess the interpersonal problems listed in the third column of Table 26.3. The PA octant, for example, includes items such as "I try to control other people too much."

Impact Message Inventory

The Impact Message Inventory (IMI; Kiesler & Schmidt, 1993)is a highly original and promising method of assessment that is based on Kiesler's (1988) theory of interpersonal communication in psychotherapy. The theory postulates that disordered individuals are unaware of the unintended, inappropriate, and ambiguous messages they repetitively "send" to others and that they are therefore confused and distressed by the pattern of negative responses they consistently evoke or "pull" from others (Kiesler, Schmidt, & Wagner, 1997). The IMI attempts to identify the location within the interpersonal circumplex of these patterns of negative response evoked in others, as a means of gaining insight into a client's own maladaptive transactional behavior.

Items were generated from a content analysis of free responses to 15 interpersonal vignettes that described characters enacting 15 different interpersonal styles, similar to those found in the second column of Table 26.3. Respondents were asked to imagine themselves in the company of each of these characters and to record their covert reactions using the stem, "*He makes me feel. . . .* " Content analysis of responses suggested three categories of covert reaction: (1) direct feelings, (2) action tendencies, and (3) perceived evoking messages. The Octant Version of the IMI consists of six items for each of the target stimuli listed in the fourth column of Table 26.3. For each octant, there are two items for each of the three categories of covert reaction to the target stimulus. Thus, for example, the PA scale includes two items each for "direct feelings" (e.g., "bossed around"), "action tendencies" (e.g., "I want to tell him to give someone else a chance to make a decision"), and "perceived evoking messages" (e.g., "He thinks he's always in control of things"). Respondents (e.g., psychotherapists) are asked to imagine themselves in the company of a particular person (e.g., a psychotherapy patient) and to indicate the extent to which they experience the covert reactions on a four-place scale. Covert reactions to a target person (e.g., feeling "bossed around") are thus revealing of the personality and the interpersonal impact of that target person (e.g., rigidly dominant [PA]).

Utility and Generalizability of the Circumplex Structure

As Gurtman (1992) has emphasized, the interpersonal circumplex itself functions as a nomological net in which the construct validity of other interpersonal measures may be evaluated. Wiggins and Broughton (1985, 1991) have similarly emphasized the integrative function of the circumplex model in providing a single framework for interpreting personality scales from a variety of research traditions in personality, clinical, and social psychology. Circumplex representations of the interpersonal field have proven to be of considerable heuristic value in both the conceptualization and measurement of a variety of interpersonal phenomena, as is evident from the approximately 1,000 references that appear in Kiesler's (1996) comprehensive survey of that literature. Research topics to which the model has proven particularly applicable include: personality assessment (e.g., Wiggins & Trobst, 1997a), psychotherapy (e.g., Anchin & Kiesler, 1982), psychiatric diagnosis (e.g., Widiger & Hagemoser, 1997), complementarity (e.g., Kiesler, 1983), nonverbal behavior (e.g., Gifford, 1991), manipulation tactics (e.g., Buss, Gomes, Higgins, & Lauterbach, 1987), agentic and communal situations (e.g., Moskowitz, 1994), and attachment styles (e.g., Bartholomew & Horowitz, 1991).

Additional Dimensions

Our emphasis on the metaconcepts of agency and communion, and their operationalization in personality measurement by the dimensions of dominance and nurturance, is not incompatible with the first two dimensions of the five-factor model of personality (FFM; McCrae & Costa, Chapter 5, this volume). The Extraversion and Agreeableness domains of the FFM are rotational variants of dominance and nurturance; and circumplex and FFM interpretations of these dimensions are complementary rather than competitive (Trapnell & Wiggins, 1990; McCrae & Costa, 1989). However, we assign conceptual priority to the first two factors of the FFM as indicants of the metaconcepts of agency and communion, and view the remaining three factors of Neuroticism, Conscientiousness, and Openness to Experience as dimensions that either facilitate or interfere with the development and maintenance of agentic and communal enterprises within a social group (Wiggins & Trapnell, 1996).

Digman's (1997) comprehensive investigation of two "higher-order factors" in the FFM provides some support for the foregoing interpretation. When he extracted factors from the intercorrelations among measures of the five domains in fourteen widely differing samples of respondents, Digman consistently obtained two higher-order factors. The two higher-order factors were labelled *alpha* (Agreeableness, Emotional Stability, and Conscientiousness) and *beta* (Extraversion and Intellect/Openness). From a societal perspective, alpha was thought to reflect the *socialization* process and beta the process of *personal growth*. Higher-order constructs are required to interpret these "super factors," and Digman was clearly sympathetic to agency and communion as useful metaconcepts in both personality theory (e.g., Wiggins, 1991) and personality data (e.g., Tellegen & Waller, in press). However, Digman's findings in no way diminish the utility of the full FFM as a widely agreed upon "working model" that can be interpreted from a variety of theoretical perspectives (Wiggins, 1996).

CONCLUSIONS

The concept of electromagnetic "fields" had a revolutionary impact on physical theory in the late 19th century, and it has influenced subsequent formulations in the social and behavioral sciences as well. The present chapter framed the history of interpersonal psychology within the distinction between interactionism (person–environment relations) and interpersonalism (focus on recurrent interpersonal situations). Field theory figured prominently in the "interactionist" writings of Kurt Lewin and in the creative theorizing and experimentation of his many students in social psychology. Interactionism was also the focus of the trait-situation controversy within the personality psychology of the 1970s and 1980s.

The radical "interpersonalism" of Harry Stack Sullivan was also influenced by field-theoretical conceptions. Sullivan focused on the relatively enduring pattern of recurrent interpersonal situations over time and challenged individualist thought concerning "persons" in environments. Subsequent operationalization of Sullivan's concepts resulted in the discovery of a structural model that integrated research on interpersonal fields from diverse areas of psychological investigation. Foa's suggestion that social exchange was the common element in these investigations provided a conceptual basis for interpreting the structural model that was common to these investigations. Bakan's metaconcepts of agency and communion provided a broader framework for interpretation that was easily generalized to cognate social and behavioral sciences.

The utility and generalizability of the interpersonal circumplex model are sufficient to suggest that continued efforts to provide a conceptual account of the reasons for its ubiquitous applicability should be encouraged. Considerable progress has been made in understanding the operation of the model in a surprising variety of contexts to which the model has been found applicable. A deeper understanding of the structural relations among interpersonal fields in different "contexts" would surely advance the conceptual underpinnings of this field of investigation.

Until quite recently, empirical research on interpersonal behavior has not greatly advanced our understanding of the relatively *enduring* nature of the recurrent interpersonal situations that characterize human lives. Instead, the focus has been on the dynamics of microanalytic action–reaction sequences of "complementarity" in dyadic relationships in psychotherapy or in initial encounters between college students participating in psychology experiments. The conceptually based, methodologically elegant, and impressively labor-intensive efforts of Moskowitz (e.g., Brown & Moskowitz, 1998; Moskowitz, 1994) to study the "stasis and flow" (Pervin, 1983) of interpersonal behavior *over time* is a welcome exception to this earlier trend.

It is our admittedly optimistic opinion that continued efforts to explore the structural relations among interpersonal fields in different contexts and to explore the parameters of interpersonal situations over time will eventually more than justify the bold extrapolations from physics that earlier psychologists made to the "fields" of interpersonal behavior.

ACKNOWLEDGMENTS

We would like to thank Michael Gurtman, Leonard Horowitz, and Lawrence Pervin for their most helpful comments on an earlier version of the present chapter. We are especially grateful to Oliver John for "editorial assistance" above and beyond the call of duty.

NOTES

1. Perhaps Michael Gurtman and Aaron Pincus will be the Maxwells of the next decade (e.g., Pincus, Gurtman, & Ruiz, 1998).

2. The latter three domains correspond to current conceptualizations of Neuroticism, Conscientiousness, and Openness to Experience.

REFERENCES

Alden, L. E., Wiggins, J. S., & Pincus, A. L. (1990). Construction of circumplex scales for the Inventory of Interpersonal Problems. *Journal of Personality Assessment, 55,* 521–536.

Anchin, J. C., & Kiesler, D. J. (1982). *Handbook of interpersonal psychotherapy.* Elmsford, NY: Pergamon Press.

Asimov, I. (1966), *Understanding physics: Light, magnetism, and electricity.* New York: Barnes & Noble.

Bakan, D. (1966). *The duality of human existence: Isolation and communion in Western man.* Boston: Beacon Press.

Bartholomew, K., & Horowitz, L. M. (1991). Attachment styles among young adults: A test of a model. *Journal of Personality and Social Psychology, 61,* 226–244.

Bowers, K. S. (1973). Situationism in psychology: An analysis and a critique. *Psychological Review, 80,* 307–336.

Brown, K. W., & Moskowitz, D. S. (1998). Dynamic stability of behavior: The rhythms of our interpersonal lives. *Journal of Personality, 66,* 105–134.

Browne, M. W. (1992). Circumplex models for correlation matrices. *Psychometrika, 57,* 469–497.

Buss, D. M. (1991a). Conflict in married couples: Personality predictors of anger and upset. *Journal of Personality, 59,* 663–688.

Buss, D. M. (1991b). Evolutionary personality psychology. *Annual Review of Psychology, 41,* 459–491.

Buss, D. M., Gomes, M., Higgins, D. S., & Lauterbach, K. (1987). Tactics of manipulation. *Journal of Personality and Social Psychology, 52,* 1219–1229.

Cartwright, D. (1959). Lewinian theory as a contemporary systematic framework. In S. Koch (Ed.), *Psychology: A study of science* (Vol. 2, pp. 7–91). New York: McGraw-Hill.

Deutsch, M. (1968). Field theory in social psychology. In G. Lindzey & E. Aronson (Eds.), *Handbook of social psychology* (2nd ed., Vol. 21, pp. 412–487). Reading, MA: Addison-Wesley.

Digman, J. M. (1997). Higher-order factors of the Big Five. *Journal of Personality and Social Psychology, 73,* 1246–1256.

Einstein, A. (1933). *On the method of theoretical physics.* New York: Oxford University Press.

Einstein, A. & Infeld, L. (1938). *The evolution of physics.* New York: Simon & Schuster.

Ekehammer, B. (1974). Interactionism in personality from a historical perspective. *Psychological Bulletin, 81,* 1026–1048.

Eldridge, S. (1925). *The organization of life.* New York: Crowell.

Endler, N. S. (1975). The case for person-situation interactions. *Canadian Psychological Review, 16,* 12–21.

Estes, W. K. (1954). Kurt Lewin. In W. K. Estes, S. Koch, K. MacCorquodale, P. E. Meehl, C. G. Mueller, W. N. Schoenfeld, & W. W. Verplank, *Modern learning theory* (pp. 317–344). New York: Appleton-Century-Crofts.

Foa, U. G. (1961). Convergences in the analysis of the structure of interpersonal behavior. *Psychological Review, 68,* 341–353.

Foa, U. G. (1965). New developments in facet design and analysis. *Psychological Review, 72,* 262–274.

Foa, U. G., & Foa, E. B. (1974). *Societal structures of the mind.* Springfield, IL: Charles C Thomas.

Freedman, M. B., Leary, T. F., Ossorio, A. G., & Coffey, H. S. (1951). The interpersonal dimension of personality. *Journal of Personality, 20,* 143–161.

Gifford, R. (1991). Mapping nonverbal behavior on the Interpersonal Circle. *Journal of Personality and Social Psychology, 61,* 279–288.

Goldberg, L. R. (1977, August). *Language and personality: Developing a taxonomy of trait descriptive terms.* Invited address to the Division of Evaluation and Measurement at the 86th convention of the American Psychological Association, San Francisco.

Gurtman, M. B. (1992). Construct validity of interpersonal personality measures: The Interpersonal Circumplex as a nomological net. *Journal of Personality and Social Psychology, 63,* 105–118.

Gurtman, M. B. (1994). The circumplex as a tool for studying normal and abnormal personality: A methodological primer. In S. Strack & M. Lorr (Eds.), *Differentiating normal and abnormal personality* (pp. 243–263). New York: Springer.

Guttman, L. (1954). A new approach to factor analysis: The radex. In P. F. Lazarsfeld (Ed.), *Mathematical thinking in the social sciences* (pp. 258–348). Glencoe, IL: Free Press.

Helgeson, V. S. (1994). Relation of agency and communion to psychological well-being: Evidence and potential applications. *Psychological Bulletin, 116,* 412–428.

Hilgard, E. R. (1987). *Psychology in America: A historical survey.* New York: Harcourt Brace Jovanovich.

Hogan, R., Jones, W. H., & Cheek, J. M. (1985). Socioanalytic theory: An alternative to armadillo psychology. In B. R. Schlenker (Ed.), *The self and social life* (pp. 175–198). New York: McGraw-Hill.

Horowitz, L. M. (1979). On the cognitive structure of interpersonal problems treated in psychotherapy. *Journal of Consulting and Clinical Psychology, 47,* 5–15.

Horowitz, L. M., Rosenberg, S. E., Baer, B. A., Ureno, G., & Villasenor, V. S. (1988). The Inventory of Interpersonal Problems: Psychometric properties and clinical applications. *Journal of Consulting and Clinical Psychology, 56,* 885–892.

Jessor, R. (1958). The problem of reductionism in psychology. *Psychological Review, 65,* 170–178.

Jones, D. C. (1984). Dominance and affiliation as factors in the social organization of same-sex groups of elementary school children. *Ethology and Sociobiology, 5,* 193–204.

Kantor, J. R. (1924–1926). *Principles of psychology* (2 vols.). Bloomington, IN: Principia Press.

Kantor, J. R. (1953). *The logic of modern science.* Bloomington, IN: Principia Press.

Kantor, J. R. (1959). *Interbehavioral psychology.* Granville, OH: Principia Press.

Kiesler, D. J. (1983). The 1982 Interpersonal Circle: A taxonomy for complementarity in human transactions. *Psychological Review, 90,* 185–214.

Kiesler, D. J. (1988). *Therapeutic metacommunication: Therapist impact disclosure as feedback in psychotherapy.* Palo Alto, CA: Consulting Psychologists Press.

Kiesler, D. J. (1996). *Contemporary interpersonal theory and research: Personality, psychopathology, and psychotherapy.* New York: Wiley.

Kiesler, D. J., & Schmidt, J. A. (1993). *The Impact Message Inventory: Form IIA Octant Scale Version.* Palo Alto, CA: Mind Garden (Consulting Psychologists Press).

Kiesler, D. J., Schmidt, J. A., & Wagner, C. (1997). A circumplex inventory of impact messages: An operational bridge between emotion and interpersonal behavior. In R. Plutchik & H. R. Conte (Eds.), *Circumplex models of personality and emotions* (pp. 221–244). Washington, DC: American Psychological Association.

Koffka, K. (1935). *Principles of Gestalt psychology.* New York: Harcourt, Brace.

Koehler, W. (1920). *Die physischen Gestalten in Ruhe und im stationaren Zustand.* Brunswick, Germany: Vieweg.

Koehler, W. (1929). *Gestalt psychology.* New York: Liveright Publishing Co.

Leary, T. (1957). *Interpersonal diagnosis of personality: A functional theory and methodology for personality evaluation.* New York: Ronald Press.

Lewin, K. (1935). *A dynamic theory of personality* (D. K. Adams & K. E. Zener, Trans.). New York: McGraw-Hill.

Lewin, K. (1997a). Behavior and development as a function of the total situation. In D. Cartwright (Ed.), *Field theory in social science: Selected theoretical papers* (pp. 337–381). Washington, DC: American Psychological Association. (Original work published 1939)

Lewin, K. (1997b). Field theory and experiment in social psychology. In D. Cartwright (Ed.), *Field theory in social science: Selected theoretical papers* (pp. 262–278). Washington, DC: American Psychological Association. (Original work published 1939)

Lewin, K. (1997c). The background of conflict in marriage. In G. W. Lewin (Ed.), *Resolving social conflicts: Selected papers on group dynamics* (pp. 68–79). Washington, DC: American Psychological Association. (Original work published 1940)

Magnusson, D. (1990). Personality development from an interactional perspective. In L. A. Pervin (Ed.), *Handbook of personality: Theory and research* (pp. 193–222). New York: Guilford Press.

McAdams, D. P. (1993). *The stories we live by: Personal myths and the making of self.* New York: William Morrow.

McCrae, R. R., & Costa, P. T., Jr. (1989). The structure of interpersonal traits: Wiggins' circumplex and the

five-factor model. *Journal of Personality and Social Psychology, 56,* 586–595.
Mischel, W. (1973). Toward a cognitive social learning reconceptualization of personality. *Psychological Review, 80,* 252–283.
Moskowitz, D. S. (1994). Cross-situational generality and the interpersonal circumplex. *Journal of Personality and Social Psychology, 66,* 921–933.
Parsons, T. , & Bales, R. F. (1955). *Family, socialization, and interaction process.* Glencoe, IL: Free Press.
Perry, H. S. (1964). Commentary. In H. S. Sullivan, *The fusion of psychiatry and social science* (p. 227–228). New York: Norton.
Perry, H. S. (1982). *Psychiatrist of America: The life of Harry Stack Sullivan.* Cambridge, MA: The Belknap Press of Harvard University Press.
Pervin, L. A. (1968). Performance and satisfaction as a function of individual-environmental fit. *Psychological Bulletin, 69,* 56–68.
Pervin, L. A. (1983). The stasis and flow of behavior: Toward a theory of goals. In M. M. Page (Ed.), *Nebraska Symposium on Motivation* (pp. 1–53). Lincoln, NE: University of Nebraska Press.
Pickering, A. (1997, August 1). Science warriors and enemies of reason. *Times Literary Supplement,* No. 4922, 8–9.
Pincus, A. L. (1994). The interpersonal circumplex and the interpersonal theory: Perspectives on personality and its pathology. In S. Strack & M. Lorr (Eds.), *Differentiating normal and abnormal personality* (pp. 114–135). New York: Springer.
Pincus, A. L., Gurtman, M. B., & Ruiz, M. A. (1998). Structural Analysis of Social Behavior (SASB): Circumplex analyses and structural relations with the interpersonal circle and the five-factor model of personality. *Journal of Personality and Social Psychology, 74,* 1629–1645.
Plutchik, R. (1980). *Emotion: A psychoevolutionay synthesis.* New York: Harper & Row.
Plutchik, R., & Conte, H. R. (Eds.). (1997). *Circumplex models of personality and emotions.* Washington, DC: American Psychological Association.
Redfield, R. (1960). How society operates. In H. L. Shapiro (Ed.), *Man, culture and society* (pp. 345–368). New York: Oxford University Press.
Rotter, J. B. (1954). *Social learning and clinical psychology.* New York: Prentice Hall.
Silver, B. L. (1998). *The ascent of science.* New York: Oxford University Press.
Sokal, A. (1996). Transgressing the boundaries: Toward a transformative hermeneutics of quantum gravity. *Social Text, 14,* 217–252.
Strickland, B. (1997). Clinical psychology: Is the future back to Boulder? *Contemporary Psychology, 42,* 386–388.
Sullivan, H. S. (1940). Conceptions of modern psychiatry: The first William Alanson White Memorial Lectures. *Psychiatry, 3,* 1–117.
Sullivan, H. S. (1948). The meaning of anxiety in psychiatry and in life. *Psychiatry, 11,* 1–13.
Sullivan, H. S. (1950). The illusion of personal individuality. *Psychiatry, 13,* 317–332. [Reprinted in H. S. Sullivan (1964), *The fusion of psychiatry and social science* (pp. 198–226). New York: Norton.]
Sullivan, H. S. (1953). *The interpersonal theory of psychiatry.* New York: Norton.
Sullivan, H. S. (1964). *The fusion of psychiatry and social science.* New York: Norton.
Tellegen, A., & Waller, N. G. (in press). Exploring personality through test construction: Development of the Multidimensional Personality Questionnaire. In S. R. Briggs & J. M. Cheek (Eds.)., *Personality measures: Development and evaluation* (Vol. 1). Greenwich, CT: JAI Press.
Tellis-Nayak, V. (1983). Power and solidarity: Clientage in domestic service. *Current Anthropology, 24,* 67–79.
Thompson, C. (1957). *Psychoanalysis: Evolution and development.* New York: Grove Press.
Trapnell, P. D., & Wiggins, J. S. (1990). Extension of the Interpersonal Adjective Scales to include the Big Five dimensions of personality. *Journal of Personality and Social Psychology, 59,* 781–790.
Triandis, H. C. (1995). *Individualism and collectivism.* Boulder, CO: Westview Press.
Trobst, K. K. (in press). An interpersonal conceptualization and quantification of social support transactions. *Personality and Social Psychology Bulletin.*
Wertheimer, M. (1912). Experimentelle Studien uber das Sehen von Bewegung. *Zeitschrift für Psychologie, 61,* 161–265.
Widiger, T. A., & Hagemoser, S. (1997). Personality disorders and the interpersonal circumplex. In R. Plutchik & H. R. Conte (Eds.), *Circumplex models of personality and emotions* (pp. 299–325). Washington, DC: American Psychological Association.
Wiggins, J. S. (1979). A psychological taxonomy of trait-descriptive terms: The interpersonal domain. *Journal of Personality and Social Psychology, 37,* 395–412.
Wiggins, J. S. (1982). Circumplex models of interpersonal behavior in clinical psychology. In P. C. Kendall & J. N. Butcher (Eds.), *Handbook of research methods in clinical psychology* (pp. 183–221). New York: Wiley.
Wiggins, J. S. (1991). Agency and communion as conceptual coordinates for the understanding and measurement of interpersonal behavior. In W. Grove & D. Cicchetti (Eds.), *Thinking clearly about psychology: Essays in honor of Paul E. Meehl* (Vol. 2, pp. 89–113). Minneapolis: University of Minnesota Press.
Wiggins, J. S. (1995). *Interpersonal Adjective Scales: Professional manual.* Odessa, FL: Psychological Assessment Resources.
Wiggins, J. S. (Ed.). (1996). *The five-factor model of personality: Theoretical perspectives.* New York: Guilford Press.
Wiggins, J. S., & Broughton, R. (1991). A geometric taxonomy of personality scales. *European Journal of Personality, 5,* 343–365.

Wiggins, J. S., & Broughton, R. (1985). The Interpersonal Circle: A structural model for the integration of personality research. In R. Hogan & W. H. Jones (Eds.), *Perspectives in personality: A research annual* (Vol. 1, pp. 1–47). Greenwich, CT: JAI Press.

Wiggins, J. S., Phillips, N., & Trapnell, P. D. (1989). Circular reasoning about interpersonal behavior: Evidence concerning some untested assumptions underlying diagnostic classification. *Journal of Personality and Social Psychology, 56,* 296–305.

Wiggins, J. S., Steiger, J. H., & Gaelick, L. (1981). Evaluating circumplexity in personality data. *Multivariate Behavioral Research, 16,* 263–289.

Wiggins, J. S., & Trapnell, P. D. (1996). A dyadic–interactional perspective on the five-factor model. In J. S. Wiggins (Ed.), *The five-factor model of personality: Theoretical perspectives* (pp. 88–162). New York: Guilford Press.

Wiggins, J. S., & Trobst, K. K. (1997a). Prospects for the assessment of normal and abnormal behavior. In J. A. Schinka & R. L. Greene (Eds.), *Emerging issues and methods in personality assessment* (pp. 113–129). Mahwah, NJ: Erlbaum.

Wiggins, J. S., & Trobst, K. K. (1997b). When is a circumplex an "interpersonal circumplex"? In R. Plutchik & H. R. Conte (1997). *Circumplex models of personality and emotions* (pp. 57–80). Washington, DC: American Psychological Association.

Woodworth, R. S. (1931). *Contemporary schools of psychology* (rev. ed.). New York: Ronald Press.

Chapter 27

Four Principles for Personality Assessment

Daniel J. Ozer
University of California, Riverside

"Personality assessment" refers to a broad multitude of interrelated, partially overlapping ideas, activities, and products. Goldberg (1972) successfully subsumed much of this domain by focusing on three personality assessment goals: (1) Identifying the important personality characteristics that ought to be measured, (2) developing measures that best assess these characteristics, and (3) establishing procedures for effectively using assessment results in research and practice. If my own questions and those of students and colleagues are any guide, progress toward the second of these goals, the development of good measures, sharply lags progress in the other two. The first assessment goal has been partially attained by the factorial resolution of traits into five broad dimensions (John, 1990; and Chapter 4, this volume), providing a map of this domain of personality without slowing the identification of other kinds of personality characteristics (Ozer & Reise, 1994). New technology has lead to progress toward the achievement of the third personality assessment goal. The advent of the information age has importantly influenced the use of assessment outcomes: Computer hardware and software enable researchers to use the latest quantitative methods and practitioners to be informed by automated interpretations. Yet these advances do not speak to the most frequently asked question put to anyone professing interest in personality assessment: "Do you know a good, short measure of ____?"

The purpose of this chapter is to elucidate what makes a personality assessment method or instrument "good." In brief, a good measure of personality is one that possesses strong evidence of construct validity for the intended assessment purpose. Thus, the four principles to be discussed below ultimately reduce to a conception of construct validity that follows largely from Cronbach and Meehl's (1955) original formulation and Hogan and Nicholson's (1988) affirmation of the centrality of construct validity issues in the interpretation and evaluation of assessment outcomes. Despite numerous discussions of construct validity that ought to dispel such efforts, algorithmic procedures for establishing the validity of a measure continue to be sought. It should become clear that construct validity is not an attribute of a measure but a characteristic of an inductive inference. Although heuristics for guiding inferences have been and will continue to be developed, a general purpose algorithm for construct validation would require the unlikely invention of a method for accomplishing inductive inference with certainty.

PRINCIPLES OF PERSONALITY ASSESSMENT

There are a variety of ways to describe the desirable attributes of a measure of personality. One way is to produce a rather long list of positive characteristics (e.g., Robinson, Shaver & Wrightsman, 1991). This "checklist" approach has appeal because it permits the inclusion of any and all positive measurement properties. But an unintegrated list makes it hard to see how different items on the list interrelate, and the items are unlinked to fundamental principles, so that the relevance of specific items to specific assessment circumstances is hard to identify.

Another approach, especially useful for introducing applied personality assessment procedures, is to separate more psychometric considerations (reliability and validity) from a detailed discussion of specific instruments and their interpretation (e.g., Beutler & Berren, 1995; Lanyon & Goodstein, 1997). Unfortunately, a sufficient definition of the "good measure" is not possible in purely psychometric terms. Wiggins (1973) provides an alternative model: Identify the fundamental principles underlying psychological measurement and link the principles to numerous personality assessment examples. Wiggins's thoroughness cannot be duplicated in a chapter, and the absence of an appropriate successor volume suggests that it is not merely space limitations that prevents an updating of this landmark volume.

Meehl (1972) offered a very brief description of seven characteristics of the "ideal" self-report item. These characteristics can be reworded to be applicable to any measure of personality, utilizing any kind of data, and the four principles proffered below constitute a condensation (from seven to four) and elaboration (from a few paragraphs to a full chapter) of Meehl's criteria. In brief, the four principles proposed here are:

1. The measure's "content" is fully rational within a psychological theory and is appropriate to specific, defined, assessment circumstances.
2. The internal structure of items in a measure should match the requirements of both the relevant psychological theory and the measurement model.
3. The measure has demonstrably high validity for the most theoretically relevant inferences, and this validity is not derived through theoretically unwarranted channels.
4. The implicative relations of the measure are well explored, and the internal structure of the measure and important validity inferences are invariant over theoretically and pragmatically defined generalization criteria.

This emphasis on principles will leave much important content out. Specific assessment tools, each with their own justification, technical development, and sometimes vast validity literatures, will be mentioned only occasionally. The expert personality assessor will find little that is new here (though perhaps the framing of the issues will stimulate critical reflection). The goal is not so much to identify the basic problems of personality assessment and the methods used to overcome them (though such concerns will be apparent), but to identify the origin of such problems and methods as they arise in the logic of the construct validation process.

Principle 1. The measure's "content" is fully rational within a psychological theory and is appropriate to specific, defined, assessment circumstances.

The elaboration of this assessment principle requires a focus on three components: the measure's "content," the relation of the measure to theory, and the part played by the specific circumstances of usage. Although there are important separable aspects of each of these components, they converge in crucial ways whenever an individual is assessed.

Measurement Content

The term "content" is unfortunately vague, covering several considerations generally considered apart. Included in considering the content of a measure is the meaning of the measure to the assessor (i.e., the psychological construct) and to the assessee. Specification of this meaning requires a consideration not just of the construct but also of the kind of data provided by measurement operations. The content of an assessment measure defines what is being assessed and how the assessment is accomplished.

Personality psychologists lack a widely accepted taxonomy of either constructs or data. Many constructs that psychologists seek to assess are terms in personality theory; others are "folk" concepts (Gough, 1996; Tellegen, 1991) derived from everyday social experience. Rather than consider the origin of units as a basis for characterizing them, McAdams (1995) has recently proposed a taxonomy of units based on their function in providing an answer to the question: "What do we know when we know a person?" McAdams proposed three different levels of units useful in answering these questions. Level I units are broad, comparative, decontextualized, and nonconditional. Personality traits are prototypic of this level. Level II units are contextualized in time, place, or role, and include motives, coping strategies, and domain-specific skills. Identity and the individual's own evolving life story provide units for McAdams's Level III units.

The data provided by assessment methods come in many variants, including direct self-ratings of trait descriptive adjectives, latency of response to a particular stimulus, and even a biography written centuries after the death of the subject. Fiske (1971) provides a taxonomy of six assessment modes: self-description (past), current experiencing, capabilities, prior behavior, observation of behavior, and psychophysiology. These modes are defined by the source of the raw data (self, other, or instrument), the "index producer" (self, other, or experimenter), whether or not the subject is aware of measurement, and the task given to the data producer. Although these distinctions are important, Fiske's taxonomy places some very similar methods (e.g., a self-report of current mood and a self-report of typical mood) in different modes, and very different methods (interview and projective test) appear in the same behavioral observation mode. In addition, important kinds of data (e.g., real life outcomes, such as occupational choice and attainment) are excluded. This evaluation presupposes certain a priori notions of what such a taxonomy ought to accomplish: Provide a beginning for (1) justifying the use of a method for assessing a particular type of psychological unit, (2) evaluating the appropriateness of the method in particular circumstances, and (3) more generally identifying likely sources of invalid variance (see below). A taxonomy that focuses solely and more exhaustively on the data source seems more likely to accomplish these ends.

Block's (1977, 1993) elaboration of Cattell's (1957) classification of data types provides a useful beginning for characterizing types of assessment methods. Four broad types of data are included: life outcomes (L), observer ratings (O), situational tests (T), and self-reports (S). L-data, such as age, education, occupation, and income are generally insufficient for personality assessment, though they may provide important validity information (e.g., artists should score higher than accountants on a measure of Openness to Experience) and generalization criteria (e.g., the validity of an Extraversion scale should not be dependent on subjects' income). O- and S-data, the description of the thoughts, feelings, actions, and attributes of other or self, are the most commonly employed types of data for personality assessment. T-data are the most heterogeneous of these four types, including not only physiological and direct behavioral measures, where data do not, in practice, require a human transducer (except perhaps to mechanically record results) but also data arising from measures like projective tests, where elaborate scoring or coding rules substitute for mechanical data production. The difference in the role of the observer in O- and T-data is sometimes unclear, but in O-data, the observer is usually asked to make some kind of inference guided by definitions of terms and examples; in T-data, an observer "codes" what is observed according to ideally exhaustive rules. In O-data, observers may legitimately disagree; in T-data, disagreement means that one or more observer is in error.

The content of a personality measure is most clear in S- and O-data, where the response format and meaning of the words constituting the items are the "content." The content of T-data is not verbal, but behavioral: It is the specific situated actions that lead to an individuals' score. In L-data, content is much harder to envision, but it is the entire sequence of real-world circumstances and behaviors that lead to a particular, assessed outcome. Thus, L-data are inherently multidimensional. Consider a variable like "income." Persons strive (or not) for high income for different reasons, in different ways, and in different contexts. The specific actions that create income are highly variable from person to person, and the content of all L-data will contain this idiosyncratic character.

Assessment and Psychological Theory

It is probably impossible to fully define or enumerate all the different ways in which a measure may be rational within a theory. In part, it is a matter of common sense: If one wishes to measure "hostility," a question like "I like most people I meet" (keyed false) seems more rational than "My favorite color is red" (keyed true). Obvious items generally work better than subtle items (Holden & Jackson, 1979, 1981), but this is not quite the issue. If it turned out that the

"My favorite color is red" item did, in fact, replicably relate to hostility, then a unified theory of hostility and color preference could, in fact, rationalize this item. The degree to which a measure's content is close to key theoretical elements also bears on its rationality. The Strange Situation (Ainsworth, Blehar, Waters, & Wall, 1978) has content closely resembling crucial elements of attachment theory in a way that a lemon juice test of Extraversion (Eysenck, 1967) does not. The chain of inferences from the cortical arousal theory of Extraversion to lemon juice salivation is considerably longer than the comparable chain from attachment theory to the Strange Situation. As a result, the Strange Situation provides a measure of secure attachment, but the lemon juice procedure, though implicitly a measure of Extraversion, better serves as test of the validity of the cortical arousal theory. Because of the inferential distance between Extraversion and salivation, few would comfortably refer to this as a "good" Extraversion measure, regardless of its psychometric properties.

In both of these examples, the substantive psychological theory leads to specific behavioral predictions that are then measured in a straightforward fashion often characteristic of T-data. In this instance, little in the way of what Meehl (1978) refers to as a "theory of the instrument" is required beyond the substantive psychological theory. The case would be rather different if, for example, a self-report Extraversion scale of the kind developed by Goldberg (1992) is considered. Here, the items are trait descriptive adjectives and subjects must evaluate the degree to which they believe each adjective describes them. Just how do respondents accomplish this? For this and virtually all S- and O-data measures, an explicit theory of the instrument is missing, though there are a few noteworthy beginnings toward the development of such theory in both S- (e.g., Helmes & Jackson, 1989) and O-data (e.g., Funder, 1995; Kenny, 1991; Lamiell, Foss, Larsen, & Hempel, 1983).

Consider what is required for a theory of the instrument in the domain of O-data. Knowledge of the general processes involved in social perception will not be sufficient. Principles of social perception only now being discovered must be applied to specific instruments. Funder (1995) points to "information" as one of several important determinants of judge accuracy. To achieve some specified level of agreement, how much and what kind of information is needed by judges when rating a particular item on the observer form of the NEO (Costa & McCrae, 1992)? To what extent do items vary on this parameter? What determines this variation? The answers to these, and quite a number of other questions about other social judgment parameters will constitute a theory of the NEO as observer instrument. When comparing the accomplishments of contemporary efforts to the idealized standards discussed in this chapter, no greater discrepancy between accomplishment and standard exists than in instrumentation theories for S- and O-data.

Assessment Circumstances

The quality of item content is also conditional on the purposes and context of assessment. This is true in many trivial ways: The words in a self-report scale must be understood by respondents, measures with obvious undesirable content will be problematic when respondents have good reason to manipulate the impression they make, and situational tests may have no generality beyond the artificial circumstances of assessment. But such contextual effects are not always so obvious. The values and standpoint of the informant may importantly influence O-data. For example, Gough (1987) reports that males scoring high (i.e., "feminine") on the California Psychological Inventory (CPI) F/M scale are described by spouses as relatively self-pitying, submissive, and complaining, whereas psychology assessment staff members described high scorers (in a different sample) as artistic, sensitive, and reflective. Is there really a contradiction here, or are the values and role relations of the observers providing different images and impressions of the same psychological attributes? A psychologically sensitive understanding of the particular circumstances of assessment is necessary to interpret the measurement outcomes.

Considerations of the kind discussed above (with the exception of types of data) are often unmentioned in most discussions of personality assessment. Rather than confront these issues directly, personality assessment has achieved implicit solutions to the problem of integrating units, data types, theory, and consideration of circumstances. These implicit solutions are recognizable in what Craik (1986) has labeled assessment guilds. Historically, applied and scientific "guilds" have formed around conjunctions of interests in particular units, questions about persons, and beliefs and values toward particular types of data. A more explicit confrontation of these issues may lead to alternative, innovative solutions for coordinating units, data, and theory.

Principle 2. The internal structure of items in a measure should match the requirements of both the relevant psychological theory and the measurement model.

Both Cronbach and Meehl (1955) and Loevinger (1957) note that the internal structure of a measure (i.e., the matrix of item intercorrelations and resultant factor structure) must match the requirements of psychological theory. Whether a construct is uni- or multidimensional and whether the items defining a dimension are strongly or weakly related is specified by theory, and the measure should mirror the theoretical specifications. It is exceedingly difficult to achieve this kind of structural validity (as it is described by Loevinger) because most constructs are theoretically defined as unidimensional, but item responses, as individual behaviors in their own right, are usually multiply determined. Overlap among these multiple determinants is difficult to avoid. In such circumstances, multiple factors typically emerge. One of the several positive consequences of the growing use of structural equation modeling (SEM) is that it forces explicit attention to a measurement model, and recent work (Bollen & Lennox, 1991) within this approach has lead to the recognition that the common factor model, which so long provided the measurement model in personality assessment, is not the only measurement model available. This discussion of internal structure will focus on two issues: (1) an elaboration of latent and emergent variable measurement models, and (2) how to work with multidimensional measures where theory requires unidimensional constructs.

Measurement Models

Classical test theory regards the items of a measure as effects of a latent, causal variable. In this view, positive item intercorrelations are expected because at least some of the item covariance arises from the common, causal latent variable. In a unidimensional scale, the items have a single common causal latent variable, and factor analytic methods are generally used to evaluate claims for unidimensionality. Bollen and Lennox (1991) compare this traditional, "effect indicator" measurement model to a less frequently adopted "causal indicator" measurement model. In a causal indicator model, the items are viewed as causes of a higher-order, emergent variable (see Figure 27.1, next page). The difference between these two models has enormous theoretical import and practical consequences (see, for example, Cohen, Cohen, Teresi, Marchi, & Velez, 1990, for a discussion of how these measurement models impact estimation in SEM).

The decision to adopt one or the other type of measurement model is dictated by whether the construct being measured is understood as a latent trait (requiring an effect indicator model) or as an emergent trait (requiring a causal indicator model). Most psychological constructs have been conceptualized as latent traits, though it is unclear whether this is by design or arises from uncertainty with respect to any alternative. The most frequently used emergent trait in psychological research is socioeconomic status (SES), an example discussed by Bollen and Lennox (1991). Education and income are surely indicators of SES. But years of education and high income are not caused by one's SES. Rather, education and income are the cause of SES. Emergent traits may provide a better model for understanding the assessment programs that led to the development of self-report scales by empirical, criterion-keying methods. For example, Gough (1996) indicates that the assessment approach of the CPI is committed to two goals: "(a) to predict with reasonable accuracy what people will say and do in defined situations, and (b) to identify people who will be described in meaningful and differentiated ways by those who know them well" (p. 2). Such a statement is certainly congenial with construing CPI scale scores as estimates of emergent rather than latent variables, and it stands in marked contrast to the explicit latent variable approach of Costa and McCrae (1992): "The NEO PI-R embodies a conceptual model that distills decades of factor analytic research on the structure of personality" (p. 1). Gough is trying to predict external variables, and the scale scores represent emergent variables summarizing the relation between the sampled item responses and their behavioral and reputational implications. Costa and McCrae seek measures of personality dimensions, where scale scores represent latent factors that cause both item responses and external outcomes.

The primary concern for present purposes is the implications of these different models for principles of measurement. Virtually all discussions of measurement criteria related to internal structure apply to effect indicator measurement

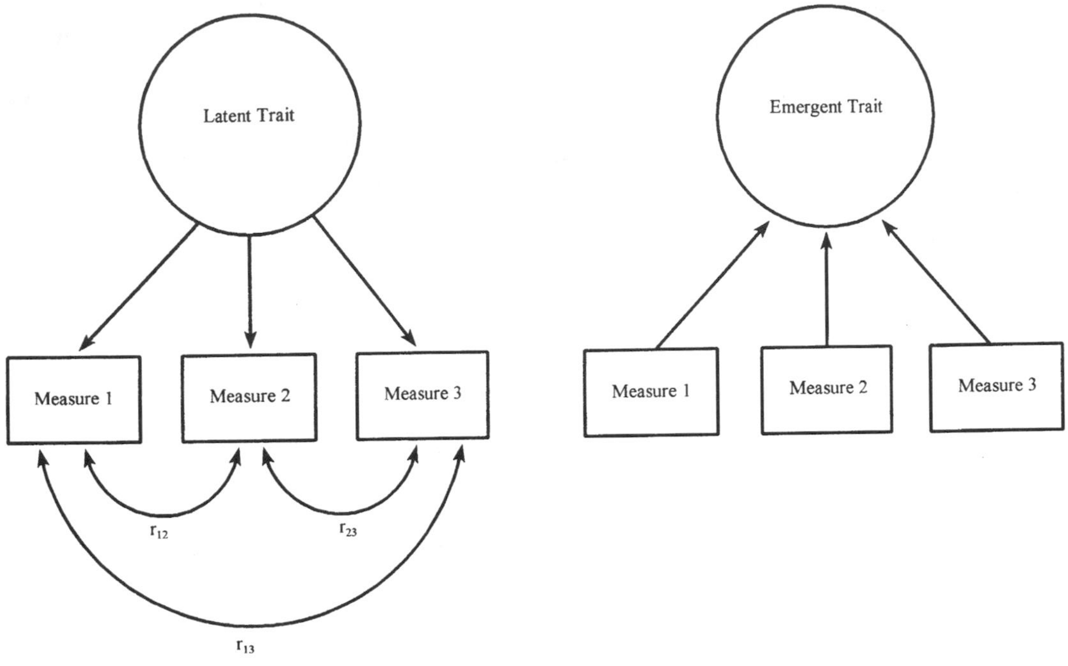

FIGURE 27.1. Bollen and Lennox's (1991) representation of the latent variable measurement model (left) with effect indicators and the emergent variable measurement model (right) with causal indicators. Intercorrelations among measures are depicted in the former because the model explicitly requires their existence.

models. However, criteria so established are generally irrelevant, if not misleading, for causal indicator measurement models. The effect indicator measurement model demands positive interitem correlations. The latent trait (or traits, if the scale is multidimensional) provides an explanation of these intercorrelations. The form of this explanation is: Observed individual differences in the measured variables, and their intercorrelations, arise from differences on the latent trait. One may evaluate the quality of model fit through standard SEM statistics, but excellent fit statistics are not sufficient: The fitted model must be in accord with theoretical expectations. If one defines a construct of interest to be quite narrow, then the causal paths from latent to measured variables in the good-fitting model should include comparatively large coefficients. For broader constructs, smaller coefficients are fully acceptable (see John & Benet-Martinez, in press, for a parallel discussion of this bandwidth–fidelity trade-off in the context of measurement reliability). In any case, parameter estimates in accord with the expectations provided by psychological theory are as important, perhaps more important, than model fit.

As Bollen and Lennox (1991) make clear, these internal structure considerations are irrelevant in causal indicator measurement models. Correlations among indicators are not required by the measurement model, nor are they in any sense "explained" if they are present. Explanation, in so far as it exists in this type measurement model, is from measured variable to emergent trait: Observed individual differences on the measured variables create differences on the emergent variable.

Because the causal indicator measurement model makes no claims about the intercorrelations of measured variables, it would seem an "easier" model because it makes no demands on the empirical world. This is certainly true in a formal sense. However, the causal indicator model requires a careful sampling of measures (Bollen & Lennox, 1991). Because the causal indicators define the emergent variable, omission of a key facet will create an emergent variable misaligned to its intended meaning. With effect indicator models, sampling of measures is important, but less crucial: The measures are all regarded as equivalent and interchangeable. Just as model fit and appropriate parameter estimates are the key evaluative standards for evaluating effect indicator measurement models, appropriate justification and implementation of measure sampling is a key evaluative standard whenever causal indicator measurement models are invoked.

Multidimensional Measures

As noted above, there are few, if any, unambiguously unidimensional measures of personality with multiple (more than two) indicators. In practice, there are any number of measures assessing narrowly defined constructs that may approach this ideal, but a determined factor analytic assault on the items will sooner or later reveal a replicable second factor or component; and the more indicators there are, the easier it will be to find a second (or third . . .) dimension. Briggs and Cheek's (1988) analysis of Snyder's (1974) self-monitoring scale, and subsequent discussion of this scale (e.g., Gangestad & Snyder, 1991; John, Cheek, & Klonen, 1996) illustrates how, under the best of circumstances, a focus on a scale's dimensionality may assist in refining theory and improving measurement. Nevertheless, the more general measurement problem of how to use multidimensional measures remains unresolved. It is important to note that multidimensionality is not a problem if a causal indicator model can be justified. The internal dimensionality of a measure is not a part of what causal indicator models seek to explain.

Carver (1989) and Hull, Lehn, and Tedlie (1991) both address multidimensionality in measurement and come to a similar conclusion: One should avoid working with a multidimensional aggregate of items and instead focus on unidimensional facets. Although this conclusion has much to recommend it, there is reason to hold out against adopting this strategy as a single general approach to solving the problem, though there exist quite a number of circumstances where this may indeed be the most desirable solution.

Hull, Lehn, and Tedlie (1991) clearly state the problem posed by multidimensional measures: If one aggregates over more homogeneous facets, any differential relations these facets may have to important external variables will be obscured. However, if facets are treated separately, the consideration of multiple correlated dimensions may lead to an even more rapid multiplication of measures and an even more bewildering array of findings than is already characteristic of the assessment literature. Indeed, if multiple indicator measures are always multidimensional to some degree, where might the disaggregation stop (Carver, 1989)? In practice, there are four ways (described in Hull, Lehn, and Tedlie, 1991) of analyzing multidimensional measures: (1) a total score approach (i.e., act as if the items are unidimensional) with the virtue of simplicity and often higher reliability but a subsequent loss of information about the contributions of individual facets; (2) a facet score approach with the opposite set of strengths and weaknesses; (3) a regression-based facet score approach where facets are treated as a set of predictors; and (4) latent variable structural equation modeling of the facets. Hull, Lehn, and Tedlie (1991) advocate this fourth alternative largely because the advantages of the regression approach (the ability to examine both individual facet contributions by examining regression coefficients and total effects with the multiple correlation) are preserved in the form of parameter estimates and measures of model fit in the SEM context, but, unlike the regression approach, measurement error is explicitly incorporated into the model.

The latent variable SEM approach described by Hull, Lehn, and Tedlie (1991) seems quite appropriate for the purpose of testing the adequacy of construct measurement and evaluating the psychological theory in which the construct is embedded. These purposes do not exhaust the functions of personality assessment. Personality assessment methods are used most often to make decisions about persons in work, counseling, and clinical settings. It is very difficult to see how assessment practitioners in applied settings could make use of assessment research if such research uniformly used only SEM methods. The changing values of measurement model parameter estimates from study to study implies that the latent trait's relation to its indicators is not constant, a problem separate from that associated with the indeterminacy of factors scores. Bollen (1989) observes that because of this latter problem "researchers should refrain from too fine comparisons of standings on factor scores, for they may be asking more from the factor score estimates than they can provide" (pp. 305–306). Assessment practitioners can either ignore assessment research using latent variable SEM or ignore Bollen's advice. Practitioners should not be forced to face this dilemma.

One solution would be to use latent variable SEM relatively early in the development of a measure for the purposes of defining relevant facets and from this research develop scoring keys for total score and facet scores that have proven valuable. Subsequent research could then use these scoring keys for manifest variables to develop the needed validity literature for applied assessment situations. Unless this, or some similar solution evolves, the increasing and deserved popularity of latent variable SEM will eventually sever ties between the research community that develops and evaluates measures and the community of applied personality assessors who use the measures.

Principle 3. The measure has demonstrably high validity for the most theoretically relevant inferences, and this validity is not derived through theoretically unwarranted channels.

Validity is the sine qua non of personality assessment. Regardless of a measure's other properties, if there are no valid inferences from the measure's scores, assessment has been pointless. Reliability is a necessary but not sufficient condition for validity so the meaning and estimation of reliability will constitute the initial topic of this discussion. A summary account of the meaning of validity, and the kind of evidence needed for valid inference from measurement outcomes will follow. Finally, common threats to validity inferences will be discussed.

Reliability in Personality Assessment

Measurement operations that yield inconsistent results have little value. Psychometric theory provides a set of definitions and equations for quantifying the degree of consistency in a set of scores. The most common method of expressing the degree of consistency is the reliability coefficient, a coefficient that has several alternate (but commensurate) definitions and several (not necessarily commensurate) estimation methods. One version of classical test theory, the theory of true and error scores, assumes that each measurement result (X_i) is the sum of two quantities: the true score and error. The error component is understood as a value randomly sampled from a distribution with mean of 0 and variance of σ_e^2. In a set of measurement results (e.g., persons' scores on a trait scale), the variance of the observed scores will equal the sum of the true score variance and error variance ($\sigma_x^2 = \sigma_t^2 + \sigma_e^2$) due to the variance sum law and the assumption that specific e_i values have been randomly and independently sampled. The ratio of true score variance to observed score variance provides a definition of reliability: $\rho_{xt}^2 = \sigma_t^2/\sigma_x^2$. If two independently obtained observed scores are available in a sample, then r_{xx} (the correlation between the two observed scores) is a reliability estimate ($\rho_{xx} = \rho_{xt}^2$). This is the rationale of "test–retest" reliability. This method of reliability estimation assumes that true scores do not change and that individuals can be independently measured twice (i.e., measurement must be nonreactive).

The stability of personality characteristics is often a theoretical concern, and in some circumstances, test–retest methods are inappropriate for assessing reliability but are of considerable substantive interest. Much hinges on the rate of change or fluctuation in the attribute being assessed and the test–retest interval. For example, if a highly stable trait (e.g., Extraversion in adults) is assessed with a 2-week interval between test and retest, then the correlation between the two observed scores (quite high, one hopes) informs the evaluation of the measure's reliability. A 2-week interval between the test and retest of a mood variable (that may fluctuate rapidly) is too long to be informative of the measure's reliability. Substantive theory and prior empiricism are required to properly interpret a test–retest coefficient. If the interval between test and retest is shorter than the interval required for true change on the construct, the test–retest correlation is pertinent to reliability; otherwise, the test–retest correlation may be descriptive of meaningful change. To the extent that theory cannot specify a rate of change, interpretation of test–retest correlations will necessarily be ambiguous.

Alternative conceptualizations of reliability avoid this interpretational problem. The theory of parallel tests provides a set of assumptions leading to an equivalent definition of reliability ($\rho_{xx} = \rho_{xt}^2 = \sigma_t^2 / \sigma_x^2$) but implying a rather different method for estimating ρ_{xx}. Here, a set of tests (A, B, C, etc.) are defined such that all persons have the same true score on each test in the set, and that the observed score means and standard deviations of the tests are equal. From these assumptions, it is possible to show that $\rho_{AB} = \rho_{AC} = \rho_{BC} = \rho_{xx}$. The reliability of a set of scores

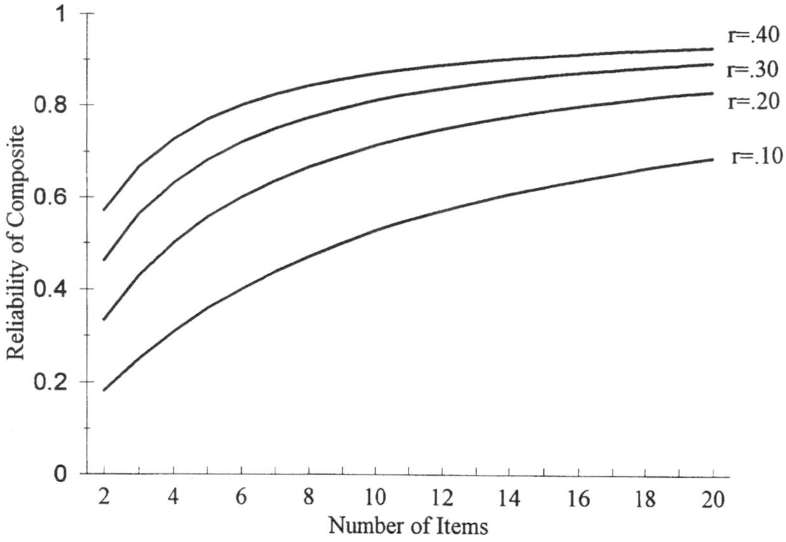

FIGURE 27.2. The Spearman–Brown formula can be represented by examining the reliability of a composite as a function of the average interitem correlation (r) and the number of items in the composite.

is given by their correlation to scores on a parallel test. Creating a parallel test that meets the stringent criteria described above is a severe impediment to applying this method. However, any multi-item measure contains within it a number of candidates for parallel half tests. Thus "split-half" reliability could be computed by correlating scores on half-tests (and obtaining the reliability of each half-test) and using the Spearman–Brown formula to estimate the reliability of the full set of items. Pushing this logic further, one might imagine each item as a test, creating as many parallel tests as their are items. The average interitem correlation provides an internal consistency estimate of the reliability of each of these "parallel tests"; application of the generalized Spearman–Brown formula provides an estimate of the internal consistency reliability of the full measure:

$$r_{xx} = \frac{k\bar{r}_{ij}}{1 + (k - 1)\bar{r}_{ij}}$$

where k is the number of items and $\bar{r}_{ij}$ is the average interitem correlation.

Cronbach (1951) provided an alternative method for estimating reliability in terms of internal consistency named coefficient alpha (α):

$$\alpha = \frac{k}{k-1}\ (1 - \Sigma\, \sigma_i^2/\sigma_x^2)$$

where k is the number of items, $\Sigma\, \sigma_i^2$ is the sum of the item variances, and σ_X^2 is the variance of the sum of item scores (i.e., the total scores). If items are standardized, these two equations yield equal values, so that in some instances, the Spearman–Brown reliability estimate is referred to as the standardized item alpha.

The Spearman–Brown formula shows that the reliability of a composite variable is a function of the intercorrelations of the indicators entering the composite and the number of indicators. This functional relation is depicted in Figure 27.2. From Figure 27.2, it is clear that if one can add indicators to a composite without reducing $\bar{r}_{ij}$, the reliability of the composite will increase.

Internal consistency methods will underestimate reliability in the presence of any degree of multidimensionality. This is easily seen in an extreme case. Consider a composite variable, in adults, of weight plus IQ. The correlation of weight with IQ would be low (and lower than the reliability of either variable), and so the Spearman–Brown formula would severely underestimate the reliability of the composite of these two highly reliable measures.

Reliability estimates have two important uses. First, reliability places a ceiling on validity. The maximum correlation between any two variables is the geometric mean (square root of the product) of the two reliability coefficients. If a predictor variable is correlated to an external criterion with a reliability of 1.00, then the maximum possible value of the correlation between predictor and criterion is the square root of the reliability of the predictor. Second, the reliability coefficient figures prominently in the formula for estimating the standard error of measurement[1] (the expected standard deviation of observed scores among individuals with equal true scores): $\sigma_{meas} = \sigma_x (1 - r_{xx})^{1/2}$. Thus, if scores are standardized ($\sigma_x = 1$) and reliability is .9, the standard error of measurement is .316. The 95% confidence interval (1.96 σ_{meas}) is then .62, or nearly two-thirds of a standard deviation in the distribution of scores on the measure.

These two uses of the reliability coefficient suggest two very different standards for how high a reliability coefficient "ought" to be. When decisions about individuals will be made on the basis of a measure of personality, reliability should be very high. As the example above suggests, even a reliability of .90 may not be high enough for this purpose (though it is important to remember that reliability estimates are lower-bound estimates). In research contexts, where decisions about individuals are not made, very much lower values of reliability are fully acceptable and setting some lower limit of "acceptability" is impossible. When working with manifest variables, low reliability will make negative results difficult to interpret, because other things being equal, power is a positive function of reliability. It is these power and attenuation concerns that make reliability an important consideration in research contexts. If results are "positive" in other respects, then reliability is sufficiently high. SEM latent variable models allow the consideration of relations among variables accounting for measurement error and provide an important strategy for avoiding attenuation effects created by low reliability.

Validity in Personality Assessment

The traditional, or "trinitarian" view identifies three forms of validity: content, criterion, and construct validity. In content validity, the concern is with the adequate sampling of the content and/or process to be assessed; in criterion validity, the focus is on the degree to which a measure predicts an important, definitional outcome; and construct validity addresses the degree to which the assessment results provide a measure of the underlying theoretical construct. Although the ideas distinguishing these validity types remain meaningful and important, a "unitarian" conception of all validity as construct validity seems to better characterize current thinking and practice (Messick, 1980; 1995).

This broader interpretation of construct validity recognizes that validity is a property of an inference based on assessment outcomes rather than a property of the measurement operation itself. Different kinds of information are relevant to various inferences that might follow from assessment outcomes. Kane (1992) considers validity as an attribute of an inference, discussing the kinds of evidence and the nature of interpretative arguments that bear on the evaluation of inferences drawn from measurement operations. This distinction between validity as a property of an inference rather than a property of a measure is subtle but important. Statements like "measure *x* is valid" must be recognized as shorthand expressions that are misleading if taken literally. A valid inference is one that is true if the inference's premises are true. In the construct validity case, these premises are theory-derived expectations concerning both the properties of a measure (e.g., internal consistency) and the relation between the theoretical construct of interest and other constructs and outcomes. The construct validation process is the verification of the truth of these premises. Only if the full set of premises are verified can the "measure *x* is valid" statement serve to represent the claim that the properties expected of the given theoretical construct are realized in measure *x* for the present purpose.

As noted at the outset of this chapter, virtually all of the issues discussed here pertain to the evaluation of a measure's construct validity. But at the very core of all validity arguments is the presentation of evidence that the assessment results are related to theoretically important external variables. In describing the concept of construct validity, Cronbach and Meehl (1955) listed various kinds of relevant evidence: differences between group (including age groups), correlations to other measures, the internal structure of the measure, factor analysis (i.e., correlations to known factors), stability (or change) over time, and analysis of the psychological processes engaged in the assessment procedure. Several of these considerations have been discussed, above, and are important construct validity considerations. But no argument for construct validity should depend solely on considerations internal to the measure itself. If the case for construct validity is based solely on the analysis of the response process and the internal structure of the measure, there emerges a kind of test-centered solipsism out of touch with the world outside the specific assessment context.

Construct validity arguments must have a hard criterion core. Although there will rarely, if ever, be a single unequivocal external criterion for test validation purposes, there will nearly always exist a set of external variables, be they behavioral outcomes, group memberships, age changes, or assessment results using quite different types of data (e.g., relation of a self-report scale to observer ratings), that collectively constitute a set of appropriate criteria. Demonstrating a substantial empirical relation between an assessment outcome and a sample of appropriate criteria is crucial for any construct validity inference.

Insisting that there be evidence of appropriate relations to external criteria as part of any construct validity argument is fully consistent with Cronbach and Meehl's (1955) original notion: "Numerous successful predictions dealing with phenotypically diverse 'criteria' give greater weight to the claim of construct validity than do fewer predictions, or predictions involving very similar behavior" (p. 295). If my emphasis on the importance of external criteria is stronger than that in the original formulation, it is because there is an alternative conceptualization now arising in the literature on latent variable SEM that denies the relevance of external variables. In this view, a measure's validity is given by the magnitude of the direct effect of a latent variable on this measured variable (see, e.g., Bollen, 1989, pp. 194–206). As shown in the effect indicator model in Figure 27.1, the validity of each of the three measures would be given by the coefficient associated with the causal path from the latent to the respective measured variable. Such an approach leaves open the possibility of "valid" measures that relate only to other such measures, but nothing else (imagine entire batteries of "valid" IQ tests that consistently fail, singly and collectively, to predict school grades).

Although examination of a measure's content and internal structure are undoubtably important, and are emphasized here in the first two assessment principles discussed above, these considerations do not provide a sufficient evidentiary foundation for justifying inferences about an individual's personality or for examining the nature of constructs in personality theory. In the absence of evidence that an assessment procedure adequately permits inferences about other characteristics in the "criterion set," little can be asserted firmly about the meaning of the measure. The converse of this claim is also true: Simply demonstrating appropriate relations to external variables does not satisfy construct validity requirements.

Threats to Validity in Personality Assessment

Since Thorndike (1920), concerns about systematic bias in measurement have provided reasons for caution in the interpretation of construct validity evidence. Bias and systematic error, especially in S- and O-data measures of personality, have been studied by generations of psychologists, and a thorough discussion of issues is provided by Cook and Campbell (1979), though findings and methods for identifying and controlling bias have accumulated since their review. For evaluating personality assessment findings, the most important concerns are those arising from monomethod studies of construct validity.

Response sets and response styles are among the most studied forms of bias in the S-data of personality assessment. The former (set) refers to a temporary reaction of the respondent to the assessment situation; the latter (style) refers to more general characteristics of the individual that may lead to biased responses. In studies relying solely on self-report measures of personality, it is often difficult to accept substantive findings because an alternative account based on common response biases across measures cannot be ruled out. Paulhus (1991) discusses acquiescence and extremity response biases, describing relatively easy ways to control these biases in personality assessment (i.e., counterbalancing item content and standardizing scores to subjects' own mean, respectively). The response bias of social desirability (individual differences in the tendency to claim virtues regardless of item content) presents a more serious problem in personality assessment, and the measurement and means of controlling social desirability are reviewed by Paulhus. Crucial to Paulhus's discussion is the distinction between self- and other-deception in social desirability. Other-deception is a form of impression management, and Paulhus suggests that controlling this bias is likely to be advantageous where there are explicit or implicit evaluative standards in the assessment context creating situational pressure to appear "good." Self-deception is linked to many substantive personality characteristics, and controlling this form of social desirability may decrease rather than increase validity in assessment.

Similar sorts of systematic bias are of concern in O-data, though Funder (1995) has assembled considerable evidence pointing to accuracy in the judgements of knowledgeable observers. The possibility of systematic bias in T- and L-data is a largely unconsidered question.

Because of the problem of shared biases in the monomethod assessment of personality, the use of multimethod assessment procedures is often preferred. Campbell and Fiske (1959) introduced the multitrait–multimethod matrix (MTMM) as a data structure for evaluating construct validity. This data structure contains the correlations among two or more traits, each measured by two or more methods (e.g., the traits Openness to Experience and intelligence each assessed by a self-report scale and peer ratings). Campbell and Fiske assert that both convergent validation (assessments of the same trait with different methods yield comparatively large correlations) and discriminant validation (assessments of different traits using the same method yield comparatively low correlations) are important, though there is some basis for questioning that the latter is as consequential as the former (Ozer, 1989).

Fundamental to both the logic and methods of the Campbell and Fiske's (1959) approach is that the trait- method unit that constitutes any psychological measure may be decomposed into separable trait and method components. A variety of alternative methods for analyzing MTMM matrices have been introduced (Kenny & Kashy, 1992; Millsap, 1995a), and most of these methods follow Campbell and Fiske in regarding the actual trait–method unit of assessment as decomposable into separate trait and method elements. Although the various methods for the analysis of MTMM matrices have each scored some successes, no generally appropriate procedure has been identified. Millsap (1995a) suggests that without knowledge of relations among methods (e.g., when are method effects likely to be independent?), distinguishing between the effects of shared method and appropriate trait correlations may be forever elusive.

It is difficult to imagine that reliable knowledge about relations between methods can be achieved without some sort of theory of method effects. Campbell and Fiske (1959) recognized the desirability of such a theory, and Ozer (1989) suggested the need to psychologize method, proposing that we abandon the assumption that the trait–method unit can be usefully decomposed. In this view, it is the trait–method unit as a whole that is the subject of the construct validation process. The expected empirical correlates of the same trait assessed by different methods need not be the same, and such a method difference need not generalize to other traits. Cronbach (1995) suggests that convergent validity will be achieved only when the psychological theory of the construct and knowledge of method effects within that construct lead to the inclusion of controls for specific method effects. For example, John and Robins (1994) found that individual differences in self-enhancement effects in performance evaluation (as independently assessed) were systematically related to measures of Narcissism. This specific instance of a method-within-construct effect provides insight into the psychological processes of self-evaluation that would be missed by a search for a global S-data method factor. As discussed by Ozer (1989), strong convergence of results across methods is an unrealistic expectation,[2] and global method factors resist interpretation when they can be identified. Contrary to the conventional view of trait and method effects as "crossed," it now seems apparent that regarding method effects as nested within trait effects offers greater promise.

There is, then, no formulaic means of avoiding fundamental threats in interpreting validity evidence in personality assessment. Successful construct validation efforts proceed by using both mono- and multimethod approaches. Monomethod findings must be cautiously interpreted, with a wary concern for shared biases offering an alternative to substantive explanations. Multimethod results must also be approached with care, recognizing that important substantive relations may be missed, or even suppressed, by method effects. Because of this need for interpretive vigilance, it is difficult to imagine the construct validation process reduced to formal procedures, rules, and definitions (as has been achieved in the analysis of reliability); the "rules," such as they can be expressed, are those of rational argument.

Principle 4. The implicative relations of the measure are well explored, and the internal structure of the measure and important validity inferences are invariant over theoretically and pragmatically defined generalization criteria.

Identification and testing the limits of generalization from assessment results is the focus of this final assessment principle. Conceived broadly, this involves two quite different kinds of activities: First, wide-ranging exploratory analyses are needed to formulate the full meaning of the measure and, second, the applicability of this meaning must be examined in various populations and assessment contexts. Because a very large body of evidence is needed to fully satisfy generalization requirements, this ideal will be realized only with assessment instruments that are widely researched over a period of years.

Exploring Implicative Relations

The need to fully explore the implicative meanings of assessment outcomes arises from two related phenomena. As discussed above, virtually all measures of personality are to some degree multidimensional. Initial construct validation efforts are aimed at the primary dimension to assure that it is appropriately pointed toward the desired construct. The implications of lesser dimensions go unrecorded in such analyses. Additionally, most meaningful measures of personality have implications beyond the dimensions actually assessed. Height, for example, has implications for "value as a basketball player." How shall such implications be uncovered in the realm of personality?

Gough (1965) describes a research strategy for fully exploring the interpretive meaning of assessment results. This conceptual analysis approach is divided into three evaluation stages. The first two cover issues already discussed, but Gough's description of tertiary evaluation provides the model for meaning expansion needed to fully interpret measurement results. Gough starts from the presumption that the assessment process must ultimately be concerned with making inferences about persons, and the goal of tertiary evaluation is to provide a basis for inferences that go beyond the original meaning of the scale. The method for accomplishing tertiary evaluation is straightforward: The measure of interest is correlated to as broad an array of variables as possible in as many diverse samples as can be obtained. Those most comfortable with the experimental testing of null hypotheses will regard such research as a "fishing expedition," though the pejorative implications of such a characterization do not follow. The goal is not to assemble a listing of statistically significant correlations, but to form a replicable, coherent interpretation of diverse results.

The potential yield of this approach is best portrayed by example. Gough (1965) provides a sample conceptual analysis of the CPI Socialization scale. By design, the scale assesses internalization of social norms, and Gough first provides evidence supporting this interpretation, noting, for example, that the scale discriminates between delinquent and nondelinquent youth in several cultures and that the socially valued implications of being high on socialization are realized in the scale correlates. But an important, unanticipated result emerged when especially creative individuals were compared to representative samples in several professional groups: The creative individuals scored lower on the Socialization scale. Apparently, given a degree of professional achievement, violating conventional norms is an element of the creative process and the scale is sensitive to this effect.

This kind of expansion of scale meaning accrues by design, as Gough (1965) demonstrates, but also arises in the accumulated findings of substantive research involving a scale or other assessment procedure. The construct validation process does not end with the publication of a scale but continues on through the usage of the measure in both scientific and applied contexts.

Measurement and Predictive Invariance

A measure that works well with one population or in one setting may not perform as successfully in another, and some measurement correlates may be contingent on other, third variables. Such circumstances necessarily limit generalizations from personality assessment. Measurement invariance refers to a constant relation between observed and latent variable scores across populations, whereas predictive invariance refers to constant relations between a predictor and a criterion over populations. Although "populations" are usually defined in terms of identifiable group differences (e.g., age, gender, or culture), alternative definitions referring to groups assessed in different circumstances or having different life experiences may also be appropriate.

Whether one wishes to assert that groups differ on a measure or that a measure has different correlates in different groups, it is first necessary to demonstrate that the same attribute has been measured in the same way across groups. The relevance of measurement invariance to construct validity should be clear at this point: Demonstrating that predicted group differences exist on a measure is often a crucial element of testing the criterion validity of a measure. Showing the absence of such differences where they are unexpected by construct definitions is important both for discriminant validity considerations and for justifying the use of the measure in new populations not included in the normative sample.

Measurement invariance is most simply assessed by comparing the factor structure of indicators across groups. Persons in different groups who have equal latent trait scores should have the same expected score on the measured variable, and this hypothesis of measurement invariance is falsified if the factor structure varies across groups. Explicit testing of measurement invariance can be accomplished with both confirmatory factor analysis and item response theory. Reise, Widaman, and Pugh (1993) describe and compare these methods.

Construct validity considerations always demand some consideration of a measure's relation to other variables. The substantive theory of the construct will demand constancy of such relations over some populations, settings, or third variables but not over others. Explicit tests of construct validity hypotheses of this form are tests of predictive invariance. Traditional moderator variable approaches are one form of test for predictive invariance for manifest variables, though latent variable SEM approaches can be adapted to this purpose (Millsap, 1995b). A measure's relation to important core criterion variables should not be moderated by extraneous third, or nuisance, variables.[3]

CONCLUDING OBSERVATIONS

My remarks in this chapter have focused on criteria for evaluating personality assessment methods. All too often, when asked "Do you know a good measure of _____?" I feel obligated to respond in the negative. This is often followed by a query asking for guidance in the task of constructing such a measure. Omitted from this chapter are specific suggestions for constructing measures of personality. Guidance for those choosing this alternative is not hard to find: Burisch (1984) offers an outline and comparative review of different strategies of scale construction; Wolfe (1993) gives straightforward advice; and Tellegen and Waller (in press) provides thorough and thoughtful discussion of an integrative approach that seeks to capitalize on the advantages of several different scale construction strategies. Although state of the art procedures utilize technical methods (e.g., item response theory) requiring considerable training, I have seen numerous beginning students develop personality scales with minimal resources in very little time. Such scales, on occasion, perform reasonably well. It seems that it is relatively easy to develop a measure of personality of middling quality (Ashton & Goldberg, 1973), and then it is terribly difficult to improve it. Creating a measure of personality that satisfies the assessment principles described here requires time, energy, and expertise. Distressingly few measures satisfy these principles.

Given the ease of doing a passable job and the difficulty of doing it well, one may wonder: Why not settle for less than the best that can be done? But the methods of personality assessment are consequential: Decisions about people are made on the basis of scores on self-report scales and on the impressions they make in interviews. The issue cannot be finessed by claiming that a measure is "for research purposes only," because personality theory demands sharp distinctions between constructs like anxiety and depression or between self-esteem and self-confidence, and these cannot be drawn with blunt instruments.

ACKNOWLEDGMENTS

I thank Lawrence Pervin and Oliver John for their editorial assistance in developing this chapter and Jacob Hershey for providing feedback as ideas developed and assistance in producing the figures.

NOTES

1. Item Response Theory (IRT; Embretson, 1996) enables estimation of a standard error of measurement for each subject. With IRT methods, some individuals may be "reliably" evaluated even if the measure's reliability (in the sense of classical test theory) is low. Conversely, high reliability does not guarantee precision in the evaluation of all scores.

2. Cattell (1979) summarizes the results of more than 30 years of effort to identify personality factors independent of data type and claims some success for the venture, but even he notes that "more remains to be aligned than has yet been brought into alignment" (p. 123).

3. Problematically, Millsap's analysis of predictive and measurement invariance indicates that these two desirable qualities can co-occur only in unusual circumstances, so that direct affirmative evidence for one form of invariance indirectly suggests at least some small degree of absence (bias) in the other. The extent to which this "duality paradox" undermines actual construct validation efforts remains an open question.

REFERENCES

Ainsworth, M. D. S., Blehar, M. C., Waters, E., & Wall, S. (1978). *Patterns of attachment: A psychological study of the Strange Situation.* Hillsdale, NJ: Erlbaum.

Ashton, S. G., & Goldberg, L. R. (1973). In response to Jackson's challenge: The comparative validity of personality scales constructed by the external (empirical) strategy and scales developed intuitively by experts, novices, and laymen. *Journal of Research in Personality, 7,* 1–20.

Beutler, L. E., & Berren, M. (Eds.). (1995). *Integrative assessment of adult personality.* New York: Guilford Press.

Block, J. (1977). Advancing the psychology of personality: Paradigmatic shift or improving the quality of research. In D. Magnusson & N. S. Endler (Eds.), *Personality at the crossroads* (pp. 37–63). Hillsdale, NJ: Erlbaum.

Block, J. (1993). Studying personality the long way. In D. C. Funder, R. D. Parke, C. Tomlinson-Keasey, & K. Widaman (Eds.), *Studying lives through time* (pp. 9–41). Washington, DC: American Psychological Association.

Bollen, K. A. (1989). *Structural equations with latent variables.* New York: John Wiley & Sons.

Bollen, K. A., & Lennox, R. (1991). Conventional wisdom on measurement: A structural equation perspective. *Psychological Bulletin, 110,* 305–314.

Briggs, S. R., & Cheek J. M. (1988). On the nature of self-monitoring: Problems with assessment, problems with validity. *Journal of Personality and Social Psychology, 54,* 663–678.

Burisch, M. (1984). Approaches to personality inventory construction: A comparison of merits. *American Psychologist, 39,* 214–227.

Campbell D. T. & Fiske D. W. (1959). Convergent and discriminant validation by the multitrait-multimethod matrix. *Psychological Bulletin, 56,* 81–105.

Carver, C. S. (1989). How should multifaceted personality constructs be tested? Issues illustrated by self-monitoring, attributional style, and hardiness. *Journal of Personality and Social Psychology, 56,* 577–585.

Cattell, R. B. (1957). *Personality and motivation structure and measurement.* Yonkers-on-Hudson, NY: World Book Co.

Cattell, R. B. (1979). *Personality and learning theory: Vol. 1. The structure of personality in its environment.* New York: Springer.

Cohen, P., Cohen J., Teresi, J., Marchi, M., & Velez, N. C. (1990). Problems in the measurement of latent variables in structural equations causal models. *Applied Psychological Measurement, 14,* 183–196.

Cook, T. D. & Campbell, D. T. (1979). Quasi-experimentation: *Design and analysis issues for field settings.* Chicago: Rand-McNally.

Costa, P. T. & McCrae R. R. (1992). *NEO PI-R professional manual.* Odessa, FL.: Psychological Assessment Resources, Inc

Craik, K. H. (1986). Personality research methods: An historical perspective. *Journal of Personality, 54,* 18–51.

Cronbach, L. J. (1951). Coefficient alpha and the internal structure of tests. *Psychometrika, 16,* 297–334.

Cronbach, L. J. (1995). Giving method variance its due. In P. E. Shrout & S. T. Fiske (Eds.), *Personality research, methods, and theory: A festschrift honoring Donald W. Fiske* (pp. 145–157). Hillsdale, NJ: Erlbaum.

Cronbach, L. J., & Meehl, P. E. (1955). Construct validity in psychological tests. *Psychological Bulletin, 52,* 281–302.

Embretson, S. E. (1996). The new rules of measurement. *Psychological Assessment, 8,* 341–349.

Eysenck, H. J. (1967). *The biological basis of personality.* Springfield, IL: Charles C Thomas.

Fiske, D. W. (1971). *Measuring the concepts of personality.* Chicago: Aldine.

Funder, D. C. (1995). On the accuracy of personality judgment: A realistic approach. *Psychological Review, 102,* 652–670.

Gangestad, S. W., & Snyder, M. (1991). Taxonomic analysis redux: Some statistical considerations for testing a latent class model. *Journal of Personality and Social Psychology, 61,* 141–161.

Goldberg, L. R. (1972). Some recent trends in personality assessment. *Journal of Personality Assessment, 36,* 547–560.

Goldberg, L. R. (1992). The development of markers for the big-five factor structure. *Psychological Assessment, 4,* 26–42

Gough, H. G. (1965). Conceptual analysis of psychological test scores and other diagnostic variables. *Journal of Abnormal Psychology, 70,* 294–302.

Gough, H. G. (1987). *California Psychological Inventory administrator's guide.* Palo Alto, CA: Consulting Psychologists Press.

Gough, H. G. (1996). *CPI manual* (3rd ed.). Palo Alto, CA: Consulting Psychologists Press.

Helmes, E., & Jackson, D. N. (1989). Prediction models of personality item responding. *Multivariate Behavioral Research, 24,* 71–91.

Hogan, R., & Nicholson, R. A. (1988). The meaning of personality test scores. *American Psychologist, 43,* 621–626.

Holden, R. R., & Jackson, D. N. (1979). Item subtlety and face validity in personality assessment. *Journal of Consulting and Clinical Psychology, 47,* 459–468.

Holden, R. R., & Jackson, D. N. (1981). Subtlety, information, and faking effects in personality assessment. *Journal of Clinical Psychology, 37,* 379–386.

Hull, J. G., Lehn, D. A., & Tedlie, J. C. (1991). A general approach to testing multifaceted personality constructs. *Journal of Personality and Social Psychology, 61,* 932–945.

John, O. P. (1990). The Big Five factor taxonomy: Dimensions of personality in the natural language and in questionnaires. In L. A. Pervin (Ed.), *Handbook of personality: Theory and research* (pp. 66–100). New York: Guilford Press.

John, O. P., & Benet-Martinez, V. (in press). Measurement, reliability, and construct validation. In H. T. Reis & C. M. Judd (Eds.), *Handbook of research methods in social psychology.* Cambridge, UK: Cambridge University Press.

John, O. P., Cheek, J. M., & Klonen, E. C. (1996). On the nature of self-monitoring: Construct explication via Q-sort ratings. *Journal of Personality and Social Psychology, 71,* 763–776.

John, O. P., & Robins, R. W. (1994). Accuracy and bias in self-perception: Individual differences in self-enhancement and the role of narcissism. *Journal of Personality and Social Psychology, 66,* 206–219.

Kane, M. (1992). An argument-based approach to validity. *Psychological Bulletin, 112,* 527–535.

Kenny, D. A. (1991). A general model of consensus and accuracy in interpersonal perception. *Psychological Review, 98,* 55–163.

Kenny, D. A., & Kashy, D. A. (1992). Analysis of the multitrait–multimethod matrix by confirmatory factor analysis. *Psychological Bulletin, 112,* 165–172.

Lamiell, J. T., Foss, M. A., Larsen, R. J., & Hempel, A. M. (1983). Studies in intuitive personology from an idiothetic point of view: Implications for personality theory. *Journal of Personality, 51,* 438–467.

Lanyon, R. I., & Goodstein, L. D. (1997). *Personality assessment* (3rd. ed.). New York: Wiley.

Loevinger, J. (1957). Objective tests as instruments of psychological theory. *Psychological Reports, 3,* 635–694.

McAdams, D. P. (1995). What do we know when we know a person? *Journal of Personality, 63,* 365–396.

Meehl, P. E. (1972). Reactions, reflections, projections. In J. N. Butcher (Ed.), *Objective personality assessment: Changing perspectives* (pp. 131–189). New York: Academic Press.

Meehl, P. E. (1978). Theoretical risks and tabular asterisks: Sir Karl, Sir Ronald, and the slow progress of soft psychology. *Journal of Consulting & Clinical Psychology, 46,* 806–834.

Messick, S. (1980). Test validity and the ethics of assessment. *American Psychologist, 35,* 1012–1027.

Messick, S. (1995). Validity of psychological assessment: Validation of inferences from persons' responses and performances as scientific inquiry into score meaning. *American Psychologist, 50,* 741–749.

Millsap, R. E. (1995a). The statistical analysis of method effects in multitrait- multimethod data: A review. In P. E. Shrout & S. T. Fiske (Eds.). *Personality research, methods, and theory: A festschrift honoring Donald W. Fiske* (pp. 93–109). Hillsdale, NJ: Erlbaum.

Millsap, R. E. (1995b). Measurement invariance, predictive invariance, and the duality paradox. *Multivariate Behavioral Research, 30,* 577–605.

Ozer, D. J. (1989). Construct validity in personality assessment. In D. M. Buss & N. Cantor (Eds.), *Personality psychology: Recent trends and emerging directions* (pp. 224–234). New York: Springer-Verlag.

Ozer, D. J., & Reise, S. P. (1994). Personality assessment. *Annual Review of Psychology, 45,* 357–388.

Paulhus, D. L. (1991). Measurement and control of response bias. In J. P. Robinson, P. R. Shaver, & L. S. Wrightsman (Eds.), *Measures of personality and social psychological attitudes* (pp. 17–59). San Diego, CA: Academic Press.

Reise, S. P., Widaman, K. F., & Pugh, R. H. (1993). Confirmatory factor analysis and item response theory: Two approaches for exploring measurement invariance. *Psychological Bulletin, 114,* 552–566.

Robinson, J. P., Shaver, P. R., & Wrightsman, L. S. (1991). Criteria for scale selection and evaluation. In J. P. Robinson, P. R. Shaver, & L. S. Wrightsman (Eds.), *Measures of personality and social psychological attitudes* (pp. 17–59). San Diego, CA: Academic Press.

Snyder, M. (1974). Self-monitoring of expressive behavior. *Journal of Personality and Social Psychology, 30,* 526–537.

Tellegen, A. (1991). Personality traits: Issues of definition, evidence, and assessment. In W. M. Grove & D. Cicchetti (Eds.), *Thinking clearly about psychology: Vol. 2. Personality and psychopathology* (pp. 10–35). Minneapolis: University of Minnesota Press.

Tellegen, A., & Waller, N. G. (in press). Exploring personality through test construction: Development of the Multidimensional Personality Questionnaire. In S. R. Briggs, J. M. Cheek, & E. M. Donahue (Eds.), *Handbook of adult personality inventories.* New York: Plenum Press.

Thorndike, E. L. (1920). A constant error in psychological ratings. *Journal of Applied Psychology, 4,* 25–29.

Wiggins, J. S. (1973). *Personality and prediction: Principles of personality assessment.* Reading, MA: Addison-Wesley.

Wolfe, R. N. (1993). A commonsense approach to personality measurement. In K. H. Craik, R. Hogan, & R. N. Wolfe (Eds.), *Fifty years of personality psychology* (pp. 269–290). New York: Plenum Press.

PART FIVE
OVERVIEW

Chapter 28

Epilogue: Constancy and Change in Personality Theory and Research

Lawrence A. Pervin
Rutgers—The State University of New Jersey

A few years ago I received an invitation to contribute to a special issue of the *Journal of Research in Personality* on "The Future of Personality." Thoughts about the future led me to reflect on the past, in particular on the relation between issues addressed in my graduate education during the late 1950s and issues facing the field today. My sense is that many of the earlier issues remain; for example, issues concerning construct validity, the disciplines of psychology, and the search for universal principles of personality system functioning (Pervin, 1996). Publication of the second edition of the *Handbook of Personality* offers an opportunity for further consideration of these issues as well as consideration of changes that are occurring in the field. Just as we can consider the stasis and flow of behavior to be central to the field of personality psychology (Pervin, 1983), we can consider constancy and change as central to our consideration of developments in the field.

CONSTANCY IN PERSONALITY PSYCHOLOGY: UNRESOLVED ISSUES IN THE FIELD

It is clear that progress has been made in the field of personality psychology in terms of sophistication of research methodologies and techniques of data analysis, as well as in awareness of the range of variables that need to be considered to understand complex personality functioning. At the same time, a reading of the history of the field suggests that fundamental problems and issues remain. Which problems are most central to the field? Would workers in the personality field agree about the content of the major issues? My own list of the top 10 issues follows. Although treated separately, in fact they are overlapping and interlocking.

1. Measurement: The Value of Self-Report Data and Relations among Measures

> There is often a minimal correlation, or none at all, between an empirical index of a concept like anxiety based on overt behavior, cognitive functioning, symptoms or physiology, on the one hand, and one based on answers in an interview or on a questionnaire.
>
> —KAGAN (1988, p. 614)

No scientific field can advance in the absence of methods for assessing or measuring relevant variables. Current advances in the life sciences are based in good part on technological advances that provide for the identification and measurement of phenomena previously inaccessible. To a great extent research in the personality field relies upon self-report data. Views on the merit of self-report measures vary (Hogan & Nicholson, 1988; Holtzman & Kagan, 1995; Kagan, 1988; Robins & John, 1997; Schwarz, 1999; Wilson, 1994). At times one finds strange bedfellows. Thus, although for different reasons and emphasizing different kinds of self-report measures, both social cognitive and trait theorists find merit in them (Bandura, 1986; Funder, 1993; McCrae & Costa, 1990). In some cases such measures are valued for the accuracy of the information they provide, whereas in other cases they are valued purely for their predictive power, without regard to whether the responses are "accurate" self-descriptions. Such supporters can be contrasted with most psychoanalytic researchers who eschew reliance on such measures. Recall Murray's statement: "Children perceive inaccurately, are very little conscious of their inner states and retain fallacious recollections of occurrences. Many adults are hardly better" (1938, p. 15). In addition, many social psychologists point to discrepancies between attitudes and behavior as well as the importance of nonconscious influences to similarly raise questions concerning a reliance on self-report measures (Greenwald & Banaji, 1995).

A global evaluation of the merit of self-report measures of personality is impossible, their accuracy being related to the variable being considered, the goals of the investigator, the measure of accuracy used, the degree of defensiveness of the individual, etc. However, my reading of the literature suggests a number of problems with a reliance on self-report data. In the main, these problems involve less than satisfactory relations between self-ratings and ratings by others and less than satisfactory relations between self-report measures and other measures of the same variables.

Relations between Self-Ratings and Ratings by Others

Proponents of the use of self-report measures, in particular those using questionnaires to measure trait variables, point to the agreement between self-ratings and ratings by observers to establish their validity (Funder, 1980; Funder, Kolar, & Blackman, 1995; John & Robins, 1993). In addition, it is suggested that observers in different contexts (i.e., observations derived from different contexts) more or less know the same person (Funder et al., 1995).

Do the correlations observed (i.e., interjudge agreement on the general order of .4 to .5) indicate that actors and observers more or less know the same person and that such knowledge is not only shared but accurate? What magnitude of correlation qualifies as a standard for "high" level of agreement?[1] If knowledge of a person involves relations among characteristics—that is, a profile of characteristics—do discrepancies between self- and observer ratings become enlarged when profiles rather than individual scores are considered? What are we to conclude from data suggesting that the magnitude of self–observer agreement varies depending on the trait and observer considered? And, what are we to conclude from data suggesting that although judges from different contexts tend to agree with one another, on average their agreement is approximately 60% of that of judges from the same context?

Other questions can be raised concerning the basis for self–other agreement but let us turn to the question of whether such agreement reflects accuracy. Does evidence that people often perceive themselves as others do mean that they perceive themselves accurately and that self-report data can be a foundation for a science of personality? Kenny (1994) has conducted considerable research on the question of agreement and accuracy in social perception. He suggests that the data "strongly support the conclusion that people do indeed see themselves as others do" (p. 189) but also suggests that "self-ratings carry a great deal of excess baggage; that is, they measure other things besides how the person truly is" (p. 202) and that the data "should lead researchers to question seriously the orientation that views personality as the study of self-report inventories" (p. 194).[2] One may note here as well recent findings suggesting that confidence in perception of the other in no way corresponds with greater accuracy (Gill, Swann, & Silvera, 1998; Swann & Gill, 1997). In other words, there is no reason to believe that limiting ratings to those in which there is high confidence would enhance accuracy.[3]

Data from studies in which self-report data and observer ratings are used as criterion variables (e.g., measures of depression) further lead us to question the near exclusive reliance on self-report data. Such studies consistently find different relationships between predictor and criterion variables depending on whether the criterion consists of self-ratings, peer ratings, parent ratings, or an independent observer (Kazdin, 1994). Although in some cases such differential relations make good theoretical sense, more often they are experienced as noise and a source of confusion.

Relations between Self-Ratings and Other Measures

Aside from how self-ratings correlate with ratings by others, how do self-report data correlate with other measures? In general, the literature suggests that when self-report data are compared with personality measures that do not share method variance (e.g., fantasy, physiological, and objective measures of overt behavior), considerable divergence emerges (Bornstein, 1998; Derakshan & Eysenck, 1997; Hedlund & Rude, 1995; King, 1995; McClelland, Koestner, & Weinberger, 1989). In addition, there is evidence that retrospective reports of behavior do not correspond well with actual measures of behavior taken at an earlier point in time (Henry, Moffitt, Caspi, Langley, & Silva, 1994).

In sum, although personality psychologists differ in their overall assessment of the utility of self-report data, an analysis of studies of self–other agreement and self-independent measure agreement raises serious questions about the use of self-report data as a foundation for a science of personality. The problem of lack of agreement among measures may be particularly critical where alternative measures are used to assess the predicted criterion. This is not to argue that self-report data are never of value but rather that their value must be established rather than assumed. Discrepancies among measures are not problematic if they can be understood in a theoretically meaningful way. Thus, for example, discrepancies between self-report measures of affect and physiological measures of affect make sense in terms of the concept of repression (Derakshan & Eysenck, 1997; Newton & Contrada, 1992; Shedler, Mayman, & Manis, 1993). Similarly, contradictions between overt and projective measures can be understood as a function of defensiveness (Wallach, Green, Lipsitt, & Minehart, 1962). However, as noted, often discrepancies among personality measures, particularly among those that do not share common method variance, represent a source of confusion more than a source of conceptual meaning.

In pointing to a lack of agreement between self-report and other measures it is recognized that this does not necessarily mean that the former is less accurate than the latter. In some cases this is demonstrably the case (e.g., self-reports of behaviors such as legal offenses or drinking as opposed to objective measures of such behaviors) but in other cases it need not be. However, clearly such lack of agreement indicates that self-reports can not automatically be assumed to be valid measures of the variable of interest. More research is needed to understand the conditions, contexts, and concepts for which self-reports are likely to be valid and useful.

2. Construct Validity

> A necessary condition for a construct to be scientifically admissible is that it occurs in a nomological net, at least some of whose laws involve observables.
>
> —CRONBACH AND MEEHL (1955, p. 290)

Inevitably the problem of measurement brings us to the question of construct validity, and thereby to the classic papers of Cronbach and Meehl (1955) on construct validity and Campbell and Fiske (1959) on convergent and discriminant validity. In the former, Cronbach and Meehl (1955) considered the problem of proceeding in the absence of a criterion to define and measure the personality variable of interest. They specifically suggested that a measure or test correlating with other tests did not necessarily establish construct validity because they might all be measuring the same thing. Factor analysis was recognized as an important type of validation both in terms of consistency of the trait underlying different tests and the unity of the construct as defined by a particular test. However, their greatest emphasis was on the theoretical status of the construct, its "nomological network" and "relational fertility." Of particular value in building construct validity were successful predictions involving phenotypically diverse criteria.[4]

In their classic paper on convergent and discriminant validity, Campbell and Fiske (1959) were particularly concerned with the adequacy of tests as measures of a construct rather than the nomological network or theoretical status of the construct. The suggested method for establishing such kinds of validity was the multitrait–multimethod matrix, that is, the representation of intercorrelations among several traits measured by several methods. Of particular importance was the use of methods that were independent of one another so as to avoid the contaminating problem of common method variance (e.g., self-ratings and inventory scores). Such multitrait–multimethod matrices were noted to be rare in the literature.

To what extent have we demonstrated evidence of construct validity and the associated evidence of convergent and discriminant validity for major personality constructs? Typically we have evidence of agreement among measures that share method variance, evidence of some independent variance accounted for in a regression equation, and occasionally evidence of the lack of agreement (i.e., "low" correlations) with other measures considered to be different from the proposed construct and measure. Rarely do we see the development of a nomological network, with explicit predictions derived theoretically, of the order considered by Cronbach and Meehl (1955) and the presentation of a multitrait–multimethod matrix of the nature suggested by Campbell and Fiske (1959).[5] Frequently the relations among what appear to be similar constructs (e.g., optimism, emotional stability, emotional well-being, self-esteem, hope), and their associated measures, remain unclear (Compton, Smith, Cornish, & Qualls, 1996; Scheier, Carver, & Bridges, 1994).

Block (1996) has articulated the problem well with his description of the jangle and jingle fallacies. According to Block, the "jangle fallacy" consists of using different terms for the same concept whereas the "jingle fallacy" consists of using the same term for different concepts. Implied in these fallacies are the problems of measures that correlate although they are presumed to measure different constructs and measures that do not correlate, or show differing patterns of relationships with criterion variables, although they are presumed to measure the same construct. At times the situation is further complicated by our not even knowing whether the problem is a jangle fallacy or a jingle fallacy. That is, the correlations among measures are such (e.g., .4–.5) that the case can be made either that the same construct is being measured by different instruments despite different terms being used, or that different concepts are involved despite the instruments being identified as measures of the same construct.

Finally, one may note the problem of lack of stability of relationships across studies, populations, measures, etc. In part this is due to unreliable observations and chance findings, what Meehl (1978, 1990) has labeled the "crud factor." In other cases, however, reliably significant findings are reported that are unstable because of slight shifts in instructions given to subjects or in context (Gigerenzer & Hoffrage, 1995; Kagan, 1988). In still other cases unstable relationships are due to differences in population characteristics (e.g., differences in age, gender, and culture). Varying results concerning the structure of personality and the functioning of processes are frequent and problematic for the field unless accounted for in a theoretically meaningful way. At this point evidence of the stability of findings across populations and settings, or an explanation for the varying relationships, in most cases remains problematic.

3. The Three Disciplines of Personality

> I shall discuss the past and future place within psychology of two historic streams of method, thought, and affiliation which run the last century of our science. One stream is experimental psychology; the other correlational psychology. Psychology continues to this day to be limited by the dedication of its investigators to one or the other method of inquiry rather than to scientific psychology as a whole.
>
> —CRONBACH (1957, p. 671)

Throughout the history of modern psychology, observers of the field have commented on the existence of different streams of method, thought, and affiliation (Cronbach, 1957; Hogan, 1982). These different streams or disciplines generally fall under the labels of "clinical," "correlational," and "experimental." Throughout my career as a personality and clinical psychologist I have been impressed with three things: First, different theoretical approaches to personality tend to be associated with different kinds of data. Second, the same person considered from the standpoint of the various theories and data looks different. For example, typically a person appears much more disturbed on projective tests and when viewed from a psychoanalytic perspective than when considered from a humanist or trait perspective using interview and questionnaire data. Because often there is no firm basis for viewing one set of data as more accurate or valid than another, a fundamental task for the field is to understand these differences and develop theories that are able to encompass such diversity in individual functioning. Third, often proponents of the various theories and associated assessment methods at best talk at cross purposes to one another and at worst are completely dismissive of each other.

Clearly this is not an issue of good theory versus bad theory or of good research versus bad research. Rather, it is an issue of three disciplines, each with its adherents committed to a particular approach to theory and research. Perhaps all that can be done realistically is to leave the situation as it is. Perhaps ultimately one of the approaches and associated theory will prevail. However, I suspect that at some point we will have to recognize that the problem is fundamental and cannot be ignored. At that point, the members of the various disciplines will have to speak to one another to establish what is valuable in each, to establish where research and theory must go to incorporate the different forms of data and associated representations of the person, and perhaps even to develop some common language to use in the endeavor.

4. Parts versus Wholes (Systems)

> Personality is the architecture of the whole, not a list of adjectives descriptive of those parts or aspects which most impresses observers.
>
> —MURRAY AND KLUCKHOHN (1953, p. 11)

The issue of parts versus wholes is a longstanding one and occurs in other disciplines as well (Mayr, 1997). One might wonder just why there should be an issue here as undoubtedly all personality psychologists would agree that one must have both units (i.e., parts) and organizations of units (i.e., wholes) for any adequate understanding of personality. However, clearly the issue goes beyond this to include conceptual focus and approach to research. In terms of conceptual focus, historically both trait and social cognitive approaches have shown a disregard of the system properties of person functioning. Such important system concepts as degree of differentiation, degree of conflict versus integration, and fluidity versus rigidity of system functioning are noteworthy in their absence from both of these approaches. Yet, it is hard to imagine how a comprehensive approach to personality could neglect such important aspects of system functioning.

Traditionally it was clinicians who were most concerned with the functioning of the person from a holistic or system perspective. As clinical psychology became more behavioral and then more cognitive, both involving a focus on isolated parts relative to the functioning of the system as a whole, there was a decrease in interest in personality as an organized system. Recent theoretical presentations by trait theorists (e.g., McCrae & Costa, Chapter 5, this volume) and social cognitive theorists (e.g., Mischel & Shoda, Chapter 7, this volume, and 1995) suggest a dynamic systems perspective. However, I believe that both fail to give adequate emphasis either to the dynamic or the system aspects of personality functioning.

Magnusson (1995, and Chapter 8, this volume) is the most articulate current spokesperson for a holistic, systems approach to personality, spelling out in detail its theoretical and methodological implications. What is most significant about a systems approach is that it emphasizes the *dynamic* interconnections among parts and the *multidetermination* of complex behavior. Such an approach also provides for the principles of "equipotentiality," in which multiple outcomes are possible from the same starting point, and "equifinality," whereby the same end-point can be reached from multiple paths. Such systems principles would appear to be necessary to appreciate the complexity of human personality functioning. For example, rather than some units standing in isolation from one another, as suggested by the trait hierarchical model, it is possible to imagine a model of multiple linkages among the units, with some units having greater interconnectedness than others. From this standpoint, some personalities would be viewed as more differentiated and organized to a greater degree of complexity than others, rather than all being organized according to the same hierarchical formula.

Some personality psychologists, sympathetic to the holistic approach, remain skeptical because of past disappointments with related efforts. Other personality psychologists are more rejecting, suggesting that terms such as "dynamic" and "system" are meaningless, associated with the old view of clinical prediction, which was demonstrated to be inferior to statistical prediction and best dropped from the field. Thus, the issue of parts versus wholes and the value of a systems perspective remains.

5. Idiographic versus Nomothetic Points of View

> There is little doubt that scientific personality research must ultimately strive for nomothetic principles, but there can be utility in approaching some issues with idiographic as well as nomothetic procedures.
>
> —WIDIGER (1993, p. 89)

> TOLMAN: I know I should be more idiographic in my research, but I just don't know how to be.
> ALLPORT: Let's learn.
>
> —ALLPORT (1962, p. 414)

Not unrelated to the discussion of parts versus wholes, although not identical to it, is the issue of idiographic versus nomothetic approaches to personality. Unfortunately, the term "idiographic" has been used in different ways, at various times being used to refer to an approach to prediction, a conception of personality, a view of science, and a research method (Pervin, 1984). The issue in psychology goes back at least to the 1930s. Lewin (1935) addressed the issue and cautioned against settling for "validity in general" or what is true "on the average," suggesting that instead we look at the individual in specific situations to understand what is true for all. Allport's (1937) discussion of the issue led to widespread debate, with some psychologists suggesting that both approaches were scientific and could be integrated with one another whereas others suggested that they stood in opposition to one another and could not be reconciled. Interestingly, Eysenck (1954) suggested that if being an idiographic psychologist meant studying traits in combination and interaction in relation to the particular personality, then he considered himself to be one rather than the "hard-bitten nomothetical psychologist" (p. 340) he always thought he was: "To the scientist, the unique individual is simply the point of interaction of a number of quantitative variables" (Eysenck, 1954, p. 8). However, others questioned whether an individual differences approach, based on trait dimensions or factors, could sustain a psychology of individuality (Lamiell, 1996; Tyler, 1981).

My view is that it is best to consider the term idiographic in terms of a research strategy, one that permits idiosyncratic aspects of the individual to emerge and looks at patterns or configurations of relationships in the service of formulating general laws or principles that hold for all humans. In this sense, I do not see idiographic approaches to personality as involving unique units or principles, or as following principles of science fundamentally different from those of the natural sciences. However, I do see the approach as orienting the researcher toward the use of different instruments and analyses than might otherwise be the case. It is possible to do systematic research involving the use of varied instruments or sources of data on the same subjects (Murray, 1938), the use of a test such as the Role Construct Repertory (Rep) test that provides both for unique constructs and the testing of formal hypotheses, and the use of free-response data that similarly generate data unique for the individual but are directed toward formulating general principles (Pervin, 1976). It also is possible to gather comparable data for many subjects but where intrasubject rather than intersubject analyses are conducted (Epstein, 1983; Pelham, 1993). The use of idiographic methods, in terms of the nature of the data obtained and ways in which data are analyzed, offers the opportunity to discover principles that may only appear when data relevant to the individual are obtained, to discover patterns of relationships that can not be observed when single variables are considered, and to discover subgroups of subjects that function differently as a function of differing relationships among the variables of interest. All of this can be done within the context of an empirical science of personality.[6]

6. Universals versus Cultural Specificity

> It may be that the psychology which European and American investigators, and those trained in these contexts, have jointly elaborated in the past

> 50 years, is a psychology rooted in one set of largely unexamined ontological assumptions about what it means to be a person.
>
> —MARKUS, KITAYAMA, AND HEIMAN (1996, p. 858)

Over the years recognition of the importance of cultural differences has waxed and waned. During my graduate student days, during the late 1950s, there was considerable interest in the area of culture and personality. Over time such interest declined and there was a hiatus during which the personality field was largely untouched by cross-cultural research. More recently, this has changed in two somewhat opposing directions. First, from a trait standpoint, there has been an interest in demonstrating the cultural universality of the five-factor model (McCrae & Costa, 1997). Second, from a social cognitive standpoint, recognition of cultural differences has led to the questioning of what were thought to be basic, universal processes (Markus et al., 1996; Miller, 1984; Morris & Peng, 1994; Rhee, Uleman, & Lee, 1996). Illustrative here is the conclusion that "self-knowledge or self-referent thought does not appear to be universally organized by trait attributes and is often situationally variable" (Markus et al., 1996, p. 884). Views concerning the importance of cultural differences range from the suggestion that cross-cultural replications of research are probably unwise (Messick, 1988) to Shweder's (1990) questioning whether it is possible to say anything of importance about psychological functioning that is not embedded in a cultural context.

My own view is that cross-cultural research is an enormously important check on our assumptions concerning the universality of principles of personality functioning and itself a potential basis for suggestions concerning such principles. This is so much the case that sometimes I have had the belief that no article suggestive of universal personality units or processes should be published in the absence of corroborating evidence from at least one other culture that is fundamentally different in language and worldview. This would be an enormously difficult task for most researchers, but it might foster greater cross-cultural collaboration and the short-circuiting of extended examination of principles believed to be universal that in reality are context bound.

7. Consistency and Variability in Individual Functioning: The Stasis and Flow of Behavior

> I am exactly the same person I was before, but my situation in life is different and I behave as differently as if I were another person.
>
> —S. KRIM (*New York Times,* November 18, 1974)

Although some suggest that we have learned our lessons from the person–situation controversy and that debate is over (Kenrick & Funder, 1988), others continue to question the "pleasing idea" of broad generalizability of psychological processes across contexts (Kagan, 1996). The point here is not to renew the person–situation controversy. My sense is that it was necessary for the field to examine some of the issues, that views often were distorted and painted in extremes, and that the important underlying issue was neither appropriately addressed nor resolved. The issue as I see it is the following: What kind of conceptualization of the person is best able to capture both the consistency and the variability characteristic of individual behavior—what I have called the stasis and flow of behavior (Pervin, 1983)?

As with the nature–nurture issue, we have gone from debate whether person or situation is more important, to how much of each contributes to behavior, to recognition that both are always interacting. So, if we are one big, happy family now, what's the problem? The problem, as we all know, is that we are not one happy family and, I believe, we are without an adequate model for conceptualizing the consistencies, the variability, and the inconsistencies so characteristic of most individual behavior. I am reminded of a patient who could be characterized by the traits of Neuroticism and Conscientiousness, was quite variable in how Agreeable, Extraverted, and Open to Experience he was, and in one session divulged to me something he had never told anyone else—he loved to listen to *Imus* on the radio and to watch the *A-Team* and *World Championship Wrestling* on television. He noted how much his radio and television preferences would surprise people because they were such a contrast with his meek, inhibited, cultured daily functioning. According to him, they played out the macho, impulsive, irreverent part of him that was inhibited in his public life. To characterize this as part of his Neuroticism and leave it at that seems to miss something fundamental about personality functioning.

So what kinds of models of personality functioning that address the consistency and variability of behavior are possible? One model might suggest that different responses are associated with different situations, that is, we learn different behaviors in different situations. In a sense, we are made up of habits or stimulus–response bonds, with a cognitive element added to address the issue of categorizations of situations and stimuli. The task for such a model is to account for the organized, patterned functioning of the person. Don't the parts, habits, or whatever relate to one another in some way?

A second model might suggest that the same core characteristics are always entering into behavior, with variability in functioning having to do with situational constraint or minor shifts in the relevance of particular characteristics. Such a model addresses broad consistencies in personality functioning but may offer inadequate explanations for variability in functioning and certainly seems to have problems with inconsistencies. A third model focuses on system functioning, with some parts of the system applying more broadly than others and different parts of the system operating in greater or lesser integration (or conflict) with one another. It is this model that has the greatest appeal to me.

Do any theories currently exist that approximate such a model? Kelly's (1955) personal construct theory offers a close approximation. Kelly suggested that people function in terms of their construct system. Constructs have a range of convenience and a focus of convenience. People behave consistently in terms of the operation of their system and to the extent that events are presumed to fall within the range of convenience of the same constructs. At the same time, different constructs might apply to different situations; or what was previously a superordinate construct might, under certain circumstances, become a subordinate construct, in both cases resulting in differences in behavior. Inconsistencies in behavior might reflect conflict in system functioning or might only appear to be inconsistencies from the standpoint of the other's construct system. Perhaps other explanations are possible from a Kellyian perspective, but the point I wish to make is that personal construct theory offers one possible model for addressing the issue of consistency and variability in functioning. My own preference is for a model based on goals rather than constructs as units (Pervin, 1983), and I believe that a lattice network rather than a hierarchical model better captures the complexity of the personality system. Nevertheless, I find personal construct theory to address better the issue of concern than other current alternatives.

8. The Nature of Development and Change

> One of the more important components of Darwin's evolutionary program was continuity. Evolution proceeds by gradual change. Yet, when one looked at living nature, all one saw was discontinuity.
>
> —MAYR (1997, p. 70)

Of late there have been an increasing number of longitudinal studies of personality, what Block (1993) calls studying personality the long way. Such studies, and more generally the research into stability and change of personality over the life course, raise many important questions, some mirroring those suggested in the previous section as well as some new ones. They include the relation between genetic and environmental determinants of behavior, where greater insight into the direct and indirect effects of genes has been obtained, and questions concerning the importance of early experience for later development, where Kagan (1996) and Lewis (1997) have forcefully challenged the view that early experiences have lasting influences on personality development and where a number of studies suggest that temperament and maintaining conditions in the environment play an important role in the continuity that is observed (Lewis, 1997; Thompson, 1998).

The literature suggests that it is very difficult to predict the unfolding of personality development between childhood and adulthood (Lewis, 1997). At the same time, for many important aspects of personality functioning one can find evidence of continuity between childhood and adulthood as well as throughout adulthood (Pervin, 1996, Chap. 6; Costa & McCrae, 1994). These two themes, of evidence of continuity of personality over time and the difficulty of predicting the unfolding of personality over the life course, are clearly played out in the developmental chapters in this volume. The interesting question, I believe, is how to conceptualize the development of personality structure over time and the nature of the processes that make change more or less likely. Just as the effort in the previous section was to consider a model of personality that provides for an appreciation of both consistency and variability, attention in this section can be drawn to the need for a model of personality development that provides for an appreciation of both stability and change, as well as for distinctions such as between phenotypic and genotypic change and between quantitative change and qualitative change.[7]

Outside of the area of clinical psychology, and with the exception of a few developmental psychologists, relatively little attention is given to the question of processes leading to change and, of equal importance, resistance to change. Bandura (1961), in a paper unfortunately lost from the literature, considered psychotherapy as a learning process. The paper is of particular significance, despite the fact that Bandura no longer references it, both because it focuses on an understanding of the process of personality change and because it relates the relevant processes (e.g., positive reinforcement, extinction, counterconditioning) to basic learning processes. A more current paper might give greater attention to cognitive processes but, I believe, would still include the processes outlined by Bandura in this paper. And, one could build upon such an analysis to consider the question of resistance to change.

In sum, just as consideration of person functioning across situations raises fundamental questions concerning personality structure and process, so too is this the case with consideration of personality over time. In both cases we can get caught up in debate concerning whether change does or does not occur, or how much change occurs, or whether it is due to internal or external determinants, but the more fundamental issues are those of models of structure and process that account for stability and change across situations and over time.

9. Person–Environment Interaction

> The organism which adapts well under one condition would not survive under another. If for each environment there is a best organism, for every organism there is a best environment.
>
> —CRONBACH (1957, p. 679)

As a graduate student I listened to Henry Murray tell the story of a Harvard undergraduate who dropped out of college after suffering psychological difficulties associated with college stress. Following this, he became a jet pilot on an aircraft carrier, distinguished himself in what most consider to be an extremely stressful enterprise, and felt psychologically well. Upon discharge he returned to Harvard, reexperienced his early psychological difficulties, and was hospitalized. The story was a simple one with a profound message concerning individual–environment interaction: what is stress for one person is different from that which is stress for another. More generally, Murray suggested that human functioning could best be understood in terms of dynamic relationships between individual and environment characteristics. It was this emphasis that influenced my early research on student–college interaction and led to a review of the literature on performance and satisfaction as a function of individual–environment fit that concluded: "In one way or another, the history of psychology reflects systems based upon an exaggerated emphasis on the individual or the environment. . . . There is now sufficient literature to indicate that these are useless controversies since there is either truth in both points of view or in neither" (Pervin, 1968, p. 65). As noted in that review, however, what is left to be considered are three major questions: Should one consider the perceived or "actual" environment? What units shall we employ, and should they be the same units of analysis for individuals and environments? What is the nature of the processes involved in individual–environment relationships?[8]

One can think of many areas in which the person–environment approach has relevance (e.g., psychological vulnerability and matching stressors, cognitive style and educational tasks, interpersonal relationships, and organizational performance). At the same time, although supportive studies can be found in each of these areas, the general conclusion can be reached that the promise of the approach remains to be fulfilled and that the search for a general model remains.

10. "The Unconscious"

> After 100 years of neglect, suspicion, and frustration, unconscious processes have now taken a firm hold on the collective mind of psychologists.
>
> —KIHLSTROM (1992, p. 788)

Last, but certainly not least, we come to the question of unconscious aspects of personality functioning. As I stated in *The Science of Personality* (Pervin, 1996), "This topic is central to our research on, and understanding of, personality. In fact, significant progress in the field will be difficult to achieve until we have some way of assessing the importance of unconscious processes in the psychological functioning of individuals" (p. 199). In a sense, with this final issue we come full circle as the nature and importance of unconscious processes in personality functioning is of critical importance in relation to issues of measurement, in particular in relation to the use of self-report measures. The literature suggests the following conclusions: (1) There is general agreement that unconscious processes are important in psychological functioning, including influences on affect and motivation; (2) There remains skepticism concerning aspects of the psychoanalytic view of the unconscious, in particular the concept of repression. Although there is varied evidence of the use of defensive mechanisms, it has been difficult to produce evidence of repression experimentally.

Where do these conclusions leave us in terms of their implications for personality? First, as noted by Greenwald and Banaji (1995), what is needed is the development of indirect measures of functioning in such areas. Second, there is the need for greater attention to the role of unconscious processes in affect and motivation. Illustrative of such research would be the work of Higgins (1987, 1989) on chronically accessible constructs and the work of Andersen (Andersen & Baum, 1994; Andersen, Reznik, & Manzella, 1996; Hinkley & Andersen, 1996) on the role of unconscious representations in interpersonal functioning. Clearly these areas are so fundamental that one could argue that a comprehensive theory of personality must give attention to the role of unconscious processes in all aspects of personality functioning.

CHANGE IN PERSONALITY THEORY AND RESEARCH

If the above represent issues that remain unresolved, is there evidence of change in the field since publication of the first edition of this handbook in 1990? Three important areas of progress seem noteworthy. First, I believe that the field is moving toward a different model of the person than has been true for the past few decades, particularly since the cognitive revolution in psychology. Personality psychologists now are emphasizing an active, purposive view of the person. Within this view there is an emphasis on motivational and affective variables as well as cognitive variables. No longer is the person "left in thought," the charge made against Tolman in his emphasis on cognitive maps. The person now is seen as actively striving toward something, with cognitive processes being influenced by motivation and affect as well as serving a critical function in the pursuit of goals. In addition, this emphasis provides for consideration of self-regulatory aspects of organismic functioning, including breakdowns in self-regulation.

A second noteworthy development in the field is the interest on the part of theorists of different persuasions in concepts emphasized by other theoretical perspectives (Winter, John, Stewart, Klohnen, & Duncan, 1998). Recently, Mischel and Shoda (1998) attempted to reconcile trait theory, with its emphasis on dispositions or stability in personality functioning, with social cognitive theory, with its emphasis on cognitive processes associated with intra-individual variability across situations. Addressing the historical divide between the two theoretical perspectives, the authors describe the field as at a choice point where, absent a reconciliation, "personality is likely to split itself in half, as the partitions that separate basic processes and individual differences in its mainstream journal already institutionalize, at best indifferent to each other, at worst undermining each other, and in either case risking making it more difficult to become a cumulative coherent science" (Mischel & Shoda, 1998, p. 232). A number of papers in this handbook suggest an interest in such a reconciliation. At the same time, despite the shared emphasis on dispositions as well as dynamic processes, it remains to be seen whether a true reconciliation is on the horizon. Rather than merely accepting that both consistency and variability exist, what is needed is an integrative framework that accounts for both the stasis and flow of personality.

The third noteworthy development in the field is the emphasis on biological developments. The grand synthesis in biology and remarkable developments in neuroscience have heightened interest in evolutionary models, behavioral genetics, and brain functioning as they relate to personality. Attempts to relate findings in biology-neuroscience to aspects of personality functioning run the gamut from temperament to the concept of the self (Klein & Kihlstrom, 1998). Clearly there is much to be learned from these breathtaking developments as well as from the use of brain-imaging techniques that are adapted to the study of questions of interest to personality psychologists. At the same time, it is important to note that the questions asked by biologists and neuroscientists differ from those typically asked by personality psychologists. Thus, we will need to find ways of asking and addressing the questions of import to us rather than merely extrapolating from findings from these other areas.

WHERE DO WE GO FROM HERE?

> More and more clearly I began to see that biology was a quite different kind of science from the physical sciences. . . . The classical physical sciences, on which the classical philosophy of science was based, were dominated by a set of ideas inappropriate to the study of organisms: these included essentialism, determinism, universalism, and reductionism. Biology, properly understood, comprises population thinking, probability, chance, pluralism, emergence, and historical narratives.
>
> —Mayr (1997, p. xiii)

A short time ago I learned of a small book that I understand has become somewhat of an underground classic among social psychologists. The book, *The June Bug: A Study of Hysterical Contagion* (Kerckhoff & Back, 1968), details the study of a social psychological and personality phenomenon—the spread of a set of symptoms among some workers in a clothing factory that was without physical explanation. The set of symptoms included reports of sickness, "poisonous insect bites," and, in some cases, actual fainting. The study, conducted in a naturalistic environment, is complex and not all of the details will be given. However, sufficient detail can be presented to appreciate the fundamental points to be made.

The task of Kerckhoff and Back (1968) was to understand the phenomenon of hysterical contagion both in terms of the general phenomenon as well as in terms of individual differences. In terms of timing of the phenomenon, it occurred during June, the month of peak production and greatest stress. In terms of who was affected, there were gender differences and context or setting differences: a much higher percentage of females than males was affected, the effects were greater on the day shift than on the evening shift, and greater in the dressmaking department than in other departments. In addition, the effects were greater among those working overtime, and presumably experiencing the greatest stress, than among those not working overtime. Social ties also were found to be important in that individuals who knew others who had been affected were more likely to themselves report being affected than others who did not have such relationships. Finally, what of personality characteristics? The authors rejected a trait of general suggestibility. Rather, they suggested that the affected individuals were those who experienced stress and had a pattern of coping through denial of external sources of strain and internal experiences. The importance of the defense of denial was viewed as particularly important in relation to the most serious symptom, that of fainting: "There is thus a kind of interactive effect of social or situational influence with the personal characteristic of denial to produce a high probability of becoming affected" (p. 155).

In sum, the explanation arrived at included both environmental and personality factors. That is, the authors suggested that the hysterical contagion was a result of job stress that did not provide for acceptable solution, a network of social relationships, and individual differences in degree of stress and how stress is handled: "All of this leads to the conclusion that there is undoubtedly some pattern of interaction among personality, social structure, and situational characteristics which influences how the diffusion of the pattern of behavior will occur" (p. 38). . . . Personal and social characteristics interact to affect the tendency to exhibit the most extreme symptoms" (p. 155). In other words, an interactionist or systems perspective was necessary to understand the phenomenon. As they further noted, "multiple factors must be considered if we are to account for the women's behavior during the epidemic and that different combinations of the same factors lead to very different outcomes" (p. 153).

In relation to other points made in this paper, we can note that self-report of stress, without taking into consideration the defense of denial, was inadequate to understand the phenomenon. Also, in addition to the gender and setting or context effects, we can note that different relationships were observed depending on the time period of the epidemic during which the symptoms appeared and on whether the criterion used consisted of visits to the medical office or reports of symptoms without such visits. In other words, the relationships depended, in a theoretically meaningful way, on a specific set of interactions among social and personality factors, personality assessments, and criterion measures. Were one or another of these components to be missing, the same results would not have been obtained. That is, the results were stable only within the context of this interaction among the variables. And, as noted, a dynamic systems perspective, both in terms of the individual (i.e., the interplay between stress and coping) and the relation of the person to the environment, was necessary to understand how the phenomenon occurred and individual differences in who was affected.

Are there lessons to be learned from this research as to where we as personality psychologists go from here? First, let me say that we are not alone in many of the problems we face. Our social psychologist friends also struggle with some of these issues, as well as with the problem of research fads that appear to come and go without explanation (Jones, 1985; Shaver & Kirk, 1996). And, even our friends in the natural sciences struggle with disagreements that seem to go on endlessly. As described by one biologist:

> Once, in my younger, more naive (and perhaps more idealistic) days, I was describing elements of High Table discussion to a gathering of mathematicians, chemists, and physicists. I told them that it must seem strange to them that such persistent disagreement, without any real prospect of a definitive solution one way or another, could go on seemingly forever in evolutionary biology. After all, I said, in chemistry and physics everything is resolved as the truth is steadily revealed in an endless series of elegant experiments. Or something like that.
>
> I was nearly laughed out of the house, and after a quickly dissipated spurt of embarrassment, I was delighted to drop the myth that there is something wrong, something imprecise, something somehow unscientific about the messy field of evolutionary biology. Physicists can't agree among themselves either! (Eldredge, 1995, pp. 221–222)

Is there anything that can be done about these problems in relation to personality psychology? First, in agreement with Kagan (1988), we can not place complete reliance on self-report as the basis for a science of personality. We need to make use of multiple methods of data collection. In fact, one of the most interesting aspects of personality assessment is how different the person may appear on different assessment instruments. Second, we need more research that demonstrates the reliability of findings across gender, setting, and culture unless differences can be understood in theoretically meaningful ways. Third, what is needed is further use of multitrait–multimethod research (Campbell & Fiske, 1959). This is important not only in terms of demonstrating convergent and discriminant validity but also in terms of exploring complex relationships among variables. Fourth, there is the importance of a dynamic, systems perspective. In this regard, there is a place for the intensive study of individuals in as naturalistic a setting as possible and involving the use of diverse assessment methods. Intensive studies of individuals provide for the study of processes over time. And, such research can provide for a much needed focus on the operations of the system aspects of personality (e.g., self-regulation, conflict resolution, system stress).[9]

The final chapter of the first edition of this handbook concluded with the hope that the next edition would trace its roots to the contributions of that edition. In reflecting upon the contributions in that edition, there is evidence of both constancy and change in the field. Many of the old issues remain, some of which perhaps will never be solved. Others have not been solved but progress has been made. In this sense, the field may be at the point of becoming a cumulative science. Finally, new areas of challenge, areas of interest, and technological developments have emerged, most significantly in areas related to the biological sciences. Hopefully a future edition of this handbook will once again reflect both constancy and change, constancy in the sense of addressing questions of historical interest to personality psychologists and change in the sense of new insights into these questions as well as the raising of new questions.

ACKNOWLEDGMENTS

My appreciation to the following individuals who commented on a draft of this chapter: Richard Contrada, Oliver John, Michael Lewis, David Magnusson, Dan McAdams, Irving Sigel, and Lawrence Stricker.

NOTES

1. Others consider a correlation of .4 between self- and other ratings as reflective of a lack of concordance (Tiffany, 1990). It may also be of interest to note that Cronbach (1989) views self- and peer ratings as distinct constructs, self-concept and reputa-

tion respectively, and therefore finds high correlations between them troublesome rather than assuring.

2. An illustration of such excess baggage might be the positivity bias in self-reports associated with narcissism (John & Robins, 1994).

3. In commenting on this section, Oliver John makes two important points. First, observers have difficulty in reliably coding behavioral acts (Gosling, John, Craik, & Robins, 1998), suggesting that they face difficulties similar to those faced by self- and peer raters in parsing behavior. Second, some personality characteristics are rated with greater accuracy than others, with emotional biases appearing to account for some of this variation.

4. More recent analyses of some of the complexities associated with the concept of construct validity and multitrait–multimethod data analyses can be found in Barrett (1992), Byrne and Goffin (1993), Cronbach (1989), and Marsh (1989).

5. Jackson (1994) presents an excellent multimethod factor analysis in the Jackson PRI manual, demonstrating that the predicted measures load highly on the respective factors. In relation to the earlier discussion of self–other rating agreement, it can be noted that correlations between Jackson Personality Inventory scale scores and peer ratings averaged .25 to .38.

6. Idiographic analyses can also serve as a check on the veridicality of data averaged across subjects. In the period when stimulus–response learning theory was the predominant model, researchers suggested caution in concluding that average learning curves reflect the learning of individual organisms. Similarly, questions can be raised concerning the extent to which trait categories and groupings of trait adjectives derived from factor analyses reflect the categories and associated adjectives used by individuals.

7. The relevance of the discussion of cross-situational consistency to the current discussion is reflected in Mischel and Shoda's (1998) note that trait conceptions emphasize stability over the life course whereas social cognitive conceptions emphasize malleability.

8. Although generally similarity appears to be an important ingredient of "fit" or "match," we are still in need of better process models of individual–environment transactions. At this point, an emphasis on the relation between personal goals and situation affordances seems the most promising to me in this regard. That is, similar to Murray's (1938) need-press model, individual–environment transactions can be considered in terms of the process of engagement between individual goals and situation affordances (Sanderson & Cantor, 1997).

9. At times I have thought that it might be useful for subjects to be studied intensively in different laboratories, with each laboratory making use of instruments suggested by other laboratories and sharing data with one another. In this way we might try to relate our theories and findings to one another, with the hope of establishing a more comprehensive picture of the person.

REFERENCES

Allport, G. W. (1937). *Personality: A psychological interpretation.* New York: Holt, Rinehart & Winston.

Allport, G. W. (1962). The general and the unique in psychological science. *Journal of Personality, 30,* 405–422.

Andersen, S. M., & Baum, A. (1994). Transference in interpersonal relations: Inferences and affect based on significant-other representations. *Journal of Personality, 62,* 459–498.

Andersen, S. M., Reznik, I., & Manzella, L. M. (1996). Eliciting facial affect, motivation, and expectancies in transference: Significant-other representations in social situations. *Journal of Personality and Social Psychology, 71,* 1108–1129.

Bandura, A. (1961). Psychotherapy as a learning process. *Psychological Bulletin, 58,* 143–159.

Bandura, A. (1986). *Social foundations of thought and action.* Englewood Cliffs, NJ: Prentice Hall.

Barrett, G. V. (1992). Clarifying construct validity: Definitions, processes, and models. *Human Performance, 5,* 13–58.

Block, J. (1993). Studying personality the long way. In D. C. Funder, R. D. Parke, C. Tomlinson-Keasey, & K. Widaman (Eds.), *Studying lives through time* (pp.9-41). Washington, DC: American Psychological Association.

Block, J. (1996). Some jangly remarks on Baumeister and Heatherton. *Psychological Inquiry, 7,* 28–32.

Bornstein, R. F. (1998). Implicit and self-attributed dependency strivings: Differential relationships to laboratory and field measures of help seeking. *Journal of Personality and Social Psychology, 75,* 778–787.

Byrne, B. M., & Goffin, R. D. (1993). Modeling MTMM data from additive and multiplicative covariance structures: An audit of construct validity concordance. *Multivariate Behavioral Research, 28,* 67–96.

Campbell, D. T., & Fiske, D. W. (1959). Convergent and discriminant validation by the multitrait–multimethod matrix. *Psychological Bulletin, 56,* 81–105.

Compton, W. C., Smith, M. L., Cornish, K. A., & Qualls, D. L. (1996). Factor structure of mental health measures. *Journal of Personality and Social Psychology, 71,* 406–413.

Costa, P. T., Jr., & McCrae, R. R. (1994). "Set like plaster?" Evidence for the stability of adult personality. In T. Heatherton & J. Weinberger (Eds.), *Can per-*

sonality change? (pp. 21–40). Washington, DC: American Psychological Association.

Cronbach, L. J. (1957). The two disciplines of scientific psychology. *American Psychologist, 12,* 671–684.

Cronbach, L. J. (1989). Construct validation after thirty years. In R. L. Linn (Ed.), *Intelligence: Measurment, theory, and public policy* (pp. 147–171). Urbana: University of Illinois Press.

Cronbach, L. J., & Meehl, P. E. (1955). Construct validity in psychological tests. *Psychological Bulletin, 52,* 281–302.

Derakshan, N., & Eysenck, M. W. (1997). Interpretive biases for one's own behavior and physiology in high-trait-anxious individuals and repressors. *Journal of Personality and Social Psychology, 73,* 816–825.

Eldredge, N. (1995). *Reinventing Darwin: The great debate at the high table of evolutionary theory.* New York: Wiley.

Epstein, S. (1983). A research paradigm for the study of personality and emotions. In M. M. Page (Ed.), *Personality: Current theory and research* (pp. 91–154). Lincoln, NE: University of Nebraska Press.

Eysenck, H. J. (1954). The science of personality: Nomothetic. *Psychological Review, 61,* 339–342.

Funder, D. C. (1980). On seeing ourselves as others see us: Self–other agreement and discrepancy in personality ratings. *Journal of Personality, 48,* 473–493.

Funder, D. C. (1993). Judgments of personality and personality itself. In K. M. Craik, R. Hogan, & R. N. Wolfe (Eds.), *Fifty years of personality psychology* (pp. 207–214). New York: Plenum Press.

Funder, D. C., Kolar, D. C., & Blackman, M. C. (1995). Agreement among judges of personality: Interpersonal relations, similarity, and acquaintanceship. *Journal of Personality and Social Psychology, 69,* 656–672.

Gigerenzer, G., & Hoffrage, U. (1995). How to improve Bayesian reasoning without instruction: Frequency formats. *Psychological Review, 102,* 684–704.

Gill, M. J., Swann, W. B., Jr., & Silvera, D. H. (1998). On the genesis of confidence. *Journal of Personality and Social Psychology, 75,* 1101–1114.

Gosling, S. D., John, O. P., Craik, K. H., & Robins, R. W. (1998). Do people know how they behave? Self-reported act frequencies compared with on-line codings by observers. *Journal of Personality and Social Psychology, 74,* 1337–1349.

Greenwald, A. G., & Banaji, M. M. R. (1995). Implicit social cognition: Attitudes, self-esteem, and stereotypes. *Psychological Review, 102,* 4–27.

Hedlund, S., & Rude, S. (1995). Evidence of latent depressive schemas in formerly depressed individuals. *Journal of Abnormal Psychology, 104,* 517–525.

Henry, B., Moffitt, T. E., Caspi, A., Langley, J., & Silva, P. A. (1994). On the "remembrance of things past": A longitudinal evaluation of the retrosopective method. *Psychological Assessment, 6,* 92–101.

Higgins, E. T. (1987). Self-discrepancy: A theory relating self and affect. *Psychological Review, 94,* 319–340.

Higgins, E. T. (1989). Continuities and discontinuities in self-regulatory self-evaluative processes: A developmental theory relating self and affect. *Journal of Personality, 57,* 407–444.

Hinkley, K., & Andersen, S. M. (1996). The working of self-concept in transference: Significant-other activiation and self change. *Journal of Personality and Social Psychology, 71,* 1279–1295.

Hogan, R. (1982). On adding apples and oranges in personality psychology. *Contemporary Psychology, 27,* 851–852.

Hogan, R., & Nicholson, R. A. (1988). The meaning of personality test scores. *American Psychologist, 43,* 621–626.

Holtzman, P., & Kagan, J. (1995). Whither or wither personality research. In P. E. Shrout & S. T. Fiske (Eds.), *Personality research, methods and theory* (pp. 3–12). Mahwah, NJ: Erlbaum.

Jackson, D. N. (1994). *Jackson Personality Inventory—revised manual.* Port Huron, MI: Sigma Assessment Systems, Inc.

John, O. P., & Robins, R. W. (1993). Determinants of interjudge agreement on personality traits: The big five domains, observability, evaluativeness, and the unique aspects of the self. *Journal of Personality, 61,* 521–551.

John, O. P., & Robins, R. W. (1994). Accuracy and bias in self-perception: Individual differences in self-enhancement and the role of narcissism. *Journal of Personality and Social Psychology, 66,* 206–219.

Jones, E. E. (1985). Major developments in social psychology during the past five decades. In G. Lindzey & E. Aronson (Eds.), *Handbook of social psychology* (3rd ed., Vol. 1, pp. 47–107). New York: Random House.

Kagan, J. (1988). The meanings of personality predicates. *American Psychologist, 43,* 614–620.

Kagan, J. (1996). Three pleasing ideas. *American Psychologist, 51,* 901–908.

Kazdin, A. (1994). Informant variability in the assessment of childhood depression. In W. M. Reynolds & H. F. Johnston (Eds.), *Handbook of depression in children and adolescents* (pp. 249–271). New York: Plenum Press.

Kelly, G. A. (1955). *The psychology of personal constructs.* New York: Norton.

Kenny, D. A. (1994). *Interpersonal perception.* New York: Guilford Press.

Kenrick, D. T., & Funder, D. C. (1988). Profiting from controversy: Lessons from the person–situation debate. *American Psychologist, 43,* 23–34.

Kerchkoff, A. C., & Back, K. W. (1968). *The June bug: A study of hysterical contagion.* New York: Appleton-Century-Crofts.

Kihlstrom, J. F. (1992). Dissociation and dissociations: A commentary on consciousness and cognition. *Consciousness and Cognition, 1,* 47–53.

King, L. A. (1995). Wishes, motives, goals and personal memories: Relations of measures of human motivation. *Journal of Personality, 63,* 985–1007.

Klein, S. B., & Kihlstrom, J. F. (1998). On bridging the gap between social–personality psychology and neuropsychology. *Personality and Social Psychology Review, 2,* 228–242.
Lamiell, J. T. (1996). One step forward, two steps back. *Psychological Inquiry, 7,* 330–334.
Lewin, K. (1935). *A dynamic theory of personality.* New York: McGraw-Hill.
Lewis, M. (1997). *Altering fate: Why the past does not predict the future.* New York: Guilford Press.
Magnusson, D. (1995). Individual development: A holistic integrated model. In P. Moen, G. H. Elder Jr., & K. Luscher (Eds.), *Explaining lives in context* (pp. 19-60). Washington, DC: American Psychological Association.
Markus, H. R., Kitayama, S., & Heiman, R. J. (1996). Culture and "basic" psychological principles. In E. T. Higgins & A. Kruglanski (Eds.), *Social psychology: Handbook of basic principles* (pp. 867–913). New York: Guilford Press.
Marsh, H. W. (1989). Confirmatory factor analyses of multitrait–multimethod data: Many problems and a few solutions. *Applied Psychological Measurement, 13,* 335–361.
Mayr, E. (1997). *This is biology.* Cambridge, MA: Belknap Press.
McClelland, D. C., Koestner, R., & Weinberger, J. (1989). How do self-attributed and implicit motives differ? *Psychological Review, 96,* 690–702.
McCrae, R. R., & Costa, P. T., Jr. (1990). *Personality in adulthood.* New York: Guilford Press.
McCrae, R. R., & Costa, P. T., Jr. (1997). Personality trait structure as a human universal. *American Psychologist, 52,* 509–516.
Meehl, P. E. (1978). Theoretical risks and tabular asterisks: Sir Karl, Sir Ronald, and the slow progress of soft psychology. *Journal of Consulting and Clinical Psychology, 46,* 806–834.
Meehl, P. E. (1990). Appraising and amending theories: The strategy of Lakatosian defense and two principles that warrant using it. *Psychological Inquiry, 1,* 108–141, 173–180.
Messick, D. (1988). On the limitations of cross-cultural research in social psychology. In M. H. Bond (Ed.), *The cross-cultural challenge to social psychology* (pp. 41–47). Newbury Park, CA: Sage.
Miller, J. G. (1984). Culture and the development of everyday social explanation. *Journal of Personality and Social Psychology, 46,* 961–978.
Mischel, W., & Shoda, Y. (1995). A cognitive-affective system theory of personality: Reconceptualizing the invariances of personality and the role of situations. *Psychological Review, 102,* 246–286.
Mischel, W., & Shoda, Y. (1998). Reconciling processing dynamics and personality dispositions. *Annual Review of Psychology, 49,* 229–258.
Morris, M. W., & Peng, K. (1994). Culture and cause: American and Chinese attributions for social and physical events. *Journal of Personality and Social Psychology, 67,* 949–971.
Murray, H. A. (1938). *Explorations in personality.* New York: Oxford University Press.
Murray, H. A., & Kluckhohn, C. (1953). Outline of a conception of personality. In C. Kluckhohn, H. A. Murray, & D. Schneider (Eds.), *Personality in nature, society, and culture* (pp. 3–52). New York: Knopf.
Newton, T. L., & Contrada, R. J. (1992). Repressive coping and verbal-autonomic response dissociation: The influence of social context. *Journal of Personality and Social Psychology, 62,* 159–167.
Pelham, B. W. (1993). The idiographic nature of human personality: Examples of the idiographic self-concept. *Journal of Personality and Social Psychology, 64,* 665–677.
Pervin, L. A. (1968). Performance and satisfaction as a function of individual–environment fit. *Psychological Bulletin, 69,* 56–68.
Pervin, L. A. (1976). A free-response description approach to the analysis of person–situation interaction. *Journal of Personality and Social Psychology, 34,* 465–474.
Pervin, L. A. (1983). The stasis and flow of behavior: Toward a theory of goals. In M. M. Page (Ed.), *Personality: Current theory and research* (pp. 1–53). Lincoln, NE: University of Nebraska Press.
Pervin, L. A. (1984). Idiographic approaches to personality. In N. Endler & J. McV. Hunt (Eds.), *Personality and the behavioral disorders* (pp. 261–282). New York: Wiley.
Pervin, L. A. (1996). *The science of personality.* New York: Wiley.
Rhee, E., Uleman, J. S., & Lee, H. K. (1996). Variations in collectivism and individualism by ingroup and culture: Confirmatory factor analyses. *Journal of Personality and Social Psychology, 71,* 1037–1054.
Robins, R. W., & John, O. P. (1997). The quest for self-insight: Theory and research on accuracy and bias in self-perception. In R. Hogan, J. Johnson, & S. Briggs (Eds.), *Handbook of personality psychology* (pp. 649–679). New York: Academic Press.
Sanderson, C. A., & Cantor, N. (1997). Creating satisfaction in steady dating relationships: The role of personal goals and situational affordances. *Journal of Personality and Social Psychology, 73,* 1424–1433.
Scheier, M. F., Carver, C. S., & Bridges, M. W. (1994). Distinguishing optimism from neuroticism (and trait anxiety, self-mastery, and self-esteem): A reevaluation of the Life Orientation Test. *Journal of Personality and Social Psychology, 67,* 1063–1078.
Schwarz, N. (1999). Self-reports: How the questions shape the answers. *American Psychologist, 54,* 93–105.
Schwartz, N. (1999). Self-reports: How the questions shpae the answers. *American Psychologist, 54,* 93–105.
Shaver, K. G., & Kirk, D. L. (1996). The quest for meaning in social behavior. *Contemporary Psychology, 41,* 423–426.

Shedler, J., Mayman, M., & Manis, M. (1993). The illusion of mental health. *American Psychologist, 48,* 1117–1131.

Shweder, R. A. (1990). Cultural psychology—What is it? In J. W. Stigler, R. A. Shweder, & G. Herdt (Eds.), *Cultural psychology: Essays on comparative human development* (pp. 1–43). Cambridge, UK: Cambridge University Press.

Swann, W. B., Jr., & Gill, M. J. (1997). Confidence and accuracy in person perception: Do we know what we think we know about our relationship partners? *Journal of Personality and Social Psychology, 73,* 747–757.

Thompson, R. A. (1998). Early socialization and personality development. In N. Eisenberg (Ed.), *Handbook of child psychology* (5th ed., Vol. 3, pp. 25–104). New York: Wiley.

Tiffany, S. T. (1990). A cognitive model of drug urges and drug-use behaviors: Role of automatic and nonautomatic processes. *Psychological Review, 97,* 147–168.

Tyler, L. E. (1981). More stately mansions—Psychology extends its boundaries. *Annual Review of Psychology, 32,* 1–20.

Wallach, M. A., Green, L. R., Lipsitt, P. D., & Minehart, J. B. (1962). Contradiction between overt and projective personality indicators as a function of defensiveness. *Psychological Monographs, 76*(Whole No. 1).

Widiger, T. A. (1993). Personality and depression: Assessment issues. In M. H. Klein, D. J. Kupfer, & M. T. Shea (Eds.), *Personality and depression: A current view* (pp. 77–118). New York: Guilford Press.

Wilson, T. D. (1994). The proper protocol: Validity and completeness of verbal reports. *Psychological Science, 5,* 249–252.

Winter, D. G., John, O. P., Stewart, A. J., Klohnen, E. C., & Duncan, L. E. (1998). Traits and motives: Toward an integration of two traditions in personality research. *Psychological Review, 105,* 230–250.

Author Index

Subject Index

Figure numbers are indicated by *f*. Table numbers are indicated by *t*.